PENGUIN REFERENCE BOOKS

ROGET'S THESAURUS

ROGET'S THESAURUS

OF ENGLISH WORDS AND PHRASES

NEW EDITION COMPLETELY
REVISED, MODERNIZED AND ABRIDGED
BY ROBERT A. DUTCH

PENGUIN BOOKS

Penguin Books Ltd, Harmondsworth, Middlesex, England
Penguin Books Australia Ltd, Ringwood, Victoria, Australia

—

First published 1852
Published in Penguin Books 1953
Reprinted twelve times
This new edition first published by Longmans 1962
Published in Penguin Books 1966
Reprinted 1968, 1969, 1970

—

—

Made and printed in Great Britain
by Hazell Watson & Viney Ltd,
Aylesbury, Bucks
Set in Monotype Times

PREFACE TO THE PENGUIN EDITION

FAMOUS as it is, *Roget's Thesaurus* lives not by the praises of past generations but by its enduring reputation for usefulness. This seems natural enough when we remember that the book itself was born of a practical need. As a young and busy doctor, already much given to lecturing, Peter Mark Roget felt the need to improve his powers of expression. Being of a practical and inventive turn of mind, he devised his own instrument for the purpose, which he describes as a 'classed catalogue of words' – quite a fair definition of what we nowadays mean by a thesaurus; but it was on a small scale and for his own use only. That was in 1805, when Roget was about twenty-six years of age. It was not until 1852, when he was well into his seventies, that he published his *Thesaurus*, expanded and developed from its first beginnings but framed on the original principles that he had tried and tested during a long and exceptionally crowded career involving incessant literary composition. His hope that what had helped him would help others was immediately and signally justified. During the remainder of Roget's life (he died in 1869, aged ninety-one), his *Thesaurus* went through twenty-eight editions, and it has never gone out of print to the present day. Over and over again it has been reproduced, copied and remodelled; sometimes it was pirated. In the English-speaking countries it has long been a cherished work of reference, and it has inspired similar thesauruses in other languages. It has undergone many revisions but these, while modifying the detail, have not shaken the principles of the original compilation. It is for very good reason that Roget's name is inseparable from his *Thesaurus*.

Roget's Thesaurus is a vocabulary on a large scale, categorized by topics. With such an arrangement it offers a choice of words to fit any given context. This, indeed, is its main function, and is the reason why it is so often alluded to as an aid to composition. In this edition the whole vocabulary is grouped under no less than 990 heads or topics. Each head, for the further definition of its contents, bears what may be called a descriptive title, e.g., Existence, Non-existence, Identity, Difference (in the class of Abstract Relations); Ship, Vehicle, Land, Lake, Ocean (among concrete objects); Love, Hate, Joy, Sorrow (representing the feelings), and so on. Under the totality of these heads is listed a substantial part of the working vocabulary of the English language, leaving aside merely technical terms. What is more important, these 990 heads, thanks to Roget's original classification, subsume pretty adequately the whole range of ideas that the vocabulary is normally used to express. Thus almost any idea or meaning that is likely to require expression in literary composition can be referred to one or more of these heads; somewhere in the vocabulary listed thereunder will be found relevant words and phrases from which a choice may be made of the expression most apt for rendering the idea or meaning in question.

A writer, or other user of words, in the throes of composition, conscious of what he wants to say but at a loss for the word that will best express it, gratefully turns for help to the work of reference which has what he needs – a rich and accessible vocabulary, assorted, graded and labelled. In other words, he consults a thesaurus. The present edition is designed to make such a consultation rapid, easy and fruitful. The inquirer refers to the head or heads closest to the meaning he wishes to express. There he finds a sizeable vocabulary classified into nouns, adjectives and verbs (sometimes, also, into adverbs), and further subdivided into paragraphs, each furnished with a defining keyword which will narrow down his area of search. If he has chosen the appropriate head he can hardly fail to find the expression he wants, either in that very place, or in some other part of the text to which the numerous cross-references will guide him. The procedure thus stated is perfectly straight-forward but of course the inquirer will want to know how he is to locate the appropriate head among all the 990 heads that constitute the text. Roget's own answer, almost certainly, would have been: Get to know the classification. That is perfectly sound advice. The heads are not set down haphazardly. They issue logically from larger categories which themselves form part of six major and very general classes. The classification really can be learnt. Once he has mastered it, the user will be able to lay his finger infallibly on the vocabulary relating to any given topic. But this is a skill only to be acquired by experience. For beginners, the advice would invariably be to use the index. The index references of the present edition are specially constructed to provide immediate and unambiguous information. The rules are simple and the required guidance will be found in the instructions How To Use This Book. In this place it is only necessary to stress the fact that the index has one purpose only – to lead the inquirer as expeditiously as possible from his first tentative approximation (i.e., the word he looks up in the index) to his final, deliberate choice elicited from the body of the text. The index – or rather that part of it consisting of the alphabetical list of words – is not, and is not intended to be, a reproduction of the text vocabulary reduced to alphabetical order. It has no direct business with the text at all. It is simply a selection of the possible words which may occur to the inquirer as the first step towards finding a reference to the right place in the text.

This edition is an abridgement of the revised and much enlarged edition published by Longmans Green & Co. in 1962. It is here reduced to the dimensions which can be compassed in a paperback. Text and index have been substantially lightened. Wordy expressions and long phrases have, on the whole, been dropped in preference to single words and concise entries. Old-fashioned and time-worn idioms have frequently been removed. Duplicated contexts which appeared under several different heads are now mainly confined to a single head, with references, where necessary, to the other heads under which they formerly occurred. A number of subheads have been totally cancelled, usually where the vocabulary thus suppressed could be derived without difficulty from that retained under the remaining subheads. Adverbial subheads, as being the most easily dispensed with, have to a large extent disappeared. In shortening the index, the guiding principle was to remove from the alphabetical list the rarer or more recondite words for which common alternatives existed and which therefore were less likely to be used as the starting point in the search for a reference. Conjugate forms of words already listed have generally been dropped. Among the sub-entries, those references which relied on the more oblique or far-fetched significations of the word indexed have been eliminated: it should not of course be supposed that the index contains the full vocabulary of the text, nor that the references in the sub-entry indicate every occurrence in the text of the word constituting the main entry.

New features which distinguish the main edition are marks of this abridgement also, namely: the close ordering of the vocabulary into a logical sequence of related contexts, with smooth transitions; the use of italicized keywords at the head of each paragraph to denote the general theme and to facilitate reference; the multiplicity of unambiguous, self-explanatory references, with the triple notation of keyword, number and part of speech; the same form of reference being also used in the index; and lastly, the printing of the text in double column, which permits the inclusion of more words to the page. With respect to its predecessor in the Penguin series, this new edition may fairly be designated 'revised and enlarged'.

R.A.D.

HOW TO USE THIS BOOK

IT is assumed you have an idea or meaning to express but cannot think of a satisfactory word for it. You therefore desire access to a wider range of vocabulary which may contain or at least suggest the word you are looking for. You turn to your *Thesaurus*. You know it has the relevant vocabulary. Your problem is to locate it. For this you will need the index. Think of some word allied in meaning to the meaning you have to express. It need not be at all a close approximation, so long as it has some connexion. Most likely it will be one of the words you have already rejected as not suitable. That is quite good enough to start with, provided it is not a rare or recondite word – for the index contains mostly plain ordinary words in their plain ordinary sense. Look up this word in the index, where you will find it, in its alphabetical place, associated with one or more references. All the references in the index (and in the text, too) consist of a keyword (in italics), a number and a part of speech, (n.=noun, adj.=adjective, vb.=verb, adv.=adverb). The keyword reflects some aspect of meaning inherent in the main entry with which it is associated and distinguishes its own context from the context of the other references. Having looked up your word, and considered the references, you select that reference whose keyword best covers the meaning you have in mind. That reference is your clue to the text. Turn to the head in the text that bears the number given by the reference; look thereunder in the division corresponding to the part of speech; there you will find a paragraph headed by the same keyword as in your reference. That is your subhead, and there you begin your search. All the words in the subhead have meanings which are related, usually in a very obvious way, to the meaning of the keyword and will therefore, in all probability, contain a word or expression which exactly hits what you are aiming at. Usually, but not invariably, the same subhead will contain the word you originally looked up, but its presence or absence is of no concern to you, as by definition, you do not require it. Once engaged with the text, you will find it easy to extend your search if you wish. You can follow up any promising cross-references you come across (they are in the same form as in the index); other paragraphs of the same head will bear on the same general topic and may well suggest an appropriate word. It is well to remember that the whole scheme of classification enables adjacent heads to deal with allied topics. Thus you will find that your range of relevant vocabulary is easily and rapidly extended in an ever-widening orbit. The resources of *Roget*, in fact, are very considerable, easily focused and profitable to explore.

A specific example will make the process clearer. Suppose the inquirer is concerned with the idea of being indignant, but this is the word that eludes him, and all he can think of, on the spur of the moment, is 'cross'. This word is close enough to his meaning to serve for the beginning of a search. He looks up 'cross' in the index and finds it indexed with no less than eight references, which the keywords enable him to distinguish. Obviously, he will not want *hybrid* 43 n., or *counteract* 182 vb., or *decoration* 729 n. But *angry* 891 adj. is right on the mark. He turns to the head numbered 891, looks in the subdivision for adjectives (Adj.) and finds his paragraph headed '*angry*'. All the words in this paragraph are in adjectival form and express some aspect of the notion of 'angry', and among them is 'indignant', which we have assumed was the word that eluded him. If he wishes to look further, he may consult the other subheads, (*resentful*, for instance, under which he will also find 'indignant'); or he may follow up the two cross-references (834 adj. *serious*, 503 adj. *frenzied*). He will also notice that the two following heads, 892 and 893, deal with Irascibility and Sullenness, both very close to the idea of anger.

THESAURUS
OF ENGLISH WORDS AND PHRASES

Class One
ABSTRACT RELATIONS

Section 1: Existence

1. Existence – N. *existence*, esse, being, absoluteness, givenness; aseity, self-existence; monad, Platonic form; a being, entity, ens; subsistence 360 n. *life*; survival, eternity 115 n. *perpetuity*; pre-existence 119 n. *priority*; co-existence 121 n. *present time*; presence, currency, prevalence 189 n. *presence*; becoming, evolution 147 n. *conversion*; potentiality 469 n. *possibility*; ontology, metaphysics, existentialism, realism.

reality, realness, actuality; thatness 80 n. *speciality*; positiveness; historicity, factuality 494 n. *truth*; fact, matter of f., brute f., stubborn f., fait accompli; real thing, no joke, no kidding; realities, fundamentals, bedrock, brass tacks 638 n. *important matter*.

essence, nature, quiddity, hypostasis, substance 3 n. *substantiality*; sum and substance 5 n. *intrinsicality*; soul, heart, core, centre 224 n. *interiority*.

Adj. *existing*, existent, ontal; existential; essential 5 adj. *intrinsic*; absolute, given, self-existing, uncreated; being, in existence, under the sun; subsistent, living, undying, immortal, eternal 115 adj. *perpetual*; present, standing, surviving, extant; current, rife, prevalent, in vogue; ontological, metaphysical.

real, essential, quidditative; substantive 3 adj. *substantial*; actual, positive, factual, historical, grounded 494 adj. *true*; natural, physical, of flesh and blood 319 adj. *material*.

Vb. *be*, exist, have being, be the case; consist in, inhere in, reside in 5 vb. *be intrinsic*; subsist, abide, continue 146 vb. *go on*; endure, stand 113 vb. *last*; vegetate 360 vb. *live*; be found, be met, stand, lie 186 vb. *be situate*; obtain, prevail, reign, spread, be rife 189 vb. *pervade*; occur 154 vb. *happen*; represent, stand for 13 vb. *be identical*.

become, come to be, take flesh; arise 68 vb. *begin*; unfold, develop, grow, take shape 316 vb. *evolve*; turn out, change into 147 vb. *be turned to*.

2. Non-existence – N. *non-existence*, (in time) 109 n. *neverness*; (in space) nullibiety 190 n. *absence*; blank, vacuum 190 n. *emptiness*; nothing 103 n. *zero*; a nothing 4 n. *insubstantial thing*; no such thing 190 n. *nobody*; negative result 728 n. *failure*.

extinction, nirvana; no life 361 n. *death*; obsolescence 127 n. *oldness*; annihilation 165 n. *destruction*; abolition 752 n. *abrogation*; amnesty 506 n. *oblivion*; cancellation, sponge, clean slate 550 n. *obliteration*.

Adj. *non-existent*, inexistent, without being; null, minus; nowhere, missing, omitted 190 adj. *absent*.

unreal, baseless, groundless, unfounded 495 adj. *erroneous*; visionary, fabulous 513 adj. *imaginary*, 4 adj. *insubstantial*; unrealized, potential 469 adj. *possible*; hypothetical 512 adj. *suppositional*.

unborn, uncreated, unmade; unbegotten, unconceived; undiscovered, uninvented, unimagined; yet to come 124 adj. *future*.

extinct, died out, vanished; no more, defunct 361 adj. *dead*; obsolete; functus officio, over and done with.

Vb. *pass away*, die out, perish from the earth 361 vb. *die, perish*; come to nothing, go, vanish, leave no trace; dematerialize, melt into thin air 446 vb. *disappear*; evaporate 338 vb. *vaporize*; dissolve 337 vb. *liquefy*.

nullify, reduce to nothing, annihilate, snuff out; render null and void 752 vb. *abrogate*; negative 533 vb. *negate*; cancel 550 vb. *obliterate*; abolish, wipe out 165 vb. *destroy*.

3. Substantiality – N. *substantiality*, essentiality 1 n. *reality*; substantivity, objectivity; corporeity, visibility, tangibility, palpability, concreteness, solidity 319 n. *materiality*; ponderability, weight 322 n. *gravity*; stuff, world-s., hyle 319 n. *matter*; plenum, world 321 n. *universe*.

substance, subsistent entity, hypostasis; substratum; thing, something, somebody 319 n. *object*; body, flesh and blood; solid, concretion 324 n. *solid body*; pith, marrow, meat; gist 514 n. *meaning*.

Adj. *substantial*, hypostatic, personal; real, objective, natural, physical 319 adj. *material*; concrete, solid, tangible, palpable 324 adj. *dense*; considerable 638 adj. *important*; bulky 195 adj. *large*, 322 adj. *weighty*; pithy, meaty, full of substance.

4. Unsubstantiality – N. *insubstantiality*, nothingness, nothing 103 n. *zero*; abstraction, incorporeality 320 n. *immateriality*; imponderability 323 n. *levity*; tenuity 206 n. *thinness*; sparseness 325 n. *rarity*; superficiality 212 adj. *shallowness*; intangibility, vanity, vacancy, void 190 n. *emptiness*; pointlessness 10 n. *irrelevance*; hallucination, fantasy 513 n. *imagination*; maya, unreality.

insubstantial thing, emblem, token, symbol 547 n. *indication*; abstraction, shadow, dream; ghost, spirit, optical illusion, will-o'-the-wisp 440 n. *visual fallacy*; air, wind, breath, vapour, mist; bubble, gossamer 163 n. *weak thing*; wisp, straw 639 n. *trifle*; vain thing, vanity, inanity, fatuity, fool's paradise 499 n. *folly*; fancy, figment, pipe-dream 513 n. *fantasy*; moonshine, cock and bull story; gossip, rumour 515 n. *empty talk*; tall talk 546 n. *exaggeration*; mockery, pretence, chimera, courtesy title; nine days' wonder, flash in the pan, damp squib, blank cartridge; cry of 'wolf' 665 n. *false alarm*; figurehead, lay figure, dummy, man of straw; stuffed shirt 639 n. *nonentity*.

Adj. *insubstantial*, abstract; nonphysical 320 adj. *immaterial*; bodiless, bloodless, incorporeal; airy, etherial; thin, tenuous, gauzy, gossamer 422 adj. *transparent*; fragile 330 adj. *brittle*; ghostly, spectral 970 adj. *spooky*; fleeting, shadowy, vague 446 adj. *disappearing*; vacuous, vacant, hollow, void 190 adj. *empty*; vain, inane; nominal, paper, fictitious; symbolic, token 547 adj. *indicating*; groundless, unfounded; visionary, dreamy, chimerical 513 adj. *imaginary*; pointless, meaningless 515 adj. *unmeaning*; superficial 212 adj. *shallow*.

5. Intrinsicality – N. *intrinsicality*, inbeing, inherence, immanence, inwardness; virtuality, potentiality 160 n. *power*; subjectivism, self-reference; ego, personality 80 n. *self*.

essential part, essence, prime constituent; principle, quintessence, stuff; life, life-blood, sap; heart, soul, backbone, marrow, pith; core, kernel; gist, nub 638 n. *chief thing*.

character, nature, quality; constitution, diathesis, ethos; type, make, stamp, breed; characteristics, cast, colour, hue; aspects, features.

temperament, temper, humour, disposition, mood, spirit 817 n. *affections*; crasis, idiosyncrasy; grain, vein, streak, strain, trait 179 n. *tendency*; habit, peculiarity 80 n. *speciality*.

heredity, endowment; gene, allelomorph, inherited characteristic, original sin; ancestry 169 n. *genealogy*; telegony, atavism 106 n. *recurrence*; Galton's law, Mendelian ratio.

Adj. *intrinsic*, immanent, deep down; inherent 58 adj. *ingredient*; inward 224 adj. *interior*; inwrought, implicit; autistic, subjective, introversive, inwardlooking, introverted; characteristic, personal, intimate, native; basic, fundamental, radical; virtual, potential.

genetic, inherited, hereditary, atavistic, inborn; native, congenital; inbred, ingrained, bred in the bone.

characteristic 80 adj. *special*; characterizing, diagnostic, idiomorphic, proper; ineradicable, invariable.

Vb. *be intrinsic*, — immanent etc. adj.; inexist, inhere 773 vb. *belong*; inherit, take after, run in the blood; involve, mean 523 vb. *imply*.

6. Extrinsicality – **N.** *extrinsicality*, objectiveness, objectivity; transcendence, otherness, the other, non-ego 59 n. *extraneousness*; externality, outwardness 223 n. *exteriority*; objectification, externalization; projection, extrapolation; extraversion, extravert; accident, contingency 159 n. *chance*; accrual, accessory, acquired characteristic 40 n. *adjunct*.

Adj. *extrinsic*, transcendent, outward, external 223 adj. *exterior*; outwardlooking, extroitive, extraverted; derived, acquired; accessory 38 adj. *additional*; incidental, accidental, contingent 159 adj. *casual*.

Vb. *be extrinsic*, lie without, not belong; transcend; supervene 38 vb. *accrue*.

make extrinsic, objectify, realize, project, extrapolate, body forth 223 vb. *externalize*.

7. State: absolute condition – **N.** *state*, modal existence, suchness; case, way, plight, pickle 8 n. *circumstance*; position, status, standing, rank; condition, trim, fettle; habit, diathesis 5 n. *temperament*.

modality, mode, fashion, style; stamp, set, fit, mould 243 n. *form*; aspect, phase, light, complexion, guise 445 n. *appearance*; tenor 179 n. *tendency*.

Adj. *conditionate*, conditional, such; modal, formal 243 adj. *formative*; in a state of; in condition, in form 694 adj. *skilful*; in bad form 695 adj. *clumsy*.

Vb. *be in a state of*, be such, be so; stand, lie, labour under; do, fare.

8. Circumstance – **N.** *circumstance*, circumstances, factors, situation; environment, milieu 230 n. *circumjacence*; context 9 n. *relation*; posture, look of things, appearances 445 n. *appearance*; lay of the land 186 n. *bearings*; footing, standing, status 27 n. *degree*, 9 n. *relation*; plight, pickle, pass, pinch, corner 700 n. *predicament*.

juncture, stage, point 154 n. *eventuality*; crossroads, turning point; moment, hour, opportunity 137 n. *occasion*; emergency 137 n. *crisis*.

Adj. *circumstantial*, given, modal 7 adj. *conditionate*; surrounding, environmental, contextual 230 adj. *circumjacent*; contingent, incidental, adventitious 154 adj. *eventful*; appropriate, convenient 642 adj. *expedient*.

Section 2: Relation

9. Relation – **N.** *relation*, relatedness, 'rapport', reference, respect, regard; bearing, direction; concern, interest 638 n. *importance*; involvement, implication 5 n. *intrinsicality*; relationship, affinity, kinship 11 n. *consanguinity*; classification, classifiability 62 n. *arrangement*; association, alliance, intimacy; liaison, linkage, connexion, link, tie-up 47 n. *bond*; common reference, common source, common denominator; context, milieu, environment.

relativeness, relativity; mutual relation, function 12 n. *correlation*; homology, correspondence 13 n. *identity*, 28 n. *equality*; analogy 18 n. *similarity*; comparability 462 n. *comparison*; approximation 200 n. *nearness*; proportionality, perspective, proportion, ratio, scale;

cause and effect 156 n. *cause*; logical relation (see *relevance*); relative position 27 n. *degree*; serial order 65 n. *sequence*.

relevance, logical relation, logicality 475 n. *reasoning*; chain of reasoning 475 n. *argumentation*; fitness, suitability 24 n. *agreement*; point, application, applicability, appositeness, pertinence; case in point, palmary instance 83 n. *example*.

referral, referment, reference; allusion, mention; citation, quotation; frame of reference, referent; referendary, referee.

Adj. *relative*, not absolute; relational, respective; relativistic; referable; en rapport, related, connected; bearing upon, concerning; belonging, appertaining; in common, mutual, reciprocal 12 adj. *correlative*; classifiable 62 adj. *arranged*; affiliated, cognate, kindred 11 adj. *akin*; analogous, like 18 adj. *similar*; comparative 462 adj. *compared*; approximating, approaching 200 adj. *near*; collateral 219 adj. *parallel*; proportional, varying as, in ratio, to scale; proportionable, commensurate 245 adj. *symmetrical*; perspectival, in perspective.

relevant, logical, in context; apposite, pertinent, applicable; to the point, well-directed, proper, appropriate 24 adj. *apt*.

Vb. *be related*, have a relation, tie in with; have a reference, refer to, have to do with; bear upon, be a factor 178 vb. *influence*; touch, concern, deal with, interest, affect; belong, pertain; answer to, correspond, reciprocate 12 vb. *correlate*; be proportionate, vary as; be relevant, have point; come to the point, get down to brass tacks.

relate, bring into relation, put in perspective; connect with, gear to; apply, bear upon; link, tie up with 45 vb. *tie*; frame, provide a background; compare 18 vb. *liken*; parallel, balance 28 vb. *equalize*; refer to, touch on; index, reference.

Adv. *relatively*, not absolutely, in a context, contextually; in its degree, comparatively; in ratio, to scale, in perspective.

concerning, touching, regarding; as to, as regards, with respect to; with reference

to, about, on, in connexion with; speaking of, à propos, by the way, by the bye, on the subject of; in the matter of, in re.

10. Irrelation: absence of relation – **N.** *irrelation*, absoluteness; independence 744 n. *freedom*; arbitrariness, unilaterality; insularity, isolation 46 n. *separation*; unclassifiability, singularity 80 n. *speciality*; lack of connexion, no context; inconsequence (see *irrelevance*); disproportion, asymmetry 246 n. *distortion*; incommensurability 29 n. *inequality*; diversity 15 n. *difference*, 17 n. *non-uniformity*, 82 n. *multiformity*, 84 n. *unconformity*; irreconcilability 14 n. *contrariety*; untimeliness 138 n. *intempestivity*; no concern, no business; square peg in a round hole 25 n. *misfit*; exotic, intruder 59 n. *extraneousness*.

irrelevance, illogicality 477 n. *sophistry*; pointlessness, inapplicability; inconsequence, non sequitur; parenthesis 231 n. *interjacence*; diversion, red herring; inessential 639 n. *unimportance*.

Adj. *irrelative*, unrelated, absolute; independent 744 adj. *unconfined*; owing nothing to, original 21 adj. *unimitated*; unilateral, arbitrary; unclassified, unidentified; unclassifiable, rootless, homeless; isolated, insular 88 adj. *alone*; unconcerned, uninvolved 860 adj. *indifferent*; unconnected, without context; digressive, parenthetic; singular, individual 80 adj. *special*; private, of no concern; exotic, foreign 59 adj. *extraneous*; intrusive, untimely 138 adj. *ill-timed*; inappropriate 25 adj. *unapt*; incommensurable, disparate 29 adj. *unequal*; disproportionate 246 adj. *distorted*; incongruent 84 adj. *unconformable*; heterogeneous 17 adj. *non-uniform*; multifarious 82 adj. *multiform*.

irrelevant, illogical; inapposite, inapplicable, pointless; out of order, misapplied, misplaced, misdirected 495 adj. *erroneous*; off-target, off-centre, peripheral; beside the point, neither here nor there; inconsequent, inconsequential; parenthetic, episodic; academic, impractical.

Vb. *be unrelated*, have no concern with, owe nothing to; not be one's business, not concern; be off the point, avoid the issue, draw a red herring; force, strain; lose the thread 570 vb. *be diffuse.*

11. Consanguinity: relations of kindred – N. *consanguinity*, relationship, kinship, kindred, blood 169 n. *parentage*; filiation, apparentation, affinity; agnation, cognation; ancestry, lineage, descent; nepotism; atavism.

kinsman, kinswoman; kindred, kith and kin, brethren, relations; relative, next of kin; children, offspring, issue, one's flesh and blood; agnate, cognate, congener, affine; twin, brother, sister; cousin german; uncle, aunt; nephew, niece; father, mother 169 n. *parent*; clansman, tribesman, compatriot, fellow.

family, matriarch, patriarch; motherhood, fatherhood, brotherhood, sisterhood; fraternity, sorority, phratry; gens, gotra, one's people; foster son, godson, stepson; godparents, gossip, in-laws; circle, family c. 882 n. *sociality*; household, homefolks; tribe, horde.

race, stock, generation, breed, strain, line, side; tribe, phyle, clan, sept, blood group; tribalism, nationality, gentility.

Adj. *akin*, sib, kindred, consanguineous, twin-born; matrilinear, out of; patrilinear, by; maternal, paternal; fraternal, brotherly, sisterly, cousinly; avuncular; novercal; related, family, collateral, allied, affined; agnate, cognate, german, uterine; near, related; next-of-kin; step-.

ethnic, racial, tribal, phyletic, clannish, gentile 371 adj. *national*; inter-racial, inter-tribal.

Vb. *be akin*, share the blood of; father, sire, dam 164 vb. *generate*; affiliate, adopt, bring into the family.

12. Correlation: double or reciprocal relation – N. *correlation*, correlativity, functionality 9 n. *relation*; proportion 245 n. *symmetry*; grid 222 n. *network*; correspondence, opposite number; mutuality, interrelation, interconnexion, interdependence; interaction, interplay; alternation 317 n. *oscillation*; reciprocity, reciprocation 151 n. *interchange*; each, each other, one another; lex talionis 714 n. *retaliation.*

Adj. *correlative*, reciprocal, functional 9 adj. *relative*; corresponding, answering to; proportional, proportionate 245 adj. *symmetrical*; mutual, reciprocating, reacting; alternating, alternate, see-saw 317 adj. *oscillating*; interlocking, geared, interacting; interchangeable, exchangeable; inter-, two-way.

Vb. *correlate*, interrelate, interconnect, interlock, interplay, interact; vary as, be a function of; proportion, symmetrize; reciprocate, correspond, answer to; react 280 vb. *recoil*; exchange, counterchange, chop, swop, barter 791 vb. *trade*; balance 28 vb. *equalize*; set off 31 vb. *compensate.*

Adv. *correlatively*, proportionately, as ... so ...; mutually, reciprocally, alternately, turn and turn about, vice versa.

13. Identity – N. *identity*, sameness, oneness 88 n. *unity*; the same, no other; genuineness 494 n. *authenticity*; the real thing, it 21 n. *no imitation*; ipsissima verba, ditto 106 n. *repetition*; oneself, myself 80 n. *self*; other self, alter ego, double; oneness with, identification, coalescence, absorption 299 n. *reception*; interchangeability, equivalence 28 n. *equality*; same kind, homogeneity 16 n. *uniformity*; no change, invariability, invariant, constant 153 n. *fixture.*

Adj. *identical*, same, selfsame; one and the same, one and only 88 adj. *one*; identified with, indistinguishable; invariable, constant 153 adj. *unchangeable*; homogeneous, monolithic 16 adj. *uniform.*

Vb. *be identical*, show no difference, ditto 106 vb. *repeat*; coincide, coalesce, merge, be one with, sink one's identity.

identify, treat as one, not distinguish 464 vb. *not discriminate*; equate 28 vb. *equalize*; assimilate, match, pair 18 vb.

liken; classify 561 vb. *name*, 80 vb. *specify*.

14. Contrariety – N. *contrariety*, absolute difference, world of d. 15 n. *difference*; mutual exclusiveness, irreconcilability 10 n. *irrelation*; antipathy 888 n. *hatred*; adverseness, contrariness, antagonism 704 n. *opposition*; antidote 182 n. *counteraction*; conflict, clash 279 n. *collision*; discord 25 n. *disagreement*; contradistinction, contrast, relief, variation 463 n. *discrimination*; contradiction 533 n. *negation*; contra-indication, counter-symptom 467 n. *counter-evidence*; counterterm, antonym 514 n. *meaning*; inconsistency, two voices 17 n. *non-uniformity*; antithesis, direct opposite, antipodes, opposite pole, other extreme 240 n. *contraposition*; reverse, wrong side 238 n. *rear*; converse, reverse image 417 n. *reflection*; opposing tendencies, polarity.

Adj. *contrary*, as different as chalk from cheese, anything but 15 adj. *different*; contrasting 25 adj. *disagreeing*; inconsistent 17 adj. *non-uniform*; ambivalent, bitter sweet; contradictory, antithetic 533 adj. *negative*; diametrically opposite, poles asunder, antipodal, antipodean 240 adj. *opposite*; reverse, converse, inverse; antipathetic, repugnant 888 adj. *hating*; adverse, antagonistic 704 adj. *opposing*; counter-active, antidotal 182 adj. *counteracting*; counter-, anti-.

Vb. *be contrary*, have nothing in common 10 vb. *be unrelated*, 15 vb. *differ*, 57 vb. *exclude*; contrast, stand out 25 vb. *disagree*; clash, discord; run counter 240 vb. *be opposite*; contravene, fly in the face of 704 vb. *oppose*, 738 vb. *disobey*; contradict 533 vb. *negate*; counteract 658 vb. *remedy*; reverse, turn the tables 221 vb. *invert*.

Adv. *contrarily*, contra, per c., on the other hand, on the contrary, contrariwise; topsy-turvy, upside down, invertedly, inversely.

15. Difference – N. *difference*, unlikeness 19 n. *dissimilarity*; disparity, odds 29 n. *inequality*; margin, differential, minus, plus 41 n. *remainder*; variety, diversity, mixed bag 17 n. *non-uniformity*; divergence 282 n. *deviation*; discrepancy, incongruity, incompatibility, antipathy 25 n. *disagreement*; discord, variance 709 n. *dissension*; non-conformity 84 n. *unconformity*; variation, modification, alteration 143 n. *change*, 147 n. *conversion*.

differentiation 463 n. *discrimination*; specification 80 n. *speciality*; distinction, nuance, shade of difference.

variant, differential, different thing; another story, another version; special case 80 n. *speciality*.

Adj. *different*, unlike 19 adj. *dissimilar*; original 21 adj. *unimitated*; various, variform, diverse, heterogeneous 17 adj. *non-uniform*; multifarious 82 adj. *multiform*; divergent 282 adj. *deviating*; discrepant, discordant, incongruous 25 adj. *disagreeing*; disparate 29 adj. *unequal*; contrasting, far from it, poles asunder, anything but 14 adj. *contrary*; other, peculiar 80 adj. *special*.

distinctive, diagnostic 5 adj. *characteristic*; differentiating, distinguishing; elative, comparative, superlative, augmentative.

Vb. *differ*, diverge from, depart f. 282 vb. *deviate*; contrast, clash 25 vb. *disagree*, 709 vb. *quarrel*; modify, vary.

differentiate, distinguish, severalize 463 vb. *discriminate*; shade, refine, particularize 80 vb. *specify*.

16. Uniformity – N. *uniformity*, consistency, constancy, steadiness 153 n. *stability*; regularity, centralization 60 n. *order*; homogeneity, monolithic quality; unity, unison 24 n. *agreement*; sameness, invariability, monotony, even tenor, mixture as before; even pace, rhythm; daily round, routine 610 n. *habit*; monotone, greyness; monolith; assimilation, standardization, mass-production 83 n. *conformity*.

Adj. *uniform*, all of a piece, one-piece, monolithic; of a piece, of a pattern 18 adj. *similar*; same, consistent, constant, steady, stable 153 adj. *fixed*; undeviating, unchanging, unvarying, invariable, undiversified, undifferentiated, unrelieved, unbroken, uncontrasting; uniformed, liveried; characterless, featureless, faceless, blank; monotonous, monotone; standard, normal 83 adj. *typical*; patterned, standardized, stereotyped, mass-produced; sized, drilled, dressed, aligned; regular, square, equilateral, circular 245 adj. *symmetrical*; straight, level, even, flush, flat 258 adj. *smooth*.

Vb. *be uniform*, follow routine 610 vb. *be wont*; sing in unison, chorus 24 vb. *accord*; dress, fall in.

make uniform, stamp, characterize, run through 547 vb. *mark*; assimilate, level, tar with the same brush 18 vb. *liken*; size, drill, dress, align; standardize, stereotype, pattern; normalize, regularize 83 vb. *make conform*.

17. Non-uniformity – N. *non-uniformity*, variability, patchiness 72 n. *discontinuity*; unpredictability 152 n. *changeableness*; inconstancy, inconsistency 604 n. *caprice*; irregularity, chaos 61 n. *disorder*; untidiness 63 n. *derangement*; ruggedness, asymmetry 244 n. *amorphism*; raggedness, unevenness 259 n. *roughness*; heterogeneity 15 n. *difference*; contrast 19 n. *dissimilarity*; diversity, variety 82 n. *multiformity*; all sorts and conditions, mixed bag, lucky dip, odds and ends 43 n. *mixture*; patchwork, motley, mosaic; abnormality 84 n. *unconformity*; odd man out, lone wolf 59 n. *extraneousness*; uniqueness, nonce word; decentralization.

Adj. *non-uniform*, variable, unpredictable 152 adj. *changeful*; inconsistent 604 adj. *capricious*; irregular, unsystematic; patternless, patchy, shapeless 244 adj. *amorphous*; untidy, chaotic 61 adj. *orderless*; uneven 259 adj. *rough*; erratic, out of step, out of time, gaining, losing; heterogeneous 15 adj. *different*, 19 adj. *dissimilar*; multifarious 82 adj. *multiform*; divergent 282 adj. *deviating*; aberrant, atypical 84 adj. *unconformable*;

exceptional 84 adj. *abnormal*; unique, lone 59 adj. *extraneous*.

18. Similarity – N. *similarity*, resemblance, likeness, similitude; semblance, seeming, look, fashion 445 n. *appearance*, 243 n. *form*; affinity, kinship; comparability, analogy, parallelism 12 n. *correlation*; equivalence 28 n. *equality*; proportionality 245 n. *symmetry*; general resemblance, family likeness; approximation, adumbration, hint; fair comparison, the size of it.

assimilation, reduction to, likening 462 n. *comparison*; simulation, camouflage, disguise 20 n. *imitation*; portrayal 590 n. *description*, 551 n. *representation*; alliteration, assonance.

analogue, congener, the like, likes of; type 83 n. *example*; simile, parallel, equivalent; brother, sister, twin; match, fellow, mate, companion, pair, double; complement, counterpart; likeness, reflection 551 n. *image*; another edition of, dead spit, living image; twins, two peas, couple, two of a kind; reproduction 22 n. *duplicate*.

Adj. *similar*, resembling, like; alike, twin, matching; of a piece 16 adj. *uniform*; analogical; analogous, parallel, equivalent 28 adj. *equal*; cognate 11 adj. *akin*; close, approximate 200 adj. *near*; typical, representative 551 n. *representing*; such as, quasi.

lifelike, realistic, photographic, exact, faithful, natural, typical; true to life, true to nature, true to type.

simulating, 20 adj. *imitative*; seeming, deceptive, camouflaged 542 adj. *deceiving*; mock, pseudo 542 adj. *spurious*; artificial, ersatz 150 adj. *substituted*.

Vb. *resemble*, pass for; mirror, reflect 20 vb. *imitate*; seem, look like, take after; savour of, smack of; approximate to 289 vb. *approach*; match, correspond to 9 vb. *relate*; assonate, rhyme; run in pairs.

liken, assimilate to, reduce to 13 vb. *identify*; match, twin, bracket with 28 vb. *equalize*; portray 20 vb. *imitate*; alliterate, rhyme 106 vb. *repeat*.

19. Dissimilarity – N. *dissimilarity*, unlikeness; disparity 29 n. *inequality*; diversity, variation, variety 17 n. *nonuniformity*, 82 n. *multiformity*; contrast 14 n. *contrariety*; little in common, no match, uniqueness 21 n. *non-imitation*; dissimilation, camouflage 527 n. *disguise*; caricature, bad likeness, false copy 552 n. *misrepresentation*; foreign body, alien element 59 n. *intruder*.

Adj. *dissimilar*, unlike, unalike, diverse 15 adj. *different*; various 82 adj. *multiform*; disparate 29 adj. *unequal*; unique, one and only, original 21 adj. *unimitated*; incongruent 25 adj. *disagreeing*; untypical, exotic 84 adj. *unconformable*; unprecedented 126 adj. *new*.

Vb. *be unlike*, etc. adj.; have nothing in common 15 vb. *differ*; stand out 34 vb. *be superior*, 35 vb. *be inferior*.

make unlike, discriminate 15 vb. *differentiate*; change 143 vb. *modify*, 147 vb. *convert*; caricature 552 vb. *misrepresent*, 246 vb. *distort*; dissemble 542 vb. *deceive*; disguise 525 vb. *conceal*; camouflage 541 vb. *fake*.

20. Imitation – N. *imitation*, copying etc. vb.; rivalry, emulation, competition 911 n. *jealousy*; conventionality, traditionalism 83 n. *conformity*; imitativeness, (see *mimicry*); affectedness 850 n. *affectation*; mimesis 551 n. *representation*; reflection, mirror, echo, shadow 18 n. *assimilation*; paraphrase, translation 520 n. *interpretation*; cribbing, plagiarism; forgery, counterfeit, fake 541 n. *falsehood*; copying, transcription, transliteration; duplication, multiplication 166 n. *reproduction*.

mimicry, mimesis, noises off 594 n. *dramaturgy*; mime, pantomime, sign language 547 n. *gesture*; ventriloquism; portraiture; realism 494 n. *accuracy*; caricature, parody 851 n. *satire*; travesty 552 n. *misrepresentation*; imitativeness, parrotry; conjuring, illusionism; simulation, disguise, camouflage, dissimulation 18 n. *similarity*, 19 n. *dissimilarity*; pretence, mockery, simulacrum, shadow 542 n. *sham*, 4 n. *insubstantiality*.

imitator, copycat, ape; mocking-bird, parrot, echo; sheep 83 n. *conformist*; poseur 850 n. *affector*; yes-man 925 n. *flatterer*; mime, mimic, impersonator, ventriloquist, conjuror, illusionist 594 n. *entertainer*; actor, portrayer; copyist, copy-typist; translator, paraphraser 520 n. *interpreter*; simulator, hypocrite 545 n. *impostor*; borrower, plagiarist; counterfeiter, forger, faker.

Adj. *imitative*, apish, parrot-like; pseudo, sham, phony, counterfeit 541 adj. *false*; ersatz, synthetic 150 adj. *substituted*; unoriginal, derivative, secondhand, conventional 83 adj. *conformable*; paraphrastic, slavish, literal; easy to copy, imitable.

Vb. *imitate*, ape, parrot, flatter, echo, mirror, reflect 18 vb. *resemble*; pose 850 vb. *be affected*; pretend, make-believe; act, mimic, mime, portray 551 vb. *represent*; parody, caricature, burlesque, travesty 851 vb. *ridicule*; sham, simulate, put on 541 vb. *dissemble*; disguise, camouflage 525 vb. *conceal*.

copy, draw, counterdraw, trace; catch, realize; quote, cite 106 vb. *repeat*; reprint, duplicate; reduplicate, multiply, reel off 166 vb. *reproduce*; copy out, transcribe, type out; paraphrase, translate 520 vb. *interpret*; crib, plagiarize, borrow; counterfeit, forge 541 vb. *fake*.

do likewise, do as the Romans do, mould *or* pattern oneself on, understudy; follow suit, follow my leader; do after, say a., echo, chorus; join in the cry, hunt with the hounds, jump on the bandwagon 83 vb. *conform*; emulate, compete, take a leaf out of another's book.

Adv. *imitatively*, emulously; literally, word for word, verbatim, literatim; sic, as per copy.

21. Non-imitation – N. *non-imitation*, creativeness, inventiveness; creation, all my own work; originality, uniqueness, the one and only; inimitability, transcendence; independence, line of one's own; precedent 23 n. *prototype*; novelty, freshness 126 n. *newness*; eccentricity, individuality 84 n. *unconformity*; unlikeness 19 n. *dissimilarity*.

no imitation, genuineness, real thing, genuine article, it, absolutely it 494 n. *authenticity*; autograph, holograph.

Adj. *unimitative*, creative, inventive, original, not derivative; prototypal, archetypal; first-hand 119 adj. *prior*; fresh 126 adj. *new*; individual, personal 80 adj. *special*; independent, eccentric 84 adj. *unconformable*.

unimitated, inimitable, transcendent, incomparable; unhackneyed, unplagiarized; unique, one and only.

22. Copy – **N.** *copy*, reproduction, replica, facsimile, tracing; apograph, transcript, ectype, stamp, seal, impress, impression, squeeze; stereotype 555 n. *engraving*; an imitation, dummy; forgery, plagiarism, crib 20 n. *imitation*; a likeness, antitype 18 n. *similarity*; study, portrait 553 n. *picture*; image, form, model, effigy 554 n. *sculpture*; echo, mirror 417 n. *reflection*; apology for, mockery of 552 n. *misrepresentation*; caricature, cartoon, travesty, parody 851 n. *ridicule*; adumbration, shadow, silhouette, outline.

duplicate, counterpart, reproduction, cast; carbon copy, stencil, transfer, rubbing; photograph, photoprint, print 551 n. *photography*; proof, pull, revise; reprint; model, specimen, show copy 83 n. *example*.

23. Prototype – **N.** *prototype*, archetype; common type, everyman; primitive form, protoplasm, original; first occurrence, precedent, test case 119 n. *priority*; guide, standard, criterion, frame of reference; ideal, cynosure 646 n. *paragon*; keynote; specimen, sample 83 n. *example*; model, subject; exemplar, pattern, paradigm; dummy, mock-up; blueprint, design, master-plan 623 n. *plan*.

living model, model, poser, sitter, subject; mannequin; fugleman, stroke, band-leader, conductor, drum-major, drill master 690 n. *leader*.

mould, matrix, mint; plate, shell; frame, wax figure, lay-f., tailor's dummy; last; boot-tree; die, stamp, punch, seal.

Vb. *be an example*, serve as a model, model, sit for, pose.

24. Agreement – **N.** *agreement*, consent 488 n. *assent*; accord, accordance, chorus, unison; harmony, consonance, attunement; concert, understanding, entente; convention, pact 765 n. *compact*; unanimity 488 n. *consensus*; peace 710 n. *concord*.

conformance 83 n. *conformity*; congruence, coincidence; consistency 16 n. *uniformity*; consequence, logical conclusion 475 n. *reasoning*; correspondence, parallelism 18 n. *similarity*.

fitness, aptness, qualification, capability 694 n. *aptitude*; suitability, propriety 642 n. *expedience*; perfect candidate, the very thing; relevancy, pertinence, admissibility, appositeness, case in point, good example 9 n. *relevance*; timeliness 137 n. *occasion*.

adaptation, conformation, harmonization, synchronization, matching 18 n. *assimilation*; reconciliation; accommodation, attunement, adjustment; compatibility, congeniality; good fit, perfect f.

Adj. *agreeing*, right, accordant; corresponding, answering; coinciding, congruent 28 adj. *equal*; on all fours, consistent 83 adj. *conformable*; in step, in phase, in tune, synchronized 123 adj. *synchronous*; consonant, concordant; combining, suiting, matching; congenial, sympathetic; reconcilable, compatible, coexisting, symbiotic; agreeable, acquiescent 488 adj. *assenting*; concurrent, in chorus, unanimous, like-minded, bipartisan; in treaty, negotiating 765 adj. *contractual*.

apt, applicable, germane, appropriate, pertinent, in point 9 adj. *relevant*; pat, in place, right, happy, felicitous; seasonable, opportune 137 adj. *timely*.

fit, suitable, suited, well-adapted, adaptable; capable, qualified, cut out for.

adjusted, timed, synchronized; tuned, strung, pitched, attuned; trimmed, balanced; well-cut, fitting, snug, comfortable.

Vb. *accord*, agree, concur 488 vb. *assent*, 758 vb. *consent*; echo, chorus, chime in, ditto 106 vb. *repeat*; coincide, register, square with, dove-tail, fit; tally, match, go with, tone in w., harmonize; comport with, come natural; fit in, belong; answer, meet, suit, do 642 vb. *be expedient*; fall pat, fit the occasion, befit; keep together, hunt t. 706 vb. *cooperate*; be logical 475 vb. *be reasonable*; concert, treat, negotiate 766 vb. *make terms*; get on with, hit it off, fraternize 880 vb. *befriend*; sing together, choir.

adjust, fit, suit, adapt, accommodate, conform, synchronize; attune, tune, pitch, string; modulate, tune in; regulate; graduate, proportion 12 vb. *correlate*; size 62 vb. *arrange*; balance, trim; tailor, make to measure.

25. Disagreement – N. *disagreement*, disaccord 489 n. *dissent*; dissidence 84 n. *unconformity*; controversy 475 n. *argument*; wrangle, bickering 709 n. *quarrel*; disunion, faction 709 n. *dissension*; clash 279 n. *collision*; rupture, breach 718 n. *war*; discrepancy 15 n. *difference*; two voices, ambiguity 518 n. *equivocalness*; variety 437 n. *variegation*; opposition 14 n. *contrariety*; dissonance, tunelessness 411 n. *discord*; incongruence 10 n. *irrelation*; disparity 29 n. *inequality*; asymmetry 246 n. *distortion*; incompatibility, irreconcilability 861 n. *dislike*, 881 n. *enmity*; interference 702 n. *hindrance*.

inaptitude, unfitness, incapacity, incompetence 695 n. *unskilfulness*; impropriety 643 n. *inexpedience*; intrusion, interruption, untimeliness 138 n. *intempestivity*.

misfit, maladjustment, bad fit; bad match, misalliance; misjoinder; false note, jar 411 n. *discord*; fish out of water, square peg in a round hole; outsider 59 n. *intruder*; odd man out, sport 84 n. *abnormality*; eccentric, oddity.

Adj. *disagreeing*, unagreed 489 adj. *dissenting*; at odds, at variance, at loggerheads 718 adj. *warring*; hostile, antagonistic 881 adj. *inimical*; uncongenial, antipathetic; contradictory 14 adj. *contrary*; unnatural; inconsistent 17 adj. *non-uniform*; incompatible 84 adj. *unconformable*; exceptional 84 adj. *abnormal*; foreign 59 adj. *extraneous*; incommensurable 10 adj. *irrelative*; disproportionate, unsymmetrical 246 adj. *distorted*; grating 411 adj. *discordant*; mismatched, mis-allied, misjoined; ill-matched; discrepant 15 adj. *different*; incongruous 497 adj. *absurd*.

unapt, inept, incapable, incompetent 695 adj. *unskilful*; wrong, unfitting, unsuitable, unbecoming, improper 643 adj. *inexpedient*; impracticable 470 adj. *impossible*; ineligible 607 adj. *rejected*; not wanted, inopportune 138 adj. *ill-timed*; mal-à-propos 10 adj. *irrelevant*; out of character, out of keeping, misplaced, out of place.

Vb. *disagree* 489 vb. *dissent*; dispute 475 vb. *argue*; jangle, bicker 709 vb. *quarrel*; clash, conflict 14 vb. *be contrary*; not play, non-cooperate 702 vb. *hinder*; come amiss, intrude 138 vb. *mistime*.

mismatch, mismate, misjoin; misadapt, misfit, misadjust; miscast; mistime.

Section 3: Quantity

26. Quantity – N. *quantity*, amount, sum 38 n. *addition*; magnitude, amplitude, extent 465 n. *measurement*; mass, bulk 195 n. *size*; dimensions 203 n. *length*, 205 n. *breadth*, 209 n. *height*, 211 n. *depth*; area, volume 183 n. *space*; weight 322 n. *gravity*; force 160 n. *energy*; numbers 104 n. *multitude*; quotient, fraction, multiple 85 n. *number*, 86 n. *mathematics*, 101 n. *plurality*, 102 n. *fraction*, 103 n. *zero*, 107 n. *infinity*; mean 30 n. *average*.

finite quantity, lower limit, upper 1., ceiling 236 n. *limit*; quantum, quota, quorum; measure, dose 465 n. *measurement*; avoirdupois 322 n. *weighment*; ration 783 n. *portion*; pittance, driblet; lot, batch, boiling; lock, stock, and barrel

52 n. *whole*; masses, heaps 32 n. *great quantity*; bit 33 n. *small quantity*; majority 104 n. *greater number*; less 37 n. *decrease*, 39 n. *subduction*, 105 n. *fewness*; stint, piece, task 682 n. *labour*.

Adj. *quantitative*, quantified, measured.

Vb. *quantify*, allot, rate, ration 783 vb. *apportion*.

27. Degree: relative quantity – N. *degree*, proportion, ratio, scale 12 n. *correlation*, 462 n. *comparison*; standard; amplitude, extent, intensity, frequency, magnitude, size 26 n. *quantity*; level, pitch; reach, compass, scope 183 n. *range*; rate, speed 265 n. *motion*; gradation, graduation, calibration 15 n. *differentiation*; differential, shade, nuance; grade, remove, stepping-stone; step, rung 308 n. *ascent*; point, stage, milestone 8 n. *juncture*; climax 725 n. *completion*; mark, peg, notch, score 547 n. *indicator*; valuation 465 n. *measurement*; rank, grade 73 n. *serial place*; place 187 n. *location*.

Adj. *gradational*, hierarchical, graduated, scalar, calibrated, graded, scaled; gradual, shading off, tapering, fading.

comparative, relative, proportional, in scale 9 adj. *relative*.

Vb. *graduate*, grade, rate, class, rank; scale, calibrate; compare, measure.

shade off, taper, die away, pass into, melt into, dissolve, fade; whittle, pare, trim 204 vb. *shorten*.

Adv. *by degrees*, gradually, little by little, step by step, drop by drop, bit by bit, inch by inch, by inches.

28. Equality: sameness of quantity or degree – N. *equality*, parity, co-extension; symmetry, balance; evenness, level; roundness 250 n. *circularity*; equability, monotony 16 n. *uniformity*; impartiality 913 n. *justice*.

equivalence, sameness 13 n. *identity*; interchangeability 151 n. *interchange*; synonymity; reciprocation, fair exchange; equivalent, fair value; not a pin to choose, six of one and half a dozen of

the other, distinction without a difference; equation.

equilibrium, equipoise, balance; even keel, steadiness; deadlock, stalemate; status quo, equilibration, homeostasis; sea-legs, seat; equilibrist, tight-rope walker.

equalization, equation; weighing 322 n. *weighment*; coordination, adjustment, levelling up or down 31 n. *compensation*; reciprocity 12 n. *correlation*; tit for tat 714 n. *retaliation*; counterpoise 31 n. *offset*; equator 92 n. *dividing line*; standardizer, bed of Procrustes.

draw, drawn game, ding-dong, level-pegging; tie, dead heat; no decision, stalemate; love all, fifteen all, etc. deuce.

compeer, peer, equal, match, fellow 18 n. *analogue*; equivalent, parallel, opposite number; rival, competitor 716 n. *contender*.

Adj. *equal*, equi-, iso-, co-; same 13 adj. *identical*; like 18 adj. *similar*; neither more nor less, coextensive, congruent 24 adj. *agreeing*; equidistant; isotropic; homeostatic, steady, stable 153 adj. *fixed*; even, level, round, square, flush 258 vb. *smooth*; symmetrical, even-sided, equilateral, regular 16 adj. *uniform*; equable, unvarying, ding-dong 153 adj. *unchangeable*; competitive, rival 716 adj. *contending*; matched, parallel, level-pegging, running level, abreast, neck-and-neck; equalized, bracketed; sharing, half-and-half, fifty-fifty; on a par, on a level; par, quits.

equivalent, comparable, parallel, interchangeable, synonymous; corresponding, reciprocal 12 adj. *correlative*; as good as, tantamount, virtually the same, indistinguishable; all one, as broad as it is long 18 adj. *similar*; worth, valued at 809 adj. *priced*.

Vb. *be equal*, equal, counterpoise 31 vb. *set off*; add nothing, come to the same thing, coincide 24 vb. *accord*; measure up to, reach; cope with, make the grade 635 vb. *suffice*; hold one's own, keep up with; parallel; tie, draw, halve the match; break even; go halves 775 vb. *participate*.

equalize, equiparate, equate; bracket, match; parallel 462 vb. *compare*; balance, poise; trim, dress, square 16 vb. *make uniform*; counterpoise 31 vb. *set off*; give points to, handicap 31 vb. *compensate*; equilibrate 153 vb. *stabilize*; right oneself, keep one's balance.

Adv. *equally* etc. adj.; pari passu, ceteris paribus; au pair, on equal terms.

29. Inequality: difference of degree or quality – **N.** *inequality*, difference of degree 34 n. *superiority*, 35 n. *inferiority*; irregularity 17 n. *non-uniformity*; variability, patchiness 437 n. *variegation*; disproportion, asymmetry 246 n. *distortion*; skewness, lop-sidedness 220 n. *obliquity*; disparity 15 n. *difference*; disequilibrium, instability, imbalance; preponderance, overweight, top-hamper 322 n. *gravity*; short weight 323 n. *levity*; defect, shortcoming 636 n. *insufficiency*; odds 15 n. *difference*; makeweight 31 n. *offset*.

Adj. *unequal*, disparate 15 adj. *different*; disproportionate, asymmetrical 246 adj. *distorted*; irregular, scalene, lop-sided 17 adj. *non-uniform*; askew, awry 220 adj. *sloping*; odd, uneven; variable, patchy 437 adj. *variegated*; deficient, inadequate 636 adj. *insufficient*; underweight 323 adj. *light*; overweight 322 adj. *heavy*; unbalanced, untrimmed, unballasted, uncompensated; top-heavy; biased, listing 220 adj. *oblique*; overbalanced, dizzy, toppling 309 adj. *descending*.

Vb. *be unequal*, fall short 35 vb. *be inferior*, 636 vb. *not suffice*; preponderate, give points to, overtop, outclass, outrank 34 vb. *be superior*; outstrip; lag 136 vb. *be late*; overcompensate, overweigh, tip the scale 322 vb. *weigh*; overbalance, capsize 221 vb. *be inverted*; list, tilt, lean 220 vb. *be oblique*; rock, swing, sway.

30. Mean – N. *average*, medium, mean, median; intermedium, middle term; happy medium, golden mean 177 n. *moderation*; ruck, run of the mill 732 n. *mediocrity*.

middle point, mediety, half way 70 n.

middle; middle distance, middle age; middle of the road, mid-way 625 n. *midcourse*.

middle class, bourgeoisie, bourgeois, black-coat worker, white-collar w.

common man, 869 n. *commoner*; man-in-the-street, little man 79 n. *everyman*.

Adj. *median*, mean, average, medial 70 adj. *middle*, 225 adj. *central*; lukewarm, intermediate, grey; normal, standard, ordinary, commonplace, middling, fifty-fifty, much of a muchness, mediocre; moderate, neutral, middle-of-the-road; middle-class, middle-grade, bourgeois.

Vb. *average out*, average, take the mean, keep to the middle; split the difference, go half way 770 vb. *compromise*.

31. Compensation – N. *compensation*, weighting 28 n. *equalization*; retrieval, recovery, break-back, come-b.; reaction, neutralization 182 n. *counteraction*; indemnification, reparation 787 n. *restitution*; amends, expiation 941 n. *atonement*; recompense, repayment 962 n. *reward*; measure for measure 714 n. *retaliation*.

offset, set-off, allowance, makeweight, balance, counterweight, counterpoise, counterbalance, ballast 28 n. *equalization*; indemnity, reparations, costs, damages 787 n. *restitution*; quid pro quo, cover, collateral 150 n. *substitute*; concession 770 n. *compromise*.

Adj. *compensatory*, compensating, countervailing, balancing 28 adj. *equivalent*; indemnificatory, restitutory 787 adj. *restoring*.

Vb. *compensate*, make amends; do penance 941 vb. *atone*; indemnify 787 vb. *restitute*; make up for, do instead 150 vb. *substitute*; add a makeweight, ballast; overcompensate, lean over backwards.

set off, offset, allow for; counterpoise, countervail, balance 28 vb. *equalize*; neutralize 182 vb. *counteract*; cover, hedge 858 vb. *be cautious*; give and take, concede 770 vb. *compromise*.

recoup, recover 656 vb. *retrieve*; indemnify oneself, take back; make up leeway, take up the slack; make a come-back 656 vb. *be restored.*

32. Greatness – N. *greatness,* largeness, bigness 195 n. *size;* large scale, vastness, enormousness, gigantism 195 n. *hugeness;* amplitude, fullness, plenitude, maximum 54 n. *completeness,* 637 n. redundance, exorbitance, excess 546 n. *exaggeration;* enormity, immensity 107 n. *infinity;* dimensions, magnitude 26 n. *quantity,* 27 n. *degree;* spaciousness 183 n. *room;* mightiness, might, strength, intensity 160 n. *power,* 178 n. *influence;* intensification, magnification, multiplication 197 n. *expansion;* aggrandizement 36 n. *increase;* seriousness 638 n. *importance;* eminence 34 n. *superiority;* grandeur 868 n. *nobility;* majesty 733 n. *authority.*

great quantity, muchness, galore 635 n. *plenty;* profusion, abundance 171 n. *productiveness;* superfluity, superabundance, spate 637 n. *redundance;* sight of, world of, power of; much, lot, great deal; stock, mint, mine 632 n. *store;* quantities, lots, lashings, oodles, scads, wads, pots, bags; heaps, loads, masses, stacks; oceans, seas, floods, streams; volumes, reams, pages; numbers, crowds, masses, hosts, swarms 104 n. *multitude;* all, entirety 52 n. *whole.*

main part, almost all, best part 52 n. *chief part;* majority 104 n. *greater number;* body, bulk, mass 3 n. *substance.*

Adj. *great,* main, most, major; maximum 34 adj. *supreme;* grand, big 195 adj. *large;* substantial, considerable; sizeable, full-size, man-s.; bulky, massy, massive 322 adj. *weighty;* ample, voluminous, capacious 183 adj. *spacious;* profound 211 adj. *deep;* tall, lofty, towering, mountainous 209 adj. *high;* Herculean 162 adj. *strong;* mighty 160 adj. *powerful,* 178 adj. *influential;* intense 174 adj. *vigorous;* soaring, mounting 308 adj. *ascending,* 197 adj. *expanded;* culminating, at the maximum, at the peak, at its height 213 adj. *topmost;* plentiful, abundant, overflowing 635

adj. *plenteous;* many, swarming, teeming 104 adj. *multitudinous;* imperial, august 868 adj. *noble;* sublime, exalted 821 adj. *impressive;* glorious, worshipful 866 adj. *renowned;* grave, solemn, serious 638 adj. *important;* excellent 306 adj. *surpassing,* 644 adj. *best;* flagrant, unconscionable; remarkable 638 adj. *notable;* unspeakable 517 adj. *inexpressible;* exorbitant 735 adj. *oppressive;* consummate 54 adj. *complete,* 646 adj. *perfect;* absolute 44 adj. *unmixed.*

extensive, ranging, far-flying, far-flung, far-reaching, far-stretching 183 adj. *spacious;* wide-spread, prevalent, epidemic; world-wide, universal, cosmic; mass, indiscriminate, wholesale, whole-hogging, all-embracing, comprehensive 78 adj. *inclusive.*

enormous, immense, vast, colossal, monumental 195 adj. *huge;* record-breaking 306 adj. *surpassing.*

prodigious, marvellous, astounding 864 adj. *wonderful;* fabulous, incredible 486 adj. *unbelieved,* 472 adj. *improbable,* 470 adj. *impossible;* stupendous 854 adj. *frightening;* remarkable, breath-taking, overwhelming, out of this world 821 adj. *impressive.*

whopping, whacking, thumping, thundering, rattling, howling, screaming, swingeing; father and mother of.

Vb. *be great,* — large etc. adj.; bulk, loom; stretch 183 n. *extend;* tower, soar, mount; transcend 34 vb. *be superior;* exceed, know no bounds 306 vb. *overstep;* swamp, overwhelm.

Adv. *greatly,* much, well; passing, very, right; mighty, ever so; fully, entirely, utterly, unreservedly 52 adv. *wholly,* 54 adv. *completely;* widely, extensively, universally; largely, mainly, mostly; more than ever, doubly, trebly; on a large scale, in a big way; vastly, hugely, enormously; heavily, strongly, powerfully, mightily; actively, strenuously, intensely; closely, narrowly, intensively; zealously, fanatically, hotly, bitterly, fiercely; acutely, sharply, shrewdly, exquisitely; generously, richly; supremely, pre-eminently, superlatively; rarely, strangely; immeasurably, incalculably, infinitely, unspeakably, ineffably; awfully, badly.

extremely, ultra, to extremes, to the limit, no end of; beyond measure, beyond all bounds; overly, unduly, to a fault, out of all proportion; unconscionably, with a vengeance; immoderately, uncontrollably, desperately, madly, frantically, furiously, fiercely, violently; exceedingly, excessively, exorbitantly, inordinately; foully, abominably, grossly, beastly, monstrously, horribly; confoundedly, deucedly, devilishly, damnably, hellishly; tremendously, terribly, fearfully; unforgiveably, mortally.

remarkably, noticeably, markedly, pointedly; sensibly, feelingly; notably, strikingly, signally, emphatically, prominently, glaringly, flagrantly, blatantly; eminently, egregriously; singularly, peculiarly, oddly, specially; surprisingly, astonishingly, amazingly, incredibly, marvellously, magically.

painfully, unsparingly, till it hurts; badly, bitterly, hard; seriously, sorely, grievously; sadly, miserably, wretchedly; distressingly, pitiably, piteously, woefully, lamentably; shrewdly, cruelly; savagely; exquisitely, excruciatingly, shockingly, frightfully; banefully, mortally.

33. Smallness – N.

smallness, exiguousness, scantiness; diminutiveness, minuteness 196 n. *littleness*; brevity 204 n. *shortness*; meagreness 206 n. *thinness*; briefness 114 n. *transientness*; paucity 105 n. *fewness*; rareness, sparsity 140 n. *infrequency*; scarcity 636 n. *insufficiency*; pettiness, insignificance 639 n. *unimportance*, 35 n. *inferiority*; tenuity 4 n. *insubstantiality*; compression, abbreviation 198 n. *contraction*; diminution 37 n. *decrease*; vanishing point, nothingness 103 n. *zero*, 444 n. *invisibility*.

small quantity, modicum, minimum 26 n. *finite quantity*; detail; nutshell 592 n. *compendium*; drop in the ocean; homoeopathic dose 639 n. *trifle*; thimbleful, spoonful; trickle, dribble, sprinkling, dash, splash; tinge, tincture, trace, spice, smack, smell, lick; nuance, soupçon, thought, suggestion, shade, shadow, touch, cast; spark, scintilla, gleam, flash; pinch, snatch; snack, sip, bite, mite, morsel, sop; scantling, fragment 53 n. *piece*; whit, bit, mite; iota, jot, tittle; ounce, pennyweight, grain, scruple, minim 322 n. *weighment*; vanishing point, next to nothing, just enough to swear by.

small thing, 196 n. *miniature*; dot, stop, point, pinpoint; dab, spot, fleck, speck, mote, smut; grain, granule, seed, crumb; drop, droplet, driblet; thread, shred, rag, fragment 53 n. *piece*; scrap, smithereens; flake, snip, snippet, gobbet, finger; chip, clipping, paring, shaving; shiver, sliver, slip; pinprick; corpuscle, particle, atom, electron 319 n. *element*.

Adj. *small*, exiguous, homoeopathic, minimal, infinitesimal; microscopic 444 adj. *invisible*; tiny, wee, minute, diminutive, miniature 196 adj. *little*; least, minimum; small-sized, under-sized 196 adj. *dwarfish*; slim, slender, meagre; slight 163 adj. *weak*; delicate, dainty, minikin; fine, subtle, rarefied 325 adj. *rare*; squat 210 adj. *low*; brief, skimpy, abbreviated 204 adj. *short*; cut, compact, compendious, thumbnail 198 adj. *contracted*; scanty, scant, scarce 636 adj. *insufficient*; declining, ebbing 37 adj. *decreasing*.

inconsiderable, minor, light-weight, trifling, petty, paltry, insignificant 639 adj. *unimportant*; inappreciable, unnoticeable 444 adj. *invisible*; shadowy, tenuous, evanescent 446 adj. *disappearing*, 114 adj. *transient*; marginal, negligible; slight, superficial, cursory 4 adj. *insubstantial*; skin-deep 212 adj. *shallow*; moderate, modest, humble 732 adj. *mediocre*; not much of a, no great shakes 35 adj. *inferior*; no more than, just, only, mere, bare.

Adv. *slightly*, exiguously, little; lightly, softly, faintly; superficially, cursorily, grazingly; gradually, imperceptibly, insensibly, invisibly; on a small scale, in a small way, modestly, humbly; indifferently, hardly, scarcely, barely, only just; only, merely.

partially, to a certain extent; somehow, after a fashion, in a manner; restrictedly, within bounds 55 adv. *incompletely*; not wholly, in part.

almost, all but, within an ace of, within an inch of, on the brink of, on the verge of, within sight of, in a fair way to, approximately 200 adv. *nearly*; not quite, hardly, scarcely, barely.

in no way, by no means, in no respect, not at all, not in the least, not a bit, not a whit, not a jot, on no account.

34. Superiority – N. *superiority*, loftiness, sublimity, transcendence 32 n. *greatness*; the tops, quality, excellence, ne plus ultra 646 n. *perfection*; preferability 605 n. *choice*; primacy, pride of place, seniority 119 n. *priority*; eminence, pre-e. 866 n. *prestige*; overlordship, paramountcy, supremacy, sovereignty, imperium 733 n. *authority*; preponderance, predominance, hegemony, leadership 178 n. *influence*; directorship, win, championship 727 n. *victory*; prominence 638 n. *importance*; one-upmanship 727 n. *success*; maximum, top, peak, crest; record, high 213 n. *summit*.

vantage, advantage, privilege, prerogative, favour; start, lead, one up, winning position; odds, points, pull, edge, bulge; command, upper hand, whip-h.; majority, vantage ground, coign of vantage.

superior, superior person 644 n. *exceller*; better man, first choice 890 n. *favourite*; high-up, top people, best p. 638 n. *bigwig*; one's betters 868 n. *upper class*; overlord 741 n. *master*; commander, chief, boss 690 n. *leader*; primate, president, chairman, prime minister, primus inter pares 690 n. *director*; model 646 n. *paragon*; star, topsawyer 696 n. *proficient*; specialist 696 n. *expert*; world-beater, winner, prizeman, champion 727 n. *victor*; prima donna, first lady, head boy; first-born, elder.

Adj. *superior*, more so; elative, comparative, superlative; major, greater;

overlying, upper, higher; senior, over, super; super-normal, above the average, in a different class; better, a cut above, outstanding 644 adj. *excellent*; competitive, more than a match for; one up, ahead 64 adj. *preceding*; prior, preferable 605 adj. *chosen*; outmatching 306 adj. *surpassing*; on top, winning 727 adj. *successful*; top-level, high-l. 689 adj. *directing*, 638 adj. *important*; commanding 733 adj. *ruling*; reformed, bettered, all the better for 654 adj. *improved*.

supreme, arch-, greatest 32 adj. *great*; uppermost 213 adj. *topmost*; first, chief, foremost; main, principal, leading, overruling, overriding, cardinal, capital 638 adj. *important*; excellent, best; superlative, super, champion, tip-top, first-rate, first-class, A1, front-rank, world-beating 644 adj. *best*; on top, top of the class, second to none; dominant, paramount, pre-eminent, sovereign; incomparable, unrivalled, matchless, peerless, unapproachable, inimitable, unsurpassed, beyond compare, beyond criticism 646 adj. *perfect*; transcendent, out of this world.

Vb. *be superior*, transcend, rise above, overtop, tower over, overlook, command 209 vb. *be high*; outrange, outreach 306 vb. *overstep*; exceed, out-Herod Herod, beat the limit; pass, surpass, beat the record; improve on, better, cap, trump, overtrump; assert one's superiority, be too much for; steal the show, outshine, eclipse, overshadow, throw into the shade, cut out; score off, have the laugh on 851 n. *ridicule*; best, outrival, outmatch, outclass, outrank 277 vb. *outstrip*; outplay, outpoint, outmanoeuvre, outwit; get the better of, worst, beat 727 vb. *defeat*; rise to the occasion; predominate, have the edge on.

Adv. *beyond*, more, over, far and away; above par, over the average; upwards of; on the crest, at its height, at the peak.

eminently, egregiously, pre-eminently, superlatively, supremely; above all, of all things; to crown all, to cap all; par excellence; principally, especially, particularly, peculiarly; a fortiori, even more, all the m.

35. Inferiority – N. *inferiority*, minority 105 n. *fewness*; littleness 33 n. *smallness*; no record, second best; subordination, dependence 745 n. *subjection*; secondariness, supporting role, second fiddle 639 n. *unimportance*; lowliness 872 n. *humility*; second rank, back seat; commonness 869 n. *commonalty*; disadvantage, handicap 702 n. *hindrance*; faultiness, blemish 647 n. *imperfection*; deficiency 307 n. *shortcoming*, 636 n. *insufficiency*; failure 728 n. *defeat*; poor quality 645 n. *badness*; decline 655 n. *deterioration*; minimum, nadir, the bottom 214 n. *base*; averageness 732 n. *mediocrity*.

inferior, subordinate, subaltern, sub, underling, understrapper, assistant, subsidiary 707 n. *auxiliary*; tool, pawn, retainer 742 n. *dependant*; menial 742 n. *servant*; poor relation 639 n. *nonentity*; subject, underdog 742 n. *slave*; backbencher, private, other ranks, lower classes 869 n. *commonalty*; second, second best, second string, second fiddle, second-rater; bad second, also-ran; failure, reject 607 n. *rejection*; younger, junior.

Adj. *lesser*, less, minor 639 adj. *unimportant*; reduced 198 adj. *contracted*; least, smallest, minimal, minimum; lowest, bottommost 214 adj. *undermost*; minus 307 adj. *deficient*.

inferior, lower, junior, under-, sub-; subject, unfree, dependent, parasitical; subordinate, secondary, subsidiary, auxiliary 639 adj. *unimportant*; second, second-best, second-rate, second-rank; humble, lowly, low-level, menial; low-ranking, unclassified; sub-normal, substandard, subgrade, C3 607 adj. *rejected*; unsound, defective 647 adj. *imperfect*; low, common, low-caste 869 adj. *plebeian*; scratch, makeshift 670 adj. *unprepared*; unworthy, not a patch on.

Vb. *be inferior*; not come up to, fall below 307 vb. *fall short*; lag, fall behind, trail 284 vb. *follow*; want, lack 636 vb.

not suffice; bow to 739 vb. *obey*; yield, cede, hand it to 721 vb. *submit*; play second fiddle, take a back seat; lose face, lose caste 867 vb. *lose repute*.

36. Increase – N. *increase*, augmentation, crescendo; advance, progress 285 n. *progression*; growth, build-up, development; extension, prolongation, protraction 203 n. *lengthening*; amplification, inflation 197 n. *expansion*; proliferation, swarming 166 n. *reproduction*; multiplication 86 n. *numerical operation*; adding 38 n. *addition*; enlargement, magnification, aggrandizement; enhancement; intensification, stepping up; acceleration 277 n. *spurt*; hotting up 381 n. *heating*; excitation 174 n. *stimulation*; exacerbation 832 n. *aggravation*; advancement, rise, uprush, upsurge, upward curve, upward trend, anabasis 308 n. *ascent*, 654 n. *improvement*; flood, tide, swell, surge 350 n. *wave*; progressiveness, cumulative effect, snowball 74 n. *accumulation*; ascending order 71 n. *series*.

increment, augment, bulge; accretion, access, accession, accrual, addition, contribution 40 n. *adjunct*; supplement 40 n. *extra*; padding, stuffing 303 n. *insertion*; interest, gain, profit 771 n. *acquisition*.

Adj. *increasing*, spreading, greater than ever; crescent, on the increase, anabatic; ever-increasing, snowballing, cumulative 285 adj. *progressive*; augmentative, elative, comparative, intensive; prolific, fruitful 164 adj. *productive*.

Vb. *grow*, increase, gain; dilate, swell, bulge, wax, fill 197 vb. *expand*; fill out, thicken 205 vb. *be broad*; sprout, flower, blossom, 164 vb. *reproduce itself*; breed, spread, swarm, proliferate, multiply 104 vb. *be many*, 171 vb. *be fruitful*; flare up 417 vb. *shine*; improve 654 vb. *get better*; gain ground, advance, snowball, accumulate 285 vb. *progress*; appreciate, rise in price; exceed, overflow 637 vb. *superabound*, 32 vb. *be great*.

augment, increase, bump up, double, triple 94 vb. *treble*, 97 vb. *quadruple*; redouble, square, cube; duplicate 106 vb. *repeat*; multiply 164 vb. *produce*; enlarge, magnify, distend, inflate 197 vb. *expand*; amplify, develop, build up; supplement, superadd, repay with interest; accrue 38 vb. *add*; prolong, stretch 203 vb. *lengthen*; broaden, widen, thicken, deepen; heighten, enhance, send up; exalt 310 vb. *elevate*; speed up 277 vb. *accelerate*; intensify, redouble, step up, screw up, stimulate, energize 174 vb. *invigorate*; recruit, reinforce, revive 685 vb. *refresh*, 656 vb. *restore*, 162 vb. *strengthen*; glorify 546 vb. *exaggerate*; stoke, add fuel to the flame, exacerbate 832 vb. *aggravate*; maximize, bring to a head 725 vb. *climax*.

Adv. *crescendo*, increasingly etc. adj.; more so, with a vengeance, with knobs on; up and up, more and more.

37. Decrease: non-increase – N. *decrease*, fade-out, dimming, obscuration; wane, ebb 286 vb. *regression*; descending order 71 n. *series*; sinking, decline, catabasis, downward curve, fall, drop, plunge 309 n. *descent*; deflation, recession, slump 655 n. *deterioration*; loss of value, depreciation; enfeeblement 163 n. *weakness*; impoverishment 801 n. *poverty*; diminishing returns, exhaustion; shortage, shrinkage, evaporation, erosion, decay 655 n. *dilapidation*; spoilage, leakage, wastage, damage, loss, wear and tear 42 n. *decrement*; using up, consumption 634 n. *waste*; non-increase, anticlimax; limitation, limit, bound 747 n. *restriction*; forfeit, sacrifice 963 n. *penalty*, 772 n. *loss*.

diminution, abatement, deduction 39 n. *subtraction*; reduction, restriction 747 n. *restraint*; deceleration 278 n. *slowness*; retrenchment, cut 814 n. *economy*; pruning, paring, curtailment, abridgement, abbreviation 204 n. *shortening*; compression, squeeze 198 n. *contraction*; attrition, abrasion, erosion 333 vb. *friction*; scattering, dispersal 75 n. *dispersion*; elimination 300 n. *voidance*; extenuation, mitigation, minimization; belittlement, undervaluation.

Adj. *decreasing*, dwindling; decrescent,

waning, fading, catabatic; bated, decreased, diminished etc. vb.

Vb. *bate*, diminish, decrease, lessen; take away, detract from, deduct 39 vb. *subtract*; except 57 vb. *exclude*; reduce, step down, scale d., whittle, pare, scrape 206 vb. *make thin*; shrink, abridge 204 vb. *shorten*; squeeze, compress 198 vb. *make smaller*; limit 747 vb. *restrain*; cut back, retrench 814 vb. *economize*; minimize, mitigate, extenuate 177 vb. *moderate*; deflate, puncture; belittle, depreciate 483 vb. *underestimate*, 812 vb. *cheapen*, 926 vb. *detract*; degrade, demote 872 vb. *humiliate*; unload, throw overboard 323 vb. *lighten*; run down, empty, drain, exhaust 300 vb. *void*; use up, consume 634 vb. *waste*; abrade, gnaw, nibble at, erode, rust; strip, denude 229 vb. *uncover*; dilute, water; thin, thin out, depopulate 105 vb. *render few*; eliminate, expel 300 vb. *eject*; decimate, wipe out, annihilate 165 vb. *destroy*; hush, quiet 399 vb. *silence*; quell 745 vb. *subjugate*.

decrease, lessen, suffer loss; abate, die down; dwindle, shrink 198 vb. *become small*; wane, set; waste, decay, languish, fade 655 vb. *deteriorate*; run low, ebb, drain away, dry up, tail off, fail 636 vb. *not suffice*; subside, come down, decline, fall, drop, slump, collapse 309 vb. *descend*; melt 337 vb. *liquefy*; evaporate 338 vb. *vaporize*; lose numbers 105 vb. *be few*, 75 vb. *disperse*; bant, diet, reduce, lose, shed, rid oneself 229 vb. *doff*; forfeit, sacrifice 963 vb. *be punished*.

Adv. *diminuendo*, decrescendo, less and less, in decline, on the wane, at low ebb.

38. Addition – N. *addition*, adding to, annexation; imposition 187 n. *location*; prefixion, suffixion, affixation; supplementation 725 n. *completion*; contribution, reinforcement, accession, accretion, accrual; increment, supplement, addendum, appendage, appendix 40 n. *adjunct*; summation, adding up, total, toll 86 n. *numeration*.

Adj. *additional*, additive; adopted, adscititious 59 adj. *extraneous*; supplementary 725 adj. *completive*; auxiliary, contributory 703 adj. *aiding*; supernumerary, supererogatory; extra, spare; epenthetic, prosthetic.

Vb. *add*, add up, sum, total, do the addition 86 vb. *do sums*; carry over 272 vb. *transfer*; annex, append, subjoin; attach, pin to, clip to, tack on 45 vb. *join, tie*; preface, prefix, affix, suffix, postfix, infix; introduce, interpose, interject; read into, import; engraft, let in 303 vb. *insert*; contribute to, add one's share 36 vb. *augment*; supplement 54 vb. *complete*; impose, clap on, saddle with; superadd, superimpose, pile on, heap on.

accrue, supervene; accede, adhere, join; make one more, swell the ranks, reinforce, recruit 162 vb. *strengthen*.

Adv. *in addition*, additionally, more, plus, extra; with interest, with a vengeance, with knobs on; and, too, also, item, furthermore, further, to boot; else, besides; et cetera; moreover, into the bargain, over and above, including, inclusive of; with, as well as, not to mention, let alone, not forgetting; together with, along w., coupled w., in conjunction w.

39. Subduction: non-addition – **N.** *subtraction*, deduction 86 n. *numerical operation*; abstraction, removal, withdrawal 786 n. *taking*; clearance 300 n. *voidance*; unloading 188 n. *displacement*; retrenchment, curtailment 204 n. *shortening*; severance, detruncation, amputation, excision 46 n. *disjunction*; expurgation, bowdlerization, garbling 648 n. *cleansing*; deletion 550 n. *obliteration*; minuend 85 n. *numerical element*; subtrahend, discount 42 n. *decrement*.

Adj. *subtracted*, subtractive; beheaded, headless; minus, without.

Vb. *subtract*, take away, subduct, deduct; detract from 37 vb. *bate*; except, leave out 57 vb. *exclude*; abstract, withdraw, remove; unload, unpack 188 vb. *displace*; abrade, erode; eradicate 304 vb. *extract*; cross out, delete 550 n. *obliterate*; expurgate, bowdlerize, garble, mutilate; sever, amputate, excise 46 vb.

disjoin; retrench, cut back, prune, pare, whittle; decapitate, behead, dock, curtail, abridge, abbreviate 204 vb. *shorten*; geld, castrate 161 vb. *unman*; strip, divest, denude 229 vb. *uncover*.

Adv. *in deduction*, less, short of, minus, without, except, barring, bar, save, exclusive of, save and except.

40. Adjunct: thing added – **N.** *adjunct*, addition, contribution 38 n. *addition*; addendum, carry-over; attachment, fixture; annexure; inflexion, affix, suffix, prefix, infix, postfix, subscript; preposition, postposition; adjective, adverb 564 n. *part of speech*; appendage, tail, train 67 n. *sequel*; appendix, postscript; codicil, rider 468 n. *qualification*; corollary, complement 725 n. *completion*; appurtenance, pendant, concomitant 89 n. *accompaniment*; extension, supplement, continuation; annexe, wing (of a house); increment, augment; patch, darn, insertion, reinforcement 656 n. *repair*; padding, stuffing 227 n. *lining*; item, oddment, accessory; fringe, frill 234 n. *edge*; embroidery 844 n. *ornamentation*; garnish 389 n. *condiment*; frills, trimmings, all that goes with it.

extra, additive, addendum, something over and above, by-product; percentage, interest 771 n. *gain*; refresher, bonus, tip, solatium, something on the side 962 n. *reward*; gratuity, grace marks 781 n. *gift*; supernumerary; reserves, spare parts 633 n. *provision*; fifth wheel of the coach 641 n. *inutility*; luxury 637 n. *superfluity*.

41. Remainder: thing remaining – **N.** *remainder*, residue, residuum; residuals, result, resultant 157 n. *effect*; margin, outstanding, balance, surplus, carryover; overplus, overtrick, excess 637 n. *superfluity*; relic, rest, remnant; rump, stump, scrag end 69 n. *extremity*; frustum, torso, trunk 53 n. *piece*; track, trace 548 n. *record*; vestige, remains.

leavings, left-overs; precipitate, deposit; alluvium, silt 344 n. *soil*; sediment; drift, loess, moraine, detritus, debris; grounds, lees, heel-taps, dregs; scum, skimmings, dross, scoria, slag, sludge; bilge; dottle; husks, bran, chaff, stubble; peel, peelings; slough, scurf; parings, combings; shorts, trimmings, clippings, garbage, remnants; scraps, odds and ends, lumber 641 n. *rubbish*; rejects 779 n. *derelict*; sweepings, scourings, offscourings; refuse, waste, sewage 649 n. *dirt*, 302 n. *excrement*.

survivor, finisher; inheritor, heir, successor 776 n. *beneficiary*; widower, widow, relict 896 n. *widowed spouse*; orphan 779 n. *derelict*; descendant 170 n. *posterity*.

Adj. *remaining*, surviving, left, vestigial; resting, resultant; residual; left behind, sedimentary, precipitated 779 adj. *not retained*; left over, odd; net, surplus; unspent, unexpended, unexpired, unconsumed; outstanding, carried over; spare, to s., superfluous 637 adj. *redundant*; cast-off, pariah, outcast 607 adj. *rejected*; orphaned, orphan, widowed.

42. Decrement: thing deducted – N. *decrement*, deduction, cut 37 n. *diminution*; allowance, free a.; rebate 810 n. *discount*; reprise, tare, drawback, shortage, defect 307 n. *shortcoming*, 636 n. *insufficiency*; loss, sacrifice, forfeit 963 n. *penalty*; leak, leakage, primage, escape 298 n. *egress*; shrinkage 204 n. *shortening*; spoilage, wastage; off-take, consumption 634 n. *waste*; subtrahend, rake-off 786 n. *taking*.

43. Mixture – N. *mixture*, mingling, mixing, stirring; blending, harmonization; intermixture, interlarding, interpolation 231 n. *interjacence*; interlacing 222 n. *crossing*; merger, amalgamation, integration 50 n. *combination*; syncretism, eclecticism; fusion, interfusion, alloyage; adulteration, sophistication; contamination, infection; infiltration, permeation 297 n. *ingress*; interbreeding, miscegenation, intermarriage; hybridization, mongrelism; solubility 337 n. *liquefaction*; crucible, melting-pot.

tincture, admixture, infusion; tinge 33 n. *small quantity*; seasoning 389 n. *condiment*; stain, dye 425 n. *hue*.

a mixture, mélange, blend, composition; amalgam, alloy, compound 50 n. *combination*; cento, pastiche, pasticcio; salad, stew, hash, mishmash; cocktail, brew.

medley, motley, patchwork, mosaic 437 n. *variegation*; miscellany, old curiosity shop; farrago, hotch-potch; potpourri; jumble, mess, tangle 61 n. *confusion*; Noah's ark 369 n. *zoo*; multiracial state; all sorts, odds and ends, paraphernalia, oddments.

hybrid, bigener, cross, cross-breed, mongrel; half-blood, half-breed, half-caste, mestizo, mulatto, quadroon, octaroon; mule, hinny.

Adj. *mixed*, in the melting pot, stirred; blended, syncretic, eclectic; adulterated, sophisticated; composite, half-and-half, fifty-fifty; jumbled, unclassified, unsorted; heterogeneous, kaleidoscopic 82 adj. *multiform*; patched, motley 437 adj. *variegated*; shot 437 adj. *iridescent*; miscellaneous, hotch-potch, promiscuous 464 adj. *indiscriminate*; infectious; hybrid, bigenerous, cross-bred, crossed; half-blooded, mongrel; interbred; intermixed, multi-racial.

Vb. *mix*, stir, shake; shuffle 272 vb. *transpose*, 63 vb. *jumble*; brew, compound 56 vb. *compose*; fuse, alloy, merge, amalgamate 45 vb. *join*; blend, harmonize 24 vb. *adjust*; mingle, intermingle, intersperse 437 n. *variegate*; lace, intermix, interlard, interleave 303 vb. *insert*; intertwine, interlace, interweave 222 vb. *weave*; tinge, dye 425 vb. *colour*; water, adulterate, sophisticate 163 vb. *weaken*; temper, doctor, medicate 468 vb. *qualify*; season, spice 390 vb. *appetize*; hybridize, mongrelize, cross, cross-breed 164 vb. *generate*.

be mixed, pervade, permeate, run through, overrun 297 vb. *infiltrate*; infect, contaminate; tinge, dye, stain 425 vb. *colour*; miscegenate, intermarry, interbreed, cross with 164 vb. *reproduce itself*.

44. Simpleness: freedom from mixture – N. *simpleness* etc. adj.; homogeneity 16 n. *uniformity*; purity; oneness; atomicity, indivisibility; lack of complication, simplicity 516 n. *intelligibility*, 573 n. *plainness*, 699 n. *artlessness*; not a trace of, not a hint of 190 n. *absence*; simplification; elimination.

Adj. *simple*, homogeneous, monolithic, of a piece 16 adj. *uniform*; absolute, sheer, mere, nothing but; undifferentiated, asexual; single, unified 88 adj. *one*; elemental, atomic, indivisible 52 adj. *whole*; primary, irreducible, fundamental, basic 5 adj. *intrinsic*; elementary, uncomplicated; unsophisticated; homespun 573 adj. *plain*, 699 adj. *artless*.

unmixed, pure and simple, without alloy; clear, pure 648 adj. *clean*; whole-blooded, thoroughbred 868 adj. *noble*; unmingled, unalloyed; undiluted, unadulterated, neat; unqualified; unmedicated; untinged, undyed.

Vb. *simplify*, unmix, unscramble; render simple 16 vb. *make uniform*; narrow down, factorize, reduce; disentangle, unravel 46 vb. *disjoin*; unify, make one, unite.

45. Junction – N. *junction*, meeting, concurrence, conjunction 293 n. *convergence*, 279 n. *collision*; contact 202 n. *contiguity*, 378 n. *touch*; congress 74 n. *assembly*; confluence, meeting-point 76 n. *focus*; coalescence, symphysis; cohesion, inextricability 48 n. *coherence*; concretion, consolidation 324 n. *condensation*; closeness, tightness; union, coalition 706 n. *association*; connexion, linkage, tie-up, hook-up 47 n. *bond*; communication, intercommunication, intercourse, commerce, traffic 791 n. *trade*.

joinder, bringing together 74 n. *assemblage*; unification 50 n. *combination*; articulation 331 n. *structure*; joining, stringing together, concatenation; suture, stitching; tightening, astriction 264 n. *closure*; knotting, tying, fastening, infibulation; attachment, annexure 38 n. *addition*; connecting, earthing; affixa-

tion, suffixion, prefixion; fixture, grafting 303 n. *insertion*; agglutination 48 n. *coherence*; coupling, yoking; hyphenization 547 n. *punctuation*; joiner, coupler, riveter, welder.

coition, coitus, copulation, sexual intercourse, intimacy, carnal knowledge; pairing, mating, coupling; union 894 n. *marriage*; enjoyment, consummation; violation, ravishment 951 n. *rape*.

joint, joining, juncture, commissure; suture, seam 47 n. *bond*; weld, splice; hinge, ginglymus, knee, elbow; finger, wrist, ankle, knuckle; node; junction, intersection, crossways 222 n. *crossing*.

Adj. *conjunct*, joined etc. vb.; partnered, participant 775 adj. *sharing*; rolled into one, united; joint, incorporated 708 adj. *corporate*; handfast, hand in hand, arm in arm; coalescent, symphysian 48 adj. *cohesive*; composite 50 adj. *combined*; stitched up, sutural.

conjunctive, subjunctive, adjunctive, copulative; adhesive 48 adj. *cohesive*; coagulate, astringent; coital, venereal.

firm-set, firm, close, fast, secure 153 adj. *fixed*; set, solidified 324 adj. *dense*, 48 adj. *cohesive*; put, pat; rooted, ingrown, impacted; tight, wedged, jammed, stuck, inextricable.

Vb. *join*, conjoin, couple, yoke, hyphenate, harness together, partner, pair, match; bracket, assemble, unite 50 vb. *combine*; mobilize, mass 74 vb. *bring together*; associate, ally, merge; embody, incorporate; lump together, roll into one 464 vb. *not discriminate*; hinge, articulate, dovetail, mortise, rabbet; fit, set, interlock, engage, gear to; weld, solder, braze, fuse, cement 48 vb. *agglutinate*; draw together, lace, knit, sew, stitch; pin, infibulate, buckle; do up, button up 264 vb. *close*.

connect, attach, annex (see *affix*); tag, clip; thread together, concatenate; contact 378 vb. *touch*; make contact, plug in, earth; interconnect, open into; link, bridge, span; communicate, intercommunicate, hook up with.

affix, attach, fix, fasten; fix on, yoke, leash, harness, limber, saddle, bridle, bit;

tie up, moor, anchor; tether, picket; stick on 48 vb. *agglutinate*; suffix, prefix, infix; set, frame 235 vb. *enclose*; drive in, wedge, jam; screw, nail, rivet, bolt, clamp, clinch.

tie, secure; knot, hitch, bend; lash, belay; knit, cast on, sew, stitch, suture; tack, baste; braid, plait, crochet, twine, twist, thread, reeve; truss, string, rope, strap; lace, frap, trice up, brail; tether, picket, moor; pinion, manacle, handcuff; hobble, shackle 747 vb. *fetter*; bind, splice, gird, girdle, cinch; bandage, swathe, swaddle, wrap; enfold, embrace, clinch, grip, grapple 235 vb. *enclose*, 778 vb. *retain*.

unite with; join, meet 293 vb. *converge*; adhere, hang together; interlock, engage, grip, grapple, embrace, entwine, clinch; marry 894 vb. *wed*; live with, cohabit, bed; lie with, sleep w., have intercourse, have carnal knowledge; consummate a union know, enjoy, have, do; board, tumble; deflower, rape, ravish, violate, force 951 vb. *debauch*; copulate, couple, mate, pair; mount, tup; cross with, breed w.

46. Disjunction – N. *disjunction*, disconnexion, disconnectedness, unthreading, break, ladder, run 72 n. *discontinuity*; looseness, separability, fissionability 49 n. *non-coherence*, 335 n. *fluidity*; scattering 75 n. *dispersion*; dissociation, withdrawal, disengagement, retirement 621 n. *relinquishment*, 753 n. *resignation*; moving apart 294 n. *divergence*; detachment, non-attachment; disunion 709 n. *dissension*; dissilience 280 n. *recoil*; immiscibility, separateness, isolationism, separatism 80 n. *particularism*; no connexion, asyndeton 10 n. *irrelation*; distance apart 199 n. *farness*; interval, space, breach 201 n. *gap*.

separation, severance, parting 896 n. *divorce*; unravelment, laddering; loosening, freeing 746 n. *liberation*; isolation, quarantine, segregation 883 n. *seclusion*; boycott 620 n. *avoidance*; expulsion 300 n. *ejection*; taking away 39 n. *subtraction*; abstraction, deprivation 786 n.

taking; detachment, removal, transfer 188 n. *displacement*; dislocation, luxation; dissolution, resolution, disintegration, break-up 51 n. *decomposition*; dissection, analysis, breakdown; splitting, fission; rupture, fracture 330 n. *brittleness*; dividing line, caesura; wall 231 n. *partition*; boundary 236 n. *limit*.

scission, section, cleavage; division, dichotomy 92 n. *bisection*; subdivision, segmentation; abscission, decapitation 204 n. *shortening*; resection, circumcision; incision 658 n. *surgery*; dissection; rending, clawing, laceration, avulsion; biting etc. vb.

Adj. *disjunct*, disjoined etc. vb.; broken, interrupted 72 adj. *discontinuous*; in pieces, quartered, dismembered; torn, rent, riven, cleft, cloven; fugitive, uncollected 75 adj. *unassembled*; loose, free, open-ended.

separate, apart, asunder; adrift, lost; free-standing, unfastened, unattached; distinct, discrete, differentiated, distinguishable; unassimilated, alien, foreign 59 adj. *extraneous*; external 223 adj. *exterior*; insular, self-sufficient, lonely, isolated 88 adj. *alone*, 883 adj. *friendless*; disjunctive, separative; dichotomous.

severable, separable, detachable; partible, divisible, fissionable, scissile, tearable; dissoluble.

Vb. *be disjoined*, stand apart, not mix 620 vb. *avoid*; radiate 294 vb. *diverge*, 282 vb. *deviate*; separate, part, part company, cut adrift, split off, hive off; get loose, disengage, unclinch, break away; cast off, unmoor; scatter, break it up 75 vb. *disperse*, 280 vb. *recoil*; disintegrate 51 vb. *decompose*; unravel, ladder, run; shear; start, split, crack 263 vb. *open*.

disjoin, disunite, dissociate, divorce; part, separate, sunder, sever, dissever; uncouple, unhitch, disconnect, unplug; cast off (knitting); disengage, ungear; disjoint, dislocate, wrench; remove, detach, unseat, dismount 49 vb. *unstick*; skin, pluck 229 vb. *uncover*; undo, unbutton, unhook, unclasp, unlock, unlatch 263 vb. *open*; unstring, untie, unknot, disentangle 62 vb. *unravel*; loosen

21

177 vb. *moderate*; unbind, unchain, unfetter, unloose, loose, free, release 746 vb. *liberate*; unharness, unsaddle, unbridle 701 vb. *disencumber*; unload, unpack 188 vb. *displace*; dispel, disband, demobilize 75 vb. *disperse*; unstitch, unpick, unthread.

set apart, put aside 632 vb. *store*; mark out, distinguish 463 vb. *discriminate*; single out 605 vb. *select*; except 57 vb. *exclude*; taboo, boycott 620 vb. *avoid*; insulate, isolate, zone 232 vb. *circumscribe*; segregate, sequester 883 vb. *seclude*; drive a wedge between, set against 881 vb. *make enemies*, 888 vb. *excite hate*.

sunder (see *disjoin*); divide, keep apart; subdivide, fragment, chunk, segment, sectionalize, fractionize; dissect, anatomize 51 vb. *decompose*; dichotomize 92 vb. *bisect*; disbranch (see *cut*); behead 204 vb. *shorten*; take apart, cannibalize, dismantle, break up; cleave 263 vb. *pierce* (see *break*).

cut (see *rend*); hew, hack, slash, gash 655 vb. *wound*; prick, stab, knife 263 vb. *pierce*; cleave, rive, saw, chop; slit, make an incision, incise; carve, slice; pare, whittle, chip, bevel, skive; clip, snick, snip; shave, scythe, mow; lop, prune, dock, curtail, behead, decapitate, amputate, circumcise (see *sunder*); bite, plough 262 vb. *groove*; nick 260 vb. *notch*.

rend, rive (see *sunder*); tear, scratch, claw, scarify, score; gnaw, fret, fray; strip, flay, skin, peel, pluck 229 vb. *uncover*; rip, slash, slit (see *cut*); lacerate, quarter, dismember; pluck to pieces, divellicate, scramble; mince, grind, crunch, scrunch 301 vb. *chew*, 332 vb. *pulverize*.

break, fracture, rupture; split, burst, blow up, explode; shear, snap, knap; smash, shatter, splinter, shiver 165 vb. *demolish*; fragment, comminute, crumble 332 vb. *pulverize*; disintegrate 51 vb. *decompose*; break up (see *sunder*); chip, crack, damage 655 vb. *impair*.

Adv. *separately*, apart, severally, singly, one by one, bit by bit, piecemeal.

47. Bond: connecting medium – N. *bond*, connecting medium, vinculum, chain, tie, band, hoop, yoke; nexus, connexion, link, liaison 9 n. *relation*; hinge 45 n. *joint*; connective, copula; hyphen 547 n. *punctuation*; intermedium, cement (see *adhesive*); bondstone, binder; tie-beam 218 n. *beam*; interconnexion, intercommunication, channel, passage, corridor 624 n. *way*; stepping-stone 624 n. *bridge*; span, arch; isthmus, neck; stair 308 n. *ascent*; life-line.

cable, line, hawser, painter, moorings; tow-line, ripcord, lanyard, communication cord; rope, cord, string, strand, thread 208 n. *fibre*; chain, wire.

tackling, tackle, cordage; rigging, shroud, ratline; sheets, guy, stay; clew line, garnet, halliard, bowline, lanyard; harness.

ligature, binding, end-paper; ligament, tendon, muscle; tendril; bast, raffia 208 n. *fibre*; lashing, string, cord, thread, tape, inkle; band, fillet, ribbon; bandage, roller, tourniquet 198 n. *compressor*; drawstring, thong, latchet, lace; braid, plait; tie 228 n. *neckwear*; knot, hitch, clinch, bend; Gordian knot, running k., slip k., granny k., reef k., sailor's k.; half-hitch, clove h.; sheepshank, Turk's head.

fastening 45 n. *joinder*; fastener, snap, f., press f., zip f.; drawstring, ripcord; button, buttonhook, buttonhole, frog; hook and eye; eyelet; stud, cufflink; garter, suspender, braces; tiepin, stickpin; brooch, fibula; ouch 844 n. *jewellery*; clip, grip, slide, curlers; hairpin, hatpin; skewer, spit, brochette; pin, linch p., king p.; peg, dowel, trennel; nail, brad, tack, tintack, hobnail, blakey 256 n. *sharp point*; holdfast, staple, clamp, batten, cramp, rivet; nut, bolt, screw; buckle, clasp, morse; hasp, hinge 45 n. *joint*; catch, safety-c., pawl, click, detent; latch, bolt; lock 264 n. *closure*; padlock, handcuffs 748 n. *fetter*; bollard, cleat, bitt.

coupling, yoke; coupler, draw-bar, traces; grappling iron, hook, claw; anchor 662 n. *safeguard*.

girdle, band 228 n. *belt*; cincture; waist-band, waist-string, cummerbund, bellyband, girth, roller, cinch, surcingle; cestus, zone; sash, shoulder-belt, bandoleer; neckband 228 n. *neckwear*; bandeau, fillet, tiara; hatband; banderole; equator, zodiac.

halter, collar, noose; tether, lead, leash, jess, trash-cord, reins, ribbons; lasso, lariat; shackle 748 n. *fetter*.

adhesive, glue, lime, gum, fixative, brilliantine, grease; solder; paste, size, lute, clay, cement, putty, mortar, stucco, plaster, grout 226 n. *facing*; wafer, sealing-wax; plaster, scotch tape, fly-paper.

48. Coherence – N. *coherence*, connectedness 71 n. *continuity*; cohesion, cohesiveness; tenaciousness 778 n. *retention*; adhesiveness; cementation, agglutination 45 n. *junction*; consolidation, set 324 n. *condensation*; inseparability, indivisibility; phalanx, agglomerate 324 n. *solid body*; sticker, burr, leech, limpet, remora, barnacle, parasite; gum 47 n. *adhesive*; stickjaw; toffee.

Adj. *cohesive*, adhesive; clinging, tenacious; sticky, gummy, gluey 354 adj. *viscid*; compact, well-knit, solid 324 adj. *dense*; infrangible, indivisible, inseparable, inextricable; close, tight, fitting.

Vb. *cohere*, hang together, hold, hold fast; bunch, close the ranks, stand shoulder to shoulder, rally 74 vb. *congregate*; grip, hug, clasp, embrace, clinch 778 vb. *retain*; fit tight, mould the figure; adhere, cling, stick, cleave to, come off on, rub off on; freeze on to, stick like a leech; cake, coagulate, solidify 324 vb. *be dense*.

agglutinate, conglutinate, glue, gum, paste, lute, cement, weld, braze 45 vb. *join*.

49. Non-coherence – N. *non-coherence*, incoherence 72 n. *discontinuity*; chaos 51 n. *decomposition*; scattering 75 n. *dispersion*; separability; looseness, bagginess; wateriness 335 n. *fluidity*; slipperiness 258 n. *smoothness*; frangibility 330 n. *brittleness*.

Adj. *non-adhesive*, slippery 258 adj.

smooth; incoherent, unconsolidated, loose; loose-knit, lax, slack, baggy, floppy, flapping, flying, streaming; watery, runny 335 adj. *fluid*; open-ended 217 adj. *pendent*; uncombined 51 adj. *decomposed*.

Vb. *unstick*, unglue, peel off; detach, unpin 46 vb. *disjoin*; shake off, unseat, dismount; shed, slough 229 vb. *doff*.

come unstuck, peel off; melt, thaw, run 337 vb. *liquefy*; totter, slip 309 vb. *tumble*; dangle, flap 217 vb. *hang*; rattle, shake.

50. Combination – N. *combination*, 56 n. *composition*; coalescence, symphysis 45 n. *junction*; fusion, crasis, blending, conflation, synthesis, syncretism 43 n. *mixture*; amalgamation, merger, assimilation; unification, integration, centralization 88 n. *unity*; union, incorporation, embodiment, incarnation; synchronization 123 n. *synchronism*, 706 n. *cooperation*; coagency 181 n. *concurrence*; league 706 n. *association*; conspiracy 623 n. *plot*; orchestration 710 n. *concord*; synopsis, conspectus 438 n. *view*; mosaic, jigsaw; compound, alloy 43 n. *a mixture*.

Adj. *combined* etc. vb.; unified 88 adj. *one*; integrated, centralized; incorporate; inbred 5 adj. *intrinsic*; fused 43 adj. *mixed*; coalescent, symphysical; synchronized 123 vb. *synchronous*; conspiratorial; coagent 181 adj. *concurrent*.

Vb. *combine*, put together 45 vb. *join*; make up 56 vb. *compose*; interweave 222 vb. *weave*; harmonize, synchronize 24 vb. *accord*; unify, centralize; incorporate, merge, amalgamate; compound 43 vb. *mix*; fuse, conflate; lump together 38 vb. *add*; embody, group 74 vb. *bring together*; brigade, associate; league with, partner, team up with 706 vb. *cooperate*; mate, couple 90 vb. *pair*; cabal, conspire 623 vb. *plot*; have an affinity, combine with.

51. Decomposition – N. *decomposition*, 46 n. *disjunction*; resolution, diaeresis; partition, dissection, analysis, breakdown, factorization, syllabification, simplification; parsing 564 n. *grammar*; dissolution 337 n. *liquefaction*; decentralization; disintegration, chaos.

decay, 655 n. *dilapidation*; erosion, wear and tear 37 n. *diminution*; corruption, putrefaction, mortification, necrosis, gangrene 649 n. *uncleanness*; rot, rust, mould 659 n. *blight*; carrion 363 n. *corpse*.

Adj. *decomposed* etc. vb.; uncombined, chaotic 46 adj. *disjunct*; mouldering, rotten, bad, off, high, rancid 649 adj. *unclean*.

Vb. *decompose*, resolve, reduce, factorize 44 vb. *simplify*; separate out, parse, dissect; break down, analyse 46 vb. *disjoin*; disband 75 vb. *disperse*; decentralize; disturb, confuse 63 vb. *derange*; dissolve 337 vb. *liquefy*; erode 37 vb. *bate*; rot, rust, moulder, decay, crumble, perish 655 vb. *deteriorate*; corrupt, putrefy 649 vb. *make unclean*; disintegrate 165 vb. *be destroyed*.

52. Whole: principal part – N. *whole*, wholeness, fullness 54 n. *completeness*; a whole, entirety, ensemble, corpus, complex, four corners of; totality (see *all*); universalization 79 n. *generality*; comprehensivity, inclusiveness 78 n. *inclusion*; collectivity, world 321 n. *universe*; grand view, bird's eye v., panorama, conspectus, synopsis 438 n. *view*; round, circuit 314 n. *circuition*.

all, no omissions, one and all, everybody, everyone; the whole, total, aggregate, gross amount, sum, sum total; ensemble, tout e., length and breadth, lock, stock, and barrel, hook, line, and sinker; unit, set, outfit, pack; inventory 87 n. *list*; lot, the whole caboodle.

chief part, best part 638 n. *chief thing*; ninety-nine per cent, bulk, mass, substance; tissue, staple; lion's share; gist, sum and substance, the long and the short; majority 104 n. *greater number*.

Adj. *whole*, total, universal, holistic; integral 44 adj. *unmixed*; entire, ungelded 646 adj. *perfect*; grand, gross, full 54 adj. *complete*; single, integrated 88 adj. *one*; in one piece, seamless.

intact, untouched, unaffected; undivided, unbroken, unimpaired; uncut, unabridged, uncensored, unexpurgated; undamaged 646 adj. *perfect*.

indivisible, impartible, indissoluble; indiscerptible, inseparable; monolithic 16 adj. *uniform*.

comprehensive, omnibus, encyclopedic, all-embracing, full-length 78 adj. *inclusive*; wholesale, sweeping 32 adj. *great*; wide-spread, epidemic 79 adj. *general*; international, world-wide, cosmic 79 adj. *universal*, 189 adj. *ubiquitous*.

Adv. *wholly*, integrally, body and soul, as a whole; every inch, without deduction, one hundred per cent, in extenso; bodily, en masse, en bloc; all in all.

53. Part – N. *part*, portion, proportion; majority 104 n. *greater number*; minority 105 n. *fewness*; fraction, half, moiety, tithe, percentage; balance 41 n. *remainder*; quota, contingent, share 783 n. *portion*; item 80 n. *particulars*; ingredient, member, constituent, factor, element 58 n. *component*; excerpt, extract, passage, quotation; arc 248 n. *curve*; hemisphere 252 n. *sphere*; instalment, advance, earnest money, sample, foretaste; fragment (see *piece*).

subdivision, segment, sector, section 46 n. *scission*; division, compartment; group, sub-g., species, sub-s., family 74 n. *group*; department 184 n. *district*; chapter, paragraph, clause, sub-clause, phrase, verse; fascicle, part, number, issue, instalment, book, volume 589 n. *edition*; canto 593 n. *poem*.

branch, sub-b., ramification, offshoot 40 n. *adjunct*; bough, limb, spur 366 n. *foliage*.

piece, frustum, torso, trunk 41 n. *remainder*; limb, segment, section (see *part*); patch, insertion; strip, length, roll 222 n. *textile*; fragment, unfinished symphony 55 n. *incompleteness*; bit, scrap, shred, wisp, rag 33 n. *small thing*; morsel 33 n. *small quantity*; splinter, sliver, chip, snip; cantle, cut, wedge, finger, slice, rasher; gobbet, collop, cutlet, chop, steak; hunk, chunk; potsherd, brickbat; dollop, dose; bits and pieces 43 n. *medley*; shreds, rags, tatters; piece of land, parcel.

Adj. *fragmentary*, broken, brashy, crumbly; in bits, in pieces 46 adj. *disjunct*; limbless, armless, legless, in torso 647 adj. *imperfect*; partial, bitty, scrappy 636 adj. *insufficient*; half-finished, unfinished; fractional, half, semi, hemi, aliquot; sectional, departmentalized, compartmentalized; shredded 33 adj. *small*.

Adv. *piecemeal*, part by part, limb from limb; by instalments, by snatches, by inches, by driblets; bit by bit, inch by inch, foot by foot, drop by drop; in detail, in lots.

54. Completeness – N. *completeness*, nothing lacking, nothing to add 52 n. *whole*; integration, solidarity 88 n. *unity*; self-sufficiency 635 n. *sufficiency*; universality, comprehensivity 79 n. *generality*; the ideal 646 n. *perfection*; ne plus ultra, the limit, peak, culmination, crown 213 n. *summit*; finish, last touch 725 n. *completion*; whole hog, nothing less than, the utmost.

plenitude, fullness, capacity, maximum, one's fill, saturation 635 n. *sufficiency*; saturation point 863 n. *satiety*; completion, replenishment, refill; overfulfilment 637 n. *redundance*; complement, full measure, brimmer; bumper; bellyful, sickener.

Adj. *complete*, plenary, full; utter, total; integral, entire 52 adj. *whole*; self-contained, self-sufficient, self-sufficing 635 adj. *sufficient*; comprehensive 78 adj. *inclusive*; exhaustive, circumstantial, detailed; absolute, extreme, radical; thorough, thoroughgoing, whole-hogging, sweeping, wholesale, regular, unmitigated; crowning 725 adj. *completive*; unqualified 744 adj. *unconditional*.

full, replete, topped up, well-filled, well-lined, bulging; brim-full, top-f., brimming; overfull, overflowing, slopping, swamped, drowned; saturated 637 adj. *redundant*; bursting at the seams; crop-full, gorged 863 adj. *sated*; chock-full, cram-full, crammed; laden, freighted, fraught; infested, overrun; full of, rolling in; inexhaustible 146 adj. *unceasing*.

Vb. *be complete*, make a whole; reach perfection, have everything; culminate 725 vb. *climax*; come to a close 69 vb. *end*; reach maturity 669 vb. *mature*; fill up, brim, hold no more, run over, slop o., overflow 637 vb. *superabound*.

make complete, complete, integrate; piece together 56 vb. *compose*; eke out, supplement, supply, fill a gap 38 vb. *add*; make good 31 vb. *compensate*; do thoroughly 725 vb. *carry through*; put the finishing touch 69 vb. *terminate*.

fill, fill up, brim, top: soak, saturate 341 vb. *drench*; overfill, swamp, drown, overwhelm; top up, replenish 633 vb. *provide*; cram, pack, stuff, line, ram in, jam in 303 vb. *insert*; stow, charge; lade, freight 193 vb. *load*; occupy 226 vb. *cover*; overrun 189 vb. *pervade*; fill in, enter 38 vb. *add*.

Adv. *completely*, fully, wholly, totally, entirely, utterly, extremely 32 adv. *greatly*; effectually, virtually, as good as; to all intents and purposes; quite, altogether; outright, downright; thoroughly, clean; out and out, all out, heart and soul, up to the hilt, hook, line, and sinker; root and branch; with a vengeance, and then some; as . . . as can be.

throughout, from first to last, from beginning to end, from end to end, fore and aft; from top to bottom; from top to toe, from head to foot, cap-à-pie; to the bitter end, to the end of the chapter, for good and all.

55. Incompleteness – N. *incompleteness*, defectiveness; growing pains, unreadiness; immaturity 670 n. *undevelopment*; sketch, outline 623 n. *plan*; torso 53 n. *piece*; half-measures, a lick and a promise 726 n. *non-completion*; perfunctoriness, superficiality 458 n. *negligence*; deficiency 307 n. *shortcoming*, 636 n. *insufficiency*; mutilation 655 n. *deterioration*; omission, missing link 201 n.

interval, semi-, half, quarter; instalment 53 n. *part.*

deficit, missing link, omission, caret 190 n. *absence*; defect, shortfall; default, want, lack, need 627 n. *requirement.*

Adj. *incomplete*, defective 307 adj. *deficient;* short, scant 636 adj. *insufficient*; short of, shy of; maimed, lame, limping; without, -less; garbled; docked, truncated 204 adj. *short*; flawed 647 adj. *imperfect*; half, semi-, partial, 53 adj. *fragmentary*; left unfinished 726 adj. *uncompleted*; unready 670 adj. *unprepared*; unripe 670 adj. *immature*; raw, crude, rough-hewn 244 adj. *amorphous*; sketchy, scrappy, bitty; superficial, perfunctory, half-done; interrupted 72 adj. *discontinuous*; in default, in arrears; in progress, in hand, in preparation, on the stocks 68 adj. *beginning.*

Adv. *incompletely*, partially, by halves, in instalments.

56. Composition – N. *composition*, constitution, set-up, make-up; make, conformation, formation, construction, build-up, build, organization 331 n. *structure*; temper, crasis, nature, character, condition 5 n. *temperament*; compound 43 n. *mixture*, 50 n. *combination*; syntax, sentence, period 563 n. *phrase*; composing, typography 587 n. *print*; compilation 74 n. *assemblage*; choreography 837 n. *dancing*; orchestration, instrumentation, score 412 n. *musical piece*; pattern, design.

Vb. *constitute*, compose, form, make; make up, add up to, build up to; inhere, belong to, go to the making of, enter into.

compose, compound 43 vb. *mix*, 50 vb. *combine*; synthesize, organize 62 vb. *arrange*; compile, assemble 74 vb. *bring together*; compose, set up 587 vb. *print*; draft, indite 586 vb. *write*; orchestrate, score 413 vb. *compose music*; construct, build, make 164 vb. *produce*; pattern, design 12 vb. *correlate.*

57. Exclusion – N. *exclusion*, preemption, forestalling 702 n. *hindrance*;

possessiveness, monopoly, dog-in-the-manger policy, exclusiveness, closed shop 932 n. *selfishness*; exception, exemption, dispensation; omission 607 n. *rejection*; non-admission, black-ball; closed door, lock-out; ban, bar, taboo 757 n. *prohibition*; ostracism, boycott 620 n. *avoidance*; segregation, quarantine, colour-bar, apartheid, casteism 883 n. *seclusion*; intolerance 481 n. *prejudice*; extrusion, expulsion, disbarment, dismissal, deportation, exile, expatriation; cancellation 550 n. *obliteration*; screen, partition, pale, curtain, iron c., barrier; ghetto, outer darkness 223 n. *exteriority.*

Adj. *excluding*, exclusive, exclusory, exemptive; preventive, interdictive, prohibitive 757 n. *prohibiting*; preclusive, pre-emptive.

excluded, barred etc. vb.; peripheral, half in, half out; disbarred, struck off 550 adj. *obliterated*; shut out, outcaste 607 adj. *rejected*; inadmissible, beyond the pale 470 adj. *impossible.*

Vb. *exclude*, preclude, preoccupy, pre-empt, forestall 64 vb. *come before*; keep out, warn off 747 vb. *restrain*; black-ball, bar, ban, taboo, black, disallow 757 vb. *prohibit*; ostracize, cold-shoulder, boycott, outcaste, send to Coventry 620 vb. *avoid*; leave out, count o.; dispense 919 vb. *exempt*; except, omit, miss out, pass over, disregard 458 vb. *neglect*; cancel 550 vb. *obliterate*; disbar, strike off, remove, disqualify 963 vb. *punish*; rule out, draw the line; wall off, curtain off, quarantine, excommunicate, segregate, sequester 883 vb. *seclude*; thrust out, extrude, dismiss, deport, exile, banish, outlaw, expatriate; sort out, declassify; expurgate, censor 648 vb. *purify.*

Adv. *exclusive of*, barring, not counting, except, save; let alone, apart from.

58. Component – N. *component*, element; constituent, part and parcel 53 n. *part*; factor, leaven 178 n. *influence*; appurtenance, feature 40 n. *adjunct*; one of; member; ingredient 193 n. *contents*;

components, set, outfit 88 n. *unit*; complete set, complement.

Adj. *ingredient*, belonging, inherent 5 adj. *intrinsic*; component, constituent; built-in, appurtenant 45 adj. *conjunct*; part of, one of, on the staff.

59. Extraneousness – N. *extraneousness*, foreignness 6 n. *extrinsicality*, 223 n. *exteriority*; foreign parts 199 n. *farness*; foreign body, alien element 84 n. *unconformity*; alienism.

foreigner, alien, stranger; continental, barbarian, Celtic fringe, lime-juicer, greaser, dago, wog; paleface, gringo; Martian; resident alien, metic, uitlander, expatriate; migrant, emigrant, immigrant, declarant; refugee, déraciné, displaced person, D.P. 268 n. *wanderer*; diaspora, ten lost tribes.

intruder, interloper, cuckoo, squatter; uninvited guest, gate-crasher, stowaway; outsider, novus homo, upstart; newcomer 297 n. *incomer*; trespasser, invader 712 n. *attacker*.

Adj. *extraneous*, ulterior 223 adj. *exterior*, 6 adj. *extrinsic*; imported, foreign-made; foreign, alien, strange, outlandish, barbarian; oversea, continental; exotic, hot-house, unacclimatized; nomad, wandering 267 adj. *travelling*; unassimilated 84 adj. *unconformable*; immigrant 297 adj. *incoming*; intrusive; exceptional 84 adj. *unusual*; un-American, un-English 84 adj. *abnormal*; unnatural, supernatural 983 adj. *magical*.

Adv. *abroad*, in foreign parts, overseas; from outer space.

Section 4: Order

60. Order – N. *order*, state of order, orderliness, tidiness, neatness; harmony 710 n. *concord*; economy, system, method, methodicalness, methodology, systematization, rule, regularity 16 n. *uniformity*; routine 610 n. *habit*; discipline 739 n. *obedience*; due order, gradation, rank, place 73 n. *serial place*; course, even tenor 71 n. *continuity*; organiza-

tion, disposition, array 62 n. *arrangement*.

Adj. *orderly*, harmonious 710 adj. *concordant*; well-behaved, disciplined 739 adj. *obedient*; well-regulated, under control, schematic, methodical, systematic, businesslike; correct, shipshape, trim, neat, tidy, dinky 62 adj. *arranged*; unruffled, unrumpled 258 adj. *smooth*.

Vb. *be in order*, harmonize, synchronize 24 vb. *accord*; fall in, range oneself, line up; fall into place, find one's level; take station, take one's place 187 vb. *place oneself*; keep one's place.

Adv. *in order*, strictly, just so, by the book, by order, as directed; in turn, seriatim; orderly, methodically; all correct, O.K.

61. Disorder – N. *disorder*, random order, incoordination, muddle, chaos, anarchy 734 n. *laxity*; anomaly, irregularity, ectopia; disharmony 411 n. *discord*; disorderliness, unruliness 738 n. *disobedience*; untidiness, littering, sluttishness, slovenliness 649 n. *uncleanness*; discomposure, disarray, dishevelment 63 n. *derangement*.

confusion (see *disorder*); welter, jumble, mix-up, medley, imbroglio; wilderness, jungle; chaos, huddle, seething mass, scramble, shambles 74 n. *crowd*; muddle, litter, clutter, lumber 641 n. *rubbish*; farrago, mess, hash, hotchpotch, witch's brew, jumble sale, lucky dip; confusion worse confounded (see *turmoil*).

complexity, complication 700 n. *predicament*; imbroglio, embroilment; intricacy, interlocking, maze, labyrinth, web 222 n. *network*; coil, tangle, twist, tangled skein, ravelment; knot, Gordian k. 47 n. *ligature*; wheels within wheels, puzzle 517 n. *unintelligibility*.

turmoil, turbulence, tumult, frenzy, ferment, storm, upheaval, convulsion 176 n. *violence*; pandemonium, inferno; hullabaloo, row, riot, uproar 400 n. *loudness*; affray, fight, fracas, mêlée 718 n. *battle*; to-do, rumpus, ruction, pother 318 n. *agitation*; whirlwind 352 n.

gale; beargarden, shambles, madhouse, Bedlam; Saturnalia, rough house, rough and tumble, free for all, hell broke loose, bull in a china shop.

Adj. *orderless*, in disorder, in disarray, disordered, disorganized, jumbled; unclassified, ungraded, unsorted; out of order, not in working order 641 adj. *useless*; out of joint, dislocated 46 adj. *disjunct*; irregular, ectopic 188 adj. *displaced*; awry, snafu; topsy-turvy 221 adj. *inverted*; straggling 75 adj. *unassembled*; random, unarranged, unorganized, uncoordinated; unschematic, planless; incoherent, skimble-skamble; irregular, anomalous 17 adj. *nonuniform*; unsystematic, unmethodical, desultory, aimless, casual; promiscuous, indiscriminate 463 adj. *indiscriminating*; confused, chaotic, in a mess, messy, haywire; unkempt, dishevelled, tumbled, windswept, tousled, discomposed; untidy, slovenly, sluttish, slatternly, bedraggled 649 adj. *dirty*; sloppy, slipshod 456 adj. *inattentive*.

complex, intricate, involved, complicated, over-c.; mazy, winding, inextricable 251 adj. *labyrinthine*; entangled, balled up, snarled 702 adj. *hindered*.

disorderly, undisciplined, tumultuous, rumbustious 738 adj. *riotous*; frantic 503 adj. *frenzied*; orgiastic, Saturnalian, Bacchic, Dionysiac 949 adj. *drunken*; tempestuous 176 adj. *violent*, 318 adj. *agitated*; anarchical, lawless 954 adj. *lawbreaking*; wild, harum-scarum, scatter-brained 456 adj. *light-minded*.

Vb. *rampage*, storm 176 vb. *be violent*; rush, mob, break the cordon; roister, riot 738 vb. *revolt*; romp 837 vb. *amuse oneself*; play the fool; fête, maffick 886 vb. *gratulate*.

Adv. *confusedly*, in disorder, anyhow; irregularly, chaotically, pell-mell, higgledy-piggledy, helter-skelter; at sixes and sevens, at cross purposes; topsy-turvy, upside down 221 adv. *inversely*.

62. Arrangement: reduction to order –
N. *arrangement*, reduction to order; ordering, disposal, disposition, marshal-

ling 187 n. *location*; collocation, grouping 74 n. *assemblage*; method, systematization, organization, reorganization; rationalization; streamlining 654 n. *improvement*; centralization, decentralization; administration, staff-work 689 n. *management*; planning 669 n. *preparation*; taxonomy, codification, categorization 77 n. *classification*; grading, graduation, calibration 465 n. *measurement*, 71 n. *series*; formulation, construction 56 n. *composition*; result of arrangement, array, system, form 60 n. *order*; orchestration 412 n. *music*; lay-out, pattern 331 n. *structure*; schematic arrangement, schematism; register, file 548 n. *record*; catalogue 87 n. *list*; syntagma, code, digest 592 n. *compendium*; scheme 623 n. *plan*.

sorting, grading, seeding; reference system, cross-reference 12 n. *correlation*; file, filing system, card index, pigeonhole; sieve, strainer 263 n. *porosity*; sorter, sifter.

Adj. *arranged*, disposed etc. vb.; ordered, schematic, tabular; methodical, systematic, organizational; classified, seeded, assorted; unravelled, disentangled, unscrambled, straightened out.

Vb. *arrange*, set, dispose, set up, set out; formulate, form, put into shape, orchestrate, score 56 vb. *compose*; range, align; marshal, array; grade, size, group, space; collocate 45 vb. *connect*; arrange for, make arrangements 669 vb. *prepare*, 623 vb. *plan*, 689 vb. *manage*.

regularize, reduce to order, straighten out, put to rights 654 vb. *rectify*, 24 vb. *adjust*; regulate, coordinate, phase; organize, systematize, methodize, schematize; standardize, normalize, centralize 16 vb. *make uniform*.

class, classify, subsume, group; specify 561 vb. *name*; analyse, dissect 51 vb. *decompose*; rate, rank, grade; sort, sift, seed; file, pigeon-hole; index, reference, cross-r.; tabulate, alphabeticize; catalogue 87 vb. *list*; register 548 vb. *record*; codify, digest.

unravel, untangle, disentangle, card, comb out, unweave, uncoil, untwist, untwine 316 vb. *evolve*; uncrease, iron out 258 vb. *smooth*; unscramble, straighten out, neaten.

63. Derangement – N. *derangement*, shuffling 151 n. *interchange*, 272 n. *transference*; sabotage 702 n. *hindrance*; disarrangement, disorganization, discomposure, dishevelment; dislocation 46 n. *separation*; displacement, disturbance, interruption 138 n. *intempestivity*; convulsion 176 n. *violence*, 318 n. *agitation*, 61 n. *disorder*.

Vb. *derange*, disarrange, disorder, tumble; disturb, touch 265 vb. *move*; meddle, interfere 702 vb. *hinder*; mislay 188 vb. *misplace*; disorganize, muddle, confound, confuse, convulse, make havoc, scramble; tamper 655 vb. *impair*; unhinge, dislocate, sprain, rick 188 vb. *displace*; unseat, dislodge, derail; unbalance, upset, overturn, capsize 221 vb. *invert*; unsettle, shake 318 vb. *agitate*; trouble, perturb, discompose, disconcert, ruffle, rattle, flurry, fluster 456 vb. *distract*; interrupt 138 vb. *mistime*; misdirect, disorientate 495 vb. *mislead*; dement 503 vb. *make mad*.

jumble, shuffle 151 vb. *interchange*, 272 vb. *transpose*; mix up 43 vb. *mix*; toss, tumble 318 vb. *agitate*; ruffle, dishevel, tousle, fluff; rumple, crumple, crease, crush; untidy, mess, muck up; muddle, huddle, mess up, litter, clutter; scatter, fling about 75 vb. *disperse*.

bedevil, confuse, confound, complicate, perplex, involve, ravel, ball up, entangle, tangle, embroil.

64. Precedence – N. *precedence*, antecedence 283 n. *precession*; anteriority 119 n. *priority*; anteposition, prefixion, prothesis 237 n. *front*; pride of place 34 n. *superiority*; pre-eminence 638 n. *importance*; hegemony 733 n. *authority*; the lead; precedent 66 n. *precursor*.

Adj. *preceding* etc. vb.; precedent, prodromic; antecedent, foregoing, outgoing; anterior 119 adj. *prior*; beforementioned, aforesaid; precursory, leading; preliminary, prefatory, introductory;

prelusive, prelusory; proemial, preparatory, anacrustic; prepositive, prosthetic, prefixed, prepositional 237 adj. *fore*.

Vb. *come before*, go first, run ahead, jump the queue 283 vb. *precede*; lead, guide, conduct, show the way, point the trail 547 vb. *indicate*; forerun, pioneer, clear the way, blaze the trail 484 vb. *discover*; head, take the lead 237 vb. *be in front*; outrank 34 vb. *be superior*; open, lead off, 68 vb. *begin*; preamble, prelude, preface, prologize; introduce, usher in, ring in 68 vb. *auspicate*.

prepose, prefix 38 vb. *add*; front, face, tip, top 237 vb. *be in front*; preface, prelude.

65. Sequence – N. *sequence*; going after 284 n. *following*; inference 475 n. *reasoning*; postposition, suffixion, suffixment; succession, Elijah's mantle 780 n. *transfer*; series 71 n. *continuity*; successiveness, alternation, serialization; continuation, prolongation 146 n. *continuance*; consequence 67 n. *sequel*, 157 n. *effect*.

Adj. *sequent*, following, succeeding, incoming; ensuing, proximate, next 200 adj. *near*; posterior 120 adj. *subsequent*; successive, consecutive 71 adj. *continuous*; postpositional 238 adj. *back*; consequent 157 adj. *caused*.

Vb. *come after*, come next, ensue 284 vb. *follow*; tread on the heels 200 vb. *be near*; succeed, inherit, supplant 150 vb. *substitute*; alternate, turn and turn about 141 vb. *be periodic*; relieve, take over.

place after, suffix, append; subscribe, subjoin 38 vb. *add*.

Adv. *after*, following; afterwards 120 adv. *subsequently*, 238 adv. *rearward*; successively; next, later; infra, below.

66. Precursor – N. *precursor*, predecessor, ancestor, forbear, 169 n. *parent*; eldest, firstborn; discoverer, inventor 461 n. *experimenter*; pioneer, pathfinder, explorer 690 n. *leader*; vanguard, avantgarde; forerunner, herald, harbinger 531 n. *messenger*; dawn, prefigurement, foretaste, preview, premonition, forewarning 511 n. *omen*; precedent 83 n. *example*; antecedent, prefix, preposition 40 n. *adjunct*; eve 119 n. *priority*.

prelude, preliminary, anacrusis, preamble, preface, prologue, foreword; proem, overture, opening, exordium, prolegomena, introduction 68 n. *beginning*; premiss, presupposition 512 n. *supposition*.

Adj. *precursory*, preliminary, exploratory 669 adj. *preparatory*; prelusive, prelusory, anacrustic; proemial, introductory, prefatory 68 adj. *beginning*; inaugural, foundational; precedent 64 adj. *preceding*.

67. Sequel – N. *sequel*, consequence, result, by-product 157 n. *effect*; conclusion 69 n. *end*; sequela, after-effect, hangover; after-taste; afterglow; aftermath; afterbirth; inheritance, legacy 777 n. *dower*; afterthought, esprit d'escalier; afterpiece, postlude, epilogue, postscript; peroration, envoi, last words; follow-through 725 n. *completion*; continuation, sequel, tag, tailpiece, heelpiece, colophon, coda 238 n. *rear*; appendage, appendix, codicil, supplement 40 n. *adjunct*; suffix, affix, afterpart, tail, queue, retinue 284 n. *follower*; dessert 301 n. *dish*.

aftercomer, after-generations, epigoni, the unborn 170 n. *posterity*; heir 776 n. *beneficiary*; successor; replacement 150 n. *substitute*; relief 707 n. *auxiliary*; fresh blood, new broom; new arrival 297 n. *incomer*; gleaner, jackal.

68. Beginning – N. *beginning*, rise (see *origin*); infancy 130 n. *youth*; primitiveness 127 n. *oldness*; commencement; onset 295 n. *arrival*; inception, foundation; origination, invention 484 n. *discovery*; exordium, introduction, curtain-raiser 66 n. *prelude*; van, forefront 237 n. *front*; dawn 128 n. *morning*; teething troubles; first blush, first glance; primer, rudiments, elements, principia, first principles, alphabet, ABC; débutant, starter 538 n. *beginner*; preliminaries 669 n. *preparation*.

début, coming out, inauguration, opening, unveiling; première, first offence; premier pas, first step, gambit; maiden voyage, maiden speech.

start, outset; starting point, zero hour, D-day; send-off 296 n. *departure*; kick-off; resumption 148 n. *reversion*; new departure, precedent; threshold 263 n. *doorway*.

origin, derivation; genesis, birth, nativity; provenance, ancestry 169 n. *parentage*; fount, fons et origo; rise 156 n. *source*; bud, germ, egg, protoplasm; cradle, incunabula 192 n. *home*.

Adj. *beginning*, initiatory, inchoative; introductory 66 adj. *precursory*; inaugural, foundational; elemental 156 adj. *fundamental*; aboriginal 127 adj. *primal*; rudimentary, elementary 670 adj. *immature*; embryonic, nascent, budding, incipient, inchoate, raw 726 adj. *uncompleted*; launched.

first, initial, maiden, starting, natal; original 21 adj. *unimitated*; unprecedented 126 adj. *new*; foremost, front 237 adj. *fore*.

Vb. *begin*, commence; set in, open, dawn, break out, burst forth, spring up, crop up; arise, come into existence; make one's début, come out; start, enter upon, embark on 296 vb. *start out*; clock in; handsel, run in; resume, make a fresh start 148 vb. *revert*; recommence, re-open; set about, attack, tackle, go to it 672 vb. *undertake*.

initiate, found, launch; originate, invent 484 vb. *discover*; usher in, introduce; start up, switch on, set going, set on foot; take the initiative, lead off, pioneer, open up; broach, open, break the ice, set the ball rolling; take the plunge, cross the Rubicon; touch off, spark off, set off.

auspicate, inaugurate, open; institute, lay the foundations, found, set up, establish 156 vb. *cause*; baptize, christen, launch 561 vb. *name*; initiate, blood, flesh.

Adv. *initially*, originally; in the bud, in embryo; ab initio, ab ovo; firstly, imprimis.

69. End – N. *end*, close, conclusion, consummation 725 n. *completion*; pay-off, result 157 n. *effect*; termination, closure; finishing stroke, death blow, quietus, coup de grâce; ending, finish, finale, curtain; term, period, stop, halt 145 n. *cessation*; final stage, latter end; peroration, last words, swansong 67 n. *sequel*; last lap, home stretch; last breath, last gasp; see *finality*.

extremity, final point, omega; extreme, ne plus ultra; farthest point, pole, world's end 199 n. *farness*; verge, brink, frontier 236 n. *limit*; terminus, terminal 295 n. *goal*; heel, toe, bottom, nadir 214 n. *base*; tip, vertex, peak, top 213 n. *summit*; tail 67 n. *sequel*; end, fag-e. 238 n. *rear*; epilogue, postscript, appendix 40 n. *adjunct*.

finality, bitter end; time up; conclusion, end of the matter 54 n. *completeness*; drop of the curtain, dissolution 361 n. *death*; eschatology, last things, last trump, Day of Judgement, end of the world 124 n. *future state*.

Adj. *ending*, final, terminal, last, ultimate; extreme, polar; definitive, conclusive, crowning 725 adj. *completive*; at an end, settled, set at rest; off, cancelled; penultimate, antepenultimate; hindmost, caudal 238 n. *back*.

Vb. *end*, come to an end, expire, run out 111 vb. *elapse*; close (see *terminate*); die out 361 vb. *die*; come to a close, have run its course; stop, clock out 145 vb. *cease*.

terminate, conclude, close, determine, decide, settle; apply the closure, bring to an end, put paid to; finish, achieve, consummate, get through 725 vb. *carry through*; ring down the curtain, switch off, stop 145 vb. *halt*.

Adv. *finally*, in conclusion, in fine; at last; once for all.

70. Middle – N. *middle*, midst, mediety; mean 30 n. *average*; medium, middle term; thick of things; heart, hub 225 n. *centre*; midweek, midwinter, half-tide 625 n. *mid-course*; bisection, midline,

equator; middle distance, equidistance, halfway house.

Adj. *middle*, medial, mean, mid; mediate, middlemost, midmost 225 adj. *central*; middling 177 adj. *moderate*, 625 adj. *neutral*; intermediate 231 adj. *interjacent*; equidistant; mediterranean, equatorial.

Adv. *midway*, in the middle, in the thick, halfway; midships.

71. Continuity: uninterrupted sequence – N. *continuity*, monotony 16 n. *uniformity*; overlap; consecutiveness, successiveness; line, one thing after another, serialization 65 n. *sequence*; endlessness 115 n. *perpetuity*; repetitiveness 106 n. *repetition*; cumulativeness, snowball 36 n. *increase*; gradualism; flow, trend 179 n. *tendency*; daily round, routine 610 n. *habit*; concatenation, chain-reaction, chain-letter; circle 250 n. *circularity*.

series, gradation 27 n. *degree*; succession, run, progression; count, count down; ascending order, descending o.; pedigree 169 n. *genealogy*; chain, line; array 62 n. *arrangement*; row, colonnade; ladder, steps 308 n. *ascent*; range, tier, storey 207 n. *layer*; set, suite, suit (of cards), assortment 77 n. *classification*; team 74 n. *band*; gamut, scale; stepping stones 624 n. *bridge*; hierarchy.

procession 267 n. *marching*; cavalcade 875 n. *pageant*; crocodile, queue, tail, cortège, train, suite, retinue; caravan, file, single f.

Adj. *continuous*, consecutive, running, successive 65 adj. *sequent*; serial, serialized; progressive 179 adj. *tending*; overlapping, unbroken, uninterrupted, circular; direct, immediate, unmediated; continual, non-stop 115 adj. *perpetual*; rhythmic, recurrent 106 adj. *repeated*, 16 adj. *uniform*; linear 249 adj. *straight*.

Vb. *run on*, continue, succeed, overlap 65 vb. *come after*; file, defile; circle 626 vb. *circuit*.

continuate, run on 203 vb. *lengthen*; serialize, thread, string 45 vb. *connect*.

Adv. *continuously* etc. adj.; serially, seriatim; successively, in succession, in turn; at a stretch, running; step by step, hand over hand; in file, in column, in line ahead, nose to tail.

72. Discontinuity: interrupted sequence – N. *discontinuity*, solution of continuity, intermittence; discontinuance 145 n. *cessation*; interval, intermission, pause 145 n. *lull*; randomness 61 n. *disorder*; interruption, intervention; parenthesis, episode 231 n. *interjection*; caesura, division 46 n. *separation*, 547 n. *punctuation*; break, fault, crack 201 n. *gap*; missing link, broken thread, anacoluthon, non sequitur; alternation 141 n. *periodicity*; irregularity 142 n. *fitfulness*.

Adj. *discontinuous*, non-recurrent, unrepeated; interrupted, stopping; disconnected 46 adj. *disjunct*; few and far between 140 adj. *infrequent*; patchy 437 adj. *variegated*, 17 adj. *non-uniform*; desultory, intermittent 142 adj. *fitful*; spasmodic, jerky, uneven; incoherent, anacoluthic 477 adj. *illogical*; parenthetic, episodic, not belonging.

Vb. *be discontinuous*, pause 145 vb. *stop*; alternate, intermit.

discontinue, interrupt, intervene; interpose, interject, punctuate 231 vb. *put between*; disconnect 46 vb. *disjoin*.

Adv. *discontinuously*, at intervals, occasionally, irregularly, by snatches, desultorily.

73. Term: serial position – N. *serial place*, term, order, remove 27 n. *degree*; rank, ranking, grade, gradation; station, place, position, pitch; status, standing, footing; point, mark, pitch, level, storey; stage, milestone, climacteric, climax.

74. Assemblage – N. *assemblage*, bringing together, collection 50 n. *combination*; collocation, juxtaposition 202 n. *contiguity*; contesseration 45 n. *joinder*; compilation 56 n. *composition*; gathering, ingathering, reaping 771 n. *earnings*; concentration, mobilization, levy 718 n. *war measures*; muster, review, parade

875 n. *pageant*; rally, round-up; collectivization.

assembly, mutual attraction 291 n. *attraction*; congregation, concourse, conflux, concurrence 293 n. *convergence*; gathering, meeting, mass-m., meet, coven; conventicle, convention; conclave 692 n. *council*; eisteddfod, festival 876 n. *celebration*; company 882 n. *social gathering*; circle, symposium 584 n. *conference*.

group, constellation, galaxy, cluster; bevy, flock, herd; drove, team; pack, kennel; stable, string; nest, eyrie; brood, hatch; gaggle, flight, covey; shoal, school; unit, brigade 722 n. *formation*; batch, lot, clutch; brace, pair, span, pride of lions; leash, four-in-hand; set, class, genus, species 77 n. *sort*; breed, tribe, clan, household 11 n. *family*; brotherhood, fellowship, college 706 n. *association*; movement 708 n. *party*; sphere, quarter, circle; social group, the classes 868 n. *nobility*, 869 n. *commonalty*; age-group, stream; hand (at cards), set 71 n. *series*.

band, company, circus; troupe, cast 594 n. *actor*; team, string, eleven, eight; knot, bunch; set, coterie, ring; gang, party; committee, commission 754 n. *consignee*; crew, establishment, cadre, staff 686 n. *personnel*; unit, regiment 722 n. *formation*; squad, posse; force, body, host 722 n. *armed force*, 104 n. *multitude*; brotherhood, band of brothers, merry men; panel 87 n. *list*.

crowd, throng 104 n. *multitude*; huddle, swarm, colony; knot, bunch; mass, mob, rout 869 n. *rabble*; sea of faces, full house; congestion, press, squash, jam, scrum, rush, crush, rush-hour; flood 32 n. *great quantity*; condensation, populousness, over-population 324 n. *density*; infestation; herd instinct, crowd psychology, mass emotion.

bunch, lot, mixed l. 43 n. *medley*; clump, tuft, wisp, handful; bag, bundle, packet, package, parcel, budget; file 548 n. *record*; bale, roll, bolt; shock, sheaf, stook, truss, heap; bouquet, nosegay, posy; clue, skein, hank.

accumulation, agglomeration, conglomeration, aggregation; amassment, concentration; pile-up 279 n. *collision*; mass, pile; congeries, heap; drift, snowdrift; snowball 36 n. *increment*; dump, shoot 641 n. *rubbish*; store 632 n. *storage*, 633 n. *provision*; magazine 723 n. *arsenal*; kit, stock; range, selection, assortment 795 n. *merchandise*; display 522 n. *exhibit*; museum 632 n. *collection*; menagerie 369 n. *zoo*.

Adj. *assembled*, met, convened, etc. vb., collectivized; crowded, huddled 324 adj. *dense*; populous, swarming 104 adj. *multitudinous*; in a crowd, seething, milling; in formation, serried.

Vb. *congregate*, meet, forgather, rendezvous, assemble; associate, come together, get t., join t., flock t., pig t.; gather, collect, troop, rally, roll up; resort to, make for 293 vb. *converge*; band, gang up; huddle, cluster, bunch, crowd, nest; throng, swarm, seethe, mill around.

bring together, assemble, put together 45 vb. *join*, 291 vb. *attract*; gather, collect, rally, muster, call up, mobilize; concentrate, consolidate; lump together, group, brigade, unite; focus, centre; convene, convoke, hold a meeting; herd, shepherd, get in, whip in, call in, round up, corral 235 vb. *enclose*; mass, aggregate; accumulate, heap, pile, amass; catch, rake in, net 771 vb. *acquire*; scrape together 632 vb. *store*; truss, bundle, parcel, package; bunch, bind; pack, cram, stuff 54 vb. *fill*.

75. Non-assemblage. Dispersion – N.
dispersion, scattering, diffraction; spread, scatter, radiation 294 n. *divergence*; disintegration 51 n. *decomposition*; evaporation; dissipation; circulation, diffusion; dissemination, broadcasting; dispersal, sprawl; disbandment, demobilization; diaspora.

Adj. *unassembled*, dispersed etc. vb.; strung out, sporadic 140 n. *infrequent*; widespread 183 adj. *spacious*; epidemic 79 adj. *universal*; spread, dispread 46 adj. *separate*; dishevelled, streaming 61

adj. *orderless*; decentralized; centrifugal 294 adj. *divergent*.

Vb. *be dispersed*, disperse, scatter, spread, rarefy 325 vb. *be rare*; radiate 294 vb. *diverge*; break ranks, fall out, dismiss; hive off 267 vb. *wander*; drift apart, straggle, trail 282 vb. *stray*; sprawl over 226 vb. *overlie*; explode, blow up, burst; evaporate, melt; disintegrate 51 vb. *decompose*.

disperse, scatter, diffract; separate 46 vb. *sunder*; thin out, string o.; disseminate, broadcast, sow, strew, spread; dissipate, dispel, disintegrate; decentralize; break up, disband, disembody, demobilize, send home; draft off, detach 272 vb. *send*; diffuse, spatter 341 vb. *moisten*; circulate, utter; rout 727 vb. *defeat*.

Adv. *sporadically*, here and there, sparsely, in twos and threes.

76. Focus: place of meeting – N. *focus*,
corradiation, focal point; crossways, crossroads; hub 70 n. *middle*; hall, civic centre, village hall, village green; campus; market place, forum 796 n. *mart*; resort, retreat, haunt, stamping ground; club, pub, local 192 n. *tavern*; headquarters, depot; rallying point, standard; rendezvous, meeting place; nest, fireside 192 n. *home*; cynosure, centre of attraction, honey-pot 291 n. *magnet*; place of pilgrimage, Mecca, Rome, promised land 295 n. *goal*.

Vb. *focus*, centre, corradiate 293 vb. *converge*; centralize, concentrate, focus upon.

77. Class – N. *classification*, categorization; diagnosis, specification; designation, category, class, bracket; cadre; head, heading, sub-head, section, subsection 53 n. *subdivision*; division, branch, department; pigeon-hole 194 n. *compartment*; sex, gender; stream 74 n. *group*.

sort, order, type, variety, kind; manner, genre, style; quality, grade 5 n. *character*; mark, brand 547 n. *label*; kidney, feather, colour; stamp, mould, shape, make 243 n. *form*; assortment, set, suit, lot.

breed, strain, blood, family, kin, tribe, clan, sept, line 11 n. *race*, 169 n. *genealogy*; caste, phylum, genus, species, subspecies; genotype, monotype.

Adj. *generic*, sexual, masculine, feminine, neuter.

classificatory, classificational, taxonomic; sectional, denominational 978 adj. *sectarian*.

78. Inclusion – N. *inclusion*, comprisal; incorporation, embodiment, assimilation; admission 299 n. *reception*; admissibility, eligibility; membership 775 n. *participation*; inclusiveness, coverage 79 n. *generality*; comprehensiveness, set, packages 52 n. *whole*; accommodation, capacity, volume 183 n. *space*.

Adj. *inclusive*, comprising etc. vb.; incorporating, accommodating; overall, all-embracing 52 adj. *comprehensive*; wholesale, sweeping, total, global, world-wide, universal; synoptical 79 adj. *general*; broad-based.

included, admitted, admissible, eligible; constituent, component; inherent 58 adj. *ingredient*; inner 224 adj. *interior*.

Vb. *be included*, make one of; swell the ranks 708 vb. *join a party*; come under, appertain to; come in 297 vb. *enter*; constitute 56 vb. *compose*; inhere 5 vb. *be intrinsic*.

comprise, include, contain, consist of, hold, have, count, boast; take, measure; accommodate, find room for; comprehend, incapsulate 226 vb. *cover*; embody, incorporate; embrace 235 vb. *enclose*; have everything; involve, imply.

number with, count w., reckon among; subsume, place under; not omit, take into account.

Adv. *including*, inclusively; from A to Z; et cetera.

79. Generality – N. *generality*, universality, catholicity, ecumenicalism; generalization, the universals; panorama, synopsis, conspectus 438 n. *view*; in-

clusiveness, something for everybody; currency, prevalence, ubiquity 189 n. *presence*; broadness, looseness 495 n. *inexactness*, 464 n. *indiscrimination*; commonness 30 n. *average*, 732 n. *mediocrity*; internationalism, cosmopolitanism 901 n. *philanthropy*; impersonality.

everyman, man in the street, little man; common type 30 n. *common man*; everybody, one and all, all and sundry, every mother's son, all hands 52 n. *all*; all the world and his wife, Tom, Dick, and Harry 869 n. *commonalty*; anyone, whosoever, N or M 562 n. *no name*.

Adj. *general*, generic, typical, representative, standard; encyclopedic, broad-based; collective, all-embracing, pan-; blanket 52 adj. *comprehensive*; broad, sweeping, panoramic, synoptic; usual 610 adj. *habitual*; loose, indefinite 495 adj. *inexact*; impersonal 10 adj. *irrelative*; average 30 adj. *median*; popular, mass 869 adj. *plebeian*; for everybody, multipurpose.

universal, catholic, ecumenical, cosmopolitan, international, global, worldwide; epidemic, pandemic 189 adj. *ubiquitous*.

Vb. *be general*, cover all cases 78 vb. *comprise*; prevail, obtain 610 vb. *be wont*; penetrate 189 vb. *pervade*.

generalize, broaden, widen, universalize.

80. Speciality – N. *speciality*, specific quality, specificity, idiom, uniqueness; singularity; originality, individuality, particularity; personality, personal equation, make-up 5 n. *character*; idiosyncrasy, peculiarity, characteristic, mannerism; trait, mark, feature, attribute; specialization 694 n. *skill*.

particulars, details, minutiae, items, counts, special points, specification; circumstances; the ins and outs of.

particularism, chosen race, Peculiar People; exclusiveness, class consciousness, caste; nationality, nationalism, individualism, private enterprise.

self, subjectivity; ego, id-ego, identity, selfhood, personality; I, myself, yours truly, number one; we-group, in-g.; a person 371 n. *person.*

Adj. *special*, specific, respective, particular; sui generis, peculiar, singular, unique; individual, idiosyncratic, idiomatic, original 21 adj. *unimitated*; native, proper, personal, private, selfish; typical, diagnostic 5 adj. *characteristic*; distinctive, uncommon 84 adj. *unusual.*

Vb. *specify*, be specific, enumerate, quantify 86 vb. *number*; particularize, itemize, detail, inventorize 87 vb. *list*; define, determine 236 vb. *limit*, 463 vb. *discriminate*; pin-point, locate 187 vb. *place*; denote 514 vb. *mean*; individualize, personalize 15 vb. *differentiate.*

Adv. *namely*, that is to say, videlicet, viz., to wit, i.e., e.g.

81. Rule – **N.** *rule*, norm, formula, principle 693 n. *precept*; code 953 n. *law*; regulation, order, standing o., party line; guide, precedent, model, pattern; form, standard, keynote 83 n. *example*; regularity 16 n. *uniformity*, 60 n. *order*, 610 n. *habit*; system, method 62 n. *arrangement.*

Adj. *regular*, constant, steady 141 adj. *periodical*; even 258 adj. *smooth*; circular, square; regulated, according to rule 60 adj. *orderly*; regulative, normative; normal 83 adj. *typical*; customary 610 adj. *usual*; conforming, conventional 83 adj. *conformable.*

82. Multiformity – **N.** *multiformity*, heterogeneity, variety, diversity 17 n. *non-uniformity*; multifariousness, many-sidedness, polymorphism; variability 152 n. *changeableness*, 604 n. *caprice*; all-rounder; Proteus, Jekyll and Hyde; kaleidoscope.

Adj. *multiform*, polymorphic; multifarious, multiplex, manifold, many-headed, many-sided; metamorphic; protean, versatile, all-round; variform, heterogeneous, motley 17 adj. *non-uniform*; irregular, diversified 437 adj. *variegated*; diverse, sundry, 15 adj. *different*; variable 152 adj. *changeful*, 604 adj. *capricious*; schizophrenic.

83. Conformity – **N.** *conformity*, conformation 24 n. *conformance*; adjustment 24 n. *agreement*, *adaptation*; pliancy 327 n. *softness*; acquiescence 721 n. *submission*; assimilation, acclimatization, naturalization; conventionality 848 n. *etiquette*; traditionalism, orthodoxism 976 n. *orthodoxy*; convention 848 n. *fashion*, 610 n. *practice.*

example, exemplar, precedent, type, pattern, model 23 n. *prototype*; exemplification, stock example, locus classicus; case, instance; illustration, object lesson; sample, specimen, cross section.

conformist, conventionalist, formalist, traditionalist; copycat 20 n. *imitator*; loyalist.

Adj. *conformable*, adaptable, adjustable, consistent with; malleable 327 adj. *flexible*; agreeable 24 adj. *agreeing*; faithful, loyal 768 adj. *observant*; conforming, conventional 976 adj. *orthodox*; slavish 20 adj. *imitative.*

typical, normal, natural, of daily occurrence, everyday, ordinary, common, common or garden; average 30 adj. *median*; true to type; commonplace; representative, stock, standard.

Vb. *conform*, adapt oneself, accommodate o.; fit in, know one's place; bend, yield, fall into line 721 vb. *submit*; comply with 768 vb. *observe*; rubber-stamp, echo 106 vb. *repeat*; follow precedent 739 vb. *obey*; keep in step, do as others do, jump on the band-wagon, swim with the stream; follow in the steps of, keep to the beaten track.

make conform, conform, assimilate, naturalize, acclimatize 610 vb. *habituate*; bring under rule, systematize 62 vb. *regularize*; normalize, standardize; bend 740 vb. *compel*; accommodate 24 vb. *adjust*; square, trim, rub off the corners 258 vb. *smooth.*

exemplify, illustrate, cite, quote, instance; produce an example, give an instance.

84. Unconformity – **N.** *unconformity*, inconsistency 25 n. *disagreement*; contrast, oasis 14 n. *contrariety*; exceptionality

59 n. *extraneousness*; nonconformity, unorthodoxy 977 n. *heterodoxy*, 489 n. *dissent*, 769 n. *non-observance*; deviationism, Titoism 744 n. *independence*; anomalousness, eccentricity, irregularity 282 n. *deviation*; informality, unconventionality, angularity, awkwardness; bizarrerie, piquancy, freakishness, oddity; infringement, infraction 954 n. *illegality*; anomaly, ectopia; exception 57 n. *exclusion*; exemption 919 n. *non-liability*; special case, isolated instance; individuality 80 n. *speciality*.

abnormality, aberration 282 n. *deviation*; abortion, miscreation, monstrous birth, teratogenesis, monstrosity, monster; sexual abnormality, homosexualism, lesbianism; nymphomania, andromania, necrophilia, sadism, masochism; transvestism; virilism, viraginity, gynandry 372 n. *male*; androgyny 373 n. *female*; hermaphroditism 161 n. *impotence*.

nonconformist, dissident, dissenter 489 n. *dissentient*; sectarian 978 n. *sectarist*; deviationist, Titoist 603 n. *tergiversator*; blackleg, scab 938 n. *cad*; unconventionalist, Bohemian; rebel, angry young man; fanatic 504 n. *crank*; outsider 904 n. *offender*; pariah 883 n. *outcaste*; hermit 883 n. *solitary*; nomad 268 n. *wanderer*; odd man out, joker; square peg in a round hole 25 n. *misfit*; sport, freak, lusus naturae; oddity, original, character, card, queer fish 851 n. *laughing stock*; curiosity, rarity, one in a million; homosexual, lesbian, pansy, fairy, queer, pervert; sadist, masochist.

rara avis, unicorn, phoenix, griffin, wyvern, roc, liver; sphinx, hippogriff, manticore, chimera, centaur; minotaur, dragon, hydra; cockatrice, basilisk, salamander; kraken, sea-serpent, Loch Ness monster; Cerberus, Gorgon, Snark; Cyclops; merman, mermaid, siren, Lorelei.

Adj. *unconformable*, inadjustable 25 adj. *unapt*; unmalleable, stiff 326 adj. *rigid*; recalcitrant 711 adj. *defiant*; awkward, all edges 893 adj. *sullen*; arbitrary, a law to oneself 744 adj. *independent*;

egregious, sui generis, unique 80 adj. *special*; nonconformist 489 adj. *dissenting*, 978 adj. *sectarian*; unorthodox 977 adj. *heterodox*; non-practising 769 adj. *non-observant*; unconventional, Bohemian, informal, unfashionable; off-side, not done 924 adj. *disapproved*; aberrant, astray 282 adj. *deviating*; misplaced 188 adj. *displaced*; incongruous, out of step 25 adj. *disagreeing*; exotic 59 adj. *extraneous*; unidentifiable, unclassifiable, hard to place, nondescript, nameless 491 adj. *unknown*; nomadic 267 adj. *travelling*.

unusual, uncustomary 611 adj. *unaccustomed*; unfamiliar 491 adj. *unknown*; new-fangled, outlandish 59 adj. *extraneous*; extraordinary, unparalleled, unexampled; singular, unique 80 adj. *special*, 140 adj. *infrequent*; strange, bizarre, curious, odd, queer, rum, rummy; funny, peculiar, fantastic, grotesque 849 adj. *ridiculous*; surprising, astonishing, mysterious, miraculous 864 adj. *wonderful*; monstrous, outsize 32 adj. *enormous*; outré 546 adj. *exaggerated*.

abnormal, unnatural, supernatural, preternatural (see *unusual*); aberrant, freakish; untypical, atypical, unrepresentative, exceptional; eccentric, anomalous, anomalistic 17 adj. *non-uniform*; homosexual, lesbian, queer; epicene, androgenous, gynandrous; irregular, heteroclite; unidiomatic, solecistic 565 adj. *ungrammatical*; non-standard, subnormal.

Section 5: Number

85. Number – **N.** *number*, round n., numeric, numeral, serial; integer; cipher, digit, figure, algorism, Arabic numerals, Roman n.; X, symbol; function, variable; surd; expression, algebraism; formula, series.

numerical element, subtrahend; multiplicand; multiplier; coefficient; multiple, dividend, divisor, aliquant, quotient, factor, sub-multiple, fraction; numerator, denominator; decimal system, decimal, recurring d., repetend; reciprocal, complement; power, root; exponent, index; logarithm, antilogarithm; modulus, differential, integral; operator, sign.

ratio, proportion; progression, arithmetical progression, geometrical p., harmonical p.; trigonometrical ratio, sine, tangent, secant; cosine, cotangent, cosecant; percentage, per cent, per mil, per hour.

numerical result, answer, product, equation; sum, total, aggregate 52 n. *whole*; difference, residual 41 n. *remainder*; score, tally 38 n. *addition*.

Adj. *numerical*, numerary, numeral; arithmetical; cardinal, ordinal; round, whole; even, odd; prime; figurate; positive, negative, surd, radical; divisible, aliquot; multiple; reciprocal, complementary; fractional, decimal; proportional; exponential, logarithmic, logometric, differential, integral, rational, irrational.

86. Numeration – N. *numeration*, numbering, enumeration, census, counting, ciphering, figuring, reckoning; sum, tale, tally, score, break, runs, points; count, recount; figure-work, summation, calculation, computation 465 n. *measurement*; pagination; dactylonomy; accountancy 808 n. *accounts*; counting heads, poll, head-count, hand-c.

mathematics, arithmetic, algebra; differential calculus, integral c., infinitesimal c.; geometry, trigonometry; graphs, logarithms; rhabdology; Napier's bones.

numerical operation, figure-work, notation; addition, subtraction, multiplication, division, proportion, rule of three, practice, equations, analysis, extraction of roots, reduction, involution, evolution, approximation, interpolation; differentiation, integration, permutation, combination, variation.

statistics, figures, tables, averages; census, capitation; roll-call, muster, muster-roll, account 87 n. *list*; demography, birth rate, death r., vital statistics.

counting instrument, abacus, swanpan, quipu; ready reckoner, multiplication table; logometer, scale measure, tape-m., yardstick 465 n. *gauge*; slide rule; tallies, counters, Napier's bones; comptometer, calculating machine, computer; cash register, totalizator, tote.

computer, enumerator, census-taker; abacist; calculator, counter, teller, pollster; mathematician, wrangler; arithmetician, geometrician, algebraist; statistician, statist, bookkeeper 808 n. *accountant*; actuary.

Adj. *numerable*, numberable, countable; calculable, computable, measureable, mensurable 465 adj. *metric*.

statistical, expressed in numbers, ciphered, numbered, figured out; mathematical, arithmetical, algebraical; geometrical, trigonometrical; in ratio, in proportion, percentile.

Vb. *number*, cast, count, tell, score; foliate, paginate; enumerate, census, poll; muster, call over, call the roll; take stock, inventorize 87 vb. *list*; audit, keep accounts 808 vb. *account*.

do sums, cast up, carry over, totalize, tot up; take away, subtract; multiply; divide; algebraize, geometrize, square, cube, extract roots; figure, cipher; work out, reduce; compute, calculate, reckon, reckon up 465 vb. *measure*; estimate, appraise.

87. List – N. *list*, enumeration, items; inventory, stock list; table, catalogue; portfolio; statement, schedule, manifest, bill of lading; check-list; invoice; score; price-list, tariff, bill, account; registry, cartulary; cadastre, terrier, Domesday Book; file, register 548 n. *record*; table of contents, bill of fare, menu, diet-sheet 301 n. *eating*; playbill, programme, prospectus; synopsis, syllabus 592 n. *compendium*; roll, electoral r. 605 n. *electorate*; muster-roll, check-r., payroll; statistical list, census l., returns 86 n. *numeration*; index, thumb i., bibliography; rota, roster, panel; string of names, visitors' book; family tree, pedigree 169 n. *genealogy*; scroll, roll of honour; questionnaire; thesaurus 559 n. *dictionary*; directory 524 n. *guide book*; calendar 117 n. *chronology*.

Vb. *list*, enumerate; itemize, inventory, catalogue, calendar, index, tabulate; file, docket, schedule, enter, book, post 548 vb. *register*; enlist, matriculate, enrol, empanel, inscribe; score, keep s., keep count 86 vb. *number*.

88. Unity – N. *unity*, oneness, absoluteness 44 n. *simpleness*; unification, integration, wholeness 52 n. *whole*; uniqueness, singularity 80 n. *speciality*; singleness, isolation, solitude 883 n. *seclusion*; union, indivisibility, solidarity 706 n. *association*.

unit, integer, one, ace, item, piece; individual, point, atom, monad, entity, a being; monolith; singleton, monotype, nonce-word; solo; package deal.

Adj. *one*, not plural, singular, sole, single; unique, only, lone, one and only; unrepeated, only-begotten; individual 80 adj. *special*; absolute, universal 79 adj. *general*; indivisible, unitary; unilateral; mono-; monotonous, monolithic 16 adj. *uniform*; unified, rolled into one 324 adj. *dense*.

alone, lonely, homeless, rootless, orphaned, kithless 883 adj. *friendless*; lonesome, solitary, lone, eremitical 883 adj. *unsociable*; isolable, isolated 46 adj. *disjunct*; single-handed, on one's own, unaccompanied; unpaired, fellowless; monadic.

Adv. *singly*, one by one, one at a time; once, for the nonce, never again, only, solely, simply; in the singular.

89. Accompaniment – N. *accompaniment*, concomitance, togetherness 71 n. *continuity*, 45 n. *junction*; inseparability; society, companionship, partnership, association 706 n. *cooperation*; coincidence, simultaneity 123 n. *synchronism*; fellow-travelling, escort, company, attendance; parallel course; life with, coexistence.

concomitant, attribute, sine qua non; coefficient, accessory, appurtenance, fix-

ture 40 n. *adjunct*; symptom 547 n. *indication*; coincidence 159 n. *chance*; context, circumstance 7 n. *state*; background, noises off; accompaniment, obbligato; attendant, train; convoy, escort 690 n. *leader*; chaperon 660 n. *protector*, 749 n. *keeper*; tracker 619 n. *hunter*; inseparable, shadow, Mary's little lamb 284 n. *follower*; consort 894 n. *spouse*; comrade 880 n. *friend*; partner 707 n. *colleague*; fellow-traveller 707 n. *collaborator*; fellow 18 n. *analogue*; satellite 742 n. *dependant*.

Adj. *accompanying*, with, concomitant, attendant, background; inseparable, built-in; hand-in-glove; accessory, belonging 58 adj. *ingredient*; satellitic 745 adj. *subject*; symptomatic 547 adj. *indicating*; incidental, coincidental 159 adj. *casual*; co-existent, contemporaneous, contemporary, simultaneous.

Vb. *accompany*, be found with; co-exist; cohabit, live with; attend, wait on 284 vb. *follow*; squire, chaperon 660 vb. *safeguard*; convoy, escort, conduct; track, dog, shadow 619 vb. *pursue*; associate, partner 706 vb. *cooperate*; coincide, keep time with 123 vb. *synchronize*; belong, go together 9 vb. *be related*.

Adv. *with*, in company w., in convoy, hand in hand, arm in arm, side by side; jointly, in a body, collectively, inseparably, unitedly.

90. Duality – N. *duality*, dualism; double-sidedness; dyad, two, deuce; twain, couple, brace, pair, fellows; doublets, twins, Tweedledum and Tweedledee; yoke, span; couplet, distich; double harness, twosome; duel, duet, tandem.

Adj. *dual*, dualistic; dyadic, binary; bilateral, bicameral; twin; paired, coupled etc. vb.; in twos, both; tête-à-tête; double-sided, bipartisan; amphibious; biform, bifrontal, two-faced; di-, bi-.

Vb. *pair*, couple, match, bracket, yoke; conduplicate, mate; pair off.

91. Duplication – N. *duplication*; doubling 261 n. *fold*; gemination, reduplication, encore, repeat; iteration 106 n. *repetition*; copy 22 n. *duplicate*.

Adj. *double*, doubled, twice; duplex, bifarious; twofold, two-sided, two-edged; bifacial, double-faced; amphibious, ambidextrous; double-sided; twin, duplicate.

Vb. *double*, redouble, square; ingeminate, encore 106 vb. *repeat*; duplicate, twin; reduplicate 22 vb. *copy*.

Adv. *twice*, once more; over again 106 adv. *again*; as much again, twofold.

92. Bisection – N. *bisection*, bipartition, dichotomy; halving, dimidiation; half, moiety 53 n. *part*; hemisphere 252 n. *sphere*; bifurcation 294 n. *divergence*.

dividing line, diameter, diagonal, equator; parting, suture, seam; date-line; party-wall 231 n. *partition*.

Adj. *bisected*, dimidiate, bifid; bipartite, biconjugate, bicuspid; bifurcated; dichotomous; semi-, demi-, hemi-; cloven, cleft 46 adj. *disjunct*.

Vb. *bisect*, transect; divide, split 46 vb. *sunder*; halve, dimidiate, dichotomize, share, go halves, go fifty-fifty 783 vb. *apportion*; bifurcate 294 vb. *diverge*.

93. Triality – N. *triality*, trinity, trimurti; triunity; triplicity 94 n. *triplication*.

three, triad, trine; threesome, triumvirate, leash; troika; triplet, trey, trio, ternion; trimester, triennium; trefoil, triangle, trident, tripod; tricorn, triphthong, triptych, trilogy.

Adj. *three*, trinal, triform, trinomial; tertiary; triune, tripartite; tridimensional; triangular, trilateral; three-pointed, trinacrian; trimestrial; tri-.

94. Triplication – N. *triplication*, triplicity; trebleness; hat-trick.

Adj. *treble*, triple; trine, tern, ternary; triplex, triplicate, threefold; third, trinal; trihedral; trilateral.

Vb. *treble*, triple, triplicate, cube.

95. Trisection – N. *trisection*, tripartition, trichotomy; third, third part; tierce.

Adj. *trifid*, trisected; tripartite, trichotomous, trisulcate.

Vb. *trisect*, trifurcate.

96. Quaternity – N. *quaternity*, four, tetrad, tetractys; square, tetragon, quadrilateral, quadrangle, quad; quadrature, quarter; tetrastich, tetrapod, tetrameter; tetragrammaton; quaternion, quartet, foursome; four-in-hand, quadriga; quatrefoil; quadruplet, quad; quadruped; quadrennium; quadrilateral; four corners of 52 n. *whole*.

Adj. *four*, quaternary, quaternal; quartite; quartic, tetractic, quadratic, quadrate, square, quadrilateral, tetrahedral, four-square; quadrennial; quadrilateral; quadri-.

97. Quadruplication – N. *quadruplication*, quadruplicity; squaring.

Adj. *fourfold*, quadruplicate, quadruplex; squared; quadrable.

Vb. *quadruple*, quadruplicate; square, biquadrate.

98. Quadrisection – N. *quadrisection*, quadripartition; quartering etc. vb.; fourth, fourth part; quart, quarter, quartern; farthing.

Adj. *quartered*; quadrifid, quadripartite.

Vb. *quadrisect*, quarter, divide by four.

99. Five and over – N. *five*; five, cinque, quint, quintuplet; pentad, fiver; quincunx; pentagon; pentameter; Pentateuch, pentacle; pentapolis; pentarchy.

over five, six, half-a-dozen, sextet, hexad, sixer; hexagon; seven, heptad, week; septennium; heptarchy; eight, octave, octet, octad; octagon; nine, three times three; ennead; novena; double figures; ten, tenner, decade, decad; decury, decemvirate; eleven, hendecasyllable; twelve, dozen; teens; thirteen, baker's dozen, long d.; a score.

over twenty, twenty-five, pony; half a hundred, jubilee; three score; sexagenarian; three score and ten, septuagenarian; four score, octogenarian; nonagenarian.

hundred, century, centenary; hecatomb; hundredweight; centurion; centenarian; centipede; treble figures.

over one hundred, a gross; thousand, chiliad, grand; millennium; ten thousand, myriad; hundred thousand, plum, lakh; million; ten million, crore; thousand million, milliard; billion; trillion, quadrillion, centillion, multimillion; millionaire, billionaire, milliardaire.

Adj. *fifth and over*, five, quinary, quintuple; fifth; senary, sextuple; octuple; ninefold, ninth; tenfold, decimal, denary, decuple, tenth; duodenary, duodenal; vigesimal, twentieth; centesimal, centuple, centuplicate, centennial, centenary, centenarian, centurial; secular, hundredth; thousandth, millenary.

100. Multisection – N. *multisection*, quinquesection, decimation, centesimation.

Adj. *multifid*, quinquefid, quinquepartite; octifid; decimal, tenth, tithe; duodecimal; sexagesimal, sexagenary; centesimal; millesimal.

Vb. *multisect*, decimate, quinquesect.

101. Plurality – N. *plurality*, plural; multiplicity 104 n. *multitude*; a number, some, several; majority 104 n. *greater number*.

Adj. *plural*, in the p., not singular; composite, pluralistic, multiple; more than one, some, certain; upwards of, more 104 adj. *many*.

102. Fraction: less than one – N. *fraction*, fractional part, fragment 53 n. *part*, 783 n. *portion*; shred 33 n. *small quantity*.

Adj. *fractional*, portional, partial 53 adj. *fragmentary*, 33 adj. *small*.

103. Zero – N. *zero*, nil, nothing; naught, nought, nix; no score, love, duck; blank, cipher; nullity, nothingness 2 n. *nonexistence*; none, nobody, not a soul 190 n. *absence;* zero level, nadir.

Adj. *not one*, not any, zero; null 4 adj. *insubstantial*, 2 adj. *non-existent*.

104. Multitude – N. *multitude*, numerosity, multiplicity; multimillion 99 n. *over one hundred*; a quantity, clutter, hantle, lots, loads, heaps 32 n. *great quantity*; numbers, umpteen, scores, myriads, millions; a world of, a sight of; host, array, legion, phalanx 722 n. *army*; throng, mob, rout, all the world and his wife 74 n. *crowd*; swarm, tribe, horde 74 n. *group*.

greater number, weight of numbers, majority, mass, bulk, mainstream 32 n. *main part*; multiplication, multiple 101 n. *plurality*.

Adj. *many*, several, sundry, various, umpteen, a thousand and one; not a few, considerable, numerous; uncounted 107 adj. *infinite*; many-headed 82 adj. *multiform*; much, ample, multiple, multiplied; profuse, abundant, overflowing, galore 635 adj. *plenteous*, 32 adj. *great*.

multitudinous, massed, crowded, thronged, studded with 54 adj. *full*; populous, peopled 324 adj. *dense*; multiferous, teeming, alive with 171 adj. *prolific*; thick, thick on the ground; thick and fast 139 adj. *frequent*; incalculable, innumerable, inexhaustible 107 adj. *infinite*.

Vb. *be many*, — various etc. adj.; swarm with, crawl w., hum w., bristle w., teem w. 54 vb. *fill*; pullulate, multiply 171 vb. *be fruitful*; crowd, throng, swarm, mass, flock, troop 74 vb. *congregate*; flood, overflow, swamp, overwhelm 341 vb. *drench*; infest, overrun 297 vb. *infiltrate*; swell the ranks 36 vb. *augment*; overweigh, outnumber, make a majority 32 vb. *be great*.

105. Fewness – N. *fewness*, paucity, underpopulation; thinness, sparseness, rarity 140 n. *infrequency*; a few, a handful; thin house; trickle 33 n. *small quantity*; limited number, too few, no quorum; minority, remnant.

Adj. *few*, weak in numbers, scanty 636 adj. *scarce*; thin, thin on the ground, sparse, rare, few and far between 140 adj. *infrequent*; soon counted; too few, in a minority, without a quorum.

Vb. *render few*, reduce, diminish, pare 198 vb. *make smaller*; scale down, decimate; weed, thin 300 vb. *eject*; underman, understaff.

106. Repetition – N. *repetition*, iteration, reiteration; ditto, reduplication 91 n. *duplication*; recapitulation, rehearsal 610 n. *practice*; renewal, resumption 68 n. *beginning*; harping, tautology 570 n. *diffuseness*; a repetition, repeat, reprise, encore; replay, return match, revenge; chorus, refrain 412 n. *vocal music*; echo 404 n. *resonance*; cliché, quotation, citation, plagiarism; twice-told tale, old story 838 n. *tedium*; rehandling, restatement; reprint, reissue 589 n. *edition*; rehash 656 n. *restoration*; repeater, gramophone record, cuckoo, parrot; creature of habit.

recurrence, repetitiveness 139 n. *frequency*; cycle, round 141 n. *regular return*; run, series 71 n. *continuity*; throw-back, atavism 5 n. *heredity*; reappearance, curtain call, return; rhythm, drumming 141 n. *periodicity*; alliteration 593 n. *prosody*; monotony, dingdong 16 n. *uniformity*, 838 n. *tedium*; mixture as before 610 n. *habit*.

Adj. *repeated*, repetitional; repeatable, quotable; rhythmical, recurrent 141 adj. *periodical*; haunting 505 adj. *remembered*; repetitive, repetitious, iterative; stale, cliché-ridden 572 adj. *feeble*; alliterative, assonant 18 adj. *similar*; monotonous 16 adj. *uniform*; incessant, habitual 139 adj. *frequent*; retold, twice-told; above-mentioned, aforesaid 66 adj. *precursory*.

Vb. *repeat*, do again, iterate, cut and come again; reduplicate 91 vb. *double*; multiply 166 vb. *reproduce*; reiterate, recapitulate, go over; retell, restate, reword, rephrase; always say, trot out; say one's piece, recite, say after; echo, ditto, parrot, plagiarize 20 vb. *copy*; quote, cite 505 vb. *remember*; practise, rehearse; play back (a record); restart, resume 68 vb. *begin*; republish; rehash, revive 656 vb. *restore*.

repeat oneself, reverberate 404 vb.

resound; drum, beat a tattoo; chant, chorus; give an encore; quote oneself 570 vb. *be diffuse*; plug, labour, harp on; din into, go on at, hammer at; revert to 505 vb. *remember*; commute 610 vb. *be wont*; return 139 vb. *recur*.

Adv. *again*, afresh, anew, over again, once more; ditto; encore, bis; de novo, da capo; re-.

107. Infinity – N. *Infinity*, infinitude, boundlessness; eternity 115 n. *perpetuity*.

Adj. *infinite*, immense, measureless; eternal 115 adj. *perpetual*; numberless, countless, sumless, innumerable, immeasurable, illimitable, interminable; incalculable, unfathomable; inexhaustible, no end of; limitless, endless, boundless; untold, unnumbered 104 adj. *many*; unbounded, unlimited.

Adv. *infinitely*, to infinity, ad infinitum; without end, indefinitely 32 adv. *greatly*.

Section 6: Time

108. Time – N. *time*, tide; tense 564 n. *grammar*; duration, extent 183 n. *space*; season, term, semester, tenancy, tenure; spell, stint, span 110 n. *period*; a bit, a while; lapse 111 n. *course of time*; life, life-time; years, days; fourth dimension; aorist, past tense 125 n. *preterition*; prospective time 124 n. *futurity*; contemporaneity 121 n. *present time*; recent time 126 n. *newness*; antiquity 127 n. *oldness*, interim 145 n. *lull*.

date, day, age, reign 110 n. *era*; vintage, year, regnal y. 117 n. *chronology*; birthday 141 n. *anniversary*; day of the week, kalends, ides, nones; moment 116 n. *instant*; target date, zero hour, D-day; term, fixed day.

Adj. *dated*, calendared 117 adj. *chronological*; temporal 141 adj. *periodical*.

Vb. *pass time*, pass 111 vb. *elapse*; vegetate, subsist 360 vb. *live*; age, grow old; spend time 678 vb. *be busy*; while away t., kill t., summer, winter, weekend 681 vb. *have leisure*; mark time, tide over, take time, wait; have one's day, enjoy a spell.

Adv. *while*, during, pending; day by day; in the course of; for the time being, meantime, meanwhile; between whiles, in the meantime, in the interim; hourly 139 adv. *often*; for a time, for a season; till, until, up to, yet.

when, one day, once upon a time, one fine morning; in the days of, in the time of, in the year of.

109. Neverness – N. *neverness*, Greek Kalends; Tib's eve; blue moon; dies non; no time, datelessness, eternity 115 n. *perpetuity*.

Adv. *never*, not ever, at no time, on no occasion, not in donkey's years; nevermore, never again; over one's dead body; never before, never in one's born days; without date, sine die; out of time.

110. Period – N. *period*, matter of time; long run 113 n. *diuturnity*; short run 114 n. *transientness*; season; close season 145 n. *lull*; time of day, time of year, spring, summer, autumn, winter 128 n. *morning*, 129 n. *evening*; one's time, term; notice, warning, ultimatum 766 n. *conditions*; time up 69 n. *finality*; spell, stint, shift, span, stretch, sentence; innings, turn; round, chukker, bout, lap; vigil, watch, nightwatch, dogwatch; second, minute, hour; pause, interval; day, weekd., working d.; week, sennight, octave, novena; fortnight, month, moon, lunation; quarter, trimester; semester; twelve month, year; Olympiad, lustrum, quinquennium; decade, decennium; indiction; jubilee 141 n. *anniversary*; century, millennium; one's born days; life, lifetime, life-sentence.

era, time, age, days; epoch, samvat; cycle, Sothic c., Metonic c.; Platonic year, Great Year, Annus Magnus, Yuga, Kalpa; geological period, Ice Age, Stone A.

Adj. *periodic*, seasonal; hourly, horary; annual, biennial, quinquennial, decennial, centennial.

secular, epochal, millennial; archaean, primary, palaeozoic; secondary, mesozoic; tertiary, cainozoic; quaternary, recent; eocene, miocene, pliocene, pleistocene, neocene; eolithic, palaeolithic, mesolithic, neolithic, chalcolithic.

111. Course: indefinite duration – N. *course of time*, matter of t., process of t., lapse of t., flow of t., flux of t., stream of t., march of t., flight of t.; duration 108 n. *time*, 146 n. *continuance*.

Vb. *elapse*, pass, lapse, flow, run, roll, proceed, advance 285 vb. *progress*; run its course, expire 69 vb. *end*; go by, pass by 125 vb. *be past*; have one's day, enjoy a spell 108 vb. *pass time*.

Adv. *in time*, in due time, in due season; in course of time, in the fulness of t., with the years.

112. Contingent duration – Adv. *during pleasure*, during good behaviour; provisionally, precariously, by favour; for the present; so long as it lasts; as *or* so long as.

113. Diuturnity: long duration – N. *diuturnity*, length of time, unconscionable t.; a week of Sundays, years on end; a lifetime, life sentence; generations, a century, an age, ages, aeons 115 n. *perpetuity*; length of days, cat's nine lives, longevity 131 n. *age*; antiquity 125 n. *preterition*.

durability, lasting quality, endurance, survival 146 n. *continuance*; permanence 153 n. *stability*; inveteracy, long standing 127 n. *oldness*.

protraction, prolongation, extension 203 n. *lengthening*; interminability 136 n. *delay*, 278 n. *slowness*; extra time, overtime, long innings, long run.

Adj. *lasting*, abiding, diuturnal 146 adj. *continuing*; secular, agelong, lifelong, livelong; longstanding, inveterate, deep-seated, deep-rooted; long-term, long-service, marathon 203 adj. *long*; too long, unconscionable; durable 162 adj. *strong*; longeval 131 adj. *aged*; evergreen, unfading; eternal, perennial 115 adj. *perpetual*; persistent, chronic 602 adj. *obstinate*; permanent 153 adj. *unchangeable*.

Vb. *last*, endure, stand, stay, remain, abide, never end 146 vb. *go on*; spin out 136 vb. *put off*; wear, wear well 162 vb. *be strong*.

outlast, outlive, outwear, outstay, survive, remain; live to fight another day; have nine lives.

Adv. *for long*, long, for ages, for years, many a long day; for good, for all time, for better for worse.

all along, all day long, the livelong day; all the year round, round the clock; ever since.

114. Transientness – N. *transientness*, transience, ephemerality, impermanence; evanescence 446 n. *disappearance*; fugacity 277 n. *velocity*; fragility 330 n. *brittleness*; mortality 361 n. *death*; mutability 152 n. *changeableness*; fickleness 604 n. *caprice*; suddenness 116 n. *instantaneity*; provisionality, makeshift 150 n. *substitute*; interregnum.

brief span, briefness 204 n. *shortness*; mortal span, short life and a merry one; summer lightning, flash in the pan, nine days' wonder; April shower, summer cloud 4 n. *insubstantial thing*; short run 110 n. *period*; moment 116 n. *instant*.

Adj. *transient*, time-bound, temporal, impermanent, transitory, fading, passing 4 adj. *insubstantial*; fair-weather, summer; cursory, flying, fleeting, fugitive 277 adj. *speedy*; precarious, volatile; evanescent 446 adj. *disappearing*; flickering 152 adj. *changeful*; fickle, flighty 604 adj. *capricious*.

ephemeral, of a day, short-lived, non-durable; perishable, mortal; deciduous, frail 330 adj. *brittle*; impermanent, temporary, acting, provisional, for the time being; doomed, under sentence.

brief, short-term, short-service 204 adj. *short*; summary, short and sweet 569 adj. *concise*; momentary 116 adj. *instantaneous*; at short notice 609 adj. *spontaneous*.

Vb. *be transient*, — transitory etc. adj.;

flit, fleet, fly 277 vb. *move fast*; fade, flicker 446 vb. *disappear*; have no roots.

Adv. *transiently*, temporarily, provisionally; for the moment, easy come, easy go; here today and gone tomorrow; touch and go.

115. Perpetuity: endless duration – N. *perpetuity*, sempiternity, everlastingness; eternity, timelessness; interminability 113 n. *diuturnity*; immortality 146 n. *continuance*; perpetuation, immortalization; lasting monument 505 n. *reminder*.

Adj. *perpetual*, long-lasting, durable 113 adj. *lasting*; aeonian, agelong 127 adj. *immemorial*; non-stop 146 adj. *unceasing*; dateless, ageless 144 adj. *permanent*; evergreen, unfading, amaranthine, incorruptible; imperishable, undying, deathless, immortal; unending, never-ending, interminable, endless, without end; timeless, eternal.

Vb. *perpetuate*, establish; immortalize, eternalize, eternize.

Adv. *forever*, in perpetuity, on and on; ever and always, evermore, ever and ever; for keeps, for better for worse; to infinity; non-stop.

116. Instantaneity: point of time – N. *instantaneity*, instantaneousness, simultaneity 121 n. *present time*; suddenness, abruptness 508 n. *inexpectation*; momentariness 114 n. *transientness*.

instant, moment, point of time; second, split s., tick, jiffy; breath; burst, crack; stroke, coup; flash, twinkling; two shakes; the very moment, the stroke of.

Adj. *instantaneous*, simultaneous, immediate, instant, sudden, abrupt; flickering, like a flash 277 adj. *speedy*; on time, punctual 135 adj. *early*.

Adv. *instantaneously*, instantly, immediately; punctually, promptly; without warning, overnight, all at once; slap; in the same breath; at one swoop; in a moment, in a tick; at the drop of a hat, on the spot, on the dot; extempore, impromptu, on the spur of the moment, slapdash, off-hand; like a shot, no sooner said than done.

117. Chronometry – N. *chronometry*, chronoscopy, horometry, horology, horography; timing, dating; timekeeping, watching.

clock time, right time, true t., solar t., sidereal t., Greenwich t., mean t., standard t., local t.; the hour, time of day, time of night; summer time, daylight saving.

timekeeper, chronometer, marine c., ship's c.; timepiece, clock, dial, face, hand; bob, pendulum 317 n. *oscillation*; clock, pendulum c., grandfather c., alarm c.; alarum; water-clock, clepsydra; watch, ticker; fob-watch, hunter, repeater; wrist-watch; sundial, gnomon; hour-glass, sand-glass, egg-glass; chronograph; time-signal, pip, siren, hooter, gong, bell; minute-gun, time-ball; timer, stopwatch, parking-meter 305 n. *traffic control*; time-fuse, time-switch; metronome, conductor, bandleader; watchmaker, clock-maker, horologer.

chronology, dendrochronology; carbon 14; dating, chronogram; date, age, epoch, style 110 n. *era*; almanac, Old Moore, calendar; ephemeris, Nautical Almanac; menology, chronicle, annals, diary, journal 548 n. *record*; date list, time-chart; timetable.

chronologist, chronographer, chronologer, calendarist, datary, chronogrammatist; chronicler, annalist, diarist 549 n. *recorder*.

Adj. *chronological*, chronometrical, horological, timekeeping; chronographic; annalistic 548 adj. *recording*; calendarial, chronogrammatical, datal, temporal; isochronous 123 adj. *synchronous*.

Vb. *time*, clock; fix the time; match times 123 vb. *synchronize*; phase 24 vb. *adjust*; put the clock forward *or* back 135 vb. *be early*, 136 vb. *be late*; set the alarm 669 vb. *make ready*; calendar, chronologize, chronicle, diarize 548 vb. *record*; date, be dated, bear date; measure time, mark t., beat t., keep t.; count the minutes, watch the clock; clock in; clock out.

118. Anachronism – N. *anachronism*, metachronism, parachronism, prochron-

ism; wrong date, chronological error, antichronism; mistiming, previousness 135 n. *anticipation*; untimeliness, wrong moment 138 n. *intempestivity*.

Adj. *anachronistic*, misdated, undated; antedated, foredated, prochronous, previous 135 adj. *early*; metachronous, post-dated 136 adj. *late*; slow, losing; fast, gaining; out of season, out of date.

Vb. *misdate*, 138 vb. *mistime*; antedate, foredate 135 vb. *be early*; postdate 136 vb. *be late*; be fast, gain; be slow, lose.

119. Priority – N. *priority*, antecedence, anteriority, pre-occurrence, pre-existence; primogeniture, birthright; eldest, first-born, son and heir; the past 125 n. *preterition*; eve, vigil, day before; precedent, antecedent; foretaste, preview, pre-release; aperitif 66 n. *precursor*.

Adj. *prior*, pre-, fore; earliest, first, first in the field, precedent 64 adj. *preceding*; previous, earlier, anterior, antecedent; prewar, prenatal, predeceased; pre-existing, pre-existent; elder, first-born; former, ci-devant, one-time, whilom, erstwhile, ex-, retired; foregoing, above-mentioned; aforesaid, said; introductory 66 adj. *precursory*; premised 512 adj. *supposed*.

Vb. *be before*, 135 vb. *be early*, come before 283 vb. *precede*; forerun, antecede; pre-exist.

Adv. *before*, pre-, prior to, beforehand; on the eve of; ultimo, ult.; already, in anticipation.

120. Posteriority – N. *posteriority*, subsequence; ultimogeniture, succession 65 n. *sequence*; lineage, descent 170 n. *posterity*; postnatus, cadet; remainder, reversion; aftermath 67 n. *sequel*.

Adj. *subsequent*, post-, posterior, following, next, after, later; puisné, junior, cadet, younger, youngest 130 adj. *young*; designate, to be 124 adj. *future*; postnate; postdiluvian; posthumous; postprandial, after-dinner 65 adj. *sequent*.

Vb. *ensue*, supervene 65 vb. *come*

after, 284 vb. *follow*; succeed 771 vb. *inherit*.

Adv. *subsequently*, later, next time; after, afterwards; next, in the sequel; thereupon, upon which; since, from that time.

121. The present time – N. *present time*, contemporaneity, topicality 126 n. *modernism*; time being, the present, the now; present day; juncture 137 n. *occasion*; the times, modern t.; today, twentieth century; this date, current d., even d.; one's age; present generation, one's contemporaries 123 n. *contemporary*.

Adj. *present*, actual, instant, current; topical, contemporary, contemporaneous; present-day, latest 126 adj. *modern*.

Adv. *at present*, now, at this time; contemporaneously; today, nowadays; now or never.

122. Different time – N. *different time*, other times; not now, any time but this; jam yesterday, and jam tomorrow, but never jam today 124 n. *futurity*; parachronism 118 n. *anachronism*.

Adv. *not now*, ago, earlier, later; one of these days; sometime, somewhen; some time or other, sooner or later; otherwhiles; once, one day.

123. Synchronism – N. *synchronism*, co-existence, coincidence, concomitance 89 n. *accompaniment*; simultaneity 116 n. *instantaneity*; contemporaneity 121 n. *present time*; same age, twin birth; level time, dead heat 28 n. *draw*; synchronization, isochronism.

contemporary, coeval, twin 28 n. *compeer*; one's contemporaries, one's own generation; age-group, stream, class, year 74 n. *group*.

Adj. *synchronous*, contemporary, contemporaneous 121 adj. *present*, 126 adj. *modern*; simultaneous, coincident, co-existent, co-eternal; level, neck and neck 28 adj. *equal*; matched in age, coeval, twin, of the same vintage; synchronized, isochronous, on the beat, punctual.

Vb. *synchronize*, coexist 89 vb. *accompany*; encounter, coincide 295 vb. *meet*; keep time, watch the beat 284 vb. *follow*; tune, phase 24 vb. *adjust*; pace, keep in step with.

Adv. *synchronously*, concurrently, pari passu, in time, on the beat.

124. Futurity: prospective time – N. *futurity*, future tense; womb of time; morrow 120 n. *posteriority*; future, prospect, outlook 507 n. *expectation*; coming events, fate 155 n. *destiny*; advent 289 n. *approach*; distant future, after ages; descendants 170 n. *posterity*; successorship, shadow cabinet.

future state, latter end 69 n. *finality*; doomsday, judgement day, resurrection d.; post-existence, after-life, life to come, hereafter, kingdom come 971 n. *heaven*; good time coming, millennium 730 n. *prosperity*.

Adj. *future*, to be, to come; about to be 289 n. *approaching*; nigh, close at hand 200 adj. *near*; due, imminent, overhanging 155 adj. *impending*; in the future, ahead, yet to come; prospective, designate, ear-marked 605 adj. *chosen*; promised 507 adj. *expected*; predictable, foreseeable, sure 473 adj. *certain*; later 120 adj. *subsequent*.

Vb. *be to come*, lie ahead, lie in the future, be for tomorrow; threaten, overhang 155 vb. *impend*; draw nigh 289 vb. *approach*; be just round the corner, cast its shadow before, stare one in the face 200 vb. *be near*.

Adv. *prospectively*, eventually, ultimately, later; in fulness of time, hereafter, in due course, in the long run; tomorrow.

henceforth, in future, from now on; thenceforward.

125. Preterition: restrospective time – N. *preterition*, 119 n. *priority*; retrospection 505 n. *remembrance*; past tense, preterite, perfect, pluperfect; the past, history, antiquity, old story, matter of history 127 n. *oldness*; past times, olden days; auld lang syne, yesterday, former times; ancien régime, part of history.

antiquity, eld; creation, when time began, time immemorial, remote ages; prehistory, geological times, palaeolithic age, stone a.; the ancients, ancientry; relic, fossil 127 n. *archaism*; ruin, ancient monument 548 n. *monument*; antiquarium, museum 632 n. *collection*; ancient lineage 169 n. *genealogy*.

palaetiology, palaeontology, palaeozoology, palaeology, palaeography, archaeography; archaeology, digging up the past; antiquarianism; medievalism.

antiquarian, palaeontologist, archaeologist; palaeologist; antiquary 492 n. *scholar*; historian, prehistorian; medievalist 549 n. *chronicler*.

Adj. *past*, in the p., historical; ancient, prehistoric, Ogygian 127 adj. *olden*; early, primitive, proto-, dawn 127 adj. *primal*; gone, bygone, lost, irrecoverable, dead and buried; no more 2 adj. *extinct*; passé, has-been 127 adj. *antiquated*; foregoing 64 adj. *preceding*; over, behind one; lapsed, expired, run out 69 adj. *ending*.

former, late, pristine, quondam, erstwhile; whilom, sometime, one-time, ci-devant, ex-; retired, outgoing 753 adj. *resigning*; ancestral 127 adj. *immemorial*.

Vb. *be past*, have run its course, have had its day; pass, elapse, blow over, pass off; be a dead letter; hark back, archaize 505 vb. *retrospect*.

Adv. *formerly*, aforetime, of old, of yore; erst, whilom, time was, ago; yesterday, yestreen, yestereve, yesternight; yesterweek, yesteryear.

retrospectively; retroactively; historically speaking, hitherto, heretofore, no longer; in the memory of man; time out of mind.

126. Newness – **N.** *newness*, recency, recent date 125 n. *preterition*; novelty, neonomianism, innovation, neoterism 560 n. *neology*; gloss, freshness, greenness, immaturity, rawness 130 n. *youth*; renovation 656 n. *restoration*.

modernism, modernity, moderniza-

tion; contemporaneity 121 n. *present time*; the latest, the last word, dernier cri; new look 848 n. *fashion*.

modernist, neologist, neoteric, futurist; avant-garde, neonomian; bright young thing; modern generation.

upstart, novus homo, mushroom, parvenu, nouveau riche 847 n. *vulgarian*.

Adj. *new*, recent; upstart, mushroom; novel, original, unhackneyed, unprecedented, unheard of; brand-new; like new, in mint condition; green, evergreen, dewy, juicy, sappy 128 adj. *vernal*; fresh, fresh as paint; virgin, maiden, fledgeling; new-born 130 adj. *young*; raw, unripe, unfledged 670 adj. *immature*; untried, untrodden 491 adj. *unknown*; untested 461 adj. *experimental*; unhandseled, unbroken, not broken in, not yet run in; unfleshed, new-fledged; budding, prentice.

modern, late, latter-day; contemporary, topical 121 adj. *present*; up-to-the-minute, up-to-date, à la mode, ultramodern, advanced, avant-garde, futuristic, untraditional; neoteric, newfangled, new-fashioned, revolutionary, neonomian.

Vb. *modernize*, bring up to date; have the new look, go contemporary; move with the times 285 vb. *progress*.

Adv. *newly*, afresh, anew, like new; recently, just now, lately, latterly, of late.

127. Oldness – **N.** *oldness*, primitiveness, the prime 68 n. *beginning*; age, eld, cobwebs, dust of ages, ruins 125 n. *antiquity*; rust 51 n. *decay*; senility 131 n. *age*.

archaism, antiquities 125 n. *antiquity*; thing of the past, relic; ancien régime; vieux jeu; museum piece, antique, fossil; fogy, old timer, has-been, back number, extinct volcano.

tradition, lore, folklore, mythology; inveteracy, custom, prescription 610 n. *habit*.

Adj. *olden*, old, ancient, antique, of historical interest; venerable, patriarchal; archaic, ancient, old-world; time-worn, ruined; prehistoric, mythological, heroic, feudal, medieval; first-born 131 adj. *older*; historical 125 adj. *past*.

primal, prime, primitive, primeval, primordial, aboriginal 68 adj. *beginning*; geological, palaeocrystic, palaeozoic, fossil, preglacial, palaeolithic; early, proto-, dawn-, eo-; antemundane, pre-Adamite, antediluvian; diluvian, out of the Ark, patriarchal; Cronian, Saturnian, Ogygian.

immemorial, ancestral, traditional, time-honoured, customary 610 adj. *habitual*; inveterate, long-standing 153 adj. *fixed*; old as time, age-old 131 adj. *aged*.

antiquated, of other times, archaic; last-century, Victorian, pre-war; fossilized, ossified, static; behind the times, out of date, out of fashion, antediluvian, out of the Ark; conservative, old-fashioned, old-school; passé, outworn 125 adj. *past*; rusty, moth-eaten, crumbling; mildewed, moss-grown, mouldering, rotten; fusty, stale, second-hand; obsolete, over-age, obsolescent; superseded, superannuated, on the shelf 674 adj. *disused*.

128. Morning. Spring. Summer – N. *morning*, morn, forenoon, a.m.; small hours 135 n. *earliness*; matins, prime; dawn, morning twilight, cockcrow 66 n. *precursor*; sunrise, sun-up, daybreak 417 n. *light*; peep of day, break of d.; full day, prime of the morning; Aurora, Eos.

noon, high noon, meridian, midday, noonday, noontide; eight bells, twelve o'clock.

spring, springtime, springtide, vernal season, spring s., seed-time; vernal equinox, first point of Aries.

summer, 379 n. *heat*; summertime, summertide, midsummer, solstice, high summer; Indian summer, St Luke's s., St Martin's s.

Adj. *matinal*, matutinal, morning; auroral, dawning, fresh, dewy 135 adj. *early*; antemeridian; noon.

vernal, equinoctial, spring; springlike, sappy, florescent 130 adj. *young*.

summery, summer, aestival 379 adj. *warm*.

129. Evening. Autumn. Winter – N. *evening*, eventide, even, eve; evensong, vespers, afternoon, p.m.; matinée (theatre); dog-watches, sunset, sundown; dusk, twilight 419 n. *half-light*; close of day, nightfall, dark, night-time 418 n. *darkness*.

midnight, dead of night, night's high noon; witching time; night-watch, small hours.

autumn, fall, harvest-time; autumnal equinox.

winter, 380 n. *wintriness*; winter-time, winter-tide; midwinter, winter solstice 70 n. *middle*.

Adj. *vespertine*, afternoon, post-meridian; evening; dusky, crepuscular 418 adj. *dark*, 419 adj. *dim*; nocturnal, noctivagant; benighted, late.

autumnal, equinoctial.

wintry, winter, brumal, hiemal, winter-bound 380 adj. *cold*.

130. Youth – N. *youth*, freshness, salad days 126 n. *newness*; young blood, youthfulness, juvenility, juvenescence; juniority 35 n. *inferiority*; infancy, babyhood, childhood, childish years, tender age 68 n. *beginning*; puppyhood, puppy fat; boyhood, girlhood, school-going age; one's teens, teenage, adolescence, age of puberty, boyishness, girlishness, awkward age, growing pains; younger generation, rising g. 132 n. *youngster*.

nonage, tender age, immaturity, minority, infancy, pupilage, wardship, leading strings, status pupillaris, cradle, nursery, kindergarten.

Adj. *young*, youthful, boyish, girlish; teenage, juvenile, adolescent, pubescent; budding, flowering; beardless, unripe, green, callow, awkward, raw, unfledged 670 adj. *immature*; under-age, minor, infant, in statu pupillari; younger, minor, junior, puisné, cadet; youngest, minimus; childish 132 adj. *infantine*; ever-green, unwrinkled, ageless.

131. Age – N. *age*, eld 127 n. *oldness*; time of life, years; middle age, riper a.; pensionable age, superannuation 753 n. *resignation*; old age, grey hairs; senescence, declining years; senility, anility, second childhood, dotage 51 n. *decay*; longevity, green old age.

seniority, old man's privilege 64 n. *precedence*; primogeniture 119 n. *priority*; eldership, deanship, doyen; elders 692 n. *council*.

gerontology, nostology, gerontotherapy, geriatrics, care of the aged 658 n. *therapy*.

Adj. *aged*, old, elderly, matronly; middle-aged; not so young as one was, no chicken; balding, greying, hoary-headed; ageing, senescent, moribund 361 adj. *dying*; wrinkled, lined, rheumy-eyed, toothless, palsied; drivelling, doddering, doting 499 adj. *foolish*; senile, anile, failing; in years, with one foot in the grave; venerable, patriarchal 920 adj. *respected*; so many years old, turned of, rising; too old, past it; superannuated 127 adj. *antiquated*.

older, big, major; elder, senior 34 adj. *superior*; first-born, eldest, primogenital 119 adj. *prior*.

Vb. *grow old*, age; show one's years, wrinkle, go grey, turn white.

132. Young person. Young animal. Young plant – N. *child*, children, nursery; man child, babe, baby; infant, nursling, suckling, weanling, fosterling; bairn, little one, mite, tiny, toddler, bantling; brat, kid, kidlet; papoose, bambino, pickaninny, cherub, imp, changeling. See *youngling*.

youngster, juvenile, young person, hopeful; boy, schoolboy, stripling, adolescent; youth, callant, lad, laddie; urchin, nipper, shaver, whipper-snapper; cub; hobbledehoy, Teddy-boy; minor, master, junior, cadet; girl, schoolgirl, lass, lassie, missie, wench, maid; chit, miss, junior m.; teenager, bobbysoxer, flapper, tomboy, hoyden, romp; giglet, minx, baggage; colleen, damsel. See *youngling*.

youngling, yearling, lamb, lambkin, ewelamb, kid, calf, heifer; pigling, piglet; fawn, colt, foal, filly; kit, kitten; puppy, pup, whelp, cub; chick, chicken, pullet; duckling, gosling, cygnet 365 n. *animal, bird*; fledgeling, nestling, eyas, squab; fry, litter, farrow, clutch, spawn, spat, brood; larva, pupa, nymph; chrysalis, cocoon, tadpole; embryo, foetus 156 n. *source*.

young plant, seedling, set; sucker, shoot, sprout, slip; twig, sprig, scion, sapling 366 n. *plant*.

Adj. *infantine*, baby, infantile, babyish, childish, childlike; juvenile, boyish, girlish 130 adj. *young*; kittenish, coltish, hoydenish; new-born, new-fledged, fledgy, unfledged, unbreeched; in the cradle, in arms, in long clothes, in leading strings; small, knee-high 196 adj. *little*.

133. Old person – N. *old man*, elder, senior, sir; oldster, greybeard, gaffer; dotard; veteran; old 'un, old hand, dugout; old stager, old timer 696 n. *expert*; fossil, old fogy 501 n. *fool*; grandsire, patriarch; elders 169 n. *parent*; centenarian, Methuselah.

old woman, granny, grandam, beldam; no chicken, gammer, crone; old dutch 894 n. *spouse*.

134. Adultness – N. *adultness*, adulthood, riper years, years of discretion; legal age, majority, full age, man's estate; manhood, womanhood; beard, toga virilis; maturity, prime; meridian of life, floruit.

adult, grown-up, big boy, big girl; man 372 n. *male*; woman, matron 373 n. *female*.

Adj. *grown up*, adult, major, of age, responsible; full grown 669 adj. *matured*; nubile 894 adj. *marriageable*; virile, manly 372 adj. *male*; womanly, matronly 373 adj. *female*; full-fledged, in one's prime 130 adj. *young*.

Vb. *come of age*, reach man's estate, attain majority, have the key of the door; put one's hair up; sow one's wild oats.

135. Earliness – N. *earliness*, early hour, prime 128 n. *morning*; primitiveness 68

n. *beginning*; early riser, early bird; primitive, aborigine, earliest inhabitant 191 n. *native*.

punctuality, timeliness 137 n. *occasion*; dispatch, promptitude 678 n. *activity*; suddenness 116 n. *instantaneity*.

anticipation, prevenience, a stitch in time 510 n. *foresight*; prematurity, precocity; forestalling 64 n. *precedence*.

Adj. *early*, prime, in the small hours; prevenient, previous 119 adj. *prior*; timely, punctual; forward, precocious, rare-ripe 126 adj. *new*; immediate 116 adj. *instantaneous*; forthcoming, ready 669 adj. *prepared*; imminent 200 adj. *near*; over-early, premature, abortive, 670 adj. *immature*; in advance.

Vb. *be early*; anticipate, draw on futurity; forestall, take time by the forelock; gain the start, steal a march on; engage, book, pre-empt, reserve, bespeak; expedite 277 vb. *accelerate*; jump the queue, jump the gun; put the clock forward, gain time, gain, go fast.

Adv. *betimes*, early, soon, beforehand, ere long; first thing, at the first opportunity.

136. Lateness – N. *lateness*, late hour, small hours; high time, eleventh hour, last minute; backwardness 670 n. *nonpreparation*; tardiness, lagging, hysteresis 278 n. *slowness*; afterthought, delayed reaction 67 n. *sequel*; latecomer; slow starter, late riser 278 n. *slowcoach*; laggard 679 n. *idler*.

delay, Fabian policy, 'wait and see' 858 n. *caution*; gaining time, obstruction, filibuster 702 n. *hindrance*; retardation, check 278 n. *slowness*; detention, hold-up; postponement, adjournment; prorogation, remand, pause, truce 145 n. *lull*; deferment, moratorium, respite, days of grace; suspension, stay, reprieve; procrastination, mañana; dilatoriness, red-tape, shelving, pigeon-hole, cold storage 679 n. *inactivity*.

Adj. *late*, late in the day, eleventh-hour, last-minute, deathbed; overdue, belated, benighted; behindhand, backward 278 adj. *slow*; cunctatory 858 adj. *cautious*;

unready, unpunctual, never on time; procrastinating, dilatory 679 adj. *inactive*.

Vb. *be late*, keep late hours, burn the midnight oil; lag, stay, tarry, take time, be long about it, linger, dawdle, saunter, loiter 278 vb. *move slowly*; dilly-dally, oversleep 138 vb. *lose a chance*; be losing, lose, stop (clock); stay, pend, lie over.

put off, defer, prorogue, postpone, adjourn, lay over; keep, reserve, hold over; file, pigeonhole; table, lay on the t.; shelve, put in cold storage, keep on ice; remand, send back; stay, suspend, hold in abeyance, respite; procrastinate, protract, delay, retard, hold up, talk out, gain time, filibuster; temporize, tide over; stall, keep one waiting.

Adv. *late*; after time, behind t.; at the eleventh hour, last thing; at length, at last, ultimately; till all hours.

137. Occasion: timeliness – **N.** *occasion*, event, juncture 154 n. *eventuality*, 181 n. *concurrence*; timeliness, opportuneness; right time, suitable season, auspicious hour, moment, nick of time, eleventh hour 136 n. *lateness*.

opportunity, time's forelock, golden opportunity 469 n. *possibility*; one's chance, luck 159 n. *chance*; best chance, only c.; opening, room, field 183 n. *space*; liberty 744 n. *freedom*; convenience, spare time 681 n. *leisure*; handle, lever 630 n. *tool*, 629 n. *means*.

crisis, critical time, key moment; turning point, psychological moment, emergency, crunch, pinch, push; eleventh hour, last minute 136 n. *lateness*.

Adj. *timely*, timeous, in time; on time, punctual 135 adj. *early*; seasonable, well-timed, in the nick of time, at the eleventh hour.

opportune, favourable, providential, heaven-sent, auspicious, propitious, lucky; for the occasion, occasional.

crucial, critical, key, momentous, decisive 638 adj. *important*.

Vb. *profit by*, improve the occasion, take the opportunity, make an opening; cash in on, capitalize.

Adv. *opportunely*, in due time; all in good time; in the nick of time, at the eleventh hour, now or never.

138. Intempestivity – N. *intempestivity*, wrong time, untimeliness, unseasonableness 643 n. *inexpedience*; evil hour 731 n. *ill fortune*; intrusion, interruption, disturbance; mistiming.

Adj. *ill-timed*, mistimed, ill-advised 481 adj. *misjudging*; unseasonable, untimely, interrupting, intrusive; mal à propos, inconvenient, unsuited 25 adj. *unapt*, 643 adj. *inexpedient*; unpunctual 136 adj. *late*; premature 135 adj. *early*.

inopportune, untoward, inauspicious, unpropitious, unfavourable, ill-omened 731 adj. *unfortunate*.

Vb. *mistime*, time it badly 481 vb. *misjudge*; intrude, disturb, break in upon.

lose a chance, waste time, miss the bus 728 vb. *fail*; drop a sitter 695 vb. *be unskilful*; oversleep, let slip 458 vb. *neglect*; spoil a good chance, stand in one's own light 695 vb. *stultify oneself*.

139. Frequency – N. *frequency*, rapid succession 71 n. *continuity*; oftenness, hourliness 141 n. *periodicity*.

Adj. *frequent*, recurrent 106 adj. *repeated*; common, not rare 104 adj. *many*; thick-coming 104 adj. *multitudinous*; incessant, non-stop 146 adj. *unceasing*; regular, hourly 141 adj. *periodical*; haunting, frequenting, assiduous 610 adj. *habitual*.

Vb. *recur*, redouble, do nothing but 146 vb. *go on*; frequent, haunt 882 vb. *visit*; obsess; plague, pester 827 vb. *incommode*.

Adv. *often*, frequently, commonly, not once or twice, again and again; in quick succession, regularly, daily, hourly; ad lib.

perpetually; at all times, night and day, day after day, morning, noon, and night.

sometimes, occasionally, every so often, at times, now and then, from time to time.

140. Infrequency – N. *infrequency*, rarity, uncommonness 105 n. *fewness*; intermittence; phoenix 84 n. *rara avis*.

Adj. *infrequent*, uncommon, sporadic, occasional; intermittent 72 adj. *discontinuous*; scarce, rare 105 adj. *few*; unprecedented 84 adj. *unusual*; not to be repeated.

Adv. *seldom*, once in a way; rarely, scarcely, hardly, only sometimes; infrequently, scarcely ever, once in a blue moon.

141. Periodicity: regularity of recurrence – N. *periodicity*, regularity, steadiness, evenness 16 n. *uniformity*; timing, phasing, serialization 71 n. *continuity*; alternation, in and out system (politics); alternating current, wave movement, tidal m. 317 n. *fluctuation*; pulsation, pulse, beat, rhythm, pendulum 317 n. *oscillation*; chorus, refrain 106 n. *recurrence*; drum-beat 403 n. *roll*; frequency, wave f.; shift, relay 110 n. *period*.

regular return, rota, cycle, circuit, revolution, life cycle 314 n. *circulation*, 315 n. *rotation*; yearly cycle, seasons; routine, daily round 60 n. *order*, 610 n. *habit*; menses 302 n. *haemorrhage*.

anniversary, birthday, jubilee, silver wedding, golden w.; centenary, bi-centenary, tercentenary, quater-centenary.

Adj. *periodical*, periodic, cyclic, revolving 315 adj. *rotary*; tidal, undulatory 317 adj. *oscillating*; measured, rhythmical, beating; pulsating, pulsatory; recurrent, recurring, repeating, remittent 106 adj. *repeated*; alternating 12 adj. *correlative*; serialized 65 adj. *sequent*, 71 adj. *continuous*.

seasonal, anniversary; at fixed intervals, hourly, daily, nightly, diurnal, quotidian, tertian, weekly, hebdomadal, hebdomadary, fortnightly, monthly; menstrual, catamenial; yearly, annual, biennial, triennial, quadrennial, quinquennial, decennial; bissextile, centennial, secular.

Vb. *be periodic*, recur, repeat; serialize; revolve 315 vb. *rotate*; return, come round again; turn and turn about, alter-

nate; reciprocate 12 vb. *correlate*; fluctuate, undulate 317 vb. *oscillate*; beat,
pulse, pulsate, throb 318 vb. *be agitated*;
heave, pant 352 vb. *breathe*; swing 217
vb. *hang*; ply, commute 610 vb. *be wont*.

Adv. *periodically* etc. adj.; regularly,
at regular intervals, at stated times; sea-
sonally, hourly, daily, weekly, monthly,
yearly; per diem, per annum; ever and
anon.

by turns; in turn, in rotation, turn and
turn about, alternately, every other day.

142. Fitfulness: irregularity of recurrence – **N.** *fitfulness*, irregularity 61 n.
disorder; jerkiness, fits and starts 17 n.
non-uniformity, 318 n. *spasm*; remittency
72 n. *discontinuity*; unsteadiness, inconstancy, variability 152 adj. *changeableness*; capriciousness 604 n. *caprice*.

Adj. *fitful*, remittent, intermittent;
irregular, uneven; occasional 140 adj.
infrequent; unrhythmical, unsteady, flut-
tering 17 adj. *non-uniform*; inconstant,
uncertain, unpunctual; spasmodic, jerky
318 adj. *agitated*; wavering, flickering,
guttering; desultory, unsystematic 61
adj. *orderless*; erratic 604 adj. *capricious*.

Section 7: Change

143. Change: difference at different times
– **N.** *change*, alteration, variation 15 n.
difference; mutation, permutation,
modulation; mutability 152 n. *changeableness*; modification, adjustment, process, treatment 468 n. *qualification*;
break, innovation 126 n. *newness*; reformation 654 n. *improvement*; change for
the worse 655 n. *deterioration*; diversion,
shift, turn 282 n. *deviation*, 286 n. *regression*; transition, metastasis 305 n. *passage*; catalysis, leavening; change of
opinion 603 n. *tergiversation*.

transformation, metamorphosis, transfiguration, transfiguration; unrecogniz-
ability, transmogrification; transmutation, transubstantiation 147 n. *conversion*; transmigration, metempsychosis;
reincarnation, avatar.

alterer, alterant, changer; converter,
transformer; catalytic agent, catalyst,
enzyme, ferment, leaven; adapter, modi-
fier, reviser; censor, bowdlerizer; alchemist, chemist; magician 983 n. *sorcerer*;
improver 654 n. *reformer*.

Adj. *changeable*, variable 152 adj.
changeful; affected, changed etc. vb.;
transitional, provisional, modifiable,
qualifiable; alternative, transmutative.

Vb. *change*, be changed 152 vb. *vary*.
modify, alter, vary, modulate, diversify,
shift the scene 437 vb. *variegate*; superinduce, superimpose 38 vb. *add*; change,
make a c., innovate, bring in new blood
126 vb. *modernize*; turn upside down 149
vb. *revolutionize*, 221 vb. *invert*; rearrange, reorder, reset 62 vb. *arrange*;
adapt 24 vb. *adjust*; recast 243 vb. *efform*;
process, treat; revise, correct 654 vb.
rectify; reform 654 vb. *improve*; tamper
with, mar 655 vb. *impair*; deform 246 vb.
distort; adulterate 163 vb. *weaken*;
disguise 525 vb. *conceal*; change round
151 vb. *interchange*, 272 vb. *transpose*;
leaven 156 vb. *cause*; affect, 178 vb.
influence; metamorphose 147 vb. *transform*.

144. Permanence: absence of change –
N. *permanence*, no change, status quo;
invariability, unchangeability, immutability 153 n. *stability*; endurance, duration 113 n. *durability*, 115 n. *perpetuity*;
sustenance, maintenance, conservation
666 n. *preservation*, 146 n. *continuance*;
law, rule, regularity; standing, long
s., inveteracy 127 n. *oldness*; tradition
610 n. *habit*; conservatism, Bourbonism,
die-hardism; routine, standing order 60
n. *order*; unprogressiveness 266 n. *quiescence*; traditionalist, Bourbon, conservative, stick-in-the-mud, die-hard 602 n.
opinionist.

Adj. *permanent*, enduring, durable 113
adj. *lasting*; persistent, unfailing, sustained 146 adj. *unceasing*, 115 adj. *perpetual*; inveterate, prescriptive, long-
standing 127 adj. *immemorial*; established, entrenched, unchangeable, immutable, unrepealable 153 adj. *vested*;

intact, inviolate, living 666 adj. *pre-served*; unchanging, conservative 602 adj. *obstinate*; unprogressive 266 adj. *quiescent*; unaltered, uninfluenced, unaffected, still the same.

Vb. *stay*, come to stay, set in 146 vb. *go on*; abide, outlive, survive, outlast 113 vb. *last*; persist, hold; keep on 146 vb. *go on*; remain, live 192 vb. *dwell*; stand fast 600 vb. *persevere*; stand pat, stand one's ground; stand still, stick in the mud 266 vb. *be quiescent*; not change one's spots.

145. Cessation: change from action to rest – **N.** *cessation*, surcease; discontinuation 72 n. *discontinuity*; arrest 747 n. *restraint*; withdrawal 753 n. *resignation*.

stop, halt, stand; dead stop, standstill, deadlock, stalemate; checkmate 728 n. *defeat*; breakdown 728 n. *failure*; discontinuance, stoppage, stall; shut-down, non-resumption 69 n. *end*; check 702 n. *hindrance*; blockage 264 n. *closure*; interruption 72 n. *discontinuity*; closure of debate, guillotine 399 n. *silence*; full stop 547 n. *punctuation*.

strike, general strike, hartal; slow down, working to rule; stoppage, walk-out, sit-down strike; unofficial strike, mutiny; lockout 57 n. *exclusion*.

lull, rest, interval (mus.) 410 n. *tempo*; pause, remission, recess, break 685 n. *refreshment*; holiday, day off 681 n. *leisure*; intermission, interlude, interregnum; interim, abeyance, suspense, suspension; close season, respite, moratorium, truce, armistice, cease-fire, standstill 136 n. *delay*.

stopping place, port of call, port, harbour 192 n. *stable*; lay-by, park, car park, parking place; stop, halt, pull-up, whistle-stop, station; bus-stop, request s.; terminus, terminal, air t. 271 n. *air travel*; dead end, blind alley, cul-de-sac.

Vb. *cease*, stay, desist, refrain, hold; stop, halt, stand, rest, rest on one's oars 683 vb. *repose*; have done with, see the last of, end, finish 69 vb. *terminate*; leave off, knock o.; break o., let up 72 vb.

discontinue; down tools, strike, come out 715 vb. *resist*; lock out 57 vb. *exclude*; come to an end, dry up, peter out 634 vb. *waste*; fade out 446 vb. *disappear*; come off, end its run; fold up, collapse 728 vb. *fail*; blow over, clear up 125 vb. *be past*; retire 753 vb. *resign*; give up 621 vb. *relinquish*; shut up, shut down, close, wind up; shut off steam, switch off; call it a day.

halt, stop, put a stop to; arrest, check, dam 702 vb. *obstruct*; hold up, call off; pull up, cut short, call a halt 747 vb. *restrain*; call out, stage a strike, bring to a standstill, freeze 679 vb. *make inactive*; checkmate, stalemate, thwart 702 vb. *hinder*; stop short, drop in one's tracks; seize up, stall, jam, stick, catch; brake 278 vb. *retard*.

pause, halt for a moment, stop for breath; wait awhile, allow an interval, intermit; recess, relax, rest 683 vb. *repose*.

146. Continuance in action – N. *continuance*, continuation 71 n. *continuity*, 144 n. *permanence*, 179 n. *tendency*; maintenance, perpetuation 115 n. *perpetuity*; sustained action, persistence 600 n. *perseverance*; break, run, rally 71 n. *series*; recurrence 106 n. *repetition*.

Adj. *unceasing*, incessant; continual, steady, sustained, non-stop, uninterrupted, unremitting; unreversed, unvaried 153 adj. *fixed*; undying 115 n. *perpetual*; unfailing, ever-running, inexhaustible 635 adj. *plenteous*; persistent 600 adj. *persevering*; obsessive, haunting, recurrent 106 adj. *repeated*.

Vb. *go on*, keep going, march on, drive on 285 vb. *progress*; run on, never end; — and — (e.g. rain and rain, pour and pour); pursue its course, trend 179 vb. *tend*; endure, stick, hold, abide, rest, remain 144 vb. *stay*; obsess, haunt, frequent; keep at it, persist, carry on 600 vb. *persevere*; sit it out 725 vb. *carry through*.

sustain, maintain, uphold 218 vb. *support*; follow up, follow through; keep up, keep alive 666 vb. *preserve*; keep on, harp on 106 vb. *repeat*; keep it up, keep the pot boiling, keep the ball rolling; laisser faire, let it rip 756 vb. *permit*.

147. Conversion: change to something different – N. *conversion*, making into; processing 164 n. *production*; fermentation, ferment, leaven; chemistry, alchemy; crucible, melting pot 461 n. *testing agent*; transfiguration 143 n. *transformation*; bewitchment 983 n. *sorcery*; development 36 n. *increase*; regeneration 654 n. *improvement*; assimilation, naturalization 78 n. *inclusion*; brainwashing, evangelization, proselytization 534 n. *teaching*; transition 305 n. *passage*; convertibility 469 n. *possibility*.

changed person, new man; convert, neophyte, catechumen, proselyte, disciple 538 n. *learner*; apostate, turncoat 603 n. *tergiversator*; pervert, degenerate 938 n. *bad man*.

Adj. *converted*, turned into, made i. etc. vb.; reborn, regenerate; becoming, transitional; transformed, unrecognizable 15 adj. *different*; convertible.

Vb. *be turned to*, become, get, turn to; ferment, develop into 316 vb. *evolve*; fall into, pass i., elapse 305 vb. *pass*; melt into, merge i. 43 vb. *be mixed*; mellow 669 vb. *mature*; degenerate 655 vb. *deteriorate*; take the impress of, take the shape of; be transformed, not know oneself; enter a phase.

convert, reduce, ferment, leaven; make into, reduce to, turn into, conjure i. 983 vb. *bewitch*; transmute, alchemize; render, process; mould, shape 243 vb. *efform*; brainwash 178 vb. *influence*; proselytize, evangelize, missionize 534 vb. *teach*; regenerate 656 vb. *revive*.

transform, transfigure; camouflage, disguise 525 vb. *conceal*; reshape, deform 246 vb. *distort*; change the face of, change out of recognition 149 vb. *revolutionize*; reform 654 vb. *make better*; new-model, reorganize 656 vb. *restore*; assimilate, absorb, naturalize, Americanize, Anglicize; detribalize, denaturalize, alienize.

148. Reversion – N. *reversion*, reverting, changing back, return; regress 286 n. *regression*; atavism, throwback 5 n. *heredity*; reaction 182 n. *counteraction*; repercussion 280 n. *recoil*; revulsion, disenchantment 830 n. *regret*; counter-revolution, reversal; volte face 240 n. *contraposition*; backsliding, recidivism 657 n. *relapse*; reconversion 656 n. *restoration*; replacement, reinstatement 787 n. *restitution*; getting back, recovery, retrieval 771 n. *acquisition*; turning point, turn of the tide, swing of the pendulum 317 n. *oscillation*; round trip, there and back, out and home; back where one started, status quo; resumption, recommencement 68 n. *start*.

Adj. *reverted*, reversionary, recessive, reflexive 286 adj. *regressive*; reactionary, atavistic 5 adj. *genetic*.

Vb. *revert*, turn, return, retrace 286 vb. *regress*; face about 221 vb. *invert*; ebb 290 vb. *recede*; kick 280 vb. *recoil*; backslide 657 vb. *relapse*; hark back, archaize; undo, unmake 68 vb. *begin*; restore the status quo, change back 656 vb. *restore*; derestrict, decontrol 746 vb. *liberate*; reconvert, disenchant 656 vb. *cure*; recover 656 vb. *retrieve*; reinstate, replace 787 vb. *restitute*.

149. Revolution: sudden or violent change – N. *revolution*, full circle 315 n. *rotation*; radical change, clean sweep 550 n. *obliteration*; catastrophe, peripeteia 508 n. *inexpectation*; débâcle, landslide, upset, overthrow, subversion 221 n. *overturning*; convulsion, shake-up, upheaval, eruption, explosion, cataclysm; revulsion, counter-revolution 148 n. *reversion*; abolition 752 n. *abrogation*.

revolutionist, abolitionist, radical, revolutionary, Marxist, Red 738 n. *revolter*; anarchist 168 n. *destroyer*.

Adj. *revolutionary* 126 adj. *new*; radical, thoroughgoing, root and branch 54 adj. *complete*; cataclysmic, catastrophic, seismic, world-shaking 165 adj. *destructive*; seditious, subversive, Marxist, red 738 adj. *disobedient*; anarchistic 176 adj. *violent*.

Vb. *revolutionize*, subvert, overturn 221 vb. *invert*; uproot, eradicate, make a clean sweep 550 vb. *obliterate*, 165 vb. *demolish*; break with the past 126 vb. *modernize*; change the face of 147 vb. *transform*.

150. Substitution: change of one thing for another – N. *substitution*, commutation, exchange, switch, shuffle 151 n. *interchange*; supersession, replacement, transfer 272 n. *transference*; metonymy 519 n. *trope*; vicariousness; compensation 941 n. *atonement*; compounding, composition.

substitute, succedaneum; proxy, alternate 755 n. *deputy*; understudy, stand-in; ghost-writer; locum tenens, locum; reserve, twelfth man 707 n. *auxiliary*; replacement, remount; relief, successor, supplanter 67 n. *aftercomer*; changeling 545 n. *impostor*; dummy; synonym, doublet; alternative, second best, pis aller; whipping-boy, chopping-block, scape-goat; makeshift, stopgap.

quid pro quo, equivalent, consideration, value, worth 809 n. *price*; payment in lieu, composition, redemption 804 n. *payment*; new lamps for old, replacement.

Adj. *substituted*, substitutional; vicarious 941 adj. *atoning*; substitutable, interchangeable, commutable 28 adj. *equivalent*; dummy, imitation, mock, ersatz 35 adj. *inferior*; makeshift, stopgap, provisional, temporary 114 adj. *ephemeral*.

Vb. *substitute*, change for, commute, exchange 151 vb. *interchange*; compound 770 vb. *compromise*; make do with, count as, treat as, regard as; replace, step into the shoes of, succeed 65 vb. *come after*; supersede, supplant; do duty for, stand in f., understudy f., ghost 755 vb. *deputize*.

Adv. *instead*, in place, in lieu, in the room of; by proxy; alternatively: in default of, for want of better.

151. Interchange: double or mutual change – N. *interchange*, interchange-ability; swap, counterchange, exchange, commutation 791 n. *barter*; transposal, transposition, mutual transfer; castling (chess), shuffle 272 n. *transference*; interplay, two-way traffic, reciprocation 12 n. *correlation*; quid pro quo; rally (tennis), battledore and shuttlecock, give and take; tit for tat 714 n. *retaliation*.

Adj. *interchanged*, counter-changed etc. vb.; in exchange, au pair; reciprocating, mutual, two-way 12 adj. *correlative*; inter-, interchangeable, substitutable, convertible, commutable 28 adj. *equivalent*.

Vb. *interchange*, exchange, counterchange; change money, convert; chop, swap, barter 791 vb. *trade*; permute, commute; switch, shuffle, castle (chess) 272 vb. *transpose*; give and take 770 vb. *compromise*; return the compliment, rejoin 460 vb. *answer*.

Adv. *in exchange*, vice versa, mutatis mutandis; in kind; au pair; interchangeably, conversely.

152. Changeableness – N. *changeableness*, changeability, mutability, changefulness 143 n. *change*; variability, variety 17 n. *non-uniformity*, 437 n. *variegation*; inconsistency, inconstancy, irregularity; instability 29 n. *inequality*; unfixity 335 n. *fluidity*; mobility, restlessness, inquietude 318 n. *agitation*; fluctuation, alternation 317 n. *oscillation*; chopping and changing 142 n. *fitfulness*; impermanence 114 n. *transientness*; vacillation, wavering, yea and nay, floating vote 601 n. *irresolution*; flightiness, fickleness 604 n. *caprice*; versatility 694 n. *aptitude*.

changeable thing, moon, Proteus, chameleon; shifting scene, kaleidoscope; mercury, quicksilver 335 n. *fluid*; wind, weathercock; wheel, whirligig; fortune, vicissitude, luck 159 n. *chance*; a variable, phase.

Adj. *changeful*, changing, mutable, alterable, phased 143 adj. *changeable*; variable 17 adj. *non-uniform*; kaleidoscopic, protean 82 adj. *multiform*; quick-change, versatile 694 adj. *skilful*; unreliable 601 adj. *irresolute*; unpredictable, unaccountable 508 adj. *unexpected*; never the same, unstaid, mercurial 15 adj. *different*; wayward 604 adj. *capricious*; giddy, dizzy, flighty 456 adj. *light-minded*; shifty 603 adj. *tergiversating*.

unstable, unsteady, unstaid; rocky, tottering, staggery; mobile, unquiet, restless, fidgety 318 adj. *agitated*; desultory, spasmodic, flickering 142 adj. *fitful*; touch and go 114 adj. *transient*; unsettled, unfixed, loose, unattached, floating; erratic, mercurial; rootless, homeless, vagrant 267 adj. *travelling*; alterable, plastic 327 adj. *soft*; running 335 adj. *fluid*.

Vb. *vary*, show variety 437 vb. *variegate*; ring the changes, go through phases 143 vb. *modify*; chop and change; shuffle, be shifty 518 vb. *be equivocal*; flicker, gutter 417 vb. *shine*; wave, flutter, flap, shake, tremble 318 vb. *be agitated*; wobble, stagger, rock, reel 317 vb. *oscillate*; ebb and flow, wax and wane, fluctuate; veer, tack 282 vb. *deviate*, 269 vb. *navigate*; vacillate, waver 601 vb. *be irresolute*; blow hot and cold.

153. Stability – N. *stability*, immutability; irreversibility. invariability, constancy 16 n. *uniformity*; firmness, fixity, rootedness; indelibility 144 n. *permanence*; rest, immobility 266 n. *quiescence*; steadiness, stabilization, stable equilibrium, homeostatis 28 n. *equality*; stiffness, inflexibility 326 n. *hardness*; solidarity.

fixture, establishment, firm foundation, rock, bedrock; invariant, constant; leopard's spots; laws of the Medes and Persians, entrenched clause 953 n. *legality*.

stabilizer, fin, centre-board, keel; counterweight, ballast 31 n. *offset*; stabilimeter.

Adj. *unchangeable*, unsusceptible, stiff, inflexible; unwavering 599 adj. *resolute*; reliable 473 adj. *certain*; immutable, inconvertible; irreducible, indissoluble; changeless, inalterable, irreversible; stereotyped, invariable, constant 16 adj.

uniform; steady, undeviating; perennial, evergreen 115 adj. *perpetual*. See *fixed*.

vested, established, entrenched, settled; inveterate, prescriptive; irrevocable, irreversible; incontrovertible, indefeasible, of right.

fixed, steadfast, firm, immovable, irremovable; steady, stable, balanced, homeostatic; fast, in grain, indelible; ineradicable, rooted; deep-seated; stranded, grounded, high and dry; pinned down, transfixed; immobile 266 adj. *still*.

Vb. *stabilize*, root, entrench, found, establish 115 vb. *perpetuate*; erect, set up 215 vb. *render vertical*; fix, set. stereotype; validate 488 vb. *endorse*; stand, hold.

154. Eventuality: present events – N. *eventuality*, incidence, realization; event, phenomenon, incidental; occurrence, hap, happening, incident, adventure 137 n. *occasion*; accident 159 n. *chance*; misadventure, mishap 731 n. *ill fortune*; emergency 137 n. *crisis*; coincidence; encounter; proceeding, see *affairs*; result 157 n. *effect*; dénouement, peripeteia, catastrophe 69 n. *end*.

affairs, matters, doings, transactions 676 n. *deed*; agenda, order of the day; involvement, concern, interests, irons in the fire, axes to grind 622 n. *business*; world, life, situation, state of affairs 8 n. *circumstance*; course of events 111 n. *course of time*; chapter of accidents, vicissitudes.

Adj. *happening*, incidental, accidental, occasional; doing, current, on foot, afloat, in the wind, on the agenda; circumstantial, contingent.

eventful, stirring, bustling, busy 678 adj. *active*; momentous, critical 638 adj. *important*.

Vb. *happen*, become, materialize, be realized, come off, take place, occur, come about; befall, betide 159 vb. *chance*; turn up, pop up, crop up, arise, appear; supervene 284 vb. *follow*; eventuate, issue 157 vb. *result*; turn out, fall o.; fall to one's lot.

meet with, incur, encounter 295 vb. *meet*; realize, find 484 vb. *discover*; experience, pass through, go t.; endure, undergo 825 vb. *suffer*.

155. Destiny: future events – N. *destiny*, what's to come, one's stars 596 n. *fate*; horoscope 511 n. *prediction*; prospect, outlook 507 n. *expectation*; coming events 124 n. *futurity*; something in store 900 n. *threat*; imminence 289 n. *approach*; hereafter 124 n. *future state*; foredoom, predestination 596 n. *necessity*.

Adj. *impending*, hanging over, lowering, imminent 900 adj. *threatening*; preparing, brewing 669 adj. *preparatory*; destined, in the stars; forthcoming, forecast 511 adj. *predicting*; inescapable, inevitable 473 adj. *certain*; due, owing 596 adj. *necessary*; on the agenda, in prospect, in view, in the offing, on the horizon; in the future, to come 124 adj. *future*; about to be, on the point of; pregnant with 511 adj. *presageful*; in store, in reserve, in pickle 669 adj. *prepared*.

Vb. *impend* 124 vb. *be to come*; hang over, hover, loom 900 vb. *threaten*; stare one in the face 237 vb. *be in front*; breathe down one's neck 200 vb. *be near*; ripen 669 vb. *mature*.

predestine, foredoom, pre-ordain, foreordain 596 vb. *necessitate*; foreshadow 511 vb. *predict*; have in store, have in pickle 669 vb. *make ready*; intend 608 vb. *predetermine*.

Section 8: Causation

156. Cause: constant antecedent – N. *causation*, causality, cause and effect, ground and consequent; aetiology 158 n. *attribution*; authorship, origination, invention 484 n. *discovery*; inspiration 178 n. *influence*; generation, evocation, provocation; encouragement, motivation 612 n. *motive*; reason why.

cause, first c., final c., causa causans; primum mobile 965 n. *the Deity*; creator

167 n. *producer*; begetter, only b. 169 n. *parent*; author, originator, founder; inventor, agent; leaven, stimulus 174 n. *stimulant*; contributor, factor, moment, determinant; inspirer, mainspring 612 n. *motivator*; hidden hand 178 n. *influence*; stars 155 n. *destiny*; fate 596 n. *necessity*; force 740 n. *compulsion*; causal means, appliance 629 n. *means*, 630 n. *tool*.

source, fountain, fount, fons et origo 68 n. *origin*; head-waters, spring, well; mine, quarry 632 n. *store*; birthplace 192 n. *home*; genesis, descent 169 n. *parentage*; progenitor; rudiment, element, principle, germ, seed, sperm; egg, foetus, embryo; chrysalis, cocoon 194 n. *receptacle*; taproot, root; foundation, bedrock 214 n. *base*; groundwork 68 n. *beginning*; raw material 631 n. *materials*.

seedbed, hotbed, nidus 192 n. *nest*; cradle, nursery 68 n. *origin*; breeding place, incubator, womb 164 n. *propagation*.

Adj. *causal*, causative, formative, effective, effectual; pivotal, determinant, decisive; seminal, germinal 164 adj. *productive*; suggestive, inspiring 178 adj. *influential*; impelling 740 adj. *compelling*; answerable, responsible; at the bottom of, original; creative, inventive 21 adj. *unimitated*.

fundamental, primary, elemental; foundational, radical, basic; crucial, central 638 adj. *important*.

Vb. *cause*, originate, create, make 164 vb. *produce*; beget 164 vb. *generate*; invent 484 vb. *discover*; be the reason 158 vb. *account for*; underlie, be *or* lie at the bottom of; institute, found 68 vb. *auspicate*; set afoot, set going, spark off, touch o. 68 vb. *initiate*; sow, plant, water 370 vb. *cultivate*; effect, bring about, bring off, bring to pass; procure, engineer 623 vb. *plan*; bring on, superinduce, precipitate 680 vb. *hasten*; kindle, evoke, elicit, provoke, arouse 821 vb. *excite*; inspire; occasion, give occasion for 612 vb. *motivate*; have an effect, show its result, make or mar 178 vb. *influence*; decide, turn the scale, prevail.

conduce, tend to 179 vb. *tend*; lead to;

contribute to, operate to 703 vb. *minister to*; involve 523 vb. *imply*; have the effect, entail, draw down, give rise to, open the door to 68 vb. *initiate*; promote, foster, foment 703 vb. *aid.*

157. Effect: constant sequel – **N.** *effect*, consequence 65 n. *sequence*; derivation, derivative, precipitate 41 n. *remainder*; result, upshot, outcome, issue, dénouement 154 n. *eventuality*; mark, print, impress 548 n. *trace*; after-effect, legacy, backwash, wake, repercussion 67 n. *sequel*; response 460 n. *answer*; reaction 182 n. *counteraction.*

Adj. *caused*, owing to, due to 158 adj. *attributed*; consequential, resulting, consequent 65 adj. *sequent*; contingent, dependent on 745 adj. *subject*; resultant, derivable, derivative, descended; born of, out of, by; ending in, issuing in.

inherited, heritable, hereditary, Mendelian.

Vb. *result*, come of; follow, be due to; owe everything to, borrow from; derive from, descend f., originate f., originate in, come from; issue, proceed 298 vb. *emerge*; begin from, grow f., spring f., arise f.; develop, unfold 316 vb. *evolve*; show a trace, bear the stamp 522 vb. *show.*

depend, hang upon, hinge on, pivot on, turn on 12 vb. *correlate*, 745 vb. *be subject.*

158. Attribution: assignment of cause – **N.** *attribution*, assignment, reference to, imputation, ascription; aetiology 459 n. *inquiry*; basis, reason why, rationale; apparentation, filiation; derivation 156 n. *source*; credit, acknowledgement 915 n. *dueness.*

Adj. *attributed* etc. vb.; attributable, assignable, imputable, referable; imputed, putative 512 adj. *supposed*; inferable, derivable, traceable; owing to, explained by 157 adj. *caused*; aetiological, explanatory.

Vb. *attribute*, ascribe, impute; say of, predicate 532 vb. *affirm*; put *or* set down to, assign to, refer to, point to, trace to,

derive from 9 vb. *relate*; lay at the door of, filiate, father upon; charge on, saddle on; make responsible, blame for 928 vb. *accuse*; bring home to 478 vb. *demonstrate*; credit with, acknowledge 915 vb. *grant claims.*

account for, explain 520 vb. *interpret*; theorize, hypothesize, assume 512 vb. *suppose.*

Adv. *hence*, therefore, wherefore; for, since, on account of, because, owing to, thanks to.

159. Chance: no assignable cause – **N.** *chance*, blind c., fortuity, indeterminacy; randomness; uncertainty principle, unpredictability 474 n. *uncertainty*; unaccountability, inexplicability 517 n. *unintelligibility*; lot, fortune 596 n. *fate*; whatever comes, potluck; luck 730 n. *prosperity*, 731 n. *ill fortune*; hap, hazard, accident, casualty, contingency, coincidence, chapter of accidents 154 n. *eventuality*; lucky shot, fluke 618 n. *nondesign*; serendipity 484 n. *discovery*; fifty-fifty 28 n. *equality*; toss-up 618 n. *gambling.*

calculation of chance, odds, theory of probabilities, actuarial calculation, mathematical probability; risk-taking, insurance, underwriting 672 n. *undertaking*; bookmaking 618 n. *gambling.*

Adj. *casual*, fortuitous, chance, haphazard, random, stray 618 n. *designless*; adventitious, accidental, incidental, contingent 154 adj. *happening*; non-causal, epiphenomenal, coincidental 89 n. *accompanying*; chancy, fluky, dicey, incalculable 474 adj. *uncertain.*

causeless, groundless, uncaused, unforeseeable, unpredictable, indeterminate 474 adj. *uncertain*; unmotivated 618 adj. *unintentional*; unaccountable, inexplicable 517 adj. *puzzling.*

Vb. *chance*, hap, fall to one's lot, so happen 154 vb. *happen*; chance upon, stumble u., blunder u. 484 vb. *discover*; risk it 618 vb. *gamble.*

Adv. *by chance*, by accident, casually, unintentionally, fortuitously, randomly; whatever happens, in any event.

160. Power – N. *power*, potency, puissance, mightiness 32 n. *greatness*; prevalence, predominance 34 n. *superiority*; omnipotence, almightiness 733 n. *authority*; control, sway 733 n. *governance*; ascendancy 178 n. *influence*; staying power, endurance 153 n. *stability*; might, right arm 162 n. *strength*; might and main, effort 682 n. *exertion*; force 740 n. *compulsion*; weight 322 n. *gravity*; manpower 686 n. *personnel*; vantage ground 34 n. *vantage*; cogency, emphasis 532 n. *affirmation*; extra power, overdrive.

ability, capability, potentiality 469 n. *possibility*; competency, efficiency, efficacy 694 n. *skill*; capacity, faculty, virtue, property, qualification 24 n. *fitness*; gift 694 n. *aptitude*; compass, reach, grasp 183 n. *range*; susceptibility 180 n. *liability*; enablement, authorization 756 n. *permission*.

energy, liveliness, vigour, dynamism 174 n. *vigorousness*; engine power, horse-power; force, field of f.; compression, spring 328 n. *elasticity*; pressure, head, charge, steam; full pressure, steam up; tension, high t.; pulling power 288 n. *traction*; thrust, jet propulsion 287 n. *propulsion*, 279 n. *impulse*; potential function, potential; erg, action; foot-pound, poundal.

electricity, active e., static e.; positive electricity, negative e.; lightning, spark; electro-dynamics, electrostatics, electromagnetism; electrification, inductance, capacitance, voltaism, galvanism; amperage, current; circuit, short c., closed c., open c.; lightning conductor, live wire; cable, pylon, grid; generator, dynamo; battery, cell; volt, watt, kilo-watt, megawatt; resistance, ohm; ampere, amp, milliamp; potential, voltage.

nucleonics, electronics, nuclear physics; atomic fission, nuclear f., thermonuclear f.; cyclotron, atom-smasher, betatron, cosmotron, high-energy accelerator; atomic pile, reactor, chain-reactor, breeder-r.; moderator, Zeta; mushroom, fall-out, radioactive cloud 417 n. *radiation*.

Adj. *powerful*, potent 162 adj. *strong*; puissant, mighty, overmighty 32 adj. *great*; rising, in the ascendant 36 adj. *increasing*; prevalent, prevailing, predominant 178 adj. *influential*; almighty, omnipotent, irresistible 34 adj. *supreme*; empowered; competent, capable, able; omnicompetent, multicompetent 694 adj. *expert*; efficacious, effectual, effective 727 adj. *successful*; operative, workable, having teeth; in force, valid 153 adj. *vested*; cogent, compulsive 740 adj. *compelling*; forcible 176 adj. *violent*; armipotent, bellicose 718 adj. *warlike*.

dynamic, energetic 174 adj. *vigorous*; high-potential, high-tension, super-charged; locomotive, kinetic 265 adj. *moving*; powered, engined; live, electric; atomic, electronic, nuclear, thermonuclear; radioactive.

Vb. *be able*, — powerful etc. adj.; can, have it in one; compass, manage 676 vb. *do*; measure up to 635 vb. *suffice*; control 733 vb. *dominate*; force 740 vb. *compel*.

empower, enable, authorize; put teeth into, arm 162 vb. *strengthen*; electrify, charge; power, engine.

161. Impotence – N. *impotence*, no authority, power vacuum; inability, incapacity; incapability, incompetence, inefficiency 728 n. *failure*, 695 n. *unskilfulness*; decrepitude 131 n. *age*; invalidation, disqualification; sterility, sterilization 172 n. *unproductivity*; disarmament, demilitarization 719 n. *pacification*.

helplessness, defencelessness 661 n. *vulnerability*; powerlessness 745 n. *subjection*; unconsciousness 375 n. *insensibility*; stroke, apoplexy 651 n. *disease*; cramp; torpor 677 n. *inaction*; atrophy; palsy 131 n. *age*; loss of control, incontinence; imbecility 499 n. *unintelligence*; legal incapacity, minority 130 n. *nonage*; infancy 130 n. *youth*; invalid 651 n. *sick person*, 163 n. *weakling*.

eunuch, castrato; no-man; gelding, capon, bullock, steer, neuter, it; free-martin, hermaphrodite.

ineffectuality, ineffectiveness, futility 497 n. *absurdity*; vanity 4 n. *insubstantiality*; uselessness 641 n. *inutility*; dead letter 752 n. *abrogation*; dummy 4 n. *insubstantial thing.*

Adj. *powerless*, unable; unempowered, unauthorized; nominal 4 adj. *insubstantial*; nugatory, invalid, null and void; without a leg to stand on 163 adj. *weak*; inoperative 679 adj. *inactive*; in abeyance 752 adj. *abrogated*; obsolete 127 adj. *antiquated*; disabled, unqualified, unfit 25 adj. *unapt*; unworkable, dud 641 adj. *useless*; inadequate 636 adj. *insufficient*; ineffective, ineffectual; incapable 695 adj. *unskilful*; unpowered, unengined.

defenceless, helpless, without resource; bereaved, bereft, unfriended 883 adj. *friendless*; harmless 935 adj. *innocent*; barehanded, weaponless, unarmed, disarmed; unfortified, exposed 661 adj. *vulnerable.*

impotent, powerless, feeble 163 adj. *weak*; emasculated (see **Vb.** *unman*); sexless, neuter; sterile, barren, infertile 172 adj. *unproductive*; worn out, effete; senile 131 adj. *aged*; unconscious 375 adj. *insensible*; without self-control, incontinent; dead-beat 684 adj. *fatigued*; nerveless, spineless 601 adj. *irresolute*; hors de combat, out of the running 728 adj. *defeated*; helpless, rudderless; baffled, thwarted.

Vb. *be impotent,* — defenceless etc.adj.; cannot, not help 641 vb. *be useless*; avail nothing 728 vb. *fail*; feel helpless, shrug, wring one's hands; look on, stand by; not have a leg to stand on; faint, swoon, pass out; collapse 163 vb. *be weak.*

disable, incapacitate, unfit; disqualify 916 vb. *disentitle*; invalidate, decontrol 752 vb. *abrogate*; disarm, demilitarize 163 vb. *weaken*; neutralize 182 vb. *counteract*; undermine, sap 255 vb. *make concave*; exhaust, use up 634 vb. *waste*; double up, wind, prostrate, bowl over, knock out 279 vb. *strike*; paralyse 679 vb. *make inactive*; sprain, dislocate; cripple, lame, maim 702 vb. *hinder*, 655 vb. *impair*; stifle, suffocate 362 vb. *kill*;

muzzle 399 vb. *silence*; spike the guns, draw the teeth, clip the wings, scotch the snake; tie the hands, cramp one's style; sabotage; put out of action 674 vb. *disuse.*

unman, unnerve, enervate, palsy, cowardize 854 vb. *frighten*; devitalize 163 vb. *weaken*; emasculate, castrate, spay, geld, caponize, effeminate 172 vb. *sterilize.*

162. Strength – N.

strength, might, potency, horse-power, engine-p. 160 n. *power*; energy 174 n. *vigorousness*; force 735 n. *brute force*; tone, tonicity, tension, temper, capacity to bear, tolerance; iron, adamant 326 n. *hardness*; oak, heart of oak 329 n. *toughness*; grip 778 n. *retention*; grit 600 n. *stamina.*

vitality, 650 n. *health*; liveliness 360 n. *life*; animal spirits 833 n. *cheerfulness*; virility, red blood 855 n. *manliness*, 372 n. *male*; physique, muscularity, muscle, biceps, sinews, beef, brawn 195 n. *size.*

athletics, 837 n. *sport*; athleticism, gymnastics, feats of strength, callisthenics 682 n. *exercise*; acrobatics, aerobatics; agonism 716 n. *contest*; palaestra 724 n. *arena.*

athlete, gymnast, acrobat; circus animal, performing flea; agonist, Blue, all-rounder, pancratiast 716 n. *contender*; wrestler 716 n. *wrestling*; heavyweight 722 n. *pugilist*; weight-lifter, strong man; he-man 372 n. *male*; strongarm man, bully, bruiser 857 n. *desperado*; chucker-out, bouncer 300 n. *ejector*; amazon, virago; matador 362 n. *killer*; giant refreshed 195 n. *giant.*

strengthening etc. vb.; reinforcement 703 n. *aid*; stiffening 326 n. *hardening*; invigoration 174 n. *stimulation*; reanimation, revival 656 n. *restoration*; emphasis, stress 532 n. *affirmation.*

Adj. *strong*, lusty, youthful 130 adj. *young*; mighty, puissant, potent, armed 160 adj. *powerful*; high-powered; all-powerful, omnipotent, overpowering, overwhelming 34 adj. *superior*; irresistible, more than a match for 727 adj. *unbeaten*; valid, in full force; strongarm; forceful, forcible 735 adj. *severe*;

urgent 740 adj. *compelling*; emphatic 532 adj. *assertive*; tempered, iron-hard, steely 326 adj. *hard*; case-hardened 329 adj. *tough*; firm, stable 153 adj. *fixed*; well-built, stout; strong as brandy, heady, double-strength 949 adj. *intoxicating*.

unyielding, staunch 599 adj. *resolute*; stubborn 602 adj. *obstinate*; persistent 600 adj. *persevering*; inelastic 326 adj. *rigid*; shatter-proof, unbreakable, solid 324 adj. *dense*; impregnable 660 adj. *invulnerable*; invincible 727 adj. *unbeaten*; unflagging 678 adj. *industrious*; proof, of proof, sound; waterproof, impermeable; bullet-proof, bomb-p.

stalwart, stout, sturdy, hardy, rugged, robust 174 adj. *vigorous*; able-bodied, muscular, brawny; sinewy, wiry 678 adj. *active*; strapping, well-knit, well set-up, broad-shouldered, thickset, burly, beefy, husky, hefty 195 adj. *large*; gigantic 195 adj. *huge*.

athletic, gymnastic, acrobatic, agonistic, palaestric 716 adj. *contending*; exercised, fit, fighting f., in training, in condition 650 adj. *healthy*.

manly, masculine 372 adj. *male*; amazonian; virile, red-blooded 855 adj. *courageous*.

Vb. *be strong*, — mighty etc. adj.; have what it takes; come in force; overpower, overwhelm 727 vb. *overmaster*; convalesce, recover 656 vb. *be restored*, 685 vb. *be refreshed*.

strengthen, confirm, lend force to 36 vb. *augment*; underline, stress 532 vb. *emphasize*; reinforce, fortify; stuff 227 vb. *line*; buttress, prop 218 vb. *support*; nerve, brace, steel 855 vb. *give courage*; temper 326 vb. *harden*; energize 174 vb. *invigorate*; quicken 821 vb. *excite*; vivify 656 vb. *revive*; recruit 685 vb. *refresh*; build up, power 160 vb. *empower*.

163. Weakness – N. *weakness*, feebleness; helplessness 161 n. *impotence*; incapacity to bear, intolerance; flimsiness, fragility, frailness 330 n. *brittleness*; delicacy, tenderness 327 n. *softness*; effeminacy, womanishness; feet of clay,

instability 152 n. *changeableness*; weakliness, debility, infirmity, decrepitude 131 n. *age*; invalidism 651 n. *ill-health*; atony, flaccidity, flabbiness, floppiness, anaemia, bloodlessness; enervation, inanition, faintness, languor 679 n. *sluggishness*; exhaustion 684 n. *fatigue*; swoon 375 n. *insensibility*; decline 655 n. *deterioration*; adulteration, dilution 43 n. *mixture*; emasculation; invalidation 752 n. *abrogation*; crack, fault, flaw 845 n. *blemish*.

weakling, effeminate, pansy; softy, sissy, milksop; invalid, hypochondriac 651 n. *sick person*; lame dog, lame duck 731 n. *unlucky person*; babe 132 n. *child*; cry-baby 856 n. *coward*; mother's darling 890 n. *favourite*; doormat, jelly-fish 825 n. *sufferer*; gull 544 n. *dupe*.

weak thing, broken reed, rope of sand; sandcastle, house built on sand, house of cards, cobweb, gossamer 4 n. *insubstantial thing*; matchwood 330 n. *brittleness*; dishwater, slops, milk and water.

Adj. *weak*, powerless, strengthless, invalid 161 adj. *impotent*; under-strength, under-proof; helpless 161 adj. *defenceless*; harmless 935 adj. *innocent*; babyish 132 adj. *infantine*; delicate 4 adj. *insubstantial*; flimsy, sleazy 330 adj. *brittle*; feeble, slight, puny 33 adj. *small*; lightweight 323 adj. *light*; thin 206 adj. *lean*; sheepish, gutless 601 adj. *irresolute*; spineless, invertebrate; bloodless, anaemic; weakly, seedy 651 adj. *unhealthy*; untempered, limp, flaccid 327 adj. *soft*; slack, loose 734 adj. *lax*; watery, wishy-washy, milk-and-water, insipid 387 adj. *tasteless*; decrepit, old 131 adj. *aged*; groggy, rocky, rickety 152 adj. *unstable*; infant 68 adj. *beginning*, 126 adj. *new*, 130 adj. *young*.

weakened, deflated 37 adj. *decreasing*; wasted, spent, effete, used up, burnt out 673 adj. *used*; faint, flagging 684 adj. *fatigued*; strained, overstrained 246 adj. *distorted*; weather-beaten, worn 655 adj. *dilapidated*; rotten, withered 51 adj. *decomposed*; deactivated, neutralized 175 adj. *inert*; diluted 43 adj. *mixed*. See *crippled*.

crippled, halt, lame, game, limping, hobbling; hamstrung, hipshot; arthritic, rheumatic, gouty; legless, armless, handless, eyeless 647 adj. *imperfect*.

Vb. *be weak*, weaken; sicken 651 vb. *be ill*; faint, fail, languish, flag 684 vb. *be fatigued*; decline 655 vb. *deteriorate*; droop, wilt; soften 327 vb. *soften*; yield, give, sag; totter 317 vb. *oscillate*; halt, limp, go lame 278 vb. *move slowly*.

weaken, enfeeble, debilitate, enervate; relax, slacken, loosen 46 vb. *disjoin*; shake, soften up 327 vb. *soften*; strain, cripple, lame 161 vb. *disable*; disarm, take the edge off 257 vb. *blunt*; impoverish, starve; reduce, extenuate, thin 37 vb. *bate*; dilute, water, adulterate 43 vb. *mix*; denature, devitalize; neutralize 182 vb. *counteract*; invalidate 752 vb. *abrogate*; dismantle 165 vb. *demolish*; sap, undermine; hurt, injure 655 vb. *wound*.

164. Production – N. *production*, creation; origination, invention, original work 21 n. *non-imitation*, 484 n. *discovery*; creative urge, productivity 171 n. *productiveness*; performance, output, out-turn, through-put 676 n. *action*; concoction, brewing 669 n. *preparation*; formation; tectonics, building, architecture; construction, establishment; making, fabrication, manufacture; industry 622 n. *business*; processing, process 147 n. *conversion*; assembly-line, production l. 630 n. *machine*; industrialization, mass-production, automation; farming 370 n. *agriculture*; breeding 369 n. *animal husbandry*; development 316 n. *evolution*.

product, creature, creation; result 157 n. *effect*; output, out-turn; end-product, by-p.; extract, essence, confection; work of one's hands, handiwork, artifact; manufacture, article, thing 319 n. *object*; ware 795 n. *merchandise*, production, work, opus, piece 56 n. *composition*; chef d'œuvre 694 n. *masterpiece*; fruit, flower, produce, yield, harvest, crop; interest, increase, return 771 n. *gain*; mental product, brain-child 451 n. *idea*.

edifice, piece of architecture, building, structure, fabric, erection; pile, dome, tower, skyscraper 209 n. *high structure*; pyramid 548 n. *monument*; mansion 192 n. *house*; stonework, brickwork, bricks and mortar.

propagation 166 n. *reproduction*; fertility, fecundity, proliferation, multiplication 171 n. *productiveness*; breeding, hatching, incubation; copulation 45 n. *coition*; generation, procreation, genesis, biogenesis; parthenogenesis, virgin birth; autogenesis, abiogenesis, spontaneous generation; fertilization, fecundation, superfecundation; impregnation, insemination, artificial i., pollination; conception, pregnancy, germination, gestation; birth 68 n. *origin*; parenthood 169 n. *parentage*; genesiology.

obstetrics, midwifery, maternity work; parturition, birth, childbirth, childbed, confinement, lying-in, accouchement, labour, travail, throe, birth-pang, pains; delivery, caesarian operation; omentum, caul, umbilical cord, placenta, afterbirth; obstetrician; midwife, accoucheur, accoucheuse 658 n. *nurse*; stork, gooseberry bush.

genitalia, loins, womb 156 n. *source*; genitals, organs of generation, parts, private p.; parts of shame, pudenda; intromittent organ, male o., member, penis; testicle, scrotum; vulva, vagina, uterus, ovary, seed, pollen; seminal fluid, sperm, spermatozoa; phallus, phallic emblem, lingam ; yoni.

Adj. *productive*, creative, inventive; shaping, constructive, architectonic 331 adj. *structural*; manufacturing, industrial 243 adj. *formative*; genesial, genesiological; fertile 171 adj. *prolific*; potent 171 adj. *generative*; polliniferous; pregnant, breeding, broody; expecting, carrying, heavy with, big w.; with child, with young, in the family way; parturient, in the straw; obstetrical 658 adj. *medical*; puerperal, puerperous; viviparous, oviparous, autogenous, abiogenetic; parthenogenetic; genital, vulvar, vaginal, phallic, priapic.

Vb. *produce*, create, originate; invent

484 vb. *discover*; make 243 vb. *efform*; forge, chisel, carve, sculpt, cast; coin 797 vb. *mint*; manufacture, fabricate, prefabricate, process, machine; mass-produce, churn out, multiply; construct, build, raise, rear, erect, set up, run up 310 vb. *elevate*; mine 304 vb. *extract*; engineer, contrive 623 vb. *plan*; yield results, effect 156 vb. *cause*. See *generate*.

reproduce itself, yield, give increase, flower, seed, sprout, blossom, bud, bloom, be out; burgeon 197 vb. *expand*; fruit, bear fruit, fructify 669 vb. *mature*; multiply, breed, hatch, teem, spawn, spat, pullulate 104 vb. *be many*; carry, bear, bring forth, give birth; ean, yean, farrow, lamb, foal, drop, calve, pup, whelp, kitten, lay, seed; lie in, be brought to bed of.

generate, evolve, produce; fecundate, cover, impregnate, inseminate, pollinate; copulate 45 vb. *unite with*; procreate, propagate; beget, get, engender; father, sire, dam; call into being, incubate 369 vb. *breed stock*; farm, grow 370 vb. *cultivate*.

165. Destruction: non-production – N. *destruction*, unmaking, undoing; blotting out 550 n. *obliteration*; annihilation, nullification 2 n. *extinction*; abolition, suppression 752 n. *abrogation*; subversion, overthrow 221 n. *overturning*; dissolution 51 n. *decomposition*; demolition, demolishment; disruption, pulverization; liquidation, elimination, extirpation, eradication 300 n. *ejection*; mass murder, genocide 362 n. *slaughter*; doing in, spifflication; destructiveness, mischief, iconoclasm, vandalism; wrecking activities, sabotage 702 n. *hindrance*.

havoc, scene of destruction, desolation, scorched earth 172 n. *desert*; carnage, shambles 362 n. *slaughter-house*; upheaval, cataclysm 176 n. *violence*; devastation, ravages; blitz 712 n. *bombardment*; holocaust, hecatomb. See 168 n. *destroyer*.

ruin, downfall, ruination, perdition,

one's undoing; catastrophe 731 n. *adversity*; collapse, débâcle, landslide 149 n. *revolution*; wreck, shipwreck, wreckage, wrack; loss, total l.; knock-out blow, K.O. 279 n. *knock*; beginning of the end, road to ruin 655 n. *deterioration*; doom, knell 69 n. *finality*; ruins 127 n. *oldness*.

Adj. *destructive*, internecine, annihilating etc. vb.; ruinous, sacrificial, costly 811 adj. *dear*; apocalyptic, cataclysmic, overwhelming 176 adj. *violent*; raging, furious, mortal, suicidal, cut-throat 362 adj. *deadly*; subversive 149 adj. *revolutionary*; mischievous, pernicious 645 adj. *harmful*.

Vb. *destroy*, undo, unmake 148 vb. *revert*; abolish, annihilate, liquidate, exterminate; devour, swallow up, engulf 299 vb. *absorb*; swamp, overwhelm, drown 341 vb. *drench*; incinerate, gut 381 vb. *burn*; wreck, sink, torpedo, scupper 313 vb. *plunge*; end 69 vb. *terminate*; do for, do in, put down, put away, do away with, make away w., 362 vb. *kill*; decimate, spare none 362 vb. *slaughter*, 906 vb. *be pitiless*; remove, extirpate, eradicate, uproot 300 vb. *eject*; wipe out, efface, blot out 550 vb. *obliterate*; annul, revoke 752 vb. *abrogate*; deface; knock out, spifflicate; make short work of, mop up; sabotage 702 vb. *obstruct*; ruin, be the ruin of.

demolish, slight 655 vb. *impair*; dismantle, knock down, tear d., level, raze 216 vb. *flatten*; throw down, prostrate, steam-roller, bull-doze 311 vb. *fell*; blow away; subvert, overthrow, overturn 221 vb. *invert*; undermine, sap, mine, blow up; bombard. bomb, blitz, blow to pieces 712 vb. *fire at*; smash, shatter, shiver 46 vb. *break*; pulp, crush, grind 332 vb. *pulverize*; atomize, make mincemeat of; rend, tear up, tear to bits 46 vb. *sunder*; beat down, batter, ram 279 vb. *strike*; strip, bare, unwall, unroof 229 vb. *uncover*.

suppress, quench, blow out, put o., snuff o. 382 vb. *extinguish*; nip in the bud; quell, put down, stamp out 735 vb. *oppress*; stamp on, sit on, squash 216 vb.

flatten; blanket, stifle, suffocate, burke; keep under, repress 525 vb. *conceal*; drown, submerge, sink, scuttle, scupper, torpedo.

lay waste, waste, desolate, devastate, depopulate 300 vb. *void*; despoil, depredate 788 vb. *rob*; spoil, mar, ruin 655 vb. *impair*; ravage, run amok, make havoc 176 vb. *be violent*; consume, devour 634 vb. *waste*.

be destroyed, go west, go under, sink 361 vb. *perish*, 313 vb. *plunge*; go on the rocks, break up, split, crumple up; go to rack and ruin, crumble 655 vb. *deteriorate*; go to the wall, succumb; go to pot, go to the dogs.

166. Reproduction – N. *reproduction*, procreation 164 n. *production*; remaking, reconstruction; rediscovery 484 n. *discovery*; redoing 106 n. *repetition*; duplication, reduplication, mass-production 171 n. *productiveness*; renovation 656 n. *restoration*; regeneration, reanimation 656 n. *revival*; resurrection, resurgence; reincarnation, palingenesis, metempsychosis 124 n. *future state*; Phoenix.

Adj. *reproductive*, progenitive; resurrectional; renascent, resurgent; Hydra-headed, Phoenix-like.

Vb. *reproduce*, remake, refashion, recoin, reconstruct; rebuild, refound, reestablish, rediscover; duplicate 20 vb. *copy*, 106 vb. *repeat*; take after, throw back to, inherit 18 vb. *resemble*, 148 vb. *revert*; renovate, renew 656 vb. *restore*; regenerate, resurrect, resuscitate 656 vb. *revive*; mass-produce, multiply; print off, reel o. 587 vb. *print*.

167. Producer – N. *producer*, creator, maker; originator, inventor, discoverer, mover, instigator 612 n. *motivator*; founder, establisher; generator, fertilizer; inseminator, donor; begetter 169 n. *parent*; creative worker 556 n. *artist*; constructor, builder, architect, engineer; manufacturer, industrialist 686 n. *agent*; artificer, craftsman 686 n. *artisan*; farmer 370 n. *husbandman*, 369 n. *breeder*; miner, extractor.

168. Destroyer – N. *destroyer*, remover, leveller, abolitionist, iconoclast, nihilist, anarchist 149 n. *revolutionist*; saboteur, wrecker, pyromaniac 381 n. *incendiarism*; spoiler, ravager; defacer, eraser 550 n. *obliteration*; assassin 362 n. *murderer*; executioner 963 n. *punisher*; barbarian, Hun, Tartar, Vandal; time 111 n. *course of time*; destructive agency, locust, moth, worm, rust, erosion 51 n. *decay*; corrosive, acid, cankerworm, mildew, blight, poison 659 n. *bane*; sword 723 n. *weapon*; dynamite 723 n. *explosive*; torpedo 723 n. *bomb*.

169. Parentage – N. *parentage*, paternity, maternity; parenthood, fatherhood, motherhood; loins, womb 156 n. *source*; kinship 11 n. *consanguinity*.

parent, father, sire, dad, papa, pop, governor, the old man; head of the family, paterfamilias; progenitor, procreator, begetter, author of one's existence; grandfather 133 n. *old man*; ancestor, forefather, forbear, patriarch 66 n. *precursor*; first parents, Adam and Eve 371 n. *mankind*; foster-father, stepfather.

genealogy, family tree, lineage 11 n. *family*; pedigree, heredity; line, blood, strain; stock, stem, tribe, house, race, clan, sept 11 n. *race*; descent, extraction, birth, ancestry 68 n. *origin*.

maternity, motherhood; mother, dam, mamma, momma, ma, mummy, mum; grandmother, grandam, grandma, gran, granny; materfamilias, matron, matriarch; beldam 133 n. *old woman*; foster-mother, stepmother, mother-in-law.

Adj. *parental*, paternal; maternal, matronly; fatherly, fatherlike; motherly, step-motherly; family, linear, patrilinear, matrilinear; ancestral; hereditary; patriarchal 127 adj. *immemorial*; racial, phyletic 11 adj. *ethnic*.

170. Posterity – N. *posterity*, progeny, issue, offspring, young, little ones 132 n. *child*; breed 11 n. *race*; brood 132 n. *youngling*; fruit of the womb, children, grandchildren 11 n. *family*; aftercomers,

succession, heirs; rising generation 130 n. *youth.*

descendant, son, daughter, pledge; child, bantling, chip of the old block 132 n. *child*; seed, scion 132 n. *young plant*; heir, heiress, heir of the body 776 n. *beneficiary*; branch, daughter-house, daughter-nation, colony; graft, offshoot.

sonship, filiation, descent, male d. 169 n. *parentage*; collaterality, ramification; illegitimacy 954 n. *bastardy*; succession, heirship; primogeniture 119 n. *priority.*

Adj. *filial*, daughterly; descended, lineal; collateral; primogenital 119 n. *prior*; adopted, adoptive; step-; hereditary.

171. Productiveness – N. *productiveness*,

productivity, mass-production; booming economy 730 n. *prosperity*; overproductivity 637 n. *redundance*; high birthrate, fecundity, fertility, luxuriance, lushness, exuberance, richness, uberty 635 n. *plenty*; productive capacity, biotic potential; procreation 164 n. *propagation*; fructification 669 n. *maturation*; inventiveness, resourcefulness 513 n. *imagination.*

fertilizer, manure, artificial m., fish-m., guano, dung, mould, silt, compost 370 n. *agriculture*; semen, sperm, seed, roe, milt; spermatic fluid.

abundance, wealth, riot, foison, harvest 32 n. *great quantity*; teeming womb, mother earth, rich soil; hotbed, nursery 68 n. *origin*; cornucopia, land flowing with milk and honey; warren, ant heap 104 n. *multitude*; milch cow; rabbit.

Adj. *prolific*, fruitful, fertile, fecund; teeming, multiparous, spawning 164 adj. *productive*; exuberant, lush, luxuriant, rich, fat, uberous 635 adj. *plenteous*; creative, inventive, resourceful.

generative, procreant, procreative, philoprogenitive, potent; life-giving, spermatic, seminal, germinal; originative, all-creating.

Vb. *make fruitful*, plant, fertilize 370 vb. *cultivate*; impregnate, fecundate 164 vb. *generate.*

be fruitful, conceive, germinate, bud,

blossom; bear, give birth, have children; teem, proliferate, pullulate, swarm, multiply, propagate 104 vb. *be many*; send up the birthrate; populate.

172. Unproductiveness – N. *unproductivity*,

dearth, famine 636 n. *scarcity*; sterility, barrenness, infertility; contraception, sterilization 161 n. *impotence*; dying race, falling birthrate 37 vb. *decrease*; virginity 895 n. *celibacy*; unprofitability 772 n. *loss*; stagnation, maiden over 641 n. *lost labour.*

desert, 342 n. *dryness*; desolation, waste, wild, wilderness; sand, dustbowl; desert island 883 n. *seclusion.*

Adj. *unproductive*, dried up, exhausted, waste, desert, desolate; poor, stony, shallow; unprolific, barren, infertile, sterile; unfruitful, acarpous; rootless, seedless, ungerminating; arid 342 adj. *dry*; fallow 674 adj. *disused*; unsown, uncultivated, unharvested; childless, issueless; celibate 895 adj. *unwedded*; fruitless, unprofitable 641 adj. *profitless*; addled, abortive.

Vb. *be unproductive*, rust, stagnate, lie fallow 679 vb. *be inactive*; bury one's talent 674 vb. *not use*, 728 vb. *fail*; abort 728 vb. *miscarry.*

sterilize, castrate, geld 161 vb. *unman*; sow with salt 165 vb. *lay waste*; addle 51 vb. *decompose*; disinfect 652 vb. *sanitate.*

173. Agency – N. *agency*, operation,

work 676 n. *action*; exercise 673 n. *use*; force, play 160 n. *power*; procuration 689 n. *management*; service 628 n. *instrumentality*; efficiency 156 n. *causation*; co-agency 706 n. *cooperation*; process, treatment, handling.

Adj. *operative*, efficient 727 adj. *successful*; drastic 735 adj. *severe*; executive, operational, functional; in action, in operation 676 adj. *doing*; on the active list 678 adj. *active*; live 160 adj. *dynamic*; practical, workable 642 adj. *expedient*; serviceable 640 adj. *useful.*

Vb. *operate*, play, act, work, go, run 676 vb. *do*; serve 622 vb. *function*; take effect, act upon 178 vb. *influence*; bring into play, wind up, turn on, switch on; actuate, power, drive 265 vb. *move*; manipulate, handle, wield, brandish 673 vb. *use*.

174. Vigour: physical energy – N. *vigorousness*, lustiness, energy 571 n. *vigour*; dynamism, pressure, force 160 n. *energy*; intensity, high pressure 162 n. *strength*; dash, élan, spurt, impetuosity 680 n. *haste*; zest 824 n. *joy*; liveliness, life, spirit, vim, fire, mettle; ginger, fizz, verve, pep, drive, go; enterprise, initiative 672 n. *undertaking*; vehemence 176 n. *violence*; aggressiveness, thrust, push, kick, punch 712 n. *attack*; grip, bite, teeth, backbone 599 n. *resolution*; live wire, dynamo, dynamite, quicksilver.

stimulation, activation, tonic effect; intensification, boost 36 n. *increase*; excitement 821 n. *excitation*; ferment, fermentation, leaven; ebullience 318 n. *commotion*.

stimulant, energizer, activator, booster; stimulus, fillip, shot; crack of the whip, lash 612 n. *incentive*; hormone, restorative, tonic; bracer, pick-me-up 390 n. *savouriness*; spice, sauce; aphrodisiac, love philtre; pep talk 821 n. *excitant*.

Adj. *vigorous*, energetic 678 adj. *active*; forcible 571 adj. *forceful*; vehement 176 adj. *violent*; vivid, vibrant 160 n. *dynamic*; high-pressure, intense 678 adj. *industrious*; go-ahead 672 adj. *enterprising*; aggressive, pushful, thrustful 712 adj. *attacking*; keen 597 adj. *willing*; double-edged, double-shotted, double-distilled, potent 160 adj. *powerful*; hearty, full-blooded; peppy, zestful, lusty, mettlesome, brisk, live 819 adj. *lively*; nippy, snappy; fizzy, heady, racy; tonic, bracing 821 adj. *exciting*; drastic, punishing 735 n. *severe*.

Vb. *invigorate*, energize, activate; intensify, double, redouble; wind up, step up, bump up, pep up, ginger up, boost 162 vb. *strengthen*; rouse, kindle, enflame, stimulate, enliven, quicken 821 vb. *excite*; act like a tonic, hearten, animate 833 vb. *cheer*; go to one's head,

intoxicate 949 vb. *inebriate*; freshen, recruit 685 vb. *refresh*; give an edge to 256 vb. *sharpen*; force, fertilize 370 vb. *cultivate*.

Adv. *vigorously*, forcibly, with telling effect.

175. Inertness – N. *inertness*, inertia 677 n. *inaction*; lifelessness, languor, paralysis, torpor 375 n. *insensibility*; rest, stagnation, passivity 266 n. *quiescence*; dormancy 523 n. *latency*; dullness, sloth 679 n. *sluggishness*; immobility, impassiveness 823 n. *inexcitability*; spent fires, extinct volcano.

Adj. *inert*, passive, dead 677 adj. *nonacting*; lifeless, languid, torpid, numb 375 adj. *insensible*; heavy, lumpish, sluggish 278 adj. *slow*, 679 adj. *inactive*; stagnant 266 adj. *quiescent*; slack, low-pressure, untensed 734 adj. *lax*; apathetic 860 adj. *indifferent*; pacific 717 adj. *peaceful*; in abeyance 752 adj. *abrogated*; smouldering, dormant 523 adj. *latent*.

Vb. *be inert*, slumber 679 vb. *sleep*; hang fire, not catch; smoulder 523 vb. *lurk*; lie, stagnate, vegetate 266 vb. *be quiescent*.

176. Violence – N. *violence*, vehemence, impetuosity 174 n. *vigorousness*; destructiveness 165 n. *destruction*; boisterousness, turbulence, storminess 318 n. *commotion*; outburst, outbreak, eruption; uproar 61 n. *turmoil*; roughness 735 n. *severity*; high hand, strong-arm work, terrorism 735 n. *brute force*; barbarity 898 n. *inhumanity*; paroxysm 318 n. *spasm*.

storm, turmoil, ferment; weather, dirty w., inclemency; tempest, gale force, hurricane 352 n. *gale*; thunder, lightning, fulguration; rainstorm, cloudburst 350 n. *rain*; hailstorm, snowstorm, blizzard 380 n. *wintriness*; sandstorm, dust-storm.

violent creature, brute, beast, wild b.; dragon, tiger, wolf, mad dog; demon, devil, hell-hound, hell-cat, fury 938 n. *monster*; savage, barbarian, Vandal, iconoclast 168 n. *destroyer*; man of blood, butcher 362 n. *murderer*; homicidal maniac 504 n. *madman*; rough 904 n. *ruffian*, Herod 735 n. *tyrant*; fire-eater, bravo 877 n. *boaster*; fire-brand 738 n. *agitator*; revolutionary, anarchist, nihilist, terrorist 149 n. *revolutionist*; virago, termagant, Amazon; spitfire, scold 892 n. *shrew*.

Adj. *violent*, vehement, forcible 162 adj. *strong*; acute 256 adj. *sharp*; rude, ungentle; extreme, severe, tyrannical, heavy-handed 735 adj. *oppressive*; brutal, bloody 898 adj. *cruel*; hot-blooded 892 adj. *irascible*; aggressive, bellicose 718 adj. *warlike*; rough, boisterous, wild, stormy 352 adj. *windy*; uproarious, rowdy, turbulent, tumultuous 738 adj. *riotous*; incendiary, anarchistic, nihilistic 149 adj. *revolutionary*; intemperate, immoderate, unbridled; ungovernable, unruly, uncontrollable 738 adj. *disobedient*; furious, frenzied 891 adj. *angry*; hot, red-hot, inflamed, burning, molten 379 adj. *fiery*; eruptive, explosive, cataclysmic, overwhelming, volcanic, seismic 165 adj. *destructive*; disturbed, troublous, stirring.

Vb. *be violent*, break bounds, run wild, run riot, run amuck, rampage; tear, rush; 277 vb. *move fast*; surge forward, mob 712 vb. *charge*; break the peace, riot, take to arms 718 vb. *go to war*; see red, go berserk 891 vb. *be angry*; storm, rage, roar, bluster, come in like a lion 352 vb. *blow*; foam, fume, run high; burst its banks, flood, overwhelm 350 vb. *flow*; explode, go off, blow up, detonate, burst; let fly, let off, fulminate; erupt, break out; struggle, lash out 715 vb. *resist*; savage, maul 655 vb. *wound*; tyrannize, out-Herod Herod 735 vb. *oppress*.

force, use f., smash 46 vb. *break*; strain, wrench, torture 246 vb. *distort*; force open, prize o. 263 vb. *open*; do violence to, abuse, violate 951 vb. *debauch*.

make violent, goad, lash, whip 612 vb. *incite*; fan, inflame, foment, exacerbate, exasperate 832 vb. *aggravate*; irritate, infuriate 891 vb. *enrage*; madden 503 vb. *make mad*.

177. Moderation – N. *moderation*, nonviolence, gentleness 736 n. *lenity*; reasonableness, measure, golden mean 732 n. *mediocrity*; control, check 747 n. *restraint*; self-control 942 n. *temperance*, 948 n. *sobriety*; correction, adjustment, modulation; mitigation, alleviation, mollification 831 n. *relief*; relaxation 734 n. *laxity*; appeasement, assuagement, détente 719 n. *pacification*; tranquillization, sedation.

moderator, palliative, stopgap, solvent 658 n. *remedy*; lenitive, demulcent 658 n. *balm*; soothing syrup, oil; sedative, tranquillizer 679 n. *soporific*; anodyne, opiate 375 n. *anaesthetic*; cold water, wet blanket damper 613 n. *dissuasion*; brake 747 n. *restraint*; neutralizer 658 n. *antidote*; cushion, shockabsorber; mollifier, peacemaker 720 n. *mediator*; controller, restraining hand, rein.

Adj. *moderate*, unextreme, non-violent, reasonable, judicious 480 adj. *judicial*; tame, gentle 736 adj. *lenient*; measured, 747 adj. *restrained*; chastened, self-controlled 942 adj. *temperate*, 948 adj. *sober*; peaceable, pacific 717 adj. *peaceful*; leftish, pink, non-extreme.

lenitive, abirritant 658 adj. *remedial*; alleviative, anodyne, calmative, sedative 679 adj. *somnific*; soothing, bland, emollient; disarming 719 adj. *pacificatory*.

Vb. *be moderate*, — gentle etc. adj.; hold a mean, keep within bounds 942 vb. *be temperate*; keep the peace; not resist, go quietly, go out like a lamb.

moderate, mitigate, temper; correct 24 vb. *adjust*; tame, check, curb, control 747 vb. *restrain*; palliate, qualify 927 vb. *extenuate*; take the edge off 257 vb. *blunt*; break the fall, cushion 218 vb. *support*; tone down, chasten, euphemize 648 vb. *purify*; cool, throw cold water on 613 vb. *dissuade*.

assuage, ease, pour balm, mollify, lenify, alleviate, allay, lay, deaden 831 vb. *relieve*; take the sting out 182 vb. *counteract*; soothe, calm, compose, tranquillize, still, quiet, hush, lull, rock, cradle; disarm, appease, smooth over 719 vb. *pacify.*

Adv. *moderately,* within bounds, within reason.

178. Influence – N. *influence,* predominance 34 n. *superiority;* mightiness, over-mightiness 32 n. *greatness,* 638 n. *importance;* position of influence, vantage, leverage, hold, grip; weight, pressure 322 n. *gravity;* magnetism 291 n. *attraction;* counter-attraction 292 n. *repulsion,* 182 n. *counteraction;* impact 279 n. *impulse;* leaven, contagion, infection; magic, spell 983 n. *sorcery;* stars 596 n. *fate;* fascination, hypnotism; malign influence, curse, ruin 659 n. *bane;* persuasion, insinuation 612 n. *motive;* personality, credit, repute 866 n. *prestige;* hegemony, ascendancy 733 n. *authority;* factor, contributing f., vital role, leading part 156 n. *cause;* patronage, interest, favour, pull, friend at court, wire-pulling; strings, wires, lever 630 n. *tool;* hidden hand, power behind the throne, Grey Eminence 523 n. *latency;* manipulator, wire-puller 612 n. *motivator;* uncrowned king 638 n. *bigwig;* atmosphere, climate.

Adj. *influential,* dominant, prevailing 34 adj. *supreme;* in power, commanding, listened to; recognized 733 adj. *authoritative;* rising, ascendant, mighty, overmighty 32 adj. *great,* 160 adj. *powerful;* leading, hegemonical 689 adj. *directing;* contributing 156 adj. *causal;* key, momentous, decisive 638 adj. *important;* telling, moving 821 adj. *impressive;* appealing 291 adj. *attracting;* gripping, fascinating; irresistible, hypnotic 740 adj. *compelling;* persuasive 612 adj. *inducive;* habit-forming; catching, contagious 653 adj. *infectious.*

Vb. *influence,* have a pull, carry weight, have a hold on, have the ear of, be listened to 737 vb. *command;* dominate, tower over, bestride; make oneself felt, assert oneself, pull one's weight; put pressure on, lobby, pull strings 612 vb. *motivate;* affect, tell 821 vb. *impress;* tempt, inspire, work upon, induce, dispose, persuade, prevail upon, convince; force 740 vb. *compel;* colour, prejudice 481 vb. *bias;* appeal, allure, fascinate, mesmerize 291 vb. *attract;* make, be the making of 654 vb. *make better;* make or mar 147 vb. *transform;* infect, leaven, colour 143 vb. *modify.*

179. Tendency – N. *tendency,* trend, tenor; tempo, set, drift 281 n. *direction;* main stream, zeitgeist, spirit of the age; conatus, nisus; affinity, aptness, instinct for 694 n. *aptitude;* proneness, proclivity, propensity, predisposition, readiness, inclination, penchant, liking, leaning, bias, prejudice; weakness 180 n. *liability;* cast, bent, turn, grain.

Adj. *tending,* trending, conducive; tendentious 617 adj. *intending;* in a fair way to, calculated to 471 adj. *probable.*

Vb. *tend,* trend, verge, lean, incline; set, set towards, gravitate t. 289 vb. *approach;* point to, lead to 156 vb. *conduce;* bid fair to 471 vb. *be likely;* redound to, contribute to 285 vb. *promote.*

180. Liability – N. *liability,* liableness, weakness 179 n. *tendency;* susceptibility, impressibility; potentiality 469 n. *possibility;* likelihood 471 n. *probability;* responsibility 917 n. *duty.*

Adj. *liable,* apt to 179 adj. *tending;* subject to, obnoxious to, the prey of, at the mercy of 745 adj. *subject;* open to, exposed to, in danger of 661 adj. *vulnerable;* on the cards 469 adj. *possible;* susceptible 819 adj. *impressible;* answerable, accountable 917 adj. *dutied.*

Vb. *be liable,* — subject to etc. adj.; be responsible 917 vb. *incur a duty;* incur, lay oneself open, run the chance of; stand to, expose oneself 661 vb. *be in danger;* lie under, labour u. 745 vb. *be subject.*

181. Concurrence: combination of causes – N. *concurrence,* combined operation, joint effort, collaboration, co-agency, synergy, synergism 706 n. *co-operation;* compliance 758 n. *consent;* concert, joint planning, collusion, conspiracy 623 n. *plot*; partnership 706 n. *association*.

Adj. *concurrent*, concurring etc. vb.; coagent, synergic 706 adj. *cooperative*; joint, combined 45 adj. *conjunct*; colluding, contributing, involved 703 adj. *aiding*.

Vb. *concur*, acquiesce 488 vb. *assent*; collude, conspire 623 vb. *plot*; agree, harmonize 24 vb. *accord*; hang together, pull t. 706 vb. *cooperate*; contribute, help, aid, abet, serve 703 vb. *minister to*; promote, subserve 156 vb. *conduce*.

182. Counteraction – **N.** *counteraction*, opposing causes, action and reaction; polarity 240 n. *contraposition*; antagonism, antipathy, clash 14 n. *contrariety*, 279 n. *collision*; retroaction, repercussion 280 n. *recoil*; renitency, recalcitrance 715 n. *resistance*, 704 n. *opposition*; inertia, vis inertiae, friction, drag, check 702 n. *hindrance*; interference, counterpressure, 747 n. *restraint*; neutralization, deactivation 177 n. *moderation*; cross-current, counter-sea, head-wind 702 n. *obstacle*; counter-charm, counter-irritant, neutralizer 658 n. *antidote*; counterweight 31 n. *offset*; counter-blast, counter-move 688 n. *tactics*; deterrent 713 n. *defence*; prevention, preventive, inhibitor 757 n. *prohibition*.

Adj. *counteracting*, counter, counteractive; antipathetic, antagonistic 881 adj. *inimical*; resistant, recalcitrant, renitent 715 adj. *resisting*; reactionary 280 adj. *recoiling*; frictional, retarding 747 adj. *restraining*; preventive, antidotal, corrective 658 adj. *remedial*.

Vb. *counteract*, counter, run c., cross, traverse, work against, go a., militate a.; not conduce to 702 vb. *hinder*; react 280 vb. *recoil*; resist, withstand 704 vb. *oppose*; antagonize, conflict with 14 vb. *be contrary*; clash 279 vb. *collide*; interfere 678 vb. *meddle*; countervail, cancel out, counterpoise 31 vb. *set off*; repress 165 vb. *suppress*; undo 752 vb. *abrogate*; neutralize, deactivate; recover 656 vb. *retrieve*; prevent, inhibit 757 vb. *prohibit*.

Class Two

SPACE

Section 1: Space in General

183. Space: indefinite space – N. *space*, expanse, extension, extent, surface, area, acreage; volume, cubic content; continuum, stretch 71 n. *continuity*; empty space 190 n. *emptiness*; depth of space, abyss 211 n. *depth*; outer space 321 n. *heavens*; world, horizon, length and breadth of the land 348 n. *plain*, *grassland*; wilderness 172 n. *desert*; everywhere, ubiquity 189 n. *presence*; measure, dimensions 203 n. *length*, 205 n. *breadth*, 209 n. *height*.

range, reach, carry, compass, coverage; stretch, grasp; radius, latitude, amplitude; sweep, spread, ramification; play, swing 744 n. *scope*; sphere, field 724 n. *arena*; purview, prospect 438 n. *view*; perspective 199 n. *distance*; telescopic range, light-grasp.

room, space, accommodation; capacity, roomage 632 n. *storage*; seating capacity, seating; margin, free space, clearance, windage; headroom 263 n. *opening*; living space, Lebensraum, development area; elbow room, room to swing a cat in.

Adj. *spatial*, space; spatio-temporal; volumetric, cubic, three-dimensional; flat, superficial, two-dimensional.

spacious, extensive; expansive, roomy; ample, vast, capacious, broad, deep, wide; amplitudinous, voluminous, baggy 195 adj. *large*; far-reaching, widespread, world-wide, global, world 79 adj. *general*; uncircumscribed, boundless, shoreless 107 adj. *infinite*.

Vb. *extend*, spread, range, cover; span, straddle, bestride 226 vb. *overlie*; extend to, reach to 202 vb. *be contiguous*; branch, ramify.

Adv. *widely*, extensively, everywhere, wherever; far and near, far and wide, all over; from end to end, from pole to pole.

184. Region: definite space – N. *region*, locality, parts 185 n. *place*; sphere, orb, hemisphere; zone, belt; latitude, parallel, meridian; clime, climate; tract, terrain, country 344 n. *land*; geographical unit, island, peninsula, continent, land-mass; sea 343 n. *ocean*; compass, circumference 233 n. *outline*; boundaries 236 n. *limit*; pale, precincts 235 n. *enclosure*; salient; corridor 624 n. *access*; area, field, theatre 724 n. *arena*; exclusive area, charmed circle. See *territory*.

territory, sphere, zone; beat, pitch, ground; lot, holding, claim 235 n. *enclosure*; domain, grounds, park 777 n. *estate*; territorial waters, twelve-mile limit, continental shelf; air-space; motherland 192 n. *home*; commonwealth 733 n. *polity*; debatable territory, no-man's land, Tom Tiddler's ground 774 n. *non-ownership*.

district, purlieus, ins and outs, haunt; locality, highways and byways; subregion, quarter, division 53 n. *subdivision*; state, province, county, shire, riding; diocese, bishopric, parish, ward, constituency; borough, township, urban district, rural d., metropolitan area; village, town, city, conurbation; canton, department, arrondissement, commune; deme, nome; suburb, suburbia, down town, up t., City; clubland, theatreland, dockland; neighbourhood, environs, milieu.

Adj. *regional*, territorial, continental, peninsular, insular; national, state; subdivisional, local, municipal, parochial, provincial, red-brick; suburban, urban, rural, up-country; district, town, country.

185. Place: limited space – N. *place*, site, location 187 n. *station*; assigned place, pitch, beat, billet, socket, groove; centre 76 n. *focus*; birthplace 192 n.

home; address 192 n. *abode*; premises 192 n. *house*, spot, plot; point, dot, pinpoint; niche, nook, corner 194 n. *compartment*; baseline, crease (cricket) 236 n. *limit*; precinct, bailey, garth, enclosure, paddock, compound, pen, close, quadrangle, square; yard, area, areaway, backyard, courtyard, court, patio, atrium 235 n. *enclosure*.

186. Situation – N. *situation*, position, setting; time and place, when and where; location, address, whereabouts; point, stage, milestone 27 n. *degree*; site 185 n. *place*; post, station; side, aspect 445 n. *appearance*; place in a book, reference, chapter and verse; topography 321 n. *geography*.

bearings, compass direction, latitude and longitude, declination, right ascension, northing, southing 281 n. *direction*; radio-location 187 n. *location*.

Adj. *situated*, situate, located at, living at, to be found at, occupying; local, topical; topographical, geographical.

Vb. *be situate*, be situated, centre on; be, lie, stand; live, live at 192 vb. *dwell*; touch 200 vb. *be near*.

Adv. *in place*, in situ, in loco, here, there; hereabout, thereabout; whereabout; at the sign of.

187. Location – N. *location*, placing, placement, emplacement, collocation, disposition; locating, pinpointing; centring, localization 200 n. *nearness*; domestication, naturalization, indenization; settling, colonization; settlement, lodgement, establishment, fixation, installation.

station, seat, site, emplacement, position 186 n. *situation*; depot, base; factory, colony, settlement; anchorage 662 n. *shelter*; cantonment, camp-site 192 n. *abode*; halt 145 n. *stopping place*.

Adj. *located*, placed etc. vb.; ensconced, embedded; settled 153 adj. *fixed*; camping 192 adj. *residing*; at anchor 266 adj. *quiescent*; vested in, in the hands of 773 adj. *possessed*.

Vb. *place*, collocate, assign a place; situate, position, site, locate; base, centre, localize, pinpoint; find the place, put one's finger on; place right, hit 281 vb. *aim*; put, lay, set, seat; station, post, park; install, ensconce, set up, establish, fix 153 vb. *stabilize*; root, plant, implant, embed 303 vb. *insert*; bed, bed down, tuck in; accommodate, find a place for, lodge, house, quarter, billet, quarter upon; moor, anchor, dock, berth; deposit, lay down; stand, put up, erect 310 vb. *elevate*; place with, transfer, bestow, invest 780 vb. *convey*; stow 193 vb. *load*; array, deploy.

replace, put back, sheathe; bring back, reinstate 656 vb. *restore*.

place oneself, stand, take one's place; anchor; settle, strike root, gain a footing, entrench, dig in; perch, alight, sit, squat, park; pitch on, encamp, camp, bivouac; stop at, lodge, put up; hive, burrow; ensconce oneself, locate oneself, establish o., find a home; settle, colonize, populate, people 192 vb. *dwell*.

188. Displacement – N. *displacement*, dislocation, derailment 63 n. *derangement*; misplacement, wrong place 84 n. *abnormality*; shift, move 265 n. *motion*; aberration 282 n. *deviation*; transfer 272 n. *transference*; mutual transfer 151 n. *interchange*; supersession 150 n. *substitution*; removal 304 n. *extraction*; unloading, unpacking, unshipment; disencumbrance 831 n. *relief*; ejectment 300 n. *ejection*; eradication 300 n. *voidance*; exile, banishment 883 n. *seclusion*; refugee 268 n. *wanderer*; unloader, remover, removal man.

Adj. *displaced* etc. vb.; unplaced, unhoused, unharboured; unestablished, rootless, unsettled; roofless, houseless, homeless.

misplaced, ectopic 84 adj. *abnormal*; out of one's element, out of place, inappropriate 10 adj. *irrelevant*; mislaid 190 adj. *absent*.

Vb. *displace*, disturb, disorientate, derail, dislocate; dislodge, unseat, unfix, unstick 46 vb. *disjoin*; dispel, scatter, send flying 75 vb. *disperse*; shift, remove, translate, transport 272 vb. *transfer*; change round, transpose 151 vb. *interchange*; ablegate, relegate, banish, exile; supersede 752 vb. *depose*; uproot 300 vb. *eject*; discharge, unload, off-load 300 vb. *void*; clear away 648 vb. *clean*; take away, cart off.

misplace, mislay, lose, lose touch with, lose track of.

189. Presence – N. *presence*, being there, existence; ubiquity, omnipresence; permeation, pervasion; availability, bird in the hand; attendance 89 n. *accompaniment*; residence, occupancy, occupation, lodgement 773 n. *possession*; visit, stay; man on the spot; witness, spectator, bystander 441 n. *onlookers*.

Adj. *on the spot*, present, existent; resident 192 adj. *residing*; attendant, waiting, ready, on tap, available, at hand, within reach, on call; under one's nose, before one's eyes 443 adj. *well-seen*.

ubiquitous, omnipresent, pervasive, diffused through.

Vb. *be present*, exist, be; occupy, hold 773 vb. *possess*; stand, lie 186 vb. *be situate*; look on, stand by, witness; sojourn 882 vb. *visit*; attend, assist at, grace the occasion; answer one's name; turn up, present oneself 295 vb. *arrive*; show one's face, put in an appearance; face, confront; present, introduce 522 vb. *show*.

pervade, permeate 54 vb. *fill*; impregnate, soak, run through; overrun, meet one at every turn 297 vb. *infiltrate*.

190. Absence: nullibiety – N. *absence*, disappearing trick 446 n. *disappearance*; nullibiety 2 n. *non-existence*; being elsewhere, alibi; non-residence, living away; non-attendance, truancy, absenteeism 620 n. *avoidance*; absentee, truant 620 n. *avoider*; deprivation 772 n. *loss*.

emptiness, bareness, void, vacuity, vacancy; hollowness, shell; vacuum, air-pocket; virgin territory, no-man's land; waste, desolation 172 n. *desert*.

nobody, no one, nobody on earth, not

a soul, not a living thing; empty house, no audience.

Adj. *absent*, not found, unrepresented; away, not resident; out, not at home; lacking, minus, to seek, wanting, lost, missing, wanted; truant, absentee 667 adj. *escaped*; unavailable, unprocurable 636 adj. *unprovided*; inexistent 2 adj. *non-existent*; on leave; left out 57 adj. *excluded*.

empty, vacant, vacuous, inane; void, devoid, bare; blank, clean; without content, hollow; vacant, unoccupied, uninhabited, tenantless; unstaffed, unmanned; unpeopled, depopulated; desert, godforsaken, lonely; unhabitable, uninhabitable.

Vb. *be absent*, take no part in, spare one's presence; stay away, play truant 620 vb. *avoid*; be missed, leave a gap; vacate 296 vb. *depart*.

Adv. *without*, minus, sans; in default of, for want of; in vacuo.

191. Inhabitant – N. *dweller*, inhabitant, habitant, denizen, indweller; sojourner, commorant, parasite; mainlander, Continental; insular, islander; isthmian; landsman, landlubber; mountaineer, hillman, hill-billy, dalesman, highlander, lowlander, plainsman; backwoodsman; frontiersman, borderer, marcher; city-dweller, town-d., suburbanite; countryman, rustic, villager; peasant 370 n. *husbandman*; steppe-dweller, tent-d., bedouin; cave-dweller, troglodyte. See *native*.

resident, householder, goodman; housewife, chatelaine, housekeeper; cottager; addressee, occupier, occupant, incumbent, residentiary 776 n. *possession*; tenant, inmate, inpatient; indoor servant 742 n. *domestic*; houseman 658 n. *doctor*; garrison, crew 686 n. *personnel*; lodger, boarder, roomer, paying guest, p.g.; guest, visitor, someone to stay; squatter 59 n. *intruder*.

native, aboriginal, aborigines, autochthones, first-comers 66 n. *precursor*; tribe 371 n. *nation*; local, local inhabitant, tribal; parishioner, townsman, townee, city man, cit, oppidan, cockney, suburbanite, yokel; compatriot, fellow-countryman, fellow-citizen; national, citizen, burgess, burgher, voter; earth-dweller, terrestrial, tellurian.

settler, pioneer; immigrant, colonist, colonial, creole; squatter 59 n. *intruder*; planter 370 n. *husbandman*; inquiline, metic, resident alien 59 n. *foreigner*; parasite.

habitancy, population, townspeople, country folk; populace, people, citizenry, tenantry, peasantry, yeomanry; villadom, suburbia; household, ménage 11 n. *family*; settlement, colony, plantation, community.

Adj. *native*, vernacular, popular, national, swadeshi; indigenous, autochthonous, aboriginal, enchorial, terrigenous; earthbound, terrestrial, tellurian; home, home-made; domestic, domiciliary, domesticated, naturalized.

192. Abode: place of habitation or resort – **N.** *abode*, abiding place, habitat, haunt; place, province, sphere; habitation, street, house, home; address, house-number; domicile, residence, residency; town, city, capital, metropolis; headquarters 187 n. *station*; hang-out, camp; holiday home, resort, watering place, hill-station; bivouac, encampment, castrametation.

quarters, accommodation, billet, berth; barrack, casemate, casern; bunkhouse, lodging, rooms, chambers, diggings, digs, chummery; guest house, boarding h., lodging h., pension, hostel, dormitory.

dwelling, roof over one's head; tower, keep; cave, hut, kraal, igloo; wigwam, tepee, wicky-up, tent; lair, den, hole; hive, burrow, warren, earth, set 662 n. *shelter*; menagerie 369 n. *zoo*.

nest, branch 366 n. *tree*; aerie, eyry, perch, roost; covert, gullery, rookery, swannery, hatchery, aviary, apiary, wasp's nest, ant-heap, ant-hill; chrysalis, cocoon 226 n. *wrapping*; cradle 68 n. *origin*.

home, hearth, fireside, rooftree, roof,

homestead; birthplace 68 n. *origin*; motherland, fatherland, homeland, one's country, God's own country, the Old Country; native heath, home ground, home town.

house, home, residence, dwelling-house; bungalow, ranchhouse, villa, chalet; seat, place, mansion, hall; château, castle, keep, tower; manor, grange, lodge, priory, abbey; retreat, cloister; palace, palatial residence; steading, farmstead.

small house, bijou residence, flatlet; snuggery, chalet, lodge, box, cottage, cot; cabin, hut, shebang, adobe; hovel, shed, shanty, shack, lean-to, penthouse, outhouse; shelter, tent, booth, bothy, stall, sheiling; houseboat, budgerow 275 n. *boat*; caravan, trailer, house-t. See *flat*.

housing, bricks and mortar, built-up area; housing estate, hutments; urbanization, conurbation; city, town, borough, suburb, satellite town, dormitory; crescent, terrace, circus, square; block, court, row, mansions, villas, buildings; houses, tenements; slum, condemned building; hamlet, village, villadom, suburbia.

street, avenue 624 n. *road*; lane, alley, wynd, by-street, back street, side s., passage, arcade 624 n. *path*; mall, grove, walk, parade, esplanade, promenade, boulevard.

flat, penthouse; apartment, suite, chambers 194 n. *chamber*; maisonette, duplex, walkup; apartment house, block of flats, mews, tenements, rents.

stable, byre, cowshed, cowhouse, kennel, doghouse, sty, pigpen, fold, dovecote 235 n. *enclosure*; stall, cage, coop, hencoop, hutch; stabling, mews, coachhouse, garage, hangar; boathouse; marina, dock; wharf, roads, roadstead, port, interport 662 n. *shelter*; berth, lay-by, quay, jetty, pier.

inn, hotel, hostelry, hospice, motel; doss-house, bunk-h., kip, flophouse; caravanserai, khan; rest-house, rest-room, waiting-room.

tavern, alehouse, pothouse; public

house, pub, local, roadhouse; gin palace, grog-shop, dram-s., toddy-s.; speakeasy, dive, honky-tonk, shebeen; beer hall, brauhaus; bar, saloon, tap-room.

café, restaurant, cafeteria, automat; eating-house, chop-house; beanery, diner, dinette, luncheonette; brasserie, bistro; grill-room, rôtisserie; coffee house, milk-bar, soda-fountain; lunch-counter, snack-bar; teahouse, teashop, tea-room, refreshment r.; buffet, canteen, Naafi; coffee stall; pull-up, carman's rest.

Adj. *residing*, at home, in residence; residential, fit for habitation; parasitical.

urban, towny, oppidan, metropolitan, cosmopolitan, suburban; built-up, citified, urbanized, suburbanized.

provincial, parochial, regional, local, domestic; up-country, countrified, rural, rustic.

architectural, architectonic, edificial; Gothic, classical; cottage-style, bungalow type; palatial, grand; detached, semi-d.; double-fronted.

Vb. *dwell*, inhabit, populate, people 187 vb. *place oneself*; settle, colonize 786 vb. *appropriate*; frequent, haunt 882 vb. *visit*; reside, remain, abide, sojourn, live; move in, put up at, stay, keep, lodge, lie, sleep at; have an address, hang out; tenant, occupy, squat 773 vb. *possess*; bunk, room, chum with, p.g.; stable, nestle, perch, roost, nest, hive, burrow; camp, encamp, bivouac, pitch, pitch one's tent, make one's quarters; tent, tabernacle, shelter; berth, dock, anchor.

urbanize, citify, suburbanize, conurbate, town-plan, develop, build up.

193. Contents: things contained – N.
contents, ingredients, items, components, constituents, parts 58 n. *component*; inventory 87 n. *list*; furnishings, equipment 633 n. *provision*; load, payload, cargo, lading, freight, shipment, cartload, busload, shipload 272 n. *thing transferred*; stuffing, filling 227 n. *lining*.

Vb. *load*, lade, freight, charge, burden; take in, take on board, ship; stow, pack,

fit in, tuck in 303 vb. *insert*; squeeze in, cram, stuff 54 vb. *fill*; pad, wad 227 vb. *line*; hide, conceal 78 vb. *comprise*.

194. Receptacle – N. *receptacle*, container; tray, recipient, holder; frame 218 n. *supporter*; cage 748 n. *prison*; folder, wrapper, envelope, cover, file 235 n. *enclosure*; net, 222 n. *network*; sheath, chrysalis, cocoon 226 n. *wrapping*; capsule, ampoule; socket; slot 262 n. *furrow*; hole, cave, cavity 263 n. *opening*; bosom, lap 261 n. *fold*; catch-all, trap; well, reservoir, hold 632 n. *store*; drain 649 n. *sink*.

bladder, air-bladder, water-wings; balloon, gas-bag; sac, cyst, vesicle, utricle, bubble 253 n. *swelling*; udder 253 n. *bosom*.

maw, stomach, tummy, breadbasket, little Mary; abdomen, belly, paunch, venter 224 n. *insides*; gizzard, gullet, weasand, crop, craw, jaws, mouth, oesophagus 263 n. *orifice*.

compartment, cell, cellule, follicle; tray; cage, cubicle (see *chamber*); sentry-box; box 594 n. *theatre*; pew, stall 990 n. *church interior*; niche, nook, cranny, recess, bay; pigeon-hole, cubby-h., drawer; storey, floor 207 n. *layer*.

cabinet, closet, commode, wardrobe, press, chest of drawers, tallboy, highboy; cupboard, dresser; buffet, sideboard 218 n. *stand*; chiffonier, cellaret, dumb-waiter; secrétaire, davenport, bureau, desk; bookcase.

basket, cran, creel; hamper; bread-basket, canister; pannier, dosser, dorser; trug, maund, punnet, frail; crib, cradle, bassinet, whisket; clothes basket, buck-basket; wickerwork, basket-work.

box, chest, ark; coffer, locker; case, canteen; safe 799 n. *treasury*; boot, imperial; coffin, cist 364 n. *tomb*; tuck-box; attaché case, dispatch c., dispatch box; suitcase, trunk, valise, portmanteau, uniform case; sea-chest, ditty-box; band-box, hat-b.; canister, caisson 723 n. *ammunition*; luggage; brake-van, luggage v.

small box, pill b., snuff b., match-b.,

carton, packet; metal box, can, tin; caddy, tea-caddy, canister; casket, pyx, reliquary; pepper-box, caster; nest of boxes.

bag, sack; handbag, vanity bag, reticule, tidy; cornet, twist; Gladstone bag, carpet b., travelling-b., last-minute b.; sleeping-bag, flea-b.; bedding-roll; holdall, grip-sack, grip, haversack, knapsack, rucksack, kitbag, ditty-bag, saddlebag, nosebag; satchel, budget, scrip, bundle, swag.

case, étui, housewife, wallet, scripcase; billfold, note-case, card case, compact, vasculum; brief-case, portfolio; scabbard, sheath; holster; quiver 632 n. *store*.

pocket, side-p., hip-p., trouser-p., breastpocket; fob, placket; purse, pouch, poke, money-bag; sleeve.

vat, dye-v., butt, cask, barrel, tun, tub, keg, breaker; wine-cask, puncheon, pipe 465 n. *metrology*; hopper, cistern, tank 632 n. *store*.

vessel, vase, urn, jar, amphora, ampulla, cruse, crock, pot; pipkin, gugglet, pitcher, ewer, jug, toby-jug; gourd, calabash; carafe, decanter, bottle, water-b.; blackjack, wineskin; demijohn, magnum, jeroboam; flask, flagon, vial, phial; cruet; gallipot, crucible, retort, receiver, alembic 461 n. *testing agent*; cupping-glass; chamber-pot, potty, jerry, bed-pan, commode, thunder-box 302 n. *excretion*; trough, trug; pail, bucket, piggin, skeel; can, watering c.; bin, dust-b., garbage can, trash c., gubbins 649 n. *sink*; scuttle, coal-s., perdonium.

cauldron 383 n. *heater*; boiler, copper, kettle, skillet, dixie, pan, casserole, messtin; teapot, samovar, coffee-pot, percolator, biggin; censer, cassolette; hot-water bottle, warming pan.

cup, tea-service, tea-set; chalice, goblet, beaker; drinking-cup, loving c.; quaich; horn, drinking-h., tankard, stoup, can, cannikin, mug, stein, toby, noggin, rummer; tumbler, glass, wine-glass; cupel.

bowl, basin, hand-b., wash-b., laver; slop-bowl; mixing-bowl, crater, punch-bowl, drinking-b., jorum; soup-plate, porringer; manger, trough; colander, vegetable dish, tureen, sauce-boat; spittoon, cuspidor.

plate, salver, tray, paten, platter, trencher, charger, dish; saucer; palette; mortar-board, hod.

ladle, dipper, baler, scoop, cupped hands; spoon, spade, trowel 274 n. *shovel*.

chamber, room, apartment 192 n. *flat*; cockpit, cubicle, cab; cabin, stateroom; roundhouse, cuddy; cabinet, closet, study, den, sanctum, adytum; studio, atelier, workroom, office 687 n. *workshop*; playroom, nursery, schoolroom; drawing room, sitting r., reception r.; living room, lounge, parlour, saloon, boudoir; bedroom, dormitory; dressing room; bathroom, bath-house; dining room, messroom, mess, hall, refectory, canteen 192 n. *café*; gunroom, wardroom, smoking room; bar, tap-room; cook-house, galley, kitchen; scullery, pantry, larder, still-room; dairy, laundry, offices, outhouse; store-room, lumber r., glory hole 632 n. *storage*; retiring room, cloakroom 649 n. *latrine*. See *compartment*.

lobby, vestibule, foyer, anteroom, waiting-room 263 n. *doorway*; corridor, passage; verandah, piazza, loggia, balcony, portico, porch, stoa.

cellar, cellarage, vault, crypt, basement 214 n. *base*; coal-hole, bunker 632 n. *storage*; dust-hole, dust-bin 649 n. *sink*; hold, dungeon 748 n. *prison*.

attic, loft, hayloft, cockloft; penthouse, garret, top storey 213 n. *summit*.

arbour, alcove, bower, grotto, grot, summer-house, gazebo, pergola, pavilion; conservatory, greenhouse, glass-house 370 n. *garden*.

Adj. *cellular*, multicellular, camerated, compartmentalized; locular, multilocular, marsupial, polygastric, ventricular; abdominal, gastral, ventral 253 adj. *convex*.

capsular, saccular, sacculated, cystic; vascular, vesicular.

Section 2: Dimensions

195. Size – N. *size*, magnitude, order of m.; proportions, dimensions, measurements, measure; area 183 n. *space*; extension 203 n. *length*, 209 n. *height*, 211 n. *depth*; width 205 n. *breadth*; volume, cubature; girth, circumference 233 n. *outline*; bulk, mass, weight 322 n. *gravity*; capacity, intake, tonnage; calibre 465 n. *measurement*; full size, life size; magnum; excessive size, hypertrophy.

hugeness, bigness, grandiosity 32 n. *greatness*; enormity, enormousness, immensity, vastness, giantship; gigantism 209 n. *height*.

bulk, mass, weight 322 n. *gravity*; lump, block 324 n. *solid body*; massiveness, bulkiness; girthrate, obesity, corpulence, fatness, plumpness, fleshiness; corporation, gorbelly 253 n. *swelling*.

giant, colossus, mountain of a man; ogre, monster; leviathan, behemoth, whale; elephant; mammoth; giantry, Gargantua, Goliath.

whopper, spanker, thumper, strapper; a mountain of a —

Adj. *large*, big 32 adj. *great*; large size, king s., jumbo; bulky, massive, massy 322 adj. *weighty*; ample 205 adj. *broad*, 183 adj. *spacious*; monumental 209 adj. *tall*; whacking 32 adj. *whopping*; man-size, life-s., large as life; well-grown, large-limbed, elephantine; macroscopic, large-scale, megalithic.

huge, immense, enormous, vast, mighty, grandiose, monstrous 32 adj. *prodigious*; colossal, gigantic, mountainous; Brobdingnagian, Titanic, Herculean, Gargantuan; Cyclopean, megalithic; outsize, oversize; limitless 107 adj. *infinite*.

fleshy, meaty, fat, stout, obese, heavy, overweight; plump, chubby, podgy; dumpy, chunky; tubby, portly, corpulent, paunchy, pot-bellied, gorbellied; pursy, bloated, bosomy 197 adj. *expanded*; full, double-chinned, dimpled, dimply; hulking, strapping, beefy, brawny 162 adj. *stalwart*.

196. Littleness – N. *littleness* etc. adj.; lack of height 204 n. *shortness*; diminutiveness, dwarfishness, stuntedness 33 n. *smallness*; exiguity 105 n. *fewness*; meagreness 206 n. *thinness*; —kin, —let.

minuteness, point, vanishing p.; pinpoint, pinhead; crystal; atom; drop, droplet, dust, grain 33 n. *small thing*.

miniature 553 n. *picture*; microphotograph, reduction 551 n. *photography*; thumbnail sketch, epitome 592 n. *compendium*; model, microcosm.

dwarf, midget, pigmy, elf, atomy, Lilliputian; chit, urchin, cock-sparrow, pipsqueak; mannikin, doll, puppet; Tom Thumb, Hop-o'-my-thumb, homunculus; shrimp, runt, miserable specimen.

animalcule, micro-organism, microzoon; amoeba, protozoon, bacillus, bacteria, microbe, germ, virus; mite, tick, nit, maggot, grub, worm; insect, ant; midge, gnat, fly, tit; fingerling, small fry, shrimp, sprat; mouse; whippet, bantam, runt.

micrology, microscopy, micrography, microphotography; microscope, microspectroscope, micrometer, Vernier scale.

Adj. *little*, exiguous 33 adj. *small*; petite, dainty, dinky, dolly, elfin; diminutive, pigmy, Lilliputian; wee, titchy, tiny, teeny; toy, baby, pocket, pocket-size, pint-size, duodecimo; miniature, model; runty, puny 163 adj. *weak*; petty 33 adj. *inconsiderable*; meagre, slight, scraggy 206 adj. *lean*.

dwarfish, dwarf, pigmy, undersized, stunted, wizened, shrunk 198 adj. *contracted*; squat, dumpy 204 adj. *short*; knee-high, knee-high to a grasshopper.

minute, minimal; micro-, microscopic, ultramicroscopic, infinitesimal; atomic, molecular; miniature; imperceptible, intangible 444 adj. *invisible*.

197. Expansion – N. *expansion*, increase of size, enlargement, augmentation, aggrandizement 36 n. *increase*; amplification, supplementation, reinforcement 38 n. *addition*; dilatation, distension, diastole; inflation, reflation 352 n. *sufflation*; turgescence, tumescence 253 n.

swelling; hyperbole 546 n. *exaggeration*; stretching, pandiculation; upgrowth, development; overstaffing, Parkinson's law 637 n. *superfluity*; extensibility 328 n. *elasticity*.

Adj. *expanded* etc. vb.; expanding 36 adj. *increasing*; expansive 183 adj. *spacious*; spread, fan-shaped, flabelliform 205 adj. *broad*; tumescent, budding, bursting, flowering, out 134 adj. *adult*; full-blown 669 adj. *matured*; bloated, fat 195 adj. *fleshy*; padded out; distended, stretched, tight; swollen, bulbous 253 adj. *convex*; puffy, pouchy.

Vb. *expand*, greaten 36 vb. *grow*; broaden 205 vb. *be broad*; spread, fan out, deploy, extend, take open order 75 vb. *be dispersed*; spread over, overrun, mantle 226 vb. *cover*; rise, prove (e.g. dough); gather, swell, distend, dilate, fill out; balloon, belly 253 vb. *be convex*; get fat, gain flesh, put on weight; germinate, bud, burgeon, shoot, sprout, open, blossom, flower, floresce, blow, bloom, be out 171 vb. *be fruitful*; stretch oneself, pandiculate.

enlarge, greaten, aggrandize; make larger, expand; leaven 310 vb. *elevate*; bore, ream; widen, broaden, let out; stretch, extend 203 vb. *lengthen*; intensify, heighten, deepen; amplify 38 vb. *add*; develop, build up 36 vb. *augment* ; distend, inflate, reflate, pump up, blow up 352 vb. *sufflate*; stuff, pad 227 vb. *line*; cram 54 vb. *fill*; feed up, fatten, plump up, bloat 301 vb. *feed*; enlarge, blow up 551 vb. *photograph*; magnify, over-enlarge, over-develop 546 vb. *exaggerate*.

198. Contraction – N. *contraction*, reduction, deflation 37 n. *diminution*; shrinkage 42 n. *decrement*; curtailment 204 n. *shortening*; condensation, freezing; attenuation, emaciation, consumption, marasmus, withering, atrophy; bottleneck 206 n. *narrowness*; epitome 592 n. *compendium*.

compression, coarctation, pressure, squeeze, stenosis, strangulation, constriction; compressibility.

compressor, squeezer, mangle, roller 258 n. *smoother*; constrictor, astringent; bandage, binder, tourniquet 658 n. *surgical dressing*; belt 47 n. *girdle*; corset 228 n. *underwear*; straitjacket, iron boot 964 n. *instrument of torture*; bear, python, boa-constrictor.

Adj. *contracted*, shrunk, shrunken, smaller 33 adj. *small*; constricted, strangled; unexpanded, deflated; condensed 324 adj. *dense*; compact, compressed; pinched 206 adj. *narrow*; compressible, contractile; wasting, consumptive 655 adj. *deteriorated*.

compressive, contractional, astringent, binding, constipating.

Vb. *become small*, lessen, fall away 37 vb. *decrease*; wither, waste 51 vb. *decompose*; contract, shrink, narrow, taper, draw in 293 vb. *converge*; condense 324 vb. *be dense*.

make smaller, lessen, reduce 37 vb. *bate*; contract, shrink, abridge, take in; dwarf 204 vb. *shorten*; bant, diet, slim 323 vb. *lighten*; taper, narrow, attenuate 206 vb. *make thin*; deflate 325 vb. *rarefy*; drain 300 vb. *void*; boil down 338 vb. *vaporize*; constrict, pinch, nip, squeeze, bind, bandage, garter, corset; draw in, draw tight, strain, tauten; compress, wring, hug, crush, strangle, strangulate; condense, nucleate 324 vb. *be dense*; huddle, crowd; squeeze in, pack tight 193 vb. *load*; whittle, shear, clip 46 vb. *cut*; pucker, purse 261 vb. *fold*.

199. Distance – N. *distance*, astronomical d., depths of space 183 n. *space*; mileage, footage 203 n. *length*; longinquity, elongation, aphelion, apogee; far distance, horizon, skyline; background 238 n. *rear*; periphery, circumference 233 n. *outline*; reach, grasp 183 n. *range*; far cry, long run, marathon.

farness, far distance, remoteness, aloofness; antipodes, pole 240 n. *contraposition*; world's end, back of beyond; outpost 883 n. *seclusion*; outskirts 223 n. *exteriority*; frontier 236 n. *limit*.

Adj. *distant*, far, farther, distal, peripheral, terminal, ultimate, furthermost; long-distance, long-range; offshore; remote, aloof; hyperborean, antipodean, out of range, telescopic; out of sight 444 adj. *invisible.*

removed, inaccessible, unapproachable; overseas, transmarine, transpontine, transoceanic, transatlantic.

Adv. *afar,* away, not locally; far afield, far off, way o., at a distance, a far cry to; at the limit of vision, out of sight; to the ends of the earth, to the back of beyond; far and wide.

beyond, farther on, ahead, in front; clear of, wide of; below the horizon, hull down; up over, down under.

too far, out of reach, out of range, out of sight, out of hearing, out of earshot, out of bounds.

200. Nearness – N. *nearness,* proximity, propinquity, closeness, near distance, foreground 237 n. *front;* vicinage, neighbourhood 230 n. *circumjacence;* brink, verge 234 n. *edge;* adjacency 202 n. *contiguity;* approximation 289 n. *approach.*

short distance, bee-line, short cut, step, no distance, walking d.; striking distance, close quarters; close range, earshot, stone's throw, spitting distance; short span, hair's breadth 201 n. *gap;* close-up, near approach; perigee, perihelion.

near place, vicinage, neighbourhood, purlieus, environs, suburbs, confines; approaches, borderlands; ringside seat, next door 202 n. *contiguity;* second place, proxime accessit 65 n. *sequence.*

Adj. *near,* proximate, approximate; getting warm 289 adj. *approaching;* near-by, wayside, roadside 289 adj. *accessible;* hard by, inshore; at hand 189 adj. *on the spot;* home, local; neighbouring, adjacent, adjoining 202 adj. *contiguous;* inseparable 45 adj. *conjunct;* close-run, neck-and-neck 716 adj. *contending.*

Vb. *be near,* be around, be about 189 vb. *be present;* approximate, draw near, get warm 289 vb. *approach;* meet 293 vb. *converge;* neighbour, abut, adjoin,

border, verge upon 202 vb. *be contiguous;* trench upon 306 vb. *encroach;* hug, skirt, graze, shave, brush, skim, hedge-hop, hover over; jostle, buzz, get in the way 702 vb. *obstruct;* sit on one's tail 284 vb. *follow;* huddle, crowd, close up 202 vb. *juxtapose.*

Adv. *nigh,* locally; near, hard by, fast by, close to; at close range, at close quarters; within call, within hearing; at one's door, at one's elbow, under one's nose; face to face; next door, side by side, cheek by jowl, beside, alongside.

nearly, practically, almost, all but; more or less, near enough, roughly, around, in the region of; nearabout, circa; closely, approximately; wellnigh, as good as, within an ace of.

201. Interval – N. *interval,* distance between, space; hair space 200 n. *short distance;* interspace, daylight, head, length; clearance, margin, freeboard 183 n. *room;* interregnum; time-interval 145 n. *lull;* interruption, hiatus, jump, leap.

gap, interstice 222 n. *network;* hole 263 n. *orifice;* pass, defile 305 n. *passage;* ditch, trench 351 n. *drain;* ravine, intervale 255 n. *valley;* cleft, crevice, chink, crack, rift, rime, scissure, cut, gash, tear, rent, slit; fault, breach, break, split, fracture, rupture, fissure 46 n. *separation;* slot 262 n. *furrow;* indentation 260 n. *notch;* inlet 345 n. *gulf.*

Adj. *spaced,* spaced out, leaded; gappy, fatiscent, split, cloven, cleft 46 adj. *disjunct;* dehiscent, gaping 263 adj. *open;* far between; interstitial, reticulated.

Vb. *space,* stagger, space out, lead (typography); seam, crack, split, start, gape 263 vb. *open;* clear, show daylight between; lattice, mesh, reticulate.

202. Contiguity – N. *contiguity,* juxtaposition, apposition, proximity 200 n. *nearness;* no interval 71 n. *continuity;* contact, tangency; abutment; intercommunication; conjunction (astron.) 45 n. *junction;* cohesion 48 n. *coherence;* tangent; border, borderland, frontier 236 n. *limit.*

Adj. *contiguous*, touching, in contact; intercommunicating; tangential, abutting, end to end, conterminous 71 adj. *continuous*.

Vb. *be contiguous*, overlap 378 vb. *touch*; make contact, brush, rub, skim scrape, graze, kiss; meet 293 vb. *converge*; abut, adjoin, reach to 183 vb. *extend*; rub shoulders, crowd, jostle 200 vb. *be near*; skirt 234 vb. *hem*; osculate, intercommunicate 45 vb. *connect*.

juxtapose, set side by side, range together, bring into contact, knock persons' heads together.

Adv. *contiguously*, tangentially; end to end; cheek by jowl; hand in hand, arm in arm.

203. Length. Longimetry – N. *length*,

longitude; extent, extension; reach, long arm; full length, over-all l.; stretch, span, mileage, footage 199 n. *distance*; perspective 211 n. *depth*.

lengthening etc. vb.; prolongation, extension 113 n. *protraction*; stretching, tension.

line, bar, rule, strip, stripe, streak; single file, line ahead 65 n. *sequence*; cord, thread 208 n. *fibre*.

long measure, linear m., longimetry, micrometry 465 n. *measurement*; finger, hand, palm, span, cubit; fathom; head, length; pace, step; ell; rod, pole, perch; chain, furlong, stade; mile, statute m. sea m., nautical m., knot, league; kos, verst, parasang; degree of latitude *or* longitude; micron, wavelength; astronomical unit, light-year, parsec.

Adj. *long*, lengthy, extensive, longsome; long-drawn, protracted; elongated, outstretched, extended, strung out; wire-drawn, lank 206 adj. *lean*; lanky 209 adj. *tall*; interminable, no end to 838 adj. *tedious*; sesquipedalian 570 adj. *prolix*; unabridged, full-length 54 adj. *complete*.

longitudinal, oblong, lineal, linear; one-dimensional.

Vb. *be long*, —lengthy etc. adj.; outstretch, stretch out; make a long arm; reach 183 vb. *extend*; drag, trail.

lengthen, stretch, elongate, draw out, wiredraw 206 vb. *make thin*; spreadeagle; stretch oneself, pandiculate 197 vb. *expand*; string out, deploy 75 vb. *disperse*; extend, pay out, uncoil, unfurl, unroll, unfold 316 vb. *evolve*; let out, drop the hem; produce, continue, prolong, protract; drawl 580 vb. *stammer*.

Adv. *longwise*, longways, lengthwise; along, endlong; longitudinally, radially, in line ahead, in single file; tandem; in perspective; end to end, overall; fore and aft, head to tail, stem to stern.

204. Shortness – N. *shortness* etc. adj.;

brevity; transience 114 n. *brief span*; low stature, dwarfishness, duck's disease 196 n. *littleness*; no height 210 n. *lowness*; concision 569 n. *conciseness*.

shortening, abridgement, abbreviation, curtailment, cut-back, reduction 37 n. *diminution*; contraction 198 n. *compression*; retrenchment 814 n. *economy*; ellision, ellipsis; abridger 592 n. *epitomizer*.

Adj. *short*, brief 114 adj. *transient*; not big, dwarfish 196 adj. *little*; squat, dumpy, stumpy, stocky, thick-set, stubby 195 adj. *fleshy*; flat 210 adj. *low*; skimpy, scanty, scrimpy, revealing (of dress) 636 adj. *insufficient*; foreshortened 246 adj. *distorted*; half-length, catalectic; cut, curtailed, docked, headless; shaven, shorn, mown; terse 569 adj. *concise*; elliptical (of style); potted, compact 592 adj. *compendious*.

Vb. *shorten*, abridge, abbreviate; pot, epitomize, boil down 592 vb. *abstract*; sum up 569 vb. *be concise*; compress, contract, telescope 198 vb. *make smaller*; reduce 37 vb. *bate*; foreshorten 246 vb. *distort*; take in, raise the hem, tuck up, kilt; behead 46 vb. *cut*; cut short, dock, curtail, truncate; cut back, cut down, lop, poll, pollard, prune; shear, shave, trim, clip, bob, shingle; whittle, pare, taper; mow, crop; nip, snub; stunt; scrimp, skimp, scant 636 vb. *make insufficient*; retrench 814 vb. *economize*.

205. Breadth. Thickness – N. *breadth*,

width, latitude; diameter, radius, semi-diameter; gauge, bore, calibre; broadness, expanse 183 n. *range*; fullness, bagginess.

thickness, crassitude, stoutness, corpulence 195 n. *size*.

Adj. *broad*, wide, expansive, ample 183 adj. *spacious*; wide-cut, full, baggy; outspread, outstretched; broad-based; callipygic, wide-hipped; broad in the beam, beamy; non-specific 79 adj. *general*.

thick, stout, dumpy, squat, squab, thickset, tubby, stubby 195 adj. *fleshy*; solid 324 adj. *dense*; semi-liquid, ropy, to be cut with a knife 354 adj. *viscid*.

Vb. *be broad*, — thick etc. adj.; get broad, broaden, widen, fatten, thicken; straddle, bestride, span 226 vb. *overlie*.

206. Narrowness. Thinness – N. *narrowness* etc. adj.; tight squeeze, hair's breadth 200 n. *short distance*; length without breadth 203 n. *line*; knife-edge, razor's edge; eye of a needle, bottleneck; narrows, strait 345 n. *gulf*; gully 255 n. *valley*; neck, isthmus 624 n. *bridge*.

thinness etc. adj.; lack of thickness, tenuity, emaciation, consumption; scrag, skin and bone, skeleton, anatomy; scarecrow, rake, shadow, wraith; haggardness; paper, tissue 422 n. *transparency*; shaving, slip.

narrowing, angustation, coarctation, compression 198 n. *contraction*; taper 293 n. *convergence*; constriction, waistline; waist, wasp-w., hour-glass.

Adj. *narrow*, narrow-gauge; strait, tight, close; pinched 198 adj. *contracted*; fine, thin 422 adj. *transparent*; tight-drawn, wire-d., spun, fine-s. 203 adj. *long*; thread-like 208 adj. *fibrous*; tapering 293 adj. *convergent*; slender, slim, svelte, slinky, sylph-like; willowy, arrowy, rangy, lanky.

lean, thin, spare, meagre, skinny, bony; cadaverous, fleshless, skin-and-bone, skeletal, bare-boned, raw-b.; haggard, gaunt; spindly, spindle-shanked, spidery; undersized, weedy, scrawny, scrub, scraggy, rickety; consumptive, emaciated, wasted, withered, wizened, pinched,

peaky 651 adj. *sick*; sere, shrivelled 131 adj. *aged*; starved, starveling 636 adj. *underfed*; miserable, herring-gutted; jejune.

Vb. *be narrow*, —thin etc. adj.; straiten, narrow, taper 293 vb. *converge*.

make thin, compress 198 vb. *make smaller*; starve, underfeed, bant, reduce, take off weight; slenderize, slim; wiredraw 203 vb. *lengthen*; attenuate 325 vb. *rarefy*.

207. Layer – N. *layer*, stratum, substratum, underlayer, floor 214 n. *base*; bed, course, range, row; zone, vein, seam, lode; thickness, ply; storey, tier, floor, landing; deck, top-d., bridge; film 423 n. *opacity*; bloom, dross, scum; patina, coating, coat, top-layer 226 n. *covering*; scale, scab, membrane, peel, pellicle, sheath, bark, integument 226 n. *skin*; level, table, water-t.

lamina, sheet, plate, slab, foil, strip, latten; plank, board, clapboard; slat, lath, leaf, table; tablet, plaque, panel; slab, flag, flagstone, slate, shale; shingle, tile; brick, domino; slide; wafer, shaving, flake, slice; page, folio; card; disk.

stratification, stratigraphy; layering, lamination; laminability, flakiness, schistosity, scaliness, squamation; overlapping, overlap; nest of boxes, Chinese b., sandwich.

Adj. *layered*, lamellar, lamelliform, laminiferous; laminal, laminable, flaky; schistous, slaty, shaly; foliate, membranous; bedded, stratified, stratiform; overlapping, clinker-built; tabular, decked, storied; scaly.

Vb. *laminate*, lay, deck, layer, shingle, overlap 226 vb. *overlay*; zone, stratify, sandwich; plate, veneer, 226 vb. *coat*; delaminate, flake off; shave, slice.

208. Filament – N. *filament*, capillament, cilium, lash, eyelash, down 259 n. *hair*; flock, lock, wisp, curl; list, thrum 234 n. *edging*; fibril, funicle, barb, tendril 778 n. *nippers*; whisker, antenna 378 n. *feeler*; gossamer, cobweb 222 n. *network*;

capillary 351 n. *conduit*; wire, element, wick 420 n. *torch.*

fibre, hair, camel-h., rabbit-h.; Angora, mohair, cashmere; alpaca, vicuna; wool, merino; mungo, shoddy; silk, tussore; cotton, cotton wool, silk-cotton; linen, flax; hemp, cannabis; jute, sisal, coir, kapok; harl, hards; tow, oakum; bast, raffia; worsted, sewing-silk; yarn, staple; thread, pack t.; twine, twist, strand, cord, whipcord, string, line, rope, ropework 47 n. *cable*; rayon, nylon 222 n. *textile.*

strip, fascia, band, bandage, linen; tape, strap, ribbon, fillet 47 n. *girdle*; lath, slat, batten, spline 207 n. *lamina*; shaving, wafer; splinter, shiver 53 n. *piece*; streak, strake.

Adj. *fibrous*, fibrillous; woolly, cottony, silky; filamentous, filiform; whiskery, downy, fleecy 259 adj. *hairy*; wiry, threadlike, funicular; capillary, capilliform; fine-spun, wire-drawn 206 adj. *narrow*; stringy, ropy 205 adj. *thick*; anguilliform 251 adj. *convoluted*; flagelliform, lashlike; antennary, antennal.

209. Height – N. *height*, perpendicular length, vertical range, altitude, elevation; ceiling, pitch 213 n. *summit*; loftiness, steepness; tallness, stature; eminence, sublimity.

high land, surface relief, height, highlands, heights, uplands, wold, moor, downs, rolling country; rise, bank, brae, slope, climb; knap, hill, eminence, mount, mountain; fell, scar, tor; mountain range, sierra, massif; ridge, hog's back, col, saddle; hilltop 213 n. *summit*; precipice, cliff; crag, bluff, steep, escarpment; chine 255 n. *valley*; mesa, plateau, tableland.

monticle, knoll, hillock, hummock, hump, dune; barrow 364 n. *tomb*; mound, heap; tell 548 n. *monument*; molehill, tussock, pimple.

high structure, column, pillar, turret, tower; dome, pile, skyscraper; steeple, spire, belfry, campanile; minaret, muezzin's tower; colossus; pyramid, pagoda, ziggurat, Tower of Babel; pole, maypole; lamp-post; pylon, radio-mast; masthead, truck 213 n. *summit*; watchtower, crow's nest, eyrie 438 n. *view.*

altimetry, altimeter, height-finder, hypsometer, barograph.

Adj. *high*, high-up, sky-high, overhead; eminent, exalted, lofty, sublime, supernal 310 adj. *elevated*; aloft, aerial, air-borne; soaring 308 adj. *ascending*; towering, steep, dizzy, vertiginous; knee-high, shoulder-h.; altitudinal, altimetric.

tall, lanky, rangy, long-legged, long-necked, giraffelike; statuesque, colossal, gigantic, monumental 195 adj. *huge.*

alpine, alpestrine, Andean, Himalayan; mountainous, hilly; rolling; monticolous, hill-dwelling; orogenical.

Vb. *be high*, — tall etc. adj.; tower, soar; surmount, clear, overtop, overlook, dominate, command; overhang, overshadow 226 vb. *cover*; beetle, impend 254 vb. *jut*; hover, hang over 217 vb. *hang*; culminate, north 725 vb. *climax*; upgrow; rise 308 vb. *ascend*; heighten 310 vb. *elevate.*

Adv. *aloft*, up, on high, high up, in the clouds; atop, on top, on the crest; above, overhead; upwards, skyward, heavenward; on stilts.

210. Lowness – N. *lowness*, debasement 311 n. *depression*; prostration, recumbency; sea-level, flatness 216 n. *horizontality*; level, Flatland, steppe 348 n. *plain*; lowlands 209 n. *monticle*; subjacency, lower level, foothill; bottom, hollow, depression 255 n. *valley*; sea-floor, benthos 343 n. *ocean*; subterraneity, depths 211 n. *depth*; floor, foot 214 n. *base*; underside, undersurface, underbelly; nadir; low water 350 n. *current.*

Adj. *low*, squat 204 adj. *short*; unerect, crouched, stooping; laid low 216 adj. *supine*; low-lying, flat 216 adj. *horizontal*; underfoot, lower, under, nether 35 adj. *inferior*; lowered 311 adj. *depressed*; subterranean, underground, submarine 523 adj. *latent*, 211 adj. *deep.*

Vb. *be low*, — flat etc. adj.; lie low, lie flat 216 vb. *be horizontal*; crouch 311 vb.

stoop; grovel 721 vb. *knuckle under*;
lower, debase, depress.

Adv. *under*, beneath, underneath; below, at the foot of; downwards, down,
face-down; underfoot, underground,
downstairs.

211. Depth – N. *depth*, perspective 203
n. *length*; vertical range, profundity,
lowest depth, nadir; deeps 343 n. *ocean*;
depression, bottom 255 n. *valley, cavity*;
abyss, abysm, chasm 345 n. *gulf*; cellarage 194 n. *cellar*; bowels of the earth;
underworld, bottomless pit 972 n. *hell*;
soundings, sounding line, plummet, lead,
313 n. *diver*; draught, displacement,
sinkage; bathymeter, bathymetry.

Adj. *deep*, steep, plunging, profound;
abysmal, yawning, cavernous; abyssal,
deep-sea; deep-seated, deep-rooted 153
adj. *fixed*; unplumbed, bottomless,
reachless, fathomless, unsoundable, unfathomable; subterranean, underground,
hypogeal; under-water, undersea, sub-
aqueous, submarine; buried, deep in,
immersed, submerged; sunk, foundered,
drowned; deepish, navigable; knee-deep,
ankle-d.; infernal, deep as hell; depth-
haunting, bathyphilous; bathymetric.

Vb. *be deep*, deepen; hollow 255 vb.
make concave; plumb, go deep, plumb
the depth, touch bottom, reach one's
nadir 210 vb. *be low*; sink, plunge 313 vb.
founder; gape, yawn.

Adv. *deeply*, deep down, out of one's
depth, deep in, over one's head, up to
the eyes.

212. Shallowness – N. *shallowness* etc.
adj.; no depth, superficiality; veneer,
thin coat 226 n. *skin*; surface injury,
scratch, pin-prick, graze 639 n. *trifle*;
soundings, shoals, shallows; puddle 346
n. *lake*; ripple, catspaw 350 n. *wave*; light
soil 344 n. *soil*.

Adj. *shallow*, slight, superficial 4 adj.
insubstantial; surface, skin-deep; ankle-
deep; shoaly, unnavigable; light, thin,
thinly spread.

213. Summit – N. *summit*, sky, heaven;
pole; top, peak, crest, apex, pinnacle,

crown; maximum height, pitch; zenith,
meridian, high noon; culmination,
acme, ne plus ultra 646 n. *perfection*;
climax, crest of the wave, top of the tree;
highwater mark 236 n. *limit*; coping,
capstone, keystone; lintel, pediment,
capital, entablature, architrave, epi-
style.

vertex, apex, crown, cap, brow, head;
tip, cusp, spike, nib, end 69 n. *extremity*;
spire, finial 990 n. *church exterior*;
stair-head, landing 308 n. *ascent*; summit level, hilltop, plateau, tableland 209
n. *highland*; tree-top, house-t., roof-t.;
ceiling 226 n. *roof*; garret 194 n. *attic*;
top storey; topside, upperdeck, quarter-
d., hurricane d., boat d., bridge 275 n.
ship; topmast, topgallant mast; masthead, crow's nest, truck; upper works,
top-hamper.

head, headpiece, pate, poll, sconce;
noddle, nob, nut, crumpet, bean; upper
storey, belfry; brow, dome, forehead;
loaf; brain, grey matter 498 n. *intelligence*; scalp, crown; skull, cranium,
brainpan; occiput, sinciput; fontanelle;
craniology, craniognomy, cranioscopy,
craniometry.

Adj. *topmost*, top, highest 209 adj.
high; uppermost, overmost 34 adj. *supreme*; polar, apical, crowning; capital,
head; cephalic, cranial, occipital, sinci-
pital; culminating, zenithal, meridian,
meridional; tip-top, super 644 adj. *topping*.

Vb. *crown*, cap, head, top, tip, surmount, crest, overtop 209 vb. *be high*;
culminate, consummate 725 vb. *climax*.

214. Base – N. *base*, foot, toe, skirt 210
n. *lowness*; bottom, fundament; lowest
point, rock-bottom, nadir, low water;
footing, foundation 218 n. *basis*; root,
fundamental 68 n. *origin*; groundwork,
substructure; substratum, floor, underlayer, bed, bedrock; ground, earth,
foundations; baseline; base-level, basement, ground floor 194 n. *cellar*; flooring 226 n. *paving*; baseboard, wainscot,
plinth, dado; keel; hold, orlop, bilge;
sump 649 n. *sink*.

foot, feet, pedal extremities; forefoot, hindfoot; sole, pad; heel, instep, arch; toe, toe-nail, great toe, hallux; trotter, hoof; paw, pug; claw, talon 778 n. *nippers*; ankle, ankle-bone, fetlock, pastern.

Adj. *undermost*, lowermost, nethermost, bottom, rock-b. 210 adj. *low*; basic, basal, fundamental; grounded; underlying 218 adj. *supporting*.

footed, pedal; hoofed, ungulated; soled, heeled, shod, shoed; toed, five-t.

215. Verticality – N. *verticality*, the vertical, erectness, uprightness, upright carriage; steepness, sheerness, precipitousness 209 n. *height*; perpendicularity, plumbline, plummet; sheer face, precipice, steep 209 n. *high land*.

Adj. *vertical*, upright, erect, upstanding, standing; perpendicular; sheer, abrupt, steep, precipitous 209 adj. *high*; plumb, straight up *or* down; standing up, on one's feet, on one's legs; bolt upright, stiff as a ramrod, unbowed, head-up; rampant, rearing; on end.

Vb. *be vertical*, stick up, cock up, bristle, stand on end; hold oneself straight; rise, stand, ramp, rear.

make vertical, erect, rear, raise, pitch 310 vb. *elevate*; up-end, stand, set up, stick up.

Adv. *vertically* etc. adj.; palewise (heraldry); upright, on end; at right angles, perpendicularly.

216. Horizontality – N. *horizontality*, horizontal, azimuth; horizontal line, ruling, rule; flatness 258 n. *smoothness*; level, plane, dead level; stratum 207 n. *layer*; steppe 348 n. *plain*; flats 347 n. *marsh*; platform, ledge 254 n. *projection*; plateau, tableland 209 n. *high land*; bowling green 728 n. *arena*; billiard table; pancake; spirit-level 465 n. *gauge*; flattener 258 n. *smoother*.

Adj. *flat*, horizontal, level, plane, even, flush; trodden, beaten; flat as a pancake; unwrinkled 258 adj. *smooth*.

supine, flat on one's back; prone, face down, prostrate; recumbent, procum-

bent, lying down, couchant; abed, laid out; sprawling, lolling.

Vb. *be horizontal*, lie, lie down, lie flat; recline, couch, sprawl, loll 311 vb. *sit down*; grovel 311 vb. *stoop*; straighten out, level o.

flatten, lay out, roll o., lay down, spread; lay flat, stamp down, trample d., squash; make flush, align, level, even, plane 28 vb. *equalize*; iron out 258 vb. *smooth*; smooth down, plaster d.; prostrate, knock down, floor, gravel, ground 311 vb. *fell*.

217. Pendency – N. *pendency*, pensility, dependence; suspension, dangle; set, hang.

pendant, dangler, eardrop, earring 844 n. *jewellery*; tassel, bobble, tag 844 n. *trimming*; hangings, draperies, drapes, curtains 226 n. *covering*; train, skirt, flap 228 n. *dress*; pendulum, bob, swing, hammock 317 n. *oscillation*; chandelier, 420 n. *lamp*; icicle, stalactite.

hanger, coat-h., curtain-rod, runner; hook, tenterhook, staple, peg, knob, nail, yoke 218 n. *supporter*; suspender; clothes-line 47 n. *cable*; davit; gallows, gibbet, crucifix 964 n. *pillory*.

Adj. *pendent*, hanging, pendulous, pensile; suspended, dangling etc. vb.; overhanging, beetling 254 adj. *salient*; open-ended, loose 46 adj. *disjunct*.

Vb. *hang*, be pendent, drape, set; hang down, depend, trail, flow; hang on to, swing from; swing, sway, dangle, bob; hang the head, nod, weep, droop, sag, hang in the wind, stream, wave, float, ripple, flap; hang over, hover; overhang, lower 226 vb. *overlie*; suspend, hang up, sling, hook up; curtain 226 vb. *cover*.

218. Support – N. *support*, uplift, sustenance, maintenance, upkeep, nurture 633 n. *provision*; point d'appui, locus standi, footing, ground, leg to stand on; hold, foothold, handhold, toe-hold 778 n. *retention*.

supporter, carriage, carrier; support, mounting, bearing; underframe, chassis; buttress; abutment, embankment, wall, retaining w.; underpinning, shore, jack, prop; flagstaff, jackstaff; brace, strut; stay, mainstay, guy, shrouds, rigging 47 n. *tackling*; trunk, stem, stalk 366 n. *plant*; arch, ogive 248 n. *curve*; keystone, head-stone, corner-stone, springer; cantilever; pier (see *pillar*); bandage, jockstrap, truss, splint; stiffener, whalebone, stays 228 n. *underwear*; rest, headrest, backrest, footrest, stirrup; skid, chock, sprag, wedge 702 n. *obstacle*; staff, stick, cane, alpenstock, crutch; leg-support, irons; bracket (see *shelf*); hob (see *stand*); arm, back, shoulder, broad shoulders; backbone, spine, neck, cervix; world-bearer, Atlas.

handle, holder 194 n. *receptacle*; hold, grip, hilt, pommel, haft; knob, door-handle; lug, ear, loop; railing, handrail, rail, taffrail, balustrade; shaft, oar-s., loom; handlebar, tiller; lever, trigger 630 n. *tool*.

basis, foundation; sleeper; stereobate, substratum 207 n. *layer*; ground, groundwork, floor, bed, bedrock, rock bottom 214 n. *base*; flooring, pavement 226 n. *paving*; terra firma 344 n. *land*; perch, footing, foothold.

stand, tripod, trivet, hob; wine-stand, coaster; lampstand, lamp-post, standard; anvil, block, bench; table, board; console, console table; sideboard, dresser 194 n. *cabinet*; desk, counter; pedestal, plinth, socle; stylobate, podium; platform, gantry; emplacement, banquette; footplate; landing, half-l.; landing-stage, pier; dais, pulpit, stage 539 n. *rostrum*; step, stair, tread, rung, round 308 n. *ascent*; stilt 310 n. *lifter*; shank 267 n. *leg*.

seat, throne, woolsack; bench, form, settle; window-seat, rumble s., dickey; pew 990 n. *church interior*; stall, fauteuil 594 n. *theatre*; chair, armchair, easy c., elbow c., rocking c., high c., chaise longue; triclinium, sofa, settee, divan, couch, ottoman, Chesterfield, sociable, loveseat; stool, footstool, campstool, faldstool; tabouret, pouffe; priedieu, kneeler, cushion; saddle, pillion; howdah, pad 964 n. *pillory*; lap, knees.

bed, cot, crib, cradle, bassinet; couch, tester, four-poster; truckle bed, camp-b., pallet, shake-down, bunk, hammock; litter, hurdle, stretcher 658 n. *hospital*; bedding 226 n. *coverlet*; bedstead; bier 364 n. *funeral*.

cushion, pillow; bolster, Dutch wife; mattress, palliasse; squab, hassock, kneeler; prayer-mat.

beam, baulk, joist, girder, rafter, raft, tree 47 n. *bond*; summer, cross-beam, transom, cross-bar, traverse; architrave, lintel.

pillar, shaft, pier, pile, post, kingpost, stock; jamb, door-j.; newel-post, bannister, balustrade, baluster; pilaster, column, portico, stoa; caryatid, telamon, Atlantes.

pivot, fulcrum, fulciment, lever, purchase; hinge 45 n. *joint*; pole, axis; axle, axle-tree, spindle, arbor, pintle 315 n. *rotator*; gudgeon, trunnion; rowlock, thole-pin.

shelf, ledge, offset 254 n. *projection*; corbel, bracket, console; retable, niche 194 n. *compartment*; sill, window-s., mantelpiece, mantelshelf, rack, cupboard, dresser 194 n. *cabinet*; plank 207 n. *lamina*.

frame, bony f., skeleton, ribs; framework, scaffolding 331 n. *structure*; chassis, fuselage, body (of a car), undercarriage; trestle; easel, clothes-horse; cage 235 n. *enclosure*; picture-frame, window f., sash, window-s. 233 n. *outline*.

Adj. *supporting*, sustentative, sustaining; fundamental, basal; columellar, columnar; cervical, spinal; structural, skeletal; framing, holding.

Vb. *support*, sustain, bear, carry, hold, shoulder; uphold, upbear, buoy up; prop, shore up, underprop, underpin, jack up 310 vb. *elevate*; bolster, cushion; reinforce, underset 162 vb. *strengthen*; bandage, brace, truss; steady, stay; cradle, pillow, cup one's chin; nourish 301 vb. *feed*; maintain, keep on foot 804 vb. *pay*; back up 703 vb. *aid*; frame, set, mount 235 vb. *enclose*; bottom, ground, found, base 153 vb. *stabilize*;

stand, endure, stand up to, take the strain.

219. Parallelism – N. *parallelism*, nonconvergence, equidistance, concentricity; parallel, correspondence 28 n. *equality*; tramlines; parallelogram, parallelepiped.

Adj. *parallel*, concurrent, concentric; equidistant 28 adj. *equal*; corresponding 18 adj. *similar*.

220. Obliquity – N. *obliquity*, obliqueness, skewness; diagonal; rhomboid 247 n. *angular figure*; inclination 247 n. *angularity*; side-pressure; indirectness, squint; curvature, skewback 248 n. *curve*; crookedness, scoliosis, zigzag, chevron; switchback 251 n. *meandering*; knight's move, digression, swerve 282 n. *deviation*; bias 246 n. *distortion*; list, tip, cant; slopeness, slope, slant, tilt, rake, rakish angle; sloping face, batter; sloping edge, bevel, bezel; inclined plane, ramp, chute, slide.

acclivity, rise, ascent; ramp, incline, gradient; hill 209 n. *monticle*; hillside, bank 239 n. *laterality*; declivity, fall, dip, downhill, devexity, shelving beach 309 n. *descent*; steepness 215 n. *verticality*; escarpment, scarp, glacis 713 n. *fortification*.

Adj. *oblique*, inclined, abaxial, plagihedral; bevel, bezel; tipsy, tilted, rakish; biased, askew, skew, aslant; out of the perpendicular, battered, clinal, leaning, stooping; cater-cornered, rhomboidal 247 adj. *angular*; wry, awry, wonky, skew-whiff, crooked, squinting, cockeyed, knock-kneed 246 adj. *distorted*; diagonal, transverse; thwart, cross 222 adj. *crossed*; indirect, zigzag, herringbone; stepped, in echelon; divergent, non-parallel 282 adj. *deviating*.

sloping, acclivous, uphill 308 adj. *ascending*; declivous, downhill 309 adj. *descending*; anticlinal, anaclinal, synclinal, cataclinal; steep 215 adj. *vertical*; rounded 248 adj. *curved*.

Vb. *be oblique*, —tilted etc. adj.; incline, lean; tilt, slope, slant, shelve,

decline 309 vb. *descend*; rise, climb 308 vb. *ascend*; diagonalize, transect 222 vb. *cross*; lean, tip, bank, heel, careen, cant; bend, sag, give; edge, sidle, sidestep; squint; zigzag; jink, swerve; diverge, converge.

render oblique, incline, lean, slant, slope, cant, tilt, tip, rake; splay, bend, crook, twist, warp 246 vb. *distort*; bevel; bias, divert 282 vb. *deflect*; camber 248 vb. *make curved*.

Adv. *obliquely* etc. adj.; diagonally, crosswise, on the cross, on the bias; askew, aslant; askance, asquint; edgewise, sidelong, sideways.

221. Inversion – N. *inversion*, turning back to front, palindrome, hysteron proteron; turning inside out, eversion; turning backwards, retroversion 148 n. *reversion*; turning inward, introversion, invagination; capsizal (see *overturning*); inverted order (linguistic), chiasmus 519 n. *trope*.

overturning, capsizal, upset, spill, overset; somersault, cartwheel, hand-spring; subversion, undermining 149 n. *revolution*; pronation, supination.

Adj. *inverted*, inverse, back-to-front; palindromic; everted, invaginated, inside out; upside down, bottom up; capsizing, topheavy; topsy-turvy, head over heels; chiastic, antithetic.

Vb. *be inverted*, turn round 286 vb. *turn back*; turn over, heel o., capsize, turn turtle, stand on one's head; reverse, back 286 vb. *regress*.

invert, transpose, put the cart before the horse 151 vb. *interchange*; reverse, turn the tables; retrovert, turn back; turn down 261 vb. *fold*; introvert, invaginate; turn inside out, evaginate; upturn, overturn, tip over, spill, upset, capsize.

Adv. *inversely* etc. adj.; vice versa; contrariwise, other way round; arsyversy, topsy-turvy, head over heels; face down.

222. Crossing: intertexture – N. *crossing*, crossing over and under, plain weaving;

criss-cross, transversion, transection, intersection; decussation, X-shape; intertexture, interlacement; arabesque; interdigitation; braid, wreath, plait 251 n. *convolution*; entanglement, intricacy, skein, sleave, cat's cradle 61 n. *complexity*; cross-roads, road-junction 624 n. *road*.

cross, crux, rood, crucifix; pectoral 989 n. *vestments*; ansate cross, Lorraine c., Greek c., Maltese c., Celtic c., St Andrew's c.; saltire 547 n. *heraldry*; swastika, fylfot, tau.

network, reticulation, meshwork, netting, webbing, matting, wickerwork, mokes, trellis, wattle; lattice, grating, grid, grill, gridiron; tracery, fretwork, filigree 844 n. *ornamental art*; crewelwork, lace, crochet, knitting; web, cobweb; net, fishnet, seine, drag-net, trawl, mesh, moke, reticle.

textile, weave, web, loom; woven stuff, piecegoods, dry goods; bolt, roll, length, piece, cloth, stuff, material; broadcloth, fabric, tissue, suiting; jute, burlap, hessian, gunny, sacking, sackcloth; linen, lawn, cambric; duck; tapestry, towelling, crash; mohair, cashmere; alpaca, vicuna, Angora; wool, merino, worsted; frieze, felt; jersey, stockinette; homespun, khadi, khaddar, duffle, hodden, kersey, tweed, serge, shalloon, baize; flannel, flannelette; cotton, drill, nankeen, muslin, mull, nainsook, jaconet; calico, dowlas, long-cloth, fustian, moleskin, sharkskin, dimity, gingham, voile, madras, percale, rep, seersucker, poplin; chintz, cretonne, holland, silk, foulard, georgette, grosgraine, damask, brocade, samite, satin, sateen, ninon, taffeta, tussah, tussore, sarcenet, shantung, chiffon; velvet, velveteen, velours; corduroy; tulle, organdie; lace, bullion, chenille.

weaving, texture, weftage; web, warp, weft, woof; frame, loom, shuttle; weaver, stockinger, knitter; spinning wheel, distaff, whorl; spinner, spinster; spider.

Adj. *crossed*, cross, criss-cross; quadrivial; diagonal, transverse 220 adj. *oblique*; decussated, X-shaped, chiastic,

quincunxial; cross-legged, cruciform, forked, furcate 247 adj. *angular*; textile, woven, tweedy.

reticular, reticulated, retiform, webbed, webby; meshed 201 adj. *spaced*.

Vb. *cross*, 305 vb. *pass*; intersect, cut, diagonalize 220 vb. *be oblique*; decussate, interdigitate; reticulate, mesh, net, knot; fork, bifurcate 247 vb. *angulate*.

weave, loom; pleach, plait, braid; knit, crochet.

enlace, interlace, interlink, interlock, interdigitate, intertwine, interweave; enmesh, engage gear; twine, entwine, twist, wreathe, pleach; mat, ravel, tangle, entangle, dishevel 63 vb. *derange*.

223. Exteriority – N. *exteriority*, exterior; outwardness, externality 230 n. *circumjacence*; surface, crust, cortex, shell 226 n. *skin*; façade 237 n. *front*; outside, out of doors, open air; extraterritoriality 57 n. *exclusion*; outsider 84 n. *non-conformist*.

Adj. *exterior*, outward, extra-; external 10 adj. *irrelative*; outer, outermost, outlying 199 adj. *distant*; outside, outboard; outdoor, extramural; foreign 59 adj. *extraneous*; extraterritorial 57 adj. *excluding*; extravert 6 adj. *extrinsic*; exogenous; superficial, epidermic, cortical; skin-deep 212 adj. *shallow*; frontal, facial 237 adj. *fore*.

Vb. *be exterior*, lie beyond etc. adj.; frame, enclose 230 vb. *surround*.

externalize, body forth, objectify 6 vb. *make extrinsic*; project, extrapolate; extern 300 vb. *eject*.

Adv. *externally*, outwardly, outwards, superficially, on the surface; on the face of it; outside, extra muros; out, out of doors in the open, al fresco.

224. Interiority – N. *interiority*, interior, inside, indoors; inner surface, undersurface; inmost being, heart's blood, soul; marrow, pith; heart, centre, breast, bosom 225 n. *centrality*; inland, heartland, hinterland, up-country; seamy side, penetralia, recesses 211 n. *depth*; in-

troversion 5 n. *intrinsicality*; internee 750 n. *prisoner*.

insides, 193 n. *contents*; inner man, internal organs, vitals; heart, ticker; bowels, entrails, guts, pluck, tripe; intestines, colon, rectum; viscera, liver and lights; spleen; milt; abdomen, belly, paunch, underbelly; womb, uterus; stomach, tummy 194 n. *maw*; gland; endocrine; cell 358 n. *organism*; offal, chitterlings, haslet, kidney, liver.

Adj. *interior*, internal, inward 5 adj. *intrinsic*; inner, innermost, midmost 225 adj. *central*; inland, up-country, landlocked; domestic, home; intimate 490 adj. *known*; indoor, intramural, enclosed; inboard, built-in, inwrought; endemic 192 adj. *residing*; deep, deep-seated, ingrown; intestinal, visceral; intravenous, subcutaneous; interstitial 231 adj. *interjacent*; introvert; endo-, endogamous; endogenous.

Vb. *be inside*, — internal etc. adj.; lie beneath, be at the bottom of; show through 443 vb. *be visible*.

Adv. *inside*, within, in, deep in, deep down; inly, intimately; heart, inwardly.

225. Centrality – N. *centrality*, 70 n. *middle*; centripetence; centralization, focalization. central position 231 n. *interjacence*; waist, centre-line, parting 231 n. *partition*.

centre, dead c.; centroid; centre of gravity; centre of buoyancy, metacentre, epicentre; storm-centre, hot-bed; heart, core, kernel, nub, hub, nave, nucleus; navel, umbilicus; fesse-point 547 n. *heraldry*; bull's-eye, blank 617 n. *objective*.

Adj. *central*, centro-, centric, centrical, centroidal; centremost, midmost 70 adj. *middle*; focal; mesogastric, umbilical; homocentric, concentric; geocentric; heliocentric; centripetal; metropolitan 34 adj. *supreme*.

Vb. *centralize*, centre, take c.; focus, centre upon, concentrate 324 vb. *be dense*.

226. Covering – N. *covering*, superimposition; overlap, imbrication; cover, lid; flap, shutter 421 n. *screen*; cap, top, plug, bung, cork 264 n. *stopper*; carapace, shell; mail, plate 713 n. *armour*; shield, cowl, cowling, bonnet, hood (of a car); crust, fur 649 n. *dirt*; sheath, envelope 194 n. *receptacle*; hangings, curtains, drapes, arras, tapestry, wallpaper 217 n. *pendant*; mask 527 n. *disguise*.

roof, cupola 253 n. *dome*; housetop, rooftop, roof-ridge 213 n. *vertex*; leads, slates, tiles, pantile, shingle, thatch; gable; eaves 234 n. *edge*; ceiling, rafters; deck.

canopy, ciborium, baldachin; tilt, awning, sun-blind 421 n. *screen*; marquee, shamiana, pavilion, tent, bell-tent; tent-cloth, canvas.

shade, cover, film; hood, eyelid, eyelash; blind, shutters, slats 421 n. *screen*; curtain, veil; umbrella, gamp, bumbershoot, brolly; parasol, sunshade; sunbonnet 228 n. *headgear*; peak (of a cap).

wrapping, wrapper; bandage, roll, cast 658 n. *surgical dressing*; book-cover, binding, boards, covers, dust-jacket; mantle 228 n. *cloak*; cocoon, chrysalis; shroud 364 n. *grave clothes*.

skin, scarf-s., cuticle, epidermis; cutis, derm, corium; integument, peel, bark, crust, rind, coat, cortex; husk, hull, shell, pod, cod, shuck, jacket; pellicle, film; scalp 213 n. *head*; scale 207 n. *lamina*; pelt, peltry, fleece, fell, fur; leather, hide, rawhide; shagreen, calf, morocco, pigskin, kid, sealskin, deerskin; sheepskin, woolfell; chinchilla; sable, mink; vair, ermine, miniver, marten; feathers, coverts 259 n. *plumage*.

paving, flooring, floor, parquet; deck, floorboards, duck-b.; pavement, flags, paving-stone; sett, cobble, cobblestone; tarmac 624 n. *road*.

coverlet, bedspread, counterpane, bedding, bed-clothes, sheet, quilt, eiderdown, blanket, rug; caparison, housings, trappings; saddlecloth, horsecloth.

floor-cover, carpet, pile c.; mat, doormat, rug; drugget; linoleum, oilcloth; matting.

facing, revetment 162 n. *strengthening*; veneer, coating, varnish, japan, lacquer, enamel, glaze; incrustation, rough-cast, pebble-dash; stucco, compo, plaster, parget, rendering; wash, whitewash, distemper, stain, polish; paint 425n *pigment*.

Adj. *covered*, roofed, ceiled, wall-papered, carpeted; tented, garaged, under cover, under canvas; armour-plated, iron-clad; metalled, paved; over-built, built over; inundated, flooded.

dermal, cutaneous, cortical, cuticular; tegumentary; scaly, squamous; epidermic, epidermoid.

Vb. *cover*, superpose, superimpose; roof, cap, tip; spread, lay (a table); overlay, smother; lap, wrap 235 vb. *enclose*; blanket, mantle, muffle, hood, veil 525 vb. *conceal*; case, bind, cover (books); bandage, swathe, dress 658 vb. *doctor*; sheathe, incapsulate, encase 303 vb. *insert*; wall up; keep under cover, garage.

overlie, overarch, overhang, overlap; span, bestride, straddle, bestraddle 205 vb. *be broad*; inundate 341 vb. *drench*; skin over, crust, scab.

overlay, pave, floor; ceil, roof, dome, overarch, deck; paper 227 vb. *line*; overspread, top-dress, mulch; spread, smear; butter, anoint; powder, dust, sand.

coat, revet, face, do over; grout, rough-cast, incrust, shingle; stucco, plaster, parget, render; veneer, varnish, lacquer, japan, enamel, glaze; paint 425 vb. *colour*; tar, pitch, pay; daub, bedaub, scumble, overpaint, grease, lay it on thick; gild, plate, silver, electroplate, silverplate; waterproof 660 vb. *safeguard*.

227. Lining – N. *lining*, interlining 231 n. *interjacence*; coating, inner c.; stuffing, wadding, padding, bombast; inlay; backing, facing; doublure; upholstery; papering, wallpaper; panelling, wainscot; metal lining, bushing; packing, pack, dunnage; filling, stopping (dentistry); washer, shim.

Vb. *line*, interlard, inlay; back, face, paper, wall-p.; upholster, cushion; stuff, pad, wad; fill, pack; bush.

228. Dressing – N. *dressing*, investment, investiture; clothing, dressing up, toilet; overdressing, foppishness 848 n. *fashion*; vesture, dress, garb, attire, trim; accoutrement, caparison, harness, housing, trappings; rigging, rig; rig-out, turn-out; tailoring, millinery, mercery.

clothing, wear; raiment, linen; apparel, clothes, garments, weeds, things, doings; gear, vestments, habiliments; wardrobe, outfit, trousseau; layette, baby linen; togs, toggery, duds, traps; old clothes, slops; reach-me-downs, rags, tatters; best, best clothes, fine raiment; party dress, glad rags; pearlies, frippery 844 n. *finery*; fancy dress, masquerade; woollens, cottons. See *dress*.

dress, frock, gown, creation; garment, costume, habit; suiting, suit, lounge s., boiler s., siren s., track s.; civvies, mufti.

formal dress, correct d., regalia, court dress, full d.; grande toilette, evening dress, tails; morning dress; mourning, black, weepers, widow's weeds.

uniform, regimentals, accoutrement; full dress, undress, mess kit; battle dress, fatigues; khaki, jungle green, field grey, red coat 547 n. *livery*; robes, vestments 989 n. *canonicals*; academicals, cap and gown.

informal dress, undress, mufti, déshabille, négligé, boudoir dress, dressing gown, peignoir, bathrobe, wrapper; housecoat, kimono; tuxedo, dinner jacket, smoking j.; slippers, slacks.

robe, robes; long clothes, drapery; sari; himation; pallium, peplum, peplos; sheet, shroud 364 n. *grave clothes*.

tunic, coat, tail c., frock c.; coatee, jacket, reefer j.; dinner jacket, smoking j., tuxedo; monkey jacket, pea-j., pilot j., Eton j., mess j., blazer; parka, windbreaker; leotard; gym dress, drill d.; jerkin, doublet; cassock, soutane; toga, chiton.

vest, waistcoat, bolero; stomacher, jumper, jersey, guernsey, cardigan, spencer, pullover, sweater, singlet, zephyr.

trousers, pants, long p., peg-p.; trews, breeks, pantaloons, pantalettes; bloomers, bag-trousers, salwar; slacks, bags; chaparejos, chaps, dungarees, overalls, denims, jeans, levis, sweat pants; drawers, shorts, half-pants.

breeches, knee b., riding b., jodhpurs; buckskins, unmentionables, inexpressibles; small-clothes, smalls; knickerbockers, knickers; galligaskins, plus fours; toreador pants; rompers, crawlers.

skirt, outer petticoat, kirtle; grass skirt, Hawaian s., hobble s.; crinoline, hoop-skirt, farthingale, pannier, hoop; ballet skirt, tutu; kilt, filibeg; overskirt, peplum; sporran; bustle, tournure.

apron, pinafore, pinner, jumper, overall; bib, tucker, front, false shirt, dickey; fichu.

loincloth, breechcloth, breechclout; loin-guard; diaper, nappy.

bodywear, linen, lingerie; shirt, vest, singlet; smock, shift, chemise, slip, petticoat; blouse, waist, shirt-waist, basque; stomacher, bodice, camisole, chemisette, corsage; corslet.

underwear, undies, dessous, lingerie, frillies; underclothes, underlinen, undershirt, underskirt, underpants; pants, combinations; drawers, knickers, bloomers, pettipants; panties, scanties, briefs, step-ins, camiknickers, camibockers; foundation garment, corset, stays, whalebone; roll-on, girdle, pantie-girdle; brassière, bra; suspender belt, garter; shoulder-straps.

nightwear, sleeping suit, nightgown, nightshirt, nighty; pyjamas, shorties; bedsocks, bed-jacket, nightcap.

beachwear, play-suit, bikini; bathing costume, swim-suit, bathing drawers, bathing-suit, trunks.

overcoat, coat, warm c., greatcoat, uniform coat; trench-coat, riding coat; duffel coat, loden c.; waterproof, mackintosh, raincoat; sou'wester, oilskins; slicker, pea-jacket, windcheater; spencer, raglan, burberry.

cloak, mantle, cape, mantua, pelisse, roquelaure, cardinal, tippet, pelerine; burnous, yashmak; domino 527 n. *disguise*.

shawl, mantilla; stole, scarf, wrapper, choker; comforter, muffler, plaid; prayer-scarf, tallith.

headgear, head-dress, mantilla; plumes, feathers; crown, coronet, tiara 743 n. *regalia*; fillet, snood, coif, wimple 47 n. *girdle*; bandeau, kerchief; turban, puggree; fez, tarboosh; hood, cowl; helmet, busby, bearskin, shako, képi, forage cap, side-c., pill-box; casque, morion, steel hat 713 n. *armour*; cap, skull-c., smoking c., jockey c.; fast-cap, stocking c.; beret, tam-o'shanter, tam; Balmoral, glengarry; hat, tile, lid, beany; crown, peak, brim; soft hat, homburg, trilby; pork pie hat, billycock; fedora, felt hat; slouch hat, terai h.; stetson, ten-gallon hat; wideawake, petasus; bowler hat, derby; topper, top-hat; opera hat, crush h., gibus; straw hat, boater, panama, astrakhan, leghorn; bonnet, sun-bonnet, mobcap; toque, cloche hat; tricorne; witch's hat, dunce's cap; biretta 989 n. *canonicals*.

wig, peruke, periwig, full-bottomed w., bagwig, curled wig, tie-w., barrister's w.; false hair, toupee; coiffure 259 n. *hair*.

footwear, footgear, buskin, sock; bootee, footlet, bootikin; boot, top-b., jack-b., Wellington, Hessian; thigh-boot, gambado; hipboot, waders; shoe, clog, sabot, patten; brogues, moccasin, sandal; rope shoe, espadrilles; gumshoe, rubbers, plimsol, sneakers, loafers; overshoe, galosh; slipper, mule, pump; ballet shoe, toe-slipper; snowshoe, ski-boot; boot-tree, stretcher.

legwear, hosiery; stockings, nylons; tights, fleshings; trunks, hose, gaskins; half-hose, socks; leggings, gaiters, cutikins, galligaskins; spatter-dashes, spats; puttees, antigropelos; greaves 713 n. *armour*; garter; waders. See *footwear*.

neckwear, ruff, collar; dog-collar 989 n. *canonicals*; neckband, choker, cravat, stock, tie; neckerchief, neckcloth, bandana; boa, scarf (see *shawl*); necklace 844 n. *finery*.

belt, waistband; cummerbund, sash, obi; armlet, armband; bandolier, bellyband, girth 47 n. *girdle*.

glove, gauntlet, long gloves; mitten, bootikin; muff, muffettee.

sleeve, arm, armhole; leg-of-mutton sleeve, raglan s.; wristband, cuff.

clothier, rag trade; outfitter, costumier; tailor, snip, cutter, couturier; dressmaker, sempstress, seamstress, modiste; cobbler, cordwainer; hosier, hatter, milliner, draper, linen-draper, haberdasher, mercer; valet, tirewoman 742 n. *domestic*; dresser, mistress of the wardrobe 594 n. *stage hand*; slopshop.

Adj. *dressed*, clad, dight; rigged out, invested; uniformed, liveried; shod, gloved, hatted; well-dressed, soigné; tailored; wearable, sartorial.

Vb. *dress*, clothe, breech; array, apparel, garment, dight, garb, habit, attire; robe, drape, sheet, cloak, mantle; accoutre, uniform, equip, rig out, harness, caparison 669 vb. *make ready*; dress up, bedizen 843 vb. *primp*; envelop, wrap, lap, enfold, muffle, roll up in, swaddle, swathe 226 vb. *cover*.

wear, put on, assume, don, slip on, slip into, get i., huddle i.; get one's clothes on; have on, dress in, carry, sport; dress up 875 vb. *be ostentatious*; change, change into.

229. Uncovering – N. *uncovering*, divestment; undressing etc. vb.; exposure, nudism, naturism; striptease 594 n. *stage show*; undress, déshabillé 228 n. *informal dress*; decortication, exfoliation, excoriation; depilation, shaving; denudation 165 n. *havoc*.

bareness, décolleté, décolletage, plunging neckline; nudity, nakedness, state of nature, birthday suit, the altogether, the buff, the raw, not a stitch on; baldness, hairlessness, alopecia, acomia; tonsure; shaveling, baldhead.

stripper, nudist, naturist, ecdysiast, stripteaser; skinner, furrier, flayer, peeler; nude.

Adj. *uncovered*, bared; exposed, unveiled, showing 522 adj. *manifest*; divested, debagged; stripped, unclad, undressed; décolleté, bare-necked, low-n., bare-legged, barefoot, unshod, discalced;

hatless, bareheaded; underdressed, bare, naked, nude, raw; au naturel, in one's birthday suit; stark, starkers; acomous, leafless; moulting, unfeathered, unfledged; threadbare, out-at-elbows, ragged 801 adj. *poor*; drawn, unsheathed 304 adj. *extracted*.

hairless, bald, baldheaded, smooth, beardless, shaved, shaven, clean-s., tonsured; napless, threadbare; mangy 651 adj. *diseased*; balding, thin on top.

Vb. *uncover*, unveil, undrape, unrobe, undress, unclothe; divest, debag; strip, skin, scalp, flay, tear off; pluck, peel, bark, decorticate, excoriate, exfoliate, desquamate; hull, shuck, shell, stone; bone, fillet 300 vb. *void*; denude, denudate 165 vb. *lay waste*; expose, bare, lay open 526 vb. *disclose*; unsheathe, draw (a sword) 304 vb. *extract*; unwrap, unfold, unpack.

doff, uncap, uncover, raise one's hat; take off, change; shed, cast, moult, mew, cast its skin; undress, disrobe, uncase, peel, strip; undo, unbutton, unlace, untie 46 vb. *disjoin*.

230. Circumjacence – N. *circumjacence*, ambience, medium, atmosphere, aura, halo; encompassment, containment 235 n. *enclosure*; circumference 233 n. *outline*; surrounding, environment, entourage; background, setting, scene 594 n. *stage set*; environs, suburbs, precincts; hem, confines 234 n. *edge*; wall 235 n. *fence*.

Adj. *circumjacent*, circum-; circumambient, circumfluent, ambient; circumferential, peripheral; roundabout 314 adj. *circuitous*.

Vb. *surround*, lie around, compass, encompass, environ, lap; girdle, encircle 235 vb. *enclose*; contain 232 vb. *circumscribe*.

Adv. *around*, about, round about, all round.

231. Interjacence – N. *interjacence*, intermediacy, interlocation; intervenience, intervention, intercurrence, interpenetration, permeation 189 n. *presence*; dovetailing 45 n. *junction*; intermediary 720 n. *mediator*; link; buffer, buffer state, shock absorber 177 n. *moderator*.

partition, curtain 421 n. *screen*; wall, party-w., bulk-head 235 n. *fence*; divide, watershed, parting 46 n. *separation*; interface, septum, diaphragm, midriff; common frontier 236 n. *limit*.

interjection, interposition, sandwiching; interpolation, intercalation, interlineation 303 n. *insertion*; interruption, obtrusion; interference 702 n. *hindrance*; thing inserted, obiter dictum 40 n. *adjunct*; infix, insert, flyleaf, wedge; interjector, interpolator; interloper 702 n. *hinderer*.

Adj. *interjacent*, interposed, sandwiched; episodic, parenthetical, in brackets; intercurrent, intermediary, intervenient, intervening etc. vb.; intercessory 720 n. *mediatory*; intercalary; inter-, intermediate; median 70 adj. *middle*; partitioning, septal.

Vb. *put between*, sandwich; cushion 227 vb. *line*; interpose, interject; interpolate, intercalate, interline; interleave, interlard, intersperse; interweave, interdigitate 222 vb. *enlace*; bracket, parenthesize; come between, intervene.

Adv. *between*, betwixt; among, amid; sandwich-wise, parenthetically.

232. Circumscription – N. *circumscription*, ringing round, enclosing 235 n. *enclosure*; drawing round, ring, circle, balloon; circumvallation, investment 712 n. *attack*; envelopment, encirclement, containment.

Adj. *circumscribed* etc. vb.

Vb. *circumscribe*, describe a circle, ring round, encircle, encompass; envelop, close in, cut off, circumvallate, invest, blockade 712 vb. *besiege*; hem in, corral, enclose 235 vb. *enclose*; frame 230 vb. *surround*; edge, border 234 vb. *hem*; delimit 236 vb. *limit*.

233. Outline – N. *outline*, circumference, perimeter, periphery 230 n. *circumjacence*; surround, frame, rim 234 n. *edge*; ambit, compass, circuit 250 n.

circle; delineation, lines, lineaments 445 n. *feature*; profile, relief 239 n. *laterality*; silhouette; sketch 623 n. *plan*; skeleton, framework 331 n. *structure*; tournure, contour 243 n. *form*; loop, balloon, circle 232 n. *circumscription*; ring, cordon; figure, diagram; trace, tracing.

Adj. *outlined*, framed etc. vb.; in outline, etched; peripheral, perimetric, circumferential.

Vb. *outline*, describe a circle, construct a figure 232 vb. *circumscribe*; frame 230 vb. *surround*; delineate, silhouette, trace 551 vb. *represent*; etch 555 vb. *engrave*; sketch, diagrammatize, not fill in.

234. Edge – N. *edge*, verge, brim; hoist, fly (of a flag); tip, brink, skirt, fringe, margin, margent 69 n. *extremity*; confines, bounds 236 n. *limit*; littoral, land-line, water's edge, front 344 n. *shore*; side, kerb, wayside, roadside, riverside, bank 239 n. *laterality*; lip, ledge, eave, rim, welt, flange, gunwale 254 n. *projection*; coping, coaming; horizon, sky-line 199 n. *farness*.

edging, thrum, list, selvedge; hem, hemline, border; skirting, purfling, piping; basque, fringe, frill, flounce, furbelow, valance 844 n. *trimming*; exergue; milling 260 n. *notch*; scallop 251 n. *coil*.

Adj. *marginal*, liminal, border, skirting, marginated; riverine, coastal; riverside, roadside, wayside.

Vb. *hem*, edge, border, trim, fringe, purfle; mill, crenellate 260 vb. *notch*; bound, confine 236 vb. *limit*.

235. Enclosure – N. *enclosure*, inclosure, envelope, case 194 n. *receptacle*; wrapper 226 n. *wrapping*; frame 233 n. *outline*; enceinte, precinct; enclave, reserve 883 n. *seclusion*; fold, pen, corral 369 n. *cattle pen*; park 370 n. *garden*; compound, yard, pound, paddock, field; parking lot, car-park 192 n. *stable*; stockade, palisade, circumvallation, lines 713 n. *defences*; fish-trap 542 n. *trap*; cell 748 n. *prison*.

fence, ring f., sunk f., ha-ha, hedge, hedgerow; rails, paling, railing; pale, wall; moat, dike, ditch, fosse, trench, vallum, curtain 713 n. *defences*.

Vb. *enclose*, inclose, fence in, cordon, surround; pen, hem, ring 232 vb. *circumscribe*; cloister, immure, cage 747 vb. *imprison*; wrap, lap, enwrap, enfold 261 vb. *fold*; hug, embrace 889 vb. *caress*; frame, set, mount, embox.

236. Limit – N. *limit*, limitation 747 n. *restriction*; definition, delimitation, demarcation; upper limit, ceiling, highwater mark 213 n. *summit*; lower limit, threshold, low-water mark 214 n. *base*; uttermost, extreme, furthest point, farthest reach 69 n. *extremity*; ends of the earth 199 n. *farness*; terminus 295 n. *goal*; target 617 n. *objective*; turning-point 137 n. *crisis*; borderline, outside edge 233 n. *outline*; landmark, boundary stone; bourne, boundary, verge; frontier, border, marches 234 n. *edge*; line, demarcation l., date-l.; divide, parting 231 n. *partition*; horizon, equator, terminator; deadline, time-limit, term 110 n. *period*.

Adj. *limited*, definite, finite; limitable; limitary, terminal; frontier, border, borderline, bordering, boundary.

Vb. *limit*, bound, border 234 vb. *hem*; define, confine, condition 468 vb. *qualify*; restrict 747 vb. *restrain*; draw the line, delimit, demarcate, stake out; mark out, chalk o. 547 vb. *mark*.

237. Front – N. *front*, fore, forefront, forepart; prefix, frontispiece; forelock 259 n. *hair*; forecourt, anteroom, entrance 263 n. *doorway*; foreground, proscenium; anteposition, front rank, first line; forward line, centre forward; avant garde, vanguard, van; spearhead, forlorn hope 712 n. *attacker*.

face, frontage, façade, facia; face of a coin, obverse, head; right side, outer s.; front elevation; brow, forehead; chin, mentum; physiognomy, features, visage, countenance, frontispiece, figurehead, phiz, map, mug, pan, kisser, dial 445 n. *feature*; prominent feature, nose 254 n. *protuberance*.

prow, nose, beak, figurehead; bow, bowsprit; jib, foremast, forecastle 275 n. *ship*.

Adj. *fore*, forward, front, obverse; frontal, head-on, oncoming, facing 240 adj. *opposite*; anterior, prepositional, prosthetic, prefixed 64 adj. *preceding*.

Vb. *be in front*, front, confront, face, face up to 240 vb. *be opposite*; come to the fore, take the lead, head 64 vb. *come before*.

Adv. *in front*, before, in advance, in the lead, in the van, vanward; ahead, infra, further on 199 adv. *beyond*.

238. Rear – N. *rear*, rearward, afterpart, back end, tail e., stern 69 n. *extremity*; tail-piece, heel, colophon; coda 412 n. *musical piece*; tail, brush, scut, pigtail queue 67 n. *sequel*; wake, train; last place, rear rank, back seat 35 n. *inferiority*; rearguard 67 n. *aftercomer*; background, hinterland, depths, far corner; behind, backstage, back side; reverse side, wrong s., verso 240 n. *contraposition*; backdoor, postern 263 n. *doorway*; back (of the body), dorsum, chine; backbone, spine, rachis 218 n. *supporter*; nape, scruff, short hairs; occiput 213 n. *head*.

buttocks, breech, backside, posterior, posteriors; bottom, seat, sit-me-down; bum, arse; rear, stern, tail; fanny, hips; hindquarters, croup, crupper, haunches, haunch, ham, hunkers; rump, loin; dorsal region, lumbar r., lower back, coccyx; fundament, vent, anus.

poop, stern, stern-sheets, afterpart, quarter, counter, rudderpost, rudder, rear-mast, mizen-mast 275 n. *ship*.

Adj. *back*, rear, postern; posterior, after, hind, hinder, hindermost, rearmost; mizen; backswept 253 adj. *convex*; reverse 240 adj. *opposite*; spinal, vertebral, retral, dorsal, lumbar, gluteal, popliteal; anal; caudal, caudate, caudiform.

Vb. *be behind*, back on, back; bring up the rear 284 vb. *follow*; drop behind, fall astern 278 vb. *move slowly*; tail, shadow, dog 619 vb. *pursue*.

Adv. *rearward*, behind, back of; in the rear; in the background; behind one's back; after, aftermost, sternmost; aft, abaft, astern, aback; to the rear, hindward, backward, retro; back to back.

239. Laterality – N. *laterality*, sidedness; side movement 317 n. *oscillation*; sidestep 282 n. *deviation*; side-line, side, bank 234 n. *edge*, 344 n. *shore*; siding, side-entrance, side-door; broadside; beam; quarter 238 n. *poop*; flank, ribs, pleura; cheek, jowl, chops, chaps, gill; temples, side-face, half-face; profile, side elevation; lee, lee-side, leeward; weather-side, windward 281 n. *direction*; offside, on-s., near s. 241 n. *dextrality*, 242 n. *sinistrality*.

Adj. *lateral*, laparo-; side 234 adj. *marginal*; sidelong, glancing; parietal, buccal, side-face; costal, pleural; flanking, skirting; flanked, sided; many-sided, multilateral, bilateral, trilateral, quadrilateral; collateral 219 adj. *parallel*.

Vb. *flank*, side 234 vb. *hem*; coast; move sideways, passage, sidle; sideslip, sidestep 282 vb. *deviate*; deploy, outflank 306 vb. *overstep*.

Adv. *sideways*, laterally; askance, asquint; sidelong, broadside on; abreast, abeam, alongside; aside, beside; side by side, cheek by jowl 200 adv. *nigh*; coastwise.

240. Contraposition – N. *contraposition*, antithesis, opposition, antipodes 14 n. *contrariety*; opposite side, other s.; reverse, back 238 n. *rear*; polarity, polarization, opposite poles.

Adj. *opposite*, reverse, inverse 221 adj. *inverted*, 14 adj. *contrary*; oncoming 237 adj. *fore*; diametrically opposite, antipodal, antipodean; polarized; antarctic, arctic 281 adj. *directed*.

Vb. *be opposite* etc. adj.; subtend; face, confront 237 vb. *be in front*; oppose, contrapose.

Adv. *against*, over against; facing, face to face, vis à vis; back to back; contrariwise, vice versa.

241. Dextrality – N. *dextrality*, right hand, right-handedness; ambidexterity 694 n. *skill*; right, dexter; offside, starboard; right-hand page, recto; right wing, right-winger.

Adj. *dextral*, right-hand, starboard, offside; right-handed; ambidextrous; dextrorsal, dextrad; right-wing.

Adv. *dextrally*, on the right; rightwards, dextrad, a-starboard.

242. Sinistrality – N. *sinistrality*, left hand, left-handedness; left, sinister, nearside, on-s.; larboard, port; left wing, left-winger; laevogyration.

Adj. *sinistral*, sinister, sinistrous, left, left-handed, sinistro-manual, gauche; offside, nearside, sinistrad, sinistrorse, sinistrorsal; laevogyrate; laevogyrous.

Adv. *sinistrally*, on the left, a-port, offside; leftwards.

Section 3: Form

243. Form – N. *form*, Platonic f., idea; significant form, inner f., inscape; shape, turn, lines, architecture; make, formation, conformation, formulation, expression; fashion, style, design 331 n. *structure*; contour, silhouette, relief, profile, frame, outline; figure, cut, set, trim, build, lineament 445 n. *feature*; physiognomy 237 n. *face*; look, expression, appearance 445 n. *mien*; posture, attitude, stance; type, kind, pattern, stamp, cast, mould, blank 23 n. *prototype*; format 587 n. *print*; morphology, morphography, isomorphism.

Adj. *formed* etc. vb.; receiving form, plastic, fictile; shaped, fashioned, fully f., styled, stylized; ready-made.

formative, plasmic, informing, normative, formal; plastic, glyptic, architectural 331 adj. *structural*.

Vb. *efform*, inform, form; create, make 164 vb. *produce*; shape, fashion, figure, pattern; turn, round, square; cut, style, tailor; cut out, silhouette 233 vb. *outline*; sketch, draw 551 vb. *represent*; model, carve, chisel 554 vb. *sculpt*; hew, rough-

h. 46 vb. *cut*; mould, cast; stamp, coin, mint; hammer out, block o.; carpenter, mason; forge, smith; knead, work, work up into; construct, build, frame; express, formulate, put into shape, pull into s., lick into s., knock into s.

244. Amorphism: absence of form – N. *amorphism*, prime matter, chaos 61 n. *confusion*; amorphousness, shapelessness; vagueness, fuzziness; rawness, uncouthness 670 n. *undevelopment*; disfigurement 246 n. *distortion*.

Adj. *amorphous*, formless, unformed; liquid 335 adj. *fluid*; shapeless, featureless, characterless; messy, chaotic 61 adj. *orderless*; undefined, ill-defined, lacking definition, vague, fuzzy, blurred 419 adj. *shadowy*; unfashioned, unshapen; embryonic 68 adj. *beginning*; raw, unlicked 670 adj. *immature*; unhewn, in the rough 55 adj. *incomplete*; rude, inchoate, uncouth 699 adj. *artless*; rugged 259 adj. *rough*; unshapely 842 adj. *unsightly*; malformed, misshapen 246 adj. *deformed*.

245. Symmetry: regularity of form – N. *symmetry*, correspondence, proportion 12 n. *correlation*; balance 28 n. *equilibrium*; regularity, evenness 16 n. *uniformity*, 219 n. *parallelism*; shapeliness, regular features 841 n. *beauty*; harmony, eurhythmy; rhythm 141 n. *periodicity*.

Adj. *symmetrical*, balanced 28 adj. *equal*; proportioned, well-p. 12 adj. *correlative*; rhythmical, harmonious, congruent 24 adj. *agreeing*; corresponding 219 adj. *parallel*; smooth, even 16 adj. *uniform*; round, evensided, isosceles, equilateral; undeformed, well set-up 249 adj. *straight*; undistorted, unwarped, unbiased 494 adj. *true*.

246. Distortion: irregularity of form – N. *distortion*, asymmetry, disproportion 10 n. *irrelation*; imbalance, disequilibrium 29 n. *inequality*; lop-sidedness, crookedness 220 n. *obliquity*; anamorphosis, projection; stress, strain; bias, warp; screw, twist 251 n. *convolution*; contortion, grimace, scowl, mop, mow,

moue, snarl, rictus; perversion 552 n. *misrepresentation*.

deformity, malformation, monstrosity, abortion 84 n. *abnormality*, 845 n. *blemish*; ugliness, hideosity 842 n. *eyesore*; teratology.

Adj. *distorted* etc. vb.; irregular, asymmetric, unsymmetrical, disproportionate 17 adj. *non-uniform*; grotesque; out of shape 244 adj. *amorphous*; gnarled 251 adj. *convoluted*; wry, askew, crazy, crooked, cock-eyed 220 adj. *oblique*; contortive, scowling.

deformed, ugly 842 adj. *unsightly*; misproportioned, ill-proportioned, scalene; ill-made, misshapen, misbegotten; rickety; humpbacked, crook-backed, wrynecked; bandy, knock-kneed 845 adj. *blemished*; haggard, gaunt 206 adj. *lean*; bloated 195 adj. *fleshy*.

Vb. *distort*, disproportion, weight, bias; contort, screw, twist 251 vb. *twine*; bend, warp 251 vb. *crinkle*; buckle, crumple; dislocate; strain, sprain, wrest, rack, torture; misshape, botch, batter, knock out of shape; pervert 552 vb. *misrepresent*; misconstrue 521 vb. *misinterpret*; writhe, grimace, make faces, mop and mow; snarl, scowl 893 vb. *be sullen*.

247. Angularity – N. *angularity*, angulation; crotchet, bracket, hook; angle, bend 248 n. *curvature*; zigzag 220 n. *obliquity*; V-shape, elbow, knee; knuckle 45 n. *joint*; crutch, crotch, fluke 222 n. *cross*; fork, bifurcation; corner; wedge 256 n. *sharp edge*; indentation 260 n. *notch*.

angular measure, goniometry, trigonometry, altimetry; second, degree, minute; radian; goniometer, altimeter; clinometer, graphometer; level, theodolite; transit circle; sextant, quadrant; protractor.

angular figure, triangle, trigon; parallelogram, rectangle, square, quadrangle, quadrature; quadrilateral, lozenge, diamond; rhomb, rhombus, rhomboid; tetragon, polygon, pentagon, hexagon, heptagon, octagon, decagon, decahedron, polyhedron; cube, pyramid, wedge; prism, parallelepiped; Platonic bodies.

Adj. *angular*, aduncous, aduncate, hooked; hook-nosed, aquiline, rostrate; angled, cornered; zigzag 220 adj. *oblique*; jagged 260 adj. *notched*; jointed, geniculated, elbowed; akimbo; forked, bifurcate, furcular, V-shaped.

angulated, triangular, trigonal, trilateral; wedge-shaped, cuneate, cuneiform; rectangular, right-angled, orthogonal; square, four-square, quadrangular, quadrilateral, four-sided, squared; multilateral, polygonal; cubical, rhomboidal, pyramidal.

Vb. *angulate*, angle, corner; hook, crook, bend 248 vb. *make curved*; zigzag 220 vb. *be oblique*; fork, bifurcate, divaricate 294 vb. *diverge*.

248. Curvature – N. *curvature*, 255 n. *concavity*, 253 n. *convexity*; flexure, flexion 261 n. *fold*; arcuation, sweep; bending down, deflexion; detour 282 n. *deviation*; devexity 309 n. *descent*; retroflexion 221 n. *inversion*; curling, curliness, sinuosity 251 n. *convolution*.

curve, camber; turn, bend, hairpin **b.** U-turn; bay 345 n. *gulf*; figure of eight 250 n. *loop*; tracery, curl, festoon 251 n. *convolution*; bow 250 n. *arc*; arch, arcade, vault; crescent, lunule, half-moon, horseshoe, meniscus, lens; catenary, parabola, hyperbola, conic section; caustic line, caustic, diacaustic, catacaustic, cardioid, conchoid; arch (of the foot), instep; crane-neck; swan-n.

Adj. *curved*, cambered etc. vb.; flexed, bent, re-entrant 220 adj. *oblique*; bowed, stooping 311 adj. *depressed*; sweeping, curviform, curvilinear; rounded, curvaceous, bosomy; wavy, billowy 251 adj. *undulatory*; aquiline, hook-nosed, parrot-beaked 247 adj. *angular*; rostrate, beaked; retroussé, turned-up, tip-tilted 221 adj. *inverted*; circumflex; arched, archiform, vaulted, arcuate; devex 309 adj. *descending*; hooked, falciform; semicircular 250 adj. *circular*; crescentic, luniform, lunular, lunate, semilunar, horned; meniscal, lentiform,

lenticular, reniform; cordiform, cordated, cardioidal, heart-shaped, bell-s., pear-s., fig-s.; conchoidal.

Vb. *be curved*, — bent etc. adj.; curve, bend, loop, camber, arch, sweep, sag, swag, give 217 vb. *hang*; re-enter, recurve, curvet 312 vb. *leap*.

make curved, bend, crook 247 vb. *angulate*; turn, round; recurve, retroflect 221 vb. *invert*; bow, incline 311 vb. *stoop*; arcuate, arch, concamerate; coil 251 vb. *twine*; loop, curl, wave, frizzle 251 vb. *crinkle*; loop the loop, make figures-of-eight.

249. Straightness – N. *straightness*, directness, rectilinearity; perpendicularity 215 n. *verticality*; inflexibility 326 n. *hardness*; chord, straight line, bee-l.; Roman road; straight stretch, straight, reach.

Adj. *straight*, direct, even, right, true; linear, rectilinear; perpendicular 215 adj. *vertical*; unbent, unwarped; stiff, inflexible 326 adj. *rigid*; uncurled, out of curl; straightened, unfrizzed, dekinked; dead straight, undeviating, unswerving, undeflected, on the beam.

Vb. *straighten*, make straight 654 vb. *rectify*; iron out 216 vb. *flatten*; unbend (a bow); dekink, uncurl 258 vb. *smooth*; uncoil, unroll, unfurl, unfold 316 vb. *evolve*.

250. Circularity: simple circularity – N. *circularity*, orbicularity, roundness, rondure 252 *rotundity*; annulation, annularity; orbit 314 n. *circuition*.

circle, full c., circumference 233 n. *outline*; great circle, equator; orb, annulus; roundel, roundlet; areola; saucer; round, disc, disk, discus; hoop, ring, quoit; eye, iris; eyelet 263 n. *orifice*; circuit, roundabout; zodiac; ring formation, annulation.

loop, figure-of-eight 251 n. *convolution*; ringlet, curl 259 n. *hair*; bracelet, armlet 844 n. *jewellery*; crown, coronet 743 n. *regalia*; corona, aureole, halo; wreath, garland, fillet, chaplet, snood, fascia 228 n. *headgear*; collar 228 n. *neck-*

wear; cincture 228 n. *belt*, 47 n. *girdle*; lasso 47 n. *halter*; knot, tie.

wheel, truckle, pulley, caster; truck; hub, nave-plate; felloe, felly, tyre; tubeless t., inner tube, outer t.; roller 252 n. *rotundity*; fly-wheel 315 n. *rotator*.

arc, semicircle, half-circle, hemicycle, half-moon, crescent, rainbow 248 n. *curve*; sector, quadrant, sextant; ellipse, oval, ovule; ellipsoid, cycloid, epicycloid.

Adj. *round*, rounded, circular, cyclic, discoid; orbicular, annular, semicircular, hemicyclic; oval, ovate; elliptic, ovoid, egg-shaped, crescent-s., pear-s. 248 adj. *curved*; cycloidal, spherical 252 adj. *rotund*; fusiform, spindle-shaped.

Vb. *make round* etc. adj.; round, turn.

251. Convolution: complex circularity – **N.** *convolution*, involution, circumvolution; intricacy; flexuosity, anfractuosity, sinuosity; tortility, torsion; ripple 350 n. *wave*; wrinkle 261 n. *fold*; indentation, 260 n. *notch*; waviness, undulation.

coil, roll, twist; turban 228 n. *headgear*; spiral, cochlea, helix; screw, screwthread, worm, corkscrew; spring; armature; whorl, snailshell, ammonite; whirlpool 315 n. *vortex*; tendril; scollop, scallop 234 n. *edging*; kink, curl; ringlet, lovelock 259 n. *hair*; scroll, volute, fiddlehead, flourish, curlicue, squiggle 844 n. *ornamentation*; Cupid's bow; hairpin.

meandering, meander, winding course, crankiness; winding, twists and turns, ambages, circumbendibus 282 n. *deviation*; labyrinth, maze 530 n. *enigma*.

Adj. *convoluted*, involved, intricate 61 adj. *complex*; tortile; cranky, ambagious; winding, anfractuous, sinuous, tortuous, flexuous.

labyrinthine, mazy, meandering, serpentine.

snaky, serpentine, serpentiform; anguilliform, vermiform, vermicular; squirming, wriggling, peristaltic, sigmoidal.

undulatory, undulating, rolling, heaving; up-and-down, switchback; wavy, curly, frizzy, kinky, crinkly, woolly, crimped; scolloped, wrinkled; flamboyant.

coiled, spiral, helical, turbinated, cochlear; wormed, turbinate, whorled, verticillate; wound, wound up.

Vb. *twine*, twist, twirl, roll, coil, corkscrew; spire, spiral 315 vb. *rotate*; wreathe, entwine 222 vb. *enlace*; turn and twist 248 vb. *be curved*.

crinkle, crimp, frizz, crape, crisp, curl; wave, undulate, ripple, popple; wrinkle, corrugate 261 vb. *fold*; indent, scallop, scollop 260 vb. *notch*; crumple 246 vb. *distort*.

meander, snake, crank, crankle, twist and turn, zigzag, corkscrew. See *twine*.

wriggle, writhe, squirm, shimmy, shake; worm, serpentine.

252. Rotundity – **N.** *rotundity*, rondure, roundness, orbicularity 250 n. *circularity*; sphericity, spheroidicity; globosity, gibbosity 253 n. *convexity*.

sphere, globe, spheroid, ellipsoid, globoid, geoid; balloon; bubble; ball, wood (bowls), marble, alley, taw; cannon-ball, bullet; bead, pill, pea, boll; spherule, globule; drop, droplet, dewdrop; thread-ball, clew; hemisphere, hump 253 n. *dome*.

cylinder, roll, roller, rolling-pin 258 n. *smoother*; rod; round, rung; column; bole, trunk, stalk 218 n. *supporter*; pipe 263 n. *tube*; drum 194 n. *vessel*.

cone, conoid; shadow-cone, penumbra 419 n. *half-light*; sugarloaf 253 n. *dome*; cornet, horn; top, peg-t.; pear-shape, bell-s., egg-s.

Adj. *rotund*, orbicular 250 adj. *round*; spherical, sphery, spherular; globular, globy, globulous, global; bullet-headed; beady, globulitic; hemispheric; spheroidal, ovoid, oviform, egg-shaped; cylindrical, columnar, tubular, lumbriciform; conical, conoidal; bell-shaped, campaniform, napiform, pyriform, pear-shaped, egg-s.; fungiform, moniliform; humped, gibbous, bulbous 253 adj. *convex*; pot-bellied 195 adj. *fleshy*.

Vb. *round*, make spherical; sphere, globe, ball; balloon; mushroom; clew, coil up, roll.

253. Convexity – N. *convexity*, lordosis, arcuation, camber 248 n. *curve*; sphericity 252 n. *rotundity*; gibbosity, bulginess, bulge; protuberance 254 n. *prominence*; excrescency, tumescence, tumidity, turgidity 197 n. *expansion*; paunchiness 195 n. *bulk*; pimpliness, wart-hog; lens 442 n. *optical device*.

swelling, growth, excrescence, knot, nodosity, node, nodule; exostosis, oedema, emphysema; bubo, bump, gall, carbuncle, bunion, corn, blain, wart, wen; boil, furuncle, stye, pimple, papula, blister, vesicle; polypus, adenoids, haemorrhoids, piles; proud flesh, wheal; bleb 355 n. *bubble*; boss, torus, knob, bullion, nub; bulb, button, bud; belly, pot-belly, corporation, paunch 195 n. *bulk*; billow, swell 350 n. *wave*; bulge, bunt.

bosom, bust, breast, breasts, bubs; mamma, mamilla, papilla, nipple, pap, dug, teat, udder; thorax, chest; cuirass, breastplate.

dome, cupola, vault 226 n. *roof*; beehive 192 n. *nest*; brow 237 n. *face*; skull, cranium 213 n. *head*; mound, barrow, hummock, mamelon 209 n. *monticle*; mushroom, umbrella.

Adj. *convex*, out-bowed, protruding 254 adj. *salient*; hemispheric 252 adj. *rotund*; lentiform, lenticular; gibbous, humpy; swollen 197 adj. *expanded*; bloated 195 adj. *fleshy*; turgid, tumid, tumescent; verrucose, warty, papulous, pimply; verruciform, blistery, vesicular.

Vb. *be convex*, camber, arch, bow; swell, belly, bulge, balloon, mushroom; bag, bunt, pout.

254. Prominence – N. *prominence*, eminence 209 n. *high land*; solar prominence, solar flare; tongue, tongue of flame.

projection, salient, salient angle; tongue of land, spit, point, mull, promontory, foreland, headland 344 n. *land*; peninsula, chersonese 349 n. *island*; spur, foothill; jetty, mole 662 n. *shelter*; outwork 713 n. *fortification*; shelf, sill, ledge, soffit; eaves 226 n. *roof*; over-hang, forerake, sternrake 220 n. *obliquity*; tang, tongue; tenon 45 n. *joint*; outcrop.

protuberance, bump 253 n. *swelling*; prominent feature, nose, snout, conk; beak, rostrum; muzzle, proboscis, trunk; antenna 378 n. *feeler*; chin, mentum, jaw, brow, beetle-brow 237 n. *face*.

rilievo, relief, basso rilievo, alto r., mezzo r., low relief, bas r., high r.; embossment 844 vb. *ornamental art*; cameo 554 n. *sculpture*.

Adj. *salient*, bold, jutting, prominent, protuberant; emissile, protruding, popping; overhung, beetle-browed; underhung, undershot; repoussé, embossed, in relief.

Vb. *jut*, project, protrude, pout, pop out, start o.; stand out, stick o., poke o., hang o. 443 vb. *be visible*; bristle up, cock up 259 vb. *roughen*; shoot up 197 vb. *expand*; overhang, beetle over 217 vb. *hang*.

255. Concavity – N. *concavity*, incurvation 248 n. *curvature*; hollowness 190 n. *emptiness*; depression, dint, dent; impression, footprint 548 n. *trace*; intaglio 555 n. *engraving*; indentation 260 n. *notch*.

cavity, hollow, niche, recess, corner 194 n. *compartment*; hole, den, burrow, warren 192 n. *dwelling*; pit, chasm, abyss 211 n. *depth*; cave, cavern, hypogeum; grot, grotto, alcove 194 n. *arbour*; basin, trough 194 n. *vessel*; cell, pore 263 n. *orifice*; dimple, pockmark; honeycomb, sponge 263 n. *porosity*; funnel, tunnel 263 n. *tube*; socket 262 n. *furrow*; antrum, sinus; inlet 345 n. *gulf*; channel 351 n. *conduit*; dip, depression, pot-hole, crater.

valley, vale, dell, dingle, combe, cwm, U-valley, strath; glen, glade, dip, depression, dene; ravine, gorge, crevasse, barranca, canyon, gully 201 n. *gap*.

excavation, dug-out, grave, grave-pit 364 n. *tomb*; shaft, mine, pit, colliery, quarry 632 n. *store*; gallery, adit; sap, trench, tunnel, burrow, warren 263 n. *tunnel*; underground railway, tube;

archaeological excavation, dig; cutting, cut.

excavator, miner, quarrier; digger, dredger; sapper, burrower, tunneller; grave-digger, fossor.

Adj. *concave*, hollow, cavernous, speluncar; depressed, sunken; funnel-shaped, infundibular; cellular, alveolar; honeycombed, porous 263 adj. *perforated*.

Vb. *make concave*, depress, press in, stamp, impress; buckle, dent, dint, stave in; excavate, hollow, dig, spade, delve, scrape; trench 262 vb. *groove*; mine, sap, undermine, burrow, tunnel, bore; honeycomb, perforate 263 vb. *pierce*; scoop out, gouge o. 300 vb. *eject*; hole, pit, pockmark; indent 260 vb. *notch*.

256. Sharpness – N. *sharpness*, acuity, acuteness, serration, saw-edge 260 n. *notch*; spinosity, thorniness, prickliness.

sharp point, sting, prick; point, cusp 213 n. *vertex*; nail, tack, staple 47 n. *fastening*; nib, tag, pin, needle, bodkin, skewer, skiver, spit, broach, brochette; lancet, fleam, awl, bradawl, drill, borer, auger 263 n. *perforator*; arrow-head, barb 723 n. *missile weapon*; sword-point 723 n. *spear*; harpoon; dagger, poniard, stiletto 723 n. *weapon*; spike, caltrop, chevaux-de-frise, barbed wire 713 n. *defences*; spur, rowel; goad 612 n. *incentive*; fork, prong, tine, pick, pick-axe; claw, talon, nails 778 n. *nippers*.

prickle, spine, needle, thorn, brier, bramble, thistle, nettle, cactus; bristle 259 n. *hair*; beard, awn, spica; porcupine, hedgehog.

tooth, tuck, tush, fang; milktooth; canine tooth, incisor, grinder, molar, premolar teeth; pearls, ivories; dentition, front teeth, back t., cheek t.; set of teeth, denture, false teeth, plate, bridge; comb, saw; denticulation 260 n. *notch*.

sharp edge, cutting e., blade, edge-tool; razor's edge, knife-e.; cutlery, steel, razor; share, plough-s., coulter 370 n. *farm tool*; spade, mattock; scythe, sickle, hook; scissors, barber's s., pinking s., aesculap; shears, clippers,

secateurs; scalpel, bistoury, catling; chisel, plane, spokeshave 258 n. *smoother*; knife, carver, slicer; pen-knife, sheath-k., clasp-k., jack-k., bowie-k., shive-k., flick-k.; gully, whittle; machete, dao, dah, kukri, kris, creese, parang, panger; chopper, cleaver, wedge; hatchet, axe, adze; battle-axe 723 n. *axe*; sword, 723 n. *side arms*.

sharpener, knife-s., oilstone, whetstone, grindstone, rubstone; hone, steel, file, strop; emery-paper, sand-p.

Adj. *sharp*, stinging, keen, acute; edged, cutting; pointed, unblunted, unbated; sharp-pointed, cuspidate, mucronate; sagittal, arrowy; spiked, spiky, spiny, thorny, brambly, briery, thistly; needlelike, aciform; aculeiform, prickly, bristly 259 adj. *hairy*; jagged 259 adj. *rough*; set, razor-sharp.

toothed, odontoid; toothy; tusky, fanged, dental, denticulate, dentiform; cogged, serrated, saw-edged, pectinated 260 adj. *notched*.

Vb. *be sharp*, —stinging etc. adj.; have a point, prick, sting; bite 46 vb. *cut*; taper 293 vb. *converge*.

sharpen, edge, put an edge on, whet, hone, oilstone, grind, file, strop, set; barb, spur, point, stud.

257. Bluntness – N. *bluntness*, flatness, bluffness; curves, hard c., flat c.; toothlessness, lack of bite; blunt instrument, foil; blunt edge, blade, flat.

Adj. *unsharpened*, unwhetted; blunt, blunted, unpointed, bated (of a sword); rusty, dull; toothless, edentate; stub, stubby, snub, square; round 248 adj. *curved*; flat, bluff; obtundent.

Vb. *blunt*, make blunt, turn, turn the edge, disedge; bate (a foil); obtund, dull, rust; draw the teeth 161 vb. *disable*; be blunt, not cut, pull, scrape, tear.

258. Smoothness – N. *smoothness* etc. adj.; silkiness, silk, satin, velvet; sleekness; smooth surface, marble, glass, ice; flatness 216 n. *horizontality*; levigation, polish, varnish, gloss, glaze, shine, finish; slipperiness, slip-way, slide; oiliness, greasiness 334 n. *lubrication*; smooth water, calm 266 n. *quiescence*.

smoother, roller, bulldozer; rolling-pin; iron, flat-i., tailor's goose; mangle, wringer, press; plane 256 n. *sharp edge*; sand-paper, emery-p., file; polish, varnish, enamel; lubricator 334 n. *lubricant*.

Adj. *smooth*, non-friction, non-adhesive, stream-lined; slithery, slippery, skiddy; oily, greasy, buttery, soapy; polished (see Vb. *smooth*); soft, suave, bland, soothing 177 adj. *lenitive*; silky, silken, satiny, velvety; downy; marble, glassy; bald; sleek, well-brushed, unruffled; unwrinkled, uncrumpled; rolled, plumb 216 adj. *horizontal*; calm 266 adj. *still*; rounded 248 adj. *curved*; blunt 257 adj. *unsharpened*.

Vb. *smooth*, remove friction, streamline; butter 334 vb. *lubricate*; plane, even, level; file, rub down 333 vb. *rub*; roll, calender, steam-roll; press, uncrease, iron, mangle 216 vb. *flatten*; mow, shave 204 vb. *shorten*; shine, burnish 417 vb. *make bright*; levigate, buff, polish, glaze, wax, varnish 226 vb. *coat*; pave, macadamize, tarmac 226 vb. *overlay*.

go smoothly, glide, float, roll, bowl along, run on rails; slip, slide, skid 265 vb. *be in motion*; skate, ski; feel no friction, coast, free-wheel.

259. Roughness – N. *roughness*, asperity, harshness 735 n. *severity*; surface relief; choppiness 350 n. *wave*; jaggedness, serration, saw-edge 260 n. *notch*; ruggedness, cragginess; unevenness, joltiness, bumpiness; corrugation, rugosity, wrinkling 261 n. *fold*; rut 262 n. *furrow*; coarseness, coarse grain, knobbliness, nodosity 253 n. *convexity*; washboard, grater, file, sand-paper; goose-flesh, horripilation; bristliness, shagginess, hairiness; undergrowth 366 n. *wood*; stubble, bristle, scrubbing-brush 256 n. *prickle*.

hair, head of h., matted h.; shock, mop, mane, fleece, shag; bristle, stubble; locks, tresses, curls, ringlet; kiss-curl; strand, plait; pigtail, pony-tail; topknot, forelock, elflock, lovelock, scalplock;

cowlick, quiff; pompadour, roll; fringe, bang, fuzz, earphones, bun, chignon; false hair, switch, wig, toupée 228 n. *headgear*; thin hair, wisp; beard, beaver, goatee, imperial, Van Dyke; whiskers, mutton-chops; moustache, toothbrush, handlebars; eyebrows, eyelashes, cilia 208 n. *filament*; woolliness, fleeciness, fluffiness; down, pubescence, pappus, wool, fur, budge 226 n. *skin*; tuft, flock; pile, nap; floss, fluff, fuzz, thistledown 323 n. *levity*; horsehair 227 n. *lining*.

plumage, pinion 271 n. *wing*; feathering, feathers, coverts; hackle; plume, panache, crest; quill.

Adj. *rough*, uneven, broken; choppy, storm-tossed; rutty, pitted, potholed, poached; bumpy, jolting, bonebreaking; lumpy, stony, nodular, knobbly, studded; knotted, gnarled; coarse-grained, coarse; lined, wrinkled 262 adj. *furrowed*; craggy, jagged; horripilant, creeping; ruffled, unkempt.

hairy, crinose, crinite; woolly, fleecy, furry; hirsute, shaggy, tufty, matted, shock-headed; hispid, bristly, bristling; wispy, filamentous, ciliated; bewhiskered, bearded, moustached; unshaven, unshorn; unplucked; curly, frizzy, fuzzy, tight-curled, woolly.

downy, nappy, pilose; pubescent, tomentous, pappous; velvety, peachy; fleecy, woolly, fluffy, feathery, fledged.

Vb. *be rough*, — hairy etc. adj.; bristle 254 vb. *jut*; creep (of flesh), horripilate; scratch, catch; jolt, bump, jerk 278 vb. *move slowly*.

roughen, mill, serrate 260 vb. *notch*; stud, boss; corrugate, wrinkle 262 vb. *groove*; ruffle, tousle 63 vb. *derange*; rumple, crumple 261 vb. *fold*; rub up the wrong way, set on edge.

260. Notch – N. *notch*, serration, serrulation, saw-edge, ragged e. 256 n. *sharpness*; indentation, deckle-edge; machicolation, crenellation; nick, cut, gash; crenation 201 n. *gap*; dog-tooth 844 n. *pattern*; cog, ratchet, cog-wheel; saw, hacksaw, circular saw; battlement, embrasure, crenelle.

Adj. *notched*, notchy 256 adj. *sharp*; crenellated; toothed, denticulated; serrated, palmate, emarginated.

Vb. *notch*, serrate, tooth, cog; snip, nick, score, scratch, scotch, scarify 46 vb. *cut*; crenellate, machicolate; indent, scallop; jag, pink, slash; dent, mill, knurl.

261. Fold – N. *fold*, plication, flexure, doubling; lapel, cuff, turn-up; pleat, tuck, gather, pucker, ruche, ruffle; flounce, frounce; crease, wrinkle, frown; crow's feet 131 n. *age*; crinkle.

Adj. *folded*, doubled; gathered; creasy, wrinkly, puckery; dog-eared; turn-down, turn-over, rolled.

Vb. *fold*, plicate, double, turn over, roll; crease, pleat; corrugate, furrow, wrinkle 262 vb. *groove*; rumple, crumple 63 vb. *derange*; curl, frizzle, frizz 251 vb. *crinkle*; ruffle, pucker, cockle up, gather, frounce, ruck, shirr, smock, twill; tuck, tuck up, kilt; hem, cuff; turn up, turn down; enfold, wrap, swathe 235 vb. *enclose*; fold up, roll up, furl, reef.

262. Furrow – N. *furrow*, groove, chase, bore; slot, slit 201 n. *gap*; engraving, glyph, triglyph; fluting, goffering, rifling; gash, scratch, score 46 vb. *scission*; wake, rut 548 n. *trace*; gutter, ditch 351 n. *conduit*; ravine 255 n. *valley*; corduroy, whipcord, corrugated iron, washboard, ripple, catspaw 350 n. *wave*.

Adj. *furrowed*, ploughed etc. vb.; sulcated, bisulcous, trisulcate, canaliculate; channelled, rutty; wrinkled, lined 261 adj. *folded*.

Vb. *groove*, slot, flute, bore, rifle; chase; gash, scratch, score 46 vb. *cut*; striate, streak 437 vb. *variegate*; grave, carve, enchase, bite in, etch 555 vb. *engrave*; furrow, plough, channel, rut, wrinkle, line; corrugate, goffer 261 vb. *fold*.

263. Opening – N. *opening*, patefaction; pandiculation, stretching 197 n. *expansion*; yawn, yawning, oscitation; hiatus,

lacuna, space, interval 201 n. *gap*; split, crack, leak 46 n. *disjunction*; hole, hollow 255 n. *cavity*.

perforation, empalement, puncture, acupuncture, venepuncture; terebration, trephining; boring, borehole, bore, calibre; pin-hole, eyelet.

porosity, porousness, sponge; sieve, sifter, cribble, riddle, screen; strainer, colander; honeycomb, warren.

orifice, aperture, slot; oral cavity, mouth, gob, trap, clap, jaws, muzzle; throat, gullet, weasand, oesophagus 194 n. *maw*; mouthpiece 353 n. *air-pipe*; nozzle, spout, vent, vomitory, blower, blowhole, spiracle; nasal cavity, nostril; inlet, outlet; river-mouth, embouchure; ostiole, foramen, pore, stomata; hole 255 n. *cavity*; touch-hole, pin-h., button-h., arm-h., key-h.; manhole, pigeonhole 194 n. *compartment*; eye, eyelet, dead-eye.

window, fenestration; casement, embrasure, loophole 713 n. *fortification*; lattice, grill; oriel, dormer; light, lightwell, fan-light, skylight, transom, companion, window-frame; deadlight, port, porthole; peep-h., hagioscope, squint 990 n. *church interior*; window pane 422 n. *transparency*.

doorway, archway; doorstep; threshold, drive in, entry 297 n. *ingress*; exit; gate, door, portal, porch, propylaeum; lychgate; back door, postern 238 n. *rear*; wicket; scuttle, hatch, hatchway; trapdoor, companion-way; door-jamb, gatepost, lintel; door-keeper.

open space, yard, court 185 n. *place*; opening, clearing, glade; landscape, champaign 348 n. *plain*; thoroughfare 305 n. *passage*; estuary 345 n. *gulf*.

tunnel, boring; subway, underpass, underground, tube; mine, shaft, pit, gallery, adit 255 n. *excavation*; bolt hole, rabbit-h., fox-h., mouse-h.; funnel 252 n. *cone*; sewer 351 n. *drain*.

tube, pipe, artery 351 n. *conduit*; main, tap, faucet; tubule, pipette, cannula; tubing, piping, pipe-line, hose; colon, gut 224 n. *insides*.

chimney, factory c., smoke-stack,

funnel; smoke-duct, flue; volcano, fuma-role, smoke-hole 383 n. *furnace*.

opener, key, master-k., skeleton-k., passe-partout; corkscrew, tin-opener, bottle-o.; aperient, purgative, pull-through; pass, ticket 756 n. *permit*.

perforator, borer, corer; gimlet, wimble, corkscrew; auger, drill; bur, bit, brace and b.; reamer, rimer; trepan, trephine; probe, lancet, fleam, stylet, trocar; bodkin, needle, awl, pin, nail, skewer, spit 256 n. *sharp point*; punch, puncheon, stapler; dibble; digging-stick; pickaxe, pick.

Adj. *open*, patent 522 adj. *manifest*; unclosed, unshut, ajar; open to 289 adj. *accessible*; agape, gaping; yawning; open-mouthed, slack-jawed.

perforated etc. vb.; honeycombed, riddled; cribriform, foraminous, holey; windowed, fenestrated.

porous, permeable, pervious, spongy, percolating, leachy, leaky, leaking.

tubular, tubulous, tubulated, canalular, piped; cylindrical 252 adj. *rotund*; infundibular; fistulous; vascular, capillary.

Vb. *open*, unclose, unfold; unlock, unlatch; pull out (a drawer); uncover, bare 229 vb. *doff*; unstop, uncork; unseam 46 vb. *disjoin*; enlarge a hole, ream; fly open, split, gape, yawn; burst, explode; crack, start, leak; space out 201 vb. *space*; open out, deploy 75 vb. *be dispersed*; unclench; bloom, be out.

pierce, transfix; gore, run through, stick, pink, lance, bayonet, spear 655 vb. *wound*; spike, skewer, spit; prick, puncture, tattoo; probe, stab, poke, inject; perforate, hole, riddle, pepper, honeycomb; pin, nail, impale, punch full of holes, hull (a ship), scuttle, stave in; tap, broach; bore, drill, wimble; trephine, trepan; burrow, tunnel 255 vb. *make concave*; penetrate 297 vb. *enter*.

264. Closure – N. *closure*, closing etc. vb.; occlusion, stoppage; contraction 198 n. *compression*; blockade 235 n. *enclosure*; obstruction, obturation; constipation, strangury; dead-end, cul-de-

sac, impasse, blank wall; imperviousness, impermeability.

stopper, stopple, cork, plug, fid, bung, peg, spill, spigot, spike (of a gun); wedge, embolus, wad, dossil, pledget, tampon, stopping 227 n. *lining*; gag 748 n. *fetter*; shutter 421 n. *screen*; tourniquet 198 n. *compressor*; damper, choke, cut-out; vent-peg, tap, faucet, stopcock; top, lid 226 n. *covering*; lock, key, bolt, bar, staple 47 n. *fastening*.

janitor, doorkeeper, gatekeeper, porter, durwan, ostiary; commissionaire, concierge; watchman 660 n. *protector*; turnkey 749 n. *gaoler*.

Adj. *closed*, unopened; shut etc. vb.; unpierced, non-porous, imperforate, unholed; impervious, impermeable 324 adj. *dense*; impenetrable 470 adj. *impracticable*; caecal, dead-end, blank; infarcted, bunged up; strangurious 198 adj. *contracted*.

sealed off, sealed; cloistered, claustral; close, unventilated; staunch, tight, air-t., gas-t.; proof 660 adj. *invulnerable*.

Vb. *close*, shut, occlude, seal, make all tight; clap to, slam, bang (a door); lock, fasten, snap to; plug, fother; bung, cork, obturate, spike (a gun); button, do up 45 vb. *join*; block, dam, stanch, choke, throttle, strangle; blockade 712 vb. *besiege*; shut in, seal off 232 vb. *circumscribe*; trap, bolt, bar, lock in 747 vb. *imprison*.

Section 4: Motion

265. Motion: successive change of place – N. *motion*, movement, going, move, march; speed-rate 277 n. *velocity*; mobility, kinetic energy; advance, progress, headway 285 n. *progression*; sternway 286 n. *regression*, 290 n. *recession*; motion towards 289 n. *approach*, 293 n. *convergence*; driftway 294 n. *divergence*, 282 n. *deviation*; rising 308 n. *ascent*; sinking 309 n. *descent*, 313 n. *plunge*; axial motion 315 n. *rotation*; fluctuation 317 n. *oscillation*, 318 n. *agitation*; stir, bustle, unrest, restlessness 678 n. *activ-*

ity; speed 277 n. *velocity*; slow motion 278 n. *slowness*; rhythm 141 n. *periodicity*; process 316 n. *evolution*; conduction 272 n. *transference*; current 350 n. *stream*; course, career, run; locomotion, traffic 305 n. *passing along*; transit 305 n. *passage*; transportation 272 n. *transport*; running, walking 267 n. *pedestrianism*; riding 267 n. *equitation*; travel 267 n. *land travel*, 269 n. *water travel*, 271 n. *air travel*; manoeuvre 688 n. *tactics*; exercise 162 n. *athletics*; gesticulation 547 n. *gesture*; cinematography, motion picture 445 n. *cinema*; laws of motion, kinematics, kinetics, dynamics.

gait, walk, port, carriage; tread, tramp, footfall, stamp; pace, step, stride; run, lope; jog-trot, dog-t.; dance-step, hop, skip, jump 312 n. *leap*; waddle, shuffle; swagger, proud step, stalk, strut, goose-step; march, slow m., quick m., double; trot, piaffer, amble, canter, gallop 267 n. *equitation*.

Adj. *moving* etc. vb.; in motion; motive, motor; movable, mobile; locomotive, automotive; mercurial 152 adj. *changeful*; unquiet, restless 678 adj. *active*; nomadic 267 adj. *travelling*; erratic, runaway 282 adj. *deviating*; kinetic; cinematographic.

Vb. *be in motion*, move, go, hie, gang, wend, trail; gather way 269 vb. *navigate*; budge, stir; flutter, wave, flap 217 vb. *hang*; tread, tramp 267 vb. *walk*; trip, dance 312 vb. *leap*; roll, taxi; stream, drift 350 vb. *flow*; paddle 269 vb. *row*; skitter, slide, slither, skate, ski, toboggan, glide 258 vb. *go smoothly*; fly, frisk, flit, flitter, dart, hover; cruise, steam, chug; make one's way 285 vb. *progress*; pass through, wade t. 305 vb. *pass*; dodge 620 vb. *avoid*; tack, manoeuvre 282 vb. *deviate*; remove, move house, change one's address; change places 151 vb. *interchange*; travel 267 vb. *wander*; motion 547 vb. *gesticulate*.

move, impart motion, set going, power; actuate 173 vb. *operate*; stir, jerk, pluck, twitch 318 vb. *agitate*; budge, shift, manhandle, trundle, roll, wheel; shove 279 vb. *impel*; tug, pull 288 vb.

draw; convey, transport 272 vb. *transfer*; dispatch 272 vb. *send*; scatter 75 vb. *disperse*; transpose 151 vb. *interchange*.

266. Quiescence – N. *quiescence*, subsidence 145 n. *cessation*; rest, stillness; deathliness, deadness; stagnation 679 n. *inactivity*; truce 145 n. *lull*; stand, stoppage, halt 145 n. *stop*; immobility, fixity, steadiness, equilibrium 153 n. *stability*; numbness, trance 375 n. *insensibility*.

quietude, quiet, quietness, stillness, hush 399 n. *silence*; tranquillity, peacefulness 717 n. *peace*; rest 683 n. *repose*; slumber 679 n. *sleep*; calm 258 n. *smoothness*; windlessness, not a breath of air; dead quiet, not a mouse stirring; homekeeping, domesticity; passivity, quietism; quietist 717 n. *pacifist*.

Adj. *quiescent*, quiet, still; asleep 679 adj. *sleepy*; at rest, becalmed; at anchor, moored, docked; at a standstill 679 adj. *inactive*; unemployed 674 adj. *unused*; dormant, stagnant, vegetating, unprogressive, static 175 adj. *inert*; settled, stay-at-home, domesticated 828 adj. *content*.

tranquil, undisturbed, sequestered 883 adj. *secluded*; peaceful, restful; uneventful 16 adj. *uniform*; calm, windless, airless; sunny, halcyon 730 adj. *palmy*; comfortable, relaxed 683 adj. *reposeful*; unruffled, serene 823 adj. *inexcitable*.

still, unmoving, standing, flat 387 adj. *tasteless*; stock-still, immobile, motionless, gestureless; expressionless, dead-pan, poker-faced 820 adj. *impassive*; steady, unwinking, unblinking; rooted 153 adj. *fixed*; immoveable, stuck; stiff, frozen 326 adj. *rigid*; benumbed 375 adj. *insensible*; quiet 399 adj. *silent*.

Vb. *be quiescent* etc. adj.; quiesce, subside, die down 37 vb. *decrease*; pipe down; stand still, keep quiet; stagnate, vegetate 175 vb. *be inert*; stand, mark time; stay put, sit tight, stand pat 144 vb. *stay*; stand to, lie to, ride at anchor; rest 683 vb. *repose*; go to bed 679 vb. *sleep*; ground, stick 145 vb. *halt*.

267. Land travel – N. *land travel*, travel, itinerancy, wayfaring; globe-trotting, tourism; riding, driving, coaching, motoring, cycling; journey, voyage, trip, course, passage; peregrination, pilgrimage; expedition, safari, trek; business trip, errand 917 n. *duty*; progress, tour, grand t.; jaunt, hop; ride, joy-r., drive; excursion, outing, airing, ramble, constitutional, promenade; ambulation, perambulation, walk, heel and toe; stroll, saunter, hike, march, run; conveyance, lift 273 n. *horse*, 274 n. *vehicle*.

wandering, errantry, wanderlust, nomadism; vagrancy, vagabondage; no fixed address; roving, rambling, waltzing Matilda (see Vb. *wander*).

pedestrianism, walking, shanks's mare, heel and toe; ambulation, perambulation; walk, promenade, constitutional; stroll, saunter, amble, ramble; hike, tramp, march, walking-tour; run, trot; 265 n. *gait*; walking about, peripateticism; prowling, loitering; sleep-walking, somnambulism 375 n. *insensibility*; all fours, crawl.

marching, campaigning, campaign; manoeuvres, marching and countermarching; march, route-m., night-m.; quick march, slow m.; cavalcade, procession, parade, march past 875 n. *formality*; column, file, cortège, train, caravan.

equitation, riding, equestrianism, horsemanship, manège, dressage 694 n. *skill*; show-jumping, steeplechasing 716 n. *contest*; horse-racing; haute école, caracol, piaffer, curvet 265 n. *gait*.

leg, foreleg, hindleg; limb, nether l.; shank, knee, shin, calf; thigh, ham, hock, hough; popliteal tendons, hamstrings; legs, pegs, pins, underpinnings 218 n. *supporter*; stump, wooden leg; long legs, spindle shanks; thick legs, piano l.; shank bone, shin bone, tibia.

itinerary, route 624 n. *way*; march, course 281 n. *direction*; route-map, road m. 551 n. *map*; guide, road-book, handbook, timetable, Bradshaw 524 n. *guide book*; milestone, finger-post 547 n. *signpost*; stop-over, terminus 145 n. *stopping place*.

Adj. *travelling* etc. vb.; journeying, itinerant, wayfaring, travelled, travel-stained; stopping over, visiting; nomadic, floating, unsettled; homeless, rootless, déraciné 59 adj. *extraneous*; footloose, on the road, roving, errant, wandering, ambulant, strolling, circumforaneous, peripatetic, vagabond; pedestrian, foot-slogging; self-driven, self-drive; noctivagrant, somnambular, sleep-walking.

crural, genual, femoral, popliteal, gluteal; long-legged, leggy, leggity 209 adj. *tall*; spindly, spindle-shanked, calfless 206 adj. *lean*; piano-legged, thick-ankled.

Vb. *travel*, fare, journey, peregrinate; tour, see the world, visit, explore 484 vb. *discover*; go places, sightsee, rubberneck; pilgrimage, go on a p.; go on safari, trek, hump bluey; traverse, transit 305 vb. *pass*; fare forth, take wing 296 vb. *depart*; migrate, emigrate, immigrate, settle 187 vb. *place oneself*; go, betake oneself to 882 vb. *visit*; cruise 269 vb. *voyage*; wend, wend one's way, bend one's steps, follow the road; post 277 vb. *move fast*; proceed 285 vb. *progress*, 265 vb. *be in motion*.

wander, nomadize, migrate; rove, roam; knock around, bum, ramble, stroll, saunter; gad, trapes, gallivant, gad about, hover 265 vb. *be in motion*; prowl, skulk 523 vb. *lurk*; straggle, trail 75 vb. *be dispersed*; lose the way 282 vb. *stray*.

walk, step, tread, pace, stride; stride out 277 vb. *move fast*; strut, stalk, prance 871 vb. *be proud*; tiptoe, trip, dance, curvet 312 vb. *leap*; stamp, tramp, goose-step; toddle, patter; stagger, lurch; halt, limp; waddle, straddle; shuffle, dawdle 278 vb. *move slowly*; paddle, wade; foot it, hoof it, stump, hike, plod, trudge, jog; go for a walk, ambulate, perambulate; peripateticize, pace up and down; take the air, take one's constitutional; march, quick march, double, slow-march; file, file off, defile.

ride, mount, back (horse), take horse; trot, amble, tittup, canter, gallop; prance, curvet, piaff, caracol, passage; cycle, bicycle, push-bike, motor-cycle; drive, motor, taxi, cab; take a lift, thumb a l., hitch-hike.

268. Traveller – N. *traveller*, itinerant, wayfarer; voyager 270 n. *mariner*; space-traveller, space-man 271 n. *aeronaut*; pilgrim, palmer, haji; walker, hiker, trekker; globe-trotter, tourist 441 n. *spectator*; tripper, excursionist; holiday-maker, visitor; pioneer, pathfinder, explorer 66 n. *precursor*, roundsman, hawker 794 n. *pedlar*; commercial traveller 793 n. *seller*; passenger, commuter, season-ticket holder.

wanderer, migrant, bird of passage, visitant; floating population, nomad, gypsy, bedouin, rover, ranger, rambler; straggler; stroller; strolling player, wandering minstrel; rolling stone, drifter, vagrant, vagabond, tramp, swagman, sundowner, hobo, bum, landloper; loafer, beachcomber 679 n. *idler*; emigrant, immigrant, émigré 59 n. *foreigner*; refugee, displaced person, D.P.; runaway, fugitive, escapee 620 n. *avoider*; waif, stray, street-arab 801 n. *poor man.*

pedestrian, foot-passenger, walker, hoofer, tramper; pacer; runner; skater, skier; peripatetic; hiker, hitch-h.; marcher, foot-slogger; footman 722 n. *infantry*; noctambulist, somnambulist, sleepwalker; toddler.

rider, horse-rider, cameleer; mahout, horseman, horsewoman, equestrian, equestrienne; postilion, post-boy 531 n. *courier*; cavalier, knight, chivalry 722 n. *cavalry*; jockey, show-jumper 716 n. *contender*; rough-rider, bronco-buster, cowboy, cow-puncher, gaucho, centaur; cyclist, wheelman, pedal-pusher; circus-rider, trick-rider 162 n. *athlete*; back-seat driver; passenger, strap-hanger, commuter.

driver, drover, teamster, muleteer; mahout, cameleer; charioteer, coachman, whip; postilion, post-boy; carter, waggoner, drayman, truckman; cabman, cabby, hackie, jarvey; chauffeur, motorist, scorcher 277 n. *speeder*; joy-rider; taxi-driver, taximan; motorman, engine-driver, shunter; stoker, footplate man; guard, conductor, brakeman.

269. Water travel – N. *water travel*, seafaring, sea service; coasting, gutter-crawling; boating (see *aquatics*); voyage, cruise, sail, steam; course, run, passage, crossing; circumnavigation, periplus 314 n. *circuition*; breath of sea air 685 n. *refreshment*; way, headway, steerage way, sternway, seaway 265 n. *motion*; leeway, driftway 282 n. *deviation*; wake, track, wash, backwash 350 n. *eddy*; sea-path, ocean track, steamer route, sea lane 624 n. *route* 275 n. *ship*; sailor 270 n. *mariner.*

navigation, plane sailing, plain s.; compass reading, dead reckoning 465 n. *measurement*; pilotship, helmsmanship, seamanship 694 n. *skill*; nautical experience, weather eye, sea legs; naval exercises, fleet operations, naval tactics, weather gauge 688 n. *tactics.*

aquatics, water-sports 837 n. *sport*; boating, sailing, yachting, cruising; rowing, sculling, canoeing; water-skiing, aquaplaning, surf-riding; natation, swimming, floating; diving 313 n. *plunge*; wading, paddling; swimsuit 228 n. *beachwear*; bathing machine.

sailing aid, navigational instrument, sextant, quadrant, backstaff; chronometer, ship's c. 117 n. *timekeeper*; log, line, lead, plummet 313 n. *diver*; compass, needle, card, compass c.; binnacle; gyrocompass; radar 689 n. *directorship*; helm, wheel, tiller, rudder, steering oar; sea-mark, buoy, lighthouse, pharos, lightship 547 n. *signpost*; chart, Admiralty c., portolano 551 n. *map*; nautical almanac, ephemeris 524 n. *guide-book.*

Adj. *seafaring*, sea, salty, deep-sea; sailor-like, sailorly 270 adj. *seamanlike*; nautical, naval 275 adj. *marine*; navigational, sailing, steaming, plying, coasting, ferrying; sea-going, ocean-g.; at sea, on the high seas, afloat, water-borne, on board; seaworthy, tight, snug; navigable, boatable.

swimming, natatory, floating; launched, afloat, buoyant; natatorial, aquatic, like a duck.

Vb. *go to sea*, follow the s., join the navy; be in sail, sail before the mast; go sailing, boat, yacht.

voyage, sail, go by sea, take ship, embark, go on board, put to sea, set sail 296 vb. *start out*; cruise, steam, ply, run, tramp, ferry; coast, hug the shore, gutter-crawl.

navigate, man a ship, work a s., crew; put to sea, set sail; launch, push off, boom off; unmoor, cast off, weigh anchor; hoist sail, spread canvas; get under way, carry sail 265 vb. *be in motion*; drop the pilot; set a course, make for, head for; go by the card 281 vb. *orientate*; pilot, steer, hold the helm, captain 689 vb. *direct*; trim the sails, square away; change course, veer, gybe, yaw 282 vb. *deviate*; put about, wear ship; run before the wind, scud 277 vb. *move fast*; put the helm up, fall to leeward, pay off; put the helm down, luff, bring into the wind; beat to windward, tack, weather; round, double a point, circumnavigate 314 vb. *circle*; ride out the storm, weather the s. 667 vb. *escape*; lie to, lay to, heave to; take soundings, heave the lead; tide over 507 vb. *await*; tow, haul, warp, kedge, clubhaul 288 vb. *draw*; ground, run aground, wreck, cast away; sight land, raise, make a landfall 289 vb. *approach*; make port; cast anchor, drop a.; moor, tie up, dock, disembark 295 vb. *land*; cross one's bows, take the wind out of one's sails, gain the weather gauge 702 vb. *obstruct*; foul 279 vb. *collide*; surface, break water 298 vb. *emerge*; flood the tanks, dive 313 vb. *plunge*; shoot, shoot a bridge, shoot the rapids 305 vb. *pass*.

row, ply the oar, get the sweeps out; pull, stroke, scull; feather; punt; paddle, canoe; boat.

swim, float, sail, ride; scud, skim, skitter; surf-ride, surf-board, water-ski, aquaplane; strike out; tread water; dive 313 vb. *plunge*; bathe, dip, duck; wade, paddle 341 vb. *be wet*.

270. Mariner – N. *mariner*, sailor, sailor-man, seaman, seafarer; salt, sea-dog, shellback, tar; shipman, skipper, captain, master mariner, master; mate, boatswain, coxswain; able seaman, A.B.; deckhand, swabbie, lascar; steward, cabin boy 742 n. *servant*; crew, complement 686 n. *personnel*; whaler, deep-sea fisherman; sea-rover, privateer, sea-king, Viking, pirate 789 n. *robber*; sea-scout; argonaut.

navigator, pilot, sailing master, helmsman, steersman, man at the wheel, quartermaster; coxswain, cox 690 n. *leader*; leadsman, look-out man; foretopman, reefer; circumnavigator 314 n. *circler*.

boatman, waterman; rower, rowing man, wet bob; gigsman; galley-slave; oar, oarsman, sculler, punter; yachtsman, yachter; canoer, canoeist; ferryman, gondolier; wherryman, bargee, lighterman; stevedore, docker, longshoreman.

Adj. *seamanlike*, sailorly, like a sailor 694 adj. *expert*; nautical, naval 275 adj. *marine*.

271. Aeronautics – N. *aeronautics*, aeromechanics, aerodynamics, aerostatics; ballooning; rocketry 276 n. *rocket*; volitation, flight; aviation, flying, night f., blind f., instrument f.; aerobatics 875 n. *ostentation*; gliding, planing; spin, roll, side-slip; nose-dive, pull-out; crash-dive, crash, prang 309 n. *descent*; pancake, crash-landing, forced l.

air travel, space t.; air transport, airlift 272 n. *transport*; air service, airline, airways; airlane, air route 624 n. *route*; take off, touch-down, landing; landing ground, airstrip, runway, tarmac, airfield, aerodrome, airport, heliport; terminal, air-t. 295 n. *goal*; hangar 192 n. *stable*.

aeronaut, aerostat, balloonist; glider; parachutist; paratrooper 722 n. *soldier*; aviator, airman, birdman; astronaut, spaceman; air-hostess; flier, flying-man, pilot, air-p., jet-p.; air-crew, navigator, observer, bombardier 722 n. *air force*;

ground staff 686 n. *personnel*; Icarus, Daedalus.

wing, pinion, feathers, wing-feather, wing-spread 259 n. *plumage*; backswept wing, Delta-w., variable w.; aileron, flaps; talaria, winged heels.

Adj. *flying*, on the wing; winged, alar, pinnate, feathered; aerial 340 adj. *airy*; air-worthy, air-borne 308 adj. *ascending*; air-sick; aeronautical, aviational; aerodynamic, aerostatic; aerobatic.

Vb. *fly*, flight, wing, wing one's way, be wafted, cross the sky; soar, rise 308 vb. *ascend*; hover 217 vb. *hang*; flutter; taxi, take off 296 vb. *depart*; glide, plane; stunt, spin, roll, side-slip, loop the loop; hedge-hop, buzz 200 vb. *be near*; stall, dive, nose-d., spiral 313 vb. *plunge*; crash, prang, force-land 309 vb. *tumble*; pull out, flatten o.; touch down 295 vb. *land*; bale out, jump, parachute, hit the silk; orbit, go into o. 314 vb. *circle*.

272. Transference – N. *transference*, change of place, transplantation, trans-shipment, transfer; shift, drift 282 n. *deviation*; translation (to a post), posting, cross-p. 751 n. *mandate*; transposition 151 n. *interchange*; removal, relegation, deportation, expulsion 300 n. *ejection*; unpacking, unloading 188 n. *displacement*; exportation, export 791 n. *trade*; importation, import 299 n. *reception*; transmittal, remittance, dispatch; recall 752 n. *abrogation*; extradition 304 n. *extraction*; recovery, retrieval; delivery, hand-over, take-o.; conveyance 780 n. *transfer*; committal, trust 751 n. *commission*; transition, trajection, ferriage 305 n. *passage*; transmigration, metempsychosis; transmission, throughput; conduction, convection; transfusion, perfusion; decantation; communication, contact 378 n. *touch*; contagion, infection, contamination 178 n. *influence*; helping oneself 788 n. *stealing*.

transport, transportation, vection; conveyance, carriage, waftage, shipment; portage, porterage, haulage, draught 288 n. *traction*; carting, cartage, freightage, air freight, airlift.

thing transferred, carry-over 40 n. *extra*; flotsam, jetsam, driftwood, drift; alluvium, detritus, scree, moraine 53 n. *piece*; sediment, deposit 649 n. *dirt*; pledge, hostage, trust 767 n. *security*; gift, legacy, bequest 781 n. *gift*; cargo, load, payload, freight, consignment, shipment 193 n. *contents*; goods, mails; luggage, baggage, impedimenta; passenger 268 n. *traveller*.

transferrer, transferor, testator, conveyancer 781 n. *giver*; sender, remitter, dispatcher, dispatch clerk, consignor; shipper, transporter; exporter, importer 794 n. *merchant*; conveyor 273 n. *carrier*; post office 531 n. *mails*; communicator, transmitter, diffuser; vector, carrier (of a disease); pipe-line, tap 632 n. *store*; decanter, siphon.

Adj. *transferable*, conveyable, assignable, negotiable, devisable; transportable, movable, portable, carriageable; roadworthy, airworthy, seaworthy; transmissive, conductive; transmissible, communicable; contagious 653 adj. *infectious*.

Vb. *transfer*, hand over, deliver 780 vb. *convey*; devise 780 vb. *bequeath*; commit, assign, entrust 751 vb. *commission*; transmit, hand down, hand on, pass on; make over, turn o., hand to, pass, pass the buck; export, transport 273 vb. *carry*; ferry, set across; put across, put over 524 vb. *communicate*; infect, contaminate 178 vb. *influence*; conduct, convect; transfer itself, come off (e.g. wet paint) 48 vb. *cohere*.

transpose, shift, move 188 vb. *displace*; switch 151 vb. *interchange*; draft, transfer, post, translate; deport, expel 300 vb. *eject*; transfuse, decant, strain off, siphon 300 vb. *void*; unload, remove.

send, remit, transmit, dispatch; ship, rail, truck; direct, consign, address; post, mail; redirect, re-address, post on, forward; send away, detach, detail.

273. Carrier – N. *carrier*, common c., haulier, carter, wagoner, tranter; shipper 272 n. *transferrer*; gondolier, ferryman 270 n. *boatman*; lorry-driver 268 n. *driver*; delivery van 274 n. *vehicle*; freighter, tramp 275 n. *ship*; carrier bag 194 n. *bag*; escalator 274 n. *conveyor*.

bearer, stretcher-b.; caddy, gold-c.; shield-bearer, cup-bearer 742 n. *retainer*; porter, red-cap, coolie; bummaree, stevedore; letter-carrier 531 n. *courier*.

beast of burden, pack-horse, sumpter-horse; ass, donkey, moke, Neddy; sledge-dog, husky; reindeer, llama; camel, dromedary, elephant 365 n. *animal*.

horse, equine species, quadruped, horseflesh; courser, steed; stallion, gelding, mare, colt, filly, foal; stud-horse, brood-mare, stud, stable; roan, grey, bay, chestnut, sorrel, liver-chestnut, black, piebald, skewbald, pinto, paint, dun, palamino, buckskin; dobbin, Rosinante.

thoroughbred, blood-horse, bloodstock; Arab, Barbary horse, barb; pacer, stepper, high-s., trotter; courser, racehorse, racer, goer, stayer; steeplechaser, hurdler, fencer, jumper, hunter.

drafthorse, draught-horse, cart-h., dray-h.; shaft-horse, trace-h.; carriage-horse, post-h.; plough-h., shire-h., punch, Percheron; pit-pony.

war-horse, cavalry h., remount; charger 722 n. *cavalry*; Bucephalus, Bayard, Copenhagen, Marengo, Rosinante.

saddle-horse, riding-h., mount, hack, roaster; pony, cob; jade, tit, screw, nag; pad-nag, pad, ambler; mustang, bronco; palfrey, genet; riding mule, alborak.

Adj. *bearing*, carrier, shouldering, burdened, freighted, loaded, overloaded, hag-ridden; pick-a-back.

equine, horsy, horse-faced; roan, grey (see *horse*); asinine; mulish.

Vb. *carry*, bear 218 vb. *support*; hump, heave, tote; caddy; stoop one's back to, shoulder; fetch and carry, trant; transport, cart, vehicle, truck, rail, railroad; ship, waft, raft; lift, fly 272 vb. *transfer*; traject, ferry; have a rider, be ridden, be mounted.

274. Vehicle – N. *vehicle*, conveyance, transport, vehicular traffic; sedan-chair,

palanquin, litter; stretcher, hurdle, crate; hearse; tractor, tracked vehicle; hobbyhorse.

sled, sledge, sleigh; bob-sleigh, toboggan, luge, coaster, ice-yacht; skate, iceskate; snowshoes, skis, runners.

bicycle, velocipede, cycle, pedal-c., bike, push-b., safety-bicycle, safety, sit-up-and-beg, tandem; penny-farthing, bone-breaker; monocycle, unicycle, tricycle, quadricycle; moped; scooter, motor-cycle; motorcycle combination, side-car; invalid carriage; cycle-rickshaw.

pushcart, perambulator, pram, baby-carriage, kiddy-cart, bassinet; Bathchair, wheel-c., invalid-c.; jinricksha, rickshaw; barrow, wheel-b., hand-b., coster-b.; hand-cart; trolley, lawn-mower, grass-cutter.

cart, ox-c., bullock-c., hackery; horse-and-cart, horse-cart, dog-c., gig; van, furniture-v., removal-v., pantechnicon; dray, milkfloat; farm-cart, hay-wagon; wain, wagon, covered w., prairie-schooner, Cape-cart; caravan, trailer; limber, gun-carriage; tumbril, dead-cart, dust-c.

carriage, horse-c., equipage, turn-out, rig; chariot, coach, state c., coach and four; riding-carriage, landau, landau-lette, berlin, victoria, brougham, barouche, phaeton, clarence, sociable, coupé; surrey, buckboard, buggy, wagonette; travelling carriage, chaise, shay, calashe, droshky, kibitzka, tarantass; racing chariot, quadriga; four-in-hand, drag, tally-ho, brake, char-à-banc; two-wheeler, cabriolet, curricle, tilbury, whiskey, whitechapel, vis-à-vis, outside car, jaunting-c., beachwagon; ekka, tonga, hackery; trap, gig, pony-cart, dog-c., governess-c.; carriole, sulky, désobligeant; shandrydan, rattle-trap; house on wheels, caravan, trailer, house-t. 192 n. *small house*.

war-chariot, scythed c., weapon carrier; gun-carriage, caisson, limber, ammunition wagon; tank, armoured car 722 n. *cavalry*; jeep, staff car.

stage-coach, stage-wagon, stage, tally-ho, mail-coach, mail-phaeton;

diligence, post-chaise, omnibus, horse-bus. See *bus*.

cab, hackney-carriage, horse-cab, four-wheeler, growler, hansom, fly; fiacre, droshky, thika-gharry; taxi-cab, taxi; rickshaw.

bus, horse-b., steam-b., motor-b.; omnibus, double-decker, single-d.; autobus, trolley-bus, motor-coach, coach.

tram, horse-t., tram-car, trolley-c., trolley, street-car, cable-c.

automobile, horseless carriage, motorcar; motor, auto, car; limousine, landaulette, sedan, saloon, hard-top, open-car, tourer, sports car, racing c.; convertible; coupé, two-seater, two-door, four-door; jeep; roadster, runabout; station-wagon, beachwagon, estate-car, shooting-brake; motor-van, lorry, truck, bowser, tanker; flivver, model-T, tin Lizzie; rattletrap, old crock, bus, jalopy; hotrod, souped-up car; autocar, tricar; bubblecar, minicar.

train, railway train, boat-t., corridor t.; express train, through t.; stopping train, local t., omnibus t., passenger t., workmen's t., goods t., freight t., milk t., mail t.; Pullman, wagon-lit, sleeping-car, sleeper; club-car, observation c.; restaurant car, dining c., diner; smoker, non-smoker, ladies only; rolling stock, coach, car, carriage, compartment, coupé; caboose; brake-van, guard's v., brake, luggage van; truck, goods t., flat-car, freight c.; bogie; railway, railroad, railway line, line, track, rails, sleepers, fish-plate; underground, tube, metro, subway; elevator, monorail, funicular.

locomotive, steam-engine, pony-e., shunter, tanker; choo-choo, puff-puff, puffer; traction engine, steam-roller; diesel.

conveyor; conveyor belt, escalator, moving staircase, travolator, moving pavement.

shovel, spoon, spatula 194 n. *ladle*; spade, spud, spaddle, hoe, trowel, hod; pitchfork, hay-fork; knife and fork, chop-sticks.

Adj. *vehicular*, wheeled, on wheels; on rails, on runners, on sleds, on skates; automobile, automotive, loco-motive.

275. Ship – N. *ship*, vessel, boat, craft; great ship, tall s.; little ship, cockboat, cockle-shell; bottom, keel, sail; tub, hull; hulk, prison-ship; Argo, Ark, Noah's Ark; steamer, steamship, motor-ship; paddle-boat, stern-wheeler, river-boat, showboat; liner; ferry, train-f.; deck unit; mail-ship, packet; dredger, hopper; transport, storeship, tender, escort vessel; pilot vessel; tug, launch; lightship, cable-s.; cog, galleon, dromond, carrack, caravel, gallivat, grab, junk; submarine 722 n. *warship*; fireship.

galley, war-g., galley-foist, foist, galliass, galliot, lymphad; catur; pirate-ship, Viking-s., corsair; penteconter, bireme, trireme, quadrireme, quinquereme.

merchant ship, merchantman, merchant, trader; cog, galleon, argosy, levanter, dromond, carrack, polacca; caraval, galliot; Indiaman; cargo-boat, freighter, tramp; coaster, hoy, crumster, bilander, hooker; collier, tanker; banana-boat, tea-clipper; slaver, slave-ship.

fishing-boat, whaler, sealer, trawler, dogger, drifter, dory, fishing smack, herring-fisher, trow, buss, coble.

sailing-ship, sailboat, sailer; wind-jammer, clipper, ship, tall s., full-rigged s., square-rigged s., fore-and-aft-rigged s., schooner-rigged s., lateen-rigged s.; bark, barque, barquentine; brig, brigantine, schooner, pinnace; frigate, sloop, corvette 722 n. *warship*; cutter, ketch, yawl, lugger; xebec, felucca, caique, dhow, gallivat, junk, sampan; sailing barge, smack, hoy, hooker; yacht, skiff.

sail, sail-cloth, canvas; square sail, lug-s., lug, lateen-s., fore-and-aft s., leg-of-mutton s., spanker; course, mainsail, main-course, foresail, fore-course; topsail, topgallant s., royal, skysail; jib, staysail, spinnaker, balloon-s., studding-s., stud-s., boomsail.

boat, skiff, cockle-shell, foldboat, cockboat; lifeboat; ship's boat, long-b., jolly-b., fly-b., bumboat; picket boat, pinnace; cutter, gig, whale-g.; barge, trow, lighter; state-barge, bucentaur; wherry, ferry-boat; towboat tug; launch, motorboat, motor launch, cris-craft, speedboat, cabin-cruiser; yacht, pleasure boat; house boat, budge-row.

rowboat, rowing boat, galley; eight, racing e.; sculler, shell, funny, randan; dinghy; outrigger, punt, gondola, cora-cle, currach; canoe, trow; dug-out; piragua, proa, prahu, kayak, umiak.

raft, balsa r., float, log, catamaran, jangada.

shipping, craft; argosy, fleet, flotilla, squadron 722 n. *navy*; marine, mercan-tile marine, merchant navy, shipping line.

Adj. *marine*, maritime, naval, nautical, sea-going, ocean-g. 269 adj. *seafaring*; sea-worthy, water-w., weatherly; snug, tight, shipshape; rigged, square-r. (see N. *sailing-ship*); clinker-built, cruiser-b., flush-decked.

276. Aircraft – N. *aircraft*, 271 n. *aero-nautics*; aerodyne, flying machine, heavier-than-air m.; aeroplane, plane, monoplane, biplane, triplane; hydro-plane, sea-plane, flying-boat; warplane, fighter, bomber 722 n. *air force*; strato-cruiser, jet-plane, jet, turbo-j., turbo-prop; helicopter, autogiro, rotodyne; hovercraft; glider, sailplane; flying in-struments, controls, joystick, rudder, tail, wings, flaps, aileron; cockpit, cat-walk, under-carriage, landing gear; parachute, ejector-seat; flight simu-lator; aerodrome 271 n. *air travel*.

airship, aerostat, balloon, gas-b., fire-b.; captive balloon, observation b., blimp; dirigible, Zeppelin; kite, box-k.; parachute; magic carpet; balloon-basket, nacelle, car, gondola.

rocket, rocketry, sky-rocket; guided missile, intercontinental ballistic m. 723 n. *missile weapon*; doodlebug, V2.

space-ship, flying saucer; satellite, artificial s., sputnik, arknik, lunik; com-munications satellite, radio-mirror, echo balloon; space-station.

Adj. *aviational*, aeronautical, aero-dynamic, aerostatic; balloonistic, astro-nautical 271 adj. *flying*; air-worthy.

277. Velocity – N. *velocity*, celerity, rapidity, swiftness, quickness, liveliness; instantaneousness 116 n. *instantaneity*; promptness, expedition, dispatch; speed, tempo, rate, pace, bat 265 n. *motion*; speed-rate, miles per hour, ton, knots; maximum speed, full s., full steam; pre-cipitation, hurry 680 n. *haste*; type of speed, streak, flash; lightning, greased l.; speed measurement, velocimeter, tacho-meter, speedometer 465 n. *gauge*; speed-trap 542 n. *trap*.

spurt, acceleration, speed-up, over-taking; burst, impetus, charge; jump, spring, bound, pounce 312 n. *leap*; whizz, swoop, swoosh, uprush, zoom; down rush, dive, power-d.; flying start, rush, dash, scamper, run, sprint, gallop.

speeding, hard driving, overdriving; scorching, racing; course, race, career, full c.; full speed, full lick, full bat; pace, smart p., spanking rate; forced march, post-haste 680 n. *haste*; race-course, speed-track 716 n. *racing*.

speeder, hustler, speed merchant, ton-up, scorcher, racing-driver, Jehu 268 n. *driver*; runner, racer; galloper, jockey; courser, racehorse 273 n. *thoroughbred*; greyhound, hunting leopard; hare, deer; arrow 287 n. *missile*; rocket; clipper 275 n. *ship*; express 531 n. *courier*; magic carpet, seven-league boots.

Adj. *speedy*, swift, fast, quick, rapid; dashing, lively, smart, snappy, zippy; expeditious, hustling 680 adj. *hasty*; prompt 135 adj. *early*; immediate 116 adj. *instantaneous*; high-speed, stream-lined; runaway, tempestuous, break-neck, headlong, precipitate 857 adj. *rash*; fleet, light-footed; agile, nimble, winged, arrowy; like a flash, like the wind, quick as lightning, quick as thought, like a bat out of hell; meteoric, electric, transonic, supersonic, hypersonic.

Vb. *move fast*, move, shift, travel, speed; drive, pelt, streak, flash, flare, scorch; do a ton; scud, careen; skim, nip, cut; bowl along 258 vb. *go smoothly*;

sweep, tear, rip, zip, rush, dash; fly, wing, whizz, hurtle; zoom, dive; run, trot, double, lope, gallop; bolt, scoot, scurry 620 vb. *run away*; hare, run like mad; start, dart; pounce 312 vb. *leap*; ride, spur, put one's best foot forward, step out; hurry, post 680 vb. *hasten*; charge, career, go full pelt.

accelerate, raise the tempo, spurt, sprint, put on speed, pick up s., step on it, crowd canvas; mend one's pace, get a move on; make up time, make forced marches; quicken, drive, spur, urge on, lend wings to, expedite 680 vb. *hasten*.

outstrip, overtake, overhaul, catch up, lap, outpace, outrun, outmarch, outsail, outwalk, outdrive; lead, head, gain on, distance, outdistance, leave behind, leave standing; make the running, have the legs of, romp home, win the race 34 vb. *be superior*.

Adv. *swiftly* etc. adj.; trippingly, apace; post haste, full tilt; in full career, all out, flat out, ventre à terre; helter-skelter, headlong; like a shot, like an arrow, in double-quick time, nineteen to the dozen; by leaps and bounds.

278. Slowness – **N.** *slowness*, slackness, languor 679 n. *sluggishness*; deliberation, tentativeness, gradualism, Fabianism; hesitation 858 n. *caution*; reluctance 598 n. *unwillingness*; go-slow 145 n. *strike*; deceleration, retardation, drag 333 n. *friction*; brake, curb 747 n. *restraint*; leisureliness, no hurry, easy stages 681 n. *leisure*; slow motion, slow march, dead m.; slow pace, foot-p., snail's p., lag.

slowcoach, snail, slug, tortoise; stopping train, omnibus t.; dawdler, loiterer, lingerer, slow starter, non-starter, laggard, sloucher 679 n. *idler*.

Adj. *slow*, go-slow; slow-paced, andante, low-geared, slow-motion; snail-like, tortoise-l.; slow-moving 695 adj. *clumsy*; dilatory 136 adj. *late*; long about it, unhurried 681 adj. *leisurely*; deliberate 823 adj. *patient*; hesitant 858 adj. *cautious*; tentative 461 adj. *experi-*

mental; languid 679 adj. *lazy*; gradual, imperceptible, stealthy.

Vb. *move slowly*, go slow, amble, crawl, creep, inch; ooze, drip, trickle 350 vb. *flow*; shamble, slouch, shuffle; plod, trudge, lumber; totter, stagger; struggle, chug, jolt, bump, creak; halt, limp, hobble, go lame, drag, flag, falter 684 vb. *be fatigued*; trail, lag, fall behind 284 vb. *follow*; drag one's feet 598 vb. *be loth*; tarry, linger, take one's time 136 vb. *be late*; stroll, saunter, dawdle 267 vb. *walk*; grope 461 vb. *be tentative*; hesitate 858 vb. *be cautious*; drawl 580 vb. *stammer*.

decelerate, slow down, lose momentum, reduce speed; smell the ground (of ships); ease off 145 vb. *pause*.

retard, check, curb, rein in, throttle down 177 vb. *moderate*; reef, shorten sail 269 vb. *navigate*; brake 747 vb. *restrain*; back-pedal, back-water 286 vb. *regress*; handicap, clip the wings 702 vb. *hinder*.

Adv. *slowly* etc. adj.; lazily, sluggishly; at a snail's p., at a funeral p.; slower than molasses; in slow time, adagio, largo.

gradatim, gradually etc. adj.; by degrees, little by little, bit by bit, inch by inch, step by step, by easy stages.

279. Impulse – **N.** *impulse*, impulsion, pressure; impetus, momentum; boost 174 n. *stimulant*; drive, thrust, push, shove, heave; batting (cricket); throw 287 n. *propulsion*; lunge, riposte, kick; percussion, beat 403 n. *roll*; ramming, butt (see *collision*); concussion, shock, impact; slam, bang; tap 378 n. *touch*; shake, rattle, jolt, jerk, wrench 318 n. *agitation*; transmission (mechanics); mechanics, dynamics.

collision, head-on c., frontal c.; scrape 333 n. *friction*; clash 14 n. *contrariety*; cannon, carambole; impact, bump, shock, crash, smash, encounter, meeting; brunt, charge 712 n. *attack*; collision course 293 n. *convergence*; pile-up 74 n. *accumulation*.

hammer, sledge-h., sledge; hammer-head, peen; punch; bat, beetle, maul, mall, mallet; flail; knocker, door-k.; cudgel 723 n. *club*; pestle, anvil.

ram, battering-r., bulldozer; pile-driver, monkey; ramrod; rammer, tamper, tamp, stemmer; cue, billiard c., pusher; shover.

knock, dint, dent 255 n. *concavity*; rap, tap, clap; dab, pat, fillip, flip, flick; nudge, dig 547 n. *gesture*; blow, stroke (see Vb. *strike*); hit, crack, cut, drive (cricket); punch, left, right, straight left, uppercut, jab, hook; haymaker, swipe; stamp, kick; whap, swat; spanking, etc. (see Vb. *strike*); rain of blows, hiding 963 n. *corporal punishment*; assault 712 n. *attack*; fisticuffs, cut and thrust, hammer and tongs 61 n. *turmoil*; innings (cricket).

Adj. *impelling* etc. vb., impellent, impulsive; dynamic, thrustful.

Vb. *impel*, fling 287 vb. *propel*; give an impetus, impart momentum; slam, bang 264 vb. *close*; press, push, thrust, shove; ram, tamp; boom, punt; prod, urge, spur 277 vb. *accelerate*; fillip, flip, flick; jerk 318 vb. *agitate*; shoulder, elbow 282 vb. *deflect*; expel 300 vb. *eject*; frog-march; goad 612 vb. *incite*; drive, start, run 173 vb. *operate*.

collide, make impact 378 vb. *touch*; impinge 306 vb. *encroach*; come into collision 293 vb. *converge*; meet, encounter, clash; ram, butt, bunt, batter, dint, dent; batter at, bulldoze; bump into, run over; graze 333 vb. *rub*; foul, fall foul of; run against 712 vb. *charge*; bark one's shins, stub one's toe; trip 309 vb. *tumble*.

strike, smite, hit, land *or* plant a blow; hit out at, lunge, swing, flail, beat the air; slam, bang, knock; floor 311 vb. *fell*; pat, flip, tickle; tap, rap, clap; slap, smack, skelp; cuff, clump, clout, box the ears; box, spar 716 vb. *fight*; buffet, punch, thump, whack, rain blows, pummel, trounce, belabour, beat up; pound, batter 332 vb. *pulverize*; biff, bash, slosh, sock, slug, cosh, cudgel, club; sandbag, brain, crown; concuss, stun, knock out; spank, paddle, thrash, beat, whip, cane 963 vb. *flog*; dust, tan, hide, leather, strap 963 vb. *punish*; hammer, thresh, flail; flap, squash, swat 216 vb. *flatten*; scratch, maul 655 vb. *wound*; run through 263 vb. *pierce*; tear 46 vb. *cut*; stone, pelt, snowball 712 vb. *lapidate*; head (a football); bat, strike a ball, swipe, drive, turn, glance, cut, crack, lift (at cricket); smash, volley (tennis).

kick, spurn, boot, knee, calcitrate; trample, tread on, stamp on, kneel on; ride over, ride roughshod; spur, dig in one's heels; heel, punt, dribble, shoot (a football).

280. Recoil – N. *recoil*, revulsion, revulsion of feeling; reaction, repercussion, reverberation, echo 404 n. *resonance*; reflex 417 n. *reflection*; kick, kick-back, back-lash; ricochet, cannon; rebound, bounce, spring, springboard 328 n. *elasticity*; swing-back, swing of the pendulum 317 n. *oscillation*; return (at tennis), boomerang; rebuff 292 n. *repulsion*; reactionary, reactionist.

Adj. *recoiling*, recalcitrant, repercussive, revulsive; reactionary 148 adj. *reverted*.

Vb. *recoil*, react 182 vb. *counteract*; shrink, wince, flinch 620 vb. *avoid*; recalcitrate, kick back; ricochet, cannon off; uncoil, spring back, rebound; have repercussions; boomerang 714 vb. *retaliate*.

281. Direction – N. *direction*, bearing, compass reading 186 n. *bearings*; lie of the land 186 n. *situation*; orientation, collimation, alignment; set, drift 350 n. *current*; tenor 179 n. *tendency*; course, tack, line, track 624 n. *route*; steering, aim, target 295 n. *goal*; compass 269 n. *sailing aid*; collimator, sights 442 n. *optical device*; fingerpost 547 n. *signpost*; direction-finder, range f. 465 n. *gauge*.

compass point, cardinal points, half points, quarter points; quarter, north, east, south, west; magnetic north; rhumb, azimuth, line of collimation.

Adj. *directed* etc. vb.; orientated, signposted; well-directed, well-placed; bound for 617 adj. *intending*; cross-country, axial, diagonal 220 adj. *oblique*; direct, one-way 249 adj. *straight*; northern, northerly, southerly, meridional; western, occidental; eastern, oriental; 240 adj. *opposite*.

Vb. *orientate*, orientate oneself, box the compass, take one's bearings, shoot the sun; have a direction, bear; direct, show the way, signpost 547 vb. *indicate*; pinpoint 187 vb. *place*.

aim, level, point; take aim, aim at; train one's sights, draw a bead on, level at; collimate, sight, set one's sights.

Adv. *towards*, versus, facing; on the road to; through, via, by way of; straight, direct, point blank; as the crow flies; upstream, downstream; upwind, downwind; against the w., in the wind's eye, hither, thither; clockwise, anticlockwise, counter-clockwise, widdershins.

282. Deviation – N. *deviation*, disorientation, misdirection, wrong course, wrong turning; aberration, aberrancy, deflection; exorbitation, short circuit; diversion, digression, tangent; departure, declension 220 n. *obliquity*; swerve 248 n. *curvature*; divarication 294 n. *divergence*; deviousness, detour, bypath 626 n. *circuit*; lapse 495 n. *error*; drift, leeway; passaging, crab-walk, sidestep, sideslip; break, googly (cricket).

Adj. *deviating*, aberrant, deviant 84 adj. *unconformable*; eccentric, off-centre; excursive, out of orbit, tangential; errant 267 adj. *travelling*; undirected, unguided, random, erratic 495 adj. *inexact*; disorientated, off-course, offbeam, lost, astray; misdirected, misaimed, off-target, wide; devious, roundabout 314 adj. *circuitous*; indirect, zigzag 220 adj. *oblique*.

Vb. *deviate*, leave the straight, digress; divaricate 294 vb. *diverge*; turn, filter, turn a corner, swerve; step aside, alter course, change direction, yaw, tack; veer, back (wind); bend, curve; lurch, stagger, zigzag 251 vb. *meander*; sidle, passage; slide, skid, sideslip; glance, fly off at a tangent 220 vb. *be oblique*; shy, jib, sidestep 620 vb. *avoid*.

stray, err, ramble, rove, drift, divagate, straggle 267 vb. *wander*; lose the way, get lost, lose one's bearings; lose track of, lose the thread 456 vb. *be inattentive*.

deflect, bend, crook 220 vb. *render oblique*; put off the scent, misdirect 495 vb. *mislead*; avert 713 vb. *parry*; divert, draw aside, bias, put screw on (billiards); slice, pull, shank (golf); hook, glance, bowl a break, bowl wide (cricket); sidetrack, sidestep.

283. Precession: going before – N. *precession*, 119 n. *priority*, 64 n. *precedence*; prevention, queue-jumping; leading, heading, flying start; pride of place; lead, leading role 34 n. *superiority*; pioneer 66 n. *precursor*; van, vanguard 237 n. *front*.

Adj. *foremost*, first; leading etc. vb.

Vb. *precede*, go before, forerun, herald; usher in, introduce; head, lead; clear the way, lead the w. 689 vb. *direct*; take the lead, steal a march, get in front, jump the queue; get ahead of, lap 277 vb. *outstrip*; be beforehand 135 vb. *be early*; take precedence 64 vb. *come before*.

Adv. *ahead*, before, in advance, in the van.

284. Following: going after – N. *following*, 65 n. *sequence*; run, suit 71 n. *series*; one after another, O.D.T.A.A.; subsequence 120 n. *posterity*; pursuance 619 n. *chase*; succession, reversion 780 n. *transfer*; last place 238 n. *rear*.

follower, attendant, hanger-on, dangler, client 742 n. *dependant*; train, tail, wake, cortège, suite; following, party, adherent, supporter 707 n. *auxiliary*; satellite, moon; tender 275 n. *ship*.

Adj. *following*, subsequent 65 adj. *sequent*.

Vb. *follow*, succeed, follow on; sit on one's tail, tread on the heels of, tread in the steps of 65 vb. *come after*; tag after, attend, wait on 742 vb. *serve*; dog, shadow, trail, tail, track 619 vb. *pursue*; drop behind, lag, trail 278 vb. *move* *slowly*; bring up the rear 238 vb. *be behind*.

285. Progression: motion forwards –
N. *progression*, arithmetical p. 71 n. *series*; march, course, career; march of time 111 n. *course of time*; progress, stride, leaps and bounds 277 n. *spurt*; gain, advance, headway 654 n. *improvement*; overtaking 306 n. *overstepping*; next step, development, evolution; furtherance, promotion, advancement, preferment; progressiveness, 'onward and upward department' 654 n. *reformism*; enterprise, go-getting 672 n. *undertaking*; achievement 727 n. *success*; progressive, improver 654 n. *reformer*; go-getter, coming man 730 n. *made man*.

Adj. *progressive*, enterprising, go-getting, forward-looking, reformist; advancing etc. vb.; unbroken, irreversible; advanced, up-to-date 126 adj. *modern*.

Vb. *progress*, proceed 265 vb. *be in motion*; advance, come on, develop 316 vb. *evolve*; show promise 654 vb. *improve*; get on 730 vb. *prosper*; march on 146 vb. *go on*; move with the times 126 vb. *modernize*; never look back, hold one's lead; press on 680 vb. *hasten*; start well, break the back of; gain ground, make headway, make strides 277 vb. *move fast*; get ahead, forge a.; gain on, outdistance 277 vb. *outstrip*; recover 31 vb. *recoup*.

promote, further, contribute to, advance 703 vb. *aid*; prefer, move up, raise, lift, bounce up, jump up 310 vb. *elevate*; bring forward, force, develop 36 vb. *augment*; favour, make for, bring on, conduce 156 vb. *cause*.

Adv. *forward*, onward, forth, on, ahead; progressively, by leaps and bounds; in progress, in sight of.

286. Regression: motion backwards –
N. *regression*, regress, infinite r.; retrogression, retrogradation, backward step 148 n. *reversion*; retreat, withdrawal, retirement, disengagement 290 n. *recession*; reversing, backing; falling away, decline 655 n. *deterioration*.

return, remigration, homeward journey; home-coming 295 n. *arrival*; turn of the tide, reflux, refluence, ebb, regurgitation 350 n. *current*; relapse, backsliding, recidivation 603 n. *tergiversation*; U-turn, volte-face, about-turn 148 n. *reversion*; turning point 137 n. *crisis*.

Adj. *regressive*, retrogressive, retrograde, backward; backward-looking, retrospective; reactionary 280 adj. *recoiling*; backing, anticlockwise, counterclockwise; reverse, reversible 148 adj. *reverted*; homing, homeward-bound.

Vb. *regress*, recede, retrogress, retrograde, retrocede; retreat, retire 290 vb. *recede*, 620 vb. *run away*; disengage, back out, back down 753 vb. *resign*; give ground, lose g.; fall behind 278 vb. *move slowly*; reverse, back, go backwards, back-water; not hold, slip back; ebb, slump, fall, drop, decline 309 vb. *descend*.

turn back, put b., retrace one's steps; remigrate, go back, home, return 148 vb. *revert*; look back, look over one's shoulder, hark back 505 vb. *retrospect*; veer round, wheel r., about face, execute a volte-face 603 vb. *tergiversate*; double back, counter-march.

Adv. *backwards*, back, astern, in reverse; back to where one started.

287. Propulsion – N. *propulsion*, drive; impulsion, push 279 n. *impulse*; projection, precipitation; defenestration 300 n. *ejection*; cast, throw, chuck, toss, pitch and t.; fling, shy, cock-shy; pot-shot, pot, shot; discharge, volley 712 n. *bombardment*; bowling, full toss, yorker, lob (cricket); kick, punt, dribble (football); stroke, drive, swipe 279 n. *knock*; pull, slice (golf); service, return, rally, volley, kill, smash (tennis); ballistics, gunnery, musketry; archery, toxophily; marksmanship 694 n. *skill*.

missile, projectile, shell, rocket; cannon-ball 723 n. *ammunition*; brickbat, stone; arrow, dart 723 n. *missile weapon*; ball, football, leather; quoit, discus; javelin, hammer, caber.

propellant, thrust, driving force, jet,

steam 160 n. *energy*; thruster, pusher, shover; lever, pedal ; oar, sweep, paddle; screw, blade, paddle-wheel, propeller; coal, petrol, oil 385 n. *fuel*; gunpowder 723 n. *explosive*; rifle, revolver 723 n. *firearm*, 723 n. *pistol*, 723 n. *toy gun*; blow-pipe, pea-shooter; catapult 723 n. *missile weapon*.

shooter, gunman, rifleman, musketeer, pistoleer; gunner, gun-layer; archer, bowman, toxophilite, slinger 722 n. *soldier*; gun, marksman, sharpshooter, sniper, shot 696 n. *proficient*.

thrower, launcher, slinger; bowler, pitcher, curler; server, striker (tennis); pitchfork; projector.

Adj. *propulsive*, propellant, propelling etc. vb., expulsive, explosive; propelled etc. vb.

Vb. *propel*, launch, project; flight, throw, cast, heave, pitch, toss, cant, chuck, shy; bowl, lob, york; hurl, fling, sling, catapult; dart, flick; pelt, stone, shower, snowball 712 vb. *lapidate*; precipitate, send flying, defenestrate; pitchfork 300 vb. *eject*; blow away, blow up, fulminate; serve, return, volley, smash, kill (tennis); bat, slog; sky, loft; drive, cut, pull, hook, glance (cricket); shank, slice 279 vb. *strike*; kick, dribble, punt (football); push 279 vb. *impel*; wheel, pedal, roll, bowl, trundle 315 vb. *rotate*; sweep, drive like leaves.

shoot, fire, open fire, volley; discharge, let off, bombard 712 vb. *fire at*; snipe, pot at; pepper 263 vb. *pierce*.

288. Traction – N. *traction*, drawing etc. vb., pulling back, retractiveness, retraction; towage, haulage; draught, pull, haul; tug, tow; tow-line, tow-rope; drawer, puller, hauler; retractor; windlass 310 n. *lifter*; tug, tugboat 275 n. *ship*; tractor, traction engine; loadstone 291 n. *magnet*; strain, tug of war 716 n. *contest*; thing drawn, trailer, train.

Adj. *drawing* etc. vb., tractive, retractive, retractile, retractable; magnetic 291 adj. *attracting*; tractile, ductile; drawn, horse-d.

Vb. *draw*, pull, haul, hale, trice; warp,

kedge 269 vb. *navigate*; tug, tow, take in tow; lug, drag, train, trail, trawl; rake; wind in, wind up; pull out 304 vb. *extract*; pull towards 291 vb. *attract*; pull back, retract.

289. Approach: motion towards – **N.** *approach*, near approach, approximation, appulse 200 n. *nearness*; afflux 350 n. *stream*; confluence 293 n. *convergence*; onset, advent, coming 295 n. *arrival*; advances, overture 759 n. *offer*; accessibility, approaches 624 n. *access*.

Adj. *approaching*, nearing, getting warm etc. vb.; close, approximative 200 adj. *near*; meeting 293 adj. *convergent*; imminent 155 adj. *impending*; oncoming 295 adj. *arriving*.

accessible, approachable, get-at-able; within reach, attainable 469 adj. *possible*; available, obtainable 189 adj. *on the spot*; wayside, roadside, near-by 200 adj. *near*; welcoming, inviting 291 adj. *attracting*.

Vb. *approach*, approximate, verge on; appropinquate 200 vb. *be near*; come closer, meet 293 vb. *converge*; near, draw n., step up to, sidle up to; roll up 74 vb. *congregate*; accost 884 vb. *greet*; incline, trend 179 vb. *tend*; advance upon, bear down on 712 vb. *attack*; close, close in 232 vb. *circumscribe*; gain upon, catch up with, overtake 277 vb. *outstrip*; follow hard, narrow the gap, run one close 295 vb. *land*; accede, adhere, join 38 vb. *accrue*.

290. Recession: motion from – **N.** *recession*, retirement, withdrawal, retreat 286 n. *regression*; leak 298 n. *outflow*; emigration, evacuation 296 n. *departure*; flight 667 n. *escape*.

Adj. *receding* etc. vb.; retreating 286 adj. *regressive*.

Vb. *recede*, retire, withdraw, fall back, draw b., retreat 286 vb. *regress*; ebb, subside, shrink 37 vb. *decrease*; go, leave, evacuate, emigrate 296 vb. *depart*; leak out 298 vb. *flow out*; move off, stand off, put space between, widen the gap; stand aside, make way, sheer off

282 vb. *deviate*; back away, flinch 620 vb. *avoid*; flee 620 vb. *run away*; go back 286 vb. *turn back*.

291. Attraction – N. *attraction*, adduction, pull, drag, tug; magnetization, magnetism, force of gravity; itch for 859 n. *desire*; affinity, sympathy; attractiveness, appeal, allure 612 n. *inducement*; charmer 612 n. *motivator*; draw, centre of attraction, cynosure 890 n. *favourite*.

magnet, bar m.; coil magnet, solenoid; magnetite, siderite, loadstone; lodestar 520 n. *guide*; magnetizer.

Adj. *attracting* etc. vb.; attractive, magnetic, magnetized; centripetal.

Vb. *attract*, magnetize, pull, drag, tug 288 vb. *draw*; adduct, exercise a pull; appeal, lure, allure, bait 612 vb. *tempt*; decoy 542 vb. *ensnare*.

292. Repulsion – N. *repulsion*, repellance; repulsive force, centrifugal f.; repulsiveness 842 n. *ugliness*; reflection 280 n. *recoil*; repulse, rebuff 607 n. *rejection*.

Adj. *repellent*, repelling etc. vb.; repulsive 842 adj. *ugly*; off-putting, antipathetic 861 adj. *disliked*; centrifugal.

Vb. *repel*, push away, butt a., repulse, beat off, fend off 713 vb. *parry*; dispel 75 vb. *disperse*; turn away, reflect 282 vb. *deflect*; rebuff, snub, brush off 607 vb. *reject*; hold off, keep at arm's length; put off 861 vb. *cause dislike*.

293. Convergence – N. *convergence*, mutual approach 289 n. *approach*; narrowing gap; collision course 279 n. *collision*; concourse, confluence, conflux, meeting 45 n. *junction*; pincer movement 232 n. *circumscription*; centring, corradiation, focalization 76 n. *focus*; tapering, taper 206 n. *narrowness*; convergent view, perspective, vanishing point 438 vb. *view*.

Adj. *convergent*, converging etc. vb.; focused; centripetal, confluent, concurrent; asymptotical, tangential; pointed, tapering, conical, pyramidal.

Vb. *converge*, narrow the gap; fall in with 295 vb. *meet*; unite, gather, roll up 74 vb. *congregate*; intercept, head off, close in 232 vb. *circumscribe*; pinch, nip 198 vb. *make smaller*; concentrate, corradiate, focus; toe in; centre, centre on 225 vb. *centralize*; taper, come to a point 206 vb. *be narrow*.

294. Divergence – N. *divergence*, centrifugence, divarication; spread, deployment 75 n. *dispersion*; parting of the ways, fork, bifurcation 222 n. *crossing*; radiation, ramification; rays, spokes.

Adj. *divergent*, diverging etc. vb.; divaricate, separated; radiating, radiant; centrifugal.

Vb. *diverge*, radiate, star; ramify, branch out; fork, bifurcate; part ways 46 vb. *be disjoined*; glance off, fly off at a tangent 282 vb. *deviate*; deploy, fan out, spread, scatter 75 vb. *be dispersed*; divaricate, straddle; spread-eagle; splay.

295. Arrival – N. *arrival*, coming, advent, accession 289 n. *approach*, 189 n. *presence*; onset 68 n. *beginning*; landfall, landing, touch-down, docking, mooring; disembarkation 298 n. *egress*; last lap, home stretch; meeting; home-coming 286 n. *return*; reception, welcome 876 n. *celebration*; visitor, homing pigeon 297 n. *incomer*.

goal, 617 n. *objective*; bourne 192 n. *home*; terminus, journey's end 69 n. *end*; billet, resting place; port, harbour, haven, anchorage, roadstead 662 n. *shelter*; dock, berth 192 n. *stable*; airport 271 n. *air travel*; rendezvous.

Adj. *arriving* etc. vb.; homing, homeward-bound; terminal; nearing 289 adj. *approaching*, 155 adj. *impending*.

Vb. *arrive*, come, reach, fetch up at, get there; make land, sight, raise; make port, dock, berth, tie up, moor, drop anchor (see *land*); unharness, unhitch, outspan; home, come h. 286 vb. *regress*; hit, make, win to, gain. attain; enter, show up, pop up, turn up, drop in 882 vb. *visit*; put in, stop at, stop over, break journey 145 vb. *pause*; clock in 135 vb. *be early*; come to hand.

land, beach, ground, touch down, make a landing; disembark 298 vb. *emerge*; surrender one's ticket, detrain, debus; get down, alight, perch 309 vb. *descend*; dismount, set foot to ground.

meet, join, rejoin, see again; greet, welcome 882 vb. *be sociable*; go to meet, keep a date, rendezvous; come upon, encounter 154 vb. *meet with*; bump into 279 vb. *collide*; assemble 74 vb. *congregate*.

296. Departure – N. *departure*, leaving, parting, removal; walk-out, exit 298 n. *egress*; emigration, migration, exodus, Hejira; flight, decampment, elopement, get-away 667 n. *escape*; embarkation 297 n. *ingress*; zero hour, setting out 68 n. *start*; take-off 308 n. *ascent*; port of embarkation, departure platform; starting-point, starting-post, stake-boat.

valediction, valedictory, last post, funeral oration 364 n. *obsequies*; leave-taking, congé, dismissal; goodbye, good night, farewell, adieu; send-off; last words, parting shot; stirrup-cup, one for the road.

Adj. *departing* etc. vb.; valedictory, farewell; outward bound; emigrational.

Vb. *depart*, quit, leave 621 vb. *relinquish*; retire, withdraw 286 vb. *turn back*; remove, leave home, emigrate, expatriate oneself; take wing, take a ticket; take one's leave, be going, have one for the road; bid farewell, say goodbye, make one's adieus, tear oneself away; quit the scene, leave the stage, exit.

decamp, up sticks, strike tents, break camp; march out, pack up; clear out, evacuate; make tracks, sling one's hook; be off, beetle o., buzz o.; vamoose, skedaddle, beat it, hop it, scram; cut and run, flee, take flight 620 vb. *run away*; leave no trace 446 vb. *disappear*; elope, welsh, abscond, give one the slip 667 vb. *escape*.

start out, be off, get going, set out 68 vb. *begin*; set forth, sally f. 298 vb. *emerge*; gird oneself, warm up 669 vb. *make ready*; unmoor, cast off 269 vb. *navigate*; mount, harness, saddle 267 vb.

ride; hitch up, inspan; emplane, entrain; catch (a train); take off, be on one's way; see off, speed the parting guest.

297. Ingress: motion into – N. *ingress*, entry, entrance 263 n. *doorway*, 624 n. *access*; re-entry, re-entrance; inflow, influx 350 n. *stream*; inrush; invasion, forced entry, inroad, raid, irruption, incursion 712 n. *attack*; penetration, infiltration, insinuation 303 n. *insertion*; immigration; indraught, intake 299 n. *reception*; import, importation 272 n. *transference*; right of entry, admission, admittance, access, entrée 756 n. *permission*; free trade, open-door policy 791 n. *trade*; ticket, pass 756 n. *permit*.

incomer, newcomer, new arrival, new face; new boy 538 n. *beginner*; visitor 882 n. *social person*; immigrant, migrant, colonist, settler 59 n. *foreigner*; stowaway 59 n. *intruder*; invader, raider 712 n. *attacker*; entrant, competitor 716 n. *contender*; ticket-holder; audience, house, gate 441 n. *onlookers*.

Adj. *incoming*, ingressive, ingoing, inward, inward bound, homing; irruptive; allowed in, imported.

Vb. *enter*, turn into, go in; cross the threshold, darken the doors; let oneself in 263 n. *open*; gain admittance, have the entrée; look in, drop in, call 882 vb. *visit*; board, get in, hop in, squeeze into; creep in, steal in; work oneself into, insinuate oneself, worm into; tread in, fall into 309 vb. *tumble*; sink into, dive i. 313 vb. *plunge*; join, enlist in, enroll oneself; immigrate, settle in 187 vb. *place oneself*; enter for 716 vb. *contend*.

infiltrate, percolate, seep, soak through, go t.; sink in, penetrate, interpenetrate, interfuse 43 vb. *mix*; taint, infect.

irrupt, rush in, burst in, charge in 176 vb. *force*; flood, flow in, pour in 350 vb. *flow*; crowd in, roll in 74 vb. *congregate*; invade, raid, lay aboard, storm, escalade 712 vb. *attack*.

intrude, trespass, gate-crash, outstay one's welcome; horn in, barge in, interrupt 63 vb. *derange*; break in, housebreak 788 vb. *steal*.

298. Egress: motion out of – N. *egress*, exit, walk-off; walk-out, exodus, evacuation 296 n. *departure*; emigration, expatriation, exile; emergence, debouchment; emanation (see *outflow*); eruption, outburst, outbreak; break-out 667 n. *escape*; outcome, issue 157 n. *effect*; exportation 272 n. *transference*.

outflow, effluence, efflux, effusion; issue, outpouring; exudation; extravasation; bleeding 302 n. *haemorrhage*; transudation, perspiration, sweating, sweat; leak, escape, leakage, seepage 634 n. *waste*; drain, running sore 772 n. *loss*; outfall, discharge, disemboguement 300 n. *voidance*; overflow, spill 350 n. *waterfall*; jet, fountain, spring 156 n. *source*; gusher, well.

outlet, vent, chute, exhaust; spout, tap; pore 263 n. *orifice*, 352 n. *respiration*; sluice, flood-gate 351 n. *conduit*, *drain*; exit, way out 624 n. *access*; outgate, sally-port 263 n. *doorway*; escape, loophole 667 n. *means of escape*.

Adj. *outgoing*, outward bound; emergent, emanating; oozy, runny, leaky; extravasated; eruptive, explosive 300 adj. *expulsive*.

Vb. *emerge*, pop out, project 254 vb. *jut*; surface, break water 308 vb. *ascend*; emanate, transpire 528 vb. *be published*; issue, debouch, sally; jump out, bale o. 312 vb. *leap*; erupt, break out 667 vb. *escape*.

flow out, 350 vb. *flow*; gush, spurt, spout, jet; drain out, run, drip, dribble, trickle, ooze; rise, well up, boil over; overflow, spill, slop over; run off, escape, leak, vent itself, discharge i.; bleed, weep, effuse, extravasate.

exude, transude, perspire, sweat, steam 379 vb. *be hot*; ooze, seep, percolate, distil; run, dribble, drivel, drool, slaver, slabber, slobber, salivate; transpire, exhale 352 vb. *breathe*.

299. Reception – N. *reception*, admission, admittance, entrée, access; invitation 759 n. *offer*; receptivity, acceptance; open arms, welcome 876 n. *celebration*; enlistment, enrolment, naturalization 78

n. *inclusion*; initiation, baptism 534 n. *teaching*; asylum 660 n. *protection*; suction; assimilation, digestion, absorption; engulfment, ingurgitation; ingestion (of food) 301 n. *eating*; intake, consumption 634 n. *waste*; admissibility.

Adj. *admitting*, receptive, introceptive; welcoming 289 adj. *accessible*; receivable, admissible, acceptable; absorptive, absorbent; ingestive; digestive, assimilative.

Vb. *admit*, receive, accept, naturalize; take in, shelter 660 vb. *safeguard*; welcome; invite, call in 759 vb. *offer*; enlist, enrol, take on 622 vb. *employ*; pass in, allow in; import, land 272 vb. *transfer*; let in, show in, usher in, introduce; initiate, baptize 534 vb. *teach*; avow 526 vb. *confess*.

absorb, incorporate, engross, assimilate, digest; suck in; soak up, sponge, mop up, blot 342 vb. *dry*; ingest, ingurgitate, imbibe; lap up, swallow, engulf 301 vb. *eat, drink*; inhale 352 vb. *breathe*; sniff, snuff 394 vb. *smell*.

300. Ejection – N. *ejection*, extrusion, expulsion; precipitation, defenestration 287 n. *propulsion*; disbarment, disqualification 57 n. *exclusion*; dismissal, discharge, sack, boot, push, bounce; externment, deportation, extradition; relegation, exile, banishment 883 n. *seclusion*; eviction, dislodgement 188 n. *displacement*; ejectment, dispossession, deprivation, ouster 786 n. *expropriation*; clean sweep, elimination 165 n. *destruction*; expellee, deportee, refugee 883 n. *outcaste*.

ejector, evicter, dispossessor 786 n. *taker*; supplanter 150 n. *substitute*; chucker-out, bouncer; expellant, emetic, sickener; aperient 658 n. *cathartic*; propellant 723 n. *explosive*; emitter, radiator; ejector-seat 276 n. *aircraft*.

voidance, clearance, drainage; eruption; egestion, regurgitation, disgorgement; vomiting, nausea, vomit; eructation, gas, wind, burp, belch; crepitation, belching, collywobbles; blood-letting, cupping, bleeding, venesection, phlebotomy, paracentesis, tapping; elimination 302 n. *excretion.*

Adj. *expulsive*, expellent, extrusive; eruptive, effusive; radiating, emitting; salivant, secretory, salivary; emetic; cathartic, emeto-cathartic.

vomiting, sick, sickened, nauseated; sea-sick, air-s., car-s., train-s.

Vb. *eject*, expel, send down 963 vb. *punish*; strike off, disbar 57 vb. *exclude*; deport, extern, expatriate, exile, banish, transport 883 vb. *seclude*; throw up, cast up; spit out, spew o.; extrude, put out, push o., turf o., throw o., bounce; kick out, boot o., drum o.; defenestrate, precipitate 287 vb. *propel*; root out, weed o., uproot, eradicate 165 vb. *destroy*; rub out 550 vb. *obliterate*; exorcise, rid, get shot of; dispossess, expropriate 786 vb. *deprive*; out, oust, evict, dislodge, unhouse, turn out; hunt out, smoke o.; jettison, discard 779 vb. *not retain*; supplant, supersede 150 vb. *substitute.*

dismiss, discharge, lay off, turn off, axe, sack, fire; turn away, send packing, see off, shoo o., exorcize, order off.

void, evacuate, eliminate 302 vb. *excrete*; vent, disgorge, discharge; empty, drain; pour out, decant 272 vb. *transpose*; strain off, bail; run off, siphon o.; draw off, bleed, cup, let blood 304 vb. *extract*; clear, sweep away 648 vb. *clean*; unload, break bulk 188 vb. *displace*; exenterate, disembowel, eviscerate, gut, clean, bone, fillet 229 vb. *uncover*; disinfest 648 vb. *purify*; desolate, depopulate, dispeople, unpeople 105 vb. *render few.*

emit, send out 272 vb. *send*; emit rays 417 vb. *radiate*; give off, exhale, breathe out 394 vb. *smell*; vapour, fume, smoke, steam, puff 338 vb. *vaporize*; spit, spatter, sputter, splutter; effuse, pour, spend, spill, shed, sprinkle 341 vb. *moisten*; squirt 298 vb. *flow out*; salivate 298 vb. *exude*; egest, pass 302 vb. *excrete.*

vomit, be sick, bring up, throw up, cast up, disgorge, retch, keck; spew, puke, cat; feel nausea, heave.

eruct, eructate, crepitate, rumble; belch, burp, gurk; break wind, blow off, fart; hiccup, cough, hawk, clear the throat, expectorate, spit, gob.

301. Food: eating and drinking – N. *eating* etc. vb.; ingestion; alimentation, nutrition, feeding; deglutition; mastication; rumination, digestion; animal feeding, pasture; table, diet; overeating, overindulgence 947 n. *gluttony*; appetite, voracity, wolfishness 859 n. *hunger*; omnivorousness; eating habits, table manners; carnivorousness, cannibalism; herbivorousness, vegetarianism; edibility, digestibility.

feasting, eating and drinking, banqueting, epulation; regalement, orgy, feast, banquet, bump-supper, spree, beanfeast; blow-out, spread (see *meal*); good table, festal cheer, groaning board; fleshpots, milk and honey 635 n. *plenty.*

dieting, dietetics 658 n. *therapy*; diet, balanced d.; regimen, régime, course, dietary, diet sheet; calories, vitamins, proteins, carbohydrates, roughage; dietician, nutritionist.

gastronomy, gastronomics, gastrology, epicureanism, epicurism 944 n. *sensualism*; gourmandise, good living 947 n. *gluttony*; dainty palate 463 n. *discrimination*; epicure, gourmet, Lucullus (see *eater*).

cookery, domestic science, home economics, catering 633 n. *provision*; culinary department, cuisine; baker, cook, chef, cuisinier; cookshop, bakery, rotisserie, restaurant 192 n. *café*; kitchen, galley, cook-house, bake-h.; oven 383 n. *furnace*; cookery book, cookbook 589 n. *textbook*; recipe, receipt 496 n. *maxim.*

eater, feeder, consumer, partaker, taster, nibbler; boarder, messer, messmate; breakfaster, luncher, diner; banqueter, feaster, picnicker, diner-out, dining club 882 n. *sociability*; dainty feeder, connoisseur, gourmet, epicure, trencherman, gourmand, bon viveur, epicure, Lucullus 947 n. *glutton*; flesh-eater, carnivore; man-eater, cannibal; vegetarian, herbivore.

provisions, stores, commissariat: provender, foodstuff, groceries; keep, board, entertainment 633 n. *provision*; commons, sizing, provend, ration, helping 783 n. *portion*; buttery, buffet, pantry, larder, still-room 632 n. *storage*; hot-box, meat-safe; ice-box, frigidaire 384 n. *refrigerator.*

provender, animal food fodder, feed, pasture, pasturage, forage; corn, oats, grain, barley, hay, grass, mast, seed; dry feed, winter f.; saltlick.

food, meat, bread, staff of life; aliment, nutriment; alimentation, nutrition; nurture, sustenance, nourishment, food and drink, pabulum, pap; food for the gods, nectar and ambrosia; one's daily bread, one's bread-and-butter 622 n. *vocation*; foodstuffs, comestibles, edibles, eatables, eats, victuals, viands, provender; belly-timber, grub, tuck, prog, scoff, tack, biscuit, dogsbody, pemmican; bad food, carrion, offal; cheer, good c., good table, regular meals, fleshpots, fat of the land; creature comforts, cakes and ale; dainties, titbits, luxuries 637 n. *superfluity*; flavouring, sauce 389 n. *condiment*.

mouthful, bite, nibble, morsel 33 n. *small quantity*; sop, sip, swallow; gobbet, slice, titbit, sandwich, snack, crust; cud, quid; tablet, pill 658 n. *drug*; sweetmeat 392 n. *sweet*.

meal, refreshment, fare; light meal, snack, sandwich, club-s.; heavy meal, square m.; repast, collation, refection, spread, blow-out, bust, beanfeast, beano (see *feasting*); picnic, fête champêtre, barbecue, cookout, clambake; junket 837 n. *festivity*; pot-luck; breakfast, brunch, elevenses, luncheon, lunch, tiffin; tea, five o'clock t., high t.; dinner, supper, fork s., buffet s.; ordinary, table d'hôte; à la carte; menu, bill of fare, diet-sheet, dietary (see *dieting*); cover, table, place; helping 783 n. *portion*.

dish, cover, course; mess; hors d'œuvre, main dish, side-d., dessert, savoury; sweet, pudding; speciality, pièce de résistance, plat du jour; fritters; mixed grill; curry and rice, pilau, pilaff;

hotchpotch, hash, stew; risotto, ragout, fricassee, casserole, goulash; made-up dish, réchauffé; compote, soufflé, mousse, crumble.

soup, thick s., clear s.; broth, brew, potage, consommé; stock, bouillon, bisque, purée; gumbo, skilly.

meat, flesh; roast; red meat, beef, mutton, pork, venison; white meat, game 365 n. *poultry*; kebab; cut, joint, leg, fillet end, shank e.; baron of beef, sirloin; saddle, undercut, shoulder, neck, collar, chuck, skirt, knuckle; aitchbone, scrag end, breast, brisket; shin, loin, flank, ribs, rolled r., topside, silver s.; chop, loin c., chump c.; steak, fillet s., rump s., porterhouse s., ham s., hamburger; ham, bacon, gammon; fried bacon, rasher; tongue, knuckle, oxtail, cow-heel, calf's head; pig's trotters, chitterlings, haslet, pig's fry; offal, tripe, giblets, kidney, liver, heart, brain, sweetbread; sausage, banger, salami; hot dog, wiener, frankfurter, cocktail sausage; grease, lard, bard, dripping; bacon fat, bacon rind.

fruit, soft f.; stone-fruit, drupe; orange, tangerine, mandarin; apple, pippin, medlar; pear, avocado p., alligator p.; peach, apricot; banana, plantain; grape, muscat, raisin; plum, prune, damson, currant; berry, gooseberry, cape-g.; bilberry, dewberry, elderberry, blackberry, strawberry, raspberry, redberry, loganberry, blueberry, whortleberry, cranberry, huckleberry; paw-paw, papaya; melon, water-m., cantaloupe, honeydew melon, musk-m.; nut, coconut, almond, chestnut, walnut; filbert, hazel nut, Brazil n., pea-n., monkey-n., ground-n., cashew n., Barcelona n., pistachio n.

tuber, root, rhizome; ginger; artichoke, Jerusalem a.; truffle; potato, spud, sweet potato, yam, turnip, swede, nalkal, parsnip, beetroot; carrot.

vegetable 366 n. *plant*; greens, vegetables, garden-stuff; cabbage, red c., pickled c., sauerkraut, slaw, coleslaw, cauliflower, kale, seakale, curly kale, cole, colewort, broccoli, sprouts, Brussels s.; beans, haricot b., string b., runner b., scarlet runner; broad beans, lima b., waxed b., soya b.; lettuce, cabbage l., cos l.; egg plant, aubergine, brinjal; chicory, endive; leek, chive, garlic, onion, shallot; marrow, courgette; cucumber, pumpkin, gourd; pulse, edible fungus, boletus edilis, bolet, mushroom, truffle.

potherb, herb, culinary h., sweet h., marjoram, rosemary, mint, thyme, bay, dill, mace, sage, sorrel, fennel; parsley, cress, water-c.; clove, caper, chicory, borage, hops.

cereal, gruel, skilly, brewis, brose; porridge, stirabout, oatmeal; bread, black b., pumpernickel; loaf, roll, croissant, rusk; crust; toast; flapjack, waffle, succotash; crumpet, muffin; grain 366 n. *corn*; meal, flour, atta.

pastry, bakemeat, patty, pasty, turnover, crumble; tart, flan, puff, pie; cake, delicatessen, confectionary; shortbread, gingerbread; biscuit, snap, cracker, wafer; bannock, scone; crumpet, muffin, English m.; bun, doughnut, cruller.

milk product, butter, cream, curds, junket, yogurt; whey, cheese; ripe cheese, toasted cheese, Welsh rabbit.

drinking, imbibing, imbibition, fluid intake; potation; wine-tasting 463 n. *discrimination*; one's cups, bibbing, wine-b. 949 n. *drunkenness*; libation 981 n. *oblation*; drinker, bibber, swiller, sipper, quaffer.

potion, something to drink, thirst-quencher; drink, draught, dram, drench; gulp, sop, sup; noggin, bottle, bowl, glass 194 n. *vessel*; glassful, bumper; swig, nip, tot, peg, wallop, snorter, snifter, chaser, long drink, short d.; snort; backhander; nightcap, stirrup-cup, one for the road; health, toast; beverage, posset; cocktail 43 n. *mixture*; decoction, infusion (see *liquor*).

soft drink, teetotal d., non-alcoholic beverage, thirst-quencher, water, soda; table-water, mineral, barley water; milk, milkshake, frappé, float; fizz, pop, lemonade, orangeade; cordial, fruit juice; coconut milk, dab-juice; tea,

Indian tea, China t., green t., Russian t., maté; coffee, Turkish c., chocolate, cocoa; sherbet, syrup. See *milk*.

liquor, liquid 335 n. *fluid*; nectar, soma; booze, stimulant; brew, fermented liquor (see *wine*); alcohol, malt-liquor, hops, beer, small b., swipes; ale, nog; stout, lager, bitter, porter, home-brew; cider, perry, mead, brose; arrack, raki, toddy; spirits, ardent s., raw s., firewater, hooch; brandy, cognac, eau-de-vie; gin, schnapps, mother's ruin, blue r.; whisky, scotch; rye, bourbon; whiskey, Irish w., potheen; rum, grog, punch, eggnog; cordial, spiced wine, negus, posset, hippocras; mulled wine, caudle; cup, claret-c.; shandy, stingo, highball; julep, cocktail; apéritif; liqueur.

wine, the grape; red wine, tawny w., white w., vin rosé; spumante, sparkling wine, still w., sweet w., dry w.; vintage w.; vin ordinaire, vin du pays; sherry, sack, port, madaire; claret, lal shrub; champagne, fizz, bubbly; hock; chianti, rezina.

milk, top of the m., cream; cow's milk, beestings; koumiss; mother's milk, breast m.; curds, junket. See *milk product*.

Adj. *feeding*, eating, grazing etc. vb.; carnivorous, creophagous, cannibalistic; omophagous; herbivorous, graminivorous, frugivorous; vegetarian; omnivorous 464 adj. *indiscriminating*; greedy, wolfish 947 adj. *gluttonous*; teetotal, tea-drinking 942 adj. *temperate*; liquorish, bibulous, tippling 949 adj. *drunken*; well-fed, well-nourished; at the breast; breast-fed; full up 863 adj. *sated*.

edible, eatable; ritually pure, kosher; esculent, comestible; digestible, predigested; potable, drinkable; milky, lactic; palatable, succulent 386 adj. *tasty*, 390 adj. *savoury*; fermented, spirituous, alcoholic, hard 949 adj. *intoxicating* non-alcoholic, soft.

nourishing, sustaining; nutritious, nutritive, nutritional; alimentary; vitaminous, dietetic; rich, calorific; body-building, bone-b.

culinary, dressed, oven-ready, made-up; underdone, red, rare, raw; done, well-d.; over-cooked, burnt; roasted etc. vb. (see *cook*); gastronomic, epicurean.

mensal, prandial, commensal; messing, dining, lunching; pre-prandial, after-dinner, post-prandial; self-service.

Vb. *eat*, feed, fare, board, mess, keep hall; partake, discuss 386 vb. *taste*; break one's fast, break bread; breakfast, lunch, dine, sup; dine out, regale, feast, banquet, carouse 837 vb. *revel*; water at the mouth, raven 859 vb. *be hungry*; fall to, set to, tuck in, lay in, cram 863 vb. *sate*; guzzle, gormandize 947 vb. *gluttonize*; eat up, make a clean plate; swallow, gulp down, snap up, devour, dispatch, bolt, wolf; fatten on, batten on, prey on; nibble, peck, lick, play with one's food; ingest, digest 299 vb. *absorb*.

chew, masticate, champ, munch, crunch, scrunch; mumble, mouth, worry, gnaw; bite, tear 46 vb. *cut*.

graze, browse, pasture, crop, feed; ruminate, chew the cud.

drink, imbibe, ingest, suck 299 vb. *absorb*; quaff, drink up, slake one's thirst; lap, sip, sup; wet one's whistle, soak, wash down; swill, swig, tipple, tope 949 vb. *get drunk*; drink to, pledge 876 vb. *toast*; refill 633 vb. *replenish*; give to drink, wine, water, drench; posset, caudle.

feed, nourish, vitaminize; nurture, sustain, board; victual, cater 633 vb *provide*; nurse, breast-feed, suckle, give suck; pasture, graze, put out to grass; fatten 197 vb. *enlarge*; dine, wine, feast, banquet, have to dinner 882 vb. *be hospitable*.

cook, do to a turn; bake, scallop; roast, spit; broil, grill, griddle, devil, curry; sauté, fry; scramble, poach; boil, parboil; coddle, seethe, simmer, steam; casserole, stew; baste, lard; mince, dice; stuff, dress, garnish; sauce, flavour, spice.

302. Excretion – N. *excretion*, discharge, secretion, extrusion 300 n. *ejection*; exudation, sudation, perspiration, induced sweat, diaphoresis 298 n. *outflow*;

cold, catarrh, hay fever; salivation, expectoration; urination, micturition.

haemorrhage, bleeding, extravasation of blood, haemophilia 335 n. *blood*; period, menstruation, monthlies, menses, catamenia, flowers, leucorrhoea.

cacation, defecation, evacuation, elimination, clearance 300 n. *voidance*; movement, motion; regular motion, one's daily functions; frequency, trots, bowel hurry, diarrhoea, dysentery.

excrement, faeces, stool, excreta, ordure; dung, horse-dung, cow-pat; droppings, guano; piss, urine, water; spittle, spit, sputum; saliva, slaver, froth, foam; rheum, phlegm; slough, cast, exuviae; feculence 649 n. *dirt*.

Adj. *excretory*, secretory; purgative, eliminant; ejective, diuretic; diaphoretic, sudorific, perspiratory; faecal, feculent; rheumy, watery; cast-off, exuvial; stercoraceous 649 adj. *unclean*.

Vb. *excrete*, secrete; pass, move; defecate, ease oneself, stool, go to s.; urinate, piddle, wet; make water, spend a penny; piss, stale; sweat, perspire 379 vb. *be hot*; salivate, slobber 298 vb. *exude*; cast, slough 229 vb. *doff*.

303. Insertion: forcible ingress – N. *insertion*, intromission; interpolation 231 n. *interjection*; introduction, insinuation 297 n. *ingress*; infixion, impaction; planting 370 n. *agriculture*; inoculation, injection 263 n. *perforation*; immersion 313 n. *plunge*; thing inserted, insert, inset; stuffing 227 n. *lining*.

Adj. *inserted* etc. vb.

Vb. *insert*, intromit, introduce; put into, thrust i., intrude; pocket, purse 782 vb. *receive*; knock into, hammer i., drive i. 279 vb. *impel*; inlay, inset 227 vb. *line*; mount, frame 232 vb. *circumscribe*; interject 231 vb. *put between*; drop in, put in the slot 311 vb. *let fall*; putt, hole out; pot, hole; bury 364 vb. *inter*; sheathe, incapsulate, embox, encase 235 vb. *enclose*, 226 vb. *cover*; immerse 313 vb. *plunge*.

infuse, instil, pour in 43 vb. *mix*; imbue, imbrue, impregnate; transfuse, decant 272 vb. *transpose*; squirt in, inject 263 vb. *pierce*.

implant, plant, transplant, plant out 187 vb. *place*; graft, ingraft, imp, bud; inoculate; embed, bury; infix, wedge in, impact, dovetail 45 vb. *join*.

304. Extraction: forcible egress – N. *extraction*, withdrawal, removal 188 n. *displacement*; eradication 300 n. *ejection*; extrication, disengagement 668 n. *deliverance*; cutting out, exsection; exsuction, sucking out; drawing out, pull, tug, wrench 288 n. *traction*; excavation, extractive industry, mining, quarrying, fishery; distillation 338 n. *vaporization*; essence, extract.

extractor, gouger; miner, quarrier; forceps, pincers 778 n. *nippers*; corkscrew 263 n. *opener*; scoop 274 n. *shovel*; pick, pickaxe; excavator, dredger.

Adj. *extracted* etc. vb; extractive.

Vb. *extract*, pull 288 vb. *draw*; draw out, elicit; pull out, pluck; withdraw, unsheathe; exsect, cut out, whip o.; excavate, mine, quarry, dig out; dredge; lever out, winkle o. 300 vb. *eject*; extort, wring; force out, press out, squeeze o., gouge o.; draw off, milk, tap, suck; pull up, weed, grub up; uproot, eradicate 165 vb. *destroy*; distil 338 vb. *vaporize*; extricate, unravel, free 746 vb. *liberate*; eviscerate, gut, shuck, shell 229 vb. *uncover*; pick out 605 vb. *select*.

305. Passage: motion through – N. *passage*, passing, traversing; transit, traverse, crossing, journey, voyage, perambulation, patrol 267 n. *land travel*; penetration 297 n. *ingress*; pass, defile, tunnel 624 n. *access*; track 624 n. *path*; intersection, cross-road 222 n. *crossing*; channel 351 n. *conduit*.

passing along, thoroughfare; traffic, pedestrian t., vehicular t.; traffic movement, flow of traffic, circulation; traffic pattern, walking, crossing, cycling, driving, carrying; loading, unloading; waiting, parking; traffic load, traffic density; traffic jam, procession, queue.

traffic control, traffic engineering; traffic rules, highway code, rule of the road; traffic lane, one-way street, flyover, underpass; clearway 624 n. *road*; diversion, alternative route 282 n. *deviation*; street furniture, white line, traffic lights, roundabout; clover leaf, pedestrian crossing, zebra c., Belisha beacon, refuge, island; car-park, parking place, parking area *or* zone; parking meter, lay-by; traffic police, traffic cop, road patrol; traffic engineer; traffic warden.

Adj. *passing* etc. vb.

Vb. *pass*, pass by, leave on one side, skirt, coast 200 vb. *be near*; join the traffic, circulate, weave; pass through, shoot, transit, traverse; come out the other side 298 vb. *emerge*; go through, percolate 189 vb. *pervade*; patrol, work over, beat, scour, sweep; penetrate 297 vb. *enter*; bore 263 vb. *pierce*; thread 45 vb. *connect*; enfilade; force a passage 297 vb. *irrupt*; cross, cross over, ford; cross one's bows 702 vb. *obstruct*; skip 458 vb. *disregard*; pass beyond 306 vb. *overstep*.

306. Overstepping: motion beyond – N. *overstepping*, transilience, leap-frog 305 n. *passage*; transcendence 34 n. *superiority*; extravagation 282 n. *deviation*; transgression 936 n. *guilt*; infringement, encroachment 916 n. *arrogation*; expansionism, over-extension, ribbon development 197 n. *expansion*.

Adj. *surpassing* etc. vb.; one up on 34 adj. *superior*; over-extended, overlong, overhigh; out of bounds, out of reach.

Vb. *overstep*, overpass, leave behind; go too far, exceed the limit, overrun, overshoot; overlap 226 vb. *overlie*; jump over, leap-frog 312 vb. *leap*; step over 305 vb. *pass*; cross the Rubicon, pass the point of no return; over-fulfil 637 vb. *superabound*; stretch a point; overbid 482 vb. *overrate*; overstay, oversleep 136 vb. *be late*; outdo, go one better 34 vb. *be superior*, 277 vb. *outstrip*.

encroach, break bounds, make inroads 712 vb. *attack*; infringe, transgress, trespass 914 vb. *do wrong*; squat, usurp 786 vb. *appropriate*; overlap, impinge, trench upon; overflow, flood 341 vb. *drench*.

307. Shortcoming – N. *shortcoming*, falling short, inadequacy 636 n. *insufficiency*; a minus, deficit, short measure, shortage, shortfall, loss 42 vb. *decrement*; unfinished state 55 n. *incompleteness*; nonfulfilment, default 726 n. *non-completion*; no go 728 n. *failure*; defect 647 n. *imperfection*, 845 n. *blemish*; something missing, want, lack, need 627 n. *requirement*.

Adj. *deficient*, short, short of, minus, wanting, lacking, missing; catalectic; underpowered, substandard; perfunctory 55 adj. *incomplete*.

Vb. *fall short*, run s. 636 vb. *not suffice*; not stretch, not reach to; miss, lack, want 627 vb. *require*; lag 136 vb. *be late*; fall by the way, not stay the course; lose ground, slip back 286 vb. *regress*; fizzle out, fail 728 vb. *miscarry*; tantalize, not come up to expectations 509 vb. *disappoint*.

308. Ascent: motion upwards – N. *ascent*, ascension, upward motion, gaining height; defiance of gravity, levitation; take-off 296 n. *departure*; zoom 271 n. *aeronautics*; culmination 213 n. *summit*; surfacing; rise, uprise, uprush, upsurge 36 n. *increase*; updraught; climbing, skylarking, mountaineering, Alpinism; escalade 712 n. *attack*; jump 312 n. *leap*; bounce 280 n. *recoil*; gradient, slope, ramp 220 n. *acclivity*; stairs, steps, flight, staircase, stairway, landing; ladder, step-l., accommodation l., Jacob's l., companion way; rope-ladder, ratlin; stair, step, tread, rung; lift, elevator 310 n. *lifter*.

climber, mountaineer, alpinist, cragsman, Alpine Club; stegophilist; cat-burglar; foretopman, steeple-jack; excelsior-figure; rocket, sky-r.; soarer, lark.

Adj. *ascending*, rising etc. vb.; scansorial, scandent; air-borne, gaining height; excelsior; anabatic; uphill 215 n. *vertical*; scalable, climbable.

Vb. *ascend*, rise, uprise, leave the ground; levitate; take off, fly up 271 vb. *fly*; gain height, mount, soar, spiral, zoom, climb; zenith, culminate; bob up, surface, break water; bounce, spring 312 vb. *leap*; upheave, tower 209 vb. *be high*; stand up, rear up, ramp 215 vb. *be vertical*; steepen 220 vb. *be oblique*; go up, blow up.

climb, struggle up; mount, work one's way up; go climbing, mountaineer; skylark; clamber, swarm up, shin up, monkey up, climb hand over fist; surmount, top, breast, scale 209 vb. *be high*; go over the top, escalade 712 vb. *attack*.

Adv. *up*, uphill, upstairs; excelsior; ever higher; hand over fist.

309. Descent – N. *descent*, declension; declination 282 n. *deviation*; decline, drop, slump 37 n. *decrease*; come-down 872 n. *humiliation*; downfall, débâcle, collapse 165 n. *ruin*; fall, tumble, cropper, crash, spill; downrush, swoop, stoop, pounce; dive, header 313 n. *plunge*; nose-dive, power-d. 271 n. *aeronautics*; glissade; subsidence, landslide, avalanche; cascade 350 n. *waterfall*; declivity, dip 220 n. *acclivity*; submergence 311 n. *depression*; speleology, potholing; plunger 313 n. *diver*; parachutist 271 n. *aeronaut*; paratrooper 722 n. *soldier*; speleologist, pot-holer.

Adj. *descending* etc. vb.; declivitous 220 adj. *sloping*; deciduous; tumble-down, nodding to its fall; submersible, sinkable.

Vb. *descend*, come down, go d., dip d.; go downhill, slump 655 vb. *deteriorate*; fall, drop, sink; seep down 297 vb. *infiltrate*; touch bottom 210 vb. *be low*; gravitate, precipitate, settle; subside, cave in, collapse; draw, have draught; submerge, dive 313 vb. *plunge*; drown 313 vb. *founder*; burrow, tunnel, undermine 255 vb. *make concave*; drop from the sky, parachute, swoop, stoop, pounce; lose height, drop down; touch down, alight, perch 295 vb. *land*; get down, dismount; slide down, glissade, toboggan; shower, pour, cascade 350 vb. *rain*; bow down, dip, duck 311 vb. *stoop*; flop, plop.

tumble, fall; topple, overbalance, capsize 221 vb. *be inverted*; miss one's footing, slip, trip, stumble; stagger, totter 220 vb. *be oblique*; rise and fall, pitch, toss, roll; take a header 313 vb. *plunge*; take a fall, come a cropper, go for a Burton, bite the dust, measure one's length; plop, plump down, slump, sprawl 311 vb. *sit down*; spiral down, nose-dive, crash, prang.

310. Elevation – N. *elevation*, raising etc. vb.; erection, upheaval; lift, uplift, leg-up 703 n. *aid*; sublimation, exaltation; upswing 308 n. *ascent*; defiance of gravity, levitation.

lifter, erector, builder, spiderman; yeast 323 n. *leaven*; lever, jack 218 n. *pivot*; crane, derrick, hoist, windlass; winch, capstan; rope and pulley, block and tackle; lift, ski-l., elevator; escalator 274 n. *conveyor*; gas, hydrogen, helium; spring, springboard, trampoline.

Adj. *elevated* etc. vb.; exalted, uplifted; erectile; upright, erect, upstanding, rampant 215 adj. *vertical*; mounted, on high; lofty, sublime 209 adj. *high*.

Vb. *elevate*, heighten; puff up, blow up, swell, leaven 197 vb. *enlarge*; raise, erect, set up, run up, build; lift, pick up, heave up; up-end, unlift, upraise; jack up, prop 218 vb. *support*; hold up, bear up, upbear, buoy up; hoist, haul up; pull up, wind up; weight, trip (anchor); fish up, dredge up 304 vb. *extract*; exalt, sublimate; chair, shoulder, put on a pedestal; put on top, mount; jump up, bounce up 285 vb. *promote*; throw up, toss; sky, loft, lob 287 vb. *propel*; perk up (one's head); prick up (one's ears); bristle up.

Adv. *on*, on stilts, on tiptoe.

311. Depression – N. *depression*, lowering etc. vb.; detrusion; debasement 655 n. *deterioration*; demotion 872 n. *humiliation*; overthrow; upset 221 n. *overturning*; keeping under, suppression; a depression 255 n. *cavity*; low pressure 340 n. *weather*.

Adj. *depressed* etc. vb.; at a low ebb 210 adj. *low*; prostrate 216 adj. *supine*; sessile, sedentary, sitting, sit-down; depressive, detrusive; submersible.

Vb. *depress*, detrude, push down; shut down (a lid) 264 vb. *close*; hold down 165 vb. *suppress*; lower, let down, take d.; dip, half-mast, haul down, strike; pitch, precipitate, defenestrate, fling down; sink, scuttle 313 vb. *plunge*; weigh on, press on 322 vb. *weigh*; crush, stave in 255 vb. *make concave*.

let fall, drop, shed; pour, decant 300 vb. *void*; spill, slop 341 vb. *moisten*; sprinkle, shower, scatter, dust; lay down, put d. (see *fell*); pitch *or* chuck overboard.

fell, trip, topple, tumble, overthrow; prostrate, lay low 216 vb. *flatten*; knock down 279 vb. *strike*; bowl over, floor, drop, down; pull down, tear d., raze, slight, level, pull about one's ears, trample in the dust 165 vb. *demolish*; undermine; bring down, shoot d. 287 vb. *shoot*.

sit down, sit, be seated, squat; kneel, recline, couch, stretch oneself out 216 vb. *be horizontal*; roost, nest 683 vb. *repose*; take a seat, perch, alight 309 vb. *descend*.

stoop, bend, lean, bend down; cringe, crouch, cower 721 vb. *knuckle under*; bow, scrape, arch one's back 884 vb. *greet*; nod 488 vb. *assent*; bow down 920 vb. *show respect*; kneel, genuflect.

312. Leap – N. *leap*, saltation, leapfrog; jump, hop, skip; spring, bound, vault; high jump, long j., running j.; caper, gambol, frolic; kick, high k.; prance, curvet, caracole, capriole, demivolt, gambade, buck; dance step 837 n. *dancing*.

jumper, high-j., pole-vaulter, hurdler, steeplechaser; skipper, hopper, leapfrogger; caperer, prancer; dancer 837 n. *dance*; dancing man; dancing girl, nautch girl 594 n. *entertainer*; kangaroo, springbok, jumping-mouse; frog, flea;

bucking horse, bucker; jumping cracker, jumping bean; jumping jack, Jack-in-the-box 837 n. *plaything*.

Adj. *leaping* etc. vb.; saltatory, saltatorial; skittish, frisky 819 adj. *lively*.

Vb. *leap*, jump, take a running j.; spring, bound, vault, hurdle, steeple-chase, take one's fences; skip, hop, leap-frog, bob, bounce, buck; tread a measure 837 vb. *dance*; caper, gambol, frisk; prance, paw the ground, ramp, rear, backjump, plunge; cavort, curvet, cara-cole; start, startle, give a jump; jump over, clear; flounder 318 vb. *be agitated*; writhe 251 vb. *wriggle*.

313. Plunge – **N.** *plunge*, swoop, pounce, stoop 309 n. *descent*; nose-dive 271 n. *aeronautics*; dive, header, belly-flop; dip, ducking; immersion, submergence.

diver, frogman, under-water swimmer; submariner; submarine, bathyscaph, bathysphere, sinker, diving-bell; plunger, lead, plummet; fathometer.

Vb. *plunge*, dip, duck, bathe 341 vb. *be wet*; dive, take a header; welter, wallow, pitch and toss; souse, immerse, drown; submerge, flood the tanks, crash-dive 309 vb. *descend*; sink, scuttle, send to the bottom; sound, fathom, plumb the depths, heave the lead 465 vb. *measure*.

founder, go down 309 vb. *descend*; get out of one's depth; drown, settle down, go to the bottom, sink, sink like lead.

314. Circuition: curvilinear motion – **N.** *circuition*, circulation, circumambulation, circumnavigation, gyre, spiral 315 n. *rotation*; cornering, turn, U-turn; orbit, ambit, compass, lap; circuit, tour, round trip, full circle.

circler, girdler, circumambulator; circumnavigator 270 n. *mariner*; roundsman 794 n. *tradesman*; moon, satellite 321 n. *planet*.

Adj. *circuitous*, turning etc. vb.; circumfluent, circumambient; circumnavigable; devious 626 adj. *roundabout*; orbital.

Vb. *circle*, circulate, go the round; compass, circuit, lap; tour, do the round

trip; go round, skirt; circumambulate, circumnavigate, circumaviate; turn, round, double a point; corner, turn a c.; wheel, revolve, orbit 315 vb. *rotate*; wind, twist 251 vb. *meander*; make a detour 626 vb. *circuit*.

315. Rotation: motion in a continued circle – **N.** *rotation*, orbit, cycle, epicycle; revolution, full circle; verticity, gyration, circulation, circumfluence; spin, circumvolution, turbination; rolling, volutation; spiral, roll, turn, twirl, waltz, pirouette, reel; whirlabout, whirl; dizziness, vertigo; gyrostatics, trochilics.

vortex, whirl; whirlwind, whirlblast, tornado, cyclone 352 n. *gale*; waterspout, whirlpool, swirl 350 n. *eddy*; maelstrom, Charybdis.

rotator, rotor, spinner; whirligig, teetotum, yo-yo, top, spinning t.; roundabout, merry-go-round; churn, whisk; potter's wheel, lathe; spinning wheel, whorl; fly-wheel, prayer-w., roulette-w. 250 n. *wheel*; gyroscope, gyrostat; turntable; windmill, fan, sail; propeller, prop, screw; winder, capstan 310 n. *lifter*; spindle, axle, axis 218 n. *pivot*; reel, roller 252 n. *cylinder*.

Adj. *rotary*, trochilic; spinning etc. vb.; rotary, gyratory; gyral; circling, cyclic; vortical, vorticular; cyclonic, turbinated; vertiginous, dizzy.

Vb. *rotate*, revolve, orbit 314 vb. *circle*; box the compass, chase one's own tail; spin, twirl, pirouette; gyrate, waltz, wheel, whirl; swirl, eddy 350 vb. *flow*; roll, bowl, trundle, troll; churn, whisk; turn, crank, wind, reel, spin, yarn; slew, swing round; roll up, furl 261 vb. *fold*; roll itself up, scroll.

316. Evolution: motion in a reverse circle – **N.** *evolution*, unrolling, unfolding, unfurling; explication, dénouement; counter-spin, eversion 221 n. *inversion*; development, evolutionism, Darwinism.

Adj. *evolving*, unwinding etc. vb.; evolutionary, evolutionistic.

Vb. *evolve*, unfold, unfurl, unroll, unwind, uncoil, uncurl, untwist, untwine, explicate, unravel, disentangle; evolute, develop, grow into 147 vb. *be turned to*; roll back 263 vb. *open*.

317. Oscillation: reciprocating motion – **N.** *oscillation*, libration, nutation; harmonic motion, swing of the pendulum; vibration, tremor; vibrancy, resonance 141 n. *periodicity*; pulsation, drumming, pulse, beat, throb; flutter, palpitation 318 n. *agitation*; undulation, wave-motion, frequency, wave-length 417 n. *radiation*, 350 n. *wave*; seismic disturbance, earthquake, ground wave, tremor 176 n. *violence*; seismology, seismograph; oscillator, vibrator; pendulum, bob 217 n. *pendant*. See *fluctuation*.

fluctuation, wave motion (see *oscillation*); alternation, reciprocation 12 n. *correlation*; to and fro movement, coming and going, shuttle service; ups and downs, boom and bust, ebb and flow, flux and reflux, systole and diastole; roll, pitch, lurch, stagger, reel; shake; swing, see-saw; rocker, rocking-chair, rocking-horse; shuttlecock, shuttle; wavering, vacillation 601 n. *irresolution*.

Adj. *oscillating* etc. vb.; oscillatory, undulatory, libratory; pulsatory, palpitating, vibratory, vibratile; earth-shaking, seismic; pendular; reeling, staggery, groggy.

Vb. *oscillate*, emit waves 417 vb. *radiate*; fluctuate, undulate; vibrate, pulsate, pulse, beat, drum; tick, throb, palpitate; respire 352 vb. *breathe*; nutate, librate; play, sway, nod; swing, dangle 217 vb. *hang*; see-saw, rock; hunt, lurch, reel, stagger, totter, teeter, wobble, wiggle, waggle, wag; bob bounce 312 vb. *leap*; toss, roll, pitch, tumble, wallow; brandish, flourish, wave, flutter; shake 318 vb. *be agitated*; flicker 417 vb. *shine*.

318. Agitation: irregular motion – **N.** *agitation*, irregular motion, jerkiness, fits and starts, unsteadiness 152 n. *changeableness*; joltiness, bumpiness, choppiness 259 n. *roughness*; start, jump 508 n. *inexpectation*; succussion, shake; shock, jar, jolt, jerk, bounce, bump,

rock 279 n. *knock*; vibration, thrill, throb, pit-a-pat, palpitation, flutter 317 n. *oscillation*; shudder, shiver, frisson; quiver, quaver, tremor; tremulousness, trembling, palsy (see *spasm*); restlessness, feverishness, fever; tossing, turning; jiving, twist, shimmy 837 n. *dancing*; itchiness, itch 378 n. *formication*; twitchiness, twitch; disquiet 825 n. *worry*; trepidation, jumpiness, twitter, flap 854 n. *nervousness*; the shakes, jumps, jitters, shivers, fidgets, aspen-leaf.

spasm, ague, rigor, chattering; palsy; twitch, subsultus; tic, chorea, St Vitus's dance, the jerks; tarantism; cramp, the cramps; throe 377 n. *pang*; convulsion, paroxysm, access, orgasm 503 n. *frenzy*; staggers, megrims; fit, epilepsy, falling sickness; pulse, throb 317 n. *oscillation*; attack, turn, seizure, stroke.

commotion, turmoil, turbulence, tumult, hurly-burly, hubbub; fever, rush, rout 680 n. *haste*; furore 503 n. *frenzy*; stir, ferment 355 n. *bubble*; tempest 176 n. *storm*; disturbance, atmospherics.

Adj. *agitated*, shaken, shaking, succussive; feverish, fevered, restless; scratchy, jittery, jumpy 854 adj. *nervous*; breathless, panting; subsultory, twitching, itchy; convulsive, spasmodic, spastic; saltatory, choreic; shaky, tremulous, a-tremble.

Vb. *be agitated*, boil 355 vb. *bubble*; chatter, rattle; shake, tremble, quiver, quaver, shiver, throw a fit; writhe, squirm, itch, twitch 251 vb. *wriggle*; toss, turn; thresh, kick, plunge 176 vb. *be violent*; flounder, flop, wallow; pulse, beat, thrill, vibrate 317 vb. *oscillate*; jump about, hop 312 vb. *leap*; flicker, twinkle 417 vb. *shine*; flap, flutter, twitter, start, jump; throb, pant, palpitate, go pit-a-pat; bustle, rush, mill around.

agitate, disturb 63 vb. *derange*; discompose 827 vb. *displease*; ripple, puddle, muddy; stir, whisk, whip, beat, churn 315 vb. *rotate*; shake; wag, waggle, wave, flourish, brandish; jog, joggle, jiggle, jolt; jerk, pluck, twitch 378 vb. *touch*.

Class 3

MATTER

Section 1: Matter in General

319. Materiality – N. *materiality*, empirical world, world of experience; corporeality; world of nature 3 n. *substantiality*; concreteness, tangibility, palpability, solidity 324 n. *density*; embodiment, incarnation, reincarnation, metempsychosis; realization, materialization; hylism, positivism, materialism, Marxism; unspirituality, worldliness 944 n. *sensualism*; materialist, realist, positivist.

matter, brute m., stuff; plenum; hyle, prime matter; mass, material, body, frame 331 n. *structure*; substance, corpus; organic matter, flesh, flesh and blood; real world, Nature.

object, tangible o., bird in the hand; flesh and blood 371 n. *person*; thing, gadget, something, commodity, article, item; stocks and stones 359 n. *mineral*.

element, elementary unit, sense datum; principle, first p. 68 n. *origin*; unit of being, monad; factor, ingredient 58 n. *component*; atom, molecule; fundamental particle, sub-atom, electron, beta-particle, negatron, positron, neutron, meson, proton, nucleus, nucleon; alpha-particle; mucon, neutrino, hyperion; anti-particle, anti-electron; photon; quantum; ion.

physics, physical science, science of matter; science of bodies, somatics, somatology; applied physics, technology; natural philosophy, experimental p. 490 n. *science*.

Adj. *material*, hylic; real, natural; massy, solid, concrete, palpable, tangible, ponderable, sensible; somatoscopic, somatic; physical, spatiotemporal; hypostatic 3 adj. *substantial*; incarnate, incorporate; corporeal, bodily, fleshy, of flesh and blood; materialistic, mundane, worldly, earthbound, unspiritual 944 adj. *sensual*.

Vb. *materialize*, substantialize, hypostatize, corporealize; objectify 223 vb. *externalize*; realize, body forth; embody, incorporate; incarnate, personify; substantiate.

320. Immateriality – N. *immateriality*, unreality 4 n. *insubstantiality*; incorporeality, dematerialization, disembodiment, inextension, imponderability, intangibility, ghostliness, shadowiness; superficiality 639 n. *unimportance*; immaterialism, idealism, Platonism; spirituality, otherworldliness; animism; spiritualism, psychism 984 n. *occultism*; other world, world of spirits, astral plane; animist; spiritualist 984 n. *occultist*; idealist 449 n. *philosopher*; astral body 970 n. *ghost*.

Adj. *immaterial*, without mass; incorporeal, asomatous; ghostly, shadowy 4 adj. *insubstantial*; imponderable, intangible; superficial 639 adj. *unimportant*; bodiless, discarnate, disembodied; extramundane, unearthly, supersensory, psychic, spiritistic, astral 984 adj. *psychical*; spiritual, otherworldly 973 adj. *religious*.

Vb. *disembody*, spiritualize, dematerialize, disincarnate.

321. Universe – N. *universe*, omneity 52 n. *whole*; world, creation, all c.; sum of things, plenum, matter and anti-matter; cosmos, macrocosm, microcosm; space-time continuum.

world, wide w., four corners of the earth; home of man, sublunary sphere; earth, globe, sphere, terrestrial s., terraqueous globe, geoid; terrestrial surface, crust, sub-crust, moho; atlas, world map 551 n. *map*; personal world, idioverse, life space, total situation 8 n. *circumstance*.

heavens, sky, welkin, empyrean, ether, etherial sphere; firmament; night-sky, aurora borealis, northern lights, aurora australis; zodiacal light, counterglow, gegenschein.

star, heavenly body; sidereal sphere; asterism, constellation; starlight, star-shine; double star, binary, primary, secondary, component, comes; multiple star; giant, supergiant, sub-giant, dwarf, red d., white d.; new star, nova, super-nova; pole star, Polaris, Milky Way, star cloud; nebula, star cluster, globular c., open c.; galaxy, super-g., island universe; stellar motion, star stream.

zodiac, signs of the z., Aries (the Ram), Taurus (the Bull), Gemini (the Twins), Cancer (the Crab), Leo (the Lion), Virgo (the Virgin), Libra (the Balance), Scorpius *or* Scorpio (the Scorpion), Sagittarius (the Archer), Capricornus (the Goat), Aquarius (the Man with the Watering-pot), Pisces (the Fish); ecliptic; house, mansion, lunar m.

planet, major p., minor p., asteroid, planetoid; Mercury; Venus, morning star, evening s.; Mars, red planet; Earth, Jupiter, Saturn, Uranus, Neptune, Pluto; comet.

meteor, falling star, shooting s., fireball, meteorite, aerolite, bolide, chondrite; meteoroid; micrometeorite; meteor shower; radiant point.

sun, day-star, orb of day, midnight sun; parhelion, mock sun; sunlight, photosphere, chromosphere; sun spot, solar prominence, solar flare, corona; solar system, heliocentrics; solstice.

moon, satellite, earth s., artificial s. 276 n. *space-ship*; new moon, old moon in the young moon's arm; harvest moon, hunter's m.; paraselene, mock moon; man in the moon, lunarian; moonlight; lunistice.

astronomy, star-lore, star-gazing; radio-astronomy; astrophysics; selenography, uranography, uranology; astrology, astromancy, horoscope 511 n. *divination*; observatory, planetarium; refractor, reflector 442 n. *telescope*; orrery, astrolabe; astronomer, radio a., astro-

physicist; star-gazer, star-watcher; astrologer, astromancer.

cosmography, cosmology, cosmogony, cosmogonist, cosmographer.

geography, orography, oceanography, cosmography, physiography, geodesy, geology; geographer, geodesist, geologist; hydrology, hydrography, hydrogeology.

Adj. *cosmic*, universal, cosmical, cosmological, cosmogonic, cosmographical; interstellar, intersidereal; galactic, metagalactic.

celestial, heavenly, empyreal, sphery; starry, star-spangled; sidereal, astral, stellar; solar, heliacal, zodiacal; lunar, selenic, lunate; lunisolar; nebular, nebulous; heliocentric, geocentric, planetocentric; cometary, meteoric, meteorological; uranological, uranometrical; equinoctial, solstitial.

planetary, planetoidal, asteroidal, satellitic, planetocentric; Mercurian, Venerean, Martian, Jovian, Saturnian, Neptunian, Plutonian.

telluric, tellurian, terrestrial, terrene, terraqueous; sublunary, subastral; polar, equatorial; world-wide 79 adj. *universal*; earth-bound, worldly, earthly.

astronomic, astronomical, astrophysical, star-gazing, star-watching; astrological, astromantic; telescopic, spectroscopic.

geographic, geographical, oceanographic, orographical; geological; geodesic, geodetic, physiographic; hydrogeological, hydrographic, hydrological.

322. Gravity – N. *gravity*, gravitation, force of gravity; weight, weightiness, heaviness, ponderosity; specific gravity; displacement, sinkage, draught; load, lading, freight; ballast, makeweight, rider, counterpose 31 n. *offset*; mass 324 n. *solid body*; weight, bob, sinker, lead, stone; millstone, incubus, burden; geostatics, statics.

weighment, weighing, ponderation; balancing, equipoise 28 n. *equalization*; weights, avoirdupois weight, troy w., apothecary's w.; grain, carat, scruple, pennyweight, drachm; megaton, kiloton; axle-load, laden weight; tonnage, burthen.

scales, weighing-machine; steelyard, beam; balance, spring-b.; pan, scale, weight; platform scale, weigh-bridge.

Adj. *weighty*, heavy, ponderous, leaden; cumbersome, cumbrous; massy, massive 324 adj. *dense*; overweighted, overburdened, overloaded; gravitational.

Vb. *weigh*, have weight, balance 28 vb. *be equal*; counterpoise 31 vb. *compensate*; outweigh, overweigh, overbalance, tip the scale; gravitate, settle 309 vb. *descend*; lay in the scale 465 vb. *measure*.

make heavy, weight, hang weights on; burden, weigh on, hang like a millstone; overweight, overburden, overload 193 vb. *load*.

323. Levity – **N.** *levity*, lightness etc. adj.; thinness, air, ether 325 n. *rarity*; buoyancy; volatility 338 n. *vaporization*; weightlessness, imponderability; defiance of gravity, levitation; feather-weight, fluff, thistle-down 4 n. *insubstantial thing*; cork, buoy, bubble.

leaven, lightener; ferment, enzyme, zymogen, barm, yeast, baking-powder, self-raising flour.

Adj. *light*, underweight 307 adj. *deficient*; light-weight, feather-w.; portable, handy 196 adj. *little*; non-gravitational, weightless; imponderable, unweighable; volatile, sublimated 325 adj. *rare*; uncompressed, doughy, barmy, yeasty, zymotic, enzymic; aerated, frothy, foamy, whipped; buoyant, unsinkable; feathery, light as air.

Vb. *be light* etc. adj.; defy gravity, levitate, surface, float 308 vb. *ascend*; be outweighed, kick the beam.

lighten, buoy up; lighten ship, throw overboard, jettison 300 vb. *void*; volatilize, gasify, vaporize 340 vb. *aerify*; leaven, work.

Section 2: Inorganic Matter

324. Density – **N.** *density*, solidity; compactness, concreteness, thickness, concentration; consistence, spissitude; incompressibility 326 n. *hardness*; impenetrability, impermeability, imporosity; cohesion, solidarity 48 n. *coherence*; relative density, specific gravity; densimeter, hydrometer, aerometer.

condensation, inspissation, constipation; thickening etc. vb.; consolidation, concentration; concretion, nucleation; caseation, coagulation; solidification, consolidation; congealment, gelatination; glaciation; ossification, petrifaction, fossilization 326 n. *hardening*; crystallization; sedimentation, precipitation; condenser, compressor, thickener, curdler, gelatine, rennet.

solid body, solid; lump, mass 319 n. *matter*; knot, block; condensation, nucleus, hard core; conglomerate, concretion; concrete, cement; stone 344 n. *rock*; precipitate, deposit, sediment; coagulum, curd, clot, grume, thrombosis; solid mass, phalanx, wall 702 n. *obstacle*.

Adj. *dense*, thick, crass; close, heavy (air); foggy, murky, to be cut with a knife; lumpy, ropy, grumous, clotted, curdled; caked, caky; monolithic, firm, close-textured; massy 322 adj. *weighty*; concrete, solid, frozen; costive, constipated; compact, close-packed; thickset, thick, bushy; serried, massed; incompressible 326 adj. *rigid*; impermeable, impenetrable, impervious; indissoluble, insoluble, sedimentary; styptic, astringent.

Vb. *be dense*, —solid etc. adj.; solidify, consolidate; conglomerate, cement 48 vb. *cohere*; condense, nucleate; densen, thicken, inspissate, incrassate; precipitate, silt up; freeze 380 vb. *be cold*; set, gelatinize, jellify, jell; congeal, coagulate, clot, curdle; cake, crust; crystallize; fossilize, petrify, ossify 326 vb. *harden*; compress 198 vb. *make smaller*; bind, constipate.

325. Rarity – **N.** *rarity*, low pressure, vacuum 190 n. *emptiness*; compressibility 327 n. *softness*; fineness 206 n. *thinness*; incorporeality 320 n. *immateriality*; rarefaction, expansion, pressure-reduction, attenuation; subtilization, etherealization.

Adj. *rare*, tenuous, thin, fine, subtile; flimsy, slight 4 adj. *insubstantial*; low-pressure; compressible, spongy 328 adj. *elastic*; rarefied 336 adj. *gaseous*; void, hollow 190 adj. *empty*; incorporeal 320 adj. *immaterial*.

Vb. *rarefy*, reduce the pressure, expand; pump out 300 vb. *void*; subtilize, attenuate; dilute 163 vb. *weaken*; volatilize 338 vb. *vaporize*.

326. Hardness – N. *hardness*, intractability, resistance; starchiness, stiffness, rigidity, inflexibility, inelasticity; firmness, temper; grittiness 329 n. *toughness*; callosity, callousness; stone, granite, diamond 344 n. *rock*; adamant, metal, steel, iron, bone, gristle; a callosity, callus, corn, kibe; blain, chilblain; shell; hard core, jaw-breaker; stiffener, starch, wax; whalebone 218 n. *supporter*.

hardening, induration; stiffening, backing; starching; petrifaction, fossilization; ossification, cornification; sclerosis.

Adj. *hard*, adamantine, unbreakable, infrangible 162 adj. *strong*; steeled, proof; steely; cartilaginous, gristly 329 adj. *tough*; callous, stony, rocky, flinty, gritty; horny, corneous; bony, osseous; icy, frozen; sclerotic.

rigid, stubborn, obdurate 602 adj. *obstinate*; intractable, unmalleable, firm, inflexible, unbending 162 adj. *unyielding*; incompressible, inextensible; inelastic, unsprung; starchy, starched; muscle-bound 695 adj. *clumsy*; tense, taut, tight 45 adj. *firm-set*; stiff, stark.

Vb. *harden*, steel 162 vb. *strengthen*; indurate, temper, vulcanize, toughen; petrify, fossilize, ossify; calcify, vitrify, crystallize; glaciate 382 vb. *refrigerate*; stiffen, back, starch, wax (a moustache); tauten.

327. Softness – N. *softness*, tenderness; pliancy, pliability, flexibility, plasticity, malleability; suppleness, litheness; springiness, turfiness 328 n. *elasticity*;

impressibility, doughiness 356 n. *pulpiness*; sponginess etc. adj.; laxity, looseness 335 n. *fluidity*; sogginess 347 n. *marsh*; butter, wax, clay, dough; padding, cushion 376 n. *euphoria*; velvet, down 259 n. *hair*; light rein, velvet glove 736 n. *lenity*.

Adj. *soft*, tender 301 adj. *edible*; melting 335 adj. *fluidal*; compressible; springy, sprung 328 adj. *elastic*; pneumatic, cushiony, padded; impressible, as wax, doughy, argilaceous; spongy, soggy, mushy, squelchy 347 n. *marshy*; squashy 356 adj. *pulpy*; fleecy 259 adj. *downy*; turfy; plushy, velvety, silky 258 adj. *smooth*; unstarched, limp; flaccid, flabby, floppy; gentle, light; emollient 177 adj. *lenitive*.

flexible, whippy, pliant, pliable; ductile, tractile, malleable, plastic; stretchable 328 adj. *elastic*; lithe, supple, lissom, limber, loose-limbed, double-jointed.

Vb. *soften*, mollify 177 vb. *assuage*; tenderize; mellow 669 vb. *mature*; grease 334 vb. *lubricate*; knead, massage, mash, pulp; macerate, steep 341 vb. *drench*; cushion, pillow 177 vb. *moderate*; relax, unbend 683 vb. *repose*.

328. Elasticity – N. *elasticity*, give, stretch; spring, springiness; suspension, knee action; stretchability, extensibility; resilience, bounce 280 n. *recoil*; buoyancy, rubber, elastic; caoutchouc, gutta-percha.

Adj. *elastic*, stretchable, tensile, extensile; springy, bouncy, resilient 280 adj. *recoiling*; buoyant; sprung, well-s.

329. Toughness – N. *toughness*, durability 162 n. *strength*; tenacity 778 n. *retention*; cohesion 48 n. *coherence*; leather, gristle, cartilage 326 n. *hardness*.

Adj. *tough*, durable, close-woven 162 adj. *strong*; tenacious, retentive 48 adj. *cohesive*; untearable, shock-proof 162 adj. *unyielding*; hardboiled, overdone; stringy, fibrous; gristly, cartilaginous; rubbery, leathery; indigestible, inedible.

Vb. *toughen*, tan, case-harden; mer-cerise, vulcanize, temper, anneal 162 vb. *strengthen*.

330. Brittleness – N. *brittleness* etc. adj.; frangibility; friability 332 n. *pulverulence*; fissility 46 n. *scission*; laminability, flakiness 207 n. *lamina*; fragility, frailty, flimsiness 163 n. *weakness*; bubble, egg-shell, matchwood, piecrust; glass, china, crockery, glasshouse 163 n. *weak thing*.

Adj. *brittle*, breakable, fragile, glassy; papery, like parchment; shattery, friable, crumbly 332 adj. *powdery*; crisp, short; flaky, laminable; fissile; tearable 46 adj. *severable*; frail, delicate, flimsy 163 adj. *weak*; gimcrack 4 adj. *insubstantial*; tumble-down 655 adj. *dilapidated*; ready to burst, explosive.

Vb. *be brittle*, fracture 46 vb. *break*; crack, snap; star, craze; split, shatter, shiver, fragment; splinter, snap off; burst, explode; wear thin; crumble 332 vb. *pulverize*.

331. Structure. Texture – N. *structure*, organization, pattern, plan; complex 52 n. *whole*; fashion, mould, shape, build 243 n. *form*; constitution, set-up 56 n. *composition*; construction, make, works, workings; compaction, architecture, tectonics; fabric, brickwork, stonework, woodwork; scaffold, framework, chassis, shell 218 n. *frame*; physique, anatomy; bony structure, skeleton.

texture, intertexture, contexture 222 n. *crossing*; tissue, fabric, stuff 222 n. *textile*; staple, denier 208 n. *fibre*; web, weave 222 n. *weaving*; nap, pile 259 n. *hair*; granulation, grain, grit, surface 223 n. *exteriority*; feel 378 n. *touch*.

Adj. *structural*, organic; skeletal; anatomic, anatomical, physiological, organological; organizational, constructional; tectonic, architectural.

textural, woven 222 adj. *crossed*; ribbed, twilled; grained, granular; fine-grained, silky, satiny 258 adj. *smooth*; coarse-grained 259 adj. *rough*; fine, fine-spun; coarse, homespun, hodden, linsey-woolsey.

332. Pulverulence – N. *pulverulence*, powderiness; 'flowers' (chemistry), dustiness 649 n. *dirt*; sandiness, grittiness; granulation; friability, crumbliness 330 n. *brittleness*; pulverization, levigation, trituration; multure; abrasion 333 n. *friction*; fragmentation 46 n. *disjunction*.

powder, face-p. 843 n. *cosmetic*; pollen, spore, sporule; dust, soot, ash 649 n. *dirt*; flour, grist, meal, bran; sawdust, filings, limature; efflorescence, flowers; sand, grit, gravel; granule, grain, crumb, flake, snow f.; smoke, smoke-cloud.

pulverizer, miller, grinder; roller, crusher, masher, atomizer; mill, millstone, quern; pestle, mortar; hand-mill; grater, grindstone, file; abrasive, sandpaper, emery paper; sledge-hammer 279 n. *hammer*; bulldozer 279 n. *ram*.

Adj. *powdery*, pulverulent; dusty, sooty, smoky 649 adj. *dirty*; sandy, arenaceous; farinaceous, branny, floury; granulated, granular; gritty, gravelly; crumbly, friable 330 adj. *brittle*.

Vb. *pulverize*, powder; triturate, levigate, granulate; crush, mash, comminute, atomize, shatter, fragment 46 vb. *break*; grind, mill, mince, beat, bruise, pound, bray; knead; crumble, crumb; chip, flake, grate, rasp, file 333 vb. *rub*; weather, rust 51 vb. *decompose*.

333. Friction – N. *friction*, frictional force, drag 278 n. *slowness*; rubbing etc. vb.; attrition; erasure 550 n. *obliteration*; abrasion, limature; erosion 165 n. *destruction*; scrape etc. vb.; polish, levigation, elbow grease; shampoo, massage; eraser, rubber; masseur 843 n. *beautician*.

Adj. *rubbing*, frictional; abrasive, fricative.

Vb. *rub*, friction; rub, strike (a match); chafe, gall; graze, scratch 655 vb. *wound*; rub off, abrade; scrape, scrub, scour; brush, rub down, curry, curry-comb 648 vb. *clean*; polish, wax, buff, levigate 258 vb. *smooth*; rub out, erase 550 vb. *obliterate*; gnaw, erode, fret, fray; rasp, file, grind 332 vb. *pulverize*; knead, shampoo, massage; grate, catch, stick; stroke 889 vb. *caress*; iron 258 vb. *smooth*.

334. Lubrication – N. *lubrication*, lubrification; anointment, unction; oiling etc. vb.; lubricity 357 n. *unctuousness*; non-friction 258 n. *smoothness*.

lubricant, graphite, plumbago, black lead; glycerine, wax, grease 357 n. *oil*; soap, lather 648 n. *cleanser*; ointment, salve 357 n. *unguent*; lubricator, oil-can, grease-gun.

Adj. *lubricated* etc. vb.; well-oiled, well-greased.

Vb. *lubricate*, oil, grease, wax, soap, lather; grease leather, liquor; anoint, pour balm.

335. Fluidity – N. *fluidity*, liquidity, fluxility; wateriness, rheuminess 339 n. *water*; juiciness, sappiness 356 n. *pulpiness*; non-coagulation, haemophilia; solubility, liquidescence 337 n. *liquefaction*; bloodiness, goriness 354 n. *semiliquidity*; hydrology, hydrometry, hydrostatics, hydrodynamics; hydraulics, hydrokinetics.

fluid, elastic f. 336 n. *gas*; non-elastic fluid, liquid; water 339 n. *water*; drink 301 n. *liquor*; juice, sap, latex; gore (see *blood*); hydrocele, dropsy 651 n. *disease*.

blood, ichor, claret; life-blood 360 n. *life*; blood-stream, circulation; gore, cruor, sanies, grume; clot, thrombosis 324 n. *solid body*; haemad, corpuscle, red c., white c., platelet; lymph, plasma, serum, serosity; serolin; cruorin, haemoglobin, haematoglobulin; haematogenesis, haematosis, sanguification; blood group; blood-count; haematoscopy, haematoscope, haemometer; haematics, haematology.

Adj. *fluidal*, fluid, liquid; uncongealed, fluxive; unclotted, clear, clarified; soluble, liquescent 337 adj. *liquefied*; runny, rheumy, phlegmy 339 adj. *watery*; succulent, juicy, sappy; pussy, mattery, suppurating 653 adj. *toxic*; hydrostatic, hydrodynamic.

sanguineous, haemal, haemogenic; serous, lymphatic, plasmatic; bloody,

sanguinary 431 adj. *bloodshot*; gory, sanious, ichorous; bleeding, haemophilic.

336. Gaseity – N. *gaseity*, gaseousness, vaporousness etc. adj.; windiness, flatulence 352 n. *wind*; aeration, gasification; volatility 338 n. *vaporization*; pneumatostatics 340 n. *pneumatics*.

gas, vapour, elastic fluid; ether 340 n. *air*; effluvium, exhalation, miasma; flatus 352 n. *wind*; fume, reek, smoke; steam, water vapour 355 n. *cloud*; damp, fire d., choke d.; gasworks, gas plant, gasification p.; gas-holder, gasometer 632 n. *storage*.

Adj. *gaseous*, gasiform; vaporous, steamy, volatile 338 adj. *vaporific*; gassy, windy, flatulent; effluvial, miasmic 659 adj. *baneful*; pneumatic, aerostatic, aerodynamic.

Vb. *gasify*, aerate 340 vb. *aerify*; vapour, steam 338 vb. *vaporize*; let off steam, blow off 300 vb. *emit*.

337. Liquefaction – N. *liquefaction*, liquidization; liquescence; solubility, deliquescence, fluxibility 335 n. *fluidity*; fusion, colliquation 43 n. *mixture*; lixiviation; thaw 381 n. *heating*; solvent, flux, diluent, menstruum, alkahest, aqua fortis; anticoagulant 658 n. *antidote*.

solution, decoction, infusion, apozem; flux, lixivium, lye.

Adj. *liquefied*, molten: runny, liquescent, uncongealed; liquefacient, solvent; soluble, fluxible 335 adj. *fluidal*.

Vb. *liquefy*, liquidize, unclot 350 vb. *make flow*; dissolve, deliquesce, run 350 vb. *flow*; unfreeze, melt, thaw 381 vb. *heat*; melt down, fuse, render, clarify; leach, lixiviate; hold in solution; cast, found.

338. Vaporization – N. *vaporization*, exhalation 355 n. *cloud*; gasification, aerification; evaporation, volatilization, distillation, sublimation; fumigation, vaporability, volatility.

vaporizer, evaporator; atomizer, spray; retort, still, distillery.

Adj. *vaporific*, volatilized etc. vb.; reeking, steaming etc. vb.; vaporous, steamy, gassy, smoky; evaporable, volatile.

Vb. *vaporize*, evaporate; aerify 336 vb. *gasify*; volatilize, distil, sublimate, exhale, transpire, blow off steam; smoke, fume, reek, steam; fumigate, spray; spray, atomize.

339. Water – N. *water*, drinking water, tap w. 301 n. *soft drink*; water vapour, steam 355 n. *cloud*; rain water 350 n. *rain*; running water 350 n. *stream*; high water, low w. 350 n. *wave*; still water 346 n. *lake*; sea water, brine 343 n. *ocean*; soap and water, lotion, bath 648 n. *cleansing*; wateriness, damp, wet; watering 341 n. *moistening*; water-carrier, bheestie; water-cart 341 n. *irrigator*; tap 351 n. *conduit*; hydrometry 341 n. *hygrometry*.

Adj. *watery*, aqueous, aquatic, lymphatic; hydro-, hydrated, hydrous; hydrological, hydrographic 321 adj. *geographic;* adulterated 163 adj. *weak*; still, fizzy; wet 341 adj. *humid*; balneal 648 adj. *cleansing*; hydrotherapeutic 658 adj. *medical*.

340. Air – N. *air*, 336 n. *gas*; thin air 325 n. *rarity*; air-pocket 190 n. *emptiness*; blast 352 n. *wind*; common air, oxygen, nitrogen, neon, argon, ozone; open air, out-of-doors, exposure; airing 342 n. *desiccation*; aeration 338 n. *vaporization*; ventilation 685 n. *refreshment*; air-conditioning 382 n. *refrigeration*; ventilator, blower, fan, air-conditioner 384 n. *refrigerator*.

atmosphere, aerosphere; Heaviside Layer, Van Allen belt; ionosphere, troposphere, tropopause, stratosphere; isothermal layer.

weather, the elements; fair weather, halcyon days; doldrums; atmospheric pressure, anticyclone, high pressure; cyclone, depression, rough weather 176 n. *storm*; rise and fall of the barometer; meteorology, weather forecast 511 n.

prediction; isobar, decibar, millibar; glass, mercury, barometer; weathership; barograph, weather glass, weather gauge; vane, weathercock; hygrometer, weather-house; weather-man, meteorologist; climate, climatology, climatologist.

pneumatics, aerodynamics, aerography, aeroscopy, aerology, barometry, anemometry 352 n. *anemology*; aerometer, baroscope, barometer, aneroid b., barograph, barogram.

Adj. *airy*, ethereal 4 adj. *insubstantial*; skyey; aerial; pneumatic, aerated; inflated, blown up, flatulent 197 adj. *expanded*; oxygenated 355 adj. *bubbly*; breezy 352 adj. *windy*; well-ventilated 382 adj. *cooled*; meteorological, weather-wise; atmospheric, barometric; cyclonic, anticyclonic; high-pressure, low-pressure; climatic, climatological.

Vb. *aerify*, aerate, oxygenate; air, expose 342 vb. *dry*; ventilate, freshen, deodorize 648 vb. *clean*; fan, winnow, make a draught 352 vb. *blow*.

341. Moisture – N. *moisture*, humidity, sap, juice 335 n. *fluid*; dampness, wetness; dewiness; dankness; ooze, sogginess, swampiness 347 n. *marsh*; saturation 863 n. *satiety*; leakiness 298 n. *outflow*; pluviosity 350 n. *rain*; damp, dank, wet; froth, foam 355 n. *bubble*; drip, dew, drop, rain-d., dew-d., tear-d.; saliva 302 n. *excrement*; sop.

moistening, madefaction, humidification; bedewing, rorification; deluge 350 n. *rain*; spargefaction, sprinkle, aspersion, ducking, submersion, immersion; overflow 350 n. *waterfall*; wash, bath 648 n. *ablution*; baptism; percolation, leaching; irrigation see *irrigate*; injection; gargle; hydrotherapy.

irrigator, sprinkler, aspergillum; waterer, watering-cart; watering-pot, watering-can; spray, rose; hose, syringe; pump, fire-engine; Persian wheel, shadoof, swipe; cistern, dam, reservoir 632 n. *store*; sluice 351 n. *conduit*.

hygrometry, hydrography, hydrology; hygrometer, udometer, rain-gauge, plu-

133

viometer, Nilometer; hydroscope, weather-house.

Adj. *humid*, moistening, humective; wet 339 adj. *watery*; pluvious, pluvial 350 adj. *rainy*; undried, damp, moist, dripping; dank, misty 355 adj. *cloudy*; undrained 347 adj. *marshy*; dewy, fresh; juicy, sappy 335 adj. *fluidal*; drip-dropping, wetted, dabbled.

drenched, saturated, irriguous; sodden, wet through, wringing wet; waterlogged, awash, swamped, drowned.

Vb. *be wet*, — moist etc. adj.; be soggy, squelch, suck; salivate, sweat 298 vb. *exude*; steam 300 vb. *emit*; percolate, seep 297 vb. *infiltrate*; weep, bleed, stream; ooze, drip, leak 298 vb. *flow out*; drizzle 350 vb. *rain*; dip, duck, dive 313 vb. *plunge*; wallow. welter.

moisten, humidify, wet, dampen; dilute; lick, lap, wash; splash; spill, slop 311 vb. *let fall*; spray, syringe, sprinkle; asperge; bedew, bedabble, gargle.

drench, saturate, imbrue, imbue; soak, deluge, wet through; leach, lixiviate; wash, lave, bathe; sluice, rinse 648 vb. *clean*; immerse, dip, duck, submerge, drown; swamp, whelm, flood, inundate, flood out, waterlog; souse, steep; macerate, pickle, brine 666 vb. *preserve*.

irrigate, water, hose, pump; inundate, flood, overflow, submerge; syringe, gargle; squirt, inject.

342. Dryness – N. *dryness*, aridity; thirst 859 n. *hunger*; drought, rainlessness, desert conditions 172 n. *desert*; dry climate, sunny south; sun, sunniness 379 n. *heat*.

desiccation, arefaction; drying up; airing, evaporation 338 n. *vaporization*; drainage; dehydration; insolation, aprication, sunning 381 n. *heating*.

drier, desiccator, evaporator; absorbent, sand, blotting paper, mop, swab, sponge 648 n. *cleanser*; wringer, mangle 198 n. *compressor*.

Adj. *dry*, thirsty 859 adj. *hungry*; unirrigated, irrigable; arid, rainless, waterless, riverless; sandy, dusty, desert,

Saharan; anhydrous, dehydrated, desiccated; sapless, juiceless, mummified; sun-dried, wind-d., bleached; sunny, fine, cloudless, fair; drained; waterproof, rain-proof, damp-p., watertight; bonedry; unwetted, dry-footed, dry-shod; out of water, high and dry; unsweetened 393 adj. *sour*.

Vb. *dry*, dehumidify, desiccate; dehydrate; ditch, drain; wring out, mangle, hang out, air, evaporate, sun, insolate, apricate, sun-dry; smoke, kipper, cure; parch 381 vb. *heat*; wither, dry up 350 vb. *stanch*; blot, mop up, soak up, sponge 299 vb. *absorb*.

343. Ocean – N. *ocean*, sea, blue water, salt w., brine, briny; main, deep; high seas, great waters; herring pond, big drink; sea-lane; sea floor, ooze, benthos; the seven seas.

sea-god, Oceanus, Neptune, Varuna, Triton, Amphitrite, Tethys; old man of the sea, merman.

sea-nymph, Oceanid, Naiad, Nereid, siren; Calypso, Undine; mermaid; bathing-beauty; water-sprite 970 n. *fairy*.

oceanography, hydrography, bathymetry; sea-survey, Admiralty chart; bathysphere, bathyscaph, bathymeter; oceanographer, hydrographer.

Adj. *oceanic*, thalassic, pelagic; sea, marine, maritime; ocean-going 269 adj. *seafaring*; benthic, benthonic; hydrographic, bathymetric.

344. Land – N. *land*, dry l., terra firma; earth, ground, crust 321 n. *world*; country, continent, mainland; heart-land, hinterland; midland, inland, interior 224 n. *interiority*; peninsula, delta, promontory 254 n. *projection*; isthmus, landbridge; terrain; steppe, fields 348 n. *plain*; oasis, Fertile Crescent; zone, clime 184 n. *region*; territory, possessions, acres 777 n. *lands*; physical features 321 n. *geography*; landsman, landlubber, continental, mainlander, islander, isthmian 191 n. *dweller*.

shore, coast-line, coast; strand, beach, sands, shingle; seaboard, seashore, seaside; plage, lido, riviera; bank, riverside; continental shelf.

soil, glebe, farmland, arable land 370 n. *farm*; pasture 348 n. *grassland*; deposit, moraine, geest, silt, alluvium, loess; topsoil, subsoil; mould, humus; loam, clay, bole, marl; cledge, Fuller's earth; argil, potter's clay, China clay, kaolin 381 n. *pottery*; turf, divot, sod, clod 53 n. *piece*.

rock, cliff, scar, crag; stone, boulder; reef, skerry; igneous rock, abyssal r., volcanic r.; lava, lapilli, tuff; sedimentary rock, bedded r., metamorphic r., conglomerate, schist.

Adj. *territorial*, landed, predial, farming, agricultural 370 adj. *agrarian*; terrene 321 adj. *telluric*; earthy, alluvial, silty; loamy, humic; clayey, marly, chalky; flinty, pebbly, gravelly, stony, lithic, rocky.

coastal, coasting; littoral, riparian, riverine, riverside, seaside; on-shore.

inland, continental, midland, interior, central; landlocked.

345. Gulf: inlet – N. *gulf*, bay, bight, cove, creek, lagoon; inlet, arm of the sea, fiord; mouth, estuary 263 n. *orifice*; firth, frith, kyle; sound, strait, belt, gut, euripus, channel.

346. Lake – N. *lake*, mere, lagoon, landlocked water; loch, lough, linn; inland sea; ox-bow lake, bayou; broads; standing water, sheet of w.; mud flat, wash 347 n. *marsh*; pool, tarn, pond; millpond; dam, reservoir 632 n. *storage*; basin, tank, cistern; water-hole, puddle, sough, splash, wallow.

Adj. *lacustrine*, lake-dwelling, landlocked.

347. Marsh – N. *marsh*, marshland, slobland; fen, moorland, moor; everglade, wash; flat, salt pan, salina; sullage, silt; morass, slough, swamp, bog, moss, quagmire, quicksand; bottom; wallow, sough; thaw, slush, squash, mire, mud, ooze; forest swamp, taiga.

Adj. *marshy*, silty, paludial; moorish;

swampy, boggy, fenny; oozy, quaggy, squelchy, slushy 354 adj. *semiliquid*; muddy, miry, slabby 649 adj. *dirty*; undrained, waterlogged, uliginous.

348. Plain – N. *plain*, peneplane; dene, dale, basin, lowlands 255 n. *valley*; flats 347 n. *marsh*; delta, alluvial plain, landes; tundra; ice-plain 380 n. *ice*; grasslands, steppe, prairie, savanna, pampas; heath, common, wold, weald; upland, plateau, tableland, mesa; range, open country, rolling c., champaign; lowlands, low countries 210 n. *lowness*.

grassland, pasture, pasturage, grazing 369 n. *animal husbandry*; sheep-run, sheep-walk; field, meadow, water-m., mead, lea; chase, park, grounds; green, greensward, sward, lawn, turf, sod; green belt.

Adj. *champaign*, campestrian, campestral; flat, open, rolling.

349. Island – N. *island*, isle, islet; lagoon-island, atoll, reef, coral r.; cay, key; sandbank, bar; island continent; island universe, galaxy 321 n. *star*; archipelago; insularity 883 n. *seclusion*; insular, islander, islesman 191 n. *dweller*.

Adj. *insular*, circumfluous, sea-girt; isleted, archipelagic.

350. Stream: water in motion – N. *stream*, running water, river, waterway; tributary, branch, feeder, affluent, effluent, distributary; reach; watercourse, streamlet, rivulet, creek, brook, brooklet, bourne, burn, beck, rill, runnel; freshet, torrent, force; spring, fountain, fount 156 n. *source*; jet, spout, gush; gusher, geyser, hot spring, well 632 n. *store*.

current, flow, set; flux; confluence 293 n. *convergence*; indraught, inflow 297 n. *ingress*; outflow, reflux 286 n. *regression*; undercurrent, undertow, cross-current, rip tide 182 n. *counteraction*; tide, spring t., neap t.; tidal flow, ebb and flow 317 n. *fluctuation*; tideway, bore, eagre; race, tidal r., mill-r.; bloodstream, circulation 314 n. *circuition*.

eddy, whirlpool, swirl, maelstrom

315 n. *vortex*; surge, regurgitation 290 n. *recession*; wash, backwash, wake 67 n. *sequel*.

waterfall, cataract, catadupe, Niagara; cascade, force, overfall, rapids, watershoot, weir; flush, chute, spillway, sluice; overflow, spill; flood, inundation, cataclysm.

wave, bow-w.; wash, backwash; ripple, cat's-paw 262 n. *furrow*; swell, ground s., billow, roller, comber, beach-c.; breaker, surf, white horses, white caps; tidal wave, tsunami 176 n. *storm*; bore, eagre; rip, overfall; broken water, choppiness 259 n. *roughness*; sea, heavy s.; waviness, undulation.

rain, rainfall 341 n. *moisture*; precipitation; drizzle, mizzle; shower, downpour, drencher, soaker, cloud-burst; flurry 352 n. *gale*; raininess, wet spell, foul weather; rainy season, the rains, monsoon; hyetography; rain-gauge 341 n. *hygrometry*.

Adj. *flowing* etc. vb.; runny 335 adj. *fluidal*; fluent, streamy, fluvial, tidal; in flood, in spate; inundatory, cataclysmic; popply, choppy 259 adj. *rough*; oozy, sluggish 278 adj. *slow*.

rainy, showery, drizzly, spitting, spotting; wet 341 adj. *humid*; torrential, monsoonish.

Vb. *flow*, run, course; set, make; ebb, regurgitate 286 vb. *regress*; swirl, eddy 315 vb. *rotate*; surge, break, dash, ripple, popple; roll, swell; gush, rush, spirt, spout, jet, play, squirt, splutter; well, issue 298 vb. *emerge*; pour, stream; drip, trickle, dribble 298 vb. *exude*; plash, lap, wash, splash 341 vb. *moisten*; overflow, flood, inundate, deluge 341 vb. *drench*; drain, spill, percolate 305 vb. *pass*; ooze, wind 251 vb. *meander*.

rain, shower, stream, pour, pelt; come down, rain hard, rain in torrents, rain cats and dogs, sheet; patter, drizzle, drip, spit.

make flow, make *or* pass water 302 vb. *excrete*; pump 300 vb. *eject*; broach, tap, open the cocks 263 vb. *open*; pour, spill 311 vb. *let fall*; transfuse, decant 272 vb. *transpose*; empty, drain out 300 vb. *void*.

stanch, stop the flow 342 vb. *dry*; apply a tourniquet, compress 198 vb. *make smaller*; stop a leak, plug 264 vb. *close*; stem, dam 702 vb. *obstruct*.

351. Conduit – N. *conduit*, water channel, tideway, riverbed; ditch, dyke, trench, moat; watercourse, canal, channel, gutter, runnel; duct, aqueduct; plumbing, water-pipe, main; pipe, hose-p., hose; standpipe, hydrant, siphon, tap, spout, waterspout, gargoyle, funnel 263 n. *tube*; sluice, weir, lock, floodgate, watergate, spillway; pipeline; blood vessel, vein, artery.

drain, kennel, gutter; gargoyle, waterspout; scupper, overflow, waste-pipe, drain-p.; ajutage, efflux-tube; culvert, ditch, sewer 649 n. *sink*; emunctory, intestine, colon.

352. Wind: air in motion – N. *wind*, 340 n. *air*; draught, downdraught, updraught; windiness, weather; flatus, afflatus; blast, blow (see *breeze*, *gale*); current, air-c.; headwind, tailwind, airstream, slip-s.; air pocket; seasonal wind, monsoon, etesian winds; trade w., antitrades, Brave West Winds, Roaring Forties.

anemology, aerodynamics, anemography 340 n. *pneumatics*; wind-rose, Beaufort scale; anemometer, windgauge, weather-cock, weather-vane, wind-sock, wind-cone; wind-tunnel.

breeze, zephyr, light air; breath, whiff, puff, gust, capful of wind; sea-breeze, doctor.

gale, half g., fresh wind; blow, hard b., blast, gust, flurry, flaw, squall; storm-wind, buster, northwester, sou'wester, hurricane; whirlwind, whirlblast; cyclone, tornado, typhoon, simoom 315 n. *vortex*, 176 n. *storm*; weather, dirty w., stress of w.; gale force.

sufflation, insufflation, perflation, inflation; pump, air-p., stirrup-p.; bellows, windbag, bagpipe; blow-pipe; exhaust-pipe, exhaust 298 n. *outlet*.

ventilation, airing 340 n. *air*; draught, ventiduct, ventilator; blower, fan, punkah, pull-p., chowrie, thermantidote, air-conditioner 384 n. *refrigerator*.

respiration, breathing, inhalation, exhalation, expiration; stomach wind, eructation, belch; lungs, bellows; windpipe 353 n. *air-pipe*; sneezing, sternutation 406 n. *sibilation*; cough, whoopingc., croup, strangles; sigh, sob, gulp, hiccup; hard breathing, panting; wheeze, rattle, death r.

Adj. *windy*, airy, exposed, draughty, blowy; ventilated, fresh; blowing, breezy, puffy, gusty, squally; blusterous, blustery, dirty, foul, stormy, tempestuous, boisterous 176 adj. *violent*; windswept, storm-tossed; flatulent; fizzy, gassy; monsoonish, cyclonic.

puffing, huffing; snorting, wheezy, asthmatic, stertorous; panting, breathless; sniffy, snuffly, sneezey; pulmonary, coughy, chesty.

Vb. *blow*, puff, breeze, blast; freshen, blow hard, blow great guns, rage, storm 176 vb. *be violent*; howl 409 vb. *ululate*; whistle, pipe 407 vb. *shrill*; moan 401 vb. *sound faint*; draw, make a draught; ventilate, fan 382 vb. *refrigerate*; veer, back 282 vb. *deviate*.

breathe, respire, breathe in, inhale, draw; breathe out, exhale; aspirate, puff, huff; sniff, sniffle, snuffle, snort; breathe hard, gasp, pant, heave; wheeze, sneeze, cough 407 vb. *rasp*; sigh, sob, gulp, suck *or* catch the breath, hiccup; belch, burp 300 vb. *eruct*.

sufflate, inflate, dilate; blow up, pump up 197 vb. *enlarge*; pump out, exhaust 300 vb. *void*.

353. Air-pipe – N. *air-pipe*, air-shaft, wind-tunnel; air-tube, blow-pipe; windpipe, trachea, larynx; weasand, bronchia; throat, gullet; nose, nostril, spiracle, blow-hole, nozzle, vent, mouthpiece 263 n. *orifice*; gas-pipe; tobacco pipe 388 n. *tobacco*; smoke-stack 263 n. *chimney*; air-duct, ventilator; air-hole, smoke-duct 263 n. *window*.

354. Semiliquidity – N. *semiliquidity*, stodginess 324 n. *density*; mucosity, viscidity; clamminess, ropiness, colloidality; semiliquid, colloid, emulsion, mucus, phlegm, pituita; pus, matter; mush 356 n. *pulpiness*; slush 347 n. *marsh*; sediment, grounds 649 n. *dirt*.

viscidity, glutinosity, glueyness, gumminess, stickiness, treacliness, adhesiveness 48 n. *coherence*; glue 47 n. *adhesive*; emulsion, collodion, colloid; glair, size, paste, glaze, slip; treacle, syrup.

Adj. *semiliquid*, stodgy, thick, soupy, lumpy, ropy 324 adj. *dense*; unclarified, curdled, clotted, gelatinous; pulpy, juicy, sappy, creamy; starchy, amylaceous; emulsive; colloidal; thawing, half-frozen, half-melted 347 adj. *marshy*; slimy, silty, sedimentary. See *viscid*.

viscid, lentous, grumous, gummy, adhesive 48 adj. *cohesive*; clammy, sticky, tacky; jammy, treacly, syrupy, gluey; glairy, glaireous; mucous, mucilaginous.

Vb. *thicken*, 324 vb. *be dense*.

355. Bubble. Cloud: air and water mixed – N. *bubble*, suds, lather, foam, froth; head, top; spume, surf, spray, spindrift 341 n. *moisture*; yeast 323 n. *leaven*; effervescence, fermentation, yeastiness, fizziness, fizz.

cloud, cloudlet, scud, rack; rain-cloud, nimbus; cumulus, cirrus, stratus; mackerel sky, mare's tail; vapour, steam 338 n. *vaporization*; haze, mist, fog, fogbank, smog, London special; cloudiness, cloudbank 419 n. *dimness*; nebulosity.

Adj. *bubbly*, effervescent, fizzy, sparkling; foamy, spumy; frothy, soapy, lathery; yeasty, up, aerated 323 adj. *light*.

cloudy, overcast, overclouded; nubilous, nebulous; thick, foggy, hazy, misty 419 adj. *dim*; vaporous 338 adj. *vaporific*.

Vb. *bubble*, spume, foam, froth, lather, form a head; mantle, scum; ream, cream; boil, effervesce; ferment, fizz, sparkle; aerate 340 vb. *aerify*.

356. Pulpiness – N. *pulpiness*, doughiness, sponginess; juiciness, sappiness 327 n. *softness*; sop; poultice, pulp, pith,

137

paste, pap; mush, mash, squash; dough; pulper, pulp-digester.

Adj. *pulpy* 354 adj. *semiliquid*; mushy, pappy 327 adj. *soft*; succulent, juicy, sappy, squashy, ripe, overripe; flabby, dimply 195 adj. *fleshy*; doughy, pasty; soggy, spongy 347 adj. *marshy*.

357. Unctuousness – N. *unctuousness* etc. adj.; unctuosity, oiliness, greasiness, lubricity, soapiness 334 n. *lubrication*; fattiness, pinguescence; anointment, unction.

oil, volatile o., essential o.; lubricating oil; fuel oil, paraffin, kerosene, petroleum 385 n. *fuel*.

fat, animal f., adeps, adipocere, grease; blubber, tallow, spermaceti; sebum, cerin, wax; suet, lard, dripping; glycerine, stearine, butyrin; butter, ghee; margarine; soap 648 n. *cleanser*.

unguent, salve, unction, ointment, cerate; liniment, embrocation, lanolin, vaseline; hair-oil, brilliantine; pomade; face-cream, hand-c. 843 n. *cosmetic*.

resin, resinoid, rosin, colophony, gum arabic, tragacanth, mastic, myrrh, frankincense, camphor, labdanum; lac, amber, ambergris; pitch, tar, bitumen, asphalt; varnish, copal, megilp, shellac, lacquer, japan.

Adj. *fatty*, pinguid, pinguescent; fat, adipose 195 adj. *fleshy*; sebaceous, waxy, cerated; lardaceous, lardy; saponaceous, soapy; butyraceous, buttery, creamy, milky, rich 390 adj. *savoury*.

unctuous, unguentary, greasy, oily, oleaginous; anointed, basted; slippery 334 adj. *lubricated*.

Vb. *pinguefy*, fatten; oleaginize, grease, oil 334 vb. *lubricate*; baste; butter; resinify, resinate.

Section 3: Organic Matter

358. Organization – N. *organism*, organic matter, organization; organic nature, living beings; animal and vegetable kingdom, flora and fauna, biota; biotype, living matter, cell, protoplasm, cytoplasm, bioplasm, bioplast, nucleoplasm; chromosome, chromatin; organic remains, fossil.

biology, microbiology; natural history, nature study; biogeny, phylogeny; organic chemistry, biochemistry, plasmology; zoography 367 n. *zoology*; phytography 368 n. *botany*; ecology, bionomics; genetics, biogenetics, eugenics, cacogenics; evolution, natural selection, survival of the fittest, vitalism; Darwinism, Lamarckism, neo-Darwinism; biogenist, naturalist, biologist, zoologist; evolutionist, Darwinist.

Adj. *biological*, biogenetic; organic, physiological, zoological, palaeontological; embryological; vitalistic, evolutionary, Darwinian.

359. Mineral: inorganic matter – N. *mineral*, mineral kingdom; inorganic matter; metal, noble m., precious m., base m.; mineralogical deposit, coal measures 632 n. *store*.

mineralogy, geology; lithology, petrology; oryctology, oryctography; metallurgy, metallography.

Adj. *inorganic*, inanimate, azoic; mineral, non-animal, non-vegetable; mineralogical; metallurgical.

360. Life – N. *life*, animate existence, being 1 n. *existence*; living being, soul, spirit; birth, nativity 68 n. *origin*; revivification 656 n. *revival*; vivification, animation; vitality, force, hold on life, survival, cat's nine lives, longevity 113 n. *diuturnity*; liveliness, animation 819 n. *sensibility*; breath, vital spark, breath of life; life-blood, heart's blood 335 n. *blood*; seat of life, heart; biological function, parenthood 164 n. *propagation*; living matter 358 n. *organism*; symbiosis 706 n. *association*; lifetime, one's born days; viability 469 n. *possibility*.

Adj. *alive*, living, quick, live; animated 819 adj. *lively*; in life, incarnate, in the flesh; not dead, surviving; long-lived 113 adj. *lasting*; viable; vital, Promethean; biotic, symbiotic, biological.

born, born alive; begotten, fathered,

sired; mothered, dammed; foaled, dropped; out of, by 11 adj. *akin*; spawned, littered; laid, new-l., hatched.

Vb. *live*, be alive, have life; draw breath 352 vb. *breathe*; exist 1 n. *be*; live one's life, walk the earth; be spared, survive.

vitalize, give birth to, beget, conceive 164 vb. *generate*; vivify, quicken, enliven, breathe life into, bring to life, reanimate 656 vb. *revive*; support life, provide a living, keep body and soul together 301 vb. *feed*.

361. Death – N. *death*, no life 2 n. *extinction*; dying (see *decease*); mortality, ephemerality 114 n. *transientness*; martyrdom; sentence of death, doom, knell; deathblow 362 n. *killing*; mortification 51 n. *decay*; the beyond, deathliness, rest, long sleep, Abraham's bosom; the grave, Sheol 364 n. *tomb*; post mortem, autopsy, necropsy 364 n. *inquest*; mortuary 364 n. *cemetery*.

decease, end of life, extinction, end, departure, exit, demise; euthanasia 376 n. *euphoria*; natural death, release; fatality, sudden death; dying day, last hour; death-bed, death-watch, death scene; last agony, last gasp, last breath; swansong, death-rattle; stroke of death, article of d., death's door.

the dead, forefathers 66 n. *precursor*; loved ones, the great majority; the shades 970 n. *ghost*; dead corpses 363 n. *corpse*; next world 124 n. *future state*; underworld, netherworld, Hades; Elysium, happy hunting grounds 971 n. *mythic heaven*.

death roll, mortality, death-toll, death-rate; bill of mortality, casualty list; necrology, death register 87 n. *list*; death certificate 548 n. *record*; martyrology; obituary.

Adj. *dying* etc. vb.; mortal, ephemeral, perishable 114 adj. *transient*; moribund, half-dead, deathlike, deathly; sick unto death 651 adj. *sick*; at death's door, at the last gasp, in articulo mortis; doomed, fey 961 adj. *condemned*.

dead, deceased, no more; dead and gone, dead and buried 364 adj. *buried*; born dead, stillborn; lifeless, breathless, extinct, inanimate; stone dead, cold, stiff; defunct, late, lamented, regretted, sainted.

Vb. *die* (see *perish*); be dead, lie in the grave; end one's life, decease, demise; expire, give up the ghost, breathe one's last; pass, be taken; pay the debt of nature, go the way of all flesh; croak, peg out, kick the bucket.

perish, die out, become extinct 2 vb. *pass away*; meet one's death, get killed, fall, lose one's life, be lost; lay down one's life, become a martyr; catch one's death, drop dead; die the death, receive one's death warrant; commit suicide 362 vb. *kill oneself*.

362. Killing: destruction of life – N. *killing* etc. vb., slaying 165 n. *destruction*; blood-sports 619 n. *chase*; violent death, blood-shedding, blood-letting; vivisection; mercy-killing, euthanasia; murder, assassination (see *homicide*); poisoning (see Vb. *kill*); ritual killing, immolation, sacrifice; martyrization, martyrdom; crucifixion, execution 963 n. *capital punishment*; judicial murder, auto da fé; dispatch, deathblow, coup de grâce, final stroke, quietus.

homicide, manslaughter; murder, capital m.; assassination, thuggee; crime passionel 911 n. *jealousy*; regicide, tyrannicide, parricide, patricide, matricide, fratricide; aborticide, infanticide, exposure, exposure of infants; genocide (see *slaughter*).

suicide, self-slaughter, self-destruction, felo de se; self-devotion, suttee, hara-kiri; death-wish; race-suicide.

slaughter, bloodshed, high casualties, butchery, carnage, shambles; blood-bath, massacre, noyade, fusillade, battue, holocaust; pogrom, purge, liquidation, decimation, extermination, annihilation 165 n. *destruction*; race-murder, genocide; war, battle 718 n. *warfare*; Roman holiday.

slaughter-house, abattoir, knacker's yard, shambles; bull-ring 724 n. *arena*;

battlefield 724 n. *battleground*; Auschwitz, Belsen, gas-chamber.

killer, slayer, man of blood; mercy-killer 905 n. *pity*; slaughterer, butcher, knacker; trapper, rat-catcher, exterminator; toreador, picador, matador; executioner 963 n. *punisher*; homicide (see *murderer*); homicidal maniac, head-hunter; beast of prey, man-eater.

murderer, homicide, killer; Cain, assassin, poisoner, strangler, garrotter, thug; gangster, gunman; bravo, desperado, cut-throat, high-binder 904 n. *ruffian*; parricide, regicide, tyrannicide.

Adj. *deadly*, killing, lethal; fell, mortal, fatal, deathly; involving life, capital; death-bringing, mortiferous, asphyxiant, poisonous 653 adj. *toxic*; inoperable, incurable.

murderous, homicidal, genocidal; suicidal; internecine, slaughterous, death-dealing; sanguinary, bloody, bloodstained, red-handed; blood-guilty, bloodthirsty 898 adj. *cruel*; cannibalistic.

Vb. *kill*, slay, take life; do in, do for 165 vb. *destroy*; put down, put to sleep; hasten one's end, shorten one's life; put to death, hang, gibbet, turn off, send to the scaffold, behead, guillotine, impale 963 vb. *execute*; stone 712 vb. *lapidate*; make away with, do away w., dispatch; put one out of his misery; shed blood, sabre, spear 263 vb. *pierce*; blow the brains out 287 vb. *shoot*; strangle, wring the neck of, garrotte, bowstring; gas, choke, suffocate, smother, overlay, stifle, drown; brain, pole-axe 279 vb. *strike*; send to the stake 381 vb. *burn*; immolate, sacrifice, offer up; martyr, martyrize; condemn to death, sign the death warrant 961 vb. *condemn*.

slaughter, butcher, pole-axe, cut the throat of; do execution, massacre, put to the sword; decimate, scupper, wipe out; cut to pieces, mow down; wade in blood, give no quarter, spare none 906 vb. *be pitiless*; annihilate, exterminate, liquidate, purge, commit genocide 165 vb. *destroy*.

murder, commit m., assassinate, bump off, rub out; take for a ride, make to walk the plank; smother, burke, strangle, poison, gas.

kill oneself, do oneself in, commit suicide; commit hara-kiri, commit suttee; hang oneself, shoot oneself, blow out one's brains, cut one's throat, fall on one's sword; put one's head in the oven, gas oneself, take poison; jump overboard.

363. Corpse – N. *corpse*, dead body, body; defunct, goner, stiff; cadaver, carcass; mummy; mortal remains, relics, ashes; carrion, food for worms; fossil 125 n. *palaetiology*; zombie 970 n. *ghost*.

Adj. *cadaverous*, corpselike; deathlike, deathly; stiff, carrion.

364. Interment – N. *interment*, burial, entombment; urn burial; disposal of the dead, burial customs, inhumation, cremation, incineration; mummification, embalmment; coffin, kist, shell, casket, urn, cinerary u., funerary u.; sarcophagus, mummy-case; pyre, funeral pile, crematorium; mortuary, morgue, charnel-house; bone-urn, ossuary; funeral parlour; sexton, grave-digger; mortician, undertaker, funeral director; embalmer, pollinator.

obsequies, exequies, mourning, wake 836 n. *lamentation*; last rites, burial service, funeral, cortège; knell, passing bell, dead march, muffled drum, last post, taps; requiem, funeral oration; elegy, dirge 836 n. *lament*; inscription, epitaph, obituary, lapidary phrases, in memoriam, R.I.P.; stele, tombstone, gravestone, headstone; war memorial; cenotaph 548 n. *monument*; monumental mason.

funeral, hearse, bier, pall, catafalque, coffin; mourner, keener; mute, pallbearer (see *obsequies*).

grave clothes, cerements, cere cloth, shroud, winding sheet, mummy-wrapping.

cemetery, burial place; God's acre, garden of sleep, garden of remembrance; churchyard, graveyard, boneyard; urn cemetery, catacomb, columbarium; tower of silence; necropolis.

tomb, vault, crypt; mummy-chamber; pyramid, mastaba; tower of silence; mausoleum, sepulchre; grave, grave pit, cist; barrow, cairn 548 n. *monument*.

inquest, 459 n. *inquiry*; necropsy, autopsy, post-mortem; exhumation, disinterment, disentombment.

Adj. *buried*, interred etc. vb.; laid to rest, in the grave, below ground 361 adj. *dead*.

funereal, funerary; sombre, sad 428 adj. *black*; mourning; mortuary, cinerary, crematory, sepulchral; obsequial, obituary; lapidary, elegiac.

Vb. *inter*, inhume, bury; lay out, embalm, mummify; coffin, urn, entomb; lay to rest; cremate 381 vb. *burn*; mourn, keen, hold a wake 836 vb. *lament*.

exhume, disinter, unbury; disentomb, untomb, unsepulchre; unearth, dig up.

365. Animality. Animal – N. *animality*, animal life, animal spirits; animal kingdom, fauna, brute creation; physique, flesh, flesh and blood; animal behaviour 944 n. *sensualism*.

animal, birds, beasts and fishes; creature, brute, beast, dumb animal; protozoon, metazoon; zoophyte 196 n. *animalcule*; mammal, marsupial, batrachian, amphibian, fish, mollusc, crustacean, bird, reptile, worm, insect, arachnid; invertebrate, vertebrate, articulate, biped; quadruped, ass, donkey, moke; mule 273 n. *horse, beast of burden*; carnivore, herbivore, omnivore, man-eater; wild animal, animal ferae naturae, game, beast of prey; pack, flock, herd; livestock 369 n. *stock farm*; tame animal, pet; extinct animal, dodo, auk, moa; bear, bruin, grizzly; elephant, tusker; mammoth, mastodon; pachyderm, hippopotamus, rhinoceros; dragon, unicorn, griffin, abominable snowman, yeti 84 n. *rara avis*.

bird, winged thing, fowl; fledgeling, squab 132 n. *youngling*; avi-fauna, birdlife; migrant, winter visitor, summer v.; bird of omen, raven; cagebird, song-bird, humming-bird, songster, warbler; talking bird, parrot, polly, budgerigar; dove, cushat, culver, pigeon; woodpecker, yaffle; nightbird, owl, nightjar, bat, flying fox; scavenging bird, carrion crow, adjutant bird, vulture.

bird of prey, lammergeyer, eagle, eaglet, erne; gled, kite, harrier, osprey, buzzard; hawk, falcon, peregrine f., hobby, merlin, shrike.

waterfowl, swan, cob, pen, cygnet; duck, drake, duckling; goose, gander, gosling; teal; ousel, mallard, widgeon, moorhen, coot, diver, grebe, dabchick; merganser, goosander.

flightless bird, ratite, ostrich, emu, cassowary; apteryx, kiwi; moa, dodo, penguin.

table bird, game bird, woodcock, woodpigeon, grouse, ptarmigan, capercailzie, pheasant, partridge, duck, snipe, snippet; quail, ortolan; turkey, gobbler; guinea-fowl, goose, chicken.

poultry, hen, biddy, cock, cockerel, rooster, barnyard fowl; chicken, pullet; spring chicken, boiler, broiler, roaster, capon.

cattle, herd, livestock, neat, kine, beeves; bull, cow, calf, heifer, fatling, yearling; maverick; ox, oxen, steer, stot, stirk, bullock; beef cattle, dairy cattle, milch-cow; buffalo, bison, aurochs, urus, nilgai; yak, musk-ox; goat, billy-g., nanny-g.

sheep, baa-baa, ram, tup, wether, bell-w., ewe, lamb, ewe-l., lambkin.

pig, swine, boar, tusker; hog, sow; piglet, pigling, sucking-pig, shoat, porker.

dog, bow-wow, bitch, whelp, puppy-dog, pup, puppy, mutt; cur, hound, tyke; mongrel, pariah dog, pi-d.; watch-dog, house-d., ban-d., police d., Alsatian, bloodhound, mastiff; sheepdog, collie; bulldog, boxer, bull-terrier, greyhound, courser, whippet; hounds, pack, hunting p.; game dog, lurcher; harrier, beagle, whippet; gun-dog, retriever, pointer, setter; spaniel, terrier, show dog, toy d., lap-dog, chow, Pekinese, pug-dog, poodle; husky, sledge-dog;

wild dog, dingo; canine, wolf, barking wolf, coyote.

cat, grimalkin, puss, kitten; tom, tom-c., gib-c.; mouser; feline, lion, tiger, leopard, cheetah, panther, puma, jaguar, cougar; wildcat, bobcat, cata-mountain, lynx.

deer, cervidae; stag, hart, hind, buck, fawn, pricket; red deer, fallow d., roe d., roe, roebuck; muskdeer, reindeer, caribou; gazelle, antelope, springbok, wildebeest, gnu; elk, moose, eland.

monkey, jacko, rhesus monkey, marmoset, tamarin; ape, anthropoid a., chimpanzee, gorilla, baboon, orangoutang, mandrill; monkeydom, bandarlog.

reptile, creeping thing; ophidian, serpent, sea-s.; snake, rattlesnake, adder, asp; viper; cobra, king c., hamadryad; cerastes, mamba, anaconda, boa-constrictor, python; amphibian, crocodile, alligator, cayman, mugger, gavial; annelid, worm, earthworm; lizard, slow-worm, chameleon, iguana, gecko, salamander, polywog, amphisbaena; basilisk, cockatrice; chelonian, turtle, tortoise, terrapin; malacostracan, crab.

frog, batrachian, bull-frog, croaker, paddock, toad; eft, newt, tadpole.

marsupial, kangaroo, wallaby, opossum, wombat, marmose.

rodent, rat, bandicoot; mouse, field-m., shrewmouse; mole, hamster, guinea-pig; gopher, marmot, woodchuck; beaver; squirrel, chipmunk, prairie dog; mongoose, racoon, ichneumon; porcupine.

fly, house-fly, blue-bottle; dragonfly, butterfly, moth; caddis-fly, may-f., greenfly, blackfly; ladybird; firefly; gadfly, gnat, midge, mosquito, gallinipper, culex, anopheles; bee, honey-b., queen b., worker b., bumble-b., humble-b., drone; wasp, yellow-jacket, hornet; beetle, cockroach.

vermin, parasite; insect, chrysalis, cocoon; imago; bug, bedbug, louse, flea, nit; maggot, earwig, mite; weevil; ant, termite; pest, garden p.; locust, grasshopper, cicada; cricket; rabbit, bunny, cony; hare, leveret; Reynard, fox, dog-

f., vixen; stoat, ferret, weasel, skunk, polecat.

fish, marine animal, cetacean, whale, Leviathan, grampus; dolphin, porpoise, seal, sea-lion, walrus; shark, swordfish, sawfish, starfish, sea-urchin, sea-horse, jelly-fish, stingray, torpedo; flying fish; goldfish; cephalopod, octopus, cuttle fish, squid, sepia.

table fish, salmon, grilse; trout, bream, roach, dace, perch, bass, carp; tunny, tuna, mackerel, sturgeon, mullet, turbot, halibut, brill, cod, hake, haddock, herring, buckling, shad, dory, plaice, skate, sole, flounder, whiting, smelt, sprat, sardine, whitebait; shell-fish, lobster, langouste, crawfish, crayfish, crab; shrimp, prawn, scampi; oyster, clam, winkle, mussel, cockle, whelk; eel, sea-e., conger-e., elver, grig.

Adj. animal, animalcular; beastly, bestial, subhuman; therianthropic, theriomorphic, zoomorphic; mammalian, warm-blooded; primatial, anthropoidal; equine, asinine, mulish; cervine; bovine, taurine, ruminant; ovine, sheepish; hircine, goatish; porcine, piggy; ursine; elephantine; canine, doggy; lupine, wolfish; feline, catty, tigerish, leonine; tigroid, pantherine; vulpine, vixenish, foxy; avian, birdlike; aquiline, vulturine; passerine, columbaceous, dovelike; cold-blooded, fishy, piscine, piscatorial, molluscous; amphibian; batrachian, reptilian, ophidian, serpentine, viperish, colubrine; vermicular, wormy, weevilly; insectile, entomological.

366. Vegetability. Plant – N. *vegetability*, vegetable life, vegetable kingdom; flora, vegetation; florescence, frondescence; lushness, rankness, luxuriance 635 n. *plenty*; faun, dryad 967 n. *nymph*.

wood, timber, lumber, softwood, hardwood, heart-wood; forest, rain-forest; taiga; jungle, bush, heath, scrub, maquis; greenwood, woodland, copse, coppice, spinney; thicket, brake, covert; park, chase, game-preserve; shaw, hurst, holt; plantation, arboretum 370 n. *garden*; grove, clump, clearing; brushwood, underwood, undergrowth; bushiness, shrubbery, bushes, windbreak, hedge, hedgerow.

forestry, dendrology, silviculture, afforestation, conservation; woodman, forester, forest-guard, verderer; wood-cutter, lumberman, lumberjack; den-drologist.

tree, shrub, sapling, scion, stock; pollard; shoot, sucker, trunk, bole; limb, branch, bough, twig.

foliage, foliation, frondescence; leafi-ness, leafage, umbrage; limb, branch, bough, twig; spray, sprig; leaf, frond, flag; leaflet, foliole; fir-cone, pine-needle; leaf-stalk, petiole, stalk, stem, tigella, caulicle, radical.

plant, growing thing; sucker, wort, weed; seed, root, bulb; greenery, herb 301 n. *potherb*, *vegetable*, *tuber*: ivy, creeper, vine, bine, tendril; calabash, gourd, marrow, melon; thorn, thistle, cactus, euphorbia; spurge; heath, heath-er, ling; broom, furze, gorse, whin; fern, bracken; moss, sphagnum; lichen, fun-gus, bolet, mushroom, truffle, toadstool, puffball, spore; osier, sedge, reed, rush, bullrush; algae, conferva, seaweed, wrack, sargasso, Gulf-weed.

flower, floweret, blossom, bloom, bud; petal, sepal, calyx; annual, perennial; hot-house plant, exotic 370 n. *garden*.

grass, 348 n. *grassland*; pasture, pas-turage, herbage, verdure, turf, sod, divot; bent; hay; graminiferous plant, millet; trefoil, shamrock, clover.

corn, grain 301 n. *cereal*; wheat, oats, barley, rye, buckwheat, spelt, emmer; Indian corn, maize, mealies; rice, paddy; millet, sorghum; straw, stubble; chaff, husk; hominy, meal, flour.

Adj. *vegetal*, vegetative, vegetable, botanical; evergreen; deciduous; horti-cultural, floricultural; floral, flowery, bloomy; rank, lush, overgrown; weedy, weed-ridden; verdant, verdurous, green; grassy, mossy, turfy; graminiferous, poaceous, herbaceous, herbal; legumin-ous, vetchy; fungoid, fungiform.

arboreal, dendritic, forestal; arbores-cent, forested, timbered; woody, wood-

ed, sylvan, beechy, bosky; jungly, scrubby; bushy, shrubby; silvicultural, afforested, planted; dendrological.

wooden, wood, xyloid, ligneous, lig-nous; hard-grained, soft-grained.

367. Zoology: the science of animals – N. *zoology*, animal physiology; anatomy; anthropology; ornithology, bird lore, bird watching; ichthyology, herpetology, malacology, helminthology, ento-mology; taxidermy.

zoologist, ornithologist, ichthyologist, entomologist, anatomist; taxidermist.

368. Botany: the science of plants – N. *botany*, phytology; vegetable physiology, plant pathology; herborization, botan-ization; dendrology 366 n. *forestry*; my-cology, fungology, algology; botanical garden 370 n. *garden*; hortus siccus, herbarium, herbal.

botanist, herbalist, herborist, her-barian.

Vb. *botanize* etc. n.

369. Animal husbandry – N. *animal hus-bandry*, animal management, training, manège; domestication, breeding, stock-b.; veterinary science; stirpiculture, selective breeding; pisciculture, apicul-ture, sericulture; veterinary surgeon, vet, horse doctor 658 n. *doctor*; ostler, groom, stable boy 742 n. *servant*; farrier, blacksmith; keeper, gamekeeper, gillie.

stock farm, stud; dairy farm, cattle f.; fishery, hatchery; piscina, vivarium; piggery; beehive, hive, apiary; pasture, grazing, sheep-run; chicken farm, chicken-run, free range; hen-battery, deep litter.

cattle pen, byre 192 n. *stable*; sheep-fold, pinfold 235 n. *enclosure*; coop, hencoop, henhouse, cowshed, pigsty; aquarium, bird-cage; bear-pit, cockpit 724 n. *arena*.

zoo, zoological gardens, menagerie, circus; aviary, vivarium, terrarium, aquarium; Noah's Ark.

breeder, stock-b., horse-b.; trainer, lion-tamer; cattle-farmer, sheep-f., woolgrower, pig-keeper, bee-k., apiarist; fancier, bird-f., pigeon-f.

herdsman, herd, neatherd, cattleherd, cowherd; stockman, cattleman; rancher; cowman, cowboy, cowpuncher, broncobuster, gaucho; shepherd, shepherdess; goatherd; goose-girl; milkmaid; fodderer.

Vb. *break in*, tame, domesticate; train 534 vb. *teach*; yoke, harness; cage, corral, round up, ride, herd 747 vb. *restrain*.

breed stock, breed, grow, hatch, culture, incubate, nurture, fatten; ranch, farm 370 vb. *cultivate*; rear, raise.

groom, currycomb, rub down, stable, bed down; tend, herd, shepherd; shear, fleece; milk; drench, water, fodder 301 vb. *feed*.

370. Agriculture – N. *agriculture*, agronomics, rural economy; cultivation, growth, harvest, crop, vintage; husbandry, farming; geoponics, hydroponics; tillage, tilth, spadework; floriculture, horticulture, gardening; fruit-growing, pomiculture; olericulture, kitchen gardening; viticulture, wine-growing; arboriculture 366 n. *forestry*; landscape gardening, landscape architecture.

farm, home f., grange; ranch, hacienda; state farm, collective f., kolkhoz, kibbutz; farmland, arable land, plough-l., fallow 344 n. *soil*; grazing, pasturage, pasture, fields, meadows 348 n. *grassland*; holding, small-h., croft 777 n. *lands*; allotment, kitchen garden; market garden; tea-garden, tea-estate; nursery; vinery, vineyard; orchard.

garden, botanical g., flower-g., ornamental g., winter g.; cabbage patch, kitchen garden, allotment; orchard, orangery; arboretum, pinery 366 n. *wood*; patch, plot, grass, lawn, park, border, bed, knot, parterre; seedbed, frame, cloche, conservatory, hot-house, greenhouse, glass-house; flowerpot 194 n. *vessel*.

husbandman, farmer, farm manager, farm-bailiff, granger; cultivator, planter; agriculturist, tiller, peasant; serf, ascrip-

tus glebae; share-cropper, tenant-farmer; yeoman, smallholder, crofter; farm hand, plougher, sower, reaper, harvester, mower, gleaner; thresher, barnsman; picker, hop-p., vintager; agricultural folk, farming community, yeomanry, peasantry.

gardener, horticulturist; topiarist, landscape gardener; seedsman, nurseryman; market gardener; hop-grower, fruit-g., citriculturist, vine-grower, vinedresser; forester 366 n. *forestry*.

farm tool, plough, ploughshare, coulter; harrow; spade, hoe, rake, trowel; dibble, digging-stick; pitchfork; scythe, sickle, reaping hook, shears 256 n. *sharp edge*; flail, winnowing fan; wine-press; cutter, reaper, thresher, binder, baler, combine-harvester; tractor; hay-wagon; byre, cowshed; barn, hayloft, silo 632 n. *storage*.

Adj. *agrarian*, peasant, farming; agrestic, bucolic, pastoral, rustic; agricultural, agronomic, geoponic; arable, cultivable.

horticultural, garden; topiary; hothouse, exotic, artificial.

Vb. *cultivate*, farm, ranch, garden, grow; till, dig, delve, dibble; seed, sow, broadcast; set, plant, transplant, plant out, bed o.; plough, raft; harrow, rake, hoe; weed, prune 204 vb. *shorten*; graft, imp 303 vb. *implant*; force, fertilize, dung, manure 174 vb. *invigorate*; harvest, gather in 632 vb. *store*; glean, reap, mow, cut, scythe; bind, bale, stook; flail, thresh, winnow; crop, pluck, pick, gather; ensile, ensilate; ditch, drain 342 vb. *dry*.

371. Mankind – N. *mankind*, womankind, humankind; humanity, human nature, creaturehood; flesh, mortality; generations of man, peoples of the earth; the world, the living, ourselves; human race, human species, man; tellurian, earthling; human being, Adam, Adamite, lord of creation; zoological man, hominid, homo sapiens; ethnic type 11 n. *race*.

anthropology, anthropometry, craniometry, craniology; anthropogenesis, somatology; ethnology, ethnography, folklore, mythology; social anthropology, demography.

person, individual, human being, creature, fellow c., mortal, body; one, somebody, someone; party, customer, character, type, element; chap 372 n. *male*; personage 638 n. *bigwig*; dramatis personae 686 n. *personnel*; unit, head, hand, nose.

social group, society, community 706 n. *association*; human family 11 n. *family*; tribalism; comity of nations 654 n. *civilization*; people, persons, folk; public, man in the street, you and me; population, populace, citizenry 191 n. *native*; the classes; the masses 869 n. *commonalty*.

nation, nationality, statehood, nationalism, national consciousness; ultranationalism, chauvinism, expansionism, imperialism; civil society, body politic, Leviathan, people, demos; commonwealth 733 n. *polity*.

Adj. *human*, creaturely, Adamitical; earthborn, tellurian; anthropoid, hominal; anthropological, ethnographical, racial 11 adj. *ethnic*; anthropocentric, personal, individual.

national, state, civic, civil, public, general, communal, tribal, social, societal; cosmopolitan, international.

372. Male – N. *male*, male sex, man, he; virility, manliness, masculinity, manhood; mannishness, viraginity, gynandry; he-man, cave-m.; gentleman, sir, esquire 870 n. *title*; wight, fellow, guy, blade, bloke, beau, chap, cove, card, chappie, johnny, buffer; gaffer, goodman; male relation 11 n. *kinsman*, 169 n. *parent*, 132 n. *youngster*, 170 n. *sonship*, 894 n. *spouse*; bachelor; stag party, menfolk.

male animal, cock, cockerel, rooster; drake, gander; male swan, cob; buck, stag, hart; horse, stallion, colt, foal; bull, calf, bullock, ox, steer, stot; boar, hog; ram, tup; he-goat, billy-g.; dog, dog-fox, tom-cat; gelding, capon, neuter cat.

Adj. *male*, masculine, androcentric; manly, he, virile; mannish, unfeminine, unwomanly; viraginous, gynandrous.

373. Female – N. *female*, feminine gender, she, -ess; femininity; womanhood, womanliness, girlishness; feminism; womanishness, effeminacy, androgyny 163 n. *weakness*; gynaecology, gyniatrics.

womankind, the sex, fair s.; the distaff side, womenfolk, women, matronage; hen party; gynaeceum, women's quarters, zenana, purdah, seraglio, harem.

woman, Eve, she; petticoat, skirt; girl, virgin, maiden 895 n., ma'am *spinster*; co-ed, undergraduette; lady; bride, matron 894 n. *spouse*; mother 169 n. *parent*; wench, lass, nymph; dame 537 n. *teacher*; blonde, brunette; sweetheart, bird 887 n. *loved one*; moll, doll, broad, mistress 952 n. *loose woman*; quean; shrew, virago, Amazon.

female animal, hen, duck, goose; pen (female swan); bitch, she-dog; mare, filly; cow, heifer; sow, gilt; ewe, ewe-lamb; nanny-goat; hind, doe; vixen; tigress, lioness, she-bear.

Adj. *female*, mammiferous; she, feminine, petticoat; girlish, womanly, lady-like, maidenly, matronal, matronly; feminist, feministic; womanish, effeminate, unmanly; feminized, androgynous; thelytokous 164 adj. *productive*.

374. Physical sensibility (See 819 *Sensibility*) – **N.** *sensibility*, sensitiveness, tenderness, quick, exposed nerve; sensitivity 819 n. *moral sensibility*; hyperaesthesia, allergy; aestheticism, aesthetics; aesthete 846 n. *man of taste*; thin skin 892 n. *irascibility*.

sense, sensory process, touch, hearing, taste, smell, sight, sixth sense; sensation 818 n. *feeling*; reaction, reflex; extrasensory perception 984 n. *psychics*.

Adj. *sentient*, sensitive, sensitized; aware, sensible, affectible, susceptible 818 adj. *feeling*; tender, raw, sore, exposed; ticklish, itchy; impressionable 819 adj. *sensitive*; suggestible 822 adj. *excitable*.

Vb. see 818 vb. *feel*, 822 vb. *be excitable*, 821 vb. *impress*.

375. Physical insensibility (See 820 *Insensibility***) – N.** *insensibility*, insensitiveness, insentience, anaesthesia, hysterical a., la belle indifférence; analgesia; narcotization, hypnosis, auto-hypnosis; paralysis, numbness, narcosis; catalepsy, stupor, coma, trance, unconsciousness; sleeping-sickness 651 n. *disease*.

anaesthetic, dope 658 n. *drug*; local anaesthetic, general a.; narcotic, sleeping draught 679 n. *soporific*; opium, laudanum; pain-killer, anodyne, analgesic 177 n. *moderator*.

Adj. *insensible*, insensitive, insentient, insensate; obtuse 499 adj. *unintelligent*; imperceptive, impercipient 416 adj. *deaf*, 439 adj. *blind*; senseless, sense-bereft, unconscious; inert, stony, stiff, cold, dead 266 adj. *quiescent*; numb, frozen; paralysed; dopy, drugged; punch-drunk; tranced, comatose 679 adj. *sleepy*; unfeeling 820 adj. *impassive*.

Vb. *render insensible*, paralyse, benumb; freeze 382 vb. *refrigerate*; deaden, hypnotize 679 vb. *make inactive*; anaesthetize, chloroform; narcotize, drug, dope, stupefy; stun, concuss, brain, knock out 279 vb. *strike*; pall, cloy 863 vb. *sate*.

376. Physical pleasure – N. *pleasure,* gratification, sensuousness, sensuality, self-indulgence, luxuriousness, hedonism 944 n. *sensualism*; dissipation 943 n. *intemperance*; entertainment 837 n. *amusement*; gusto, zest; enjoyment 824 n. *joy*.

euphoria, well-being, contentment 828 n. *content*; gracious living; ease, heart's-ease; convenience, comfort, cosiness, snugness, creature comforts; luxury 637 n. *superfluity*; lap of luxury, clover 800 n. *wealth*; feather-bed, bed of roses 327 n. *softness*; peace, quiet 683 n. *repose*; painlessness, euthanasia.

Adj. *pleasant*, delightful, pleasure-giving 826 adj. *pleasurable*; congenial, welcome, grateful, gratifying, satisfying 685 adj. *refreshing*; nice, agreeable, enjoyable 837 adj. *amusing*; palatable, delicious 386 adj. *tasty*.

comfortable, comfy, homely, snug, cosy, warm, comforting, restful 683 adj. *reposeful*; convenient, easy, painless; easeful, downy 327 adj. *soft*; luxurious, de luxe; enjoying comfort, euphoric, relieved 685 adj. *refreshed*.

sensuous, of the senses, bodily, physical 319 adj. *material*; voluptuous, pleasure-loving, sybaritic, epicurean, hedonistic 944 adj. *sensual*.

Vb. *enjoy*, relish, like; feel pleasure 824 vb. *be pleased*; luxuriate in, revel in, wallow in; gloat over, get a kick out of; lick one's lips 386 vb. *taste*; bask 379 vb. *be hot*.

377. Physical pain – N. *pain*, discomfort, malaise, inconvenience; distress, thin time, hell 731 n. *adversity*; strain 825 n. *suffering*; hurt, bruise 655 n. *wound*; anguish, agony, slow death, torment, torture, cruciation; crucifixion, martyrdom, vivisection; rack 964 n. *instrument of torture*; sore 827 n. *painfulness*.

pang, smart, sting, twinge, nip, pinch; throe, thrill; stitch, cramp 318 n. *spasm*; ache, headache, splitting head, migraine; gripe, colic; neuritis, neuralgia, angina.

Adj. *painful*, excruciating, exquisite; poignant 827 adj. *distressing*; sore, raw, tender, exposed; disagreeable 827 adj. *unpleasant*.

Vb. *give pain*, ache, hurt, pain, tingle, sting; excruciate, torment, rack, wring 963 vb. *torture*; flog, crucify, martyr 963 vb. *punish*; vivisect, tear, harrow, lacerate 46 vb. *cut*; gripe, nip, pinch, tweak, shoot, throb; grate, jar, set on edge; fret, chafe, gall 333 vb. *rub*; irritate 832 vb. *aggravate*; kill by inches, prolong the agony; distress 827 vb. *incommode*.

feel pain, ache, hurt, 825 vb. *suffer*; agonize, twitch, wince, flinch, writhe, squirm 318 vb. *be agitated*; weep 836 vb. *lament*; lick one's wounds.

378. Touch: sensation of touch – N. *touch*, palpability; feeling, palpation, manipulation; massage, squeeze, pressure 333 n. *friction*; graze, contact 202 n. *contiguity*; stroke, pat, tap.

formication, titillation, tickling sensation; creeps, goose-flesh; tingle, pins-and-needles; itchiness, itch, urtication, urticaria 651 n. *skin disease*; phthiriasis, pediculosis 649 n. *uncleanness*.

feeler, organ of touch, palp, antenna, whisker; digit (see *finger*); hand, paw, palm, flipper.

finger, forefinger, index, middle finger, ring f.; thumb, pollex; hallux, great toe 214 n. *foot*; hand, fist 778 n. *nippers*.

Adj. *tactual*, tactile, palpal; lambent, licking etc. vb.; touchable, tangible, palpable 324 adj. *dense*; light-fingered; heavy-handed 695 adj. *clumsy*.

handed, with hands; thumbed, fingered; five-finger; manual, digital.

Vb. *touch*, make contact, graze, scrape, brush, kiss 202 vb. *be contiguous*; meet 279 vb. *collide*; feel, palp, palpate; finger, thumb, pinch, nip, massage, knead 333 vb. *rub*; palm, stroke; tap, pat, flick, flip, tickle, scratch; lick, tongue; handle, twiddle, fiddle with; manipulate 173 vb. *operate*; bruise, crush 377 vb. *give pain*.

itch, tickle, tingle, creep, have goose-flesh, have the creeps; prick, prickle, titillate, urticate, scratch.

379. Heat – N. *heat*, caloric, phlogiston; diathermancy; incandescence, warmth, fervour, ardour; fever heat, pyrexia, fever 651 n. *disease*; high temperature, white heat; boiling point, flash p., melting p.; swelter, high summer, flaming June, dog-days 128 n. *summer*; heat wave, scorcher; geyser, steam; insolation 381 n. *heating*.

fire, flames; bonfire, beacon f., pyre 364 n. *obsequies*; conflagration; wild-fire; blaze, flame; spark 417 n. *light*; volcano 383 n. *furnace*; fireworks, pyrotechnics; arson 381 n. *incendiarism*.

thermometry, heat measurement, thermometer, clinical t., Fahrenheit t., centigrade t., Réaumur t.; thermostat, air-conditioner; pyrostat, calorimeter;

therm, calorie; pyrology, thermodynamics.

Adj. *hot*, superheated, overheated; inflamed, fervent, fervid; molten, red-hot, white-h.; diathermic; calescent; feverish, fevered; sweltering, sudorific; on the boil, boiling, scalding; tropical, torrid; scorching etc. vb.; parched 342 adj. *dry*.

fiery, ardent, fervent, unquenched; ablaze, on fire, in flames; incandescent, molten, aglow; ignited, lit, alight; volcanic, erupting, plutonic.

warm, hypothermal, tepid, lukewarm; temperate, mild, genial, balmy; fair, sunny, sunshiny; summery, estival; tropical, equatorial; canicular, torrid, sultry; stuffy, muggy, close; overheated, unventilated; oppressive, suffocating, stifling.

Vb. *be hot*, burn, kindle, catch fire, draw; blaze, flare, flame; glow, flush; smoke, smoulder, reek, fume 300 vb. *emit*; boil, seethe; frizzle 301 vb. *cook*; get burnt, scorch, boil dry; bask, sunbathe; swelter, sweat; melt, thaw 337 vb. *liquefy*; thirst, parch, run a temperature; keep warm, wrap up.

380. Cold – N. *coldness*, etc. adj.; low temperature; frigidity, coolness, freshness; cold, zero; iciness, frostiness, chilliness, chill, rigor, shivering, shivers, frostbite, chilblains; pole, high altitude.

wintriness, winter, depth of w.; cold weather, cold front; arctic conditions, freeze, degrees of frost; frost, rime, hoarfrost.

snow, snowflake, snow-fall, avalanche, snow-drift, snow-storm, blizzard; snow-line; snowball, snowman; snow-plough, snow-shoe.

ice, dry i., ice-cube; hailstone, icicle; sleet, hail; ice-cap, ice-sheet, ice-field, floe, iceberg; glacier; shelf-ice, pack-i.; ice-yacht; ice-plough; icebox 382 n. *refrigeration*.

Adj. *cold*, impervious to heat, adiathermic; cool, temperate; shady, chilly; unheated, unwarmed; fresh, raw, keen, nipping; freezing, ice-cold; frigid, hiemal, brumal 129 adj. *wintry*; winter-bound, frosty, snowy, niveous, sleety, icy; glacial, ice-capped; polar, Arctic, Siberian.

a-cold, feeling cold, chilly, shivery, aguish; blue, perished, frozen, frost-bitten.

Vb. *be cold* etc. adj.; lose heat; feel cold, chatter, shiver, shudder; freeze, catch cold.

381. Calefaction – N. *heating*, calefaction; calorification, calorific value, thermal efficiency; inflammation; warming, aprication, insolation 342 n. *desiccation*; boiling, coction; cooking 301 n. *cookery*; anti-freeze mixture.

burning, combustion, kindling, ignition; conflagration 379 n. *fire*; incineration, carbonization, calcination; cremation 364 n. *interment*; auto-da-fé, holocaust 981 n. *oblation*; cauterization, cautery, branding; inflammability, combustibility; burner 383 n. *furnace*; cauterant, caustic; match 385 n. *lighter*; stoker, fireman; burn-mark, burn, brand, singe, scald, sunburn, tan, empyreuma.

incendiarism, arson, fire-raising, pyromania; incendiary, arsonist, fire-raiser, fire-bug; firebrand 738 n. *agitator*.

warm clothes, furs, woollens, woollies, flannel; parka, wrap, muffler, muff; warm 228 n. *overcoat*; blanket 226 n. *coverlet*; padding, wadding 227 n. *lining*.

ash, ashes, lava, tuff; carbon, soot, smut, smoke; clinker, charcoal, ember, cinder, coke.

pottery, ceramics; earthenware, lustre ware, glazed w.; majolica, faience, chinaware, porcelain; crockery, china; terracotta, tile, brick; pot 194 n. *vessel*.

Adj. *heating*, warming etc. vb.; calorific, caustic, burning; incendiary, inflammatory; diathermal, diathermanous; anti-freeze.

Vb. *heat*, raise the temperature, warm; winterize; thaw, hot up, warm up, stoke up; inflame, foment 832 vb. *aggravate*; overheat, stive, stew; insolate, sun 342 vb. *dry*; roast 301 vb. *cook*; melt, de-frost, de-ice 337 vb. *liquefy*; smelt, fuse, weld, vulcanize; cast, found.

kindle, ignite, light; set fire to, touch off; fuel, stoke, feed the flames; make the fire, rub two sticks together.

burn, gut; send to the stake; fire, incendiarize; cremate, incinerate; carbonize, calcine, oxidize; char, singe, scorch, tan; cauterize, brand, burn in; scald.

382. Refrigeration – N. *refrigeration*, reduction of temperature; icing etc. vb.; freezing up, glaciation 380 n. *ice*; cooling, ventilation, air-conditioning; deep-freeze 384 n. *refrigerator*.

incombustibility, non-inflammability, fire-resistance; asbestos, amiant.

extinguisher, fire-e.; sand, water hose, sprinkler; fire-engine, fire-brigade, fire-station; fireman, fire-fighter.

Adj. *cooled* etc. vb.; frosted, iced, glacé; cooling etc. vb.; frigorific, refrigerative, deep-freeze.

incombustible, non-inflammable; fire-proof, flame-p., burn-p.

Vb. *refrigerate*, cool, fan, air-condition 685 vb. *refresh*; ventilate, air 340 vb. *aerify*; turn off the heat; shade, shadow 421 vb. *screen*; frost, freeze, congeal, glaciate; ice, glacify; chill, benumb, nip, pinch; frost-bite.

extinguish, quench, snuff, put out, blow o.; damp down, bank d.; rake out, stub o.

383. Furnace – N. *furnace*; the stake 964 n. *means of execution*; volcano, solfatara, fumarole; touch-hole; forge, blast-furnace, reverbatory, kiln; oast, oast-house; incinerator, destructor; crematory, crematorium; cooker, stove; oven, range, kitchener; gas-ring, burner, blow-lamp; fire-box, fire-place, grate, hearth, ingle 379 n. *fire*; fireguard, fender; flue 263 vb. *chimney*.

heater, heating system, radiator, hypocaust, boiler, salamander, copper, kettle 194 n. *cauldron*; brazier, fire-pan, warming p., chafing dish, hot-water bottle; hot-case, hot-plate; still, retort

461 n. *testing agent*; blowpipe, bellows, damper; hot-house, conservatory 370 n. *garden*; sun-trap, solarium; kitchen 301 n. *cookery*; gridiron, grill, frying-pan; toaster.

384. Refrigerator – N. *refrigerator*, cooler; ventilator, fan, air-conditioner; cooling-room, frigidarium; frigidaire, deep-freeze, freezer, wine-cooler, ice-pail; coolant, snow, ice; ice-box, ice-pack; ice-cubes, rocks; cold storage 382 n. *refrigeration*.

385. Fuel – N. *fuel*, combustible, food for the flames; firing, kindling, briquette; firewood, faggot, log; turf, peak; lignite, brown coal, charcoal; oil, fuel o., petrol, gasoline, gas, paraffin, kerosene; gas, coal g.

coal, black diamond, sea-coal, steam-c., hard c., anthracite; coal dust, culm, slack; coal seam, coal deposit, coal measure, coalfield 632 n. *store*; coke; smoke-less fuel.

lighter, igniter, light; illuminant 420 n. *torch*; ember, brand; fire-barrel, fire-ship; wick, fuse, touch-paper, match, slow m.; linstock, portfire 723 n. *fire-arm*; cap, detonator; safety-match, lucifer; flint, steel, tinder, touchwood, punk, spunk, amadou; tinder-box, match-box.

Adj. *combustible*, inflammable, explosive; carboniferous, coal-bearing, coaly.

386. Taste – N. *taste*, sapor; savour, flavour, flavouring; smack, tang, after-taste; relish, palate, gustatory nerve, taste-buds; tooth, stomach; refinement 846 n. *good taste*.

Adj. *tasty*, saporous, saporific; gustatory; palatable 390 adj. *savoury*.

Vb. *taste*, find palatable, savour, sample, try; taste of, savour of, smack of, relish of 18 vb. *resemble*; taste well 390 vb. *appetize*.

387. Insipidity – N. *insipidity*, no taste, vapidity, flatness, staleness, tasteless-

ness etc. adj.; water, milk and water, pap.

Adj. *tasteless*, jejune, vapid, insipid, watery, milk-and-water; diluted 163 adj. *weakened*; wishy-washy, deadish, flat, stale, savourless, flavourless, un-flavoured, unspiced.

388. Pungency – N. *pungency*, piquancy, sting, bite, edge; spiciness; sharpness, acidity 393 n. *sourness*; roughness, harshness; strength, tang, race; salt 389 n. *condiment*; smelling salts, hartshorn.

tobacco, nicotine; the weed, tobacco-leaf; snuff, rappee, maccoboy; plug, quid, fid, twist; pipe-tobacco, shag; cigar, cheroot; cigarette, fag, gasper, reefer, nail, woodbine; tobacco-pipe, clay-p., dudeen, churchwarden; briar, corncob; meerschaum, hubble-bubble, hookah, narghile; pipe of peace, calumet; bowl, stem; snuff-taker; tobacco-chewer, smoker; tobacconist, tobacco shop, cigar divan; snuff-box, cigarette-case; pipe-rack; pipe-cleaner, reamer; smoker, smoking carriage.

Adj. *pungent*, penetrating, strong; mordant 256 adj. *sharp*; caustic, burning; harsh 259 adj. *rough*; tart, astringent 393 adj. *sour*; heady, overproof; high, gamy, off; spicy, spiced, curried; hot, peppery; smoky.

salty, salt, brackish, briny, saline, pickled.

Vb. *season*, salt, brine, pickle; flavour, sauce; spice, pepper, devil, curry; smoke, smoke-dry, kipper 666 vb. *preserve*.

smoke, use tobacco, indulge, smoke a pipe, draw, suck, inhale; puff, blow smoke, funk; chew, quid; take snuff, take a pinch.

389. Condiment – N. *condiment*, seasoning, flavouring, dressing, relish; caviar; chutney; pickles, salt, mustard; pepper, cayenne, chilli; capsicum, paprika, pimento, red pepper, green p.; black pepper, peppercorn; curry, curry powder; onion, garlic 301 n. *potherb*; spicery, spice, allspice, mace, cinnamon, turmeric, saffron, galingale, ginger, nutmeg, clove, caper, caraway; sauce, roux.

Vb. See 388 vb. *season.*

390. Savouriness – N. *savouriness*, right taste, tastiness, palatability; raciness, richness; body, bouquet; savoury, relish, appetizer; delicacy, dainty, titbit, bonne-bouche; caviar; cocktail eats, hors d'œuvre; ambrosia, nectar, epicure's delight.

Adj. *savoury*, nice, good, worth eating; flavoured, spicy, tasty; done to a turn; tempting, appetizing; palatable, toothsome, sweet; dainty, delicate, delicious, exquisite, epicurean; ambrosial, nectareous, fit for the gods; luscious, juicy, succulent; creamy, rich; generous, strong, nutty, racy; rare-flavoured, full-f., vintage.

Vb. *appetize*, spice 388 vb. *season*; tickle the palate, taste good; like, relish, savour, lap up, smack the lips, lick one's fingers.

391. Unsavouriness – N. *unsavouriness* etc. adj.; unpalatability, nasty taste, wrong t.; unwholesomeness 653 n. *insalubrity*; acerbity 393 n. *sourness*; austerity, prison fare, bread and water; bitter pill, gall and wormwood; emetic, poison 659 n. *bane.*

Adj. *unsavoury*, flat 387 adj. *tasteless*; ill-flavoured, unpalatable, unappetizing; coarse, raw, undressed, ill-cooked; uneatable, inedible; sugarless, unsweetened; rough 388 adj. *pungent*; bitter 393 adj. *sour*; undrinkable, corked; rancid 397 adj. *fetid*; nasty 827 adj. *unpleasant*; sickening 861 adj. *disliked*; poisonous 653 adj. *toxic.*

Vb. *be unpalatable* etc. adj.; nauseate, turn the stomach 861 vb. *cause dislike*; lose its savour, pall.

392. Sweetness – N. *sweetness*, sweetening, dulcification; sugariness, saccharinity; sweet smell 396 n. *fragrance*; sweet music 410 n. *melody*; saccharometer.

sweet, sweetening, honey, honeycomb, honeypot, honeydew; saccharine, sugar;

molasses, jaggery; syrup, treacle; julep, nectar, hydromel, mead, liqueur; conserve, jam; candy, sugar-c. sugar-plum; icing; sweetmeat, chocolate, toffee, fudge, butterscotch, liquorice; comfit, bonbon, jujube, caramel, lollipop, rock; confectionery, confection, cake.

Adj. *sweet*, sweetened, honied, candied, crystallized; sugary, saccharine; ambrosial, nectareous, luscious, sweet as a nut 390 adj. *savoury.*

Vb. *sweeten*, sugar, candy, crystallize, ice; sugar the pill; dulcify, saccharize.

393. Sourness – N. *sourness*, acidity, acerbity; tartness, bitterness; sharpness 388 n. *pungency*; acidosis; acid, lemon, vinegar, bitters; gall, wormwood, absinth.

Adj. *sour*, sourish, acid, acidulous, acidulated, acetous, acid-forming, tartaric; crabbed, tart, bitter, vinegary; unripe, green 670 adj. *immature*; sugarless, unsugared; unsweetened, dry.

Vb. *be sour* etc. adj.; sour, turn, turn sour; acetify, acidify; ferment; set one's teeth on edge.

394. Odour – N. *odour*, smell, aroma, bouquet; perfume 396 n. *fragrance*; stink 397 n. *fetor*; exhalation, effluvium, smoke, fume, reek; breath, whiff; odorousness, redolence; scent, trail 548 n. *trace*; olfaction, sense of smell; olfactory, nostril, nose; keen scentedness, flair.

Adj. *odorous*, aromatic, odoriferous; scented 396 adj. *fragrant*; graveolent, strong, heady, heavy 388 adj. *pungent*; redolent, reeking; malodorous 397 adj. *fetid*; olfactory, quick-scented, sharp-nosed.

Vb. *smell*, reach one's nostrils; smell of, breathe of, reek of, exhale; smell out, scent, nose, wind, get wind of 484 vb. *detect*; sniff, snuff 352 vb. *breathe*; aromatize, scent, perfume, incense, fumigate, thurify.

395. Inodorousness – N. *inodorousness*, no smell; inability to smell, anosmia;

deodorant, deodorizer, deodorization, fumigation 648 n. *cleansing*.

Adj. *odourless*, inodorous, scentless; unscented, unperfumed; deodorized; noseless, without flair.

Vb. *have no smell*, not smell; deodorize, defumigate, clear the air 648 vb. *purify*; lose the scent 495 vb. *err.*

396. Fragrance – N. *fragrance*, sweet smell, sweet savour 392 n. *sweetness*; aroma, bouquet 394 n. *odour*; violet, rose 370 n. *garden*; buttonhole, nosegay; perfumery, perfumer.

scent, perfume, aromatic gum, balm, myrrh, incense; spicery 389 n. *condiment*; breath-sweetener, cloves, pastille; musk, civet, camphor; sandalwood, attar; lavender, thyme, vanilla; toilet water, lavender w., rose-w.; patchouli, pomade 843 n. *cosmetic*; scent-bag, lavender-b., sachet, pouncet box; pomander, pot-pourri, scent-bottle, joss-stick, censer, thurible.

Adj. *fragrant*, aromatic, scented, perfumed; sweet-scented, incense-breathing, balmy, ambrosial; thuriferous, musky; spicy, fruity.

Vb. *be fragrant*, smell sweet; aromatize 394 vb. *smell*; embalm, lay up in lavender.

397. Fetor – N. *fetor*, offence to the nose, bad smell, malodour; halitosis; stink, stench, reek, mephitis; smell of death, taint 51 n. *decay*; mustiness, fustiness, frowst; skunk, polecat; stinkard, stinker, stink-bomb, bad egg; sewer 649 n. *sink*.

Adj. *fetid*, olid, graveolent, heavy, strong, malodorous, not of roses; smelly, whiffy, niffy; rank, hircine; fruity, gamy, high, tainted, rancid; stale, musty, reasty, fusty, frowsty; foul, noisome, sulphurous, mephitic 653 adj. *toxic*; acrid 388 adj. *pungent*; nasty, offensive, fulsome 827 adj. *unpleasant*.

Vb. *stink*, smell, reek; make a smell, funk, fart, blow off; smell bad, make one hold one's nose; stink out.

398. Sound – N. *sound*, auditory effect; distinctness, audibility, reception 415 n. *hearing*; stereophonic sound; radio noise 417 n. *radiation*; sonority, sonorousness; noise 400 n. *loudness*; low sound 401 n. *faintness*; tone, pitch, level, cadence; accent, intonation, twang, timbre 577 n. *voice*; tune 410 n. *melody*, 412 n. *music*; types of sound 402 n. *bang*, 403 n. *roll*, 404 n. *resonance*, 405 n. *non-resonance*, 406 n. *sibilation*, 407 n. *stridor*, 408 n. *cry*, 409 n. *ululation*, 411 n. *discord*; unit of sound, decibel, sone; sonic barrier, sound b.

acoustics, phonics; phonology, phonography; phonetics; acoustician; phonetician, phonographer; audiometer, sonometer.

speech sound, simple sound, phone, syllable, dissyllable, polysyllable; consonant, spirant, liquid, sibilant; dental, nasal, palatal, guttural, velar, labiovelar; fricative; aspirate, rough breathing, smooth b.; stop; click; plosive, semiplosive, sonant; surd; semi-vowel; glide; vowel; diphthong, triphthong 577 n. *voice*; allophone; vowel gradation, ablaut; umlaut; guna, vriddhi; assimilation, dissimilation; vocable 559 n. *word*; sound symbol, phonogram 586 n. *script*.

Adj. *sounding*, sonic; supersonic; plain, audible, distinct, heard; sonorous 404 adj. *resonant*; stentorian 400 adj. *loud*; auditory, acoustic; phonic, phonetic; sonantal, vocal, vowelled, voiced, consonantal; spirantal, surd, unvoiced.

399. Silence – N. *silence*, soundlessness, inaudibility, not a sound; stillness, hush, lull, quiet 266 n. *quiescence*; speechlessness 578 n. *aphony*.

Adj. *silent*, still, stilly, hushed, quiet 266 adj. *quiescent*; noiseless, soundless, frictionless, soundproof; speechless, mute 578 n. *voiceless*; unuttered, unspoken.

Vb. *silence*, still, lull, hush, quiet; play down, soft-pedal; stifle, muffle, gag, stop, muzzle 578 vb. *make mute*; drown the noise.

400. Loudness – N. *loudness*, distinctness, audibility 398 n. *sound*; noise, broken *or* shattered silence; report, explosion 402 n. *bang*; alarm 665 n. *danger signal*; reverberation, boom, rattle 403 n. *roll*; thunder, war in heaven 176 n. *storm*; dashing, surging 406 n. *sibilation*; gunfire 712 n. *bombardment*; stridency, blast 407 n. *stridor*; clarion call 547 n. *call*; sonority, organ notes, clang 404 n. *resonance*; peal, carillon 412 n. *campanology*; diapason, swell, crescendo, fortissimo, full blast, full chorus; vociferation 408 n. *cry*, 409 n. *ululation*; cachinnation 835 n. *laughter*; noisiness, din, row, racket, clatter, hubbub, hullabaloo, uproar, tumult, rowdiness, pandemonium, hell let loose 61 n. *turmoil*.

megaphone, amplifier, loud pedal; loud-hailer, loudspeaker, microphone; ear-trumpet 415 n. *hearing aid*; whistle, siren, hooter, horn, klaxon, bell; trumpet, brass; stentorian voice, lungs of brass, iron throat; Stentor, town-crier.

Adj. *loud*, distinct, audible, heard; noisy, rackety, uproarious, rowdy, rumbustious, riproaring, obstreperous, tumultuous; clamorous, clamant 408 adj. *crying*; big-mouthed, loud-m.; sonorous, deep, full, powerful; full-throated, stentorian; deafening, dinning; piercing, ear-splitting; thunderous, pealing, clangorous, strepitous; shrill, brassy 407 adj. *strident*; fortissimo, enough to waken the dead.

Vb. *be loud*, —noisy etc. adj.; break the silence; vociferate 408 vb. *cry*; cachinnate 835 vb. *laugh*; roar 409 vb. *ululate*; din, sound 404 vb. *resound*; rattle, thunder, volley, fulminate, storm; surge 406 vb. *hiss*; ring, peal, clang, crash; bray, blare; slam 402 vb. *bang*; explode; knock, hammer; deafen, stun; swell, fill the air; awake the echoes, awake the dead.

401. Faintness – N. *faintness*, softness, indistinctness, inaudibility; noise abatement; thud 405 n. *non-resonance*; whisper, susurration; breath, bated b., undertone; murmur, hum, sigh; scratch,

squeak; tick, click; tinkle, clink, chink; purr, purl, plash; patter, pitter-p.; quiet tone, conversation level.

silencer, mute, damper, sordine, soft pedal 414 n. *mute*; rubber; grease, oil 334 n. *lubricant*.

Adj. *muted*, distant, faint, inaudible, half-heard; weak, unemphatic, unstressed, unaccented; soft, low, gentle; piano, stealthy, whispered; muffled 407 adj. *hoarse*.

Vb. *sound faint*, drop one's voice, whisper, breathe, murmur, mutter; sing low, hum, croon, purr; purl, ripple 350 vb. *flow*; tinkle; moan, sigh 352 vb. *blow*; rustle, tremble, melt; die on the ear; squeak, creak; tick, click; clink, chink; thud 405 vb. *sound dead*.

mute, soften, dull, deaden, dampen, soft-pedal; hush, muffle, stifle 399 vb. *silence*.

Adv. *faintly*, with bated breath, sotto voce, aside; piano, pianissimo; out of earshot.

402. Bang: sudden and violent noise – N. *bang*, report, explosion, detonation, blast; crash 400 n. *loudness*; rat-tat-tat etc. see **Vb.** *crackle, bang*; knock, slam, plop, plunk; burst, volley, round, salvo, shot; cracker, squib, bomb, grenade.

Adj. *rapping* etc. vb.

Vb. *crackle*, crepitate; crack, split; click, rattle; snap, clap, rap, tap, slap, smack; plop, plump, plonk, plunk.

bang, slam, clash, crash; burst, explode, blast, detonate; back-fire.

403. Roll: repeated and protracted sounds – N. *roll*, rattle, clatter, chatter; clang, ping 404 n. *resonance*; fanfare, flourish; drumming, tattoo, rub-a-dub; tantara, peal 412 n. *campanology*; ding-dong 106 n. *repetition*; trill, tremolo 410 n. *musical note*; hum, whirr, buzz; tinnitus; drumfire, barrage.

Adj. *rolling* etc. vb.

Vb. *roll*, drum, tattoo, beat a t.; din in the ear; grumble, rumble, drone, hum, whirr; trill, chime, peal, toll; tick, beat; rattle, chatter, clatter, clack; clang, ping, ring 404 vb. *resound*; shake, tremble, vibrate; patter 401 vb. *sound faint*.

404. Resonance – N. resonance, vibration 317 n. *oscillation*; reverberation; echo 106 n. *recurrence*; ringing, tinnitus; tintinnabulation 412 n. *campanology*; sonority, boom, clang, clangour, plangency; peal, blare, bray, flourish, tucket; tinkle, jingle; ping, ring, chime; low voice, bass, baritone, contralto.

Adj. *resonant*, vibrant, reverberant; resounding etc. vb.; echoing; lingering; sonorous, plangent; ringing, tintinnabulary; basso, deep-toned, deep-mouthed; hollow, sepulchral.

Vb. *resound*, vibrate, reverberate, echo, re-echo; whirr, buzz; boom, hum, ring in the ear, sing; ping, ring, ding; drone, whine; jingle, jangle, clang, tinkle, gong, chime, tintinnabulate.

405. Non-resonance – N. *non-resonance*, non-vibration, dead sound, dull s.; thud, thump, bump; plump, plop, plonk, plunk; cracked bell 411 n. *discord*; muffled drums 401 n. *faintness*; mute, damper, sordine 401 n. *silencer*.

Adj. *non-resonant*, muffled, damped 401 adj. *muted*; dead, dull, heavy; cracked 407 adj. *hoarse*; soundproof 399 adj. *silent*.

Vb. *sound dead*, click, flap; thump, thud, bump, pound; gurgle, guggle; muffle, deaden 401 vb. *mute*.

406. Sibilation: hissing sound – N. *sibilation*, sibilance, hissing, hiss; sigmatism, sigma, sibilant; sneeze; sputter, splutter; surge, splash, plash; rustle, frou-frou 407 n. *stridor*; sucking noise, squelch; swish, swoosh, escape of air; hisser, goose, viper, adder, serpent.

Adj. *sibilant*, sibilatory, hissing, sigmatic.

Vb. *hiss*, sibilate, sigmate; sneeze, snort, wheeze, snuffle, whistle; buzz, fizz, fizzle, sizzle, sputter, splutter, spit; seethe, surge, splash, plash, boil, bubble,

effervesce; swish, swoosh, whizz; squelch, suck; rustle 407 vb. *rasp*.

407. Stridor: harsh sound – N. *stridor*, stridency, cacophony 411 n. *discord*; raucousness, hoarseness, huskiness; aspirate, guttural; squeakiness 333 n. *friction*; scrape, scratch, creak, squeak; stridulation, screechiness; shriek, screech 409 n. *ululation*; shrillness, whistle; soprano, treble, falsetto; nasality, twang, drone, skirl; brassiness, blare 400 n. *loudness*; pipe 414 n. *flute*.

Adj. *strident*, stridulous; unoiled, grating, rusty, creaking (see *hoarse*); harsh, brassy, brazen, metallic; high-pitched, acute, shrill; piercing, tinny; dry, reedy, squeaky, scratchy; cracked 405 adj. *non-resonant*.

hoarse, husky, throaty, guttural, raucous, rough, gruff; asthmatic, wheezy; snoring, stertorous.

Vb. *rasp*, stridulate, grate, crunch, scrunch, grind, saw, scrape, scratch; snore, snort; cough, hawk, clear the throat, wheeze, choke, gasp, sob, catch the breath; bray, croak, caw, screech 409 vb. *ululate*; grunt, burr, aspirate, gutturalize; crack, break (of the voice); jar, grate, jangle, twang 411 vb. *discord*.

shrill, stridulate; drone, skirl; trumpet, blare 400 vb. *be loud*; pipe 413 vb. *play music*; whistle, cat-call, caterwaul 408 vb. *cry*; scream, squeal, yelp, screech, squawk; strain, crack one's voice.

408. Human cry – N. *cry*, animal cry 409 n. *ululation*; human cry, exclamation, ejaculation 577 n. *voice*; vociferation, vociferousness, outcry, clamour 400 n. *loudness*; yodel 412 n. *vocal music*; shout etc. see **Vb.** *cry, vociferate*; shouter, rooter, cheerer; crier, barker; town-crier, Stentor.

Adj. *crying*, clamant, clamorous; loud, vocal, vociferous; stentorian, full-throated, full-lunged, lusty.

Vb. *cry*, cry out, exclaim, ejaculate 579 vb. *speak*; call, yodel; hail 884 vb. *greet*; whoop, yoiks; whistle 924 vb. *disapprove*; scream, screech, howl, groan

377 vb. *feel pain*; snigger 835 vb. *laugh*;
caterwaul, squall, boo-hoo, whine,
whimper, wail, fret, mewl, pule 836 vb.
weep; yammer, moan, sob, sigh 836 vb.
lament; squeak, squawk 409 vb. *ululate.*

vociferate, clamour, holla, shout,
bawl, yell; chant, chorus 413 vb. *sing*;
cheer, hurrah, huzza, root 835 vb. *rejoice*;
hiss, hoot, boo, shout down 924 vb.
disapprove; roar, bellow 409 vb. *ululate*;
cry out, sing o., thunder o.; strain one's
lungs, crack one's throat 400 vb. *be loud.*

409. Ululation: animal sounds – N. *ululation*, animal noise, howling, belling;
barking, baying; buzzing, humming,
drone; twittering, fritiniency; call, cry,
note, bird-call; cock-a-doodle-doo,
cuckoo, tu-whit tu-whoo; see **Vb.**
ululate.

Adj. *ululant*, mugient, blatant, latrant.

Vb. *ululate*, cry, call, pipe, flute, sing;
squawk, screech; caterwaul, yawl, howl,
wail; roar, bellow; hum, drone, buzz;
spit 406 vb. *hiss*; bark, bay; yelp, yap,
yaup; snap, snarl, gnarr, growl, whine;
trumpet, bell, troat; bray, neigh,
whinny; bleat, baa; low, moo; miaow,
mew, purr; quack, cackle, gaggle;
gobble, cluck, crow; grunt, snuffle, snort;
blatter, chatter, chirp, chirrup, cheep,
tweet, twitter, chuckle, churr, whirr,
coo; caw, croak, crunk; hoot, honk,
boom; grate, chirk, crick; stridulate,
squeak 407 vb. *rasp*; warble, carol,
whistle 413 vb. *sing*.

410. Melody: concord – N. *melody*,
musicality 412 n. *music*; melodiousness,
tune, tonality, euphony; harmonious-
ness, chime, harmony, concert, attunement 24 n. *agreement*; unison; preparation, resolution (of a discord); harmonization, counterpoint, polyphony;
thorough bass, ground b.; part, second,
chorus; orchestration, instrumentation;
phrase, passage, movement 412 n.
musical piece.

musical note, note, keys, keyboard,
manual, pedal point; black notes, white
n., sharp, flat, natural, tone, semitone,

quartertone; keynote, tonic, dominant;
diatesseron, diapason; gamut, scale,
octave; chord, tetrachord, perfect fourth,
arpeggio; grace note, grace; mordent,
shake, tremolo, trill, cadenza; tone,
tonality, register, pitch, concert p.;
undertone, overtone, harmonic; key,
modulation, mode.

notation, musical n., tonic solfa,
solmization; score; signature, clef; bar,
stave, line, shaft, space, brace; rest,
pause, interval; breve, semibreve, minim,
crotchet, quaver, semiquaver.

tempo, time, beat; rhythm 593 n.
prosody; measure, timing; syncopation;
suspension, prolongation; rallentando,
andante 412 adv. *adagio*.

Adj. *melodious*, melodic, musical,
canorous, tuneful, tuneable, singable,
catchy; musical, sweet, dulcet, mellifluous; harmonious, concordant; euphoni-
ous, euphonic, true, well-pitched.

harmonic, enharmonic, diatonic, chromatic; tonal, atonal, sharp, flat, twelve-
toned; keyed, modal, minor, major,
Doric, Lydian.

411. Discord – N. *discord*, conflict of
sounds, discordance, dissonance, disharmony 25 n. *disagreement*; atonality,
consecutive fifths; preparation (of a
discord); cacophony, Dutch concert,
marrowbones and cleavers, caterwauling
400 n. *loudness*; racket, atmospherics 61
n. *turmoil*.

Adj. *discordant*, dissonant, jarring,
harsh, raucous, cacophonous 407 adj.
strident; inharmonious, unharmonized;
unmelodious, unmusical, untuneable,
untuneful; off pitch, off key, out of tune,
sharp, flat; atonal, toneless, tuneless.

Vb. *discord*, 25 vb. *disagree*; jangle,
jar, grate, clash; saw, scrape 407 vb.
rasp; untune, unstring.

412. Music – N. *music*, harmony 410 n.
melody; minstrelsy, musicianship 413 n.
musical skill; composing, composition;
instrumental music; counterpoint; electronic music, musique concrète; recorded music, canned m.; dance music,

hot m., syncopation; ragtime, jazz, swing, bebop, bop, blues; written music, the music, score; performance, concert, smoking-c., sing-song; music festival, eisteddfod; school of music, conservatoire, tin-pan alley.

campanology, bell-ringing; ringing, chiming; peal, touch, chime; method-ringing, change-r., hunt, hunt forward, hunt backward, dodge; round, change; method, Grandsire, Plain Bob, Treble Bob, Stedman; carillon, doubles, triples, caters, cinques; minor, major, royal; maximus; bell 414 n. *gong*; bell-ringer, carilloneur, campanologist.

tune, signature t.; refrain; melodic line; air, aria, solo; melody, strain; peal, chime, carillon; flourish, sennet, tucket; phrase, passage, measure.

musical piece, piece, composition, opus, work; record, recording; orchestration, instrumentation; arrangement, adaptation, setting, transcription; voluntary, prelude, overture, intermezzo, finale; accompaniment, incidental music, background m.; étude, study; suite, fugue, toccata, toccatina; sonata, sonatina, symphony; symphonic poem, tone p.; pastorale, scherzo, rondo, jig, reel; march, dead m., dirge, pibroch, coronach; nocturne, serenade, berceuse; aubade; statement, exposition, development, variation; theme, motive, leitmotiv, signature tune; movement; passage, phrase, coda.

vocal music, singing, vocalism, lyricism; part, singing p.; opera, operetta, light opera, comic o., opéra bouffe, musical comedy, musical 594 n. *stage play*; choir-singing, oratorio, cantata, chorale; psalmody, hymnology; descant; chant, plainsong; cantillation, recitative; bel canto, coloratura, bravura; anthem, canticle, psalm 981 n. *hymn*; song, lay, carol, lyric; lieder, ballad; ditty, chanty, calypso; part song, glee, madrigal, round, catch; stave, verse; chorus, refrain, burden, undersong; choral hymn, dithyramb; boat-song, barcarole; lullaby, cradle-song, berceuse; serenade, aubade; song, bird-s., bird-call, dawn

chorus; dirge, threnody 836 n. *lament*; libretto; song-book, hymn-book, psalter.

duet, trio, quartet, quintet, sextet, septet, octet; concerto, concerto grosso, solo, monody; ensemble, tutti.

Adj. *musical,* 410 adj. *melodious*; philharmonic, symphonic; melodic, arioso, cantabile; vocal, singable; operatic, lyric, melic; choral, dithyrambic; hymnal, psalmodic; contrapuntal; orchestrated, scored; set, arranged; instrumental, orchestral; hot, jazzy, syncopated, swung.

Adv. *adagio,* lento, largo, larghetto, andante, andantino, maestoso, moderato; allegro, allegretto; spiritoso, vivace, presto; piano, pianissimo, forte, fortissimo, sforzando, con brio, scherzando; legato, sostenuto, staccato; crescendo, diminuendo, rallentando; affettuoso, arioso, cantabile; obbligato, tremolo, pizzicato, vibrato; rubato.

413. Musician – N. *musician,* artiste, virtuoso, soloist; player, executant, performer, concert artist; bard, minstrel, jongleur, troubadour, minnesinger, gleeman; composer, contrapuntist; syncopator, jazzer, swinger, bebopper, bobster, hepcat; librettist, song-writer, lyrist, lieder-writer, hymn-w.; hymnographer, psalmist; music-master, kapellmeister, master of the music, bandleader, conductor (see *orchestra*); concert-goer, opera-g.

instrumentalist, player, pianist, cembalist, accompanist; organist, accordionist; violinist, fiddler; cellist; harper, lutanist, guitarist; strummer, thrummer; piper, fifer, flautist, flutist; horn-player, trumpeter, bugler; bell-ringer, campanologist; drummer; timpanist; organ-grinder, hurdy-gurdy man.

orchestra, symphony o., quartet, quintet; strings etc. 414 n. *musical instrument*; band, German b., jazz b., brass b., skiffle-group; conductor, maestro, band-master; band-leader, leader, first violin; orchestra-player, bandsman.

vocalist, singer, songster, warbler, chanter; songstress, Siren; melodist, troubadour, gleeman, gleesinger, minstrel, nigger m., coon; serenader, crooner; prima donna, diva; cantatrice; castrato, soprano, mezzo-s., contralto, alto, tenor, counter-t., baritone, bass-b., bass; song-bird, nightingale, lark. thrush, mavis, blackbird.

choir, chorus, waits, carol-singers, glee-club; choir-festival, massed choirs, eisteddfod; chorister, choir-boy, choir-man; precentor, cantor, choir-master; the Muses, tuneful Nine.

musical skill, musical appreciation; musicianship, bardship, minstrelsy; execution, fingering, touch, expression; virtuosity, bravura 694 n. *skill*.

Adj. *musicianly*, knowing music, musical; Orphean, bardic; vocal, coloratura, lyric, melic, choral; instrumental, orchestral, symphonic, contrapuntal; songful, warbling etc. vb.; in music, to m.

Vb. *compose music*, compose, put to music, score, arrange, transpose, orchestrate, harmonize.

play music, play, perform, execute, render, interpret; conduct, beat time; syncopate; sight-read; pedal, vamp, strum; harp, thrum, twang; fiddle, bow, scrape, saw; squeeze the box; wind the horn, blow, bugle, trumpet, toot, tootle; pipe, flute, whistle; doodle, squeeze the bag; drum, tattoo, beat, tap 403 vb. *roll*; ring, peal the bells, toll, knell; tune, string, fret; strike up.

sing, vocalize, chant, hymn; intone, cantillate, descant; warble, carol, lilt, trill; croon, hum, whistle, yodel; chorus, choir; serenade; chirp, pipe 409 vb. *ululate*.

414. Musical instruments – N. *musical instrument*, band 413 n. *orchestra*; strings, brass, wind, wood-wind, percussion, batterie; sounding board, diaphragm, sound box.

harp, stringed instrument, monochord, heptachord, Aeolian harp, Jew's h.; lyre, lute, theorbo; guitar, mandoline; banjo, ukelele, balalaika; psaltery; plectrum, fret.

viol, rebeck, violin, fiddle, kit, crowd; viola, violon-cello, cello, bass-viol, double-bass; bow, fiddlestick; string, catgut.

piano, pianoforte, grand piano; upright piano, cottage p.; virginals, cymbalo, dulcimer, harpsichord, spinet, clavichord, piano-player, pianola; xylophone, marimba; keyboard, manual, keys, ivories.

organ, pipe-o., Hammond o., harmonium; mouth organ, harmonica; accordion, concertina; barrel-organ, hurdygurdy.

flute, fife, piccolo, flageolet, recorder; wood-wind, reed instrument, clarinet, basset horn; shawm, oboe, cor anglais; bassoon, ocarina, sweet potato; pipe, reed; bagpipes, musette; pan-pipes, syrinx; whistle; pitch-pipe; siren; mouthpiece.

horn, bugle, trumpet, clarion; euphonium, ophicleide, serpent, bombardon; saxophone, cornet, trombone, sackbut, tuba; conch.

gong, bell, tintinnabulum; tocsin 665 n. *danger signal*; tintinnabulation, peal, carillon, chimes, bells; knackers, bones, clappers, castanets, cymbals; rattle, sistrum; musical glasses, harmonica; glockenspiel; triangle.

drum, bass d., tenor d., side d., kettle d., tom-tom; tabor, tabouret, tambourine, timbrel; timpanum, timpani; caisse, grosse c.

gramophone, phonograph; record-player, radiogram, pick-up; record, recording, disc, long-player; musical box, juke b., nickelodeon.

mute, damper, sordine, pedal, soft p., celeste 401 n. *silencer*.

415. Hearing – N. *hearing*, audition 398 n. *acoustics*; sense of hearing, good ear; audibility, reception; earshot; earful.

listening, hearkening; auscultation; listening-in, tuning-in; lip-reading; eavesdropping, phone-tapping; audition, voice-testing 461 n. *experiment*; interview, audience, hearing 584 n. *conference*.

listener, auscultator; stethoscopist; hearer, audience, auditorium; disciple, lecture-goer 538 n. *learner*; auditor, examiner 459 n. *questioner*.

ear, lug, lobe, auricle, earhole; external ear, pinna; aural cavity, cochlea, eardrum, tympanum; auditory canal, labyrinth; otology; otoscopy.

hearing aid, stethoscope, otoscope; ear-trumpet; loud-speaker, loud-hailer, public address system 528 n. *publication*; microphone, mike, amplifier 400 n. *megaphone*; speaking-tube; telephone, receiver, earphone, radiophone 531 n. *telecommunication*; sound-tape, dictaphone 549 n. *recording instrument*.

Adj. *auditory*, auricular, aural, otological, otoscopic; auditive, acoustic; listening, all ears 455 adj. *attentive*; within earshot, audible, heard 398 adj. *sounding*.

Vb. *hear*, catch; listen, auscultate, put one's ear to; lip-read 520 vb. *interpret*; listen in; overhear, eavesdrop, tap the wires; hearken, give ear; give audience, interview; hang on the lips of 455 vb. *be attentive*; be told, hear say; bug, tap.

416. Deafness – N. *deafness*, deaf ears, deaf-mutism; deaf-and-dumb speech, dactylology; deaf-mute; inaudibility 399 n. *silence*.

Adj. *deaf*, earless, hard of hearing, stone-deaf; deaf and dumb, deaf-mute; deafened, unable to hear; deaf to, unhearing, not listening 456 adj. *inattentive*; tone-deaf, unmusical.

Vb. *deafen*, stun, split the ear-drum, drown one's hearing 400 vb. *be loud*.

417. Light – N. *light*, day-l., light of day, noonday, broad day, sunlight; half-light, twilight 419 n. *dimness*; artificial light 420 n. *lighting*; illumination, irradiation, splendour, effulgence, intensity, brightness, vividness, brilliance; albedo, luminosity, candle-power; radiance (see *glow*); glare, sheen (see *reflection*); blaze, flare, flame 379 n. *fire*; halo, nimbus, glory, corona; spectrum, iridescence 437 n. *variegation*; riot of colour 425 n. *colour*; white 427 n. *whiteness*.

flash, fulguration, coruscation; lightning, levin; beam, ray; streak; scintillation, sparkle, spark; glint, glitter, play of light; blink, twinkle, starlight; flicker, glimmer, gleam, shimmer; spangle, tinsel; firefly 420 n. *glow-worm*.

glow, flush, dawn, sunset; lambency; aurora, northern lights; radiance, incandescence 379 n. *heat*; luminescence, fluorescence, phosphorescence; ignis fatuus 420 n. *glow-worm*.

radiation, radiant energy; actinism, emission; radio-activity, fall-out, mushroom, radio-active cloud; radiation belt 340 n. *atmosphere*; ray, beam, pencil; searchlight, headlight; infra-red ray, ultra-violet r., Röntgen rays, X-ray, gamma r., beta r., cosmic r., microwave; light wave, radio w.; wavelength, beam width; photon.

reflection, refractivity, refraction; scattering, interference, polarization; albedo, polish, gloss, sheen, lustre; glare, dazzle, blink, ice-b.; moonlight, earthshine, reflector 442 n. *mirror*; mirror-image 551 n. *image*.

light contrast, chiaroscuro, clair-obscur; light and shade, black and white, half-tone, mezzotint; highlights.

optics, photics, photometry, actinometry; dioptrics, catoptrics, spectroscopy; heliography 551 n. *photography*; radioscopy, radiometry, radiology; magnifying power, light-grasp 197 n. *expansion*.

Adj. *luminous*, luminiferous, lucid; light, lit, well-lit, flood-l.; bright, gay, shining, resplendent, brilliant, vivid; garish, colourful 425 adj. *coloured*; radiant, effulgent; incandescent, aflame, aglow, ablaze 379 adj. *fiery*; auroral, orient 431 adj. *red*; luminescent, fluorescent, phosphorescent; soft, lambent, playing; glittery, rutilant, meteoric; lustrous, shiny, glossy; reflecting, catoptric; refractive, dioptric; optical, photometric.

undimmed, clear, bright, fair, set f.; cloudless, shadowless, unclouded, unshaded; sunny, sunshiny; moonlit, star-lit, starry; glassy, gleaming; pellucid 422 adj. *transparent.*

radiating, radiant, radio-active, reflec-tive, reflecting.

Vb. *shine,* burn, blaze, flame, flare 379 vb. *be hot*; glow, phosphoresce; glare, dazzle, blind; play, dance; flash, fulgur-ate, coruscate; glisten, glister, blink; glimmer, flicker, twinkle; glitter, shim-mer, glance; scintillate, sparkle, spark; reflect; take a shine, come up, gleam.

radiate, beam, shoot 300 vb. *emit*; reflect, refract; be radio-active, bombard; X-ray.

make bright, lighten, dawn; clear, brighten; ignite 381 vb. *kindle*; light up, switch on; shed lustre, illuminate, illume; polish, burnish, rub up 648 vb. *clean.*

418. Darkness – N. *darkness,* dark; black 428 n. *blackness*; night, nightfall; dead of night 129 n. *midnight*; obscurity, gloom, shadows 419 n. *dimness*; shade, shadow, umbra, penumbra; dark-room; cavern, mine, dungeon, depths.

obscuration, obfuscation, darkening; black-out, brown-o., dim-o., fade-o.; occultation, eclipse 446 n. *disappear-ance*; lights out; blackening, shading, hatching; dimmer, dipper.

Adj. *dark,* subfusc, sombre; dark-coloured 428 adj. *black*; obscure, pitch-dark, pitchy, sooty, cavernous; murky, funereal, gloomy, dismal; shady 419 adj. *shadowy*; all black, silhouetted; darkling, benighted, nocturnal; secret 523 adj. *occult.*

unlit, unlighted, unilluminated; apho-tic, lightless; sunless, moonless, starless; eclipsed, overcast 421 adj. *screened*; cloudy 423 adj. *opaque*; blacked out.

Vb. *darken,* black out, brown o., dim o.; occult, eclipse, mantle 226 vb. *cover*; veil 421 vb. *screen*; obscure, obfuscate; dim, tone down 419 vb. *bedim*; overcast, overcloud, overshadow, spread gloom; shade, hatch, fill in; over-expose, over-develop 428 vb. *blacken.*

snuff out, extinguish, quench, put out the light, blow o., switch off, dip, douse.

419. Dimness – N. *dimness,* bad seeing, obscurity, indistinctness, vagueness, fuz-ziness, blur; faintness 426 n. *achro-matism*; greyness 429 n. *grey*; cloudi-ness; mistiness 423 n. *opacity*; murk, gloom 418 n. *darkness*; fog, mist 355 n. *cloud*; shadowiness, shadow, shade.

half-light, semidarkness, bad light; glimmer; gloaming 129 n. *evening*; twi-light, dusk; penumbra, half-shadow, par-tial eclipse.

Adj. *dim,* darkish, darksome; dusky, twilight, crepuscular; wan, dun, subfusc, grey, pale 426 adj. *colourless*; faint, waning; dull, lack-lustre; filmy, hazy, foggy, misty 355 adj. *cloudy*; smoky, sooty 423 adj. *opaque*; dingy, grimy, rusty, unpolished, unburnished 649 adj. *dirty.*

shadowy, shady, overcast, overclouded; vague, indistinct, undefined, confused, fuzzy, blurry; looming; deceptive; half-seen, half-glimpsed, half-hidden 444 adj. *invisible*; dreamlike, ghosty 523 adj. *occult.*

Vb. *be dim,* — faint etc. adj.; be indis-tinct, loom; fade, wane 426 vb. *lose colour*; gloom, darkle; glimmer, flicker, gutter.

bedim, dim, dip; fade out; obscure, blur, blear; smirch, smear, sully; rust, mildew, begrime 649 vb. *make unclean*; becloud 423 vb. *make opaque*; over-shadow, shade, shadow, veil 226 vb. *cover.*

420. Luminary: source of light – N. *luminary,* illuminant 417 n. *light*; naked light, flame 379 n. *fire*; flare (see *lamp*); orb of day 321 n. *sun*; orb of night 321 n. *moon*; starlight 321 n. *star*; shooting-star, fire-ball 321 n. *meteor*; fulguration, lightning, sheet-l., fork-l., lightning flash, levin; spark 417 n. *flash.*

glow-worm, lampyrine, firefly; nocti-luca; fata morgana, ignis fatuus, will-o'-the-wisp, Friar's lantern, Jack-o'-lan-tern; fire-ball, St Elmo's fire, corposant; phosphorescent light, corpsecandle.

torch, brand, coal, ember; torchlight, link, flambeau, cresset, match 385 n. *lighter*; candle, taper; spill, wick, dip, rush-light, night-l., flare, gas-f., burner; torch-bearer, lampadist, link-boy,

lamp, lamplight; lantern, dark-l., glim, bull's-eye; safety lamp, Davy l.; oil lamp, hurricane l.; gas mantle; torch, flashlight, searchlight, arc light, head-lamp, headlight, side-light; stoplight, tail-light, reflector; bulb, flashbulb, photoflood, filament; vapour light, neon l.; chandelier, gaselier, lustre, electrolier, candelabra; lamp-post, lampstand, sconce, candlestick; lamplighter.

lighting, illumination, irradiation; artificial lighting, street-l.; floodlighting, son et lumière, limelight, spotlight, foot-light.

signal light, warning l. 665 n. *danger signal*; traffic light, stop-light, trafficator, blinker; rocket, star shell; flare, beacon; lighthouse, lightship.

fireworks, illuminations, pyrotechnics; sparkler, fizgig; thunderflash 723 n. *explosive*; Greek fire.

Adj. *luminescent* 417 adj. *luminous*.

Vb. *illuminate*, light up 417 vb. *shine, make bright.*

421. Screen – N. *screen*, shield 660 n. *protection*; covert 662 n. *shelter*; bower 194 n. *arbour*; windshield, windscreen, sunshade, parasol; awning 226 n. *canopy*; sunscreen, visor; eye-shade, blinkers, blinders; dark glasses, sun glasses; curtain, shutter, deadlight 226 n. *shade*; pall, cloud, dust, smokescreen, obfuscation 423 n. *opacity*; mask 527 n. *disguise*; hood 228 n. *cloak*.

Adj. *screened*, sunproof; shady, bowery; blindfolded, hooded 439 adj. *blind*.

Vb. *screen*, shield, shelter 660 vb. *safeguard*; be a blind, cover up for; blanket, veil, hood 226 vb. *cover*; mask 525 vb. *conceal*; blinker, blindfold 439 vb. *blind*; shade, shadow, darken; shutter, curtain, canopy; cloud, fog, mist; smoke, frost, glaze, film 423 vb. *make opaque*.

422. Transparency – N. *transparency*, transillumination; translucence, unob-structed vision; thinness, gauziness; limpidity, clearness; glassiness, vitreosity, hyalescence; hyaline, water, glass, lens, eyepiece; pane, shop-window; gauze, lace, chiffon 4 n. *insubstantial thing*.

Adj. *transparent*, seen through, pellucid, transpicuous, diaphanous, revealing, sheer; thin, fine, gauzy; translucent, liquid, limpid; crystal, crystalline, hyaline, vitreous, glassy; clear, serene; crystal-clear.

Vb. *be transparent*, — transpicuous etc. adj.; show through, transilluminate; clarify.

423. Opacity – N. *opacity*, opaqueness; solidity 324 n. *density*; filminess, frost; turbidity 649 n. *dirt*; devitrification; fog, mist 355 n. *cloud*; film, scale 421 n. *screen*; smoke-screen.

Adj. *opaque*, impervious, adiactinic, adiathermic; non-transparent, blank, windowless; clear as mud, unclarified, cloudy, filmy, turbid; foggy, hazy, misty, murky, smoky, sooty, fuliginous 419 adj. *dim*.

Vb. *make opaque*, devitrify; cloud, puddle, muddy 649 vb. *make unclean*; frost, film, smoke 419 vb. *bedim*; obfuscate; overpaint 226 vb. *coat*; be opaque 421 vb. *screen*.

424. Semitransparency – N. *semitransparency*, milkiness, lactescence; pearliness, opalescence; smoked glass, frosted g., coloured spectacles, dark glasses; horn, mica.

Adj. *semitransparent*, semidiaphanous, gauzy; translucent, opalescent, milky, lactescent, pearly; frosted, matt, misty, fumé 419 adj. *dim*, 355 adj. *cloudy*.

425. Colour – N. *colour*, monochrome; range of colour, chromatic scale; prism, spectrum, rainbow 437 n. *variegation*; coloration 553 n. *painting*; riot of colour, splash; heraldic colour, tincture, metal, fur 547 n. *heraldry*.

chromatics, chromatoscopy, chromatology, spectrum analysis; chromascope, tintometer; spectroscope, prism.

hue, colour quality, chromatism, tone, value, key; brilliance, intensity, warmth, loudness; softness, deadness, dullness; coloration, livery; pigmentation, colouring, complexion; discoloration; tint, shade, cast, grain, dye; tinge, patina; half-tone, half-light, mezzotint.

pigment, colouring matter, rouge, warpaint, peroxide 843 n. *cosmetic*; dyestuff, dye, grain; madder 431 n. *red pigment*; indigo 434 n. *purple*; woad 435 n. *blue*; stain, fixative, mordant; wash, colour-wash, whitewash, distemper; paint, medium 553 n. *art equipment*.

Adj. *coloured*, in colour, tinged etc. vb.; colorific, tinctorial; fast, unfading, constant; chromatic, polychromatic; monochromatic 16 adj. *uniform*; prismatic, spectroscopic; kaleidoscopic 437 adj. *variegated*.

florid, colourful, high-coloured; ruddy 431 adj. *red*; intense, deep, strong, emphatic; unfaded, vivid, brilliant; warm, glowing, rich, gorgeous; painted, gay, bright; gaudy, garish; lurid, loud, screaming, shrieking.

soft-hued, soft, quiet, tender, delicate; pearly, creamy 427 adj. *whitish*; light, pale, pastel; dull, flat, matt, dead; sober 573 adj. *plain*; drab, dingy, faded; patinated, weathered, mellow; matching, toning 24 adj. *agreeing*.

Vb. *colour*, lay it on, daub, scumble 553 vb. *paint*; rouge 431 vb. *redden*; pigment, tattoo; dye, dip, imbue; tinge, tint, touch up; shade, shadow 428 vb. *blacken*; wash, colour-wash, distemper 226 vb. *coat*; stain, discolour; come off (e.g. on one's fingers); tan, weather, mellow; illuminate, miniate, emblazon; whitewash 427 vb. *whiten*; yellow 433 vb. *gild*; enamel 437 vb. *variegate*.

426. Achromatism: absence of colour – **N.** *achromatism*, colourlessness; fade, discoloration, etiolation 427 n. *whiteness*; under-exposure 551 n. *photography*; pallor, paleness; no colour, anaemia, bloodlessness; pigment-deficiency, albinism; neutral tint.

bleacher, decolorant, peroxide, bleaching powder, lime; bleachery.

Adj. *colourless*, hueless, toneless, lustreless; uncoloured, achromatic; bleached, etiolated, under-exposed; faded, fading; unpigmented, albino, fair 433 adj. *yellow*; glossless, mousy; bloodless, anaemic; washed out, off-colour, pale 427 adj. *white*; ashy, ashen; pasty, sallow, sickly 651 adj. *unhealthy*; dingy, dull, leaden; lack-lustre; lurid, ghastly, wan 419 adj. *dim*; deathly, cadaverous.

Vb. *lose colour*, 419 vb. *be dim*; pale, fade, blanch, turn pale, change countenance 427 vb. *whiten*.

decolorize, fade, etiolate; blanch, bleach 427 vb. *whiten*; drain, wash out; tone down; dull, tarnish, discolour, stain 649 vb. *make unclean*.

427. Whiteness – N. *whiteness*, albescence; leucosis, albinism, leucoderma; whitishness, lactescence, creaminess, pearliness; hoariness, canescence.

white thing, alabaster, marble; snow, chalk, paper, milk, flour, ivory, lily; silver, pearl, teeth; white man, paleface, white; albino.

whiting, white lead, pipeclay; calamine, whitewash.

Adj. *white*, pure, albescent; dazzling 417 adj. *luminous*; silvery, argent; snowy, hoar, frosty; foaming, spumy; soapy, lathery; pure white, lily-white, milk-w., snow-w.; albinistic, leucodermatous.

whitish, pearly, milky, creamy 424 adj. *semitransparent*; ivory, eburnean; waxen, sallow, pale, off-white; unbleached, ecru; grizzled 429 adj. *grey*; blond, fair, ash-blond, platinum b.

Vb. *whiten*, pipeclay, whitewash, calcimine, wash 648 vb. *clean*; blanch, bleach; frost, besnow; silver, grizzle.

428. Blackness – N. *blackness*, nigrescence 418 n. *darkness*; inkiness, black, sable; melanism, swarthiness, colour; depth, deep tone.

negro, negress, mammy; nigger, black,

darky, sambo, coon, piccaninny; blackamoor, coloured man; negrito, negrillo.

black thing, coal, charcoal, soot, pitch, tar, tar-barrel; ebony, jet, ink; crow, raven; crape, mourning.

black pigment, blacking, lamp-black; ink; japan, niello; burnt cork.

Adj. *black*, sable; jetty, ebon, inky, pitchy 418 adj. *dark*; sooty, fuliginous, smoky, smudgy 649 adj. *dirty*; black-haired, raven; black-eyed, sloe-e.; dark, brunette; black-skinned, negroid; pigmented, coloured; sad, sombre 364 adj. *funereal*; coal-black, collied; jet-black, pitch-b.; deep, of the deepest dye.

blackish, nigrescent; swarthy, dark, dark-skinned, tanned; coloured, pigmented; livid, black and blue; overexposed.

Vb. *blacken*, black; ink, ink in; blot, smudge 649 vb. *make unclean*; deepen, over-develop 418 vb. *darken*; singe, char 381 vb. *burn*.

429. Grey – N. *grey*, greyness, canescence, neutral tint, pepper and salt, chiaroscuro, grisaille; oyster, gunmetal, ashes.

Adj. *grey*, neutral, sad, leaden, livid; canescent, grizzled, grizzly, hoary, hoar; glaucous; steely, pearly; powder-grey; smoky; ashen, ashy, cinereous; field-grey, iron-g., mousy, mole; charcoal-grey; pepper-and-salt, dapple grey.

430. Brownness – N. *brownness*, brown, bronze; sun-tan, sun-burn; coffee, chocolate, walnut, mahogany, amber, copper; khaki; burnt almond; brunette.

brown paint, bistre, ochre, sepia, Vandyke brown, sienna, umber.

Adj. *brown*, brownish; bronzed, tanned, sunburnt; dark, brunette; bay, bayard, dapple, roan, auburn, chestnut, sorrel; nutbrown, hazel; cinnamon; beige, fawn, bronze, buff, khaki; tawny; fuscous, tan, foxy, russet, maroon; coppery, cupreous; mahogany, puce, chocolate, coffee-coloured; rust-coloured, snuff-c., liver-c.

Vb. *embrown*, brown, bronze, tan, sunburn; singe, char, toast 381 vb. *burn*.

431. Redness – N. *redness*, flush, blush; fire-glow 417 n. *glow*; reddening, warmth, rubescence; rosiness, ruddiness, bloom; high colour, floridness, rubicundity; type of red, pink, cyclamen, rose, poppy, geranium, peony, cherry, strawberry, plum, peach; tomato; ruby, garnet, carbuncle; coral; rust; salmon, lobster; flame 379 n. *fire*; redskin; red-head, gingernob; rubric.

red pigment, grain, murex, cochineal, carmine; kermes; dragon's blood; cinnabar, vermilion; ruddle, madder; crimson lake, Indian l., Venetian red, rosaniline, solferino; corallin, paeonin; fuchsin, magenta; red lead, minium; rouge 843 n. *cosmetic*.

Adj. *red*, rose-r., rosy, roseate; reddish, pink, salmon-p., flesh-p.; flesh-coloured; coral, russet; scarlet, vermeil, vermilion; crimson, cardinal, imperial purple, Tyrian; murrey, stammel; ruddy, rubicund, sanguine, florid, blowzy; sandy, carroty, red-haired, ginger-h., rufous; auburn, Titian; rusty, rust-coloured; lateritious, brick-red; warm, hot, fiery, glowing, hectic; flushing, rubescent; cerise; tawny; lobster-red; red-hot 379 adj. *hot*.

bloodshot, bloodstained, blood-red; sanguinary, bloody, gory, incarnadine, ensanguined 335 adj. *sanguineous*.

Vb. *redden*, rubify, rubricate, miniate; rouge, raddle 843 vb. *primp*; incarnadine; flush, blush, glow; mantle, colour, crimson.

432. Greenness – N. *greenness*, green, verdancy, greenery, greenwood; verdure, viridescence; jade, emerald, malachite, beryl.

green colour, jungle green, Lincoln g., sea-g., Nile g.; bottle green, pea-g., sage g., jade g.; celadon, reseda.

green pigment, terre verte, celadonite, viridian, verditer, bice, Paris green; chlorophyl, etiolin.

Adj. *green*, viridescent, verdant,

emerald; verdurous, grassy, leafy; grass-green; olive, olivaceous, glaucous; leek-green, porraceous; greenish, bilious; lime, chartreuse.

433. Yellowness – N. *yellowness*, canary yellow; yellow metal, gold; crocus, buttercup, primrose, daffodil, saffron, mustard; topaz; lemon, honey; biliousness, jaundice; xanthodermia, xanthoma, xanthochromism.

yellow pigment, gamboge, cadmium yellow, chrome y., orpiment, yellow ochre; weld, luteolin, xanthin.

Adj. *yellow*, gold, golden, aureate, gilt, gilded; fulvous, fallow, sallow, honey-pale; yellowish, bilious, jaundiced, xanthic; luteous; sandy, flaxen, fair-haired, blond, platinum b.; creamy, cream-coloured; citrine, lemon-coloured, straw-c., butter-c.

Vb. *gild*, gilt, yellow, jaundice.

434. Purple – N. *purple*, blue and red; heliotrope, lavender, pansy, violet; amethyst; Tyrian purple, gentian violet; mulberry colour, lividness 428 n. *blackness*; mauve.

Adj. *purple*, purply, violet, violaceous; mauve, lavender, lilac, puce, plum-coloured; ianthine, hyacinthine, heliotrope; livid, mulberry; black and blue 428 adj. *black*.

Vb. *empurple*, purple.

435. Blueness – N. *blueness*, blue, sky, sea; azure, cerulean, celeste, perse, watchet; robin's egg, peacock, hyacinth, bluebell, cornflower, violet, forget-me-not; sapphire, turquoise, lapis lazuli, beryl, aquamarine; bluishness, cyanosis; lividness, lividity; cyanometer.

blue pigment, bice, indigo, woad; cyanin; saxe-b., Prussian b., ultramarine, cobalt, zaffre, smalt; cerulean, azulene; blue-bag.

Adj. *blue*, azure, cyanic; cerulean, skyey; sky-blue, air-force b., watchet-b.; light blue, Cambridge b., powder b., steel b.; royal blue, peacock b., pavonian; aquamarine, sea-b., electric b.;

ultramarine; deep blue, Oxford b., midnight b., navy b., hyacinthine, blue-black, black and blue, livid; bluish, perse; cyanosed.

436. Orange – N. *orange*, red and yellow, gold, old g.; or 547 n. *heraldry*; apricot, mandarin, tangerine, ginger, copper, bronze; ochre, cadmium, henna, helianthin.

Adj. *orange*, ochreous, cupreous, bronzy, coppery, ginger; tenné.

437. Variegation – N. *variegation*, variety, diversification, diversity 15 n. *difference*; shot colours, iridescence; nacre, mother-of-pearl; pigeon's neck; dichromatism, trichromatism, tricolour; polychrome, multi-colour 425 n. *colour*; peacock's tail, butterfly, tortoiseshell, chameleon; Joseph's coat, motley, harlequin, patchwork; riot of colour; stained glass, kaleidoscope; rainbow, rainbow effect, band of colour, spectrum, prism.

chequer, checker, chequerwork, check, pepper-and-salt; plaid, tartan; chessboard, draught-b., checker b.; mosaic, tessellation, marquetry, parquetry, crazy-paving 82 n. *multiformity*.

striation, striae; line, streak, band, bar, stripe, tricolour; zebra, tiger; streakiness, mackerel sky; crack, craze 330 n. *brittleness*.

maculation, dappling, stippling, marbling; spottiness, patchiness 17 n. *nonuniformity*; patch 845 n. *blemish*; maculae, sunspot; leopard, spotted dog.

Adj. *variegated* etc. vb., diversified, daedal; embroidered, worked 844 adj. *ornamental*; polychromatic, colourful 425 adj. *florid*; bicolour, tricolour; many-coloured, multi-c., parti-c., motley, patched, crazy; kaleidoscopic 82 adj. *multiform*; iridal, iridian; prismatic, spectral; mosaic, tessellated.

iridescent, irisated, chameleon; nacreous, mother-of-pearl; opalescent, opaline, pearly; shot, gorge-de-pigeon, pavonian, moiré, watered, chatoyant.

pied, parti-coloured, black-and-white,

pepper-and-salt, grizzled, piebald, skewbald, roan, pinto, chequered, check, dappled, patchy.

mottled, marbled; studded, maculous, spotty, patchy; speckledy, freckled; streaky, stripy, lined, barred, banded; brindled, tabby; pockmarked, fleabitten 845 adj. *blemished*; cloudy, dusty.

Vb. *variegate*, diversify, fret; punctuate; chequer, check, patch; embroider, work 844 vb. *decorate*; damascene, inlay, tessellate, tile; stud, mottle, speckle, freckle, spangle, spot; sprinkle, powder, dust; tattoo, stipple, dapple; streak, stripe; marble, jasper, vein, cloud 423 vb. *make opaque*; stain, blot, maculate, discolour 649 vb. *make unclean*; irisate; interchange colour, play.

438. Vision - N. *vision*, sight, lightgrasp; eyesight; seeing, visualization; perception, recognition; acuity (of vision), good sight; short sight 440 n. *dim sight*; second sight 984 n. *occultism*; double vision, stereoscopic v., binocular v.; magnification; oculist, optician, ophthalmologist 417 n. *optics*; dream 440 n. *visual fallacy*.

eye, organ of vision, eyeball, iris, pupil, white, cornea, retina, optic nerve; optics, orbs, lights, peepers, weepers; eyelashes, eyelid; naked eye, unaided e.; sharp eye, gimlet e., X-ray e., hawk, eagle, lynx; evil eye 983 n. *sorcery*.

look, regard, glance, side-g., squint; tail *or* corner of the eye; glint, blink; stare, gaze; glad eye, ogle 889 n. *endearment*; wink 524 n. *hint*; dirty look, scowl, evil eye; peep, peek, glimpse, half an eye; mien 445 n. *appearance*.

inspection, ocular demonstration; examination, autopsy 459 n. *inquiry*; view, preview 522 n. *manifestation*; oversight 689 n. *management*; survey, sweep, reconnaissance; sight-seeing, rubbernecking; look, look-see, once-over; review, revision; discernment, catching sight, espial, view, first sight; observation, watch; espionage; peeping, scopophilia, Peeping Tom.

view, full v., eyeful; vista, prospect, outlook, perspective; conspectus, panorama, bird's-eye view, horizon; scene, setting, stage 594 n. *theatre*; angle, slant, point of view, viewpoint 485 n. *opinion*; observation point, look-out, crow's nest, watch-tower; astrodome, conning tower; observatory; grandstand 441 n. *onlookers*; peephole 263 n. *window*.

Adj. *seeing* etc. vb.; visual; perceptible 443 adj. *visible*; panoramic, synoptic; ocular, ophthalmic; optical; stereoscopic, binocular; perspicacious, clearsighted, sharp-eyed, eagle-e., hawk-e., lynx-e.

Vb. *see* . behold, visualize, use one's eyes; perceive, discern, distinguish, make out, recognize, ken 490 vb. *know*; descry, discover 484 vb. *detect*; sight, espy, spy, spot, observe 455 vb. *notice*; clap eyes on, catch sight of; glimpse; view, have in sight; witness, look on, watch.

gaze, quiz, gaze at, look, look at; eye, stare, peer, squinny; stare, goggle, gape, gawk; focus, rivet one's eyes; glare 891 vb. *be angry*; glance, take a slant; squint, look askance; wink, blink 524 vb. *hint*; ogle, leer 889 vb. *court*; gloat 947 vb. *gluttonize*; steal a glance, peep, peek; cock one's eye; notice, look upon 455 vb. *be attentive*; look away 458 vb. *disregard*; look at each other, exchange glances.

scan, scrutinize, inspect, examine, take stock of; contemplate, pore over 536 vb. *study*; look over, look through; see, take in, sight-see, rubberneck 882 vb. *visit*; view, survey, sweep, reconnoitre, scout; peep, peek 453 vb. *be curious*; spy, pry, snoop; observe, keep under observation, watch 457 vb. *invigilate*; keep watch, look out, stand sentry; strain one's eyes, peer, squinny; crane one's neck.

439. Blindness - N. *blindness*, lack of vision; sightlessness, eyelessness; night blindness, snow b., colour b.; dimsightedness 440 n. *dim sight*; blind side, blind spot, blind eye 456 n. *inattention*; Braille 586 n. *script*; white stick.

Adj. *blind*, sightless, eyeless, visionless, dark; unseeing 456 adj. *inattentive*; blinded blindfold, blinkered; in the dark, benighted; gravel-blind, stone-b., sandblind, stark-b.

Vb. *blind*, deprive of sight; put one's eyes out; dazzle, daze; blinker, blindfold 421 vb. *screen*; hoodwink, bluff, throw dust in one's eyes 495 vb. *mislead*.

440. Dim-sightedness: imperfect vision – **N.** *dim sight*, weak s., failing s.; purblindness; half-vision, partial v.; weak eyes, eye-strain; amblyopia, short s., near s., myopia; presbyopia, long sight; double vision; astigmatism, teichopsia, cataract, film; glaucoma, iridization; scotoma; colour-blindness, Daltonism; lippitude, blearedness; ophthalmia, ophthalmitis; conjunctivitis, pink eye; cast; convergent vision, strabismus, strabism, squint, cross-eye; wall-eye, swivel e.; myosis; wink, blink, nictitation, nystagmus; blind side, blind spot 456 n. *inattention*.

visual fallacy, refraction 417 n. *reflection*; false light 552 n. *misrepresentation*; illusion, optical i., phantasmagoria; mirage 542 n. *deception*; fata morgana, ignis fatuus, will-o'-the-wisp 420 n. *glow-worm*; phantasm 970 n. *ghost*; vision, dream 513 n. *fantasy*; distorting mirror 442 n. *optical device*.

Adj. *dim-sighted*, purblind, half-blind, gravel-b.; bleary, weak-eyed, bespectacled; myopic, short-sighted, near-s.; presbyopic, long-sighted; astigmatic; colour-blind, dichromatic; hemeralopic, nyctalopic; dim-eyed, one-e., monocular; wall-eyed, squinting; strabismal, cross-eyed; myopic, nystagmic; blinking, dazzled; amaurotic, cataractous, glaucomatic.

Vb. *be dim-sighted*, —myopic etc. adj.; grope, peer, screw up the eyes, squint; blink, wink, nictitate; see double, dazzle, swim.

blur, confuse; glare, dazzle, bedazzle 417 vb. *shine*; darken, dim, mist, fog 419 vb. *bedim*.

441. Spectator – **N.** *spectator*, beholder, seer; mystic 513 n. *visionary*; looker, viewer, observer, watcher; inspector, scrutineer; witness, eye-w.; bystander, onlooker; looker-on, gaper, goggler; eyer, ogler; sightseer, rubberneck 268 n. *traveller*; spotter, look-out 484 n. *detector*; watchman, watch, sentinel, sentry 664 n. *warner*; scout, spy, snoop 459 n. *detective*.

onlookers, audience, auditorium, sea of faces; box-office, gate, house, gallery, grandstand, pit, stalls; supporters, followers, fans 707 n. *patron*; viewership.

442. Optical instrument – **N.** *optical device*, optical instrument; glass 422 n. *transparency*; lens, meniscus; eyepiece, ocular, object-glass; sunglass, burning-glass; optometer, ophthalmoscope, retinoscope; helioscope, coronograph; periscope; radar; prism, spectroscope, diffraction grating, polariscope; kaleidoscope; stereoscope, stereopticon; photometer, actinometer, radiometer; projector, epidiascope, magic lantern 445 n. *cinema*; slide.

eyeglass, spectacles, specs, glasses, goggles, gig-lamps, barnacles; sunglasses, dark glasses; pince-nez, nippers; bifocals; contact lens; lorgnette, monocle, quizzing-glass; magnifying glass, reading g.; spectacle-maker, oculist, optician, ophthalmologist; optometrist, optometry.

telescope, astronomical t., terrestrial t., achromatic t., inverting t., refractor, reflector; finder, range-f.; spy-glass, field-g., night-g.; binoculars, opera glass.

microscope, photo-m., electron m., ultra-microscope; microscopy, microphotography, microscopist.

mirror, magic m., distorting m.; flat, speculum; rear-view mirror, traffic m.; glass, hand-mirror, hand-glass, looking-g., pier-g., cheval-g.

camera, camera lucida, camera obscura, pin-hole camera; stereo-camera, telephoto lens, movie-camera, X-ray c.; microphotography 551 n. *photo-*

graphy; plate, wet p., dry p.; film, micro-f., panchromatic f.

443. Visibility – N. *visibility*, perceptibility; sight, exposure; distinctness, clearness, conspicuousness, prominence; ocular demonstration, object lesson 522 n. *manifestation*; scene 438 n. *view*; seeing, good s., bad s.; ceiling, eye-range, eye-shot 183 n. *range.*

Adj. *visible*, viewable; perceptible, perceivable, discernible, observable, detectable; noticeable, recognizable, unmistakable, palpable; apparent 445 adj. *appearing*; evident 522 adj. *manifest*; exposed, open, naked, open to view; in view, before one's eyes; macroscopic; telescopic, at the limit of vision; panoramic, stereoscopic, periscopic.

well-seen, obvious, showing, for all to see; plain, clear, clear-cut; definite, well-defined; distinct, unblurred, in focus; unclouded, undisguised, uncovered, unhidden; spectacular, conspicuous, prominent, cynosural, eye-catching; pronounced, in bold relief; eidetic, eidotropic; under one's nose, plain as plain.

Vb. *be visible*, show, show through 422 vb. *be transparent*; meet the eye; catch *or* hit the eye, stand out, act as a landmark; come to light; loom, heave in sight 445 vb. *appear*; surface, break s. 308 vb. *ascend*; show, materialize; manifest itself, betray i.; fill the eyes, dazzle, glare; have no secrets, live in a glass house.

444. Invisibility – N. *invisibility*, nonappearance 190 n. *absence*; vanishment, thin air 446 n. *disappearance*; imperceptibility, indistinctness; poor visibility, obscurity 419 n. *dimness*; submergence 523 n. *latency*; hiding 525 n. *concealment*; smoke screen, mist, pall 421 n. *screen*; blind spot, blind eye 439 n. *blindness*; blind corner 663 n. *pitfall.*

Adj. *invisible*, imperceptible, unapparent, unnoticeable, indiscernible; indistinguishable, unrecognizable; unseen,

unsighted; out of sight 446 adj. *disappearing*; sequestered 883 adj. *secluded*; delitescent 523 adj. *latent*; dark, secret, in the dark.

ill-seen, half-s., glimpsed; unclear, ill-defined, indistinct 419 adj. *dim*; faint, inconspicuous, microscopic 196 adj. *minute*; confused, vague, blurred, blurry, out of focus; fuzzy, misty, hazy.

445. Appearance – N. *appearance*, apparition, phenomenon; revelation 484 n. *discovery*; externals, outside 223 n. *exteriority*; appearances, look of things; visual impact, face value, first blush; impression, effect; show, seeming, semblance; side, aspect, guise, colour, light, outline, shape 243 n. *form*; set, hang, look; a manifestation, emanation, theophany; vision 513 n. *fantasy*; mirage 440 n. *visual fallacy*; spectre 970 n. *ghost*; reflection 551 n. *image.*

spectacle, impressiveness, impression, effect; speciousness, meretriciousness, decoration 844 n. *ornamentation*; feast for the eyes, eyeful, vision, sight, scene; panorama 438 n. *view*; display, pageantry 875 n. *ostentation*; show, exhibition 522 n. *exhibit*; peep-show, phantasmagoria; diorama, cyclorama, georama, cosmorama; staging, tableau, set, decor 594 n. *stage set*; floor show 594 n. *stage show*; television, video (see *cinema*) landmark 547 n. *signpost.*

cinema, cinematograph, bioscope, cinema-screen, silver s.; photoplay, motion picture, movie-show, film s., cinerama; movies, flickers, flicks, films; film, stereoscopic f., three-dimensional f., 3D; talkie; cartoon, newsreel, documentary, short, double feature, trailer, preview; film production, montage, continuity, cutting, scenario; cinema house, picture palace, nickelodeon 594 n. *theatre*; projector, ciné-camera 442 n. *camera.*

mien, look, face; play of feature, expression; countenance, favour; complexion, colour, cast; air, demeanour, carriage, port, presence; gesture, posture, behaviour 688 n. *conduct.*

feature, trait, mark, lineament; lines, cut, shape, fashion, figure 243 n. *form*; contour, relief, elevation, profile, silhouette; visage, physiognomy 237 n. *face*.

Adj. *appearing*, apparent, phenomenal; seeming, specious, ostensible; deceptive 542 adj. *deceiving*; outward, external 223 adj. *exterior*; on view 443 adj. *visible*; impressive, spectacular 875 adj. *showy*; revealed, theophanic 522 adj. *manifest*.

Vb. *appear*, show 443 vb. *be visible*; seem, look so 18 vb. *resemble*; exhibit the form of, take the shape of; figure in, display oneself 875 vb. *be ostentatious*; be on show, be on exhibit; dawn 68 vb. *begin*; come to light, materialize, eventuate, blow up 154 vb. *happen*.

Adv. *apparently*, ostensibly, seemingly, to all appearances, to the eye, on the face of it; in the eyes of.

446. Disappearance – N. *disappearance*, vanishment; disappearing trick 542 n. *sleight*; flight 667 n. *escape*; exit 296 n. *departure*; evanescence, dematerialization; occultation 418 n. *obscuration*; dissolving views, fade-out; vanishing point, thin air 444 n. *invisibility*.

Adj. *disappearing*, evanescent 114 adj. *transient*; lost to sight 444 adj. *invisible*.

Vb. *disappear*, vanish, do the vanishing trick; dematerialize, melt into thin air; evanesce, dissolve, melt; fade 426 vb. *lose colour*, 114 vb. *be transient*; disperse 75 vb. *be dispersed*; absent oneself, play truant 190 vb. *be absent*; hide 523 vb. *lurk*; cover one's tracks, leave no trace 525 vb. *conceal*.

Class Four

INTELLECT

DIVISION (I): FORMATION OF IDEAS

Section 1: General

447. Intellect – N. *intellect*, mind, psyche, psychic organism, mentality; understanding, intellection, conception; rationality, reasoning power; reason 475 n. *reasoning*; philosophy 449 n. *thought*; awareness, sense, consciousness, self-c., stream of c. 455 n. *attention*; cognizance, noesis, perception, apperception, insight; extra-sensory perception, instinct 476 n. *intuition*; flair, judgement 463 n. *discrimination*; noology, intellectualism, intellectuality; mental capacity, brains 498 n. *intelligence*; mental evolution, psychogenesis; sensorium, sensory 818 n. *feeling*.

psychology, science of mind, metapsychology; parapsychology 984 n. *psychics*; abnormal psychology 503 n. *psychopathy*; psychosomatics; Freudianism, Freudian psychology, Jungian p., Adlerian p.; Gestalt psychology; configurationism, behaviourism; psychography, psychometry, psychoanalysis; psychopathology, psychiatry, psychotherapy 658 n. *therapy*; psychophysiology, psychophysics, psychobiology.

psychologist, psychoanalyst, psychiatrist, psychotherapist, psychopathist, mental specialist, alienist, mad doctor 658 n. *doctor*.

spirit, soul, mind, heart, breast, bosom, inner man 224 n. *interiority*; genius 80 n. *self*; psyche, pneuma, id, ego, superego, self, subliminal s., the unconscious, the subconscious; personality, split p. 503 n. *psychopathy*; spiritualism 984 n. *occultism*.

Adj. *mental*, thinking, reasoning 475 adj. *rational*; cerebral, intellectual, noological, noetic, conceptual, abstract; theoretical 512 adj. *suppositional*; unconcrete 320 adj. *immaterial*; perceptual, percipient, perceptive; cognitive, cognizant 490 adj. *knowing*; conscious, self-c., subjective.

psychic, psychical, psychological; subconscious, subliminal; spiritualistic 984 adj. *psychical*; spiritual 320 adj. *immaterial*.

Vb. *cognize*, perceive, apperceive 490 vb. *know*; realize, sense; objectify 223 vb. *externalize*; note, advert, mark 455 vb. *notice*; ratiocinate 475 vb. *reason*; understand 498 vb. *be wise*; conceptualize, intellectualize 449 vb. *think*; conceive, invent 484 vb. *discover*; ideate 513 vb. *imagine*.

448. Non-intellect – N. *non-intellect*, unintellectuality; brute creation 365 n. *animality*, 366 n. *vegetability*; stocks and stones; instinct, brute i. 476 n. *intuition*; unreason, vacuity, brainlessness, mindlessness 450 n. *incogitance*.

Adj. *mindless*, non-intellectual, unintellectual; animal, vegetable; mineral, inanimate 359 adj. *inorganic*; unreasoning 450 adj. *unthinking*; instinctive, brute 476 adj. *intuitive*; uninventive, unidea'd 20 adj. *imitative*; brainless 499 adj. *foolish*; moronic, wanting 503 adj. *insane*.

449. Thought – N. *thought*, mental process, thinking; mental act, ideation; intellectual exercise, mentation, cogitation; cerebration, lucubration, head work, thinking-cap; brain-work, brain-fag; hard thinking, concentration 455 n. *attention*; profundity 498 n. *wisdom*; abstract thought, imageless t.; thoughts, ideas 451 n. *idea*; conception, conceit, workings of the mind 513 n. *ideality*; association of ideas 475 n. *reasoning*; brown study, reverie 456 n. *abstractedness*; excogitation (see *meditation*); inventiveness 513 n. *imagination*; after-thought, reconsideration 67 n. *sequel*; retrospection, hindsight 505 n. *memory*; forethought 510 n. *foresight*; thought transference 984 n. *psychics*.

meditation, thoughtfulness, specula-tion 459 n. *inquiry*; reflection, brooding, rumination, consideration, pondering; contemplation 438 n. *inspection*; intro-spection; religious contemplation, re-treat, mysticism 979 n. *piety*; delibera-tion 691 n. *advice*; excogitation, thinking out 480 n. *judgement*; examination, concentration, application 536 n. *study*.

philosophy, ontology, metaphysics; speculation, philosophical thought, ab-stract t., systematic t.; ideology, doc-trine, school.

philosopher, thinker, i deologist 492 n. *intellectual*; schoolman, metaphysician, Vedantist; school of philosophers, Pre-Socratics, Eleatics, Peripatetics; Aca-demy, Stoa; Garden of Epicurus, Dio-genes' tub.

Adj. *thoughtful*, conceptive, ideative, speculative (see *philosophic*); cogitative, deliberative; pensive, meditative, con-templative, reflective; self-communing, introspective; ruminant, absorbed, musing, dreamy 456 adj. *abstracted*; concentrating 455 adj. *attentive*; con-siderate 901 adj. *philanthropic*; prudent 510 adj. *foreseeing*.

philosophic, metaphysical, ontological, speculative, abstract, systematic, ra-tional, logical; ideological, doctrinal.

Vb. *think*, 512 vb. *suppose*; conceive, ideate; fancy 513 vb. *imagine*; think about, cogitate (see *meditate*); use one's brain, put on one's thinking-cap; con-centrate, collect one's thoughts, pull one's wits together 455 vb. *be attentive*; trouble one's head about, animadvert; lucubrate, cerebrate, mull 536 vb. *study*; beat one's brains, rack one's b., worry at; think out, excogitate, invent 484 vb. *discover*; devise 623 vb. *plan*; take into one's head, get a bee in one's bonnet; think on 505 vb. *remember*.

meditate, ruminate, chew over, digest, discuss; examine 459 vb. *inquire*; reflect,

contemplate, study; speculate, philoso-phize; intellectualize 447 vb. *cognize*; think about, consider; take stock of, per-pend, ponder, weigh 480 vb. *estimate*; think over, revolve, con over 505 vb. *memorize*; bethink oneself, reconsider, review, have second thoughts; take counsel, advise with, consult one's pil-low, sleep on it 691 vb. *consult*; intro-spect; brood, muse; go into retreat.

cause thought, dawn upon, occur to, make one think, strike 821 vb. *impress*; penetrate, sink in; haunt, obsess, occupy, fascinate, absorb, engross, pre-occupy, run in one's head, come upper-most.

Adv. *in mind*, in contemplation, under consideration; all things considered; on second thoughts; come to think of it.

450. Absence of thought – N. *incogitance*, mindlessness 448 n. *non-intellect*; blank mind, fallow m. 491 n. *ignorance*; vacancy, abstraction 456 n. *abstracted-ness*; inconsideration, thoughtlessness 456 n. *inattention*; conditioned reflex, automatism; instinct 476 n. *intuition*; stocks and stones.

Adj. *unthinking*, incogitant, unreflect-ing, unphilosophic, unintellectual 448 adj. *mindless*; unidea'd, unimaginative, uninventive 20 adj. *imitative*; blank, vacant, empty-headed, not thinking 456 adj. *inattentive*; thoughtless, incon-siderate; irrational 477 adj. *illogical*; stupid 499 adj. *unintelligent*; animal, vegetable, mineral.

unthought, inconceivable, uncon-sidered, undreamt, not to be thought of 470 adj. *impossible*.

451. Idea – N. *idea*, noumenon, notion, a thought; object of thought, concept; theory 512 n. *supposition*; percept, image, mental i.; Platonic idea, archetype 23 n. *prototype*; conception 447 n. *intellect*; reflection, observation 449 n. *thought*; impression, conceit, fancy, phantasy 513 n. *imagination*; figment, fiction; asso-ciated ideas, complex; invention, brain-child; brain wave, happy thought 484 n.

discovery; wheeze 623 n. *contrivance*; view, point of v., slant, attitude 485 n. *opinion*; principle.

Adj. *ideational*, ideative 449 adj. *thoughtful*; notional, ideal 513 adj. *imaginary*.

452. Topic – N. *topic*, subject of thought, food for t.; subject matter, subject; contents, chapter, section, head 53 n. *subdivision*; what it is about, argument, plot, theme; text, commonplace, burden, motif; musical topic, statement, leitmotiv 412 n. *musical piece*; concern, interest, human i.; matter, affair; shop 622 n. *business*; agenda, order paper 623 n. *policy*; problem 459 n. *question*; heart of the question, gist, pith; theorem, proposition 512 n. *supposition*; thesis, case, point 475 n. *argument*; issue, moot point, point at issue; field, field of inquiry 536 n. *study*.

Adj. *topical*, thematic; challenging, thought-provoking; obsessive, on the brain; mooted, debatable 474 adj. *uncertain*; thought about, uppermost in the mind, fit for consideration.

Section 2: Precursory Conditions and Operations

453. Curiosity: desire for knowledge – N. *curiosity*, morbid c., ghoulishness; prurience, voyeurism, scopophilia; interest, itch, inquisitiveness; quizzing 459 n. *question*; sightseeing 267 n. *land travel*.

inquisitor, censor, examiner 459 n. *inquirer*, *questioner*; pry; busybody 678 n. *meddler*; gossip, quidnunc 529 n. *newsmonger*; sightseer, globe-trotter 441 n. *spectator*; snoop 459 n. *detective*; eavesdropper 415 n. *listener*; Paul Pry, Peeping Tom, Nosy Parker.

Adj. *inquisitive*, curious, interested; avid for knowledge 536 adj. *studious*; morbidly curious, ghoulish, prurient; newsmongering; wanting to know, burning with curiosity; over-curious, nosy, snoopy; inquisitorial 459 adj. *inquiring*; meddlesome 678 adj. *meddling*.

Vb. *be curious*, want to know; seek 459 vb. *search*; feel a concern, take an interest; show interest, prick up one's ears 455 vb. *be attentive*; nose out, peep, peek, spy, snoop, pry 459 vb. *inquire*; eavesdrop, tap the line 415 vb. *hear*; quiz, question 459 vb. *interrogate*; stand and stare 438 vb. *gaze*; rubberneck, sightsee.

454. Incuriosity – N. *incuriosity*, incuriousness, no questions; uninterest, unconcern 860 n. *indifference*; apathy 820 n. *moral insensibility*; indifferentism; blunted curiosity 863 n. *satiety*.

Adj. *incurious*, uninquisitive, unreflecting 450 adj. *unthinking*; uninterested; unconcerned, uninvolved 860 adj. *indifferent*; listless, apathetic 820 adj. *impassive*.

Vb. *be incurious*, feel no concern, couldn't care less 860 vb. *be indifferent*; mind one's own business, see nothing, hear n., look the other way 458 vb. *disregard*.

455. Attention – N. *attention*, notice, regard 438 n. *look*; advertence, heed, attentiveness 457 n. *carefulness*; observation, eyes on 457 n. *surveillance*; wariness, circumspection 858 n. *caution*; contemplation 449 n. *meditation*; intentness, undivided attention, whole a.; concentration, application, studiousness 536 n. *study*; scrutiny 438 n. *inspection*; pains, trouble 678 n. *assiduity*; exclusive attention, single-mindedness; absorption, preoccupation; interest 453 n. *curiosity*.

Adj. *attentive*, intent, diligent, assiduous 678 adj. *industrious*; heedful 457 adj. *careful*; alert, open-eyed, awake; observant, sharp-eyed 457 adj. *vigilant*; interested, curious; attending, missing nothing, all eyes, all ears; single-minded, undistracted, deep in; study-bent 536 adj. *studious*; meticulous, pedantic 494 adj. *accurate*.

Vb. *be attentive*, attend, pay attention, mind 457 vb. *be careful*; advert, listen, prick up one's ears, sit up and take notice; miss nothing, watch, be all eyes 438 vb. *gaze*; be all ears, drink in, hang on the lips of 415 vb. *hear*; rivet, focus (one's mind on), concentrate on, fix on; scrutinize 438 vb. *scan*; study closely, pore, mull 536 vb. *study*; glance at, look into, dip into, leaf through.

notice, note, take n., register; mark, advert, recognize; take cognizance of; animadvert upon, comment u., remark on 584 vb. *converse*; mention, touch on 524 vb. *hint*; recall, revert to, hark back 106 vb. *repeat*; have time for, find time f. 681 vb. *have leisure*; acknowledge, salute 884 vb. *greet*.

attract notice, draw the attention, hold the a., focus the a., rivet the a.; interest, excite attention; catch the eye, fall under observation 443 vb. *be visible*; advertise 528 vb. *publish*; point out 547 vb. *indicate*; stress, underline 532 vb. *emphasize*.

456. Inattention – N. *inattention*, inadvertence, forgetfulness 506 n. *oblivion*; oversight, aberration; detachment, unconcern 860 n. *indifference*; inconsideration, heedlessness 857 n. *rashness*; aimlessness, desultoriness, superficiality; étourderie, levity, volatility 604 n. *caprice*; blind spot, blind side 439 n. *blindness*; daydream, daydreamer.

abstractedness, abstraction, absent-mindedness; wool-gathering, daydreaming, doodling; reverie, brown study; distraction, preoccupation, divided attention.

Adj. *inattentive*, careless 458 adj. *negligent*; unobservant, unnoticing 454 adj. *incurious*; unseeing, unhearing; unmindful, unheeding, inadvertent, unreflecting 450 adj. *unthinking*; not concentrating, half asleep; listless 860 adj. *indifferent*; oblivious 506 adj. *forgetful*; inconsiderate, thoughtless, heedless, regardless 857 adj. *rash*; off-hand, cursory, superficial, unthorough 212 adj. *shallow*.

abstracted, distrait, absent-minded, absent, not there; lost in thought, rapt, absorbed, in the clouds, bemused, dreamy, dreaming, day-d., wool-gathering; nodding, half-awake 679 adj. *sleepy*.

distracted, preoccupied, otherwise engaged, with divided attention; disconcerted, put out, put off one's stroke.

light-minded, unfixed, unconcentrated, wandering, desultory, trifling; frivolous, flippant, insouciant; airy, volatile, mercurial, bird-witted, flighty, giddy, dizzy; scatter-brained, hare-b.; inconstant 604 adj. *capricious*.

Vb. *be inattentive*, not attend, not register, not hear the penny drop, not click, not catch; overlook 458 vb. *neglect*; be off one's guard, be caught out; dream, drowse, nod 679 vb. *sleep*; trifle, play at; wander, go woolgathering, muse, moon, star-gaze; idle, doodle 679 vb. *be inactive*; be distracted, lose the thread, fluff one's notes 282 vb. *stray*.

distract, call away, divert one's attention, put out of one's head; disconcert, upset, fluster, flurry, rattle 318 vb. *agitate*; put one off his stroke, put one out of his stride 702 vb. *obstruct*; daze, dazzle 439 vb. *blind*; play with, amuse.

Adv. *inadvertently*, per incuriam; giddily, gaily, lightheartedly.

457. Carefulness – N. *carefulness*, mindfulness, attentiveness; diligence, pains 678 n. *assiduity*; heed, care 455 n. *attention*; anxiety, solicitude 825 n. *worry*; tidiness, neatness 60 n. *order*; attention to detail, thoroughness, meticulousness, minuteness, circumstantiality, particularity; nicety, exactness 494 n. *accuracy*; over-nicety, pedantry, perfectionism 862 n. *fastidiousness*; conscience, scruples, scrupulosity 929 n. *probity*; vigilance, wakefulness, watchfulness, alertness, readiness 669 n. *preparedness*; circumspection 858 n. *caution*.

surveillance, an eye on, guarding, watch and ward 660 n. *protection*; vigilance, invigilation, inspection; babysitting, chaperonage; look-out, weather-eye; vigil, watch; guard, sentry-go; chaperon, sentinel 749 n. *keeper*.

Adj. *careful*, mindful, regardful, heedful 455 adj. *attentive*; painstaking, solicitous, anxious; gingerly, afraid to touch; loving, tender; conscientious, scrupulous 929 adj. *honourable*; thorough, thorough-going; meticulous, minute, particular, circumstantial; exact 494 adj. *accurate*; pedantic, overcareful, perfectionist 862 adj. *fastidious*; tidy, neat 60 adj. *orderly*.

vigilant, alert, ready 669 adj. *prepared*; on guard, on the qui vive, on one's toes; watchful, wakeful, wide-awake; observant, sharp-eyed; forehanded, far-sighted 510 adj. *foreseeing*; surefooted, circumspect 858 adj. *cautious*.

Vb. *be careful*, reck, mind, heed 455 vb. *be attentive*; check, recheck 858 vb. *be cautious*; keep a look-out, mind one's step; pick one's steps, feel one's way 461 vb. *be tentative*; take pains, do with care.

look after, take care of, see to 689 vb. *manage*; take charge of, care for, mind 660 vb. *safeguard*; baby-sit, nurse, foster, cherish 889 vb. *pet*; keep a sharp eye on, keep tabs on, chaperon, play gooseberry.

invigilate, stay awake, sit up; keep vigil, watch; stand sentinel; keep watch, look out; mount guard, set watch 660 vb. *safeguard*.

Adv. *carefully*, diligently; thoroughly; lovingly, tenderly; painfully, anxiously; with care, gingerly.

458. Negligence – N. *negligence*, carelessness 456 n. *inattention*; neglectfulness, forgetfulness 506 n. *oblivion*; remissness, neglect, oversight, omission; non-observance, default, laches, culpable negligence 918 n. *dutilessness*; unguarded hour, unpreparedness 670 n. *non-preparation*; disregard, insouciance, nonchalance 860 n. *indifference*; procrastination 136 n. *delay*; supineness 679 n. *inactivity*; slovenliness 61 n. *disorder*; off-handedness, casualness 734 n. *laxity*; superficiality 212 n. *shallowness*; scamped work, loose ends 728 n. *failure*; slacker 679 n. *idler*; procrastinator, shirker; sloven, slut.

Adj. *negligent*, neglectful, careless, un-

mindful 456 adj. *inattentive*; remiss 918 adj. *dutiless*; uncaring, insouciant 860 adj. *indifferent*; casual, off-hand, unstrict 734 adj. *lax;* slapdash, unthorough, perfunctory, superficial; slack, supine 679 adj. *lazy*; sluttish, untidy, slovenly 649 adj. *dirty*; unguarded, uncircumspect 670 adj. *unprepared*.

Vb. *neglect*, omit, pretermit; lose sight of, overlook 456 vb. *be inattentive*; leave undone, do by halves 726 vb. *not complete*; skimp, scamp 204 vb. *shorten*; skip, gloss over, slur over 525 vb. *conceal*.

disregard, ignore, pass over, give the go-by 620 vb. *avoid*; wink at, connive at, take no notice 734 vb. *be lax*; dismiss, turn a blind eye to; forget it, excuse, overlook 909 vb. *forgive*; discount 483 vb. *underestimate*; slight, cold shoulder, cut 885 vb. *be rude*; turn a deaf ear to, turn one's back; laugh off, pooh-pooh 922 vb. *hold cheap*, desert, abandon 621 vb. *relinquish*.

be neglectful, nod 679 vb. *sleep*; be caught napping, oversleep; drift, procrastinate, let the grass grow under one's feet; take it easy, let things rip 679 vb. *be inactive*; shelve 136 vb. *put off*.

Adv. *negligently*, anyhow; cursorily, perfunctorily.

459. Inquiry – N. *inquiry*, asking (see *interrogation*); challenge (see *question*); taking information 524 n. *information*; witch-hunt, spy-mania (see *search*); probe, inquisition, examination, investigation, visitation; inquest, post mortem, autopsy, audit, trial 959 n. *legal trial*; poll, Gallup p., straw vote 605 n. *vote*; review, scrutiny 438 n. *inspection*; research 461 n. *experiment*; exploration, reconnaissance 484 n. *discovery*; discussion, canvassing 584 n. *conference*.

interrogation, questioning, interpellation; forensic examination, examination-in-chief; cross-examination, leading question, cross-question; re-examination; quiz, brains trust; interrogatory; catechism; inquisition, third degree, grilling; dialogue, dialectic, question and answer; Socratic method, Socratic elenchus; question time.

question, question mark, note of interrogation 547 n. *punctuation*; query, questionnaire, question paper; interrogatory, interpellation; challenge; awkward question, catch; feeler; moot point, point at issue 475 n. *argument*; problem, poser, stumper 530 n. *enigma*.

exam, examination, oral e., viva; interview, audition 415 n. *hearing*; test, intelligence t.; catechumen 460 n. *respondent*; examinee 461 n. *testee*.

search, probe; quest, hunt, witch-h., treasure-h. 619 n. *pursuit*; house-search, perquisition, domiciliary visit; search of one's person, frisking; exploration, excavation, digging, dig; search-party; search-warrant.

secret service, espionage, counter-e., spying, intelligence, M.I.5; informer, spy, undercover agent, double a., cloak-and-dagger man; spy-ring.

detective, investigator, criminologist; plain-clothes man; inquiry agent, private eye; Federal agent, G-man, C.I.D. man; tec, sleuth, bloodhound, gumshoes; snooper, snoop, spy 524 n. *informer*.

inquirer, investigator, prober, workparty; asker (see *questioner*); quidnunc 529 n. *newsmonger*; seeker, searcher, rummager, search-party; dowser, water-diviner 484 n. *detector*; prospector; talent scout; scout, spy, surveyor, reconnoitrer; inspector, visitor 438 n. *inspection*; checker, scrutineer; examiner; tester, researcher 461 n. *experimenter*; sampler, pollster, canvasser; explorer 268 n. *traveller*; advertiser.

questioner, cross-examiner; interrogator, querist, interpellator, interlocutor interviewer; catechizer 453 n. *inquisitor*; quizzer, enfant terrible; riddler, enigmatist.

Adj. *inquiring*, prying, nosy 453 adj. *inquisitive*; quizzical; interrogatory, interrogative; examining, catechetical, inquisitional; dialectic, maieutic, heuristic,

zetetic; fact-finding, exploratory; empirical, tentative 461 adj. *experimental*.

Vb. *inquire*, ask, want to know; demand 761 vb. *request*; canvass, agitate, air, ventilate, discuss, bring in question 475 vb. *argue*; seek, search, hunt 619 vb. *pursue*; sound, probe, delve into, investigate, conduct an inquiry, try, hear 959 vb. *try a case*; review, audit, scrutinize, monitor; research, study, consider, examine; check, check on; get to the bottom of, fathom, see into, X-ray 438 vb. *scan*; snoop, spy, pry 453 vb. *be curious*; survey, reconnoitre, explore; test 461 vb. *experiment*.

interrogate, ask questions, interpellate, question; cross-question, cross-examine; interview, hold a viva; examine, sound, probe, quiz, catechize, grill, give the third degree; put to the question 963 vb. *torture*; pump, pick the brains; pop the question, put the q.; pose, moot.

search, seek, quest, look for; conduct a search, rummage, ransack, comb; scour, turn out, rake through, go t.; pry into, peer i.; overhaul, frisk, go over; search for, feel for, grope for, hunt for, fish for; cast about, seek a clue 619 vb. *pursue*; prospect, dowse.

460. Answer – N. *answer*, replication, reaction; reply, response; answer by post, acknowledgement, return 588 n. *correspondence*; official reply, rescript 496 n. *maxim*; returns, results 548 n. *record*; echo, antiphon 106 n. *repetition*; password, countersign; backchat, repartee; retort, counterblast, riposte 714 n. *retaliation*; question and answer, dialogue 584 n. *interlocution*; last word, Parthian shot; clue, key, right answer 520 n. *interpretation*; oracle 530 n. *enigma*.

rejoinder, counter-statement, reply, rebuttal, rebutter, surrejoinder; defence 467 n. *counter-evidence*; countercharge, tu quoque 928 n. *accusation*.

respondent, defendant; answerer, responder, replier, correspondent; examinee 461 n. *testee*; candidate 716 n. *contender*.

Adj. *answering*, responsive, echoic 106 adj. *repeated*; counter 182 adj. *counteracting*; antiphonic, antiphonal; corresponding to 28 adj. *equal*; oracular.

Vb. *answer*, reply, write back, acknowledge, respond; echo 106 vb. *repeat*; react, answer back, retort, riposte 714 vb. *retaliate*; rejoin, rebut, counter 479 vb. *confute*; contradict 533 vb. *negate*; defend, have the right of reply; solve 520 vb. *interpret*; suit the requirements 642 vb. *be expedient*.

461. Experiment – **N.** *experiment*, experimentalism, experimentation, experimental method, verification; exploration, probe 459 n. *inquiry*; assay 480 n. *estimate*; testability; check, test, crucial t., acid t., test case; trial, trials, try-out, work-out, trial run, practice r. 671 n. *essay*; ranging shot; ordeal 959 n. *legal trial*; pilot scheme, first steps, teething troubles 68 n. *début*.

empiricism, speculation, guesswork 512 n. *conjecture*; tentativeness, experience, rule of thumb, trial, hit and miss; random shot, shot in the dark, leap in the d., gamble 618 n. *gambling*; sampling; feeler 378 n. *touch*; kite-flying, ballon d'essai.

experimenter, experimentalist, empiricist, researcher, research worker, analyst; pollster, assayer; tester; test-driver, test-pilot; speculator, prospector; adventurer 459 n. *inquirer*; gamester 618 n. *gambler*.

testing agent, criterion, touchstone; standard, yardstick 465 n. *gauge*; control; reagent, litmus paper, crucible, cupel, retort, test-tube; proving ground, wind-tunnel, flight-simulator.

testee, examinee 460 n. *respondent*; candidate, entrant, sitter 716 n. *contender*; subject, patient; guinea-pig, rabbit, mouse, hamster, monkey.

Adj. *experimental*, analytical, verificatory, probationary; provisional, tentative 618 adj. *speculative*; exploratory 459 adj. *inquiring*; empirical; testable, verifiable, in the experimental stage 474 adj. *uncertain*.

Vb. *experiment*, experimentalize, make experiments; check, check on, verify; prove, put to the proof, assay, analyse; research; experiment upon, practise upon; test, try, try out 671 vb. *essay*; sample 386 vb. *taste*.

be tentative, be empirical, feel one's way; probe, grope, fumble; get the feel of 536 vb. *learn*; throw out a feeler, fly a kite, feel the pulse; wait and see, try it on, try one's luck, speculate 618 vb. *gamble*; venture; explore, prospect 672 vb. *undertake*; probe, sound 459 vb. *inquire*.

Adv. *experimentally*, on test, on trial, on probation, on approval; empirically, by rule of thumb, by guess and God; on spec.

462. Comparison – **N.** *comparison*, analogical procedure; confrontation, collation, juxtaposition; check 459 n. *inquiry*; comparability, analogy 18 n. *similarity*; contrast 15 n. *differentiation*; simile, allegory 519 n. *metaphor*; criterion, pattern, model, check-list, control 23 n. *prototype*; comparer, collator.

Adj. *compared*, collated; compared with, likened, contrasted; comparative, comparable, analogical.

Vb. *compare*, collate, confront; set side by side 202 vb. *juxtapose*; draw a comparison, parallel; contrast 15 n. *differentiate*; compare and contrast 463 vb. *discriminate*; match 28 vb. *equalize*; check with 12 vb. *correlate*; compare notes, match ideas.

463. Discrimination – **N.** *discrimination*, distinction, diorism 15 n. *differentiation*; insight, flair 498 n. *intelligence*; appreciation, critical appraisal 480 n. *estimate*; sensitivity 494 n. *accuracy*; delicacy 846 n. *good taste*; tact, feel 378 n. *touch*; timing, sense of the occasion; diagnosis, diagnostics 520 n. *interpretation*; nicety 862 n. *fastidiousness*; hair-splitting, logic-chopping 475 n. *reasoning*; sifting 62 n. *sorting*; selection 605 n. *choice*; nuance.

Adj. *discriminating*, selective, discreet,

judicious, discerning; accurate, sensitive 494 adj. *exact*; fine, delicate, nice 862 adj. *fastidious*; tactful 513 adj. *imaginative*; critical 480 adj. *judicial*; diagnostic 15 adj. *distinctive*.

Vb. *discriminate*, distinguish, diagnose 15 vb. *differentiate*; compare and contrast 462 vb. *compare*; sort, sieve, bolt, sift, van, winnow; severalize, separate 46 vb. *set apart*; pick out 605 vb. *select*; see the difference, draw the line 468 vb. *qualify*; split hairs, chop logic 475 vb. *reason*; criticize, appraise 480 vb. *estimate*; discern, have insight.

464. Indiscrimination – N. *indiscrimination*, promiscuity, universality 79 n. *generality*, 499 n. *unintelligence*; tactlessness, insensitiveness 820 n. *moral insensibility*; tastelessness, unrefinement 847 n. *bad taste*; inaccuracy 495 n. *inexactness*.

Adj. *indiscriminate*, unsorted 61 adj. *orderless*; rolled into one, undistinguished, undifferentiated, average 16 adj. *uniform*; random, undefined, promiscuous, haphazard, wholesale, blanket 79 adj. *general*.

indiscriminating, unselective, undiscerning, uncritical 499 adj. *unintelligent*; muddled; tactless, insensitive 820 adj. *impassive*; unrefined 847 adj. *vulgar*; tone-deaf 416 adj. *deaf*; colour-blind 439 adj. *blind*; inaccurate 495 adj. *inexact*.

Vb. *not discriminate*, make no distinction, see no difference, swallow whole; roll into one, lump everything together; muddle, confound 63 vb. *derange*; average, smooth out 30 vb. *average out*.

465. Measurement – N. *measurement*, quantification; mensuration, triangulation, cadastral survey; weighment; posology, dosage 26 n. *finite quantity*; rating, valuation; appraisal 480 n. *estimate*; calculation .computation, reckoning 86 n. *numeration*; check; reading off; metrics, longimetry, micrometry 203 n. *long measure*; trigonometry 247 n. *angular measure*; cubature.

geometry, plane g., planimetry; solid geometry, stereometry; altimetry, hypsometry; geometer.

metrology, dimensions, length, breadth, height, depth, thickness; weights and measures, metric system; weights 322 n. *weighment*; linear measure 203 n. *long measure*; measure of capacity, volume, cubature, cubic contents 183 n. *space*; liquid measure, gill, pint, imperial p., quart, gallon, imperial g.; barrel, pipe, hogshead 194 n. *vessel*; litre; minim, dram; dry measure, peck, bushel, quarter; unit of energy, ohm, watt 160 n. *electricity*; poundal 160 n. *energy*; candle-power 417 n. *light*; decibel, sone 398 n. *sound*.

coordinate, ordinate and abscissa, polar coordinates, latitude and longitude, right ascension and declension, altitude and azimuth.

gauge, meter; measure, scale; time scale 117 n. *chronometry*; balance 322 n. *scales*; nonius, vernier; footrule, yardstick; pace-stick; yard measure, tape m., metre bar; lead, log; fathometer; ruler, slide-rule; straight-edge, T-square, set-s.; dividers, callipers, compass, protractor; sextant, quadrant 247 n. *angular measure*; theodolite; index 547 n. *indication*; high-water mark 236 n. *limit*; milestone 547 n. *signpost*.

surveyor, topographer, cartographer, oceanographer, hydrographer, geodesist; geometer.

Adj. *metric*, metrical, mensural, dimensional, three-d., four-d.; cubic, volumetric, linear, longimetrical, micrometric; cadastral, topographical; geodetical.

measured, graduated, calibrated; mensurable, measurable, meterable, assessable, computable, calculable.

Vb. *measure*, mete, mensurate, survey; compute, calculate, count, reckon, quantize 86 vb. *number*; quantify, size; pace out, count one's steps; tape, span; sound, fathom, plumb 313 vb. *plunge*; pace 117 vb. *time*; balance 322 vb. *weigh*.

gauge, meter, take a reading, read off; standardize 16 vb. *make uniform*; grade, mark off, calibrate 27 vb. *graduate*; reduce to scale, map 551 vb. *represent*.

Section 3: Materials for Reasoning

466. Evidence – N. *evidence*, facts, data, case-history; grounds, reasons; hearsay, what the soldier said 524 n. *report*; proof 478 n. *demonstration*; corroboration, confirmation 473 n. *certainty*; rebutting evidence 467 n. *counter-evidence*; piece of evidence, fact, relevant f.; document, exhibit, finger-prints 548 n. *record*; clue, symptom, sign 547 n. *indication*; reference, chapter and verse, documentation; authority, scripturality, canonicity.

testimony, witness; statement, evidence in chief; admission, confession 526 n. *disclosure*; one's case, plea 614 n. *pretext*; word, assertion, allegation 532 n. *affirmation*; Bible evidence, sworn e., deposition, affidavit, attestation 532 n. *oath*; case record, dossier 548 n. *record*.

credential, testimonial, chit, character, recommendation, references; seal, signature 488 n. *assent*; voucher, warranty 767 n. *security*; ticket, passport, visa 756 n. *permit*; authority, scripture.

witness, eye-w. 441 n. *spectator*; informant, tell-tale 524 n. *informer*; deponent, attestant 765 n. *signatory*.

Adj. *evidential*, evidentiary, testificatory; prima facie 445 adj. *appearing*; suggestive, significant 514 adj. *meaningful*; indicative, symptomatic 547 adj. *indicating*; indirect, secondary, circumstantial; first-hand, direct; constructive 512 adj. *suppositional*; cumulative, corroborative; probative, demonstrative, conclusive 478 adj. *demonstrating*; factual, documentary 473 adj. *positive*; authentic 494 adj. *true*; biblical, scriptural, canonical 976 adj. *orthodox*; in evidence 548 adj. *recorded*.

Vb. *evidence*, show, evince; show signs of, have the makings of 852 vb. *give hope*; betoken 551 vb. *represent*; lend colour to 471 vb. *make likely*; tell its own tale, speak for itself, speak volumes;

suggest 547 vb. *indicate*; argue, involve 523 vb. *imply*.

testify, witness; take one's oath, swear 532 vb. *affirm*; bear witness, depose, swear to; authenticate, certify, attest, subscribe, countersign 488 vb. *endorse*; admit 526 vb. *confess*; testimonialize.

corroborate, support, buttress 162 vb. *strengthen*; sustain 927 vb. *vindicate*; bear out, circumstantiate, verify; validate, confirm, make good, prove 478 vb. *demonstrate*; lead evidence, adduce e.; document.

467. Counter-evidence – N. *counter-evidence*, adverse symptom, contra-indication 14 n. *contrariety*; evidence against, defence, rebuttal 460 n. *answer*; refutation 479 n. *confutation*; oath against oath, counter-oath, tu quoque argument, reverse of the shield; hostile witness 603 n. *tergiversation*.

Adj. *countervailing*, rebutting 460 adj. *answering*; counteractive 182 adj. *counteracting*; ambiguous 518 adj. *equivocal*; in the opposite scale 14 adj. *contrary*; damaging; refutatory; qualificatory 468 adj. *qualifying*.

Vb. *tell against*, damage the case; weigh against, countervail; traverse, run counter, contradict, contra-indicate; rebut 479 vb. *confute*; point the other way 14 vb. *be contrary*; cancel out 182 vb. *counteract*; cut both ways 518 vb. *be equivocal*; tell another story, alter the case; not improve, weaken; turn the tables.

468. Qualification – N. *qualification*, specification 80 n. *speciality*; modification 143 n. *change*; mitigation 177 n. *moderation*; limitation 747 n. *restriction*; proviso, reservation; exception, salvo, saving clause, escape c.; demur, objection, but 704 n. *opposition*; allowance, grains of a.; extenuating circumstances; redeeming feature 31 n. *offset*.

Adj. *qualifying*, qualificatory; mitigatory 177 adj. *lenitive*; contingent, provisional 766 adj. *conditional*; saving, excepting; qualified, not absolute.

Vb. *qualify*, condition, limit, restrict 747 vb. *restrain*; colour, leaven; temper, palliate, mitigate 177 vb. *moderate*; excuse 927 vb. *extenuate*; make allowance for 810 n. *discount*; make exceptions 919 vb. *exempt*; object, demur 762 vb. *deprecate*.

Adv. *provided*, with the proviso, subject to, conditionally, saving.

469. Possibility – N. *possibility*, potentiality, virtuality; capacity, viability, workability 160 n. *ability*; the might-have-been 125 n. *preterition*; best one can do; contingency, a possibility, off-chance 159 n. *chance*; bare possibility, ghost of a chance; likelihood 471 n. *probability*; credibility 485 n. *belief*; practicability, operability, feasibility 701 n. *facility*; availability, accessibility; risk of.

Adj. *possible*, virtual, potential, of power, able, capable, viable; arguable, tenable; feasible, practicable, negotiable 701 adj. *easy*; workable, performable, achievable; operable; attainable, approachable, accessible, obtainable, realizable; superable, surmountable; available, still open, not excluded; conceivable, thinkable, credible, imaginable; practical 642 adj. *expedient*; on the cards 471 adj. *probable*; not inevitable, revocable 620 adj. *avoidable*; liable, tending.

Vb. *be possible*, may, might, maybe, might be, might have been; enable, empower, admit of 756 vb. *permit*.

470. Impossibility – N. *impossibility* etc. adj.; no chance 853 n. *hopelessness*; irrevocability, the might-have-been; impasse, deadlock 702 n. *obstacle*; impracticability 643 n. *inexpedience*; unavailability, inaccessibility; insuperability, no go.

Adj. *impossible*, not allowed, ruled out 757 adj. *prohibited*; out of the question, hopeless; unnatural, against nature;

self-contradictory 477 adj. *illogical*; too improbable, incredible, inconceivable, unthinkable, unimaginable 486 adj. *unbelieved*; miraculous 864 adj. *wonderful*; irrevocable .

impracticable, unfeasible, not to be done; unworkable, unviable; unachievable, unrealizable, unsolvable, insoluble, inextricable, too hard 700 adj. *difficult*; incurable, inoperable; insuperable, insurmountable, impassable, unbridgeable, impervious, unnavigable, unmotorable; unapproachable, inaccessible, unobtainable, unavailable; elusive 667 adj. *escaped*.

Vb. *make impossible*, rule out, exclude 757 vb. *prohibit*; put out of reach, tantalize; deny the possibility, eat one's hat if 533 vb. *negate*.

471. Probability – N. *probability*, likelihood, likeliness 159 n. *chance*; good chance 469 n. *possibility*; prospect, excellent p. 507 n. *expectation*; real risk 661 n. *danger*; liability, natural course 179 n. *tendency*; presumption, presumptive evidence 466 n. *evidence*; plausibility, likely belief 485 n. *belief*; verisimilitude, colour, show of, semblance 445 n. *appearance*.

Adj. *probable*, likely 180 adj. *liable*; on the cards; natural, to be expected, foreseeable; presumable, presumptive; reliable 473 adj. *certain*; hopeful, promising 507 adj. *expected*.

plausible, specious, colourable; logical 475 adj. *rational*; convincing, persuasive, believable 485 adj. *credible*; well-grounded 494 adj. *true*; ben trovato 24 adj. *apt*.

Vb. *be likely*, — probable etc. adj., bid fair, be in danger of; show signs, have the makings of 852 vb. *give hope*.

make likely, increase the chances; involve 523 vb. *imply*; entail 156 vb. *conduce*; put in the way to, promote 703 vb. *aid*; lend colour to 466 vb. *evidence*; assume, dare say.

Adv. *probably*, in all probability, as is to be expected; very likely, ten to one, by all odds; belike, as likely as not.

472. Improbability – N. *improbability*, unlikelihood, doubt 474 n. *uncertainty*; chance in a million 470 n. *impossibility*; long odds, bare possibility; pious hopes, poor prospect 508 n. *inexpectation*; rarity 140 n. *infrequency*; implausibility, traveller's tale 541 n. *falsehood*.

Adj. *improbable*, unlikely, more than doubtful 474 adj. *uncertain*; unforeseeable 508 adj. *unexpected*; unconvincing, implausible 474 adj. *uncertified*; incredible, too good to be true 486 adj. *unbelieved*.

473. Certainty – N. *certainty*, certitude, certain knowledge 490 n. *knowledge*; sureness, inevitability, inexorability, irrevocability, necessity 596 n. *fate*; inerrancy, infallibility; indubitability, reliability 494 n. *truth*; indisputability, proof 478 n. *demonstration*; certification, verification, confirmation, ascertainment 484 n. *discovery*; dead certainty, cert, sure thing, safe bet, cinch, open and shut case; fact, matter of f.; gospel, Bible 511 n. *oracle*; dogma 976 n. *orthodoxy*; dictum, ipse dixit, axiom 496 n. *maxim*.

positiveness, moral certainty; confidence, conviction 485 n. *belief*; idée fixe, obsession; dogmatism, bigotry 602 n. *opiniatry*; infallibility, air of i., self-confidence, pontification.

doctrinaire, self-opinionated person 602 n. *opinionist*; dogmatist, infallibilist; bigot, fanatic, zealot; oracle, Sir Oracle, know-all 500 n. *wiseacre*.

Adj. *certain*, sure, reliable, solid, unshakable, well-founded, well-grounded 3 adj. *substantial*; authoritative, official 494 adj. *genuine*; factual, historical 494 adj. *true*; ascertained, certified; tested, foolproof 660 adj. *safe*; infallible, unerring, inerrant 540 adj. *veracious*; taken for granted, self-evident, axiomatic, evident; unequivocal, unambiguous, unmistakable 443 adj. *well-seen*; inevitable, unavoidable, necessary; bound to be, sure as fate, sure as death and taxes 124 adj. *future*; verifiable, demonstrable 478 adj. *demonstrated*.

positive, confident, sure 485 adj. *believing*; cocksure, opinionated, dictatorial, pontifical; dogmatic, doctrinaire 976 adj. *orthodox*; fanatical 481 adj. *biased*; unshaken 153 adj. *unchangeable*.

undisputed, beyond doubt, axiomatic, uncontroversial; uncontested, indubitable, unquestionable, incontrovertible, incontestable, unchallengeable, unimpeachable, undeniable, irrefutable, irrefragable, indefeasible.

Vb. *dogmatize*, pontificate, lay down the law, play the oracle, know all the answers.

make certain, certify, authenticate 488 vb. *endorse*; guarantee, warrant, assure; remove doubt 485 vb. *convince*; make sure, ascertain, check, verify, confirm, clinch 466 vb. *corroborate*; reassure oneself, re-check; ensure 596 vb. *necessitate*.

474. Uncertainty – N. *uncertainty*, unverifiability, doubtfulness, dubiousness; ambiguity 518 n. *equivocalness*; vagueness, haziness, obscurity 418 n. *darkness*; mist, haze, fog 355 n. *cloud*; indeterminacy, borderline case; query 459 n. *question*; open question, anybody's guess; guesswork 512 n. *conjecture*; gamble 618 n. *gambling*; leap in the dark, pig in a poke, blind date.

dubiety, incertitude 486 n. *doubt*; open mind, suspended judgement, open verdict; suspense; indecision 601 n. *irresolution*; perplexity, bewilderment, bafflement, nonplus, quandary; dilemma, cleft stick 530 n. *enigma*.

unreliability, fallibility 495 n. *error*; insecurity, precariousness, touch and go 661 n. *danger*; untrustworthiness, treacherousness; fluidity 152 n. *changeableness*; unpredictability; fickleness 604 n. *caprice*; slipperiness 930 n. *improbity*, perfidy, 603 n. *tergiversation*; bare word, dicer's oath, scrap of paper.

Adj. *uncertain*, unsure, doubtful, dubious; unverifiable (see *uncertified*); insecure, chancy, risky 661 adj. *unsafe*; treacherous (see *unreliable*); fluid 152 adj. *unstable*; contingent 766 adj. *conditional*; unpredictable, unforeseeable 508 adj. *unexpected*; indeterminate, undefined; random 61 adj. *orderless*; indecisive, undecided, open, in suspense; moot, questionable, arguable, debatable, disputable, controvertible, controversial; problematical 512 adj. *suppositional*; undefinable, borderline; ambiguous 518 adj. *equivocal*; oracular, enigmatic, cryptic, obscure 517 adj. *puzzling*; vague, hazy 419 adj. *shadowy*; perplexing, bewildering.

unreliable, undependable, untrustworthy; slippery 930 adj. *dishonest*; treacherous 930 adj. *perfidious*; unsteady, unstable 152 adj. *changeful*; unpredictable, fickle, whimsical 604 adj. *capricious*; fallible, open to error 495 adj. *erroneous*; precarious, ticklish, touch and go.

doubting, doubtful, dubious; agnostic, sceptical 486 adj. *unbelieving*; in suspense, open-minded; distrustful, mistrustful 858 adj. *cautious*; uncertain, unconfident; hesitant, undecided, wavering 601 adj. *irresolute*; unable to say; perplexed; guessing, at a loss, clueless 491 adj. *ignorant*.

uncertified, unverifiable, unverified, unchecked; uncorroborated, unauthenticated, unratified, unsigned, unattested; unofficial, apocryphal; unproved; unascertained; untried, untested, in the experimental stage.

Vb. *be uncertain*, hinge on 157 vb. *depend*; tremble in the balance; non liquet; be ambiguous 518 vb. *be equivocal*; have one's doubts, doubt; wait and see 507 vb. *await*; have a suspicion, suspect, wonder whether; dither, be in two minds, sit on the fence, waver, vacillate, hesitate 601 vb. *be irresolute*; flounder, drift, grope, fumble 461 vb. *be tentative*; lose the scent; not know which way to turn.

puzzle, perplex, confuse, daze, bewilder, baffle, nonplus, flummox, stump, gravel 727 vb. *defeat*; mystify, keep one guessing.

Section 4: Reasoning Processes

475. Reasoning – N. *reasoning*, ratiocination, force of argument; reason, discursive r.; sweet reason, reasonableness, rationality; dialectics, logic; logical sequence, inference, generalization; apriorism, deduction; induction, Baconian method; rationalism, euhemerism; dialecticism, dialectic; plain reason, simple arithmetic.

argumentation, rules of pleading; dialectic, Socratic elenchus, dialogue, logical disputation; sorites, syllogism, elench, prosyllogism, enthymeme, major premiss, minor p.; proposition, thesis, theorem, problem; predication, lemma, predicate; dilemma; conclusion, Q.E.D. 478 n. *demonstration*; paradox, reductio ad absurdum.

argument, discussion, symposium, dialogue; disputation, controversy, debate 489 n. *dissent*; appeal to reason, plea, thesis, case; reasons, submission; grounds 614 n. *pretext*; point, point well taken, clincher 478 n. *demonstration*; apologetics, defence; polemic; logomachy, war of words 709 n. *quarrel*; propaganda, pamphleteering 534 n. *teaching*; controversialism, argumentativeness, ergotism, contentiousness 709 n. *dissension*; sophism 477 n. *sophistry*; legal argument, pleadings 959 n. *litigation*; argumentum ad hominem, play on the feelings; argumentum ad baculum 740 n. *compulsion*; argument by analogy, parity of reasoning; tu quoque argument, same to you.

reasoner, logician, dialectician, syllogist; rationalist, euhemerist, sophister 477 n. *sophist*; casuist; polemicist, apologist, controversialist, eristic; arguer, debater, disputant; pleader 958 n. *lawyer*; sea-lawyer, logomachist, quibbler; scholastic, schoolman 492 n. *intellectual*; mathematician.

Adj. *rational*, clear-headed, reasoning, reasonable; rationalistic, euhemeristic; ratiocinative, logical; analytic, synthetic; consistent, systematic; dialectic, discursive, deductive, inductive, inferential, a posteriori, a priori; tenable 469 adj. *possible*.

arguing, polemical, irenic, apologetic; controversial, disputatious, eristic, argumentative; quibbling 477 adj. *sophistical*.

Vb. *be reasonable*, 471 vb. *be likely*; stand to reason, follow, hang together, hold water; appeal to reason, listen to reason; have a case.

reason, philosophize 449 vb. *think*; syllogize, ratiocinate; rationalize, explain away; put two and two together; infer, deduce, induct; assume, postulate.

argue, argufy, bandy arguments, give and take, cut and thrust; exchange opinions, discuss, canvass; debate, dispute; quibble, split hairs, chop logic; put one's case, plead; propagandize, pamphleteer 534 vb. *teach*; take up the case, defend; attack, polemicize; join issue 489 vb. *dissent*; out-argue 479 vb. *confute*; wrangle 709 vb. *bicker*; propose, bring up, moot.

476. Intuition: absence of reason – **N.** *intuition*, instinct, automatic reaction, association, conditioned reflex; light of nature, sixth sense, insight; direct apprehension, unmediated perception, a priori knowledge; clairvoyance 511 n. *divination*, 984 n. *psychics*; inspiration, presentiment, impulse 818 n. *feeling*; hunch, impression, guesswork; illogic, feminine reason; unreason 503 n. *insanity*.

Adj. *intuitive*, instinctive, impulsive; non-discursive; unknown to logic, inspirational, clairvoyant.

Vb. *intuit*, know by instinct, have a sixth sense; sense, feel in one's bones; guess, work on a hunch.

477. Sophistry: false reasoning – **N.** *sophistry*, affective logic, rationalization; illogicalness, illogic; equivocation, mystification; casuistry, jesuitry; special pleading, hair-splitting, logic-chopping; debating point, quibbling, quibble; evasion 614 n. *pretext*.

sophism, a sophistry, specious argument; illogicality, fallacy, paralogism; bad logic, loose thinking; begging the question, ignoratio elenchi; circular reasoning, petitio principii; non sequitur,

post hoc ergo propter hoc; contradiction in terms, antilogy.

sophist, sophister, casuist, quibbler, equivocator; caviller, devil's advocate; captious critic.

Adj. *sophistical*, specious, plausible, ad captandum; evasive, insincere; deceptive, illusive, illusory; pettifogging, captious, quibbling; tortuous; casuistical, jesuitical.

illogical, irrational, unreasonable; unreasoned, arbitrary; paralogistic, fallacious, fallible; inconsistent; invalid, untenable, unsound; inconsequential; unscientific 495 adj. *erroneous*; unrigorous, inconclusive, unproved; wishful, instinctive.

Vb. *reason ill*, paralogize, mistake one's logic, argue in a circle, beg the question, not see the wood for the trees; rush to conclusions.

478. Demonstration – **N.** *demonstration*, logic of facts 494 n. *truth*; certain conclusion, proof, establishment 473 n. *certainty*; verification, ascertainment, experimentum crucis 461 n. *experiment*; clarification 522 n. *manifestation*; burden of proof, onus.

Adj. *demonstrating*, demonstrative, probative 466 adj. *evidential*, 9 adj. *relevant*; conclusive, decisive, crucial.

demonstrated, evident; unconfuted, unrefuted, unanswered; open and shut, unanswerable 473 adj. *certain*; capable of proof, demonstrable, testable, discoverable.

Vb. *demonstrate*, prove, show; justify 927 vb. *vindicate*; bear out 466 vb. *corroborate*; substantiate, establish, verify 466 vb. *evidence*; make out a case, prove one's point, clinch an argument 485 vb. *convince*; avoid confutation, save.

479. Confutation – **N.** *confutation*, refutation, disproof, invalidation; successful cross-examination, exposure; rebuttal, complete answer 460 n. *answer*; clincher, finisher, knock-down argument, reductio ad absurdum 851 n. *ridicule*; exploded argument, proved fallacy 477 n. *sophism*.

Adj. *confuted*, disproved etc. vb.; without a leg to stand on; convicted 961 adj. *condemned*; disprovable, refutable, refutatory; not proven, inconclusive.

Vb. *confute*, refute, disprove, invalidate; rebut, have an answer, explain away; argue against, controvert; give the lie to, force to withdraw; confound, silence, floor, gravel, nonplus; show up, expose; convict 961 vb. *condemn*; outargue, triumph in argument, score off.

be confuted, fail in argument; fall to the ground, have not a leg to stand on; have no answer.

Section 5: Results of Reasoning

480. Judgement: conclusion – **N.** *judgement*, judging (see *estimate*); discretion 463 n. *discrimination*; arbitrament 733 n. *authority*; arbitration, arbitrage, umpirage; judgement on facts, verdict, finding; sentence 963 n. *punishment*; decision, adjudication, award, order, ruling 737 n. *decree*; settled decision, res judicata; moral 496 n. *maxim*; deduction, inference, corollary 475 n. *reasoning*.

estimate, estimation, consideration, view 485 n. *opinion*; assessment, valuation, evaluation, calculation 465 n. *measurement*; appreciation, appraisal, appraisement; criticism, critique, review, notice, comment 591 n. *dissertation*; summing up, recapitulation; survey 438 n. *inspection*; inspection report 524 n. *report*; opinion 691 n. *advice*.

estimator, judge, adjudicator; arbitrator, umpire, referee; assessor, surveyor, valuer, appraiser; inspector, referendary, reporter, examiner 459 n. *inquirer*; censor, critic; reviewer, commentator 591 n. *dissertator*; juror 957 n. *jury*.

Adj. *judicial*, judicious, judgematic 463 adj. *discriminating*; unbiased, dispassionate 913 adj. *just*; juridical, juristic, arbitral; judicatory, decretal; determinative, conclusive; moralistic, sententious; critical, appreciative.

Vb. *judge*, sit in judgement, hold the scales; arbitrate, umpire, referee; hear,

try; rule, pronounce; find, decree, award, adjudge, adjudicate; decide, settle, conclude, confirm; pass judgement, sentence 961 vb. *condemn*; infer 475 vb. *reason*; sum up, recapitulate; moralize 534 vb. *teach*.

estimate, measure, calculate, make 465 vb. *gauge*; value, evaluate, appraise; rate, rank; sum up, size up; cast up, take stock 808 vb. *account*; consider, weigh, ponder, perpend 449 vb. *meditate*; examine, investigate, check, vet 459 vb. *inquire*; report on, comment, criticize, review 591 vb. *dissert*; survey 438 vb. *scan*; censor, censure 924 vb. *disapprove*.

481. Misjudgement: prejudice – **N.** *misjudgement*, miscalculation, misreckoning, misconception, wrong impression 495 n. *error*; loose thinking 495 n. *inexactness*; fallibility, gullibility 499 n. *unintelligence*; misconstruction 521 n. *misinterpretation*; miscarriage of justice 914 n. *injustice*; overvaluation 482 n. *overestimation*; undervaluation 483 n. *underestimation*; wishful thinking 542 n. *deception*; fool's paradise 513 n. *fantasy*.

prejudgement, foregone conclusion 608 n. *predetermination*; preconception, parti pris, mind made up; idée fixe, infatuation, obsession, monomania 503 n. *mania*.

prejudice, prepossession, predilection; partiality, favouritism 914 n. *injustice*; bias, jaundiced eye; blind spot, blind side; party spirit, partisanship, clannishness, cliquism, esprit de corps; sectionalism, parochialism, provincialism, insularity; chauvinism, xenophobia, my country right or wrong; snobbishness, class war, racialism, Aryanism; colourprejudice, negrophobia; intolerance 888 n. *hatred*.

narrow mind, narrow-mindedness; closed mind, one-track m.; one-sidedness, over-specialization; legalism, pedantry, donnishness; bigotry, fanaticism, odium theologicum 602 n. *opiniatry*; legalist, pedant, stickler; zealot, bigot, fanatic 473 n. *doctrinaire*.

Adj. *misjudging*, in error, out 495 adj. *mistaken*; fallible, gullible 499 adj. *foolish*; muddled; wrong, wrong-headed; misguided 487 adj. *credulous*; subjective, unrealistic, visionary, impractical; crankish 503 adj. *crazed*.

narrow-minded, narrow, confined, cramped; parochial, provincial, insular; pedantic, donnish; legalistic, literal, literal-minded, unimaginative, matter-of-fact; hypercritical 862 adj. *fastidious*; dogmatic 473 adj. *positive*.

biased, viewy; jaundiced, embittered; prejudiced, closed; snobbish, clannish, cliquish 708 adj. *sectional*; partisan, one-sided, party-minded 978 adj. *sectarian*; nationalistic, chauvinistic, xenophobic; illiberal, intolerant 735 adj. *oppressive*; bigoted, fanatic 602 adj. *obstinate*; class-prejudiced, colour-p.

Vb. *misjudge*, miscalculate 495 vb. *blunder*; undervalue, minimize 483 vb. *underestimate*; overestimate, overvalue 482 vb. *overrate*; rush to conclusions, precondemn 608 vb. *predetermine*; misconceive 521 vb. *misinterpret*; overreach oneself, reckon without one's host 695 vb. *stultify oneself*; over-specialize, not see the wood for the trees.

bias, warp, twist, bend; jaundice, prejudice; prepossess, predispose 178 vb. *influence*; infatuate, haunt, obsess; blind oneself, take sides.

482. Overestimation – N. *overestimation*, overestimate, overvaluation 481 n. *misjudgement*; ballyhoo, build-up 528 n. *advertisement*; overpraise, panegyric 515 n. *empty talk*; storm in a teacup, much ado about nothing; megalomania 871 n. *pride*; over-confidence 857 n. *rashness*; over-optimism; defeatism 853 n. *hopelessness*; optimist, prisoner of hope 852 n. *hope*.

Adj. *optimistic*, sanguine, over-sanguine, over-confident; high-pitched, over-p.; over-enthusiastic, raving.

Vb. *overrate*, overreckon, overestimate; overvalue, overprice 811 vb. *overcharge*; idealize, overprize, overpraise, think too much of; make too much of

546 vb. *exaggerate*; cry up, puff, panegyrize; maximize, make the most of.

483. Underestimation – N. *underestimation*, underestimate, undervaluation, minimization; conservative estimate 177 n. *moderation*; depreciation 926 n. *detraction*; understatement, litotes, meiosis; false modesty 850 n. *affectation*; pessimist, pessimism 853 n. *hopelessness*.

Adj. *depreciating*, depreciatory, pejorative 926 adj. *detracting*; minimizing, conservative 177 adj. *moderate*; modest 872 adj. *humble*; pessimistic 853 adj. *hopeless*; euphemistic 541 adj. *hypocritical*.

Vb. *underestimate*, underrate, undervalue, underprice; belittle, depreciate, underpraise 926 vb. *detract*; slight, pooh-pooh 922 vb. *hold cheap*; misprize, not do justice to 481 vb. *misjudge*; understate, spare one's blushes; euphemize, gloze; play down, soft-pedal, slur over; make the least of, minimize.

484. Discovery – N. *discovery*, finding; breakthrough; invention; exploration; detective instinct, nose, flair 619 n. *pursuit*; detection 438 n. *inspection*; dowsing, radiesthesia; ascertainment 473 n. *certainty*; exposure, revelation 522 n. *manifestation*; eye-opener, illumination, realization, disenchantment; accidental discovery, serendipity; strike, find, trover, treasure-trove.

detector, lie-d., sound d., Asdic, sonar; radar; finder 442 n. *telescope*; dowser; discoverer, inventor; explorer 268 n. *traveller*,

Adj. *discovering*, exploratory 461 adj. *experimental*; on the scent, warm, getting w.

Vb. *discover*, rediscover, invent, explore 461 vb. *experiment*; find out, hit it, have it; strike, hit upon 154 vb. *meet with*; realize, tumble to 516 vb. *understand*; find, locate 187 vb. *place*.

detect, expose, show up 522 vb. *show*; get at the facts, unearth, disinter, bring to light; elicit, worm out, ferret o.; spot, sight, raise 438 vb. *see*; sense, trace, pick up; smell a rat, nose, scent, wind; track down 619 vb. *hunt*; trap 542 vb. *ensnare*.

485. Belief – N. *belief*, suspension of disbelief; credence, credit; assurance, conviction, persuasion; confidence, reliance, trust, faith; ignorance of, doubt 487 n. *credulity*; obsession, blind belief 481 n. *prejudice*; expectation 852 n. *hope*; credibility 471 n. *probability*; one's credit, one's troth 929 n. *probity*; token of credit, pledge.

creed, credo, dogma, doxy 976 n. *orthodoxy*; principles, tenets, articles; catechism, articles of faith, credenda; profession, confession, ideology, doctrine, system, school, ism 449 n. *philosophy*.

opinion, sentiment, mind, view; viewpoint, stand, position, angle; impression 818 n. *feeling*; thought 451 n. *idea*; thinking, Anschauung 449 n. *philosophy*; principle, premiss, theory 512 n. *supposition*; surmise 512 n. *conjecture*; conclusion 480 n. *judgement*.

Adj. *believing* etc. vb.; confident, assured 473 adj. *certain*; cocksure 473 adj. *positive*; convinced, converted; sold on, wedded to; confiding, trustful, unhesitating, undoubting, unquestioning 487 adj. *credulous*; loyal 976 adj. *orthodox*; viewy 481 adj. *biased*.

credible, plausible, believable, tenable, reasonable 469 adj. *possible*; likely 471 adj. *probable*; reliable, trustworthy, worthy of credence, persuasive, convincing 178 adj. *influential*; supposed, putative 512 adj. *suppositional*.

credal, taught, doctrinal, dogmatic, confessional; canonical, orthodox, authoritative, accredited, ex cathedra; of faith; undeniable 473 adj. *undisputed*.

Vb. *believe*, be a believer 976 vb. *be orthodox*; credit, put faith in, hold, maintain, declare 532 vb. *affirm*; take for gospel, profess, confess; receive, accept, admit 488 vb. *assent*; take on trust, swallow; assume, postulate; have no doubt; confide, trust, rely on, depend on, take one at his word; pin

one's faith on, have faith in, swear by; be told, understand, know; be converted; realize 484 vb. *discover*.

opine, conceive, fancy; deem, assume, surmise 512 vb. *suppose*; suspect, be under the impression 818 vb. *feel*; embrace an opinion, get it into one's head; have views, view as, take as, regard as.

convince, assure, satisfy; make realize, bring home to; convert, win over, wean from; evangelize, spread the gospel, propagandize, indoctrinate 534 vb. *teach*; sell an idea to, put over, persuade 612 vb. *induce*; gain one's confidence 178 vb. *influence*.

be believed, be received; go down well, be swallowed; find credence.

Adv. *credibly*, believably, supposedly, to the best of one's knowledge and belief; on the strength of.

486. Unbelief. Doubt – N. *unbelief*, disbelief, incredulity; disagreement 489 n. *dissent*; non-belief, agnosticism; conviction to the contrary 704 n. *opposition*; unfaith, infidelity, misbelief, miscreance; atheism, nullifidianism 974 n. *irreligion*; loss of faith, retraction 603 n. *recantation*; incredibility, implausibility 472 n. *improbability*.

doubt, 474 n. *dubiety*; half-belief, critical attitude, hesitation, uncertainty; misgiving, distrust, mistrust; suspiciousness, scepticism, pyrrhonism; reservation, scruple 468 n. *qualification*.

unbeliever, no believer, disbeliever; misbeliever, infidel, miscreant, heretic; pagan, atheist 974 n. *irreligionist*; sceptic, pyrrhonist, agnostic; doubter, doubting Thomas; dissenter 489 n. *dissentient*; nullifidian; scoffer 926 n. *detractor*.

Adj. *unbelieving*, disbelieving, incredulous, sceptical; unfaithful, lapsed 603 adj. *tergiversating*; doubtful 474 adj. *doubting*; slow to believe, distrustful, mistrustful; nullifidian, creedless.

unbelieved, disbelieved, discredited, exploded; incredible, unbelievable 470 adj. *impossible*; untenable, unworthy of credit; open to doubt, unreliable, suspect 474 adj. *uncertified*; so-called, pretended.

Vb. *disbelieve*, be incredulous, ignore, explain away; discredit, greet with scepticism, disagree 489 vb. *dissent*; scoff at 851 vb. *ridicule*; deny 533 vb. *negate*; retract, lapse 603 vb. *recant*; misbelieve; doubt, have doubts, scent a fallacy 474 vb. *be uncertain*.

487. Credulity – N. *credulity*, credulousness; simplicity, gullibility; rash belief, uncritical acceptance 485 n. *belief*; will to believe, blind faith 612 n. *persuasibility*; infatuation, self-deception, wishful thinking; superstition 481 n. *misjudgement*; simpleton, sucker 544 n. *dupe*.

Adj. *credulous*, believing, persuasible, amenable; hoaxable, gullible; naïve, simple; doting, infatuated; superstitious 481 adj. *misjudging*; confiding, unsuspecting.

488. Assent – N. *assent*, yes, yea, amen; hearty assent, welcome; agreement, concurrence 758 n. *consent*; acceptance, agreement in principle 597 n. *willingness*; acquiescence 721 n. *submission*; no denial, admission; sanction, nod, O.K., imprimatur, green light 756 n. *permission*; corroboration 466 n. *evidence*; confirmation, validation, ratification; authentication, certification, endorsement, seal, signature, mark, cross; stamp, rubber s.; assentation 925 n. *flattery*.

consensus, consentience, same mind 24 n. *agreement*; concordance, harmony 710 n. *concord*; unanimity, solid vote, general consent; consentaneity, general voice, chorus; likemindedness, mutual sympathy, bipartisanship; bargain 765 n. *compact*.

assenter, follower 83 n. *conformist*; fellow-traveller, cooperator 707 n. *collaborator*; assentator, yes-man 925 n. *flatterer*; the ayes; supporter, abettor; seconder, assentor; ratifier, authenticator; subscriber, endorser 765 n. *signatory*; party, consenting p., covenanter.

Adj. *assenting*, concurrent, party to 758 adj. *consenting*; fellow-travelling, collaborating 706 adj. *cooperative*; like-minded, sympathetic; unanimous, solid, with one voice, in chorus; acquiescent 597 adj. *willing*; delighted 824 adj. *pleased*; ratificatory; not opposed.

assented, voted, carried; unopposed, unanimous; uncontradicted, uncontested, unchallenged 473 adj. *undisputed*; uncontroversial, non-party, bipartisan.

Vb. *assent*, concur, agree with 24 vb. *agree*; welcome, hail, cheer, acclaim 923 vb. *applaud*; go all the way with, have no reservations; accept, agree in principle, like the idea; not deny, concede, admit, grant; plead guilty 526 vb. *confess*; nod, say yes 758 vb. *consent*; sanction 756 vb. *permit*; ratify (see *endorse*); chime in with, echo, ditto, say amen, hear hear; say the same, chorus; be a yes-man, rubber-stamp 925 vb. *flatter*; accede, adhere, side with 708 vb. *join a party*; covenant 765 vb. *contract*.

acquiesce, not oppose, accept, abide by 739 vb. *obey*; tolerate, not mind, put up with; sign on the dotted line, toe the l. 721 vb. *submit*; yield, defer to; let the ayes have it, allow 756 vb. *permit*; join in the chorus 83 vb. *conform*.

endorse, second, support, vote for 703 vb. *patronize*; subscribe to, attest 547 vb. *sign*; seal, stamp, rubber-stamp, confirm, ratify, sanction 758 vb. *consent*; authenticate, countersign.

489. Dissent – N. *dissent*, agreement to disagree; dissidence, difference; no brief for; difference of opinion, disagreement, discordance, controversy 709 n. *dissension*; faction 708 n. *party*; dissatisfaction, disapproval 924 n. *disapprobation*; repudiation 607 n. *rejection*; non-conformism, schism 978 n. *sectarianism*; withdrawal, secession; recusancy 738 n. *disobedience*; denial 760 n. *refusal*; contradiction 533 n. *negation*; objection, demurrer, reservation 468 n. *qualification*; protest 762 n. *deprecation*; challenge 711 n. *defiance*; passive resistance, non-cooperation.

dissentient, objector, caviller, critic 926 n. *detractor*; interrupter, heckler 702 n. *hinderer*; dissident, dissenter,

recusant, non-juror, protestant 84 n.
nonconformist; sectary 978 n. *sectarist*;
separatist, seceder 978 n. *schismatic*;
rebel 738 n. *revolter*; grouser 829 n.
malcontent; odd man out, minority;
splinter-group, cave, faction 708 n.
party; the noes, the opposition 704 n.
opposition; non-cooperator, conscientious objector, passive resister 705 n.
opponent.

Adj. *dissenting*, dissentient, differing,
dissident 709 adj. *quarrelling*; sceptical,
unconvinced, unconverted 486 adj. *unbelieving*; separatist, schismatic 978 adj.
sectarian; non-conformist 84 adj. *unconformable*; dissatisfied 829 adj. *discontented*; apostate 603 adj. *tergiversating*; protesting 762 adj. *deprecatory*;
non-compliant 769 adj. *non-observant*;
reluctant 598 adj. *unwilling*; intolerant
735 adj. *oppressive*.

Vb. *dissent*, differ, agree to d. 25 vb.
disagree; beg to differ; demur, object,
cavil, boggle, scruple 468 vb. *qualify*;
protest 762 vb. *deprecate*; resist 704 vb.
oppose; challenge 711 vb. *defy*; say no,
shake one's head.760 vb. *refuse*; repudiate, hold no brief for; go one's own way,
secede, withdraw.

490. Knowledge – N. *knowledge*, ken;
cognition, cognizance, recognition, realization; apprehension, comprehension,
understanding, grasp, mastery 447 n.
intellect; consciousness, awareness; precognition 510 n. *foresight*; illumination,
lights, enlightenment, insight 498 n.
wisdom; learning, lore (see *erudition*);
experience, acquaintance, familiarity,
intimacy; private knowledge, privity
524 n. *information*; notoriety, common
knowledge, open secret 528 n. *publicity*;
omniscience; intimation, sidelight,
glimpse, inkling 524 n. *hint*; specialism,
know-how, expertise 694 n. *skilfulness*;
half-knowledge, semi-ignorance, smattering 491 n. *sciolism*; cognizability 516
n. *intelligibility*; epistemology.

erudition, lore, wisdom, scholarship,
letters 536 n. *learning*; smattering, dilettantism 491 n. *sciolism*; reading, book-

learning, bookishness, bibliomania; pedantry, donnishness; information, mine
of i., encyclopedia 589 n. *library*;
department of learning, faculty 539 n.
academy.

culture, letters, literature; the humanities, the arts; education, instruction 534
n. *teaching*; civilization, cultivation,
sophistication, acquirements, attainments, accomplishments, proficiency,
mastery.

science, exact s., natural s., etiology,
metascience; natural philosophy, experimental p.; technology; tree of knowledge, circle of the sciences, ologies and
isms.

Adj. *knowing*, all-k., encyclopedic,
omniscient 498 adj. *wise*; cognizant,
cognitive 447 adj. *mental*; conscious,
aware 455 adj. *attentive*; alive to 819 adj.
sensitive; experienced, no stranger to, at
home with, acquainted, familiar with
610 adj. *habituated*; intimate, privy to,
in the know, behind the scenes 524 adj.
informed; conversant, proficient 694 adj.
expert.

instructed, briefed, primed 524 adj.
informed; trained, bred to; clerkly,
lettered, literate; scribal, literary; schooled, educated; learned, bookish; erudite,
scholarly; read in, well-read, knowledg-
able; donnish, scholastic, pedantic;
highbrow, intellectual, cultured, cultivated, sophisticated; strong in, well-
qualified; professional, specialized 694
adj. *expert*.

known, seen, heard; ascertained,
verified 473 adj. *certain*; discovered, ex-
plored; celebrated 866 adj. *renowned*; no
secret, public, notorious; familiar, intimate, dear; hackneyed, trite; proverbial,
household, commonplace, corny 610 adj.
habitual; memorized 505 adj. *remembered*; knowable, cognizable.

Vb. *know*, ken, wot of; realize, apprehend, conceive, catch, grasp 516 vb.
understand; possess, comprehend; appreciate; know again, recognize; discern
463 vb. *discriminate*; know well, see
through, know inside out, know down
to the ground; be in the know *or* secret;

know by heart 505 vb. *memorize*; know backwards 694 vb. *be expert*; smatter 491 vb. *not know*; experience, learn one's lesson 536 vb. *learn*; know all the answers, know what's what 498 vb. *be wise*.

491. Ignorance – N. *ignorance*, unknowing, nescience; lack of news, no word of; unawareness, unconsciousness 375 n. *insensibility*; incomprehension, obscurantism; superstition 495 n. *error*; lack of knowledge, no science; uneducation, no schools; untaught state, blankness, blank mind; unacquaintance, unfamiliarity, inexperience, gaucherie; inexpertness 695 n. *unskilfulness*; innocence, simplicity, naïveté 699 n. *artlessness*; nothing to go on, anybody's guess 474 n. *uncertainty*; darkness, benightedness, unenlightenment; imperfect knowledge (see *sciolism*); illiterate 493 n. *ignoramus*; layman, non-expert 697 n. *bungler*; obscurantist; Philistine.

unknown thing, obstacle to knowledge; unknown quantity, sealed book, Greek; terra incognita, virgin soil; dark horse, enigma, mystery 530 n. *secret*; unknown person, Mr X, anonymity 562 n. *no name*.

sciolism, smattering, a little learning; glimmering, glimpse 524 n. *hint*; superficiality 212 n. *shallowness*; shallow profundity, pedantry, quackery, charlatanry 850 n. *affectation*; smatterer 493 n. *sciolist*.

Adj. *ignorant*, nescient, unknowing, blank; in ignorance, unwitting; unaware, unconscious 375 adj. *insensible*; unhearing, unseeing; unfamiliar with, a stranger to; in the dark (see *uninstructed*); mystified 474 adj. *uncertain*; clueless, blindfolded 439 adj. *blind*; lay, amateurish, unqualified 695 adj. *unskilful*; unversed, not conversant, inexperienced, uninitiated, green, raw; naïve, simple 699 adj. *artless*; knowing no better, gauche, awkward; unenlightened, benighted; backward, unteachable 499 adj. *unintelligent*; obscurantist, unscientific; dark, superstitious, pre-scientific; unretentive 506 adj. *forgetful*.

uninstructed, unbriefed, not told, no wiser, kept in the dark; misinformed, misled; vague about 474 adj. *uncertain*; unschooled, untaught, untutored, untrained; unlettered, illiterate, uneducated; unlearned, bookless; uncultured, low-brow; unscholarly, unread, Philistine.

unknown, unbeknown, untold, unheard; unspoken, unseen, never seen 444 adj. *invisible*; veiled 525 adj. *concealed*; unrecognized; unrealized, unperceived; dark, enigmatic, mysterious 523 adj. *occult*; strange, unfamiliar 126 adj. *new*; unnamed; unidentified, unclassified 562 adj. *anonymous*; undiscovered, unexplored, uncharted, unplumbed, unfathomed; untried, untested; unknowable, undiscoverable, unpredictable; obscure 639 adj. *unimportant*; out of mind 506 adj. *forgotten*.

smattering, sciolistic; unqualified, quack 850 adj. *affected*; half-educated, half-baked, semi-literate; shallow, superficial, dilettante.

Vb. *not know*, be in the dark, have nothing to go on; be innocent of, know no better; know not, wist not, cannot say 582 vb. *be taciturn*; know nothing, wallow in ignorance, have everything to learn 695 vb. *be unskilful*; smatter, dabble in, coquette with; guess, suspect, wonder 512 vb. *suppose*; unlearn 506 vb. *forget*; ignore 458 vb. *disregard*.

492. Scholar – N. *scholar*, savant, philologer, learned man; don, professor, pedagogue 537 n. *teacher*; doctor, clerk, scribe, pedant, bookworm; polymath, encyclopedist; prodigy of learning, mine of information, walking encyclopedia, talking dictionary; graduate, student; specialist 696 n. *proficient*; academic circles, clerisy, professoriate; connoisseur 846 n. *man of taste*.

intellectual, scholastic, schoolman, clerk 449 n. *philosopher*; brain-worker; mastermind, wise man, brain, genius, prodigy 500 n. *sage*; publicist; know-all, brains trust; highbrow, egghead, bluestocking; intelligentsia, literati, illuminati, philosophe; scientist; academist, academician, Immortal.

493. Ignoramus – N. *ignoramus*, know-nothing, illiterate, no scholar, lowbrow; duffer 501 n. *dunce*; greenhorn, novice 538 n. *beginner*; simpleton, babe, innocent 544 n. *dupe*.

sciolist, smatterer, half-scholar, pedant 500 n. *wiseacre*; dabbler, dilettante; quack, charlatan 545 n. *impostor*.

494. Truth – N. *truth*, verity, sooth; rightness, intrinsic truth; accordance with fact, honest truth, dinkum, fair d.; light, gospel, Bible 975 n. *revelation*; facts of life 1 n. *existence*; actuality, historicity 1 n. *reality*; factualness, fact 3 n. *substantiality*; no lie, home-truth, truthfulness 540 n. *veracity*; verisimilitude 471 n. *probability*.

authenticity, validity, realness, genuineness; real Simon Pure, the real thing, it 13 n. *identity*; no fake 21 n. *no imitation*.

accuracy, attention to fact; verisimilitude, local colour, realism, 'warts and all'; fine adjustment, sensitivity, fidelity, high f., exactitude, exactness, preciseness, precision; orthology, mot juste; meticulousness 455 n. *attention*; pedantry, rigour, letter of the law; literality, literalness 514 n. *meaning*; ipsissima verba 540 n. *veracity*; chapter and verse 466 n. *evidence*.

Adj. *true*, very, veritable; correct, right, so; real, tangible 3 adj. *substantial*; actual, factual, historical; well-grounded, well-founded 478 adj. *demonstrated*; literal, truthful 540 adj. *veracious*; true to the facts, true to scale (see *accurate*); ascertained 473 adj. *certain*; unimpeachable 473 adj. *undisputed*; consistent, self-c. 475 adj. *rational*; natural, true to life, unflattering, faithful; realistic, objective; unromantic, unideal, down to earth.

genuine, no other, as represented; authentic, valid, guaranteed, official, pukka; reliable, honest 929 adj. *trustworthy*; natural, pure, sterling; true-bred, legitimate; unadulterated, unvarnished, uncoloured, undisguised.

accurate, exact, precise, definite, defined; well-adjusted, high-fidelity, dead-on 24 adj. *adjusted*; well-aimed, dead-centre 281 adj. *directed*; unerring, undeviating; punctual, right, correct, true; never wrong, infallible; close, faithful, photographic; fine, delicate, sensitive; mathematical, scientific, micrometer-minded; meticulous 455 adj. *attentive*; word for word, literal; literal-minded, pedantic, just so 862 adj. *fastidious*.

Adv. *truly*, verily, undeniably, really, genuinely, actually, indeed; plumb, right, to an inch, to a hair, to a nicety, to a T.

495. Error – N. *error*, erroneousness, wrongness; unreality, non-objectivity; falsity, non-historicity 2 n. *non-existence*; fallacy, self-contradiction 477 n. *sophism*; unorthodoxy 977 n. *heterodoxy*; mists of error, superstition; fallibility 481 n. *misjudgement*; subjectivity, unrealism, wishful thinking, self-deception; misunderstanding, misconstruction 521 n. *misinterpretation*; misguidance 535 n. *misteaching*; bad memory; falseness, untruthfulness 541 n. *falsehood*; hallucination 440 n. *visual fallacy*; delusion 503 n. *insanity*; wrong idea (see *mistake*).

inexactness, inexactitude, inaccuracy, imprecision, wildness, non-adjustment; faultiness, systematic error; looseness, broadness, generalization 79 n. *generality*; loose thinking 477 n. *sophistry*; mistiming 118 n. *anachronism*; misstatement 552 n. *misrepresentation*.

mistake, bad idea (see *error*); miscalculation 481 n. *misjudgement*; blunder 695 n. *bungling*; bloomer, boner, clanger, howler 497 n. *absurdity*; mishit, bosh shot 728 n. *failure*; faux pas, slip, slip of the pen, slip of the tongue, malapropism 565 n. *solecism*; clerical error, printer's e., misprint, erratum, corrigendum; inadvertency, oversight 456 n. *inattention*.

Adj. *erroneous*, erring, wrong; solecistica 565 adj. *ungrammatical*; in error (see *mistaken*); unfactual, unhistorical, mythological 2 adj. *unreal*; wide of the truth 543 adj. *untrue*; unsound, unscientific, self-contradictory 477 adj. *illogical*; unfounded, disproved 479 adj. *confuted*; exploded 924 adj. *disapproved*; fallacious, misleading; unauthentic, apocryphal, unscriptural, unbiblical; heretical 977 adj. *heterodox*; untruthful 541 adj. *false*; hallucinatory, deceptive 542 adj. *deceiving*; subjective, unrealistic 513 adj. *imaginary*; fallible, wrong-headed 481 adj. *biased*; superstitious 491 adj. *ignorant*.

mistaken, wrongly taken, misunderstood; miscalculated 481 adj. *misjudging*; in error, misled, misguided; misinformed, deluded 491 adj. *uninstructed*.

inexact, inaccurate, unstrict; unrigorous, broad, generalized 79 adj. *general*; imprecise, erratic, wild, hit or miss; insensitive, clumsy; out, off-target, off-beam; maladjusted, out of register; untuned, unsynchronized; uncorrected, unrevised, uncompared; faulty 695 adj. *bungled*; misprinted, misread, mistranslated.

Vb. *err*, go wrong, mistake; be in the wrong, be mistaken; misunderstand, get it wrong 517 vb. *not understand*; miscalculate, miscount, misreckon 482 vb. *overrate*, 483 vb. *underestimate*; go astray 282 vb. *stray*.

blunder, trip, stumble, miss, fault 695 vb. *be clumsy*; slip up, drop a brick; blot one's copy-book, flaw, bungle 728 vb. *fail*; play into one's hands 695 vb. *stultify oneself*; mistake the meaning 521 vb. *misinterpret*.

mislead, misdirect, misinform, lead into error, pervert, start a heresy 535 vb. *misteach*; beguile, befool, lead one up the garden path 542 vb. *deceive*; falsify, garble 541 vb. *dissemble*; gloze 925 vb. *flatter*.

496. Maxim – **N.** *maxim*, apothegm, gnome, adage, saw, proverb, byword, aphorism; dictum, saying, truth; epigram 839 n. *witticism*; truism, cliché, commonplace, banality, glimpse of the obvious, bromide; motto, slogan, catchword; text 693 n. *precept*; comment,

observation 532 n. *affirmation*; moral, pious fiction 979 n. *piety*.

axiom, self-evident truth, truism; principle, postulate, theorem, formula.

Adj. *aphoristic*, gnomic, sententious, proverbial, moralizing 498 adj. *wise*; epigrammatic 839 adj. *witty*; enigmatic, oracular 517 adj. *puzzling*; commonplace, stock 610 adj. *usual*; axiomatic 693 adj. *preceptive*.

497. Absurdity – **N.** *absurdity*, height of a. 849 n. *ridiculousness*; ineptitude 10 n. *irrelevance*; silliness, silly season 499 n. *folly*; senselessness, futility, fatuity 641 n. *inutility*; nonsense-verse, amphigory; twaddle 515 n. *silly talk*; rhapsody, bombast 546 n. *exaggeration*; Irish bull, Hibernicism, malapropism, howler, screamer 495 n. *mistake*; spoonerism, joke 839 n. *witticism*; anticlimax, bathos.

foolery, antics, silliness, asininity, tomfoolery; vagary, whimsicality 604 n. *whim*; extravaganza, silly symphony; escapade, scrape 700 n. *predicament*; practical joke, monkey trick, piece of nonsense; drollery, comicality 849 n. *ridiculousness*; clowning, buffoonery 851 n. *ridicule*; farce, mummery 850 n. *affectation*; exhibition 875 n. *ostentation*.

Adj. *absurd*, inept 25 adj. *unapt*; ludicrous 849 adj. *ridiculous*; silly, asinine 499 adj. *foolish*; Pickwickian, nonsensical, senseless 515 adj. *unmeaning*; preposterous, without rhyme or reason 477 adj. *illogical*; wild, extravagant 546 adj. *exaggerated*; fanastic 513 adj. *imaginative*; futile, fatuous 641 adj. *useless*.

498. Intelligence. Wisdom – **N.** *intelligence*, thinking power, intellectualism 447 n. *intellect*; brains, grey matter, head, headpiece; nous, wit, mother-w., common sense; lights, understanding, sense, good s., horse s., gumption; wits, quick thinking, readiness, esprit; capacity, calibre, mental c., I.Q.; forwardness, brightness; cleverness, brilliance, talent, genius; ideas, inspiration 476 n. *intuition*; brainwave, bright idea 451 n. *idea*.

sagacity, judgement, discretion, discernment 463 n. *discrimination*; perception, perspicacity, clear thinking; acumen, sharpness, acuteness; shrewdness, long-headedness; level-headedness, balance 502 n. *sanity*; prudence, forethought, far-sightedness 510 n. *foresight*; subtlety, craftiness 698 n. *cunning*; policy, statesmanship 688 n. *tactics*.

wisdom, sageness, wise understanding, sapience; profundity 449 n. *thought*; depth, breadth of mind, reach, enlargement; experience 490 n. *knowledge*; tolerance, enlarged views; soundness, ballast, sobriety, objectivity, enlightenment.

Adj. *intelligent*, brainy, clever, forward, bright; brilliant, talented, of genius 694 adj. *gifted*; capable, able, practical 694 adj. *skilful*; apt, ready, quick, acute, sharp, quick-witted, astute, shrewd, fly, smart, canny, not born yesterday; too clever by half, over-clever, clever-clever; far-sighted, clear-s. 510 adj. *foreseeing*; discerning 463 adj. *discriminating*; perspicacious, clear-headed, long-h., hard-h., calculating; subtle, crafty 698 adj. *cunning*.

wise, sage, sapient; thinking, reflecting 449 adj. *thoughtful*; reasoning 475 adj. *rational*; highbrow, intellectual, profound, deep, oracular; sound, sensible, reasonable 502 adj. *sane*; sagacious, prudent; experienced, cool, unflattered, undazzled; balanced, level-headed, realistic, objective; judicious, judgematical, impartial 913 adj. *just*; tolerant, fairminded, enlightened; unfanatical, unbigoted, unprejudiced, broad-minded; tactful, politic, statesmanlike, discreet.

Vb. *be wise*, — intelligent etc. adj.; use one's head, have brains, scintillate, shine 644 vb. *be good*; have a head on one's shoulders; show foresight 510 vb. *foresee*; grasp, fathom 516 vb. *understand*; discern, see through, penetrate; distinguish 463 vb. *discriminate*; listen to reason 475 vb. *be reasonable*.

499. Unintelligence. Folly – **N.** *unintelligence*, lack of brains, upper storey to

let; feeble-mindedness, low I.Q., low mental age, immaturity, infantilism; mental handicap, backwardness; imbecility, idiocy; slowness, dullness (see *unintelligent*), stupidity, stolidity 820 n. *moral insensibility*; incapacity, meanest capacity, incompetence 695 n. *unskilfulness*; inanity, vacuity, superficiality 212 n. *shallowness*; impercipience 464 n. *indiscrimination*.

folly, foolishness, extravagance, eccentricity 849 n. *ridiculousness*; fool's idea 497 n. *foolery*; trifling, levity, frivolity, giddiness 456 n. *inattention*; unreason, illogic 477 n. *sophistry*; unwisdom, i neptitude; fatuity, pointlessness; silliness, asininity; blind side, obsession, infatuation 481 n. *misjudgement*; puerility, childishness 130 n. *nonage*; second childhood, senility, anility, dotage 131 n. *age*; conceit 873 n. *vanity*.

Adj. *unintelligent*, unintellectual, lowbrow; ungifted, untalented, no genius; not bright, dull; handicapped, backward, retarded, feeble-minded 503 adj. *insane*; deficient, wanting, not there, vacant; limited, slow; stupid, obtuse, dense, crass, gross, heavy, stolid, bovine, blockish, oafish, doltish, owlish; dumb, dim, dim-witted; muddle-headed, puzzle-h.; cracked 503 adj .*crazed*; unteachable, impervious.

foolish, silly, idiotic, imbecile, asinine; nonsensical, pointless, senseless, fatuous, futile 497 adj. *absurd*; ludicrous 849 adj. *ridiculous*; like a fool, fallible; simple, naïve 699 adj. *artless*; soft, wet, soppy; gumptionless, gormless; goofy, gawky, sappy, dopy, dizzy, unconscious; childish, babyish, puerile, infantile 132 adj. *infantine*; gaga, senile, anile 131 adj. *aged*; besotted, fond, doting; dazed, fuddled, maudlin 949 adj. *drunk*; mindless, witless, brainless (see *unintelligent*); shallow, superficial, frivolous, birdwitted, feather-brained 456 adj. *lightminded*; extravagant, wild; scatty, nutty, dotty, daft 503 adj. *crazed*.

unwise, unblessed with wisdom, unenlightened; obscurantist, unscientific 491 adj. *ignorant*; unphilosophical, unintellectual; unreasoning 477 adj. *illogical*; indiscreet, injudicious 481 adj. *misjudging*; undiscerning 439 adj. *blind*; thoughtless 450 adj. *unthinking*; incautious 857 adj. *rash*; inconsistent, unbalanced, penny-wise, pound-foolish; unreasonable, against reason; ill-advised, illjudged, miscalculated 495 adj. *mistaken.*

Vb. *be foolish*, maunder, dote, drivel, babble 515 vb. *mean nothing*; take leave of one's senses 503 vb. *be insane*; never learn; invite ridicule 849 vb. *be ridiculous*; make a fool of oneself, play the fool; frivol, sow one's wild oats 837 vb. *amuse oneself.*

500. Sage – N. *sage*, nobody's fool; wise man, statesman; oracle, elder statesman, counsellor 691 n. *adviser*; genius, master mind; master, mentor, guide, guru 537 n. *teacher*; seer, prophet; leading light, shining l., luminary, master spirit; doctor, thinker 449 n. *philosopher*; egghead 492 n. *intellectual*; wizard 983 n. *sorcerer.*

wiseacre, know-all, smart aleck; brains trust; witling, wise fool.

501. Fool – N. *fool*, Tom fool 504 n. *madman*; perfect fool, precious f.; ass, donkey, calf; owl, goose, cuckoo, daw, gull; mooncalf, idiot, congenital i., born fool, natural; cretin, moron, imbecile; half-wit, nitwit, stupid, silly; butt, clown 851 n. *laughing-stock*; blunderer 697 n. *bungler*; witling 500 n. *wiseacre*; crackpot 504 n. *crank*; gaffer, old fogy; babbler, burbler, driveller; dotard 133 n. *old man.*

ninny, simpleton, simp, charley; tony, noodle, nincompoop, juggins, muggins, booby, boob, sap, stiff, dizzy, dope, gowk, galoot, goof; lubber, greenhorn 538 n. *beginner*; wet, drip, milksop, mollycoddle, softy, sissy, goody-goody, sawney; child, babe 935 n. *innocent*; mug, flat 544 n. *dupe*; gaper, gawker.

dunce, dullard, no conjuror; blockhead, numskull, duffer, dolt, dumb-bell; fathead, thickhead, bonehead, pin-head,

dunderhead, muttonhead; chump, clot; clod 869 n. *countryman*; block, stock, stone.

502. Sanity – N. *sanity*, saneness, soundness of mind; reasonableness; rationality, reason; mental equilibrium; sobriety, common sense; coherence 516 n. *intelligibility*; lucidity, lucid interval; normality, proper mind, senses, sober s.; sound mind, mens sana; mental hygiene, mental health.

Adj. *sane*, normal, not neurotic; mentally sound, all there; in one's senses, compos mentis, in one's right mind, rational, reasonable 498 adj. *intelligent*; common-sensical, sober; coherent 516 adj. *intelligible*; lucid, clear-headed; sane enough, not certifiable.

503. Insanity – N. *insanity*, brain damage, unsound mind, alienation, lunacy, madness, amentia; mental illness; mental instability, psychopathic condition, abnormal psychology; mental decay, senile d., dotage, softening of the brain 131 n. *age*; dementia; mental deficiency, idiocy, congenital i., imbecility, cretinism, morosis, feeblemindedness 499 n. *unintelligence*; obsession, craze; alienism, psychiatry, psychotherapy 658 n. *therapy*; mad doctor, alienist, psychiatrist 658 n. *doctor.*

psychopathy, certifiability; psychopathic condition, psychosis; neuropathy, neurosis, psychoneurosis; nerves, nervous disorder; hysteria, shell-shock; attack of nerves, nervous breakdown, brainstorm; phobia 854 n. *phobia*; the insanities; delusional insanity, paranoia, delusions, hallucinations; confusion, paraphrenia, katatonia, schizophrenia, split personality; obsession; frustration; depression; manic d., elation; mania, hypomania; hypochondriasis, hypochondria, pathoneurosis; hyp, melancholia, blues, blue devils 834 n. *melancholy.* See *mania.*

mania, monomania, hypomania, megalomania, persecution mania, religious m.; pathomania, kleptomania;

homicidal mania, suicidal m.; nymphomania, gamomania, bibliomania.

frenzy, furore, corybantiasm; rabies, canine madness, hydrophobia; paraphronesis; ecstasy, delirium, raving; distraction; delirium tremens 949 n. *alcoholism*; epilepsy, fit, turn, paroxysm 318 n. *spasm*.

eccentricity, craziness, crankiness, faddishness; queerness, oddness, strange behaviour; oddity, twist, kink, crank, fad 84 n. *abnormality*; a screw loose; obsession, monomania, ruling passion, fixed idea.

madhouse, mental home, mental hospital, hospital for mental diseases; asylum, lunatic a.; Bedlam, Colney Hatch; booby-hatch, loony-bin, nuthouse, padded cell 658 n. *hospital*.

Adj. *insane*, mad, lunatic; of unsound mind, non compos mentis, alienated, confused, deranged, demented; certifiable, mental; abnormal, psychologically a., mentally ill, brain-damaged; psychopathic; psychotic; neurasthenic, neurotic, hysterical; paranoiac, paraphrenic, schizophrenic, schizoid; manic, maniacal; katatonic, depressive, manic-d., elated; hypochondriac 834 adj. *melancholic*; monomaniac; idiotic, imbecile, moronic, cretinous, defective, subnormal, feeble-minded 499 adj. *unintelligent*; raving mad, stark staring m., mad as a hatter, mad as a March hare (see *frenzied*); certified.

crazed, wandering, mazed 456 adj. *abstracted*; not all there, not right in the head; off one's head, round the bend, up the pole; demented, driven mad, maddened (see *frenzied*); unhinged, off one's rocker; bedevilled, pixilated, deluded; infatuated, obsessed, possessed; fond, doting 887 adj. *enamoured*; drivelling, in one's second childhood; brain-sick, touched, wanting; idiotic, crack-brained 499 adj. *foolish*; bonkers, crackers, scatty, screwy, nutty, nuts, batty, bats, cuckoo, wacky, loco; crazy, daft, dippy, loony, loopy, potty, dotty; cranky, faddy, eccentric, erratic, funny, queer, odd, peculiar 84 adj. *ab-*

normal; dizzy, giddy 456 adj. *light-minded*.

frenzied, rabid, maddened; furious 891 adj. *angry*; possessed, bedevilled, bacchic, corybantic; frantic, demented, beside oneself, uncontrollable; berserk 176 adj. *violent*; epileptic, having fits; delirious, seeing things, raving, rambling, wandering, incoherent, light-headed 651 adj. *sick*.

Vb. *be insane*, — mad, — crazed etc. adj.; have a screw loose; dote, drivel 499 vb. *be foolish*; ramble, wander; babble, rave; corybantiate.

go mad, run m., go off one's head, lose one's wits; become a lunatic, have to be certified; see red 891 vb. *get angry*.

make mad, drive m., send m.; mad, madden; craze, derange, dement; turn one's brain, unhinge; infuriate 891 vb. *enrage*; infatuate, go to one's head, turn one's h. 542 vb. *befool*.

504. Madman – N. *madman*, lunatic, maddy, mental case; bedlamite; screwball, nut, loon, loony; madcap, mad dog; psychopath, sociopath; hysteric, neurotic, neuropath; psychotic; paranoiac; schizoid; manic-depressive; maenad, bacchante, corybant; raving lunatic, maniac; kleptomaniac, automaniac, pyromaniac, monomaniac, megalomaniac; dipsomaniac 949 n. *drunkard*; dope addict, dope fiend; hypochondriac, melancholic 834 n. *moper*; idiot, congenital i., natural, cretin, moron, mongol 501 n. *fool*.

crank, crackpot, nut, screwball; eccentric, oddity, fogy 851 n. *laughing-stock*; freak 84 n. *nonconformist*; fad, fanatic, extremist, lunatic fringe; fan, rhapsodist, enthusiast; knight-errant, Don Quixote.

Section 6: Extension of Thought

505. Memory – N. *memory*, retention; collective memory, race m., atavism; Mnemosyne.

remembrance, recollection, recall;

commemoration, evocation; memorization 536 n. *learning*; reminiscence, reminiscent vein, retrospection, review, retrospect, hindsight; flash-back; memorabilia, memoirs, reminiscences, recollections; history 590 n. *narrative*; memoranda.

reminder, memento, memorial, testimonial, commemoration 876 n. *celebration*; token, souvenir, keepsake, autograph; relic, monument, trophy 548 n. *record*; remembrancer, flapper, prompter; memorandum, aide-mémoire, note, notebook, diary, album, scrapbook; leading question, prompt, cue 524 n. *hint*; mnemonic, aid to memory.

Adj. *remembered*, recollected etc. vb.; unforgotten, fresh, green; of blessed memory, missed, regretted; memorable, unforgettable; haunting; indelible, stamped on one's memory.

remembering, mindful, faithful to the memory; evocative, memorial, commemorative 876 adj. *celebrative*; reminiscent, anecdotal; reminding, mnemonic.

Vb. *remember*, recognize, know again 490 vb. *know*; recollect, not forget, bottle up 666 vb. *preserve*; hold in mind, store in one's memories; never forget; recall (see *retrospect*).

retrospect, recollect, recall, recapture; reflect, review, think back, retrace, hark back, reminisce, rake up the past, live in the p.

remind, put one in mind, jog one's memory, refresh one's m., prompt 524 vb. *hint*; not allow one to forget, haunt, obsess; commemorate, raise a memorial, toast 876 vb. *celebrate*; recapitulate 106 vb. *repeat*.

memorize, commit to memory, con 490 vb. *know*; get by heart, learn by rote 536 vb. *learn*; repeat one's lesson 106 vb. *repeat*; fix in one's memory, burden the memory with.

be remembered, stay in the memory; recur, ring a bell; haunt, dwell in one's thoughts, not leave one's t.; make history, leave a name 866 vb. *have repute*.

506. Oblivion – **N.** *oblivion*, forgetfulness, absent-mindedness 456 n. *abstractedness*; loss of memory, amnesia, fugue, absence, total blank; paramnesia; memory like a sieve; effacement 550 n. *obliteration*; amnesty, absolution 909 n. *forgiveness*; Lethe; good riddance.

Adj. *forgotten*, clean f., well f., not missed; unremembered; almost remembered, on the tip of one's tongue; bygone, out of mind, sunk in oblivion.

forgetful, forgetting, oblivious; not historically minded; amnesic; amnemonic; amnestic, Lethean; unmindful 458 adj. *negligent*; absent-minded 456 adj. *abstracted*; ingrate 908 adj. *ungrateful*.

Vb. *forget*, clean f., misremember, disremember, have no recollection; think no more of, amnesty, let bygones be bygones, bury the hatchet 909 vb. *forgive*; break with the past, unlearn, efface 550 vb. *obliterate*; be forgetful, need reminding; let in one ear and out of the other; almost remember, have on the tip of one's tongue, not call to mind.

be forgotten, slip one's memory, fade from one's mind; sink into oblivion, drop out of the news.

507. Expectation – **N.** *expectation*, expectancy 455 n. *attention*; reliance, confidence, trust 473 n. *certainty*; presumption; optimism 833 n. *cheerfulness*; waiting, suspense 474 n. *uncertainty*; pessimism, apprehension 854 n. *fear*; prospect, look-out, outlook, forecast 511 n. *prediction*; expected thing, the usual 610 n. *practice*.

Adj. *expectant*, expecting, in suspense, on the waiting list; sure, confident 473 adj. *certain*; anticipatory, banking on; predicting 511 adj. *foreseeing*; unsurprised 865 adj. *unastonished*; forewarned, forearmed 669 adj. *prepared*; on the look-out, standing by, on call 457 adj. *vigilant*; tense, keyed up; tantalized, on tenterhooks 859 adj. *desiring*; optimistic, sanguine 852 adj. *hoping*; apprehensive, anxious 854 adj. *nervous*; pessimistic 853 adj. *hopeless*.

expected, long e.; up to expectation 865 adj. *unastonishing*; anticipated, foreseeable 471 adj. *probable*; prospective 155 adj. *impending*; contemplated, in view 617 adj. *intending*.

Vb. *expect*, look for, have in prospect, face; contemplate, promise oneself 617 vb. *intend*; reckon 480 vb. *estimate*; forecast 510 vb. *foresee*; see it coming 865 vb. *not wonder*; presume, assume; rely on, bank on; anticipate, forestall 669 vb. *prepare oneself*; stand by, be on call; apprehend 854 vb. *fear*; count upon, hope and believe 485 vb. *believe*.

await, be on the waiting list; dance attendance, queue up, mark time, bide one's t.; stand by, be on call; hold one's breath, be in suspense; tantalize, lead one to expect 859 vb. *cause desire*.

508. Inexpectation – **N.** *inexpectation*, no expectation 472 n. *improbability*; no hope 853 n. *hopelessness*; apathy 454 n. *incuriosity*; unpreparedness 670 n. *nonpreparation*; unexpectedness, miscalculation 495 n. *error*; surprise, surprisal; surprise packet, Jack-in-the-box, afterclap; shock, start, jolt, turn, blow; bolt from the blue, thunderclap, bombshell; revelation, eye-opener; paradox, reversal, peripeteia; amazement 864 n. *wonder*; anticlimax 509 n. *disappointment*.

Adj. *unexpected*, unanticipated, unlooked for, unguessed, unforeseen; unpredictable 472 adj. *improbable*; unheralded, unannounced; arresting, staggering 864 adj. *wonderful*; disconcerting, shocking; sudden 116 adj. *instantaneous*; dropped from the clouds; uncovenanted, unbargained for 670 adj. *unprepared*; paradoxical; out of one's ken, unprecedented 84 adj. *unusual*; freakish 84 adj. *abnormal*; full of surprises, unaccountable 517 adj. *puzzling*.

inexpectant, unsuspecting, off guard 456 adj. *inattentive*; unaware 491 adj. *ignorant*; unwarned, disconcerted, taken aback, caught napping, caught bending 670 adj. *unprepared*; thunderstruck, stunned 864 adj. *wondering*; shocked; un-

hopeful 853 adj. *hopeless*; apathetic, incurious 860 adj. *indifferent*.

Vb. *surprise*, take by s., spring something on one, catch, trap, ambush 542 vb. *ensnare*; catch unawares, catch napping, startle, jolt, make one jump, give one a turn; disconcert, take aback, stagger; knock one down with a feather, bowl one over, dumbfound 864 vb. *be wonderful*; shock, electrify 821 vb. *impress*; drop from the clouds, fall upon, pounce on.

Adv. *unexpectedly*, abruptly 116 adv. *instantaneously*; without notice, like a thief in the night.

509. Disappointment – **N.** *disappointment*, regrets 830 n. *regret*; tantalization, frustration, bafflement; much cry and little wool 482 n. *overestimation*; bad news 529 n. *news*; disillusionment 829 n. *discontent*; false dawn, fool's paradise; blow, setback 702 n. *hitch*; bad luck 731 n. *ill fortune*; anticlimax 508 n. *inexpectation*; let-down 872 n. *humiliation*; damp squib 728 n. *failure*.

Adj. *disappointed*, expecting otherwise 508 adj. *inexpectant*; thwarted; baffled, foiled 728 adj. *defeated*; dashed, disconcerted, crestfallen, out of countenance 872 adj. *humbled*; disgruntled 829 adj. *discontented*; ill-served, let down; refused 607 adj. *rejected*.

disappointing, unsatisfactory 636 adj. *insufficient*; not up to expectation, less than one's hopes; deceptive 542 adj. *deceiving*.

Vb. *be disappointed*, try in vain 728 vb. *fail*; not realize one's expectations 307 vb. *fall short*; find to one's cost 830 vb. *regret*; listen too often.

disappoint, not come up to expectations 307 vb. *fall short*; falsify *or* belie one's expectation; dash one's hopes, betray one's h.; disillusion; serve ill, fail one, let down, not come up to scratch; foil, thwart, frustrate 702 vb. *hinder*; disconcert 872 vb. *humiliate*; betray, tantalize, leave unsatisfied; disgruntle 829 vb. *cause discontent*.

Adv. *disappointingly*, tantalizingly, so near and yet so far.

510. Foresight – N. *foresight*, prevision, preview, foreglimpse; anticipation, foretaste; prenotion, precognition, foreknowledge, prescience, second sight, clairvoyancy; premonition, foreboding 511 n. *omen*; prognostication 511 n. *prediction*; forethought 498 n. *sagacity*; prudence 858 n. *caution*; readiness 669 n. *preparation*.

Adj. *foreseeing*, foresighted, prognostic 511 adj. *predicting*; clairvoyant, second-sighted, prophetic; prescient 498 adj. *wise*; looking ahead, provident 858 adj. *cautious*; anticipatory 507 adj. *expectant*.

Vb. *foresee*, foreglimpse, preview, prophesy, forecast, divine 511 vb. *predict*; forewarn 664 vb. *warn*; foreknow, read the future; see ahead, scent, feel in one's bones; anticipate, forestall 135 vb. *be early*; plan ahead 623 vb. *plan*; take precautions 858 vb. *be cautious*.

511. Prediction – N. *prediction*, foretelling, forewarning, prophecy; apocalypse 975 n. *revelation*; forecast, prognostication, prognosis; presentiment, foreboding 510 n. *foresight*; presage, prefigurement; programme, prospectus 623 n. *plan*; announcement, notice 528 n. *publication*; warning, warning shot 665 n. *danger signal*; prospect 507 n. *expectation*; shape of things to come, horoscope, fortune.

divination, clairvoyancy 984 n. *psychics*; augury, hariolation; mantology, vaticination, soothsaying; astrology, horoscopy, genethliacs; fortune-telling, palmistry, cheiromancy; crystal-gazing; sortilege, casting lots; dowsing, radiesthesia 484 n. *discovery*.

omen, portent, presage, writing on the wall; prognostic, symptom, sign 547 n. *indication*; augury, auspice; forewarning 664 n. *warning*; harbinger, herald 531 n. *messenger*; prefigurement, foretoken, type; ominousness, portentousness, signs of the times 661 n. *danger*; bird of omen, owl, raven.

oracle, consultant 500 n. *sage*; meteorologist, weather-prophet; calamity pro-

phet, Cassandra 664 n. *warner*; prophet, prophetess, seer; forecaster, soothsayer; clairvoyant, medium 984 n. *occultist*; cards, dice, lot; tripod, crystal, mirror, tea leaves, palm; Bible, Old Moore.

diviner, water-d., dowser 983 n. *sorcerer*; tipster 618 n. *gambler*; astrologer, fortune-teller, gypsy, palmist, crystal-gazer; augur, haruspex.

Adj. *predicting* etc. vb.; predictive; presentient, clairvoyant 510 adj. *foreseeing*; fortune-telling; weather-wise; prophetic, vaticinal, fatidical, apocalyptic; oracular, Sibylline; premonitory, foreboding 664 adj. *cautionary*.

presageful, significant, ominous, portentous; augurial, auspicial, haruspical; auspicious, promising, favourable 730 adj. *prosperous*; sinister 731 adj. *adverse*.

Vb. *predict*, forecast, prognosticate; foretell, prophesy, forebode, bode, augur, spell; foretoken, presage, portend; foreshow, foreshadow, prefigure, forerun, herald 64 vb. *come before*; point to, betoken 547 vb. *indicate*; give notice 528 vb. *advertise*; forewarn 664 vb. *warn*; menace 900 vb. *threaten*; promise, augur well, bid fair to 852 vb. *give hope*.

divine, auspicate, take the auspices; soothsay, vaticinate; draw a horoscope, cast a nativity; cast lots 618 vb. *gamble*; tell fortunes; read the future, read one's hand.

Section 7: Creative Thought

512. Supposition – N. *supposition*, notion, the idea of 451 n. *idea*; fancy 513 n. *ideality*; presumption, assumption, presupposition, postulate, premise; proposal, proposition 759 n. *offer*; submission 475 n. *argument*; hypothesis, theory 452 n. *topic*; thesis, position 485 n. *opinion*; suggestion 524 n. *hint*; hunch (see *conjecture*); instinct 476 n. *intuition*.

conjecture, unverified supposition, guess, surmise, suspicion; inkling, shrewd idea 476 n. *intuition*; construction, reconstruction; guesswork, guessing, speculation; shot in the dark 618 n. *gambling.*

theorist, hypothesist, theorizer, theoretician; surmiser, guesser; academic person, critic, armchair c.; doctrinarian 473 n. *doctrinaire*; speculator, thinker 449 n. *philosopher*; backroom boy 623 n. *planner.*

Adj. *suppositional,* notional, conjectural, guessing, propositional, hypothetical, theoretical, armchair, speculative, academic; unverified; suggestive, allusive, thought-provoking.

supposed etc. vb.; presumed, premissed; mooted 452 adj. *topical*; given, granted; suppositive, putative, presumptive; pretended, so-called, quasi; alleged, supposititious, fabled 543 adj. *untrue*; supposable, surmisable.

Vb. *suppose,* pretend 850 vb. *be affected*; fancy 513 vb. *imagine*; surmise, conjecture, guess; suppose so, dare say; persuade oneself 485 vb. *believe*; presume, assume, presuppose, premise; posit, lay down; take for granted, postulate 475 vb. *reason*; speculate, have a theory, hypothesize, theorize 449 vb. *meditate.*

propound, propose, mean seriously 759 vb. *offer*; moot, move; put a case, submit 475 vb. *argue*; make a suggestion, venture to say 691 vb. *advise*; suggest 524 vb. *hint.*

513. Imagination – N. *imagination,* power of i., visual i.; imaginativeness, creativeness; originality, inventiveness 21 n. *non-imitation*; fancifulness, stretch of the imagination (see *ideality*); insight, empathy, sympathy 819 n. *moral sensibility*; frenzy, ecstasy, inspiration, afflatus, divine a.; fancy, the mind's eye, visualization, objectification, image-building, imagery, word-painting.

ideality, idealization 449 n. *thought*; concept, image, conceit, fancy, brain-creation, notion 451 n. *idea*; whim, whimsey, maggot 497 n. *absurdity*, 604 n. *caprice*; figment, fiction 541 n. *falsehood*; imaginative exercise, flight of fancy, romance, extravaganza, rhapsody 546 n.

exaggeration; poetic licence 593 n. *poetry.*

fantasy, wildest dreams; vision, dream, nightmare; mirage 440 n. *visual fallacy*; hallucination, chimera 495 n. *error*; reverie 456 n. *abstractedness*; trance; delirium 503 n. *frenzy*; subjectivity, autistic distortion, auto-suggestion, wishful thinking; castle-building, make-believe, daydream, pipe-d. 859 n. *desire*; romanticism, escapism, idealism, Utopianism; Utopia, Erewhon; promised land; fairyland, wonderland; cloud-cuckoo land, dream world, castles in Spain; El Dorado; myth 543 n. *fable.*

visionary, seer 511 n. *diviner*; dreamer, day-d., somnambulist; idealist, Utopian 901 n. *philanthropist*; escapist, ostrich 620 n. *avoider*; romantic, romancer, myth-maker; enthusiast, knight-errant, fool-e., Don Quixote 504 n. *crank*; creative worker 556 n. *artist.*

Adj. *imaginative,* creative, lively, original, idea'd, inventive, fertile, ingenious; resourceful 694 adj. *skilful*; fancy-led, romantic; poetic, fictional; Utopian, idealistic; rhapsodic, enthusiastic; dreaming, tranced; extravagant, fantastical 497 adj. *absurd*; visionary, otherworldly, Quixotic; imaginal, visualizing, eidetic, eidotropic.

imaginary, unreal 4 adj. *insubstantial*; subjective, notional, chimerical, illusory 495 adj. *erroneous*; dreamy, visionary, ideal; unhistorical, fictitious, fabulous, fabled, legendary, mythic, mythological 543 adj. *untrue*; fanciful, fancy-bred, hypothetical 512 adj. *suppositional*; make-believe.

Vb. *imagine,* ideate 449 vb. *think*; fancy, dream; make up, invent, originate, create 609 vb. *improvise*; coin, hatch, concoct, fabricate 164 vb. *produce*; visualize, envisage 438 vb. *see*; conjure up, paint, word-p., objectify, realize, capture 551 vb. *represent*; pretend, make-believe, daydream 456 vb. *be inattentive*; see visions, dream dreams; idealize, romanticize, fictionalize, rhapsodize 546 vb. *exaggerate*; enter into, empathize, sympathize 516 vb. *understand.*

DIVISION (II): COMMUNICATION OF IDEAS

Section 1: Nature of Ideas Communicated

514. Meaning – N. *meaning*, idea conveyed, substance, gist, pith; contents, text, matter 452 n. *topic*; semantic content, sense, drift, tenor, purport, import, implication; value, force, effect; relevance, bearing, scope; construction 520 n. *interpretation*; context (see *connotation*); expression, diction 566 n. *style*; semantics, semasiology 557 n. *linguistics*.

connotation, denotation, signification, significance, reference, application; context; derivation 156 n. *source*; range of meaning, comprehension, extension; intention, main meaning, leading sense; idiom 80 n. *speciality*; usage, acceptance 520 n. *interpretation*; single meaning, univocity, unambiguity 516 n. *intelligibility*; double meaning, ambiguity 518 n. *equivocalness*; convertible terms, synonym, synonymity, equivalence; antonym, antonymity; countersense; changed meaning, semantic shift; literality, translationese 573 n. *plainness*; Pickwickian sense, nonsense 497 n. *absurdity*.

Adj. *meaningful*, significant 638 adj. *important*; substantial, pithy, pregnant; purporting, significatory, indicative 547 adj. *indicating*; expressive, suggestive, evocative, allusive, implicit; express, explicit 573 adj. *plain*; declaratory 532 adj. *affirmative*; interpretative 520 adj. *interpretive*.

semantic, semasiological, philological, etymological 557 adj. *linguistic*; connotational; denotational; literal, verbal 573 n. *plain*; metaphorical 519 adj. *figurative*; univocal, unambiguous 516 adj. *intelligible*; ambiguous 518 adj. *equivocal*; synonymous, homonymous 13 adj. *identical*; tautologous 106 adj. *repeated*; antonymous 14 adj. *contrary*; idiomatic 80 adj. *special*; paraphrastic 520 adj. *interpretive*; implied, constructive 523 adj. *latent*; Pickwickian, nonsensical 497

adj. *absurd*; meaningless 515 adj. *unmeaning*.

Vb. *mean*, have a meaning, bear a sense; get across 524 vb. *communicate*; typify, symbolize 547 vb. *indicate*; signify, denote, connote, stand for 551 vb. *represent*; import, purport, intend; add up to, boil down to, spell, involve 523 vb. *imply*; convey, express, declare, assert 532 vb. *affirm*; tell of, speak of, breathe of, speak volumes 466 vb. *evidence*; mean to say, come to the point, drive at, allude to, refer to; infer, understand by 516 vb. *understand*.

515. Unmeaningness – N. *unmeaningness*, meaninglessness, no meaning, no context; no bearing 10 n. *irrelevance*; nonsignificance 639 n. *unimportance*; inanity, cliché, triteness; truism, platitude; unreason, illogicality 477 n. *sophistry*; illegibility, scribble 586 n. *script*; jargon, rigmarole, hocus-pocus; gibberish, gabble 517 n. *unintelligibility*; incoherence, raving, delirium 503 n. *frenzy*; double-talk, mystification 530 n. *enigma*.

silly talk, nonsense 497 n. *absurdity*; stuff, balderdash, gammon, rubbish, rot, tommyrot; drivel, twaddle, bosh, tosh, tripe, piffle, bilge.

empty talk, idle speeches, soft nothings, wind, gas, hot air, vapouring, verbiage 570 n. *diffuseness*; rant, bombast, fustian, rodomontade 877 n. *boasting*; blether, blather, blah-blah, flap-doodle; guff, pi-jaw, claptrap, poppycock; humbug 541 n. *falsehood*; bunkum, bunk, boloney, hooey; blarney 925 n. *flattery*; prattle, prate, patter 581 n. *chatter*.

Adj. *unmeaning*, meaningless, Pickwickian; nonsensical 497 adj. *absurd*; senseless, null; unexpressive, unidiomatic 25 adj. *unapt*; insignificant, cliché-ridden, trite 639 adj. *unimportant*; fatuous, piffling; twaddling, waffling; incoherent, raving, gibbering 503 adj. *frenzied*.

195

unmeant, unintended, unimplied, un-alluded to; insincere 925 adj. *flattering*.

Vb. *mean nothing*, have no meaning; scribble, strum; talk like an idiot; babble, prattle, prate, palaver, gabble, jabber, clack 584 vb. *converse*; talk gibberish, doubletalk 517 vb. *be unintelligible*; rant 546 vb. *exaggerate*; rave, drivel, drool, blether, blat, waffle, twaddle; vapour, gas 499 vb. *be foolish*; blarney 925 vb. *flatter*.

516. Intelligibility – N. *intelligibility*, knowability, cognizability; explicability; comprehensibility; readability, legibility; lucidity 567 n. *perspicuity*; precision, un-ambiguity 473 n. *certainty*; straightfor-wardness, plain speaking, plain English, mother tongue 573 n. *plainness*; para-phrase, simplification 701 n. *facility*; popularization 520 n. *interpretation*.

Adj. *intelligible*, understandable, rea-lizable, comprehensible, apprehensible; coherent 502 adj. *sane*; distinguishable, audible, recognizable; knowable 490 adj. *known*; explicable, teachable; un-ambiguous, unequivocal 514 adj. *mean-ingful*; explicit, positive 473 adj. *certain*; plain-spoken 573 adj. *plain*; straightfor-ward, simple 701 adj. *easy*; obvious, made easy, explained, popular, for the million; clear, limpid 422 adj. *trans-parent*; lucid 567 adj. *perspicuous*; read-able, legible, decipherable.

expressive, telling, vivid, graphic, em-phatic, strong, strongly worded 590 adj. *descriptive*; illustrative, explicatory 520 adj. *interpretive*.

Vb. *be intelligible*, come alive, take on depth; be readable, read easily; make sense, add up; 514 vb. *mean*; tell its own tale, speak for itself 466 vb. *evidence*; elucidate 520 vb. *interpret*; simplify, popularize 701 vb. *facilitate*; labour the obvious 532 vb. *emphasize*.

understand, comprehend, apprehend 490 vb. *know*; master 536 vb. *learn*; have, hold, retain 505 vb. *remember*; see through, penetrate, fathom, get to the bottom of 484 vb. *detect*; discern, make out 438 vb. *see*; grasp, get hold of, seize;

get the hang of, take in, register; be with one, follow, savvy; get, catch on, twig; realize, get wise to, tumble to; see it all, be undeceived.

517. Unintelligibility – N. *unintelligibil-ity*, incomprehensibility; inexplicability, perplexity 474 n. *uncertainty*; obscurity 568 n. *imperspicuity*; ambiguity 518 n. *equivocalness*; mystification 515 n. *un-meaningness*; incoherence 503 n. *insanity*; double Dutch, gibberish; private lan-guage, slang 560 n. *dialect*; illegibility, scribble, scrawl 586 n. *lettering*; inaudi-bility 401 n. *faintness*; Greek, sealed book 530 n. *secret*; hard saying 530 n. *enigma*.

Adj. *unintelligible*, incomprehensible, inconceivable, inexplicable, unaccount-able; unknowable, unrecognizable 491 adj. *unknown*; unfathomable, unsearch-able, inscrutable, impenetrable; poker-faced, expressionless 820 adj. *impassive*; inaudible 401 adj. *muted*; crabbed, un-readable, illegible, undecipherable; dark, hidden, arcane 523 adj. *occult*; esoteric.

puzzling, recondite, abstruse, elusive; mysterious 523 adj. *occult*; clear as mud 568 adj. *imperspicuous*; ambiguous 518 adj. *equivocal*; oracular, Sphinx-like, enigmatic; paradoxical 508 adj. *unex-pected*; unexplained, insoluble 474 adj. *uncertain*.

inexpressible, unspeakable, unmen-tionable, untranslatable; unpronounce-able, unutterable, ineffable; incommuni-cable, indefinable; profound, deep; mystic, mystical, transcendental.

Vb. *be unintelligible*, present a puzzle 474 vb. *puzzle*; talk in riddles, speak oracles 518 vb. *be equivocal*; talk gib-berish 515 vb. *mean nothing*; keep one guessing; elude one's grasp, escape one; pass comprehension, baffle understand-ing; require explanation, need an inter-preter.

not understand, make nothing of, make neither head nor tail of; puzzle over, give up, be out of one's depth 491 vb. *not know*; play at cross-purposes

495 vb. *blunder*; get one wrong 481 vb. *misjudge*; not register 456 vb. *be inattentive*.

518. Equivocalness – N. *equivocalness*, two voices 14 n. *contrariety*; ambiguity, ambivalence 517 n. *unintelligibility*; doubletalk 515 n. *unmeaningness*; oracle, oracular utterance 530 n. *enigma*; mental reservation 525 n. *concealment*; prevarication, balancing act; equivocation 543 n. *untruth*; quibble 477 n. *sophistry*; word-play, paronomasia 574 n. *ornament*; pun, calembour, equivoque, double entendre 839 n. *witticism*; anagram, paragram, acrostic.

Adj. *equivocal*, not univocal, ambiguous, epicene, ambivalent; double, double-tongued, two-edged; vague, evasive, oracular.

Vb. *be equivocal*, cut both ways; play upon words, pun; have it both ways, equivocate, speak with two voices; prevaricate 541 vb. *dissemble*.

519. Metaphor: figure of speech – N. *metaphor*, mixed m.; tralatition, transference; extended metaphor, allegorization, allegory, anagoge 520 n. *interpretation*; apologue, fable, parable 534 n. *teaching*; symbolism, figurativeness, imagery 513 n. *imagination*; simile, likeness 462 n. *comparison*; personification, prosopopeia.

trope, figure, figure of speech, rhetorical figure 574 n. *ornament*; euphuism, euphemism 850 n. *affectation*.

Adj. *figurative*, metaphorical, tropical; allusive, symbolical, typical, allegorical, anagogic; parabolical; comparative, similitudinous 462 adj. *compared*; euphuistic, tortured, euphemistic 850 adj. *affected*; colloquial 573 adj. *plain*; hyperbolic 546 adj. *exaggerated*; ironical 851 adj. *derisive*; florid 574 adj. *ornate*; oratorical 574 adj. *rhetorical*.

520. Interpretation – N. *interpretation*, definition, explanation, exposition, exegesis; elucidation, light, clarification, illumination; illustration, exemplification 83 n. *example*; solution, key, clue, the secret; decipherment 484 n. *discovery*; application, twist, turn; construction, construe, reading, lection 514 n. *meaning*; allegorization 519 n. *metaphor*; usual text, vulgate; criticism, higher c., literary c., critique, review 480 n. *estimate*; insight 819 n. *moral sensibility*.

commentary, comment; scholium, gloss, footnote; inscription, caption, legend 563 n. *phrase*; motto, moral 693 n. *precept*; annotation, notes, marginalia, adversaria; apparatus criticus, critical edition; glossary, lexicon 559 n. *dictionary*.

translation, version, rendering; faithful translation, construe; key, crib, Bohn; rewording, paraphrase, metaphrase; précis, abridgement, epitomy 592 n. *compendium*; transliteration; lip-reading.

hermeneutics, exegetics, epigraphy, palaeography 557 n. *linguistics*; diagnostics, symptomatology, semeiology, semeiotics.

interpreter, exponent, expounder, expositor, exegete 537 n. *teacher*; euhemerist, demythologizer; editor 528 n. *publicizer*; textual critic, emendator; commentator, annotator, glossographer, scholiast, glossarist; critic, reviewer 480 n. *estimator*; oneirocritic 511 n. *diviner*; translator, paraphrast; solver, cipherer, coder, decoder; lip-reader; epigraphist, palaeographer 125 n. *antiquarian*; spokesman 754 n. *delegate*.

guide, precedent 83 n. *example*; dragoman, courier, man from Cook's, cicerone 690 n. *leader*; showman, demonstrator 522 n. *exhibitor*.

Adj. *interpretive*, interpretative, constructive; explanatory, explicatory, expository; exegetical, hermeneutic; defining, definitive; illustrative, exemplary; glossarial, annotative, scholiastic, editorial; paraphrastic, metaphrastic; literal, strict, word-for-word 494 adj. *accurate*; faithful 551 adj. *representing*; free 495 adj. *inexact*.

Vb. *interpret*, define, clarify; explain, unfold, expound, elucidate; illustrate

83 vb. *exemplify*; comment; edit, annotate, gloss, gloze; simplify 701 vb. *facilitate*; read, spell, spell out; construe, give a sense to; throw light on, be spokesman 551 vb. *represent*.

translate, make a version; render, do into, turn i., English; reword, rephrase, paraphrase; transliterate, transcribe; code, put into code; lip-read.

decipher, crack, decode; read hieroglyphics; read, spell out, puzzle o., find the sense of; solve, unriddle, read between the lines.

521. Misinterpretation – N. *misinterpretation*, misconstruction, wrong end of the stick; cross-purposes 495 n. *mistake*; mistranslation, misconstrue, translator's error, false construction; misapplication 246 n. *distortion*; strained sense; false reading; falsification 552 n. *misrepresentation*; parody, travesty 851 n. *ridicule*.

Adj. *misinterpreted* etc. vb.

Vb. *misinterpret*, misunderstand, misconceive 481 vb. *misjudge*; get wrong, misread, misspell 495 vb. *blunder*; misexplain 535 vb. *misteach*; mistranslate, misconstrue, pervert, strain, wrest, twist the words 246 vb. *distort*; add a meaning, read into, suppress; misquote; falsify, garble, gloze 552 vb. *misrepresent*; travesty, parody, caricature, guy 851 vb. *ridicule*.

Section 2: Modes of Communicating

522. Manifestation – N. *manifestation*, revelation, discovery, daylight, divulgence 526 n. *disclosure*; expression, formulation 532 n. *affirmation*; confrontation; presentation 551 n. *representation*; preview 438 n. *view*; demonstration, exhibition; display 875 n. *ostentation*; unconcealment, openness, flagrance 528 n. *publicity*; candour 573 n. *plainness*; apparition, vision, materialization 445 n. *appearance*; shekinah, glory 965 n. *theophany*; incarnation, avatar.

exhibit, specimen, sample 83 n. *example*; show piece, collector's p., museum p., antique, curio; display, show 445 n. *spectacle*; scene 438 n. *view*; showplace, showroom, showcase, showcard, placard, hoarding 528 n. *advertisement*; sign 547 n. *identification*; shopwindow, museum 632 n. *collection*; exhibition 796 n. *mart*; projection 551 n. *image*.

exhibitor, advertiser, publicist 528 n. *publicizer*; demonstrator, showman, pageant-maker; producer 594 n. *stage manager*; exhibitionist 873 n. *vain person*.

Adj. *manifest*, apparent 445 adj. *appearing*; plain as a pike-staff, clear as noonday; unconcealed, showing 443 adj. *visible*; conspicuous, noticeable, prominent, pronounced, striking, salient, in the foreground, in the limelight 443 adj. *well-seen*; open, patent, evident, obvious; gross, crass, palpable; self-evident, autoptical, written all over one, for all to see, unmistakable, recognizable, identifiable; eyecatching 875 adj. *showy*; glaring, flagrant.

undisguised, spoken, overt, explicit, express 532 adj. *affirmative*; on show, on display; in the open, public; exoteric; unreserved, open, candid 540 adj. *veracious*; frank, forthright, outspoken 573 adj. *plain*; brazen, shameless, barefaced; bare, naked 229 adj. *uncovered*; flaunting, unconcealed.

Vb. *manifest*, reveal, divulge 526 vb. *disclose*; evince, show signs of 466 vb. *evidence*; bring to light 484 vb. *discover*; expose, lay bare 229 vb. *uncover*; open up 263 vb. *open*; elicit 304 vb. *extract*; incarnate, personify 223 vb. *externalize*; typify, symbolize, exemplify 547 vb. *indicate*; throw light on 420 vb. *illuminate*; highlight, spotlight, set in strong relief 532 vb. *emphasize*; express, formulate 532 vb. *affirm*; proclaim, publicize 528 vb. *publish*.

show, make a spectacle, exhibit, display; set out, expose to view; dangle, flourish, brandish; sport 228 vb. *wear*; flaunt, parade 875 vb. *be ostentatious*; present, feature 551 vb. *represent*; put on, stage 594 vb. *dramatize*; show off, model (garments); demonstrate 534 vb. *teach*; bring to notice 547 vb. *indicate*; confront, bring face to face; reflect, image, mirror 20 vb. *imitate*; show up, expose 526 vb. *disclose*.

Adv. *manifestly*, openly, publicly, for all to see; externally, on the face of it; open and above-board.

523. Latency – N. *latency*, no signs of 525 n. *concealment*; insidiousness 930 n. *perfidy*; dormancy, potentiality 469 n. *possibility*; esoterism, esotericism 984 n. *occultism*; symbolism, allegory 519 n. *metaphor*; implication, adumbration, symbolization; mystery 530 n. *secret*; penetralia 224 n. *interiority*; more than meets the eye; anonymity 562 n. *no name*; snake in the grass 663 n. *pitfall*; hidden hand 178 n. *influence*; unsoundness, something rotten; innuendo 524 n. *hint*; undercurrent 401 n. *faintness*; clandestinity 525 n. *secrecy*; underground 527 n. *ambush*; cryptography.

Adj. *latent*, undercover 525 adj. *concealed*; dormant, sleeping 679 adj. *inactive*; passive 266 adj. *quiescent*; potential, undeveloped 469 adj. *possible*; unguessed, unsuspected, crypto- 491 adj. *unknown*; underlying, below the surface 211 adj. *deep*; unmanifested 444 adj. *invisible*; arcane, obscure 418 adj. *dark*; impenetrable, undiscoverable 517 adj. *unintelligible*; tucked away, sequestered 883 adj. *secluded*; awaiting discovery, unexplored.

tacit, unsaid, unspoken, half-spoken, unpronounced, unexpressed, unvoiced, unbreathed; unmentioned, unsung; unproclaimed, undeclared; unwritten, unpublished, unedited; understood, implied, implicit; implicational, suggestive; inferential, allusive, allusory.

occult, mysterious, mystic; symbolic, allegorical, anagogical 519 adj. *figurative*; cryptic, esoteric 984 adj. *cabbalistic*; covert, clandestine, secret 525 adj. *concealed*; insidious, treacherous 930 adj. *perfidious*; underhand 525 adj. *stealthy*.

Vb. *lurk*, hide, be a stowaway; burrow, stay underground; lie low, make no sign 266 vb. *be quiescent*; act behind the scenes, pull the wires; skulk 525 vb. *be stealthy*; underlie, be at the bottom of 156 vb. *cause*; smoke, smoulder.

imply, insinuate, suggest 524 vb. *hint*; understand, infer, allude; symbolize, connote, involve, spell 514 vb. *mean*.

524. Information – N. *information*, communication of knowledge, transmission, dissemination, diffusion; tradition, hearsay; instruction 534 n. *teaching*; intercommunication 531 n. *telecommunication*; narration 590 n. *narrative*; notification, announcement, intimation, warning, advice, notice, mention, tip, tip-off (see *hint*); advertisement 528 n. *publicity*; common knowledge, general information, gen; facts, the goods, documentary 494 n. *truth*; inside story, dope, lowdown, confidence, indiscretion 530 n. *secret*; dossier 548 n. *record*; word, report, intelligence 529 n. *news*, 529 n. *message*; communicativeness 581 n. *loquacity*.

report, information called for 459 n. *inquiry*; paper, command p., White Paper; account 590 n. *narrative*; statement 86 n. *statistics*; dispatch, bulletin, communiqué, hand-out 529 n. *news*; representation, case; memorial, petition 761 n. *entreaty*.

hint, whisper, aside; broad hint, signal, nod, wink, look, nudge, kick 547 n. *gesture*; prompt, cue 505 n. *reminder*; suggestion, lead, leading question 547 n. *indication*; caution 664 n. *warning*; tip, tip-off (see *information*); word in the ear 691 n. *advice*; insinuation, innuendo 926 n. *calumny*; clue, symptom 520 n. *interpretation*; sidelight, glimpse, inkling; suspicion, inference, guess 512 n. *conjecture*.

informant, teller 590 n. *narrator*; spokesman 579 n. *speaker*; mouthpiece 754 n. *delegate*; announcer, notifier, advertiser 528 n. *publicizer*; testifier 466 n. *witness*; authority, source; channel, grape-vine; go-between, contact; informed circles, information centre; communicator, correspondent, special c., reporter 529 n. *newsmonger*; blurter, 'big mouth'.

informer, common i., delator 928 n. *accuser*; spy, snoop 459 n. *detective*; stool-pigeon, nark, copper's n., snitch, fink, blabber, squealer, squeaker, peacher; approver 603 n. *tergiversator*; eavesdropper, tell-tale, tale-bearer, tattle, gossip 529 n. *newsmonger*.

guide-book, travelogue, topography; Baedeker, Murray; handbook, manual, vade mecum; timetable, Bradshaw, A.B.C.; itinerary, route map, chart, plan 551 n. *map*; gazetteer; catalogue; cicerone, courier 520 n. *guide*.

Adj. *informative*, communicative, newsy, chatty, gossipy; informatory, informational, instructive, instructional, documentary 534 adj. *educational*; expository 520 adj. *interpretive*; annunciatory 528 adj. *publishing*; monitory 664 adj. *cautionary*; over-communicative, talking, indiscreet 581 adj. *loquacious*.

informed, well-i., kept i.; posted, primed, briefed, instructed 490 adj. *knowing*; told, certified, au courant, in the know, in on, in the picture.

Vb. *inform*, certify, advise, beg to a.; intimate, impart, convey (see *communicate*); apprise, acquaint, have one know, give to understand; possess, brief, instruct, put one in the picture, enlighten; insinuate (see *hint*); confide, get confidential; put right, correct, disabuse, unbeguile, undeceive, disillusion; open one's mouth, blurt out, talk 581 vb. *be loquacious*; break the news 526 vb. *disclose*; tell, blab, split, peach, squeal, blow the gaff 526 vb. *confess*; tell tales, tell on, inform against, delate, denounce 928 vb. *accuse*.

communicate, transmit, pass on; report, cover; post, keep posted; get across, put it over; contact, get in touch; convey, bring word 588 vb. *correspond*; speak, semaphore 547 vb. *signal*; wire, telegraph, telephone, ring, call, dial; disseminate, broadcast, telecast, televise; announce, notify 528 vb. *advertise*;

carry a report, publicize 528 vb. *publish*; retail, recount, narrate 590 vb. *describe*; commune 584 vb. *converse*.

hint, drop a h., suggest; prompt, give the cue 505 vb. *remind*; caution 664 vb. *warn*; tip off 691 vb. *advise*; wink, tip the wink; nudge 547 vb. *gesticulate*; insinuate, breathe, whisper, say in one's ear, let fall, imply, leave one to gather, intimate.

525. Concealment – **N.** *concealment*, confinement, purdah 883 n. *seclusion*; latitancy 523 n. *latency*; occultation 446 n. *disappearance*; cache 527 n. *hiding-place*; camouflage 527 n. *disguise*; anonymity, incognito 562 n. *no name*; smoke screen 421 n. *screen*; reticence, discretion 582 n. *taciturnity*; evasion 518 n. *equivocalness*; mystification, obfuscation; subterfuge 542 n. *trickery*; suppression 543 n. *untruth*; dissimulation 541 n. *duplicity*.

secrecy, 399 n. *silence*; mystery 530 n. *secret*; seal of secrecy, hearing in camera, auricular confession; clandestinity, secretiveness, furtiveness, stealthiness; conspiracy 623 n. *plot*; cryptography, cipher, code 517 n. *unintelligibility*.

Adj. *concealed*, crypto-, hidden; hiding, lost, perdu; in ambush 523 adj. *latent*; incommunicado 747 adj. *imprisoned*; mysterious, recondite, arcane 517 adj. *unintelligible*; cryptic 523 adj. *occult*; private 883 adj. *secluded*; privy, confidential, off the record; reticent 582 adj. *taciturn*; secret, top-secret, hush-hush, inviolable; undisclosed, untold; incognito, unsigned, unnamed 562 adj. *anonymous*; hole-and-corner, clandestine; undercover, underground, subterranean 211 adj. *deep*; cryptographic, steganographic.

stealthy, silent, furtive, like a thief; feline, catlike, pussyfoot, on tiptoe; clandestine, hugger-mugger, conspiratorial, cloak-and-dagger; hole-and-corner, backdoor, underhand, surreptitious 930 adj. *dishonest*.

Vb. *conceal*, hide, hide away, secrete, confine, keep in purdah 883 vb. *seclude*; lock up, seal up, bottle up 632 vb. *store*;

bury 364 vb. *inter*; sweep under the mat, cover up 226 vb. *cover*; varnish, gloss over 226 vb. *overlay*; overpaint 550 vb. *obliterate*; slur, slur over 458 vb. *disregard*; smother, stifle 165 vb. *suppress*; veil, muffle, mask, disguise, camouflage; shroud 421 vb. *screen*; shade, obscure, eclipse 418 vb. *darken*; befog, becloud, obfuscate 419 vb. *bedim*; masquerade 541 vb. *dissemble*.

keep secret, keep it dark, keep close, keep under one's hat; be mum 582 vb. *be taciturn*; keep back, reserve, withhold, let it go no further; hush up, hide, suppress; blindfold, keep in the dark 542 vb. *deceive*.

be stealthy, — furtive, — evasive etc. adj.; conspire 623 vb. *plot*; snoop, sneak, slink, creep; steal along, tiptoe, pussyfoot; prowl, skulk, loiter; wear a mask 541 vb. *dissemble*; lie doggo 523 vb. *lurk*; evade, shun 620 vb. *avoid*; play hide-and-seek, leave no address, cover one's tracks, take cover; vanish 446 vb. *disappear*; lay an ambush 527 vb. *ambush*.

Adv. *secretly*, hugger-mugger, conspiratorially; confidentially, entre nous, between ourselves; aside, to oneself; sub rosa; not for publication, in camera.

526. Disclosure – N. *disclosure*, revelation, apocalypse; daylight, discovery; lid off 528 n. *publication*; exposure 522 n. *manifestation*; explanations, showdown; communication, leak, indiscretion; bewrayment, betrayal, give-away; cloven hoof, tell-tale sign; avowal, confession; confessional 939 n. *penitence*; clean breast, whole truth, cards on the table 494 n. *truth*.

Adj. *disclosing*, revelatory, apocalyptic; revealing 422 adj. *transparent*; explanatory 520 adj. *interpretive*; communicative 524 adj. *informative*; leaky, indiscreet, garrulous 581 adj. *loquacious*; tell-tale, indicative 547 adj. *indicating*.

Vb. *disclose*, reveal, expose, show up 522 vb. *manifest*; bare, lay b., denude 229 vb. *doff*; unfold, unroll, unfurl, unpack, unwrap 229 vb. *uncover*; unveil, lift the veil; unseal, unclose 263 vb. *open*; open up 484 vb. *discover*; catch out 484 vb. *detect*; bewray, not hide; give away, betray; uncloak, unmask, tear off the mask; declare oneself, drop the mask, show one's colours; show for what it is, debunk; disabuse, undeceive, disillusion, open the eyes 524 vb. *inform*.

divulge, be open about, declare, vent, ventilate, air, canvass, publicize 528 vb. *publish*; let on, repeat, blurt out, talk out of turn, spill the beans, let the cat out of the bag; let out, leak 524 vb. *communicate*; come out with; get it off one's chest, unbosom oneself; confide, let one into the secret, open one's mind; show one's hand, show one's cards; report, tell on 928 vb. *accuse*; split, peach, squeal, blab 524 vb. *inform*.

confess, admit, avow, acknowledge; own up, implicate oneself, plead guilty; come out with, come clean, tell all 540 vb. *be truthful*; make a clean breast, unburden one's conscience, go to confession, be shriven 939 vb. *be penitent*.

527. Hiding. Disguise – N. *hiding-place*, hide, hide-out, hole, hidy-h., funk-h. 662 n. *refuge*; lair, den; cache, oubliette; closet, safe place, safe 632 n. *storage*; recess, corner, nook, cranny, niche, holes and corners; cover 662 n. *shelter*; backroom, adytum, penetralia 224 n. *interiority*.

ambush, ambuscade, ambushment 525 n. *concealment*; spider's web 542 n. *trap*; deathtrap, stalking horse, Trojan h., decoy, stool-pigeon 545 n. *impostor*; underground.

disguise, blind, camouflage, protective colouring 542 n. *deception*; dummy 20 n. *imitation*; veneer 226 n. *covering*; mask, visor, veil 228 n. *cloak*; domino, masquerade dress, fancy d.; cloud, smoke-screen, cover 421 n. *screen*.

hider, lurker, skulker, stowaway; dodger 620 n. *avoider*; masker, masquerader; wolf in sheep's clothing 545 n. *impostor*.

Vb. *ambush*, waylay, lie in wait 523 vb. *lurk*; set a trap for 542 vb. *ensnare*.

528. Publication – N. *publication*, dissemination, divulgation 526 n. *disclosure*; promulgation, proclamation; edict 737 n. *decree*; cry, rallying c. 547 n. *call*; beat of drum, flourish of trumpets 400 n. *loudness*; notification, public notice, bulletin; announcement, pronouncement, pronunciamento, declaration, manifesto, programme, platform; publishing, book-trade 589 n. *book*; broadcasting 531 n. *telecommunication*; broadcast 529 n. *news*; circulation, circular, encyclical.

publicity, publicness, common knowledge 490 n. *knowledge*; open discussion, ventilation, canvass; flagrancy, blatancy 522 n. *manifestation*; cry, open secret, open scandal; notoriety, fame 866 n. *famousness*; currency, circulation; readership, viewership; public relations, propaganda; display, showmanship, salesmanship, window-dressing 875 n. *ostentation*; sensationalism, ballyhoo 546 n. *exaggeration*; publicization, advertising, sky-writing; public address system, loud speaker, loud hailer 415 n. *hearing aid*; journalism, reporting, coverage, report, write-up (see *the press*); newsreel 529 n. *news*; correspondence column, open letter; editorial 591 n. *article*; pulpit, platform, hustings, soapbox 539 n. *rostrum*; printing press 587 n. *print*; letters of fire, letters of gold.

advertisement, public notice, press n., gazette, insertion, ad, personal column, agony c.; headline, banner, streamer, screamer, spread; puff, blurb, boost, ballyhoo, build-up, limelight, spotlight; bill, affiche, poster, show-card 522 n. *exhibit*; bill-board, hoarding, placard, sandwich-board, notice b.

the press, fourth estate, Fleet Street, newspaper world, news business, the papers; newspaper, news-sheet, sheet, paper, rag, tabloid, comic strip; organ, journal, daily; issue, edition, stop-press e., extra; magazine section, serial, supplement, trade s.; leaflet, handbill, pamphlet, brochure, broadsheet, squib, open letter, newsletter.

journal, review, magazine, periodical; gazette, trade organ, house o., trade publication 589 n. *reading matter*.

publicizer, canvasser, advertiser, notifier, announcer; herald, trumpet 531 n. *messenger*; proclaimer, crier, town-crier bellman; barker, booster; bill-sticker sandwichman; publicist, printer, publisher 589 n. *bookman*; reporter 529 n. *newsmonger*; journalist 589 n. *author*; copywriter, blurb-writer, commercial artist, publicity agent, press a., advertising a.; public relations officer, P.R.O., propagandist, pamphleteer 537 n. *preacher*.

Adj. *published*, in print; in circulation, circulating, passing round, current, broadcast; in the news, public 490 adj. *known*; open, ventilated, canvassed.

publishing, promulgatory, declaratory, notificatory, annunciative.

Vb. *publish*, make public, carry a report 524 vb. *communicate*; report, cover, write up; reveal 526 vb. *divulge*; highlight, spotlight 532 vb. *emphasize*; radio, broadcast, telecast, televise, relay, diffuse 524 vb. *inform*; spread, circulate, distribute, disseminate, circularize; canvass, ventilate, discuss 475 vb. *argue*; pamphleteer, propagate 534 vb. *teach*; use the press 587 vb. *print*; serialize, edit, issue, lay before the public; spread a rumour, fly a kite; bruit, noise abroad; talk about, retail 581 vb. *be loquacious*; voice 579 vb. *speak*.

proclaim, announce, promulgate, notify, gazette; raise a hue and cry 928 vb. *accuse*; pronounce, declare 532 vb. *affirm*; celebrate, noise, trumpet, blazon, herald, cry 400 vb. *be loud*; declaim, shout from the housetops.

advertise, publicize, canvass, bill, placard, post; tell the world, put on the map, headline, splash; put in lights, spotlight, build up; make much of, feature; sell, boost, puff, cry up, write up, glorify 482 vb. *overrate*.

be published, issue, come out; hit the headlines; circulate, pass round, get about, spread abroad; find a publisher, see oneself in print, get into the papers.

529. News – N. *news*, tidings; news-packet, dispatches, diplomatic bag; intelligence, report, dispatch, word, advice; something to tell, titbit, flash 524 n. *information*; bulletin, communiqué, hand-out; fresh news, latest n., stop-press n.; sensation, scoop; copy, filler; newscast, newsreel 528 n. *publicity*; news-value.

rumour, unconfirmed report; hearsay, gossip, talk, talk of the town, tittle-tattle 581 n. *chatter*; noise, cry; hoax, canard; grape-vine; kite-flying.

message, word of mouth, word 524 n. *information*; communication 547 n. *signal*; radiogram, cablegram, cable, telegram, wire, lettergram 531 n. *telecommunication*; letter, postcard 588 n. *correspondence*; errand, embassy 751 n. *commission*.

newsmonger, quidnunc, gossip 584 n. *interlocutor*; scandalmonger 926 n. *defamer*; newsman, news-hound, pressman, reporter, sob-sister, special correspondent 589 n. *author*; news-agent, news-vendor.

530. Secret – N. *secret*, no publicity, press ban; secret lore, esoterism, arcanum, mystery 984 n. *occultism*; sealed orders, hush-hush subject, top-secret file; confidential communication, confidence; sphinx, man of mystery; Mr X 562 n. *no name*; dark horse, unknown quantity; skeleton in the cupboard; sealed book.

enigma, mystery, puzzle, Chinese p.; problem, poser, brain-twister, teaser; knotty point, vexed question, crux 700 n. *difficulty*; cipher, code, cryptogram, hieroglyphics 517 n. *unintelligibility*; word-puzzle, anagram, acrostic, crossword; riddle, riddle-me-ree, conundrum, rebus; charade, dumb c.; intricacy, labyrinth, maze 61 n. *complexity*.

531. Messenger – N. *messenger*, forerunner 66 n. *precursor*; harbinger; message-bearer (see *courier*); crier, towncrier, bellman 528 n. *publicizer*; ambassador, minister, nuncio, legate, spokesman 754

n. *envoy*; apostle, emissary; flag-bearer, parlementaire, herald, trumpet; process-server 955 n. *law-officer*; go-between, contact, contact-man.

courier, runner, King's messenger, express, dispatch-rider, estafette; post-boy, telegraph boy, messenger b., errand b., office-b., corridor girl; call-boy, bell-hop, page, buttons; carrier pigeon 273 n. *carrier*.

mails, letters 588 n. *correspondence*; mail, post, pigeon-p.; surface mail, sea-m., air-m.; mail-train, mail packet, mail plane; delivery, postal d., express d.; sorter, postman, mailman; postmaster, postmistress; post-office, mail o., G.P.O., poste restante; postbox, letter box, pillar b.; mailbag, letter-bag, diplomatic bag.

telecommunication, cable, cablegram, telegram, wire 529 n. *message*; signalling, semaphore, smoke-signal, beacon 547 n. *signal*; wireless, radio, television; radio signal, morse pip; telephone, radio t., walkie-talkie, telegraph, grape-vine t.; teleprinter; transmitter, radio mast, aerial, antenna; receiver, earphone, headphone; public address system 415 n. *hearing aid*; broadcasting, broadcast, simulcast, relay; broadcaster, radio announcer; listener-in; televiewer, looker-in.

532. Affirmation – N. *affirmation*, proposition, subject and predicate; saying, dictum 496 n. *maxim*; predication, statement, truth-claim 512 n. *supposition*; expression, formulation, one's position, one's stand; claim, declaration, profession, jactitation; allegation 928 n. *accusation*; assertion, ipse dixit, say-so; asseveration, averment, admission; confession, avowal 526 n. *disclosure*; assurance, one's word, warrant 466 n. *testimony*; insistence, stress, accent, emphasis, overstatement; challenge 711 n. *defiance*; observation, remark, interjection 579 n. *speech*; pontification, dogmatism 473 n. *positiveness*.

oath, Bible o., oath-taking, oath-giving, adjurement, solemn affirmation, statement on oath, deposition, affidavit 466 n. *testimony*; word of a gentleman, pledge, promise, warrant, guarantee 764 n. *promise*.

Adj. *affirmative*, not negative 473 adj. *positive*; predicatory, predicative; declaratory, declarative 526 adj. *disclosing*; unretracted, unretractable 473 adj. *undisputed*; solemn, sworn, on oath; affirmable, predicable.

assertive, assured, dogmatic 473 adj. *positive*; trenchant, incisive 571 adj. *forceful*; express, peremptory, categorical, absolute, emphatic, insistent, urgent; flat, broad, round, blunt, strong, outspoken, strongly-worded 573 adj. *plain*; pontifical 485 adj. *credal*; challenging 711 adj. *defiant*.

Vb. *affirm*, state, express, formulate, set down; declare, pronounce, enunciate 528 vb. *proclaim*; voice 579 vb. *speak*; remark, comment, observe, say; dare be sworn 485 vb. *opine*; vow, protest; assert, predicate; maintain, stand for, hold, contend 475 vb. *argue*; advance, urge 512 vb. *propound*; represent, put one's case, submit; claim 761 vb. *request*; allege, pretend, asseverate, avouch, aver; bear witness 466 vb. *testify*; certify 488 vb. *endorse*; commit oneself 764 vb. *promise*, 759 vb. *offer*; profess, avow; abide by, not retract; challenge 711 vb. *defy*; speak out; brook no denial, shout down; say so, lay down, pontificate 473 vb. *dogmatize*; have one's say, have the last word.

swear, be sworn, take oath; attest 466 vb. *corroborate*; outswear 533 vb. *negate*; cross one's heart, kiss the book, take God's name in vain.

emphasize, stress, lay stress on, accent, accentuate, shout; underline, put in italics, italicize, dot the i's and cross the t's; raise one's voice 400 vb. *be loud*; insist 737 vb. *command*; urge, enforce, drive home, impress on, rub in; plug, dwell on, labour 106 vb. *repeat*; highlight 638 vb. *make important*.

Adv. *affirmatively*, without fear of contradiction; seriously, joking apart; on oath, on the Bible.

533. Negation – N. *negation*, negative, nay; denial 760 n. *refusal*; disbelief 486 n. *unbelief*; disagreement 489 n. *dissent*; rebuttal 460 n. *rejoinder*; refutation 479 n. *confutation*; contradiction, gainsaying; the lie, lie direct, démenti; challenge 711 n. *defiance*; repudiation, disclaimer, disavowal, disownment 607 n. *rejection*; retractation, palinode, abjurement 603 n. *recantation*; disallowance 757 n. *prohibition*; recusancy 769 n. *non-observance*; cancellation, invalidation, revocation 752 n. *abrogation*.

Adj. *negative*, negatory; adversative, contradictory 14 adj. *contrary*; recusant 769 adj. *non-observant*; revocatory; disowned, unfathered.

Vb. *negate*, negative; deny, gainsay, give the lie to, belie, contradict, eat one's hat if; disaffirm, repudiate, disavow, disclaim, disown, leave unfathered 607 vb. *reject*; hold no brief for 860 vb. *be indifferent*; demur, object 468 vb. *qualify*; disagree 489 vb. *dissent*; dissociate oneself 704 vb. *oppose*; controvert, traverse, impugn, question, refute 479 vb. *confute*, 486 vb. *disbelieve*; challenge, 711 vb. *defy*; say no 760 vb. *refuse*; disallow 757 vb. *prohibit*; revoke 752 vb. *abrogate*; abjure, forswear, swear off 603 vb. *recant*.

534. Teaching – N. *teaching*, pedagogy, paedeutics, pedagogics; education, schooling, upbringing; tutelage, leading strings; direction, guidance, instruction, edification; spoon-feeding; tuition, preparation, coaching, tutorial; initiation, introduction; training 682 n. *exercise*; inculcation, catechization, indoctrination, preaching, pulpitry, homiletics; proselytism, propagandism; conversion; conditioning, brainwashing.

curriculum, course of study 536 n. *learning*; course; first lessons, propaedeutics, A.B.C., the three Rs; set books, prescribed text 589 n. *textbook*; set task, exercise, homework, prep; correspondence course, classes, evening c.; seminar.

lecture, reading, prelection, discourse,

disquisition; sermon, preachment, homily, lesson, apologue, parable; readership, lectureship, professorship, chair.

Adj. *educational*, pedagogic, paedeutic, tutorial; scholastic, scholarly, academic; instructional, informational; instructive 524 adj. *informative*; educative, didactic; doctrinal, normative; edifying, moralizing, homiletic, preachy; cultural, humane, scientific.

Vb. *educate*, edify (see *teach*); breed, rear, nurse, nurture, bring up, develop, form, lick into shape; put to school; tutor, teach, school; ground, coach, cram, prime 669 vb. *prepare*; instruct 524 vb. *inform*; enlighten, illumine; inculcate, indoctrinate, imbue; disabuse, unteach; chasten, sober.

teach, profess, give lessons, teach school, hold classes; lecture, tutor; preach, harangue, sermonize; moralize, point a moral; expound 520 vb. *interpret*; pamphleteer, propagandize, proselytize, condition, brainwash 178 vb. *influence*.

train, coach 669 vb. *prepare*; take in hand, initiate, tame, school 369 vb. *break in*; nurse, foster, inure, put through the mill, drill, exercise, practise, make second nature, condition 610 vb. *habituate*; house-train, teach manners 369 vb. *groom*.

535. Misteaching – **N.** *misteaching*, misinstruction, misguidance, misdirection; quackery, blind leading the blind; misinformation 552 n. *misrepresentation*; miscorrection 495 n. *mistake*; obscurantism 491 n. *ignorance*; false teaching 541 n. *falsehood*; perversion 246 n. *distortion*.

Adj. *misteaching* etc. vb.

Vb. *misteach*, miseducate, bring up wrong; misinform, misdirect, misguide 495 vb. *mislead*; not edify, corrupt, abuse, pervert 246 vb. *distort*; misdescribe 552 vb. *misrepresent*; lie 541 vb. *be false*; explain away, leave no wiser; unteach; propagandize, brainwash.

536. Learning – **N.** *learning*, lore, scholarship, attainments 490 n. *erudition*; intellectual curiosity 453 n. *curiosity*;

pupillage, tutelage, apprenticeship, novitiate, initiation 669 n. *preparation*; docility, teachability 694 n. *aptitude*, self-instruction, self-education, self-improvement.

study, application, studiousness; cramming etc. vb.; studies, course, lessons, class, class-work, desk-w.; homework, prep; revision, refresher course; perusal, reading; research 459 n. *inquiry*.

Adj. *studious*, devoted to studies, academic; bookish, well-read, scholarly, erudite, learned 490 adj. *knowing*; diligent, degree-hungry 678 adj. *industrious*; receptive, teachable, docile 597 adj. *willing*; self-taught, self-instructed, autodidact.

Vb. *learn*, go to school, take lessons, sit at the feet of, assimilate learning, imbibe, drink in; learn one's trade, serve an apprenticeship, article oneself 669 vb. *prepare oneself*; train, practise, exercise 610 vb. *be wont*; master, get by heart 505 vb. *memorize*; hear, be told.

study, prosecute one's studies, burn the midnight oil; do, take up; research into 459 vb. *inquire*; specialize, major in, graduate in; swot, cram, grind, mug, mull, get up; revise, go over, brush up; read, peruse, spell, pore, wade through.

537. Teacher – **N.** *teacher*, preceptor, mentor; guru 500 n. *sage*; instructor, tutor, munshi; crammer, coach; bearleader, governor, governess 749 n. *keeper*; educationist, pedagogue; dominie, abecedarian; master, schoolmaster, classmaster, headmaster, principal; schoolmistress, school-marm, dame; underteacher, pupil teacher, usher, don, fellow; lecturer, reader, professor, faculty member; catechist; initiator, mystagogue, coryphaeus; teaching staff, faculty, professoriate, senior common room.

trainer, instructor; coach; choirmaster; dancing-master; drill-sergeant; disciplinarian; animal trainer, breaker-in, lion-tamer 369 n. *breeder*.

preacher, lay p. 986 n. *pastor*; pulpiteer; gospeller, evangelist; apostle, missionary; seer, prophet 511 n. *oracle*; pamphleteer, propagandist 528 n. *publicizer*; proverbialist 500 n. *sage*.

538. Learner – N. *learner*, disciple, follower, chela; proselyte, convert, catechumen; do-it-yourself fan, autodidact; empiricist 461 n. *experimenter*; swotter, mugger, bookworm 492 n. *scholar*; alumnus, student, pupil, scholar, schoolboy, schoolgirl, school-miss, school-goer, day-scholar, day-boy, boarder; schoolfellow, school-mate, classmate; fellow-student, condisciple.

beginner, novice, débutant; new boy, fag, tyro, greenhorn, tenderfoot, neophyte; recruit, raw r.; initiate, catechumen; cub, colt, trainee, apprentice, 'prentice; probationer; first offender; L-driver.

college student, colleger, collegian, seminarist; undergraduate, undergraduette; freshmen, frosh, first-year man; sophomore, soph; commoner, pensioner, sizar, exhibitioner; passman, honours student, graduate.

class, standard, form, grade, remove, shell, stream; scholarship class; art class, life c.; seminar.

539. School – N. *academy*, ι nstitute, teaching institution; college, seminary, lycée, gymnasium; conservatoire; university, university college.

school, nursery s., crèche, kindergarten; infant school, dame s.; preparatory school, prep s.; primary school, secondary s., high s., grammar s., comprehensive s., public s.; reformatory, Borstal, remand home.

training school, nursery, training ground, gymnasium, palaestra 724 n. *arena*; crammer; finishing school; training ship, training college, teachers training c., normal school; medical college, teaching hospital; military college, staff college.

trade school, vocational s., technical training s.; polytechnic; research laboratory, research institute; secretarial school, business college.

classroom, schoolroom; study; lecture-room, lecture-hall, auditorium, theatre, amphitheatre; desk; schoolbook, reader, crib, hornbook, abecedary, primer 589 n. *textbook*; slate, copybook, exercise book; visual aid.

rostrum, tribune, dais, platform, stage, hustings, soap-box; chair 534 n. *lecture*; pulpit, lectern, ambo.

540. Veracity – N. *veracity*, no lie, truthfulness; verisimilitude, realism, exactitude 494 n. *accuracy*; sincerity, frankness, candour; bona fides, honour bright, no kidding; downrightness, plain speaking 573 n. *plainness*; home-truth, unvarnished tale, honest truth 494 n. *truth*; clean breast 526 n. *disclosure*; circumstantiality, full details 570 n. *diffuseness*; no liar, prophet.

Adj. *veracious*, truthful 494 adj. *true*; veridical, not lying, unperjured; as good as one's word 929 adj. *trustworthy*; factual, ungarbled, unvarnished 494 adj. *accurate*; full, particular, circumstantial 570 adj. *diffuse*; bona fide, not joking; sincere; unfeigned, candid, unreserved, forthcoming; unambiguous, free, downright, outspoken, straightforward, plain, direct, truly spoken, infallible, prophetic 511 adj. *presageful*.

Vb. *be truthful*, tell |no lie, swear true 532 vb. *swear*; stick to the facts; mean it, really mean; speak one's mind, open one's heart; make a clean breast 526 vb. *confess*.

541. Falsehood – N. *falsehood*, falseness, spuriousness, falsity; bad faith 930 n. *perfidy*; untruthfulness, mendacity, deceitfulness; lying, pathological l., mythomania; lie, perjury 543 n. *untruth*; fabrication, fiction; falsification 542 n. *deception*; disingenuousness, prevarication, equivocation, evasion 518 n. *equivocalness*; overstatement 546 n. *exaggeration*; perversion 246 n. *distortion*; misrepresentation 521 n. *misinterpretation*; humbug 515 n. *empty talk*; cant (see *duplicity*).

duplicity, double life, double-dealing

930 n. *improbity*; guile 542 n. *trickery*; hollowness, front, façade, window-dressing 875 n. *ostentation*; pretence, bluff 542 n. *sham*; hypocrisy, simulation, dissimulation, insincerity, tongue in cheek, cant; lip-homage 925 n. *flattery*; cupboard love, crocodile tears; Judas kiss, Cornish hug; fraud, legal fiction, diplomatic illness; cheat, cheating; put-up job, frame-up 930 n. *foul play*; charlatanry.

Adj. *false*, untruthful, lying, mendacious 543 adj. *untrue*; perfidious, perjured; disingenuous, uncandid, evasive 518 adj. *equivocal*; meretricious, painted; ungenuine, counterfeit, fake 542 adj. *spurious*; deceitful 542 adj. *deceiving*; covinous, collusive.

hypocritical, hollow, empty, insincere, diplomatic; put on, feigned, make-believe; double, two-faced, treacherous, double-dealing 930 adj. *perfidious*; sanctimonious, pharisaical; plausible, smooth, oily, gushing 925 adj. *flattering*.

Vb. *be false*, perjure oneself, bear false witness; forswear 603 vb. *recant*; palter, prevaricate, not give a straight answer, economize; fib, lie, tell lies, swing the lead; strain the truth 546 vb. *exaggerate*; lie hard, lie like a trooper; make believe, make up, romance 513 vb. *imagine*; garble, falsify, pervert 246 vb. *distort*; overstate, understate 552 vb. *misrepresent*; misreport, cry wolf 535 vb. *misteach*; play false 930 vb. *be dishonest*; break faith, betray.

dissemble, dissimulate, disguise 525 vb. *conceal*; simulate, counterfeit 20 vb. *imitate*; put on, assume, affect, dress up, play-act 594 vb. *act*; feign, sham, pretend; malinger 542 vb. *deceive*; play the hypocrite, cant, gloze.

fake, fabricate, coin, forge, plagiarize, counterfeit 20 vb. *imitate*; get up, trump up, frame; manipulate, rig, pack (a jury); spin, weave, concoct, hatch, invent 623 vb. *plot*.

542. Deception – N. *deception*, kidding, tongue in cheek; circumvention, outwitting; self-deception, wishful thinking 487 n. *credulity*; fallacy 477 n. *sophistry*; illusion, delusion, hallucination 495 n. *error*; deceptiveness 523 n. *latency* (see *trap*); false appearance, mirage 440 n. *visual fallacy*; show, meretriciousness, paint (see *sham*); falseness, deceit, quackery, imposture, lie 541 n. *falsehood*; deceitfulness, guile 698 n. *cunning*; hypocrisy 541 n. *duplicity*; treachery 930 n. *perfidy*; fraudulence, cozenage, cheating (see *trickery*).

trickery, swindling, skulduggery, shenanigan, jockeyship, sharp practice, chicanery; swindle, chouse, ramp, wangle, fiddle, diddle, swizzle, swiz, sell, bite, fraud, cheat 545 n. *trickster*; trick, bag of tricks, tricks of the trade, confidence trick, wile, ruse, shift, dodge, fetch, reach, blind, dust, feint 698 n. *stratagem*; bait, diversion; hocus, hoax, bluff, spoof, leg-pull; joke, practical j. 839 n. *witticism*.

sleight, pass, sleight of hand, legerdemain, prestidigitation, conjuring, hocuspocus, illusion, ventriloquism; jugglery, juggle, googly; magic 983 n. *sorcery*.

trap, deathtrap 527 n. *ambush*; catch 530 n. *enigma*; plant, frame-up 930 n. *foul play*; noose, snare, gin, net, spider's web; springe, hook, mine; diversion, blind, decoy, kill, bait, lure; fly-paper, lime-twig; booby-trap, trip-wire, deadfall 663 n. *pitfall*; fatal gift, poisoned chalice, Trojan horse.

sham, not what it seems 541 n. *duplicity*; make-believe, pretence 850 n. *affectation*; paint, whitewash; dummy 4 n. *insubstantial thing*; imitation, simulacrum, mockery, farce; counterfeit, forgery, fake; mummery, mask, disguise, borrowed plumes, false colours 525 n. *concealment*; tinsel, paste.

Adj. *deceiving*, deceitful, lying 543 adj. *untrue*; deceptive 523 adj. *latent*; hallucinatory, illusive, delusive, illusory; fraudulent, treacherous, insidious 930 adj. *perfidious*; colourable, tricky, crafty, wily, guileful, artful 698 adj. *cunning*; collusive, covinous.

spurious, illegitimate 954 adj. *bastard*; ungenuine, false, fake; sham, counterfeit; make-believe, mock, ersatz, bogus, phoney; pseudo, so-called; not natural, artificial; tinsel, meretricious, flash, catchpenny 812 adj. *cheap.*

Vb. *deceive*, delude, illude, beguile; hoodwink, blindfold 439 vb. *blind*; kid, bluff, bamboozle, hoax, humbug, hornswoggle, gammon; dazzle, throw dust in the eyes; spoof, mystify 535 vb. *misteach*; play false, betray, doublecross 930 vb. *be dishonest*; circumvent, overreach, outwit, outmanoeuvre; outsmart 698 vb. *be cunning*; trick, dupe (see *befool*); cheat, cozen, sharp, swindle, swizzle, sell, bite, do down; diddle, bubble, do out of, bilk, gyp, chouse, pluck 788 vb. *defraud*; juggle, conjure, palm off, foist o.; cog the dice, load the d., mark the cards; impose upon 541 vb. *dissemble*; counterfeit 541 vb. *fake.*

befool, fool, make an ass of; rag, pull one's leg, have one on, play a joke on; sport with, trifle w., jilt; take in, have, dupe, victimize, gull, outwit; trick, trap, catch, take advantage of; kid, spoof, bamboozle (see *deceive*); cog, cajole 925 vb. *flatter*; let down, leave in the lurch 509 vb. *disappoint*; send on a fool's errand 495 vb. *mislead.*

ensnare, snare, trap, set *or* lay a trap for, lime, enmesh, entangle, net; trip, trip up, catch, catch out, hook, sniggle; bait, lure, decoy, entice, inveigle 612 vb. *tempt*; lie in wait, waylay 527 vb. *ambush.*

543. Untruth – N. *untruth*, reverse of the truth 541 n. *falsehood*; less than the truth, understatement 483 n. *underestimation*; lie, taradiddle, fib, whopper, terminological inexactitude 545 n. *liar*; broken word, dicer's oath, lover's o., breach of promise 930 n. *perfidy*; perjury, false oath; false evidence, pack of lies, frame-up 466 n. *evidence*; invention (see *fable*); misstatement, misinformation 535 n. *misteaching*; lie factory, propaganda machine.

mental dishonesty, disingenuousness, economy of t., half-t., partial t., half-lie, white l., pious fraud; mental

reservation 468 n. *qualification*; suggestio falsi, suppressio veri 525 n. *concealment*; tongue in cheek, pretence; excuse 614 n. *pretext*; evasion 518 n. *equivocalness*; empty words 925 n. *flattery*; falsification 552 n. *misrepresentation.*

fable, invention, fiction, imaginative exercise 513 n. *ideality*; tall story, tall order, fisherman's yarn, traveller's tale 546 n. *exaggeration*; fairy tale, romance, tale, yarn, story, cock-and-bull s. 497 n. *absurdity*; canard 529 n. *rumour*; myth, mythology.

Adj. *untrue*, lying, mendacious 541 adj. *false*; far from the truth; mythological, fabulous; unfounded, empty; fictitious, make-believe, well-imagined, ben trovato; phoney, bogus, soi-disant, socalled.

544. Dupe – N. *dupe*, fool, old f., April f. 851 n. *laughing-stock*; Simple Simon 501 n. *ninny*; easy prey, victim, sucker, gull, greenhorn, innocent; puppet, cat's-paw, pawn 630 n. *tool*; admass.

Adj. *gullible* 487 adj. *credulous.*

545. Deceiver – N. *deceiver*, gay d., seducer 952 n. *libertine*; kidder, ragger, leg-puller; dissembler, actor, shammer, hypocrite; false friend, jilt, turncoat, rat 603 n. *tergiversator*; four-flusher, doublecrosser 938 n. *knave*; intrigant, conspirator 623 n. *planner*; counterfeiter, forger, faker 20 n. *imitator.*

liar, fibster, fibber, story-teller; romancer, fabulist, yarner; mythologist; pseudologist, fabricator; oath-breaker, perjurer, false witness; Ananias, father of lies.

impostor, shammer, malingerer; adventurer, usurper; ass in the lion's skin, wolf in sheep's clothing; boaster, bluffer; pretender, quack 850 n. *affector*; fake, fraud, humbug.

trickster, hoaxer, spoofer; cheat, cozener; sharper, shyster, pettifogger; swindler 789 n. *defrauder*; slicker, spieler, twister, chiseller 938 n. *knave*; con-man, magsman; crimp, decoy, stoolpigeon, decoy-duck, agent provocateur;

fiddler, manipulator; fox 698 n. *sly-boots*.

conjuror, illusionist, prestidigitator, galigali man, juggler, ventriloquist; quick-change artist; magician 983 n. *sorcerer*.

546. Exaggeration – N. *exaggeration*, over-emphasis, inflation; extravagance, exaggerated lengths, extremes; inordinacy, exorbitance, overdoing it; overacting, histrionics 875 n. *ostentation*; sensationalism, ballyhoo 528 n. *publicity*; overstatement, hyperbole 519 n. *trope*; adulation 925 n. *flattery*; colouring, high c. 574 n. *ornament*; caricature, burlesque 851 n. *satire*; exacerbation 832 n. *aggravation*; big talk 877 n. *boasting*; rant 574 n. *magniloquence*; tall story 543 n. *fable*; storm in a teacup, much ado about nothing 318 n. *commotion*; extremist, exaggerator; sensationalist, miracle-monger.

Adj. *exaggerated*, magnified 197 adj. *expanded*; strained, overdone, hyperbolical 574 adj. *rhetorical*; overacted, histrionic; bombastic 877 adj. *boastful*; extravagant, excessive, outré, extremist.

Vb. *exaggerate*, maximize, inflate 197 vb. *enlarge*; touch up, enhance, heighten, embroider 844 vb. *decorate*; lay it on thick, overdo, over-emphasize 638 vb. *make important*; overpraise 482 vb. *overrate*; caricature 851 vb. *satirize*; protest too much, speak in superlatives, hyperbolize; overact, out-Herod Herod; rant 877 vb. *boast*; run riot, go to extremes, make mountains out of molehills; intensify 832 vb. *aggravate*.

Section 3: Means of Communicating Ideas

547. Indication – N. *indication*; signification 514 n. *connotation*; notification 524 n. *information*; symbolization, symbolism 551 n. *representation*; symbol; image, type, figure; token (see *badge*); something to go by, symptom, sign 466 n. *evidence*; nudge, wink 524 n. *hint* (see

gesture); straw in the wind 511 n. *omen*; clue, scent, whiff 484 n. *detector*; symptomatology 520 n. *hermeneutics*; pointer (see *indicator*); guide, index, thumb-i.; marker, mark, guide-m.; note, underrunner, catchword (see *punctuation*); stamp, print, impression; stigma, stigmata; prick, tattoo-mark 263 n. *perforation*; inscription, epitaph; motto, cipher.

identification, naming 561 n. *nomenclature*, 77 n. *classification*; means of identification, brand, trade-mark, imprint (see *label*); name and address; autograph, signature, hand 586 n. *script*; finger-print, footprint, spoor, slot 548 n. *trace*; password, open sesame, watchword, countersign; diagnostic, markings, cloven hoof; characteristic, trait, lineament 445 n. *feature*; trick of speech, shibboleth; mole, scar, birth-mark, strawberry mark 845 n. *blemish*; criterion, mark, note.

symbology, symbolization, dactylogy; cipher, code 525 n. *secrecy*; symbolography 586 n. *script*; gypsy signs, hobo s., scout s.

gesture, gesticulation, sign-language, dactylogy; deaf-and-dumb language; sign 524 n. *hint*; pantomime, by-play, dumb-show, charade; demeanour, look, tone 445 n. *mien*; motion, move; shrug, nod, beck, wink, twinkle, glance, ogle, leer; hand-pressure, handshake; wave, hand-signal; clenched fist 711 n. *defiance*; clap 923 n. *applause*; frown, scowl 893 n. *sullenness*; pout 829 n. *discontent*.

signal, 529 n. *message*; sign, symptom 522 n. *manifestation*; flash, rocket; signalling, heliograph, semaphore, telegraph, morse 531 n. *telecommunication*; beacon; red flag; warning light, red l. 420 n. *signal light*; alarum, S.O.S. 665 n. *danger signal*; siren, hooter; doorbell, alarm-b.; time-signal, pip 117 n. *chronometry*.

indicator, index, pointer, arrow, needle, magnetic n.; finger, index-f.; hand, hour-h. 117 n. *timekeeper*; Plimsoll line 465 n. *gauge*; traffic indicator, trafficator, semaphore; white line 305 n.

traffic control; weathercock, wind sock, straw in the wind 340 n. *weather*.

signpost, direction post, finger-p., milestone, milliary column, waymark; lighthouse 662 n. *safeguard*; compass 269 n. *sailing aid*; lodestar 690 n. *leader*; cynosure, landmark, sea-mark.

call, proclamation, ban, hue-and-cry 528 n. *publication*; shout, hail; church-bell, muezzin's cry 981 n. *worship*; summons 737 n. *command*; bugle-call, re-veillé, assemble, charge, advance, rally, retreat; lights out, last post; call to arms, Fiery Cross; battle-cry, war-c., slogan, watchword; challenge, countersign.

badge, token, emblem, symbol, sign, figurehead (see *indication*); insignia (see *heraldry*); markings; badge of sovereign-ty, crown 743 n. *regalia*; badge of office 743 n. *badge of rule*; baton, stars 743 n. *badge of rank*; medal, gong, cross 729 n. *decoration*; badge of merit, laurels 729 n. *trophy*; blue, cap, oar; badge of loyalty, favour, rosette, love-knot.

livery, dress, national d. 228 n. *uni-form*; tartan, tie, old school t., blazer; regimental badge, brassard, epaulette, chevron, stripes, pips, wings; flash, hackle, cockade, rosette.

heraldry, armoury, blazonry; heral-dic register, Roll of Arms; armorial bearings, coat of arms; achievement, hatchment; shield, escutcheon; crest, mantling; supporters, motto; ordinary, chief, base, pale, fess, bend, bend sinis-ter, chevron, pile, saltire, cross; marshal-ling, quartering, impaling, dimidiating; differencing, difference; charge; national emblem, rose, thistle, leek, daffodil, shamrock, lilies, fleur-de-lys; device, national d., charkha, eagle, bear, ham-mer and sickle; swastika, fylfot; skull and crossbones; heraldic tincture, colour, gules, azure, vert, sable, purpure, tenné, murray; metal, or, gold, yellow, argent, silver, white; fur, ermine, pean, vair, potent; heraldic personnel, College of Arms, herald, pursuivant.

flag, ensign; red ensign, Red Duster; jack; colours; cavalry colours, guidon; standard, banner, gonfalon; banneret, bannerol, banderole, oriflamme; pen-nant, swallowtail, triple tail; pendant, broad p., burgee; bunting; Blue Peter, yellow flag; white flag 721 n. *submission*; eagle, Roman e.; crescent; tricolour; Union Jack; Stars and Stripes, Old Glory, star-spangled banner; Red Flag; black flag, Jolly Roger, skull and cross-bones; parts of a flag, hoist, fly, canton; flag-pole, flag-mast, colour pike.

label (see *identification*); ticket, billet, bill, docket, counterfoil, stub, duplicate; tally, counter, chip; letter, number, check, mark, countermark; tie-label, tab, tag; name-tape, name-plate, name-board, sign-b.; sign, plate, trade-mark, hall-m., cachet; earmark, brand, stigma, broad arrow; seal, signet, sigil, stamp, impression; caption, heading, title, super-scription, rubric; imprint, colophon, signation, watermark; book-plate, monomark; card, visiting c., address c.; certificate, identification papers; pass-port 756 n. *permit*; signature, sign-manual, autograph, cipher, mark, cross, initials, monogram, paraph; finger-print, thumb-print, footprint 548 n. *trace*.

punctuation, point, stop, full s., period; comma, colon, semicolon; in-verted commas, quotation marks, apos-trophe, quotes; exclamation mark, question mark, note of interrogation; parentheses, brackets, crotchet, crook, brace; hyphen, hyphenation; dash, dot, caret mark; asterisk, asterism, star; obelus, dagger, squiggle, marginal fin-ger; accent, grave a., acute a., circumflex a.; diaeresis, cedilla, tilde; diacritical mark, vowel point, macron, breve, umlaut; sigla, stroke, paragraph; under-lining, sublineation; italics 587 n. *print-type*.

Adj. *indicating*, indicative, indicatory; significative 514 adj. *meaningful*; typical, token, symbolic, emblematic, nominal, diagrammatic 551 adj. *representing*; tell-tale 526 adj. *disclosing*; symptomatic 466 adj. *evidential*; diagnostic, semeiological, symptomatological; characteristic 80 adj. *special*; explanatory 520 adj. *inter-pretive*; gesticulatory, pantomimic.

heraldic, emblematic; crested, armorial, blazoned; dexter, sinister; rampant, guardant, reguardant, forcene, couchant, statant, sejant, genuant, passant.

Vb. *indicate*, point; point out, exhibit 522 vb. *show*; blazon; mark out, blaze; register, read, tell 548 vb. *record*; name, identify, classify 80 vb. *specify*; index, reference, supply references, refer; guide 689 vb. *direct*; signify 514 vb. *mean*; symbolize, typify, betoken, stand for 551 vb. *represent*; signalize, highlight 532 vb. *emphasize*; evince, show signs of, bear the marks of 466 vb. *evidence*; intimate 524 vb. *hint*; reveal 526 vb. *disclose*; prefigure 511 vb. *predict*.

mark, mark out, demarcate, delimit 236 vb. *limit*; label, ticket, docket, tag, tab; earmark, designate; note, annotate, underline, underscore; number, letter, page; tick; nick 260 vb. *notch*; chalk, chalk up; scratch 586 vb. *write*; blot 649 vb. *make unclean*; scar 842 vb. *make ugly*; punctuate, obelize, asterisk; blaze, brand, burn in; stigmatize, prick, tattoo 263 vb. *pierce*; stamp, seal, punch, impress, emboss; crest, emblazon; impale, dimidiate, quarter, difference; marshal, charge.

sign, countersign 488 vb. *endorse*; autograph, subscribe, undersign; initial, paraph; put one's mark *or* cross; make signation; attest 466 vb. *testify*.

gesticulate, pantomime, mime, mimic, suit the action to the word 20 vb. *imitate*; saw the air, wave; gesture, motion, sign; point, thumb, beckon 455 vb. *attract notice*; nod, beck, wink, shrug; jog, nudge, poke; look, look volumes 438 vb. *gaze*; twinkle, smile 835 vb. *laugh*; gnash one's teeth 891 vb. *be angry*; snap 893 vb. *be sullen*; grimace, pout 829 vb. *be discontented*.

signal, exchange signals, speak 524 vb. *communicate*; tap out, semaphore, heliograph; flag, thumb; wave; fly the flag, break the f., dip, half-mast, salute; alert 665 vb. *raise the alarm*.

548. Record – N. *record*, recording, documentation; memoir, chronicle, annals, history 590 n. *narrative*; case history, psychic profile, histogram, psychogram 590 n. *biography*; dossier, rogues gallery; public record, gazette, official journal, Hansard, Congressional Record; minutes, transactions, acta; cuttings, press-c.; memorabilia, memorandum 505 n. *reminder*; returns, statements 524 n. *report*; tally, score-sheet, scoreboard; form, document, muniment; voucher, certificate, diploma 466 n. *credential*, 767 n. *title-deed*; copy, spare c. 22 n. *duplicate*; documentation, archives, papers, correspondence; record, roll, register, registry, cartulary; notebook, minute-b., log-b., diary, journal, scrap-book, album; ledger 808 n. *account-book*; file, index; card, microcard, microfilm; inscription 547 n. *indication*.

registration, registry, record-keeping; recording, tape-r.; epigraphy; enrolment, enlistment; booking, reservation; bookkeeping 808 n. *accounts*; filing system, docket.

monument, memorial 505 n. *reminder*; mausoleum 364 n. *tomb*; statue, bust 551 n. *image*; brass, tablet, slab, inscription 364 n. *obsequies*; column, memorial arch, obelisk; cromlech, dolmen, cairn, menhir, megalith, barrow, tell; testimonial 729 n. *trophy*.

trace, vestige, relic, remains; footprint, footmark, hoofmark, pug-mark, tread; spoor, slot; scent, smell, piste; wake, wash, trail, smoke-t., track; furrow, swathe, path; impression, finger-print, dabs 466 n. *evidence*; mark, stain, scar.

Adj. *recording* etc. vb.; annalistic, record-making; self-recording; recordable; monumental, epigraphic, inscriptional.

recorded, on record, in the file; in writing 586 adj. *written*; in print, in black and white; traceable, vestigial, extant 41 adj. *remaining*.

Vb. *record*, tape-record; document; docket, file, index, catalogue; inscribe 555 vb. *engrave*; take down 586 vb. *write*; write down, jot d.; note, mark, make a note of; minute, calendar; chronicle 590 vb. *describe*.

register, chalk up, tick off, score; tabulate, table, enrol, enlist 87 vb. *list*; fill in, enter, post, book; inscribe, inscroll, blazon; log, diarize, journalize 808 vb. *account*.

549. Recorder – N. *recorder*, registrar, record-keeper, archivist, remembrancer; notary, protonotary; amanuensis, stenographer, scribe; secretary, referencer, receptionist; clerk, record-clerk 808 n. *accountant*; filing cabinet, record room, muniment r., Record Office.

chronicler, saga-man, annalist, diarist, historian, historiographer, biographer, autobiographer 590 n. *narrator*; antiquary 125 n. *antiquarian*; reporter, columnist, gossip-writer 529 n. *newsmonger*; candid camera.

recording instrument, recorder, tape-r.; record, disc, long-player 414 n. *gramophone*; dictaphone; teleprinter, tape-machine, ticker-tape; cash register; turnstile; seismograph, speedometer 465 n. *gauge*.

550. Obliteration – N. *obliteration*, erasure, effacement; overprinting, defacement; deletion, blue pencil, censorship; cancellation; blot 649 n. *dirt*; tabula rasa, clean slate, clean sweep 149 n. *revolution*; eraser, duster, sponge, rubber; abrasive 648 n. *cleaning utensil*.

Adj. *obliterated*, out of print; leaving no trace, unrecorded, unregistered, unwritten; intestate.

Vb. *obliterate*, remove the traces, cover up 525 vb. *conceal*; overpaint, overprint, deface, make illegible; efface, erase, rase, scratch out, rub o.; expunge, blot, black out, cancel, delete, dele; strike out, cross out, score through, censor, blue-pencil; wipe off the map, bury 364 vb. *inter*; submerge 165 vb. *suppress*; drown 399 vb. *silence*.

551. Representation – N. *representation*, personification, incarnation, embodiment; typification 547 n. *indication*; conventional representation, diagram, presentation, realization, evocation 522 n.

manifestation; personation, impersonation; enactment 594 n. *acting*; mimesis, mimicry, noises off 20 n. *i mitation*; depiction, characterization 590 n. *description*; delineation, graphic d., illustration, iconography 553 n. *painting*; likeness, double, facsimile 22 n. *duplicate*; reflection (see *image*); portraiture, portrayal; pictorial equivalent, realism 553 n. *picture*; reproduction 555 n. *printing*; design, cartoon, sketch 623 n. *plan*.

image, very i. 22 n. *duplicate*; mental-image, after-image 451 n. *idea*; projection 417 n. *reflection*; idol, graven image 982 n. *idolatry*; icon; statuary 554 n. *sculpture*; effigy, figure, figurine; waxwork; dummy, lay figure; model, working m.; doll, marionette, puppet; scarecrow; type, symbol.

art, fine a., graphic a. 553 n. *painting*; plastic art 554 n. *sculpture*; architecture; the minor arts, illumination, calligraphy, weaving, tapestry, embroidery, pottery.

photography, radiography, skiagraphy; cinematography 445 n. *cinema*; photograph, photo, photostat, snapshot, snap, shot; colour photo, transparency, slide; print, photo-p., still; reduction, enlargement, blow-up, close-up; plate, film; skiagram, radiograph, X-ray; heliotype, calotype, talbotype, daguerreotype; camera obscura 442 n. *camera*; cameraman, cinematographer, photographer, snapshotter; radiographer.

map, chart, plan, outline, sketch map; Admiralty chart, portulan; ground plan, ichnography; projection, Mercator's p., Chad's p.; atlas; map-making, cartography.

Adj. *representing*, reflecting etc. vb.; representative 590 adj. *descriptive*; pictorial, graphic, vivid; emblematic, symbolic; figurative, illustrative, diagrammatic; representational, realistic, naturalistic, impressionist, surrealistic; photographic, photogenic, paintable.

Vb. *represent*, act for 755 vb. *deputize*; stand for, symbolize 514 vb. *mean*; type, typify, incarnate, embody, personify; personate, impersonate, pose as 542 vb. *deceive*; pose, model, sit for; present, enact 594 vb. *dramatize*; reflect, image, mimic, mime, copy 20 vb. *imitate*; depict, evoke 590 vb. *describe*; sketch, delineate, limn, draw, picture, portray, figure; illustrate 553 vb. *paint*; hit off, catch, realize; carve 554 vb. *sculpt*; mould, shape 243 vb. *efform*; diagrammatize 233 vb. *outline*; map, chart, survey, plot.

photograph, photo, snapshot, snap; take, shoot, film; X-ray, radiograph; expose, develop, enlarge, blow up, reduce.

552. Misrepresentation – N. *misrepresentation*, false light 541 n. *falsehood*; travesty, parody, caricature 851 n. *ridicule*; bad art, daub, botch; twist, deformation, distorted image 246 n. *distortion*; misinformation 535 n. *misteaching*.

Adj. *misrepresented* etc. vb.

Vb. *misrepresent*, misdescribe 535 vb. *misteach*; deform 246 vb. *distort*; give a twist *or* turn; tone down; overdramatize 546 vb. *exaggerate*; overdraw, caricature, guy, burlesque, parody, travesty; daub, botch; traduce 926 vb. *detract*; lie 541 vb. *be false*.

553. Painting – N. *painting*, graphic art; colouring, rubrication, illumination; daubing, finger-painting; depicting, drawing, sketching 551 n. *representation*; artistry, composition, design, technique, draughtsmanship, brushwork; treatment, tone, values, atmosphere, ambience; polychrome 425 n. *colour*; black and white, chiaroscuro, grisaille.

picture, pictorial equivalent 551 n. *representation*; tableau, mosaic, tapestry; painting, pastiche, icon, triptych, diptych; fresco, mural, wall-painting; canvas, daub; drawing, line-d.; sketch, outline, cartoon; oil-painting, watercolour, aquarelle, pastel, black-and-white drawing, pen-and-ink d.; cartoon, chad, caricature, silhouette; miniature, vignette, thumbnail sketch; old master, masterpiece; study, genre, interior, still life; view, landscape, nocturne; nude,

portrait, head, profile; print, photoprint 551 n. *photography*; photogravure, reproduction, half-tone; aquatint, woodcut 555 n. *engraving*; print, plate; illustration, picture postcard; picture book 589 n. *book*.

art equipment, palette, palette knife, paint-brush, paint-box, paint-tube; paints, oils; water-colours, tempera, distemper, gouache, gesso, varnish 226 n. *facing*; ink, crayon, pastel, chalk, charcoal; pen, pencil; canvas, easel; studio, atelier, art museum, picture-gallery; model, sitter, poser, subject; drysaltery 633 n. *provision*.

Adj. *painted* etc. vb.; graphic, pictorial, scenic, picturesque, decorative 844 adj. *ornamental*; pastel; chiaroscuro, grisaille 429 adj. *grey*; painterly, paintable 551 adj. *representing*.

Vb. *paint*, colorize 425 vb. *colour*; tint, touch up, daub; dead-colour, scumble; paint on, splash, lay it on 226 vb. *coat*; portray, do a portrait, draw, sketch, limn, cartoon 551 vb. *represent*; miniate, rubricate, illuminate; ink, shade, stipple; pinxit, delineavit, fecit.

554. Sculpture – N. *sculpture*, plastic art 551 n. *representation*; carving, stone cutting; moulding, ceroplastics; petroglyph, rock-carving, bone-c., shell-c., scrimshaw; statuary; group; statue, colossus; statuette, figurine, bust, torso, head, cast, plaster c., waxwork 551 n. *image*; ceramics; anaglyph, cameo, intaglio, relief 254 n. *relievo*; chisel, burin.

Adj. *glyptic*, sculptured, carved; statuary, statuesque, marmoreal; anaglyptic, in relief 254 adj. *salient*; ceroplastic; toreutic.

Vb. *sculpt*, sculpture, cut, carve, scrimshaw; chisel, chip; figure, model, mould, cast; sculpsit.

555. Engraving – N. *engraving*, etching, line engraving, plate e., chalcography; zincography, cerography, glyptography, gem-cutting; mezzotint, aquatint; woodcut; drypoint; steel plate, copper p., graphotype; chisel, graver, burin, bur,

bur-chisel, needle, dry-point, etching-p., style.

printing, type-p. 587 n. *print*; plate printing, lithography, photolithography, photogravure, chromolithography, colour-printing; stereotype; die, punch, stamp.

Vb. *engrave*, grave, incise, cut; etch, stipple, scrape; bite, bite in; impress, stamp; lithograph 587 vb. *print*; mezzotint, aquatint; incisit, sculpsit, imprimit.

556. Artist – N. *artist*, craftsman 686 n. *artisan*; art-master, designer, draughtsman; dress-designer, couturier; drawer, sketcher, delineator, limner; copyist; caricaturist, cartoonist; illustrator, commercial artist; painter, colourist; dauber, pavement artist, scene-painter, sign-p.; oil-painter, aquarellist, pastellist; illuminator, miniaturist; Academician, R.A., old master, modern m.

sculptor, carver, statuary, monumental mason, modeller, moulder, figurist; image-maker, idol-m.

engraver, etcher, aquatinter; lapidary, chaser, gem-engraver, enameller, typographer, type-cutter 587 n. *printer*.

557. Language – N. *language*, tongue, speech, idiom; patter, lingo 560 n. *dialect*; mother tongue; vernacular, common speech; correct speech, Queen's English; lingua franca, Koine, pidgin, pidgin English, Chinook; sign language, semeiology 547 n. *gesticulation*; artificial language, Esperanto, Ido, Volapuk; private language, idioglossia; officialese, translationese; confusion of tongues, polyglot, medley, Babel 61 n. *confusion*.

linguistics, language study, glottology, dialectology, philology; phonetics 577 n. *pronunciation*; derivation 559 n. *etymology*; morphology; semasiology, semantics 514 n. *meaning*; onomasiology 561 n. *nomenclature*; palaeography 125 n. *palaetiology*; linguistic geography, word-g.; polyglottism, bilingualism; literature 589 n. *reading matter*.

linguist, philologist, glottologist; etymologist, lexicographer 559 n. *etymo-*

logy; semasiologist, onomasiologist; grammarian 564 n. *grammar*; phonetician 398 n. *acoustics*; man of letters, belletrist 492 n. *scholar*; humanist, Hellenist, Latinist; polyglot, bilinguist.

Adj. *linguistic*, philological, etymological, grammatical, morphological; lexicographical, onomasiological, semasiological; analytic; agglutinative; monosyllabic; tonal, inflected; holophrastic; written, literary, standard; spoken, living, idiomatic; vernacular, slangy 560 adj. *dialectical*; current, common, demotic; bilingual, diglot; multilingual, polyglot.

558. Letter – N. *letter*, part of the alphabet; sign, character 586 n. *script*; alphabet, ABC, abecedary; syllabary; Chinese character, ideogram, ideograph; pictogram, hieroglyphic; cuneiform, arrowhead; ogham alphabet, runic a., futhorc; runic letter, wen; lettering, black letter, Gothic, italic; big letter, capital l., cap, majuscule; small letter, minuscule; block letter, uncial; letterpress 587 n. *print-type*; spelling, orthography; lexigraphy.

initials, first letter; monogram, cipher; anagram, acrostic.

Adj. *literal*, in letters, lettered; alphabetical, abecedarian; syllabic; Cyrillic; runic, oghamic; cuneiform, hieroglyphic 586 adj. *written*; Gothic, italic, roman, uncial; large, majuscule, capital, initial; small, minuscule; lexigraphical, spelt, orthographic; ciphered, monogrammatic.

Vb. *spell*, spell out, read, syllable; alphabetize; letter, form letters, uncialize 586 vb. *write*; initial 547 vb. *sign*; cipher, make a monogram; anagrammatize.

559. Word – N. *word*, expression, locution 563 n. *phrase*; term, vocable 561 n. *name*; phoneme, syllable 398 n. *speech sound*; semanteme 514 n. *meaning*; isogloss, synonym, homonym, homophene; homophone, pun 518 n. *equivocalness*; antonym 14 n. *contrariety*; etymon, root, back-formation; derivation, derivative, paronym, doublet; morpheme, stem, inflexion, affix, suffix, prefix, infix; part of speech 564 n. *grammar*; diminutive, pejorative, intensive; cliché, vogueword; nonce-word 560 n. *neology*; bad word, swear-word 899 n. *malediction*; jawbreaker, polysyllable; monosyllable; many words 570 n. *pleonasm*.

dictionary, rhyming d., polyglot d.; lexicon, wordbook, wordstock, wordlist, glossary, vocabulary; thesaurus, gradus; compilation, concordance.

etymology, derivation of words, philology 557 n. *linguistics*; morphology; semasiology 514 n. *meaning*; phonology, orthoepy 577 n. *pronunciation*; onomasiology, terminology 561 n. *nomenclature*; lexicology, lexicography; philologist, etymologist, lexicographer, compiler, dictionarian.

Adj. *verbal*, literal; titular, nominal; morphological, etymological, lexical, vocabular; philological, lexicographical, lexigraphical.

560. Neology – N. *neology*, neologism, neoterism 126 n. *newness*; coinage, new c., new word, nonce-w., loan-w., voguew., cliché; jargon, technical term, term of art; barbarism, hybrid, corruption; novelese, journalese, officialese, newspeak; archaism, Lallans 850 n. *affectation*; abuse of language, malapropism 565 n. *solecism*; word-play, spoonerism 839 n. *witticism*; paraphrasia 580 n. *speech defect*.

dialect, idiom, lingo, patois , brogue, vernacular 557 n. *language*; cockney, Doric, Lallans; broken English, pidgin E., pidgin, Chinook; Koine, lingua franca; Anglicism, Americanism, Scoticism, Hibernicism, Gallicism, Teutonism, Sinicism; chi-chik babuism; neologist, word-coiner; dialectology 557 n. *linguistics*.

slang, vulgarism, colloquialism; jargon, argot, cant, patter; gipsy lingo, Romany; flash tongue, thieves' Latin, pedlar's French, St Giles Greek, rhyming slang; Billingsgate; gibberish 515 n. *empty talk*.

Adj. *neological*, newfangled, newly coined, not in the dictionary; barbarous, unidiomatic, hybrid, corrupt, pidgin; archaic, obsolete; irregular, solecistic 565 adj. *ungrammatical*.

dialectical, vernacular, kailyard; Doric, Cockney, broad; provincial, local; homely, colloquial; unliterary, slangy, argotic, canting, cant; jargonistic, journalistic; technical, special.

Vb. *neologize*, coin words, invent vocabulary; talk slang, jargonize, cant.

561. Nomenclature – N. *nomenclature*, naming etc. vb.; eponymy; onomatology, terminology, orismology; description, designation, appellation, denomination; addressing, apostrophe, roll-call 583 n. *allocution*; christening; study of placenames, toponymy.

name, nomen, first name, fore-n., Christian n., prenomen; surname, patronymic, matronymic, cognomen; appellation, moniker; nickname, pet name, by-name, agnomen, kenning; epithet, description; title, handle, style; designation, appellative; name and address 547 n. *label*; term, technical t., term of art; name-child, namesake; synonym, eponym, counter-term, antonym; pseudonym 562 n. *misnomer*; noun 564 n. *part of speech*; list of names, onomasticon.

nomenclator, roll-caller, announcer, toastmaster; onomatologist; terminologist; namer, namegiver, eponym.

Adj. *named*, called etc. vb.; titled, entitled, christened; known as, alias; so-called, soi-disant; nominal, titular; named after, eponymous, theophoric; nameable.

naming, nuncupative, nuncupatory 532 adj. *affirmative*; appellative, compellative, terminological, orismological.

Vb. *name*, call, give a name, christen; give one's name to, eponymize; surname, nickname, dub; give one his title, sir, bemadam; title, entitle, style, term 80 vb. *specify*; nomenclate, announce.

562. Misnomer – N. *misnomer*, misnaming; malapropism 565 n. *solecism*; alias, assumed title; nom de guerre, nom de plume, pen-name; nom de théâtre, stage name; pseudonym, allonym; nickname, pet name 561 n. *name*; pseudonymity.

no name, anonymity; anonym, certain person, so-and-so, N or M, sir or madam; Mr X, A. N. Other; what d'ye call 'em, thingummy bob; this or that; and co.; some, any, what-have-you.

Adj. *misnamed*, self-styled, soi-disant, would-be, so-called, quasi, pseudonymous.

anonymous, unknown, nameless, without a name; incognito, innominate, unnamed, unsigned.

Vb. *misname*, miscall, misterm, mistitle; nickname, dub 561 vb. *name*; misname oneself, assume an alias.

563. Phrase – **N.** *phrase*, form of words; clause, sentence, period, paragraph; expression, locution; idiom, mannerism 80 n. *speciality*; formula, set terms; well-worn phrase, cliché, commonplace; saying 496 n. *maxim*; lapidary phrase, epitaph 364 n. *obsequies*; inscription, legend, caption 548 n. *record*; terminology 561 n. *nomenclature*; phraseology 566 n. *style*; paraphrase 520 n. *translation*.

Adj. *phraseological*, sentential, periodic, in phrases, in sentences.

Vb. *phrase*, word, articulate, syllable; reword, rephrase 520 vb. *translate*; express, put in words, find words for, formulate, state 532 vb. *affirm*; turn a sentence, round a period.

564. Grammar – **N.** *grammar*, comparative g., philology 557 n. *linguistics*; grammarianism, grammatical studies, analysis, parsing, construing; praxis, paradigm; accidence, declension; conjugation, mode, voice, tense; number, gender, accentuation, pointing 547 n. *punctuation*; syntax, word order, parataxis; bad grammar 565 n. *solecism*; good grammar, jus et norma loquendi.

part of speech, substantive, noun; adjective; adnoun; verb; adverb, pre-

position, postposition, copula, conjunction; particle, augment; augmentative, affix, suffix, postfix, infix; inflexion, case-ending; formative, morpheme, semanteme; denominative, deverbative; diminutive, intensive.

Adj. *grammatical*, correct; syntactical; inflexional; heteroclite, asymptote; substantival, adjectival, adnominal; verbal, adverbial; participial; prepositional; denominative, deverbal; conjunctive, copulative; elative, comparative, superlative.

Vb. *parse*, analyse, inflect, punctuate, conjugate, decline; construe 520 vb. *interpret*; know one's grammar.

565. Solecism – **N.** *solecism*, bad grammar; missaying, antiphrasis; misapplication, catachresis; barbarism 560 n. *neology*; malapropism, cacology, bull; slip of the tongue 495 n. *mistake*; mispronunciation 580 n. *speech defect*; misspelling, cacography.

Adj. *ungrammatical*, solecistic, solecistical.

Vb. *solecize*, ignore grammar, violate g.; murder the Queen's English; mispronounce 580 vb. *stammer*; misspell 495 vb. *blunder*.

566. Style – **N.** *style*, fashion, mode, tone, manner, vein, strain 688 n. *conduct*; idiosyncrasy, mannerism, trick 80 n. *speciality*; diction, parlance, phrasing, phraseology 563 n. *phrase*; choice of words, vocabulary, command of language, raciness, power 571 n. *vigour*; feeling for words, sprachgefühl; grace 575 n. *elegance*; word magic 579 n. *oratory*; weak style 572 n. *feebleness*; severe style 573 n. *plainness*; elaborate style 574 n. *ornament*; clumsy style 576 n. *inelegance*.

Adj. *stylistic*, literary.

567. Perspicuity – **N.** *perspicuity*, perspicuousness, clearness, clarity, lucidity, limpidity 422 n. *transparency*, *intelligibility*; directness 573 n. *plainness*; definition, exactness 494 n. *accuracy*.

Adj. *perspicuous*, lucid, limpid 422 adj. *transparent*; clean, unambiguous 516 adj. *intelligible*; explicit, clear-cut, exact 494 adj. *accurate*; uninvolved, direct 573 adj. *plain*.

568. Imperspicuity – N. *imperspicuity*, imperspicuousness, obscurity 517 n. *unintelligibility*, 423 n. *opacity*; abstruseness; complexity, involved style; hard words, Johnsonese, Carlylese 700 n. *difficulty*; imprecision, vagueness 474 n. *uncertainty*; ambiguity 518 n. *equivocalness*; oracular style 530 n. *enigma*; profundity 211 n. *depth*; over-compression 569 n. *conciseness*.

Adj. *imperspicuous*, unclear, cloudy 423 adj. *opaque*; obscure, oracular, mysterious, enigmatic 517 adj. *unintelligible*; abstruse, profound 211 adj. *deep*; allusive, indirect 523 adj. *latent*; vague, imprecise, indefinite 474 adj. *uncertain*; ambiguous 518 adj. *equivocal*; confused, tangled, involved 61 adj. *complex*; crabbed 576 adj. *inelegant*; hard 700 adj. *difficult*.

569. Conciseness – N. *conciseness*, concision, succinctness, brevity; pithiness, aphorism, epigram, witticism; verbal economy, terseness, compression, telegraphese; ellipsis, abbreviation, contraction 204 n. *shortening*; compendiousness 592 n. *compendium*; compactness, portmanteau word; monosyllabism 582 n. *taciturnity*.

Adj. *concise*, brief, not long in telling, short and sweet 204 adj. *short*; laconic, monosyllabic 582 adj. *taciturn*; irreducible, succinct; curt, brusque 885 adj. *ungracious*; compendious, compact; pithy, pregnant, sententious, pointed, aphoristic, epigrammatic, Tacitean; elliptic, telegraphic, summary.

Vb. *be concise*, put in a nutshell, come to the point, cut a long story short; telescope, compress, condense, contract, abridge 204 vb. *shorten*; summarize 592 vb. *abstract*; laconize, waste no words 582 vb. *be taciturn*; epigrammatize 839 vb. *be witty*.

570. Diffuseness – N. *diffuseness* etc. adj.; profuseness, copiousness, amplitude; amplification 197 n. *expansion*; expatiation, circumstantiality, minuteness; fertility, output, penny-a-lining, word-spinning 171 n. *productiveness*; vein, flow, outpouring; exuberance 637 n. *redundance*; rich vocabulary, wealth of terms; verbosity, wordiness, verbiage, flatulence, vapouring, cloud of words; fluency, gush 581 n. *loquacity*; long-windedness, prolixity, length; repetitiveness, reiteration 106 n. *repetition*; tirade, harangue, speeches 579 n. *oration*.

pleonasm, superfluity, redundancy 637 n. *redundance*; circumlocution, periphrasis; padding, expletive, verse-filler 40 n. *extra*; episode, digression 10 n. *irrelevance*.

Adj. *diffuse*, verbose, non-stop 581 adj. *loquacious*; profuse, copious 171 adj. *prolific*; inspired, in the vein, fluent; overflowing 637 adj. *redundant*; circumstantial, detailed, minute; flatulent, windy; polysyllabic, sesquipedalian, magniloquent 574 adj. *ornate*.

prolix, of many words, long-winded, wordy, prosy; longsome, boring 838 adj. *tedious*; lengthy, epic, never-ending 203 adj. *long*; diffusive, discursive, digressing, episodic; repetitious, pleonastic, circumlocutory, periphrastic, roundabout.

Vb. *be diffuse*, dilate, expatiate, amplify, particularize, detail, expand, enlarge upon; descant, discourse at length; repeat 106 vb. *repeat oneself*; pad out 203 vb. *lengthen*; gush, pour out 350 vb. *flow*; launch out, let oneself go, rant, harangue, perorate 579 vb. *orate*; wander, digress 282 vb. *deviate*; ramble, maunder, drivel, never end.

571. Vigour – N. *vigour* 174 n. *vigorousness*; power, drive, force, forcefulness 160 n. *energy*; incisiveness, trenchancy, punch; sparkle, verve, vivacity, vividness, raciness; spirit, fire, ardour, glow, warmth, vehemence, enthusiasm, passion 818 n. *feeling*; bite, piquancy, mordancy 388 n. *pungency*; strong language, emphasis 532 n. *affirmation*; gravity,

weight; impressiveness, grandiloquence
574 n. *magniloquence.*

Adj. *forceful*, powerful, nervous 162
adj. *strong*; energetic 174 adj. *vigorous*;
racy, idiomatic; bold, spirited, vivacious
819 adj. *lively*; fiery, impassioned 818
adj. *fervent*; vehement, emphatic, insistent 532 adj. *affirmative*; incisive, trenchant 256 adj. *sharp*; pungent, mordant,
salty 839 adj. *witty*; grave, strongly-
worded 834 adj. *serious*; crushing; vivid,
graphic, effective 551 adj. *representing*;
inspired 579 adj. *eloquent*; high-toned,
sublime 821 adj. *impressive.*

572. Feebleness – N. *feebleness* 163 n.
weakness; prosiness, frigidity etc. see
adj.; poverty, thinness; anticlimax.

Adj. *feeble*, weak, thin, flat, vapid,
insipid 387 adj. *tasteless*; wishy-washy,
watery; sloppy, sentimental; jejune, exhausted; colourless, bald 573 adj. *plain*;
languid, flaccid, nerveless, tame; un-
dramatic, uninspired, unimpassioned;
ineffective, frigid, uninspiring; prosy,
dry 838 adj. *tedious*; cliché-ridden, stale;
pretentious, flatulent; forced, forcible-
feeble; slipshod, limping; bad, poor,
trashy 847 adj. *vulgar.*

573. Plainness – N. *plainness*, naturalness, simplicity 699 n. *artlessness*; austerity, severity, baldness; matter-of-
factness 593 n. *prose*; plain *or* basic
English 516 n. *intelligibility*; vernacular,
common speech, vulgar parlance;
idiom, natural i.; frankness, coarseness,
four-letter word, Anglo-Saxon monosyllable.

Adj. *plain*, simple 699 adj. *artless*;
austere, severe, disciplined; bald, stark,
bare; unadorned, uncoloured; undra-
matic, unsensational; unpretentious 874
adj. *modest*; chaste 950 adj. *pure*; unaffected, natural, idiomatic; basic, homely, homespun, vernacular; sober 834 adj.
serious; humdrum, commonplace, unpoetical 593 adj. *prosaic.*

574. Ornament – N. *ornament*, embellishment, colour, embroidery, frills 844

n. *ornamentation*; floridness, flowers of
speech 563 n. *phrase*; prose run mad,
Gongorism, cultism; euphuism, preciosity, rhetoric, flourish, purple patch;
figure of speech 519 n. *trope*; metaphor,
simile, antithesis.

magniloquence, high tone 579 n. *eloquence*; grandiloquence, declamation,
orotundity 571 n. *vigour*; turgidity,
flatulence, inflation, swollen diction;
pomposity 875 n. *ostentation*; highfalutin, bombast, rant, fustian, rodomontade 515 n. *empty talk*; Johnsonese, long
words 559 n. *word.*

Adj. *ornate*, beautified 844 adj. *ornamented*; rich, florid; precious, gon-
goresque, euphuistic, euphemistic;
meretricious, flashy 875 adj. *showy*;
sonorous, clanging 400 adj. *loud*; tropical, alliterative, antithetical 519 adj.
figurative; overloaded, stiff, stilted; sesquipedalian, Johnsonian.

rhetorical, declamatory, oratorical 579
adj. *eloquent*; loud; mouthy, orotund;
high-pitched, high-flown, highfalutin;
grandiose, stately; bombastic, pompous,
fustian; grandiloquent, magniloquent;
inflated, turgid; antithetical, alliterative,
metaphorical, tropical 519 adj. *figurative.*

575. Elegance – N. *elegance*, style, perfect s.; grace 841 n. *beauty*; refinement,
taste 846 n. *good taste*; propriety, restraint, distinction, dignity; clarity 567 n.
perspicuity; Attic quality, purity, simplicity; idiom 573 n. *plainness*; harmony,
concinnity; ease, flow, fluency, readiness,
felicity; neatness, polish, finish; elaboration, artificiality.

stylist, classic, Atticist, purist; phrasemonger, word-spinner; rhetorician,
orator 579 n. *speaker.*

Adj. *elegant*, graceful; stylish, polite
846 adj. *tasteful*; distinguished, dignified; chaste 950 adj. *pure*; good, correct, idiomatic, sensitive; expressive,
clear 567 adj. *perspicuous*; simple,
natural, unaffected 573 adj. *plain*; un-
laboured, easy, smooth, fluent, tripping;
rhythmic, mellifluous, harmonious; neat,
felicitous, happy, right; artistic,

wrought, elaborate, artificial; soigné, manicured, chic; restrained, controlled; flawless, classic.

576. Inelegance – N. *inelegance*, inconcinnity; clumsiness, uncouthness 699 n. *artlessness*; coarseness 647 n. *imperfection*; harshness 411 n. *discord*; stiffness, stiltedness; impropriety, barbarism; incorrectness 565 n. *solecism*; vulgarity 847 n. *bad taste*; mannerism 850 n. *affectation*; unrestraint, excess 637 n. *superfluity*.

Adj. *inelegant*, ungraceful 842 adj. *ugly*; faulty, incorrect, unclassical; unpolished 647 adj. *imperfect*; coarse, crude, rude, doggerel, uncouth, barbarous 699 adj. *artless*; tasteless 847 adj. *vulgar*; meretricious; unrestrained, turgid, pompous 574 adj. *rhetorical*; forced, laboured, mannered 850 adj. *affected*; grotesque 849 adj. *ridiculous*; jarring, grating 861 adj. *disliked*; heavy, ponderous, crabbed, cramped, unfluent, clumsy; stiff, stilted 875 adj. *formal*.

577. Voice – N. *voice*, 398 n. *sound*, 579 n. *speech*; vociferation 400 n. *loudness*; tongue, vocal organs, vocal chords, lungs, bellows; larynx; vocalization, vocable, phoneme, vowel 398 n. *speech sound*; voice production, articulation, distinctness; utterance, enunciation, delivery, attack; articulate sound 408 n. *cry*; exclamation, ejaculation, gasp; mutter, whisper; tone of voice, accents, timbre, pitch, tone, intonation; ventriloquism, gastriloquism.

pronunciation, articulation, elocution, enunciation, inflexion, accentuation, stress, emphasis; accent, burr, brogue, trill, roll; mispronunciation 565 n. *solecism*, 580 n. *speech defect*.

Adj. *vocal*, voiced, oral, aloud, out loud; vocalic, sonant; phonetic, enunciative; articulate, distinct, clear; spoken, dictated, read out; accented, tonal, accentual; open, broad-vowelled, closed, close-vowelled.

Vb. *voice*, pronounce, syllable 579 vb. *speak*; mouth, give tongue, express,

utter, enunciate, articulate; labialize, palatalize, vocalize; aspirate, sound one's aitches; trill, roll, burr; stress, accent 532 n. *emphasize*; whisper, stage-w.; exclaim, ejaculate; warble 413 vb. *sing*; shout 408 vb. *vociferate*; mispronounce 580 vb. *stammer*.

578. Aphony – N. *aphony*, voicelessness, no voice, loss of v.; difficulty in speaking, disphonia, inarticulation; thick speech, hoarseness, huskiness; dumbness, mutism; changing voice, cracked v.; undertone, bated breath 401 n. *faintness*; surd, unvoiced consonant; mute, deaf-m., dummy; sign language, deaf and dumb l. 547 n. *gesticulation*.

Adj. *voiceless*, aphonic, dysphonic; unvoiced, surd; mute, dumb; breathless, speechless, wordless; inarticulate, unvocal, tongue-tied; mum 582 adj. *taciturn*; croaking 407 adj. *hoarse*.

Vb. *make mute*, strike dumb, dumbfound, take one's breath away; stick in one's throat, choke one's utterance; muffle, hush, deaden 401 vb. *mute*; shout down, drown one's voice; muzzle, gag, stifle 165 vb. *suppress*; shut one up, cut one short, hang up on; still, hush 399 vb. *silence*.

579. Speech – N. *speech*, faculty of s., organ of s., tongue, lips 557 n. *language*; oral communication, word of mouth 524 n. *report*; spoken word, accents, tones 577 n. *voice*, 559 n. *word*; verbal intercourse, conversation 584 n. *interlocution*; apostrophe 583 n. *allocation*; talkativeness, volubility 581 n. *loquacity*; mode of speech, articulation, utterance, delivery, enunciation 577 n. *pronunciation*; sign language, eye l. 547 n. *gesticulation*; thing said, say, speech, dictum, utterance, remark, observation, comment, interjection 532 n. *affirmation*.

oration, speech, effusion, one's say; discourse, address, talk; valedictory, farewell address, funeral oration 364 n. *obsequies*; broadcast, travelogue 534 n. *lecture*; recitation, recital, reading; set speech, declamation, oratorical display (see *eloquence*); pulpit eloquence, pulpitry, sermon, preachment, homily, exhortation; harangue, tub-thumping, earful, mouthful; tirade, diatribe, philippic, invective; monologue 585 n. *soliloquy*; paper, screed 591 n. *dissertation*; proemium, prologue, narration, peroration.

oratory, art of speaking, rhetoric; public speaking, speech-making, speechifying, declamation, elocution, rant; vituperation, invective.

eloquence, facundity, eloquent tongue, oratorical gifts, gift of the gab, fluency; power of speech, grandiloquence, orotundity 574 n. *magniloquence*; elocution, good delivery, burst of eloquence, storm of words, peroration, purple patch.

speaker, sayer, utterer, talker 581 n. *chatterer*; conversationalist, colloquist 584 n. *interlocutor*; speech-maker, speech-writer, rhetor, rhetorician, elocutionist; orator, public speaker, after-dinner s.; improviser, ad-libber; declaimer, ranter, platform orator, stump o., mob o., tub-thumper; word-spinner, spellbinder; lecturer, broadcaster; pulpiteer, cushion thumper 534 n. *preacher*; spokesman, mouthpiece 754 n. *delegate*; gabber, patterer, salesman 793 n. *seller*; monologuist 585 n. *soliloquist*.

Adj. *speaking*, able to speak, fluent, outspoken, free-speaking, talkative 581 adj. *loquacious*; oral 577 adj. *vocal*; audible, spoken, aloud.

eloquent, spellbinding, silver-tongued; elocutionary, oratorical 574 adj. *rhetorical*; grandiloquent, declamatory.

Vb. *speak*, mention, say; utter, articulate, syllable 577 vb. *voice*; pronounce, declare 532 vb. *affirm*; whisper, breathe 524 vb. *hint*; confabulate, talk 584 vb. *converse*; break silence, open one's mouth *or* lips, pipe up, speak up; wag one's tongue 581 vb. *be loquacious*; expatiate 570 vb. *be diffuse*; recite, read, read out, dictate; speak with tongues, sling the bat; have tongue in one's head, speak for oneself.

orate, make speeches, speechify; declaim, take the floor, hold forth, spout; preach, sermonize, homilize, harangue;

lecture, discourse, address 534 vb. *teach*; invoke, apostrophize 583 vb. *speak to*; perorate, mouth, rant; speak like an angel, spellbind.

580. Speech defect – N. *speech defect*, aphasia 578 n. *aphony*; paraphasia, paralalia, aboiement; idioglossia, idiolalia; traulism, stammer, stutter, lambdacism, lallation, lisp; dysphony, impediment, drawl; indistinctness, thick speech, plum in one's mouth, cleft palate; burr, brogue 560 n. *dialect*; accent, twang.

Adj. *stammering*, stuttering etc. vb.; nasal, adenoidal; indistinct, thick, inarticulate; tongue-tied, aphasic; breathless 578 adj. *voiceless*.

Vb. *stammer*, stutter, drawl, quaver, hum and haw; mammer, mumble, mutter; lisp, lambdacize; nasalize, drone; swallow one's words, gabble; mispronounce 565 vb. *solecize*.

581. Loquacity – N. *loquacity*, loquaciousness, garrulity, talkativeness, conversableness, communicativeness; volubility 570 n. *diffuseness*; verbosity, wordiness, prolixity; multiloquence, spate of words, logorrhoea, inexhaustible vocabulary, gift of the gab.

chatter, chinwag, gabble, gab, jabber, palaver, much talk, talkee-talkee, clack, babble, prattle; small talk, gossip, tittle-tattle; gush, prate 515 n. *empty talk*.

chatterer, non-stop talker, rattle, chatterbox; gossip, tattler 529 n. *newsmonger*; talker, gabber; proser, windbag, gasser; conversationalist 584 n. *interlocutor*.

Adj. *loquacious*, talkative, garrulous; communicative, chatty, gossipy 524 adj. *informative*; prosing, verbose, long-winded 570 adj. *prolix*; non-stop, voluble, fluent, glib, effusive, gushing.

Vb. *be loquacious*, chatter, rattle, run on, reel off; gossip, tattle 584 vb. *converse*; clack, quack, gabble, jabber, patter 515 vb. *mean nothing*; talk, jaw, gab, prate, prose, gas, waffle, haver; drone, maunder, drivel; launch out, shoot, oil one's tongue; expatiate 570 vb. *be diffuse*; out-talk, talk down; talk out time, filibuster.

582. Taciturnity – N. *taciturnity*, silent habit 399 n. *silence*; incommunicativeness, reserve, reticence 525 n. *secrecy*; brusqueness, curtness 885 n. *rudeness*; wilful silence, obmutescence; laconism 569 n. *conciseness*; clam, oyster, statue.

Adj. *taciturn*, mute 399 adj. *silent*; saying little, monosyllabic, short, curt, laconic, brusque 569 adj. *concise*; not talking, mum; inconversable, incommunicative; reticent, close, tight-lipped; non-committal 858 adj. *cautious*; inarticulate, tongue-tied 578 adj. *voiceless*.

Vb. *be taciturn*, say nothing, make no answer; refuse comment, neither confirm nor deny; keep one's counsel 525 vb. *keep secret*; hold one's tongue, pipe down, dry up; lose one's tongue; waste no words on, save one's breath.

583. Allocution – N. *allocution*, alloquy, apostrophe; address, lecture 579 n. *oration*; greeting, salutation, hail; invocation, appeal, interjection, interpellation; buttonholing, word in the ear, aside.

Adj. *vocative*, salutatory, invocatory.

Vb. *speak to*, speak at; address, talk to, lecture to; turn to, apostrophize, invoke; sir, bemadam; hail, salute 884 vb. *greet*; parley with 584 vb. *converse*; take aside, buttonhole.

584. Interlocution – N. *interlocution*, parley, colloquy, converse, conversation, causerie; chat, chit-chat, talk 581 n. *chatter*; dialogue, question and answer; exchange, repartee; confabulation, communication, intercommunication 524 n. *information*; duologue, symposium, tête-à-tête.

conference, colloquy, conversations, talks, pourparler, parley, pow-wow, palaver; discussion, debate, symposium, seminar; controversy 475 n. *argument*; exchange of views, summitry; negotiations 765 n. *treaty*; conclave, convention 74 n. *assembly*; consultation, huddle, summit 691 n. *advice*; conference room 692 n. *council*; durbar, audience-chamber; auditorium 441 n. *onlookers*.

interlocutor, collocutor, symposiast; examiner, interviewer 459 n. *inquirer*; answerer 460 n. *respondent*; addressee; conversationalist, talker 581 n. *chatterer*.

Adj. *conversing*, confabulatory, collocutory, dialogistic; conversable, conversational; chatty, gossipy 581 adj. *loquacious*; communicative 524 adj. *informative*.

Vb. *converse*, parley, talk together (see *confer*); confabulate, collogue; lead one on, draw one out; buttonhole, enter into conversation, put in a word, chat, let one's hair down; gossip, tattle 581 vb. *be loquacious*; commune with, get confidential with; whisper together, get in a huddle.

confer, talk it over, put heads together; hold conclave, pow-wow, palaver; canvass, debate 475 vb. *argue*; parley, negotiate; advise with 691 vb. *consult*.

585. Soliloquy – N. *soliloquy*, monologue, monody; apostrophe; aside.

soliloquist, soliloquizer, monologist, monodist.

Vb. *soliloquize*, talk to oneself, say aside, think aloud; have oneself for audience.

586. Writing – N. *writing*, creative w., composition, literary activities, authorship, journalism, cacoethes scribendi 590 n. *description*; output, literary o., literature; writings, works 589 n. *reading matter*; ink-slinging, inkshed; quill-driving, paper-work 548 n. *record*; handwriting, stylography, cerography; micrography; longhand, logography; shorthand, speedwriting, phonography; contraction, phonogram, phraseogram, stenography, typewriting 587 n. *print*; embossed writing, braille; secret writing, steganography, cipher, code 530 n. *secret*; picture-writing, ideography; sign-writing, sky-writing 528 n. *advertisement*; graphology.

lettering, stroke, stroke of the pen, up-stroke, down-s., pothook, pothooks and hangers; flourish, curlicue, squiggle, scroll 251 n. *convolution*; handwriting, hand, fist; calligraphy, penmanship; fair hand, clerkly h.; script writing, print-w., beacon-w., italic; cacography, clumsy hand; scribble, scrawl, script, letters, characters, alphabet 558 n. *letter*.

script, written matter, inscribed page, illuminated address; writing, screed, scrawl, scribble; manuscript 589 n. *book*; one's own hand, autograph, holograph; signature 547 n. *label*; transcript, fair copy 22 n. *duplicate*; typescript, stencil; epistle 588 n. *correspondence*; inscription, epigraph, graffito 548 n. *record*; superscription, caption, heading; letters of fire, letters of gold.

stationery, writing materials, pen and paper, ink; stylus, reed, quill, pen, fountain p., ball-point p.; nib, stylo; pencil, slate-p., crayon, chalk; papyrus, parchment, vellum; newsprint; writing paper, note-p.; notebook, pad, block, tablet, table; slate, blackboard; inkpot, ink-horn, inkstand, inkwell; blotting paper, sand; ribbon, stencil; writing room, scriptorium.

penman, calligrapher; scribbler, scrawler; writer, pen-driver, quill-d.; scrivener, scribe, clerk 549 n. *recorder*; copyist, transcriber; creative writer 589 n. *author*; letter-writer 588 n. *correspondent*; graphologist, handwriting expert 484 n. *detector*.

Adj. *written*, inscriptional, epigraphic; in black and white 548 adj. *recorded*; handwritten, manuscript, autograph, holograph; fairly written, copybook, copperplate, clerkly, literate; Gothic, uncial, cursive, roman, italic.

Vb. *write*, scribe; form characters, character, engrave, inscribe; letter, block, print; flourish, scroll; scribble, scrawl; interline, overwrite; write down 548 vb. *record*; transcribe, copy out, engross; take dictation, stenotype, type out; throw on paper, draft; compose, indite; pen, pencil, dash off; write letters 588 vb. *correspond*; subscribe 547 vb.

sign; put pen to paper, spill ink, cover reams; write books 590 vb. *describe*, 591 vb. *dissert*.

587. Print – N. *print*, typography, printing from type, block printing, plate p., offset process, lithography, photolithography 555 n. *engraving*; photocopying, varitype; typesetting, composing, make-up, setting; monotype, linotype, stereotype, electrotype; plate, shell; presswork, make-ready, printing off, machining.

letterpress, lettering, linage, printed matter, print, impression, presswork; copy, pull, proof, revise; sheet, forme, quire, signature; caption, heading, colophon, imprint; offprint.

print-type, type, movable t., fixed t., stereotype, plate; type-mould, matrix; type-matter, setting, set type, standing t., pie, printer's p.; upper case, lower c.; fount, type-face, body f., bastard type, bold type; shoulder, shank, beard, ascender, descender, serif, sanserif; lead, rule; hair-space; type bar, slug; type size, point s.

press, printing works, press-works, printers; type-foundry; composing room; hand-press, flatbed, rotary press, linotype, monotype, offset press; quoin, frame, composing stick, case, galley.

printer, pressman; setter, type-s., compositor, printer's devil; typographer, type-cutter.

Vb. *print*, stamp; set, compose; align, justify; set up, make ready, impose, machine, run off, lithograph, litho, offset, stereotype.

588. Correspondence – N. *correspondence*, exchange of letters; communication 524 n. *information*; mailing list; mail, postbag 531 n. *mails*; letter, epistle, missive, dispatch, bulletin; love-letter, billet doux, Valentine 889 n. *endearment*; postcard; business letter, favour, enclosure; open letter 528 n. *publicity*; circular, chain letter; dispatch, rescript; note, line, chit; answer, acknowledgement; envelope, cover.

correspondent, letter-writer, pen-friend, poison pen; recipient, addressee; foreign correspondent, contributor; contact 524 n. *informant*.

Adj. *epistolary*, postal, by post; under cover of, enclosed.

Vb. *correspond*, exchange letters, keep in touch with 524 vb. *communicate*; use the post, write to, send a letter to, drop a line, acknowledge 460 vb. *answer*; circularize 528 vb. *publish*; post off, forward, mail; stamp, seal, frank, address.

589. Book – N. *book*, title, volume, tome, roll; codex, manuscript, MS., palimpsest; script, typescript, unpublished work; published work, publication, bestseller, potboiler; unsold book, remainder; work, magnum opus; opuscule, slim volume; chapbook, booklet; picture book 553 n. *picture*; magazine 528 n. *journal*; brochure, pamphlet 528 n. *the press*.

reading matter, printed word, written w. 586 n. *writing*; script, copy; text, the words, libretto, scenario; proof, revise, pull 587 n. *letterpress*; writings, literature, belles lettres 593 n. *prose*, 593 n. *poetry*; fiction, history, biography, travel 590 n. *description*, 590 n. *novel*, 590 n. *biography*; essay 591 n. *dissertation*; piece 591 n. *article*; miscellanea, marginalia, jottings, thoughts; selections 592 n. *anthology*; juvenilia; remains; complete works, corpus, omnibus volume; periodical 528 n. *journal*; issue, number, back n.; part, instalment, serial, sequel, continuation.

textbook, technical literature; school book, class book, desk b., copybook; abecedary, hornbook; primer, grammar, gradus; text, reader; chrestomathy, delectus 592 n. *anthology*; handbook, manual.

reference book, work of reference, encyclopedia, cyclopedia 490 n. *erudition*; lexicon 559 n. *dictionary*; gazetteer, directory; guide 524 n. *guide-book*; notebook, diary, album 505 n. *reminder*; bibliography, publisher's catalogue, reading list.

edition, series, set, collection, library; incunabula, old edition, first e.; reissue, reprint; adaptation, abridgement 592 n. *compendium*; duodecimo, sextodecimo, octodecimo, octavo, quarto, folio; hardback, paperback; book production, layout.

library, bibliotheca, book-collection, series; national library, public l., travelling l., lending l., circulating l., book club; bookshop, book store, booksellers.

bookman, man of letters, littérateur, literary gent; reader, bookworm 492 n. *scholar*; bibliophile, book-collector, bibliomaniac; bibliographer; librarianship, librarian; bibliopole, stationer, bookseller; publisher, book-p.; editor, redactor; reviewer.

author, writer, creative w.; literary man, man of letters; belletrist, fiction-writer, novelist, historian, biographer 590 n. *narrator*; essayist, editorialist 591 n. *dissertator*; verse-writer 593 n. *poet*; playwright, librettist 594 n. *dramatist*; freelance; journalist, pressman, reporter, reporterette, sob-sister 529 n. *news-monger*; editor, contributor, correspondent, columnist, gossip-writer, diarist; scribbler, penpusher, hack, penny-a-liner; ghost, ghost-writer.

590. Description – N. *description*, account, statement, exposé, summary 524 n. *report*, 592 n. *compendium*; narration (see *narrative*); specification, characterization; portrayal; delineation, depiction; profile, prosopography 551 n. *representation*; case history 548 n. *record*; evocation, word-painting, picture, realism, Zolaism; travelogue 524 n. *guide-book*; vignette, thumbnail sketch; obituary, epitaph 364 n. *obsequies*.

narrative, argument, plot, sub-plot, scenario; historiography, history, annals, chronicle 548 n. *record*; account; story, tale, fabliau, tradition, legend, legendary, mythology, myth, saga, epic; allegory, parable; fairy-tale, fiction, yarn 543 n. *fable*; reminiscence 505 n. *remembrance*.

biography, real-life story, human

interest; life, curriculum vitae; experiences, adventures, fortunes; hagiography, martyrology; obituary; rogue's gallery, Newgate calendar; personal account, autobiography, confessions, memoirs, memorabilia 505 n. *remembrance*; letters, diary, journals 548 n. *record*.

novel, fiction, tale; novelette, short story; romance, love-story, fairy-s., Western, science fiction; 'tecker, whodunnit; thriller, shocker, penny dreadful, dime novel, horror comic.

narrator, describer, delineator; reporter, relater; raconteur, anecdotist; yarner, story-teller, fabler, fabulist, mythologist; fiction writer 589 n. *author*; romancer, novelist; biographer; aretologist, hagiographer, martyrologist, autobiographer, memoir-writer, diarist; historian 549 n. *recorder*.

Adj. *descriptive*, descriptional, graphic, vivid, representational, well-drawn, sharp 551 adj. *representing*; true to nature, natural, realistic, real-life, photographic, convincing; picturesque 821 adj. *impressive*; impressionistic, suggestive; full, detailed, circumstantial, particular 570 adj. *diffuse*; storied, traditional, legendary, mythological; epic, heroic, romantic; picaresque; narrative, historical, biographical, autobiographical; factual, documentary 494 adj. *accurate*; fictional, imaginative 513 adj. *imaginary*.

Vb. *describe*, delineate, draw, picture, depict, paint 551 vb. *represent*; evoke, bring to life, make one see; characterize, particularize, detail, enter into 80 vb. *specify*; sketch, adumbrate 233 vb. *outline*; relate, recount, rehearse, recite, report 524 vb. *communicate*; write about 548 vb. *record*; narrate, tell, yarn, spin a y.; have a plot, make a story out of; fictionalize, romance, fable 513 vb. *imagine*.

591. Dissertation – N. *dissertation*, treatise, tract, tractate; exposition, aperçu; thesis 475 n. *argument*; disquisition, essay, examination, survey 459 n. *in-quiry*; discourse, discussion; excursus, memoir, paper, monograph, study, prolegomena; screed, harangue, homily, sermon 534 n. *lecture*; commentary.

article, leading article, leader, editorial; essay, causerie; comment, commentary, review, notice, critique, criticism, write-up.

dissertator, essayist, expositor, tractarian; pamphleteer, publicist 528 n. *publicizer*; editor, leader-writer, editorialist; writer, belletrist, contributor 589 n. *author*; reviewer, critic, commentator 520 n. *interpreter*.

Adj. *discursive*, discursory, disquisitional 475 adj. *arguing*; expository, critical 520 adj. *interpretive*.

Vb. *dissert*, treat, handle, write about, deal with; descant, dissertate, discourse upon 475 vb. *argue*; go into, inquire into, survey; set out, discuss, canvass, ventilate; notice, criticize, comment upon, write up, write down; annotate, commentate 520 vb. *interpret*.

592. Compendium – N. *compendium*, epitome, résumé, summary, brief, essentials; headline; contents, heads, analysis; abstract, sum and substance, docket; consolidation, digest; breviary, textbook; multum in parvo, précis; aperçu, conspectus, synopsis; sketch, thumbnail s., outline, skeleton; syllabus, prospectus; abridgement 204 n. *shortening*; compression 569 n. *conciseness*.

anthology, treasury, flowers, beauties, best pieces; selections, delectus, chrestomathy; collectanea, miscellany; excerpts, gleanings, chapters, leaves, pages, scrapbook; anthologist.

epitomizer, abbreviator, cutter; abstractor, summarizer, potter, préciswriter.

Adj. *compendious*, pithy 569 adj. *concise*; analytical, synoptic.

Vb. *abstract*, sum up, resume, summarize, epitomize, reduce, abbreviate, abridge 204 vb. *shorten*; condense, pot 569 vb. *be concise*; collect 74 vb. *bring together*; excerpt, glean, select, anthologize; diagrammatize 233 vb. *outline*.

593. Poetry. Prose – N. *poetry*, poesy, balladry, minstrelsy, song; versification (see *prosody*); poetic art, poetics; verse, rhyme, numbers; Muses, tuneful Nine.

poem, poetic composition; versification, lines, verses, stanzas, strains; narrative verse, epic; lyric drama, verseplay; lyric verse, melic v., gnomic v.; ode, epode, palinode; dithyramb; dirge, elegy; idyll, eclogue; prothalamium, epithalamium; song, lays 412 n. *vocal music*; drinking song, anacreontic; collected poems, divan.

doggerel, lame verse, balladry; jingle, runes, nursery rhyme; cento, macaronics; satire, limerick.

verse form, sonnet, sestet; ballade, rondeau, virelay, triolet; burden, refrain, envoi; couplet, distich; triplet, terza rima, quatrain; ottava rima, Spenserian stanza; hendecasyllables; blank verse, free v., vers libre; verse, versicle, stanza, stave, laisse, strophe, antistrophe; canto, fit; stichomythia; half line, hemistich. See *prosody*.

prosody, versification, metrics, metre, measure, numbers, scansion; rhyme, assonance, alliteration; rhythm, sprung r.; prose rhythm; metrical unit, foot; arsis, thesis, ictus, beat, stress, accent.

poet, poet laureate, versemonger, poetaster; prosodist, versifier, metrist; rhymer, rhymester, jingler, bard, minstrel, skald, troubadour, minnesinger, meistersinger; lyrist, dithyrambist, elegist, sonneteer, ballad-monger; songwriter, librettist; reciter, rhapsode, jongleur.

prose, not verse, prose rhythm; prosaicism, prosiness, prose-writing; prosaist, prose-writer 589 n. *author*.

Adj. *poetic*, poetical, bardic; songful, tuneful; Castalian, Pierian; heroic, Homeric, Dantesque, Miltonic; mock-heroic, satiric; elegiac, lyrical, dithyrambic, rhapsodic; lyric, bucolic; doggerel, macaronic; prosodic, metrical; scanning, scanned; in verse, stanzaic.

prosaic, unpoetical, unversified; prosy 570 adj. *diffuse*; in prose, pedestrian.

Vb. *poetize*, sing, tune one's lyre; metrify, prosodize, scan; rhyme, jingle; versify, elegize, sonneteer; berhyme; lampoon, satirize.

594. Drama – N. *drama*, traffic of the stage; the theatre, the stage, the scene, the boards, the footlights; theatre world, stage w., theatreland; show business, dramatic entertainment; straight drama, legitimate theatre; stock, summer s., repertory, rep; theatricals; masque, charade, tableau 551 n. *representation*.

dramaturgy, dramatization, theatricals, dramatics; melodramatics, histrionics; theatricality, staginess; playwriting, stage-craft; action, movement, plot; characterization 551 n. *representation*; production, casting; rehearsal; direction, stage-management, showmanship; staging, stage directions; gagging, business; enactment, performance, première.

stage play, play, work; piece, show; libretto, scenario, script, text, playbook, prompt book; masque, mystery, miracle play; drama 551 n. *representation*; curtain-raiser, interlude, divertissement, afterpiece, postlude; monodrama; melodrama; tragedy, comedy, tragicomedy; low comedy, farce, slapstick 849 n. *ridiculousness*; pantomime, harlequinade; musical, light opera, grand opera; photoplay, screen-play, Western, horse-opera 445 n. *cinema*; radio drama, soap opera; ballet, dumb-show, mime; puppetry, puppet-show, marionettes.

stage show, 445 n. *spectacle*; variety, music hall, vaudeville, revue; Follies, leg-show, flesh-s.; floor-show, cabaret; song and dance, act, turn; star turn; transformation scene, set piece, tableau.

stage set, stagery, set, setting, décor, mise-en-scène, scenery, scene 445 n. *spectacle*; drop-scene, drop, back-cloth, side-scene, scrim; screen, tormentor, wings, flat; upstage, downstage, backstage; curtain, act-drop; properties, props; make-up, grease-paint.

theatre, amphitheatre, stadium 724 n. *arena*; cinema, passion pit, picture palace 445 n. *cinema*; showboat; theatre-house, playhouse, opera house, music hall, cabaret; stage, boards, proscenium, wings, coulisses, flies; dressing room, green r.; footlights, floats, battens, spotlight, limelight; auditorium, orchestra; pit, circle; gallery, balcony, gods; foyer; box-office, stage-door.

acting, personification, mimesis 551 n. *representation*; pantomime, miming 20 n. *mimicry*; histrionics, play-acting, overacting, staginess, theatricality; character, role, lead; part, fat p.; stage fright.

actor, play-a., actress; mimic, mime 20 n. *imitator*; mummer, guisard; player, trouper; barnstormer, ham actor; old stager, rep player; star, matinée idol 890 n. *favourite*; prima donna, diva; ballerina, danseuse, première coryphée; tragedian, tragédienne; comedian, comedienne, comic (see *entertainer*); protagonist, deuteragonist, lead, second l., leading lady; chorus, chorus girl, show g., chorine; understudy, stand-in 150 n. *substitute*; mute, figurante, super, extra; concert-party, troupe, company, cast; corps de ballet; dramatis personae, characters; presenter, narrator; prologue, compère.

entertainer, performer; artiste, artist; street artist, busker, goon, nigger minstrel; diseuse, patterer, monologist; minstrel, jongleur; crooner, pop singer; juggler 545 n. *conjuror*; tumbler 162 n. *athlete*; gladiator 722 n. *combatant*; mountebank, fool, pantaloon, harlequin, columbine, pierrot, pierrette, buffoon, clown, merry-andrew, stooge; dancing girl, nautch g., geisha g.

stage-hand, prop-man, stage carpenter, scene-painter, scene-shifter; costumier, wardrobe mistress, make-up man; prompter, callboy; usher, usherette.

stage-manager, producer, director, compère, manager, actor m.; impresario, showman; backer, angel, choregus.

dramatist, tragic poet, comic p.; mimographer; playwright, scenario writer, script-w., librettist; gag-man.

playgoer, theatre-goer, opera-g., film-g.; theatre fan, balletomane; firstnighter; stagedoor Johnny; audience, house; groundling, pittite, galleryite, gods 441 n. *spectator*; claque, claqueur; dramatic critic, play-reviewer.

Adj. *dramatic*, dramaturgical; scenic, theatrical, stagy 551 adj. *representing*; live, legitimate; Thespian, histrionic, mimetic 20 adj. *imitative*; tragic, buskined; comic, tragi-comic; farcical, knockabout, slapstick 849 adj. *funny*; operatic; melodramatic, sensational 821 adj. *exciting*; ham, hammy, barnstorming; on the stage, trouping; cast, featured, starred, billed; well-cast, all-star; stage-struck, theatre-minded.

Vb. *dramatize*, stage, produce, direct, stage-manage, rehearse; cast, give a part; star, feature, bill; present, put on, release 522 vb. *show*.

act, go on the stage, tread the boards, troupe; enact, play, play-act 551 n. *represent*; personate, take the part; mime 20 vb. *imitate*; create a role, play the lead; play opposite, support; star, steal the show; ham, barnstorm, overact 546 vb. *exaggerate*; underact, throw away; walk on; understudy, stand in.

Class Five

VOLITION

DIVISION (I): INDIVIDUAL VOLITION

Section 1: Volition in General

595. Will – N. *will*, willing, volition; velleity; disposition 597 n. *willingness*; conatus, act of will 682 n. *exertion*; will-power, determination 599 n. *resolution*; intent 617 n. *intention*; decision 608 n. *predetermination*; one's will and pleasure 737 n. *command*; appetence 859 n. *desire*; self-will 602 n. *obstinacy*; free will 744 n. *independence* 605 n. *choice*; voluntariness 597 n. *voluntary work*.

Adj. *volitional*, willing, conative; discretional 605 adj. *choosing*; minded, so m. 617 adj. *intending*; self-willed, wilful 602 adj. *obstinate*; arbitrary, dictatorial 735 adj. *authoritarian*; self-determined 744 adj. *free*; prepense, intentional, willed 608 adj. *predetermined*.

Vb. *will*, have one's way 737 vb. *command*; please oneself 744 vb. *be free*; see fit, think f. 605 vb. *choose*; purpose, determine 617 vb. *intend*; wish 859 vb. *desire*; judge for oneself 480 vb. *judge*; take the law into one's own hands 599 vb. *be resolute*; volunteer, offer 597 vb. *be willing*.

Adv. *at will*, at pleasure, ad lib.; voluntarily, of one's own accord.

596. Necessity – N. *necessity*, hard n., no alternative, Hobson's choice 606 n. *no choice*; inevitability 155 n. *destiny*; necessitation, dictation, necessitarianism, determinism, fatalism 608 n. *predetermination*; force of circumstances, act of God, fatality 154 n. *eventuality*; law of nature; force 740 n. *compulsion*; logic, necessary conclusion 478 n. *demonstration*; moral necessity, obligation 917 n. *duty*; necessitude, indispensability, a must 627 n. *requirement*; necessitousness 801 n. *poverty*; involuntariness, reflex action, impulse, blind i. 476 n. *intuition*.

fate, lot, weird, karma, kismet; doom, predestination 155 n. *destiny*; book of fate, God's will; fortune 159 n. *chance*; stars, planets.

fatalist, determinist, predestinarian, necessitarian; pawn 630 n. *tool*.

Adj. *necessary*, indispensable, requisite, unforgoable 627 adj. *required*; logical, dictated by reason; imperative 740 adj. *compelling*; binding 917 adj. *obligatory*; inevitable, unavoidable, inescapable, inexorable, irrevocable 473 adj. *certain*; fated, dictated, imposed, necessitarian, deterministic 606 adj. *choiceless*.

involuntary, instinctive 476 adj. *intuitive*; unpremeditated, unwilled 618 adj. *unintentional*; unconscious, unwitting 609 adj. *spontaneous*; unassenting 598 adj. *unwilling*; automatic, mechanical.

Vb. *necessitate*, dictate, impose, oblige 740 vb. *compel*; bind by fate, destine, doom 155 vb. *predestine*; insist, leave no choice, drive into a corner; demand 627 vb. *require*.

597. Willingness – N. *willingness*, voluntariness, spontaneousness 609 n. *spontaneity*; disposition, inclination, leaning 179 n. *tendency*; predisposition, right mood, good will 897 n. *benevolence*; acquiescence 488 n. *assent*; compliance 758 n. *consent*; alacrity, promptness, zeal, earnestness, eagerness, zealousness, ardour, enthusiasm; impatience, over-eagerness, ardour of the chase 678 n. *overactivity*; devotion, self-d. 931 n. *disinterestedness*; helpfulness 706 n. *co-operation*; pliancy, docility 612 n. *persuasibility*.

voluntary work, honorary employment, unpaid labour, labour of love, self-appointed task; gratuitous effort, work

of supererogation 637 n. *superfluity*;
freewill offering 781 n. *gift*; volunteer.

Adj. *willing*, acquiescent, compliant,
agreeable 758 adj. *consenting*; in the
mood, receptive, favourable, predis-
posed; happy, pleased, glad, charmed,
delighted; ready and willing 678 adj.
active; forward, alacritous, zealous,
eager, enthusiastic, dedicated;impatient,
spoiling for; trying, doing one's best 671
adj. *essaying*; helpful 706 adj. *cooperative*; docile, biddable; loyal 739 adj.
obedient; fain 859 adj. *desiring*; would-
be 852 adj. *hoping*.

voluntary, offered, unprompted, unasked 609 adj. *spontaneous*; unsolicited,
self-imposed; non-mandatory, discretional 605 adj. *chosen*; gratuitous 812
adj. *uncharged*.

Vb. *be willing*, feel like, have a great
mind to 595 vb. *will*; mean 617 vb. *intend*; acquiesce 488 vb. *assent*; comply
758 vb. *consent*; try, do one's best 671
vb. *essay*; go out of one's way to, lean
over backwards; collaborate 706 vb.
cooperate; swallow, jump at, catch at
859 vb. *desire*; make no bones, have no
scruple; volunteer, sacrifice oneself 759
vb. *offer oneself*.

Adv. *willingly*, with a will, heartily;
voluntarily, without asking; heart and
soul, con amore, with a good grace,
nothing loth; gladly, with pleasure.

598. Unwillingness – N. *unwillingness*,
disinclination, indisposition, reluctance;
demur, objection, protest 762 n. *deprecation*; rejection 760 n. *refusal*; unhelp-
fulness, non-cooperation; dissociation,
abstention; unenthusiasm 860 n. *indifference*; backwardness, hesitation 858 n.
caution; aversion, no stomach for 620 n.
avoidance; bashfulness 874 n. *modesty*;
refractoriness, fractiousness; sulks 893
n. *sullenness*; perfunctoriness, grudging
service.

Adj. *unwilling*, indisposed, loth, reluctant, averse; not prepared, not minded,
not in the mood 760 adj. *refusing*; un-
consenting 489 adj. *dissenting*; adverse,
704 adj. *opposing*; protesting 762 adj.

deprecatory; with regret 830 adj. *regretting*; shy, bashful 874 adj. *modest*; unenthusiastic, half-hearted; backward 278
adj. *slow*; unhelpful, uncooperative 702
adj. *hindering*; restive, recalcitrant 738
adj. *disobedient*; not trying, perfunctory,
grudging.

Vb. *be loth*, not stomach 861 vb. *dislike*;
disagree, boggle 489 vb. *dissent*; protest
762 vb. *deprecate*; recoil, not face,
blench, fight shy, duck, shirk 620 vb.
avoid; drag one's feet, hang back; slack,
not pull one's weight 679 vb. *be inactive*;
not play, non-cooperate, abstain 702 vb.
obstruct; grudge, begrudge 893 vb. *be
sullen*; drag oneself, force o.; do with
regret 830 vb. *regret*.

Adv. *unwillingly*, with a bad grace, in
spite of oneself, against the grain.

599. Resolution – N. *resolution*, sticking
point, resoluteness, determination, earnestness, seriousness; resolve, decision
608 n. *predetermination*; drive, vigour
174 n. *vigorousness*; energy, frantic e.,
desperation 678 n. *activity*; thoroughness
725 n. *completion*; fixity of purpose,
concentration, iron will 595 n. *will*;
tenacity 600 n. *perseverance*; mettle,
guts, backbone 855 n. *courage*; single-
mindedness, devotedness, dedication;
staunchness, constancy; insistence, pressure 740 n. *compulsion*; sternness, relentlessness, ruthlessness, inexorability, implacability 906 n. *pitilessness*; inflexibility, steeliness.

Adj. *resolute*, resolved, made up, determined, desperate; serious, earnest, con-
centrated; intent upon 617 adj. *intending*;
insistent, urgent 174 adj. *vigorous*; zealous, thorough, whole-hogging; steady,
staunch, constant 153 adj. *unchangeable*;
iron-willed, unbending 602 adj. *obstinate*; stern, grim, implacable 906 adj.
pitiless; undaunted 855 adj. *unfearing*;
unflinching, tenacious 600 adj. *persevering*; indomitable 727 adj. *unbeaten*;
purposeful, serious, earnest, whole-
hearted, single-minded, devoted, dedicated.

Vb. *be resolute*, steel oneself, brace o.,

set one's face; make up one's mind, will, resolve, determine, purpose 617 vb. *intend*; know one's own mind, stand no nonsense, stick at nothing, see it through 725 vb. *carry through*; outface, dare 711 vb. *defy*; endure, stick it 600 vb. *persevere*, 825 vb. *suffer*; take the bull by the horns; take the plunge, cross the Rubicon, nail one's colours to the mast.

600. Perseverance – N. *perseverance*, persistence, tenacity, pertinacity, stubbornness 602 n. *obstinacy*; staunchness, steadfastness 599 n. *resolution*; single-mindedness, concentration 455 n. *attention*; sedulity, application, tirelessness 678 n. *assiduity*; doggedness, plodding 682 n. *exertion*; endurance, patience 825 n. *suffering*; repeated efforts 106 n. *repetition*.

stamina, staying power, indefatigability 162 n. *strength*; grit, backbone, bulldog courage 855 n. *courage*; trier, stayer, willing horse 686 n. *worker*.

Adj. *persevering*, persistent, tenacious, stubborn 602 adj. *obstinate*; hard-trying, patient, plodding, dogged 678 adj. *industrious*; steady, unfaltering, unwavering, enduring, unflagging, indefatigable, unsleeping; unfailing, constant 146 adj. *unceasing*; indomitable 727 adj. *unbeaten*; undaunted, undiscouraged 599 adj. *resolute*.

Vb. *persevere*, persist, keep at it, not take 'no' for an answer; never despair, never say die 852 vb. *hope*; endure, have what it takes 825 vb. *suffer*; try, try, and try again 671 vb. *essay*; plod, slog, peg at, plug at, hammer at 682 vb. *work*; maintain, continue, keep the pot boiling, rally, keep going; hold fast 778 vb. *retain*; hang on, stick it out, be in at the death; stick to one's guns, die in the last ditch; work till one drops, die in harness.

601. Irresolution – N. *irresolution*, infirmity of purpose, faint-heartedness 856 n. *cowardice*; non-perseverance, broken promise 603 n. *tergiversation*; indecision, uncertainty, floating vote 474 n. *dubiety*;

overcaution 858 n. *caution*; inconstancy 152 n. *changeableness*; levity, irresponsibility 604 n. *caprice*; good nature, compromise 734 n. *laxity*; half-measures 726 n. *non-completion*; listlessness 860 n. *indifference*; no will of one's own 163 n. *weakness*; submissiveness, slavishness 721 n. *submission*.

waverer, wobbler, dodderer, shilly-shallyer; shuttlecock 152 n. *changeable thing*; weathercock 603 n. *tergiversator*; faintheart, compromiser.

Adj. *irresolute*, undecided, indecisive, of two minds, undetermined, unresolved 474 adj. *doubting*; squeamish 598 adj. *unwilling*; faint-hearted, unheroic 856 adj. *cowardly*; shaken, rattled 854 adj. *nervous*; half-hearted 860 adj. *indifferent*; unstaunch, unsteadfast 474 adj. *unreliable*; characterless, featureless 175 adj. *inert*; compromising, weak-kneed, easy-going 734 adj. *lax*; inconstant, temperamental, whimsical, mercurial 604 adj. *capricious*; irresponsible 456 adj. *light-minded*; impatient, unpersevering.

Vb. *be irresolute*, back away, blink, jib 620 vb. *avoid*; palter, shilly-shally 518 vb. *equivocate*; vacillate, see-saw, wobble, waver, teeter, dither 317 vb. *oscillate*; dilly-dally, hum and haw 474 vb. *be uncertain*; hesitate 858 vb. *be cautious*; falter, grow weary 684 vb. *be fatigued*; give up 621 vb. *relinquish*; yield, submit.

602. Obstinacy – N. *obstinacy*, unyielding temper; determination, will 599 n. *resolution*; stubborness, obduracy, self-will, pig-headedness; inelasticity, woodenness 326 n. *hardness*; no compromise, intransigence; stiff neck, contumacy 715 n. *resistance*; incorrigibility 940 n. *impenitence*; indocility, intractability, mulishness; wrongheadedness, bloody-mindedness.

opiniatry, self-opinion, opiniativeness 473 n. *positiveness*; dogmatism, bigotry, zealotry; rigorism, intolerance, fanaticism 735 n. *severity*; ruling passion, infatuation, obsession, monomania, idée fixe; blind side 439 n. *blindness*.

opinionist, stubborn fellow, mule;

stick-in-the-mud, Blimp; fanatic, rigorist, stickler, pedant, dogmatist, zealot, bigot, persecutor 481 n. *narrow mind*; sticker, stayer; chronic; last-ditcher, diehard, bitter-ender; fogey 504 n. *crank*.

Adj. *obstinate*, stubborn, pig-headed, mulish; unyielding 599 adj. *resolute*; dogged 600 adj. *persevering*; stiff, rigid, inelastic, wooden 326 adj. *hard*; inflexible, unbending, obdurate, hardened, case-h.; uncompromising, intransigent; set, hidebound 610 adj. *habituated*; unteachable, obscurantist, bigoted, fanatic 481 adj. *biased*; dour, grim 893 adj. *sullen*; indocile, stiff-necked, contumacious (see *wilful*); perverse, incorrigible, bloody-minded; persistent, incurable, chronic 113 adj. *lasting*.

wilful, self-willed, wayward, arbitrary; headstrong, perverse; unruly, restive, refractory; irrepressible, ungovernable, unmanageable, intractable, uncontrollable 738 adj. *disobedient*; cross-grained, crotchety 892 adj. *irascible*.

Vb. *be obstinate*, — stubborn etc. adj.; see 600 vb. *persevere*, 599 vb. *be resolute*.

603. Tergiversation – **N.** *tergiversation*, change of mind, better thoughts; afterthought, second thought 67 n. *sequel*; good resolution, break with the past, repentance 939 n. *penitence*; backsliding, recidivation, recidivism 657 n. *relapse*; resilement, volte-face, apostasy, recreancy (see *recantation*); defection, desertion 918 n. *dutilessness*; treachery 930 n. *perfidy*; secession, withdrawal 978 n. *schism*; change of mood, temperament; coquetry 604 n. *caprice*.

recantation, palinode, eating one's words, retraction; resilement, withdrawal; renunciation, abjuration, abjurement; revocation, recall 752 n. *abrogation*.

tergiversator, turncoat, rat; weathercock 152 n. *changeable thing*; timeserver, trimmer 518 n. *equivocalness*; double-dealer, Mr Facing-both-ways 545 n. *deceiver*; jilt 604 n. *caprice*; recanter, recreant, apostate, renegade, runagate; security risk, traitor 938 n.

knave; medizer, quisling, fifth columnist 707 n. *collaborator*; lost leader, deserter, quitter, ratter; tell-tale, peacher 524 n. *informer*; deviationist, secessionist 978 n. *schismatic*; recividist, backslider 904 n. *offender*.

Adj. *tergiversating*, trimming etc. vb.; shuffling 518 adj. *equivocal*; treacherous 930 adj. *perfidious*; double-dealing 541 adj. *hypocritical*; reactionary, going back 286 adj. *regressive*; fickle 604 adj. *capricious*; time-serving, time-pleasing 925 adj. *flattering*; unfaithful, disloyal 918 adj. *dutiless*.

Vb. *tergiversate*, change one's mind, think better of it, change one's tune; renege, back out, scratch, withdraw 753 vb. *resign*; apologize (see *recant*); change front; repent 939 vb. *be penitent*; backslide 657 vb. *relapse*; trim, shuffle, face both ways; ditch, jilt, throw over, desert 918 vb. *fail in duty*.

apostatize, turn one's coat, change sides, medize; let down the side, go over; blackleg, rat; betray, collaborate 930 vb. *be dishonest*; be off with the old love, jump on the band wagon.

recant, unsay, eat one's words; eat humble pie, apologize; take back, go back on, resile, withdraw, retract 533 vb. *negate*; renounce, abjure, forswear, swear off; recall, revoke, rescind 752 vb. *abrogate*.

604. Caprice – **N.** *caprice*, fancy 513 n. *fantasy*; capriciousness, arbitrariness; whimsicality, freakishness 497 n. *absurdity*; faddiness, inconsistency, fitfulness, variability, fickleness, unreliability, temperament, levity, irresponsibility 152 n. *changeableness*; inconstancy, coquetry; playfulness.

whim, caprice, whimsey, whimwam, vagary, sweet will, humour, quirk, kink, fad, craze, freak.

Adj. *capricious*, motiveless, purposeless; whimsical, fanciful; humoursome, temperamental; freakish, prankish, wanton, wayward; faddy 862 adj. *fastidious*; uncertain, unpredictable 508 adj. *unexpected*; volatile, mercurial, skittish, giddy, frivolous 456 adj. *light-minded*; inconsistent, inconstant, erratic, variable 152 adj. *unstable*; irresponsible, unreliable, fickle; flirtatious, coquettish, playful.

605. Choice – N. *choice*, election 463 n. *discrimination*; eclecticism 862 n. *fastidiousness*; cooption, cooptation; option, pre-option; discretion, pick; preference, predilection 179 n. *tendency*; range of choice, selection, list, short l.; alternative, embarras de choix; option of difficulties, dilemma 474 n. *dubiety*; Hobson's choice 606 n. *no choice*; better choice, preferability, desirability 642 n. *expedience*; one's preference, favour, fancy; thing chosen, selection; literary selection 592 n. *anthology*.

vote, voice 485 n. *opinion*; representation, proportional r.; ballot, open vote; card vote; vote-counting, show of hands, division, poll, Gallup p., plebiscite, referendum; suffrage, franchise; Parliamentary system, ballot-box, vox populi; election, general e., 'democracy's feast'; by-election; polls, voting, electioneering, canvass, hustings, candidature.

electorate, voters, balloter, elector, straw voter; electoral college; quorum; electoral roll, voting list, constituent, constituency; polling booth, ballot-box, voting paper; slate, ticket.

Adj. *choosing*, optional, discretional 595 adj. *volitional*; preferential, favouring 923 adj. *approving*; selective, eclectic; cooptative, elective, electoral; vote-catching, electioneering.

chosen, well-c.; preferable 642 adj. *expedient*; select, choice, picked, hand-p. 644 adj. *excellent*; elect, designate; preferred, favourite, fancy, pet; God's own; by appointment.

Vb. *choose*, have a voice 595 vb. *will*; eliminate the alternatives, make one's choice; accept, opt, elect, coopt, adopt 923 vb. *approve*; favour, fancy, like best; incline 179 vb. *tend*; prefer, like better, have rather; come out for, plump f.; range oneself, take sides 703 vb. *patronize*.

select, pick, pick out, seed; nominate, designate 547 vb. *mark*; pre-select, earmark, reserve; propose, second 703 vb. *patronize*; excerpt, cull, anthologize 592 vb. *abstract*; winnow, sift, bolt 463 vb. *discriminate*; cream, pick the best; indulge one's fancy, pick and choose.

vote, have a v., be enfranchised; poll, cast a vote, raise one's hand, divide; vote for, elect, return; electioneer, canvass; stand 759 vb. *offer oneself*; put to the vote, take a poll; count heads, count noses; go to the country, appeal to the electorate.

606. Absence of choice – N. *no choice*, choicelessness, no alternative, dictation, Hobson's choice 596 n. *necessity*; any, the first that comes 464 n. *indiscrimination*; no favouritism, impartiality, first come first served 913 n. *justice*; no preference 860 n. *indifference*; open mind 474 n. *dubiety*; 'don't know', floating vote 601 n. *irresolution*; refusal to vote, abstention 598 n. *unwillingness*; disfranchisement, disqualification.

Adj. *choiceless*, without alternative, unable to choose, happy either way 625 adj. *neutral*; open to conviction, undecided 601 adj. *irresolute*; uninterested 860 adj. *indifferent*; disinterested, impartial 913 adj. *just*; non-voting, voteless, disfranchised.

Vb. *be neutral*, take no sides, not vote, abstain; sit on the fence 601 vb. *be irresolute*.

have no choice, have no alternative, suffer dictation; take it or leave it, make a virtue of necessity; lose one's vote, spoil one's ballot paper.

607. Rejection – N. *rejection*, non-acceptance, waiver; disapproval 924 n. *disapprobation*; repudiation 533 n. *negation*; rebuff, repulse 760 n. *refusal*; more kicks than ha'pence; electoral defeat, hostile vote; exception, exemption 57 n. *exclusion*; discard, reject, wallflower; lost cause.

Adj. *rejected* etc. vb.; ineligible, unchosen, outvoted 860 adj. *unwanted*;

tried and found wanting, declined with thanks 924 adj. *disapproved*; out of the question 643 adj. *inexpedient*.

Vb. *reject*, not accept, decline, rebuff, repulse, spurn 760 vb. *refuse*; not pass, return, send back 924 vb. *disapprove*; pass over, ignore 458 vb. *disregard*; outvote 489 vb. *dissent*; scrap 674 vb. *disuse*; supersede 752 vb. *depose*; expel, outcaste 300 vb. *eject*; draw the line, eliminate; count out, exempt 57 vb. *exclude*; not cater for 883 vb. *make unwelcome*; disavow 533 vb. *negate*; repudiate 603 vb. *recant*; scout, scorn, disdain; sniff at, look a gift horse in the mouth 922 vb. *hold cheap*.

608. Predetermination – N. *predetermination*, predestination 596 n. *necessity*; appointment, pre-ordination 155 n. *destiny*; premeditation, predeliberation, resolve, project 617 n. *intention*; prearrangement 669 n. *preparation*; agenda 622 n. *business*; closed mind 481 n. *prejudice*; predisposal, foregone conclusion.

Adj. *predetermined* etc. vb.; appointed, fated; deliberate, aforethought, prepense 617 adj. *intending*; with a motive, designed; ready-made, prearranged 669 adj. *prepared*.

Vb. *predetermine*, destine, appoint, foreordain, predestinate 155 vb. *predestine*; premeditate, preconceive 617 vb. *intend*; preconcert; determine, will the end 595 vb. *will*; contrive, arrange, prearrange 623 vb. *plan*; frame, stack the cards 541 vb. *fake*.

609. Spontaneity – N. *spontaneity*, unpremeditation; ad hoc measures, improvisation; extemporization, ad libbing, impromptu 670 n. *non-preparation*; involuntariness, reflex, automatic r.; impulsiveness, impulse 476 n. *intuition*; inconsideration, spur of the moment; inspiration, hunch, flash 451 n. *idea*.

improviser, extemporizer, improvisatore, creature of impulse.

Adj. *spontaneous*, off-hand, ad hoc, extempore, extemporaneous, sudden,

snap; makeshift 670 adj. *unprepared*; impromptu, unrehearsed 618 adj. *unintentional*; unprompted, unprovoked; instinctive 476 adj. *intuitive*; impulsive, emotional 818 adj. *feeling*.

Vb. *improvise*, extemporize, vamp 670 vb. *be unprepared*; obey an impulse; blurt, come out with; rise to the occasion.

610. Habit – N. *habit*, native h. 5 n. *character*; habitude, force of habit; familiarity, second nature; addiction; constitutional; knack, trick, instinct 179 n. *tendency*; bad habit, cacoethes; usage, long habit, custom, one's old way; use, wont, user 146 n. *continuance*; tradition, law, precedent; beaten track, groove, rut; round, dailiness, regularity 141 n. *periodicity*; conventionalism, traditionalism, conservatism, old school 83 n. *conformity*; occupational disease.

practice, experience, custom, matter of course; conventionality 83 n. *conformity*; institution 988 n. *rite*; cultus 981 n. *cult*; mode, vogue, craze 848 n. *fashion*; convention, protocol, done thing, the usual; form 848 n. *etiquette*; manners and customs; rules and regulations, standing order, rules of business, routine; spit and polish, pipe-clay, bull 60 n. *order*.

habituation, assuefaction, training 534 n. *teaching*; inurement 669 n. *maturation*; naturalization, acclimatization; conditioning, association, reflex, conditioned r.; fixation, complex; drill, repetitive job 106 n. *repetition*.

habitué, creature of habit, addict, drug a., dope-fiend; conventionalist 83 n. *conformist*; frequenter, regular, devotee, fan.

Adj. *habitual*, customary; routine, stereotyped 81 adj. *regular*; inveterate, prescriptive, time-honoured 113 adj. *lasting*; occupational; haunting, besetting, clinging, obsessive; habit-forming 612 adj. *inducive*; ingrained, deep-seated 153 adj. *fixed*. See *usual*.

usual, accustomed, wonted, conventional, traditional; in character, natural; household, familiar 490 adj. *known*;

unoriginal, trite, hackneyed; banal, commonplace, common, ordinary 79 adj. *general*; set, stock 83 adj. *typical*; prevalent 79 adj. *universal*; monthly, daily, everyday 139 adj. *frequent*; established, professional, official; invariable 153 adj. *unchangeable*; modish 848 adj. *fashionable*.

habituated, in the habit of, accustomed to, experienced; given to, addicted to, wedded to; broken in, tame.

Vb. *be wont*, love to, be known to, be used to, be a creature of habit; haunt, frequent; become a habit, catch on, gain upon one, grow on o.; settle, take root, radicate; be the rule, obtain; come into use.

habituate, accustom oneself, get used to, take in one's stride; take to, make a habit of; catch oneself doing; keep one's hand in, practise, gain experience; condition, accustom, inure, season, harden 534 vb. *train*; domesticate, tame 369 vb. *break in*; naturalize, acclimatize.

611. Desuetude – N. *desuetude*, discontinuance, disuse 674 n. *non-use*; rust, decay 655 n. *deterioration*; lost habit, rustiness, lack of practice 695 n. *unskilfulness*; outgrowing, weaning; unwontedness, no such custom; want of habit, inexperience 491 n. *ignorance*.

Adj. *unwonted*; unused, unpractised, not done; unfashionable, old-fashioned, defunct 125 adj. *past*; outgrown, discarded 674 adj. *disused*; against custom, unconventional 84 adj. *unconformable*; unsanctified by custom, untraditional.

unhabituated, unaccustomed, not in the habit of; untrained, unbacked, unbroken, untamed, undomesticated; inexperienced, new, raw, green 491 adj. *uninstructed*; out of the habit, rusty 695 adj. *unskilful*.

Vb. *disaccustom*, wean from, cure of 656 vb. *cure*; break a habit, outgrow; throw off, shed 229 vb. *doff*.

be unused, not catch on; offend custom, infringe protocol; lapse, fall into disuse, wear off; rust 655 vb. *deteriorate*.

612. Motive – N. *motive*, cause of action 156 n. *cause*; motivation, driving force, spring, mainspring 156 n. *causation*; ideal; aspiration, ambition 859 n. *desire*; call 622 n. *vocation*; personal reasons, ulterior motive 932 n. *selfishness*; impulse 609 n. *spontaneity*.

inducement, pressure, instance; pressure group, lobby 178 n. *influence*; provocation, incitement, encouragement, instigation 821 n. *excitation*; countenance, abetment 703 n. *aid*; solicitation, invitation 761 n. *request*; temptation, enticement, allurement, tantalization, attractiveness 291 n. *attraction*; cajolery, blandishment 925 n. *flattery*; persuasion, persuasiveness, salesmanship, sales talk 579 n. *oratory*; pep-talk, challenge 547 n. *call*; exhortation, advocacy 691 n. *advice*; bribery 962 n. *reward*; honeyed words, siren song, voice of the tempter, winning ways.

persuasibility, docility, tractability, teachableness 597 adj. *willingness*; pliancy 327 n. *softness*; susceptibility, suggestibility, emotionalism 819 n. *moral sensibility*; credulousness 487 n. *credulity*.

incentive, inducement; stimulus, fillip, tickle, prod, spur, goad, whip, crop; rod, big stick, crack of the whip 900 n. *threat*; energizer, tonic, carrot, sop 174 n. *stimulant*; charm 983 n. *spell*; attraction 291 n. *magnet*; gleam, will-o'-the-wisp, lure, decoy, bait, fly, cast 542 n. *trap*; pay increase, rise, raise, bonus 804 n. *payment*; donation, donative 781 n. *gift*; gratification, tip, bribe 962 n. *reward*; forbidden fruit; tempting offer 759 n. *offer*.

motivator, mover, prime m. 156 n. *cause*; manipulator, wire-puller 178 n. *influence*; instigator, prompter; inspirer, counsellor 691 n. *adviser*; abettor, suggester; agent provocateur 545 n. *deceiver*; tempter, seducer; temptress, vamp, siren, Circe; hypnotist; orator 579 n. *speaker*; advocate, pleader; coaxer, wheedler, cozener 925 n. *flatterer*; vote-catcher, patterer, salesman, advertiser, propagandist 528 n. *publicizer*; lobbyist, lobby, pressure-group.

Adj. *inducive*, protreptic 178 adj. *in-*

fluential; provocative, tonic, peppy; hortatory, rousing, incendiary 821 adj. *exciting*; inviting, attractive 291 adj. *attracting*; fascinating 983 adj. *sorcerous*; irresistible, hypnotic; habit-forming 610 adj. *habitual*.

Vb. *motivate*, motive, move, actuate, manipulate; work upon 178 vb. *influence*; call the tune, override; appeal, challenge, shame into (see *incite*); infect, poison; interest, intrigue 821 vb. *impress*; charm, fascinate, spellbind 983 vb. *bewitch*; turn one's head 887 vb. *excite love*; pull 291 vb. *attract*; incline, dispose; predispose, prejudice 481 vb. *bias*; lead 689 n. *manage*; set the fashion, set the pace; induce, persuade, win over 485 vb. *convince*.

incite, stimulate 174 vb. *invigorate*; encourage, keep in countenance 855 vb. *give courage*; inspire, animate, provoke, rouse, rally 821 vb. *excite*; challenge, exhort, invite, urge, insist, press, put pressure on, lobby; nag, goad, prod, spur, prick, tickle; whip, lash, flog; tar on, hound on, set on, egg on; drive, hurry, hurry up 680 vb. *hasten*; instigate, prompt, put up to; abet 703 vb. *aid*; insinuate, suggest 524 vb. *hint*; advocate 691 vb. *advise*; start, kindle 68 vb. *initiate*.

tempt, lead into temptation 495 vb. *mislead*; entice, tantalize, tease; allure, lure, bait, inveigle 542 vb. *ensnare*; tickle, coax, wheedle, blandish, cajole, pander to 925 vb. *flatter*.

bribe, offer an inducement 759 vb. *offer*; suborn, seduce, tamper with, doctor, corrupt; square, buy off, buy over; oil, grease the palm; gratify 962 vb. *reward*.

613. Dissuasion – N. *dissuasion*, dehortation, contrary advice; caution 664 n. *warning*; discouragement 702 n. *hindrance*; deterrence 854 n. *intimidation*; expostulation 762 n. *deprecation*; no encouragement, disincentive; deterrent 665 n. *danger signal*; cold water, damper, wet blanket; kill-joy, spoilsport 702 n. *hinderer*.

Adj. *dissuasive*, discouraging, chilling, damping; dehortatory, expostulatory 762 adj. *deprecatory*.

Vb. *dissuade*, advise against, argue a., convince to the contrary 479 vb. *confute*; caution 664 vb. *warn*; expostulate 762 vb. *deprecate*; shake, stagger, give one pause; intimidate 900 vb. *threaten*; deter, daunt 854 vb. *frighten*; choke off, head off 282 vb. *deflect*; wean from 611 vb. *disaccustom*; act as a drag 747 vb. *restrain*; disenchant, disillusion; disaffect, set against 861 vb. *cause dislike*; dishearten 834 vb. *deject*; throw cold water on, damp the ardour; take the edge off 257 vb. *blunt*.

614. Pretext – N. *pretext*, ostensible motive; allegation, claim 532 n. *affirmation*; plea, excuse, defence, apology, apologia, justification 927 n. *vindication*; let-out, loophole, alibi 667 n. *means of escape*; special pleading, quibble 477 n. *sophism*; subterfuge 698 n. *stratagem*; pretence, previous engagement, diplomatic illness 543 n. *untruth*; bluff, blind; apology for, simulacrum, makeshift 150 n. *substitute*; sour grapes.

Adj. *ostensible*, colourable, specious, plausible.

Vb. *plead*, allege, claim, profess 532 vb. *affirm*; pretext, take the plea of 475 vb. *argue*; make excuses 927 vb. *justify*; shelter under, use as a peg; find a loophole, wriggle out of, ride off on 667 vb. *escape*; bluff, blind, throw dust in the eyes 542 vb. *befool*; pretend, affect 850 vb. *be affected*.

615. Good – N. *good*, one's g., what is good for one; the best, supreme good, summum bonum; balance of interest, greater good, lesser evil, utilitarianism 642 n. *expedience*; weal, well-being, welfare 730 n. *prosperity*; fortune, fair *or* good f. 824 n. *happiness*; blessing, benison, world of good (see *benefit*); well-wishing, benediction 897 n. *benevolence*.

benefit, something to one's advantage, advantage, interest, commodity; behalf 640 n. *utility*; profit 771 n. *gain*; edification, betterment 654 n. *improvement*; boon 781 n. *gift*; good turn 897 n. *kind act*; favour, blessing, good riddance, blessing in disguise; godsend, windfall, piece of luck; good thing 859 n. *desired object*.

Adj. *good*, goodly, fine 644 adj. *excellent*; blessed 824 adj. *happy*; advantageous, heaven-sent 644 adj. *beneficial*; worth-while 644 adj. *valuable*; praiseworthy; edifying, moral 933 adj. *virtuous*; pleasure-giving 826 adj. *pleasurable*.

Adv. *well*, aright, favourably, happily, not amiss; for the best.

616. Evil – N. *evil*, moral e., wickedness 934 n. *vice*; evil conduct, mischievousness, injuriousness, disservice 930 n. *foul play*; wrong, injury, outrage 914 n. *injustice*; crying evil, shame, abuse; curse 659 n. *bane*; ill, ills that flesh is heir to, Pandora's box; troubles 731 n. *adversity*; affliction 825 n. *suffering*; grief 825 n. *sorrow*; nuisance 827 n. *annoyance*; 731 n. *ill fortune*, fatality, catastrophe 165 n. *ruin*; tragedy, sad ending; mischief, harm, damage 772 n. *loss*; ill effect, prejudice, disadvantage; sense of injury, grievance 829 n. *discontent*.

Adj. *evil*, wicked 934 adj. *vicious*; black, foul, shameful 914 adj. *wrong*; bad, too bad 645 adj. *damnable*; injurious 645 adj. *harmful*; troublous 827 adj. *distressing*; fatal, fell 362 adj. *deadly*; disastrous 165 adj. *destructive*; catastrophic 731 adj. *unfortunate*; satanic 969 adj. *diabolic*.

Adv. *amiss*, wrong, awry; to one's cost, for one's sins; worse luck!

Section 2: Prospective Volition

617. Intention – N. *intention*, intent; deliberateness, calculation; purpose, determination, resolve 599 n. *resolution*; animus, mind; future intention, contemplation; study, pursuit 622 n. *business*; project, design 623 n. *plan*; ambition 859 n. *desire*; ultimatum 900 n. *threat*; proposal 759 n. *offer*; engagement

764 n. *promise*; teleology, final cause 156 n. *causation*; drift 514 n. *meaning*.

objective, destination, object, end, aim; by-end, axe to grind; mark, butt, target, target area, bull's-eye; tape, winning-post 295 n. *goal*; quarry 619 n. *chase*; prize 729 n. *trophy*; heart's desire 859 n. *desired object*.

Adj. *intending*, purposeful, intent, serious; hell-bent 599 n. *resolute*; out to, out for; purposive, teleological; minded 597 adj. *willing*; prospective, would-be, aspiring, ambitious 859 adj. *desiring*.

intended, for a purpose, tendential, tendentious; deliberate, intentional, aforethought 608 adj. *predetermined*.

Vb. *intend*, purpose, propose; have in mind, have in view, contemplate, study, meditate; mean to, have every intention 599 vb. *be resolute*; resolve 608 vb. *predetermine*; project, design 623 vb. *plan*; engage 764 vb. *promise*, 900 vb. *threaten*; destine, doom 155 vb. *predestine*; earmark, hold for, keep f., reserve f.; intend for oneself (see *aim at*); mean by it 514 vb. *mean*.

aim at, make one's target, go for; drive at, strive after 619 vb. *pursue*; try for, bid f. 671 vb. *essay*; be after, have an eye on, have designs on, promise oneself, aspire to, dream of 859 vb. *desire*; take aim 281 vb. *aim*.

Adv. *purposely*, on purpose, seriously, with one's eyes open, in cold blood, deliberately; designedly, advisedly, knowingly, wittingly; with malice aforethought; in order to; in pursuance of; as planned.

618. Non-design. Gamble – N. *non-design*, indeterminacy, randomness 159 n. *chance*; involuntariness, instinct 609 n. *spontaneity*; coincidence 89 n. *accompaniment*; accident, fluke, luck 154 n. *eventuality*; lottery, luck of the draw (see *gambling*); sortilegy 511 n. *divination*; lot 596 n. *fate*; mascot 983 n. *talisman*.

gambling, risk-taking; plunge, risk, hazard 661 n. *danger*; gamble, pot-luck 159 n. *chance*; venture, speculation, flutter 461 n. *experiment*; leap in the dark,

235

pig in a poke 474 n. *uncertainty*; bid, throw; toss of a coin, turn of a card; wager, bet, stake, ante, psychic bid; dice-box, dice, die, bones, ivories, craps; element of risk, game of chance 837 n. *gambling game*; betting, turf 716 n. *racing*; draw, lottery, raffle, tombola, sweepstake, premium bond, football pool; tontine.

gaming-house, hell, gambling h., betting shop, pool room, casino; totalisator, tote.

bourse, exchange, stock e., curb e., bucket shop.

gambler, gamester, player, dicer; bet-ter, layer, backer, punter; turf agent, bookmaker, bookie, tipster; risktaker; gentleman of fortune, adventurer, entre-preneur 672 n. *undertaking*; speculator, piker, plunger; bear, bull, stag.

Adj. *unintentional*, unintended, un-meant 596 adj. *involuntary*; undesigned, unpremeditated 609 adj. *spontaneous*; accidental, fortuitous, coincidental 159 adj. *casual*.

designless, aimless, planless, purpose-less; motiveless 159 n. *causeless*; ran-dom, haphazard 282 adj. *deviating*; meaningless 515 adj. *unmeaning*.

speculative, experimental 474 vb. *un-certain*; hazardous, risky, chancy, dicey, aleatory; risk-taking, venturesome, ad-venturous, enterprising.

Vb. *gamble*, game, play; throw, dice, bet, stake, wager, lay; call one's hand, overcall; take bets, make a book; back, punt; cover, hedge; play the market, speculate; hazard, risk 857 vb. *be rash*; venture, chance it, try one's luck, draw lots, cast l., stand the hazard.

619. Pursuit – N. *pursuit*, pursuance, quest 459 n. *search*; persecution, witch-hunt; enterprise 672 n. *undertaking*; avocation, profession 622 n. *business*, *vocation*.

chase, stern-c., run, run for one's money; steeplechase 716 n. *racing*; hunt, hue and cry, tally-ho, hark; beat, drive, battue; hunting and shooting 837 n. *sport*; blood sport, foxhunt; pigsticking; falconry etc. see **Vb.** *hunt*; rod and line,

bait, fly; fish-trap 542 n. *trap*; game, quarry, prey, victim 617 n. *objective*; catch 771 n. *acquisition*.

hunter, quester, seeker, searcher 459 n. *inquirer*; search-party; pursuer, tracker, trailer, shadow; huntsman, huntress; whip, whipper-in; sportsman 837 n. *player*; gun 287 n. *shooter*; head-hunter 362 n. *killer*; fox-hunter, courser, beagler, cony-catcher, rat-c., ratter, trapper, stalker, deer-s.; fowler, falconer, hawker; fisher, fisherman, angler; shrim-per; trawler, trawlerman, whaler; field, pack, hounds, cry of h.; hound 365 n. *dog*; hawk 365 n. *bird of prey*; beast of prey, man-eater 365 n. *animal*; mouser 365 n. *cat*.

Adj. *pursuing*, questing 459 adj. *in-quiring*; in quest of, sent after; in pur-suit, in full cry, on the scent, on the trail 284 adj. *following*.

Vb. *pursue*, seek, look for, cast about, be gunning for 459 vb. *search*; send after 272 vb. *send*; stalk, shadow, dog, track, trail, tail, follow the scent 284 vb. *follow*; witch-hunt, hound, harry, persecute 735 vb. *oppress*; chase, give c., hunt, halloo, hark on, cry on, raise the hunt; run down 712 vb. *charge*; make one's quarry 617 vb. *aim at*; be after 617 vb. *intend*; run after, set one's cap at, woo 889 vb. *court*.

hunt, go hunting, follow the chase, ride to hounds, pigstick; fish, angle, fly-fish; trawl; whale; shrimp; net, catch 542 vb. *ensnare*; mouse, play cat and m.; stalk, deer-s., fowl, hawk; course, beagle; start game, flush; head-hunt; kidnap 786 vb. *take away*.

620. Avoidance – N. *avoidance*, preven-tion 702 n. *hindrance*; abstinence, ab-stention 942 n. *temperance*; forbearance 177 n. *moderation*; non-involvement 860 n. *indifference*; evasiveness, evasive action, hide-and-seek, sidestep; centri-fugal force 280 n. *recoil*; withdrawal 286 n. *regression*; evasion, slip, flight 667 n. *escape*; wide berth, safe distance 199 n. *distance*; shyness 598 n. *unwillingness*; escapism.

avoider, non-drinker 942 n. *abstainer*; dodger, evader, levanter, bilker, welsher 545 n. *trickster*; quitter 856 n. *coward*; slacker, sloucher 679 n. *idler*; skulker 527 n. *hider*; truant, deserter 918 n. *dutilessness*; runaway, fugitive 667 n. *escaper*; escapist 513 n. *visionary*.

Adj. *avoiding*, aloof; evasive, elusive, slippery, hard to catch; wild, shy; backward 598 adj. *unwilling*; non-committal, unforthcoming 582 adj. *taciturn*; centrifugal; fugitive, runaway, fly-by-night 667 adj. *escaped*; defensive, abient.

avoidable, escapable, preventable; unattempted.

Vb. *avoid*, not go near, keep away; bypass, give one the go-by, look the other way; boycott, cold-shoulder 883 vb. *make unwelcome*; hold aloof, stand apart, wash one's hands of, shun, eschew, leave, let alone; fight shy, back away 290 vb. *recede*; keep one's distance, give a wide berth, make way for; forbear, spare; refrain, abstain; pull one's punches 177 vb. *moderate*; hold back, not attempt 598 vb. *be loth*; shelve 136 vb. *put off*; shirk 458 vb. *neglect*; shrink, flinch, start aside, jib, refuse, shy, blink, blench 854 vb. *be nervous*; take evasive action, play hide-and-seek; jink, sidestep, dodge, duck, deflect 713 vb. *parry*; evade 667 vb. *elude*; skulk, cower, hide 523 vb. *lurk*.

run away, desert, play truant 918 vb. *fail in duty*; abscond, welsh, flit, levant, elope 667 vb. *escape*; absent oneself 190 vb. *be absent*; withdraw, retire, retreat, beat a r., turn tail, bunk, scuttle, flee; flit, fly, take to flight; be off, make o., bolt, run, make oneself scarce 277 vb. *move fast*.

621. Relinquishment – N. *relinquishment*, abandonment; evacuation 296 n. *departure*; desertion, defection 918 n. *dutilessness*; secession 978 n. *schism*; cession 780 n. *transfer*; waiver, renunciation 779 n. *non-retention*; retirement 753 n. *resignation*; disuse 674 n. *non-use*; annulment 752 n. *abrogation*.

Adj. *relinquished*, forsaken etc. vb.

Vb. *relinquish*, drop, let go 779 vb. *not retain*; surrender, resign, give up, yield; waive, forgo; cede 780 vb. *convey*; forfeit 772 vb. *lose*; renounce, forswear, recant 603 vb. *tergiversate*; not proceed with, forget it; wean oneself 611 vb. *disaccustom*; shed, slough, cast off, divest 229 vb. *doff*; discard, write off 674 vb. *disuse*; abdicate 753 vb. *resign*; give in 721 vb. *submit*; leave, quit, vacate, tear oneself away 296 vb. *depart*; forsake, abandon, quit one's post, desert 918 vb. *fail in duty*; secede 978 vb. *schismatize*; throw over, ditch, jilt 541 vb. *be false*; annul, cancel 752 vb. *abrogate*.

622. Business – N. *business*, affairs, interests, iron in the fire; occupation, concern, care; business on hand, case, agenda; enterprise, undertaking, pursuit 678 n. *activity*; routine, round, daily r. 610 n. *practice*; business life, daily work; business world, City; art, industry, commerce; big business; cottage industry, home i.; industrialism, industrialization, industrial arts, manufacture 164 n. *production*; trade, craft, handicraft, mystery 694 n. *skill*; guild, business association 706 n. *association*; employment (see *vocation*); side-interest, hobby 837 n. *amusement*.

vocation, calling, life-work, mission, apostolate 751 n. *commission*; life, walk, walk of life, race, career; livelihood, daily bread, one's bread and butter; service, profession, métier, craft, trade; line (see *function*).

job, ploys, activities 678 n. *activity*; chores, odd jobs, work, task, set task, exercise 682 n. *labour*; duty, charge, commission, mission, errand, quest 751 n. *mandate*; employ, service, employment; hours of work, working day, work-day; occupation, situation, position, berth, incumbency, appointment, post, office; regular employment, full-time job, permanency; situation wanted, vacancy; labour exchange, employment agency.

function, what one has to do; capacity, office, portfolio, duty; realm, province, sphere; scope, field, terms of reference; department, line, line of country; role, part; business, job; concern, care, lookout, funeral.

Adj. *businesslike*, efficient 694 adj. *skilful*; industrious, busy 678 adj. *active*; vocational, professional, career; industrial, commercial, financial; occupational, functional; official, governmental; routine, systematic 60 adj. *orderly*; work-a-day 610 adj. *habitual*.

Vb. *employ*, busy, occupy, take up one's time; engage, recruit, hire, enlist, appoint, post 751 vb. *commission*; entertain, take on the payroll, wage 804 vb. *pay*; fill a vacancy, staff; industrialize.

function, work, go 173 vb. *operate*; fill a role, carry on; officiate, act, do the offices, serve as, do duty; stand in for 755 vb. *deputize*; hold office, have a job, serve; ply, drive a trade.

623. Plan – N. *plan*, scheme, design; planning, contrivance; organization, systematization, rationalization, centralization 60 n. *order*; programme, project, proposal 617 n. *intention*; master-plan, blue-print; rough scheme, pilot s., draft, memorandum; model, dummy 23 n. *prototype*; planning office, back room, staff college.

policy, forethought 510 n. *foresight*; statesmanship 498 n. *wisdom*; course of action, procedure, strategy 688 n. *tactics*; steps, measures 676 n. *action*; stroke of policy, coup d'état 676 n. *deed*; programme, prospectus, platform, plank, ticket, slate; line, party 1.

contrivance, expedient, resource, recourse, resort, card, trump 629 n. *means*; recipe, nostrum 658 n. *remedy*; loophole, way out 667 n. *means of escape*; artifice, device, gimmick 698 n. *stratagem*; wangle, fiddle 930 n. *foul play*; knack, trick 694 n. *skill*; stunt, wheeze, inspiration 451 n. *idea*; contraption, gadget 628 n. *instrument*; ad hoc measure, improvisation; makeshift 150 n. *substitute*; tour de force 676 n. *deed*.

plot, intrigue; web, web of intrigue;

practice, cabal, conspiracy, inside job; frame-up, machination; manipulation, wire-pulling; secret influence 523 n. *latency*; counterplot, countermine 713 n. *defence*.

planner, contriver, engineer, framer, inventor, originator, hatcher; promoter, projector; founder, author, builder; designer, backroom boy, boffin 696 n. *expert*; organizer, systematizer; strategist, tactician; statesman, politician; schemer, axe-grinder; careerist, go-getter 678 n. *busy person*; plotter, intriguer, intrigant, spinner, spider; cabal, conspirator.

Adj. *planned*, blueprinted, schematic 669 adj. *prepared*; strategic, tactical.

planning, contriving, resourceful, ingenious 698 adj. *cunning*; scheming, up to something; intriguing, conspiratorial.

Vb. *plan*, approach a problem, attack; make a plan, design, draft, blueprint; project, plan out, map o., lay o.; organize, systematize, rationalize, schematize, methodize; schedule, programme, phase; contrive, devise, engineer; hatch, concoct, mature 669 vb. *prepare*; arrange, prearrange 608 vb. *predetermine*; think ahead, look a. 498 vb. *be wise*; have a policy, follow a plan, work to a schedule.

plot, scheme, have designs, be up to something; manipulate, pull wires 178 vb. *influence*; cabal, intrigue, practise; conspire, concert, concoct, hatch; undermine, countermine 542 vb. *ensnare*.

624. Way – N. *way*, route 267 n. *itinerary*; manner, wise, guise; fashion, style 243 n. *form*; method, mode, line, approach, attack; procedure, process, way of doing, modus operandi 688 n. *tactics*; usual way, routine 610 n. *practice*; technique, know-how 694 n. *skill*; way of life 688 n. *conduct*. See *route*.

access, means of a., right of way, communications; way to 289 n. *approach*; entrance, door 263 n. *doorway*; adit, drive, gangway; vestibule, lobby, corridor; way through, pass, defile 305 n. *passage*; intersection see *road*; fairway, channel 351 n. *conduit*.

bridge, way over; footbridge, over-bridge, fly-over; viaduct, span; pontoon, floating bridge; drawbridge; stepping-stone, gangway, gangplank, cat-walk, duck-boards; underpass 263 n. *tunnel*; land-bridge, isthmus, neck.

route, direction, way to; line, course, march, tack, track, beat; trajectory, orbit; lane, traffic l., air l., sea l., sea-path; by-pass, détour 626 n. *circuit*.

path, pathway, footpath, sidewalk, pavement, by-path, tow-p.; bridle-path, ride, horse-track; by-way, lane, track, trail; walk, run, drive; esplanade, front 192 n. *street*; aisle, ambulatory; race-track 724 n. *arena*; channel, fairway.

road, high-r., highway, highways and by-ways; main road, turnpike, pike; thoroughfare, through road, trunk r., arterial r., artery, by-pass; motorway, speed-track; slipway, acceleration lane; clearway 305 n. *traffic control*; cross-road, crossways, junction, intersection, roundabout, clover leaf; roadway, carriageway, twin-track; metalled road 192 n. *street*; high street, side-s.; wynd, alley; pavement, sidewalk, kerb; pavé, cobbles, paving-stone, sett 226 n. *paving*; macadam, tarmac, asphalt.

railroad, railway, line; permanent way, track, lines; monorail, funicular, cable-way, ropeway; subway, tube 274 n. *train*; junction, level crossing, tunnel, cutting; siding, marshalling yard; signal, signal box, cabin; rails, points, sleepers, frog, fishplate.

Adj. *communicating*, granting access; through, main, arterial, trunk; bridged, fly-over; trafficky, busy; trodden, beaten.

625. Mid-course – N. *mid-course*, middle course, middle of the road, via media; golden mean, mediocrity 30 n. *average*; central position, half-way house, mid-stream 30 n. *middle point*; slack water, half tide; non-deviation, straight line, short cut, bee-line 249 n. *straightness*; neutrality, correctness 177 n. *moderation*; mutual concession 770 n. *compromise*.

moderate, non-extremist, Minimalist, Menshevist; middle-of-the-roader, half-and-halfer; neutral.

Adj. *neutral*, non-committal, uncommitted, unattached; moderate, non-extreme, unextreme, middle-of-the-road 225 adj. *central*; lukewarm, half-and-half 601 adj. *irresolute*; neither one thing nor the other, grey.

626. Circuit – N. *circuit*, roundabout way, longest w., circuitous route, by-pass, détour, loop 282 n. *deviation*; circulation, circumambulation, ambit, orbit, round, lap 314 n. *circuition*; circumference 250 n. *circle*.

Adj. *roundabout*, circuitous, indirect, out of the way; circulatory.

Vb. *circuit*, round, lap, go round 314 vb. *circle*; make a détour, go out of one's way 282 vb. *deviate*; turn, by-pass, short-circuit 620 vb. *avoid*; divagate, zigzag 294 vb. *diverge*; encircle 230 vb. *surround*; skirt, edge round.

627. Requirement – N. *requirement*, requisite, desideratum, want, lack, need 636 n. *insufficiency*; stipulation, prerequisite 766 n. *conditions*; essential, sine qua non, a must 596 n. *necessity*; needs, necessities, necessaries; indent, order, requisition, shopping list; demand, call for, run upon; consumption, input, intake 634 n. *waste*; balance due 803 n. *debt*; claim 761 n. *request*; injunction 737 n. *command*.

needfulness, case of need, occasion; necessity for, indispensability, desirability; necessitousness, want 801 n. *poverty*; exigence 740 n. *compulsion*; urgency, emergency 137 n. *crisis*; matter of life and death 638 n. *important matter*; obligation 917 n. *duty*; bare minimum, the least one can do; possible need, incasement.

Adj. *required*, requisite, prerequisite, needful, needed; necessary, essential, vital, indispensable, not to be spared; in request, in demand 859 adj. *desired*; wanted, missing, desiderated, to seek 190 adj. *absent*.

necessitous, in want, in need; deprived of, craving; destitute 801 adj. *poor*.

Vb. *require*, need, want, lack 636 vb. *not suffice*; stand in need of, have occasion for; miss, desiderate; crave 859 vb. *desire*; call for, demand; claim, 761 vb. *request*; consume, take 634 vb. *waste*; stipulate 766 vb. *give terms*; order, indent, requisition 633 vb. *provide*; reserve, book, earmark.

628. Instrumentality – N. *instrumentality*, operation 173 n. *agency*; occasion 156 n. *cause*; result 157 n. *effect*; pressure 178 n. *influence*; efficacy 160 n. *power*; services, help, assistance, midwifery 703 n. *aid*; support 706 n. *cooperation*; subservience 739 n. *obedience*; instrument 630 n. *tool*; medium 629 n. *means*; serviceability, handiness 640 n. *utility*; lever, leverage; instrumentation, mechanization, automation 630 n. *machine*.

Adj. *instrumental*, working, automatic, push-button 173 adj. *operative*; effective 160 adj. *powerful*; conducive 156 adj. *causal*; practical, applied; serviceable 640 adj. *useful*; helpful 703 adj. *aiding*; obstetric, maieutic; functional, agential, subservient, ministerial; mediated by.

Vb. *be instrumental*, work, act 173 vb. *operate*; perform 676 vb. *do*; minister, serve, work for, subserve, lend oneself (*or* itself) to, pander to 703 vb. *minister to*; help, assist 703 vb. *aid*; promote 703 vb. *patronize*; have a hand in 775 vb. *participate*; effect 156 vb. *cause*.

629. Means – N. *means*, ways and m., wherewithal; potential 160 n. *ability*; conveniences, facilities; appliances, bag of tricks 630 n. *tool*; technique, know-how 694 n. *skill*; equipment, supplies, stock, munitions, ammunition 633 n. *provision*; resources, raw material 631 n. *materials*; pool of labour, manpower 686 n. *personnel*; finance, sinews of war 800 n. *wealth*; assets 777 n. *property*; line of credit 802 n. *credit*; reserves, stand-by, two strings to one's bow 662 n. *safe-guard*; cure, specific 658 n. *remedy*; expedient 623 n. *contrivance*.

Vb. *find means*, provide the wherewithal, supply 633 vb. *provide*; equip, fit out 669 vb. *make ready*; finance, promote, float; have the means 160 vb. *be able*; contrive 623 vb. *plan*; beg, borrow, or steal 771 vb. *acquire*.

630. Tool – N. *tool*, precision t., implement, instrument; apparatus, appliance, organ; weapon, arm 723 n. *arms*; device, mechanical d., gadget 623 n. *contrivance*; mechanical aid, handle, trigger; leverage, lever; handmaid, hand, minister, slave 742 n. *servant*; puppet, catspaw, stooge; pawn, piece; robot; prehistoric tool, flint; tools of the trade, tool-kit, do-it-yourself k., bag of tricks.

machine, mechanical device; machinery, mechanism, works; clockwork, wheels within wheels; spring, mainspring; motor, engine; robot, automation.

mechanics, engineering, telemechanics; servo-mechanics, cybernetics; automatic control, automation; mechanical power, mechanical advantage; technicology, technology.

equipment, furniture, appointments; gear, tackle; fittings, fixture; upholstery, furnishing; outfit, kit; trappings, accoutrement, harness; utensils, impedimenta; ware, stock-in-trade 795 n. *merchandise*.

machinist, operator, driver, minder, machine-m. 686 n. *agent*; engineer, mechanic, fitter; tool-user, craftsman 686 n. *artisan*.

Adj. *mechanical*, mechanistic, powered, power-driven; automatic; robot, self-acting, instrumental; machine-minded, tool-using.

631. Materials – N. *materials*, resources 629 n. *means*; material, stuff, staple, stock; raw material, grist; meat, fodder 301 n. *food*; oil 385 n. *fuel*; ore, mineral, metal; timber, wood; cloth, fabric 222 n. *textile*.

building material, brick 381 n. *pottery*; bricks and mortar, wattle and daub, lath and plaster, slate, tile, shingle, stone, marble, ashlar, masonry, cement, concrete, ferro-concrete.

paper, rag-p., pulp, wood-p., newsprint; papier mâché, cardboard, pasteboard, straw-board, carton; sheet, foolscap, quire, ream; note-paper 586 n. *stationery*.

632. Store – N. *store*, mass, heap, load, stack, stock-pile, build-up 74 n. *accumulation*; packet, bundle, budget 26 n. *quantity*; harvest, crop, vintage 771 n. *acquisition*; haystack, rick; stock, stock-in-trade 795 n. *merchandise*; assets, capital, holding, investment 777 n. *property*; fund, reserves, something in hand, backlog; unexpended balance, savings, nest-egg; deposit, hoard, treasure; buried treasure, cache 527 n. *hiding place*; bottom drawer, hope chest, trousseau 633 n. *provision*; pool, kitty; quarry, mine, gold-m.; natural deposit, mineral d.; coal measures, coal-field, gas-f., oil-f.; coal-face, seam, stringer, lode; pipe, vein, rich v.; bonanza, strike 484 n. *discovery*; well, oil-w., gusher; fountain, fount 156 n. *source*; supply, stream; tap, pipe-line; milch-cow, cornucopia, abundance 635 n. *plenty*; repertoire, range (see *collection*).

storage, stowage 74 n. *accumulation*; conservation 666 n. *preservation*; safe deposit 660 n. *protection*; stabling, warehousing; storage, storage space, shelf-room, space, accommodation 183 n. *room*; hold, bunker 194 n. *cellar*; store-town, supply base, promptuary, store-house, store-room, stockroom; warehouse, goods-shed, go-down; dump, depository, depot, entrepôt; dock, wharf, garage 192 n. *stable*; magazine, arsenal, armoury, gun-room; treasure-house 799 n. *treasury*; bank, safe, strong-room, vault, coffer, money-box, money-bag, till; hive, honeycomb; granary, garner, barn; reservoir, cistern, tank; gas-holder, gasometer; larder 194 n. *chamber*; portmanteau, hold-all,

packing-case 194 n. *box*; container 194 n. *receptacle*.

collection, set, complete s.; archives, file 548 n. *record*; folder, bundle, portfolio 74 n. *accumulation*; museum, antiquarium, gallery, art g.; library; menagerie 369 n. *zoo*; exhibition 522 n. *exhibit*; repertory, repertoire, bag of tricks.

Adj. *stored*, in store, in deposit; in hand, in reserve, unexpended; available, in stock.

Vb. *store*, stow, pack, bundle 193 vb. *load*; lay up, dump, house, garage, stable, warehouse; garner, gather, harvest 370 n. *cultivate*; stack, heap, pile, amass, accumulate 74 vb. *bring together*; stock up, lay in, stockpile 36 vb. *augment*; fuel, coal, bunker 633 vb. *provide*; top up, refill, refuel 633 vb. *replenish*; put by, save, keep, hold, file; bottle, pickle 666 vb. *preserve*; keep in hand, reserve, put to r.; fund, bank, deposit, invest; hoard, treasure, hive; husband, save up, salt away 814 vb. *economize*; pool, put in the kitty 775 vb. *socialize*.

633. Provision – N. *provision*, logistics; equipment 669 n. *fitting out*; purveyance, catering; service, delivery; self-service; maintenance, entertainment, bed and board, board and lodging; supply, constant s., pipeline, feed; commissariat, provisioning, supplies, stores, rations; provender 301 n. *provisions*; helping, portion 301 n. *meal*; grist, fuel, budgeting, budget 808 n. *accounts*.

provider, donor 781 n. *giver*; creditor 784 n. *lender*; wet-nurse, feeder; purser 798 n. *treasurer*; steward, commissary, quartermaster, storekeeper; supplier, victualler, sutler; provision merchant; retailer 794 n. *tradesman*; procurer 952 n. *bawd*.

caterer, purveyor, hotelier, hotel-keeper, restaurateur; innkeeper, alewife, landlord, mine host, publican; house-keeper, housewife.

Adj. *provisionary*, commissarial; self-service; sufficing, all-s. 635 adj. *suffici-*

ent; available, on tap, on the menu, on 189 adj. *present*.

Vb. *provide*, afford, offer, lend 781 vb. *give*; provision, find, find one in; equip, furnish 669 vb. *make ready*; supply, keep fed; yield 164 vb. *produce*; pipe, pump in, pipeline; cater, purvey; procure, pander, pimp; service, service an order 793 vb. *sell*; deliver, make deliveries, deliver the goods; hand out, serve up, dish up; victual, feed, cook for, board, put up, maintain, keep, clothe; budget; stock up 632 vb. *store*; fuel, coal, bunker; forage, water; tap, draw, draw on, milk 304 vb. *extract*.

replenish, recruit, make good; fill up, top up, refill 54 vb. *fill*; revictual, restock, refuel, reload.

634. Waste – **N.** *waste*, wastage 42 n. *decrement*; leakage 298 n. *outflow*; inroad; consumption, intake 627 n. *requirement*; outlay, expense 806 n. *expenditure*; depletion, exhaustion, drainage 300 n. *voidance*; dissipation 75 n. *dispersion*; evaporation 338 n. *vaporization*; damage 772 n. *loss*; wear and tear 655 n. *deterioration*; wastefulness, uneconomy, extravagance 815 n. *prodigality*; mischief, destructiveness 165 n. *destruction*; waste product, refuse, exhaust 641 n. *rubbish*.

Adj. *wasteful*, extravagant, unnecessary, uneconomic 815 adj. *prodigal*; mischievous 165 adj. *destructive*.

Vb. *waste*, consume, make inroads on, wade into; swallow, devour, eat up 301 vb. *eat*; spend, lay out 806 vb. *expend*; take, use up, exhaust, deplete, drain, suck dry 300 vb. *void*; dissipate, scatter 75 vb. *disperse*; abuse, overwork, overcrop, impoverish, milk dry 675 vb. *misuse*; wear out 655 vb. *impair*; misapply, fritter away, cast before swine; make no use of 674 vb. *not use*; overspend, squander 815 vb. *be prodigal*; ruin, play havoc 165 vb. *lay waste*; leak, run low, dry up 298 vb. *flow out*; melt away 337 vb. *liquefy*; evaporate 338 vb. *vaporize*; run to seed 655 vb. *deteriorate*; run to waste, go down the drain.

635. Sufficiency – **N.** *sufficiency*, right amount; right qualities, qualification; right number, quorum; adequacy, enough, pass marks; competence, living wage; minimum, no less, least one can do; full measure, satisfaction, all that could be desired 828 n. *content*; the possible 469 n. *possibility*; fulfilment 725 n. *completion*; repletion, one's fill 863 n. *satiety*.

plenty, God's p., cornucopia 171 n. *abundance*; outpouring, flood, tide, spate, streams, lots, lashings, galore 32 n. *great quantity*; fullness, copiousness, amplitude 54 n. *plenitude*; affluence, riches 800 n. *wealth*; fat of the land, luxury 637 n. *superfluity*; orgy, riot, profusion, fertility, productivity, luxuriance, lushness, rankness 171 n. *productiveness*; harvest, bumper crop; rich vein, bonanza, more where it came from 632 n. *store*; more than enough 637 n. *redundance*.

Adj. *sufficient*, sufficing, all-s.; self-sufficient 54 adj. *complete*; enough, adequate, competent; satisfactory 828 adj. *contenting*.

plenteous, plentiful, ample, enough and to spare, more than enough 637 adj. *superfluous*; generous, lavish 813 adj. *liberal*; wholesale, without stint, unsparing, unmeasured, exhaustless, inexhaustible 32 adj. *great*; luxuriant 171 adj. *productive*; profuse, abundant, copious, overflowing 637 adj. *redundant*.

Vb. *suffice*, be enough, do, answer 642 vb. *be expedient*; qualify, make the grade, pass, pass muster; measure up to, fill the bill; rise to the occasion; prove acceptable, satisfy 828 vb. *content*; satiate, give one his bellyful 863 vb. *sate*; abound 637 vb. *superabound*.

636. Insufficiency – **N.** *insufficiency*, not enough; inadequacy, incompetence; mingeness, little enough, nothing to spare 33 n. *small quantity*; too few, no quorum 105 n. *fewness*; deficiency, imperfection 647 n. *defect*; deficit 55 n. *incompleteness*; half-measures 307 n. *shortcoming*; bankruptcy 805 n. *insolvency*;

subsistence level, pittance; stinginess 816 n. *parsimony*; short commons, iron rations, austerity, starvation diet 945 n. *asceticism*.

scarcity, scarceness, paucity 140 n. *infrequency*; dearth, leanness, seven lean years; drought, famine, starvation; shortfall 307 n. *shortcoming*; short supply, seller's market; stint, scantiness, meagreness, lack, want, need 627 n. *needfulness*; low water 212 n. *shallowness*.

Adj. *insufficient*, unsatisfactory, disappointing; meagre, not enough, inadequate; too small, cramping 33 adj. *small*; deficient, lacking, wanting, found w. 35 adj. *inferior*; incompetent 695 adj. *unskilful*; niggardly 816 adj. *parsimonious*.

unprovided; unsupplied, unfurnished, ill-furnished, ill-supplied; bare 190 adj. *empty*; empty-handed 728 adj. *unsuccessful*; unsatisfied 829 adj. *discontented*; understaffed, undermanned.

underfed, undernourished, under-vitaminized; on short commons; unfed, famished, famine-stricken, starving 946 adj. *fasting*; starveling, thin, meagre 206 adj. *lean*.

scarce, rare 140 adj. *infrequent*; sparse 105 adj. *few*; short, in short supply, hard to get, not to be had, unavailable, unprocurable, unobtainable, out of stock.

Vb. *not suffice*, not meet requirements; want, lack, leave a gap 627 vb. *require*; come short, default 307 vb. *fall short*; run out, dry up; take half measures, tinker, paper over the cracks 726 vb. *not complete*.

make insufficient, ask *or* expect too much; overcrop, impoverish 655 vb. *impair*; starve, undernourish; stint, skimp, scant, ration 816 vb. *be parsimonious*; understaff, underman; cramp 747 vb. *restrain*.

637. Redundance – N. *redundance*, overspill, overflow, inundation 298 n. *outflow*; abundance, superabundance, exuberance, luxuriance, riot, profusion 635

n. *plenty*; avalanche, spate 32 n. *great quantity*; saturation 54 n. *plenitude*; excessiveness, exorbitance, extremes, too much 546 n. *exaggeration*; overmeasure, overpayment, overweight; burden, last straw 322 n. *gravity*; over-indulgence 943 n. *intemperance*; overdose, surfeit, plethora, congestion 863 n. *satiety*; more than enough, bellyful 635 n. *satisfaction*; glut (see *superfluity*); fat, fattiness.

superfluity, more than is needed, luxury, luxuriousness, luxury article; overfulfilment, supererogation, work of s.; something over, bonus 40 n. *extra*; margin, overlap, excess, overplus, surplusage, surplus, balance 41 n. *remainder*; superfluousness, excrescence, accessory, parasite 641 n. *inutility*; redundancy, more men than jobs 679 n. *inactivity*; more jobs than men, over-employment 678 n. *activity*; too much of a good thing, glut, drug on the market; surfeit, sickener, overdose 863 n. *satiety*.

Adj. *redundant*, too many 104 adj. *many*; overmuch, excessive, unnecessary; overdone 546 adj. *exaggerated*; overfull 54 adj. *full*; saturated 341 adj. *drenched*; cloying 838 adj. *tedious*; plethoric.

superfluous, supererogatory, supernumerary; otiose, excrescent; needless, unnecessary 641 adj. *useless*; excessive, more than one asked for; luxurious; expletive, pleonastic; surplus, extra, over and above, spare, to spare 38 adj. *additional*; de trop, a-begging 860 adj. *unwanted*; dispensable, expendable, replaceable 812 adj. *cheap*.

Vb. *superabound*, riot, luxuriate, abound; run riot, overproduce, overpopulate 171 vb. *be fruitful*; outnumber 104 vb. *be many*; overflow, brim over, burst at the seams 54 vb. *be complete*; flood, inundate, burst its banks, deluge, overwhelm 350 vb. *flow*; know no bounds 306 vb. *overstep*; soak, saturate 341 vb. *drench*; gorge, cram, congest 54 vb. *fill*; overdose, glut, cloy 863 vb. *sate*; overfeed, pamper oneself 932 vb. *be intemperate*; overfulfil, oversubscribe, do more than enough; overstock, pile up;

overdo 546 vb. *exaggerate*; overload, overburden; overcharge, surcharge.

638. Importance – N. *importance*, first i., primacy, priority, urgency 64 n. *precedence*; import, consequence, significance, weight, gravity, seriousness, solemnity; materiality, substance, pith, moment 3 n. *substantiality*; interest, concern 622 n. *business*; mark, prominence, distinction, eminence 866 n. *repute*; size 32 n. *greatness*; value 644 n. *goodness*.

important matter, vital concern, breath of one's nostrils, be-all and end-all; not peanuts, no joke, no laughing matter, matter of life and death; big news, great n. 529 n. *news*; great doings, exploit 676 n. *deed*; red-letter day.

chief thing, what matters, the thing; issue, supreme i. 452 n. *topic*; fundamentals, bedrock 1 n. *reality*; essential, sine qua non 627 n. *requirement*; priority, first choice 605 n. *choice*; gist, substance 5 n. *essential part*; cream, salt, pick 644 n. *élite*; keynote, cornerstone, mainstay; head and front, spearhead; heart of the matter, heart 225 n. *centre*; hub 218 n. *pivot*; cardinal point, half the battle 32 n. *main part*.

bigwig, personage, notability 866 n. *person of repute*; great man, V.I.P., brass hat; his nibs, big shot, big noise; panjandrum; eading light 500 n. *sage*; king pin, key man 696 n. *expert*; first fiddle, prima donna, star, catch 890 n. *favourite*; lion, big game; uncrowned king, Mr Big; top people, superior person, superman, wonderman, lord of creation 34 n. *superior*.

Adj. *important*, weighty, grave, solemn, serious; pregnant, big; world-shattering, earth-shaking, seismic 178 adj. *influential*; momentous, critical, fateful 137 adj. *timely*; chief, capital, cardinal, staple, major, main, paramount 34 adj. *supreme*; essential, material, to the point 9 adj. *relevant*; pivotal 225 n. *central*; basic, fundamental, bedrock, radical; primary, prime, foremost, leading; overriding, overruling, uppermost;

worth-while, not to be sneezed at 644 adj. *valuable*; necessary, indispensable, irreplaceable, key 627 adj. *required*; pressing, insistent, urgent, high-priority; overdue 136 adj. *late*; high-level, top-l., summital 213 adj. *topmost*; top-secret; high, grand, noble 32 adj. *great*.

notable, of mark, egregious, memorable, signal, unforgettable; outstanding 34 adj. *superior*; ranking, top-rank, top-flight 644 adj. *excellent*; conspicuous, prominent, distinguished 866 adj. *noteworthy*; august 821 adj. *impressive*; bigtime, news-worthy, front-page; eventful, stirring, breath-taking, shattering, earth-shaking, seismic, epoch-making.

Vb. *be important*, matter, weigh, carry, tell, count 178 vb. *influence*; concern, interest, affect.

make important, give weight to, seize on, fasten on; bring to the fore, enhance, highlight; rub in, stress, labour 532 vb. *emphasize*; headline, splash 528 vb. *advertise*; put on the map 528 vb. *proclaim*; write in letters of gold 876 vb. *celebrate*; magnify, glorify 920 vb. *show respect*; take seriously; value, make much of, set store by 920 vb. *respect*.

639. Unimportance – N. *unimportance*, inconsequence; secondariness 35 n. *inferiority*; insignificance 515 n. *unmeaningness*; immateriality, inessentiality 4 n. *insubstantiality*; pettiness 33 n. *smallness*; paltriness 922 n. *despisedness*; worthlessness 812 n. *cheapness*; irrelevance, red herring 10 n. *irrelation*.

trifle, inessential, triviality, technicality; nothing, mere n., no matter, parish pump; secondary matter, side-show; no great shakes, nothing to boast of; tithe, fraction 53 n. *part*; bagatelle, tinker's curse, straw, pin; small item, twopence, small change, small beer, small potatoes; chicken-feed, flea-bite; pinprick, scratch; nothing to it, child's play 701 n. *easy thing*; peccadillo, venial sin; trifles, trivia, minutiae, detail, petty d. 80 n. *particulars*.

bauble, toy, rattle 837 n. *plaything*; gewgaw, knick-knack, kickshaw, bric-à-brac; trinket, tinsel, trumpery, frippery, trash, gimcrack, stuff.

nonentity, nobody, obscurity; man of straw 4 n. *insubstantial thing*; figurehead, cipher, sleeping partner; fribble, trifler; mediocrity, light-weight, small beer, tail (of a team); small fry, other ranks 869 n. *commonalty*; second fiddle 35 n. *inferior*; understrapper 742 n. *servant*; pawn, stooge, puppet 630 n. *tool*; Cinderella, pipsqueak 867 n. *object of scorn*.

Adj. *unimportant*, immaterial 4 adj. *insubstantial*; uninfluential, inconsequential; insignificant 515 adj. *unmeaning*; inessential, not vital; unnecessary, dispensable, expendable; puny, small, petty, trifling, nugatory, flimsy, paltry 33 adj. *inconsiderable*; negligible, out of the running; powerless 161 adj. *impotent*; wretched, miserable, pitiful, pitiable, pathetic, poor, mean, sorry 645 adj. *bad*; obscure, of no account, overrated, beneath notice, beneath contempt 922 adj. *contemptible*; low-level, secondary, minor, subsidiary, peripheral 35 adj. *inferior*.

trivial, trifling, piffling, fiddling; technical; footling, puerile 499 adj. *foolish*; superficial 212 adj. *shallow*; slight; light-weight; forgivable, venial; one-horse, second-rate, rubbishy, trumpery, trashy, tawdry, catchpenny, pinchbeck, pot-boiling, two-a-penny, worthless 922 adj. *contemptible*; toy, token, nominal, symbolic 547 adj. *indicating*; commonplace 610 adj. *usual*.

640. Utility – N. *utility*, use, usefulness; employability, serviceability, handiness 628 n. *instrumentality*; adaptability, applicability, suitability 642 n. *expedience*; service, avail, help, stead 703 n. *aid*; value 644 n. *goodness*; virtue, capacity, potency 160 n. *power*; advantage, benefit; profitability, earning capacity 171 n. *productiveness*; profit 771 n. *gain*; convenience, benefit; utilization 673 n. *use*.

Adj. *useful*, of use, helpful, of service 703 adj. *aiding*; sensible, practical, applied, functional; multipurpose, all-

purpose; commodious, convenient 642 adj. *expedient*; handy, serviceable, fit for, good f., adaptable, applicable, usable, employable, good, valid; efficacious, effective 160 adj. *powerful*; pragmatic, utilitarian.

profitable, paying, remunerative 771 adj. *gainful*; prolific, fertile 164 adj. *productive*; beneficial, advantageous, to one's advantage, edifying, worth-while 615 adj. *good*; invaluable, priceless 644 adj. *valuable*.

Vb. *be useful,* — of use etc. adj.; avail, stead, stand one in good s.; come in handy, perform a function; serve, serve one's turn, suit one's purpose 642 vb. *be expedient*; help 703 vb. *aid*; do service, do yeoman s. 742 vb. *serve*; benefit 644 vb. *do good*; pay, make a profit.

641. Inutility – N. *inutility*, uselessness; no function, no purpose, superfluousness 637 n. *superfluity*; futility, vanity 497 n. *absurdity*; worthlessness, unemployability; inadequacy 636 n. *insufficiency*; inefficiency, incompetence 695 n. *unskilfulness*; unserviceableness, inconvenience, unsuitability, unfitness 643 n. *inexpedience*; inapplicability, unadaptability; disservice, disadvantage.

lost labour 728 n. *failure*; waste of breath, waste of time; labour in vain, wild-goose chase, fool's errand; half-measures, tinkering.

rubbish, good riddance, trash, stuff; waste-product, waste, refuse, lumber, junk, old iron, litter; spoilage, waste paper; scourings, off-s., sweepings, dregs, lees 41 n. *leavings*; chaff, husks, bran; scraps, bits, crumbs; offal, carrion; dust, muck, débris, slag, dross, scum 649 n. *dirt*; dead wood; rags, old clothes, cast-offs; reject, throw-out; midden, rubbish-heap, dust-h., spoil-h.; dust-hole, dump; sucked orange.

Adj. *useless*, functionless, purposeless, pointless; futile, unpractical, impracticable, unworkable, effort-wasting; nonfunctional 844 adj. *ornamental*; otiose, redundant, excrescent 637 adj. *superfluous*; expendable 860 adj. *unwanted*;

unfit, inapplicable 643 adj. *inexpedient*; fit for nothing, unusable, unemployable; unqualified, inefficient 695 adj. *unskilful*; ineffective, ineffectual 161 adj. *impotent*; unserviceable, out of order; broken down, effete, past work, obsolete 127 adj. *antiquated*.

profitless, loss-making, unprofitable, wasteful, ill-spent, in vain, losing; abortive 728 adj. *unsuccessful*; unrewarding, unrewarded, thankless; barren, sterile 172 adj. *unproductive*; worthless, good for nothing, valueless; rubbishy, trashy, unsaleable, dear at any price.

Vb. *be useless*, have no use, waste one's time, achieve no purpose; not help 702 vb. *hinder*; fall by the wayside 172 vb. *be unproductive*; go a-begging.

waste effort, labour the obvious; lose one's labour, labour in vain, flog a dead horse, cry for the moon; tinker, paper over the cracks.

642. Expedience – N. *expedience*, good policy; advisability, desirability, suitability 640 n. *utility*; fitness, propriety 915 n. *dueness*; rule of expediency, convenience; pragmatism, utilitarianism, opportunism, time-serving; an expedient, pis aller 623 n. *contrivance*.

Adj. *expedient*, expediential, advisable; desirable, worth-while; suitable 24 adj. *fit*; fitting, proper 913 adj. *right*; well-timed, opportune 137 adj. *timely*; politic 498 adj. *wise*; advantageous, profitable 640 adj. *useful*; convenient, workable, practical; qualified, cut out for; to the purpose, adapted to, applicable; handy, effective.

Vb. *be expedient*, speak to one's condition, come not amiss, serve the time, suit the occasion, beseem, befit; expedite help 703 vb. *aid*; answer, produce results; work, do, serve, deliver the goods, fill the bill; profit, advantage, benefit 644 vb. *do good*.

643. Inexpedience – N. *inexpedience*, no answer, bad policy, counsel of despair, inadvisability, undesirability; unsuitability, unfitness 25 n. *inaptitude*; untimeliness 138 n. *intempestivity*; inconvenience, disadvantage, detriment.

Adj. *inexpedient*, better not, unadvisable, not recommended 924 adj. *disapproved*; ill-advised, impolitic 499 adj. *unwise*; inappropriate, unfitting, out of place, unseemly 916 adj. *undue*; unfit, unsuitable, inept 25 adj. *unapt*; unseasonable 138 adj. *ill-timed*; inconvenient, detrimental, disadvantageous 645 adj. *harmful*; unprofitable 641 adj. *useless*; unhelpful 702 adj. *hindering*.

Vb. *be inexpedient*, not fit, come amiss, won't do, won't wash, not answer; not help 641 vb. *be useless*; penalize, hurt 645 vb. *harm*; embarrass 700 vb. *be difficult*.

644. Goodness – N. *goodness*, soundness, quality, vintage; good points, redeeming feature; merit, desert, title to fame; excellence, eminence 34 n. *superiority*; virtue, worth, value; flawlessness 646 n. *perfection*; quintessence 1 n. *essence*; beneficence 897 n. *benevolence*, 933 n. *virtue*.

élite, chosen few, chosen people; pick, prime, flower; cream, salt of the earth, pick of the bunch; crack troops, corps d'élite; top people 638 n. *bigwig*; top drawer 868 n. *nobility*.

exceller, nonpareil, prodigy, genius; superman, wonderman, wonder 646 n. *paragon*; one in a thousand, treasure, jewel 844 n. *gem*; gold, pure g.; chef-d'œuvre, collector's piece 694 n. *masterpiece*; record-breaker, best-seller, best ever; the goods, winner, fizzer, corker, knockout, hit; star, idol 890 n. *favourite*; the tops, top-notcher, top seed, first-rater; champion, title-holder, world-beater 727 n. *victor*.

Adj. *excellent*, eximious; well-done, exemplary; good 933 adj. *virtuous*; above par 34 adj. *superior*; first-rate, alpha plus, surpassing; prime, quality, fine, superfine, most desirable; God's own, superlative; of the first water, rare, vintage, classic 646 adj. *perfect*; choice, select, handpicked, tested, exquisite; worthy, meritorious 915 adj. *deserving*; admirable, praiseworthy 923 adj. *ap-*

provable; famous, great; glorious, dazzling, splendid, magnificent, marvellous, wonderful, terrific, superb.

topping, top-hole (see *best*); lovely, glorious, heavenly, out of this world; fabulous, super, wizard, zingy; smashing, stunning, corking; swell, great, grand, dandy, crackajack, hunky-dory; scrumptious, delicious 826 adj. *pleasurable*.

best, optimum, A1, champion, bonzer, tip-top, top-notch, nothing like; first, first-rate, crack; second to none, unequalled, unmatched, peerless, matchless; best-ever, record.

valuable, of value, invaluable, inestimable, priceless, above price, costly, rich 811 adj. *of price*; irreplaceable, unique, rare, precious, golden, worth its weight in gold; sterling, gilt-edged.

beneficial, wholesome, salutary 652 adj. *salubrious*; edifying, worth-while 640 adj. *useful*; propitious 730 adj. *prosperous*; harmless, innocuous 935 adj. *innocent*.

not bad, tolerable, passable, fair, satisfactory 635 adj. *sufficient*; nice, decent, pretty good, all right; unexceptionable, unobjectionable; indifferent, middling 30 adj. *median*.

Vb. *be good*, have quality; have merit 915 vb. *deserve*; qualify, stand the test, pass, pass muster; challenge comparison, vie, rival 28 vb. *equal*; excel, transcend, overtop 34 vb. *be superior*.

do good, edify; be the making of 654 vb. *make better*; help, benefit; do a favour 897 vb. *be benevolent*.

645. Badness – **N.** *badness*, bad qualities, obnoxiousness, nastiness, beastliness, foulness, grossness, rottenness; demerit, unworthiness, worthlessness; low quality 35 n. *inferiority*; faultiness 647 n. *imperfection*; shoddiness 641 n. *inutility*; rankness, unsoundness, taint 655 n. *deterioration*; peccancy, morbidity 651 n. *disease*; harmfulness, injury, detriment, damage, mischief 616 n. *evil*; noxiousness, deadliness, virulence, poison, blight 659 n. *bane*; pestilence, plague spot,

hotbed 651 n. *infection*; abomination, filth 649 n. *uncleanness*; malignity, spite 898 n. *malevolence*; depravity 934 n. *wickedness*; sin 936 n. *guilt*; bad influence, evil genius; ill wind 731 n. *misfortune*; hoodoo, jinx 983 n. *sorcery*; curse 899 n. *malediction*; bad character 904 n. *evildoer*.

Adj. *bad*, arrant, vile, base, ill-conditioned; gross, black; irredeemable, as bad as bad can be; poor, mean, wretched, measly, low-grade, execrable, awful 35 adj. *inferior*; no good, worthless, shoddy, ropy, punk 641 adj. *useless*; unsatisfactory, faulty 647 adj. *imperfect*; bad at, incompetent 695 adj. *clumsy*; foul, noisome 397 adj. *fetid* (see *not nice*); rotten, rank, unsound 51 adj. *decomposed*; peccant, disordered, septic 651 adj. *diseased*; irremediable, incurable; vicious, accursed 934 adj. *wicked*; heinous, sinful 936 adj. *guilty*; wrongful 914 adj. *wrong*; sinister 616 adj. *evil* (see *harmful*); immeritorious, unworthy; shameful, scandalous 867 adj. *discreditable*; sad, melancholy, lamentable, deplorable, pitiable, pitiful 827 adj. *distressing*; unendurable 827 adj. *intolerable*.

harmful, hurtful, malefic, mischievous, wanton, outrageous 898 adj. *maleficent*; injurious, damaging, detrimental, prejudicial, disadvantageous; deleterious, corrosive 165 adj. *destructive*; pernicious, fatal 362 adj. *deadly*; costly 811 adj. *dear*; disastrous, ruinous, calamitous 731 adj. *adverse*; noxious, unwholesome 653 adj. *insalubrious*; poisonous, venomous 653 adj. *toxic*; sinister, ominous, dire, dreadful, baleful, baneful, accursed 616 adj. *evil*.

not nice, unlikeable, obnoxious, poisonous, septic; nasty, beastly, horrid, horrible, ghastly, awful, dreadful; scruffy 867 adj. *disreputable*; foul, rotten, lousy, putrid, sickening, revolting 861 adj. *disliked*; loathsome, detestable 888 adj. *hateful*; vulgar, low, improper, gross, filthy, obscene 951 adj. *impure*; shocking 924 adj. *disapproved*; plaguey 827 adj. *annoying*.

damnable, damned, blasted, confounded, blinking, blankety-blank; execrable, cursed, hellish, infernal, devilish, diabolical.

Vb. *harm*, do h., do a mischief, scathe 827 vb. *hurt*; cost one dear 811 vb. *be dear*; injure, damage, damnify 655 vb. *impair*; corrupt 655 vb. *pervert*; do no good 641 vb. *be useless*; do evil 914 vb. *do wrong*; plague, vex, trouble 827 vb. *incommode*; land one in trouble, spite 898 vb. *be malevolent*, aggrieve.

646. Perfection – N. *perfection*, finish, classic quality; the ideal; nothing wrong with, immaculacy, faultlessness, flawlessness; irreproachability, impeccability; transcendence 34 n. *superiority*; height *or* pitch of perfection, ne plus ultra, last word; chef d'œuvre 694 n. *masterpiece*.

paragon, nonesuch, nonpareil, flower, a beauty 644 n. *exceller*; ideal, prince of; classic, pattern, standard, norm, model, mirror 23 n. *prototype*; superman, wonderman 864 n. *prodigy*.

Adj. *perfect*, perfected; ripe 669 adj. *matured*; ideal, flawless, faultless, impeccable, infallible, indefectible; correct, irreproachable; unspoilt, immaculate, unblemished, unflawed, unstained; spotless, unspotted; uncontaminated, pure 44 adj. *unmixed*; sound, whole, entire, hundred per cent; complete 52 adj. *intact*; unhurt, scatheless, unscathed; beyond praise, consummate, brilliant, masterly 694 adj. *skilful*; model, classic, excellent.

Vb. *perfect*, consummate, bring to perfection; ripen 669 vb. *mature*; complete, leave nothing to be desired 725 vb. *carry through*.

647. Imperfection – N. *imperfection*, not hundred per cent; room for improvement, not one's best; faultiness, fallibility 495 n. *error*; patchiness, unevenness, curate's egg 17 n. *non-uniformity*; immaturity, unripeness 670 n. *undevelopment*; defectiveness, missing link 55 n. *incompleteness*; lack, want 627 n. *requirement*; deficiency, inadequacy 636 n.

insufficiency; unsoundness 661 n. *vulnerability*; inferior version, poor relation 35 n. *inferiority*; second best, pis aller, makeshift 150 n. *substitute*; mediocrity 30 n. *average*.

defect, fault 495 n. *error*; flaw, rift, leak, loophole, crack 201 n. *gap*; deficiency, limitation, failing, weakness 307 n. *shortcoming*; kink, twist, screw loose 503 n. *eccentricity*; weak point, soft spot, chink in one's armour, Achilles' heel 661 n. *vulnerability*; feet of clay, weak link in the chain 163 n. *weakness*; taint 845 n. *blemish*; drawback, snag, fly in the ointment 702 n. *obstacle*.

Adj. *imperfect*, open to criticism; fallible, peccable; uneven, patchy, good in parts 17 adj. *non-uniform*; faulty, botched 695 adj. *bungled*; flawed, cracked; unstaunch, leaky, not proof; unsound 661 adj. *vulnerable*; soiled, shop-s. 845 adj. *blemished*; not at one's best, below par, off form; stale 684 adj. *fatigued*; off-colour 651 adj. *unhealthy*; not good enough, inadequate 636 adj. *insufficient*; defective 55 adj. *incomplete*, 53 adj. *fragmentary*; maimed 163 adj. *crippled*; unthorough, perfunctory 456 adj. *inattentive*; undeveloped, raw, crude 670 adj. *immature*; makeshift, provisional; second-best, second-rate 35 adj. *inferior*; moderate, unheroic; tolerable, bearable, better than nothing 923 adj. *approvable*.

Vb. *be imperfect*, fail of perfection, have a fault; might be better 307 vb. *fall short*; not bear inspection, not impress.

648. Cleanness – N. *cleanness*, freedom from dirt, immaculateness 950 n. *purity*; freshness, whiteness; shine, polish, spit and polish; cleanliness, kid gloves, daintiness 862 n. *fastidiousness*.

cleansing, clean, spring-c.; washing, cleaning up, mopping up, washing up; refining, clarification, purification, epuration; sprinkling, lustration, washing out, flushing, purging; airing, ventilation, fumigation 338 n. *vaporization*; deodorization 395 n. *inodorousness*; antisepsis, sterilization, disinfection, disinfestation, delousing; sanitation, conservancy, drainage, sewerage, plumbing 652 n. *hygiene.*

ablution, washing; douche, flush, wash; bathing, dipping; soaping, scrubbing, sponging, rinsing, shampoo; dip 313 n. *plunge*; bath, tub; hip-bath, bidet; wash-basin, ewer, hot bath, vapour b., blanket b.; shower; Turkish bath, Finnish b., sauna; wash-house, lavatory, bathhouse, bathroom, washroom; wash, laundry, washing machine, launderette.

cleanser, purifier; disinfectant, deodorant; soda, lye, spirit; fuller's earth, detergent, soap, soap flakes; water, soap and w.; wash, gargle, lotion; cream, glycerine; dentifrice, toothpaste, tooth-powder; pumice stone, heart-s., holy-s.; polish, wax, varnish; whitewash, paint 427 n. *whiting*, 351 n. *drain.*

cleaning utensil, broom, besom, mop, sponge, swab, swabber; washing board; duster, feather-d., whisk, brush, scrubbing-b., toothpick; dustpan, crumbtray; dustbin, ashcan; carpet-sweeper, vacuum cleaner; fulling mill; doormat, foot-scraper; screen, sieve, riddle, strainer 263 n. *porosity*; filter; blotter 550 n. *obliteration.*

cleaning cloth, duster, dish-cloth; glass-cloth, leather, wash-l.; buff, flannel, towel, bath-t., peignoir; bib, handkerchief, tissue; face-cloth, sudary.

cleaner, refiner, distiller; dry-cleaner, launderer, laundryman, laundress, washerwoman, dhobi; fuller; scrubber, swabber; washer-up, dish-washer, scullion; charwoman, char, help; scavenger, dustman, sweeper, road-s., crossing-s.; chimney-sweep, window-cleaner; shoe-black; scavenger bird, crow, vulture, kite.

Adj. *clean*, dirt-free; white, polished, clean, bright, shiny 417 adj. *undimmed*; cleanly, dainty, nice 862 adj. *fastidious*; dewy, fresh; washed etc. vb.; laundered, starched; spruce, natty, spick and span, neat, tidy 60 adj. *orderly*; disinfected, aseptic, hygienic, sterile 652 adj. *salubrious*; pure, refined, immaculate, spotless, stainless, unsoiled, untarnished, un-

sullied 646 adj. *perfect*; untouched, blank.

cleansing, lustral, purificatory; disinfectant; hygienic; purgative; detergent; ablutionary, balneal.

Vb. *clean*, spring-clean, clean up, lay the dust; valet, spruce, neaten, trim; wash, wipe, dry, wring out; sponge, mop, swab, wash down; scrub, scour, flush, launder, starch, iron; buck, bleach, dry-clean; soap, lather, shampoo; bathe, dip, rinse, sluice, douche 341 vb. *drench*; dust, whisk, sweep; brush, comb; buff, polish; shine 417 vb. *make bright*; whitewash 427 vb. *whiten*; blot, erase 550 vb. *obliterate*; strip, pick clean, clean out, clear out, make a clean sweep.

purify, purge, clean up; bowdlerize, expurgate; sublimate, elevate 654 vb. *make better*; cleanse, lave, lustrate, asperge; wash one's hands of; freshen, ventilate, fan, deodorize, fumigate; disinfect, sterilize, chlorinate, pasteurize 652 vb. *sanitate*; depurate, refine, distil, clarify, rack, skim, scum, despumate; decarbonize; strain, filter, percolate, lixiviate, leach 341 vb. *drench*; sift, winnow, van, bolt, riddle, screen, sieve; drain.

649. Uncleanness – N. *uncleanness*, uncleanliness, dirty habits, wallowing, beastliness; dirtiness (see *dirt*); muckiness 347 n. *marsh*; soiliness; scruffiness, filthiness; lousiness, pediculosis, phthiriasis; squalor, slumminess 801 n. *poverty*; untidiness, sluttishness, slovenliness 61 n. *disorder*; pollution, defilement; corruption, putrescence 51 n. *decomposition*; contamination 651 n. *infection*; abomination, scatology, obscenity 951 n. *impurity.*

dirt, filth, stain, patch, blot; muck, mud 347 *marsh*; dung 302 n. *excrement*; dust, mote 332 n. *pulverulence*; cobweb, grime, smut, smudge, soot, smoke; sweepings, rinsings, off-scourings 41 n. *leavings*; sediment, fur; scum, off-scum, dross; cinders 381 n. *ash*; waste product; drainage, sewerage; scurf, dandruff; pus, matter, feculence; refuse, garbage 641 n.

rubbish; rot, rust, mildew, mould, fungus 51 n. *decay*; carrion, offal.

swill, pig-s., hogwash, draff; bilge, bilge-water; ditch-w., dish-w., slops; sewage, drainage; wallow, hog-w., sough.

latrine, privy, jakes, bogs, nessy, necessary house, comfort-station; closet, earth-c., water-c., W.C.; indoor sanitation, out-door sanitation, septic tank; cloakroom, lavatory, loo, toilet; urinal, convenience; close-stool, commode, thunderbox, bed-pan, jerry 302 n. *cacation*.

sink, kitchen sink, draining board; cesspool, sump, slough; gutter, sewer, main, cloaca 351 n. *drain*; laystall, dunghill, midden, rubbish-heap; dustbin, trash-can, garbage-c., gubbins 194 n. *vessel*; dust-hole 194 n. *cellar*; Augean stables, sty 192 n. *stable*; shambles 362 n. *slaughter-house*; plague-spot 651 n. *infection*; spittoon, cuspidor.

dirty person, sloven, slattern, drab, draggletail, trapes, slut; litterer, litter lout; mudlark, street-arab; beast, pig, wallower, leper.

Adj. *unclean*, unhallowed, unholy 980 adj. *profane*; obscene, corrupt 951 adj. *impure*; coarse, unrefined, unpurified; septic, festering 653 adj. *toxic*; unsterilized, non-sterile 653 adj. *infectious*; squalid, slummy 653 adj. *insalubrious*; foul, offensive, nasty, noisome, malodorous 397 adj. *fetid*; uncleanly, unfastidious, beastly, hoggish; scrofulous, scruffy, scurfy, scorbutic, impetiginous; leprous, scabby; lousy, pediculous, crawling; faecal, dungy, stercoraceous, excrementitious 302 adj. *excretory*; carious, rotting, tainted, high; flyblown, maggoty, carrion 51 adj. *decomposed*.

dirty, filthy; dusty, grimy, sooty, smoky, snuffy; thick with dust, unswept, Augean; untidy, unkempt, slovenly, sluttish, bedraggled 61 adj. *disordered*; unwashed, black, dingy, uncleaned; tarnished, stained, soiled; messy, mucky, muddy 347 adj. *marshy*; dreggy, scummy; musty, fusty, cobwebby.

Vb. *be unclean*, get dirty, collect dust, foul up, clog; rust, mildew, moulder;

fester, suppurate; gangrene, mortify, putrify, rot 51 vb. *decompose*; wallow.

make unclean, foul, befoul; dirty, soil; begrime, stain, blot, sully, tarnish; muck, mess, untidy; spot, streak; daub, smutch, smudge 419 vb. *bedim*; smear, besmear, cake, clog, bemire, muddy; bespatter 341 vb. *moisten*; poison, taint, infect, contaminate 655 vb. *impair*; corrupt, pollute, defile; profane, desecrate 980 vb. *be impious*.

650. Health – N. *health*, healthiness, good constitution, health and strength 162 n. *vitality*; fitness, condition, bloom, rosiness; well-being 376 n. *euphoria*; hygiene, healthy state, clean bill of health.

Adj. *healthy*, healthful, wholesome, hygienic, sanitary 652 adj. *salubrious*; fat and well-liking, eupeptic, euphoric; fresh, blooming, ruddy, rosy, florid; hale, hearty, sound, fit, well, fine, bobbish, full of beans; never ill, robust, hardy 162 adj. *stalwart*; fighting fit, in condition; sound as a bell, fit as a fiddle; getting well, convalescent 656 adj. *restored*.

Vb. *be healthy*, look after oneself; feel fine, bloom, flourish; wear well, keep fit; have a clean bill of health, have no mortality; convalesce 656 vb. *revive*.

651. Ill-health. Disease – N. *ill-health*, bad h., delicate h., failing h.; delicacy, weak constitution, unhealthiness, weakliness, infirmity, debility 163 n. *weakness*; seediness, loss of condition, manginess; morbidity, indisposition, cachexia; chronic complaint; allergy; invalidism, valetudinarianism, hypochondria, medicine habit.

illness, loss of health 655 n. *deterioration*; affliction, disability, handicap, infirmity 163 n. *weakness*; sickness, ailment, complaint, complication; condition, history of; bout of sickness, attack, acute a.; breakdown, collapse, prostration; last illness 361 n. *decease*; sick-bed, deathbed.

disease, malady, distemper, disorder; epidemic disease, endemic d.; congenital disease; occupational disease; deficiency disease, malnutrition, avitaminosis; degenerative disease, wasting d., marasmus, atrophy; organic disease, functional d., circulatory d., neurological d., nervous d., epilepsy, falling sickness; endocrine disease, diabetes.

plague, pest, scourge 659 n. *bane*; pestilence, murrain, infection, contagion; epidemic, pandemic; pneumonic plague, bubonic p., Black Death.

infection, contagion, miasma, pollution, taint; infectiousness, contagiousness 653 n. *insalubrity*; toxicity, sepsis, poisoning 659 n. *poison*; plague-spot, hotbed; vector, carrier, germ-c.; virus, bacillus, bacteria, germ, pathogen; blood-poisoning, toxaemia, septicaemia; pyrogenesis, pyaemia, suppuration, festering, purulence.

malaria, ague, malarial fever, remittent f., quotidian f., quartern f., tertian f., benign, tertian, subtertian, malignant s.; enlarged spleen.

dysentery, protozoal d., amoebic d., bacillary d., blood d.; diarrhoea, bowel-hurry, trots 302 n. *cacation*; diarrhoea and vomiting, gastro-enteritis; enteritis; colitis.

indigestion, fat i., steatorrhea; dyspepsia, liverishness, liver spots, dizziness, vertigo; biliousness, nausea, vomiting, retching; flatulence, wind; acidosis, heartburn; colic, gripes; gastralgia, stomach ache, belly a.; stomach ulcer, peptic u.; constipation, auto-intoxication.

respiratory disease, cough, cold, infectious catarrh, coryza; rhinitis, rhinorrhoea; sinusitis, tonsilitis, pharyngitis; laryngitis, tracheitis, perichondritis; bronchitis; asthma; pneumonia, broncho-pneumonia; diphtheria; whooping-cough, pertussis.

heart disease, cardiac d., cardiovascular d.; angina pectoris; breast-pang, heart-stroke, chest-spasm; brachycardia; tachycardia; gallop rhythm, palpitation, dyspnoea; heart block; enlarged heart, cardiac hypertrophy, athlete's heart.

blood pressure, hypertension; hypotension, low blood pressure; spasm, stroke, seizure, apoplexy; hardened arteries, arteriosclerosis; phlebitis, thrombophlebitis, thrombosis, coronary t., clot, blood-c.

phthisis, wasting disease, consumptiveness, decline, graveyard cough, tuberculosis, consumption, galloping c.

carcinosis, epithelioma, cancer; neoplasm, growth; tumour, indolent t., benign t.; malignant tumour, cancerous growth; melanoma, black cancer.

skin disease, cutaneous d.; mange; leucoderma; leprosy; albinism; dermatitis, erythema, flush; erysipelas; tetters, impetigo, herpes, shingles; eczema, serpigo, ringworm, itch 378 n. *formication*; hives, urticaria; rash, eruption, breaking out; acne, spots; pimple, wart, verruca 253 n. *swelling*; yaws, framboesia.

venereal disease, pox; syphilis, gonorrhoea, clap; venereal ulcer, chancre, syphilitic sore.

ulcer, ulceration, gathering, festering, purulence; inflammation, -itis; sore, imposthume, abscess, fistula; blain, chilblain, kibe; corn 253 n. *swelling*; gangrene, rot 51 n. *decay*; discharge, pus, matter.

animal disease, veterinary d.; distemper, foot-and-mouth disease; rinderpest, murrain; splenic disease, anthrax, sheeprot, bloat; pine; megrims, staggers; glanders, farcy, sweeny, spavin, thrush; psittacosis; hard pad; mange.

sick person, sufferer; patient, in-p., out-p.; case, stretcher-c., hospital-c.; mental case 504 n. *madman*; invalid, chronic; valetudinarian, hypochondriac, martyr to ill-health; crock, old c., cripple 163 n. *weakling*; sick-list.

pathology, case-making, diagnosis, prognosis; etiology, nosology, epidemiology, bacteriology, parasitology 658 n. *therapy*.

Adj. *unhealthy*, unsound, sickly; infirm, decrepit, weakly 163 adj. *weak*;

251

delicate, always ill; undernourished, under-vitaminized 636 adj. *underfed*; sallow, pale, bilious; invalid, valetudinarian, hypochondriac.

sick, ill, unwell, not well, indisposed, out of sorts, under the weather, off-colour; poorly, seedy, groggy, queer, ailing; sickening for, showing symptoms of; feverish, headachy; confined, laid up, bedridden; on the sick-list, invalided; seized, taken ill, taken bad; chronic, incurable, inoperable; mortally ill, moribund 361 adj. *dying*; peaky, drooping, flagging, pining, languishing, wasting away, in a decline.

diseased, pathological, disordered, distempered; affected, infected, plague-stricken; peccant, morbid, morbific, pathogenic; infectious, poisonous, festering, purulent 653 adj. *toxic*; measly, morbillous; degenerative, consumptive, phthisical, tuberculous, tubercular; diabetic, dropsical, hydrocephalic; anaemic, bloodless, leukaemic, haemophilic; arthritic, rheumatic, rheumatoid, rheumaticky; rickety, palsied, paralysed, paralytic, spastic; leprous, leucodermatous; carcinomatous, cancerous, cankered; syphilitic, venereal; swollen, oedematous; gouty; bronchial, throaty, bronchitic, croupy, coughy, coldy; asthmatic; allergic; pyretic, febrile, fevered, shivering, aguish, feverish, delirious; sore, tender; ulcerous, fistular; ulcerated, inflamed; rashy, spotty, erythematous, erysipelatous; spavined, broken-winded; mangy.

Vb. *be ill*, enjoy ill-health; ail, suffer, labour under, have treatment; not feel well, complain of; lose one's health, sicken, fall ill; catch, take an infection, contract a disease; be laid up, take to one's bed; languish, pine, peak, droop, waste away, go into a decline, fall into a consumption; gather, fester, suppurate.

652. Salubrity – N. *salubrity*, healthiness; well-being 650 n. *health*; salubriousness, healthfulness, wholesomeness; fresh air, open a., sea-a., ozone 340 n.

air; sunshine, out-doors; fine climate, genial c. 340 n. *weather*.

hygiene, sanitation, cleanliness 648 n. *cleanness*; preventive medicine, prophylaxis 658 n. *prophylactic*; quarantine, cordon sanitaire 660 n. *protection*; immunity, immunization, inoculation, auto-inoculation, vaccination, pasteurization; antisepsis, sterilization, disinfection, chlorination; sanatorium, spa 658 n. *hospital*; keeping fit, exercise; science of health, hygiology, hygienics.

sanitarian, hygienist, sanitationist, sanitary inspector, public health officer; sanitary engineer; fresh-air fiend, sun-worshipper, nudist.

Adj. *salubrious*, healthful, healthy, wholesome; pure, fresh 648 adj. *clean*; tonic, bracing, sanative 656 adj. *restorative*; hygienic, sanitary, disinfected, sterile, aseptic, antiseptic; prophylactic 658 adj. *remedial*; salutary, what the doctor ordered; nutritious, health-preserving; uninfectious, non-infectious, innocuous; immune, immunized 660 adj. *invulnerable*.

Vb. *sanitate*, disinfect, sterilize, antisepticize, chlorinate, pasteurize; immunize, inoculate, vaccinate; quarantine, put in q., isolate, segregate 883 vb. *seclude*; ventilate, freshen 648 vb. *purify*; cleanse 648 vb. *clean*; drain 342 vb. *dry*; conserve 666 vb. *preserve*.

653. Insalubrity – N. *insalubrity*, unhealthiness, unwholesomeness; uncleanliness, lack of hygiene, dirty habits, verminousness 649 n. *uncleanness*; unhealthy conditions, unwholesome surroundings, bad climate; infectiousness, contagiousness; bad drains, slum, sewer 649 n. *sink*; infectious person, carrier, germ-c., vector; plague-spot, pesthouse, contagion 651 n. *infection*.

Adj. *insalubrious*, unwholesome, unhealthy; bad for one's health, insanitary, unhygienic; noxious 645 adj. *harmful*; verminous, infested; undrained 347 adj. *marshy*; foul, polluted, undrinkable, inedible; unventilated, windowless, airless.

infectious, morbific, morbiferous,

pathogenic; infective, germ-laden; contagious, catching, communicable; pestiferous, pestilent, plague-stricken; malarious, malarial, aguish; epidemic, pandemic, endemic; unsterilized, nonsterile, infected 649 adj. *dirty*.

toxic narcotic, azotic; poisonous, mephitic, pestilential, germ-laden; venomous, envenomed, poisoned; septic, pussy, mattery, gathering, festering, purulent, suppurating; mortiferous 362 adj. *deadly*.

654. Improvement – N. *improvement*, betterment, uplift, amelioration; good influence, the making of 178 n. *influence*; change for the better, transfiguration 143 n. *transformation*; conversion, new leaf 939 n. *penitence*; revival, recovery 656 n. *restoration*; evolution, development, perfectibility; elaboration, enrichment; progress 285 n. *progression*; uptrend, upswing; enhancement 36 n. *increase*.

amendment, mending etc. vb.; mend 656 n. *repair*; reformation, reform (see *reformism*); Borstal, reformatory 539 n. *school*; purification, sublimation 648 n. *cleansing*; refining, rectification; correction, revision; recension, revised edition; second thoughts, better t., review, reconsideration, re-examination; polish, finishing touch 725 n. *completion*; perfectionism 862 n. *fastidiousness*.

civilization, culture, kultur; civility, refinement 846 n. *good taste*; training, education; cultivation, polish, menticulture; improvement of the race, eugenics.

reformism, meliorism, perfectionism, idealism; radicalism; extremism, revolution 738 n. *sedition*; minimalism, maximalism; progressivism, onward and upward department; gradualism, Fabianism; social adjustment 901 n. *sociology*.

reformer, improver; repairer 656 n. *mender*; emender, corrector, castigator, editor, reviser, second hand; progressive; minimalist, gradualist, Fabian 625 n. *moderate*; radical, extremist, maximalist, revolutionary 738 n. *agitator*; idealist, Utopian 862 n. *perfectionist*;

social worker, slummer 901 n. *philanthropist*.

Adj. *improved*, touched up 844 adj. *ornamented*; better, all the better for; improvable, curable, reformable, perfectible.

improving, reformatory; remedial, medicinal 656 adj. *restorative*; reformist, progressive, radical; civilizing, cultural; idealistic, perfectionist, Utopian, millenarian.

Vb. *get better*, improve, mend, turn the corner; pick up, rally 656 vb. *be restored*; advance, develop, evolve 285 vb. *progress*; mellow, ripen 669 vb. *mature*; rise 308 vb. *ascend*; reform, turn a new leaf, go straight 939 vb. *be penitent*; learn by experience 536 vb. *learn*.

make better, better, improve, ameliorate, reform; improve upon, refine u.; polish, elaborate, enrich, enhance; transfigure 147 vb. *transform*; be the making of, leaven 178 vb. *influence*; refine, uplift, elevate, sublimate 648 vb. *purify*; moralize, edify, civilize; mend 656 vb. *repair*; restore 656 vb. *cure*; revive 685 vb. *refresh*; mitigate, lessen an evil 177 vb. *moderate*; forward 285 vb. *promote*; foster, mellow 669 vb. *mature*; make the most of, get the best out of 673 vb. *use*; develop, open up, reclaim; tidy, neaten, spruce, valet 648 vb. *clean*; renovate, refurbish 126 vb. *modernize*; touch up 841 vb. *beautify*; embellish 844 vb. *decorate*.

rectify, refine 648 vb. *purify*; set right, straighten 24 vb. *adjust*; mend 656 vb. *repair*; correct, revise, redact, edit, amend, emend; redraft, recast, remodel, new-model, reform; reorganize, streamline 62 vb. *regularize*; review, re-examine; stop in time, think again.

655. Deterioration – N. *deterioration*, debasement, devaluation; retrogression 286 n. *regression*; throw-back 5 n. *heredity*; decline, ebb 37 n. *decrease*; twilight 419 n. *dimness*; down-trend, slump 290 n. *recession*; impoverishment 801 n. *poverty*; vitiation, corruption, perversion, prostitution, depravation, demoralization, degeneration, degeneracy, decadence 934 n. *wickedness*; downward course, primrose path; recidivism, setback 657 n. *relapse*; bad end, tragedy 731 n. *ill fortune*.

dilapidation, collapse, ruination 165 n. *destruction*; disrepair, neglect 458 n. *negligence*; wear and tear, erosion, rust, canker, corruption, rot 51 n. *decay*; mouldiness 659 n. *blight*; decrepitude 131 n. *age*; ruin, wreck, physical w., shotten herring.

impairment, spoiling 675 n. *misuse*; detriment, damage, inroad, waste 772 n. *loss*; pollution, defilement 649 n. *uncleanness*; contamination, contagion 651 n. *infection*; adulteration 43 n. *mixture*; dilaceration, demolishment 165 n. *destruction*; injury, mischief, ravage, scathe, harm 165 n. *havoc*; disablement, mutilation 163 n. *weakness*; disorganization, bedevilment, sabotage 63 n. *derangement*; exacerbation 832 n. *aggravation*.

wound, injury, trauma; sore, running s. 651 n. *ulcer*; laceration, lesion; cut, gash, incision, abrasion, scratch 46 n. *scission*; stab, prick, jab 263 n. *perforation*; contusion, bruise, bump, discoloration, black eye, thick ear 253 n. *swelling*; burn, scald; rupture, broken head, broken bones; scar, mark, cicatrice 845 n. *blemish*.

Adj. *deteriorated*, not improved, the worse for; exacerbated 832 adj. *aggravated*; spoilt, impaired etc. vb.; worn out, effete 641 adj. *useless*; stale, rotten 645 adj. *bad*; no better, deteriorating, worse and worse; failing, past one's best, on the decline, on the way out; faded, withered, sere 51 adj. *decomposed*; degenerative, retrogressive, retrograde; lapsed, recidivist 603 adj. *tergiversating*; degenerate, vitiated 934 adj. *vicious*; impoverished 801 adj. *poor*.

dilapidated, the worse for wear, in ruins, in shreds; weather-beaten, decrepit, ruinous, ramshackle, tottery, tumbledown, on its last legs; slummy, condemned; worn, well-w., frayed, shabby, tatty, holey; seedy, down at

heel 801 adj. *poor*; rusty, rotten, moss-grown, moth-eaten, worm-e., dog-eared 51 adj. *decomposed*.

Vb. *deteriorate*, not improve, get no better; worsen, go from bad to worse; slip, slide, go downhill; not maintain 657 vb. *relapse*; fall off, slump, decline, wane, ebb, sink, fail 37 vb. *decrease*; retrograde 286 vb. *regress*; lapse 603 vb. *tergiversate*; degenerate, go to the bad, spoil oneself 934 vb. *be wicked*; collapse, break down, fall, totter 309 vb. *tumble*; wear out, age 131 vb. *grow old*; fade, wither, wilt, shrivel, perish, crumble, moulder, mildew, grow moss, grow weeds; bolt, run to seed; weather, rust, rot, decay 51 vb. *decompose*; spoil, stale, fust; putrefy, fester, suppurate, gangrene, sicken 651 vb. *be ill*; make things worse 832 vb. *aggravate*.

pervert, deform, warp 246 vb. *distort*; abuse, prostitute 675 vb. *misuse*; demoralize, vitiate, corrupt 934 vb. *make wicked*; lower, degrade, debase; brutalize, dehumanize, barbarize, decivilize; denature 147 vb. *transform*; propagandize, brainwash 535 vb. *misteach*.

impair, damage, damnify, hurt, injure, sabotage 645 vb. *harm*; jumble, mess up, untidy, disorganize 63 vb. *derange*; spoil, maul, mar, botch 695 vb. *be clumsy*; tinker, tamper 678 vb. *meddle*; not improve, worsen, exacerbate, embitter 832 vb. *aggravate*; do no good, kill with kindness; stale, degrade, lower, coarsen 847 vb. *vulgarize*; devalue, debase 812 vb. *cheapen*; blacken, blot 842 vb. *make ugly*; scar 845 vb. *blemish*; deface, disfigure 246 vb. *distort*; vitiate (see *pervert*); mutilate, maim, lame, cripple, hobble, nobble 161 vb. *disable*; scotch, clip the wings, cramp, hamper 702 vb. *hinder*; castrate 161 vb. *unman*; expurgate, eviscerate, bowdlerize; cream, skim; adulterate 43 vb. *mix*; subvert, shake, sap, mine, undermine 163 vb. *weaken*; eat away, erode, corrode, rust, rot 51 vb. *decompose*; blight, blast; ravage 165 vb. *lay waste*; wreck, ruin 165 vb. *destroy*; fray, wear out; exhaust 634 vb. *waste*; infect, contaminate, poison, envenom, ulcerate; taint, canker 649 vb. *make unclean*; defile, desecrate 980 vb. *be impious*.

wound, scotch, draw blood; tear, rend, lacerate, mangle 46 vb. *disjoin*; maul, savage 176 vb. *be violent*; bite, scratch, claw; hack 46 vb. *cut*; scarify, score 262 vb. *groove*; sting, prick, pink, stab 263 vb. *pierce*; bruise, contuse, buffet 279 vb. *strike*; chafe 333 vb. *rub*; graze, pepper, wing.

656. Restoration – N. *restoration*, retrocession 787 n. *restitution*; redress, amends, reparation 941 n. *atonement*; retrieval, recovery 786 n. *taking*; reestablishment, recall, reinstatement; rehabilitation; reafforestation, reclamation; rescue, salvage, redemption 668 n. *deliverance*; reconstitution, reformation, reconstruction; readjustment; reaction, counter-reformation 182 n. *counteraction*; resumption, return to normal, derestriction; reinforcement 162 n. *strengthening*; replenishment 633 n. *provision*.

repair, reparation, repairs, renovation, renewal, reconditioning, redintegration, rectification; restoration 126 n. *newness*; mending etc. vb.; clout, patch, darn, insertion, reinforcement.

revival, recruitment, recovery 685 n. *refreshment*; sanation, cure, convalescence; renewal, reawakening, resurgence, recurrence, come-back; fresh spurt, new energy; economic miracle, boom 730 n. *prosperity*; reactivation, reanimation, resuscitation, artificial respiration; rejuvenation, rejuvenescence, second youth, Indian summer; face-lift, new look; rebirth, renaissance; regeneration 654 n. *amendment*; new life, resurrection.

mender, restorer, repairer, renovator; emendator, rectifier; rebuilder, second founder; patcher, darner, cobbler, botcher; tinker, fixer; salvor, salvager; healer 658 n. *doctor*; reformist 654 n. *reformer*.

Adj. *restored*, revived, refreshed etc. vb.; remade, reconditioned, like new; reborn, redivivus, renascent, Phoenix-like; cured, none the worse, better, convalescent, on the mend; back to normal; retrievable, recoverable; medicable, curable, operable.

restorative, reparative, analeptic, recuperative, curative, sanative, healing, medicated, medicinal 658 adj. *remedial*.

Vb. *be restored*, recover, come round, come to, revive, pick up, rally 685 vb. *be refreshed*; pull through, get well, convalesce, recuperate; weather, survive, live through; resurrect, come to life again, return from the grave; reappear, make a come-back; be oneself again, sleep off; return to normal, resume 68 vb. *begin*.

restore, give back, retrocede 787 vb. *restitute*; make amends 941 vb. *atone*; reinstate, replace; recall, reappoint; refound, re-establish, rehabilitate; reconstitute, reconstruct 654 vb. *make better*; renovate, renew, refurbish 126 vb. *modernize*; make whole, redintegrate; reafforest, replant, reclaim; reinforce, recruit 162 vb. *strengthen*; rescue, salvage 668 vb. *deliver*; release, derestrict 746 vb. *liberate*.

revive, revivify, revitalize, resuscitate, regenerate, resurrect, reanimate, rekindle; rejuvenate; freshen, recruit 685 vb. *refresh*; service; valet.

cure, heal, make well, wean of, break of; nurse 658 vb. *doctor*; cicatrize, heal over, scab o., skin o., close; right itself, work its own cure.

repair, do repairs; amend, emend, right, set to rights, put right, make all square 654 vb. *rectify*; overhaul, mend, fix; tinker, cobble, botch, thatch 226 vb. *cover*; darn, patch, patch up, clout; make over, do up, touch up, freshen up, retouch, vamp, paper over; pick up the pieces, refit, reassemble, cannibalize 45 vb. *join*; face-lift, refurbish, recondition, renovate, renew, remodel, reform.

retrieve, get back, recover, regain, retake, recapture; find again, reclaim, compensate oneself 31 vb. *recoup*.

657. Relapse – N. *relapse*, lapse, falling back; throw-back, return; retrogression 286 n. *regression*, 655 n. *deterioration*; backsliding, recidivation, recidivism, apostasy 603 n. *tergiversation*; recrudescence, reinfection, recurrence, fresh outbreak.

Vb. *relapse*, slip back, slide b.; throw back, return, retrograde 286 vb. *regress*; degenerate 655 vb. *deteriorate*; backslide, recidivate, fall from grace 603 vb. *apostatize*; return to one's vomit.

658. Remedy – N. *remedy*, succour, help, present help in time of trouble 703 n. *aid*; oil on troubled waters 177 n. *moderator*; remedial measure, corrective, correction 654 n. *amendment*; redress, amends 787 n. *restitution*; medicinal value, healing gift, healing quality; sovereign remedy, specific; prescription, recipe, receipt, nostrum; panacea, cure-all; elixir, philosopher's stone.

medicine, materia medica, pharmacopoeia; Galenical, herb, simple; medication, medicament, patent medicine, drug; tablet, tabloid, capsule, lozenge; physic, draught, potion, dose, drench; pill, purge, bolus; preparation, mixture, powder, electuary, linctus; plaster (see *surgical dressing*); medicine chest, medicine bottle.

prophylactic, preventive; sanitation, quarantine 652 n. *hygiene*; prophylaxis, immunization, inoculation, vaccination; antisepsis, disinfection, sterilization; antiseptic, disinfectant; mothball, camphor, lavender; bactericide, germicide, insecticide 659 n. *poison*.

antidote, abirritant; analgesic, painkiller; counter-irritant, urtication, beesting; counter-poison, antitoxin, mithridate, theriac; antemetic; antaphrodisiac; febrifuge, quinine; vermifuge; antigen, antibody; antibiosis, antibiotic; anticoagulant.

cathartic, purge, purgative, laxative, aperient, pull-through; agaric, castor oil, Epsom salts, calomel, senna pods; expectorant, emetic.

tonic, restorative, cordial; bracer, reviver, refresher, pick-me-up 174 n.

stimulant; spirits, smelling salts, sal volatile, hartshorn; vitamin.

drug, dope, hemp, opium, cocaine, snow, morphia, morphine, mescalin; synthetic drug, wonder d.; antibiotic; penicillin; tranquillizer, opiate, narcotic, analgesic 375 n. *anaesthetic*.

balm, balsam, oil, soothing syrup, emollient, lenitive 177 n. *moderator*; salve, ointment, cream, face-c. 843 n. *cosmetic*; liniment, embrocation; lotion, wash.

surgical dressing, dressing, lint, gauze; swab; bandage, suspensory, sling, splint, cast, tourniquet; cataplasm, plaster, mustard p., sinapism, fomentation, poultice, compress; tampon, tent, pledget; pessary, suppository.

medical art, leechcraft; therapeutics, healing touch, practice, medical p.; allopathy, homoeopathy; medicine, clinical m., preventive m., virology; diagnosis, prognosis 651 n. *pathology*; healing, faith-h., Christian Science; midwifery 164 n. *obstetrics*; geriatrics, pediatrics; psychopaedics; iatrochemistry, psychopharmacology; pharmaceutics, pharmacology, posology, dosology.

surgery, plastic s., anaplasty, rhinoplasty; manipulative surgery, chiropraxis; operation, op.; phlebotomy, venesection; bleeding, blood-letting, cupping, transfusion, perfusion; amputation, trephination; dentistry; massage.

therapy, therapeutics, medical care; treatment, medical t., clinical t.; nursing, bedside manner; first aid, after-care; course, cure, faith c., nature c., hydrotherapy; regimen, diet, dietary; chiropody, bone-setting, orthopaedy, osteopathy, osteotherapy, orthopraxy; hypnotherapy; physiotherapy, radiotherapy, phototherapy; occupational therapy; electrotherapy, shock treatment; mental treatment, clinical psychology; psychotherapy, psychiatry, psychoanalysis; acupuncture, needling; injection, shot, stab, jab; enema, clyster, purge, bowel-wash, douche; catheterization; fomentation.

hospital, infirmary, general hospital;

mental hospital 503 n. *madhouse*; dispensary, clinic; nursing home, convalescent h., rest h.; home for the dying, terminal home; lazaret, hospice, pesthouse; lazar-house, leper asylum, leper colony; stretcher, ambulance; ward, sick bay, sickroom, sick-bed; tent, oxygen t., iron lung; dressing station, casualty s.; operating theatre, operating table; consulting room, surgery, clinic; sanatorium, spa, hydro, watering-place; pump-room, baths, thermae.

doctor, medical man; leech, quack; vet, horse-doctor; herbalist, herb-doctor; faith-healer, Christian Scientist; allopath, homoeopath; witch-doctor, medicine-man 983 n. *sorcerer*; medico, medical student; houseman, intern, registrar; medical practitioner, general p., G.P.; locum tenens, locum; physician, clinician, therapeutist, healer; operator, surgeon; chirurgeon, barber, barber-surgeon, sawbones; medical officer, health o., sanitary inspector; medical adviser, consultant, specialist; diagnostician, pathologist; alienist, psychiatrist, psychoanalyst, psychopathist, brain-specialist, neurologist; anaesthetist, radiotherapist; paediatrician, geriatrician; obstetrician, accoucheur, midwife; gynaecologist; sexologist; dermatologist; orthopaedist, osteopath, bonesetter, chiropractor, masseur, masseuse; pedicurist, chiropodist, manicurist; ophthalmologist, optician, oculist; aurist; dentist, dental surgeon; nutritionist, dietician; medical profession, Harley Street; Red Cross, St John's Ambulance.

druggist, apothecary, chemist, pharmacopolist; pharmacist; dispenser, posologist, pharmacologist; drug store, pharmacy.

nurse, probationer n., pro.; sister, night s., ward s., theatre s., sister tutor, matron; Nightingale; district nurse, home-n., Sairy Gamp; nursing auxiliary, ward orderly, dresser, stretcher-bearer, ambulance-driver.

Adj. *remedial*, corrective, analeptic, curative, first-aid 656 adj. *restorative*; therapeutic, medicinal, sanative, hygienic 652 adj. *salubrious*; specific, sovereign; panacean, all-healing; soothing, paregoric, balsamic, demulcent, emollient, palliative 177 adj. *lenitive*; analgesic, narcotic, anaesthetic 375 adj. *insensible*; peptic, digestive; cathartic, emetic, vomitory, laxative; antidotal 182 adj. *counteracting*; alexipharmic, theriacal, therial; prophylactic, disinfectant, antiseptic; febrifugal, alexipyretic; tonic, stimulative, corroborant; dietetic, alimentary, nutritive, nutritional.

medical, pathological, physicianly, Aesculapian, Hippocratic, Galenic; allopathic, homoeopathic, ayurvedic; surgical, anaplastic, rhinoplastic, orthopaedic, chiropractic; obstetrical; medicable, medicinable, operable, curable.

Vb. *remedy*, fix, put right, correct 656 vb. *restore*; succour, help 703 vb. *aid*; treat, heal, work a cure 656 vb. *cure*; palliate, soothe, neutralize 831 vb. *relieve*.

doctor, practise; treat, prescribe, advise; attend 703 vb. *minister to*; tend, nurse; give first aid, hospitalize, put on the sick-list; physic, medicine, medicate, drench, dose, purge; inject, poke, stab, jab; dress, bandage; poultice, plaster, foment; set, put in splints; drug, dope, anaesthetize; operate, use the knife; trepan, trephine; cauterize; bleed, leech, cup, let blood, venesect, phlebotomize; transfuse, perfuse; draw, extract, pull, stop, fill, crown; pedicure, manicure; immunize, vaccinate, inoculate; sterilize, pasteurize, antisepticize, disinfect 652 vb. *sanitate*.

659. Bane – **N.** *bane*, curse, plague, pest, scourge, ruin 616 n. *evil*; malady 651 n. *disease*; weakness, bad habit, besetting sin 934 n. *vice*; hell, cup, visitation, affliction 731 n. *adversity*; cross, trial; bore 838 n. *tedium*; bugbear, bête noire 827 n. *annoyance*; burden, imposition, tax, white elephant; thorn in the flesh, stone round one's neck; running sore 651 n. *ulcer*; sting, serpent's tooth; hornet's nest 663 n. *pitfall*; snake 663 n. *troublemaker*; oppressor, terror 735 n. *tyrant*.

blight, blast, rust, rot, dry-r.; mildew;

moth, worm, canker, cancer; frost, nip 380 n. *coldness*; drought 342 n. *desiccation*.

poison, poisonousness, virulence, toxicity; germ, virus 651 n. *infection*; venom, toxicant, toxin; deadly poison, ratsbane, germicide, insecticide, pesticide, acaricide, vulpicide, fungicide, weed-killer; hemlock, arsenic, strychnine; asphyxiant, poison gas; foul air, mephitis, miasma, effluvium, sewer gas 653 n. *insalubrity*; fall-out, strontium-90 417 n. *radiation*; dope 658 n. *drug*; intoxicant 949 n. *alcoholism*; toxicology.

Adj. *baneful*, plaguy, pestilent, noisome 645 adj. *harmful*; deadly, poisonous, venomous 653 adj. *toxic*; accursed 616 adj. *evil*.

660. Safety – N. *safety*, safeness, security, surety; social security, welfare state 901 n. *sociology*; invulnerability, impregnability, immunity, charmed life; safe distance, wide berth 620 n. *avoidance*; all clear, coast c.; guarantee, warrant 473 n. *certainty*; sense of security, assurance, confidence; safety-valve 667 n. *means of escape*; rescue 668 n. *deliverance*.

protection, self-preservation 666 n. *preservation*; insurance 858 n. *caution*; patronage, auspices, fatherly eye; protectorate, guardianship, tutelage, custody 747 n. *restraint*; custodianship, safe-keeping, keeping, charge, safe hands 778 n. *retention*; safeguard, cushion, screen 713 n. *defence*; safe-conduct 756 n. *permit*; escort 722 n. *armed force*; bastion, bulwark, tower of strength 713 n. *defences*; asylum 662 n. *refuge*; anchor, sheet-a. 662 n. *safeguard*; shield 713 n. *armour*; wing, umbrella, aegis.

protector, guardian, tutor; guardian angel 707 n. *patron*; defender, preserver, shepherd; bodyguard, life-guard 742 n. *retainer*; conservator, custodian, curator, warden; warder, castellan, guard; chaperon 749 n. *keeper*; policeman 955 n. *police*; sentry, sentinel, garrison 722 n. *soldiery*; watch-dog.

Adj. *safe*, without risk, unhazardous; assured, secure, sure; safe and sound, spared 666 adj. *preserved*; in safety, on the safe side; out of danger, out of harm's way; clear, in the clear, unthreatened; unexposed, unhazarded; under shelter, protected etc. vb.; in safe hands, held 747 adj. *imprisoned*.

invulnerable, immune, impregnable, expugnable, unassailable; defensible, tenable 162 adj. *strong*; proof, foolproof; waterproof, bullet-p.; armoured, steel-clad, panoplied.

tutelary, custodial, guardian, protective; ready to die for 931 adj. *disinterested*; watchful 457 adj. *vigilant*.

Vb. *safeguard*, keep safe, guard, protect; spare 905 vb. *show mercy*; shield, grant asylum, afford sanctuary; cover up for 703 vb. *patronize*; treasure, hoard 632 vb. *store*; watch over, nurse, foster, cherish; take charge of, keep an eye on, chaperon 457 vb. *look after*; hide; cover, cloak 421 vb. *screen*; keep under cover, garage, lock up; house, shelter, fold; secure, fortify 162 vb. *strengthen*; shepherd, convoy, escort; flank, support; garrison; immunize, inoculate, vaccinate; disinfect 652 vb. *sanitate*; insure, warrant, guarantee 473 vb. *make certain*; keep order, police, patrol.

Adv. *under shelter*, under cover, in the lee of; out of harm's way, safely, with impunity.

661. Danger – N. *danger*, peril; dangerousness, perilousness, dragon's mouth; parlous state 700 n. *predicament*; emergency 137 n. *crisis*; insecurity, jeopardy, risk, hazard, ticklishness, precariousness, razor's edge 474 n. *uncertainty*; black spot, snag 663 n. *pitfall*; trap, death-t. 527 n. *ambush*; endangerment, hazarding, dangerous course 857 n. *rashness*; menace 900 n. *threat*; apprehension, fears 854 n. *nervousness*; cause for alarm 665 n. *danger signal*; narrow escape, close shave, near thing 667 n. *escape*.

vulnerability, non-immunity, susceptibility, danger of 180 n. *liability*; insecurity, exposure, nakedness, defencelessness 161 n. *helplessness*; vulnerable point, chink in the armour, Achilles' heel 163 n. *weakness*; unsoundness, feet of clay 647 n. *imperfection*.

Adj. *dangerous*, perilous, treacherous, snaggy; risky, hazardous, venturous, venturesome, aleatory, dicey, chancy 618 adj. *speculative*; serious, ugly, emergent, critical; menacing, ominous 900 adj. *threatening*; inflammable, explosive.

unsafe, not safe, slippery, treacherous, untrustworthy 474 adj. *unreliable*; insecure, unsecure, precarious; shaky, top-heavy, unsteady 152 adj. *unstable*; critical, ticklish, touch and go, on the edge, on the brink, on the verge; at stake.

vulnerable, expugnable, in danger of, not immune 180 adj. *liable*; open to, exposed, naked, bare 229 adj. *uncovered*; unarmoured, unfortified, unprotected 161 adj. *defenceless*; unshielded, shelterless, helpless, guideless; unguarded, unescorted; unwarned 508 adj. *inexpectant*.

Vb. *be in danger*, run the risk of 180 vb. *be liable*; enter the lion's den, walk into a trap 527 vb. *ambush*; skate on thin ice, sail too near the wind; hang by a thread, hover on the brink 474 vb. *be uncertain*.

face danger, expose oneself, lay oneself open, live in a glass house; stand in the breach 711 vb. *defy*; brave all hazards, spurn the odds; tempt providence, court disaster 857 vb. *be rash*; run the gauntlet, come under fire; venture, dare, risk it 618 vb. *gamble*.

endanger, imperil, hazard, jeopardize, compromise; risk, stake, venture 618 vb. *gamble*; threaten danger, loom, bode ill, menace 900 vb. *threaten*.

662. Refuge. Safeguard – **N.** *refuge*, sanctuary, asylum, retreat, safe place; last resort, funk-hole, bolt-hole; earth, hole, den, lair, covert, nest, lap, hearth 192 n. *home*; sanctum, cloister; ark, palladium; acropolis, citadel; wall, rampart, bulwark, bastion, stronghold 713 n. *fort*; rock, pillar, tower of strength, mainstay 218 n. *support*.

shelter, roof, cover; covert, fold; screen, lee, wind-break 235 n. *fence*; aegis, umbrella, wing, shield; haven, harbour, port 295 n. *goal*; harbourage, anchorage; quay, jetty, marina, dock 192 n. *stable*; asylum, almshouse.

safeguard, means of safety, protection 660 n. *safety*; mail 713 n. *armour*; arms, deterrent 723 n. *weapon*; buffer, bumper, fender; safety device, safety belt, safety harness, safety catch, safety-valve, lightning conductor, fuse; parachute; lifeboat; life-belt, Mae West, life-line; anchor, sheet-a.; bolt, bar, lock, key 264 n. *stopper*; ballast 31 n. *offset*; mole, breakwater.

663. Pitfall: source of danger – **N.** *pitfall*, pit, trapdoor, catch, booby-trap 542 n. *trap*, 527 n. *ambush*; thin ice, quicksands 347 n. *marsh*; reef, rock, lee shore; precipice 209 n. *high land*; vortex, maelstrom 350 n. *eddy*; squall 352 n. *gale*; volcano 383 n. *furnace*; dynamite, powder magazine, powder-keg 723 n. *explosive*; trouble-spot, danger-spot 661 n. *danger*; hornet's nest 659 n. *bane*.

trouble-maker, mischief-m., wrecker; ill-wisher 881 n. *enemy*; firebrand 738 n. *agitator*; ugly customer 904 n. *ruffian*; nigger in the woodpile, snake in the grass, viper in the bosom; hidden hand 178 n. *influence*; Nemesis 910 n. *avenger*.

664. Warning – **N.** *warning*, caution, caveat; example, lesson, object l.; notice 524 n. *information*; ultimatum 737 n. *demand*; admonishment 924 n. *reprimand*; foreboding, premonition 511 n. *prediction*; alarm, siren, foghorn 665 n. *danger signal*; signs of the times, writing on the wall, symptom, sign 547 n. *indication*; beacon, light 547 n. *signal, indicator*; menace 900 n. *threat*.

warner, admonisher 691 n. *adviser*; prophet, Cassandra 511 n. *diviner*; flagman, signaller; watchman, look-out, watch; sentinel, sentry 660 n. *protector*; watch-dog, house-d.; dun 763 n. *petitioner*.

Adj. *cautionary*, monitory, admonitory; dehortative 762 adj. *deprecatory*; exemplary, instructive 524 adj. *informative*; premonitory, ominous 511 adj. *presageful*; menacing, minatory 900 adj. *threatening*; deterrent 854 adj. *frightening*.

Vb. *warn*, caution; give fair warning, give notice 524 vb. *inform*; drop a hint 524 vb. *hint*; admonish 924 vb. *reprove*; spell danger, forewarn 511 vb. *predict*; forearm, put one on his guard 669 vb. *prepare*; lower, menace 900 vb. *threaten*; sound the alarm 665 vb. *raise the alarm*.

be warned, receive notice; beware, take heed 457 vb. *be careful*; learn one's lesson, profit by the example.

665. Danger signal – N. *danger signal*, note of warning 664 n. *warning*; writing on the wall, black cap, evil omen 511 n. *omen*; alert, alarm, alarum, alarm-bell, police whistle; fire-alarm, foghorn, motor-horn, klaxon; blast, honk, toot 400 n. *loudness*; tocsin, siren; warning light, red l., beacon; red flag; distress signal, S.O.S. 547 n. *signal*.

false alarm, cry of 'wolf', scare; scarecrow 854 n. *intimidation*; blank cartridge 4 n. *insubstantiality*; scaremonger 854 n. *alarmist*.

Vb. *raise the alarm*, alarm, alert, arouse, scare, startle 854 vb. *frighten*; honk, toot; turn out the guard, raise a hue and cry 528 vb. *proclaim*; cry wolf, cry too soon.

666. Preservation – N. *preservation*, safe-keeping; safe-conduct 660 n. *protection*; salvation 668 n. *deliverance*; conservation 144 n. *permanence*; upkeep, maintenance; saving up 632 n. *storage*; mummification, embalmment 364 n. *interment*; deep-freeze, cold pack 382 n. *refrigeration*; dehydration 342 n. *desiccation*; ensilage; canning, tinning; prophylaxis 652 n. *hygiene*.

preserver, saviour 668 n. *deliverance*; amulet, charm, mascot 983 n. *talisman*; preservative, ice, cold; camphor, moth-ball; pickle, brine 389 n. *condiment*; refrigerator, fridge 382 n. *refrigeration*;

silo; cannery; safety device 662 n. *safeguard*; embalmer, mummifier; canner, bottler.

Adj. *preserving*, preservative, conservative; prophylactic, protective, preventive 652 adj. *salubrious*.

preserved, well-p., kept, well-k., fresh, undecayed, intact, whole 646 adj. *perfect*; frozen, on ice; pickled, embalmed, laid up in lavender 632 adj. *stored*.

Vb. *preserve*, conserve, keep, keep fresh, ice, freeze, keep on ice; embalm, mummify; pickle, salt, corn, spice 388 vb. *season*; cure, smoke, kipper, dehydrate, sun-dry 342 vb. *dry*; pot, bottle, tin, can; protect, paint, coat, waterproof; maintain, service, valet 656 vb. *repair*; shore up, embank 218 vb. *support*; keep alive, feed 633 vb. *provide*; nurse, tend 658 vb. *doctor*; cherish, treasure 457 vb. *look after*; save, rescue 668 vb. *deliver*.

667. Escape – N. *escape*, leak, leakage, short circuit 298 n. *egress*; extrication, rescue 668 n. *deliverance*; riddance, good r. 831 n. *relief*; getaway, break-out; French leave 296 n. *departure*; disappearing trick 446 n. *disappearance*; elopement, runaway match; evasion, truancy 620 n. *avoidance*; close shave, narrow squeak, near thing 661 n. *danger*; immunity, impunity 919 n. *non-liability*; escapology; escapism.

means of escape, exit, way out, back-door, secret passage 298 n. *egress*; ladder, fire-escape, escape hatch; vent, safety-valve 662 n. *safeguard*; loophole, saving clause, escape c. 468 n. *qualification*.

escaper, escapee, runaway; truant, dodger; prison-breaker; fugitive, refugee; survivor; escapologist.

Adj. *escaped*, flown, missing, wanted; eloping, truant; fugitive, runaway; slippery, elusive, tip-and-run 620 adj. *avoiding*; free, at large; well out of, well rid of; exempt 919 adj. *non-liable*.

Vb. *escape*, save oneself; make a getaway, break prison; flit, elope, skip 620 vb. *run away*; extricate oneself, break out, break loose, get free, slip the collar; get away, slip through one's fingers; get off, secure an acquittal; scrape through, save one's bacon, survive; get away with it 919 vb. *be exempt*; rid oneself 831 vb. *relieve*; leak 298 vb. *flow out*.

elude, evade, welsh, abscond, dodge 620 vb. *avoid*; lie low 523 vb. *lurk*; make oneself scarce, give one the slip; play truant 190 vb. *be absent*.

668. Deliverance – N. *deliverance*, delivery, extrication 304 n. *extraction*; disburdenment, riddance 831 n. *relief*; emancipation 746 n. *liberation*; rescue, life-saving; salvage, retrieval 656 n. *restoration*; salvation, redemption 965 n. *divine function*; ransom 792 n. *purchase*; discharge, reprieve 960 n. *acquittal*.

Adj. *extricable*, deliverable, redeemable; riddable.

Vb. *deliver*, save, rescue, come to the r., throw a life-line; extricate 62 vb. *unravel*; unloose, untie, unbind 46 vb. *disjoin*; accouche 164 vb. *generate*; disburden 701 vb. *disencumber*; rid, save from 831 vb. *relieve*; release, unlock; emancipate, free 746 vb. *liberate*; get one off 960 vb. *acquit*; save oneself 667 vb. *escape*; redeem, ransom, buy off 792 vb. *purchase*; salvage, retrieve, recover 656 vb. *restore*; dispense from 919 vb. *exempt*.

669. Preparation – N. *preparation*, preliminaries, mobilization 718 n. *war measures*; trial run, trials 461 n. *experiment*; practice, rehearsal; training, inurement, novitiate 534 n. *teaching*; homework 536 n. *learning*; spadework 68 n. *beginning*; groundwork, foundation 218 n. *basis*; planning, blueprint, scheme, pilot s. 623 n. *plan*; premeditation 608 n. *predetermination*; consultation 691 n. *advice*; anticipation 510 n. *foresight*.

fitting out, provisioning, logistics 633 n. *provision*; appointment, commission, equipment, accoutrement, array, marshalling, armament.

maturation, ripening, concoction, brewing, digestion; gestation, hatching, incubation 164 n. *propagation*; nursing, nurture; cultivation 370 n. *agriculture*.

preparedness, readiness, ripeness, mellowness, maturity; puberty, nubility 134 n. *adultness*; fitness, shipshape condition, training.

preparer, trainer, coach, gymnasiarch, drill-sergeant 537 n. *trainer*; torchbearer, pioneer, bridge-builder 66 n. *precursor*; fitter, equipper, provisioner 633 n. *provider*.

Adj. *preparatory*, preparative; precautionary, preliminary 64 adj. *preceding*; provisional, stop-gap 150 adj. *substituted*; broody, gestatory, in embryo; in preparation, on foot, on the stocks, on the anvil.

prepared, ready, alert 457 adj. *vigilant*; poised, in readiness, at the ready; mobilized, standing by, on call; teed up, keyed up, spoiling for; trained, practised, in practice, at concert pitch; primed, briefed 524 adj. *informed*; forewarned, forearmed; armed, rigged, equipped, furnished, well-appointed 633 adj. *provisionary*; in reserve, ready for use; fit for use, in working order.

matured, ripe, seasoned, weathered; hardened, inured; tried, experienced, veteran 694 adj. *expert*; adult, grown, fledged 134 adj. *grown up*; overripe; well-cooked, well-done; elaborate, wrought, laboured; deep-laid.

ready-made, cut and dried, ready for wear, reach-me-down, off the peg; ready-furnished; oven-ready; predigested, ready-cooked, instant.

Vb. *prepare*, take steps, take measures; build up, mount; make ready, pave the way, bridge, pioneer 64 vb. *come before*; choose one's ground, lay *or* dig the foundations, provide the basis; predispose, incline; sow the seed 370 vb. *cultivate*, set to work, address oneself to, limber up 68 vb. *begin*; rough-hew, sketch, outline, blueprint 623 vb. *plan*; plot, concert 608 vb. *predetermine*; forearm, guard against, insure; anticipate 507 vb. *expect*.

make ready, ready, have r., finish one's

261

preparations; trim, make tight; commission, put in c.; put one's house in order, bring up to scratch; settle preliminaries, clear the decks; mobilize 74 vb. *bring together*; tee up; set, cock, prime, load; raise steam, warm up; equip, fit out, furnish, accoutre, harness, rig, dress; arm, provide with teeth 633 vb. *provide*; improvise, rustle up; rehearse, drill, groom, exercise 534 vb. *train*; inure 610 vb. *habituate*; coach, brief 524 vb. *inform.*

mature, mellow, ripen, bring to fruition 646 vb. *perfect*; force, bring on 174 vb. *invigorate*; bring to a head 725 vb. *climax*; digest, stew, brew 301 vb. *cook*; gestate, hatch, incubate, breed 369 vb. *breed stock*; grow 370 vb. *cultivate*; fledge, nurse; elaborate, work out 725 vb. *carry through*; season, weather.

prepare oneself, brace o.; qualify oneself, serve an apprenticeship; study, train, exercise, rehearse, practise 536 vb. *learn*; gird up one's loins, limber up, warm up, flex one's muscles; keep one's powder dry; anticipate, forearm, set the alarm.

670. Non-preparation – N. *non-preparation*, pot-luck; unpreparedness, unreadiness; lack of training, want of practice; rawness, immaturity, unripeness 126 n. *newness*; improvidence 458 n. *negligence*; hastiness, precipitance, rush 680 n. *haste*; improvisation, impromptu 609 n. *spontaneity*; surprise 508 n. *inexpectation.*

undevelopment, delayed maturity, backwardness; native state, virgin soil; raw material, unlicked cub, rough diamond; embryo, abortion.

Adj. *unprepared*, unready, not ready, backward, behindhand 136 adj. *late*; unorganized, makeshift; ad hoc, extemporized, improvised, impromptu, snap, catch-as-catch-can 609 adj. *spontaneous*; unstudied 699 adj. *artless*; careless 458 adj. *negligent*; rush, precipitant, overhasty 680 adj. *hasty*; unguarded, exposed 661 adj. *vulnerable*; unwarned 508 adj. *inexpectant*; shiftless, improvident,

thoughtless, happy-go-lucky 456 adj. *light-minded*; scratch, unequipped, untrained; undrilled, unpractised, unexercised, unrehearsed 611 adj. *unhabituated*; untilled, fallow, virgin 674 adj. *unused.*

immature, ungrown, half-grown, unripe, green, underripe, unmellowed; unfledged, unlicked, callow; adolescent, juvenile 130 adj. *young*; undeveloped, raw; half-baked, rare, underdone; underdeveloped, backward 136 adj. *late*; embryonic, rudimentary 68 adj. *beginning*; undigested, ill-digested; premature, abortive, at half-cock 728 adj. *unsuccessful*; untrained, prentice, undergraduate 695 adj. *unskilled*; crude, coarse 699 adj. *artless.*

Vb. *be unprepared*,—unready etc. adj.; lie fallow, rust 655 vb. *deteriorate*; want practice; not plan, offer pot-luck, extemporize 609 vb. *improvise*; go off at half-cock 135 vb. *be early*; drop one's guard 456 vb. *be inattentive.*

671. Essay – N. *essay*, attempt, bid; step, move, gambit 676 n. *deed*; endeavour, struggle, effort 682 n. *exertion*; coup d'essai, tackle, try, best one can do; set, dead s. 712 n. *attack*; trial, probation 461 n. *experiment*; go at, shot at, stab at, crack at, whack at; campaign, operation, exercise 672 n. *undertaking.*

essayer, bidder, tackler, trier 852 n. *hoper*; assayer, tester 461 n. *experimenter*; searcher, quester 459 n. *inquirer*; struggler, striver, fighter, campaigner 716 n. *contender*; undertaker, contractor, entrepreneur, jobber.

Adj. *essaying*; game, nothing daunted 599 adj. *resolute*; tentative, catch-as-catch-can; testing, probationary 461 adj. *experimental*; venturesome, daring 672 adj. *enterprising.*

Vb. *essay*, quest, seek 459 vb. *search*; aim 617 vb. *intend*; offer, bid, try, attempt, do something about; endeavour, struggle, strive, try and try again 599 vb. *be resolute*; try one's best, do one's b. 682 vb. *exert oneself*; tackle, take on, have a go 672 vb. *undertake*; take a chance, chance one's arm, try one's luck, venture, speculate 618 vb. *gamble*; test, make trial of, assay 461 vb. *be tentative*; bite off more than one can chew, die in the attempt 728 vb. *fail*.

672. Undertaking – N. *undertaking*, contract, engagement, obligation 764 n. *promise*; job, task; labour of love, pilgrimage; operation, exercise; programme, project, design 623 n. *plan*; enterprise, emprise; quest, search, adventure 459 n. *inquiry*; venture 618 n. *gambling*; occupation, matter in hand 622 n. *business*; campaign 671 n. *essay*; undertaker 671 n. *essayer*.

Adj. *enterprising*, pioneering, adventurous, venturesome, daring; go-ahead, progressive; opportunist, ambitious 859 adj. *desiring*.

Vb. *undertake*, engage in, take up, go in for, devote oneself to; venture on, take on, tackle 671 vb. *essay*; go about, take in hand, put one's hand to; broach, embark on, launch into 68 vb. *begin*; assume, take charge of 689 vb. *manage*, 917 vb. *incur a duty*; contract 764 vb. *promise*; volunteer 597 vb. *be willing*; venture, dare 661 vb. *face danger*.

673. Use – N. *use*, usufruct, enjoyment, disposal 773 n. *possession*; conversion to use, utilization, exploitation; employment, application; exercise 610 n. *practice*; treatment, usage; ill-treatment, hard usage 675 n. *misuse*; effect of use, wear, wear and tear 655 n. *dilapidation*; usefulness 640 n. *utility*; serviceability, practicality, convertibility, applicability 642 n. *expedience*; purpose, point 622 n. *function*.

Adj. *used*, availed of etc. vb.; in service, in use; worn, second-hand 655 adj. *dilapidated*; staled, vulgarized; practical 640 adj. *useful*; subservient 628 adj. *instrumental*; available, usable, employable, convertible 642 adj. *expedient*; at one's service, disposable.

Vb. *use*, employ, exercise, practise; apply, exert, bring to bear, adhibit, administer; consume, spend on, utilize,

make use of, convert, convert to use; exploit, use to the full, get the best out of, make the most of; put to use, turn to account, capitalize 137 vb. *profit by*; make play with, play off; handle, thumb 378 vb. *touch*; wield, ply, brandish; overwork, tax 684 vb. *fatigue*; over-use, stale 847 vb. *vulgarize*.

avail of, take up, adopt; avail oneself of, try; resort to, run to, betake oneself to, have recourse to, fall back on; presume on; press into service, make do with.

dispose of, command; control, have at one's command, do what one likes with; give to, devote to, spare, have to s.; call into play, deploy 612 vb. *motivate*; enjoy, have the usufruct 773 vb. *possess*.

674. Non-use – N. *non-use*, abeyance, suspension 677 n. *inaction*; non-availability 190 n. *absence*; stagnation 679 n. *inactivity*; forbearance, abstinence 620 n. *avoidance*; disuse 611 n. *desuetude*; waiver, surrender 621 n. *relinquishment*; uselessness, write-off 641 n. *inutility*; superannuation.

Adj. *unused*, out of order, unusable, unemployable 641 adj. *useless*; unutilized, unapplied, spare, extra; unspent, unconsumed 666 adj. *preserved*; unessayed, untried; in abeyance, suspended; unrequired 860 adj. *unwanted*; unemployed, idle 679 adj. *inactive*; briefless.

disused, derelict, discarded, cast-off, written off; laid up, out of commission, rusting; on the shelf, retired, superannuated; obsolete, discredited 127 adj. *antiquated*.

Vb. *not use*, hold in abeyance, have no use for; abstain, forbear 620 vb. *avoid*; dispense with, waive 621 vb. *relinquish*; overlook, disregard 458 vb. *neglect*; save, reserve, keep in hand 632 vb. *store*; decline 607 vb. *reject*.

disuse, leave off 611 vb. *disaccustom*; lay up, put in mothballs; lay aside; superannuate, pension off, put out to grass; discard, dump, ditch, scrap, write off; jettison, throw overboard 300 vb. *eject*; slough, cast off 229 vb. *doff*;

relinquish 779 vb. *not retain*; suspend 752 vb. *abrogate*; discharge, lay off 300 vb. *dismiss*; drop, supersede, replace 150 vb. *substitute*.

675. Misuse – N. *misuse*, abuse, wrong use, misapplication; misdirection, mismanagement, maladministration 695 n. *unskilfulness*; misappropriation, malversation 788 n. *peculation*; perversion, prostitution, violation; profanation, desecration 980 n. *impiety*; pollution 649 n. *uncleanness*; misusage, mishandling, ill-usage, ill-treatment, force 176 n. *violence*.

Vb. *misuse*, abuse; misapply, misemploy; divert, misappropriate 788 vb. *defraud*; violate, desecrate 980 vb. *profane*; prostitute 655 vb. *pervert*; pollute 649 vb. *make unclean*; do violence to, strain 176 vb. *force*; maltreat; ill-treat 735 vb. *oppress*; misgovern, misrule, mishandle, mismanage 695 vb. *be unskilful*; overwork, overtask 684 vb. *fatigue*; wear out, squander, throw away 634 vb. *waste*.

Section 3: Voluntary Action

676. Action – N. *action*, doing; commission; omission; measures 623 n. *policy*; transaction, enactment, performance, perpetration; dispatch, execution 725 n. *completion*; procedure, routine 610 n. *practice*; behaviour 688 n. *conduct*; movement, play, swing 265 n. *motion*; operation 173 n. *agency*; force, pressure 178 n. *influence*; work, labour 682 n. *exertion*; drama 678 n. *activity*; occupation 622 n. *business*; effort, endeavour 671 n. *essay*; implementation, administration, handling 689 n. *management*; plot 594 n. *dramaturgy*.

deed, act, overt a.; action, exploit, feat, achievement 855 n. *prowess*; crime 930 n. *foul play*; stunt, tour de force 875 n. *ostentation*; measure, step, move 623 n. *policy*; manoeuvre, evolution 688 n. *tactics*; stroke, blow, coup 623 n.

contrivance; job, task 672 n. *undertaking*; proceeding, transaction, deal, doings, dealings 154 n. *affairs*; work, handiwork.

doer, man of deeds, man of action, activist, militant; practical man, realist; hero 855 n. *brave person*; practitioner 696 n. *expert*; stunter, stunt-merchant, executant, performer, player 594 n. *actor*; perpetrator, committer; controller, manipulator 612 n. *motivator*; operator 686 n. *agent*; contractor, undertaker, entrepreneur, campaigner; executive, administrator, manager 690 n. *director*; hand, workman, operative 686 n. *worker*.

Adj. *doing*, in the act, red-handed; in operation, in harness 173 adj. *operative*; up and doing 678 adj. *active*; occupational 610 adj. *habitual*.

Vb. *do*, come into operation; perform, do one's stuff 173 vb. *operate*; militate, act upon 178 vb. *influence*; manipulate 612 vb. *motivate*; proceed, move, act, take steps; attempt, try 671 vb. *essay*; do the deed, perpetrate, commit, inflict, achieve, accomplish 725 vb. *carry through*; do the needful, dispatch, execute, implement 725 vb. *carry out*; solemnize, observe; make history 866 vb. *have repute*; practise, exercise, carry on, prosecute, wage, ply; officiate 622 vb. *function*; transact, administer, administrate 689 vb. *direct*; labour 682 vb. *work*; have a hand in 775 vb. *participate*; conduct oneself, indulge in 688 vb. *behave*.

677. Inaction – N. *inaction*, non-action, nothing doing, inertia 175 n. *inertness*, 161 n. *impotence*; neglect 458 n. *negligence*; abstention 620 n. *avoidance*; suspension, abeyance, dormancy 674 n. *non-use*; immobility, paralysis 375 n. *insensibility*; passivity, stagnation, vegetation, doldrums 266 n. *quiescence*; idle hours 681 n. *leisure*; rest 683 n. *repose*; no work, sinecure; unemployment 679 n. *inactivity*; masterly inactivity 136 n. *delay*; unprogressiveness, rust 654 n. *deterioration*; non-interference, neutrality 860 n. *indifference*; defeatism 856 n. *cowardice*.

Adj. *non-active*; inoperative, in abeyance; fallow 175 adj. *inert*; unoccupied 681 adj. *leisurely*; do-nothing, unprogressive; Fabian, cunctative, defeatist 853 adj. *hopeless*; stationary 266 adj. *quiescent*; idle, unemployed 679 adj. *inactive*; benumbed, paralysed 161 adj. *impotent*; apathetic 820 adj. *impassive*; neutral 860 adj. *indifferent*.

Vb. *not act*, hang fire 598 vb. *be loth*; refrain, abstain 620 vb. *avoid*; look on, wait and see, procrastinate 136 vb. *put off*; live and let live, laisser faire, let sleeping dogs lie, let well alone; do nothing, tolerate; not budge, not lift a finger 175 vb. *be inert*; drift, slide, coast; give it a miss 458 vb. *neglect*; have no function 641 vb. *be useless*; pause, desist 145 vb. *cease*; rust, lie idle.

678. Activity – N. *activity*, activeness, activism, militancy 676 n. *action*; interest 775 n. *participation*; activation 612 n. *motivation*; agitation, movement, mass m. 738 n. *sedition*; life, stir, animation 265 n. *motion*; briskness, alacrity 597 n. *willingness*; quickness, dispatch, expedition 277 n. *velocity*; spurt, burst, fit 318 n. *spasm*; hurry, hustle, bustle 680 n. *haste*; fuss, ado, to-do 61 n. *turmoil*; rat-race, maelstrom 315 n. *vortex*; drama, great doings, thick of things; working life; plenty to do, pressure of work, no sinecure; press, madding crowd; hive of industry 687 n. *workshop*.

restlessness, pottering, aimless activity, desultoriness 456 n. *inattention*; unquiet, fidgets, fidgetiness 318 n. *agitation*; fever, fret 503 n. *frenzy*; eagerness, enthusiasm, ardour, abandon 818 n. *warm feeling*; vigour, energy, dynamism, aggressiveness, militancy, enterprise, initiative, push, drive, go, pep 174 n. *vigorousness*; watchfulness, vigilance 457 n. *carefulness*; wakefulness, sleeplessness, insomnia.

assiduity, application, concentration, intentness 455 n. *attention*; sedulity, industriousness, industry, laboriousness,

drudgery 682 n. *labour*; determination, earnestness, empressement 599 n. *resolution*; tirelessness, indefatigability 600 n. *perseverance*; painstaking, diligence, habits of business; Stakhanovism.

overactivity, over-extension, over-expansion, excess 637 n. *redundance*; over-work; thyrotoxic condition, over-exertion, Stakhanovism; officiousness, ultra-crepidarianism, meddlesomeness, interference, finger in every pie.

busy person, new broom, enthusiast, bustler, hustler, man in a hurry; zealot, fanatic 602 n. *opinionist*; slogger, hard worker, Stakhanovite, demon for work, glutton for w. 686 n. *worker*; factotum, maid-of-all-work, drudge, fag, nigger, slave, galley-s., Trojan; horse, beaver, ant, busy bee; live wire, go-getter, pusher, thruster; careerist.

meddler, officious person, spoilsport, nosy parker, ultracrepidarian, busybody, pickthank; tamperer, intriguer 623 n. *planner*; interferer, butter-in; fusspot, nuisance.

Adj. *active*, stirring 265 adj. *moving*; incessant 146 adj. *unceasing*; quick, brisk, nippy, spry 277 adj. *speedy*; energetic, forceful, thrustful 174 adj. *vigorous*; pushing, go-getting, up-and-coming 672 adj. *enterprising*; frisky, coltish, dashing, animated 819 adj. *lively*; eager, ardent 818 adj. *fervent*; fierce, desperate 599 adj. *resolute*; enthusiastic, on one's toes 597 adj. *willing*; expeditious 622 vb. *businesslike*; alert 457 adj. *vigilant*; sleepless, tireless, restless, feverish, fretful, fidgety, jumpy, fussy 318 adj. *agitated*; overactive, thyrotoxic; aggressive, militant, up in arms 718 adj. *warlike*.

busy, bustling, coming and going; up and doing, stirring, eventful; astir, afoot, a-doing, in full swing; hard at it, in harness, at work.

industrious, studious, sedulous, assiduous 600 adj. *persevering*; hard-working, plodding, strenuous 682 adj. *laborious*; unflagging, unwearied, unsleeping, tireless, indefatigable; efficient, workmanlike 622 adj. *businesslike*.

meddling, over-busy, officious, ultra-crepidarian, interfering, meddlesome, intriguing; participating, in the business.

Vb. *be active*, show interest, trouble oneself, join in 775 vb. *participate*; stir, come and go; run riot; wake up, rouse oneself; hum, thrive 730 vb. *prosper*; keep the ball rolling 146 vb. *go on*; push, shove, thrust, drive 279 vb. *impel*; dash, fly, run 277 vb. *move fast*; take pains 455 vb. *be attentive*, 682 vb. *exert oneself*; persist 600 vb. *persevere*; polish off, dispatch, make short work of; rise to the occasion 727 vb. *be successful*; jump to it 597 vb. *be willing*; assert oneself, be up in arms, react, show fight 711 vb. *defy*.

be busy, have irons in the fire; bustle 680 vb. *hasten*; join the rat-race, run round in circles; chase one's own tail 641 vb. *waste effort*; have one's hands full; fuss, fret, fume 822 vb. *be excitable*; slave, slog 682 vb. *work*; overwork, make work; never stop, improve the shining hour.

meddle, intermeddle, interpose, intervene, interfere, not mind one's own business, have a finger in every pie; butt in 297 vb. *intrude*; pester, bother, dun, annoy 827 vb. *incommode*; tinker, tamper 655 vb. *impair*.

679. Inactivity – N. *inactivity*, inactiveness 677 n. *inaction*; inertia, heaviness, torpor 175 n. *inertness*; lull, suspension, suspended animation 145 n. *cessation*; doldrums 266 n. *quiescence*; stagnation, rust, rustiness 674 n. *non-use*; idleness, dolce far niente 681 n. *leisure*.

sluggishness, laziness, indolence, sloth; lethargy, accidie; dawdling 278 n. *slowness*; inanimation, lifelessness; languor, lentor, dullness, listlessness 820 n. *moral insensibility*; apathy 860 n. *indifference*; phlegm, impassivity 823 n. *inexcitability*; supineness, line of least resistance 721 n. *submission*.

sleepiness, tiredness 684 n. *fatigue*; somnolence, drowsiness, heaviness; yawning; heavy lids, sand in the eyes; dreaminess 513 n. *fantasy*.

sleep, slumber, bye-byes; half-sleep, drowse; first sleep, beauty s.; nap, cat-nap, forty winks, shut-eye, snooze, doze, siesta 683 n. *repose*; hibernation; unconsciousness, coma, trance 375 n. *insensibility*; sleep-walking, somnambulism; dreams, dreamland, Land of Nod; cradle, pillow, bed, shake-down.

soporific, somnifacient, sleeping draught, nightcap; sleeping pill *or* tablet; sedative, barbiturate; opiate, poppy, mandragora 375 n. *anaesthetic*; lullaby, berceuse, cradle-song.

idler, drone, lazybones, lie-abed, loafer, lounger, flâneur, sloucher, slug, sluggard; moper, mopus, sleepy-head; dawdler 278 n. *slowcoach*; hobo, bum, tramp 268 n. *wanderer*; spiv, parasite, cadger, sponger; floater, drifter; opium-eater, lotus-e.; non-worker, sinecurist, rentier; fainéant, dummy, passenger, sleeping partner, absentee landlord; dreamer, sleeper; hibernator, dormouse, marmot.

Adj. *inactive*, motionless, stationary, at a standstill, extinct 266 adj. *quiescent*; out of commission 674 adj. *disused*; inanimate, lifeless 175 adj. *inert*; torpid 375 adj. *insensible*; sluggish, stiff, rusty 677 adj. *non-active*; listless, lackadaisical 834 adj. *dejected*; languid 684 adj. *fatigued*; unresisting, supine 721 adj. *submitting*; uninterested 454 adj. *incurious*; apathetic 860 adj. *indifferent*; lethargic 823 adj. *inexcitable*; non-participating, sleeping 190 adj. *absent*; idle, empty, otiose 681 adj. *leisurely*; on strike, out.

lazy, bone-l., do-nothing; slothful, sluggish, work-shy, indolent, idle; dronish, spivvish, parasitical; tardy, laggard; slack 458 adj. *negligent*.

sleepy, ready for bed, tired 684 adj. *fatigued*; half-awake, half-asleep; slumbrous, somnolent, heavy-eyed; drowsy, dozy, nodding, yawning; asleep, dreaming, fast asleep, sound a., dead to the world; unconscious, out; dormant, hibernating, comatose.

somnific, soporific, somniferous, somnifacient, sleep-inducing, sedative, hypnotic.

Vb. *be inactive*, do nothing, rust, stagnate, vegetate, smoulder, hang fire 677 vb. *not act*; delay 136 vb. *put off*; take one's time, lag, loiter, dawdle 278 vb. *move slowly*; dally, tarry, stay 136 vb. *be late*; stand, sit, lie, lollop, loll, lounge, laze 683 vb. *repose*; not work, sit on one's hands; loaf, idle, mooch, hesitate 474 vb. *be uncertain*; discontinue, stop 145 vb. *cease*; strike, come out.

sleep, slumber, snooze, nap; aestivate, hibernate; dream; snore; drop off, fall asleep, take a nap, have forty winks; yawn, nod, doze, drowse; go to bed, turn in, doss down, roost, perch.

make inactive, put to sleep, lull, rock, cradle; soothe 177 vb. *assuage*; make lazy, sluggardize; deaden, paralyse, benumb 375 vb. *render insensible*; stiffen, cramp, immobilize 747 vb. *fetter*; pay off 300 vb. *dismiss*.

680. Haste – N. *haste*, hurry, scurry, hustle, bustle, scuttle, scramble 678 n. *activity*; rush, rush job 670 n. *nonpreparation*; race, no time to lose 136 n. *lateness*; push, drive, expedition, dispatch 277 n. *velocity*; hastening, forced march 277 n. *spurt*; overhaste, precipitance, impetuosity 857 n. *rashness*; hastiness, impatience 822 n. *excitability*; immediacy, urgency 638 n. *importance*.

Adj. *hasty*, over-h.; impetuous, precipitant 857 adj. *rash*, feverish, impatient, all impatience 818 adj. *fervent*; precipitate, headlong, breathless 277 adj. *speedy*; expeditious, prompt; in haste, hotfoot, in a hurry, unable to wait, pressed for time, driven; rush, lastminute 670 adj. *unprepared*; urgent, immediate 638 adj. *important*.

Vb. *hasten*, expedite, dispatch; urge, drive, spur, goad, whip, lash, flog 612 vb. *incite*; rush, brook no delay; haste, make haste; post, race, run 277 vb. *move fast*; catch up 277 vb. *outstrip*; spurt 277 vb. *accelerate*; hurry, scurry, hustle, bustle 678 vb. *be active*; cut corners, rush one's fences; rush through, make short work of; work against time,

do at the last moment 136 vb. *be late*; lose no time, make every minute count.

681. Leisure – N. *leisure*, spare time, convenience; vacant moments, time to kill; no work, idleness; time off, holiday, vacation, leave, furlough, sabbatical year 679 n. *inactivity*; time to spare, no hurry; rest, ease 683 n. *repose*.

Adj. *leisurely*, unhurried 278 adj. *slow*; at one's convenience; leisured, at leisure, disengaged, unoccupied; at a loose end, at ease; off duty, on holiday; in retirement; labour-saving.

Vb. *have leisure*, have time to spare; take one's ease, while away; take one's time 278 vb. *move slowly*; take a holiday 683 vb. *repose*; give up work, retire 753 vb. *resign*.

682. Exertion – N. *exertion*, effort, struggle 671 n. *essay*; strain, stress, might and main; drive, force, pressure 160 n. *energy*; ado, trouble, toil and t., mighty efforts, the hard way; muscle, elbow grease, sweat of one's brow; painstaking 678 n. *assiduity*; overwork 678 n. *overactivity*; overtime; battle, campaign.

exercise, exercitation; employment 673 n. *use*; practice, training, work-out 669 n. *preparation*; bodily exercise, gymnastics 162 n. *athletics*; eurhythmics, callisthenics; games, sports 837 n. *sport*.

labour, work, uphill w., long haul; spadework, donkey-work; manual labour, sweat of one's brow; housework, chores; toil, travail, drudgery, slavery, sweat, fag, grind, strain, treadmill, grindstone; penal work, hard labour 963 n. *penalty*; forced labour, corvée 740 n. *compulsion*; fatigue, fatigue duty 917 n. *duty*; piecework, taskwork; task, chore, job, operation, exercise 676 n. *deed*; shift, trick, stint, stretch 110 n. *period*; job of work, hand's turn; working life, working day, man-hours.

Adj. *labouring*, born to toil, hornyhanded; working etc. vb.; hard at it 678 adj. *busy*; hard-working, laborious 678 adj. *industrious*; strenuous, energetic 678 adj. *active*; painstaking, thorough 455 adj. *attentive*; palestric, gymnastic, athletic.

laborious, full of labour, involving effort; operose, fatiguing, crushing, killing, backbreaking; gruelling, punishing; toilsome, troublesome, weary, wearisome; heroic, Herculean; arduous, hard, warm, heavy, uphill 700 adj. *difficult*; hard-fought, hard-won; effort-wasting 641 adj. *useless*.

Vb. *exert oneself*, make an effort, try 671 vb. *essay*; struggle, strain, strive, sweat blood; trouble oneself, bestir oneself, put oneself out; spare no effort, do one's utmost, go to all lengths; put one's back into it, strain every nerve; slog at 600 vb. *persevere*; battle, campaign.

work, labour, toil, moil, drudge, fag, grind, slog, sweat; haul, tug, heave, ply; do the work, soil one's hands; keep at it, plod 600 vb. *persevere*; overwork, slave, work like a horse, overdo it, make work; work for 703 vb. *minister to*; task, tax 684 vb. *fatigue*.

683. Repose – **N.** *repose*, rest, rest from one's labours 679 n. *inactivity*; restfulness, ease, comfort 376 n. *euphoria*; happy dreams 679 n. *sleep*; relaxation 685 n. *refreshment*; pause, respite, recess, break 145 n. *lull*; holiday 681 n. *leisure*; day of rest, sabbath, Lord's day.

Adj. *reposeful*, restful, easeful, slippered; snug 376 adj. *comfortable*; peaceful, quiet 266 adj. *tranquil*; leisured, sabbatical, vacational, holiday 681 adj. *leisurely*.

Vb. *repose*, rest, take r., enjoy peace; take one's ease, mop one's brow, stretch one's legs; recline, lie down, loll, sprawl, perch, roost 311 vb. *sit down*; couch, go to bed 679 vb. *sleep*; relax, unbend, rest and be thankful; take a breather 685 vb. *be refreshed*; take a holiday 681 vb. *have leisure*.

684. Fatigue – **N.** *fatigue*, tiredness, weariness, lassitude, languor; aching

muscles; brain-fag, staleness; jadedness, distress; limit of endurance, exhaustion, collapse, prostration; strain, over-tiredness 682 n. *exertion*; faintness, faint, swoon 375 n. *insensibility*.

Adj. *fatigued*, ready for bed 679 adj. *sleepy*; exhausted, spent, fordone; done up, pooped, fagged, knocked up; dull, stale; strained, jaded, overworked, overtired, overdriven; dog-tired, dropping, all in, dead beat, beat, whacked, more dead than alive; aching, sore; way-worn, footsore; tired-eyed, heavy-e.; haggard, worn; faint, languid; unrefreshed; tired of 863 adj. *sated*.

panting, out of breath, short of b.; breathed, breathless, gasping, winded, blown, broken-winded 352 adj. *puffing*.

Vb. *be fatigued*, get weary, gasp, pant, puff, blow, grunt, lose one's wind 352 vb. *breathe*; languish, droop, drop, sink, flag, fail 163 vb. *be weak*; stagger, faint, swoon, swim; yawn 679 vb. *sleep*; succumb, drop, collapse, crack up, crock up, pack up; cry out for rest, can go *or* do no more; overwork, get stale.

fatigue, weary, tire, fag, exhaust, whack, knock up, prostrate; double up, wind; task, tax, strain, work, drive, overdrive, flog, overwork, overtask; distress, jade 827 vb. *incommode*; allow no rest.

685. Refreshment – **N.** *refreshment*, breather, break, recess 145 n. *lull*; renewal, recreation, recruitment, recuperation 656 n. *restoration*; reanimation, refocillation 656 n. *revival*, 831 n. *relief*; stimulation, refresher, reviver 174 n. *stimulant*; refection 301 n. *food*.

Adj. *refreshing*, cool 380 adj. *cold*; comforting 831 adj. *relieving*; bracing 656 adj. *restorative*; easy on, labour-saving.

refreshed, freshened up, breathed, recovered 656 adj. *restored*; like a giant refreshed, twice the man one was; ready for more.

Vb. *refresh*, freshen up 648 vb. *clean*; fan, ventilate 340 vb. *aerify*; shade, cool off 382 vb. *refrigerate*; brace, stimulate

174 vb. *invigorate*; recruit, recreate, revive, reanimate, recuperate 656 vb. *restore*; ease 831 vb. *relieve*; allow rest; regale 301 vb. *feed*.

be refreshed, breathe, get one's breath back, respire, clear one's head; come to, perk up, revive 656 vb. *be restored*; mop one's brow, take a breather, sleep off; go for a change 683 vb. *repose*.

686. Agent – N. *agent*, operator, actor, performer, player, executant, practitioner; perpetrator 676 n. *doer*; minister, instrument 630 n. *tool*; factor 754 n. *consignee*; representative 754 n. *delegate*; spokesman 755 n. *deputy*; proxy 150 n. *substitute*; executor, executrix, executive, administrator, dealer; employer, manufacturer, industrialist 167 n. *producer*.

worker, social worker 901 n. *philanthropist*; free-lance, self-employed person; toiler, moiler, drudge, fag, erk, hack; menial, factotum, maid-of-all-work 742 n. *servant*; hewer of wood and drawer of water, beast of burden 742 n. *slave*; ant, beaver, Stakhanovite 678 n. *busy person*; professional man, business m., breadwinner, earner, wage-e., wage-slave, employee; brain-worker, boffin; clerical worker, white-collar w., blackcoat w.; piece-worker, manual w.; labourer, day-l.; working man, workman, man, hand, operative; navvy, ganger.

artisan, artificer, tradesman, technician; skilled worker, past-master 696 n. *proficient*; journeyman, apprentice 538 n. *learner*; craftsman.

personnel, staff, force, company, gang, squad, crew, complement, cadre 74 n. *band*; dramatis personae 594 n. *actor*; co-worker, fellow-w., mate, partner 707 n. *colleague*; workpeople, hands, men, payroll; labour, labour pool, labour force, man-power, working classes.

687. Workshop – N. *workshop*, studio, atelier; workroom, study; laboratory; workhouse, sweatshop; plant, installaation; shop, workshop, yard; mill, factory, manufactory; foundry, works yard; blast-furnace, forge, smithy 383 n. *furnace*; powerhouse, power station 160 n. *energy*; quarry, mine 632 n. *store*; mint; arsenal; dockyard, shipyard, slips; shop, shop-floor, bench, production line; nursery 370 n. *farm*; office, bureau, business house, firm, company; secretariat, administrative buildings; manufacturing town, hive of industry 678 n. *activity*.

688. Conduct – N. *conduct*, behaviour, deportment; bearing, comportment, carriage, port; demeanour, attitude, posture 445 n. *mien*; aspect, look 445 n. *appearance*; motion, action, gesticulation 547 n. *gesture*; manner, guise, air; poise, dignity; pose 850 n. *affectation*; outlook 485 n. *opinion*; good behaviour 933 n. *virtue*; misbehaviour, misconduct 934 n. *wickedness*; past behaviour, record, history; deserts 915 n. *dueness*; way of life, ethos, mores, morals, ideals, customs, manners 610 n. *habit*; line of action 623 n. *policy*; career, walk of life 622 n. *vocation*; observance, routing 610 n. *practice*; procedure, method, modus operandi 624 n. *way*; direction 689 n. *management*; dealings, transactions 154 n. *affairs*; deeds 676 n. *deed*.

tactics, strategy, campaign, plan of c., programme 623 n. *plan;* line, party l. 623 n. *policy*; political science, art of the possible, politics, realpolitik, statesmanship 733 n. *governance*; lifemanship, gamesmanship, one-upmanship 698 n. *cunning*; brinkmanship, generalship 694 n. *skill*; manoeuvres, jockeying, position; shift 623 n. *contrivance*; move, gambit 676 n. *deed*; game, little g. 698 n. *stratagem*.

Adj. *behaving*, behaviourist; psychological; tactical, strategical; political, statesmanlike.

Vb. *behave*, act 676 vb. *do*; behave well 933 vb. *be virtuous*; misbehave, carry on 934 vb. *be wicked*; deserve well *or* ill; gesture 547 vb. *gesticulate*; posture, pose 850 vb. *be affected*; conduct oneself, behave o., bear o., comport o., demean o.; indulge in 678 vb. *be active*; employ tactics, manoeuvre, jockey; behave towards, treat; deal with 689 vb. *manage*.

689. Management – N. *management*, conduct of affairs, managership, stewardship, proctorship, agency 751 n. *commission*; care, charge, control 733 n. *authority*; superintendence, oversight 457 n. *surveillance*; ménage, regimen, régime, dispensation; housekeeping, housewifery; husbandry, economics, political economy; statecraft, statesmanship; government 733 n. *governance*; staff work, administration; bureaucracy, civil service; secretariat.

directorship, direction, responsibility, control 737 n. *command*; dictatorship, leadership, premiership, chairmanship, captaincy 34 n. *superiority*; guidance, steersmanship, pilotship; pole-star, lodestar 520 n. *guide*; steering instrument, steering oar, joy-stick, controls, helm, rudder, wheel, tiller 269 n. *sailing aid*; direction-finding, beam, radar 281 n. *direction*; remote control, telearchics.

Adj. *directing*, directorial, leading, hegemonic; directional, guiding, steering; gubernatorial 733 adj. *authoritative*; dictatorial 735 adj. *authoritarian*; supervisory, managerial; executive, administrative; economic, political; official, bureaucratic 733 adj. *governmental*.

Vb. *manage*, manipulate, manoeuvre, pull the strings 178 vb. *influence*; handle, conduct, run, carry on; administer, take order, deal with, cope w., see to, do the needful; supervise, superintend, oversee, caretake 457 vb. *invigilate*; keep order, police, regulate; control, govern, sway 733 vb. *rule*; know how to manage, have a way with.

direct, lead, pioneer 64 vb. *come before*; boss, dictate 737 vb. *command*; hold office 917 vb. *incur a duty*; preside, take the chair; head, captain; stroke; pilot, cox, steer, take the helm 269 vb. *navigate*; point, show the way 547 vb. *indicate*; shepherd, guide, conduct; channel, canalize; route, train, lead.

690. Director – N. *director*, governing body, boardroom, governor; steering committee; ministry, cabinet 692 n. *council*; board, chair; policy-maker, staff, brass, top b., management; manager, controller; legislator, law-giver, lawmaker; employer, capitalist, boss 741 n. *master*; headman, chief 34 n. *superior*; principal, headmaster, head, rector, moderator, vice-chancellor, chancellor; president, vice-p.; chairman, speaker; premier, prime minister; captain; master, sailing-m. 270 n. *mariner*; steersman, helmsman 270 n. *navigator*; pilot 520 n. *guide*; king-maker, wire-puller 612 n. *motivator*.

leader, charismatic l., judge (Old Testament), commander; messiah, mahdi; spearhead, centre-forward; fugleman, file-leader; pace-maker; high priest, mystagogue; coryphaeus, conductor; Führer, Duce 741 n. *autocrat*; ringleader 738 n. *agitator*; condottiere.

manager, responsible person, man in charge; administrator, executive 676 n. *doer*; statesman, statist, politician; housekeeper, husband, housewife; steward, agent, factor 754 n. *consignee*; superintendent, supervisor, inspector, overseer, foreman; party-manager, whip; custodian, caretaker 749 n. *keeper*.

official, functionary, placeman, incumbent; office-holder, office-bearer, Jack-in-office, tin god; shop steward; officer of state, high official, vizier, minister, secretary of state, secretary; bureaucrat, mandarin; magistrate 733 n. *magistrature*; commissioner, prefect, intendant; consul, proconsul.

691. Advice – N. *advice*, word of a., piece of a.; counsel, words of wisdom, rede 498 n. *wisdom*; criticism, constructive c. 480 n. *estimate*; didacticism, moralizing, moral 693 n. *precept*; suggestion, recommendation, proposition, proposal, motion 512 n. *supposition*; tip 524 n. *hint*; briefing, instruction 524 n. *information*; charge to the jury 955 n. *legal trial*; consultation, mutual c. 584 n. *conference*; seeking advice, reference.

adviser, counsellor, consultant 696 n. *expert*; referee, arbiter 480 n. *estimator*; advocate, recommender, mover, prompter; counsel 958 n. *lawyer*; guide, philosopher, and friend, mentor, confidant 537 n. *teacher*; monitor, admonisher, remembrancer 505 n. *reminder*; oracle, wise man 500 n. *sage*; committee of inquiry, consultative body 692 n. *council*.

Adj. *advising*, advisory, consultative, deliberative; hortative, recommendatory 612 adj. *inducive*; admonitory, warning 664 adj. *cautionary*; didactic; moral, moralizing.

Vb. *advise*, give advice, counsel; recommend, prescribe, advocate, commend; propose, move, put to, submit, suggest 512 vb. *propound*; prompt 524 vb. *hint*; urge, exhort 612 vb. *incite*; advise against 613 vb. *dissuade*; admonish 664 vb. *warn*.

consult, seek advice, refer, make a reference, call in; confide in; take advice, listen to, be advised, take one's cue from, submit one's judgement to another's; sit in conclave, lay heads together, deliberate, parley, compare notes 584 vb. *confer*.

692. Council – N. *council*, council board, round table; council chamber, board room; curia, consistory, Bench of Bishops; vestry; cabinet, board, consultative body; conclave, convocation 985 n. *synod*; convention, congress, summit; durbar, diet; municipal council, county c., borough c., town c., parish c.; zemstvo, soviet; council of elders, genro, sanhedrim.

parliament, Mother of Parliaments, Westminster, Upper House, House of Lords, House of Peers, 'another place'; Lower House, House of Commons; senate, senatus; legislative assembly, deliberative a., consultative a.; States-General, Cortes, witenagemot; Chambre des Députés, Reichstag, Reichsrath, Rigsdag, Storthing, Duma, Dail Eireann; Senate, Congress; Legislative Council, Lok Sabha, Majlis, Sejm, Knesset.

councillor, privy councillor; senator, conscript fathers, Areopagite, sanhedrist; peer, life-peer; representative, deputy, congressman, member of Parliament 754 n. *delegate*; back-bencher, lobby-fodder; parliamentarian, legislator; municipal councillor, mayor, alderman.

Adj. *parliamentary*, senatorial, congressional; unicameral, bicameral; curule, conciliar; convocational, synodal.

693. Precept – N. *precept*, firm advice 691 n. *advice*; injunction, charge 737 n. *command*; prescription, ordinance, regulation 737 n. *decree*; canon, formula, formulary, rubric; rule, golden r., moral 496 n. *maxim*; recipe, receipt 658 n. *remedy*; commandment, statute 953 n. *legislation*; tenet, article, set of rules, constitution; ticket, party line; Ten Commandments, Twelve Tables; rule of custom, convention 610 n. *practice*; precedent, leading case, text 83 n. *example*.

Adj. *preceptive*, prescriptive, decretal, mandatory, binding; canonical, rubrical, statutory 953 adj. *legal*; moralizing, didactic.

694. Skill – N. *skill*, skilfulness, dexterity, dexterousness, handiness, ambidexterity; grace, style 575 n. *elegance*; neatness, deftness, adroitness, address; proficiency, competence, efficiency 160 n. *ability*; many-sidedness, all-round capacity, versatility; touch, grip, control; mastery, mastership, wizardry, virtuosity, prowess 644 n. *goodness*; strong point, métier, forte, major suit; acquirement, attainment, accomplishment; experience, expertise, professionalism; specialism; technology, science, know-how, technique 490 n. *knowledge*; craftsmanship, art, artistry; craft 698 n. *cunning*; cleverness, sophistication, lifemanship 498 n. *sagacity*; savoir faire, tact 463 n. *discrimination*; feat of skill, sleight of hand 542 n. *sleight*; generalship 688 n. *tactics*.

aptitude, inborn a., innate ability; bent, natural b. 179 n. *tendency*; faculty, endowment, gift, flair, parts, natural p.; turn, knack, green fingers; genius for; aptness, fitness, qualification.

masterpiece, chef-d'œuvre, a beauty; masterstroke, coup-de-maître, feat, exploit, hat-trick 676 n. *deed*; tour de force, bravura, fireworks; ace, trump, clincher 644 n. *exceller*; work of art, collector's piece.

Adj. *skilful*, good at 644 adj. *excellent*; skilled, crack; apt, handy, dexterous, deft, adroit, slick, neat; sure-footed; cunning, ingenious; politic, statesmanlike 498 adj. *wise*; many-sided, versatile; able, competent, efficient; wizard, masterly, like a master, magisterial 646 adj. *perfect*.

gifted, taught by nature, greenfingered; of parts, talented, endowed, well-e., born for, just made for.

expert, experienced, veteran, seasoned, tried, versed in, up in 490 adj. *instructed*; skilled, trained; specialized 669 adj. *matured*; proficient, efficient, qualified, competent; professional 622 adj. *businesslike*.

well-made, well-done, craftily contrived, deep-laid; finished, artistic, stylish 575 adj. *elegant*; Daedalian, cunning; technical, scientific; shipshape, workmanlike.

Vb. *be skilful*, be good at, do well; have the knack, have the trick of, play one's cards well, not put a foot wrong; use skilfully, exploit, squeeze the last ounce out of 673 vb. *use*; know all the answers 498 vb. *be wise*.

be expert, turn professional; know one's job, have the know-how; qualify oneself 536 vb. *learn*; know the ropes, know backwards, be up to every trick, take in one's stride 490 vb. *know*.

695. Unskilfulness – N. *unskilfulness*, no gift; rustiness 674 n. *non-use*; inexperience 491 n. *ignorance*; incapacity, incompetence, inefficiency 161 n. *ineffectuality*; inexpertise, unproficiency; quackery, charlatanism 850 n. *pre-*

tension; clumsiness, unhandiness, awkwardness (see *bungling*).

bungling, half-measures, pale imitation 726 n. *non-completion*; bungle, boch; off day, botched performance, bad job 728 n. *failure*; hamhandedness, foozle, muff, miss, mishit, misfire 495 n. *mistake*; impolicy, mismanagement, misrule, misgovernment, maladministration; misdoing, misconduct, antics.

Adj. *unskilful*, ungifted, untalented; undexterous, unadroit; incompetent, inefficient, ineffectual; impolitic 499 adj. *unwise*; futile, feckless.

unskilled, skill-less, raw 670 adj. *immature*; untrained, half-baked, half-skilled, semi-s. 670 adj. *unprepared*; unqualified, inexpert, scratch, inexperienced; non-professional, lay, amateurish, bumble-puppy; unscientific, unsound, charlatan, quack, quackish.

clumsy, awkward, gauche, gawkish; lubberly, unhandy, all thumbs, butterfingered; left-handed, ham-h.; ungainly, lumbering; stiff, rusty 674 adj. *unused*; slovenly, slatternly, slapdash 458 adj. *negligent*; fumbling 461 adj. *experimental*; ungraceful, graceless, clownish 576 adj. *inelegant*; cumbersome, unwieldy, unmanageable, unsteerable.

bungled, ill-done, botched etc. vb.; unplanned 670 adj. *unprepared*; ill-contrived, ill-devised, ill-conducted; unhappy, infelicitous, ill-chosen; inartistic, home-made 699 adj. *artless*; slapdash, perfunctory.

Vb. *be unskilful*, show one's ignorance, set the wrong way about it; tinker, paper over the cracks 726 n. *not complete*; maladminister, mishandle, mismanage, misconduct, misrule, misgovern; misapply 674 vb. *misuse*; miss one's cue 506 vb. *forget*; lose one's cunning, get out of practice 611 vb. *be unused*.

stultify oneself, not know what one is about, not know one's business, stand in one's own light, cut one's own throat, make a fool of oneself; put the cart before the horse; put new wine into old bottles 495 vb. *blunder*; labour in vain, go on a fool's errand 641 vb. *waste effort*; catch a Tartar, burn one's fingers.

be clumsy, lumber, hulk, get in the way; trip, stumble; fumble, grope, flounder 461 vb. *be tentative*; muff, fluff, foozle; pull, slice, mishit, misthrow; overthrow, overshoot 306 vb. *overstep*; play into the hands of, give a catch, give a chance; bungle, drop a brick, put one's foot in it 495 vb. *blunder*; botch, spoil, mar, slubber, blot, vitiate 655 vb. *impair*; fool with 678 vb. *meddle*; make a mess of it, mash, hash 728 vb. *miscarry*; perpetrate, do a bad job 728 vb. *fail*.

696. Proficient – N. *proficient*, sound player, expert, adept, dab, dabster; all-rounder, handyman; master, past master, graduate, cordon bleu; genius, wizard 864 n. *prodigy*; magician 545 n. *conjuror*; man of parts, virtuoso; prima donna, first fiddle, top-sawyer, prize-man, prize-winner, medallist, champion, holder, cup-h. 644 n. *exceller*; crack, crack shot, dead s., marksman 287 n. *shooter*.

expert, no novice, practitioner; professional, specialist; professor 537 n. *teacher*; savant 492 n. *scholar*; veteran, old hand, old stager, old file, old soldier, seadog, shellback; man of the world, man of business, tactician, strategist; technician, skilled worker 686 n. *artisan*; right man for the job, key man; consultant 691 n. *adviser*; boffin, backroom boy 623 n. *planner*; connoisseur, fancier.

697. Bungler – N. *bungler*, failure 728 n. *loser*; duffer, bad learner, one's despair 501 n. *dunce*; botcher, blunderer, marplot; mismanager, fumbler, muff, butterfingers; hulker, lump, lout, lubber, swab, awkward squad, jaywalker; clown 501 n. *fool*; dauber, bad hand, no conjuror; novice, greenhorn, colt, raw recruit, apprentice 538 n. *beginner*; tail 35 n. *inferior*; quack 545 n. *imposter*.

698. Cunning – N. *cunning*, craft 694 n. *skill*; lore 490 n. *knowledge*; resourcefulness, inventiveness, ingenuity 513 n.

imagination; guile, gamesmanship, craftiness, artfulness, subtlety, wiliness, slyness, foxiness; sharp practice, chicanery 930 n. *foul play*; finesse, jugglery 542 n. *sleight*; policy, diplomacy, Machiavellism; underhand dealing, practice, intrigue 623 n. *plot*.

stratagem, ruse, wile, art, artifice, device, wrinkle, shift, dodge, artful d. 623 n. *contrivance*; machination, game, little g. 623 n. *plot*; subterfuge, evasion; juggle, cheat 542 n. *deception*; trick, box of tricks, tricks of the trade 542 n. *trickery*; feint, catch, net, web, ambush, Trojan horse 542 n. *trap*, 663 n. *pitfall*; blind, dust thrown in the eyes, flag of convenience 542 n. *sham*; manoeuvre, move 688 n. *tactics*.

slyboots, crafty fellow, artful dodger, snake, fox, Reynard; nigger in the woodpile 663 n. *trouble-maker*; fraud, shammer, dissembler, hypocrite 545 n. *deceiver*; cheat, sharper 545 n. *trickster*; juggler 545 n. *conjuror*; smooth citizen, glib tongue 925 n. *flatterer*; intriguer, plotter, schemer 623 n. *planner*; strategist, tactician, manoeuvrer.

Adj. *cunning*, knowledgeable 498 adj. *wise*; crafty, artful, sly, wily, guileful, subtle, snaky, foxy, feline; rusy, tricky, tricksy; scheming, intriguing 623 adj. *planning*; knowing, fly, canny, sharp, astute, shrewd, acute; too clever for, too clever by half, up to everything, not to be caught with chaff, not born yesterday 498 adj. *intelligent*; resourceful, ingenious; deep as water; deep-laid, well-l.; shifty, slippery, deceitful, flattering 542 adj. *deceiving*; knavish 930 adj. *rascally*.

Vb. *be cunning*, proceed by stratagem, play the fox, try a ruse, finesse, dodge; manoeuvre, double cross; intrigue, scheme, practise, play a deep game 623 vb. *plot*; circumvent, overreach, pull a fast one, trick 542 vb. *deceive*; outsmart, go one better, know a trick worth two of that; waylay 527 vb. *ambush*; match in cunning, see the catch.

699. Artlessness – N. *artlessness*, simplicity, simple-mindedness; naïveté, ingenuousness, guilelessness 935 n. *innocence*; unaffectedness, unsophistication, naturalness 573 n. *plainness*; sincerity, candour 540 n. *veracity*; uncivilized state, savagery; darkness, no science, no art 491 n. *ignorance*; Philistinism; no artistry 647 n. *imperfection*; uncouthness 847 n. *bad taste*.

ingenue, child of nature, savage, noble s.; enfant terrible; lamb 935 n. *innocent*; greenhorn 538 n. *beginner*; rough diamond, plain man, Philistine; hayseed, hillbilly 869 n. *countryman*.

Adj. artless, without art, without artifice, without tricks; uncomplicated 44 adj. *simple*; unadorned, unvarnished 573 adj. *plain*; native, natural, unartificial, homespun, home-made; do-it-yourself 695 adj. *unskilled*; in a state of nature, uncivilized, wild, savage, unlearned, unscientific 491 adj. *ignorant*; Arcadian, unsophisticated, ingenuous, naïve, childlike 935 adj. *innocent*; shy, inarticulate 874 adj. *modest*; guileless, unsuspicious, confiding; unaffected 609 adj. *spontaneous*; candid, frank, open 540 n. *veracious*; undesigning, honest, sincere 929 adj. *honourable*; transparent 522 adj. *undisguised*; unpoetical, prosaic, matter-of-fact; inartistic, Philistine; rude, unpolished, uncouth 847 adj. *vulgar*.

Vb. be artless, — natural etc. adj.; live in a state of nature, know no better; confide, wear one's heart upon one's sleeve.

Section 4: Antagonism

700. Difficulty – N. *difficulty*, hardness, arduousness, laboriousness, the hard way 682 n. *exertion*; impracticability, one's despair 470 n. *impossibility*; intricacy, perplexity, inextricability 61 n. *complexity*; complication 832 n. *aggravation*; obscurity 517 n. *unintelligibility*; inconvenience, awkwardness, embarrassment 643 n. *inexpedience*; hard going 259 n. *roughness*; knot, Gordian k. 251 n. *coil*; problem, crux, poser, headache 530 n. *enigma*; impediment, handicap 702 n. *hindrance*; impasse 264 n. *closure*;

stress, brunt, burden 684 n. *fatigue*; tribulation, trouble 731 n. *adversity*; difficult person, handful, one's despair, kittle cattle.

hard task, test, severe t., test of strength; labours of Hercules, Herculean task, Augean stables; task, job, work cut out, hard row to hoe; handful, tall order, tough assignment, hard work, uphill work 682 n. *labour*.

predicament, embarrassment, false position; nonplus, quandary, dilemma, cleft stick, option of difficulties, borderline case 474 n. *dubiety*; fix, jam, hole, scrape, hot water, trouble, peck of troubles, kettle of fish, pickle, stew, imbroglio, mess, muddle; pinch, strait, straits, pass, pretty p.; sticky wicket, tight corner, situation 661 n. *danger*; emergency 137 n. *crisis*.

Adj. difficult, hard, tough, formidable; steep, arduous, uphill; inconvenient, onerous, burdensome, toilsome 682 adj. *laborious*; exacting, demanding 684 adj. *fatiguing*; insuperable, impracticable 470 adj. *impossible*; delicate, ticklish; sooner said than done; unmanageable, out of hand, intractable 738 adj. *disobedient*; stubborn 602 adj. *obstinate*; ill-behaved, naughty 934 adj. *wicked*; perplexing, problematical, knotty, intricate; impassable, unnavigable; sticky, critical 661 adj. *dangerous*.

in difficulties, bested, ill-b.; labouring under difficulties; in a quandary, in a dilemma 474 adj. *doubting*; baffled, clueless; in a jam, in a spot, in a hole, in hot water, out of one's depth; up against it, hard pressed, in straits, cornered, at bay.

Vb. be difficult, make things difficult, complicate, complicate matters 63 vb. *bedevil*; trouble, inconvenience, bother, irk, plague 827 vb. *incommode*; present difficulties, set one a problem, pose, perplex, baffle, nonplus, ground, stump, gravel 474 vb. *puzzle*; encumber 702 vb. *hinder*; make things worse 832 vb. *aggravate*.

be in difficulty, have a problem; have one's hands full 678 vb. *be busy*; be at a loss 474 vb. *be uncertain*; have one's work cut out, have trouble with; run into trouble, strike a bad patch, let oneself in for; bear the brunt, feel the wind 825 vb. *suffer*; make heavy weather, flounder; try it the hard way 716 vb. *contend*; labour under difficulties.

701. Facility – N. *facility*, easiness, ease, convenience, comfort; wieldiness, ease of handling; flexibility 327 n. *softness*; feasibility 469 n. *possibility*; comprehensibility 516 n. *intelligibility*; facilitation, simplification, disencumbrance; full play, full scope 744 n. *scope*; facilities 703 n. *aid*; leave 756 n. *permission*; simplicity, straightforwardness, no difficulty; clear coast 137 n. *opportunity*; highway, primrose path 624 n. *road*; downhill 309 n. *descent*.

easy thing, no effort, child's play, holiday task, sinecure; picnic, play 837 n. *amusement*; piece of cake, money for jam; plain sailing, joy-ride; nothing to it, sitter, easy target; walk-over 727 n. *victory*; no trouble, pleasure.

Adj. *easy*, facile, undemanding; effortless, painless; uncomplicated, foolproof 44 adj. *simple*; no sooner said than done; convenient 376 adj. *comfortable*; within comprehension, for the million 516 adj. *intelligible*.

wieldy, manageable, tractable 597 adj. *willing*; yielding, soft, ductile, pliant 327 adj. *flexible*; smooth-running, well-oiled, frictionless; handy, manoeuvrable, labour-saving.

Vb. *be easy*, — simple etc. adj.; require no effort, present no difficulties, give no trouble, make no demands; have a simple answer 516 vb. *be intelligible*; work like a machine, go like clockwork, run on smoothly 258 vb. *go smoothly*.

do easily, have no trouble, see one's way; make light of, make no bones about, make short work of; have it all one's own way, carry all before one, win hands down 727 vb. *win*; be in one's element, take in one's stride.

facilitate, ease, make easy; iron out 258 vb. *smooth*; grease, oil 334 vb. *lubri-*

cate; explain, simplify, popularize 520 vb. *interpret*; enable, not stand in the way, allow 756 vb. *permit*; give a chance to, help, speed 703 vb. *aid*.

disencumber, free, liberate, unshackle, unfetter 668 vb. *deliver*; clear, clear the ground 648 vb. *clean*; derestrict, disengage, disembarrass; disentangle, extricate 62 vb. *unravel*; unknot, untie 46 vb. *disjoin*; cut the knot; ease, lighten, take off one's shoulders, unload, unburden, disburden, ease the burden, alleviate 831 vb. *relieve*.

Adv. *easily*, readily, smoothly, without friction, swimmingly; effortlessly, by the flick of a switch; without a hitch, without let or hindrance; on easy terms.

702. Hindrance – N. *hindrance*, let or h., impediment, rub; obstruction, frustration; hampering etc. vb.; limitation, restriction, control 747 n. *restraint*; arrest, check, retardation; drag 333 n. *friction*; interference, interruption, interception, interposition, intervention; obstructiveness, picketing, sabotage 704 n. *opposition*; counter-measure 182 n. *counteraction*; discouragement, disincentive 613 n. *dissuasion*; forestalling, prevention; prophylaxis, sanitation 652 n. *hygiene*; ban, embargo, estoppal 757 n. *prohibition*; nuisance value.

obstacle, impediment, drawback, inconvenience, handicap 700 n. *difficulty*; bunker, hazard; bottleneck, blockage, jam, log-j.; a hindrance, let, stay; tie 47 n. *bond*; snag, block, stop, stymie; stumbling-block, trip-wire, hurdle, hedge; something in the way, barrier, bulkhead, wall, brick w., sea-w., groyne, boom, dam, dyke, embankment 662 n. *safeguard*; bulwark 713 n. *defences*; fence, ring, blockade 235 n. *enclosure*; curtain, iron c., bamboo c. 231 n. *partition*; check, brake, clog, curb 748 n. *fetter*; impasse, deadlock, stalemate, vicious circle; cul-de-sac, blind alley, dead end.

hitch, snag, catch; contretemps, spot of trouble; teething troubles; technical hitch, breakdown, stoppage 145 n. *stop*; something wrong, spanner in the works, fly in the ointment.

encumbrance, handicap, remora; trammels, clog, shackle, chain 748 n. *fetter*; impedimenta, baggage, lumber, weight, dead-weight, millstone, weight on one's shoulders, load on one's back, last straw, incubus, white elephant; passenger.

hinderer, hindrance; red herring 10 n. *irrelevance*; wet blanket, damper, spoilsport, kill-joy, pussyfoot; marplot 697 n. *bungler*; dog in the manger, obstructionist, filibuster, saboteur; heckler, interrupter, barracker; interceptor, interferer 678 n. *meddler*; mischief-maker, gremlin 663 n. *trouble-maker*; lion in the path, challenger 705 n. *opponent*; rival, competitor 716 n. *contender*.

Adj. *hindering*, impedient, obstructive, strike-happy; thwarting etc. vb.; cross, contrary, unfavourable 731 adj. *adverse*; restrictive 747 adj. *restraining*; prohibitive, preventive 757 adj. *prohibiting*; prophylactic, counteractive 182 adj. *counteracting*; obtrusive, not wanted 59 adj. *extraneous*; in the way, in the light; inconvenient 643 adj. *inexpedient*; snaggy 700 adj. *difficult*; discouraging, unhelpful, uncooperative, against the grain 598 adj. *unwilling*.

Vb. *hinder*, let, obstruct, impede; bother, inconvenience 827 vb. *incommode*; embarrass, upset 63 vb. *derange*; trip, trip up, give one a fall; entangle, enmesh 542 vb. *ensnare*; get in the way, cross one's path; come between, intervene, interpose 678 vb. *meddle*; intercept, cut off, head off; nip, stifle, choke; gag, muzzle 578 vb. *make mute*; hamper, burden, encumber; load with, saddle w.; cramp, handicap; shackle, trammel, clog, tie one's hands 747 vb. *fetter*; restrict, circumscribe 236 vb. *limit*; check, brake, drag 747 vb. *restrain*; hold up, set one back 278 vb. *retard*; lame, cripple 161 vb. *disable*; scotch, wing 655 vb. *wound*; clip the wings; intimidate, deter 854 vb. *frighten*; discourage, dishearten 613 vb. *dissuade*; mar, spoil 655 vb. *im-*

pair; damp, throw cold water; snub, rebuff 760 vb. *refuse*.

obstruct, interpose, interfere 678 vb. *meddle*; obtrude, interlope 297 vb. *intrude*; stymie, stand in the way; buzz, jostle, crowd; stop, intercept, occlude, stop up, block 264 vb. *close*; jam, make a bottleneck; bandage 350 vb. *stanch*; dam, embank; fend off, stave off 713 vb. *parry*; barricade 235 vb. *enclose*; hedge in, blockade 232 vb. *circumscribe*; deny access 57 vb. *exclude*; prevent, inhibit 757 vb. *prohibit*.

be obstructive, make it hard for, give trouble 700 vb. *be difficult*; stall, keep one in play, occupy; not play, non-cooperate 598 vb. *be loth*; thwart, frustrate, baffle, foil, stymie, balk; counter 182 vb. *counteract*; check, put in c., checkmate; object 704 vb. *oppose*; interrupt, heckle, barrack; refuse a hearing, shout down; take evasive action 620 vb. *avoid*; talk out time, filibuster 581 vb. *be loquacious*; picket, molest; sabotage.

703. Aid – **N.** *aid*, assistance, help, helping hand, leg-up, lift; succour, rescue 668 n. *deliverance*; comfort, support, stead, backing, seconding, abetment, encouragement; reinforcement 162 n. *strengthening*; helpfulness 706 n. *cooperation*; service; good offices; patronage, auspices, sponsorship, countenance, suffrage, favour 660 n. *protection*; intercession 981 n. *prayers*; advocacy, championship; relief 685 n. *refreshment*, preferential treatment; favourable conditions; fair wind; facilitation 701 n. *facility*; helper 707 n. *auxiliary*.

subvention, economic aid, monetary help, pecuniary assistance; poor relief 901 n. *philanthropy*; benefit, sick b.; loan, accommodation 802 n. *credit*; subsidy, bounty, grant, allowance, expense account; stipend 962 n. *reward*; supplies, maintenance, support, keep 633 n. *provision*; manna.

Adj. *aiding*, helpful 706 adj. *cooperative*; well-disposed 897 adj. *benevolent*; favourable, propitious; of service 640 adj. *useful*; auxiliary, subsidiary, ancillary; in aid of, contributory; at one's beck and call, subservient 628 adj. *instrumental*.

Vb. *aid*, help, assist, lend a hand, bear a h.; take in tow, give a lift to; hold one's hand, spoonfeed; oblige, accommodate 784 vb. *lend*; subsidize; facilitate, speed, further, advance, boost 285 vb. *promote*; abet, foment, nourish; make for, contribute to 156 vb. *conduce*; second, back, back up, stand by, bolster 218 vb. *support*; comfort, sustain, succour, relieve 668 vb. *deliver*; reinforce 162 vb. *strengthen*; recruit 685 vb. *refresh*.

patronize, favour, smile on, shine on 730 vb. *be auspicious*; sponsor, back, guarantee; recommend, put up for; propose, second; countenance, connive at, protect 660 vb. *safeguard*; lend one's name 488 vb. *endorse*; take an interest in 880 vb. *befriend*; side with, champion, stick up for, stand by 713 vb. *defend*; make interest for, canvass f. 605 vb. *vote*; bestow one's custom 792 vb. *purchase*.

minister to, wait on, do for, help, oblige 742 vb. *serve*; nurse 658 vb. *doctor*; subserve 628 vb. *be instrumental*; make oneself useful 640 vb. *be useful*; pander to 925 vb. *flatter*.

Adv. *in aid of*, for the sake of, on behalf of; by the aid of, thanks to.

704. Opposition – **N.** *opposition*, oppositeness, polarity 240 n. *contraposition*; antagonism 881 n. *enmity*; dissociation, non-cooperation 598 n. *unwillingness*; contrariness, cussedness 602 n. *obstinacy*; contradiction 533 n. *negation*; confrontation, challenge 711 n. *defiance*; oppugnancy, stand 715 n. *resistance*; mutual opposition, tug of war; rivalry, emulation, competition, race 716 n. *contention*; political opposition, the Opposition, the other party; the other side, wrong s., ranks of Tuscany.

Adj. *opposing*, oppositional, opposed; in opposition, on the other side; anti, against, agin; antagonistic 881 adj. *inimical*; unpropitious 731 adj. *adverse*;

cross, thwarting 702 adj. *hindering*; contrarious 14 adj. *contrary*; recalcitrant 738 adj. *disobedient*; resistant 182 adj. *counteracting*; facing, face to face, fronting 237 adj. *fore*; rival, competitive 911 adj. *jealous*.

Vb. *oppose*, confront, face; go against, militate a. 14 vb. *be contrary*; side against, fight a. 715 vb. *resist*; object, kick, protest 762 vb. *deprecate*; vote against, vote down 924 vb. *disapprove*; dissociate oneself; contradict, belie 533 vb. *negate*; traverse, counter, work against 182 vb. *counteract*; foil 702 vb. *be obstructive*; withstand, challenge, dare 711 vb. *defy*; fly in the face of 738 vb. *disobey*; rebuff, spurn 760 vb. *refuse*; emulate, rival, play against, bid a. 716 vb. *contend*; set against, pit a., match a.

Adv. *in opposition*, against, versus, agin; against the grain, in the teeth of, in spite of, despite.

705. Opponent – **N.** *opponent*, opposer, lion in the path; adversary, antagonist 881 n. *enemy*; assailant 712 n. *attacker*; the opposition, ranks of Tuscany, opposite camp; oppositionist, radical; obstructionist, filibuster 702 n. *hinderer*; cross-benches; die-hard, irreconcilable; radical of the right, reactionary; objector 489 n. *dissentient*; non-cooperator 829 n. *malcontent*; agitator 738 n. *revolter*; challenger, other candidate, rival, emulator, competitor; entrant, the field, all comers 716 n. *contender*.

706. Cooperation – **N.** *cooperation*, helpfulness 597 n. *willingness*; contribution, coagency, symbiosis; duet, double harness, collaboration, joint effort, combined operation; team work, relay-race; team spirit, esprit de corps; concurrence, bi-partisanship 710 n. *concord*; clannishness, party spirit, cliquishness, partisanship; connivance, collusion, abetment; conspiracy 623 n. *plot*; involvement, complicity, participation; solidarity, fellowship, freemasonry, fellow-feeling, comradeship; common cause, mutual assistance; reciprocity, give and take 770

n. *compromise*; consultation 584 n. *conference*.

association, partnership 775 n. *participation*; pooling, pool; membership, affiliation 78 n. *inclusion*; connexion, hook-up 9 n. *relation*; combination 45 n. *junction*; integration, solidarity 52 n. *whole*; unification, union, synoecism 88 n. *unity*; amalgamation, fusion, merger; coalition, alliance, league, federation, confederation, confederacy; axis, united front; an association, fellowship, college, club, sodality, fraternity 708 n. *society*; set, clique, cell 708 n. *party*; company, interlocking directorship, trust, cartel, ring 708 n. *corporation*; common market 708 n. *community*.

Adj. *cooperative*, helpful 703 adj. *aiding*; frictionless 710 adj. *concordant*; symbiotic, synergic; collaborating, in double harness; married, associated, in league, hand in glove with; bi-partisan; federal 708 adj. *corporate*.

Vb. *cooperate*, collaborate, work together, pull t., go hand in hand, hunt in pairs, run in double harness; team up, partner, go into partnership 775 vb. *participate*; play ball, reciprocate, respond; join in, take part; hang together, hold t., sink or swim t.; make common cause, take in each other's washing; band, gang up, associate, league; coalesce, merge, unite 43 vb. *be mixed*; combine, club together; think alike, conspire 623 vb. *plot*; lay heads together 691 vb. *consult*; collude, connive; treat with, negotiate 766 vb. *make terms*.

707. Auxiliary – **N.** *auxiliary*, relay, recruit, reinforcement; second line 722 n. *soldiery*; ally, brother-in-arms, confederate (see *colleague*); coadjutor, assistant, helper, helpmate, helping hand; right hand, right-hand man, stand-by, stalwart, support, tower of strength; adjutant, lieutenant; midwife, handmaid 742 n. *servant*; acolyte, server; friend in need 880 n. *friend*; hanger-on, satellite, henchman, follower 742 n. *dependant*; disciple, adherent, votary, sectary 978 n. *sectarist*; instrument,

stooge, cat's-paw, puppet 630 n. *tool*; jackal, running dog, creature.

collaborator, cooperator, co-worker, fellow-w.; team-mate, yoke-fellow; sympathizer, fellow-traveller, fifth columnist.

colleague, associate, confrère, brother; co-director, partner, fellow; comrade, companion, playmate; confidant, alter ego, second self 691 n. *adviser*; mate, pal 880 n. *chum*; ally, confederate; accomplice, accessory, abettor, fellow-conspirator, particeps criminis; co-religionist; one's fellows, one's own side.

patron, defender, guardian angel, tutelary genius, special providence 660 n. *protector*; well-wisher, sympathizer; champion, advocate, friend at court; supporter, backer, guarantor; proposer, seconder, voter; favourer, partisan, votary, fan 887 n. *lover*; friend in need, deus ex machina; fairy godmother 903 n. *benefactor*; promoter, founder; Maecenas; customer, client 792 n. *purchaser*.

708. Party – **N.** *party*, movement; group, class 77 n. *classification*; sub-sect, denomination, church 978 n. *sect*; faction, cave, splinter group 489 n. *dissentient*; circle, set, clique, coterie; caucus, junta, committee, club, cell, ring, closed shop; gang, knot, bunch, outfit, push 74 n. *band*; side, camp.

political party, right, left, centre; coalition, popular front, bloc; Red, commie; socialist, labourite, Fabian, syndicalist, anarchist; right-winger, rightist; left-winger, leftist; moderate, centrist, party man, party member, politician.

society, partnership, coalition, combination, combine 706 n. *association*; league, alliance, axis; federation, confederation, confederacy; economic association, cooperative, union, customs u., common market, free trade area; secret society, Ku Klux Klan, Freemasonry, lodge, cell, club; trades union, chapel; movement, fellow; associate, member; party member, comrade; affiliate 58 n. *component*.

community, membership, fellowship, brotherhood, body, band of brothers, fraternity, confraternity, sorority, sisterhood; guild, sodality; race, tribe, clan, sect 11 n. *family*; order 77 n. *classification*; society 371 n. *social group*; state, nation-s., multi-racial s. 371 n. *nation*.

corporation, body; incorporated society, body corporate, mayor and corporation 692 n. *council*; company, livery c., joint-stock c.; firm, concern, partnership; house, establishment, organization, institute; trust, combine, monopoly, cartel, syndicate, consortium 706 n. *association*; chamber of commerce, guild, cooperative society.

Adj. *corporate*, incorporate, joint-stock; joint, leagued, federal; allied, confederate; social, clubbable 882 adj. *sociable*; fraternal, comradely 880 adj. *friendly*; cooperative, syndicalist.

sectional, denominational, Masonic 978 adj. *sectarian*; partisan, communal, clannish, cliquish, cliquey, exclusive; class-conscious; rightist, leftist, left-wing, pink, red; radical, conservative.

Vb. *join a party*, put one's name down, subscribe, take out membership; join, sign on, enlist, belong to, make one of 78 vb. *be included*; align oneself, side, take sides 706 vb. *cooperate*; club together, associate, ally, league, federate.

709. Dissension – N. *dissension*, dissentience 489 n. *dissent*; non-cooperation 704 n. *opposition*; disharmony, dissonance, jar, jarring note, rift within the lute; recrimination, bickering, cat-and-dog life; differences, odds, variance, friction, unpleasantness; no love lost 888 n. *hatred*; disunity, disunion, division in the camp 25 n. *disagreement*; rift, cleavage, parting of the ways, split, faction 978 n. *schism*; imbroglio 61 n. *confusion*; breach, rupture, severance of relations; challenge 711 n. *defiance*; ultimatum, declaration of war 718 n. *war*.

quarrelsomeness, factiousness, litigiousness; aggressiveness 718 n. *bellicosity*; provocativeness 711 n. *defiance*; cantankerousness, awkwardness, prickliness 892 n. *irascibility*; shrewishness 899 n. *scurrility*; contentiousness 716 n. *contention*; rivalry 911 n. *jealousy*; thirst for revenge 910 n. *revengefulness*; mischievousness 898 n. *malevolence*; apple of discord.

quarrel, open q.; feud, vendetta 910 n. *revenge*; war 718 n. *warfare*; strife 716 n. *contention*; clash 279 n. *collision*; controversy, polemic, paper war 475 n. *argument*; words, high w., altercation 899 n. *scurrility*; spat, tiff, squabble, jangle, breeze; scrimmage, fracas, brawl, fisticuffs 61 n. *turmoil*.

casus belli, root of dissension, breaking point; stakes; apple of discord, bone of contention; area of disagreement 724 n. *battle-ground*.

quarreller, disputer, eristic, wrangler 475 n. *reasoner*; duellist, rival; strange bedfellows, Kilkenny cats; mischief-maker 663 n. *trouble-maker*; scold 892 n. *shrew*; aggressor 712 n. *attacker*.

Adj. *quarrelling*, discordant, discrepant, ill-mated 14 adj. *contrary*; at feud, at loggerheads 881 adj. *inimical*; factious, schismatic 489 adj. *dissentient*; awkward, cantankerous 892 adj. *irascible*; litigious 959 adj. *litigating*; quarrelsome, bellicose 718 adj. *warlike*; divisive, contentious, disputatious, eristic, wrangling, polemical 475 adj. *arguing*.

Vb. *quarrel*, disagree 489 vb. *dissent*; clash, conflict 279 vb. *collide*; be at variance, have differences 15 vb. *differ*; recriminate; fall out, part company, split, break with, break away 978 vb. *schismatize*; declare war 718 vb. *go to war*; dispute, controvert 479 vb. *confute*.

make quarrels, pick q.; look for trouble, be spoiling for a fight, trail one's coat, challenge 711 vb. *defy*; irritate, rub the wrong way, tread on one's toes, provoke 891 vb. *enrage*; have a bone to pick, have a crow to pluck; embroil, set at odds 888 vb. *excite hate*; sow dissension, make mischief; divide, set against, pit a., match with; egg on, incite 612 vb. *motivate*.

bicker, spat, tiff, squabble, nag; peck,

hen-peck, jar, spar, live a cat-and-dog life; wrangle, dispute with 475 vb. *argue*; scold 899 vb. *cuss*; altercate, row with, brawl.

710. Concord – N. *concord*, harmony, unison, unity, duet 24 n. *agreement*; unanimity, bi-partisanship 488 n. *consensus*; understanding, rapport; solidarity, team-spirit 706 n. *cooperation*; reciprocity, sympathy, fellow-feeling; compatibility, coexistence, league, amity 880 n. *friendship*; rapprochement, reunion, reconciliation 719 n. *pacification*; entente cordiale, happy family 717 n. *peace*; good will, honeymoon.

Adj. *concordant*, harmonious; en rapport, eye to eye, unanimous, of one mind, bi-partisan 24 adj. *agreeing*; co-existent, compatible, united; amicable, on good terms 880 adj. *friendly*; frictionless, happy 717 adj. *peaceful*; agreeable, congenial 826 adj. *pleasurable*.

Vb. *concord*, harmonize; agree 24 vb. *accord*; see eye to eye 706 vb. *cooperate*; reciprocate, respond, run parallel; fraternize 880 vb. *be friendly*; keep the peace, work for peace.

711. Defiance – N. *defiance*, dare, challenge, cartel, gage, gauntlet, hat in the ring; bold front, brave face 855 n. *courage*; war-cry 900 n. *threat*; high tone 878 n. *insolence*; demonstration 875 n. *ostentation*.

Adj. *defiant*, proud, provocative, bellicose, militant 718 adj. *warlike*; saucy 878 adj. *insolent*; reckless, trigger-happy 857 adj. *rash*.

Vb. *defy*, challenge, take one up on 489 vb. *dissent*; stand up to 704 vb. *oppose*; throw down the gauntlet; demand satisfaction, call out, send one's seconds; dare, outdare, beard; snap one's fingers at 922 vb. *hold cheap*; bid defiance, call one's bluff; show fight, show one's fangs; take a high tone 871 vb. *be proud*; look big, slap one's chest, crow, bluster 877 vb. *boast*; cock a snook 878 vb. *be insolent*.

712. Attack – N. *attack*, best method of defence, aggressiveness 718 n. *bellicosity*; aggression, Pearl Harbor; assault, assault and battery 176 n. *violence*; offensive, drive, push, thrust; run at, dead set at; onslaught, onset, rush, shock, charge; sally, sortie; counter-attack 714 n. *retaliation*; shock tactics, blitzkrieg; encroachment 306 n. *overstepping*; invasion, inroad, incursion, irruption 297 n. *ingress*; raid, foray 788 n. *brigandage*; challenge, tilt.

bombardment, cannonade, barrage, strafe, blitz; broadside, volley, salvo; bomb-dropping, laying eggs; fire, gun-f., fusillade; enfilade; flak; gunnery, musketry, practice.

foin, thrust, home-t., lunge, pass; cut, cut and thrust; bayonet, cold steel; swipe 279 n. *knock*.

attacker, assailant, aggressor; militant, war party; spearhead, storm troops, shock t.; sharp-shooter, sniper, guerrilla; invader, raider; stormer, escalader.

Adj. *attacking*, assailing etc. vb.; combative, aggressive, offensive 718 adj. *warlike*; militant, spoiling for a fight, hostile 881 adj. *inimical*; up in arms, on the warpath 718 adj. *warring*.

Vb. *attack*, aggress, be spoiling for a fight; strike the first blow; assault, assail, go for, set on, pounce upon, fall u., pitch into, sail i., have at; savage, maul 655 vb. *wound*; launch out at, let fly at, round on; surprise, blitz; move in, invade 306 vb. *encroach*; raid, foray, overrun, infest; show fight, take the offensive; counter-attack 714 vb. *retaliate*; erupt, sally 298 vb. *emerge*; board, lay aboard, grapple; escalade, storm, carry, capture 727 vb. *overmaster*; ravage, make havoc, scorch, burn 165 vb. *lay waste*; harry, drive, beat up; challenge, enter the lists 711 vb. *defy*.

besiege, lay siege, beleaguer, sit down before, invest, surround, beset, blockade 235 vb. *enclose*; open the trenches, plant a battery; sap, mine, undermine.

strike at, raise one's hand against; lay about one, swipe, flail, hammer 279 vb. *strike*, *kick*; have at, fetch a blow, lunge; close with, grapple w., cut and thrust; push, thrust; stab, spear, lance, bayonet, run through, cut down 263 vb. *pierce*.

charge, advance against, fly a.; bear down on, come on, sail in, ram; rush, mob; rush at, run at, dash at, tilt at; go over the top.

fire at, shoot at, pop at, snipe, pick off 287 vb. *shoot*; shoot down, bring d.; torpedo, sink; soften up, strafe, bombard, blitz, cannonade, shell, fusillade, pepper; bomb, drop b., lay eggs, plaster; open fire, let fly, volley; spend powder and shot, volley and thunder, rattle, blast, rake, straddle, enfilade.

lapidate, stone, throw a stone, heave a brick; shy, sling, pelt 287 vb. *propel*.

713. Defence – N. *defence*, the defensive, self-defence 715 n. *resistance*; counterstroke 182 n. *counteraction*; defensiveness 854 n. *nervousness*; posture of defence, guard, ward; self-protection 660 n. *protection*; a defence, rampart, bulwark, buffer 662 n. *safeguard*; deterrent 723 n. *weapon*.

defences, muniment; lines, entrenchment, fieldwork, breastwork, contravallation; outwork, circumvallation; earthwork, embankment, mound; mole, boom; wall, barricade, fence; abatis, palisade, paling, stockade, moat, ditch, dyke, fosse; trench, dug-out; traverse, parallel; trip-wire, booby-trap 542 n. *trap*; barbed wire, spike, caltrop, chevaux de frise; Maginot Line, Siegfried L.; barrage, flak; minefield, mine, countermine; smoke-screen.

fortification (see *fort*); circumvallation, bulwark, rampart, wall; parapet, redan; battlement, machicolation, embrasure, casemate, loophole; vallum, scarp, counterscarp, glacis; curtain, bastion; ravelin, demilune, outwork, hornwork, demibastion.

fort, fortress, stronghold, fastness; citadel, acropolis 662 n. *refuge*; air-raid shelter 662 n. *shelter*; castle, keep, ward, tower, turret; turret, peel-house, Martello tower, pill-box, cassine; blockhouse, strong point; laager, zareba, camp 235 n. *enclosure*.

armour, harness; full armour, panoply; mail, chain m.; armour-plate; breastplate, cuirass; hauberk, habergeon, brigandine, coat of mail, corselet; helmet, helm, casque, basinet, sallet, morion; visor, beaver; siege cap, steel helmet, tin hat; greaves, gauntlet, vambrace, rerebrace; shield, buckler; carapace, shell; protective clothing, gas-mask.

defender, champion 927 n. *vindicator*; patron; knight-errant, paladin; loyalist, legitimist, patriot; house-carl, bodyguard, life-guard; watch, sentry, sentinel; garrison, picket; guard, escort; Home Guard 722 n. *soldiery*; guardian 660 n. *protector*; warder 749 n. *keeper*; custodian; deliverer, rescuer 668 n. *deliverance*; challengee.

Adj. *defending*, challenged, on the defensive 715 adj. *resisting*; defensive, protective, patriotic 660 adj. *tutelary*.

defended, armoured, plated, panoplied; heavy-armed, mail-clad, armour-c., iron-c.; moated, walled, fortified, entrenched, dug in; defensible, proof, bomb-p., bullet-p. 660 adj. *invulnerable*.

Vb. *defend*, guard, protect, keep, watch, ward 660 vb. *safeguard*; fence, hedge, moat 232 vb. *circumscribe*; palisade, barricade 235 vb. *enclose*; block 702 vb. *obstruct*; cushion, pad, shield, curtain, screen; munition, arm, accoutre, armour; reinforce, fortify, wall 162 vb. *strengthen*; garrison, man; champion 927 vb. *vindicate*; fight for, take up arms for 703 vb. *patronize*; rescue 668 vb. *deliver*.

parry, counter, riposte, fend off, ward off, fight off, hold *or* keep at bay 620 vb. *avoid*; turn, avert 282 vb. *deflect*; fence, foin; stall, stonewall, block 702 vb. *obstruct*; act on the defensive, play for a draw; fight back, show fight 715 vb. *resist*; repulse 292 vb. *repel*; fall back on 673 vb. *avail of*.

Adv. *defensively*, on the defensive, at bay.

714. Retaliation - N. *retaliation*, reprisal, lex talionis 910 n. *revenge*; requital, recompense 962 n. *reward*; deserts 915 n. *dueness*; punitive action, poetic justice, retribution, Nemesis 963 n. *punishment*; reaction, boomerang 280 n. *recoil*; counter-stroke 182 n. *counteraction*; counter-attack 712 n. *attack*; riposte, retort 460 n. *rejoinder*; reciprocation, like for like, tit for tat, quid pro quo, measure for measure, biter bit, a game at which two can play; deterrent 854 n. *intimidation*.

Adj. *retaliatory*, retaliative, retributive, punitive, like for like; rightly served.

Vb. *retaliate*, return, retort upon; serve rightly, teach one a lesson, take reprisals; pay one out, be quits, get even with, get one's own back 910 vb. *avenge*; requite; counter, riposte 713 vb. *parry*; return good for evil; heap coals of fire on one's head; reciprocate, return the compliment, give as good as one got, pay in the same coin; retort, cap 460 vb. *answer*; react, boomerang 280 vb. *recoil*; round on, kick back 715 vb. *resist*; turn the tables.

715. Resistance - N. *resistance*, front, stand 704 n. *opposition*; objection, demur 468 n. *qualification*; recalcitrance, protest 762 n. *deprecation*; non-cooperation, passive resistance, satyagraha; resistance movement 738 n. *revolt*; repulse, rebuff, bloody nose 760 n. *refusal*.

Adj. *resisting* etc. vb.; firm against 704 adj. *opposing*; recalcitrant, unsubmissive, mutinous, insurrectional 738 adj. *disobedient*; unyielding 727 adj. *unbeaten*; resistant, proof.

Vb. *resist*, withstand, give a warm reception 704 vb. *oppose*; obstruct 702 vb. *hinder*; challenge, try a fall 711 vb. *defy*; front, confront, struggle against, contend with, kick, protest 762 vb. *deprecate*; demur, object 468 vb. *qualify*; rise, not take it lying down 738 vb. *revolt*; make a stand, keep at bay 713 vb. *parry*; hold out, die hard 599 vb. *be resolute*; bear up, bear the brunt, endure 825 vb.

suffer; repel, rebuff 760 vb. *refuse*; not be tempted.

716. Contention - N. *contention*, strife, tussle, conflict, clash 709 n. *dissension*; combat 718 n. *warfare*; controversy, polemics 475 n. *argument*; altercation, words 709 n. *quarrel*; stakes, bone of contention 709 n. *casus belli*; competition, rivalry, emulation, prestige-chasing 911 n. *jealousy*; competitiveness, gamesmanship, survival of the fittest; cutthroat competition, war to the knife, no holds barred; sporting, athletics 837 n. *sport*.

contest, trial, trial of strength 461 n. *experiment*; tug-of-war 682 n. *exertion*; tussle, struggle 671 n. *essay*; competition, free-for-all; knock-out competition, tournament; tourney, joust, tilt; prize-competition, stakes, Ashes; match, test m.; concourse, rally; event, handicap, run-off; heat, final; set, game, rubber; sporting event, wager, bet 837 n. *sport*; agonism, athletics, gymnastics; gymkhana, horse-show, rodeo; games, Olympics.

racing, speed contest 277 n. *speeding*; races, race, foot r., flat r., sprint, dash; marathon; relay race, team-r.; the Turf, sport of kings; horse-race, point-to-point, steeplechase, paperchase, hurdles, sticks; regatta, eights, torpids, Henley.

pugilism, noble art of self-defence, boxing, sparring, milling, fisticuffs; boxing match, prize-fight; mill, spar, clinch, in-fighting; round, bout; the ring, the fancy 837 n. *sport*.

wrestling, ju-jitsu, judo, all-in-wrestling, catch-as-catch-can, no holds barred; catch, hold; wrestle, grapple, wrestling match.

duel, affair of honour; match, monomachy, single combat; joust, tilt, tourney, tournament; fencing, fence, swordplay, lathi-p., single-stick, quarter-s.; close quarters, close grips; bull-fight, tauromachy, dog-fight, cock-fight; cockpit 724 n. *arena*.

fight, hostilities, appeal to arms 718 n. *warfare*; battle royal, free fight, free-for-

all, rough and tumble, rough house,
horse-play, shindy, scuffle, scrum,
scrimmage, dog-fight, mêlée, fracas 61
n. *turmoil*; gang-warfare, street-fight,
riot; brawl 709 n. *quarrel*; fisticuffs,
blows, hard knocks; give and take, cut
and thrust; affray, set-to, tussle; in-
fighting, close grips, close quarters; combat, fray; encounter, scrap, brush, skirmish; engagement 718 n. *battle*; deed of
arms, passage of a.; campaign, struggle;
battlefield 724 n. *battleground*.

contender, struggler, trier, striver,
campaigner; tussler, fighter, battler,
gamecock; gladiator, bull-fighter 722 n.
combatant; prize-fighter 722 n. *pugilist*;
duellist 709 n. *quarreller*; candidate, entrant, examinee; competitor, rival, cor-
rival, emulator; challenger; starter, also-
ran, the field, all comers; contester, pot-
hunter; racer, runner, sprinter, miler 277
n. *speeder*; agonist 162 n. *athlete*.

Adj. *contending*, struggling etc. vb.;
rival, competing, in the business; agonistic, sporting; in the running; athletic,
palaestric, pugilistic, gladiatorial; contentious 709 adj. *quarrelling*; aggressive,
combative, fight-hungry 718 adj. *warlike*; belligerent 718 adj. *warring*; competitive, keen, cut-throat; keenly con-
tested, ding-dong; close run; well-
fought.

Vb. *contend*, combat, strive, struggle,
battle, fight, campaign; tussle, wrestle,
grapple 671 vb. *essay*; oppose 715 vb.
resist; argue for 475 vb. *argue*; enter
for, contest, compete, challenge, stake,
wager, bet; play, play against, match
oneself, vie with, race; emulate, rival;
take on, try a fall, try conclusions.

fight, break the peace, scuffle, row,
scrimmage, scrap, set to; mix it, pitch
into 712 vb. *attack*; lay on, lay about
one 712 vb. *strike at*; square up to,
come to blows; box, spar, pummel 279
vb. *strike*; duel, call out, meet, give
satisfaction; encounter, skirmish, engage 718 vb. *give battle*; close with,
grapple, lock horns; fence, cross swords,
appeal to arms 718 vb. *go to war*; combat, campaign 718 vb. *wage war*.

717. Peace – N. *peace*, state of p., peacefulness, peace and quiet 266 n. *quiescence*; Pax Romana, Pax Britannica; end
of hostilities, demobilization 145 n. *cessation*; truce, armistice 145 n. *lull*; cold
war, coexistence; neutrality, non-involvement 860 n. *indifference*; peace-
ability, non-aggression 177 n. *moderation*; pacifism, peace at any price,
non-violence, ahimsa; peace-making,
irenics 719 n. *pacification*; pipe of peace,
calumet.

pacifist, man of peace, peace-lover,
peacemonger; peace-party 177 n. *moderator*; neutral, non-combatant, non-bel-
ligerent; civilian, women and children;
peacemaker 720 n. *mediator*.

Adj. *peaceful*, quiet, halcyon 266 adj.
tranquil; without bloodshed, bloodless;
peaceable, law-abiding, peace-loving,
pacific, unmilitary, unwarlike, unmili-
tant, unaggressive, war-weary; pacifist,
non-violent; unarmed, non-combatant,
civilian; unresisting 721 adj. *submitting*;
peace-making, conciliatory, irenic 720
adj. *mediatory*; not at war, neutral;
post-war, pre-war.

718. War – N. *war*, arms, the sword;
appeal to arms, arbitrament of war, fortune of w., wager of battle; war of
nerves 854 n. *intimidation*; intervention,
armed i., police action; real war, hot
w.; religious war, crusade, jehad; total
war, blitzkrieg, atomic war; war of
attrition, war to the knife, pomp and
circumstance of war, chivalry, battle-
cry, war-song 711 n. *defiance*. See *warfare*.

belligerency, state of war, state of
siege; resort to arms, declaration of war,
militancy, hostilities; wartime.

bellicosity, war fever; warlike habits,
military spirit, pugnacity, combativeness,
aggressiveness, militancy 709 n. *quarrelsomeness*; militarism, Prussianism, war
policy; jingoism, chauvinism 481 n.
prejudice.

war measures, war footing, arming 669
n. *preparation*; call to arms, Fiery Cross
547 n. *call*; war effort, call-up, mobiliza-

tion, recruitment, conscription, national service, military duty.

warfare, war, warpath; warlike operations, ops.; bloodshed, battles, sieges 176 n. *violence*; soldiering, active service; chemical warfare, germ w., atomic w.; economic warfare, blockade, attrition, scorched earth, denial policy; psychological warfare, propaganda; bushfighting, guerrilla warfare; campaign, expedition; invasion, raid; warcraft, siegecraft; strategy, tactics, generalship; plan of campaign, battle-orders 623 n. *plan*.

battle, pitched b. 716 n. *fight*; array, line, firing l., front; armed conflict, action, engagement, scrap, skirmish, brush, collision, clash; offensive 712 n. *attack*; battlefield 724 n. *battleground*.

Adj. *warring*, on the warpath; campaigning etc. vb.; at war, belligerent, mobilized, under arms, at the front, on active service; militant, up in arms; arrayed, embattled; engaged, at grips; on the offensive 712 adj. *attacking*.

warlike, militaristic, bellicose, unpacific; militant, aggressive, pugnacious, combative; war-loving, bloodthirsty, fierce 898 adj. *cruel*; military, martial, veteran, battle-scarred; armigerent, knightly, chivalrous; soldierly; Napoleonic; military, naval; operational, strategical, tactical.

Vb. *go to war*, resort to arms; declare war, commit hostilities; appeal to arms 716 vb. *fight*; rise 738 vb. *revolt*; raise one's banner, set up one's standard; arm, militarize, mobilize, put on a war footing; call up, call to the colours, recruit, conscript; join up, enlist.

wage war, make w., engage in hostilities, war, campaign, take the field; go on active service, smell powder, soldier; take the offensive, invade 712 vb. *attack*; manoeuvre, march, counter-march; blockade, beleaguer 712 vb. *besiege*; shed blood 362 vb. *slaughter*; ravage, burn, scorch 165 vb. *lay waste*.

give battle, battle, join b., engage; combat, fight it out 716 vb. *fight*; stand, make a s. 715 vb. *resist*; sound the

charge, go over the top 712 vb. *charge*; open fire 712 vb. *fire at*; skirmish, brush.

719. Pacification – N. *pacification*, peace-making; conciliation, appeasement, mollification 177 n. *moderation*; reconciliation, reconcilement, détente, improved relations, rapprochement; composition 770 n. *compromise*; good offices 720 n. *mediation*; peace-treaty, peace-pact, league of peace 765 n. *treaty*; disarmament, demobilization.

irenics, irenicon, peace-offering 177 n. *moderator*; propitiation, olive-branch, overture 880 n. *friendliness*; flag of truce, white flag 717 n. *peace*; compensation 787 n. *restitution*; fair offer, easy terms 177 n. *moderation*; mercy 909 n. *forgiveness*.

Adj. *pacificatory*, conciliatory, placatory, propitiatory; irenic, disarming, emollient 177 adj. *lenitive*; peacemaking, mediatory, trucial.

Vb. *pacify*, give peace to; tranquillize, mollify, take the sting out of 177 vb. *assuage*; heal 656 vb. *cure*; conciliate, propitiate, disarm, reconcile, placate, appease, satisfy 828 vb. *content*; meet half-way 770 vb. *compromise*; bring together 720 vb. *mediate*; show mercy 736 vb. *be lenient*.

make peace, stop fighting; bury the hatchet, let bygones be bygones 506 vb. *forget*; shake hands, make it up, patch up a quarrel; lay down one's arms, demilitarize, disarm, demobilize.

720. Mediation – N. *mediation*, good offices, mediatorship, intercession; umpirage, arbitrage, arbitration; intervention, interposition 231 n. *interjacence*; parley, negotiation 584 n. *conference*.

mediator, common friend, middleman, intermediary, match-maker, go-between, negotiator; arbitrator, umpire, referee 480 n. *estimator*; diplomat, diplomatist; intercessor, propitiator; moderating influence, peace party 177 n. *moderator*; pacifier, pacificator, trouble-shooter; peacemaker, dove.

Adj. *mediatory*, mediatorial, intercessory, intercessorial, propitiatory 719 adj. *pacificatory*.

Vb. *mediate*, intervene, intermeddle 678 vb. *meddle*; intercede for, beg off, propitiate; bring together, negotiate; arbitrate, umpire 480 vb. *judge*.

721. Submission – N. *submission*, submissiveness 739 n. *obedience*; subservience, slavishness 745 n. *servitude*; acquiescence 488 n. *assent*; supineness, peace at any price, line of least resistance, passiveness, resignation, fatalism 679 n. *inactivity*; white flag, capitulation, surrender 621 n. *relinquishment*; deference 872 n. *humility*; homage 739 n. *loyalty*.

Adj. *submitting*, surrendering etc. vb.; meet, unresisting, law-abiding 717 adj. *peaceful*; submissive 739 adj. *obedient*; fatalistic, resigned 488 adj. *assenting*; weak-kneed, lying down, supine; on bended knees 872 adj. *humble*.

Vb. *submit*, yield, give in; not insist, defer to; bow to, make a virtue of necessity, admit defeat 728 vb. *be defeated*; resign oneself 488 vb. *acquiesce*; shrug 860 vb. *be indifferent*; have no fight left, give up, throw up the sponge, surrender, hold up one's hands, surrender on terms, capitulate; throw oneself on another's mercy; haul down the flag, strike one's colours.

knuckle under, succumb, take the count, show no fight, take the line of least resistance, bow before the storm; learn obedience, bow one's neck to the yoke, homage, do h. 745 vb. *be subject*; take one's medicine, swallow the pill 963 vb. *be punished*; apologize, beg pardon; not mind, take it, take it lying down, pocket the insult, suffer in patience, digest, stomach, put up with 825 vb. *suffer*; bend, bow, kneel, kowtow, crouch, cringe, crawl 311 vb. *stoop*; grovel, lick the dust, kiss the rod; beg for mercy.

722. Combatant. Army. Navy – N. *combatant*, fighter, battler, tussler, struggler 716 n. *contender*; assailant 712 n. *at-*

tacker; besieger; stormtroops; belligerent, fighting man, warrior, brave; bodyguard 713 n. *defender*; gunman, strong-arm m. 362 n. *killer*; bully, bravo 904 n. *ruffian*; fire-eater, swashbuckler, swaggerer 877 n. *boaster*; duellist 709 n. *quarreller*; swordsman, sabreur, foilsman, fencer, sword, good s.; agonist 162 n. *athlete*; gladiator, retiarius; fighting cock, gamecock; bull-fighter, toreador, matador, picador; grappler, wrestler, ju-jitsuist, judoist 716 n. *wrestling*; competitor 716 n. *contender*; champion 644 n. *exceller*; jouster, tilter; knight-errant, paladin 707 n. *patron*.

pugilist, pug, boxer, bruiser, sparring partner; prize-fighter, flyweight, bantam-w., feather-w., welter-w., middle-w., cruiser-w., heavy-w. 716 n. *pugilism*.

militarist, jingoist, chauvinist, warmonger, militant, crusader, ghazi; professional soldier, free-lance, mercenary, free companion, soldier of fortune, condottiere, war-lord; freebooter 789 n. *robber*.

soldier, army man, pongo; military man, regular; soldiery, troops (see *armed force*); campaigner, old c., conquistador; old soldier, veteran; fighting man, warrior, brave, myrmidon; man-at-arms, redcoat, legionary, centurion; vexillary, standard-bearer, colour escort, colour sergeant, ensign, cornet; hoplite, phalangist; skirmisher; sharpshooter, sniper, franc-tireur 287 n. *shooter*; auxiliary, territorial, Home Guard, militiaman, fencible; yeomanry, yeoman; irregular, guerrilla, moss-trooper, cateran, kern, gallow-glass; guardsman (see *armed force*); reservist; pressed man, conscript, recruit, rookie; serviceman, enlisted man, Tommy, G.I., doughboy, poilu, sepoy, sowar; Amazon; battlemaid, valkyrie.

soldiery, cannon fodder; private, man-at-arms; targeteer, slinger, archer, bowman, cross-b., arbalester; spearman, pikeman, pike, halberdier, hoplite, phalangist, lancer; arquebusier, musketeer, fusilier, rifleman, pistoleer, carabineer, bazookaman, grenadier, bombardier, gunner, cannoneer, artillery-man; pioneer, sapper, miner.

army, host, camp; phalanx, legion; cohorts, big battalions; horde, mass 104 n. *multitude*; nation in arms, levée en masse, general levy; militia, yeomanry; regular army, standing a., territorial a.; draft, class.

armed force, the services, all arms; forces, troops, contingents, effectives, men, personnel; armament, armada; corps d'élite, ceremonial troops, guards, household troops; janissaries; picked troops, crack t., shock t., storm t., for-lorn hope; spearhead, expeditionary force, striking f., flying column; para-troops, commando, task force; combat troops, field army, line, thin red l.; wing, van, vanguard, rear, rearguard, centre, main body; second échelon, base troops, reserves, recruits, reinforcements, draft, levy; base, staff; detachment, picket, party, detail; patrol, sentry, sentinel 660 n. *protector*; garrison, army of occupation.

formation, array, line; square, British s., schiltron, phalanx; legion, cohort; column, file, rank; unit, group, army g., corps, army c., division; brigade; bat-tery; regiment, cavalry r., squadron, troop; battalion, company, platoon, sec-tion, squad, detail, party 74 n. *band*.

infantry, bayonets, foot-regiment, infantryman, foot-soldier, foot, foot-slogger, P.B.I.

cavalry, yeomanry; sabres, horse; horseman, cameleer; mounted police, mounted infantry, horse artillery; caval-ryman, yeoman; trooper, sowar; chival-ry, knight; man-at-arms, lancer, cuiras-sier, dragoon; Ironsides; rough-rider; armour, armoured car, tank, Panzer; charger 273 n. *war-horse*.

navy, sea-power, admiralty; sail, wooden walls; fleet arm, naval arma-ment, armada; fleet, flotilla, squadron; 'little ships'.

navy man, naval service, navy, senior service, silent s.; admiral, sea-lord 741 n. *naval officer*; naval architect, Seabee; sailor 270 n. *mariner*; blue-jacket, man-

o'-war man, able seaman, rating, pressed man; fore-topman; coastguardsman; gob, swab, swabbie; marine, jolly, leatherneck, Marine Corps; submariner; privateer; naval reserve.

warship, war vessel, trireme, galleon, galleass 275 n. *ship*; man-o'-war, ship of the line, first-rater, seventy-four; armoured vessel, capital ship, battleship, dreadnought, ironclad; cruiser; raider; privateer; frigate, sloop, corvette, scout; gunboat, torpedo-boat; destroyer; fire-ship, hell-burner, bomb-vessel; block ship, mine-layer, mine-sweeper; submar-ine; aircraft carrier, flat-top; floating battery; landing-craft, duck, amphibian; transport, troopship; flagship, flotilla-leader.

air force, air arm, flying corps; squadron, flight, group, wing; warplane; battle-plane, bomber, fighter; air-troops, air-borne division; parachute troops, para-troopers; aircraftman, ground staff; air crew, bomb-aimer, weaponeer.

723. Arms – N. *arm* (see *weapon*); arma-ment, munitions; arms manufacture, armaments race; arms traffic, gun-running; ballistics, rocketry, gunnery, musketry, archery, bowmanship, ar-mourer, bowyer, fletcher.

arsenal, armoury, gun-room, gun-rack, arms chest, stand of arms; maga-zine, powder-barrel; caisson, limber-box, magazine-chamber; bullet-pouch, car-tridge-belt, bandolier, cartridge-clip; arrow-case, quiver; scabbard, sheath; holster, pistol-case 194 n. *receptacle*.

weapon, arm, deterrent; deadly weap-on; armour, plate, mail 713 n. *defence*; conventional weapon; A.B.C. weapons (atomic w., bacteriological w., chemical w.); anti-missile weapon; secret weapon, death ray; gas, poison g. 659 n. *poison*; teeth, claws, nails.

missile weapon, javelin, knobkerrie, harpoon, dart, discus; bolas, lasso; boomerang, throwstick; arrow, shaft, bolt, quarrel; brickbat; slingstone, shot, shrapnel, rocket (see *ammunition*); bow, long-b., cross-b., arbalest, balister, catapult, mangonel, sling; blow-pipe; bazooka, rocket-thrower (see *gun*); ballistic missile; thunderbolt.

club, mace, knobstick, war-hammer 279 n. *hammer*; battering-ram 279 n. *ram*; bat, staff, stave, stick, cane, ferrule, ruler, switch, rattan, quarterstaff; bludgeon, cudgel, shillelagh, sandbag, knuckle-duster, brass knuckle, cosh, truncheon.

spear, hunting s., fishing s., harpoon, gaff; lance, javelin, pike, sarissa; partisan, bill, halberd 256 n. *sharp point*.

axe, battle-axe, tomahawk, hatchet, war-h., halberd, bill, gisarme; pole-axe, chopper 256 n. *sharp edge*.

side-arms, sword, swordstick; heraldic sword, seax; dagger, bayonet; broadsword, glaive, claymore, cutlass, hanger, whinyard; sabre, scimitar, yataghan, falchion, snickersnee; blade, rapier, tuck; épée, foil; dirk, skean, poniard, dudgeon, miséricorde, stiletto 256 n. *sharp point*; machete, kukri, kris, parang, knife, flick-k., gravity-blade k., pigsticker 256 n. *sharp edge*.

fire-arm, small arms, portable gun, hand g., arquebus, hackbut; matchlock, wheel-lock, flint-l., fusil, musket; blunderbuss, muzzle-loader, smooth-bore, carbine; breechloader, needle-gun; rifle, magazine r.; fowling-piece, sporting gun, shot-g.; muzzle; trigger, lock; magazine; breech, butt, gunstock; sight, backsight; ramrod.

pistol, petronel, pistolet; six-shooter, revolver, repeater, zipgun, rod, gat, shooting-iron; automatic pistol.

toy gun, pop-g., air-g., water pistol, pea-shooter, blow-pipe 287 n. *propellant*.

gun, guns, ordnance, cannonry, artillery; horse artillery, galloping guns; battery, broadside; park, gun-p.; cannon, bombard, falconet, swivel, gingal, basilisk, petard, carronade, culverin, demi-c.; serpentine, sling; demi-cannon, saker, drake, rabonet, base, murderer, perier, mortar; stern-chaser, bow-c.; piece, field-piece, field-gun, siege-g.; heavy metal, Big Bertha; howitzer, trench-mortar, mine-thrower; anti-aircraft gun, anti-tank g., bazooka; quick-firing gun, pom-pom, machine-g., sub-machine g., Tommy g.; flammenwerfer, flame-thrower; gun-lock, gun-carriage, limber, caisson; gun-emplacement, rocket site.

ammunition, live a., round; powder and shot; shot, round s., case s., grape s., small s., buck-s.; ball, cannon b., bullet, dum-dum b.; projectile 287 n. *missile*; stone, sling-shot, slug, pellet; shell, shrapnel-s.; charge, priming, warhead; wad, cartouche, cartridge, cartridge-case, shell-c.; cap, detonator, fuse.

explosive, propellant; powder, gunpowder; saltpetre, high explosive, cordite, gun-cotton, dynamite, gelignite, T.N.T.; Greek fire; fissionable material.

bomb, explosive device; bombshell, egg; grenade; megaton bomb; blockbuster, stink-bomb, gas-b., incendiary b., napalm b.; mine, land-m., magnetic m., acoustic m.; booby-trap; depth-charge, ash-can, torpedo; flying bomb, P-plane, V.1, doodlebug, V.2; time-bomb, infernal machine.

724. Arena – N. *arena*, field, field of action; ground, terrain; centre, scene, stage, theatre; hustings, platform, floor; amphitheatre, stadium, stand, grandstand; campus, parade ground; forum, market-place 76 n. *focus*; hippodrome, circus, course, race-c., turf; track; ring, bull-r., boxing r., ropes; palaestra, gymnasium, gym; range, shooting r., butts; playground, gutter, beach, fair-ground 837 n. *pleasure-ground*; playing field, pitch; court, tennis c.; bowling-green, bowling-alley, skittle a.; lists, tilt-yard; cockpit, beargarden; chess-board, checker-board.

battle-ground, battlefield, field of battle; war theatre, front, front line, firing l., trenches, no-man's-land; sector, salient, bulge, pocket; camp, enemy's c.

Section 5: Results of Action

725. Completion – N. *completion*, conclusion, end of the matter 69 n. *end*;

issue, upshot, result, end r. 157 n. *effect*;
fulfilment 635 n. *sufficiency*; maturity,
readiness 669 n. *maturation*; consummation, culmination, climax 646 n. *perfection*; exhaustiveness, thoroughness
455 n. *attention*; top, crown, coping-
stone 213 n. *summit*; missing link; last
touch, coup de grâce; achievement, fait
accompli, finished product (see *effectuation*); boiling point, last straw 236 n.
limit; dénouement, last act 69 n. *finality*.

effectuation, carrying through, follow
t.; execution, discharge, implementation;
dispatch, performance 676 n. *action*;
accomplishment, achievement 727 n.
success.

Adj. *completive*, exhaustive, perfective;
crowning 213 adj. *topmost*; conclusive,
final, last 69 adj. *ending*; unanswerable,
crushing; thorough 599 adj. *resolute*.

Vb. *carry through*, follow t., follow up,
hole out; drive home, clinch, seal; mop
up, wipe up, finish off, polish off; dispose
of, dispatch; complete, consummate,
put the finishing touch, cast off (knitting),
top up 54 vb. *make complete*; elaborate,
hammer out 646 vb. *perfect*; ripen, bring
to a head 669 vb. *mature*; sit out, see it
through (see *carry out*); get through, get
shot of 69 vb. *terminate*.

carry out, see through, effect 676 vb.
do; dispatch, execute, discharge, implement, effectuate, realize, compass, bring
about, accomplish, consummate, achieve
727 vb. *succeed*; make short work of,
leave no ends hanging, not do by halves;
deliver the goods, bring home the bacon,
be as good as one's word.

climax, cap, crown all 213 vb. *crown*;
culminate, stand at its peak, scale the
heights; reach boiling point, come to a
head; reach the limit, touch bottom;
put the lid on, add the last straw.

726. Non-completion – N. *non-completion*, non-success 728 n. *failure*; non-
performance, neglect 458 n. *negligence*;
non-fulfilment 636 n. *insufficiency*; never-
ending task, Penelope's web 71 n.
continuity; perfunctoriness, superficiality,
a lick and a promise 456 n. *inattention*;

no result, drawn game; stalemate,
deadlock.

Adj. *uncompleted*, partial, fragmentary
55 adj. *incomplete*; unfinalized, unbegun;
undone, unexecuted, unaccomplished;
unrealized, half-done, half-finished; half-
baked, underdone 670 adj. *immature*;
unthorough, perfunctory, superficial;
inchoate, sketchy 647 adj. *imperfect*;
never-ending 71 adj. *continuous*.

Vb. *not complete*, leave undone, leave
in the air, leave hanging 458 vb. *neglect*;
skip, scamp, do by halves, tinker 636 vb.
not suffice; fall out, drop o., not stay the
course 728 vb. *fail*; postpone 136 vb.
put off.

727. Success – N. *success*, glory 866 n.
famousness; happy ending, favourable
issue; prowess, success story, time well
spent 285 n. *progression*; fresh advance,
breakthrough; one's day, run of luck
730 n. *prosperity*; advantage, lead, first
blood 34 n. *vantage*; exploit, feat,
achievement 676 n. *deed*; accomplishment 725 n. *completion*; a success,
feather in one's cap, triumph, hit, knock-
out, kill; winning hit 694 n. *skill*; lucky
stroke, fluke 618 n. *non-design*; hat-trick,
master-stroke 694 n. *masterpiece*; trump
card, winning c. 623 n. *contrivance*.

victory, infliction of defeat, beating
728 n. *defeat*; conquest, subdual 745 n.
subjection; expugnation, storm 712 n.
attack; honours of battle, the best of it,
triumph; win, game and match; outright win, checkmate; narrow win,
Pyrrhic victory; easy win, walk-over,
push-o., picnic; slam, grand s.; kill,
knock-out; mastery, ascendancy, upper
hand, whip-h., advantage, edge, winning
position 34 n. *vantage*; no defeat, stalemate 28 n. *draw*; triumph, ovation 876 n.
celebration.

victor, winner, match-winner, champion 644 n. *exceller*; winning side, the
winners; conqueror, vanquisher, subju-
gator, master; triumphator, conquering
hero.

Adj. *successful*, effective, efficacious,
efficient; well-spent, fruitful 640 adj.

profitable; happy, lucky; ever-victorious, unbeatable (see *unbeaten*); match-winning, never-failing, surefire, foolproof; unerring, infallible, sure-footed 473 adj. *certain*; victorious; winning 34 adj. *superior*; triumphant; triumphal, epinician; glorious 866 adj. *renowned*.

unbeaten, undefeated, unsubdued, unquelled, unvanquished; unbeatable, unconquerable, ever-victorious, invincible.

Vb. *succeed*, succeed in, effect, accomplish, achieve, compass 725 vb. *carry through*; make out, win one's spurs, make good; pass, make the grade, qualify, graduate; come off well, have the best of it 34 vb. *be superior*; advance, break through, make a breakthrough 285 vb. *progress*; speed well, strive to some purpose, pull it off, be as good as one's word, bring home the bacon; score a success, make a hit; hit the jackpot, break the bank; arrive, be a success.

be successful, come off, answer the purpose, do the trick, show results; turn up trumps, rise to the occasion; do wonders, do marvels; compass, manage 676 vb. *do*; work like magic, act like a charm 173 vb. *operate*; take effect, tell 178 vb. *influence*; bear fruit 171 vb. *be fruitful*; play one's hand well, not put a foot wrong.

triumph, have one's day, wear the laurels, receive an ovation 876 vb. *celebrate*; crow over 877 vb. *boast*; score, score off; reap the fruits 771 vb. *gain*.

overmaster, be too much for, be more than a match for 34 vb. *be superior*; master, overcome, overpower, overmatch, overthrow, overturn, override, overtrump; prevail, predominate; checkmate, mate, euchre, trump, ruff; conquer, vanquish, quell, subdue 745 vb. *subjugate*; capture, carry, take, storm 712 vb. *attack*.

defeat (see *overmaster*); discomfit, dash, repulse, rebuff 292 vb. *repel*; best, be too good for, get the better of 34 vb. *be superior*; worst, outplay, outpoint, outflank, outmanoeuvre, outgeneral, outclass, outshine, outdo; gravel, nonplus 474 vb. *puzzle*; beat, lick, thrash, whip,

trounce, swamp, overwhelm, crush, drub, roll in the dust; beat hollow, rout, put to flight, scatter 75 vb. *disperse*; flatten, knock out; bowl out, skittle o.

win, win the battle, gain the day (see *defeat*); erect a trophy, claim the victory; come off best, come off with flying colours; win hands down, carry all before one, romp home 701 vb. *do easily*; win on points, scrape home, survive; take the prize, gain the palm.

Adv. *successfully*, swimmingly, to some purpose, to good p.; with flying colours, in triumph.

728. Failure – N. *failure*, non-success, negative result; no luck, off day 731 n. *ill fortune*; non-fulfilment 726 n. *non-completion*; frustration 702 n. *hindrance*; inefficacy, ineffectiveness 161 n. *ineffectuality*; vain attempt, wild-goose chase 641 n. *lost labour*; bungle, foozle 695 n. *bungling*; miscarriage 172 n. *unproductivity*; wash-out, fiasco, flop, frost; anticlimax 509 n. *disappointment*; losses 772 n. *loss*; bankruptcy 805 n. *insolvency*.

defeat, bafflement 474 n. *uncertainty*; nonplus, deadlock 145 n. *stop*; lost battle, repulse, rebuff, check, reverse; the worst of it, discomfiture; retreat; flight 290 n. *recession*; rout, landslide; fall, downfall, collapse, débâcle 165 n. *ruin*; lost cause, losing game; deathblow, quietus; Waterloo 745 n. *subjection*.

loser, also-ran, non-starter; has-been, extinct volcano; foozler 697 n. *bungler*; dud, failure; victim, prey 544 n. *dupe*; underdog 35 n. *inferior*; beatnik 25 n. *misfit*; bankrupt 805 n. *non-payer*; the losers, losing side.

Adj. *unsuccessful*, ineffective, inglorious, successless, empty-handed; unlucky 731 adj. *unfortunate*; vain, negative, profitless, bankrupt; infructuous, dud, miscarried, stillborn, abortive, premature; feckless, manqué, failed, plucked, ploughed.

defeated, beaten, bested, worsted, pipped; non-suited, cast; discomfited, outmanoeuvred, outmatched, outplayed, outvoted; outclassed, outshone 35 adj.

inferior; on the losing side, among the also-rans, unplaced; routed, scattered, put to flight; sunk, lost, kaput.

Vb. *fail*, have no success; fall down on, flunk, foozle, muddle, botch, bungle 495 vb. *blunder*; not make the grade 636 vb. *not suffice*; fail one, let one down 509 vb. *disappoint*; misaim, misdirect, go wide, miss 282 vb. *deviate*; get nothing out of it, draw a blank, lose one's pains 641 vb. *waste effort*; break down, come to pieces; ground, sink 313 vb. *founder*; make losses, crash, break, go bankrupt 805 vb. *not pay*.

miscarry, abort; misfire, fizzle out; fall to the ground, crash 309 vb. *tumble*; come to naught 641 vb. *be useless*; come to grief, flop; go wrong, gang agley, take an ugly turn 509 vb. *disappoint*; do no good, make things worse 832 vb. *aggravate*; falter, limp 278 vb. *move slowly*.

be defeated, lose, lose out, take a beating, lose the day; get the worst of it, come off second best, lick one's wounds; take the count, bite the dust; succumb 745 vb. *be subject*; take to flight 620 vb. *run away*; admit defeat 721 vb. *submit*.

729. Trophy – N. *trophy*, sign of success, spoils, capture 790 n. *booty*; scalp, head; scars 655 n. *wound*; memorial 548 n. *monument*; triumph, ovation 876 n. *celebration*; prize 962 n. *reward*; sports trophy, Ashes, cup, pot, plate; award, bays, laurels, crown, wreath, palm; flying colours 875 n. *ostentation*; glory 866 n. *repute*.

decoration, honour 870 n. *title*; spurs 866 n. *honours*; citation, ribbon, blue r., cordon bleu; athletic honour, blue, oar; medal, gong, star, cross, garter, order; Victoria Cross, Congressional Medal, Medal of Honour; George Cross, civic crown.

730. Prosperity – N. *prosperity*; well-being; welfare, weal 824 n. *happiness*; thriving, health and wealth 727 n. *success*; boom, roaring trade; crest of the wave, affluence 635 n. *plenty*; luxury

800 n. *wealth*; golden touch, Midas t.; flesh-pots, fat of the land; auspiciousness, favour, smiles of fortune, blessings, godsend, crowning mercy; luck, run of l., break 159 n. *chance*; glory 866 n. *prestige*.

palmy days, heyday, floruit; halcyon days, summer, sunshine; piping times, clover, velvet, bed of roses 376 n. *euphoria*; bonanza, golden times, Golden Age, Ram Raj 824 n. *happiness*; spacious times.

made man, man of property 800 n. *rich man*; rising man, child of fortune, lucky dog; arriviste, upstart, parvenu, nouveau riche, profiteer; celebrity, lion 890 n. *favourite*.

Adj. *prosperous*, thriving 727 adj. *successful*; rising, up and coming; on the make, profiteering; well-to-do 800 adj. *moneyed*; fortunate, lucky; in clover, on velvet; fat, sleek, euphoric.

palmy, balmy, halcyon, golden; piping, blissful, blessed; providential, favourable, promising, auspicious, propitious, cloudless; glorious, spacious; euphoric 376 adj. *comfortable*.

Vb. *prosper*, thrive, flourish, have one's day; bask, make hay, live in clover, lie on velvet; batten on, grow fat 301 vb. *eat*; blossom, bloom, flower 171 vb. *be fruitful*; boom; profiteer 771 vb. *gain*; get on, rise in the world, arrive 727 vb. *succeed*; make money 800 vb. *get rich*.

have luck, have all the l.; strike lucky, strike oil, be on to a good thing; fall on one's feet, bear a charmed life, have the ball at one's feet.

be auspicious, promise well, set fair; favour, prosper, profit; smile on, shine on, bless; turn out well, turn up trumps; glorify 866 vb. *honour*.

731. Adversity – N. *adversity*, adverse circumstances, misfortune, mixed blessing (see *ill fortune*); weary way 700 n. *difficulty*; hardship, hard life, no bed of roses 825 n. *suffering*; travail, bad times, hard t., iron age, hell upon earth 616 n. *evil*; troubles, trials 825 n. *worry*; gloom, wretchedness, misery 834 n. *dejection*;

bitter pill 872 n. *humiliation*; cup, cup of sorrows 825 n. *sorrow*; curse, blight, blast, plague, scourge, infliction, visitation 659 n. *bane*; bleakness, cold wind, draught 380 n. *coldness*; blow, setback, rebuff 728 n. *defeat*; rub, pinch, plight 700 n. *predicament*; bad patch, rainy day 655 n. *deterioriation*; slump, recession 679 n. *inactivity*; decline, fall 165 n. *ruin*; distress, extremity 801 n. *poverty*.

ill fortune, misfortune, bad luck, bad cess; no luck 728 n. *failure*; evil star, malign influence; hard case, raw deal, rotten hand; hard fate, hard lines; mishap, mischance, misadvanture, disaster, calamity, catastrophe, the worst.

unlucky person, poor risk; sport of fortune, underdog 35 n. *inferior*; lame dog, lame duck, one's own worst enemy 163 n. *weakling*; scapegoat, victim, wretch 825 n. *sufferer*; prey 544 n. *dupe*.

Adj. *adverse*, hostile, frowning, ominous, sinister, inauspicious, unfavourable; bleak, cold; opposed, contrary, untoward 704 adj. *opposing*; malign 645 adj. *harmful*; dire, dreadful, ruinous 165 adj. *destructive*; disastrous, calamitous, catastrophic.

unprosperous, unblest, inglorious 728 adj. *unsuccessful*; badly off 801 adj. *poor*; in trouble, up against it, under a cloud 700 adj. *in difficulties*; declining, on the wane 655 adj. *deteriorated*; in the wars, in hard case, in extremities.

unfortunate, ill-fated, unlucky, ill-starred, star-crossed, planet-struck, blasted; unblest, luckless, hapless, poor, unhappy; stricken, doomed, devoted; out of luck, out of favour, under a cloud 924 adj. *disapproved*; accident-prone.

Vb. *have trouble*, be in t., stew in one's own juice; have no luck; be in for it, fall foul of 700 vb. *be in difficulty*; strike a bad patch 825 vb. *suffer*; come to grief 728 vb. *miscarry*; feel the pinch, feel the draught, go downhill, decline 655 vb. *deteriorate*; come to a bad end 728 vb. *fail*.

732. Mediocrity – **N.** *mediocrity*, mediety, averageness 30 n. *average*; common lot, vicissitudes, ups and downs, mixed blessing; average circumstances, a modest competence, enough to get by; respectability, bourgeoisie 30 n. *middle class*; suburbia, subtopia, villadom.

Adj. *mediocre*, average, middling; betwixt and between, ordinary, commonplace 30 adj. *median*; common, representative 83 adj. *typical*; non-extreme 177 adj. *moderate*; decent, quiet 874 adj. *modest*; not striking, undistinguished, inglorious, nothing to boast of; minor, second-rate 35 adj. *inferior*; fair, fair to middling; unobjectionable, tolerable, passable, fifty-fifty, much of a muchness; medium, colourless, grey 625 adj. *neutral*.

DIVISION (II): INTERSOCIAL VOLITION

Section 1: General

733. Authority – **N.** *authority*, power; authorities, powers that be, 'them', the establishment, ruling classes 741 n. *master*; right, divine r., prerogative, royal p.; dynasticism, legitimacy; law, lawful authority 953 n. *legality*; delegated authority, regency 751 n. *commission*; office, place (see *magistrature*); portfolio 955 n. *jurisdiction*; power behind the throne 178 n. *influence*; indirect authority, patronage, prestige, credit; leadership, hegemony 689 n. *directorship*; ascendance, preponderance, predominance, supremacy 34 n. *superiority*; lordliness, majesty, royalty, kingliness, crown 868 n. *nobility*; seapower, admiralty, trident, Britannia; seizure of power, usurpation.

governance, rule, sway, régime; direction, command 689 n. *directorship*; control, hold, grip, clutches 778 n. *retention*; domination, mastery, whiphand, reach, long arm; dominion, condominium, sovereignty, suzerainty, overlordship, supremacy 34 n. *superiority*; reign, regency, dynasty; foreign rule, empire 745 n. *subjection*; imperialism, colonialism, expansionism; state control, statism, dirigisme, paternalism; bureaucracy, civil service, officialism, red-tapism, beadledom, bumbledom; droit administratif; Parkinson's law 197 n. *expansion*.

despotism, benevolent d., paternalism; one man rule, monocracy, tyranny; dictatorship, Caesarism, kaiserism, tsarism, Stalinism; absolutism, autocracy, absolute monarchy; statism, omnicompetent state, dictatorship of the proletariat; guided democracy, totalitarianism; police state, dinarchy, rule of terror 735 n. *brute force*.

government, direction 689 n. *management*; form of government, state system, polity; constitutionalism, rule of law 953 n. *legality*; misgovernment 734 n. *anarchy*; theocracy, clericalism 985 n. *ecclesiasticism*; monarchy, kingship; republicanism, federalism; feudalism; aristocracy, meritocracy; oligarchy, minority rule; gerontocracy, senatorial government; plutocracy; representative government, parliamentary g., party system; democracy, democracy unlimited, demagogy, popular will, vox populi; isocracy, pantisocracy; collectivism, proletarianism, ergatocracy; communism, Leninism; party rule, Bolshevism, Fascism; committee rule, sovietism; imperium in imperio, stratocracy, military government, martial law; ochlocracy, mobocracy; syndicalism, socialism; statism; bureaucracy, technocracy; self-government, autonomy, home rule 744 n. *independence*; caretaker government, regency, interregnum.

magistrature, magistracy, office, place; kingship, royalty; regency, regentship; protectorship; rulership, chieftainship, sheikhdom, emirate, principate, lordship, seigniory; sultanate, caliphate; prefecture, governorship, vice-royalty, satrapy; consulate, consulship, tribunate; mayoralty, aldermanship; seat of government, capital, metropolis, palace, secretariat.

polity, body politic, state, commonwealth; country, realm, kingdom, sultanate; republic, city state; federation, confederation; principality, duchy, dukedom, palatinate; empire, dominion, colony, dependency, protectorate, mandate 184 n. *territory*; laws, constitution.

Adj. *authoritative*, empowered, competent; in office, in authority, magisterial, official, ex officio; mandatory, binding 740 adj. *compelling*; masterful, domineering; commanding, lordly, dignified, majestic; overruling, imperious, bossy; autocratic, dictatorial 735 adj. *authoritarian*; hegemonic 178 adj. *influential*; preponderant, dominant, paramount 34 adj. *supreme*.

ruling, reigning, regnant, regnal; sovereign; royal, regal, majestic, kingly, queenly, princely, lordly; dynastic; imperial.

governmental, gubernatorial, political, constitutional; administrative, ministerial, official, bureaucratic, centralized; technocratic; monarchic, feudal, aristocratic, oligarchic, plutocratic, democratic, popular, classless, republican; autonomous 744 adj. *independent*.

Vb. *rule*, bear r., sway, reign, wear the crown; govern, control 737 vb. *command*; hold office 689 vb. *direct*; be in power, have authority; tyrannize 735 vb. *oppress*; dictate, lay down the law; plan, give laws to; divide and rule; keep order, police.

dominate, domineer, lord it over, boss, rule the roost 737 vb. *command*; regiment, discipline, drill, drive 735 vb. *be severe*; dictate, coerce 740 vb. *compel*; hold down 745 vb. *subjugate*; overawe, overshadow, bestride.

734. Laxity – **N.** *laxity*, slackness, remissness 458 n. *negligence*; informality 769 n. *non-observance*; loose organization, decentralization; connivance, indulgence, toleration 736 n. *lenity*; line of least resistance 721 n. *submission*; no grip, no drive 175 n. *inertness*; no control, abdication 753 n. *resignation*.

anarchy, breakdown of administration, writ not running; disorganization, chaos 61 n. *turmoil*; licence, insubordination, indiscipline 738 n. *disobedience*; anarchism, nihilism, antinomianism 769 n. *non-observance*; interregnum, power vacuum, powerlessness 161 n. *impotence*; misrule, misgovernment; mob law, reign of terror 954 n. *lawlessness*; usurpation 916 n. *arrogation*; dethronement 752 n. *deposal*.

Adj. *lax*, loose, slack, decentralized, disorganized, unorganized 61 adj. *orderless*; feeble 163 adj. *weak*; remiss 458 adj. *negligent*; relaxed, unstrict, informal, slipshod; tolerant, undemanding, indulgent 736 adj. *lenient*; weak-kneed 601 adj. *irresolute*.

anarchic, anarchical; ungoverned, uncontrolled; unbridled, licentious 878 adj. *insolent*; rebellious 738 adj. *disobedient*; unruly 738 adj. *riotous*; unauthorized 954 adj. *illegal*; lawless, nihilistic, anarchistic, antinomian 769 adj. *non-observant*.

Vb. *be lax*, not enforce; stretch a point, connive at; tolerate; laisser faire 756 vb. *permit*; not say bo to a goose; spoonfeed, indulge 736 vb. *be lenient*; lose control 161 vb. *be impotent*; abdicate 753 vb. *resign*; misrule, misgovern 63 vb. *derange*.

735. Severity – N. *severity*, no weakness, strictness, stringency; rigidity, inflexibility 326 n. *hardness*; discipline, strong hand 733 n. *authority*; rod of iron, heavy hand, Draconian laws; harshness, rigor, extremes; letter of the law, pound of flesh; intolerance; press laws, censorship, suppression 747 n. *restraint*; blue laws, puritanism 950 n. *prudery*; persecution, harassment, oppression; victimization 910 n. *revenge*; inexorability, no appeal 906 n. *pitilessness*; hard measure, cruelty 898 n. *inhumanity*; austerity 945 n. *asceticism*.

brute force, rule of might, big battalions; coercion 740 n. *compulsion*; bloodiness 176 n. *violence*; absolutism, dictatorship 733 n. *despotism*; tyranny,

liberticide; totalitarianism; militarism; iron heel, jackboot, bludgeon.

tyrant, rigorist, pedant; extremist; petty tyrant, Jack-in-office; disciplinarian, martinet, drill-sergeant; hanging judge, Draco; Big Brother, despot, dictator 741 n. *autocrat*; boss, commissar, gauleiter; inquisitor, persecutor; oppressor, bully, slave-driver, slaver; extortioner, blood-sucker, predator, harpy, vulture, octopus; brute 938 n. *monster*.

Adj. *severe*, austere, Spartan 945 adj. *ascetic*; strict, rigorous, extreme; straitlaced, puritanical; donnish, formalistic, pedantic; hypercritical 862 adj. *fastidious*; intolerant, censorious 924 adj. *disapproving*; inflexible, uncompromising 602 adj. *obstinate*; relentless, ruthless, unsparing 906 adj. *pitiless*; punishing, stiff, exemplary, stringent, Draconian, drastic, savage.

authoritarian, masterful, domineering, lordly 878 adj. *insolent*; despotic, absolute, unfettered, arbitrary; totalitarian, Fascist, communistic; anti-democratic, undemocratic; coercive 740 adj. *compelling*; bossy, governessy.

oppressive, hard on 914 adj. *unjust*; tyrannical, despotic, arbitrary; tyrannous, harsh, exacting, grasping, extortionate, vulturine, predatory; inquisitorial; high-handed, overbearing, overmighty, domineering; heavy-handed, ungentle, bloody, brutal 898 adj. *cruel*.

Vb. *be severe*, put one's foot down, discipline; bear hard on, deal hardly with; permit no liberties 747 vb. *restrain*; have a down on (see *oppress*); not tolerate, crack down on, stamp on 165 vb. *suppress*; treat rough, get tough with, pull no punches; inflict, visit, chastise 963 vb. *punish*; proceed to extremities, have one's pound of flesh; harden one's heart 906 vb. *be pitiless*.

oppress, tyrannize, play the tyrant, strain one's authority; domineer, lord it; overawe, intimidate, terrorize 854 vb. *frighten*; bludgeon 740 vb. *compel*; shove around, put upon; bully, haze, harass 827 vb. *torment*; persecute, spite, victimize 898 vb. *be malevolent*; break, tame; task, tax, drive 684 vb. *fatigue*; overtax, extort, suck, squeeze, grind 809 vb. *tax*; trample, tread down; enslave 745 vb. *subjugate*; misgovern, misrule; whip, scourge 963 vb. *torture*; burden, crush 322 vb. *weigh*.

736. Lenity – N. *lenity*, softness 734 n. *laxity*; lenience, mildness etc. adj.; forbearance 823 n. *patience*; pardon 909 n. *forgiveness*; quarter, mercy, clemency. compassion 905 n. *pity*; humanity 897 n, *benevolence*; favour, sop, concession; indulgence, toleration; sufferance 756 n. *permission*; justice with mercy 177 n. *moderation*; light rein, velvet glove, kid gloves.

Adj. *lenient*, soft, gentle, mild; indulgent, tolerant; conniving, complaisant; unstrict, easy-going, undemanding 734 adj. *lax*; forbearing, long-suffering 823 adj. *patient*; merciful 909 adj. *forgiving*; tender 905 adj. *pitying*.

Vb. *be lenient*, show consideration, go easy, pull one's punches 177 vb. *moderate*; featherbed, spoonfeed, spoil, indulge, humour 889 vb. *pet*; tolerate, allow, connive 756 vb. *permit*; stretch a point 734 vb. *be lax*; refrain, forbear 823 vb. *be patient*; pity, spare 905 vb. *show mercy*; pardon 909 vb. *forgive*; humanize 897 vb. *be benevolent*.

737. Command – N. *command*, commandment, ordinance; injunction; dictation, bidding, behest, will and pleasure; charge 751 n. *mandate*; instructions, rules, regulations; directive, order; word of command, word, signal; summons, whip, three-line w.; dictate 740 n. *compulsion*; negative command 757 vb. *prohibition*; countermand 752 n. *abrogation*.

decree, edict, fiat, ukase, firman; law, canon, rescript, prescript, prescription 693 n. *precept*; bull, decretal; circular, encyclical; ordinance; decision, placet 480 n. *judgement*; act 953 n. *legislation*; plebiscite, electoral mandate 605 n. *vote*.

demand, demand as of right, claim 915 n. *dueness*; requisition 761 n. *request*;

notice, final demand, ultimatum; blackmail 900 n. *threat*; imposition 809 n. *tax*.

warrant, commission, brevet, authorization, written authority, letters patent, passport 756 n. *permit*; writ, summons, subpoena 959 n. *legal process*.

Adj. *commanding*, imperative; dictatorial; mandatory, obligatory, peremptory 740 adj. *compelling*; decretory, decretal 733 adj. *authoritative*.

Vb. *command*, bid, invite; order, tell; pass orders; signal, call, motion, sign 547 vb. *gesticulate*; direct, instruct, brief, circularize; rule, lay down, enjoin; give a mandate, charge 751 vb. *commission*; impose, lay upon, set 917 vb. *impose a duty*; detail, tell off; send for, summon; subpoena, dictate 740 vb. *compel*; countermand 752 vb. *abrogate*; ban, proscribe 757 vb. *prohibit*.

decree, pass a d., promulgate 528 vb. *proclaim*; say so, lay down the law 532 vb. *affirm*; prescribe, ordain, appoint 608 vb. *predetermine*; enact, legislate 953 vb. *make legal*; pass judgement, decide, rule 480 vb. *judge*.

demand, requisition 627 vb. *require*; order, indent 761 vb. *request*; make demands on, present an ultimatum, blackmail 900 vb. *threaten*; make claims 915 vb. *claim*; dun, bill, invoice, foreclose; exact, levy 809 vb. *tax*.

738. Disobedience – N. *disobedience*, indiscipline, naughtiness 598 n. *unwillingness*; insubordination 711 n. *defiance*; non-compliance 769 n. *non-observance*; disloyalty, defection, desertion 918 n. *dutilessness*; infraction, infringement, criminality, crime, sin 936 n. *guilty act*; non-cooperation, passive resistance 715 n. *resistance*; obstructionism 702 n. *hindrance*; seditiousness (see *sedition*); banditry 788 n. *brigandage*.

revolt, mutiny; direct action 145 n. *strike*; faction, breakaway, secession 978 n. *schism*; defection, Titoism 603 n. *tergiversation*; explosive situation 318 n. *agitation*; disturbance, disorder, riot, gang warfare, barricades 61 n. *turmoil*; rebellion, insurrection, rising; putsch, coup d'état; resistance movement, insurgence 715 n. *resistance*; tyrannicide 362 n. *homicide*.

sedition, seditiousness, Chartism, kulakism; agitation, cabal, intrigue 623 n. *plot*; subversion, infiltration, fifth-columnism; underground activities, terrorism, anarchism, treasonable activities, treason 930 n. *perfidy*.

revolter, awkward person, handful; mutineer, rebel; striker 705 n. *opponent*; secessionist 978 n. *schismatic*; Titoist, deviationist; blackleg, scab 84 n. *nonconformist*; traitor, Quisling, fifth-columnist 603 n. *tergiversator*; insurgent, guerrilla, partisan; tyrannicide, regicide; revolutionary, extremist, Fenian, Jacobin; counter-revolutionary, reactionary, monarchist, terrorist, anarchist, nihilist.

agitator, factionary, protester, demonstrator, marcher; tub-thumper, rabble-rouser, mob-orator, demagogue; firebrand 663 n. *trouble-maker*; seditionary, sedition-monger; ringleader.

rioter, street-r., brawler, corner-boy 904 n. *ruffian*; demonstrator, suffragette, chartist, sansculotte; saboteur, wrecker, Luddite; secret society, Ku Klux Klan.

Adj. *disobedient*, undisciplined, ill-disciplined; naughty; unfilial, undaughterly; unbiddable, self-willed, wayward 602 adj. *wilful*; insubordinate, mutinous, rebellious, bolshie; unsubmissive, uncompliant 769 adj. *non-observant*; recalcitrant 715 adj. *resisting*; contumacious 602 adj. *obstinate*; subversive, revolutionary, reactionary; seditious, trouble-making; traitorous, disloyal 918 adj. *dutiless*; antinomian 734 adj. *anarchic*; uninvited, unbidden.

riotous, rioting; anarchic, sansculottic, lawless 61 adj. *disorderly*; insurrectionary, uprisen, rebellious, up in arms 715 adj. *resisting*.

Vb. *disobey*, not listen; not conform 769 vb. *not observe*; violate, infringe, transgress, trespass 306 vb. *encroach*; turn restive, kick, play up; kick over the traces, bolt.

revolt, rebel, mutiny; down tools, strike work, come out 145 vb. *cease*; undermine, work underground; secede 978 vb. *schismatize*; betray 603 vb. *tergiversate*; agitate, demonstrate, protest 762 vb. *deprecate*.

739. Obedience – N. *obedience*, compliance 768 n. *observance*; meekness, discipline; acquiescence 721 n. *submission*; dutifulness, morale 917 n. *duty*; obsequiousness, slavishness 879 n. *servility*.

loyalty, constancy, devotion, fidelity, faithfulness, faith 929 n. *probity*; allegiance, fealty, homage, service; vote of confidence.

Adj. *obedient*, compliant 768 adj. *observant*; loyal, faithful, true-blue, devoted, dedicated, sworn; homageable, submissive 721 adj. *submitting*; law-abiding 717 adj. *peaceful*; complaisant, docile; good, well-behaved; filial, daughterly; ready 597 adj. *willing*; meek, biddable, dutiful, disciplined; at one's beck and call, under control.

Vb. *obey*, comply, do to order, act upon 768 vb. *observe*; sign on the dotted line, come to heel 83 vb. *conform*; listen, hearken, put oneself at one's service 597 vb. *be willing*; do one's bidding 742 vb. *serve*; owe loyalty, bear allegiance, homage 768 vb. *observe faith*; know one's duty 917 vb. *do one's duty*.

740. Compulsion – N. *compulsion*, spur of necessity 596 n. *necessity*; law of nature 953 n. *law*; Hobson's choice 606 n. *no choice*; coercion; blackmail 900 n. *threat*; sanction, sanctions 963 n. *penalty*; enforcement, constraint, duress, force; big stick, bludgeon 735 n. *brute force*; impressment, press-gang, conscription 718 n. *war measures*; corvée, forced labour, labour camp 745 n. *servitude*.

Adj. *compelling*, compulsive, involuntary, of necessity, unavoidable, inevitable 596 adj. *necessary*; imperative, dictatorial, peremptory 737 adj. *commanding*; compulsory, mandatory, binding 917 adj. *obligatory*; urgent, overriding, coercive; irresistible 160 adj. *powerful*; forcible, forceful, cogent.

Vb. *compel*, constrain, coerce 176 vb. *force*; enforce, dictate, necessitate, oblige, bind; make, leave no option; pin down, tie d.; press, draft, conscript; drive, dragoon, regiment, discipline; force one's hand; bludgeon 735 vb. *oppress*; requisition, commandeer 786 vb. *take*; squeeze, put the screw on 963 vb. *torture*; insist 532 vb. *emphasize*; take no denial, not take no for an answer 532 vb. *affirm*; force upon, inflict, foist, fob off on.

741. Master – N. *master*, mistress; master of, captor, possessor 776 n. *owner*; sire, lord, lady, dame; overlord, lord's lord, suzerain; master of the house, husband, goodman; senior, head, principal 34 n. *superior*; schoolmaster, dominie 537 n. *teacher*; employer, capitalist, boss; leader 690 n. *director*; cock of the walk, lord of creation 638 n. *bigwig*; the authorities, the powers that be, 'them' 733 n. *government*; staff, High Command 689 n. *directorship*.

autocrat, autarch, absolute ruler, despot, tyrant, dictator, duce, Führer; tycoon, boss, shogun; petty tyrant, gauleiter, commissar, Jack-in-office, tin god 690 n. *official*.

sovereign, suzerain, crowned head, anointed king; Majesty, Highness, Royal H.; dynasty, house, royal h., royalty; monarch, king, queen; emperor, empress; caliph, Commander of the Faithful.

potentate, dynast, ruler; chief, chieftain, sheik, cacique; prince, ruling p., princeling, tetrarch; rajah, maharajah; emir, sirdar, mehtar, sherif; nawab, archduke, duke, Elector, Prince Bishop; regent, interrex; governor, viceroy.

officer, man in office, functionary, mandarin, bureaucrat 690 n. *official*; civil servant, public s. 742 n. *servant*; gauleiter, commissar; chief officer, aga, prime minister, grand vizier, vizier, diwan; constable, marshal, seneschal, warden; burgomaster, mayor, lord m.,

lady m., mayoress, alderman, bailie, city father, councillor, syndic, sheriff, bailiff; justice 957 n. *judge*; magistrate, city m., podestà; president, doge; consul, proconsul; prefect, intendant, district officer; bumbailiff, catchpole, tipstaff 955 n. *law officer*.

naval officer, sea-lord, first s.; naval attaché; admiral of the fleet, admiral, vice-a., rear-a., port-a.; commodore, captain, post c., flag-c., commander, lieutenant-c., lieutenant, flag-l., sub-l., midshipman, middy, petty officer, warrant o., leading seaman 270 n. *mariner*; trierarch, nauarch.

army officer, staff, staff officer, brass hat, red-tab; commissioned officer, brevet o.; marshal, field m.; commander-in-chief, generalissimo, general, captain-g., lieutenant-g., major-g., brigadier, colonel, lieutenant-c., major, captain, lieutenant, subaltern, shavetail; ensign, cornet, cadet; warrant officer, non-commissioned o.; adjutant, aide-de-camp; war-lord, war minister; commanding officer, commander, commandant.

air officer, marshal of the air-force, air marshal, air commodore, group-captain, wing-commander, squadron-leader, flight-lieutenant, pilot-officer, flight-sergeant 722 n. *air force*.

742. Servant – N. *servant*, public s., civil s. 690 n. *official*; unpaid servant, fag, slave; general servant, factotum 678 n. *busy person*; menial, orderly, peon; subordinate, underling, understrapper 35 n. *inferior*; subaltern, helper, assistant, secretary, right-hand man; mercenary, hireling, creature, employee, hand, hired man; hewer of wood and drawer of water, hack, drudge, erk; steward, stewardess, cabin-boy; waiter, waitress, nippy; bar-tender, barman, barmaid, pot-boy, tapster, drawer, skinker; stable-man, ostler, groom; doorman 264 n. *janitor*; porter, night-p.; help, daily, char, charwoman; universal aunt; baby-sitter.

domestic, servantry, staff; servant's hall 686 n. *personnel*; servitor, man, serving m.; livery servant, footman, flunkey, lackey, houseman; servant girl, abigail, maid, chambermaid; maid-of-all-work, tweeny, skivvy, slavey; kitchen boy, turnspit, scullion, dish-washer; upper servant, housekeeper, steward, chaplain, governess, tutor, nurse, nanny; butler, cook, cook-general; personal servant, valet, gentleman's gentleman, batman; lady's maid, waiting woman; nursemaid, ayah, amah, bonne; gyp, scout, bedder.

retainer, follower, following, suite, train, cortège, retinue; court, courtier; bodyguard, housecarl, henchman, squire, page; major domo, chamberlain, equerry, steward, bailiff, seneschal; châtelaine, housekeeper; cellarer, butler, cup-bearer; chaplain, bedeman; lady-in-waiting, companion, confidante.

dependant, clientèle, client; hanger-on, led-captain, parasite, satellite, camp-follower, creature, jackal 284 n. *follower*; stooge, puppet 630 n. *tool*; subordinate 35 n. *inferior*; minion, lackey, flunkey (see *domestic*); man, henchman, liege-man, homager, vassal; feudary, feuda-tory; pensioner; protégé, ward, charge, nurseling, foster-child.

subject, state s., national, citizen 191 n. *native*; lieger, vassal, feudatory, homag-er, man; people, citizenry 869 n. *com-monalty*; subject population, depen-dency, colony, helot; satellite; helotry (see *slave*).

slave, thrall, bondman, bondwoman, broadwife, bondmaid, slave-girl; helot, helotry, hewer of wood and drawer of water, doormat; serf, villein; chattel, puppet, chessman, pawn, machine, robot 630 n. *tool*; captive 750 n. *prisoner*.

Adj. *serving*, ministering 703 adj. *aiding*; in service, menial; in employ-ment, on the payroll; on the staff, at one's beck and call 739 adj. *obedient*; in slavery 745 adj. *subject*.

Vb. *serve*, wait upon 703 vb. *minister to*; follow, do suit and service 739 vb. *obey*; tend, squire, valet, dress; char, do for, oblige; do service, make oneself useful 640 vb. *be useful*.

743. Badge of rule – **N.** *regalia*, royal trappings; crown, orb, sceptre; coronet, tiara, diadem; sword of state 733 n. *authority*; ermine, royal purple; throne, royal seat.

badge of rule, emblem of authority, staff, wand, rod, baton; herald's wand, caduceus; seal, privy s.; sword of state, sword of justice, mace, fasces, axes; sartorial insignia, triple crown, mitre 989 n. *canonicals*; robe, mantle, toga; royal robe, pall.

badge of rank, sword, belt, sash, spurs, cocked hat, epaulet, tab 547 n. *badge*; uniform 547 n. *livery*; brass, star, pips, crown, crossed batons; chevron, stripe, anchor, curl, brassard, armlet; garter 729 n. *decoration*.

744. Freedom – **N.** *freedom*, liberty; rights, privilege, prerogative; exemption, immunity 919 n. *non-liability*; liberal-ism, libertarianism, latitudinarianism; licence, indiscipline 738 n. *disobedience*; laisser faire, non-interference; isolation-ism 883 n. *seclusion*; emancipation 746 n. *liberation*; enfranchisement, citizenship.

independence, freedom of action, uni-laterality; freedom of choice, initiative; floating vote; emancipation, bohemian-ism 84 n. *unconformity*; individualism, self-expression, individuality 80 n. *par-ticularism*; self-determination, state-hood, nationhood, national status 371 n. *nation*; autonomy, autarchy, self-rule, home-r., dominion status; autarky, self-support, self-sufficiency.

scope, play, full p. 183 n. *range*; rope, long r.; manoeuvrability, leverage; field, room, lebensraum, elbow-room, sea-r., margin, clearance 183 n. *room*; unstrict-ness, latitude, liberty, Liberty Hall; the run of, fling; one's head, one's own devices; ball at one's feet 137 n. *oppor-tunity*; facilities, free hand, blank cheque, carte blanche.

Adj. *free*, free-born, free-bred, en-franchised; heart-whole, fancy-free; scot-free 960 adj. *acquitted*; at large, free as air; footloose, go-as-you-please, ranging 267 adj. *travelling*; licensed, chartered, privileged 756 adj. *permitted*; exempt 919 adj. *non-liable*; free-thinking, emancipated, broad, broadminded, latitudinarian; free of cost, gratis 812 adj. *uncharged*; unreserved 289 adj. *accessible*.

unconfined, untrammelled, unshackled, unfettered, unbridled, uncurbed; unchecked, unrestrained; unhindered, unimpeded, unobstructed; wandering, random, at one's own devices.

independent, uninduced, unilateral 609 adj. *spontaneous*; unattached, detached 860 adj. *indifferent*; uncommitted, uninvolved; non-partisan 625 adj. *neutral*; isolationist 883 adj. *unsociable*; unconquered, unconquerable, irrepressible 727 adj. *unbeaten*; autonomous, autarchic, self-governing; autarkic, self-sufficient, self-supporting, self-contained; ungoverned, masterless, ungovernable 734 adj. *anarchic*; free-lance; breakaway 978 adj. *schismatical*.

unconditional, unconditioned, without strings; unrestricted, unlimited, absolute; discretionary, arbitrary; freehold, allodial.

Vb. *be free*, go free, save oneself 667 vb. *escape*; have the run of, feel at home; range, have scope, have rope enough, have one's head, have one's fling, follow one's bent 179 vb. *tend*; go it alone, shift for oneself, paddle one's own canoe; have a will of one's own 595 vb. *will*; be independent, call no man master; take liberties, make free with, presume on 878 vb. *be insolent*; make bold to, permit oneself.

Adv. *freely*, liberally, ad libitum.

745. Subjection – N. *subjection*, subordination, cadetship, juniority, inferior status, satellite s. 35 n. *inferiority*; creaturehood, creatureliness; dependence, clientship, tutelage, guardianship, wardship, chancery, apron strings, leadings.; subjecthood, allegiance, vassalage, nationality, citizenship; subjugation, conquest, colonialism; loss of freedom, disfranchisement, enslavement 721 n. *submission*; yoke 748 n. *fetter*.

service, employ, employment; servantship, flunkeydom, flunkeyism; tribute, suit and service; vassalage 739 n. *loyalty*; corvée, forced labour 740 n. *compulsion*; conscription 718 n. *war measures*.

servitude, slavery, enslavement, captivity, thraldom, bondage, yoke; helotry, serfdom, villenage.

Adj. *subject*, unfree, unfranchised, unprivileged; satellite, satellitic 879 adj. *servile*; bond, bounden, tributary, colonial; owing service, vassal, feudatory 739 adj. *obedient*; under, subordinate, junior, cadet 35 adj. *inferior*; dependent, in chancery, in statu pupillari; subject to, 180 adj. *liable*; a slave to 610 adj. *habituated*; in the hands of, at the mercy of; paid, stipendiary.

Vb. *be subject*, live under, homage, pay tribute, be under 739 vb. *obey*; depend on, lean on 35 vb. *be inferior*; be a doormat; serve, live in subjection, drag a chain, grace the triumph of.

subjugate, subdue, reduce, subject 727 vb. *overmaster*; colonize, make tributary, vassalize, mediatize; take, capture, lead captive, enslave; fetter 747 vb. *imprison*; trample on, tread on, wipe one's feet on, treat like dirt 735 vb. *oppress*; keep under, repress, sit on 165 vb. *suppress*; enthral, captivate 821 vb. *impress*; dominate 178 vb. *influence*; discipline, regiment, plan; tame, quell 369 vb. *break in*; bring to heel, have at one's beck and call, do what one likes with 673 vb. *dispose of*.

746. Liberation – N. *liberation*, binding, release, discharge, enlargement 960 n. *acquittal*; unravelling, extrication 46 n. *separation*; riddance, good r. 831 n. *relief*; rescue 668 n. *deliverance*; manumission, emancipation, enfranchisement; parole; liberalization, relaxation, decontrol 734 n. *laxity*; demobilization, disbandment 75 n. *dispersion*.

Adj. *liberated*, rescued, saved 668 adj. *extricable*; rid of, relieved; paroled, freed, manumitted; unbound 744 vb. *unconfined*; released etc. vb.

Vb. *liberate*, rescue, save 668 vb. *deliver*; dispense 919 vb. *exempt*; discharge, absolve 960 vb. *acquit*; emancipate, manumit; enfranchise; release, set free, set at liberty, enlarge, let out; parole 766 vb. *give terms*; unfetter, unshackle, unchain; unlock 263 vb. *open*; loosen, unloose, extricate, disengage 62 vb. *unravel*; ungag, unmuzzle; uncage, unkennel; unleash, let slip; let loose, turn adrift; license, charter; let out, vent 300 vb. *void*; leave hold, unhand 779 vb. *not retain*; relax, liberalize 734 vb. *be lax*; decontrol, deration 752 vb. *abrogate*; disband, send home 75 vb. *disperse*; unyoke 701 vb. *disencumber*.

747. Restraint – N. *restraint*, self-r., self-control 942 n. *temperance*; repression, constraint 740 n. *compulsion*; cramp, check 702 n. *hindrance*; curb, drag, brake 748 n. *fetter*; arrest, retardation 278 n. *slowness*; veto, ban 757 n. *prohibition*; control, discipline 733 n. *authority*; censorship, press laws 735 n. *severity*.

restriction, limitation, limiting factor 236 n. *limit*; localization 232 n. *circumscription*; curfew; constriction, squeeze 198 n. *compression*; control; restrictive practice, exclusivity 57 n. *exclusion*; monopoly, ring, closed shop; protection, protectionism, mercantilism, tariff, tariff wall; retrenchment 814 n. *economy*; blockade, starving out; monopolist, protectionist.

detention, preventive d., custody; arrest, house a., open a.; custodianship, keeping, care, charge, ward; quarantine, internment; captivity, durance; immurement, impoundment, confinement, incarceration, imprisonment; remand, no bail.

Adj. *restraining* etc. vb.; restrictive, conditioned, with strings; limiting, limitary; custodial; cramping, strict, stiff 326 adj. *rigid*; strait 206 adj. *narrow*; confining, close 198 adj. *compressive*; confined, poky; repressive, inhibiting 757 adj. *prohibiting*; monopolistic, protectionist.

restrained, self-r. 942 adj. *temperate*; under discipline, under control, on a lead 739 adj. *obedient*; hidebound, straitlaced; pinned down; restricted, scant, tight; cramped, tied, bound; held up, weather-bound.

imprisoned, detained, kept in; confined, earth-bound, land-locked; in quarantine; in internment; under detention, kept close, incommunicado; under arrest, in custody; behind bars, inside, in jug, in quod; under hatches, confined to barracks; in irons, pilloried, in the stocks; serving sentence, doing time; captive, trapped.

Vb. *restrain*, hold back, arrest, check, curb, rein in, brake 278 vb. *retard*; cramp, clog, hamper 702 vb. *hinder*; call off, put a stop to 145 vb. *halt*; veto, ban, bar 757 vb. *prohibit*; bridle, discipline, control; hold in leash 778 vb. *retain*; hold in, bottle up; restrict, limit, keep within bounds, localize, draw the line 232 vb. *circumscribe*; stanch, damp down 177 vb. *moderate*; repress 165 vb. *suppress*; muzzle, gag, silence 578 vb. *make mute*; debar from, rope off, keep out 57 vb. *exclude*; keep in, blockade; police, patrol, keep order.

arrest, make an a., apprehend, lay by the heels, catch, cop, nab, collar, pinch, pick up; take, take prisoner, capture, lead captive; take into custody.

fetter, manacle, bind, pinion, tie up, handcuff, put in irons; pillory, put in the stocks; tether, picket 45 vb. *tie*; shackle, trammel, hobble; chain, load with chains; condition, attach strings.

imprison, confine, quarantine, intern; hold, detain, keep in, gate; hold incommunicado; cloister 883 vb. *seclude*; entomb, bury 364 vb. *inter*; wall up, seal up, immure; cage, kennel, impound, corral, herd, pen, mew, crib, cabin, box up, shut in, trap 235 vb. *enclose*; incarcerate, jug, lock up.

748. Prison – N. *prison*, common p., calaboose; prison-house, house of correction, penitentiary, reformatory, approved home, Borstal; prison ship, hulks; dungeon, oubliette, limbo; Bastille, Tower; debtor's prison, sponging house.

gaol, jail, quod, clink, tronk, jug, can, stir, cooler, big house, glasshouse, booby hatch.

lock-up, choky, police-station; guard-room, roundhouse; cell, dungeon, oubliette, torture-chamber; prison van, Black Maria; dock, bar; hold, hatches, hulks; pound, pen, cage, coop, kennel 235 n. *enclosure*; ghetto, reserve; stocks, pillory; lock, padlock, bolt, bar.

prison camp, detention c., internment c., stalag, oflag; concentration camp, slave c.; Belsen, Auschwitz, Buchenwald; penal settlement, convict s., Botany Bay, Devil's Island.

fetter, shackle, trammel, bond, chain, ball and c., irons, gyve, bilboes, hobble; manacle, pinion, handcuff, bracelet, darbies; strait jacket, whalebone; muzzle, gag, bit, bridle, halter; reins, ribbons, traces; yoke, collar, harness; curb, brake, skid, shoe, clog, drag 702 n. *hindrance*; tether, rope, leading string, lead, leash 47 n. *halter*.

749. Keeper – N. *keeper*, custodian, curator; archivist 549 n. *recorder*; caretaker, concierge, housekeeper; castellan, seneschal, châtelaine, warden; ranger, gamekeeper; guard, escort, convoy; watchdog, sentry, sentinel, look-out, watchman, watch 660 n. *protector*; invigilator, tutor, chaperon, duenna, governess, nurse, mammy, nanny, nurse-maid, bonne, ayah, amah, baby-sitter; foster-parent, adoptive p., guardian.

gaoler, jailer, turnkey, warder, wardress, prison guard, prison governor.

750. Prisoner – N. *prisoner*, captive, capture, prisoner of war; parolee, ticket-of-leave man; person under arrest, charge; détenue, detainee, prisoner of state; prisoner at the bar 928 n. *accused person*; gaol-bird 904 n. *offender*; gaol inmate, convict; chain-gang, galley-slave 742 n. *slave*; hostage 767 n. *security*.

751. Commission: vicarious authority – N. *commission*, committal, delegation; devolution, decentralization; deputation, ablegation; legation, mission, embassy, embassage 754 n. *envoy*; regency 733 n. *authority*; representation, procuration, proxy; card vote; agency, factorship, trusteeship 689 n. *management*.

mandate, trust, charge; commission, assignment, errand, mission; return, election 605 n. *vote*; nomination, appointment, posting; investment, investiture, installation, inauguration, ordination, enthronement, coronation; power, power of attorney 737 n. *warrant*; terms of reference 766 n. *conditions*; responsibility, care, cure (of souls); baby, ward, charge.

Adj. *commissioned*, empowered etc. vb.; deputed, accredited; vicarious, representational, agential, procuratory.

Vb. *commission*, empower, authorize, charge 756 vb. *permit*; post, accredit, appoint, assign, nominate; invest, induct, install, collate, ordain; enthrone, crown, anoint; commit, turn over to, leave it to; consign, entrust; delegate, depute, ablegate; return, elect, give a mandate 605 vb. *vote*.

752. Abrogation – N. *abrogation*, annulment, invalidation; voidance, nullification; cancellation, suppression; repeal, rescission, abolition; repudiation 603 n. *recantation*; suspension, discontinuance, disuse, dead letter 674 n. *non-use*; reversal, countermand, nolle prosequi.

deposal, deposition, dethronement; demotion, degradation; disestablishment, disendowment; discharge, dismissal, sack, removal 300 n. *ejection*; deprivation 786 n. *expropriation*; replacement, supersession, recall.

Adj. *abrogated*, voided, vacated etc. vb.; null and void; functus officio, dead; dormant 674 adj. *unused*.

Vb. *abrogate*, annul, cancel; scrub 550 vb. *obliterate*; invalidate, abolish, dissolve, nullify, void, vacate; quash, set aside, reverse, overrule; repeal, revoke, recall; rescind, tear up; countermand; repudiate, retract 603 vb. *recant*; suspend, discontinue 674 vb. *disuse*; not proceed with 621 vb. *relinquish*.

depose, uncrown, dethrone; unseat, vote out; divest 786 vb. *deprive*; unfrock, disordain; disbench, disbar, strike off the roll 57 vb. *exclude*; suspend, cashier, break 300 vb. *dismiss*; ease out, oust 300 vb. *eject*; demote, degrade; recall, relieve, supersede, remove.

753. Resignation – N. *resignation*, demission, good-bye to office; retirement, superannuation, pension, golden handshake; waiver, surrender, abdication, renunciation 621 n. *relinquishment*; declaration (of innings at cricket).

Adj. *resigning*, abdicatory, renunciatory; outgoing, former, retired, quondam, one-time, ci-devant.

Vb. *resign*, send in one's papers, demit; hand over, vacate office; stand down, stand aside; sign off, declare one's innings closed; scratch, withdraw, back out, quit, throw up, chuck it; abdicate, abandon, renounce 621 vb. *relinquish*; retire, take one's pension; waive, disclaim.

754. Consignee – N. *consignee*, committee, panel 692 n. *council*; bailee, resignee, stakeholder; nominee, appointee, licensee; trustee, executor 686 n. *agent*; factor, one's man of business, bailiff, steward 690 n. *manager*; caretaker, curator 749 n. *keeper*; representative (see *delegate*); attorney 958 n. *law agent*; procurator, proxy 755 n. *deputy*; negotiator, middleman, broker; intermediary; office-bearer 741 n. *officer*; clerk, functionary, placeman 690 n. *official*.

delegate, nominee, representative, commissary, commissioner; man on the spot, correspondent, special c., plenipotentiary (see *envoy*); delegation, mission.

envoy, emissary, legate, nuncio, resident, resident minister, ambassador, High Commissioner, chargé d'affaires; corps diplomatique, diplomatic corps; minister, diplomat; embassy, legation, mission, consulate, High Commission; diplomatist, negotiator, plenipotentiary.

755. Deputy – N. *deputy*, surrogate, alternate, proxy; scapegoat, chopping block, substitute, locum tenens, understudy, stand-in 150 n. *substitution*; pro, vice; vicar; second-in-command, right-hand man, lieutenant, secretary; alter ego, Grey Eminence; spokesman, mouthpiece, herald 531 n. *messenger*; agent, factor, attorney 754 n. *consignee*.

Adj. *deputizing*, representing, agential; vice, pro; diplomatic, ambassadorial, plenipotentiary.

Vb. *deputize*, act for; attorney, act on behalf of, represent, appear for, hold a brief f.; negotiate, broke for; replace, stand for, do duty for 150 vb. *substitute*; hold the baby.

Section 2: Special

756. Permission – N. *permission*, general p., liberty 744 n. *freedom*; leave, sanction, clearance; grant, licence, authorization, warrant; allowance, sufferance, tolerance, toleration, indulgence 736 n. *lenity*; acquiescence; connivance; blessing, approval 923 n. *approbation*.

permit, authority, law 737 n. *warrant*; brevet, grant, charter, patent; pass, password, passport, safe-conduct; ticket, licence; free hand, carte blanche, blank cheque 744 n. *scope*; all clear, green light, clearance; nihil obstat, imprimatur.

Adj. *permitting*, permissive, indulgent, complaisant, tolerant 736 adj. *lenient*.

permitted, allowed etc. vb.; licit 953 adj. *legal*; unforbidden, open, optional, discretional, without strings 744 adj. *unconditional*; permissible, allowable; printable, sayable.

Vb. *permit*, let; give permission, grant leave, grant, accord, vouchsafe 781 vb. *give*; nod, say yes 758 vb. *consent*; bless, give one's blessing; sanction, pass 923 vb. *approve*; entitle, authorize, warrant, charter, license, enable 160 vb. *empower*; legalize 953 vb. *make legal*;

decontrol; dispense 919 vb. *exempt*; clear, give clearance 746 vb. *liberate*; concede, allow 488 vb. *assent*; favour, privilege, indulge 701 vb. *facilitate*; open the door to; foster, encourage 156 vb. *conduce*; suffer, tolerate 736 vb. *be lenient*; connive, wink at 734 vb. *be lax*; laisser faire, allow a free hand, give scope, give rope enough.

757. Prohibition – N. *prohibition*, inhibition, interdiction, disallowance, injunction; countermand, counter-order; intervention, interference; interdict, veto, ban, embargo, outlawry; proscription, taboo, index expurgatorius; non-recognition, intolerance 924 n. *disapprobation*; repressive legislation, repression, suppression 735 n. *severity*; forbidden fruit, contraband article 859 n. *desired object*.

Adj. *prohibiting*, prohibitory, forbidding, prohibitive, excessive 470 adj. *impossible*; penal 963 adj. *punitive*; hostile 881 adj. *inimical*; exclusive 57 adj. *excluding*.

prohibited, forbidden, under ban; contraband, illicit, unlawful, outlawed 954 adj. *illegal*; verboten, taboo, untouchable, black; unmentionable, unsayable, unprintable; out of bounds 57 adj. *excluded*.

Vb. *prohibit*, forbid, disallow, veto 760 vb. *refuse*; countermand 752 vb. *abrogate*; inhibit, prevent, paralyse 702 vb. *hinder*; restrict, stop 747 vb. *restrain*; ban, interdict, taboo, proscribe, outlaw; bar, debar, warn off 57 vb. *exclude*; excommunicate; repress 165 vb. *suppress*; censor 550 vb. *obliterate*; frown on 924 vb. *disapprove*; draw the line, block; intervene, interpose, interfere.

758. Consent – N. *consent*, free c. 597 n. *willingness*; agreement 488 n. *assent*; acquiescence, acceptance; endorsement, ratification, confirmation.

Adj. *consenting*, agreeable, compliant, ready 597 adj. *willing*.

Vb. *consent*, entertain the idea, say yes, nod; ratify, confirm 488 vb. *endorse*;

approve; agree 488 vb. *assent*; have no objection 488 vb. *acquiesce*; yield 721 vb. *submit*; comply, do as asked; grant, accord, vouchsafe, deign, condescend, listen, hearken 415 vb. *hear*; accept, jump at; close with, settle 766 vb. *make terms*; tolerate 736 vb. *be lenient*; consent unwillingly, drag oneself, make o.

759. Offer – N. *offer*, tender, bid, take-over b.; proposition, proposal; approach, overture, advance, invitation; offering, sacrifice 781 n. *gift*; candidature, application 761 n. *request*.

Adj. *offering*, offered, advertised; open, available; on offer, on the market; to let, for sale; on bid, on auction.

Vb. *offer*, proffer, hold out, bid, tender; present, lay at one's feet 781 vb. *give*; dedicate, sacrifice to; propose, put forward, suggest 512 vb. *propound*; not wait to be asked, make overtures, make advances; nduce 612 vb. *bribe*; press, invite 882 vb. *be hospitable*; hawk, offer for sale 793 vb. *sell*; cater for 633 vb. *provide*.

offer oneself, sacrifice o.; stand, run for, enter 716 vb. *contend*; volunteer, come forward 597 vb. *be willing*; be on offer, look for takers, go begging.

760. Refusal – N. *refusal*, non-acceptance 607 n. *rejection*; denial, no, nay 533 n. *negation*; repulse, rebuff, slap in the face; withholding 778 n. *retention*; non-compliance 769 n. *non-observance*; recusancy 598 n. *unwillingness*; protest 762 n. *deprecation*; renunciation 621 n. *relinquishment*.

Adj. *refusing*, denying, withholding, etc. vb.; recusant, uncompliant 769 adj. *non-observant*.

Vb. *refuse*, say no, shake one's head; deny, negative 533 vb. *negate*; decline, turn down 607 vb. *reject*; repulse, rebuff 292 vb. *repel*; turn away 300 vb. *dismiss*; resist persuasion, harden one's heart, turn a deaf ear; not consent, will otherwise; not want, not cater for; frown on, disallow 757 vb. *prohibit*; set one's face against 715 vb. *resist*; kick, protest 762 vb. *deprecate*; grudge, begrudge, withhold 778 vb. *retain*.

761. Request – **N.** *request*, asking; negative request 762 n. *deprecation*; canvass, canvassing; demand, requisition; last time of asking, ultimatum 737 n. *demand*; blackmail 900 n. *threat*; claim, counter-c. 915 n. *dueness*; consumer demand, seller's market 627 n. *requirement*; postulate, proposal, motion, suggestion; bid, application, suit; petition, prayer, appeal, plea (see *entreaty*); pressure, instance, insistence, urgency 740 n. *compulsion*; dunning, importunity; solicitation, invitation, temptation; mendicancy, begging, begging letter, subscription list, flag day; want ad., want column.

entreaty, beseeching; submission, folded hands, bended knees, supplication, prayer; appeal, invocation; adjuration, adjurement, conjuration; imprecation.

Adj. *requesting*, asking etc. vb.; alms-hunting; claiming, insistent; importunate, pressing, urgent, instant; clamorous, dunning.

supplicatory, entreating, suppliant, prayerful; on bended knees, cap in hand; precatory, imploratory, invocatory, imprecatory; precative.

Vb. *request*, ask, invite, solicit; approach, accost 759 vb. *offer*; sue, sigh, woo 889 vb. *court*; need, have in request, call for 627 vb. *require*; crave, ask a boon, trouble one for 859 vb. *desire*; apply, make application, put in for, bid; tout, hawk, canvass 793 vb. *sell*; petition, memorialize; expect 915 vb. *claim*; make demands 737 vb. *demand*; blackmail 900 vb. *threaten*; insist 532 vb. *emphasize*; urge, persuade; importune, ply, press, dun, besiege, beset; requisition 786 vb. *take*; state one's terms 766 vb. *give terms*.

beg, cadge, crave, sponge; scrounge; panhandle, mendicate; appeal for funds, pass the hat, take a collection 786 vb. *levy*; whistle for 627 vb. *require*.

entreat, beg hard, supplicate, pray, implore, beseech, appeal, conjure, adjure, obtest, obsecrate, imprecate; invoke, appeal to; kneel to; sue, sigh.

762. Deprecation: negative request – **N.** *deprecation*, negative request, contrary advice 613 n. *dissuasion*; begging off, plea for mercy, crossed fingers; intercession 981 n. *prayers*; complaint 829 n. *discontent*; exception, demur, expostulation, remonstrance, protest 704 n. *opposition*; tut-tut, raised eyebrows, groans, jeers 924 n. *disapprobation*; round robin; demonstration, indignation meeting.

Adj. *deprecatory*, dehortative 613 adj. *dissuasive*; protesting, expostulatory; intercessory, mediatorial; averting, apotropaic.

Vb. *deprecate*, ask one not to, advise against 613 vb. *dissuade*; avert the omen, touch wood, cross one's fingers 983 vb. *practise sorcery*; beg off, intercede 720 vb. *mediate*; cry for mercy, propitiate, pray; tut-tut, raise one's eyebrows 924 vb. *disapprove*; remonstrate, expostulate 924 vb. *reprove*; jeer, groan; murmur, complain 829 vb. *be discontented*; demur, jib, kick, squeak, protest, cry blue murder 704 vb. *oppose*; demonstrate.

763. Petitioner – **N.** *petitioner*, suppliant, supplicant; appellant; claimant, pretender; asker, inquirer, advertiser; customer, bidder, tenderer; suitor, wooer; canvasser, hawker, tout; dun, dunner; pressure group, lobby, lobbyist; applicant, candidate; man with a grievance 829 n. *malcontent*.

beggar, professional b., schnorrer, panhandler; mendicant, alms-hunter; cadger, borrower, scrounger, sponger, parasite 879 n. *toady*.

Section 3: Conditional

764. Promise – **N.** *promise*, undertaking, engagement, commitment; betrothal 894 n. *marriage*; troth, plighted word, word, parole, word of honour, vow 532 n. *oath*; professions, fair words; assurance, pledge, credit, honour 767 n. *security*;

gentlemen's agreement 765 n. *compact*; bond, promise to pay 803 n. *debt*; pre-engagement 672 n. *undertaking*; promise-maker, votary.

Adj. *promissory*, promising, votive; on credit, on parole.

Vb. *promise*, say one will 532 vb. *affirm*; hold out, proffer 759 vb. *offer*; give one's word; vow 532 vb. *swear*; vouch for, go bail for, underwrite 767 vb. *give security*; pledge, stake; parole oneself, pledge one's honour, stake one's credit; engage for 672 vb. *undertake*; commit oneself, bind oneself, covenant 765 vb. *contract*; exchange vows 894 vb. *wed*.

765. Compact – N. *compact*, contract, bargain, agreement, mutual undertaking 672 n. *undertaking*; gentleman's agreement 764 n. *promise*; mutual pledge, exchange of vows; espousal 894 n. *marriage*; covenant, indenture, bond 767 n. *security*; league, alliance, cartel 706 n. *cooperation*; pact, convention, understanding; private understanding, something between them; conspiracy 623 n. *plot*; negotiation 766 n. *conditions*; deal, give and take 770 n. *compromise*; adjustment, composition; seal, signature, ratification 488 n. *assent*; seal, indenture 767 n. *title-deed*.

treaty, international agreement; pact, convention, concordat, protocol.

signatory, subscriber, the undersigned; swearer, attestant 466 n. *witness*; endorser, ratifier; adherent, party, consenting p. 488 n. *assenter*; contractor, contracting party; treaty-maker, negotiator.

Adj. *contractual*, conventional 488 adj. *assenting*; bilateral, multilateral; signed, sealed and delivered; under one's hand and seal.

Vb. *contract*, engage 672 vb. *undertake*; pre-contract 764 vb. *promise*; covenant, strike a bargain, strike hands, do a deal, league, ally 706 vb. *cooperate*; treat, negotiate 791 vb. *bargain*; agree, arrive at a formula, come to terms 766 vb. *make terms*; execute, sign, subscribe, ratify, attest, confirm 488 vb. *endorse*.

766. Conditions – N. *conditions*, treaty-making, negotiation, bargaining, collective b.; horse-dealing 791 n. *barter*; formula, terms, set t.; final terms, ultimatum 900 n. *threat*; part of the bargain, condition; set of terms, frame of reference, articles; provision, clause, entrenched c., escape c., proviso, limitation, strings, reservation, exception 468 n. *qualification*; stipulation, sine qua non 627 n. *requirement*; casus foederis, the letter of the treaty; terms of reference 751 n. *mandate*.

Adj. *conditional*, with strings attached, binding 917 adj. *obligatory*; provisional, stipulatory, qualificatory, provisory 468 adj. *qualifying*; limiting, subject to terms, conditioned, contingent.

Vb. *give terms*, propose conditions; condition, bind, tie down, attach strings; hold out for 737 vb. *demand*; stipulate 627 vb. *require*.

make terms, negotiate, treat, be in treaty, parley, hold conversations 584 vb. *confer*; make overtures 461 vb. *be tentative*; haggle, higgle 791 vb. *bargain*; proffer 759 vb. *offer*; give and take, yield a point, stretch a p. 770 vb. *compromise*; negotiate a treaty, do a deal 765 vb. *contract*.

767. Security – N. *security*, guarantee, warranty, authorization, certificate, writ 737 n. *warrant*; sponsorship, patronage 660 n. *protection*; suretyship, surety, bail, caution, replevin, recognizance, parole; bailor, cautioner, mainpernor; gage, pledge, pawn, hostage; stake, stake money, deposit, earnest, token, instalment; colour of one's money, money in advance 804 n. *payment*; insurance, underwriting 660 n. *safety*; collateral, hypothecation, mortgage, bottomry 780 n. *transfer*.

title-deed, deed, instrument; deed-poll; indenture; charter, covenant, bond 765 n. *compact*; receipt, I.O.U., voucher, acquittance, quittance; valuable security, banknote, promissory note, note of hand; paper, Government p., gilt-edged security; portfolio, scrip, share, debenture; will, testament, codicil.

Adj. *pledged*, pawned, popped, deposited; in pawn, on deposit; on lease, on mortgage; on bail, on recognizance.

Vb. *give bail*, go b., bail one out, go surety; take bail, take recognizance; hold in pledge, keep in pawn.

give security, offer collateral, hypothecate, bottomry, mortgage; pledge, impignorate, pawn, pop 785 vb. *borrow*; guarantee 473 vb. *make certain*; authenticate, verify 466 vb. *corroborate*; execute, endorse, seal, stamp, sign, counters., subscribe 488 vb. *endorse*; grant a receipt 782 vb. *receive*; secure, insure, assure, underwrite 660 vb. *safeguard*.

768. Observance – N. *observance*, adherence to, attention to; performance, discharge 676 n. *action*; compliance 739 n. *obedience*; conformance 83 n. *conformity*; attachment, fidelity, faith 739 n. *loyalty*.

Adj. *observant*, practising 676 adj. *doing*; heedful, careful of 455 adj. *attentive*; conscientious, punctual, diligent, earnest, religious, punctilious; literal, pedantic, exact 494 adj. *accurate*; responsible, reliable, dependable 929 adj. *trustworthy*; loyal, true, compliant 739 adj. *obedient*; faithful 929 adj. *honourable*.

Vb. *observe*, heed, respect, have regard to, acknowledge; keep, practise, adhere to, follow, hold by, abide by 83 vb. *conform*; comply 739 vb. *obey*; fulfil, discharge, perform 676 vb. *do*.

observe faith, keep f., be faithful to 917 vb. *do one's duty*; be as good as one's word, stand by, come up to scratch.

769. Non-observance – N. *non-observance*, no such practice; informality, indifference 734 n. *laxity*; inattention, omission, laches 458 n. *negligence*; non-conformity 84 n. *unconformity*; non-performance 726 n. *non-completion*; infringement, violation, transgression 306 n. *overstepping*; disloyalty 738 n. *disobedience*; bad faith, breach of promise

930 n. *perfidy*; repudiation, retractation 603 n. *tergiversation*; failure 805 n. *insolvency*.

Adj. *non-observant*, non-practising; nonconformist 84 adj. *unconformable*; inattentive to, neglectful 458 adj. *negligent*; unprofessional, uncanonical; indifferent, informal 734 adj. *lax*; non-compliant 738 adj. *disobedient*; transgressive 954 adj. *lawbreaking*; disloyal 918 adj. *dutiless*; unfaithful 930 adj. *perfidious*; antinomian, anarchical 734 adj. *anarchic*.

Vb. *not observe*, not practise, abhor 607 vb. *reject*; not conform, stand out; ignore 458 vb. *neglect*; disregard, slight 921 vb. *not respect*; stretch a point 734 vb. *be lax*; violate, transgress 306 vb. *overstep*; desert 918 vb. *fail in duty*; break faith, dishonour, repudiate, go back on 603 vb. *tergiversate*; palter, quibble, equivocate 518 vb. *be equivocal*.

770. Compromise – N. *compromise*, non-insistence, concession; give and take, adjustment, formula 765 n. *compact*; second best, pis aller, modus vivendi, working arrangement; middle term, balancing act.

Vb. *compromise*, find a formula, find a basis; give and take, meet half-way; live and let live, not insist, stretch a point 734 vb. *be lax*; split the difference 30 vb. *average out*; compound, commute; arbitrate, go to arbitration; take the good with the bad, make a virtue of necessity, make the best of a bad job.

Section 4: Possessive Relations

771. Acquisition – N. *acquisition*, getting, winning; bread-winning, earning; acquirement, obtainment, procurement; money-getting, money-grubbing 816 n. *avarice*; heap, stack, pile, pool, scoop, jackpot 74 n. *accumulation*; trover, finding 484 n. *discovery*; recovery, retrieval, recoupment 656 n. *restoration*; getting hold of 786 n. *taking*; inheritance, heirship, patrimony; find, windfall, treasure-trove; something for nothing 781 n. *gift*; gratuity, baksheesh 962 n. *reward*; prize, plum; plunder 790 n. *booty*.

earnings, income, earned i., wage, salary, screw, pay-packet 804 n. *pay*; rate for the job, pay-scale, differential; pension, compensation, golden handshake; remuneration, emolument 962 n. *reward*; pickings, perquisite; commission, rake-off 810 n. *discount*; return, receipts, proceeds, turnover, takings 807 n. *receipt*; harvest, vintage, crop, gleanings.

gain, thrift, savings 814 n. *economy*; no loss, credit side, profit, winnings; dividend, share-out 775 n. *participation*; interest 36 n. *increment*; paying transaction, lucrative deal, main chance; advantage, benefit.

Adj. *acquiring*, acquisitive, accumulative; on the make; hoarding, saving.

gainful, paying, profitable, lucrative, remunerative 962 adj. *rewarding*; advantageous 644 adj. *beneficial*; fruitful, fertile 164 adj. *productive*; paid, remunerated, breadwinning.

acquired, had, got, gotten, ill-gotten; inherited, patrimonial; on the credit side.

Vb. *acquire*, get, come by; earn, gain, obtain, procure, get at; find, strike, pick up 484 vb. *discover*; make one's own, annex 786 vb. *appropriate*; win, capture, catch, land, net, bag 786 vb. *take*; gather, reap, crop, harvest; derive, draw, tap, milk, mine 304 vb. *extract*; collect, accumulate, pile up 74 vb. *bring together*; raise, levy, save, hoard 632 vb. *store*; get somehow, beg, borrow or steal; win one's bread, draw a salary; gross, take 782 vb. *receive*; convert, cash, realize; recoup, get back, recover, regain, redeem, recapture 656 vb. *retrieve*; attain, reach; come in for, catch, incur, contract.

inherit, come into, be left, take one's patrimony; succeed, succeed to.

gain, profit, make a p., earn a dividend; make, win; make money, turn a pretty penny 800 vb. *get rich*; scoop,

win, win the jackpot, break the bank; credit to one's account.

772. Loss – N. *loss*, deprivation, privation, bereavement; dispossession 786 n. *expropriation*; sacrifice, forfeiture, forfeit, lapse; dead loss, perdition 165 n. *ruin*; depreciation, diminishing returns 42 n. *decrement*; bankruptcy 805 n. *insolvency*; spilt milk, wastage, leakage 634 n. *waste*; drain, running sore; riddance, good r. 746 n. *liberation*.

Adj. *losing*, unprofitable 641 adj. *profitless*; the worse for 655 adj. *deteriorated*; sacrificial; denuded, bereft, bereaved; minus, without, lacking; rid of, quit of; out of pocket, in the red, overdrawn, insolvent 805 adj. *non-paying*; non-profitmaking 931 adj. *disinterested*.

lost, gone for ever; missing, mislaid 188 adj. *misplaced*; untraceable 190 adj. *absent*; rid, off one's hands; irrecoverable, irretrievable, irredeemable; forfeit.

Vb. *lose*, not find, look in vain for; mislay 188 vb. *misplace*; miss, let slip, say good-bye to; squander 634 vb. *waste*; forfeit, sacrifice; be a loser 728 vb. *be defeated*; make no profit, incur losses, break, go bankrupt 805 vb. *not pay*; overdraw, be minus.

773. Possession – N. *possession*, ownership, proprietorship, rightful possession, enjoyment; seisin, occupancy, nine points of the law, bird in the hand; mastery, hold, grasp 778 n. *retention*; a possession 777 n. *property*, *estate*; tenure, fee, fief; long possession, prescription 610 n. *habit*; monopoly, corner, ring; pre-emption, forestalment; expectations, heirship, heirdom, inheritance, heritage, patrimony, reversion, remaindership; taking possession, impropriation, engrossment 786 n. *taking*.

Adj. *possessing*, seized of, having, holding etc. vb.; having possession, propertied; in possession; endowed with, blest w.; exclusive, monopolistic, possessive.

possessed, enjoyed, had, held; in one's grasp; in the bank, to one's credit; on hand, in store; proper, personal 80 adj. *special*; belonging, one's own, unshared, private, personal; inherent, appertaining.

Vb. *possess*, own, have; hold, grip 778 vb. *retain*; command 673 vb. *dispose of*; call oneself owner, boast of 915 vb. *claim*; contain, include 78 vb. *comprise*; fill, occupy; squat, inhabit; enjoy 673 vb. *use*; all to oneself, monopolize, engross, corner; preoccupy, forestall, preempt, reserve, book, engage; inherit, come in for, succeed 771 vb. *acquire*.

belong, vest in; inhere, attach, pertain, appertain; owe service to 745 vb. *be subject*.

774. Non-ownership – N. *non-ownership*, occupancy; tenancy at will, lease; pauperism 801 n. *poverty*; deprivation, disentitlement 772 n. *loss*; no man's land, debatable territory, Tom Tiddler's ground.

Adj. *not owning*, dependent 745 adj. *subject*; destitute, penniless, propertyless 801 adj. *poor*; unblest with, barren; lacking, minus, without 627 adj. *required*.

unpossessed, unattached, not belonging; masterless, ownerless, nobody's, no man's; international; unclaimed, disowned; unoccupied, untenanted; derelict, abandoned 779 adj. *not retained*; untaken, going begging 860 adj. *unwanted*.

775. Joint possession – N. *joint possession*, jointness, possession in common; joint ownership, public property, public domain 777 n. *property*; condominium 733 n. *polity*; joint stock, pool, kitty 632 n. *store*; cooperative system, mutualism 706 n. *cooperation*; public ownership, socialism, communism, collectivism; community of possessions; collective farm, collective, kolkhoz, kibbutz 370 n. *farm*.

participation, membership, affiliation 78 n. *inclusion*; partnership, profit-sharing 706 n. *association*; joint mess, syssitia, Dutch party; dividend, share-out; share, fair s., lot, whack 783 n.

portion; complicity, involvement, sympathy, fellow-feeling.

participator, member, partner, sharer; shareholder 776 n. *possessor*; cooperator, mutualist; collectivist, socialist, communist; sympathizer 707 n. *patron*.

Adj. *sharing*, co-sharing, joint, profit-sharing, cooperative; common, communal, international; collective, socialistic, communistic; participatory, in on; sympathetic, condoling.

Vb. *participate*, have a hand in, join in 706 vb. *cooperate*; partake of, share in; share, go shares, go halves, share and share alike 783 vb. *apportion*.

socialize, mutualize, nationalize, internationalize, communize; put in the kitty, pool, hold in common.

776. Possessor – N. *possessor*, holder, person in possession, impropriator; taker, captor; trespasser, squatter; monopolizer, dog in the manger; occupant, lodger, occupier, incumbent; mortgagee, bailee, trustee; renter, hirer, lessee, lease-holder; tenantry, tenant; householder, freeholder, yeoman.

owner, monarch; master, mistress, proprietor, proprietress; vendee, buyer 792 n. *purchaser*; lord, feoffer; landed gentry, landed interest 868 n. *aristocracy*; man of property, property-owner, landholder, landowner, landlord.

beneficiary, feoffee, releasee, grantee, patentee; impropriator 782 n. *recipient*; devisee, legatee, legatary; inheritor, successor; next of kin 11 n. *kinsman*; heir, expectant; heiress, 'lady richly left'; reversioner, remainderman; tertius gaudens.

777. Property – N. *property*, meum et tuum, suum cuique; possessions, one's all; stake, venture; personalty, personal property; chattel, real property, moveables, immoveables; goods and chattels, parcels, appurtenances, belongings, paraphernalia, effects, personal e., impedimenta, baggage, luggage, traps, things; goods, wares 795 n. *merchandise*; plant, fixtures, furniture.

estate, estate and effects, assets; circumstances, what one is worth; resources 629 n. *means*; substance 800 n. *wealth*; revenue 807 n. *receipt*; valuables, securities, portfolio; stake, holding, investment; right, title, easement, interest; lease, tenure, freehold, copyhold, fee, fee simple; tenement, hereditament.

lands, land, acres, estate, property, real estate, realty; holding, tenure, allodium, freehold, copyhold, fief, feud, manor, honour, seigniory, lordship, domain, demesne; crown lands, common land, common.

dower, dowry, dot, portion, jointure, settlement, peculium; allowance, pin-money; alimony, patrimony, birthright 915 n. *dueness*; appanage, heritage; inheritance, legacy, bequest; interest, life i.; expectations, remainder, reversion; heirloom.

Adj. *proprietary*, branded, patented; moveable, immoveable, real, personal; predial, manorial, seignorial, allodial; patrimonial, hereditary, heritable, testamentary.

Vb. *dower*, endow, possess with, bless w. 781 vb. *give*; devise 780 vb. *bequeath*; grant, assign, entail 780 vb. *convey*.

778. Retention – **N.** *retention*, prehensility, tenacity; stickiness 354 n. *viscidity*; prehension, handhold, foothold, toe-hold 218 n. *support*; clutches, grip, grasp, hold, stranglehold, half-nelson; squeeze, clinch, lock, hug; keep 747 n. *detention*; containment 235 n. *enclosure*.

nippers, pincers, tweezers, pliers, wrench, tongs, forceps, vice, clamp, fist; talon, claw, nails 256 n. *sharp point*; tentacle 378 n. *feeler*.

Adj. *retentive*, retaining 747 adj. *restraining*; clinging, adhesive, sticky, gummy, gooey 48 adj. *cohesive*; tight, strangling; costive, bound.

retained, in the grip of, fast, held; detained 747 adj. *imprisoned*; unsold, not for sale; kept back, withheld, saved, reserved; esoteric, incommunicable 523 adj. *occult*; non-transferable, inalienable; entailed.

Vb. *retain*, hold; hold up, catch, steady 218 vb. *support*; hold on, hold tight; cling to, hang on to, freeze on to, adhere 48 vb. *agglutinate*; fasten on, grip, grasp, clench, clinch, lock; hug, clip, embrace; pin down, hold d.; have by the throat, throttle, strangle 747 vb. *restrain*; dig one's toes in; keep in, detain 747 vb. *imprison*; contain, keep within limits, draw the line 235 vb. *enclose*; keep back, withhold 525 vb. *keep secret*.

779. Non-retention – **N.** *non-retention*, disposal, alienation 780 n. *transfer*; release 746 n. *liberation*; unfreezing, decontrol; dispensation, exemption 919 n. *non-liability*; dissolution (of a marriage) 896 n. *divorce*; cession, abandonment, renunciation 621 n. *relinquishment*; availability, saleability, disposability; unsoundness, leak 298 n. *outflow*.

derelict, jetsam, flotsam 641 n. *rubbish*; cast-off, slough; waif, stray, foundling, orphan, maroon; outcaste, untouchable.

Adj. *not retained*, under notice to quit; derelict, unclaimed, unappropriated; heritable, transferable; available, for sale 793 n. *saleable*; giveable, bestowable.

Vb. *not retain*, part with, alienate, transfer 780 vb. *convey*; dispose of 793 vb. *sell*; let go, unhand, leave hold of; unclinch, unclench 263 vb. *open*; forego, dispense with, spare, give up, waive, abandon, cede, yield 621 vb. *relinquish*; renounce, abjure 603 vb. *recant*; cancel, revoke 752 vb. *abrogate*; lift restrictions, derestrict, decontrol 746 vb. *liberate*; supersede 150 vb. *substitute*; wash one's hands of, disown, disclaim 533 vb. *negate*; disinherit 801 vb. *impoverish*; get rid of, ditch, jettison 300 vb. *eject*; pension off, retire; discharge, give notice to quit 300 vb. *dismiss*; withdraw 753 vb. *resign*; sit loose to 860 vb. *be indifferent*; let out, leak 300 vb. *emit*.

780. Transfer (of property) – **N.** *transfer*, transmission, consignment, delivery, hand-over 272 n. *transference*; settlement, limitation; conveyancing, conveyance; bequeathal, testamentary disposition; assignment; alienation 779 n. *non-retention*; demise, devise, bequest 781 n. *gift*; lease, let; trade 791 n. *barter*; conversion, exchange 151 n. *interchange*; change of hands, change-over 150 n. *substitution*; devolution, delegation 751 n. *commission*; succession, reversion, inheritance; pledge, pawn, hostage.

Adj. *transferred*, made over, feoffed; transferable, conveyable, alienable, exchangeable, negotiable; heritable, reversional, reversionary; giveable, bestowable.

Vb. *convey*, transfer by deed; grant, assign, sign away 781 vb. *give*; demise, let, rent, hire 784 vb. *lease*; alienate 793 vb. *sell*; barter 791 vb. *trade*; exchange, convert 151 vb. *interchange*; confer ownership, put in possession, impropriate, invest with; commit, devolve, delegate, entrust 751 vb. *commission*; deliver, transmit, hand over 272 vb. *transfer*; pledge, pawn 784 vb. *lend*; disinherit, cut off 801 vb. *impoverish*.

bequeath, will, will and bequeath, devise, demise; leave, make a bequest; make a will, put in one's will.

781. Giving – N. *giving*, bestowal, donation; alms-giving, charity 901 n. *philanthropy*; generosity 813 n. *liberality*; contribution, subscription to 703 n. *subvention*; presentation, award, 962 n. *reward*; endowment, donation, settlement 777 n. *dower*; grant, accordance, conferment; bequeathal.

gift, fairing, present; tip, gratuity 962 n. *reward*; token, consideration; prize, award, presentation 729 n. *trophy*; alms, dole, benefaction, charity 901 n. *philanthropy*; ex gratia payment; bounty, manna; largesse, donation, donative, hand-out; bonus, something extra, grant, allowance, subsidy 703 n. *subvention*; boon, grace, favour; labour of love 597 n. *voluntary work*; piece of luck, windfall; bequest, legacy 780 n. *transfer*.

offering, dedication, consecration; votive-offering, vow 979 n. *piety*; offertory, collection, sacrifice 981 n. *oblation*; widow's mite; contribution, subscription; tribute; ante, stake.

giver, donor, bestower; rewarder, tipper; grantor; awarder, prize-giver; settlor, testator, devisor; donator, subscriber, contributor; sacrificer 981 n. *worshipper*; tributary, tribute-payer 742 n. *subject*; almsgiver 903 n. *benefactor*; Lady Bountiful, Santa Claus, Father Christmas 813 n. *good giver*.

Adj. *giving*, granting etc. vb.; tributary 745 adj. *subject*; contributory 703 adj. *aiding*; alms-giving, charitable, eleemosynary 897 adj. *benevolent*; sacrificial, votive 981 adj. *worshipping*; generous, bountiful 813 adj. *liberal*.

given, bestowed, gifted; gratuitous, gratis 812 adj. *uncharged*; giveable, bestowable, concessional 756 adj. *permitted*.

Vb. *give*, bestow, lend, render; afford, provide; vouchsafe, favour with, honour w.; grant, accord 756 vb. *permit*; gift, donate, make a present of; leave, devise 780 vb. *bequeath*; present, award 962 vb. *reward*; confer, vest, invest with; dedicate 759 vb. *offer*; devote, offer up, sacrifice 981 vb. *offer worship*; gratify, tip, consider, remember; give freely, open one's hand 813 vb. *be liberal*; spare, give free, not charge; stand, treat 882 vb. *be hospitable*; contribute, subscribe, pay towards, subsidize 703 vb. *aid*; give up 621 vb. *relinquish*; hand over 780 vb. *convey*.

782. Receiving – N. *receiving*, admittance 299 n. *reception*; getting 771 n. *acquisition*; acceptance, assumption; collection, collectorship, receivership; a receipt, windfall 781 n. *gift*; toll, tribute, dues, receipts, proceeds 771 n. *earnings*; receiving end.

recipient, acceptor, taker, biter; trustee 754 n. *consignee*; addressee 588 n. *correspondent*; vendee 792 n. *purchaser*; transferee, donee, grantee, assignee, licensee, concessionnaire, lessee; inheritor, heir 776 n. *beneficiary*; payee, earner, stipendiary; pensioner, annuitant; winner, prize-w., almsman, bedesman.

receiver, official r., liquidator 798 n. *treasurer*; payee, collector, bill-c., rent-c., tax-c., tax-farmer, publican, exciseman, customs officer; rentier; oblationary.

Adj. *receiving*, receptive, welcoming; paid, stipendiary; pensionary, pensioned.

Vb. *receive*, be given, have from; get 771 vb. *acquire*; collect, take up, levy 786 vb. *take*; gross, net, pocket, pouch; accept 299 vb. *admit*; encash, draw; inherit, come into, come in for; receipt, acknowledge.

be received, be added unto 38 vb. *accrue*; come to hand, come in, roll in; stick to one's fingers, fall to one's share.

783. Apportionment – N. *apportionment*, assignment, allotment, allocation, appropriation; division, partition, sharing out; shares, fair s., distribution, deal; dispensation, administration.

portion, share, share-out, cut, split; dividend; allocation, allotment, budget a.; lot, contingent; proportion, ratio; quantum, quota; halves 53 n. *part*; deal, hand (at cards); dole, meed, modicum; ration, ration book; dose, dosage 53 n. *piece*; commission 810 n. *discount*.

Vb. *apportion*, allot, allocate, appropriate; assign; assign a part, cast; partition, zone; divide, divvy, carve up, split, cut; halve 92 vb. *bisect*; share out, distribute; dispense, portion out, dole out, parcel out; mete, measure, ration, dose.

784. Lending – N. *lending*, leasing, letting, subinfeudation; loan transaction, usury 802 n. *credit*; investment; mortgage; advance, imprest, loan, accommodation; pawnbroking; lease, let, sublet.

pawnshop, mont-de-piété, pop-shop, hock s.; house of credit, finance corporation.

lender, creditor; financier, banker, money-lender, usurer, shark; pawnbroker, uncle; mortgagee, lessor, hirer, renter; backer, angel.

Adj. *lending*, usurious, extortionate; lent, loaned, on credit.

Vb. *lend*, loan, put out at interest; advance, accommodate, allow credit 802 vb. *credit*; put up the money, back, finance.

lease, let, demise, hire out, farm out; sublet, subinfeudate.

785. Borrowing – N. *borrowing*, request for credit, loan application; loan transaction, mortgage 803 n. *debt*; hire purchase, never-never system; pledging pawning; loan, repayable amount, debenture 784 n. *lending*; infringement, plagiarism, copying 20 n. *imitation*.

Vb. *borrow*, touch for; mortgage, pawn, pledge, pop, hock; get credit, take on loan, take on tick; hire-purchase 792 vb. *purchase*; run into debt 803 vb. *be in debt*; promise to pay, float a loan; invite investment, accept deposits; beg, borrow, or steal; plagiarize, infringe 20 vb. *copy*.

hire, rent, farm, lease, take on lease, take on let, charter.

786. Taking – N. *taking*, seizure, capture, rape; grasp 778 n. *retention*; appropriation, assumption 916 n. *arrogation*; requisition, compulsory acquisition 771 n. *acquisition*; compulsory saving, postwar credit 785 n. *borrowing*; exaction, taxation, impost, levy 809 n. *tax*; recovery, retrieval, recoupment; resumption, re-entry; removal 188 n. *displacement*; conveyance 788 n. *stealing*; bodily removal, abduction, kidnapping, slave-raiding, body-snatching; take, haul, catch, capture, prize, plum 790 n. *booty*; receipts 771 n. *earnings*.

expropriation, dispossession, extortion, angary; forcible seizure, attachment, distraint, distress, foreclosure; eviction, expulsion 300 n. *ejection*; deprivation, divestment 752 n. *abrogation*; disinheritance 780 n. *transfer*; confiscation, capital levy; diversion, sequestration.

rapacity; rapaciousness, predacity; avidity, greed, insatiability 816 n. *avarice*; vampirism, blood-sucking; extortion, blackmail.

taker, appropriator; remover, conveyor; snatcher, grabber; raider, ransacker, sacker, looter, despoiler, depredator 789 n. *robber*; kidnapper, abductor, crimp, press-gang; slave-raider, slaver; captor; usurper; extortioner, blackmailer; locust 168 n. *destroyer*; bloodsucker, leech, parasite, vampire, harpy, vulture, wolf, shark; beast of prey, predator; sequestrator 782 n. *receiver*; expropriator, disseisor.

Adj. *taking*, prehensile 778 adj. *retentive*; abstractive; grasping, extortionate, rapacious, wolfish, lupine, vulturine; voracious 859 adj. *hungry*; raptorial, predatory 788 adj. *thieving*; expropriatory, confiscatory; possessive 771 adj. *acquiring*.

Vb. *take*, accept, be given 782 vb. *receive*; take to, bring, fetch 273 vb. *carry*; take in advance, anticipate 135 vb. *be early*; take hold 778 vb. *retain*; lay hands upon, seize, snatch, grab, pounce; snatch at, reach out for, make a long arm; grasp at, clutch at, grab at, scramble for, rush f.; capture, storm 727 vb. *overmaster*; apprehend, catch, nab, collar, lay by the heels 747 vb. *arrest*; hook, fish, angle, trap, snare, lime 542 vb. *ensnare*; net, land, bag, pocket, pouch; gross, have a turnover 771 vb. *acquire*; cull, pick, pluck; reap, crop, harvest, glean 370 vb. *cultivate*; scrounge, tot, pick over, ransack 459 vb. *search*; snap up, snaffle; draw off, milk, tap 304 vb. *extract*; withdraw (see *take away*).

appropriate, take to *or* for oneself, make one's own, spheterize, annex; stake one's claim; take over, assume ownership, impropriate 773 vb. *possess*; overrun, occupy, settle, colonize; take back, recover, resume 656 vb. *retrieve*; commandeer, requisition 737 vb. *demand*; nationalize, secularize 775 vb. *socialize*; usurp, arrogate, jump a claim, squat 916 vb. *be undue*; dispossess (see *deprive*);

treat as one's own, make free with; monopolize, engross, hog.

levy, raise, extort, exact, wrest from 304 vb. *extract*; make pay, lay under contribution, toll, take one's t.; raise taxes 809 vb. *tax*; wring, squeeze 735 vb. *oppress*.

take away, remove, withdraw; lift 701 vb. *disencumber*; convey, abstract, relieve of 788 vb. *steal*; remove bodily, escort 89 vb. *accompany*; kidnap, crimp, shanghai, press, abduct, ravish, carry off, bear off; run away with, elope w. 296 vb. *decamp*; loot, plunder 788 vb. *rob*.

deprive, bereave, orphan, widow; divest, unfrock, unthrone 752 vb. *depose*; dispossess, usurp 916 vb. *disentitle*; oust, evict 300 vb. *eject*; expropriate, confiscate, forfeit, sequestrate, distrain, attach, foreclose; disinherit, cut off.

fleece, pluck, skin, shear; strip bare 229 vb. *uncover*; blackmail, bleed white, sponge, suck dry; devour, eat out of house and home 301 vb. *eat*; take one's all, bankrupt 801 vb. *impoverish*.

787. Restitution – N. *restitution*, giving back, return; repatriation; reinstatement, rehabilitation 656 n. *restoration*; compensation, reparations, indemnification; repayment, refund, reimbursement; indemnity, damages 963 n. *penalty*; conscience money 941 n. *atonement*.

Adj. *restoring*, restitutory, indemnificatory, compensatory 941 adj. *atoning*.

Vb. *restitute*, make restitution, return, give back 656 vb. *restore*; disgorge 804 vb. *pay*; refund, repay, reimburse; indemnify, compensate; make reparation 941 vb. *atone*; bring back, repatriate; ransom, redeem 668 vb. *deliver*; reinstate, rehabilitate.

788. Stealing – N. *stealing*, theft, larceny; pick-pocketing, shop-lifting; burglary, house-breaking; robbery, highway r., gang r., dacoity, thuggee; stick-up, hold-up, smash and grab raid; cattle-lifting, rustling; abduction, kidnapping, slave-raiding; thievery, act of theft; job, fiddle.

brigandage, banditry, outlawry, predacity, piracy, buccaneering; raiding, raid, foray 712 n. *attack*.

spoliation, plundering, looting; direption, sack; depredation, rapine 165 n. *havoc*.

peculation, embezzlement, misappropriation, malversation, breach of trust, fraudulent conversion; fraud, fiddle, swindle 542 n. *deception*.

thievishness, thievery, light fingers, kleptomania; predacity 786 n. *rapacity*; dishonesty 930 n. *improbity*; burglarious intent; den of thieves, thieves' kitchen, Alsatia.

Adj. *thieving*, thievish, light-fingered; kleptomaniac; larcenous, burglarious; predatory, predacious, raptorial; piratical, buccaneering.

Vb. *steal*, lift, thieve, pilfer, shop-lift; burgle, house-break; rob, relieve of; rifle, sack; swipe, nobble, nick, pinch, bone, snaffle, knock off, annex 786 vb. *take*; forage, scrounge; lift cattle, rustle; abduct, kidnap, crimp, shanghai, press; abstract, convey, purloin, filch, spirit away; crib, copy, plagiarize, pirate 20 vb. *copy*; smuggle, run, poach, hijack.

defraud, embezzle, peculate, purloin; fiddle, swindle, cheat, diddle, chisel, do out of, bilk 542 vb. *deceive*; welsh, levant.

rob, rob with violence, hold up, stick up, raid; buccaneer, filibuster, pickeer, maraud; foray, forage, raid; sweep, ransack; plunder, pillage, loot, sack, despoil, depredate 165 vb. *lay waste*.

789. Thief – N. *thief*, thieving fraternity, den of thieves, Alsatia; stealer, lifter, filcher, pilferer; sneak thief, shop-lifter; pickpocket, cut-purse, bag-snatcher; cattle-lifter, rustler; burglar, house-breaker, cracksman, picklock, yegg; poacher, smuggler, runner; abductor, kidnapper, crimp 786 n. *taker*; slaver, slave-raider; fence, receiver; plagiarist, infringer.

robber, robber band, forty thieves; brigand, klepht; bush-ranger, bandit, outlaw; footpad, highwayman, road agent, hold-up man; thug, dacoit; sea-robber, sea-rover, Viking, pirate, buccaneer, corsair; reaver, marauder, raider, night-rider, freebooter; plunderer, pillager, sacker, ravager, spoiler, depredator; wrecker.

defrauder, embezzler, peculator, fiddler; defaulter, levanter, welsher, bilker; swindler, sharper 545 n. *deceiver*; forger, counterfeiter, coin-clipper.

790. Booty – N. *booty*, spoil, spoils 729 n. *trophy*; plunder, loot, pillage; capture, prize; hot money, stolen goods, swag, boodle; contraband; illicit gains, graft; spoils system, pork barrel 703 n. *subvention*.

791. Barter – N. *barter*, exchange, chop, swap 151 n. *interchange*; truck, truck system; traffic, trading, buying and selling, negotiation, bargaining, higgling, haggling, horse dealing.

trade, commercial intercourse; free trade, black market; market 796 n. *mart*; trading, traffic; capitalism, free economy, laisser faire; market economy, boom and bust 317 n. *fluctuation*; profit-making, mutual profit; commerce, business affairs 622 n. *business*; private enterprise, state e.; private sector, public s.; transaction, deal, bargain 765 n. *compact*.

Adj. *trading*, in trade; commercial, commercialistic, mercantile; mercantilist; marketable 793 adj. *saleable*.

Vb. *trade*, exchange 151 vb. *interchange*; barter, chop, swap, truck; traffic, merchandise; buy and sell, export and import; deal in, handle; commercialize, put on a business footing; trade with, do business w., deal w.

speculate, venture, risk 618 vb. *gamble*; invest, sink one's capital in, rig the market, racketeer, profiteer; play the market, operate, bull, bear, stag.

bargain, negotiate, chaffer; beat up, beat down; merchant, huckster, haggle, higgle 766 vb. *make terms*; bid for, make a take-over bid; raise the bid, outbid, overbid; ask for, charge 766 vb.

give terms; drive a bargain, do a deal, settle for, take.

792. Purchase – N. *purchase*, emption; co-emption, pre-emption; redemption, ransom 668 n. *deliverance*; purchase on credit, hire purchase, never-never system; buying, shopping, shopping spree 806 n. *expenditure*; regular buying, custom, patronage, demand 627 n. *requirement*; bid 759 n. *offer*; first refusal, option; a purchase, buy, bargain; purchases, shopping list.

purchaser, buyer, vendee, transferee, consignee; hire purchaser; marketer, shopper; customer, patron, client, clientèle, consumer; offerer, bidder; taker, acceptor; bargainer, haggler; ransomer, redeemer; share-buyer, bull, stag.

Adj. *buying*, co-emptive, pre-emptive, redemptive; bidding, bargaining, haggling; bullish.

Vb. *purchase*, make a p., pay for; buy, acquire by purchase 771 vb. *acquire*; shop, window-s., market, go shopping; get one's money's worth; buy on credit, hire-purchase; buy in 632 vb. *store*; buy up, pre-empt, regrate, corner; monopolize, engross; buy over, suborn 612 vb. *bribe*; buy back, redeem, ransom 668 vb. *deliver*; 785 vb. *hire*; bid for 759 vb. *offer*; buy shares, bull, stag.

793. Sale – N. *sale*, selling, vent; clearance, sell-out; clearance sale, summer s., bazaar; public sale, auction, roup, Dutch auction, American a.; good market, market for; salesmanship, service, sales talk; saleability, vendibility, marketability; vendible, seller, best s., selling line 795 n. *merchandise*.

seller, vendor; share-seller, bear; auctioneer, crier, rouper; huckster, hawker, monger 794 n. *pedlar*; shopman, dealer 633 n. *caterer*; wholesaler, retailer 794 n. *tradesman*; salesman, traveller, commercial t., commission agent, canvasser, tout; roundsman; shop-walker, counter-jumper; shop-assistant, sales woman.

Adj. *saleable*, vendible, marketable,

on sale; in demand, sold out; available, in the market, up for sale; bearish; on auction, under the hammer.

Vb. *sell*, vend, make a sale; flog, dispose of; market, put on sale, dump; hawk, peddle; canvass, tout; cater 633 vb. *provide*; auction, bring under the hammer, knock down to; regrate, wholesale; retail, sell over the counter; turn over 791 vb. *trade*; undercut 812 vb. *cheapen*; sell off, remainder; sell up 145 vb. *cease*; clear stock, hold a sale.

be sold, be on sale, sell, have a market, meet a demand, sell well, sell out.

794. Merchant – N. *merchant*, merchant prince, merchant adventurer; liveryman, livery company; guild, chamber of commerce, concern, firm 708 n. *corporation*; business man, trader, trafficker; importer, exporter; wholesaler, regrater; merchandiser, dealer, chandler; middleman, broker; stock-jobber, share-pusher; estate agent, realtor; financier, company promoter; banker 784 n. *lender*.

tradesman, tradespeople, tradesfolk; retailer, middleman, regrater, tallyman; shopkeeper, storekeeper, shopman, storesman 793 n. *seller*; monger 633 n. *caterer*.

pedlar, peddler 793 n. *seller*; stallkeeper, huckster, itinerant tradesman, street-seller, hawker, tinker, colporteur, bagman, chapman, cheapjack; coster, costermonger, barrow-boy; sutler, vivandière 633 n. *caterer*.

795. Merchandise – N. *merchandise*, article of commerce, line; article, commodity, vendible, stock, stock-in-trade, range 632 n. *store*; freight, cargo 193 n. *contents*; stuff, supplies, ware, goods, capital g., durables; consumer goods.

796. Mart – N. *mart*, market; open market, free m.; black market, grey m.; market-place, staple, forum, agora; auction room, fair, motor show; exhibition, exposition, shop-window; exchange, stock e., bourse, kerb-market.

emporium, free port, entrepôt, depot,

warehouse 632 n. *storage*; trading centre, trading post; general market, bazaar, arcade, supermarket, shopping centre.

shop, retailer's; store, multiple s., department s., chain s.; emporium, bazaar, supermarket; concern, establishment, house, trading h.; stall, booth, stand, newsstand, kiosk, barrow; counter, bargain c.; shop-floor, shop-window; premises, place of business 687 n. *workshop*.

797. Money – N. *money*, numismatics, chrysology; lucre, pelf, Mammon 800 n. *wealth*; medium of exchange, currency, sound c., honest money; money of account; precious metal, gold, silver; ready money, the ready, the best, blunt, cash, spot c., hard c.; change, small c., coppers; pocket money, pin m.

dibs, shekels, spondulics, brass, tin, dough, lolly; 'ackers, oof, boodle; palm oil, palm grease.

funds, temporary f., hot money; liquidity, account, bank a.; wherewithal, the needful 629 n. *means*; sinews of war, financial provision, cash supplies, treasure 633 n. *provision*; funds for investment, capital; reserves, balances; fiver, tenner, pony, monkey, grand; money-bags, purse.

finance, high f., financial world, the City; financial control, money power, purse-strings, power of the purse, almighty dollar; money dealings, cash transaction; money market, exchange; exchange rate, valuta, parity, par 28 n. *equality*; devaluation, depreciation, falling exchange 655 n. *deterioration*; bi-metallism; gold standard; managed currency, equalization fund; deficit finance, inflation, spiral; disinflation, deflation.

coinage, minting, issue; metallic currency, stamped coinage, decimal c.; specie, coin, coin of the realm; monetary unit, monetary denomination, guinea, sovereign, pound, quid, shiner, chip; crown, cartwheel; shilling, bob; sixpence, tanner; shell money, cowrie, wampum.

paper money, fiat m., fiduciary currency, assignat, shinplaster; note, banknote, treasury note, smacker; bill, dollar b., greenback, buck, ten-dollar bill, sawbuck; bill of exchange, exchequer bill, negotiable instrument; draft, sight d., order, money o., postal o., check, cheque, traveller's c., letter of credit; promissory note, note of hand.

false money, bad m., counterfeit m., base coin, snide, rap; forged note, flash n., slip, kite; dud cheque; clipped coinage, depreciated currency, devalued c.

bullion, bar, gold b., ingot, nugget; solid gold, solid silver; precious metal, yellow m., platinum, gold, white g., electrum, silver, billon.

moneyer, minter, mint master; numismatist; coiner, forger, penman; bullionist; bullioner, money-dealer, money-changer, cambist 794 n. *merchant*; cashier 798 n. *treasurer*; financier, capitalist; moneyed man 800 n. *rich man*.

Adj. *monetary*, numismatical, chrysological; pecuniary, financial, fiscal, budgetary, sumptuary; nummary, fiduciary; gold-based, sterling, inflationary, deflationary; withdrawn, demonetized; touching the pocket, crumenal.

Vb. *mint*, coin, stamp; monetize, issue, circulate; pass, utter; forge, counterfeit.

demonetize, withdraw, call in; clip, debase the coinage; devalue, depreciate, inflate 812 vb. *cheapen*.

798. Treasurer – N. *treasurer*, purse-bearer, bursar, purser, quaestor; cashier, teller, croupier; stakeholder, pawnee, pledgee, trustee, steward 754 n. *consignee*; liquidator 782 n. *receiver*; book-keeper 808 n. *accountant*; banker; paymaster, almoner, budgeteer, mint master 797 n. *moneyer*.

799. Treasury – N. *treasury*, treasure-house, thesaurus; exchequer, fisc, public purse, pork barrel; counting-house, custom-house; bursary, almonry; bank; coffer, treasure chest; strong room, strong box, safe, safe deposit, cash box, money-box, stocking; till, cash register, cash desk, slot-machine; receipt of custom, box office, gate, turnstile; purse, wallet, bill-fold.

800. Wealth – N. *wealth*, Mammon, lucre, pelf, tin, moneybags 797 n. *money*; money-making, golden touch, Midas t.; riches, luxury; opulence, affluence 730 n. *prosperity*; solidity, substance 3 n. *substantiality*; independence, competence 635 n. *sufficiency*; high income, super-tax bracket; resources, long purse, bottomless p., capital 629 n. *means*; tidy sum, pile, scads, wad, packet 32 n. *great quantity*; fortune, handsome f., ample endowment, great possessions 777 n. *property*; bonanza, mine, gold-m. 632 n. *store*; El Dorado.

rich man, man of means; money-baron, nabob, moneybags, millionaire; Croesus, Midas, Dives, Plutus; money-maker, money-spinner, capitalist, plutocrat; the haves, moneyed class, jeunesse dorée; new rich, nouveau riche, parvenu 730 n. *made man*; plutocracy, timocracy.

Adj. *rich*, fat, fertile 164 adj. *productive*; luxurious, upholstered, plush, plushy, ritzy, slap-up; diamond-studded 875 adj. *ostentatious*; wealthy, blest with this world's goods, opulent, affluent 730 adj. *prosperous*; well-off, well-to-do, warm, well-feathered, over-paid 376 adj. *comfortable*.

moneyed, monied, worth a lot, made of money; high-income, millionaire; in funds, in cash, in credit, on the right side; tinny, well-heeled, flush; credit-worthy, solvent.

Vb. *afford*, have the means, be able to pay, be solvent, make both ends meet, keep up with the Joneses.

get rich, come into money 771 vb. *inherit*; enrich oneself, make money, mint m., coin m., spin m., make a fortune, feather one's nest, line one's pocket, strike oil 771 vb. *gain*.

801. Poverty – N. *poverty*, Lady Poverty 945 n. *asceticism*; poorness, meagreness 645 n. *badness*; impecuniosity, hardup-

ness, Queer Street 805 n. *insolvency*; impoverishment, beggary, mendicancy; penury, pennilessness, pauperism, destitution; indigence, neediness 627 n. *requirement*; slender means, reduced circumstances, low water 636 n. *insufficiency*; grinding poverty, subsistence level; seediness, beggarliness, raggedness, shreds and tatters; slump, depression 655 n. *deterioration*; squalor, slum, back street 655 n. *dilapidation*.

poor man, broken man, bankrupt, insolvent 805 n. *non-payer*; pauper, indigent, mendicant, beggarman 763 n. *beggar*; slum-dweller 869 n. *rabble*; the have-nots, the under-privileged; Cinderella 867 n. *object of scorn*.

Adj. *poor*, not well-off, badly o., not blest with this world's goods; hard up, impecunious; broke, stony b., bankrupt, insolvent 805 adj. *non-paying*; penurious, poverty-stricken; needy, indigent, in want 627 adj. *necessitous*; dowerless, portionless; penniless, moneyless, destitute; down to one's last penny, without a bean; poor in quality 645 adj. *bad*.

beggarly, starveling, seedy, down at heel, down and out, barefoot, threadbare, tatty 655 adj. *dilapidated*; scuffy, squalid, slummy, back-street 649 adj. *dirty*; poverty-stricken, poor as a church mouse.

Vb. *impoverish*, reduce to poverty, leave destitute, beggar, pauperize; ruin, cripple; rob, strip 786 vb. *fleece*; dispossess, disinherit, disendow, cut off with a shilling 786 vb. *deprive*.

802. Credit – N. *credit*, repute 866 n. *prestige*; credit-worthiness, reliability 929 n. *probity*; borrowing capacity, limit of credit; line of credit, tick; credit account, right side; credits, balances, credit balance 807 n. *receipt*; unpaid bill, account 808 n. *accounts*; sum voted, vote.

creditor, mortgagee, pledgee, pawnee 784 n. *lender*; depositor, investor.

Vb. *credit*, extend c., forgo repayment, grant a loan 784 vb. *lend*; place to one's credit, credit one's account; grant, vote;

take credit, open an account, run up a bill 785 vb. *borrow.*

803. Debt – N. *debt,* indebtedness 785 n. *borrowing*; liability, obligation, commitment; encumbrance, mortgage 767 n. *security*; something owing, debit, charge; debts, bills; promise to pay, debt of honour 764 n. *promise*; bad debt, write-off 772 n. *loss*; account owing, deficit, overdraft; inability to pay 805 n. *insolvency*; frozen balance, blocked account 805 n. *non-payment*; deferred payment 802 n. *credit*; arrears, no more credit, foreclosure.

interest, simple i., compound i.; usury, pound of flesh 784 n. *lending*; rate of interest, bank rate.

debtor, debitor; loanee, borrower; obligor, drawee; mortgagor, pledgor; bad debtor, defaulter 805 n. *non-payer.*

Adj. *indebted,* in debt, debt-ridden; debited, liable; owing, overdrawn, in the red, minus; encumbered, mortgaged; defaulting, involvent 805 adj. *non-paying.*

owed, unpaid, owing, due, overdue, in arrear; outstanding, unbalanced; chargeable, payable, debited, repayable; bearing, payable on delivery.

Vb. *be in debt,* owe, owe money, pay interest; get credit, overdraw (one's account); go on tick 785 vb. *borrow*; live on credit, run up an account, run into debt; bilk, welsh, levant 805 vb. *not pay.*

804. Payment – N. *payment,* defrayment; discharge, quittance, liquidation, clearance, settlement; receipt in full 807 n. *receipt*; cash payment, down p.; first payment, earnest, deposit, instalment; deferred payment, hire purchase 785 n. *borrowing*; payment in lieu, composition; repayment, compensation, indemnity 787 n. *restitution*; disbursement, remittance 806 n. *expenditure.*

pay, pay-out, pay-off, pay packet; pay day, wages bill 771 n. *earnings*; grant-in-aid, subsidy 703 n. *subvention*; salary, pension, annuity, remuneration, emolu-ment, fee, bribe 962 n. *reward*; brokerage 810 n. *discount*; something paid, contribution, subscription, collection, tribute 809 n. *tax*; compensation, golden handshake; payer, paymaster 798 n. *treasurer.*

Adj. *paying,* disbursing 806 adj. *expending*; out of debt, owing nothing.

Vb. *pay,* disburse 806 vb. *expend*; pay towards, contribute 781 vb. *give*; pay in kind, barter 791 vb. *trade*; make payment, pay out, shell o., fork o., stump up, cough up; come across, open one's purse; pay back, disgorge, repay, reimburse, compensate 787 vb. *restitute*; gratify, tip 612 vb. *bribe*; remunerate, wage 962 vb. *reward*; pay on the nail, pay down; meet, honour (a bill), pay up, redeem, get a receipt; clear, liquidate, settle 808 vb. *account*; settle a score, pay one out 714 vb. *retaliate.*

defray, pay for, bear the cost; foot the bill, pay the piper; pay sauce for all, stand treat 781 vb. *give.*

805. Non-payment – N. *non-payment,* default; defalcation 930 n. *improbity*; stoppage, deduction 963 n. *penalty*; moratorium, embargo, freeze; dishonouring, protest, repudiation 760 n. *refusal*; forgiveness of debts, seisachtheia 752 n. *abrogation*; waste paper bonds, protested bill, dishonoured cheque, dud c.

insolvency, inability to pay, crash, failure; failure of credit, run on a bank; bankruptcy; overdrawn account, overdraft 636 n. *insufficiency.*

non-payer, defaulter; defalcator, embezzler 789 n. *defrauder*; bilker, welsher, levanter; bankrupt, insolvent debtor.

Adj. *non-paying,* defaulting, behindhand, in arrear; insolvent, bankrupt, gazetted; beggared, ruined 801 adj. *poor.*

Vb. *not pay,* default, embezzle 788 vb. *defraud*; fall into arrears; stop payment, freeze, block; protest a bill; divert, sequester 786 vb. *deprive*; bounce one's cheque, dishonour, repudiate; go bankrupt, fail, break, go bust, crash, go into liquidation; welsh, bilk, levant.

806. Expenditure – N. *expenditure*, disbursement 804 n. *payment*; outgoings, costs, expenses; expense, outlay, investment; dissaving, disinvestment, run on savings; extravagance, spending spree 815 n. *prodigality*.

Adj. *expending*, spending, sumptuary; generous 813 adj. *liberal*; extravagant 815 adj. *prodigal*; out of pocket, lighter in one's purse.

Vb. *expend*, spend; shop, buy 792 vb. *purchase*; lay out, invest, sink money; be out of pocket, incur costs; meet charges, disburse 804 vb. *pay*; run down one's account, dissave, disinvest, unhoard; donate 781 vb. *give*; spare no expense 813 vb. *be liberal*; use up, consume, run through 634 vb. *waste*.

807. Receipt – N. *receipt*, accountable r., voucher, acknowledgement; money received, credits, revenue, royalty, rents, rent-roll, dues; turnover, takings, proceeds, returns, receipts, box office, gate-money, gate; income, privy purse; emolument, pay, salary, wages 771 n. *earnings*; remuneration 962 n. *reward*; pension, annuity; allowance, pocket-money, pin-m.; pittance; alimony, maintenance; exhibition, sizarship, perquisite 771 n. *acquisition*; rake-off 810 n. *discount*; interest, return; winnings, profits 771 n. *gain*; bonus, premium 40 n. *extra*; legacy 777 n. *dower*.

Adj. *received*, paid, receipted.

Vb. see 771 vb. *acquire*, 782 vb. *receive, be received*, 786 vb. *take*.

808. Accounts – N. *accounts*, accountancy, commercial arithmetic; bookkeeping, entry, double e., single e.; audit, inspection of accounts; account, profit and loss a., balance sheet, debit and credit; budgeting, budget, budget estimates 633 n. *provision*; running account, current a., suspense a., expense a.; account rendered, statement, bill, invoice, manifest 87 n. *list*; computation, score, tally, facts and figures 86 n. *numeration*.

account book, pass b., cheque b.; cash book, day-b., cost-b., journal, ledger, register, books 548 n. *record*.

accountant, chartered a., certified public a.; bookkeeper, storekeeper; accounting party, cashier 798 n. *treasurer*; auditor; actuary, statistician.

Adj. *accounting*, actuarial, inventorial, budgetary; accountable.

Vb. *account*, keep the books, keep the cash; budget; cost, value, write up, write down 480 vb. *estimate*; book, bring to book, enter, journalize, post, carry over, debit, credit 548 vb. *register*; prepare a balance sheet, balance accounts, finalize a.; present an account, charge, bill, invoice; cook the accounts, fiddle 788 vb. *defraud*; audit, go through the books; take stock 87 vb. *list*.

809. Price – *price*, selling p., world p., market p., standard p., list p., price current; rate, rate for the job; high rate 811 n. *dearness*; low rate 812 n. *cheapness*; price control, fixed price 747 n. *restraint*; value, face v., fair v., worth, money's w., what it will fetch; price list, tariff; quoted price, quotation; demand, charge; surcharge, supplement 40 n. *extra*; overcharge, extortion; fare, hire, rental, rent; charges, freightage, wharfage, lighterage; salvage; bill, invoice, reckoning, shot.

cost, purchase price; damage, costs, expenses 806 n. *expenditure*; running costs, overheads; wages, wage bill; damages 963 n. *penalty*; cost of living, cost of living index.

tax, taxes, dues; taxation, tax demand 737 n. *demand*; rating, assessment 480 n. *estimate*; cess, rate; levy, toll, duty; imposition, impost; exaction, compulsory savings, post-war credits; punitive tax, collective t. 963 n. *penalty*; tribute, danegeld, blackmail, ransom 804 n. *payment*; Peter's pence, tithe, tenths; poll tax, capitation t.; property tax, schedule A, death duty; direct taxation, income tax, surtax, super-tax; capital levy, capital gains tax 786 n. *expropriation*; indirect taxation, excise, customs, tariff; local tax, octroi; purchase tax, sales t.

Adj. *priced*, charged; chargeable, leviable, taxable, assessable, rateable, customable, dutiable, excisable; ad valorem; to the tune of, for the price of.

Vb. *price*, cost, assess, value, rate 480 vb. *estimate*; set a price on, fix a price for; ask a price, charge 737 vb. *demand*; bill, invoice.

cost, be worth, fetch; amount to, come to; bear a price, have its p.; sell for, go f.

tax, lay a tax on, fix a tariff, levy a rate, toll, excise, subject to duty; raise taxes 786 vb. *levy*.

810. Discount – N. *discount*, something off, reduction, rebate, cut 42 n. *decrement*; deduction; concession, allowance, margin, special price; tare, rate and tret; drawback, rebatement, backwardation; cut price 812 n. *cheapness*; poundage, percentage, brokerage; something for oneself, rake-off.

Vb. *discount*, deduct 39 vb. *subtract*; allow a margin, tare; abate, rebate 37 vb. *bate*; mark down 812 vb. *cheapen*; get one's rake-off; take one's percentage.

811. Dearness – N. *dearness*, costliness, expensiveness; value, high worth, pricelessness; famine price, scarcity value 636 n. *scarcity*; exorbitance, extortion, overcharge, bad value; high price, fancy p., luxury p.; cost, heavy c., pretty penny; Pyrrhic victory, white elephant; tax on one's pocket, rising costs, inflation, inflationary pressure.

Adj. *dear*, high-priced, expensive, ritzy; costly, multimillion; extravagant, dear-bought, Pyrrhic; dear at the price, overpriced, overpaid; exorbitant, excessive, extortionate; beyond one's means, not affordable, prohibitive.

of price, 644 adj. *valuable*; priceless, beyond price, above p.; unpayable; inestimable, precious.

Vb. *be dear*, cost much; rise in price, harden; go up, appreciate, soar, mount, climb; price itself out of the market.

overcharge, overprice, ask too much;

profiteer, soak, sting, bleed, skin, extort, rack-rent, hold to ransom 786 vb. *fleece*.

812. Cheapness – N. *cheapness*, inexpensiveness, affordability; good value, value for money, bargain; reasonable charge, reasonableness; nominal price, reduced p., sale p., sacrificial p.; peppercorn rent, easy terms; falling prices, bearishness, depreciation, fall, slump, deflation; glut 635 n. *plenty*.

no charge, nominal c. 781 n. *gift*; gratuitousness, labour of love 597 n. *voluntary work*; everything for nothing.

Adj. *cheap*, inexpensive, moderate, reasonable, fair; affordable, within one's means; economical, economy size; worth its price, low-priced, dirt-cheap; bargain-rate, cut-price, concessional, half-price; easy to buy, two-a-penny; worth nothing, cheap and nasty 641 adj. *useless*; unsaleable, unmarketable; underpaid, underpriced.

uncharged, gratuitous, complimentary; gratis, for nothing; free, scot-f., free of cost; untaxed, tax-free, rent-f., post-f., unpaid, honorary 597 adj. *voluntary*.

Vb. *be cheap*, — inexpensive etc. adj.; cost nothing, be had for the asking; cheapen, fall in price, depreciate, come down.

cheapen, lower the price, price low, mark down, cut, slash; undercharge, let go for a song, sacrifice, give away 781 vb. *give*; beat down, undercut, undersell, dump.

813. Liberality – N. *liberality*; liberalness, bounteousness, bountifulness, munificence, generosity 931 n. *disinterestedness*; open-handedness, open house 882 n. *sociability*; lavishness 815 n. *prodigality*; bounty, largesse 781 n. *gift*; handsome offer 759 n. *offer*; benefaction, charity 897 n. *kind act*.

good giver, princely g., liberal donor; good spender, good tipper; Lady Bountiful, Father Christmas, Santa Claus, rich uncle 903 n. *benefactor*.

Adj. *liberal*, free, freely spending, lavish 815 adj. *prodigal*; large-hearted

931 adj. *disinterested*; bountiful, charitable 897 adj. *benevolent*; hospitable 882 adj. *sociable*; handsome, generous, munificent; lordly, princely, royal 868 adj. *noble*; ungrudging, unstinting, unsparing; ample, bounteous, profuse 635 adj. *plenteous*.

Vb. *be liberal*, — generous etc. adj.; lavish, shower largesse 781 vb. *give*; give with both hands, give till it hurts 897 vb. *philanthropize*; overpay, tip well; keep open house 882 vb. *be hospitable*; do it proud, spare no expense, spend freely 815 vb. *be prodigal*.

814. Economy – N. *economy*, thrift, thriftiness, frugality; carefulness, husbandry, good housekeeping, good housewifery, sound stewardship; economy drive, sumptuary law, credit squeeze 747 n. *restriction*; time-saving, labour-s., time and motion study; economizing, cheese-paring; retrenchment, economies, savings; economizer, save-all 816 n. *niggard*.

Adj. *economical*, time-saving, labour-s., money-s., cost-reducing; money-conscious 816 adj. *parsimonious*; thrifty, frugal; unlavish, meagre; marginal, with nothing to spare.

Vb. *economize*, keep costs down, waste nothing; keep within one's budget, cut one's coat according to one's cloth, make both ends meet; make economies, retrench; save 632 vb. *store*; plough back, make every penny work.

815. Prodigality – N. *prodigality*, lavishness, profusion 637 n. *redundance*; extravagance, wastefulness, dissipation, squandermania, spending spree 634 n. *waste*; unthriftiness, uneconomy, deficit finance.

prodigal, prodigal son, spender, waster, spendthrift, squanderer, squandermaniac.

Adj. *prodigal*, lavish 813 adj. *liberal*; profuse, overlavish; extravagant, regardless of cost; unthrifty, thriftless, spendthrift, improvident.

Vb. *be prodigal*, squander 634 vb. *waste*; go the pace, go a bust, blow; overspend, spend money like water, spend to the last farthing, blow everything, play ducks and drakes; fritter away, gamble a., dissipate; not count the cost, misspend; throw good money after bad.

816. Parsimony – N. *parsimony*, parsimoniousness; credit squeeze 814 n. *economy*; false economy, policy of penny wise and pound foolish; cheeseparing, niggardliness, meanness, minginess, stinginess, miserliness; illiberality, grudging hand.

avarice, cupidity, acquisitiveness, possessiveness, monopoly; money-grubbing, rapacity, avidity, greed 859 n. *desire*; mercenariness, venality, hireling character.

niggard, skinflint, screw, scrimp, tightwad, no tipper; miser, money-grubber, lickpenny; save-all, hoarder; usurer 784 n. *lender*.

Adj. *parsimonious*, penurious 814 adj. *economical*; money-conscious, pennywise, miserly, mean, mingy, stingy, near, close, tight; tight-fisted, close-f.; grudging, illiberal, empty-handed, giftless; pinching, scraping.

avaricious, grasping, monopolistic 932 adj. *selfish*; possessive, acquisitive; miserly, money-conscious, covetous 859 adj. *greedy*; usurious, rapacious, extortionate; mercenary, venal.

Vb. *be parsimonious*, — niggardly etc. adj.; grudge, begrudge 760 vb. *refuse*; dole out, stint, skimp, starve 636 vb. *make insufficient*; scrape, pinch, screw, rack-rent, skin a flint 786 vb. *fleece*; be penny-wise, spoil the ship for a ha'porth of tar, stop one hole in a sieve; cadge, beg, borrow; hoard, sit on.

Class Six

AFFECTIONS

Section 1: Affections Generally

817. Affections – **N.** *affections*, qualities, instincts; passions, emotional life; nature, disposition 5 n. *character*; spirit, temper, tone 5 n. *temperament*; personality, psychology, mental and spiritual make-up 5 n. *heredity*; being, breast, bosom, heart, soul, inner man 5 n. *essential part*; animus, attitude, frame of mind, vein, strain, humour, mood; predilection, predisposition 179 n. *tendency*; passion, ruling p. 481 n. *prejudice*.

Adj. *with affections*, affected, characterized, moulded, tempered, inborn, inbred, congenital 5 adj. *genetic*; emotional 818 adj. *feeling*.

818. Feeling – **N.** *feeling*, experience, emotional life; sentience, sensation, sense of 374 n. *sense*; sensory perception, sense p. 378 n. *touch*; relish, gusto 386 n. *taste*; emotion, sentiment; impulse 609 n. *spontaneity*; responsiveness, response, reaction, fellow-feeling, sympathy, involvement 880 n. *friendliness*; realization, understanding 490 n. *knowledge*; impression 819 n. *moral sensibility*; finer feelings 897 n. *benevolence*; hard feelings 891 n. *resentment*; thrill, kick 318 n. *spasm*; pathos 825 n. *suffering*; animus, emotionality, emotionalism, affectivity 822 n. *excitability*; demonstration, demonstrativeness; expression, play of feature 547 n. *gesture*; tremor, quiver, flutter, palpitation 318 n. *agitation*.

warm feeling, cordiality, empressement, effusiveness, heartiness; hot head, impatience; unction, earnestness 834 n. *seriousness*; eagerness, fervour, ardour, vehemence, enthusiasm, dash, fire 174 n. *vigorousness*; fanaticism, mania 481 n. *prejudice*; emotion, passion, ecstasy 822 n. *excitable state*.

Adj. *feeling*, affective, sensible, sensorial, sensory 374 adj. *sentient*; vivacious, lively 819 adj. *sensitive*; sensuous 944 adj. *sensual*; experiencing, living; enduring 825 adj. *suffering*; responsive, involved, sympathetic 775 adj. *sharing*; emotional, passionate, unctuous, soulful; cordial, hearty, gushing, effusive; sentimental, romantic; mawkish.

fervent, fervid, perfervid, passionate, tense, intense; eager, breathless, impassioned, earnest; hot-headed, impetuous 822 adj. *excitable*; warm, fiery 379 n. *hot*; hysterical, delirious, overwrought, feverish, hectic 503 adj. *frenzied*; strong, uncontrollable 176 adj. *violent*.

felt, experienced, lived; heartfelt, cordial, hearty, sincere; deeply-felt, profound; emotive, impressive, overwhelming 821 adj. *impressive*; penetrating, absorbing; thrilling, rapturous, ecstatic 826 adj. *pleasurable*; pathetic, affecting 827 adj. *distressing*.

Vb. *feel*, sense; entertain, feel deeply, take to heart; know the feeling, experience, live, live through, got., taste, prove; bear, endure, undergo, smart under 825 vb. *suffer*; sympathize, condole 775 vb. *participate*; respond, react, warm to, kindle, catch.

show feeling, show signs of emotion; demonstrate, not hide one's feelings 522 vb. *manifest*; go into ecstasies 824 vb. *be pleased*; turn colour, look blue, look black; blench; colour, blush, flush; quiver, wince; flutter 318 vb. *be agitated*; tingle, thrill, throb.

Adv. *feelingly*, unctuously, earnestly, con amore, heart and soul; devoutly, sincerely, from the bottom of one's heart.

819. Sensibility – **N.** *moral sensibility*, sensitivity, sensitiveness; touchiness 892 n. *irascibility*; raw feelings, tender spot, quick; sore point, where the shoe pinches 891 n. *resentment*; impressibility, affectibility, susceptibility; finer feelings, sentimentality, sentimentalism; tenderness 887 n. *love*; spirit, vivacity, liveliness, verve 571 n. *vigour*; emotionalism 822 n. *excitability*; fastidiousness, aestheticism 463 n. *discrimination*; temperament, mobility, changeability 152 n. *changeableness*; physical sensitivity, allergy 374 n. *sensibility*; touchy person, sensitive plant, mass of nerves.

Adj. *impressible*, malleable, plastic 327 adj. *soft*; sensible, aware, conscious of, awake to, alive to, responsive 374 adj. *sentient*; persuasible, impressionable 822 adj. *excitable*; susceptible; romantic, sentimental; emotional, warm-hearted; tender, compassionate 905 adj. *pitying*.

sensitive, sensitized; tingling, sore, raw, tender, allergic; aesthetic, fastidious 463 adj. *discriminating*; oversensitive, all feeling 822 adj. *excitable*; touchy, thin-skinned 892 adj. *irascible*.

lively, alive, vital, vivacious, animated; gamesome, skittish; irrepressible, ebullient, effervescent; mettlesome, spirited; alert, aware 455 adj. *attentive*; nervous, highly-strung, temperamental; mobile, changeable; enthusiastic.

Adv. *on the raw*, to the quick, where the shoe pinches, where it hurts most.

820. Insensibility – N. *moral insensibility*, insentience, numbness, stupor 375 n. *insensibility*; lethargy 679 n. *inactivity*; quietism, stagnation, vegetation 266 n. *quiescence*; slowness, delayed reaction; uninterest 454 n. *incuriosity*; nonchalance, insouciance 860 n. *indifference*; no nerves, phlegm 823 n. *inexcitability*; no feelings, aloofness, impassivity, poker-face, dead pan; insensitivity, coarseness, Philistinism 699 n. *artlessness*; imperception, thick skin, rhinoceros hide; cold heart, frigidity; unimpressibility, dourness; unsentimentality, cynicism.

unfeeling person, iceberg, icicle, cold fish, cold heart, cold-blooded animal; stoic, ascetic; stock, stone, block, marble.

Adj. *impassive*, unconscious 375 adj. *insensible*; unsusceptible, insensitive, unimaginative; unresponsive, unimpressionable 823 adj. *inexcitable*; phlegmatic, stolid; wooden, blockish; dull, slow 499 adj. *unintelligent*; unemotional, passionless, proof against, steeled a.; stoical, ascetic; unconcerned, aloof 860 adj. *indifferent*; unaffected, steady, unruffled, unshaken, unshocked; imperturbable, cool; inscrutable, blank, expressionless, dead-pan, poker-faced; unsentimental, cynical; impersonal, dispassionate, frigid; unfeeling, heartless, soulless, inhuman; unsmitten, heart-free, fancy-f., heart-whole; unloving, unaffectionate, undemonstrative.

apathetic, unenthusiastic, unambitious; unimpassioned, uninspired, unmoved, unstirred; half-hearted 860 adj. *indifferent*; uninterested 454 adj. *incurious*; nonchalant, insouciant; spiritless, lackadaisical; lotus-eating, vegetative 266 adj. *quiescent*; sluggish, supine 679 adj. *inactive*; cloyed 863 adj. *sated*; torpid 375 adj. *insensible*.

thick-skinned, pachydermatous; impenetrable, impervious; blind to, deaf to, dead to; obtuse, unimaginative, insensitive; callous, insensate, tough, hardened 326 adj. *hard*; shameless, unblushing.

Vb. *make insensitive*, benumb 375 vb. *render insensible*; steel, toughen 326 vb. *harden*; sear, dry up 342 vb. *dry*; deafen 399 vb. *silence*; brutalize 655 vb. *pervert*; stale, coarsen 847 vb. *vulgarize*; satiate, cloy 863 vb. *sate*; deaden, obtund, take the edge off 257 vb. *blunt*.

821. Excitation – N. *excitation*, galvanization, galvanism, electrification 174 n. *stimulation*; possession, inspiration, afflatus, exhilaration, intoxication, headiness; encouragement, animation, incitement 612 n. *inducement*; provocation, irritation, casus belli; impact 178 n. *influence*; fascination 983 n. *sorcery*; rapture, ravishment 824 n. *joy*; emotional appeal, human interest, sentiment, sentimentalism, sob-stuff, pathos; sensationalism, melodrama; excitement 822 n. *excitable state*; shock, thrill 318 n. *spasm*; climax, pitch of excitement 503 n. *frenzy*; fuss, drama; temper, fury, rage 891 n. *anger*.

excitant, stimulator, agent-provocateur, rabble-rouser, tub-thumper 738 n. *agitator*; sensationalist, scandal-monger; headline 528 n. *publicity*; fillip, ginger, tonic, pick-me-up 174 n. *stimulant*; sting, prick, goad, spur, whip, lash 612 n. *incentive*; fan; irritant, gadfly.

Adj. *excited* 822 adj. *excitable*.

exciting, stimulating, sparkling, intoxicating, heady, exhilarating; provocative, piquant, tantalizing; evocative, suggestive; sensational, dramatic, melodramatic, interesting, gripping.

impressive, imposing, grand, stately; dignified, majestic, regal, royal, kingly, queenly 868 adj. *noble*; awe-inspiring, soul-subduing, sublime, humbling; overwhelming, overpowering; picturesque, scenic; dramatic; telling, forceful 178 adj. *influential*.

Vb. *excite*, affect, infect 178 vb. *influence*; touch, move, impassion, quicken; arouse, startle, electrify, galvanize; warm, raise the temperature 381 vb. *heat*; enflame, enkindle, sting, pique, irritate 891 vb. *enrage*; tantalize, tease 827 vb. *torment*; touch on the raw, cut to the quick; enthuse, inspire, possess; stir, rouse (see *animate*); evoke, summon up, call forth; thrill, exhilarate, intoxicate; transport 826 vb. *delight*.

animate, vivify, enliven, quicken 360 vb. *vitalize*; revive, rekindle, resuscitate, breathe fresh life into 656 vb. *restore*; inspire, inspirit 855 vb. *give courage*; urge, nag, spur, goad, lash; stimulate, ginger 174 vb. *invigorate*; intensify, fan 832 vb. *aggravate*.

impress, sink in, leave an impression; project *or* present an image; interest, hold, grip, absorb; intrigue, strike 455 vb. *attract notice*; affect 178 vb. *influence*; bring home to, drive home 532 vb. *emphasize*; make one realize, penetrate 516 vb. *be intelligible*; arrest, shake, stun, stagger 508 vb. *surprise*; sensation-

alize, stupefy 864 vb. *be wonderful*; dazzle; inspire with awe, humble; overwhelm 727 vb. *overmaster*.

822. Excitability – N. *excitability*, excitableness, explosiveness, inflammability; instability, temperament, emotionalism; hot blood, irritability 892 n. *irascibility*; impatience, incontinence; passionateness, impetuosity, recklessness 857 n. *rashness*; hastiness 680 n. *haste*.

excitable state, exhilaration, elevation, intoxication, abandon; thrill, transport, ecstasy; fever, fret, fume, whirl 318 n. *agitation*; warmth 379 n. *heat*; ferment, stew; turbulence, boisterousness; effervescence, ebullition, outburst, outbreak, explosion, scene 318 n. *commotion*; brainstorm, hysterics, delirium, agony 503 n. *frenzy*; distraction, madness 503 n. *insanity*; rage, fury; rampage 891 n. *anger*.

Adj. *excitable*, over-sensitive 819 adj. *sensitive*; passionate, emotional; out for thrills, agog with; inflammable, like tinder; unstable, impressionable; temperamental, mercurial, volatile 152 adj. *changeful*; restless, unquiet, a-tremble, a-quiver, a-twitter; nervy, fidgety, edgy 318 adj. *agitated*; highly-strung, overwrought; nervous, skittish, mettlesome 819 adj. *lively*; irritable, fiery 892 adj. *irascible*; impatient; impetuous, impulsive 857 adj. *rash*; restive, uncontrollable; effervescent, seething; volcanic, explosive; feverish, febrile, hectic, frantic, hysterical 503 adj. *frenzied*; beside oneself; tense, electric, atmospheric; raving, lyrical.

Vb. *be excitable*, fret, fume, stamp; dance, shuffle; have nerves, flap 318 vb. *be agitated*; start, jump 854 vb. *be nervous*; have a temper; foam, froth, throw fits, have hysterics 503 vb. *go mad*; abandon oneself, let oneself go, run riot, run amok, see red; ramp, rage, explode, create 891 vb. *get angry*.

823. Inexcitability – N. *inexcitability*, imperturbability, good temper; calmness, steadiness, composure; coolness, sang froid, nonchalance; frigidity 820 n. *moral insensibility*; tranquillity; serenity, placidity 828 n. *content*; equanimity, balance, poise 28 n. *equilibrium*; self-possession, self-command 942 n. *temperance*; repression, stoicism; detachment, non-attachment, dispassionateness 860 n. *indifference*; gravity, staidness, demureness, sobriety 834 n. *seriousness*; quietism 679 n. *inactivity*; tameness, meekness.

patience, forbearance, endurance, long-suffering, longanimity; tolerance, toleration, sufferance, resignation, acquiescence 721 n. *submission*.

Adj. *inexcitable*, stable 153 adj. *unchangeable*; unworried, cool, imperturbable, unflappable; steady, composed, controlled; inscrutable, dead-pan 820 adj. *impassive*; deliberate, unhurried 278 adj. *slow*; good-tempered, sunny; staid, sedate, sober, grave 834 adj. *serious*; quiet, unemphatic; placid, unruffled, calm, serene 266 adj. *tranquil*; philosophic, unambitious 860 adj. *indifferent*; unlively, unspirited, spiritless, lackadaisical, torpid, passive 175 adj. *inert*; unenthusiastic, unsentimental, unromantic, unpoetic 593 adj. *prosaic*.

patient, meek, patient as Job; tolerant, long-suffering, forbearing, stoic, stoical, philosophic, uncomplaining.

Vb. *keep calm*, compose oneself, keep cool; master one's feelings, keep one's hair on; not turn a hair, not bat an eyelid; relax, stop worrying 683 vb. *repose*; resign oneself, take in good part 721 vb. *submit*.

be patient, show restraint, forbear; put up with, stand, tolerate, bear, endure, support, suffer, abide; grin and bear it; brook, take it from, swallow, digest, stomach, pocket 721 vb. *knuckle under*; allow 756 vb. *permit*.

Section 2: Personal

824. Joy – N. *joy* 376 n. *pleasure*; sensation of pleasure, enjoyment, thrill, kick 826 n. *pleasurableness*; joyfulness, joyous-ness 835 n. *rejoicing*; delight, gladness, rapture, exaltation, exhilaration, transport, abandonment, ecstasy, enchantment, bewitchment, ravishment; unholy joy, gloating, schadenfreude 898 n. *malevolence*; pleasant time, halcyon days, holidays, honeymoon 730 n. *palmy days*.

happiness, felicity, good fortune, well-being, snugness, comfort, ease 376 n. *euphoria*; palmy days, golden age 730 n. *prosperity*; blessedness, bliss, beatitude, summum bonum; seventh heaven, paradise, happy home.

enjoyment, fruition, gratification, satisfaction, fulfilment 725 n. *completion*; usufruct 773 n. *possession*; delectation, relish, zest, gusto; indulgence, luxuriation, hedonism, full life, Epicureanism 944 n. *sensualism*; glee, merry-making, lark, frolic, gambol 833 n. *merriment*; fun, treat 837 n. *amusement*; refreshment, good cheer 301 n. *eating*.

Adj. *pleased*, glad, not sorry; satisfied, happy 828 adj. *content*; gratified, pleased as Punch; enjoying, loving it, tickled to death 837 adj. *amused*; exhilarated 833 adj. *gay*; delighted, enraptured, rapturous, ecstatic, raving 923 adj. *approving*; charmed, enchanted, gloating.

happy, happy as a king; blithe, joyful, joyous, gladsome, merry 833 adj. *gay*; radiant, sparkling, starry-eyed; felicitous, lucky, fortunate, to be congratulated 730 adj. *prosperous*; blissful, blessed; in bliss, in paradise.

Vb. *be pleased* etc. adj.; have the pleasure; hug oneself, congratulate o.; purr 833 vb. *be cheerful*; laugh, smile 835 vb. *rejoice*; get a kick out of, take pleasure in, delight in; go into ecstasies, rave 821 vb. *show feeling*; bask in, wallow 376 vb. *enjoy*; have fun 837 vb. *amuse oneself*; gloat; appreciate, relish 386 vb. *taste*; take a fancy to, like 887 vb. *love*.

825. Suffering – N. *suffering*, inconvenience, discomfort, disagreeableness, malaise; sufferance, endurance; heartache, welt-schmerz, lacrimae rerum 834 n. *dejection*; affliction, dolour, anguish, angst, agony, passion, torture, torment, 377 n. *pain*; twinge, stab, smart, sting 377 n. *pang*; crucifixion, martyrdom; rack 963 n. *punishment*; purgatory, hell, pains of h. 961 n. *condemnation*; unpleasantness, mauvais quart d'heure; the hard way, trial, ordeal; shock, blow, infliction, tribulation 659 n. *bane*; living death, death in life 616 n. *evil*; evil days, iron age 731 n. *adversity*.

sorrow, grief, sadness, mournfulness 834 n. *melancholy*; dole, woe, wretchedness, misery, depths of m.; prostration, despair, desolation 853 n. *hopelessness*; unhappiness, tale of woe 731 n. *adversity*; aching heart, broken h.; displeasure, dissatisfaction 829 n. *discontent*; vexation, bitterness, mortification, remorse 830 n. *regret*.

worry, uneasiness, discomfort, disquiet, fretting 318 n. *agitation*; discomposure, dismay; something on one's mind, anxiety, concern, solicitude, thought, care; incubus, load, burden, nightmare; a worry, cares, troubles 616 n. *evil*; bother, botheration 659 n. *bane*, 838 n. *bore*; headache, problem 530 n. *enigma*.

sufferer, victim, scapegoat, sacrifice; prey 544 n. *dupe*; willing sacrifice, martyr; object of compassion, wretch, poor w., misery 731 n. *unlucky person*.

Adj. *suffering*, ill 1651 adj. *sick*; agonizing, writhing, bleeding, harrowed, on the rack; inconvenienced, uncomfortable, ill at ease; anxious, unhappy about, apprehensive 854 adj. *nervous*; ill-used, maltreated, downtrodden 745 adj. *subject*; stricken, wounded; heavy-laden 684 adj. *fatigued*; care-worn, woebegone, haggard, wild-eyed.

unhappy, unlucky, accursed 731 adj. *unfortunate*; doomed 961 adj. *condemned*; pitiable, poor, wretched; sad, despondent 834 adj. *melancholic*; cut up, heart-broken, sorrowful, woebegone 834 adj. *dejected*; weeping, tearful 836 adj. *lamenting*; displeased, disappointed 829 adj. *discontented*; chagrined, mortified 891 adj. *resentful*; sorry, remorseful, regretful 830 adj. *regretting*.

Vb. *suffer*, undergo, endure 818 vb. *feel*; bear, put up with; bear pain; suffer torment, bleed; smart, ache 377 vb. *feel pain*; wince, flinch, agonize, writhe, squirm; have a thin time, go through it 731 vb. *have trouble*; trouble oneself, distress o., worry, fret 318 vb. *be agitated*; mind, take it badly; sorrow, passion, grieve 836 vb. *lament*; pity oneself, despond 834 vb. *be dejected*; kick oneself 830 vb. *regret*.

826. Pleasurableness – N. *pleasurableness*, pleasures of, pleasantness, niceness, delightfulness, amenity, sunny side, bright s.; invitingness, attractiveness, appeal; winning ways, amiability, charm, fascination, witchery; loveliness, sight for sore eyes 841 n. *beauty*; honeymoon 824 n. *joy*; something nice, a delight, a treat, a joy; pastime, fun 837 n. *amusement*; melody, harmony 412 n. *music*; deliciousness 390 n. *savouriness*; dainty 392 n. *sweetness*; manna in the wilderness, balm 685 n. *refreshment*; peace, perfect p., tranquillity 266 n. *quietude*.

Adj. *pleasurable*, pleasant, nice, pleasure-giving 837 adj. *amusing*; pleasing, agreeable, grateful, acceptable, welcome; sweet, to one's taste; frictionless, painless 376 adj. *comfortable*; peaceful, quiet 266 adj. *tranquil*; bowery, luxurious, voluptuous 376 adj. *sensuous*; genial, warm, sunny; delightful, delectable, delicious; luscious, juicy; delicate, tasty 390 adj. *savoury*; dulcet, musical 410 adj. *melodious*; picturesque, scenic, lovely 841 adj. *beautiful*; dear, winning, endearing 887 adj. *lovable*; seductive, enticing, inviting; haunting, thrilling; pastoral, idyllic; elysian, paradisical, heavenly, out of this world; blissful 824 adj. *happy*.

Vb. *please*, give pleasure, agree with; lull, soothe 177 vb. *assuage*; comfort 833 vb. *cheer*; pet, coddle 889 vb. *caress*; charm, interest 837 vb. *amuse*; rejoice, gladden, gratify.

delight, rejoice, exhilarate, elate; thrill, intoxicate, ravish; transport, fetch, send 821 vb. *excite*; take one's fancy 887 vb.

excite love; tickle, titillate, tantalize; entrance, enrapture; enchant 983 vb. *bewitch*.

827. Painfulness – N. *painfulness*, painful treatment, harshness, roughness, harassment, persecution 735 n. *severity*; disagreeableness, unpleasantness; friction, irritation, ulceration, inflammation, exacerbation 832 n. *aggravation*; soreness, tenderness 377 n. *pain*; sore point, rub, soft spot 819 n. *sensibility*; sore, thorn in the flesh, where the shoe pinches 659 n. *bane*; unpalatability, sickener 391 n. *unsavouriness*; bitterness, bitter pill, gall and wormwood 393 n. *sourness*; affliction 731 n. *adversity*; tribulation, ordeal 825 n. *suffering*; pitifulness, pathos; sorry sight, sad spectacle; heavy news 825 n. *sorrow*; disenchantment, disillusionment 509 n. *disappointment*.

annoyance, vexation, pain and grief, death of, pest, curse, plague, botheration, embarrassment 825 n. *worry*; nuisance, pin-prick; last straw, limit, outside edge; offence, affront 921 n. *indignity*; molestation 898 n. *malevolence*; displeasure, mortification 891 n. *resentment*.

Adj. *paining*, sore, tender; agonizing, purgatorial 377 adj. *painful*; searing, scalding, burning, sharp, biting; harsh, cruel 735 adj. *severe*; searching, exquisite, extreme.

unpleasant, unpleasing, disagreeable; uncomfortable, comfortless 834 adj. *cheerless*; unattractive, uninviting; unwelcome 860 adj. *unwanted*; distasteful, unpalatable 391 adj. *unsavoury*; foul 645 adj. *not nice*; fulsome 397 adj. *fetid*; bitter 393 adj. *sour*; invidious, obnoxious, offensive, odious 861 adj. *disliked*.

annoying, too bad; troublesome, bothersome, boring 838 adj. *tedious*; impossible, pesky, plaguy; importunate, pestering; trying, irritating, vexatious, provoking, maddening; galling, mortifying.

distressing, afflicting, heavy, grievous; moving, affecting, tear-jerking; pathetic,

tragic, pitiful 905 adj. *pitiable*; grim, dreadful, shocking, appalling, nerve-racking 854 adj. *frightening*.

intolerable, insufferable, impossible, insupportable, unendurable, unbearable, past bearing, not to be borne; extreme, more than flesh and blood can bear.

Vb. *hurt*, disagree with, injure 645 vb. *harm*; pain 377 vb. *give pain*; knock out, wind, double up 279 vb. *strike*; gall, pique, nettle, mortify 891 vb. *huff*; rub the wrong way, tread on one's corns; cut to the quick; afflict, distress 834 vb. *sadden*; corrode, embitter, exacerbate, chafe, rankle, fester 832 vb. *aggravate*; affront 921 vb. *not respect*.

torment, excruciate, martyr; harrow, rack 963 vb. *torture*; maltreat, bait, bully, rag 735 vb. *oppress*; haunt, obsess; annoy, do it to a., pin-prick; tease, pester, plague, nag, badger, wherret, worry, try, chivvy, harass, harry, heckle; molest, bother, vex, provoke 891 vb. *enrage*.

incommode, discomfort, disquiet, disturb, discompose, upset 63 vb. *derange*; worry, embarrass, trouble; weary, bore 838 vb. *be tedious*; obsess, haunt, bedevil; prey on the mind, depress 834 vb. *deject*; infest, get in one's hair.

displease, not please, find no favour 924 vb. *incur blame*; grate, jar, go against the grain; disenchant, disillusion, undeceive 509 vb. *disappoint*; dissatisfy, aggrieve 829 vb. *discontent*; offend, shock, horrify, scandalize, disgust, revolt, sicken, nauseate 861 vb. *cause dislike*.

828. Content – N. *content*, contentment, contentedness, satisfaction, complacency; self-satisfaction, smugness 873 n. *vanity*; serenity 266 n. *quietude*; ease of mind, nothing left to worry about 376 n. *euphoria*; reconciliation 719 n. *pacification*; wish-fulfilment, ambition achieved 730 n. *prosperity*; resignation 721 n. *submission*.

Adj. *content*, contented, satisfied 824 adj. *happy*; cushy 376 adj. *comfortable*; at ease 683 adj. *reposeful*; flattered 824 adj. *pleased*; having nothing to grumble at; unrepining, uncomplaining, with no regrets, without complaints; unenvious, unjealous 931 adj. *disinterested*; philosophic 823 adj. *inexcitable*; secure 660 adj. *safe*; thankful, gratified 907 adj. *grateful*.

contenting, satisfying 635 adj. *sufficient*; tolerable, bearable, endurable, liveable; desirable, all that is wished for 859 adj. *desired*.

Vb. *be content,* — satisfied etc. adj.; purr, purr with content 824 vb. *be pleased*; have much to be thankful for; have all one asks for, have one's wish 730 vb. *prosper*; congratulate oneself, hug o. 835 vb. *rejoice*; sit pat, sit pretty 376 vb. *enjoy*; be reconciled 719 vb. *make peace*; complain of nothing, have no complaints, not repine.

content, satisfy, gratify, make one's day 826 vb. *please*; meet with approval, go down well; comfort 833 vb. *cheer*; lull, set at ease, set at rest; propitiate, disarm, reconcile 719 vb. *pacify*.

829. Discontent – N. *discontent*, discontentment, disgruntlement, slow burn; displeasure, pain, dissatisfaction 924 n. *disapprobation*; cold comfort, not what one expected 509 n. *disappointment*; soreness, chagrin, mortification, heartburning 891 n. *resentment*; uneasiness 825 n. *worry*; strain, tension; unrest 738 n. *disobedience*; hypercriticism, perfectionism 862 n. *fastidiousness*; chip on one's shoulder, grievance, grudge, complain; sulkiness, sulks, dirty look 893 n. *sullenness*; cheep, squeak, murmur.

malcontent, grumbler, grouser, croaker, complainer, whiner, bleater, bellyacher, Jonah; faultfinder, critic; sorehead, man with a grievance, angry young man; laudator temporis acti; indignation meeting, protest m. 762 n. *deprecation*; irreconcilable 705 n. *opponent*.

Adj. *discontented*, displeased, not best pleased; dissatisfied 924 adj. *disapproving*; ungratified 509 adj. *disappointed*; malcontent, dissident 489 adj. *dissenting*; restless, restive 738 adj. *disobedient*; disgruntled, ill content, browned off 825 adj. *unhappy*; uncomforted, unconsoled 834 adj. *dejected*; grudging, jealous, envious; embittered, soured 393 adj. *sour*; cross, sulky 893 adj. *sullen*; grouchy, grumbling, grousing 899 adj. *maledicent*; protesting 762 adj. *deprecatory*; unflattered, smarting, sore, mortified 891 adj. *resentful*; hard to please, never satisfied 862 adj. *fastidious*; fault-finding, critical, hypercritical 926 adj. *detracting*; irreconcilable, hostile 881 adj. *inimical*.

Vb. *be discontented,* — dissatisfied etc. adj.; crab, criticize, find fault; lack, miss 627 vb. *require*; sneer 924 vb. *disapprove*; mind, take offence, take amiss, take ill, smart under 891 vb. *resent*; get the hump, sulk 893 vb. *be sullen*; look blue 834 vb. *be dejected*; murmur, whine, bleat, beef, protest, complain, object, cry blue murder 762 vb. *deprecate*; bellyache, grumble, grouse; join the opposition 704 vb. *oppose*; grudge 912 vb. *envy*; not know when one is well off, look a gift horse in the mouth; ask for one's money back, return 607 vb. *reject*; repine, moan 830 vb. *regret*.

cause discontent, dissatisfy, leave room for complaint 509 vb. *disappoint*; spoil one's pleasure 834 vb. *deject*; dishearten, discourage 613 vb. *dissuade*; sour, embitter, disgruntle; mortify 872 vb. *humiliate*; offend 827 vb. *displease*; disgust 861 vb. *cause dislike*; make trouble, agitate 738 vb. *revolt*.

830. Regret – N. *regret*, regretfulness; mortification, heart-burning 891 n. *resentment*; crying over spilt milk; soul-searching, self-reproach, remorse, contrition, compunction, regrets, apologies 939 n. *penitence*; disillusion, second thoughts 67 n. *sequel*; longing, nostalgia 859 n. *desire*; matter of regret, pity of it.

Adj. *regretting*, irreconcilable, inconsolable 836 adj. *lamenting*; compunctious, regretful, remorseful, rueful, sorry, full of regrets, apologetic, penitent 939 adj. *repentant*; undeceived, disillusioned, sadder and wiser.

regretted, regrettable, deplorable, much to be deplored, too bad.

Vb. *regret*, rue, deplore; curse one's folly, blame oneself, reproach o., kick o.; unwish, wish undone, repine 836 vb. *lament*; miss, sadly m., want back; long for, be homesick 859 vb. *desire*; apologize, feel remorse, be sorry 939 vb. *be penitent*; deplore, deprecate, lament 924 vb. *disapprove*; feel mortified, gnash one's teeth 891 vb. *resent*; have had one's lesson, smart for it 963 vb. *be punished*.

831. Relief – N. *relief*, recruitment 685 n. *refreshment*; alleviation, mitigation, palliation, abatement 177 n. *moderation*; good riddance; exemption 668 n. *deliverance*; solace, consolation, comfort, ray of c.; blue streak, rift in the clouds; load off one's mind, sigh of relief 656 n. *revival*; soothing syrup, lenitive 177 n. *moderator*; pain-killer, analgesic 375 n. *anaesthetic*; sleeping draught 679 n. *soporific*; comforter, consoler, ray of sunshine.

Adj. *relieving*, soothing, balsamic 685 adj. *refreshing*; analgesic, anodyne 177 adj. *lenitive*; curative, restorative 658 adj. *remedial*; consoling, consolatory.

Vb. *relieve*, ease, soften, cushion; relax, lessen the strain; temper 177 vb. *moderate*; lift, rake off, lighten, unburden 701 vb. *disencumber*; spare, exempt from 919 vb. *exempt*; console, solace, comfort; cheer up, buck up 833 vb. *cheer*; cool, fan 685 vb. *refresh*; bandage, bind up 658 vb. *doctor*; calm, soothe, pour balm, palliate, mitigate, moderate, alleviate, deaden 177 vb. *assuage*; anaesthetize 375 vb. *render insensible*; put one out of his misery 905 vb. *pity*.

be relieved, relieve oneself, ease o., obtain relief; take comfort, feel better 833 vb. *be cheerful*; recover, get over it, snap out of it, buck up, perk up, sleep off 656 vb. *be restored*.

832. Aggravation – N. *aggravation*, exacerbation, exasperation, irritation, embitterment; enhancement 36 n. *increase*; intensification 162 n. *strengthening*; heightening, deepening, adding to; complication 700 n. *difficulty*; irritant 821 n. *excitant*; previous offence 936 n. *guilt*.

Adj. *aggravated*, intensified; unrelieved, made worse, not improved 655 adj. *deteriorated*.

Vb. *aggravate*, intensify 162 vb. *strengthen*; enhance, heighten, deepen; increase 36 vb. *augment*; worsen, make worse, make things w., not improve matters 655 vb. *deteriorate*; exacerbate, embitter, sour, envenom, inflame 821 vb. *excite*; exasperate, irritate 891 vb. *enrage*; add fuel to the flame; complicate, make bad worse.

833. Cheerfulness – N. *cheerfulness*, alacrity 597 n. *willingness*; optimism 852 n. *hope*; cheeriness, happiness 824 n. *joy*; geniality, sunniness, breeziness, smiles, good humour; vitality, spirits, animal s., joie de vivre 360 n. *life;* lightheartedness, liveliness, sparkle, vivacity, animation, exhilaration; life and soul of the party, party spirit 882 n. *sociality*; optimist, perennial o., Pollyanna.

merriment, laughter and joy; cheer, good c.; exhilaration, high spirits, abandon; jollity, joviality, jocularity, gaiety, glee, mirth, hilarity 835 n. *laughter*; levity, frivolity 499 n. *folly*; merry-making, fun, fun and games, sport 837 n. *amusement*; marriage bells, jubilee 876 n. *celebration*.

Adj. *cheerful*, cheery, blithe 824 adj. *happy*; hearty, genial 882 adj. *sociable*; smiling, sunny, bright, beaming, radiant 835 adj. *laughing*; breezy, in spirits, in a good humour; unrepining, optimistic, hopeful, buoyant, resilient, irrepressible; carefree, light-hearted, debonair; bouncing, pert, jaunty, perky, chirpy, spirited, sprightly, vivacious, animated, vital, sparkling 819 adj. *lively*; alacritous 597 adj. *willing*.

gay, light, frivolous 456 adj. *lightminded*; joyous, joyful; sparkling, mirth-loving, waggish, jocular 839 adj. *witty*; playful, sportive, frisky, gamesome, frolicsome 837 adj. *amusing*; merry, merry-making, mirthful, jocund, jovial, jolly; wild, rackety, hilarious, uproarious, rollicking 837 adj. *amused*.

jubilant, jubilating, gleeful 824 adj. *pleased*; elate, flushed, exultant, triumphant, cock-a-hoop 727 adj. *successful*, 876 adj. *celebrative*.

Vb. *be cheerful*, look on the bright side 852 vb. *hope*; grin and bear it, put a good face upon it 599 vb. *be resolute*; take heart, cheer up, perk up, buck up 831 vb. *be relieved*; brighten, liven up, let oneself go, abandon oneself; smile, beam, sparkle; dance, sing, laugh 835 vb. *rejoice*; whoop, cheer 876 vb. *celebrate*; have fun, frisk, frolic, rollick, romp, sport 837 vb. *amuse oneself*.

cheer, gladden, warm the heart 828 vb. *content*; comfort, console 831 vb. *relieve*; inspire, enliven 821 vb. *animate*; exhilarate, elate 826 vb. *delight*; encourage, inspirit, buck up, jolly along 855 vb. *give courage*; act like a tonic, energize 174 vb. *invigorate*.

834. Dejection. Seriousness – N. *dejection*, joylessness, unhappiness, cheerlessness, dreariness, low spirits, dumps, doldrums; droopiness, dispiritedness, heart-sinking; disillusion 509 n. *disappointment*; despondency, defeatism, pessimism, despair, death-wish, suicidal tendency 853 n. *hopelessness*; weariness, oppression 684 n. *fatigue*; heart-ache, heaviness, sadness, misery, wretchedness, dolefulness 825 n. *sorrow*; gloominess, gloom; glumness, dejected look, haggardness, funereal aspect, long face, lack-lustre eye.

melancholy, melancholia, hypochondria, hypochondriasis; black mood, blue devils, blues, horrors, mopes, mopiness, sighing, sigh; disgust of life, taedium vitae, weltschmerz, angst, nostalgia 825 n. *suffering*.

seriousness, earnestness; gravity, solemnity, sobriety, demureness, staidness; grimness 893 n. *sullenness*; primness, humourlessness; straight face, dead pan; sternness, heavy stuff; earnest,

dead e.; no laughing matter, chastening thought.

moper, croaker, complainer, Jonah 829 n. *malcontent*; damper, wet blanket, Job's comforter, misery; sobersides, death's-head; hypochondriac.

Adj. *dejected*, joyless, dreary, cheerless, unhappy, sad (see *melancholic*); gloomy, despondent, unhopeful, pessimistic, defeatist 853 adj. *hopeless*; dispirited, unnerved 854 adj. *nervous*; downcast, droopy, low, down, depressed; lack-lustre, unlively, out of sorts, sluggish, listless, lackadaisical 679 adj. *inactive*; discountenanced, crestfallen, ready to cry 509 adj. *disappointed*; sobered, sadder and wiser 830 adj. *regretting*; subdued, piano.

melancholic, in the blues, atrabilious, vapourish, hypochondriacal; jaundiced, hipped, hippish; thoughtful, pensive, melancholy, sad, triste; heavy, heavy-hearted, heart-sick 825 adj. *unhappy*; mournful doleful 836 adj. *lamenting*; miserable, wretched, disconsolate; moody, sulky 893 adj. *sullen*; mopish, dull, dismal, gloomy, glum; woebegone, wan, haggard, care-worn.

serious, sober, solemn, sedate, staid, demure, grave, stern 735 adj. *severe*; sour, Puritan, grim, grim-visaged, dark, forbidding, saturnine 893 adj. *sullen*; earnest, unsmiling; straight-faced, poker-f., dead-pan; prim, humourless; unfunny, without a laugh in it 838 adj. *tedious*.

cheerless, comfortless, out of comfort; uncongenial, uninviting; depressing, unrelieved, dreary, dull, flat 838 adj. *tedious*; dismal, lugubrious, funereal, gloomy, dark, forbidding; drab, grey, sombre, overcast.

Vb. *be dejected*, despond, admit defeat 853 vb. *despair*; languish, sink, droop, sag, wilt, flag, give up 684 vb. *be fatigued*; mope, brood; sulk 893 vb. *be sullen*; eat one's heart out, yearn 859 vb. *desire*; sigh, grieve 829 vb. *be discontented*.

be serious, not smile, keep a straight face, maintain one's gravity, sober up, look grave; not see the joke, take oneself seriously 838 vb. *be tedious*.

sadden, grieve, bring sorrow, cut up; break one's heart, draw tears 821 vb. *impress*; spoil one's pleasure 829 vb. *cause discontent*; drive to despair 853 vb. *leave no hope*.

deject, depress, get one down; cause alarm and despondency, dishearten, discourage, dispirit 854 vb. *frighten*; spoil the fun, take the joy out of, cast a shadow 418 vb. *darken*; damp, throw cold water 613 vb. *dissuade*; disgust 827 vb. *displease*; bore 838 vb. *be tedious*; chasten, sober 534 vb. *teach*.

835. Rejoicing – N. *rejoicing*, 837 n. *festivity*; jubilation, jubilee, exultation 876 n. *celebration*; felicitation, self-congratulation 886 n. *congratulation*; cheers, hurrah, hosanna, hallelujah 923 n. *praise*; thanksgiving 907 n. *thanks*; paean 981 n. *hymn*; revels 837 n. *revel*; merrymaking, abandon 833 n. *merriment*.

laughter, risibility; loud laughter, Homeric l., cachinnation; derision 851 n. *ridicule*; laugh, horse l., guffaw; chuckle, chortle, gurgle, crow, coo; giggle, snigger, snicker, titter, tee-hee; the giggles; smile, simper, smirk, grin; laughingness, twinkle, half-smile; laughableness, laughing matter, comedy, farce 497 n. *absurdity*.

laugher, giggler, cackler, sniggerer, titterer; smiler, smirker, simperer, Cheshire cat; mocker, derider 926 n. *detractor*.

Adj. *rejoicing*, rollicking etc. vb.; exultant 833 adj. *jubilant*; lyrical, ecstatic 923 adj. *approving*.

laughing, guffawing etc. vb.; splitting one's sides, humorous; mocking 851 adj. *derisive*; laughable, derisory 849 adj. *ridiculous*; comic, farcical 497 adj. *absurd*.

Vb. *rejoice*, be joyful, sing for joy, dance, skip 312 vb. *leap*; clap, whoop, cheer 923 vb. *applaud*; sing paeans, shout hosannahs 923 vb. *praise*; exult, triumph, jubilate 876 vb. *celebrate*;

felicitate 886 vb. *gratulate*; give thanks 907 vb. *thank*; abandon oneself, let oneself go, riot, maffick; make merry 833 vb. *be cheerful*, 837 vb. *revel*; have a party, celebrate 882 vb. *be sociable*; congratulate oneself, hug o., gloat 824 vb. *be pleased*; purr, coo 409 vb. *ululate*.

laugh, get the giggles; hoot, chuckle, chortle, giggle, snigger, snicker, titter, tee-hee; laugh at, mock, deride 851 vb. *ridicule*; shake, hold one's sides.

smile, grin, show one's teeth; grimace, smirk, simper; twinkle, beam, flash a smile.

836. Lamentation – N. *lamentation*, wail, wail of woe; plangency, weeping and wailing, mourning 364 n. *obsequies*; sackcloth and ashes; widow's weeds, weepers, crape, black; tears, tearfulness, dolefulness; tenderness, melting mood; wet eyes, red e.; breakdown, hysterics; cry, good c.; sob, sigh, whimper, whine.

lament, complaint, dirge, knell, requiem, threnody, elegy, swan-song, funeral oration 364 n. *obsequies*; keen, coronach, wake 905 n. *condolence*; sob-stuff, sob-story, hard-luck s., tale of woe, jeremiad; cri de cœur.

weeper, wailer, keener, threnodist, elegist; mourner, mute 364 n. *funeral*; sniveller, whiner, cry-baby.

Adj. *lamenting*, crying etc. vb.; lachrymatory, tear-shedding; in tears, tearful, lachrymose, in melting mood; wet-eyed, red-e., mournful, doleful 825 adj. *unhappy*; plaining, plaintive; elegiac, epecedial, threnodic 364 adj. *funereal*; condoling, in mourning, in black; half-masted, at half-mast; querulous, querimonious; pathetic, pitiful, lamentable, tear-jerking 905 adj. *pitiable*.

Vb. *lament*, grieve, sorrow, sigh 825 vb. *suffer*; deplore 830 vb. *regret*; condole, grieve for, plain, weep over, bewail, bemoan, elegize, threnodize; mourn, wail, keen, sit at the wake; go into mourning, wring one's hands, beat the breast; complain, bellyache 829 vb. *be discontented*.

weep, wail, pipe one's eye; shed tears,

melt; cry, break down, boo-hoo, cry one's eyes out; howl, squall 409 vb. *ululate*; sob, sigh, moan, groan 825 vb. *suffer*; snivel, grizzle, blubber, pule, whine, whimper.

837. Amusement – N. *amusement*, pleasure, interest, delight 826 n. *pleasurableness*; diversion, divertissement, entertainment; pastime, hobby, labour of love 597 n. *voluntary work*; solace, recreation 685 n. *refreshment*; relaxation, holiday 681 n. *leisure*; gala day, redletter d., banner d. 876 n. *special day*; play, sport, fun 833 n. *merriment*; occasion, do, show, rout 876 n. *celebration*; outing, excursion, jaunt, pleasure trip; treat, wayzgoose, fête champêtre, picnic (see *festivity*); garden party, bun-fight, fête; game.

festivity, playtime, holiday-making, fun, whirl, round of pleasure, seeing life, high life, good time, time of one's life; a short life and a merry one 943 n. *intemperance*; festival, fair, fun-f., fun of the fair, kermesse, carnival, fiesta, mi-carême, gala; festivities, fun and games, merry-making, revels, Saturnalia, Yule-tide 833 n. *merriment*; wassail 301 n. *feasting*; conviviality, party 882 n. *social gathering*; orgy, debauch, carouse 949 n. *drunkenness*; bust, binge, beano; barbecue, cookout, clambake, banquet 301 n. *meal*.

revel, rout, jollification, whoopee, fun fast and furious, high jinks, spree, junket, night out; play, game, caper, romp, rollick, frolic, lark, skylarking, escapade, prank 497 n. *foolery*.

pleasure-ground, park, green; arbour, gardens, pleasure-g., pleasance; seaside, lido, bathing-beach, holiday camp; playground, recreation ground; field, playing-f., links, golf course; rink; circus, fair, funfair, carousel, wonderland.

place of amusement, amusement park, fun-fair, shooting-gallery, skittle-alley, bowling a., billiard room, card-r., assembly r., pump-r., concert r.; picturehouse 445 n. *cinema*; playhouse 594 n. *theatre*; ballroom, dance-floor; dance-

hall, palais de danse; cabaret, night club, casino, kursaal 618 n. *gaming house*.

sport, outdoor life; sportsmanship, gamesmanship 694 n. *skill*; sports, field s.; agonism, games, gymnastics 162 n. *athletics*, 716 n. *contest*, *racing*, *pugilism*, *wrestling*; camping, picnicking; riding, hacking; archery, hunting, shooting, fishing; water sports 269 n. *aquatics*; climbing, mountaineering, Alpinism; exploring, speleology; winter sports; curling; tourism, travelling 267 n. *land travel*.

ball game, pat-ball, bat and ball game; King Willow, cricket; baseball, soft-ball, rounders; tennis, real t., table t., ping-pong; badminton, battledore and shuttlecock; squash, rackets; fives, pelota; lacrosse, pallone; wall-game, net-ball, volley-b., basket-b.; football, soccer, rugger; hockey, polo; croquet, golf; skittles, nine-pins, bowls, curling; marbles, dibs; quoits, hoop-la, discus-throwing; billiards.

indoor game, nursery g., parlour g., round g., party g.; word game, spelling-bee, Scrabble, lexicon, riddles, crosswords, acrostics.

board game, chess, draughts, checkers; pachisi; backgammon; race-game, ludo, snakes and ladders, crown and anchor.

card game, cards, game of cards, rubber; boston, whist, bridge, euchre, écarté, loo, picquet, cribbage, quadrille, ombre, bezique, pinocle, quinze; rummy, gin r., canasta; solo, solitaire, patience; drag, poker; banker, baccarat, faro, fantan, chemin de fer, chemmy.

gambling game, dice g., craps, dice, lie d.; roulette, rouge et noir; bingo, housey-housey.

dancing, dance, ball, nautch; bal masqué, masquerade; bal costumé, fancy dress dance, pagal nautch; hop, jam session; ballet, ballet dancing, classical d., ball-room d.; choreography; eurhythmics.

dance, war-dance, sword-d., corroboree; shuffle, double-s., cakewalk, solo dance, pas seul; clog-dance, step-d., tap-d.; fan dance, skirt-d., hula-hula; high kicks, cancan; gypsy dance, flamenco; folk-dance, country d., morris d.; hornpipe, keel row; mazurka; jig, Irish j., fling, Highland f.; square dance, reel, eightsome, foursome; waltz, fox-trot, tango, rumba, samba, mambo, conga, shimmy, twist, jive, jitterbug, rock 'n' roll, creep; excuse-me dance, Paul Jones; dancer, ballet d., ballerina, corps de ballet; nautch-girl; high-kicker, cancanière; waltzer, foxtrotter, shuffler, hoofer, jiver, twister 312 n. *jumper.*

plaything knick-knack, souvenir, trinket, toy 639 n. *bauble*; five-stones, marbles; ball, bowl, wood 252 n. *sphere*; model, model yacht; card, cards, pack, stack, deck; domino, tile; draught, draughtsman.

chessman, man, piece, pawn, knight, bishop; castle, rook; queen, king.

player, sportsman, sporting man; pothunter 716 n. *contender*; gamesman, games-player, all-rounder; toxophilite 287 n. *shooter*; dicer, gamester 618 n. *gambler*; card-player, chess-p.; fellow-sportsman, playmate.

reveller, merry-maker, roisterer, skylarker, ragger; drinker, drunk 949 n. *drunkard*; feaster, diner-out 301 n. *eater*; pleasure-seeker, playboy, good-time girl; holiday-maker, excursionist, tripper, tourist 268 n. *traveller*; King of Misrule, master of the revels, symposiarch.

Adj. *amusing*, entertaining, diverting etc. vb.; fun-making, sportive 833 adj. *gay*; pleasant 826 adj. *pleasurable*; laughable, ridiculous, clownish 849 adj. *funny*; recreational 685 adj. *refreshing*; festal, festive, holiday.

amused, entertained 824 adj. *pleased*; having fun, festive, sportive, rompish, rollicking, gamesome, prankish, playful, kittenish, roguish, waggish, jolly, jovial; out to enjoy oneself, in festal mood, in holiday spirit 835 adj. *rejoicing*; horsy, sporty, sporting, games-playing 162 adj. *athletic*; entertainable, ready to be amused.

Vb. *amuse*, interest, entertain, divert, tickle, make one laugh, take one out of

oneself; titillate, please 826 vb. *delight*; recreate 685 vb. *refresh*; solace, enliven 833 vb. *cheer*; treat, regale, take out; raise a smile, wake laughter, lay them in the aisles, be the death of one 849 vb. *be ridiculous*; humour, keep amused; play the host 882 vb. *be hospitable*; be a sport, be great fun.

amuse oneself, kill time, pass the t. 681 vb. *have leisure*; ride one's hobby, dabble, trifle, fribble; play, have fun 833 vb. *be cheerful*; make holiday, disport oneself; take one's pleasure, dally, toy, wanton; frisk, frolic, rollick, romp, gambol, caper; fool about 849 vb. *be ridiculous*; live the outdoor life, camp, picnic.

dance, go dancing; tap-dance, waltz, foxtrot, tango, rumba, twist, jive, jitterbug, rock 'n' roll; cavort, caper, shuffle, hoof, trip, tread a measure.

revel, make merry, make whoopee, celebrate 835 vb. *rejoice*; make it a party, have a good time; beat it up, paint the town red; junket, roister; feast, banquet, quaff, carouse, wassail; go on a binge 301 vb. *drink*; drown one's sorrows 949 vb. *get drunk*; wanton, run a rig, sow one's wild oats.

838. Tedium – N. *tedium*, taedium vitae, world-weariness 834 n. *melancholy*; uninterest 860 n. *indifference*; wearisomeness, tediousness, irksomeness; dryness, stodginess; too much of a good thing 863 n. *satiety*; disgust 861 n. *dislike*; flatness, staleness 387 n. *insipidity*; monotony 106 n. *repetition*; leaden hours 679 n. *inactivity*.

bore, utter b., no fun; twice-told tale; irk, bind; grindstone, treadmill 682 n. *labour*; dry-as-dust, proser, buttonholer, club bore; drip, wet blanket, misery.

Adj. *tedious*, uninteresting, unenjoyable, unentertaining, unamusing, unfunny; slow, dragging, leaden, heavy; dry, dry-as-dust, arid; flat, stale, insipid 387 adj. *tasteless*; dreary, stuffy 840 adj. *dull*; stodgy, prosaic, uninspired, unreadable; prosy 570 adj. *prolix*; drowsy, soporific 679 adj. *somnific*; boring, wearisome, tiresome, irksome; same, unvarying, monotonous 16 adj. *uniform*; cloying, satiating.

Vb. *be tedious*, pall, cloy, glut, jade, satiate 863 vb. *sate*; nauseate, sicken, disgust 861 vb. *cause dislike*; bore, irk, try, weary 684 vb. *fatigue*; try one's patience, outstay one's welcome; make one yawn, send one to sleep; drag 278 vb. *move slowly*; buttonhole, be prolix 570 vb. *be diffuse*.

839. Wit – **N.** *wit*, wittiness, point, smartness, epigrammatism; esprit, ready wit; saltiness, salt 575 n. *elegance*; scintillation 498 n. *intelligence*; humour, sense of h.; pawkiness, dryness, slyness, drollery, pleasantry, waggishness, waggery, facetiousness; jocosity, jocoseness 833 n. *merriment*; comicality 849 n. *ridiculousness*; trifling, flippancy; joking, jesting, tomfoolery, buffoonery 497 n. *foolery*; farce, broad f., slapstick, ham, harlequinade 594 n. *dramaturgy*; whimsicality, fancy 604 n. *whim*; biting wit, satire, sarcasm 851 n. *ridicule*; irony 850 n. *affectation*; word-fence 477 n. *sophistry*; word-play, equivocation 518 n. *equivocalness*.

witticism, piece of humour, stroke of wit, sally, bon mot; Wellerism, Spoonerism; epigram, conceit; pun, play upon words 518 n. *equivocalness*; point of the joke, cream of the jest; chaff, banter, ribbing, badinage, persiflage; retort, repartee 460 n. *rejoinder*; joke, practical j.; quip, jape, gag, crack, wisecrack; chestnut, Joe Miller; story, funny s.

humorist, wit, epigrammatist; joker, japer; life of the party, wag; joker; jokesmith, wisecracker, gagsman, gagster, punster; banterer, persifleur, quizzer, leg-puller, ragger, teaser; ironist 850 n. *affector*; mocker, scoffer, satirist, lampooner 926 n. *detractor*; comedian, comic 594 n. *entertainer*; comic writer, cartoonist, caricaturist; burlesquer, parodist 20 n. *imitator*; jester, court j., motley fool, clown, farceur, buffoon 501 n. *fool*.

Adj. *witty*, nimble-witted, quick;

Attic, salty 575 adj. *elegant*; pointed, ben trovato, epigrammatic; smart 498 adj. *intelligent*; biting, pungent, keen, sharp, sarcastic; dry, sly, pawky; unserious, facetious 456 adj. *light-minded*; jocular, jocose, waggish, roguish; lively, pleasant, merry, merry and wise 833 adj. *gay*; comic 849 adj. *funny*; humorous, droll; playful, sportive.

Vb. *be witty*, scintillate, sparkle, flash; jest, joke, gag, wisecrack; tell a good story, lay them in the aisles 837 vb. *amuse*; pun, equivocate 518 *be equivocal*; fool, jape; tease, chaff, rag, banter, quip, quiz, twit, pull one's leg, make fun of 851 vb. *ridicule*; caricature, burlesque 851 vb. *satirize*; retort, flash back 460 vb. *answer*.

840. Dullness – **N.** *dullness*, heaviness 834 *dejection*; stuffiness, dreariness, deadliness; boringness 838 n. *tedium*; colourlessness, drabness; stodginess, unreadability, prosiness; staleness, flatness 387 n. *insipidity*; banality, triteness; gravity 834 n. *seriousness*.

Adj. *dull*, unamusing, uninteresting, unentertaining; unfunny, uncomical, straight; stuffy, dreary, deadly 838 adj. *tedious*; colourless, drab; flat, insipid 387 adj. *tasteless*; stupid 499 adj. *unintelligent*; humourless, grave, prim 834 adj. *serious*; heavy, ponderous, sluggish 278 adj. *slow*; stodgy, prosaic, pedestrian, unreadable; stale, banal, commonplace 610 adj. *usual*.

841. Beauty – **N.** *beauty*, pulchritude, the beautiful; sublimity, grandeur, magnificence 868 n. *nobility*; splendour, gorgeousness, brilliance, brightness, radiance 417 n. *light*; transfiguration 843 n. *beautification*; ornament 844 n. *ornamentation*; scenery, view, landscape 445 n. *spectacle*; form, fair proportions 245 n. *symmetry*; loveliness, comeliness, fairness, prettiness; attractiveness, agreeableness, charm, appeal, glamour; attractions, charms, graces, perfections, good looks, beaux yeux; shapeliness, curves, curvaceousness, vital statistics;

gracefulness, grace 575 n. *elegance*; chic, style 848 n. *fashion*; delicacy, refinement 846 n. *good taste*; aesthetics, callaesthetics, aestheticism.

a beauty, thing of beauty, work of art, masterpiece 644 n. *exceller*; jewel, pearl, treasure 646 n. *paragon*; fair, fair one, belle, raving beauty, toast, idol 890 n. *favourite*; beau idéal, dream girl; beauty queen; pin-up girl, cover g.; dream, vision, picture, sight for sore eyes; charmer, dazzler; enchantress, femme fatale, witch 983 n. *sorceress*; smasher, scorcher, lovely, cutie; Adonis, Prince Charming.

Adj. *beautiful*, pulchritudinous, beauteous, of beauty; lovely, fair, bright, radiant; comely, goodly, bonny, pretty; sweet, pretty-pretty; paintable, photogenic; handsome, good-looking, well-favoured; stately, statuesque, majestic; leonine, manly; picturesque, scenic, ornamental; artistic, cunning, curious, quaint 694 adj. *well-made*; aesthetic 846 adj. *tasteful*; exquisite, choice 605 adj. *chosen*.

splendid, sublime, superb, fine 644 adj. *excellent*; grand 868 adj. *noble*; rich, gorgeous 425 adj. *florid*; bright, resplendent, dazzling 417 adj. *radiating*; glossy, polished, magnificent, specious 875 adj. *showy*; ornate 844 adj. *ornamented*.

shapely, well-proportioned, regular, classic 245 adj. *symmetrical*; well-turned, rounded, buxom, curvaceous, callipygic; clean-limbed, straight, slender, slim, svelte, willowy 206 adj. *lean*; petite, dainty, delicate.

personable, prepossessing, agreeable; attractive, fetching, appealing; snappy, cute, kissable; charming, enchanting, glamorous; lovesome, winsome 887 adj. *lovable*; blooming; rosy, peachy; bright, bright-eyed; sightly, becoming; presentable, neat, natty, tidy, trim; spruce, dapper, glossy, sleek; smart, stylish 848 adj. *fashionable*; elegant, dainty, delicate 846 adj. *tasteful*.

Vb. *beautify*, trim, neaten; brighten 417 vb. *make bright*; prettify, bejewel 844 vb.

decorate; set (a jewel); set off, grace, suit, fit, become, go well, show one off, flatter; glamorize, transfigure, face-lift; prink, prank, titivate 843 vb. *primp*.

842. Ugliness

N. *ugliness*, unsightliness, hideousness, repulsiveness; gracelessness, clumsiness 576 n. *inelegance*; unshapeliness 246 n. *deformity*; mutilation, disfigurement; uglification, disfiguration, defacement; homeliness, plainness; no beauty, no oil painting; forbidding countenance, vinegar aspect 893 n. *sullenness*; haggardness; fading beauty, wrinkles 131 n. *age*.

eyesore, hideosity, blot 845 n. *blemish*; aesthetic crime; blot on the landscape, slum; ugly person, fright, sight, figure, object, not one's type; scarecrow, horror, death's-head, gargoyle, grotesque; monster, abortion; harridan, witch; satyr.

Adj. *ugly*, unlovely, unhandsome; hideous, foul; shocking, monstrous; repulsive, repellent, odious, loathsome 861 adj. *disliked*; homely, plain, plain-featured; forbidding, unprepossessing, ill-favoured, villainous, grim-visaged, saturnine 893 adj. *sullen*.

unsightly, worn, ravaged, wrinkled 131 adj. *aged*; not fit to be seen, unseemly; unshapely, irregular, asymmetrical 244 adj. *amorphous*; disfigured 246 adj. *distorted*; ill-made, ill-shaped, disproportioned, misshapen, misbegotten; ghastly, wan, grisly, gruesome.

graceless, ungraced, ungraceful 576 adj. *inelegant*; inartistic, unaesthetic; unbecoming, unpicturesque; squalid, dingy, poky; gross, indelicate, coarse 847 adj. *vulgar*; dowdy, ill-dressed; rude, uncouth 699 adj. *artless*; clumsy, awkward, ungainly.

Vb. *make ugly*, uglify; discolour 426 vb. *decolorize*; spoil 655 vb. *deteriorate*; deface, disfigure, blemish, blot; misshape; mutilate 655 vb. *impair*.

843. Beautification

N. *beautification*, 844 n. *ornamentation*; transfiguration 143 n. *transformation*; scenic improvement, landscape gardening, landscape architecture; plastic surgery, face-lift 658 n. *surgery*; beauty treatment, pack, face p., facial; massage, manicure, pedicure, chiropody; tattooing 844 n. *ornamental art*; toilet, make-up, cosmetology; wash and brush up.

hair-dressing, trichology, hair-treatment, scalp massage; barbering; depilation, plucking; shave, haircut, clip, trim, singe, tidy-up; hair-style, coiffure, crop; styling, hair-s.; hair-do, set, wave; bang, fringe, pony-tail, chignon, bun, Pompadour, cowlick, quiff 259 n. *hair*; false hair, switch 228 n. *wig*; curling-iron, tongs, curlers, rollers, crackers, rags; slide, hair-s., barette, grip.

cosmetic, glamorizer, aid to beauty, patch, beauty spot; make-up, paint, greasepaint, warpaint, rouge, fard, pomade, cream, lipstick, lipsalve; nail polish, nail varnish; powder, face-p.; kohl, collyrium, mascara, eye-shadow; scented soap, bath salts 648 n. *cleanser*; scent, perfume, essence, toilet water, cologne stick; powder puff, compact, flapjack, beauty case; make-up set, manicure s.; toiletry, toiletries.

beauty parlour, beauty shop, beauty salon; parfumerie; boudoir, make-up room.

beautician, beauty specialist, beauty doctor; face-lifter, plastic surgeon; make-up artist, glamorizer, tattooer; cosmetician, cosmetologist; barber, hairdresser, hair-stylist; trichologist; manicurist, pedicurist, chiropodist.

Vb. *primp*, prettify, doll up, dress up, bedizen, bejewel; prink, prank, trick out; preen; titivate, make up, apply cosmetics, rouge, paint, shadow; powder; scent oneself; dye, curl, wave.

844. Ornamentation – **N.** *ornamentation*, decoration, adornment, garnish; ornateness 574 n. *ornament*; prettyism, pretty-pretty; gaudiness, richness, gilt 875 n. *ostentation*; enhancement, enrichment, embellishment; setting, background; floral decoration, flower arrangement, wreath, coronal, crown, bouquet, nosegay, posy, buttonhole.

ornamental art, gardening, landscape g., topiarism; architecture, landscape a.; interior decoration, house-painting; statuary 554 n. *sculpture*; moulding, beading, fluting, fretting, tracery; pargeting, veneering, panelling, graining; ormolu, gilding, gilt, gold leaf; lettering, illumination, illustration; heraldic art 547 n. *heraldry*; tattooing; strap-work, coquillage; etching 555 n. *engraving*; work, fancy-w., woodwork, fretwork; poker-work, pyrography; open-work, filigree; mosaic 437 n. *variegation*; wrought-work, toreutics.

pattern, key-p., motif, print, design, composition 331 n. *structure*; detail, elaborate d.; tracery, scrollwork, fiddle-head, arabesque, flourish 251 n. *coil*; weave, diaper 331 n. *texture*; check 437 n. *chequer*; water-pattern, watermark 547 n. *identification*.

needlework, stitchery, tapestry, sampler; laid-work, patchwork, appliqué work, open w.; embroidery, broidery, crochet, lace; smocking, tatting, knitting; stitch, purl, plain, gros point, petit p., needle p.; cross stitch, chain s., cable s., moss s., garter s., hem s., French knotting, lazy-daisy.

trimming, passementerie, piping, valance, border, fringe, frieze, frill, galloon, gimp 234 n. *edging*; feather, panache 259 n. *plumage*; streamer, ribbon.

finery, togs, braws, Sunday best 228 n. *clothing*; fal-de-lal, frippery, ribbons, chiffon; gaudery, gaud, trinket, knick-knack, gewgaw, bric-à-brac, tinsel, spangle, sequin, costume jewellery, glass, paste 639 n. *bauble*.

jewellery, bijouterie, jewel-work; diadem, tiara 743 n. *regalia*; drop, locket 217 n. *pendant*; rope, string, necklet, necklace, chain, watch-c., albert 250 n. *loop*; torque, armlet, anklet, bracelet; wristlet, bangle, ring, earring, nose-ring, signet r.; ouch, brooch, fibula, badge, crest; stud, pin; medal, medallion.

gem, jewel, bijou; stone, precious s., semi-precious s.; brilliant, sparkler, diamond, rock, ice; solitaire; coral, jade, lapis lazuli.

Adj. *ornamental*, decorative, non-functional, fancy; glamorous, picturesque, pretty-pretty; scenic, landscape, topiary; baroque, rococo; daedal, quaint.

ornamented, decorated, embellished, polished 574 adj. *ornate*; picked out 437 adj. *variegated*; inlaid, enamelled; worked, embroidered, trimmed; over-decorated, overloaded 847 adj. *vulgar*; gilt, begilt, gilded 800 adj. *rich*; gorgeous, garish, glittering, flashy, gaudy, meretricious 875 adj. *showy*.

Vb. *decorate*, embellish, enhance, enrich; adorn, load; grace, set off, ornament; paint, bedizen, bejewel; adonize, glamorize, prettify 841 vb. *beautify*; garnish, trim; shape, topiarize; array, deck, bedeck, dight 228 vb. *dress*; prank, preen, titivate 843 vb. *primp*; freshen, smarten, spruce up; bemedal, beribbon, garland, crown 866 vb. *dignify*; stud, spangle 437 vb. *variegate*; enamel, gilt, silver; emblazon, illuminate, illustrate 553 vb. *paint*; colourize 425 vb. *colour*; border, trim 234 vb. *hem*; work, pick out, broider, embroider, tapestry; chase, tool 555 vb. *engrave*; emboss, bead, mould; fret, carve; wreathe, festoon, trace, scroll 251 vb. *twine*.

845. Blemish – N. *blemish*, no ornament; scar, weal, welt, mark, pock-m.; injury, flaw, crack, defect 647 n. *imperfection*; disfigurement, deformity 246 n. *distortion*; stigma, blot 842 n. *eyesore*; blur, blotch, smudge 550 n. *obliteration*; patch, smear, stain, tarnish, rust 649 n. *dirt*; spot, speck 437 n. *maculation*; excrescence 253 n. *swelling*.

Adj. *blemished*, defective, flawed 647 adj. *imperfect*; shop-soiled, spoilt 655 adj. *deteriorated*; marked, scarred; spotted, pitted, pock-marked, maculate.

Vb. *blemish*, flaw, crack, injure, damage 655 vb. *impair*; blot, smudge, stain, smear, soil 649 vb. *make unclean*; scar, pit, pock; spoil 842 vb. *make ugly*; disfigure, deface, deform.

846. Good taste – N. *good taste*, tastefulness, taste, simplicity 573 n. *plainness*; best of taste, choiceness 644 n. *goodness*; refinement, delicacy, euphemism 950 n. *purity*; fine feeling, nicety, palate 463 n. *discrimination*; daintiness 862 n. *fastidiousness*; decency, seemliness; dignity, urbanity 884 n. *courtesy*; correctness, propriety, decorum; grace, polish, sophistication, gracious living 575 n. *elegance*; cultivation, culture, connoisseurship, amateurship, dilettantism; aestheticism, aesthetics 480 n. *judgement*; artistry, virtuosity 694 n. *skill*.

man of taste, sophisticate, connoisseur, amateur, dilettante; aesthete, critic 480 n. *estimator*; arbiter of taste, arbiter elegantiarum 848 n. *fop*; purist, precisian.

Adj. *tasteful*, gracious, dignified; choice, exquisite 644 adj. *excellent*; unmeretricious 573 adj. *plain*; graceful 575 adj. *elegant*; chaste, refined, delicate 950 n. *pure*; aesthetic, artistic 819 n. *sensitive*; discriminatory 463 adj. *discriminating*; nice, dainty, choosy, finicky 862 adj. *fastidious*; critical, appreciative 480 adj. *judicial*; decent, seemly; house-trained, sophisticated 848 adj. *well-bred*.

847. Bad taste – N. *bad taste*, tastelessness, ill taste, no taste; bad art, commercial a.; unrefinement, coarseness, barbarism; vulgarity, gaudiness, loudness; tawdriness, shoddiness; shoddy, frippery, tinsel 639 n. *bauble*; grossness, indelicacy, impropriety, unseemliness; nastiness 951 n. *impurity*; unfashionableness, dowdiness, frumpishness.

ill-breeding, vulgarity, commonness; rusticity, jungliness; inurbanity, incivility; bad form, incorrectness; no manners, gaucherie, boorishness 885 n. *discourtesy*; misbehaviour, indecorum, ribaldry.

vulgarian, cad, bounder; rough diamond, unlicked cub; arriviste, parvenu; Vandal, Philistine, Babbitt; barbarian, savage.

Adj. *vulgar*, undignified; tasteless, unrefined, unpolished 576 adj. *inelegant*; gross, crass, coarse, coarse-grained;

Philistine, barbarian 699 adj. *artless*; commercial, commercialized; tawdry, cheap; flashy, meretricious 875 adj. *showy*; obtrusive, blatant, loud, gaudy, garish; not respectable, common, low, gutter 867 adj. *disreputable*; improper, indelicate; ribald, obscene.

ill-bred, underbred, unhousetrained; unpresentable; ungentlemanly, unlady-like; unfeminine, hoydenish; ungenteel, non-U 869 adj. *plebeian*; loud, hearty; uncourtly, mannerless 885 adj. *discourteous*; unfashionable, unsmart, dowdy, rustic, provincial, countrified; rude, boorish, clownish, uncouth, unrefined; awkward, gauche, lubberly 695 adj. *clumsy*; misbehaving 61 adj. *disorderly*.

Vb. *vulgarize*, cheapen, coarsen, lower; commercialize.

848. Fashion – N. *fashion*, style, mode, cut 243 n. *form*; vogue, cult, rage, fad, craze, cry; new look, the latest 126 n. *newness*; dernier cri, last word; fashion-ableness, ton; haute couture, elegance, foppishness, dressiness; foppery 850 n. *affectation*; world of fashion, Vanity Fair.

etiquette, punctilio, pundonor 875 n. *formality*; protocol, convention, custom 610 n. *practice*; snobbery, done thing, good form; proprieties, appearances, Mrs Grundy; right note, correctness 846 n. *good taste*; breeding, good b., polish; manners, good m., court m., best behaviour; grand air, poise, dignity, savoir faire, savvy.

beau monde, society, good s., high s., civilization; town, West End; court, drawing-room, salon; right people, best p., upper ten 868 n. *nobility*; cream, upper crust 644 n. *élite*; café society, jeunesse dorée; man of fashion, woman of f., high stepper, classy dame; socialite, cosmopolitan 882 n. *social person*.

fop, fine gentleman, macaroni, buck, pearly king; fine lady, belle, pearly queen; débutante, deb; dandy, beau, exquisite, curled darling, popinjay, peacock, clothes-horse, fashion plate,

tailor's dummy, man milliner; swell, toff, dude, masher, filbert, knut, nob; Teddy-boy; spark, blood, blade.

Adj. *fashionable*, modish, stylish, bon ton; correct, à la mode; chic, well-dressed, well-groomed 846 adj. *tasteful*; clothes-conscious, foppish, dressy; high-stepping, dashing, dandy, smart, classy, toney, swanky, posh; up-to-the-minute 126 adj. *modern*; groomed, dandified, braw, dressed to the nines, en grande tenue 228 adj. *dressed*; in society, in the swim 83 adj. *conformable*.

well-bred, thoroughbred, blue-blooded 868 adj. *noble*; cosmopolitan, sophisticated, civilized, urbane; house-trained; U, gentlemanlike, ladylike 868 adj. *genteel*; civil, well-mannered, well-spoken 884 adj. *courteous*; courtly, stately, distingué, dignified 875 adj. *formal*; poised, dégagé, easy, unembarrassed; punctilious 929 adj. *honourable*.

849. Ridiculousness – N. *ridiculousness*, ludicrousness, laughability, height of absurdity 497 n. *absurdity*; pricelessness, comicality, drollery 839 n. *wit*; quaintness, eccentricity 84 n. *abnormality*; bathos, anticlimax 509 n. *disappointment*; comic interlude, light relief; light verse, doggerel, limerick, spoonerism 839 n. *witticism*; comedy, farce, burlesque, slapstick, knock-about, clowning, buffoonery; Gilbertian situation 508 n. *inexpectation*.

Adj. *ridiculous*, ludicrous, preposterous, grotesque, fantastic 497 adj. *absurd*; awkward, clownish 695 n. *clumsy*; derisory, contemptible 639 adj. *unimportant*; laughable, risible; bizarre, rum, quaint 84 adj. *unusual*; whimsical 604 adj. *capricious*; paradoxical.

funny, funny-peculiar 84 adj. *abnormal*; funny-ha-ha, laughter-making 837 adj. *amusing*; comical, droll, humorous, waggish 839 adj. *witty*; rich, priceless, side-splitting; light, comic, burlesque, mock-heroic; farcical, slapstick, clownish, knock-about.

Vb. *be ridiculous*, raise a laugh; tickle, shake *or* disturb one's gravity, give one the giggles; look silly, play the fool; descend to bathos, pass from the sublime to the ridiculous.

850. Affectation – N. *affectation*, cult, fad 848 n. *fashion*; affectedness, pretentiousness, airs and graces, ostentation; pose, attitude; artificiality, mannerism, trick; literary affectation, tushery, prestige terms 574 n. *magniloquence*; preciosity, euphuism, cultism 574 n. *ornament*; coquetry 604 n. *caprice*; conceit, foppery, dandyism, coxcombry 873 n. *vanity*; euphemism, mock modesty 874 n. *modesty*; irony 851 n. *ridicule*; insincerity, play-acting, tongue in cheek 541 n. *duplicity*; theatricality, histrionics.

pretension, assumption, pretensions 916 n. *arrogation*; artifice, pretence 614 n. *pretext*; humbug, quackery, charlatanism 542 n. *deception*; superficiality, shallow profundity 4 n. *insubstantiality*; pedantry, purism, precisianism; demureness, prunes and prisms 950 n. *prudery*; sanctimony 979 n. *pietism*.

affector, pretender, false claimant; humbug, quack, charlatan 545 n. *impostor*; play-actor 594 n. *actor*; hypocrite, flatterer 545 n. *deceiver*; bluffer 877 n. *boaster*; coquette, flirt; mass of affectation, attitudinizer, poseur; ironist 839 n. *humorist*; dandy 848 n. *fop*; prig 950 n. *prude*; mannerist 575 n. *stylist*.

Adj. *affected*, full of affectations, self-conscious; overdone 546 adj. *exaggerated*; mannered, precious, chi-chi 574 adj. *ornate*; artificial, unnatural, stilted 875 adj. *formal*; prim, priggish, euphemistic, sanctimonious 979 adj. *pietistic*; coquettish, coy, mock-modest; canting, hypocritical, tongue-in-cheek, ironical 542 adj. *deceiving*; shallow, specious, pretentious, stagy, theatrical 875 adj. *ostentatious*; foppish, conceited, posturing 873 adj. *vain*; snobbish; for effect, sought, put on.

Vb. *be affected*, affect, air, put on, assume; pretend, feign, go through the motions, make a show of, bluff 541 vb. *dissemble*; play-act 594 vb. *act*; play to the gallery; dramatize oneself, attitudinize, posture, pose 875 vb. *be ostentatious*; put on airs, swank, show off 873 vb. *be vain*; talk big 877 vb. *boast*; simper, smirk 835 vb. *smile*; coquette, flirt, languish 887 vb. *excite love*; cant, euphemize.

851. Ridicule – N. *ridicule*, derision, derisiveness, mockery, scoffing 921 n. *disrespect*; raillery, banter, persiflage, badinage, leg-pulling, chaff; irony, sarcasm, barbed shaft; ribaldry 839 n. *witticism*.

satire, denunciation 928 n. *accusation*; parody, burlesque, travesty, caricature, cartoon 552 n. *misrepresentation*; skit, take-off 20 n. *mimicry*; squib, lampoon 926 n. *detraction*.

laughing-stock, object of ridicule, figure of fun, butt, common jest, byword; mock, sport, game, fair g.; cockshy, Aunt Sally; April fool, clown, zany 501 n. *fool*; guy, caricature, mockery of, apology for; fogy, square, geezer, museum piece, moss-back; victim 728 n. *loser*.

Adj. *derisive*, ridiculing etc. vb.; sardonic, sarcastic; ironical, quizzical; satirical, Hudibrastic 839 adj. *witty*; ribald 847 adj. *vulgar*; burlesque, mock-heroic.

Vb. *ridicule*, deride, laugh at; snigger, sniff; banter, chaff, rally, twit, josh, rag, pull one's leg, poke fun, make merry with, make fun of, have one on, fool 542 vb. *befool*; mock, scoff, jeer 926 vb. *detract*; take down, deflate, debunk 872 vb. *humiliate*.

satirize, lampoon 921 vb. *not respect*; mock, jibe, scold 899 vb. *curse*; mimic, take off 20 vb. *imitate*; parody, travesty, burlesque, caricature, guy 552 vb. *misrepresent*; denounce, pillory 928 vb. *accuse*.

852. Hope – N. *hope*, expectations, presumption 507 n. *expectation*; hope and belief, conviction 485 n. *belief*; safe hope, anchor, staff 218 n. *support*; favourable auspices, promise 511 n. *omen*; silver lining 831 n. *relief*; hopefulness, buoy-

ancy, optimism 833 n. *cheerfulness*;
wishful thinking, rosy picture.

aspiration, ambition 617 n. *intention*;
pious hope, vision, pipe-dream; Messianism; castles in Spain, fool's paradise
513 n. *fantasy*; utopia, millennium, the
day 617 n. *objective*.

hoper, aspirant, candidate, waiting list;
hopeful, young h.; optimist, prisoner of
hope; utopian, millenarian, chiliast 513
n. *visionary*; Micawber.

Adj. *hoping*, aspiring, starry-eyed;
ambitious, wishful, would-be 617 adj.
intending; hopeful, in hopes 507 adj.
expectant; in high hopes, sanguine, confident 473 adj. *certain*; buoyant, optimistic; ever-hoping, undespairing 855
adj. *unfearing*.

promising, favourable, auspicious, propitious 730 adj. *prosperous*; bright, fair,
golden, rosy, couleur de rose; hopeful,
encouraging; visionary 513 adj. *imaginary*.

Vb. *hope*, trust, confide; hope in, pin
one's hopes on 485 vb. *believe*; presume;
dream of, aspire, promise oneself 617 vb.
intend; live in hopes; not despair, hope
against hope, catch at a straw, look on
the bright side, hope for the best 833 vb.
be cheerful; anticipate, count one's
chickens before they are hatched; dream
513 vb. *imagine*.

give hope, inspire h., comfort 833 vb.
cheer; show signs of, have the makings
of, promise well, shape w., bid fair 471
vb. *be likely*.

853. Hopelessness – N. *hopelessness*, no
hope, defeatism, despondency 834 n. *dejection*; pessimism, despair, desperation;
chimera, vain hope 513 n. *fantasy*; message of despair, hopeless situation 700 n.
predicament; counsel of despair, Job's
comforter, defeatist 834 n. *moper*.

Adj. *hopeless*, without hope, des-
pairing, desperate; unhopeful, pessimistic; defeatist, disconsolate, comfortless
834 adj. *dejected*.

unpromising, hopeless, comfortless 834
adj. *cheerless*; desperate 661 adj. *dangerous*; unpropitious, inauspicious 731

adj. *adverse*; ill-omened, ominous 511
adj. *presageful*; irremediable, remediless,
incurable, inoperable; past cure, past
hope; irrevocable, irredeemable, irreclaimable; irreversible, inevitable.

Vb. *despair*, lose hope; despond,
wring one's hands 834 vb. *be dejected*;
hope for nothing more from, write off
674 vb. *disuse*.

leave no hope, drive to despair, shatter
one's last hope 509 vb. *disappoint*.

854. Fear – N. *fear*, healthy f., dread,
awe 920 n. *respect*; abject fear 856 n.
cowardice; fright, stage-f.; affright,
funk, wind up; terror, mortal t., trepidation, alarm; scare, stampede, panic,
flight, sauve qui peut; horror, hair on
end, cold sweat; consternation, dismay
853 n. *hopelessness*.

nervousness, want of courage, lack of
confidence, cowardliness 856 n. *cowardice*; self-distrust, shyness 874 n.
modesty; timidity, fearfulness, hesitation
620 n. *avoidance*; loss of nerve, cold feet,
fears, misgiving, apprehensiveness 825
n. *worry*; defeatism 853 n. *hopelessness*;
trepidation, flutter, tremor, nerves,
willies, butterflies, qualms, needles,
creeps, shivers, jumps, jitters 318 n.
agitation; gooseflesh, hair on end, knees
knocking.

phobia, claustrophobia, agoraphobia,
acrophobia, pyrophobia; fear of death;
anti-semitism, negrophobia, xenophobia
888 n. *hatred*; spy-mania, witch-hunting.

intimidation, deterrence, war of nerves,
sabre-rattling, rocket-r., fee, faw, fum
900 n. *threat*; terror, terrorization, terrorism, reign of terror 735 n. *severity*;
alarmism, scaremongering; deterrent
723 n. *weapon*; bogyman, goblin 970 n.
demon; bugbear, bugaboo, ogre 938 n.
monster; death's head, raw-head,
bloody-bones.

alarmist, scaremonger, defeatist, pessimist; terrorist, intimidator, sabre-rattler.

Adj. *fearing*, afraid, frightened, funky,
panicky; overawed 920 adj. *respectful*;
in fear, in trepidation, in a flap, in a
panic; terror-crazed, panic-stricken; dis-

mayed, flabbergasted; frozen, petrified, stunned; appalled, horrified, aghast, horror-struck, awe-s.; unmanned, frightened to death, white as a sheet.

nervous, defensive, on the d.; defeatist 853 adj. *hopeless*; timid, timorous, shy, diffident 874 adj. *modest*; coy, wary 858 adj. *cautious*; suspicious 474 adj. *doubting*; windy, faint-hearted 601 adj. *irresolute*; apprehensive, fearful, dreading 825 adj. *unhappy*; haunted, terror-ridden, jittery, jumpy, nervy; cowering, cringing 856 adj. *cowardly*.

frightening, shocking etc. vb.; formidable, redoubtable 661 adj. *dangerous*; dreadful, numinous, fearsome, awesome 821 adj. *impressive*; grim, grisly, ghastly, horrific, horrible, terrible, appalling; hair-raising; weird, eerie, creepy, ghoulish, gruesome, macabre, sinister; ominous, direful 511 adj. *presageful*; terroristic, sabre-rattling, minatory, menacing 900 adj. *threatening*; nerve-racking.

Vb. *fear*, funk; stand in fear *or* awe, dread 920 vb. *respect*; flap, have the wind up; take fright, panic, stampede 620 vb. *run away*; start, jump 318 vb. *be agitated*.

quake, shake, tremble, quiver, shiver, shudder, stutter, quaver; fear for one's life, be scared out of one's wits, change colour, blench; wince, flinch, shrink, shy 620 vb. *avoid*; quail, cower 721 vb. *knuckle under*; stand aghast, feel one's blood run cold.

be nervous, — apprehensive etc. adj.; feel shy 874 vb. *be modest*; suspect, mistrust; funk it, not face it; dread, hesitate, think twice 858 vb. *be cautious*.

frighten, fright, affright; scare, panic, stampede; intimidate, put in fear 900 vb. *threaten*; alarm, cry wolf; make one jump, give one a turn, startle 318 vb. *agitate*; perturb, prey on the mind, haunt 827 vb. *incommode*; rattle, shake, unnerve; unman, cowardize; put the fear of God into, overawe, cow; flabbergast, stun 508 vb. *surprise*; dismay, daunt, deter, discourage 613 vb. *dissuade*; terrorize 735 vb. *oppress*; browbeat, bully 827 vb. *torment*; terrify, horrify, harrow, chill, freeze, petrify 375 vb. *render insensible*; appal, chill the spine, make one's blood run cold, make one's flesh creep.

855. Courage – N. *courage*, bravery, valiance, valour; heroism, gallantry, chivalry; self-reliance, fearlessness, intrepidity, daring, nerve; boldness, hardihood, audacity 857 n. *rashness*; spirit 174 n. *vigorousness*; undauntedness, high morale 599 n. *resolution*; gameness, pluck, spunk, guts, heart, great h., stout h. 600 n. *stamina*; Dutch courage, potvaliance; courage of despair; brave face, bold front 711 n. *defiance*; encouragement 612 n. *inducement*.

manliness, manhood, feelings of a man; virtue, chivalry; manly spirit, heroic qualities; aggressiveness, fierceness 718 n. *bellicosity*; endurance, stiff upper lip 599 n. *resolution*.

prowess, derring-do, chivalry, knightliness; heroic achievement, gallant act, soldierly conduct; feat, feat of arms, emprise 676 n. *deed*; aristeia, heroics.

brave person, heroic figure, hero, heroine, V.C.; knight, paladin, stout fellow, brave, fighting man 722 n. *soldier*; man, true m., he-m., game dog, bulldog; dare-devil, fire-eater 857 n. *desperado*; band of heroes, gallant company; lion, tiger, game-cock, fighting c.

Adj. *courageous*, brave, valorous, valiant, gallant, heroic; chivalrous, knightly, yeomanly, soldierly, martial, Amazonian 718 adj. *warlike*; stout, doughty, tall, bonny, manful, manly, tough, two-fisted, red-blooded; fierce, bloody 898 adj. *cruel*; bold 711 adj. *defiant*; hardy, audacious, daring, venturesome 857 adj. *rash*; adventurous 672 adj. *enterprising*; mettlesome, spirited, high-hearted, stout-h., lion-h.; full of fight, spunky, pot-valiant; dogged, indomitable 600 adj. *persevering*; desperate, determined 599 adj. *resolute*; game, plucky, ready for anything, unflinching, unshrinking, first in the breach 597 adj. *willing*.

unfearing, unafraid, intrepid, danger-loving; self-reliant; fearless, dauntless, unshrinking, undismayed, undaunted, unshaken, unshakable.

Vb. *be courageous*, — bold etc. adj.; fight with the best 716 vb. *fight*; venture, bell the cat 672 vb. *undertake*; dare 661 vb. *face danger*; show fight, brave, face, outface, outdare, beard 711 vb. *defy*; confront, look in the face, win one's spurs; keep one's head 823 vb. *keep calm*; grin and bear it 825 vb. *suffer*.

take courage, pluck up c., muster c., nerve oneself, put a bold face on it 599 vb. *be resolute*; rally, stand.

give courage, animate, put heart into, nerve, make a man of; embolden, encourage 612 vb. *incite*; rally 833 vb. *cheer*; reassure, give confidence.

856. Cowardice – **N.** *cowardice*, abject fear, funk, sheer f. 854 n. *fear*; cowardliness, craven spirit; pusillanimity, timidity, faint-heartedness, chicken-heartedness; unmanliness, poltroonery, dastardy; desertion 918 n. *dutifulness*; white feather, yellow streak, faint heart, discretion, better part of valour; safety first, overcaution 858 n. *caution*.

coward, no hero; funk, poltroon, craven; dastard, sneak, rat; runaway; sissy, milksop, baby, cry-b. 163 n. *weakling*; quitter, shirker, flincher, deserter; cur, skunk, chicken, rabbit, hare, mouse, deer, jellyfish, doormat; faint-heart, scaremonger, defeatist 854 n. *alarmist*.

Adj. *cowardly*, coward, craven, poltroonish; not so brave, pusillanimous, timid, unable to say bo to a goose 854 adj. *nervous*; womanish, babyish, unmanly, sissy 163 adj. *weak*; spiritless, spunkless, poor-spirited; faint-hearted, dastardly, yellow; unsoldierly, unmartial 717 adj. *peaceful*; unheroic, unvaliant, easily frightened, funky.

Vb. *be cowardly*, lack courage, have no heart *or* stomach for 601 vb. *be irresolute*; have cold feet 854 vb. *be nervous*; shrink, funk; quail, cower, cringe 721 vb. *knuckle under*; show the white feather, panic, stampede, scuttle, desert 620 vb. *run away*.

857. Rashness – **N.** *rashness*, incautiousness, unwariness, heedlessness 456 n. *inattention*; imprudence, indiscretion 499 n. *folly*; inconsideration, irresponsibility, frivolity, flippancy, levity; recklessness, foolhardiness, temerity, audacity, presumption, over-confidence; fieriness, impatience, impetuosity, precipitance, over-haste 680 n. *haste*; over-enthusiasm, Quixotry; dangerous game, playing with fire, brinkmanship; last throw, desperation, courage of despair; needless risk 661 n. *danger*.

desperado, dare-devil, madcap, hot-head, fire-eater; brinkman, adventurer, plunger 618 n. *gambler*; harum-scarum, scape-grace; dynamitard; bully, bravo 904 n. *ruffian*.

Adj. *rash*, ill-considered, ill-advised, wildcat 499 adj. *unwise*; careless, hit-and-miss, slapdash, accident-prone 458 adj. *negligent*; uncircumspect, incautious, unwary, heedless, inconsiderate, uncalculating 456 adj. *inattentive*; frivolous, flippant, giddy, devil-may-care, harum-scarum, trigger-happy, slap-h. 456 adj. *light-minded*; irresponsible, reckless, regardless, couldn't-care-less, don't-care; temerarious, audacious; madcap, dare-devil, breakneck, suicidal; arrogant 878 adj. *insolent*; precipitate, headlong, hell-bent, desperate 680 adj. *hasty*; headstrong 602 adj. *wilful*; impatient, hot-headed, fire-eating 822 adj. *excitable*; risk-taking 672 adj. *enterprising*; thriftless 815 adj. *prodigal*.

Vb. *be rash*, — reckless etc. adj.; expose oneself, stick one's neck out; take a leap in the dark, buy a pig in a poke; ignore the consequences, damn the c.; play with fire, burn one's fingers; court disaster, ask for trouble, tempt providence.

858. Caution – **N.** *caution*, cautiousness, wariness, heedfulness 457 n. *carefulness*; hesitation, doubt, second thoughts 854 n. *nervousness*; instinct of self-preservation 932 n. *selfishness*; circumspection; guardedness; calculation, safety first; prudence, discretion, worldly wisdom 498 n. *wisdom*; insurance 662 n. *safeguard*; wait-and-see policy 136 n. *delay*.

Adj. *cautious*, wary, watchful, heedful 457 adj. *careful*; taking no risks, insured, hedging; guarded, secretive; once bitten, twice shy 669 adj. *prepared*; on one's guard, circumspect; gingerly, tentative 461 adj. *experimental*; conservative 660 adj. *safe*; prudential, discreet 498 adj. *wise*; canny, counting the risk.

Vb. *be cautious*, want to be sure, take no risks, play safe, play for safety; look, look out, feel one's way 461 vb. *be tentative*; tread warily, watch one's step, look twice; calculate, count the cost; know when to stop, let well alone; look a gift horse in the mouth 480 vb. *estimate*; make sure 473 vb. *make certain*; cover oneself, insure, hedge; leave nothing to chance 669 vb. *prepare*.

859. Desire – N. *desire*, wish, will and pleasure 595 n. *will*, 737 n. *command*; desideration, want, need 627 n. *requirement*; claim 915 n. *dueness*; desiderium, nostalgia, homesickness 830 n. *regret*; wistfulness, longing, sheep's eyes; daydream 513 n. *fantasy*; ambition, aspiration 852 n. *hope*; horme, appetence, appetition; yen, urge 279 n. *impulse*; itch, prurience 378 n. *formication*; curiousness 453 n. *curiosity*; avidity, eagerness 597 n. *willingness*; passion, ardour 822 n. *excitability*; craving, appetite (see *hunger*); covetousness, cupidity 816 n. *avarice*; greed 786 n. *rapacity*; voracity, wolfishness, insatiability 947 n. *gluttony*; concupiscence (see *libido*); incontinence 943 n. *intemperance*.

hunger, famine, famished condition, empty stomach, hungry look 946 n. *fasting*; appetite, good a., sharp a., keen a., edge of a.; thirst, thirstiness, drought, drouth 342 n. *dryness*; dipsomania 949 n. *alcoholism*.

liking, fancy, fondness, infatuation 887 n. *love*; stomach, appetite, zest; relish 386 n. *taste*; leaning, propensity

179 n. *tendency*; weakness, partiality; affinity, sympathy 775 n. *participation*; inclination, predilection, favour 605 n. *choice*; fascination 612 n. *inducement*.

libido, Eros, life instinct; concupiscence, sexual desire, carnal d., rut, heat, oestrus; ruttishness, mating season; eroticism, libidinousness, prurience, lust 951 n. *impurity*; nymphomania, priapism, satyriasis 84 n. *abnormality*.

desired object, wish, desire, desideratum 627 n. *requirement*; catch, prize, plum 729 n. *trophy*; forbidden fruit; magnet, lure, draw 291 n. *attraction*; aim, goal, star, ambition, aspiration, dream 617 n. *objective*; ideal 646 n. *perfection*.

desirer, coveter, envier; glutton, sucker for; fancier, amateur, dilettante, collector; devotee, votary 981 n. *worshipper*; aspirant 852 n. *hoper*; claimant, candidate 763 n. *petitioner*.

Adj. *desiring*, desirous, wishful, tempted, unable to resist; lustful, on heat 951 adj. *lecherous*; covetous (see *greedy*); missing, nostalgic 830 adj. *regretting*; fain, inclined, minded, bent upon 617 adj. *intending*; aspiring, would-be, wistful, longing; curious, solicitous; eager, keen, agog, dying for; itching, spoiling for; clamant, vocal; avid, mad for, mad after; liking, fond, partial to.

greedy, acquisitive, possessive 932 adj. *selfish*; ambitious; voracious 947 adj. *gluttonous*; unsated, unsatisfied, unslaked, unquenchable, insatiable, insatiate; rapacious 816 adj. *avaricious*.

hungry, esurient, hungering; foodless, supperless, dinnerless 946 adj. *fasting*; starving, famished 636 adj. *underfed*; ravenous, peckish, sharp-set; thirsty, thirsting, athirst, dry, parched.

desired, desirable, worth having, enviable; acceptable, welcome; appetizing 826 adj. *pleasurable*; fetching, catchy, attractive, appealing 291 adj. *attracting*; self-sought, invited.

Vb. *desire*, want, desiderate, miss 627 vb. *require*; ask for 737 vb. *demand*; wish, pray; wish otherwise, unwish 830 vb. *regret*; covet 912 vb. *envy*; promise oneself, set one's mind on, have at heart 617 vb. *intend*; aspire, raise one's eyes to, dream of 852 vb. *hope*; think one deserves 915 vb. *claim*; intercede, invoke, wish on, call down on; welcome, jump at 786 vb. *take*; favour, prefer 605 vb. *choose*; crave, itch for, hanker after, long for; long, yearn, pine, languish; thirst for (see *be hungry*); can't wait, must have; like, affect, care for 887 vb. *love*; solicit, woo 889 vb. *court*; set one's cap at, run after, chase 619 vb. *pursue*; lust for 951 vb. *be impure*.

be hungry, hunger, famish, starve; have a good appetite, gape for, raven 301 vb. *eat*; thirst, be dry.

cause desire, incline 612 vb. *motivate*; fill with longing 887 vb. *excite love*; stimulate 821 vb. *excite*; smell good, whet the appetite, parch, raise a thirst 390 vb. *appetize*; dangle, tease, titillate, tantalize 612 vb. *tempt*; allure 291 vb. *attract*.

860. Indifference – N. *indifference*, unconcern, uninterest 454 n. *incuriosity*; half-heartedness, lukewarmness, Laodiceanism 598 n. *unwillingness*; coolness, faint praise, two cheers 823 n. *inexcitability*; desirelessness, lovelessness; anorexy, inappetency; apathy 679 n. *inactivity*; nonchalance, insouciance 458 n. *negligence*; amorality, indifferentism; open mind 913 n. *justice*; nil admirari; indifferentist, neutralist, neutral 625 n. *moderate*; Laodicean.

Adj. *indifferent*, uncaring, unconcerned, uninterested 454 adj. *incurious*; lukewarm, Laodicean, half-hearted 598 adj. *unwilling*; impersonal, passionless 820 adj. *impassive*; unimpressed 865 adj. *unastonished*; cool, cold 823 adj. *inexcitable*; nonchalant, insouciant 458 adj. *negligent*; lackadaisical, listless 679 adj. *inactive*; undesirous, unambitious; don't-care, easy-going 734 adj. *lax*; unresponsive, untempted; loveless, heart-whole, fancy-free, uninvolved; disenchanted, disillusioned, out of love, sitting loose; impartial, inflexible 913 adj. *just*; pro-

miscuous 464 adj. *indiscriminating*; amoral, cynical.

unwanted, undesired, unwished, uninvited, unbidden; loveless, unmissed; all one to 606 adj. *choiceless*; unattractive, untempting, undesirable; unwelcome 861 adj. *disliked*.

Vb. *be indifferent*, not mind; couldn't care less, take it or leave it; shrug off, make light of 922 vb. *hold cheap*; not defend, hold no brief for, take neither side 606 vb. *be neutral*; fall out of love, cool off, sit loose to; leave one cold.

861. Dislike – N. *dislike*, disinclination, no fancy for, no stomach for; displeasure, dissatisfaction 829 n. *discontent*; aversion, antipathy, allergy; distaste, disrelish; repugnance, disgust, abomination, abhorrence, detestation, loathing; xenophobia 854 n. *phobia*; prejudice, bias; animosity, bad blood 888 n. *hatred*; nausea, queasiness 300 n. *voidance*; sickener, one's fill 863 n. *satiety*; bitterness 393 n. *sourness*; object of dislike, not one's type, bête noire, pet aversion, Dr Fell.

Adj. *disliking*, displeased 829 adj. *discontented*; squeamish, qualmish, queasy; allergic, antipathetic, averse, hostile 881 adj. *inimical*; unfriendly, unloverlike, loveless, unsympathetic; disenchanted 860 adj. *indifferent*; sick of 863 adj. *sated*.

disliked, unwished 860 adj. *unwanted*; unpopular, out of favour; not to one's taste, unrelished; repugnant, antipathetic, rebarbative, repulsive 292 adj. *repellent*; revolting, abhorrent 888 adj. *hateful*; disgusting, nauseous, sickening 391 adj. *unsavoury*; disagreeable, insufferable 827 adj. *intolerable*; unloveable, unsympathetic.

Vb. *dislike*, disrelish, not care for, have no stomach for; object 762 vb. *deprecate*; mind 891 vb. *resent*; take a dislike to, react against 280 vb. *recoil*; want to heave 300 vb. *vomit*; shun 620 vb. *avoid*; look askance at 924 vb. *disapprove*; sniff at 922 vb. *despise*; not endure, can't stand, detest 888 vb. *hate*;

shudder at 854 vb. *fear*; unwish, wish undone 830 vb. *regret*.

cause dislike, disincline 854 vb. *frighten*; rub the wrong way, antagonize 891 vb. *enrage*; set against, make bad blood 888 vb. *excite hate*; pall, cloy 863 vb. *sate*; disagree with, upset; put off, revolt 292 vb. *repel*; offend, grate, jar 827 vb. *displease*; disgust, nauseate, sicken, turn one's stomach; shock, scandalize 924 vb. *incur blame*.

862. Fastidiousness – N.

fastidiousness, niceness, daintiness, finicality, delicacy; discernment 463 n. *discrimination*; refinement 846 n. *good taste*; dilettantism, connoisseurship; meticulosity 457 n. *carefulness*; idealism, artistic conscience; perfectionism, fussiness, hypercriticism, pedantry.

perfectionist, idealist, purist, precisian, fuss-pot, pedant, hard taskmaster; picker and chooser, gourmet, epicure.

Adj. *fastidious*, quality-minded; nice, dainty, delicate; discerning 463 adj. *discriminating*; particular, choosy, picksome, finicky; overnice, scrupulous, meticulous, squeamish; critical, hypercritical, fussy, pernickety, fault-finding 924 adj. *disapproving*; pedantic, donnish, precise, rigorous, exacting 735 adj. *severe*; puritanical 950 adj. *pure*.

863. Satiety – N.

satiety, fullness, repletion 54 n. *plenitude*; plethora, engorgement, saturation, saturation point 637 n. *redundance*; surfeit, jadedness, too much of a good thing; overdose 637 n. *superfluity*.

Adj. *sated*, satiated; surfeited, gorged, cloyed, sick of; jaded, blasé.

Vb. *sate*, satiate; quench, slake 635 vb. *suffice*; saturate 54 vb. *fill*; soak 341 vb. *drench*; stuff, gorge, glut, surfeit, cloy, jade, pall; overdose, overfeed.

864. Wonder – N.

wonder, wonderment, admiration; hero-worship 887 n. *love*; awe, cry of wonder, gasp of admiration; shock 508 n. *inexpectation*; astonishment, astoundment, amazement; stupor, stupefaction.

thaumaturgy, wonder-working, miracle-making, spellbinding, magic 983 n. *sorcery*; wonderful works, thaumatology, teratology, aretalogy; stroke of genius, 676 n. *deed*; coup de théâtre 594 n. *dramaturgy*.

prodigy, portent, sign 511 n. *omen*; prodigiosity, phenomenon, miracle, marvel, wonder; drama, sensation, cause célèbre, nine-days' wonder; wonderland, fairyland 513 n. *fantasy*; sight, breathtaker 445 n. *spectacle*; miracle-worker, thaumaturge 983 n. *sorcerer*; hero, wonder man 646 n. *paragon*; freak, sport, monster, monstrosity 84 n. *rara avis*.

Adj. *wondering*, marvelling, admiring etc. vb.; awed, awe-struck; in wonderment, unable to believe one's eyes *or* senses; wide-eyed, spell-bound, dumbstruck, speechless, wordless; thunderstruck, aghast; scandalized 924 adj. *disapproving*.

wonderful, wondrous, marvellous, miraculous, monstrous, prodigious, phenomenal; stupendous 854 adj. *frightening*; admirable 644 adj. *excellent*; overwhelming, awesome, awe-inspiring, breath-taking 821 adj. *impressive*; dramatic, sensational; shocking, scandalizing; extraordinary, unprecedented 84 adj. *unusual*; weird, weird and wonderful, unaccountable, mysterious 517 adj. *puzzling*; fantastic, impossible 472 adj. *improbable*; unbelievable, fabulous; unutterable, ineffable 517 adj. *inexpressible*; wonder-working, thaumaturgic; magic, like m. 983 adj. *magical*.

Vb. *wonder*, marvel, admire, whistle, hold one's breath; hero-worship 887 vb. *love*; stare, open one's eyes, rub one's e. 508 vb. *not expect*.

be wonderful, do wonders, work miracles; surpass belief, beggar all description, beat everything; spellbind 983 vb. *bewitch*; dazzle, turn one's head 887 vb. *excite love*; strike dumb, awe, electrify 821 vb. *impress*; bowl over, stagger; stun, daze, dumbfound, as-

tound, astonish, amaze, flabbergast 508
vb. *surprise*; startle; shock, scandalize.

865. Non-wonder – N. *non-wonder*, un-
amazement, unsurprise; awelessness,
irreverence; nil admirari; blankness 860
n. *indifference*; imperturbability 820 n.
moral insensibility; unimaginativeness;
disbelief 486 n. *unbelief*; matter of
course, just what one thought.

Adj. *unastonished*, unamazed, unsurprised; unawed 855 adj. *unfearing*; unimpressionable, impassive 820 adj. *apathetic*; undazzled, unimpressed, unadmir-
ing 860 adj. *indifferent*; expecting 507
adj. *expectant*.

unastonishing, unsurprising, foreseen
507 adj. *expected*; customary, common,
ordinary, all in the day's work, nothing
wonderful 610 adj. *usual*.

Vb. *not wonder*, not believe, see
through 516 vb. *understand*; take for
granted; see it coming 507 vb. *expect*.

866. Repute – N. *repute*, reputation,
report, good r.; title to fame, name;
character, good references, reputability,
respectability, credit; regard, esteem 920
n. *respect*; good odour, favour, popularity; approval, stamp of a., cachet 923
n. *approbation*.

prestige, aura, mystique, magic; glamour, dazzle, éclat, lustre, splendour;
brilliance, prowess; kudos, glory, honour
(see *famousness*); face, izzat, caste;
degree, rank, standing, status; condition,
position; stardom 34 n. *superiority*;
prominence, eminence; distinction,
greatness, exaltedness, majesty 868 n.
nobility; impressiveness, dignity, stateliness, grandeur, sublimity, awesomeness; name to conjure with 178 n. *influence*; hegemony, primacy 733 n.
authority; prestige consideration, snob
value.

famousness, title to fame, celebrity;
illustriousness, renown, fame, name,
note; glory; notoriety 867 n. *disrepute*;
talk of the town 528 n. *publicity*; place
in history 505 n. *memory*; immortality,
deathlessness.

honours, honour, blaze of glory, crown,
halo, aureole, nimbus, glory; blushing
honours, battle h.; laurels, bays, wreath,
garland, favour; ribbon, medal 729 n.
decoration; an honour, accolade, award
962 n. *reward*; compliment, praise, incense; memorial 505 n. *reminder*; patent
of nobility 868 n. *nobility*; fount of
honour, College of Arms; honours list,
roll of honour.

dignification, glorification, honorifica-
tion, lionization; commemoration, coronation 876 n. *celebration*; sanctification,
dedication, consecration, canonization,
beatification; deification, apotheosis;
enshrinement, enthronement; advancement, aggrandizement, exaltation 310 n.
elevation; ennoblement, knighting.

person of repute, honoured sir, gentle
reader; worthy, sound man, loyal subject, pillar; man of honour 929 n. *gentleman*; somebody, great man, V.I.P. 638
n. *bigwig*; man of mark, notable, celebrity, figure; star, rising sun, man of the
hour, hero, idol, boast 890 n. *favourite*;
cream 644 n. *élite*; choice spirit, master s.
690 n. *leader*; grand old man 500 n. *sage*.

Adj. *reputable*, of repute, of credit;
creditworthy 929 adj. *trustworthy*; gentlemanly 929 adj. *honourable*; respectable, well thought of 920 adj. *respected*;
in good odour, in favour; popular,
modish 848 adj. *fashionable*.

worshipful, reverend, honourable;
admirable 864 adj. *wonderful*; heroic;
imposing, dignified, august, stately,
grand, sublime 821 adj. *impressive*;
mighty 32 adj. *great*; lordly, princely,
kingly, queenly, majestic, royal, regal
868 adj. *noble*; high-caste, heaven-born;
glorious, full of honours; time-honoured
127 adj. *immemorial*; sacrosanct, sacred
979 adj. *sanctified*; proud, honorific.

noteworthy, notable, remarkable 84
adj. *unusual*; of mark, of distinction, distingué 638 adj. *important*; prominent,
public, eminent 34 adj. *superior*; ranking, starring, leading, brilliant, illustrious, splendid, glorious.

renowned, celebrated, sung; of renown, of name, of fame; famous, fabled;

historic, illustrious; notorious 867 adj. *disreputable*; resounding, on every tongue, in the news 528 adj. *published*; imperishable, immortal 115 adj. *perpetual*.

Vb. *have repute*, have a reputation, wear a halo; have a name to lose; rank, stand high, enjoy consideration 920 vb. *command respect*; stand well with, do oneself credit, earn a name, improve one's credit; win one's spurs, gain the laurels 727 vb. *succeed*; cut a figure, cover oneself with glory 875 vb. *be ostentatious*; play first fiddle, star; make history, live in h. 505 vb. *be remembered*.

honour, revere, regard, look up to 920 vb. *respect*; stand in awe of 854 vb. *fear*; bow down to 981 vb. *worship*; know how to value, appreciate, prize, value, tender, treasure 887 vb. *love*; compliment 925 vb. *flatter*; dedicate to, inscribe to; praise, glorify 923 vb. *applaud*; make much of, lionize, chair; credit, give c. 907 vb. *thank*; immortalize, commemorate 505 vb. *remember*; celebrate, blazon 528 vb. *proclaim*; shed lustre, be a credit to.

dignify, glorify, exalt; canonize, deify, consecrate 979 vb. *sanctify*; enthrone, crown 751 vb. *commission*; signalize, distinguish; aggrandize, advance, upgrade 285 vb. *promote*; honour, bemedal, beribbon; create, elevate, ennoble; dub, knight, give the accolade; sir, bemadam 561 vb. *name*.

867. Disrepute – N. *disrepute*, disreputability, no repute, bad name, bad character, shady reputation, past; disesteem 921 n. *disrespect*; notoriety, infamy, ill fame; no standing, ingloriousness, obscurity; bad odour, disfavour, discredit, black books, bad light 888 n. *odium*; dishonour (see *slur*); ignominy, loss of honour, withered laurels; departed glory, Ichabod; demotion, degradation 872 n. *humiliation*; abjectness 934 n. *wickedness*.

slur, reproach 924 n. *censure*; imputation 926 n. *calumny*; insult 921 n. *indignity*; scandal, disgrace, shame, crying s.;

defilement, pollution 649 n. *uncleanness*; stain, smear; stigma, brand, taint 845 n. *blemish*; dirty linen; blot on one's scutcheon, badge of infamy, mark of Cain.

object of scorn, reproach, a hissing and a reproach, by-word, discredit 938 n. *bad man*; the bottom 645 n. *badness*; Cinderella, poor relation 639 n. *nonentity*.

Adj. *disreputable*, of no repute, characterless, without references; notorious, infamous, nefarious; shady, doubtful, questionable, objectionable 645 adj. *not nice*, 951 adj. *impure*; not thought much of 922 adj. *contemptible*; beggarly, pitiful 639 adj. *unimportant*; outcast 607 adj. *rejected*; shabby, squalid 649 adj. *unclean*; in a bad light, under a cloud (see *inglorious*); unpopular 861 adj. *disliked*.

discreditable, no credit to, damaging, compromising; ignoble, unworthy; unbecoming, dishonourable, despicable 922 adj. *contemptible*; censurable 924 adj. *blameworthy*; shameful, disgraceful, unedifying, scandalous, shocking, outrageous.

degrading, lowering, demeaning, ignominious, derogatory, beneath one, infra dig.

inglorious, unheroic 879 adj. *servile*; unambitious 874 adj. *modest*; unrenowned, unknown to fame, nameless, obscure 491 adj. *unknown*; unhymned, unsung; undecorated, titleless 869 adj. *plebeian*; deflated, cut down to size, debunked 872 adj. *humbled*; faded, withered, tarnished; discredited, creditless, in eclipse.

Vb. *lose repute*, fall *or* go out of fashion; fade, wither; achieve notoriety 924 vb. *incur blame*; spoil one's record, disgrace oneself, risk one's reputation; forfeit one's honour, lose one's halo; suffer in reputation, lose prestige, lose face, lose caste; look silly, blush for shame.

demean oneself, lower o., degrade o.; derogate, condescend, stoop; make oneself cheap, sacrifice one's pride, have no pride, feel no shame, think no s.

shame, put to s., pillory, expose, show

up, post; scorn, mock 851 vb. *ridicule*;
snub 872 vb. *humiliate*; deflate, cut down
to size, debunk; disparage 926 vb. *defame*; put in a bad light, reflect upon,
breathe u., taint; sully, blacken, tarnish,
stain, blot 649 vb. *make unclean*; defile,
desecrate, profane 980 vb. *be impious*;
stigmatize, brand, cast a slur, tar; dishonour, disgrace, discredit, bring shame
upon, scandalize 924 vb. *incur blame*;
drag through the mire; make one blush,
not spare one's blushes.

868. Nobility – N. *nobility*, nobleness
933 n. *virtue*; distinction, quality 644 n.
goodness; rank, titled r., station, order;
royalty, kingliness, queenliness, prince-
liness, majesty 733 n. *authority*; birth,
gentle b., gentility; descent, ancestry,
line, lineage, pedigree 169 n. *genealogy*;
noble family, dynasty 11 n. *family*;
blood, blue b.; bloodstock, caste; coat
of arms, crest, 'boast of heraldry' 547 n.
heraldry.

aristocracy, patriciate, grandeeship,
optimacy; nobility, ancien régime; lordship, lords, peerage, dukedom, earldom,
viscounty, baronage, baronetcy; knight-
age, chivalry; landed interest, squirearchy, squiredom; county family, gentry,
gentlefolk; life peerage.

upper class, upper ten, upper crust, top
layer; first families, best people 644 n.
élite; high society, social register 848 n.
beau monde; ruling class, the twice-
born, the Establishment 733 n. *authority*;
high-ups, Olympians; the haves 800 n.
rich man; salaried class, salariat.

aristocrat, patrician, Olympian;
bloodstock, thoroughbred; optimate,
senator, magnifico, magnate, dignitary;
don, grandee; gentleman, gentlewoman,
armiger; squire, squireen, buckeen, laird,
bog-lord; Junker; cadet; emperor, king,
prince, crown, sovereign; nob, swell,
gent, superior person 638 n. *bigwig*.

nobleman, man of rank, titled person,
noble, lady; lording, lordship, milord;
peer, life p.; duke, grand d., archduke,
duchess; marquis, marquess, marquise,
marchioness, margrave, margravine,

count, countess; earl, viscount, baron,
thane, baronet, knight.

Adj. *noble* 933 adj. *virtuous*; chivalrous, knightly; gentlemanly (see *genteel*);
majestic, royal, regal, every inch a king;
kingly, queenly, princely; ducal,
baronial, seigneurial; generous, gentle,
pedigreed, well-born, born in the purple;
thoroughbred, pur sang, blue-blooded;
ennobled, titled.

genteel, patrician, senatorial; aristocratic, Olympian; superior, top-drawer,
high-class, upper-c., cabin-c., classy, U,
gentlemanly, ladylike 848 adj. *well-bred*.

869. Commonalty – N. *commonalty*,
commons, third estate, bourgeoisie;
plebs, plebeians; citizenry, demos,
democracy, King Mob; populace, the
people, common sort; vulgar herd, great
unwashed; the many, hoi polloi; the
masses, admass, proletariat, proles; the
general, rank and file, rag, tag, and bobtail, hoc genus omne, Tom, Dick, and
Harry.

rabble, rabblement, mob, horde 74 n.
crowd; rout, varletry; riff-raff, scum, off-
scourings, canaille.

lower classes, lower orders, one's in-
feriors 35 n. *inferior*; common sort,
small fry; lesser breed, working class;
steerage, lower deck; second-class citi-
zens, the have-nots, the under-privileged;
proletariat, proles; sans-culottes, submerged tenth, slum population; down-
and-outs, outcasts, poor whites, white
trash; demi-monde, underworld, low
company; dunghill, slum 649 n. *sink*.

commoner, bourgeois, plebeian, plain
Mr; one of the people, man of the p.;
proletarian, prole; little man, man in
the street, everyman; common person 35
n. *inferior*; back-bencher, private; underling 742 n. *servant*; ranker, upstart, parvenu, mushroom; nobody 639 n. *nonentity*.

countryman, yeoman, rustic, Hodge,
swain, gaffer, peasant, cultivator 370 n.
husbandman; serf, villein 742 n. *slave*;
boor, churl, kern, bog-trotter; yokel,
hind, chawbacon, pot-walloper, clod,

clod-hopper, ploughman, hobnail, hob, rube, hay-seed, hick; bumpkin, country cousin, hillbilly; clown 501 n. *fool*.

Adj. *plebeian*, common, simple, untitled, unennobled, without rank, titleless; ignoble, below the salt; belowstairs, servant-class; mean, low 867 adj. *disreputable*; base-born, low-born, lowcaste; slave-born, servile; humble, of low estate 35 adj. *inferior*; second-class, lowclass, non-U, proletarian; homely, homespun 573 adj. *plain*; unfashionable, provincial; parvenu 847 adj. *vulgar*.

barbaric, barbarous, barbarian, wild, savage, brutish; uncivilized, uncultured, without arts, primitive, neolithic 699 adj. *artless*.

870. Title – N. *title*, entitlement, claim 915 n. *dueness*; title of honour, courtesy title, honorific, handle; honour, order 866 n. *honours*; dignified style, plural of dignity, royal we, editorial we 875 n. *formality*.

871. Pride – N. *pride*, proudness, proud heart; respect, self-r.; self-admiration, conceit, swelled head, swank, side, chest 873 n. *vanity*; snobbery 850 n. *affectation*; stateliness, loftiness, high mightiness; condescension, hauteur, haughtiness, disdain 922 n. *contempt*; arrogance, hubris 878 n. *insolence*; swelling pride, pomposity, grandiosity 875 n. *ostentation*; self-praise, vainglory 877 n. *boasting*; class-consciousness, race-prejudice 481 n. *prejudice*; object of pride, boast 890 n. *favourite*.

proud man, snob, mass of pride, pride incarnate; swank, swanker; lord of creation 638 n. *bigwig*; fine gentleman, grande dame 848 n. *fop*; swaggerer, bragger 877 n. *boaster*.

Adj. *proud*, haughty, lofty, sublime 209 adj. *high*; fine, grand, grandiose, dignified, stately, statuesque 821 adj. *impressive*; majestic, royal, lordly 868 adj. *noble*; self-respecting, high-souled 855 adj. *courageous*; stiff-necked 602 adj. *obstinate*; imperious, commanding 733 adj. *authoritative*; overweening, over-

bearing, hubristical, arrogant 878 adj. *insolent*.

prideful, full of pride, puffed-up, swollen; overproud, high and mighty, stuck-up, high-hatted, snobbish; uppish, on one's dignity; haughty, disdainful, superior, holier than thou, supercilious, patronizing, condescending 922 adj. *despising*; stand-offish, distant, unbending, undemocratic 885 adj. *ungracious*; proud of, bursting with pride, inches taller; strutting, swaggering 877 adj. *boastful*; cocky, bumptious 873 adj. *vain*; pretentious 850 adj. *affected*; swanky, pompous 875 adj. *showy*.

Vb. *be proud*, have one's pride, hold one's head high, stand on one's dignity, mount one's high horse; swank, show off, swagger, strut 875 vb. *be ostentatious*; condescend, patronize; disdain 922 vb. *despise*; lord it, queen it, throw one's weight about.

872. Humility. Humiliation – N. *humility*, humbleness, humble spirit 874 n. *modesty*; lowliness; unpretentiousness, meekness, resignation; self-knowledge, self-depreciation, self-effacement 931 n. *disinterestedness*; condescension 884 n. *courtesy*; no boaster, mouse, violet.

humiliation, abasement, humbling, letdown, climb-d., come-d.; shame 867 n. *disrepute*; chastening thought, mortification, hurt pride 891 n. *resentment*.

Adj. *humble*, unproud, humbleminded, poor in spirit, lowly; meek, self-effacing 931 adj. *disinterested*; mouselike, harmless, inoffensive 935 adj. *innocent*; unassuming, unpretentious, without airs 874 adj. *modest*; mean, low 639 adj. *unimportant*.

humbled, broken-spirited, bowed down; chastened, crushed, dashed, crestfallen 834 adj. *dejected*; not proud of, shamed, blushing 867 adj. *inglorious*.

Vb. *be humble*, humble oneself 867 vb. *demean oneself*; condescend, unbend 884 vb. *be courteous*; stoop, crawl, sing small, eat humble pie 721 vb. *knuckle under*; turn the other cheek, stomach, pocket 909 vb. *forgive*.

humiliate, humble, chasten, abash, disconcert; lower, take down a peg, debunk, deflate; make one feel small, teach one his place, make one crawl; snub, crush 885 vb. *be rude*; mortify, hurt one's pride, put to shame 867 vb. *shame*; score off 542 vb. *befool*; triumph over, crow o. 727 vb. *overmaster*.

873. Vanity – N. *vanity*, emptiness 4 n. *insubstantiality*; vain pride 871 n. *pride*; immodesty, conceit, conceitedness, self-importance; swank, side, chest, swelled head; cockiness, bumptiousness, self-consequence, good opinion of oneself, self-conceit, self-esteem, amour-propre, narcissism; vain-glory 877 n. *boasting*; exhibitionism, self-display 875 n. *ostentation*; airs 850 n. *affectation*; Vanity Fair 848 n. *beau monde*.

vain person, self-admirer, Narcissus; egotist, only pebble on the beach; coxcomb 848 n. *fop*; exhibitionist, peacock, show-off; know-all, smarty-boots, cleverstick, Sir Oracle.

Adj. *vain*, conceited, stuck-up 871 n. *prideful*; self-satisfied, full of oneself, self-important 932 adj. *selfish*; narcissistic; swelled-headed, too big for one's boots, bumptious, cocky, perky; immodest, blatant; vainglorious 877 adj. *boastful*; pompous 875 adj. *ostentatious*; pretentious, soi-disant.

Vb. *be vain*, — conceited etc. adj.; have one's head turned, think too much of oneself, blow one's own trumpet 877 vb. *boast*; admire oneself, flatter o., plume o., preen o., pride o.; swank, show off, put on airs, push oneself forward 875 vb. *be ostentatious*; fish for compliments; give oneself airs 850 vb. *be affected*.

874. Modesty – N. *modesty*, shyness, retiring disposition; diffidence, self-distrust 854 n. *nervousness*; mauvaise honte, over-modesty 950 n. *prudery*; bashfulness, pudency, shamefastness; chastity 950 n. *purity*; self-depreciation, self-effacement 872 n. *humility*; unpretentiousness, unassuming nature; demureness, reserve; modest person, shy thing, violet.

Adj. *modest*, unvain, without vanity; self-effacing, unobtrusive, unseen, unheard 872 adj. *humble*; unboastful; unambitious, unassuming, unpretentious; unimposing, mediocre 639 adj. *unimportant*; shy, retiring, shrinking, timid, diffident 854 adj. *nervous*; bashful, blushful, blushing, rosy; reserved, demure, coy; shockable, prudish; chaste 950 adj. *pure*.

Vb. *be modest*, show moderation, ration oneself 942 vb. *be temperate*; efface oneself 872 vb. *be humble*; play second fiddle, keep in the background, take a back seat, know one's place; blush unseen, shun the limelight; retire, shrink, be coy 620 vb. *avoid*; show bashfulness, blush, colour, crimson, mantle 431 vb. *redden*.

875. Ostentation – N. *ostentation*, demonstration, display, parade, show 522 n. *manifestation*; unconcealment, blatancy, flagrancy, shamelessness, brazenness 528 n. *publicity*; ostentatiousness, showiness, magnificence, grandiosity; splendour, brilliance; pomposity, swagger; swank, side, chest, strut; bravado, heroics 877 n. *boast*; theatricality, histrionics, dramatics, sensationalism 546 n. *exaggeration*; demonstrativeness 882 n. *sociability*; showmanship, effect, window-dressing; solemnity (see *formality*); grandeur, dignity, stateliness, impressiveness; declamation, rhetoric 574 n. *magniloquence*; flourish, big drum 528 n. *publication*; pageantry, pomp, bravery, pride, panache, gaudiness, glitter, tinsel 844 n. *ornamentation*; mummery, mockery 4 n. *insubstantiality*; exterior, gloss, veneer 223 n. *exteriority*.

formality, state, stateliness, dignity, ceremoniousness; plural of dignity, royal we, editorial we 870 n. *title*; ceremony, ceremonial 988 n. *ritual*; drill, spit and polish, bull; correctness, protocol, form 848 n. *etiquette*; punctilio; solemnity, formal occasion, function 876

n. *celebration*; full dress, finery 228 n. *formal dress*.

pageant, show 522 n. *exhibit*; fête, gala, gala performance, tournament, tattoo; field day, great doings 876 n. *celebration*, 445 n. *spectacle*; set piece, stage effect, stage trick 594 n. *stage set*; display, bravura, stunt; pyrotechnics 420 n. *fireworks*; carnival 837 n. *festivity*, *revel*; procession, promenade, march-past, fly-past; turn-out, review 74 n. *assembly*.

Adj. *ostentatious*, showy, pompous; aiming at effect, done for e.; for show, specious, seeming, hollow 542 adj. *spurious*; consequential, self-important; pretentious, would-be 850 adj. *affected*; showing off 873 adj. *vain*; inflated, magniloquent, declamatory, high-sounding 574 adj. *rhetorical*; grand, highfalutin, splendiferous, splendid, brilliant, magnificent, grandiose; superb, royal 813 adj. *liberal*; sumptuous, diamond-studded, luxurious 811 adj. *dear*; painted, glorified.

showy, dressy, foppish 848 adj. *fashionable*; colourful, gaudy, gorgeous 425 adj. *florid*; tinsel, garish 847 adj. *vulgar*; brave, dashing, gallant, gay; spectacular, scenic, dramatic, histrionic, theatrical, stagy; sensational, daring; exhibitionist, stunting.

formal, dignified, solemn, stately, majestic; ceremonious, punctilious, stickling, correct, stiff, starchy; of state, public, official; ceremonial, ritual 988 adj. *ritualistic*.

Vb. *be ostentatious*, keep state, stand on ceremony; cut a dash, make a figure; glitter, dazzle 417 vb. *shine*; flaunt, sport 228 vb. *wear*; beat the big drum 528 vb. *proclaim*; exhibit 522 vb. *show*; act the showman, make the most of, put on a front, window-dress; strive for effect, sensationalize; stand in the limelight 455 vb. *attract notice*; advertise oneself, dramatize o.; play to the gallery, fish for compliments; show off, stunt, show one's paces, prance; parade, strut 873 vb. *be vain*.

876. Celebration – N. *celebration*, performance, solemnization 676 n. *action*; commemoration 505 n. *remembrance*; observance 988 n. *ritual*; ceremony, function, occasion, do; welcome, hero's w., official reception 923 n. *applause*; festive occasion, fête 837 n. *festivity*; ovation, triumph, salute, salvo, tattoo, fanfare, flourish of trumpets 835 n. *rejoicing*; illuminations 420 n. *fireworks*; bonfire 379 n. *fire*; triumphal arch 729 n. *trophy*; paean, hosannah, hallelujah 886 n. *congratulation*; health, toast.

special day, day to remember, great day, red-letter d., banner d., gala d., flag d., field d.; Saint's day, feast d., fast d. 988 n. *holy-day*; anniversary, centenary, bicentenary, tercentenary, quatercentenary, sesquicentenary.

Adj. *celebrative*, commemorative 505 adj. *remembering*; occasional, anniversary, centennial, bicentennial, millennial 141 adj. *seasonal*; triumphant, triumphal; honorific 886 adj. *gratulatory*.

Vb. *celebrate*, solemnize, perform 676 vb. *do*; hallow, keep holy 979 vb. *sanctify*; commemorate 505 vb. *remember*; honour, observe, keep, maintain; signalize, make an occasion; make much of, welcome, kill the fatted calf 882 vb. *be hospitable*; do honour to, fête; garland, wreathe, crown 962 vb. *reward*; lionize, give a hero's welcome, fling wide the gates 884 vb. *pay respects*; jubilate, triumph 835 vb. *rejoice*.

toast, pledge, clink glasses; drink to, raise one's glass to, drink a health 301 vb. *drink*.

877. Boasting – N. *boasting*, bragging, boastfulness, vainglory, gasconism, braggadocio, braggartism; self-glory, self-advertisement, swagger, swank, bounce 873 n. *vanity*; puffery 482 n. *overestimation*; grandiloquence, rodomontade 515 n. *empty talk*; heroics, bravado; chauvinism, jingoism, spread-eagleism; blustering, bluster 854 n. *nervousness*; sabre-rattling 900 n. *threat*.

boast, brag, vaunt; puff 528 n. *advertisement*; gasconade, bravado, bombast 546 n. *exaggeration*; hot air, much cry and little wool 515 n. *empty talk*; bluff, bounce 542 n. *deception*; big talk, bluster 900 n. *threat*.

boaster, braggart, brag, big mouth, shouter, blusterer; charlatan, pretender 545 n. *impostor*; bluffer 545 n. *liar*; swank 873 n. *vain person*; gasconader, miles gloriosus; advertiser, puffer 528 n. *publicizer*; trumpeter; jingoist, chauvinist; sabre-rattler.

Adj. *boastful*, big-mouthed; braggart, self-glorious 873 adj. *vain*; jingoistic, chauvinistic 718 adj. *warlike*; bluffing, 542 adj. *spurious*; bombastic 546 adj. *exaggerated*.

Vb. *boast*, brag, vaunt, talk big, shoot one's mouth, bluff, bluster, shout; enlarge, magnify 546 vb. *exaggerate*; trumpet, puff, crack up, cry one's wares 528 vb. *advertise*; sell oneself, blow one's trumpet 875 vb. *be ostentatious*; play the jingo, make the eagle scream 900 vb. *threaten*; show off, strut, swagger, prance 873 vb. *be vain*; boast of, plume oneself 871 vb. *be proud*; glory, crow over 727 vb. *triumph*.

878. Insolence – N. *insolence*, hubris, arrogance, haughtiness, loftiness 871 n. *pride*; high tone 711 n. *defiance*; bluster 900 n. *threat*; disdain 922 n. *contempt*; sneer 926 n. *detraction*; contumely 899 n. *scurrility*; assurance, self-a., self-assertion, bumptiousness, cockiness, brashness; presumption 916 n. *arrogation*; audacity, hardihood, effrontery, shamelessness.

sauciness, disrespect, impertinence, impudence; pertness, nerve, brass, cheek, lip, sauce, snooks; taunt 921 n. *indignity*; rudeness 885 n. *discourtesy*; petulance, defiance, answering back, backtalk 460 n. *rejoinder*.

insolent person, sauce-box, malapert, impertinent, pup, puppy; upstart, Jack-in-office, tin god; blusterer 877 n. *boaster*; bantam-cock, cockalorum; bully, swashbuckler, fire-eater 904 n. *ruffian*.

Adj. *insolent*, insulting, contumelious 921 adj. *disrespectful*; injurious, scurrilous 899 adj. *maledicent*; disdainful,

contemptuous 922 adj. *despising*; haughty, snotty, up-stage, high-hat, high and mighty 871 n. *proud*; hubristic, arrogant, presumptuous; brash, bumptious 873 adj. *vain*; shameless, unblushing, unabashed, brazen; audacious 857 adj. *rash*; overweening, imperious, lordly, dictatorial.

impertinent, pert, malapert, impudent, saucy, cheeky, jaunty, cocky; cavalier, off-hand, familiar, over-f., free-and-easy, breezy, airy 921 adj. *disrespectful*; impolite 885 adj. *discourteous*; defiant, provocative, offensive, personal.

Vb. *be insolent*, forget one's manners 885 vb. *be rude*; have a nerve, cheek, sauce, give lip, taunt, provoke 891 vb. *enrage*; answer back 460 vb. *answer*; presume, take on oneself, make bold, make free with; sneer at 922 vb. *despise*; snort; cock a snook, put one's tongue out 711 vb. *defy*; outstare, outface, brazen it out; take a high tone, lord it; tempt providence.

879. Servility – N. *servility*; slavishness, abject spirit 856 n. *cowardice*; subservience 721 n. *submission*; submissiveness, obsequiousness 739 n. *obedience*; prostration, prosternation, bent back, bow, scrape, obeisance; toadyism, sycophancy, ingratiation 925 n. *flattery*; flunkeyism 745 n. *service*; slavery 745 n. *servitude*.

toady, toad, toad-eater, pickthank, yes-man 488 n. *assenter*; lickspittle, bootlicker, backscratcher, fawner 925 n. *flatterer*; sycophant, parasite, sponger, jackal, hanger-on; flunkey 742 n. *retainer*; born slave, cat's-paw 630 n. *tool*.

Adj. *servile*, not free 745 adj. *subject*; slavish 856 adj. *cowardly*; mean-spirited, mean, abject, tame, boot-licking; subservient 739 adj. *obedient*; time-serving 603 adj. *tergiversating*; deferential, truckling etc. vb.; sycophantic, parasitical; obsequious, over-civil, ingratiating 925 adj. *flattering*.

Vb. *be servile*, stoop to anything 867 vb. *demean oneself*; squirm, cringe, crouch, crawl, grovel, truckle, lick the boots of 721 vb. *knuckle under*; bow, scrape, bend, kowtow, kneel 311 vb. *stoop*; make up to, toady, fawn, ingratiate oneself 925 vb. *flatter*; fetch and carry for, jackal for 742 vb. *serve*; do one's dirty work, pander to, stooge for 628 vb. *be instrumental*; whine 761 vb. *beg*; sponge on.

Section 3: Sympathetic

880. Friendship – N. *friendship*, amity 710 n. *concord*; compatibility, friendly relations, intercourse, hobnobbing 882 n. *sociality*; fellowship, comradeship 706 n. *association*; solidarity 706 n. *cooperation*; acquaintanceship, acquaintance, familiarity, intimacy 490 n. *knowledge*; honeymoon 887 n. *love*; reconciliation 719 n. *pacification*.

friendliness, amicability, kindness 884 n. *courtesy*; cordiality, warmth 897 n. *benevolence*; fraternization, camaraderie, mateyness; hospitality 882 n. *sociability*; greeting, welcome, open arms; goodwill, fellow-feeling, sympathy 775 n. *participation*; understanding, entente, honeymoon 710 n. *concord*; partiality, favouritism 914 n. *injustice*.

friend, girl-f., boy-f. 887 n. *loved one*; acquaintance, intimate a.; gossip, crony (see *chum*); neighbour, fellow-townsman, fellow-countryman; well-wisher 707 n. *patron*; fellow, brother 707 n. *colleague*; ally, brother-in-arms 707 n. *auxiliary*; friend in need; invitee, guest, persona grata; host 882 n. *social person*.

close friend, best f., next f.; best man 894 n. *bridesman*; dear friend, intimate, bosom friend, confidant; alter ego, other self, shadow; comrade, companion, boon c.; good friends all, happy family; inseparables, band of brothers; birds of a feather.

chum, gossip, crony; pal, mate, bully, buddy, sidekick; fellow, comrade, shipmate, messmate 707 n. *colleague*; playmate, schoolfellow.

Adj. *friendly*, non-hostile, amicable, well-affected; devoted, loyal, faithful, staunch, fast, firm 929 adj. *trustworthy*; fraternal, brotherly, sisterly, cousinly; xenophile; compatible, sympathetic; well-intentioned 897 adj. *benevolent*; hearty, cordial, warm, welcoming, hospitable 882 adj. *sociable*; comradely, chummy, pally, matey; acquainted 490 adj. *knowing*; neighbourly, on the best of terms; intimate, inseparable, thick, thick as thieves.

Vb. *be friendly*, fraternize, hobnob 882 vb. *be sociable*; welcome, entertain 882 vb. *be hospitable*; sympathize 516 vb. *understand*; like, warm to, cotton on to 887 vb. *love*; have the friendliest feelings 897 vb. *be benevolent*.

befriend, acknowledge, know; take up, favour, protect 703 vb. *patronize*; strike an acquaintance; break the ice, make overtures 289 vb. *approach*; take to, warm to, cotton on to; fraternize with, frat, hobnob, get pally with, chum up w.; make acquainted, introduce.

881. Enmity – N. *enmity*, inimicality, hostility, antagonism 704 n. *opposition*; no love lost, unfriendliness, incompatibility, antipathy 861 n. *dislike*; loathing 888 n. *hatred*; animosity, animus, spite, grudge, ill-feeling, ill-will 898 n. *malevolence*; jealousy 912 n. *envy*; coolness, estrangement, alienation 709 n. *dissension*; bitterness, rancour 891 n. *resentment*; breach, open b. 709 n. *quarrel*; hostilities, state of war 718 n. *belligerency*; vendetta, feud.

enemy, no friend, bad f., ill-wisher; antagonist, opposite side, other s. 705 n. *opponent*; rival 716 n. *contender*; foe, foeman, hostile 722 n. *combatant*; archenemy, Amalekite; xenophobe; persona non grata, pet aversion, bête noire, Dr Fell 888 n. *hateful object*; aggressor 712 n. *attacker*.

Adj. *inimical*, unfriendly, disaffected, disloyal 738 adj. *disobedient*; cool, icy 380 adj. *cold*; antipathetic, incompatible, unsympathetic 861 n. *disliking*; hostile 704 adj. *opposing*; antagonized, estranged, irreconcilable; rancorous 891 adj. *resentful*; jealous 912 adj. *envious*; spiteful 898 adj. *malevolent*; at feud, at enmity 709 adj. *quarrelling*; aggressive, militant, belligerent 718 adj. *warring*; intolerant 735 adj. *oppressive*.

Vb. *be inimical*, — unfriendly etc. adj.; bear malice 898 vb. *be malevolent*; grudge 912 vb. *envy*; hound, persecute 735 vb. *oppress*; war, make w. 718 vb. *wage war*; conflict, collide, clash 14 vb. *be contrary*.

make enemies, get across, antagonize 891 vb. *enrage*; estrange, alienate, make bad blood, set at odds 709 vb. *make quarrels*.

882. Sociality – N. *sociality*, membership, intercommunity 706 n. *association*; clubbism, esprit de corps; fellowship, comradeship, companionship, society; camaraderie, fraternization; intercourse, social i. 880 n. *friendship*; social circle, family c., one's friends and acquaintances 880 n. *friend*; social demands, the world.

sociability, social activity, group a.; social adjustment, compatibility 83 n. *conformity*; gregariousness, fondness for company 880 n. *friendliness*; social success, popularity; social tact, common touch; social graces, savoir vivre 884 n. *courtesy*; urbanity 846 n. *good taste*; clubbability; affability, conversability 584 n. *interlocution*; greeting, glad hand, handshake 884 n. *courteous act*; hospitality, home from home 813 n. *liberality*; good fellowship, geniality, cordiality, heartiness, back-slapping, bonhomie, conviviality, joviality 824 n. *enjoyment*.

social gathering, meeting 74 n. *assembly*; reunion, get-together, conversazione, social, squash, reception, salon, drawing-room; at home, soirée, levee; symposium, party; housewarming, house party; social meal, feast 301 n. *feasting*.

social round, social whirl, season; calling list, round of visits; stay, visit, call, visiting terms 880 n. *friendship*; social demand, engagement, dating, rendezvous, assignation, date.

social person, active member; caller,

visitor, dropper-in, frequenter, habitué; bon vivant; good mixer, good company, life and soul of the party; social success 890 n. *favourite*; boon companion, clubman; good neighbour 880 n. *friend*; hostess, host; guest, one of the family; socialite, social climber 848 n. *beau monde*.

Adj. *sociable*, gregarious, social, fond of company, party-minded; companionable, affable, conversable; clubbable, clubby; folksy; neighbourly 880 adj. *friendly*; hospitable, cordial, hearty, back-slapping, hail-fellow-well-met; convivial, festive, Christmassy 833 adj. *gay*; unbuttoned, post-prandial, after-dinner 683 adj. *reposeful*.

Vb. *be sociable*, like company; mix well, get around, go out, dine o., gatecrash; beat it up 837 vb. *amuse oneself*; join in, get together, make it a party, carouse 837 vb. *revel*; make oneself at home, make one of the family; date, date up; make friends 880 vb. *befriend*; keep up with, keep in w.

visit, see people, guest with, stay, weekend, see one's friends; look one up, call, wait on, look in, drop in.

be hospitable, keep open house 813 vb. *be liberal*; invite, have, be at home, receive; welcome 884 vb. *greet*; act the host, do the honours, preside; have company, entertain 301 vb. *feed*; give a party 837 vb. *revel*; accept, cater for 633 vb. *provide*.

883. Unsociability. Seclusion – N. *unsociability*, unsociableness, shyness 620 n. *avoidance*; domesticity; singleness 895 n. *celibacy*; inhospitality; stand-offishness, unapproachability, distance, aloofness; unfriendliness, moroseness, savageness; silence, inconversability 582 n. *taciturnity*; ostracism, boycott 57 n. *exclusion*.

seclusion, privacy, private world, world on its own; peace and quiet 266 n. *quietude*; home life, domesticity; loneliness, solitude; retirement, withdrawal; confinement, purdah 525 n. *concealment*; isolation 744 n. *independence*; renunciation of the world 985 n. *monasticism*; self-exile, expatriation; sequestration, segregation, rustication, excommunication, quarantine 57 n. *exclusion*; reserve, reservation, ghetto, native quarter; backwater, god-forsaken hole, back of beyond; island, desert; cloister, cell, hermitage, retreat; ivory tower, private quarters, shell.

solitary, unsocial person, iceberg; lone wolf; isolationist, island; recluse, stay-at-home; cenobite, anchorite, hermit; stylite, pillarmonk; maroon, castaway 779 n. *derelict*.

outcaste, outcast, pariah, leper, outsider; expatriate 59 n. *foreigner*; exile, expellee, deportee, evacuee, refugee, displaced person, stateless p.; outlaw, bandit; Ishmael, vagabond 268 n. *wanderer*; waif, stray, orphan 779 n. *derelict*; flotsam and jetsam 641 n. *rubbish*.

Adj. *unsociable*, unsocial, antisocial, morose, not fit to live with; unassimilated 59 adj. *extraneous*; unclubbable, stay-at-home, home-keeping, domestic; inhospitable, unwelcoming, forbidding, hostile, savage; distant, stand-offish; unforthcoming, in one's shell; unaffable 582 adj. *taciturn*; impersonal 860 adj. *indifferent*; solitary, lone 88 adj. *alone*; shy, misanthropic; anchoretic, eremetic, retiring.

friendless, unfriended, lorn, forlorn, desolate, god-forsaken; lonely, lonesome, solitary; on one's own 88 adj. *alone*; uninvited, without introductions; unpopular 860 adj. *unwanted*.

secluded, private, sequestered, retired, hidden, buried, tucked away 523 adj. *latent*; behind the veil, behind the purdah 421 adj. *screened*; quiet, lonely, isolated, enisled; god-forsaken, unvisited, unexplored, off the beaten track 491 adj. *unknown*; uninhabited, desert, desolate 190 adj. *empty*.

Vb. *be unsocial*, keep one's own company, keep oneself to oneself; go it alone, stew in one's own juice; stay in one's shell, remain private, stand aloof 620 vb. *avoid*; leave the world, take the veil.

make unwelcome, frown on 924 vb.

disapprove; repel, keep at arm's length, ignore, cut, cut dead 885 vb. *be rude*; cold-shoulder, turn one's back on; ostracize, boycott 57 vb. *exclude*; refuse to meet, have nothing to do with, treat as a leper 620 vb. *avoid*; excommunicate, 963 vb. *punish*.

seclude, sequester, island, isolate, quarantine; bury, keep in purdah; confine 747 vb. *imprison*.

884. Courtesy – N. *courtesy*, chivalry, gallantry; deference 920 n. *respect*; consideration, condescension 872 n. *humility*; graciousness, politeness, civility, manners, good behaviour, best b.; courtliness 875 n. *formality*; amiability, sweetness, niceness, obligingness; good humour, agreeableness, affability, suavity, blandness, common touch, social tact 882 n. *sociability*; smooth address 925 n. *flattery*.

courteous act, act of courtesy, graceful gesture, courtesy, civility, favour 897 n. *kind act*; compliment 886 n. *congratulation*; welcome, reception, invitation; salutation, salute, greeting, smile, kiss, handshake 920 n. *respects*; capping, salaam, bow, obeisance.

Adj. *courteous*, chivalrous, knightly, courtly, gallant, oldworld; polite, civil, urbane, dignified, well-mannered 848 adj. *well-bred*; gracious, condescending; mannerly 920 adj. *respectful*; on one's best behaviour, anxious to please 455 adj. *attentive*; agreeable, suave, bland, smooth, ingratiating, well-spoken 925 adj. *flattering*.

amiable, nice, sweet, winning 887 adj. *lovable*; affable, conversable, friendly 882 adj. *sociable*; kind 897 adj. *benevolent*; gentle, mild, good-tempered; well-behaved, good 739 adj. *obedient*.

Vb. *be courteous*, mind one's manners, show courtesy 920 vb. *respect*; condescend 872 vb. *be humble*; conciliate, speak fair 719 vb. *pacify*; take in good part 823 vb. *be patient*; mend one's manners.

pay respects, give one's regards, pay one's devoirs, offer one's duty; send one's compliments; drink to, pledge 876 vb. *toast*; homage, pay h. 920 vb. *show respect*; honour 876 n. *celebrate*.

greet, send greetings (see *pay respects*); flag, speak 547 vb. *signal*; accost, sidle up 289 vb. *approach*; hold out one's hand 455 vb. *notice*; hail 408 vb. *vociferate*; wave, smile; say hallo 583 vb. *speak to*; salute, raise one's hat, uncap, uncover; shake hands, press *or* squeeze *or* wring *or* pump the hand; escort 89 vb. *accompany*; present arms, parade, turn out; welcome 882 vb. *be sociable*; open one's arms, embrace, hug 889 vb. *caress*.

885. Discourtesy – N. *discourtesy*, impoliteness, bad manners, no manners, mannerlessness, scant courtesy, incivility, boorishness 847 n. *ill-breeding*; unpleasantness, nastiness, beastliness; tactlessness, inconsiderateness.

rudeness, ungraciousness, gruffness, bluntness, bluffness; ungentleness 735 n. *severity*; offhandedness 456 n. *inattention*; brusquerie, shortness, short answer 569 n. *conciseness*; unparliamentary language, bad l. 899 n. *scurrility*; insult 921 n. *indignity*; personality, impertinence, truculence 878 n. *insolence*; interruption, shouting; piece of bad manners, rudery; boor, curmudgeon, bear.

Adj. *discourteous*, unknightly, ungallant, unchivalrous; uncourtly, unceremonious, ungentlemanly, impolite, uncivil, rude; mannerless, unmannerly, ill-mannered, boorish, loutish, uncouth, brutish, beastly, savage 847 adj. *ill-bred*; insolent 878 adj. *impertinent*; unpleasant, disagreeable; off-handed, cavalier, airy, breezy, tactless, inconsiderate 456 adj. *inattentive*.

ungracious, unsmiling, grim 834 adj. *serious*; gruff, bearish 893 adj. *sullen*; grudging; difficult, surly, churlish, unfriendly, unneighbourly 883 adj. *unsociable*; ungentle, rough, rugged; scant of courtesy, brusque, short 569 adj. *concise*; sarcastic, uncomplimentary, unflattering 926 adj. *detracting*; abusive 899 adj. *maledicent*; truculent 921 adj. *disrespectful*.

Vb. *be rude*, want manners, flout etiquette; know no better 699 vb. *be artless*; be beastly to, snub, show one the door 300 vb. *eject*; insult 921 vb. *not respect*; take liberties; lose one's temper, shout, interrupt 891 vb. *get angry*; scowl, pout, sulk 893 vb. *be sullen*.

886. Congratulation – N. *congratulation*, felicitation, gratulation, congratulations, compliments, compliments of the season; good wishes, best w., happy returns; salute, toast; welcome, hero's w. 876 n. *celebration*.

Adj. *gratulatory*, congratulatory, complimentary; honorific, triumphal 876 adj. *celebrative*.

Vb. *gratulate*, congratulate, felicitate, compliment; offer one's congratulations, wish one joy, give one joy; sanction a triumph, vote an ovation, accord an o.; fête, mob, rush, lionize 876 vb. *celebrate*; congratulate oneself, hug o., thank one's stars 824 vb. *be pleased*.

887. Love – N. *love*, affection, friendship, charity, Eros; agapism; true love, real thing; mother-love, baby-worship; possessiveness 911 n. *jealousy*; uxoriousness; sentiment 818 n. *feeling*; kindness, tenderness; fondness, liking, predilection, inclination 179 n. *tendency*; fancy 604 n. *caprice*; attachment, devotion, patriotism 739 n. *loyalty*; sentimentality, susceptibility, amorousness 819 n. *moral sensibility*; lovesickness, Cupid's sting, yearning, longing 859 n. *desire*; eroticism, prurience, lust 859 n. *libido*; admiration, hero-worship 864 n. *wonder*; first love, calf l., young l.; crush, pash, infatuation; worship 982 n. *idolatry*; passion, tender p., rapture, transport 822 n. *excitable state*; erotomania 84 n. *abnormality*; love-hate, odi et amo.

lovableness, amiability, attractiveness, popularity, gift of pleasing; winsomeness, charm, fascination, appeal, sex-a., attractions, winning ways; coquetry, flirtatiousness; sentimental value.

love affair, romance, love and the world well lost; flirtation, amour, amourette, entanglement; loves, amours; liaison, intrigue 951 n. *illicit love*; course of love, the old old story.

love-making, courtship, courting, walking out 889 n. *wooing*; pursuit of love, flirting, coquetry, philandering; gallantry, dalliance 951 n. *unchastity*; favours.

lover, love, true l., sweetheart; young man, boy, boy-friend, Romeo; swain, beau, gallant, squire, escort, date; steady, fiancé; wooer, courter, suitor, follower, admirer, hero-worshipper, votary, worshipper; fan, fan-mail; sugar-daddy, dotard; ladies' man, lady-killer; paramour, amorist 952 n. *libertine*; flirt, coquette, philanderer.

loved one, beloved object, beloved, love 890 n. *darling*; favoured suitor, lucky man, intended, betrothed, fiancé, fiancée, bride-to-be 894 n. *spouse*; conquest, inamorata, lady-love, flame, sweetheart, darling, babe, dear; idol, hero; heart-throb, dream man, dream girl; favourite, mistress 952 n. *kept woman*.

love god, goddess of love, Venus, Aphrodite, Astarte, Freya; Amor, Eros, Kama, Cupid, blind boy; cupidon, amoretto.

Adj. *loving*, agapistic; loyal, patriotic 931 adj. *disinterested*; wooing 889 adj. *caressing*; affectionate, cuddlesome, demonstrative; tender, motherly, wifely, conjugal; loverlike, gallant, sentimental, lovesick; love-lorn, languishing 834 adj. *dejected*; fond, uxorious, doting; possessive 911 adj. *jealous*; flirtatious, coquettish 604 adj. *capricious*; amatory, amorous, amative, ardent, passionate 818 adj. *fervent*; liking, desirous 859 adj. *desiring*; concupiscent 951 adj. *lecherous*.

enamoured, in love, sweet on, keen on, set on, sold on; smitten, bitten, caught, hooked; charmed 983 adj. *bewitched*; mad on, infatuated, besotted, dippy, crazy about, rapturous, ecstatic.

lovable, desirable, likeable, congenial, sympathetic, after one's heart 859 adj. *desired*; winsome 884 adj. *amiable*; sweet, angelic, divine, adorable, lovely 841 adj. *beautiful*; intriguing, attractive,

seductive, alluring 291 adj. *attracting*; prepossessing, appealing, engaging, winning, endearing, captivating, irresistible; bewitching 983 adj. *sorcerous*; endeared to, dear, darling, pet, fancy favourite.

erotic, aphrodisiac, erotogenic; amatory, amatorious, amatorial.

Vb. *love*, like, care, affect, be partial to; bear love, hold dear, care for, be tender, cherish; appreciate, value, prize, treasure, think the world of, regard, admire, revere 920 vb. *respect*; adore, worship, idolize 982 vb. *idolatrize*; make love, poodle-fake, honey, bestow one's favours; make much of, spoil, pet, fondle 889 vb. *caress*.

be in love, burn, sweat, die of *or* for love 361 vb. *die*; love to distraction, dote 503 vb. *be insane*; take to, warm to, look sweet on 859 vb. *desire*; fall for, fall in love, lose one's heart; woo, sue, sigh 889 vb. *court*; set one's cap at, chase 619 vb. *pursue*; honeymoon 894 vb. *wed*.

excite love 859 vb. *cause desire*; warm, inflame 381 vb. *heat*; rouse, stir, flutter, enrapture, enthral 821 vb. *excite*; dazzle, bedazzle, charm, enchant, fascinate 983 vb. *bewitch*; allure, draw 291 vb. *attract*; make oneself attractive 843 vb. *primp*; tantalize, seduce 612 vb. *tempt*; lead on, flirt, coquette, philander; toy, vamp 889 vb. *caress*; make eyes, ogle 889 vb. *court*; enamour, take one's fancy, make a hit, sweep off one's feet, infatuate; captivate 745 vb. *subjugate*; endear oneself, ingratiate o.

888. Hatred – N. *hatred*, hate, no love lost; love-hate, odi et amo; revulsion of feeling, disillusion; aversion, antipathy, allergy, nausea 861 n. *dislike*; repugnance, detestation, loathing, abhorrence, abomination; disfavour (see *odium*); disaffection 709 n. *dissension*; antagonism 881 n. *enmity*; animosity, ill-feeling, bad blood, bitterness 891 n. *resentment*; malice 898 n. *malevolence*; jealousy 912 n. *envy*; execration, hymn of hate 899 n. *malediction*; phobia, xenophobia 481 n. *prejudice*.

odium, disfavour, unpopularity 924 n. *disapprobation*; discredit, black books ¿67 n. *disrepute*; bad odour, malodour; odiousness, hatefulness, loathsomeness, obnoxiousness; contemptibility 922 n. *despisedness*.

hateful object, unwelcome necessity, bitter pill; abomination, one's hate 881 n. *enemy*; not one's type, one's aversion, pet a., bête noire, Dr Fell, nobody's darling; pest, menace, good riddance 659 n. *bane*; outsider 938 n. *cad*.

Adj. *hating*, loathing etc. vb.; loveless; antipathetic 861 adj. *disliking*; averse, antagonistic, hostile, antagonized 881 adj. *inimical*; envious, malicious, malignant, fell 898 adj. *malevolent*; rancorous 891 adj. *resentful*; implacable, vindictive 910 adj. *revengeful*; out of love, disillusioned 509 adj. *disappointed*.

hateful, odious, unlovable, unloved; invidious, antagonizing, obnoxious, pestilential 659 adj. *baneful*; beastly 645 adj. *not nice*; abhorrent, loathsome, abominable; accursed, execrable; offensive, repulsive, repellent, nauseous 861 adj. *disliked*; unwelcome 860 adj. *unwanted*.

hated, loathed etc. vb.; out of favour, unpopular 861 adj. *disliked*; discredited 924 adj. *disapproved*; loveless, unloved; unregretted, unlamented; spurned, condemned 607 adj. *rejected*.

Vb. *hate*, bear hatred, have no love for, loathe, abominate, detest, abhor, revolt from 280 vb. *recoil*; disrelish 861 vb. *dislike*; spurn, contemn 922 vb. *despise*; execrate, denounce 899 vb. *curse*; bear malice 898 vb. *be malevolent*; feel envy 912 vb. *envy*; bear a grudge; scowl, growl, snap 893 vb. *be sullen*.

excite hate, grate, jar 292 vb. *repel*; disgust, nauseate, stink in the nostrils 861 vb. *cause dislike*; shock, horrify, antagonize; estrange, alienate, create bad blood 881 vb. *make enemies*; poison, envenom 832 vb. *aggravate*; exasperate, incense 891 vb. *enrage*.

soft nothings, lovers' vows; dalliance, billing and cooing, fondling, petting, caress, embrace, clip, cuddle, squeeze; salute, kiss, buss, smacker; stroke, tickle, slap, tap, pat, pinch, nip 378 n. *touch*; familiarity, advances, pass.

wooing, courting, spooning, flirting; play, love-p., love-making; glad eye, come-hither look, ogle, sheep's eyes, fond look, sigh; flirtation, philandering, coquetry, gallantry, amorous intentions; courtship, suit, addresses; tale of love, serenade, love-song; love-letter, billet-doux; engagement, betrothal 894 n. *marriage*.

love-token, favour, glove; ring; valentine; arrow, heart, bleeding h.

Adj. *caressing*, toying etc. vb.; demonstrative, affectionate 887 adj. *loving*; spoony, cuddlesome, flirtatious, coquettish.

Vb. *pet*, pamper, spoil, mother, kill with kindness; cosset, cocker, coddle; make much of, treasure, tender 887 vb. *love*; cherish, foster, nurse, lap, rock, cradle, baby; sing to, croon over; coax, wheedle 925 vb. *flatter*.

caress, love, fondle, dandle; play with, stroke, pat, chuck under the chin; kiss, buss; embrace, fold in one's arms, hang on one's neck; clip, hug, cling 778 vb. *retain*; clasp, squeeze, press, cuddle; snuggle, nestle, nuzzle; wanton, toy, trifle, dally, spark; make love, poodle-fake, carry on, spoon, bill and coo, hold hands, slap and tickle, pet, neck; vamp 887 vb. *excite love*; (of animals) lick, fawn; (of a crowd) mob, rush.

court, make advances, give the glad eye, accept a pass; make eyes, ogle, leer 438 vb. *gaze*; get off, make passes; gallivant, philander, flirt, coquette 887 vb. *excite love*; squire, escort 89 vb. *accompany*; walk out with; sue, woo, pay court to, serenade; sigh, pine, languish 887 vb. *love*; propose marriage, pop the question, make a match 894 vb. *wed*.

889. Endearment – **N.** *endearment*, blandishment, compliment 925 n. *flattery*; loving words, pretty speeches, pet names;

890. Darling. Favourite – **N.** *darling*, dear, dearest, dear one, only one; love, beloved 887 n. *loved one*; sweetheart, fancy, sweeting, sweetie, sugar, honey, honeybunch; precious, jewel, treasure; mavourneen, babe; angel, cherub; poppet, popsy, pet, lamb; ducks, ducky, dearie, lovey.

favourite, darling, mignon; spoiled darling, mother's darling, teacher's pet; jewel, apple of one's eye, blue-eyed boy; persona grata, one of the best, the tops, sport; first choice, top seed 644 n. *exceller*; someone to be proud of, boast; hero, idol, star, top-liner, hit, knockout; general favourite, cynosure, toast; world's sweetheart, Queen of Hearts; centre of attraction, honey-pot 291 n. *attraction*; catch, lion 859 n. *desired object*.

891. Resentment. Anger – N. *resentment*, displeasure 829 n. *discontent*; huffiness, ill-humour 893 n. *sullenness*; heart-burning, rancour, soreness; slow burn, growing impatience; indignation (see *anger*); umbrage, offence, huff, tiff, pique; bile, spleen, gall; bitterness, hard feelings; virulence, hate 888 n. *hatred*; animosity, grudge, bone to pick, crow to pluck 881 n. *enmity*; vindictiveness, revengefulness, spite 910 n. *revenge*; malice 898 n. *malevolence*; cause of offence, red rag to a bull, sore point, dangerous subject; pin-prick, irritation 827 n. *annoyance*; provocation, aggravation, last straw 921 n. *indignity*.

anger, wrathfulness, irritation, exasperation, vexation, indignation; dudgeon, wrath, ire, dander, wax; rage, fury, passion 822 n. *excitable state*; crossness, temper, tantrum, paddy, paddywhack, fume, fret, pet, explosion 318 n. *agitation*; rampage, fire and fury, roar 400 n. *loudness*; fierceness, angry look, glare, frown, scowl; growl, snarl 893 n. *sullenness*; warmth, heat, high words 709 n. *quarrel*.

Adj. *resentful*, piqued, stung, hurt, sore, smarting 829 adj. *discontented*; warm, indignant; reproachful 924 adj. *disapproving*; bitter, embittered, acrimonious, rancorous, virulent 888 adj. *hating*; spiteful 898 adj. *malevolent*; vin-

dictive 910 adj. *revengeful*; jealous 912 adj. *envious*.

angry, displeased, not amused 834 adj. *serious*; impatient, cross, waxy, ratty, wild; wroth, wrathy, ireful, irate; worked up, het up, hot under the collar; indignant, incensed, infuriated; shirty, in a temper, in a taking; furious; apoplectic, rabid, mad, hopping m. 503 adj. *frenzied*; seeing red, berserk; red-eyed, bloodshot.

Vb. *resent*, be piqued, — offended etc. adj.; feel, mind, smart under 829 vb. *be discontented*; take amiss, take offence, take umbrage, take exception 709 vb. *quarrel*; get sore, cut up rough; burn, smoulder, boil with indignation; take to heart, let it rankle, bear malice, cherish a grudge.

get angry, get cross, get mad; kindle, grow warm, flush with anger; flare up, rear up, ramp; bridle up, bristle up, raise one's hackles, arch one's back; lose one's temper, forget oneself, fly off the handle; let off steam, blow one's top, explode; see red, go berserk.

be angry, show impatience, chafe, fret, fume, fuss, dance, ramp, stamp; carry on, create, make a scene; turn nasty, cut up rough, raise Cain; rage, rant, roar, bellow, bluster, storm, thunder, fulminate 400 vb. *be loud*; look like thunder, glare, glower 893 vb. *be sullen*; swell with fury, burst with indignation, lash one's tail; breathe fire and fury, out-Lear Lear.

huff, pique, sting, nettle, rankle; wound 827 vb. *hurt*; antagonize, put one's back up, get across, give umbrage, offend 888 vb. *excite hate*; affront, insult, outrage 921 vb. *not respect*.

enrage, upset, discompose, ruffle, irritate, rile, peeve; annoy, put out, vex, pester 827 vb. *incommode*; tease, bait, pinprick, needle 827 vb. *torment*; bite, fret, nag; try one's patience, push too far, work into a passion; anger, incense, infuriate, madden; goad, sting, taunt, rouse one's ire, kindle one's wrath, stir one's bile, get one's dander up; make one's blood boil, make one see red; embitter, ulcerate, envenom, poison;

exasperate 832 vb. *aggravate*; embroil 709 vb. *make quarrels.*

892. Irascibility – N. *irascibility*, quick passions, irritability, impatience 822 n. *excitability*; grumpiness, gruffness 883 n. *unsociability*; sharpness, tartness, asperity 393 n. *sourness*; sensitivity 819 n. *moral sensibility*; huffiness, touchiness, prickliness, bellicosity 709 n. *quarrelsomeness*; temperament, testiness, peevishness, petulance; hot temper, limited patience, snappishness, a word and a blow; fierceness, fieriness.

shrew, scold, fishwife, spitfire, termagant, virago, vixen, battle-axe, fury; Tartar, hornet; bear 902 n. *misanthrope*; crosspatch, mad dog.

Adj. *irascible*, impatient, choleric, irritable, peppery, testy, crusty, peevish, cross-grained; short-tempered, hot-t., sharp-t.; prickly, touchy, tetchy, huffy 819 adj. *sensitive*; inflammable, hot-blooded, fierce, fiery 822 adj. *excitable*; quick, hasty, trigger-happy 857 adj. *rash*; dangerous 709 adj. *quarrelling*; shrewish, vixenish, curst; cantankerous, querulous; bitter, vinegary 393 adj. *sour*; splenetic, liverish; scratchy, snappish, waspish; tart, sharp, short; fractious, fretful, moody, temperamental; gruff, grumpy, pettish, ratty 829 adj. *discontented*; ill-humoured, currish 893 adj. *sullen.*

893. Sullenness – N. *sullenness*, sternness, grimness 834 n. *seriousness*; sulkiness, ill-humour, pettishness; morosity, churlishness 883 n. *unsociability*; gruffness 885 n. *discourtesy*; peevishness, ill-temper 892 n. *irascibility*; sulks, the pouts, mulligrubs, moodiness, temperament; the blues 834 n. *melancholy*; black look, glare, glower, frown, scowl; snort, growl, snarl, snap.

Adj. *sullen*, forbidding, ugly; black, gloomy, overcast 418 adj. *dark*; stern, unsmiling, grim 834 adj. *serious*; sulky, cross, out of humour, misanthropic 883 adj. *unsociable*; morose, crabbed, crusty, cross-grained, ill-conditioned, difficult; snappish, pettish 709 adj. *quarrelling*;

grouchy, grumpy 829 adj. *discontented*; acid, tart, vinegary 393 adj. *sour*; gruff 885 adj. *discourteous*; temperamental, moody, humoursome; jaundiced, blue 834 adj. *melancholic*; petulant, peevish, currish, curst, shirty 892 adj. *irascible*; smouldering, sultry.

Vb. *be sullen*, gloom, look black, scowl, frown; spit, snap, snarl, growl, snort; make a face, grimace, pout, sulk 883 vb. *be unsocial*; mope 834 vb. *be dejected*; grouch, grouse 829 vb. *be discontented.*

894. Marriage – N. *marriage*, matrimony, wedlock, conjugal bliss; match, union, alliance; conjugality, nuptial bond, marriage tie, marriage bed, life together; wifehood, matronage, matronhood; banns, marriage certificate, marriage lines.

type of marriage, matrimonial arrangement, monogamy, monandry, polygamy, polygyny, polyandry; bigamy, gamomania; remarriage, widow r.; leviration, levirate; arranged match, love-match, intermarriage, miscegenation; mismarriage, mésalliance, morganatic marriage; spiritual marriage, syneisaktism; companionate marriage, free love, concubinage; shotgun wedding; abduction, Sabine rape.

wedding, getting married, match, match-making; nuptial vows, betrothal, espousal; nuptials, marriage rites, wedding service, nuptial mass, nuptial benediction; church wedding, civil marriage; run-away match, elopement; prothalamium, epithalamium; marriage feast, wedding breakfast, reception; honeymoon.

bridesman, groomsman, best man, paranymph, bridal party; matron of honour, bridesmaid, page, train-bearer; attendant, usher.

spouse, man, wife; man and wife, Mr and Mrs, Darby and Joan; married couple, bridal pair, newlyweds, honeymooners; bride, bridegroom, consort, partner, mate, affinity; husband, lord and master; married woman, wedded wife, lady, matron, wife of one's bosom, helpmate, better half, woman, old w., missus, rib; squaw, broadwife; monogamist.

polygamist, polygynist, much-married man, Mormon, Solomon; Bluebeard; bigamist.

matchmaker, matrimonial agent, marriage-broker, go-between; marriage adviser 720 n. *mediator*.

nubility, marriageable age, marriageability; eligibility, good match; welcome suitor 887 n. *lover*.

Adj. *married*, partnered, paired, mated, matched; wived, husbanded; handfast, spliced, in double harness; united, made man and wife; monogamous; polygamous, polyandrous; much-married; remarried, bigamous; newly-wed, honeymooning.

marriageable, nubile, concubitant, of age, of marriageable a.; eligible, suitable.

matrimonial, marital, connubial, concubinary; nuptial, bridal, hymeneal, epithalamial; conjugal, wifely, matronly, husbandly; digamous, bigamous; polygamous, polygynous, polyandrous; morganatic; gamomaniac; syneisaktical.

Vb. *marry*, marry off, match, mate; matchmake; betroth, affiance, espouse; give in marriage, give away; join in marriage, declare man and wife; join, couple, handfast, splice, hitch, tie the knot.

wed, marry, espouse; wive, take to oneself a wife, find a husband; get married, mate with, bestow one's hand; lead to the altar, take for better or worse, be made one; pair off, mate, couple; honeymoon, cohabit, set up house together; mismarry, repent at leisure; marry in haste, elope; contract matrimony, make one an honest woman; remarry, commit bigamy; intermarry, miscegenate.

895. Celibacy – N. *celibacy*, singleness, single state, single blessedness 744 n. *independence*; bachelorhood; misogamy, misogyny 883 n. *unsociability*; spinster-

hood; monkhood, the veil 985 n. *monasticism*; maidenhood 950 n. *purity*.

celibate, unmarried man, single m., bachelor; confirmed bachelor, not the marrying kind; misogynist 902 n. *misanthrope*; celibatarian, encratite, monastic 986 n. *monk*; hermit 883 n. *solitary*; monastic order.

spinster, unmarried woman, femme sole, bachelor girl; débutante; maid, maiden, virgo intacta; maiden aunt, old maid; Vestal 986 n. *nun*.

Adj. *unwedded*, unwed, unmarried; single, unmated; spouseless, wifeless; husbandless; unwooed, unasked; maidenly, virginal, vestal 950 adj. *pure*; spinsterish, old-maidish; celibate, celibatarian, monkish 986 adj. *monastic*.

896. Divorce. Widowhood – N. *divorce*, dissolution of marriage, divorcement, repudiation; bill of divorcement, divorce decree; separation, judicial s., separatio a mensa et thoro, separatio a vinculo matrimonii; annulment, decree of nullity; no marriage, non-consummation; nullity, impediment, prohibited degree; desertion, separate maintenance, alimony; divorce court, divorce case, matrimonial cause; divorcé, divorcée.

widowhood, widowerhood, viduage, dowagerism; grass widowhood.

widowed spouse, widower, widow, widow woman, relict; dowager; grass widow.

Adj. *divorced*, separated, living apart; dissolved.

widowed, husbandless, wifeless; vidual.

Vb. *divorce*, separate, live apart, desert; unmarry, untie the knot; put away, banish from bed and board; sue for divorce, get a divorce, regain one's freedom; put asunder, dissolve marriage; widow.

897. Benevolence – N. *benevolence*, good will, helpfulness 880 n. *friendliness*; ahimsa, harmlessness 935 n. *innocence*; benignity, heart of gold; milk of human kindness, goodness of nature, kindheartedness, kindliness, kindness, loving-

k., goodness and mercy, charity 887
n. *love*; tenderness, consideration 736 n.
lenity; fellow-feeling, sympathy 818 n.
feeling; decent feeling, humanity, humanitarianism 901 n. *philanthropy*; utilitarianism 901 n. *sociology*; charitableness,
hospitality, beneficence, unselfishness,
generosity 813 n. *liberality*; placability,
mercy 909 n. *forgiveness*.

kind act, kindness, favour, service;
good deed, charity, relief, alms, alms-
giving 781 n. *giving*; good turn 703 n.
aid; labour of love 597 n. *voluntary work*.

kind person, bon enfant, Christian;
good neighbour, good Samaritan 880 n.
friend; altruist 901 n. *philanthropist*.

Adj. *benevolent*, well-meant, well-
intentioned, for the best 880 adj. *friendly*;
out of kindness, to oblige; out of charity,
eleemosynary; sympathetic, kindly disposed, benign, benignant, kindly, kind-
hearted, warm-hearted; kind, good,
human, decent, Christian; affectionate
887 adj. *loving*; fatherly, paternal; motherly, maternal; brotherly, fraternal;
sisterly, cousinly; placable, merciful 909
adj. *forgiving*; tolerant, indulgent 734
adj. *lax*; humane, considerate 736 adj.
lenient; soft-hearted, tender 905 adj.
pitying; genial, hospitable, bountiful 813
adj. *liberal*; generous, unselfish, altruistic 931 adj. *disinterested*; beneficent,
charitable, humanitarian 901 adj. *philanthropic*; gallant, chivalrous 884 adj.
courteous.

Vb. *be benevolent*, — kind etc. adj.;
have one's heart in the right place;
sympathize, understand, do as one would
be done by; return good for evil 909 vb.
forgive; wish well, pray for, bless; bear
good will, mean well; favour 703 vb.
patronize; do a good turn, render a
service, oblige 703 vb. *aid*.

philanthropize, do good, have a social
conscience, show public spirit; reform,
humanize; go slumming; visit, nurse 703
vb. *minister to*.

898. Malevolence – N. *malevolence*, ill
nature, ill will 881 n. *enmity*; truculency,
cussedness, beastliness, worst intentions;

spite, gall, spitefulness, viciousness,
malignity, malignancy, malice; venom,
virulence 659 n. *bane*; bitterness, acrimony 393 n. *sourness*; rancour 891 n.
resentment; gloating, schadenfreude,
unholy joy 912 n. *envy*; evil eye 983 n.
spell.

inhumanity, uncharitableness; intolerance, persecution 735 n. *severity*; mercilessness, implacability 906 n. *pitilessness*;
unkindness, stepmotherly treatment;
callousness 326 n. *hardness*; cruelty,
barbarity, blood-thirstiness, bloodlust;
barbarism, savagery, ferocity; atrocious-
ness, outrageousness, immanity; ghoulishness, sadism, devilishness 934 n.
wickedness; brutality, ruffianism.

cruel act, truculence, brutality; victimization, 'tender mercies' 735 n. *severity*;
excess, extremes, extremity; atrocity,
outrage, devilry; cruelties, tortures,
barbarities; mass murder, genocide 362
n. *slaughter*.

Adj. *malevolent*, ill-wishing, meaning
harm 661 adj. *dangerous*; ill-natured,
ill-conditioned 893 adj. *sullen*; nasty,
vicious, bitchy, cussed 602 adj. *wilful*;
malicious, catty, spiteful 926 adj. *detracting*; mischievous (see *maleficent*);
baleful, malign, malignant 645 adj.
harmful; jealous 912 adj. *envious*; disloyal, treacherous 930 adj. *perfidious*;
rancorous 891 adj. *resentful*; implacable
906 adj. *pitiless*; vindictive 910 adj.
revengeful; hostile, fell 881 adj. *inimical*;
intolerant 735 adj. *oppressive*.

maleficent, hurtful 645 adj. *harmful*;
poisonous, venomous, virulent, caustic
659 adj. *baneful*; working ill, mischief-
making.

unkind, unamiable 893 adj. *sullen*;
unkindly, unloving, unaffectionate, un-
tender, stepmotherly, unmaternal, unfilial; unfriendly, hostile 881 adj.
inimical; inhospitable 883 adj. *unsociable*; ungenerous, uncharitable, unforgiving; stern 735 adj. *severe*; unsqueamish, tough, hardboiled, hardbitten 326
adj. *hard*; inhumane, unnatural.

cruel, grim, fell; steely, grim-faced,
hard-hearted; ruthless 906 adj. *pitiless*;

tyrannical 735 adj. *oppressive*; gloating, sadistic; bloodthirsty; bloody 176 adj. *violent*; excessive, extreme; atrocious, outrageous; unnatural, dehumanized, brutalized; brutal, rough, truculent, fierce, ferocious; savage, barbarous; inhuman, ghoulish, fiendish, devilish, diabolical, demoniacal, satanic, hellish, infernal.

Vb. *be malevolent*, bear malice 888 vb. *hate*; betray the cloven hoof; show envy 912 vb. *envy*; disoblige, spite, do one a bad turn; do one's worst; victimize, gloat; take it out of one, bully, maltreat; molest 645 vb. *harm*; malign 926 vb. *detract*; harry, hound, persecute, tyrannize, torture 735 vb. *oppress*; rankle, fester, poison; blight, blast; cast the evil eye 983 vb. *bewitch*.

899. Malediction – N. *malediction*, malison, curse, imprecation, anathema; evil eye 983 n. *spell*; ill wishes 898 n. *malevolence*; execration, denunciation, commination 900 n. *threat*; fulmination, thunder; exorcism, bell, book and candle.

scurrility, ribaldry, profanity, swearing; evil speaking, bad language, unparliamentary l., Limehouse, Billingsgate; naughty word, expletive, swearword, oath, swear, damn, curse; invective, vituperation, abuse; slanging match, stormy exchange; no compliment, aspersion, vilification 926 n. *calumny*; cheek 878 n. *sauciness*; personality 921 n. *indignity*; tongue-lashing 924 n. *reproach*.

Adj. *maledictory*, imprecatory, anathematizing, comminatory, fulminatory, denunciatory, damnatory.

maledicent, evil-speaking, profane, foul-mouthed, foul-spoken, unparliamentary, scurrilous, ribald 847 n. *vulgar*; sulphurous, blue; vituperative, abusive, vitriolic, vilipendious 924 adj. *disapproving*.

Vb. *curse*, cast the evil eye 983 vb. *bewitch*; accurse, wish on, call down on; wish one joy of; anathematize, imprecate, execrate; fulminate, inveigh 924 vb. *reprove*; denounce 928 vb. *accuse*; ex-

communicate, damn 961 vb. *condemn*; round upon, send to blazes; abuse, vituperate, revile, rail, heap abuse, pour vitriol 924 vb. *exprobate*.

cuss, curse, swear, damn, blast, swear like a trooper; slang, abuse, blackguard 924 vb. *exprobate*; rail, scold.

900. Threat – N. *threat*, menace; threatfulness, ominousness; challenge 711 n. *defiance*; blackmail 737 n. *demand*; war of nerves 854 n. *intimidation*; deterrent 723 n. *weapon*; sword of Damocles 661 n. *danger*; danger signal, writing on the wall 664 n. *warning*; bluster 877 n. *boast*; bark, snarl.

Adj. *threatening*, menacing, minatory, threatful; sabre-rattling 711 adj. *defiant*; bodeful, portentous, ominous 511 adj. *presageful*; in terrorem, deterrent 854 adj. *frightening*.

Vb. *threaten*, threat, menace, use threats, blackmail 737 vb. *demand*; deter, intimidate 854 vb. *frighten*; fulminate, thunder 899 vb. *curse*; bark, talk big, bluster, hector 877 vb. *boast*; snarl, growl 893 vb. *be sullen*; bristle, spit, look daggers 891 vb. *get angry*; bode, presage, promise ill, spell danger 511 vb. *predict*; breathe revenge, threaten reprisals 714 vb. *retaliate*.

901. Philanthropy – N. *philanthropy*, humanitarianism, humanity, the golden rule 897 n. *benevolence*; humanism, cosmopolitanism, internationalism; altruism 931 n. *disinterestedness*; universal benevolence, utilitarianism, Benthamism; 'onward and upward department' 654 n. *reformism*; dedication, crusading spirit, missionary s., nonconformist conscience, social c.; good works, mission; Holy War, crusade 689 n. *directorship*.

sociology, social science, social engineering, socialism; Poplarism, poor relief, social services, welfare state; social service, welfare work, slumming, good works.

patriotism, civism, civic ideals, good citizenship, public spirit, love of country; local patriotism, parochialism; nationalism, chauvinism, my country right or wrong; irredentism, Zionism.

philanthropist, friend of all the world 903 n. *benefactor*; humanitarian, do-gooder, social worker, slummer 897 n. *kind person*; paladin, champion, crusader, knight errant; Messiah 690 n. *leader*; missionary, man with a mission; visionary, ideologist; idealist, altruist; reformist 654 n. *reformer*; utilitarian, Benthamite; Utopian, millenarian, chiliast; humanist, cosmopolitan, citizen of the world, internationalist.

patriot, lover of his country, pater patriae, father of his people; nationalist, irredentist, chauvinist, Zionist.

Adj. *philanthropic*, humanitarian 897 adj. *benevolent*; enlightened, humanistic; idealistic, altruistic 931 adj. *disinterested*; visionary, dedicated; sociological, socialistic; utilitarian.

patriotic, public spirited; irredentist, nationalistic, chauvinistic; loyal, true, true-blue.

Vb. See 897 vb. *philanthropize*.

902. Misanthropy – N. *misanthropy*, hatred of mankind, cynicism, unsociality 883 n. *unsociability*; moroseness 893 n. *sullenness*.

misanthrope, man-hater, woman-h., misogynist, misogamist; cynic, Diogenes, Timon; world-hater, unsocial animal 883 n. *solitary*; bear, cross-patch.

Adj. *misanthropic*, inhuman, antisocial 883 adj. *unsociable*; cynical, uncivic, unpatriotic, defeatist.

903. Benefactor – N. *benefactor*, benefactress 901 n. *philanthropist*; Lady Bountiful, donor, fairy godmother 781 n. *giver*; guardian angel, good genius 660 n. *protector*; founder, foundress, supporter 707 n. *patron*; saviour, ransomer, redeemer, deliverer, rescuer 668 n. *deliverance*; champion 713 n. *defender*; salt of the earth, saint 937 n. *good man*.

904. Evildoer – N. *evildoer*, worker of iniquity, wrongdoer, sinner 934 n. *wick-*

edness; villain, blackguard, bad lot; mischief-maker 663 n. *trouble-maker*; marplot 702 n. *hinderer*; spoiler, despoiler, wrecker, Vandal 168 n. *destroyer*.

ruffian, blackguard, rogue 938 n. *knave*; lout, hooligan, hoodlum, larrikin, layabout; terror, holy t.; rough, tough, rowdy, ugly customer, plug-ugly, desperado, bully, bravo, assassin, cut-throat, gunman, thug, killer 362 n. *murderer*; plague, scourge 659 n. *bane*; brute, beast, savage, barbarian, homicidal maniac 504 n. *madman*.

offender, sinner, black sheep 938 n. *bad man*; suspect; culprit, guilty man, law-breaker; wrongdoer, tortfeasor; criminal, misdemeanant, felon; delinquent; recidivist, backslider, old offender, lag, convict, gaol-bird; lifer, gallows-bird; parolee, probationer, ticket-of-leave man; malefactor, gangster, racketeer 789 n. *robber*; outlaw, public enemy; trespasser; underworld 934 n. *wickedness*.

hell-hag, hell-hound, hell-kite; cat, hell-c., bitch, virago 892 n. *shrew*; she-devil, fury, harpy 938 n. *monster*.

noxious animal, brute, beast, wild b.; beast of prey, predator; tiger, man-eater, wolf, werewolf, hyena, jackal; kite, vulture, vampire 365 n. *bird of prey*; snake, serpent, viper, adder 365 n. *reptile*; scorpion, wasp, hornet; pest, locust 365 n. *vermin*; rat 365 n. *rodent*; mad dog, rogue elephant.

905. Pity – N. *pity*, ruth; remorse, compunction 830 n. *regret*; compassion, bowels of c., humanity 897 n. *benevolence*; soft heart, gentleness, squeamishness 736 n. *lenity*; commiseration, melting mood, sympathy (**see** *condolence*); plea for pity, argumentum ad misericordiam.

condolence, sympathy and c.; consolation, comfort 831 n. *relief*; commiseration, sympathy, fellow-feeling 775 n. *participation*; professional condolence, keen, coronach, wake 836 n. *lament*.

mercy, tender mercies, clemency, quarter, grace; locus paenitentiae, second

chance; mercifulness, placability, forbearance 909 n. *forgiveness*.

Adj. *pitying*, compassionate, sympathetic, understanding, condolent; pitiful, ruthful, merciful, clement, full of
mercy 736 adj. *lenient*; melting, tender;
unhardened, squeamish, easily touched;
placable 909 adj. *forgiving*; remorseful,
compunctious.

pitiable, compassionate, pitiful, pite-
ous, deserving pity.

Vb. *pity*, feel p., weep for p., bleed;
compassionate, take pity, take compassion; sympathize, feel for, share the
grief of 775 vb. *participate*; feel sorry for,
weep f., commiserate, condole, testify
one's pity 836 vb. *lament*; console, comfort, offer consolation 833 vb. *cheer*;
have pity, melt, thaw, relent 909 vb.
forgive.

show mercy, have m., spare, give quarter; be slow to anger, forbear; indulge
736 vb. *be lenient*; relax, relent, show
consideration, not be too hard upon, let
one down gently; put one out of his
misery, be cruel to be kind.

906. Pitilessness – N. *pitilessness*, ruthlessness, mercilessness; inclemency, intolerance, rigour 735 n. *severity*; callousness, hardness of heart 898 n. *malevolence*; inflexibility 326 n. *hardness*; inexorability, relentlessness, remorseless-
ness 910 n. *revengefulness*; letter of the
law, pound of flesh; short shrift, no
quarter.

Adj. *pitiless*, unpitying, unconsoling,
unfeeling 820 adj. *impassive*; unsym-
pathizing, unsympathetic; unmoved,
tearless, dry-eyed; unsqueamish, callous,
tough, hardened 326 adj. *hard*; harsh,
rigorous, intolerant 735 adj. *severe*;
brutal 898 adj. *cruel*; merciless, ruthless,
bowelless; inclement, unmerciful, unrelenting, relentless, remorseless, inflexible, inexorable, implacable; unforgiving, vindictive 910 adj. *revengeful*.

Vb. *be pitiless*, have no pity, know no
p.; give no quarter, spare none; shut the
gates of mercy, harden one's heart, admit no excuse; not tolerate 735 vb. *be

severe; insist on one's pound of flesh;
take one's revenge 910 vb. *avenge*.

907. Gratitude – N. *gratitude*, gratefulness, thankfulness, feeling of obligation,
appreciativeness, appreciation.

thanks, hearty t.; thanksgiving, benediction, blessing; praises, paean, Te
Deum 876 n. *celebration*; grace, bis-
millah; grace before meat, grace after
m., bread-and-butter letter, Collins;
credit, acknowledgement, recognition,
full praise, tribute; thank-offering, parting present, tip 962 n. *reward*; requital,
return 714 n. *retaliation*.

Adj. *grateful*, thankful, appreciative;
blessing, praising; obliged, under obligation, beholden, indebted.

Vb. *thank*, give thanks, render t.,
praise, bless; acknowledge, express
acknowledgements, credit 158 vb. *attribute*; appreciate; tip 962 vb. *reward*;
return a favour, requite, repay 714 vb.
retaliate.

908. Ingratitude – N. *ingratitude*, un-
gratefulness, unthankfulness, thankless-
ness; grudging thanks, more kicks than
ha'pence; no sense of obligation, 'bene-
fits forgot' 506 n. *oblivion*; no reward,
thankless task; ingrate, ungrateful
wretch.

Adj. *ungrateful*, unthankful, ingrate;
not obliged, unbeholden; unmindful 506
adj. *forgetful*; incapable of gratitude.

unthanked, thankless, unacknow-
ledged, forgotten; rewardless, bootless,
unrewarding; unrewarded, untipped.

Vb. *be ungrateful*, show ingratitude,
take for granted, take as one's due; not
thank, look a gift-horse in the mouth.

909. Forgiveness – N. *forgiveness*, pardon, free p., full p., reprieve, amnesty;
indemnity, act of i.; grace, indulgence,
plenary i.; remission, absolution, shrift
960 n. *acquittal*; condonation; justification, exoneration 927 n. *vindication*;
mutual forgiveness, reconciliation 719 n.

pacification; placability 905 n. *pity*; long-suffering, forbearance 823 n. *patience*.

Adj. *forgiving*, placable, condoning; unresentful, forbearing, long-suffering 823 adj. *patient*; more in sorrow than in anger.

forgiven, pardoned; absolved, shriven; unresented, unavenged, unpunished; pardonable, forgivable, venial, excusable.

Vb. *forgive*, pardon, reprieve, forgive and forget, amnesty 506 n. *forget*; remit, absolve, assoil, shrive; relent, accept an apology 736 vb. *be lenient*; be merciful, 905 vb. *show mercy*; bear with, forbear, tolerate 823 vb. *be patient*; take no offence, pocket, stomach, turn the other cheek; return good for evil, heap coals of fire 897 vb. *be benevolent*; connive, wink at, condone 458 vb. *disregard*; excuse 927 vb. *justify*; intercede 720 vb. *mediate*; exonerate 960 vb. *acquit*; bury the hatchet, make it up, kiss and be friends, be reconciled 880 vb. *be friendly*.

910. Revenge – N. *revengefulness*, revanchism; vindictiveness, spitefulness, spite 898 n. *malevolence*; implacability, irreconcilability, unappeasability.

revenge, 'wild justice'; crime passionel 911 n. *jealousy*; vengeance, avengement, day of reckoning, Nemesis 963 n. *punishment*; victimization, reprisals, punitive expedition 714 n. *retaliation*; lex talionis, eye for an eye, tooth for a tooth, blood for blood; vendetta, feud, 881 n. *enmity*.

avenger, vindicator, punisher, revanchist.

Adj. *revengeful*, vengeful, breathing vengeance; retaliative 714 adj. *retaliatory*; at feud 881 adj. *inimical*; unforgiving, implacable, unappeasable, unrelenting 906 adj. *pitiless*; grudgeful, vindictive, spiteful 898 adj. *malevolent*; rancorous 891 adj. *resentful*; gloating.

Vb. *avenge*, take vengeance, wreak v., victimize; exact retribution, get one's own back, repay, pay out 714 vb. *retaliate*; glut one's revenge, gloat.

911. Jealousy – N. *jealousy*, jealousness; jaundiced eye, green-eyed monster; distrust, mistrust 486 n. *doubt*; heart-burning 891 n. *resentment*; enviousness 912 n. *envy*; inferiority complex, prestige-chasing, emulation, competitiveness, rivalry 716 n. *contention*; possessiveness 887 n. *love*; sexual jealousy, crime passionel 910 n. *revenge*; sour grapes.

Adj. *jealous*, green-eyed, jaundiced, envying 912 adj. *envious*; possessive 887 adj. *loving*; suspicious, distrustful 474 adj. *doubting*; emulative, competitive, rival.

912. Envy – N. *envy*, envious eye, enviousness, covetousness 859 n. *desire*; rivalry 716 n. *contention*; jalousie de métier; mortification; grudging praise.

Adj. *envious*, green with envy; covetous 859 adj. *desiring*; grudging; mortified 891 adj. *resentful*.

Vb. *envy*, view with e., cast envious looks; covet, must have for oneself 859 vb. *desire*.

Section 4: Moral

913. Right – N. *right*, rightfulness, rightness, good case for; freedom from error 494 n. *accuracy*; fittingness, propriety 24 n. *fitness*; normality 83 n. *conformity*; rules and regulations 693 n. *precept*; what ought to be 917 n. *duty*; morality 917 n. *morals*; righteousness 933 n. *virtue*, 929 n. *probity*; suum cuique, one's right, one's due, deserts, merits, claim 915 n. *dueness*; prerogative, privilege 919 n. *non-liability*; rights, interest, birthright 777 n. *property*.

justice, freedom from wrong, justifiability; redress; reform 654 n. *reformism*; scales of justice 953 n. *legality*; fair-mindedness, objectivity, indifference, detachment, impartiality; equity, equitableness, reasonableness, fairness; fair deal, square d., fair play, fair field and no favour.

Adj. *right*, rightful, proper, meet and right; on the right lines, fitting, suitable

24 adj. *fit*; put right, redressed, reformed 654 adj. *improved*.

just, upright, righteous, right-minded, on the side of the angels 933 adj. *virtuous*; fair-minded, disinterested, unprejudiced, unbiased, unswerving; dispassionate, objective; equal, indifferent, impartial, even-handed; fair, square, equitable, reasonable; in the right, justifiable, unchallengeable, unimpeachable; legitimate 953 adj. *legal*; sporting 929 adj. *honourable*; deserved, well-d. 915 adj. *due*; overdue, claimable 627 adj. *required*.

Vb. *be just*, — impartial etc. adj.; play the game; do justice, give the devil his due, give full marks to, hand it to 915 vb. *grant claims*; see fair play, hold the scales even 480 vb. *judge*; right wrongs, redress, remedy 654 vb. *rectify*; serve one right 714 vb. *retaliate*; try to be fair, lean over backwards, over-compensate.

914. Wrong – **N.** *wrong*, wrongness, something wrong, oddness, queerness 84 n. *abnormality*; something rotten, scandal 645 n. *badness*; disgrace, shame 867 n. *slur*; impropriety 643 n. *inexpedience*; incorrectness, wrong lines 495 n. *error*; wrongheadedness 481 n. *misjudgement*; unreason 477 n. *sophistry*; unjustifiability 916 n. *undueness*; culpability, guiltiness 936 n. *guilt*; immorality 934 n. *wickedness*; unrighteousness 930 n. *improbity*; irregularity, illegitimacy, criminality 954 n. *illegality*; wrongfulness, misdoing, tortiousness, misfeasance, transgression 930 n. *foul play*; sense of wrong, complaint, charge 928 n. *accusation*; grievance 891 n. *resentment*.

injustice, no justice; miscarriage of justice 481 n. *misjudgement*; uneven scales, packed jury; one-sidedness, inequity, unfairness; partiality, leaning, favouritism, favour, nepotism; preferential treatment, discrimination; partisanship, party spirit 481 n. *prejudice*; unlawfulness, no law 954 n. *illegality*; justice denied 916 n. *undueness*; not cricket 930 n. *foul play*.

Adj. *wrong*, not right 645 adj. *bad*; odd, queer, suspect 84 adj. *abnormal*; unfitting, unseemly, unfit, improper, inappropriate 643 adj. *inexpedient*; false, incorrect 495 adj. *erroneous*; inaccurate 495 adj. *inexact*; on the wrong lines, ill-advised, wrongheaded 481 adj. *misjudging*; wrong from the start, out of court, inadmissible; irregular, unauthorized, unwarranted 757 adj. *prohibited*; bad in law, illegitimate, illicit, criminal 954 adj. *illegal*; culpable 936 adj. *guilty*; unwarrantable, inexcusable, unpardonable, unforgivable, unjustifiable (see *unjust*); objectionable, scandalous 861 n. *disliked*; wrongous, wrongful, injurious 645 adj. *harmful*; unrighteous 930 adj. *dishonest*; sinful 934 adj. *wicked*.

unjust, unjustifiable; inequitable, iniquitous, unfair; hard, hard on 735 adj. *severe*; foul, below the belt, unsportsmanlike; discriminatory, one-sided, partial, partisan 481 adj. *biased*.

Vb. *do wrong*, wrong, hurt, injure, do an injury 645 vb. *harm*; be hard on, have a down on 735 vb. *be severe*; not play the game, hit below the belt; break the rules, commit a foul; break the law; transgress, infringe, trespass 306 vb. *encroach*; do less than justice, load the scales, pack *or* rig the jury; discriminate against; favour 703 vb. *patronize*; commit, perpetrate.

915. Dueness – **N.** *dueness*, onus; accountability, responsibility, obligation 917 n. *duty*; the least one can do, bare minimum; expectations; payability, dues 804 n. *payment*; indebtedness 803 n. *debt*; tribute, credit 158 n. *attribution*; recognition, acknowledgement; deserts, merits; justification, entitlement, claim, title 913 n. *right*; birthright 777 n. *dower*; interest, vested i., right, civil rights, bill of r.; privilege 919 n. *non-liability*; prerogative, charter 756 n. *permit*; bond, security 767 n. *title-deed*; patent, copyright; restoration, compensation 787 n. *restitution*; title-holder, 776 n. *possessor*; heir 776 n. *beneficiary*; claimant, plaintiff, appellant.

Adj. *due*, owing, payable 803 adj. *owed*; ascribable, attributable, assignable; merited, deserved, condign, earned, well-e.; licit, lawful 756 adj. *permitted*; constitutional, entrenched, inviolable; privileged, sacrosanct; prescriptive, inalienable, imprescriptible; legitimate, rightful, of right, de jure 953 adj. *legal*; claimable, heritable, earmarked, reserved.

deserving, worthy of, meritorious, emeritus; grant-worthy, credit-w.; justifiable, justified; entitled.

Vb. *be due*, — owing etc. adj.; ought, ought to be; be due to, have it coming; behove 917 vb. *be one's duty*.

claim, lay a claim, stake a c. 786 vb. *appropriate*; arrogate, demand one's rights 927 vb. *vindicate*; lay under contribution, take one's toll 786 vb. *levy*; call in (debts), reclaim 656 vb. *retrieve*; sue, demand redress 761 vb. *request*; patent, copyright.

deserve, merit, be worthy, claim, expect, have a claim on; earn, meet with one's deserts; have it coming to one, have only oneself to thank.

grant claims, give every man his due 913 vb. *be just*; ascribe, assign, credit 158 vb. *attribute*; hand it to, acknowledge, recognize; warrant, authorize 756 vb. *permit*; pay one's dues, honour, meet an obligation 804 vb. *pay*; privilege, entitle; legalize, legitimize 953 vb. *make legal*; confirm, validate 488 vb. *endorse*.

916. Undueness – N. *undueness*, not what one expects *or* would expect 508 n. *inexpectation*; unseemliness, unfittingness 643 n. *inexpedience*; unworthiness, demerit 934 n. *vice*; no thanks to 908 n. *ingratitude*; want of title, non-entitlement; no claim, no title, weak t., courtesy t.; gratuitousness, gratuity, bonus, grace marks, unearned increment; too much, overpayment 637 n. *redundance*; lion's share 32 n. *main part*; violation, infringement 306 n. *overstepping*; profanation, desecration 980 n. *impiety*.

arrogation, assumption, presumption, unwarranted p., swollen claims; pretendership, usurpation, tyranny; encroachment, trespass 306 n. *overstepping*.

loss of right, disentitlement, disfranchisement, disqualification; forfeiture 772 n. *loss*; deprivation, dethronement 752 n. *deposal*; ouster, dispossession 786 n. *expropriation*; waiver, abdication 621 n. *relinquishment*.

usurper, arrogator 735 n. *tyrant*; pretender 545 n. *impostor*; desecrator; violator, infringer, encroacher, trespasser, squatter.

Adj. *undue*, not owing, unattributable; unowed, gratuitous, by favour; uncalled for 508 adj. *unexpected*; improper, unmeet, unfitting 643 adj. *inexpedient*.

unwarranted, unwarrantable; unauthorized, unsanctioned, unlicensed, unconstitutional; illicit, illegitimate, ultra vires 954 adj. *illegal*; usurped, stolen; presumptuous, assuming 878 adj. *insolent*; unjustifiable 914 adj. *wrong*; undeserved, unmerited, unearned.

unentitled, without title, uncrowned; unqualified, soi-disant, would-be; unempowered, incompetent; unworthy, undeserving, meritless; unprivileged, unfranchised, voteless; disentitled, disqualified; invalidated, forfeited, forfeit.

Vb. *be undue*, presume, arrogate 878 vb. *be insolent*; usurp, borrow 788 vb. *steal*; trespass, squat 306 vb. *encroach*; infringe, violate 914 vb. *do wrong*; desecrate, profane 980 vb. *be impious*.

disentitle, uncrown 752 vb. *depose*; disqualify, unfrock, disfranchise, alienize, denaturalize; invalidate 752 vb. *abrogate*; disallow 757 vb. *prohibit*; dispossess 786 vb. *deprive*; forfeit; illegalize 954 vb. *make illegal*; bastardize, debase.

917. Duty – N. *duty*, what is up to one, the right thing; obligation, liability, onus, responsibility, accountability 915 n. *dueness*; fealty, allegiance, loyalty 739 n. *obedience*; sense of duty, dutifulness 597 n. *willingness*; performance, acquittal, discharge 768 n. *observance*; claims of conscience, bond, tie, engagement, commitment, word, pledge 764 n. *promise*; task, office, charge 751 n. *commission*.

conscience, professional c., tender c., nonconformist c.; code of honour, unwritten law; categorical imperative, inward monitor, inner voice.

morals, morality 933 n. *virtue*; honour 929 n. *probity*; moral principles, ideals, standards; ethics, ethology, moral philosophy, moral science, idealism.

Adj. *dutied*, on duty, duty-bound, bounden, beholden, under obligation; unexempted, liable, amenable, chargeable, answerable, responsible, accountable; in honour bound; consciencestruck 939 adj. *repentant*; conscientious, duteous, dutiful 739 adj. *obedient*; vowed, under a vow.

obligatory, incumbent, behoving, up to one; binding, de rigueur, peremptory 740 adj. *compelling*; inescapable, unavoidable; strict, unconditional, categorical.

ethical, moral 933 adj. *virtuous*; honest, decent 929 adj. *honourable*; moralistic, ethological, casuistical; moralizing; idealistic.

Vb. *be one's duty*, be incumbent, behove 915 vb. *be due*; devolve on, belong to, fall to, arise from one's functions; rest on one's shoulders.

incur a duty, make it one's d., take on oneself, commit oneself, pledge o., engage for 764 vb. *promise*; enter upon one's office, receive a posting; owe it to oneself, feel it up to one; submit to one's vocation.

do one's duty, discharge, acquit, perform 676 vb. *do*; do one's office, be on duty, stay at one's post; not be found wanting; redeem a pledge; honour, meet, pay up 804 vb. *pay*.

impose a duty, require, oblige, look to, call upon; devolve 751 vb. *commission*; saddle with, order 737 vb. *command*; tax, task 684 vb. *fatigue*; bind, condition 766 vb. *give terms*; bind over, take security.

918. Dutilessness – **N.** *dutilessness*, default, dereliction; neglect, laches,

culpable negligence 458 n. *negligence*; undutifulness 921 n. *disrespect*; malingering, evasion 620 n. *avoidance*; truancy, absenteeism 190 n. *absence*; breach of orders, indiscipline, mutiny, rebellion 738 n. *disobedience*; sabotage 702 n. *hindrance*; desertion, defection 603 n. *tergiversation*; disloyalty, defection, treachery 930 n. *perfidy*; secession 978 n. *schism*; irresponsibility; truant, absentee, malingerer, defaulter 620 n. *avoider*; deserter, absconder 667 n. *escaper*; traitor 603 n. *tergiversator*; mutineer, rebel 738 n. *revolter*; saboteur; seceder 978 n. *schismatic*.

Adj. *dutiless*, uncooperative 598 adj. *unwilling*; undutiful, unfilial 921 adj. *disrespectful*; mutinous, rebellious 738 adj. *disobedient*; disloyal, treacherous 930 adj. *perfidious*; truant, absentee 190 adj. *absent*.

Vb. *fail in duty*, commit laches 458 vb. *neglect*; oversleep 679 vb. *sleep*; default, let one down 728 vb. *fail*; shirk, evade, wriggle out of, malinger, dodge the column 620 vb. *avoid*; play truant, overstay leave 190 vb. *be absent*; quit, scuttle, desert; break orders, exceed one's instructions 738 vb. *disobey*; mutiny, rebel 738 vb. *revolt*; defect, betray 603 vb. *tergiversate*; sabotage 702 vb. *obstruct*; break away, secede 978 vb. *schismatize*.

919. Non-liability – **N.** *non-liability*, exemption, dispensation; conscienceclause, escape-c. 468 n. *qualification*; immunity, impunity, privilege, clergiability, benefit of clergy; extra-territoriality, capitulations; licence, leave 756 n. *permission*; excuse, exoneration, exculpation 960 n. *acquittal*; discharge, release 746 n. *liberation*.

Adj. *non-liable*, not answerable, unpunishable; clergiable; untouched, exempt, immune; unaffected, well out of; independent, scot-free 744 adj. *free*; tax-free, post-f., duty-f. 812 adj. *uncharged*.

Vb. *exempt*, eliminate, count out, rule o. 57 vb. *exclude*; excuse, exonerate, exculpate 960 vb. *acquit*; pardon 909 vb. *forgive*; spare 905 vb. *show mercy*; privilege, charter 756 vb. *permit*; license, dispense, give dispensation; enfranchise, manumit 746 vb. *liberate*; pass over, stretch a point 736 vb. *be lenient.*

be exempt, have one's withers unwrung, have no liability; enjoy immunity 744 vb. *be free*; spare oneself the necessity, excuse oneself, pass the buck, shift the blame; get away with, wash one's hands of.

920. Respect – N. *respect*, regard, consideration, esteem, estimation, honour 866 n. *repute*; polite regard, attentions, flattering a. 884 n. *courtesy*; respectfulness, deference; obsequiousness 879 n. *servility*; admiration, awe 864 n. *wonder*; reverence, veneration, adoration 981 n. *worship.*

respects, regards, duty, devoirs, greetings 884 n. *courteous act*; address of welcome, illuminated address, salutation, salaam; nod, bob, duck, bow, scrape, curtsy, genuflexion, on one's knees, prostration, kowtow; reverence, homage; salute, presenting arms; honours of war, flags flying.

Adj. *respectful*, deferential 872 adj. *humble*; obsequious 879 adj. *servile*; reverent, reverential 981 adj. *worshipping*; admiring, awe-struck 864 adj. *wondering*; polite 884 adj. *courteous*; ceremonious, cap in hand, bare-headed; on one's knees, prostrate; bowing, scraping.

respected, respectable, reverend, venerable; time-honoured 866 adj. *worshipful*; imposing 821 adj. *impressive.*

Vb. *respect*, hold in honour, think well of, look up to, esteem, regard, value; admire 864 vb. *wonder*; reverence, venerate, exalt, magnify 866 vb. *honour*; adore 981 vb. *worship*; idolize 982 vb. *idolatrize*; revere, stand in awe 854 vb. *fear*; know one's place, defer to.

show respect, render honour, homage, do the honours 884 vb. *pay respects*; go to meet, welcome, hail, salute, present arms 884 vb. *greet*; bob, duck, bow, scrape, make a leg, curtsy, kneel, kowtow, prostrate oneself 311 vb. *stoop*; observe decorum, stand on ceremony, rise.

command respect, awe, overawe, impose 821 vb. *impress*; enjoy a reputation 866 vb. *have repute*; extort admiration 864 vb. *be wonderful.*

921. Disrespect – N. *disrespect*, scant respect, disrespectfulness, irreverence, impoliteness, discourtesy 885 n. *rudeness*; disesteem 924 n. *disapprobation*; neglect, undervaluation 483 n. *underestimation*; depreciation, disparagement 926 n. *detraction*; contumely 899 n. *scurrility*; scorn 922 n. *contempt*; mockery 851 n. *ridicule*; desecration 980 n. *impiety.*

indignity, humiliation, affront, insult, slight, snub, outrage 878 n. *insolence*; snooks 878 n. *sauciness*; gibe, taunt 922 n. *contempt*; hiss, hoot, boo, catcall 924 n. *disapprobation.*

Adj. *disrespectful*, neglectful 458 adj. *negligent*; irreverent, aweless 865 adj. *unastonished*; sacrilegious 980 adj. *profane*; overcandid 573 adj. *plain*; rude, impolite 885 adj. *discourteous*; airy, breezy, off-handed, cavalier, familiar, cheeky, saucy 878 adj. *impertinent*; outrageous 878 adj. *insolent*; satirical, cynical, sarcastic 851 adj. *derisive*; contumelious, scurrilous 899 adj. *maledicent*; depreciative, pejorative 483 adj. *depreciating*; scornful 922 adj. *despising*; unflattering, uncomplimentary 924 adj. *disapproving.*

unrespected, of no account 867 adj. *disreputable*; ignored, unregarded; unenvied, unadmired, unworshipped.

Vb. *not respect*, disrespect; have no respect for, have no use f. 924 vb. *disapprove*; misprize, undervalue, underrate 483 vb. *underestimate*; look down on 922 vb. *despise*; disparage 926 vb. *defame*; show disrespect, fail in courtesy 885 vb. *be rude*; ignore 458 vb. *disregard*; snub, slight, insult, affront, outrage 872 vb. *humiliate*; put to shame, drag in the mud 867 vb. *shame*; trifle with 922 vb.

hold cheap; cheapen, lower, degrade 847 vb. *vulgarize*; desecrate, profane 980 vb. *be impious*; call names, taunt, twit 878 vb. *be insolent*; deride 851 vb. *ridicule*; jeer 924 vb. *exprobate*.

922. Contempt – N. *contempt*, supreme c., scorn, disdain; disdainfulness, superiority, loftiness 871 n. *pride*; contemptuousness, sniffiness; superciliousness, snobbishness 850 n. *affectation*; superior airs; snort; slight 921 n. *disrespect*; sneer 926 n. *detraction*; scoff 851 n. *ridicule*.

despisedness, unworthiness, contemptibility, insignificance 639 n. *unimportance*; pettiness, meanness, littleness, paltriness 33 n. *smallness*; reproach, by-word of reproach 867 n. *object of scorn*.

Adj. *despising*, full of contempt, contemptuous, disdainful, holier than thou, snooty, sniffy, snobbish; haughty, lofty, supercilious 871 adj. *proud*; scornful 924 adj. *disapproving*; disrespectful 878 adj. *insolent*.

contemptible, despicable, beneath contempt; abject, worthless 645 adj. *bad*; petty, paltry, little, mean 33 adj. *small*; of no account 921 adj. *unrespected*; pitiable, futile 639 adj. *unimportant*.

Vb. *despise*, contemn, hold in contempt, have no use for 921 vb. *not respect*; look down on, hold beneath one 871 vb. *be proud*; disdain, spurn, sniff at, snort at 607 vb. *reject*; come it over, turn up one's nose; scorn, hiss, boo 924 vb. *exprobate*; laugh at, turn to scorn, scoff, scout, flout, gibe, jeer, mock, deride 851 vb. *ridicule*; trample on 735 vb. *oppress*.

hold cheap, disesteem, misprize 921 vb. *not respect*; minimize, belittle, disparage, underrate 483 vb. *underestimate*; decry 926 vb. *detract*; set no store by, think nothing of; set at naught, shrug away, pooh-pooh; slight, trifle with, lower, degrade 872 vb. *humiliate*.

923. Approbation – N. *approbation*, approval; satisfaction 828 n. *content*; appreciation, recognition 907 n. *gratitude*; golden opinions, kudos, credit 866 n. *prestige*; admiration, esteem 920 n. *respect*; good books, good graces, grace, favour, popularity; adoption, acceptance 299 n. *reception*; sançtion 756 n. *permission*; blessing; countenance, patronage 703 n. *aid*; testimonial, commendation 466 n. *credential*.

praise, laud, laudation, blessing; compliment, high c., encomium, eulogy, panegyric, glorification, adulation; hero-worship 864 n. *wonder*; modified rapture, faint praise, two cheers; hosannah, praises, paean, dithyramb, doxology; tribute, credit, meed of praise 907 n. *thanks*; complimentary reference, bouquet, citation, commendation; blurb 528 n. *advertisement*.

applause, acclaim; warm reception, hero's welcome 876 n. *celebration*; acclamation, plaudits; clapping, claque; clap, three cheers, paean, hosannah; ovation; encore, curtain call; pat on the back.

commender, praiser, encomiast, eulogist, panegyrist; clapper, claqueur, claque; approver, friendly critic, admirer, hero-worshipper; advocate, recommender, supporter 707 n. *patron*; advertiser, blurb-writer, puffer, booster, barker 528 n. *publicizer*; canvasser, electioneerer, election agent.

Adj. *approving*, uncensorious, uncomplaining 828 adj. *content*; benedictory 907 adj. *grateful*; favourable, well-inclined; appreciative, complimentary, commendatory, laudatory, eulogistic, encomiastic, panegyrical, lyrical; fulsome, uncritical; dithyrambic, ecstatic.

approvable, admissible, acceptable; worth-while 640 adj. *useful*; deserving, meritorious, commendable, laudable, estimable, worthy, praiseworthy, creditable, admirable, beyond all praise 646 adj. *perfect*; enviable, desirable 859 adj. *desired*.

Vb. *approve*, see nothing wrong with, sound pleased, have no fault to find, have nothing but praise for; like well; think well of, admire 866 vb. *honour*;

appreciate, give credit, salute, take one's hat off to, hand it to, give full marks; think no worse of, think the better of; award the palm; seal *or* stamp with approval; accept, pass; sanction, give one's blessing 756 vb. *permit*; ratify 488 vb. *endorse*; recommend, advocate, support, back, favour, countenance 703 vb. *patronize.*

praise, compliment 925 vb. *flatter*; speak well of, speak highly, swear by; salute, pay tribute to; commend, be-praise, laud, eulogize, panegyrize, hymn, doxologize, exalt, extol, glorify, magnify; not spare one's blushes 546 vb. *exaggerate*; puff, overpraise 482 vb. *overrate*; trumpet, write up, cry up, crack up, boost 528 vb. *advertise.*

applaud, welcome, hail; acclaim, clap, give a hand; cheer, give three times three; shout for, root; pat on the back; garland, chair, lionize 876 vb. *celebrate.*

Adv. *approvingly,* admiringly, with compliments; ungrudgingly; enviously.

924. Disapprobation – N. *disapprobation,* disapproval, dissatisfaction 829 n. *discontent*; non-approval, return 607 n. *rejection*; disfavour, displeasure, unpopularity 861 n. *dislike*; poor opinion 867 n. *disrepute*; disparagement 926 n. *detraction*; censoriousness, fault-finding 862 n. *fastidiousness*; hostility 881 n. *enmity*; complaint, protest, tut-tut 762 n. *deprecation*; indignation 891 n. *anger*; hissing, hiss, boo, countercheer 851 n. *ridicule*; ostracism, boycott, bar 57 n. *exclusion*; blacklist, bad books; index expurgatorius.

censure, dispraise, blame, inculpation 928 n. *accusation*; home-truth, no compliment; criticism, stricture; hypercriticism, fault-finding; onslaught 712 n. *attack*; bad press, slating; tirade, philippic, diatribe; condemnation, brand, stigma.

reproach, reproaches, exprobation; objurgation, rixation 709 n. *quarrel*; home-truths, invective, vituperation 899 n. *scurrility*; personalities 921 n. *indignity*; taunt, sneer 878 n. *insolence*;

sarcasm, hit, home-thrust 851 n. *ridicule*; rough side of one's tongue (see *reprimand*); silent reproach, dirty look 893 n. *sullenness.*

reprimand, remonstrance 762 n. *deprecation*; stricture, animadversion, reprehension, reprobation; censure, rebuke, reproof, snub; rocket, raspberry, black mark; castigation, correction, rap over the knuckles 963 n. *punishment*; admonishment, tongue-lashing, scolding, rating, slating, strafing; piece of one's mind, talking to, lecture.

disapprover, no friend, no admirer; damper, death's head, spoilsport, misery 834 n. *moper*; opposer 705 n. *opponent*; critic, hostile c., knocker, fault-finder; reprover, censurer, censor; satirist 926 n. *detractor*; man with a grievance 829 n. *malcontent.*

Adj. *disapproving,* unapproving, not amused, unamused; shocked, scandalized; unimpressed; disillusioned 509 adj. *disappointed*; unfavourable, expectoratory; hostile 881 adj. *inimical*; reproachful, vituperative, objurgatory 899 adj. *maledictory*; critical, unflattering, uncomplimentary; withering, hard-hitting, strongly worded; hypercritical, captious, fault-finding, niggling, carping; caustic, sharp, bitter, venomous, trenchant, mordant; sarcastic, cynical 851 adj. *derisive*; censorious, holier than thou; recriminative, denunciatory, damning 928 adj. *accusing.*

disapproved, unapproved, blacklisted, blackballed 607 adj. *rejected*; unsatisfactory, found wanting 636 adj. *insufficient*; censored 550 adj. *obliterated*; out of favour, under a cloud; unpraised, dispraised, criticized, shot at; henpecked, scolded, chidden; unregretted, unlamented 861 adj. *disliked*; discredited, disowned, out; in bad odour, in one's bad books 867 adj. *disreputable.*

blameworthy, not good enough, too bad; open to criticism, censurable; reprehensible, unjustifiable 867 adj. *discreditable*; unpraiseworthy, uncommendable; culpable, to blame 928 adj. *accused.*

Vb. *disapprove*, not hold with, hold no brief for, fail to appreciate, have no praise for, not think much of; think the worse of; not pass, fail, plough, pluck; return 607 vb. *reject*; censor 550 vb. *obliterate*; disfavour, reprehend, lament, deplore 830 vb. *regret*; abhor, reprobate 861 vb. *dislike*; disown, look askance; draw the line, ostracize, ban, bar, blacklist 57 vb. *exclude*; protest, tut-tut, remonstrate 762 vb. *deprecate*; discountenance, exclaim, hoot, boo, countercheer, hiss, whistle, explode; hound, chase, mob, lynch; look black 893 vb. *be sullen*.

dispraise, discommend, give no marks to, damn 961 vb. *condemn*; criticize, fault, pick holes, crab, cavil, depreciate, run down, belittle 926 vb. *detract*; attack, weigh in, hit hard, savage, maul, slash, slate, scourge, flay; slang, call names, gird, rail, revile, abuse, execrate 899 vb. *curse*; vilify 926 vb. *defame*; stigmatize, brand, pillory, gibbet, expose; denounce 928 vb. *accuse*.

reprove, reprehend, rebuke, snub; call to order, caution 664 vb. *warn*; notice, take severe n., book; censure, reprimand, take to task, rap over the knuckles; tick off, tell off, have one's head for; carpet, have on the mat, haul over the coals; remonstrate, expostulate, admonish, castigate; lecture, chide, dress down, trounce, trim, give one a wigging, browbeat, blow up, tear strips off (see *exprobate*).

blame, find fault, carp, pick holes in; hit at, peck at, henpeck 709 vb. *bicker*; hold to blame, pick on; throw the first stone, inculpate, incriminate 928 vb. *accuse*.

exprobate, exprobrate, fall foul of, reproach, reprobate, upbraid, slate, rate, berate, rail, strafe, shend, revile, abuse, blackguard 899 vb. *curse*; go for, inveigh, scold, give one a piece of one's mind, not pull one's punches.

incur blame, take the blame, take the rap, stand the racket; be open to criticism, blot one's copy book, get a bad name 867 vb. *lose repute*; stand corrected; scandalize, shock, revolt 861 vb. *cause dislike*.

925. Flattery – N. *flattery*, cajolery, wheedling, taffy, blarney, blandiloquence, blandishment; soft soap, rosewater, incense, adulation; voice of the charmer, compliment, pretty speeches; unctuousness, euphemism, glozing; fawning, backscratching; obsequiousness, flunkeyism, sycophancy, toadying 879 n. *servility*; insincerity, tongue in cheek, claque 542 n. *sham*.

flatterer, adulator, blarneyman, cajoler, wheedler; claqueur 923 n. *commender*; courtier, yes-man 488 n. *assenter*; pickthank, fawner, sycophant, parasite, hanger-on 879 n. *toady*; fairweather friend, hypocrite 545 n. *deceiver*.

Adj. *flattering*, overdone 546 adj. *exaggerated*; over-complimentary, fulsome, adulatory, incense-breathing; blandiloquent, smooth-tongued; smooth, oily, unctuous, soapy, slimy, smarmy; obsequious, sycophantic 879 adj. *servile*; ingratiating, insinuating; vote-catching, vote-snatching; insincere, tongue-in-cheek 541 adj. *hypocritical*.

Vb. *flatter*, overpraise, lay it on thick, not spare one's blushes, turn one's head; butter up, soap; coo, blarney, flannel; wheedle, coax, cajole; humour, gloze, blandish, smooth, smarm; fawn, cultivate, court; curry favour, suck up to; toady to, pander to 879 vb. *be servile*; insinuate oneself, ingratiate o.

926. Detraction – N. *detraction*, faint praise, two cheers, understatement 483 n. *underestimation*; criticism, destructive c. 924 n. *disapprobation*; decrial, disparagement, depreciation; slighting language, scorn 922 n. *contempt*; evil speaking, obloquy 899 n. *malediction*; vilification 899 n. *scurrility*; calumniation, defamation, traducement 543 n. *untruth*; backbiting, cattiness, spite 898 n. *malevolence*; aspersion, reflection (see *calumny*); whisper, innuendo, insinuation, whispering campaign; mudslinging, denigration; brand, stigma;

muck-raking, scandal-mongering, chronique scandaleuse; cynicism 865 n. *non-wonder.*

calumny, slander, libel, false report, roorback 543 n. *untruth*; a defamation, defamatory remark; smear, smear-word 867 n. *slur*; personality, insult, taunt 921 n. *indignity*; sneer, sniff; caricature 851 n. *satire*; scandal, gossip.

detractor, decrier, disparager, depreciator; non-admirer, laudator temporis acti; debunker, deflater, cynic; mocker, scoffer, satirist, lampooner; no respecter of persons, no flatterer, candid critic; arch-critic, captious critic, knocker, fault-finder, carper, caviller, niggler.

defamer, calumniator, traducer, destroyer of reputations; smircher, slanderer, libeller; backbiter, gossiper, scandalmonger, muck-raker; denigrator, mudslinger; poison pen.

Adj. *detracting,* derogatory, pejorative; disparaging, depreciatory, contemptuous 922 adj. *despising*; denigratory, mud-slinging; compromising, damaging; scandalous, calumnious, defamatory, slanderous, libellous; insulting 921 adj. *disrespectful*; contumelious, injurious, shrewish, caustic, venomous 924 adj. *disapproving*; sarcastic, cynical 851 adj. *derisive*; catty, spiteful 898 adj. *malevolent*; unflattering, candid 573 n. *plain.*

Vb. *detract,* depreciate, disparage, run down; debunk, deflate, cut down to size 921 vb. *not respect*; minimize, belittle, slight 922 vb. *hold cheap*; sneer at, sniff at 922 vb. *despise*; decry, cry down, damn with faint praise 924 vb. *disapprove*; criticize, crab, gird, fault, pick holes in 924 vb. *dispraise*; caricature, guy 552 vb. *misrepresent*; lampoon 851 vb. *satirize*; scoff, mock 851 vb. *ridicule*; whisper, insinuate.

defame, damage, compromise, scandalize 867 vb. *shame*; give a dog a bad name, destroy one's reputation; pillory, stigmatize, brand 928 vb. *accuse*; calumniate, libel, slander, traduce, malign; vilify, denigrate, blacken, tarnish, sully, breathe upon, blow u.; cast aspersions, put in a bad light; speak evil, gossip;

smear, smirch, spatter, throw mud, drag in the gutter; hound, witch-hunt, muckrake.

927. Vindication – N. *vindication,* rehabilitation 787 n. *restitution*; exoneration, exculpation 960 n. *acquitted*; justification, good grounds, just cause, every excuse; compurgation, apologetics; plea, excuse 614 n. *pretext*; excuse, extenuation, palliation 468 n. *qualification*; rebuttal 460 n. *rejoinder.*

vindicator, punisher 910 n. *avenger*; apologist, advocate, defender, champion; compurgator, oath-helper 466 n. *witness.*

Adj. *vindicating,* vindicatory, avenging; apologetic, exculpatory; extenuatory, mitigating.

vindicable, justifiable, maintainable, defensible, arguable; specious, plausible; allowable, warrantable, unobjectionable 756 adj. *permitted*; excusable, pardonable, forgivable, venial, expiable; vindicated, within one's rights, not guilty 935 adj. *innocent.*

Vb. *vindicate,* revenge 910 vb. *avenge*; rescue, deliver 746 vb. *liberate*; do justice to, set right, restore, rehabilitate 787 vb. *restitute*; maintain, advocate 475 vb. *argue*; bear out, confirm, make good, prove 478 vb. *demonstrate*; champion 713 vb. *defend.*

justify, warrant, give grounds for, give a handle, give one cause; put one in the clear, clear, exonerate, exculpate 960 vb. *acquit*; salve one's conscience, justify oneself 614 vb. *plead*; take a plea, rebut the charge.

extenuate, excuse, make excuses for, make allowance for; palliate, mitigate, soften, soft-pedal, slur over; take the will for the deed 736 vb. *be lenient.*

928. Accusation – N. *accusation,* complaint, charge, home-truth; blame, stricture 924 n. *reproach*; inculpation, crimination; countercharge, recrimination, tu quoque argument 460 n. *rejoinder*; twit, taunt 921 n. *indignity*; imputation, allegation, information, delation, denunciation; plaint, suit, action 959 n. *litigation*; prosecution, impeachment, attainder, arraignment, indictment, true bill; gravamen, head and front of one's offending; case, case to answer; items in the indictment, count 466 n. *evidence*.

false charge, faked c., put-up job, frame-up, plant; vexatious prosecution; libel, slander; scandal, stigma 926 n. *calumny*.

accuser, complainant, plaintiff, petitioner, appellant, litigant; denouncer, approver, peacher, nark 524 n. *informer*; common informer, delator; prosecutor, public p., libeller, slanderer 926 n. *detractor*.

accused person, the accused, prisoner, prisoner at the bar; defendant, respondent; culprit; suspect; libellee.

Adj. *accusing*, accusatory, denunciatory, criminatory; incriminating, pointing to, imputative; delatory, sycophantic, calumnious, defamatory 926 adj. *detracting*.

accusable, imputable; actionable, suable, chargeable, justiciable, liable to prosecution; inexcusable, unpardonable, unforgiveable, indefensible, unjustifiable 924 adj. *blameworthy*; condemnable 934 adj. *heinous*.

Vb. *accuse*, taunt, twit 878 vb. *be insolent*; throw in one's teeth, reproach 924 vb. *reprove*; stigmatize, brand, pillory, gibbet, calumniate 926 vb. *defame*; impute, charge with, tax w., hold against, lay to one's charge, pick on, fix on, pin on, bring home to 924 vb. *blame*; point at, expose, show up, name 526 vb. *divulge*; denounce, delate, inform against, tell on 524 vb. *inform*; involve, implicate, inculpate, incriminate; shift the blame, pass the buck.

indict, impeach, attaint, arraign, lodge a complaint, lay an information; complain, charge 959 vb. *litigate*; book, prosecute, sue, bring an action; haul up, put on trial; frame, trump up, plant 541 vb. *fake*.

929. Probity – N. *probity*, rectitude, uprightness, goodness, sanctity 933 n. *vir-*

tue; character, honesty, incorruptibility, integrity; decent feelings, tender conscience; honour, sense of h., principles; conscientiousness, scrupulousness; ingenuousness, singleheartedness; reliability, sense of responsibility; truthfulness 540 n. *veracity*; candour 573 n. *plainness*; sincerity, good faith, bona fides 494 n. *truth*; fidelity, faith, faithfulness, constancy 739 n. *loyalty*; clean hands 935 n. *innocence*; impartiality, fairness, sportsmanship 913 n. *justice*; respectability 866 n. *repute*; code of honour 913 n. *right*.

gentleman, honest man, man of honour, true man; squarepusher, squareshooter, knight, fair fighter, fair player, good loser, sportsman; trump, brick, sport.

Adj. *honourable*, upright, erect 933 adj. *virtuous*; law-abiding, honest, principled, scrupulous, squeamish, soulsearching; incorruptible, unbribable; stainless 648 adj. *clean*; ingenuous, unworldly 699 adj. *artless*; good, white, straight, square; fair, equitable, impartial 913 adj. *just*; manly, sporting, sportsmanlike; respectable 866 adj. *reputable*.

trustworthy, creditworthy, sterling; reliable, dependable, tried, tested, proven; trusty, sure, staunch, constant, faithful, loyal 739 adj. *obedient*; responsible, dutiful 768 adj. *observant*; conscientious, religious, scrupulous, meticulous, punctilious 457 adj. *careful*; candid, frank, open, transparent 494 adj. *true*; ingenuous, straightforward, truthful, as good as one's word 540 adj. *veracious*.

930. Improbity – N. *improbity*, dishonesty; lack of conscience, laxity; unscrupulousness, opportunism; insincerity, disingenuousness, unreliability; unfairness 914 n. *injustice*; fishiness, shadiness, obliquity, deviousness, crooked ways; corruption, venality, graft, jobbery, nepotism, simony, barratry; Tammany; baseness, dishonour, shame 867 n. *disrepute*; worthlessness, good-for-nothingness, scoundrelism, villainy, knavery, roguery, rascality, spivvery, skulduggery, racketeering; criminality, crime, complicity 954 n. *lawbreaking*; turpitude 934 n. *wickedness*.

perfidy, faithlessness, unfaithfulness, infidelity, unfaith 543 n. *untruth*; bad faith, Punic f.; disloyalty 738 n. *disobedience*; practice, double-dealing, double-crossing, Judas kiss 541 n. *duplicity*; defection, desertion 918 n. *dutilessness*; betrayal, treachery, stab in the back; treason, high t. 738 n. *sedition*; fifth column, Trojan horse; mala fides, breach of faith, scrap of paper.

foul play, dirty trick, stab in the back; foul 914 n. *wrong*; trick, chicanery 542 n. *trickery*; practice, sharp p.; dirty work, job, deal, ramp, racket; fiddle, wangle, hanky-panky; crime 954 n. *lawbreaking*.

Adj. *dishonest*, misdealing 914 adj. *wrong*; not particular, unfastidious, unsqueamish; unprincipled, unscrupulous, conscienceless; shameless, dead to honour; unethical, immoral 934 adj. *wicked*; shaky, untrustworthy, unreliable, undependable; disingenuous, unstraightforward, insincere 541 adj. *hypocritical*; opportunist, slippery, snaky, foxy 698 adj. *cunning*; underhand 523 adj. *latent*; not straight, indirect, crooked, devious, oblique; shady, suspicious, fishy; fraudulent 542 adj. *spurious*; illicit 954 adj. *illegal*; foul; dishonourable 867 adj. *disreputable*; ignoble, ungentlemanly, unmanly, unhandsome.

rascally, criminal, felonious 954 adj. *lawless*; knavish, picaresque, spivvish, scampish; infamous, villainous; scurvy, scabby, arrant, low, low-down, yellow, base, vile, mean, shabby, paltry, little, pettifogging, abject, contemptible 639 adj. *unimportant*.

venal, corruptible, bribable, for hire, hireling, mercenary; corrupt, grafting, simoniacal, nepotistic; barratrous.

perfidious, treacherous, unfaithful, faithless 541 adj. *false*; double-crossing 541 adj. *hypocritical*; traitorous, treasonous, treasonable, disloyal, unpatriotic 738 adj. *disobedient*; insidious.

Vb. *be dishonest*, —dishonourable etc. adj.; forget one's principles, yield to temptation; fiddle, wangle, racketeer; defalcate 788 vb. *defraud*; swindle, chisel 542 vb. *deceive*; betray, play false, stab in the back; double-cross 541 vb. *dissemble*; break faith 541 vb. *be false*; sell down the river; seal one's infamy 867 vb. *lose repute*.

931. Disinterestedness – N. *disinterestedness*, impartiality, indifference 913 n. *justice*; detachment, non-involvement, neutrality 625 n. *mid-course*; unselfishness, selflessness, self-effacement 872 n. *humility*; self-denial, self-sacrifice, martyrdom; nobility, magnanimity; chivalry, knight-errantry; generosity 897 n. *benevolence*; devotion, dedication; loyalty 929 n. *probity*; patriotism 901 n. *philanthropy*; altruism, thought for others; compassion 905 n. *pity*; charity 887 n. *love*.

Adj. *disinterested*, dispassionate, impersonal, uninvolved, detached, neutral, impartial, indifferent 913 adj. *just*; uncorrupted, honest 929 adj. *honourable*; self-effacing, modest 872 adj. *humble*; unjealous, unpossessive, unenvious; unselfish, selfless, self-forgetful; self-denying, self-sacrificing; devoted, dedicated, consecrated; loyal, faithful; thoughtful, considerate; altruistic, philanthropic, patriotic 897 adj. *benevolent*; undesigning; unmercenary, for love, non-profit-making; idealistic, high-minded, generous, magnanimous 868 adj. *noble*.

Vb. *be disinterested*, —unselfish etc. adj.; sacrifice, make a s., sacrifice oneself, devote o., live for, die f.

932. Selfishness – N. *selfishness*, self-consideration; self-love, narcissism, self-praise 873 n. *vanity*; self-pity, self-indulgence 943 n. *intemperance*; self-absorption, ego-centrism, autism; egoism, egotism, individualism, particularism; self-preservation, each man for himself; axe to grind, personal motives, private ends, self-interest, concern for number one; cupboard love; greed, acquisitiveness 816 n. *avarice*; possessiveness 911 n. *jealousy*; worldliness, worldly wisdom; careerism.

egotist, egoist; narcissist 873 n. *vain person*; individualist; mass of selfishness; self-seeker; axe-grinder; careerist, fortune-hunter; monopolist, dog in the manger; opportunist, time-server, worldling.

Adj. *selfish*, egocentric, autistic, self-absorbed; egoistic, egotistical; personal, individualistic; self-interested; narcissistic 873 adj. *vain*; non-altruistic, interested; illiberal, ungenerous 816 adj. *parsimonious*; acquisitive, mercenary 816 adj. *avaricious*; covetous 912 adj. *envious*; hoggish, monopolistic 859 adj. *greedy*; possessive; self-seeking, designing, axe-grinding; on the make, opportunist, time-serving, careerist; materialistic, mundane, worldly.

Vb. *be selfish*, — egoistic etc. adj.; put oneself first, take care of number one; feather one's nest, look out for oneself, keep for oneself, hog, monopolize 778 vb. *retain*; grind one's axe.

933. Virtue – **N.** *virtue*, virtuousness, state of grace; moral strength, moral tone; goodness, saintliness 979 n. *sanctity*; righteousness 913 n. *justice*; rectitude, character, integrity 929 n. *probity*; stainlessness, irreproachability; morality, ethics 917 n. *morals*; sexual morality, chastity 950 n. *purity*; straight and narrow path, good behaviour, well-spent life, good conscience.

virtues, moral v., moral laws; theological virtues, cardinal v.; saving grace; a virtue, good fault, fault on the right side; worth, merit, desert.

Adj. *virtuous*, moral 917 adj. *ethical*; good 644 adj. *excellent*; irreproachable, impeccable, above temptation 646 adj. *perfect*; saint-like, angelic, saintly 979 adj. *sanctified*; principled, on the side of the angels 913 adj. *right*; righteous 913 adj. *just*; upright, sterling 929 adj. *honourable*; dutiful 739 adj. *obedient*; chaste, virginal; proper, edifying, improving.

Vb. *be virtuous*,—good etc. adj.; have all the virtues; resist temptation 942 vb. *be temperate*; walk humbly with one's God, fight the good fight; go straight, edify, set a good example, shame the devil 644 vb. *do good*.

934. Wickedness – **N.** *wickedness*, principle of evil 616 n. *evil*; Devil, cloven hoof 969 n. *Satan*; fallen nature, Old Adam; unrighteousness, iniquity, sinfulness, sin 914 n. *wrong*, 936 n. *guilt*; moral illiteracy, amorality, amoralism 860 n. *indifference*; naughtiness 738 n. *disobedience*; immorality, turpitude, moral t.; loose morals 951 n. *impurity*; demoralization, degeneration, degeneracy 655 n. *deterioriation*; corruption, depravity 645 n. *badness*; flagitiousness, heinousness, shamelessness; bad character, viciousness, vice, villainy 930 n. *foul play*; obliquity 930 n. *improbity*; devilry 898 n. *inhumanity*; enormity, infamy 867 n. *disrepute*; infamous conduct, misbehaviour, delinquency, wrongdoing, evildoing, transgression, evil courses, career of crime; den of vice, sink of iniquity, hell-broth.

vice, fault, demerit; human weakness, infirmity, frailty, foible 163 n. *weakness*; imperfection, failing, weak side, weakness of the flesh; sin, capital s., deadly s.; venial sin, small fault, peccadillo, scrape; crime 954 n. *illegality*.

Adj. *wicked*, bad, unvirtuous, immoral; amoral, amoralistic 860 adj. *indifferent*; unprincipled, conscienceless 930 adj. *dishonest*; irreligious, profane 980 adj. *impious*; unrighteous 914 adj. *unjust*; evil 645 adj. *bad*; evil-minded, bad-hearted 898 adj. *malevolent*; weak (see *frail*); peccant, erring, sinful, sin-laden 936 adj. *guilty*; graceless, reprobate; incorrigible, irreclaimable, irredeemable; accursed, hellish, infernal, satanic 969 adj. *diabolic*.

vicious, steeped in vice, sunk in iniquity; good-for-nothing, ne'er-do-well; worthless 924 adj. *disapproved*; villainous, knavish, double-dyed 930 adj. *rascally*; indecent, profligate, abandoned, lost 867 adj. *disreputable*; vitiated, corrupt, degraded, demoralized, debauched, depraved, perverted, degenerate, rotten 655 adj. *deteriorated*.

frail, infirm, feeble 163 adj. *weak*; human, only h. 734 adj. *lax*; not above temptation 647 adj. *imperfect*; recidivous 603 adj. *tergiversating*.

heinous, heavy, grave, serious, deadly; black, scarlet, of deepest dye; hellish, infernal; unedifying, contra bonos mores; nefarious 954 adj. *lawbreaking*; flagitious, monstrous, flagrant, scandalous, infamous, shameful, disgraceful, shocking, outrageous; gross, foul, rank; base, vile, abominable, accursed; atrocious, unforgivable, unpardonable, inexcusable, inexpiable.

Vb. *be wicked*, fall from grace, spoil one's record, lapse, backslide 603 vb. *tergiversate*; go to the bad 655 vb. *deteriorate*; do amiss, transgress, misbehave; carry on, trespass, offend, sin, err, stray, fall.

make wicked, corrupt, demoralize, brutalize 655 vb. *pervert*; mislead, lead astray, seduce 612 vb. *tempt*; teach wickedness, dehumanize, brutalize.

935. Innocence – **N.** *innocence*, guiltlessness, clean hands; clear conscience, irreproachability; nothing to declare, nothing to confess; blamelessness, every excuse; inexperience, unworldliness 699 n. *artlessness*; playfulness, harmlessness, inoffensiveness; state of grace 933 n. *virtue*; stainlessness 950 n. *purity*; incorruption, incorruptibility 929 n. *probity*.

innocent, babe, new-born babe; child, ingénue; lamb, dove; milksop, goodygoody; innocent party, injured p., not the culprit.

Adj. *innocent*, pure, unspotted, stainless, spotless, immaculate, white 648 adj. *clean*; incorrupt, undefiled; unfallen, sinless, impeccable 646 adj. *perfect*; green, inexperienced, unhardened 491 adj. *ignorant*; guileless 699 adj. *artless*; well-meaning 897 n. *benevolent*; innocuous, harmless, inoffensive, playful, gentle, angelic; shockable, goody-goody.

guiltless, not responsible, not guilty 960 adj. *acquitted*; misunderstood; cleanhanded, blameless, faultless; irreproachable, above suspicion; unimpeachable, with every excuse 923 adj. *approvable*; pardonable, forgivable, excusable, venial.

Vb. *be innocent*, have every excuse, have no need to blush, have nothing to confess; mean no harm, know no better 699 vb. *be artless*; salve one's conscience, wash one's hands.

936. Guilt – **N.** *guilt*, guiltiness, redhandedness; culpability; criminality, delinquency 954 n. *illegality*; sinfulness 934 n. *wickedness*; involvement, complicity; charge, onus; blame, censure 924 n. *reproach*; guilty feeling, bad conscience, suspicious conduct; confession 526 n. *disclosure*.

guilty act, sin 934 n. *vice*; misdeed, misdoing, transgression, trespass, offence, crime, corpus delicti 954 n. *illegality*; misdemeanour, felony; misconduct, misbehaviour, malpractice, infamous conduct, unprofessional c.; indiscretion, impropriety, peccadillo; naughtiness, scrape; culpable omission, laches; fault, dereliction 918 n. *dutilessness*; injustice, tort, injury 914 n. *wrong*; enormity 898 n. *cruel act*.

Adj. *guilty*, convicted 961 adj. *condemned*; suspected, blamed 924 adj. *disapproved*; responsible, liable; in the wrong, at fault, to blame, culpable, chargeable, reprehensible 924 adj. *blameworthy*; unjustifiable, inexcusable, unpardonable, unforgivable; inexpiable, mortal, deadly 934 adj. *heinous*; peccant, sinful 934 adj. *wicked*; criminal 954 adj. *illegal*; blood-guilty 362 adj. *murderous*; red-handed, caught in the act.

937. Good man – **N.** *good man*, perfect gentleman 929 n. *gentleman*; good example, model of virtue, salt of the earth, perfection 646 n. *paragon*; saint 979 n. *pietist*; seraph, angel 935 n. *innocent*; benefactor 897 n. *kind person*; idealist 901 n. *philanthropist*; hero 855 n. *brave* *person*; good sort, brick, trump, sport; rough diamond.

938. Bad man – N. *bad man*, no saint, sinner, limb of Satan, Antichrist 904 n. *evildoer*; fallen angel, backslider, recidivist, lost sheep, lost soul; immoralist; reprobate, scapegrace, good-for-nothing, ne'er-do-well, black sheep, the despair of; scalawag, scamp, spalpeen; rake 952 n. *libertine*; wastrel, waster 815 n. *prodigal*; reproach, outcast, dregs 867 n. *object of scorn*; ugly customer, undesirable, wrong 'un, thug 904 n. *ruffian*; bad lot, bad egg, bad hat; bad influence, bad example.

knave, varlet, vagabond, caitiff, wretch, rascal, rapscallion, rogue, prince of rogues; criminal 904 n. *offender*; villain, blackguard, scoundrel; cheat, liar, crook; chiseller, impostor, twister, shyster 545 n. *trickster*; renegade, recreant 603 n. *tergiversator*; traitor, felon.

cad, nasty bit of work, rotter, blighter, heel, scab; stinker, skunk; bastard, twerp, pimp, pandar, pervert, degenerate; cur, hound, swine, worm, the bottom; louse, insect 365 n. *vermin*.

monster, shocker, horror, unspeakable villain; brute, savage, sadist; ogre 735 n. *tyrant*; fiend, demon, ghoul 969 n. *devil*; hell-hound 904 n. *hell-hag*; devil incarnate, fiend i.; bogy, terror, raw-head, bloody-bones.

939. Penitence – N. *penitence*, repentance, contrition, compunction, remorse, self-reproach 830 n. *regret*; self-accusation, self-condemnation, humble confession 526 n. *disclosure*; guilt-feeling, voice of conscience, bad c., qualms of c. 936 n. *guilt*; white sheet 941 n. *penance*; apology 941 n. *atonement*.

penitent, penitential, flagellant 945 n. *ascetic*; magdalen, prodigal son, a sadder and a wiser man; reformed character, brand plucked from the burning.

Adj. *repentant*, contrite, remorseful, regretful, sorry, apologetic, full of regrets 830 adj. *regretting*; compunctious, conscience-stricken; self-reproachful, confessing, penitent 941 adj. *atoning*; chastened, sobered; reclaimed, reformed, regenerate.

Vb. *be penitent*, repent, feel shame, blush, feel sorry, express regrets, apologize; reproach oneself, condemn o.; shrive oneself 526 vb. *confess*; do penance, wear a white sheet 941 vb. *atone*; rue, kick oneself, wish undone 830 vb. *regret*; learn one's lesson 536 vb. *learn*; turn over a new leaf 654 vb. *get better*; see the light; recant one's error 603 vb. *recant*.

940. Impenitence – N. *impenitence*, non-contrition; contumacy 602 n. *obstinacy*; hardness of heart; no apologies, no regrets 906 n. *pitilessness*; incorrigibility, hardened sinner, despair of 938 n. *bad man*.

Adj. *impenitent*, unregretting, unrecanting, recusant; contumacious 602 adj. *obstinate*; unrepentant, uncontrite; without regrets; hardened, case-h.; conscienceless, unashamed, unblushing, brazen; incorrigible, irreclaimable, irredeemable, hopeless, despaired of, lost 934 adj. *wicked*; graceless, unshriven; unreformed, unreclaimed.

Vb. *be impenitent*, make no excuses, have no regrets, would do it again; abide in one's error, not see the light; die in one's sins; harden one's heart.

941. Atonement – N. *atonement*, amends, amende honorable, apology, satisfaction; reparation, compensation, indemnity, indemnification, blood-money, conscience money 787 n. *restitution*.

propitiation, expiation, satisfaction, reconciliation 719 n. *pacification*; sacrifice, offering 981 n. *oblation*; scapegoat, whipping-boy, chopping-block 150 n. *substitute*.

penance, shrift, confession 939 n. *penitence*; penitential exercise, austerities 945 n. *asceticism*; lustration, purgation 648 n. *cleansing*; purgatory; penitent form, anxious seat, stool of repentance, corner, white sheet 964 n. *pillory*.

Adj. *atoning*, 939 adj. *repentant*; compensatory, indemnificatory 787 adj. *restoring*; conciliatory, apologetic; propitiatory, expiatory, piacular, purgatorial, lustral 648 adj. *cleansing*; sacrificial 759 adj. *offering*; penitential, penitentiary 963 adj. *punitive*.

Vb. *atone*, salve one's conscience, make amends, make reparation, indemnify, compensate; apologize; propitiate, conciliate 719 vb. *pacify*; give satisfaction 787 vb. *restitute*; redeem one's error; expiate, pay the penalty, smart for it 963 vb. *be punished*.

do penance, pray, fast, flagellate oneself; purge one's contempt; suffer purgatory; stand in a white sheet, swallow one's medicine 963 vb. *be punished*; salve one's conscience, shrive oneself 526 vb. *confess*.

942. Temperance – N. *temperance*, nothing in excess 177 n. *moderation*; self-denial, self-restraint, self-control, self-discipline 747 n. *restraint*; continence, encratism; soberness 948 n. *sobriety*; abstemiousness, abstinence, teetotalism; prohibition, prohibitionism, pussyfootism 747 n. *restriction*; vegetarianism, Pythagoreanism; plain living 945 n. *asceticism*.

abstainer, total a., teetotaller 948 n. *sober person*; prohibitionist, pussyfoot; vegetarian, fruitarian, Pythagorean.

Adj. *temperate*, within bounds 177 adj. *moderate*; plain, Spartan 814 adj. *economical*; frugal 816 adj. *parsimonious*; abstemious 620 adj. *avoiding*; dry, teetotal 948 adj. *sober*; ungreedy, continent 747 adj. *restrained*; self-denying 945 adj. *ascetic*; hardy, unpampered.

Vb. *be temperate*, moderate, temper, keep within bounds, observe a limit, avoid excess, know when to stop 177 vb. *be moderate*; keep sober 948 vb. *be sober*; refrain, abstain 620 vb *avoid*; control oneself 747 vb. *restrain*; deny oneself; go dry, take the pledge; ration oneself 946 vb. *fast*; diet, bant 206 vb. *make thin*.

943. Intemperance – N. *intemperance*, immoderation, unrestraint; excess, excessiveness, luxury 637 n. *redundance*; indiscipline, incontinence; indulgence; addiction, bad habit 610 n. *habit*; full life, dissipation 944 n. *sensualism*; intoxication 949 n. *drunkenness*.

Adj. *intemperate*, immoderate, exceeding, excessive 637 adj. *redundant*; untempered, unmeasured, unlimited; spendthrift 815 adj. *prodigal*; unascetic, unspartan, indulgent, unrestrained, uncontrolled, incontinent; unsober, wet 949 adj. *drunk*.

Vb. *be intemperate*, luxuriate, wallow; deny oneself nothing, indulge oneself; have one's fling, sow one's wild oats 815 vb. *be prodigal*; run riot, exceed 637 vb. *superabound*; go the limit, stick at nothing, not know when to stop; drink to excess 949 vb. *get drunk*; eat to excess 947 vb. *gluttonize*; addict oneself 610 vb. *be wont*.

944. Sensualism – N. *sensualism*, life of the senses, unspirituality, earthiness, materialism 319 n. *materiality*; sensuality, carnality, the flesh; grossness, beastliness, animalism, hoggishness; hedonism, epicurism, epicureanism 376 n. *pleasure*; sybaritism, voluptuousness, luxuriousness; luxury, lap of l. 637 n. *superfluity*; full life, high living, fast l. 824 n. *enjoyment*; incontinence, dissipation 943 n. *intemperance*; debauchery 951 n. *impurity*; indulgence, self-i., over-i. 947 n. *gluttony*; orgy, debauch, saturnalia 837 n. *revel*.

sensualist, animal, swine, hog, wallower; hedonist, pleasure-lover, thrill-seeker; sybarite, voluptuary; epicurean, epicure, gourmand 947 n. *glutton*; hard drinker 949 n. *drunkard*; loose liver, debauchee 952 *libertine*.

Adj. *sensual*, earthy, gross, unspiritual 319 adj. *material*; fleshly, carnal, bodily; animal, bestial, beastly, brutish, swinish, wallowing; Circean, sybaritic, voluptuous, hedonistic, epicurean; luxurious; pampered, indulged; overfed 947 adj. *gluttonous*; high-living, incontinent 943 adj. *intemperate*; licentious 951 adj. *impure*; riotous, orgiastic, Bacchanalian 949 adj. *drunken*.

945. Asceticism – N. *asceticism*, austerity, mortification, self-torture, self-mutilation; maceration, flagellation 941 n. *penance*; anchoritism, eremitism 883 n. *seclusion*; plain living, Spartan fare, Lenten f., fast-day 946 n. *fast*; self-denial 942 n. *temperance*; sackcloth, hair-shirt, cilice.

ascetic, spiritual athlete, yogi, sannyasi, fakir, dervish; hermit, anchorite, recluse 883 n. *solitary*; flagellant 939 n. *penitent*; water-drinker 948 n. *sober person*; faster, vegetarian 942 n. *abstainer*; spoilsport, kill-joy, pussyfoot.

Adj. *ascetic*, eremitical, anchoretic; puritanical; sabbatarian; austere, rigorous 735 adj. *severe*; Spartan, unpampered 942 adj. *temperate*; plain, wholesome 652 adj. *salubrious*.

946. Fasting – N. *fasting*, abstinence from food; dieting, banting; lenten entertainment, Barmecide feast; lenten fare, bread and water, spare diet, starvation d., iron rations, short commons 636 n. *scarcity*; starvation, famishment 859 n. *hunger*.

fast, fast-day, Friday, Lent; day of abstinence, meatless day, fish d. 945 n. *asceticism*; hunger-strike 145 n. *strike*.

Adj. *fasting*, off one's food; abstinent 942 adj. *temperate*; unfed, empty, foodless, dinnerless, supperless; half-starved 636 adj. *underfed*; starving, famished; meagre, thin, poor, Spartan; Lenten, quadragesimal.

Vb. *starve*, famish 859 vb. *be hungry*; waste with hunger, show one's bones; live on water, live on air; fast, keep Lent; lay off food, eat nothing, go on hunger-strike; diet, bant, reduce 37 vb. *bate*; tighten one's belt; eat sparingly, make two bites of a cherry 942 vb. *be temperate*.

947. Gluttony – N. *gluttony*, greediness, greed, rapacity, insatiability, gulosity, voracity, wolfishness; edacity, insatiable appetite 859 n. *hunger*; good living, indulgence, over-i., over-eating 943 n. *intemperance*; guzzling etc. vb.; pampered appetite, belly-worship, gourmandise, epicureanism 301 n. *gastronomy*; blow-out 301 n. *feasting*.

glutton, guzzler, gormandizer; locust, wolf, vulture, cormorant, pig, hog; trencherman 301 n. *eater*; coarse feeder, pantophagist; greedy-guts; belly-god, gourmand, gastronome, gourmet, epicure, Lucullus.

Adj. *gluttonous*, gluttonish, rapacious 859 adj. *greedy*; devouring, voracious, wolfish; omnivorous, pantophagous; insatiable 859 adj. *hungry*; pampered, full-fed, overfed 301 adj. *feeding*; belly-worshipping, gastronomic, epicurean.

Vb. *gluttonize*, gormandize; guzzle, bolt, wolf, gobble, engulf; fill oneself, gorge, cram, stuff; glut oneself, overeat 301 vb. *eat*; eat like a pig, make a beast of oneself; indulge one's appetite, tickle one's palate; water at the mouth; like one's food, worship one's belly.

948. Sobriety – N. *sobriety*, soberness 942 n. *temperance*; teetotalism, prohibition, pussyfootism; clear head, unfuddled brain, no hangover; dry zone.

sober person, moderate drinker, no toper; water-drinker, tea-d., teetotaller, total abstainer 942 n. *abstainer*; Temperance League; prohibitionist, pussyfoot; sobersides 834 n. *moper*.

Adj. *sober*, abstinent, abstemious 942 adj. *temperate*; off drink, on the water-wagon; teetotal, prohibitionist, dry, unintoxicated, unfuddled, clear-headed, sober as a judge, stone-cold sober; sobered; unfermented, non-alcoholic, soft.

Vb. *be sober*, —abstemious etc. adj.; not drink, not imbibe 942 vb. *be temperate*; go on the water-wagon, sign the pledge; go dry, turn prohibitionist; carry one's liquor, hold one's l.; sober up, clear one's head, sleep off.

949. Drunkenness – N. *drunkenness* 943 n. *intemperance*; insobriety, wine-bibbing, worship of Bacchus; sottishness, beeriness, vinousness; Dutch courage; intoxication, inebriation, befuddlement; hiccup, stammer, thick speech 580 n. *speech defect*; tipsiness; one over the eight, drop too much; hard drinking 301 n. *drinking*; libations, one's cups, flowing bowl 301 n. *liquor, wine*; drinking bout, jag, lush, blind, debauch, pubcrawl 837 n. *revel*.

crapulence, crapulousness; next-morning feeling, hangover, head, sick headache.

alcoholism, alcoholic addiction, dipsomania; delirium tremens, D.T.s, the horrors, heebiejeebies, jim-jams, pink elephants; grog-blossom, red nose, blue n.

drunkard, inebriate, drunk, tight; slave to drink, addict, drink a., alcoholic, dipsomaniac, pathological drunk; drinker, hard d., dram-d.; bibber, toper, boozer, soaker, soak, sponge, tun; sot, toss-pot; frothblower, thirsty soul; carouser, pub-crawler 837 n. *reveller*.

Adj. *drunk*, inebriated, intoxicated, under the influence of liquor; in one's cups, in liquor, the worse for l.; halfseas over, three sheets in the wind; gilded, boozed up, ginned up, lit up, flushed, happy, nappy, high, elevated; nicely thank you, mellow, ripe, full; potvaliant.

tipsy, squiffy, tight, fresh, flush, lushy, foxed; sozzled, soused, soaked; pickled, oiled, boiled, canned; overcome, disguised; maudlin, fuddled, muzzy, woozy; bottled, glassy-eyed, pie-e., gravy-e., seeing double; hiccupping 580 adj. *stammering*.

dead drunk, stinking d., stinko, blind drunk, blotto; gone, shot, stiff, out; under the table; drunk as a lord.

crapulous, crapulent, with a hangover, with a head; dizzy, giddy, sick.

drunken, inebriate 943 adj. *intemperate*; never sober; sottish, sodden, boozy, beery, vinous; thirsty, bibulous, bibbing, toping, tippling, hard-drinking; pubcrawling, carousing; red-nosed, blue-n., bottle-n.; bloodshot, gouty, liverish; alcoholic, dipsomaniac.

intoxicating, poisonous, inebriating; exhilarating, heady, winy 821 adj. *exciting*; alcoholic, spirituous, vinous, beery; hard, potent, double-strength, over-proof 162 adj. *strong*; neat 44 adj. *unmixed*.

Vb. *get drunk*, see double; drink deep, drink hard, drink like a fish; liquor up, tipple, booze, tope, guzzle, swig, swill, soak, souse, hit the bottle 301 vb. *drink*; go on a blind, pub-crawl; drown one's sorrows, quaff, carouse, wassail 837 n. *revel*.

inebriate, exhilarate, elevate 821 vb. *excite*; go to one's head, fuddle, stupefy; make drunk, tipsify, pickle, stew; drink one under the table.

950. Purity – **N.** *purity*, non-mixture 44 n. *simpleness*; immaculacy 935 n. *innocence*; morals, morality 933 n. *virtue*; decency, delicacy 846 n. *good taste*; pudicity 874 n. *modesty*; chastity, continence, encratism 942 n. *temperance*; honour, woman's h., virginity, maidenhood, maidenhead.

prudery, prudishness, squeamishness, shockability, Victorianism; overmodesty, false shame 874 n. *modesty*; primness, coyness 850 n. *affectation*; sanctimony 979 n. *pietism*; Puritanism, blue laws 735 n. *severity*; euphemism, genteelism; censorship, expurgation, bowdlerization 550 n. *obliteration*.

virgin, maiden, vestal, virgo intacta 895 n. *celibate*; encratite, religious celibate 986 n. *monk, nun*; pure woman, maid, old m.

prude, prig, Victorian, euphemist 850 n. *affector*; Puritan, guardian of morality, Watch Committee, Mrs Grundy; censor, Bowdler.

Adj. *pure*, unadulterated 44 adj. *unmixed*; undefiled 935 adj. *innocent*; maidenly, virginal, vestal; coy, shy 874 adj. *modest*; chaste, continent 942 adj. *temperate*; frigid 380 adj. *cold*; immaculate, spotless 427 adj. *white*; good 929 adj. *honourable*; moral 933 adj. *virtuous*; Platonic, sublimated; decent, delicate, refined 846 adj. *tasteful*; edifying, clean, printable, quotable, repeatable, mentionable, virginibus puerisque.

prudish, squeamish, shockable, Victorian; overdelicate, old-maidish, straitlaced, puritan, priggish; holy, sanctimonious 979 adj. *pietistic*.

951. Impurity – N. *impurity*, impure thoughts, filthiness, defilement 649 n. *uncleanness*; indelicacy 847 n. *bad taste*; indecency, immodesty, impudicity, shamelessness, exhibitionism; coarseness, grossness, nastiness; ribaldry, bawdry, bawdiness, salaciousness; loose talk, blue story, smoking-room s., Milesian s., limerick, double entendre; sex, smut, dirt, filth, obscenity, obscene literature, curious l., pornography; pornogram; banned book; blue cinema; prurience, voyeurism, scopophilia, skeptophilia.

unchastity, lightness, folly, wantonness; incontinence, easy virtue; immorality, sexual delinquency; roving eye, lickerishness, prurience, concupiscence, lust 859 n. *libido*; carnality, sexuality, the flesh 944 n. *sensualism*; sex-indulgence, lasciviousness, lewdness, salacity, lubricity; dissoluteness, dissipation, debauchery, licentiousness, libertinism, gallantry; seduction, stupration; venery, lechery, priapism, fornication, wenching, womanizing, whoring; promiscuity, harlotry, whorishness, whoredom.

illicit love, guilty l., unlawful desires; extramarital relations, criminal conversation, unlawful carnal knowledge; incest, sodomy, homosexualism, Lesbianism, bestiality 84 n. *abnormality*; adultery, unfaithfulness, infidelity, cuckoldry; eternal triangle, liaison, intrigue, amour 887 n. *love affair*; free love, irregular union, concubinage 894 n. *type of marriage*.

rape, ravishment, violation, forcing, stupration; indecent assault; sex crime, sex murder.

social evil, harlotry, whoredom; streetwalking, prostitution; pimping, pandering, bawd's trade, brothel-keeping,

living on immoral earnings, white slave traffic.

brothel, bagnio, seraglio, stew; bawdyhouse, house, tolerated h., disorderly h., house of ill-fame; kip, dive, knocking shop; red-light district.

Adj. *impure*, defiling, unclean, nasty 649 adj. *dirty*; indelicate, not for the squeamish; vulgar, coarse, gross; ribald, broad, free, loose; strong, racy, bawdy, Fescennine, Rabelaisian; uncensored, unexpurgated, unbowdlerized; suggestive, provocative, piquant, titillating; spicy, juicy; immoral, risqué, daring, naughty, wicked, blue, lurid; unmentionable, unquotable, unprintable; smutty, filthy, scabrous, scatological; indecent, obscene, lewd, salacious, lubricious; licentious, Milesian, pornographic, porny; prurient, erotic, phallic; priapic; sexual, sexy, hot.

unchaste, unvirtuous 934 adj. *vicious*; frail, fallen; moralless, immoral; incontinent, light, wanton, loose, fast, free, gay, skittish, riggish, naughty; immodest, revealing; shameless, flaunting, scarlet, meretricious, whorish, tarty; promiscuous, pandemic, streetwalking; brothelkeeping, pimping, procuring.

lecherous, carnal, voluptuous 944 adj. *sensual*; libidinous, lustful, goatish; prurient, concupiscent 859 adj. *desiring*; rampant, on heat, rutting, ruttish, must; hot, sexed-up, skittish, randy, riggish; sex-conscious; priapic, woman-crazy; sex-mad, sex-crazy, nymphomaniac; lewd, licentious, loose, rakish, gallant; debauched, dissolute, whoremongering, brothel-haunting.

extramarital, irregular, concubinary; unlawful, incestuous, homosexual, Lesbian, bestial 84 adj. *abnormal*; adulterous, unfaithful; bed-hopping.

Vb. *be impure*, — unchaste etc. adj.; commit adultery, cuckold; fornicate, womanize, whore, wench, concubinize; lust, rut 859 vb. *desire*; wanton, rig; street-walk, be on the streets; pimp, pander, procure.

debauch, dishonour, seduce, deflower, wreck, ruin; prostitute, make a whore of;

lay, tumble, copulate 45 vb. *unite with*; rape, ravish, violate, force; outrage, assault.

952. Libertine – N. *libertine*, no Joseph; gay bachelor, not the marrying kind; philanderer, flirt; free-lover, loose liver, fast man, rip, rake, roué, debauchee, profligate; lady-killer, gallant, squire of dames; fancy-man, gigolo, mignon; seducer, deceiver, gay d., false lover; co-respondent, adulterer, cuckolder, bed-hopper; Don Juan, wolf, chaser; womanizer, fornicator, whore-monger, whoremaster; voyeur; lecher, satyr, goat; rapist, ravisher; homosexual, homo, paederast, sodomite, pansy, fairy, pervert; protector, ponce, bully.

cuckold, deceived husband, injured h., complaisant h..

loose woman, light w., light o' love, wanton, hot stuff; woman of easy virtue, demi-rep, one no better than she should be; flirt, piece, wench, jade, hussy, minx, nymphet; baggage, trollop, trull, drab, slut; mantrap, adventuress, temptress, seductress, scarlet woman, Jezebel; adultress; nymphomaniac, Messalina.

kept woman, mistress, paramour, leman, hetaera, concubine, unofficial wife; favourite 887 n. *loved one*; bit of fluff, floosie, moll, mopsy, doxy.

prostitute, white slave, fallen woman, erring sister; frail sisterhood, demi-monde; harlot, trollop, whore, strumpet; street-walker, brothel-inmate; tart, punk, chippy, broad; pick-up, casual conquest, call-girl; courtesan; demi-mondaine, demi-rep, hetaera.

bawd, go-between, pimp, pandar, procurer, procuress, brothel-keeper, madam; white slaver, ponce.

953. Legality – N. *legality*, formality, form, formula, rite, due process 959 n. *litigation*; constitutionality, constitutionalism; lawfulness, legitimacy, validity.

legislation, law-giving, law-making, constitution-m.; codification; legalization, legitimization, enactment, regulation; plebiscite 605 n. *vote*; plebiscitum, psephism, popular decree; law, statute, ordinance, order, by-law 737 n. *decree*; edict, rescript 693 n. *precept*; legislator, law-giver, law-maker.

law, law and equity, the law; body of law, corpus juris, constitution, charter; codification, codified law, statute book, legal code, pandect; penal code, civil c., written law, statute l., common l.; international law, jus gentium, law of nations, arm of the law, legal process 959 n. *legal trial*.

jurisprudence, nomology, science of law, legal learning; law-book; law consultancy, legal advice.

Adj. *legal*, lawful 913 adj. *just*; law-abiding 739 adj. *obedient*; legitimate, competent; licit 756 adj. *permitted*; within the law, de jure, good in law; statutable, statutory, constitutional; nomothetic, law-giving, legislatorial, legislative, decretal; amenable to law, actionable, justiciable, triable, cognizable 928 adj. *accusable*; jurisprudential, nomological, learned in the law.

Vb. *make legal*, legalize, legitimize, validate, confirm, ratify 488 vb. *endorse*; legislate, make laws, pass, enact, ordain, enforce 737 vb. *decree*.

954. Illegality – N. *illegality*, bad law, legal flaw, irregularity, informality; wrong verdict 481 vb. *misjudgement*; miscarriage of justice 914 n. *injustice*; wrong side of the law, unlawfulness; incompetence, illicitness, illegitimacy 757 n. *prohibition*.

lawbreaking, breach of law, transgression, contravention, infringement, encroachment 306 n. *overstepping*; trespass, offence, tort, civil wrong; dishonesty 930 n. *improbity*; criminality 936 n. *guilt*; criminal activity, crime, capital c., misdemeanour, felony; misprision, misfeasance, wrongdoing 914 n. *wrong*; criminology.

lawlessness, antinomianism; outlawry, disfranchisement; breakdown of law and order, crime wave 734 n. *anarchy*; kangaroo court, gang rule,

mob law, lynch l., usurpation 916 n.
arrogation; arbitrary rule, mailed fist 735
n. *brute force*.

bastardy, bastardism, baseness; bas-
tardization, illegitimacy; bastard, illegitimate child, natural c., love c., by-
blow.

Adj. *illegal*, illegitimate, illicit, contraband, black-market; impermissible 757
adj. *prohibited*; unauthorized, incompetent, without authority, unwarrantable;
unlawful 914 adj. *wrong*; unlegislated,
bad in law; unconstitutional, unstatu-
tory; null and void 752 adj. *abrogated*;
irregular, contrary to law; extrajudicial;
outside the law, outlawed; out of bounds,
offside; tortious, actionable, cognizable,
justiciable, triable, punishable 928 adj.
accusable.

lawbreaking, offending 936 adj. *guilty*;
criminal, criminous, misdemeanant,
felonious.

lawless, antinomian, without law,
chaotic 734 adj. *anarchic*; ungovernable,
licentious 738 adj. *riotous*; violent, summary; arbitrary, irresponsible, unaccountable; above the law, overmighty;
despotic, tyrannical 735 adj. *oppressive*.

bastard, illegitimate, spurious, base;
misbegotten, adulterine, baseborn;
without a father, without a name.

Vb. *make illegal*, put outside the law,
outlaw; illegalize 757 vb. *prohibit*; forbid
by law, penalize 963 vb. *punish*; bastardize, illegitimize; annul, cancel 752 vb.
abrogate.

955. Jurisdiction – N. *jurisdiction*, portfolio 622 n. *function*; judicature, magistracy, commission of the peace; competence, legal authority, arm of the law
733 n. *authority*; legal administration,
Ministry of Justice; local authority, corporation, municipality, bailiwick 692 n.
council; office, secretariat.

law officer, legal administrator, Minister of Justice, Lord Chancellor; Crown
Counsel, public prosecutor, Procurator
Fiscal, district attorney 957 n. *judge*;
mayor, sheriff 733 n. *magistrature*;
court officer, clerk of the court, tipstaff,

bailiff, bum-bailiff; summoner, process-
server, catchpoll, Bow-street runner;
apparitor, beadle.

police, forces of law and order; police
force, the force, Scotland Yard; constabulary, gendarmerie, military police;
peace officer, police officer, limb of the
law, policeman, constable, special c.;
copper, cop; bluebottle, Peeler, bobby,
flatfoot, dick; watch, posse comitatus;
plain-clothes man 459 n. *detective*.

Adj. *jurisdictional*, competent; executive, administrative, administrational
689 adj. *directing*; justiciary, judiciary,
juridical, causidical; original, appellate;
justiciable, liable to the law.

956. Tribunal – N. *tribunal*, seat of justice, woolsack, throne; judgement seat,
bar; court of conscience, tribunal of
penance, confessional; judicatory, bench,
board, judge and jury; judicial committee, King's Council; Justices in Eyre,
commission of the peace; original side,
appellate s.

lawcourt, court of law, court of justice, criminal court, civil c.; appellate
court, Court of Appeal; small cause
court; Star Chamber; High Court of
Parliament; High Court of Judicature,
Queen's Bench; circuit court; assize;
sessions, court of session, quarter sessions, petty s.; Old Bailey; magistrate's
court, police c.; coroner's court; court-
martial, summary court; durbar, divan
692 n. *council*.

courtroom, court-house, law-courts;
bench, woolsack, jury-box; dock; witness-box, chair.

Adj. *curial*, judicatory, judicial, justiciary, inquisitional; original, appellate
955 adj. *jurisdictional*.

957. Judge – N. *judge*, justice, his Lordship; bencher, justicer, justiciar, justiciary; deemster, doomster, doomsman;
Exchequer judge, baron; Judge Advocate; chief justice, puisné judge, county
court j., recorder, common serjeant;
sessions judge, assize j., magistrate,
beak, his Worship; stipendiary magis-

trate; coroner; honorary magistrate, justice of the peace, the great unpaid; bench, judiciary, magistracy.

jury, twelve good men and true, twelve men in a box; grand jury, special j., petty j., trial j., coroner's j.; juror's panel, jury list, jurors' book; juror, juryman, assessor; foreman of the jury, chancellor.

958. Lawyer – N. *lawyer*, legal practitioner, man of law; common lawyer, canon l., civil l., criminal l.; barrister, barrister-at-law, advocate, counsel, learned c.; stuff gown, junior counsel; senior barrister, bencher; silk, leading counsel, Queen's C.; sergeant, serjeant at law, prime s., postman, tubman; circuit barrister, circuiteer; shyster, pettifogger, crook lawyer.

law agent, attorney, public a., attorney at law, proctor, procurator; writer to the signet, solicitor before the Supreme Court; solicitor, legal adviser; legal representative, legal agent, pleader, advocate; equity draftsman; conveyancer.

notary, notary public, commissioner for oaths; scrivener, petition-writer; clerk of the court, cursitor, articler; solicitor's clerk, barrister's c., barrister's devil.

jurist, jurisconsult, legal adviser, legal expert, legal light, legist, legalist, civilian, canonist; law student, legal apprentice, devil.

bar, civil b., criminal b., English b., Scottish b.; Inns of Chancery, Inns of Court, Sergeants' Inn, Gray's I., Lincoln's I., Inner Temple, Middle T.; legal profession, the long robe; barristership, advocacy, pleading; solicitorship, attorneyship; legal consultancy.

Adj. *jurisprudential*, learned in the law, called to the bar, barristerial, forensic; solicitorial, notarial.

959. Litigation – N. *litigation*, going to law, litigiousness 709 n. *quarrelsomeness*; legal dispute, issue, legal i., matter for judgement, case for decision; lawsuit, suit at law, suit, case, cause, action; prosecution, charge 928 n. *accusation*;

plea, petition, affidavit, written statement, averment, pleading, demurrer 532 n. *affirmation*.

legal process, proceedings, legal procedure, course of law 955 n. *jurisdiction*; citation, subpoena, summons, search warrant 737 n. *warrant*; arrest, apprehension, detention, committal; habeas corpus, bail, surety, security, recognizance; injunction, stay order.

legal trial, trial, trial by law, trial by jury, assize, sessions; inquest 459 n. *inquiry*; hearing, prosecution, defence; pleadings, arguments, rebutter, rebuttal; summing up, charge to the jury; ruling, finding, decision, verdict 480 n. *judgement*, 960 n. *acquittal*, 961 n. *condemnation*; execution of judgment 963 n. *punishment*; appeal, motion, writ of error; precedent, case-law; law reports, Newgate Calendar; cause-list.

litigant, party, suitor 763 n. *petitioner*; claimant, plaintiff, defendant, appellant, respondent, objector, intervener; accused, prisoner at the bar 928 n. *accused person*; sycophant, common informer 524 n. *informer*; prosecutor 928 n. *accuser*.

Adj. *litigating*, at law with, litigant; litigious 709 adj. *quarrelling*; vexatious, sycophantic.

litigated, on trial, coram judice; up for trial, submitted for judgement; sub judice, down for hearing; litigable, suable, actionable, justiciable 928 adj. *accusable*.

Vb. *litigate*, go to law, appeal to l., set the law in motion; prepare a case, brief counsel; file a claim 915 vb. *claim*; have the law on one, make one a party, implead 928 vb. *indict*; cite, summon; prosecute, bring to trial.

try a case, take cognizance, hear a cause; sit in judgement, rule, find, adjudicate 480 vb. *judge*; sum up, charge the jury; bring in a verdict, pronounce sentence; commit for trial.

960. Acquittal – N. *acquittal*, favourable verdict, benefit of doubt; clearance, exculpation, exoneration 935 n. *innocence*;

absolution, discharge; let-off, thumbs up 746 n. *liberation*; justification 927 n. *vindication*; successful defence, no case; reprieve, pardon 909 n. *forgiveness*.

Adj. *acquitted*, not guilty 935 adj. *guiltless*; clear, in the clear, exonerated; uncondemned; let off, without a stain on one's character.

Vb. *acquit*, find *or* pronounce not guilty, justify, compurgate, whitewash, get one off 927 vb. *vindicate*; clear, absolve, exonerate, exculpate; discharge 746 vb. *liberate*; reprieve, respite, pardon, remit the penalty 909 vb. *forgive*; quash, allow an appeal 752 vb. *abrogate*.

961. Condemnation – N. *condemnation*, unfavourable verdict, conviction; successful prosecution, final condemnation, damnation; excommunication 899 n. *malediction*; doom 963 n. *punishment*; writing on the wall 511 n. *omen*; outlawry, price on one's head, proscription, attainder; death-warrant, condemned cell, execution chamber, Death Row; thumbs down; black cap; knell.

Adj. *condemned*, convicted, sentenced; self-convicted, confessing; non-suited 924 adj. *disapproved*.

Vb. *condemn*, bring home the charge; find against, non-suit, cast one in his suit; find guilty, convict, sentence; proscribe, attaint, outlaw, bar, put a price on one's head; blacklist, put on the index 924 vb. *disapprove*; damn, excommunicate 899 vb. *curse*.

962. Reward – N. *reward*, guerdon, remuneration, recompense; meed, deserts 913 n. *justice*; thanks 907 n. *gratitude*; tribute 923 n. *praise*; prizegiving, award, presentation, prize 729 n. *trophy*; honours 870 n. *title*; prize-money, talent m., bursary, stipend, exhibition, demyship; fee, retainer, honorarium, remuneration, emolument, pension, salary, wage, wage scale 804 n. *pay*; perquisite, perks, expense account; return, profit 771 n. *gain*; compensation, consideration, quid pro quo, requital 714 n. *retaliation*; reparation 787 n. *restitution*;

bounty, honorarium, gratuity, golden handshake, tip, solatium, gratification, douceur 781 n. *gift*; bait, lure, bribe 612 n. *inducement*.

Adj. *rewarding*, generous, open-handed 813 adj. *liberal*; paying, profitable, remunerative 771 adj. *gainful*.

Vb. *reward*, guerdon, recompense; award, present; recognize, pay tribute, thank; yield a profit; remunerate, fee 804 vb. *pay*; satisfy, gratify, tip 781 vb. *give*; repay, requite 714 vb. *retaliate*; compensate 787 vb. *restitute*; gain over 612 vb. *bribe*.

963. Punishment – N. *punishment*, sentence 961 n. *condemnation*; penalization, victimization; execution, punition, chastisement, heads rolling; castigation 924 n. *reprimand*; disciplinary action, discipline; infliction, trial, visitation; doom, day of reckoning 913 n. *justice*; poetic justice, retribution, Nemesis; requital, reprisal 714 n. *retaliation*; avengement 910 n. *revenge*; penance, self-punishment 941 n. *atonement*; penology, penologist.

corporal punishment, trouncing, hiding, dusting, beating, fustigation; caning, whipping, flogging, scourging, flagellation, bastinado, running the gauntlet; slap, smack, rap, rap over the knuckles, box on the ear; drubbing, blow, buffet, cuff, clout, stroke, stripe 279 n. *knock*; third degree, torture, peine forte et dure, racking, strappado, breaking on the wheel.

capital punishment, extreme penalty 361 n. *death*; death sentence, death warrant; execution 362 n. *killing*; decapitation, beheading; traitor's death, hanging, drawing, and quartering; strangulation, garrotte, bow-stringing; hanging, high jump, long drop; electrocution; stoning, lapidation; crucifixion, impalement, flaying; burning, auto da fé; drowning, noyade; massacre, mass murder, purge, genocide 362 n. *slaughter*; martyrdom; lynching, lynch law; judicial murder.

penalty, penal character, penality; damage 772 n. *loss*; infliction, imposition, task, lines; sentence, penalization, pains and penalties, penal code, penology; devil to pay, liability 915 n. *dueness*; damages, costs, compensation 787 n. *restitution*; amercement, fining, fine, sconce 804 n. *payment*; ransom 809 n. *price*; forfeit, forfeiture 786 n. *expropriation*; penal servitude, hard labour, galleys; transportation; banishment, exile, proscription, ban, outlawing 57 n. *exclusion*; reprisal 714 n. *retaliation*.

punisher, vindicator 910 n. *avenger*; inflicter, chastiser, castigator, corrector, persecutor; flogger, scourger, flagellator; torturer, inquisitor; executioner, headsman, hangman, garotter, bow-stringer; fire-party; lyncher 362 n. *murderer*.

Adj. *punitive*, penological, penal; castigatory, disciplinary, corrective; retributive, vindictive 910 adj. *revengeful*; in reprisal 714 adj. *retaliatory*; mulctuary, amercing; confiscatory, expropriatory 786 adj. *taking*.

punishable, liable, amerceable, mulctable; inflictable.

Vb. *punish*, visit, afflict; persecute, victimize, make an example of 735 vb. *be severe*; inflict, impose; give one a lesson, chasten, discipline, correct, chastise, castigate; penalize, sentence 961 vb. *condemn*; settle with, get even w., pay one out 714 vb. *retaliate*; revenge oneself 910 vb. *avenge*; amerce, mulct, fine, forfeit 786 vb. *take away*; pillory, set in the stocks, stand one in a corner; masthead; duck, keelhaul; transport.

spank, paddle, slap, smack, slipper; cuff, clout, box on the ears, rap over the knuckles; drub, trounce, beat, belt, strap, leather, larrup, wallop, welt, tan, cane, birch, switch, whack, dust 279 vb. *strike*.

flog, whip, horsewhip, thrash, hide, belabour, cudgel, fustigate 279 vb. *strike*; scourge, give one the cat; lash, flay, lay one's back open; flail, flagellate, bastinado.

torture, give the third degree; give one the works; thumbscrew, rack, break on the wheel; mutilate; persecute, martyrize 827 vb. *torment*.

execute, put to death 362 vb. *kill*;

lynch 362 vb. *murder*; dismember, tear limb from limb; decimate; crucify, impale; flay, stone, shoot, fusillade, send to the stake; bow-string, garrotte, strangle; gibbet, hang, string up, stretch, turn off, bring to the gallows; hang, draw, and quarter; send to the scaffold, bring to the block, behead, guillotine; electrocute; gas; purge, massacre 362 vb. *slaughter*.

be punished, take the consequences, catch it; take the rap, face the music; take one's medicine, hold one's hand out; get what is coming, get one's deserts; regret it, smart for it; come to the gallows, swing, take the high jump, dance upon nothing, kick the air; die the death.

964. Means of punishment – **N.** *scourge*, birch, cat, cat-o'-nine-tails, rope's end, knout, sjambok; whip, horsewhip; lash, belt; cane, stick, big s., rod, ferrule, cudgel, ruler 723 n. *club*.

pillory, stocks, whipping post, ducking stool, scold's bridle, branks; stool of repentance, penitent form, white sheet; prison house 748 n. *gaol*; corner.

instrument of torture, rack, thumbscrew, iron boot, pilliwinks; maiden, wooden horse, triangle, wheel, treadmill; torture chamber.

means of execution, scaffold, block, gallows, gibbet, Tyburn tree, tumbril; cross; stake; Tarpeian rock; hemlock; bullet, wall; axe, guillotine; halter, rope, noose, drop; garrotte, bow-string; electric chair, hot seat; death chamber, lethal c., gas c.; condemned cell, Death Row 961 n. *condemnation*.

Section 5: Religion

965. Divineness – **N.** *divineness*, divinity, deity, godhead, god-ship; numen, numinousness, mana; divine essence, perfection, the Good, the True, and the Beautiful; holiness, sanctity; Brahmahood, nirvana; divine nature, God's ways, Providence.

the Deity, God, personal god, Supreme Being, Divine B.; the Infinite, the Eternal, the All-wise, the Almighty, the All-holy, the All-merciful; Maker of all things, Creator, Preserver; Demiurge; All-Father, great spirit.

Trinity, triad, Hindu Triad, Brahma, Shiva, Vishnu; Holy Trinity, Hypostatic Union; Triune God, Three Persons in one God, Three in One and One in Three; God the Father, God the Son, God the Holy Ghost.

Holy Ghost, third person of the Trinity; Holy Spirit, Paraclete, Comforter, Consoler; Dove.

God the Son, second person of the Trinity, Word, Logos, Son of God, the Only Begotten, Word made flesh, Incarnate Son; Messiah, Son of David, the Anointed, Christ; Son of Mary, Jesus, Jesus of Nazareth, the Nazarene, the Galilean; the Good Shepherd, Saviour, Redeemer, Atoner, Mediator, Intercessor, Judge.

divine function, creation, preservation, judgement; mercy, uncovenanted mercies; inspiration, unction, regeneration, grace, prevenient g.; propitiation, atonement, redemption, justification, salvation, mediation, intercession.

theophany, divine manifestation, divine emanation, descent, incarnation; transfiguration; Shekinah, Glory of the Lord; avatar.

theocracy, divine government, divine dispensation, God's law, Kingdom of God; God's ways, God's dealings, providence, special p., deus ex machina.

Adj. *divine*, holy, hallowed, sanctified, sacred, sacrosanct, heavenly, celestial; transcendental, sublime, ineffable; numinous, mystical, religious, ghostly, spiritual, superhuman, supraphysical, supernatural; unearthly, supramundane, extramundane, not of this world; providential; theophanic; theocratic.

godlike, divine, superhuman; deistic, theistic; transcendent, immanent; absolute, undefined, self-existent, living 1 adj. *existing*; timeless, eternal, everlasting, immortal 115 adj. *perpetual*; providen-

tial 510 adj. *foreseeing*; omniscient, all-knowing 490 adj. *knowing*; fatherly 887 adj. *loving*; holy, all-h., worshipped 979 adj. *sanctified*; theomorphic, incarnate, in the image of God, deified; messianic, anointed.

redemptive, intercessional, mediatory, propitiatory; incarnational, avatarik; soteriological, messianic.

966. Gods in general – N. *god*, goddess, deva, devi; the gods, the immortals; Olympian 967 n. *Olympian god*; idol; godling; demi-god, divine hero, deified person, divine king; object of worship, fetish, totem; numinous presence, mumbo jumbo; theogony; theotechny; pantheon.

Adj. *theotechnic*, theogonic, mythological, mythical; deiform, theomorphic, deific, deified; anthropomorphic, theriomorphic.

967. Pantheon: classical and non-classical gods – N. *classical gods*, gods of Greece and Rome, Graeco-Roman pantheon; Homeric gods, Hesiodic theogony; primeval gods, Chaos, Erebus, Nox; Ge, Gaia, Tellus, Terra; Uranus, Coelus, Kronos, Saturn, Rhea, Ops; Oceanus, Tethys, Nereus; Helios, Sol, Hyperion, Phaethon; Titan, Prometheus, Epimetheus, Typho, Enceladus; the Fates, Parcae, Clotho, Lachesis, Atropos.

Olympian god, Olympian, Zeus, Jupiter, Jove, president of the immortals; Pluto, Hades, Dis; Poseidon, Neptune; Apollo; Hermes, Mercury; Ares, Enyalios, Mars; Hephaestus, Vulcan; Dionysus, Bacchus; Hera, Juno; Demeter, Ceres; Persephone, Proserpina; Athena, Minerva; Aphrodite, Venus; Artemis, Diana; Eros, Cupid; Iris; Hebe.

Chthonian god, Chthonians, Ge, Gaia, Hades, Pluto, Persephone; Osiris; Cerberus, Charon, Styx; Erectheus, Trophonius, Pytho; Eumenides, Furies; Manes, Shades, spirits of the dead.

nymph, wood n., tree n., dryad, oread; water nymph, naiad; sea nymph, nereid, Oceanid; Thetis, Circe, Calypso; siren,

Parthenope, Scylla, Charybdis 970 n. *mythical being*; Leto, Maia.

968. Angel – N. *angel*, archangel; heavenly host, choir invisible; heavenly hierarchy, thrones, principalities and powers; seraph, cherub; ministering spirit; saint, patron s., angelophany; angelolatry; angelology.

Adj. *angelic*, angelical, archangelical, seraphic, cherubic; saintly, glorified, celestial.

969. Devil – N. *Satan*, Lucifer, archfiend, Prince of Darkness, Prince of this world; serpent, Old S., Tempter, Adversary, Antichrist; Diabolus, Father of Lies; the Devil, the Evil One; spirit of evil, Ahriman.

Mephisto, Mephistopheles, His Satanic Majesty, the Old Gentleman, Old Nick, Old Horny, Old Clootie, cloven hoof.

devil, fiend; familiar, imp, imp of Satan, devil's spawn 970 n. *demon*; unclean spirit; powers of darkness; damned spirit, fallen angel; devildom, demonry.

diabolism, devilry, diablerie 898 n. *inhumanity*; Satanism, devil-worship, demonism, demonolatry, demonomania, demonopathy, demoniac possession; demonomancy, black magic, Black Mass 983 n. *sorcery*; demonology.

diabolist, Satanist, devil-worshipper, demonolater; demonologist.

Adj. *diabolic*, diabolical, satanic, fiendish, demoniacal, devilish 898 adj. *malevolent*; abysmal, infernal, hellish, hell-born; devil-worshipping, demonolatrous; demonomanic, possessed; daemonic, demonological.

970. Fairy – N. *fairy*, fairyland, faerie; fairy folk, good f., little people; fay, peri; good fairy, fairy godmother, Santa Claus, Father Christmas 903 n. *benefactor*; bad fairy, witch, weird sister 983 n. *sorceress*; Puck, Robin Goodfellow; Ariel; elemental spirit, sylph; genius; fairy-ring, pixie r.; fairy-lore, folk-l.

elf, elves, hidden folk; pixie, brownie; dwarf, Hobbit; troll; gnome, goblin, hobgoblin, kobold, flibbertigibbet; imp, sprite, urchin, hob, oaf, changeling; leprechaun, clurichaun; pigwidgeon; poltergeist, gremlin; elvishness, goblinry.

ghost, spirit, departed s.; shades, souls of the dead, Manes, Lemures; revived corpse, zombie, duffy; haunter, walker, poltergeist; spook, spectre, apparition, phantom, phantasm, shape, shade, wraith, presence, doppelganger, fetch 440 n. *visual fallacy*; control 984 n. *spiritualism*.

demon, cacodemon, flibbertigibbet, Friar Rush; imp, familiar 969 n. *devil*; Afrit, Jinn, genie; she-demon, lamia; kelpie, banshee; troll; ogre, ogress, giant; bugbear, bugaboo, bogy, bogyman, raw-head, bloody-bones 938 n. *monster*; ghoul, vampire, lycanthrope, werewolf, werefolk; incubus, succubus, succuba, nightmare; fury, harpy; Gorgon; ogreism, ogreishness, demonry.

mythical being, 968 n. *angel*, 969 n. *devil*; Valkyrie, battle-maid; Oceanid, Naiad 967 n. *nymph*; nix, nixie; merfolk, merman, mermaid, merwife, Lorelei, Siren; water-spirit, Undine.

Adj. *fairy-like*, fairy, nymphean; ogreish, devilish, demonic 969 adj. *diabolic*; vampirish, lycanthropic; gorgonian, Scyllan; elfin, elvish, impish, Puckish 898 adj. *maleficent*; magic 983 adj. *magical*; mythical, mythic, folklorish 513 adj. *imaginary*.

spooky, ghostly; haunted, ghosted, hag-ridden; nightmarish, macabre 854 adj. *frightening*; weird, uncanny, unearthly, eldritch 84 adj. *abnormal*; eerie, numinous, supernatural; spectral, mopping and mowing; ectoplasmic, astral, spiritualistic, mediumistic 984 adj. *psychical*.

Vb. *goblinize*, haunt, visit, walk; gibber, mop and mow.

971. Heaven – N. *heaven*, presence of God, kingdom of heaven, kingdom come; Paradise, abode of the blest; Abraham's bosom, eternal home, celestial bliss, blessed state; nirvana; seventh heaven; the Millennium, earthly Paradise; after-life 124 n. *future state*; resurrection; assumption, translation, glorification; deification, apotheosis.

mythic heaven, Olympus; Valhalla, Asgard; Elysium, Elysian fields, happy hunting grounds; Islands of the Blest, Isle of Avalon.

Adj. *paradisiac*, paradisal; heavenly, celestial, supernal; beatific 824 adj. *happy*; resurrectional, glorified; Elysian, Olympian; millennial.

972. Hell – N. *hell*, place of the dead, lower world, nether regions, underworld; grave, limbo, Sheol, Hades; inferno, Pandemonium; abyss, bottomless pit, hellfire.

mythic hell, Hades, Tartarus, Avernus, Erebus; Charon; Cerberus; Minos, Rhadamanthus; nether gods, Chthonians.

Adj. *infernal*, chthonian; hellish, Tartarean; Stygian, Lethean; devilish 969 adj. *diabolic*.

973. Religion – N. *religion*, religious instinct, religious bias, religious feeling 979 n. *piety*; natural religion, deism; paganism 982 n. *idolatry*; nature religion, orgiastic r., mystery r., mysteries; dharma, revealed religion, historical r., incarnational r., sacramental r.; mysticism, sufism; theosophy; theolatry 981 n. *worship*; religious cult 981 n. *cult*; untheological religion, creedless r.

deism, belief in a god, theism; animism, pantheism, polytheism, henotheism, monotheism, dualism; gnosticism.

religious faith, faith 485 n. *belief*; Christianity, Cross; Judaism; Islam, Crescent; Zoroastrianism, Mazdaism, Zarathustrianism; Dharma; Brahmanism, Hinduism, Vedantism; Jainism; Buddhism, Hinayana, Mahayana, Brahmaism; Sikhism; Shintoism; Taoism, Confucianism; Theosophy.

theology, science of religion, natural theology, revealed t.; divinity; scholasticism, Thomism; Rabbinism; typology; demythologization; soteriology, theodicy; hagiology, hagiography, iconology; dogmatics, symbolics; tradition, deposit of faith; teaching, doctrine, defined d.; doxy, dogma, tenet; articles of faith, confession, credenda, credo 485 n. *creed*; Bibliology, higher criticism.

theologian, divine; doctor, doctor of the Church; doctor of the Law, rabbi, scribe, mufti; schoolman, scholastic, Thomist, Talmudist, canonist; theogonist, hagiologist, hagiographer, iconologist; psalmist, hymnwriter; textualist, Masorete; Bible critic, higher c.; scripturalist, fundamentalist.

religious teacher, prophet, rishi, inspired writer; evangelist, apostle, missionary; founder of religion, Messiah; expounder, hierophant, gospeller, catechist 520 n. *interpreter*.

religionist, deist, theist; monotheist, henotheist, polytheist, pantheist; animist, fetishist 982 n. *idolator*; star-worshipper, Sabaist; pagan, gentile 974 n. *heathen*; people of the book; believer, true b. 976 n. *the orthodox*.

Adj. *religious*, divine, holy, sacred, spiritual, sacramental; deistic, theistic, animistic, pantheistic, henotheistic, monotheistic, dualistic; yogic, mystic; devotional, devout 981 adj. *worshipping*.

theological, theosophical, scholastic, rabbinic, rabbinical; doctrinal, dogmatic, credal, canonical; Christological, soteriological; doxological 988 adj. *ritualistic*; hagiological, iconological.

974. Irreligion – N. *irreligion*, indevotion, unspirituality, leanness of soul; profaneness, ungodliness, godlessness 980 n. *impiety*; false religion, heathenism 982 n. *idolatry*; no religion, atheism, nullifidianism 486 n. *unbelief*; agnosticism, scepticism, Pyrrhonism 486 n. *doubt*; lack of faith, infidelity; lapse, recidivism 603 n. *tergiversation*; paganization, de-Christianization.

antichristianity, antichristianism 704 n. *opposition*; paganism, heathenism, heathendom, gentilism; Satanism 969 n. *diabolism*; free thought, rationalism;

materialism, dialectical m., Marxism, nihilism; secularism, worldliness; Mammonism 816 n. *avarice*.

irreligionist, Antichrist; nullifidian, dissenter from all creeds, no believer, atheist 486 n. *unbeliever*; rationalist, free thinker; agnostic, sceptic; Marxist; materialist; secularist, worldling, amoralist, indifferentist.

heathen, non-Christian, pagan, paynim; misbeliever, infidel, kafir, gentile, the uncircumcised, the unbaptized, the unconverted; backslider 603 n. *tergiversator*.

Adj. *irreligious*, godless, altarless, profane 980 adj. *impious*; atheistic; creedless, nullifidian, agnostic, sceptical 486 adj. *unbelieving*; free-thinking, rationalistic, euhemeristic; non-practising, nontheological, non-credal 769 adj. *nonobservant*; undevout, ungodly 934 adj. *wicked*; secular, mundane 944 adj. *sensual*; materialistic, Marxist; lapsed, paganized, post-Christian 603 adj. *tergiversating*; anti-Christian, anti-clerical.

heathenish, unholy, unhallowed 980 adj. *profane*; unchristian, unbaptized; gentile, gentilic, uncircumcised; heathen, pagan, infidel.

Vb. *paganize*, heathenize, de-Christianize; deconsecrate, secularize.

975. Revelation – N. *revelation*, divine r., apocalypse 526 n. *disclosure*; illumination 417 n. *light*; afflatus, inspiration, theopneustia; prophecy; mysticism; the Law, Mosaic L., Ten Commandments; divine message, God's word, gospel; theophany, epiphany, incarnation, Word made flesh; avatar, emanation, divine e.

scripture, word of God, inspired text, sacred t., sacred writings; Holy Scripture, Bible, the Book; Septuagint; canonical writings, canon; Apocrypha, Agrapha, Logia, sayings; psalter; breviary, missal; prayer-book 981 n. *prayers*; fundamentalism, scripturalism.

Adj. *revelational*, inspirational, theopneustic, mystic; inspired, prophetic; revealed; apocalyptic; prophetic, evangelical, evangelic; mystagogic.

scriptural, sacred, holy; hierographic, hieratic; revealed, inspired, prophetic; canonical 733 adj. *authoritative*; biblical, gospel, evangelistic, apostolic; sub-apostolic, patristic; Talmudic, Mishnaic; Koranic, uncreated; Vedic, Upanishadic, Puranic; textual, Masoretic.

976. Orthodoxy – N. *orthodoxy*, correct opinion, right belief; religious truth, gospel t., pure Gospel 494 n. *truth*; scripturality, canonicity; the Faith, the true faith; primitive faith, early Church, Apostolic age; ecumenicalism, catholicity, Catholicism, credo 485 n. *creed*; confession; textuary, catechism.

orthodoxism, strict interpretation; scripturalism, bibliodulia, fundamentalism, literalism, precisianism; traditionalism, institutionalism, ecclesiasticism, churchianity 985 n. *churchdom*; sound churchmanship 83 n. *conformity*; Christian practice 768 n. *observance*; guaranteed orthodoxy, imprimatur 923 n. *approbation*.

the Church, Christian world, Christendom, undivided Church; Christian fellowship, communion of saints; Holy Church, Mother C.; Body of Christ, universal Church; Church Militant, Church on earth, visible Church; invisible Church, Church Triumphant.

Catholicism, Orthodoxy, Eastern O.; Roman Catholicism, Romanism, popery, papalism, papistry, ultramontanism, Scarlet Woman; Counter-Reformation; Old Catholicism; Anglicanism, Episcopalianism, prelacy; Anglo-Catholicism, High Church, High-Churchmanship, spikiness; Laudianism, Tractarianism, Oxford Movement.

Protestantism, the Reformation, Anglicanism, Lutheranism, Zwinglianism, Calvinism; Presbyterianism, Congregationalism, Baptism; Quakerism, Quakery, Society of Friends; Wesleyanism, Methodism, Wesleyan M., Primitive M.

church member, pillar of the church; the baptized, the confirmed; practising Christian, communicant 981 n. *worship-*

per; the saints, the faithful; church people, chapel p.; congregation, co-religionist, fellow-worshipper, pew-fellow.

the orthodox, the believing, the faithful, believer, true b.; conformer 83 n. *conformist*; traditionalist, scripturalist, literalist, fundamentalist.

Adj. *orthodox*, holding the faith 485 adj. *believing*; non-heretical, unschismatical 488 adj. *assenting*; undivided, seamless 52 adj. *whole*; practising, conforming 83 adj. *conformable*; precise, strict, pedantic; hyper-orthodox, over-religious, holier than thou; intolerant, witch-hunting, heresy-h., inquisitional 459 adj. *inquiring*; of faith, doctrinal 485 adj. *credal*; authoritative, defined, canonical, biblical, scriptural, evangelical, gospel 494 adj. *genuine*; fundamentalistic; catholic, ecumenical, universal.

977. Heterodoxy – N. *heterodoxy*, other men's doxy; heresy, heresiarchy; unorthodoxy, unauthorized belief, unauthorized doubts, personal judgement; false creed, superstition 495 n. *error*; perversion 535 n. *misteaching*; unscripturality, noncatholicity, partial truth; heretic, heresiarch, arch-heretic.

Adj. *heterodox*, differing, unconventional 15 n. *different*; dissentient 489 adj. *dissenting*; non-doctrinaire, nonconformist 84 adj. *unconformable*; uncatholic, antipapal; unorthodox, unbiblical, unscriptural, unauthorized, unsanctioned, proscribed 757 adj. *prohibited*; heretical, anathematized, damnable 961 adj. *condemned*.

Vb. *hereticate*, declare heretical, anathematize 961 vb. *condemn*.

be heretical, — unorthodox etc. adj.; Arianize, Pelagianize, Socianize, Erastianize.

978. Sectarianism – N. *sectarianism*, sectarism, sectism; particularism, exclusiveness, clannishness, sectionalism 481 n. *prejudice*; party-spirit, factiousness 709 n. *quarrelsomeness*; independence, separatism 738 n. *disobedience*;

denominationalism, nonconformism, nonconformity, dissent 489 n. *dissent*.

schism, division, differences 709 n. *quarrel*; dissociation, breakaway, secession, withdrawal 46 n. *separation*; non-recognition, mutual excommunication 883 n. *seclusion*; religious schism, Donatism, Great Schism, Great Western S.

sect, division, off-shoot, branch, group, faction 708 n. *party*; order, religious o., brotherhood, sisterhood 708 n. *community*; chapel, conventicle 976 n. *Protestantism*.

sectarist, sectist, sectarian, particularist; follower, party-man; sectary, Independant; Puritan, wowser; Presbyterian, Covenanter; Quaker, Friend; Salvationist; Buchmanite, grouper.

schismatic, separated brother; separatist, separationist; seceder, secessionist; factioneer, factionist 709 n. *quarreller*; rebel 738 n. *revolter*; dissident, dissenter, nonconformist 489 n. *dissentient*; apostate 603 n. *tergiversator*.

Adj. *sectarian*, particularist; party-minded, partisan 481 adj. *biased*; clannish, exclusive 708 adj. *sectional*; sectarial.

schismatical, schismatic, secessionist, seceding, breakaway; divided, separated 46 adj. *separate*; excommunicated, excommunicable; dissentient, nonconformist 489 adj. *dissenting*; non-juring, recusant 769 adj. *non-observant*; rebel 738 adj. *disobedient*; apostate 603 adj. *tergiversating*.

Vb. *schismatize*, commit schism, separate, divide, withdraw, secede, break away, hive off 603 vb. *apostatize*.

979. Piety – N. *piety*, goodness 933 n. *virtue*; reverence, veneration, honour, decent respect 920 n. *respect*; dutifulness, loyalty, conformity 768 n. *observance*; churchmanship 976 n. *orthodoxy*; religiousness, religion 973 n. *deism*; religious feeling, pious sentiment, fear of God, godly fear 854 n. *fear*; pious belief, faith, trust 485 n. *belief*; devotion, dedication, devoutness, unction; adoration 981 n. *worship*; prayerfulness, meditation, retreat; contemplation, mysticism, mystic communion 973 n. *religion*; pious duty, charity 901 n. *philanthropy*; pious fiction 496 n. *maxim*; pilgrimage, hajji.

sanctity, holiness, hallowedness, sacredness, sacrosanctity; goodness 933 n. *virtue*; cooperation with grace, synergism; state of grace, odour of sanctity 950 n. *purity*; godliness, sanctimony, saintliness, holy character; spirituality, otherworldliness; spiritual life, life in God; sainthood, blessedness; conversion, regeneration 656 n. *revival*; edification, sanctification, justification, adoption; canonization, beatification, consecration, dedication.

pietism, show of piety, sanctimony; sanctimoniousness, unction, cant 542 n. *sham*; religiosity, religious mania; scrupulosity, tender conscience; formalism, precisianism, Puritanism 481 n. *narrow mind*; fundamentalism, Bible-worship, bibliolatry, bibliodulia 494 n. *accuracy*; sabbatarianism 978 n. *sectarianism*; churchianity, churchiness, sacerdotalism, ritualism, spikiness 985 n. *ecclesiasticism*; preachiness, unctuousness; odium theologicum, bigotry, fanaticism 481 n. *prejudice*; persecution, witchhunting, heresy-h. 735 n. *severity*; crusading spirit, missionary s., salvationism 901 n. *philanthropy*.

pietist, real saint 937 n. *good man*; conformist 488 n. *assenter*; professing *or* practising Christian, communicant 981 n. *worshipper*; confessor, martyr; saint; man of prayer, contemplative, mystic, sufi; hermit, anchorite 883 n. *solitary*; monk 986 n. *clergy*; devotee, votary; convert, believer 976 n. *church member*; pilgrim, palmer, hajji.

religionist, euchite; enthusiast, wowser, fanatic, bigot, zealot, image-breaker, iconoclast 678 n. *busy person*; formalist, precisian, Puritan; Pharisee, scribe; fundamentalist, bibliolater, Sabbatarian 978 n. *sectarist*; sermonizer, pulpiteer 537 n. *preacher*; salvationist, hotgospeller; missionary 901 n. *philanthropist*; crusader, ghazi.

Adj. *pious*, reverent 920 adj. *respect-*ful; faithful, devoted 739 adj. *obedient*; conforming, traditional 768 adj. *observant*, 976 adj. *orthodox*; professing, confessing; pure in heart, holy-minded, unworldly, otherworldly, spiritual; godly, religious, devout; prayerful, psalmsinging 981 adj. *worshipping*; meditative, contemplative, mystic; saintly, sainted.

pietistic, fervent, seraphic; enthusiastic, inspired; austere 945 adj. *ascetic*; anchoretic; pi, religiose, holier than thou; precise, Puritan; formalistic, Pharisaic, ritualistic 978 adj. *sectarian*; priest-ridden, churchy, spiky; psalmsinging, hymn-s.; preachy, sanctimonious, canting 850 adj. *affected*.

sanctified, made holy, consecrated; reverend, holy, sacred, solemn, sacrosanct 866 adj. *worshipful*; haloed, sainted, canonized, beatified; regenerate, reborn 656 adj. *restored*; adopted, justified.

Vb. *be pious*, fear God, have one's religion 485 vb. *believe*; keep the faith, fight the good fight 162 vb. *be strong*, go to church, attend divine worship; pray, say one's prayers 981 vb. *worship*; revere, show reverence 920 vb. *show respect*; sermonize, preachify, preach at 534 vb. *teach*.

make pious, bring religion to, bring to God, convert 485 vb. *convince*; christianize, win for Christ, baptize, receive into the church 299 vb. *admit*; depaganize, spiritualize 648 vb. *purify*; edify, confirm.

sanctify, hallow, make holy, keep h. 866 vb. *honour*; spiritualize, consecrate, dedicate, enshrine 866 vb. *dignify*; saint, canonize, beatify.

980. Impiety – N. *impiety*, impiousness; irreverence 921 n. *disrespect*; undutifulness 918 n. *dutilessness*; godlessness 974 n. *irreligion*; scoffing 851 n. *ridicule*; sacrilegiousness, profanity; blasphemy, evil-speaking 899 n. *malediction*; sacrilege, desecration, violation, profanation 675 n. *misuse*; sin, immoralism 934 n. *wickedness*, 940 n. *impenitence*; profaneness, worldliness 319 n. *materiality*; amoralism, indifferentism 464 n. *indiscrimination*.

false piety, pious fraud 541 n. *falsehood*; sanctimony, sanctimoniousness 979 n.*pietism*; cant,snuffling, holy horror 850 n. *affectation*.

impious person, blasphemer, curser, swearer 899 n. *malediction*; mocker, scorner 926 n. *detractor*; desecrator, violator, profaner 904 n. *offender*; profane person, gentile, pagan, infidel, unbeliever 974 n. *heathen*; indifferentist, amoralist; worldling, materialist, immoralist 944 n. *sensualist*; sinner, reprobate, sons of Belial 938 n. *bad man*; backslider, apostate, adulterous generation 603 n. *tergiversator*.

Adj. *impious*, anti-religious, antiChristian, anti-church 704 adj. *opposing*; unbelieving, atheistical, godless 974 adj. *irreligious*; non-worshipping, undevout, non-practising 769 adj. *non-observant*; misbelieving 982 adj. *idolatrous*; blasphemous, evil-speaking 899 adj. *maledicent*; irreverent 921 adj. *disrespectful*; sacrilegious, unawed; sinning, sinful, hardened, reprobate, unregenerate 934 adj. *wicked*; backsliding, recidivous, apostate 603 adj. *tergiversating*.

profane, unholy, unhallowed, unsanctified, unblest, sacrilegious; godforsaken, accursed; infidel, pagan, gentile.

Vb. *be impious*, sin 934 vb. *be wicked*; swear, blaspheme 899 vb. *curse*; profane, desecrate, violate 675 vb. *misuse*; sin against the light, harden one's heart 655 vb. *deteriorate*.

981. Worship – N. *worship*, honour, reverence, homage 920 n. *respect*; holy fear 854 n. *fear*; veneration, adoration, prostration; devotion 979 n. *piety*; prayer, one's devotions, retreat, quiet time, meditation, contemplation, communion.

cult, mystique; type of worship, service 917 n. *duty*; service of God, supreme worship, latria; iconolatry, image-worship; false worship 982 n. *idolatry*.

act of worship, rites, mysteries 988 n. *rite*; laud, laudation, praises, doxology 923 n. *praise*; glorification; hymn-singing, psalmody; thanksgiving, blessing, benediction 907 n. *thanks*; oblation, almsgiving, sacrifice (see *oblation*); praying.

prayers, orisons, devotions; private devotion, retreat, contemplation 449 n. *meditation*; prayer, orison, petition, invocation; intercession, suffrage, prayers for the dead, vigils; intention; rogation, supplication, litany; benediction, benedicite, benison, grace 907 n. *thanks*; prayer for the day, collect; rosary, beads, beadroll; prayerwheel; prayerbook, missal, breviary, book of hours; call to prayer, muezzin's cry 547 n. *call*.

hymn, song, religious lyric, psalm; processional hymn, recessional; chant, descant; anthem, cantata; antiphon, response; canticle, doxology, Gloria; paean, Hallelujah, Hosanna; hymnody; psalmody; hymn-book, hymnal, psalter; hymnology, hymnography.

oblation, tribute, Peter's pence, mass money; offertory, collection, alms and oblations 781 n. *offering*; libation, incense 988 n. *rite*; votive offering, de voto o.; thank-offering; sin-offering, victim, scapegoat; burnt-offering, holocaust; sacrifice, devotion; immolation, hecatomb 362 n. *slaughter*; human sacrifice 362 n. *homicide*; self-sacrifice 931 n. *disinterestedness*; self-immolation, suttee, sutteeism 362 n. *suicide*.

public worship, common prayer, intercommunion; agape, love-feast; service, divine service, mass, matins, evensong, benediction 988 n. *rite*; church, churchgoing, chapel-g. 979 n. *piety*; prayermeeting, revivalist m.; evangelism, revivalism; temple worship, state religion 973 n. *religion*.

worshipper, fellow-w., co-religionist, pew-fellow 976 n. *church member*; adorer, votary, devotee 979 n. *pietist*; imageworshipper, iconolater 982 n. *idolater*; sacrificer; invocator, supplicant, suppliant 763 n. *petitioner*; pray-er, man of prayer, bedesman, intercessor; contemplative, mystic, visionary; dervish, marabout, enthusiast, revivalist, prophet 973 n. *religious teacher*; celebrant, officiant 986 n. *clergy*; communicant, churchgoer, chapel-g., worshipping, church, congregation; psalmist, hymn-writer, hymnologist 988 n. *ritualist*; pilgrim, palmer, hajji 268 n. *traveller*.

Adj. *worshipping*, devout, devoted 979 adj. *pious*; reverent, reverential 920 adj. *respectful*; prayerful 761 adj. *supplicatory*; on one's knees, at one's prayers, at one's devotions, in retreat.

devotional, appertaining to worship, latreutic 988 adj. *ritualistic*; worshipful, solemn, sacred, holy 979 adj. *sanctified*; sacramental, mystic, mystical; invocatory, precatory, intercessory, petitionary 761 adj. *supplicatory*; sacrificatory, sacrificial; oblationary, votive, ex voto 759 adj. *offering*; doxological.

Vb. *worship*, honour, revere, venerate, adore 920 vb. *respect*; pay homage to, homage 917 vb. *do one's duty*; pay divine honours to, deify, apotheosize 982 vb. *idolatrize*; bow, kneel, genuflect; extol, laud, magnify, glorify, doxologize 923 vb. *praise*; hymn, anthem 413 vb. *sing*; intercede, pray, say one's prayers, recite the rosary, tell one's beads; meditate, contemplate, commune 979 vb. *be pious*.

offer worship, celebrate, officiate, minister, administer the sacraments 988 vb. *perform ritual*; sacrifice, make s., offer up 781 vb. *pacify*; vow, make vows 764 vb. *promise*; take vows 986 vb. *take orders*; go to service, hear Mass, communicate, hymnodize, psalmodize, anthem, chant 413 vb. *sing*.

982. Idolatry – N. *idolatry*, idolatrousness, false worship, superstition 981 n. *worship*; heathenism, paganism 973 n. *religion*; fetishism, anthropomorphism, zoomorphism; iconolatry, image-worship; idol-worship, idolomania; idolomancy, mumbo-jumbo, hocus-pocus 983 n. *sorcery*; heliolatry, sun-worship; star-worship, Sabaism; demonolatry, devil-

worship 969 n. *diabolism*; idol-offering, idolothyte.

deification, god-making, apotheosis, apocolocyntosis; idolization 920 n. *respect*; king-worship, emperor-w.

idol, statue 554 n. *sculpture*; image, graven i., molten i.; cult image, fetish, totem-pole; golden calf 966 n. *god*; godling, thakur, joss; totem.

idolater, idol-worshipper, fetishist, fetisheer; totemist; iconolater, image-worshipper; star-worshipper, sabaist; fire-worshipper, guebre; demonist, devil-worshipper 969 n. *diabolist*; pagan, heathendom 974 n. *heathen*; idol-maker, image-m.

Adj. *idolatrous*, pagan, heathen 974 n. *heathenish*; idolatric, serving images; fetishistic; anthropomorphic, theriomorphic; devil-worshipping 969 adj. *diabolic*; idolothyte.

Vb. *idolatrize*, anthropomorphize, make God in one's own image; deify, apotheosize 979 vb. *sanctify*; idolize, put on a pedestal; heathenize 974 vb. *paganize*.

983. Sorcery – N. *sorcery*, spellbinding, witchery, magic arts, enchantments; witchcraft, sortilege; magianism, gramarye, magic lore; wizardry 694 n. *skill*; thaumaturgics, wonder-working, miracle-mongering 864 n. *thaumaturgy*; magic, jugglery, illusionism 542 n. *sleight*; white magic, theurgy; black magic, necromancy 969 n. *diabolism*; priestcraft, superstition, shamanism, obeah, voodooism, voodoo, hoodoo; psychomancy, spirit-raising 511 n. *divination*; spirit-laying, exorcism, exsufflation 988 n. *rite*; magic rite, conjuration, invocation, incantation; coven, witches' sabbath; Walpurgisnacht; witching hour.

spell, charm, glamour, enchantment, cantrip, hoodoo, curse; evil eye, jinx, influence; bewitchment, fascination 291 n. *attraction*; possession, demoniacal p., bedevilment; incantation, rune; open sesame, abracadabra; hocus-pocus, mumbo-jumbo, fee faw fum 515 n. *un-*

meaningness; philtre, love-potion (see *magic instrument*).

talisman, charm, counter-c.; cross, demonifuge 662 n. *safeguard*; amulet, mascot, lucky charm; swastika, fylfot, pentacle; scarab, relic.

magic instrument, bell, book, and candle; broomstick; witch-broth, witches' cauldron; philtre, potion; magic wheel, rhomb; wand; magic ring, Solomon's seal, Aladdin's lamp, Alf's button; flying carpet, seven-league boots; wishing-well, wish-bone, merry-thought.

sorcerer, wise man, seer, soothsayer, Chaldean 511 n. *diviner*; astrologer 984 n. *occultist*; mage, magian; thaumaturgist, wonder-worker, miracle-w. 864 n. *thaumaturgy*; shaman, witch-doctor, medicine-man, figure-flinger, fetisheer 982 n. *idolater*; obi-man, voodooist, hoodooist, spirit-raiser; conjuror, exorcist; charmer, juggler 545 n. *conjuror*; spellbinder, enchanter, wizard, warlock; magician, theurgist; necromancer 969 n. *diabolist*; familiar, imp 969 n. *devil*; sorcerer's apprentice.

sorceress, wise woman, Sibyl 511 n. *diviner*; enchantress, witch, weird sister; hag, hellcat; night-hag; lamia; vampire; fairy godmother 970 n. *fairy*.

Adj. *sorcerous*, sortilegious; Circean; magicianly, Chaldean; thaumaturgic 864 adj. *wonderful*; goetic, necromantic 969 adj. *diabolic*; shamanistic, voodooistic; incantatory, runic; witching, spellbinding 291 adj. *attracting*; occult, esoteric 984 adj. *cabbalistic*.

magical, witching; supernatural, uncanny, eldritch, weird 970 adj. *fairy-like*; amuletic, talismanic 660 adj. *tutelary*.

bewitched, ensorcelled, enchanted, charmed, fey; fascinated, spellbound, under a curse, hag-ridden, haunted.

Vb. *practise sorcery*, cast horoscopes 511 vb. *divine*; do magic, weave spells; speak mystically, cabbalize; say the magic word, make passes; conjure, call up; raise spirits, shamanize; exorcize, lay ghosts; wave a wand.

bewitch, charm, enchant, fascinate, take 291 vb. *attract*; spellbind, cast a spell on, overlook, cast the evil eye 898 vb. *be malevolent*; haunt, walk 970 vb. *goblinize*.

984. Occultism – N. *occultism*, esoterism, mysticism; cabbalism, cabbala, gematria; theosophy, reincarnationism; hyperphysics, metapsychics; supernaturalism, psychism, pseudo-psychology; secret art, esoteric science, alchemy, astrology, psychomancy, spiritualism, magic 983 n. *sorcery*; sortilege 511 n. *divination*; fortune-telling, crystal-gazing, palmistry, chiromancy 511 n. *prediction*; clairvoyance, second sight 438 n. *vision*; sixth sense 476 n. *intuition*.

psychics, parapsychology, psychism 447 n. *psychology*; psychical research; paranormal perception, extrasensory p.; telegnosis, telesthesia, cryptesthesia, clairaudience, clairvoyance, second sight 476 n. *intuition*; telepathy, telergy; thought transference; precognition, psi faculty.

spiritualism, spiritism; spirit communication, psychomancy 983 n. *sorcery*; mediumship; séance, sitting; astral body, spirit b. 320 n. *immateriality*; materialization, ectoplasm, teleplasm 319 n. *materiality*; apport, telekinesis; poltergeistery; spirit-rapping, table-turning; automatism, automatic writing, spirit w.; spirit message, psychogram; psychograph, planchette, ouija board; control; guide.

occultist, mystic, transcendentalist, supernaturalist; esoteric, cabbalist; theosophist, seer of the real; spiritualist; alchemist 983 n. *sorcerer*; astrologer, fortune-teller, crystal-gazer, palmist 511 n. *diviner*.

psychic, clairvoyant, clairaudient; telepath; mind-reader, thought-r.; medium, spirit-rapper.

psychist, parapsychologist, metapsychologist, psychophysicist, psychical researcher.

Adj. *cabbalistic*, esoteric, cryptic, hidden 523 adj. *occult*; mystic, transcendental, supernatural; theosophical; astrological, alchemistic 983 adj. *sorcerous.*

psychical, psychic, fey, second-sighted; mantological, prophetic 511 adj. *predicting;* telepathic, clairvoyant, clairaudient; spiritualistic, mediumistic; ectoplasmic, telekinetic.

paranormal, parapsychological, metapsychological, hyperpsychological, supernatural, hyperphysical.

Vb. *practise occultism,* mysticize, eso terize; theosophize; cabbalize; astrologize, mantologize 511 vb. *divine;* hold a séance, attend séances; go into a trance, materialize, dematerialize.

985. Churchdom – **N.** *churchdom,* the church, pale of the c., Christendom 976 n. *the Church;* priestly government, hierocracy, theocracy; obedience, Roman o.; rule of the saints 733 n. *authority;* church government; ecclesiastical order, hierarchy; papacy, popedom; popishness, ultramontanism; cardinalism; bishopdom, prelacy; presbyterianism, congregationalism 978 n. *sectarianism;* ecclesiology, ecclesiologist.

ecclesiasticism, clericalism, sacerdotalism; priestliness, priesthood, brahminhood; priestdom, priestcraft; brahminism; benefit of clergy, clergiability 919 n. *non-liability.*

monasticism, monastic life, monachism 895 n. *celibacy;* cenobitism 883 n. *seclusion;* monkhood, monkishness, friarhood 945 n. *asceticism.*

church ministry, ecclesiastical vocation, call 622 n. *vocation;* apostleship, apostolate, mission; pastorship, cure of souls; spiritual guidance, confession, absolution, shrift 988 n. *ministration;* preaching office, preaching, homiletics 534 n. *teaching.*

church office, priesthood, priestliness; apostolate, apostleship; pontificate, papacy, Holy See, Vatican; cardinalate, cardinalship; patriarchate, patriarchship; exarchate, metropolitanate; primacy, primateship; archiepiscopate; see, bishopric, episcopate, episcopacy, prelacy; abbotship, abbacy; priorate,

priorship; archdeaconry, deanery; canonry, canonicate; prebendaryship; deaconship; diaconate, subdiaconate; presbyterate, presbytership, eldership, moderatorship, pastorate; rectorship, vicarship; curacy, cure, cure of souls; chaplaincy, chaplainry; incumbency, tenure, benefice 773 n. *possession;* preferment, appointment, translation.

parish, deanery; presbytery; diocese, bishopric, see, archbishopric; metropolitanate, patriarchate, province 184 n. *district.*

benefice, incumbency, tenure; living, rectorship, parsonage; glebe, tithe; prebend, prebendal stall, canonry; temporalities, church endowments 777 n. *property;* patronage, advowson.

synod, provincial s., convocation, general council, ecumenical c. 692 n. *council;* conciliar movement; college of cardinals, consistory, conclave; bench of bishops; chapter, vestry; kirk session, presbytery 956 n. *tribunal.*

Adj. *ecclesiastical,* ecclesiastic, churchly, ecclesiological, theocratic; obediental, infallible 733 adj. *authoritative;* hierocratic, priest-ridden, ultramontane; apostolic; hierarchical, pontifical, papal, popish; patriarchal, metropolitan; episcopal, prelatical 986 adj. *clerical;* episcopalian, presbyterian; prioral, abbatical, abbatial; conciliar, synodic, presbyteral, capitular; sanhedral, consistorial; provincial, diocesan, parochial.

priestly, sacerdotal, hieratic, Aaronic, Levitical; brahminic; sacramental, apostolic, pastoral.

Vb. *ecclesiasticize,* episcopize, prelatize; frock, ordain, order, consecrate, enthrone; nominate, present; benefice, prefer; translate, elevate.

986. Clergy – **N.** *clergy,* hierarchy; the cloth, the ministry; sacerdotal order, priesthood, secular clergy, regular clergy, religious.

cleric, clerk in holy orders, priest, deacon, subdeacon; churchman, ecclesiastic, divine; clergyman, reverend;

father, father in God; padre, sky-pilot, Holy Joe; parson, rector, incumbent, pluralist 776 n. *possessor*; hedgepriest, priestling; ordinand, seminarist.

pastor, shepherd, minister, parish priest, rector, vicar, perpetual curate, curate; chaplain; confessor, penitentiary; spiritual director, pardoner; friar; preaching order, predicant; preacher, pulpiteer 537 n. *preacher*; missioner, missionary, evangelist, revivalist, salvationist, hot-gospeller.

ecclesiarch, pope, Supreme Pontiff, Holy Father, Vicar of Christ; cardinal, prince of the church; patriarch, exarch, metropolitan, primate, archbishop; prelate, diocesan, bishop, suffragan, 'episcopal curate'; bench of bishops, episcopate, Lords Spiritual; archpriest, archpresbyter; archdeacon, dean, subdean, rural dean; canon, prebendary, capitular; archimandrite; superior, abbot, abbess; prior, prioress, elder, presbyter, moderator.

monk, monastic 895 n. *celibate*; hermit, cenobite, Desert Father 883 n. *solitary*; vagabond monk, circumcellion; Greek monk, caloyer; Islamic monk, santon, marabout; sufi, dervish, faqir 945 n. *ascetic*; Buddhist monk, pongye, bonze; brother, regular, conventual; novice, lay brother; cowl, shaveling; friar; monks, religious; fraternity, brotherhood, friarhood, friary; order, religious o. 708 n. *community*.

nun, cloistress, clergywoman; sister, mother; novice, postulant; lay sister; sisterhood, lay s., beguinage, beguine.

church officer, elder, presbyter, moderator; priest, chaplain, altarist; minister; lay preacher, lay reader; acolyte, server, altar-boy; crucifer, thurifer, boat-boy 988 n. *ritualist*; chorister, choirboy, choirman, precentor, cantor 413 n. *choir*; sidesman; churchwarden, vestryman, capitular; beadle, verger, pew-opener; sacristan, sexton; grave-digger, bell-ringer.

priest, chief p., high p., archpriest; priestess; Levite; pontiff, flamen; Druid, Druidess.

monastery, monkery, bonzery, lamasery; friary; priory, abbey; convent, nunnery, beguinage; ashram, hermitage; community house 192 n. *abode*; seminary 539 n. *training school*; cell 194 n. *chamber*.

parsonage, rectory, vicarage; glebe-house, manse; deanery; palace, bishop's p., Lambeth, Vatican; close, papal precincts 235 n. *enclosure*.

Adj. *clerical*, in orders, clergiable; regular; secular; ordained, consecrated; prebendal, beneficed, pluralistic; parsonical, rectorial, vicarial; pastoral, presbyteral, sacerdotal 985 adj. *priestly*; diaconal, subdiaconal, archidiaconal, prelatical, episcopal 985 adj. *ecclesiastical*.

monastic, cloistered, conventual, enclosed; monkish, celibate 895 adj. *unwedded*.

Vb. *take orders*, be ordained, enter the church, enter the ministry; take vows, take the veil.

987. Laity – **N.** *laity*, lay people, civilians 869 n. *commonalty*; cure, parish; flock, sheep, fold; congregation 976 n. *church member*; lay brethren 708 n. *community*; the profane, the worldly.

layman, laic; lay brother, lay sister; catechumen, ordinand, seminarist, novice, postulant 538 n. *learner*; parishioner, diocesan 976 n. *church member*; non-professional, amateur 695 n. *unskilfulness*; civilian 869 n. *commoner*.

Adj. *laical*, laic, lay, unordained, not in orders, non-clergiable; non-ecclesiastical, secular; temporal, in the world, of the w., profane, unholy, unconsecrated; non-professional, amateur, do-it-yourself; amateurish 695 adj. *unskilled*.

Vb. *laicize*, secularize, undedicate, deconsecrate, dishallow.

988. Ritual – **N.** *ritual*, procedure, way of doing things, method 624 n. *way*; due order, routine, drill, system 60 n. *order*; form, order, liturgy; symbolization, symbolism 519 n. *metaphor*; rituality, ceremonial, ceremony 875 n. *formality*.

ritualism, ceremonialism, ceremony, formalism, spikiness; liturgics.

rite, mode of worship 981 n. *cult*; institution, observance, ritual practice 610 n. *practice*; form, order, ordinance, rubric, formula, formulary 693 n. *precept*; ceremony, solemnity, sacrament, mystery 876 n. *celebration*; rites, mysteries 551 n. *representation*; initiatory rite, circumcision, initiation, baptism 299 n. *reception*; christening.

ministration, functioning, officiation, performance 676 n. *action*; administration, celebration, solemnization; pulpitry, predication, preaching 534 n. *teaching*; sacred rhetoric, homiletics 579 n. *oratory*; pastorship, pastoral epistle, confession, auricular c.; shrift, absolution, penance.

Holy Communion, Eucharist, Eucharistic sacrifice; mass, high m., solemn m., great m., sung m., missa cantata; low mass, little m., dry m., missa sicca; communion, the Lord's Supper; celebration, service, order of s., liturgy.

the sacrament, the Holy Sacrament; Corpus Christi, body and blood of Christ; real presence, transubstantiation, consubstantiation, impanation; the elements, bread and wine, wafer; host; reserved sacrament; viaticum.

church service, office, duty, service; liturgy, celebration, concelebration; canonical hours, matins, lauds, prime, terce, sext, none, vespers, compline; morning prayer, matins; evening prayer, evensong, benediction; tenebrae; vigil; watchnight service; novena.

ritualist, ceremonialist, sabbatarian, formalist; liturgist, liturgiologist, litanist, euchologist; sacramentarian, sacramentalist; celebrant, masser, minister 986 n. *priest*; server, acolyte; thurifer, boat-boy; crucifer, processionist, processioner.

office-book, ordinal, lectionary; book of hours, breviary; missal, mass-book; euchology, prayer-book, book of common prayer 981 n. *prayers*; beads, bead-roll, rosary.

hymnal, hymnology, hymn-book, choir-b.; psalter, psalm-book 981 n. *hymn*.

holy-day, feast, feast-day, festival 837 n. *festivity*; fast-day, meatless d. 946 n. *fast*; high day, day of observance, day of obligation 876 n. *celebration*; sabbath, day of rest 681 n. *leisure*; Lord's Day, Sunday; proper day 876 n. *special day*; saint's day 141 n. *anniversary*.

Adj. *ritual*, procedural; formal, solemn, ceremonial, liturgical; processional, recessional; symbolic, symbolical, representational 551 adj. *representing*; sacramental, eucharistic; chrismal; baptismal; sacrificial, paschal; festal, pentecostal; fasting, lenten; unleavened; kosher; consecrated, blessed.

ritualistic, ceremonious, formulistic; sabbatarian; sacramentarian; liturgiological, euchological.

Vb. *perform ritual*, do the rites, say office, celebrate, concelebrate, officiate, function; baptize, christen, confirm, ordain, lay on hands; minister, administer the sacraments, give communion, housel; sacrifice; offer prayers, bless, dedicate, consecrate, deconsecrate; purify, lustrate, asperge; thurify, cense; anoint, anele, give extreme unction; confess, absolve, pronounce absolution, shrive; take communion, receive the sacraments, housel oneself; bow, kneel, genuflect; sign oneself, cross o., sain; tell one's beads, say one's rosary; go one's stations; go in procession; fast, flagellate 941 vb. *do penance*.

ritualize, ceremonialize, institute a rite, organize a cult; sacramentalize, observe, keep holy.

989. Canonicals – N. *canonicals*, clerical dress, cloth, clerical black 228 n. *dress*; frock, soutane, cassock, scapular; gown, Geneva g. 228 n. *cloak*; robe, cowl, hood; lawn sleeves; apron, gaiters, shovel hat; cardinal's hat; priests' cap, biretta, skull-cap, calotte; Salvation Army bonnet; tonsure; prayer-cap; tallith; sanbenito, simarra.

vestments, ephod, priestly vesture; pontificals; cassock, surplice, rochet;

cope, tunicle, dalmatic, alb 228 n. *robe*; amice, chasuble; stole, deacon's s., orarion; pallium; cingulum 47 n. *girdle*; biretta 228 n. *headgear*; mitre, tiara, triple crown; papal vestment, orale, fanon; crosier, staff, pastoral s.; pectoral 222 n. *cross*; episcopal ring; altar-cloth, frontlet, pall; pyx-cloth; orphrey, orfray 844 n. *ornamentation*.

Adj. *vestimental*, vestimentary, vestiary; canonical, pontifical.

vestured, robed 228 adj. *dressed*; cowled, hooded 986 adj. *monastic*; gaitered, aproned 986 adj. *clerical*; mitred, crosiered.

990. Temple – N. *temple*, fane, pantheon; shrine, sacellum; idol house, joss-h.; house of God, tabernacle, the Temple, House of the Lord; place of worship; masjid, mosque; house of prayer, oratory; sacred edifice, pagoda, stupa, tope, dagoba; pronaos, portico, cella, naos.

holy place, holy ground, sacred precinct, temenos; sanctuary, adytum, cella, naos; Ark of the Covenant, Mercy-seat, Sanctum, Holy of Holies, oracle; martyry, sacred tomb; grave-yard, golgotha, God's acre 364 n. *cemetery*; place of pilgrimage; Holy City, Zion, Mecca, Benares, Banaras.

church, God's house; parish church, daughter c., chapel of ease; chapelry; cathedral, minister, procathedral; basilica; abbey; kirk, chapel, tabernacle, temple, bethel, ebenezer; steeple-house, conventicle, meeting-house, prayer-h.; house of prayer, oratory, chantry, chantry-chapel; synagogue, mosque.

altar, sacrarium, sanctuary; altar-stone, altar-table, Lord's t., communion t.; prothesis, credence; canopy, balda-chin, altar-piece, reredos; altar-facing, antependium; altar-stair, predella.

church utensil, font, baptistry; aumbry, stoup, piscina; cup, chalice, paten, grail, sangrail; pulpit, lectern; hassock, kneeler; salver, collection-plate; relics, sacred r., reliquary.

church interior, nave, cella, body of the kirk; aisle, apse, ambulatory, transept; chancel, choir, sanctuary; hagioscope, squint; chancel screen, rood-s., jube; stall, choir-s., sedilia, misericorde; pew; pulpit, ambo; chapel, Lady c.; confessional; clerestory, triforium, spandrel; stained-glass window, rose-w., jesse-w.; calvary, stations of the cross, Easter sepulchre; sacristy, vestry; crypt, vault; rood, cross, crucifix.

church exterior, porch, galilee, tympanum 263 n. *doorway*; tower, steeple, spire; bell-tower, belfry, campanile; cloister, ambulatory; chapter-house, presbytery 692 n. *council*; churchyard, kirkyard, lychgate; close 235 n. *enclosure*.

Adj. *churchlike*, basilican, cathedralic; cruciform; apsidal; Gothic, Romanesque, Norman, Early English, decorated, perpendicular.

A

A1
best 644 adj.

abacus
counting instrument 86 n.

abandon
relinquish 621 vb.
resign 753 vb.
not retain 779 vb.
excitable state 822 n.

abandoned
unpossessed 774 adj.
vicious 934 adj.

abasement
humiliation 872 n.

abash
humiliate 872 vb.

abate
decrease 37 vb.
discount 810 vb.

abatement
relief 831 n.

abattoir
slaughter-house 362 n.

abbey
monastery 986 n.
church 990 n.

abbot
ecclesiarch 986 n.

abbotship
church office 985 n.

abbreviate
shorten 204 vb.
abstract 592 vb.

abbreviation
smallness 33 n.

A.B.C.
beginning 68 n.
letter 558 n.

abdicate
relinquish 621 vb.
resign 753 vb.

abdication
loss of right 916 n.

abdomen
maw 194 n.
insides 224 n.

abduct
take away 786 vb.
steal 788 vb.

abeam
sideways 239 adv.

aberrant
non-uniform 17 adj.

aberration
abnormality 84 n.
deviation 282 n.
inattention 456 n.

abet
aid 703 vb.

abetment
cooperation 706 n.

abettor
colleague 707 n.

abeyance
lull 145 n.
inaction 677 n.

abhor
hate 888 vb.
disapprove 924 vb.

abide
stay 144 vb.
go on 146 vb.
dwell 192 vb.

abide by
acquiesce 488 vb.
observe 768 vb.

abiding place
abode 192 n.

ability
ability 160 n.
skill 694 n.

abirritant
antidote 658 n.

abject
servile 879 adj.
contemptible 922 adj.
rascally 930 adj.

abjure
negate 533 vb.
recant 603 vb.

able
powerful 160 adj.
possible 469 adj.
intelligent 498 adj.
skilful 694 adj.

able-bodied
stalwart 162 adj.

able seaman
mariner 270 n.

ablution
ablution 648 n.

abnormal
disagreeing 25 adj.
abnormal 84 adj.
insane 503 adj.
wrong 914 adj.

abode
abode 192 n.

abolish
destroy 165 vb.
abrogate 752 vb.

abolitionist
revolutionist 149 n.
destroyer 168 n.

abominable
hateful 888 adj.
heinous 934 adj.

abomination
badness 645 n.
hateful object 888 n.

aboriginal
primal 127 adj.
native 191 n., adj.

abort
be unproductive 172 vb.
miscarry 728 vb.

abortion
abnormality 84 n.
undevelopment 670 n.
eyesore 842 n.

abortive
immature 670 adj.
unsuccessful 728 adj.

abound
superabound 637 vb.

about
concerning 9 adv.
nearly 200 adv.
around 230 adv.

about face
turn back 286 vb.

about to be
impending 155 adj.

about turn
reversion 148 n.

above
aloft 209 adv.

above-mentioned
preceding 64 adj.

above par
excellent 644 adj.

abracadabra
spell 983 n.

abrade
rub 333 vb.

abrasion
wound 655 n.

abrasive
rubbing 333 adj.
obliteration 550 n.

abridge
shorten 204 vb.
be concise 569 vb.
abstract 592 vb.

abroad
abroad 59 adv.

abrogate
liberate 746 vb.
abrogate 752 vb.
not retain 779 vb.

abrupt
instantaneous 116 adj.
vertical 215 adj.
hasty 680 adj.

abscess
ulcer 651 n.

abscond
run away 620 vb.
elude 667 vb.

absence
non-existence 2 n.
deficit 55 n.
absence 190 n.

dutilessness 918 n.
absentee
absence 190 n.
dutilessness 918 n.
absenteeism
dutilessness 918 n.
absent-minded
abstracted 456
adj.
forgetful 506 adj.
absinth
sourness 393 n.
absolute
irrelative 10 adj.
great 32 adj.
complete 54 adj.
one 88 adj.
assertive 532 adj.
authoritarian
735 adj.
unconditional
744 adj.
godlike 965 adj.
absolution
forgiveness 909 n.
church ministry
985 n.
absolutism
despotism 733 n.
absolve
forgive 909 vb.
acquit 960 vb.
absorb
absorb 299 vb.
impress 821 vb.
absorbed
thoughtful 449 adj.
abstracted 456 adj.
absorbent
drier 342 n.
absorption
identity 13 n.
reception 299 n.
attention 455 n.
abstain
not use 674 vb.
be temperate
942 vb.
abstainer
abstainer 942 n.
abstemious
temperate 942 adj.
abstention
no choice 606 n.
avoidance 620 n.
abstinence
temperance 942 n.

abstinent
fasting 946 adj.
abstract
insubstantial 4 adj.
mental 447 adj.
compendium 592 n.
abstract 592 vb.
take away 786 vb.
abstracted
separate 46 adj.
abstracted 456 adj.
forgetful 506 adj.
abstraction
insubstantiality 4 n.
abstractedness
456 n.
abstractive
taking 786 adj.
abstruse
puzzling 517 adj.
imperspicuous
568 adj.
absurd
disagreeing 25 adj.
abnormal 84 adj.
absurd 497 adj.
unmeaning 515 adj.
abundance
great quantity 32
n.
abundance 171 n.
plenty 635 n.
redundance 637 n.
abundant
many 104 adj.
abuse
force 176 vb.
evil 616 n.
misuse 675 n., vb.
scurrility 899 n.
curse 899 vb.
exprobate 924 vb.
abusive
ungracious 885 adj.
maledicent 899 adj.
abut
be near 200 vb.
be contiguous
202 vb.
abutment
supporter 218 n.
abysmal
deep 211 adj.
abyss
depth 211 n.
cavity 255 n.
hell 972 n.

academic
suppositional
512 adj.
educational 534 adj.
studious 536 adj.
academician
intellectual 492 n.
artist 556 n.
academy
academy 539 n.
accede
accrue 38 vb.
assent 488 vb.
accelerate
accelerate 277 vb.
hasten 680 vb.
accent
sound 398 n.
prosody 593 n.
emphasize 532 vb.
punctuation 547 n.
pronunciation
577 n.
accentuate
emphasize 532 vb.
accept
admit 299 vb.
believe 485 vb.
acquiesce 488 vb.
undertake 672 vb.
receive 782 vb.
approve 923 vb.
acceptability
sufficiency 635 n.
acceptable
pleasurable 826
adj.
approvable 923 adj.
acceptance
(*see* accept)
acceptor
recipient 782 n.
purchaser 792 n.
access
approach 289 n.
spasm 318 n.
access 624 n.
accessible
near 200 adj.
accessible 289 adj.
admitting 299 adj.
accession
addition 38 n.
arrival 295 n.
accessory
extrinsic 6 adj.
adjunct 40 n.

concomitant 89 n.
superfluity 637 n.
colleague 707 n.
accidence
grammar 564 n.
accident
extrinsicality 6 n.
chance 159 n.
non-design 618 n.
accidental
casual 159 adj.
unintentional
618 adj.
accident-prone
unfortunate
731 adj.
acclaim
applaud 923 vb.
acclamation
applause 923 n.
acclimatize
habituate 610 vb.
acclivity
acclivity 220 n.
ascent 308 n.
accolade
honours 866 n.
accommodate
adjust 24 vb.
comprise 78 vb.
place 187 vb.
accommodation
room 183 n.
storage 632 n.
subvention 703 n.
accompaniment
adjunct 40 n.
accompaniment
89 n.
musical piece
412 n.
accompanist
instrumentalist
413 n.
accompany
accompany 89 vb.
synchronize 123 vb.
accomplice
colleague 707 n.
accomplish
do 676 vb.
carry out 725 vb.
succeed 727 vb.
accomplishment
culture 490 n.
skill 694 n.
(*see* accomplish)

accord
agreement 24 n.
conform 83 vb.
assent 488 vb.
concord 710 vb.
give 781 vb.

accordion
organ 414 n.

accost
approach 289 vb.
greet 884 vb.

accouchement
obstetrics 164 n.

accoucheur
obstetrics 164 n.
doctor 658 n.

account
report 524 n.
narration 590 n.
credit 802 n.
accounts 808 n.

accountability
dueness 915 n.
duty 917 n.

accountancy
numeration 86 n.
accounts 808 n.

accountant
computer 86 n.
recorder 549 n.
treasurer 798 n.
accountant 808 n.

account book
account book
808 n.

account for
cause 156 vb.
account for 158 vb.

accounts
accounts 808 n.

accoutrement
dressing 228 n.
uniform 228 n.
fitting out 669 n.

accredit
commission 751 vb.

accredited
credal 485 adj.

accretion
increment 36 n.
addition 38 n.

accrue
accrue 38 vb.
be received 782 vb.

accumulate
bring together
74 vb.

store 632 vb.

accumulative
acquiring 771 adj.

accuracy
accuracy 494 n.
veracity 540 n.

accurate
careful 457 adj.

accursed
damnable 645 adj.
bad 645 adj.
baneful 659 adj.
unhappy 825 adj.
hateful 888 adj.
heinous 934 adj.
profane 980 adj.

accusation
accusation 928 n.
litigation 959 n.

accuse
defame 926 vb.
accuse 928 vb.

accuser
informer 524 n.
accuser 928 n.
litigant 959 n.

accustom
habituate 610 vb.

accustomed
usual 610 adj.

ace
unit 88 n.
masterpiece 694 n.

acerbity
sourness 393 n.

acetose
sour 393 adj.

ache
pang 377 n.
suffer 825 vb.

achievable
possible 469 adj.

achieve
do 676 vb.
carry out 725 vb.
succeed 727 vb.

achievement
progression 285 n.
heraldry 547 n.
(see achieve)

Achilles' heel
vulnerability 661 n.

achromatism
achromatism 426 n.

acid
sourness 393 n.
poison 659 n.

acidity
pungency 388 n.
sourness 393 n.

acidosis
indigestion 651 n.

acid test
experiment 461 n.

acknowledge
attribute 158 vb.
confess 526 vb.
correspond 588
vb.
befriend 880 vb.
thank 907 vb.

acknowledgement
(see acknowledge)

acme
summit 213 n.

acne
skin disease 651 n.

acolyte
auxiliary 707 n.
ritualist 988 n.

acoustics
acoustics 398 n.
hearing 415 n.

acquaint
inform 524 vb.

acquaintance
knowledge 490 n.
friendship 880 n.

acquiesce
acquiesce 488 vb.
be willing 597 vb.

acquiescence
conformity 83 n.
patience 823 n.

acquire
acquire 771 vb.

acquired
extrinsic 6 adj.

**acquired
characteristic**
extrinsicality 6 n.

acquirement
skill 694 n.

acquisition
extra 40 n.
acquisition 771 n.

acquisitive
avaricious 816 adj.
greedy 859 adj.
selfish 932 adj.

acquit
liberate 746 vb.
forgive 909 vb.
acquit 960 vb.

acquittal
acquittal 960 n.

acquittance
title-deed 767 n.

acreage
space 183 n.

acres
lands 777 n.

acrimonious
resentful 891 adj.

acrimony
sharpness 256 n.
malevolence 898 n.

acrobat
athlete 162 n.

acrobatics
athletics 162 n.

acropolis
refuge 662 n.
fort 713 n.

across
obliquely 220 adv.

acrostic
enigma 530 n.
initials 558 n.

act
operate 173 vb.
dissemble 541 vb.
represent 551 vb.
stage show 594 n.
deed 676 n.
behave 688 vb.
decree 737 n.
be affected 850 vb.

act for
substitute 150 vb.
deputize 755 vb.

acting arrangement
transientness 114 n.

actinism
radiation 417 n.

actinometry
optics 417 n.

action
energy 160 n.
agency 173 n.
dramaturgy 594 n.
action 676 n.
conduct 688 n.
battle 718 n.
litigation 959 n.

actionable
accusable 928 adj.
litigated 959 adj.

activate
operate 173 vb.
invigorate 174 vb.

influence 178 vb.
activator
  stimulant 174 n.
active
  operative 173 adj.
  vigorous 174 adj.
  willing 597 adj.
  doing 676 adj.
  active 678 adj.
active service
  warfare 718 n.
activism
  activity 678 n.
activist
  doer 676 n.
activity
  agitation 318 n.
  business, job 622
  n.
  activity 678 n.
actor
  deceiver 545 n.
  actor 594 n.
  agent 686 n.
  affector 850 n.
actor manager
  stage-manager
  594 n.
actual
  real 1 adj.
  present 121 adj.
  true 494 adj.
actuarial
  accounting 808 adj.
actuary
  computer 86 n.
  accountant 808 n.
actuate
  move 265 vb.
  motivate 612 vb.
act upon
  operate 173 vb.
acuity
  sharpness 256 n.
acumen
  sagacity 498 n.
acute
  violent 176 adj.
  sharp 256 adj.
  strident 407 adj.
  intelligent 498 adj.
adage
  maxim 496 n.
adagio
  adagio 412 adv.
Adam
  mankind 371 n.

adamant
  strength 162 n.
  hardness 326 n.
adapt
  adjust 24 vb.
adaptable
  fit 24 adj.
  conformable 83 adj.
  useful 640 adj.
adaptation
  adaptation 24 n.
  conformity 83 n.
  musical piece 412
  n.
adapted to
  expedient 642 adj.
adapter
  alterer 143 n.
add
  add 38 vb.
  enlarge 197 vb.
  insert 303 vb.
addendum
  extra, adjunct 40 n.
adder
  reptile 365 n.
  noxious animal
  904 n.
addict
  habitué 610 n.
addiction
  habit 610 n.
  intemperance 943 n.
addition
  addition 38 n.
  adjunct 40 n.
  joinder 45 n.
  numerical result
  85 n.
  numerical
  operation 86 n.
additional
  extrinsic 6 adj.
  additional 38 adj.
additive
  extra 40 n.
addle
  sterilize 172 vb.
addled
  unproductive
  172 adj.
address
  abode 192 n.
  send 272 vb.
  oration 579 n.
  speak to 583 vb.
  skill 694 n.

addressee
  resident 191 n.
  interlocutor 584 n.
  correspondent
  588 n.
addresses
  wooing 889 n.
address oneself
  prepare 669 vb.
adduce
  corroborate 466
  vb.
add up
  be intelligible
  516 vb.
add up to
  mean 514 vb.
adenoids
  swelling 253 n.
adeps
  fat 357 n.
adept
  proficient 696 n.
adequacy
  sufficiency 635 n.
adhere
  accrue 38 vb.
  cohere 48 vb.
  assent 488 vb.
adherence
  observance 768 n.
adherent
  follower 284 n.
  auxiliary 707 n.
adhesive
  adhesive 47 n.
  viscid 354 adj.
  retentive 778 adj.
ad hoc
  spontaneous
  609 adj.
  unprepared 670
  adj.
adiactinic
  opaque 423 adj.
adiathermic
  cold 380 adj.
  opaque 423 adj.
adieu
  valediction 296 n.
adipocere
  fat 357 n.
adipose
  fatty 357 adj.
adit
  tunnel 263 n.
  access 624 n.

adjacent
  near 200 adj.
adjective
  part of speech
  564 n.
adjoin
  be near 200 vb.
  be contiguous
  202 vb.
adjourn
  put off 136 vb.
adjudge
  judge 480 vb.
adjudicate
  judge 480 vb.
  try a case 959 vb.
adjudicator
  estimator 480 n.
adjunct
  adjunct 40 n.
  component 58 n.
  concomitant 89 n.
adjure
  entreat 761 vb.
adjust
  graduate 27 vb.
  synchronize 123 vb.
  rectify 654 vb.
adjustable
  conformable
  83 adj.
adjusted
  accurate 494 adj.
  right 913 adj.
adjustment
  adaptation 24 n.
  compromise 770 n.
  (*see* adjust)
adjutant
  auxiliary 707 n.
  army officer 741 n.
ad-libbing
  spontaneity 609 n.
ad libitum, ad lib.
  freely 744 adv.
administer
  use 673 vb.
  manage 689 vb.
administration
  management 689 n.
administrative
  directing 689 adj.
  jurisdictional 955
  adj.
administrator
  agent 686 n.
  manager 690 n.

admirable
excellent 644 adj.
wonderful 864 adj.
approvable 923
adj.

admiral
navy man 722 n.

admiralty
navy 722 n.

admiration
wonder 864 n.
respect 920 n.
approbation 923 n.

admire oneself
be vain 873 vb.

admirer
lover 887 n.
commender 923 n.

admissible
approvable 923 adj.

admission
inclusion 78 n.
reception 299 n.
assent 488 n.

admit
admit 299 vb.
testify 466 vb.
assent 488 vb.
confess 526 vb.
receive 782 vb.

admit of
be possible 469 vb.

admixture
tincture 43 n.

admonish
warn 664 vb.
reprove 924 vb.

ado
activity 678 n.

adobe
small house 192 n.

adolescence
youth 130 n.

adolescent
youngster 132 n.
immature 670 adj.

adopt
choose 605 vb.
avail of 673 vb.

adopted
filial 170 adj.

adoption
approbation 923 n.

adorable
lovable 887 adj.

adoration
worship 981 n.

adore
love 887 vb.
worship 981 vb.

adorn
decorate 844 vb.

adornment
ornamentation 844
n.

adrift
separate 46 adj.
doubting 474 adj.

adroit
skilful 694 adj.

adscititious
additional 38 adj.

adulation
flattery 925 n.

adult
adult 134 n.
matured 669 adj.

adulterate
mix 43 vb.
modify 143 vb.
weaken 163 vb.

adulterer
libertine 952 n.

adulterine
bastard 954 adj.

adulterous
extramarital 951
adj.

adultery
illicit love 951 n.

adultress
loose woman 952
n.

adumbrate
describe 590 vb.

adumbration
copy 22 n.
latency 523 n.

advance
increase 36 n.
augment 36 vb.
part 53 n.
motion 265 n.
progression
285 n.
affirm 532 vb.
be expedient 642
vb.
lend 784 vb.
dignify 866 vb.

advance, in
early 135 adj.

advance against
charge 712 vb.

advanced
modern 126 adj.
progressive 285 adj.

advance notice
prediction 511 n.

advances
approach 289 n.
endearment 889 n.

advantage
utility 640 n.
expedience 642 n.
gain 771 n.

advantage of, take
befool 542 vb.

advent
approach 289 n.
arrival 295 n.

adventure
eventuality 154 n.
undertaking 672 n.

adventurer
impostor 545 n.
gambler 618 n.
desperado 857 n.

adventurous
speculative 618 adj.
enterprising 672 adj.
rash 857 adj.

adverb
part of speech
564 n.

adversaria
commentary 520 n.

adversary
opponent 705 n.

adversative
negative 533 adj.

adverse
contrary 14 adj.
unwilling 598 adj.
hindering 702 adj.
opposing 704 adj.
adverse 731 adj.
disliking 861 adj.

adversity
adversity 731 n.
suffering 825 n.

advert
notice 455 vb.

advertise
communicate
524 vb.
advertise 528 vb.
praise 923 vb.

advertisement
exhibit 522 n.
advertisement 528 n.

advertise oneself
be ostentatious
875 vb.

advertiser
exhibitor 522 n.
informant 524 n.
publicizer 528 n.

advice
hint 524 n.
news 529 n.
advice 691 n.
precept 693 n.

advisable
expedient 642 adj.

advise
inform 524 vb.
advise 691 vb.

advise against
dissuade 613 vb.

adviser
adviser 691 n.
expert 696 n.

advise with
confer 584 vb.

advisory
advising 691 adj.

advocacy
aid 703 n.
bar 958 n.

advocate
motivator 612 n.
advise 691 vb.
patron 707 n.
vindicator 927 n.
lawyer 958 n.

advowson
benefice 985 n.

adytum
chamber 194 n.
holy place 990 n.

adze
sharp edge 256 n.

aeons
diuturnity 113 n.

aerate
bubble 355 vb.
aerify 340 vb.

aerated
bubbly 355 adj.

aerial
high 209 adj.
flying 271 adj.
telecommunication
531 n.

aerify
vaporize 338 vb.
aerify 340 vb.

refresh 685 vb.
aerobatics
　aeronautics 271 n.
aerodrome
　air travel 271 n.
　aircraft 276 n.
aerodynamics
　aeronautics 271 n.
　pneumatics 340 n.
aerography
　pneumatics 340 n.
aerolite
　meteor 321 n.
aerology
　pneumatics 340 n.
aeromechanics
　aeronautics 271 n.
aeronaut
　aeronaut 271 n.
aeronautics
　aeronautics 271 n.
aeroplane
　aircraft 276 n.
aerostatics
　aeronautics 271 n.
aesculap
　sharp edge 256 n.
aesthete
　man of taste 846 n.
aesthetic
　sensitive 819 adj.
　beautiful 841 adj.
　tasteful 846 adj.
aestheticism
　moral sensibility
　　819 n.
aesthetics
　sensibility 374 n.
　beauty 841 n.
　good taste 846 n.
aetiology
　causation 156 n.
afar
　afar 199 adv.
affable
　sociable 882 adj.
　amiable 884 adj.
affair
　topic 452 n.
affairs
　affairs 154 n.
　business 622 n.
affect
　be related 9 vb.
　modify 143 vb.
　influence 178 vb.
　dissemble 541 vb.

impress 821 vb.
love 887 vb.
affectation
　imitation 20 n.
　inelegance 576 n.
　fashion 848 n.
　affectation 850 n.
affected
　diseased 651 adj.
　(*see* affect,
　　affectation)
affectibility
　moral sensibility
　　819 n.
affection
　love 887 n.
affectionate
　loving 887 adj.
　caressing 889 adj.
affections
　temperament 5 n.
　affections 817 n.
affectivity
　feeling 818 n.
affiance
　marry 894 vb.
affidavit
　testimony 466 n.
　oath 532 n.
affiliate
　be akin 11 vb.
affiliation
　association 706 n.
　participation 775 n.
affinity
　relation 9 n.
　consanguinity 11 n.
　tendency 179 n.
　attraction 291 n.
　liking 859 n.
affinity, have an
　combine 50 vb.
affirm
　affirm 532 vb.
　plead 614 vb.
　promise 764 vb.
affirmation
　testimony 466 n.
　affirmation 532 n.
affix
　affix 45 vb.
　sequel 67 n.
　part of speech
　　564 n.
afflatus
　imagination 513 n.
　revelation 975 n.

afflict
　hurt 827 vb.
　punish 963 vb.
affliction
　bane 659 n.
affluence
　plenty 635 n.
　prosperity 730 n.
affluent
　stream 350 n.
　(*see* affluence)
afford
　provide 633 vb.
　afford 800 vb.
affordable
　cheap 812 adj.
afforestation
　forestry 366 n.
affray
　fight 716 n.
affright
　fear 854 n.
affront
　huff 891 vb.
　indignity 921 n.
　not respect 921 vb.
aflame
　luminous 417 adj.
aforesaid
　preceding 64 adj.
　repeated 106 adj.
　prior 119 adj.
aforethought
　predetermined
　　608 adj.
　intended 617 adj.
a fortiori
　eminently 34 adv.
afraid
　fearing 854 adj.
aft
　rearward 238 adv.
after
　after 65 adv.
　subsequently 120
　　adv.
　rearward 238 adv.
after, be
　pursue 619 vb.
afterbirth
　obstetrics 164 n.
after-care
　therapy 658 n.
afterclap
　sequel 67 n.
aftercomer
　aftercomer 67 n.

after-effect
　sequel 67 n.
　effect 157 n.
afterglow
　sequel 67 n.
afterlife
　future state 124 n.
　Heaven 971 n.
aftermath
　sequel 67 n.
　posteriority 120 n.
afternoon
　evening 129 n.
afterpart
　rear 238 n.
after-taste
　sequel 67 n.
　taste 386 n.
afterthought
　sequel 67 n.
　tergiversation
　　603 n.
afterwards
　after 65 adv.
　subsequently 120
　　adv.
again
　again 106 adv.
again and again
　often 139 adv.
against
　opposing 704 adj.
against the grain
　unwillingly 598 adv
　hindering 702 adj.
　in opposition
　　704 adv.
agape
　open 263 adj.
Agape
　public worship
　　981 n.
agaric
　cathartic 658 n.
age
　date 108 n.
　era 110 n.
　diuturnity 113 n.
　chronology 117 n.
　oldness 127 n.
　deteriorate 655 vb.
age, full
　adultness 134 n.
age, of
　grown up 134 adj.
　marriageable
　　894 adj.

aged
aged 131 adj.
age-group
contemporary 123 n.
ageless
perpetual 115 adj.
young 130 adj.
agelong
lasting 113 adj.
perpetual 115 adj.
agency
agency 173 n.
instrumentality
628 n.
commission 751 n.
agenda
affairs 154 n.
topic 452 n.
agent
cause 156 n.
doer 676 n.
agent 686 n.
deputy 755 n.
agent provocateur
trickster 545 n.
motivator 612 n.
age-old
immemorial
127 adj.
agglomerate
coherence 48 n.
agglomeration
accumulation 74 n.
agglutinate
affix 45 vb.
agglutinate 48 vb.
agglutinative
linguistic 557 adj.
aggrandize
enlarge 197 vb.
dignify 866 vb.
aggrandizement
greatness 32 n.
aggravate
augment 36 vb.
aggravate 832 vb.
enrage 891 vb.
aggregate
all 52 n.
numerical result
85 n.
aggregation
accumulation 74 n.
aggression
attack 712 n.
aggressive
vigorous 174 adj.

active 678 adj.
attacking 712 adj.
warlike 718 adj.
aggressor
quarreller 709 n.
attacker 712 n.
aggrieve
displease 827 vb.
harm 645 vb.
aghast
fearing 854 adj.
agile
speedy 277 adj.
agitate
agitate 318 vb.
distract 456 vb.
inquire 459 vb.
cause discontent
829 vb.
frighten 854 vb.
agitation
derangement 63 n.
changeableness
152 n.
motion 265 n.
agitation 318 n.
restlessness 678 n.
revolt, sedition
738 n.
feeling 818 n.
worry 825 n.
agitator
trouble-maker
663 n.
opponent 705 n.
agitator 738 n.
excitant 821 n.
agnate
kinsman 11 n.
agnomen
name 561 n.
agnostic
doubting 474 adj.
unbeliever 486 n.
irreligious 974 adj.
ago
formerly 125 adv.
agog
desiring 859 adj.
agonize
feel pain 377 vb.
suffer 825 vb.
agony
pain 377 n.
suffering 825 n.
agrarian
agrarian 370 adj.

agree
accord 24 vb.
assent 488 vb.
concord 710 vb.
consent 758 vb.
contract 765 vb.
agreeable
agreeing 24 adj.
conformable 83 adj.
pleasant 376 adj.
pleasurable 826 adj.
agreement
relevance 9 n.
(see agree)
agrestic
agrarian 370 adj.
agriculture
agriculture 370 n.
ague
spasm 318 n.
malaria 651 n.
aguish
a-cold 380 adj.
ahead
superior 34 adj.
in front 237 adv.
ahead 283 adv.
ahimsa
peace 717 n.
benevolence 897 n.
aid
instrumentality
628 n.
aid 703 n., vb.
aide-de-camp
army officer 741 n.
aileron
aircraft 276 n.
wing 271 n.
ailment
illness 651 n.
aim
direction 281 n.
objective 617 n.
aim at
aim at 617 vb.
pursue 619 vb.
aimless
orderless 61 adj.
designless 618 adj.
air
insubstantial thing
4 n.
air 340 n.
dry 342 vb.
tune 412 n.
mien 445 n.

inquire 459 vb.
air-borne
flying 271 adj.
ascending 308 adj.
air-condition
refrigerate 382
vb.
air-conditioner
refrigerator 384 n.
aircraft
aircraft 276 n.
aircraftman
soldiery 722 n.
aircrew
air force 722 n.
airfield
air travel 271 n.
air force
air force 722 n.
air-gun
toy gun 723 n.
air-hostess
aeronaut 271 n.
airing
land travel 267 n.
ventilation 352 n.
airlane
air travel 271 n.
airless
tranquil 266 adj.
insalubrious
653 adj.
air-lift
air travel 271 n.
transport 272 n.
airline
air travel 271 n.
airmail
mails 531 n.
airman
aeronaut 271 n.
air-pipe
air-pipe 353 n.
air-pocket
emptiness 190 n.
airport
air travel 271 n.
airs
affectation 850 n.
airship
airship 276 n.
air space
territory 184 n.
air-stream
wind 352 n.
airstrip
air travel 271 n.

air-tight
  sealed off 264 adj.
air travel
  air travel 271 n.
airworthy
  aviational 276 adj.
airy
  insubstantial 4 adj.
  airy 340 adj.
  windy 352 adj.
  light-minded
    456 adj.
  disrespectful
    921 adj.
aisle
  church interior
    990 n.
ajar
  open 263 adj.
akin
  akin 11 adj.
  similar 18 adj.
alacrity
  willingness 597 n.
  activity 678 n.
Aladdin's lamp
  magic instrument
    983 n.
à la mode
  modern 126 adj.
  fashionable 848 adj.
alarm
  danger signal
    665 n.
  fear 854 n.
alarmist
  false alarm 665 n.
  alarmist 854 n.
  coward 856 n.
alarum
  timekeeper 117 n.
  signal 547 n.
alb
  vestments 989 n.
albedo
  light 417 n.
  reflection 417 n.
albescence
  whiteness 427 n.
albinism
  achromatism 426 n.
  skin disease 651 n.
album
  record 548 n.
alchemist
  alterer 143 n.
  occultist 984 n.

alchemy
  conversion 147 n.
alcohol
  liquor 301 n.
alcoholic
  drunkard 949 n.
  intoxicating
    949 adj.
alcove
  arbour 194 n.
alderman
  councillor 692 n.
aldermanship
  magistrature 733 n.
ale
  liquor 301 n.
aleatory
  speculative 618 adj.
alehouse
  tavern 192 n.
alembic
  vessel 194 n.
alert
  attentive 455 adj.
  vigilant 457 adj.
  signal 547 vb.
  danger signal 665 n.
  prepared 669 adj.
alfresco
  externally 223 adv.
algae
  plant 366 n.
algebra
  mathematics 86 n.
algology
  botany 368 n.
algorism
  number 85 n.
alias
  misnomer 562 n.
alibi
  absence 190 n.
  pretext 614 n.
alien
  foreigner 59 n.
  extraneous 59 adj.
  settler 191 n.
alienate
  not retain 779 vb.
  make enemies
    881 vb.
alienation
  transfer 780 n.
  enmity 881 n.
alienist
  psychologist 447 n.
  doctor 658 n.

alight
  place oneself
    187 vb.
  land 295 vb.
  descend 309 vb.
  sit down 311 vb.
  fiery 379 adj.
align
  make uniform 16 vb.
  arrange 62 vb.
alignment
  direction 281 n.
align oneself
  join a party 708 vb.
alike
  similar 18 adj.
aliment
  food 301 n.
alimentary
  nourishing 301 adj.
alimony
  dower 777 n.
  divorce 896 n.
alive
  alive 360 adj.
all
  all 52 n.
  universal 79 adj.
all, one's
  property 777 n.
all and sundry
  everyman 79 n.
allay
  assuage 177 vb.
all clear
  safety 660 n.
all ears
  attentive 455 adj.
allegation
  affirmation 532 n.
  pretext 614 n.
  accusation 928 n.
allegiance
  loyalty 739 n.
  duty 917 n.
allegory
  comparison 462 n.
  metaphor 519 n.
all-embracing
  comprehensive
    52 adj.
  general 79 adj.
allergy
  dislike 861 n.
  sensibility 374 n.
  ill-health 651 n.
alleviate

disencumber 701 vb.
  relieve 831 vb.
alley
  street 192 n.
  road 624 n.
alliance
  relation 9 n.
  association 706 n.
  compact 765 n.
  marriage 894 n.
alligator
  reptile 365 n.
all in
  fatigued 684 adj.
all in all
  wholly 52 adv.
alliteration
  assimilation 18 n.
  prosody 593 n.
allocate
  apportion 783 vb.
allocution
  allocution 583 n.
allodium
  lands 777 n.
all of a piece
  uniform 16 adj.
all one
  equivalent 28 adj.
allonym
  misnomer 562 n.
allopath
  doctor 658 n.
allopathy
  medical art 658 n.
allot
  apportion 783 vb.
allotment
  farm 370 n.
all out
  completely 54 adv.
  swiftly 277 adv.
allow
  acquiesce 488 vb.
  facilitate 701 vb.
  permit 756 vb.
allowance
  offset 31 n.
  qualification 468 n.
  subvention 703 n.
  permission 756 n.
  receipt 807 n.
  discount 810 n.
allow for
  set off 31 vb.
alloy
  a mixture 43 n.

combination 50 n.
all-purpose
 useful 640 adj.
all right
 not bad 644 adj.
all-round
 multiform 82 adj.
all-rounder
 athlete 162 n.
 proficient 696 n.
all sorts
 medley 43 n.
allude
 mean 514 vb.
 imply 523 vb.
allure
 influence 178 vb.
 attraction 291 n.
 tempt 612 vb.
 cause desire
  859 vb.
allusion
 referral 9 n.
allusive
 meaningful 514 adj.
 figurative 519 adj.
 imperspicuous
  568 adj.
alluvial
 territorial 344 adj.
alluvium
 leavings 41 n.
 thing transferred
  272 n.
 soil 344 n.
ally
 colleague 707 n.
 join a party 708
  vb.
 friend 880 n.
almanac
 chronology 117 n.
almighty
 powerful 160 adj.
Almighty, the
 the Deity 965 n.
almoner
 treasurer 798 n.
almonry
 treasury 799 n.
almost
 almost 33 adv.
alms
 gift 781 n.
 kind act 897 n.
almshouse
 shelter 662 n.

aloft
 aloft 209 adv.
alone
 alone 88 adj.
 friendless 883 adj.
along
 longwise 203 adv.
alongside
 nigh 200 adv.
 sideways 239 adv.
aloof
 distant 199 adj.
 impassive 820 adj.
alopecia
 bareness 229 n.
aloud
 speaking 579 adj.
 vocal 577 adj.
alpaca
 fibre 208 n.
 textile 222 n.
alpestrine
 alpine 209 adj.
alphabet
 beginning 68 n.
 letter 558 n.
alpha particle
 element 319 n.
alpha plus
 excellent 644 adj.
alpine
 alpine 209 adj.
also-ran
 inferior 35 n.
 loser 728 n.
altar
 altar 990 n.
alterable
 unstable 152 adj.
 changeful 152 adj.
alterant
 alterer 143 n.
alteration
 difference 15 n.
 change 143 n.
altercate
 bicker 709 vb.
alter course
 deviate 282 vb.
alter ego
 colleague 707 n.
 close friend 880 n.
alternate
 correlative 12 adj.
 be periodic 141 vb.
 substitute 150 n.
 deputy 755 n.

alternative
 substitute 150 n.
 choice 605 n.
alter the case
 tell against 467
  vb.
altimeter
 altimetry 209 n.
altitude
 height 209 n.
alto
 vocalist 413 n.
altogether
 wholly 52 adv.
 completely 54 adv.
altruism
 philanthropy
  901 n.
 disinterestedness
  931 n.
altruist
 kind person 897 n.
altruistic
 disinterested
  931 adj.
alumnus
 learner 538 n.
amalgam
 a mixture 43 n.
amalgamate
 combine 50 vb.
amalgamation
 association 706 n.
amanuensis
 recorder 549 n.
amass
 bring together
  74 vb.
 store 632 vb.
amateur
 bungler 697 n.
 man of taste 846 n.
 layman 987 n.
amateurish
 unskilled 695 adj.
amatory
 erotic 887 adj.
amaurotic
 dim-sighted 440
  adj.
amaze
 be wonderful
  864 vb.
amazement
 inexpectation
  508 n.
 wonder 864 n.

Amazon
 athlete 162 n.
 soldier 722 n.
ambassador
 envoy 754 n.
amber
 resin 357 n.
 brownness 430 n.
ambergris
 resin 357 n.
ambidexterity
 skill 694 n.
ambience
 circumjacence
  230 n.
ambiguity
 uncertainty 474 n.
 equivocalness
  518 n.
 imperspicuity
  568 n.
ambit
 outline 233 n.
 circuition 314 n.
ambition
 intention 617 n.
 aspiration 852 n.
 desired object
  859 n.
ambitious
 enterprising 672
  adj.
 greedy 859 adj.
ambivalence
 equivocalness 518 n.
amble
 gait 265 n.
 ride 267 vb.
 move slowly 278 vb.
ambrosia
 savouriness 390 n.
ambulance
 hospital 658 n.
ambulatory
 path 624 n.
ambush
 latency 523 n.
 ambush 527 n., vb.
 pitfall 663 n.
 stratagem 698 n.
amelioration
 improvement 654 n.
amen
 assent 488 n.
amenable
 credulous 487 adj.
 dutied 917 adj.

amend
rectify 654 vb.
amende honorable
atonement 941 n.
amends
restoration 656 n.
atonement 941 n.
amenity
pleasurableness
826 n.
amentia
insanity 503 n.
amerce
punish 963 vb.
amethyst
purple 434 n.
amiability
courtesy 884 n.
lovableness 887 n.
amicable
concordant 710
adj.
friendly 880 adj.
amid
between 231 adv.
amiss
amiss 616 adv.
amity
concord 710 n.
friendship 880 n.
ammunition
means 629 n.
ammunition 723 n.
amnesia
oblivion 506 n.
amnesty
oblivion 506 n.
forgive 909 vb.
amoeba
animalcule 196 n.
among
between 231 adv.
amoral
indifferent 860 adj.
amoralism
impiety 980 n.
amoralist
indifference 860 n.
amorous
loving 887 adj.
amorphous
incomplete 55 adj.
amorphous 244 adj.
amount
quantity 26 n.
degree 27 n.
funds 797 n.

amour
love affair 887 n.
illicit love 951 n.
ampere, amp
electricity 160 n.
amphibian
animal 365 n.
reptile 365 n.
amphibious
double 91 adj.
amphitheatre
arena 724 n.
ample
great 32 adj.
many 104 adj.
spacious 183 adj.
large 195 adj.
broad 205 adj.
plenteous 635 adj.
liberal 813 adj.
amplifier
megaphone 400 n.
hearing aid 415 n.
amplify
augment 36 vb.
enlarge 197 vb.
be diffuse 570 vb.
amplitude
range 183 n.
diffuseness 570 n.
ampoule
receptacle 194 n.
amputate
subtract 39 vb.
cut 46 vb.
amulet
preserver 666 n.
talisman 983 n.
amuse
amuse 837 vb.
amusement
enjoyment 824 n.
amusement 837 n.
amusing
amusing 837 adj.
anachronism
anachronism 118 n.
different time 122 n.
anachronistic
anachronistic
118 adj.
anacoluthon
discontinuity 72 n.
anacrusis
prelude 66 n.
anaemia
weakness 163 n.

anaesthesia
insensibility 375 n.
anaesthetic
moderator 177 n.
anaesthetic 375 n.
drug 658 n.
remedial 658 adj.
relief 831 n.
anaesthetist
doctor 658 n.
anagoge
metaphor 519 n.
anagram
enigma 530 n.
initials 558 n.
anal
back 238 adj.
analeptic
restorative 656 adj.
analgesia
insensibility 375 n.
analgesic
antidote 658 n.
relieving 831 adj.
analogue
analogue 18 n.
analogy
relativeness 9 n.
similarity 18 n.
comparison 462 n.
analyse
decompose 51 vb.
class 62 vb.
analysis
numerical
operation 86 n.
grammar 564 n.
analyst
experimenter 461
n.
analytic
rational 475 adj.
anarchic
disorderly 61 adj.
anarchic 734 adj.
lawless 954 adj.
anarchism
sedition 738 n.
anarchist
revolutionist 149 n.
revolter 738 n.
anarchy
anarchy 734 n.
anathema
malediction 899 n.
anatomic
structural 331 adj.

anatomist
zoologist 367 n.
anatomize
sunder 46 vb.
anatomy
thinness 206 n.
structure 331 n.
zoology 367 n.
ancestor
precursor 66 n.
parent 169 n.
ancestral
immemorial
127 adj.
parental 169 adj.
ancestry
heredity 5 n.
origin 68 n.
genealogy 169 n.
anchor
coupling 47 n.
navigate 269 vb.
safeguard 662 n.
anchorage
station 187 n.
shelter 662 n.
anchorite
solitary 883 n.
ascetic 945 n.
pietist 979 n.
ancien régime
preterition 125 n.
archaism 127 n.
aristocracy 868 n.
ancient
former 125 adj.
olden 127 adj.
ancients, the
antiquity 125 n.
ancillary
aiding 703 adj.
andante
slow 278 adj.
adagio 412 adv.
anecdotal
remembering
505 adj.
anemology
pneumatics 340 n.
anemology 352 n.
anemometer
anemology 352 n.
aneroid barometer
pneumatics 340 n.
anfractuosity
convolution 251
n.

angel
darling 890 n.
angel 968 n.
angelic
virtuous 933 adj.
lovable 887 adj.
angelic 968 adj.
anger
anger 891 n.
angina
pang 377 n.
angle
angularity 247 n.
opinion 485 n.
hunt 619 vb.
Anglicanism
Catholicism 976 n.
Protestantism
976 n.
Anglicism
dialect 560 n.
angry
angry 891 adj.
angry young man
nonconformist 84 n.
malcontent 829 n.
anguish
pain 377 n.
suffering 825 n.
angular
angular 247 adj.
angularity
unconformity 84 n.
obliquity 220 n.
angularity 247 n.
angular measure
angular measure
247 n.
anility
age 131 n.
folly 499 n.
animadversion
reprimand 924 n.
animadvert
notice 455 vb.
animal
animal 365 n., adj.
mindless 448 adj.
animalcule
animalcule 196 n.
animalism
sensualism 944 n.
animality
animality 365 n.
non-intellect 448 n.
animal spirits
vitality 162 n.

cheerfulness 833 n.
animate
invigorate 174 vb.
animate 821 vb.
give courage 855
vb.
animation
life 360 n.
excitation 821 n.
animism
immateriality 320
n.
deism 973 n.
animosity
dislike 861 n.
enmity 881 n.
resentment 891 n.
animus
affections 817 n.
feeling 818 n.
ankle
joint 45 n.
anklet
jewellery 844 n.
annalist
chronicler 549 n.
annals
chronology 117 n.
record 548 n.
narrative 590 n.
anneal
toughen 329 vb.
annex
connect 45 vb.
appropriate 786 vb.
annexe
adjunct 40 n.
annexure
adjunct 40 n.
annihilate
nullify 2 vb.
destroy 165 vb.
anniversary
date 108 n.
anniversary 141 n.
celebrative 876 adj.
annotate
interpret 520 vb.
annotation
commentary 520 n.
annotator
interpreter 520 n.
announce
proclaim 528 vb.
name 561 vb.
annoy
torment 827 vb.

enrage 891 vb.
annoyance
bane 659 n.
annoyance 827 n.
resentment 891 n.
annual
periodic 110 adj.
seasonal 141 adj.
annuitant
recipient 782 n.
annuity
receipt 807 n.
annul
destroy 165 vb.
abrogate 752 vb.
annularity
circularity 250 n.
annulment
abrogation 752 n.
divorce 896 n.
anodyne
lenitive 177 adj.
relieving 831 adj.
anoint
lubricate 334 vb.
commission 751 vb.
anomalous
abnormal 84 adj.
anonymity
no name 562 n.
anonymous
anonymous 562
adj.
anopheles
fly 365 n.
another
different 15 adj.
another story
variant 15 n.
answer
numerical result 85
n.
answer 460 n., vb.
argue 475 vb.
confutation 479 n.
be successful 727
vb.
answerable
causal 156 adj.
dutied 917 adj.
answer back
answer 460 vb.
be insolent 878 vb.
answer for
deputize 755 vb.
answer to
be related 9 vb.

correlate 12 vb.
ant
vermin 365 n.
busy person 678 n.
antagonism
contrariety 14 n.
counteraction 182
n.
opposition 704 n.
enmity 881 n.
antagonist
opponent 705 n.
antagonize
cause dislike 861 vb.
make enemies
881 n.
huff 891 vb.
ante
gambling 618 n.
antecedence
precedence 64 n.
priority 119 n.
antecedent
precursor 66 n.
antedate
misdate 118 vb.
antediluvian
primal 127 adj.
antelope
deer 365 n.
antenna
filament 208 n.
feeler 378 n.
telecommunication
531 n.
antepenultimate
ending 69 adj.
anterior
preceding 64 adj.
prior 119 adj.
anteroom
lobby 194 n.
anthem
hymn 981 n.
ant-hill
nest 192 n.
anthologize
abstract 592 vb.
anthology
anthology 592 n.
choice 605 n.
anthracite
coal 385 n.
anthropocentric
human 371 adj.
anthropoid
animal 365 adj.

human 371 adj.
anthropology
  anthropology 371 n.
anthropomorphic
  idolatrous 982 adj.
anti
  contrary 14 adj.
  opposing 704 adj.
antibiosis
  antidote 658 n.
antibiotic
  drug 658 n.
  antidote 658 n.
antibody
  antidote 658 n.
Antichrist
  bad man 938 n.
  Satan 969 n.
anticipate
  be early 135 vb.
  expect 507 vb.
  foresee 510 vb.
  prepare oneself
    669 vb.
anti-clerical
  irreligious 974 adj.
anticlimax
  decrease 37 n.
  absurdity 497 n.
  disappointment
    509 n.
  feebleness 572 n.
anticoagulant
  antidote 658 n.
antics
  foolery 497 n.
  bungling 695 n.
anticyclone
  weather 340 n.
antidemocratic
  authoritarian
    735 adj.
antidotal
  counteracting
    182 adj.
  remedial 658 adj.
antidote
  contrariety 14 n.
  counteraction
    182 n.
  antidote 658 n.
anti-freeze
  heating 381 adj.
antigen
  antidote 658 n.
antinomian
  anarchic 734 adj.

lawless 954 adj.
antipathy
  contrariety 14 n.
  enmity 881 n.
  hatred 888 n.
antiphon
  hymn 981 n.
antiphrasis
  solecism 565 n.
antipodes
  farness 199 n.
  contraposition
    240 n.
antiquarianism
  palaetiology 125 n.
antiquary
  antiquarian 125 n.
  chronicler 549 n.
antiquated
  past 125 adj.
  antiquated 127 adj.
  disused 674 adj.
antique
  olden 127 adj.
  exhibit 522 n.
antiquities
  archaism 127 n.
antiquity
  antiquity 125 n.
  oldness 127 n.
antisemitism
  phobia 854 n.
antiseptic
  salubrious 652 adj.
  prophylactic 658 n.
antisocial
  unsociable 883 adj.
  misanthropic
    902 adj.
antithesis
  contrariety 14 n.
  contraposition
    240 n.
  ornament 574 n.
antithetic
  inverted 221 adj.
antitoxin
  antidote 658 n.
antitype
  copy 22 n.
antonym
  contrariety 14 n.
  connotation 514 n.
antrum
  cavity 255 n.
anus
  buttocks 238 n.

anvil
  stand 218 n.
anxiety
  (*see* anxious)
anxiety neurosis
  psychopathy 503 n.
anxious
  careful 457 adj.
  expectant 507 adj.
  suffering 825 adj.
anybody's guess
  uncertainty 474 n.
anyone
  everyman 79 n.
apart
  separate 46 adj.
apartheid
  exclusion 57 n.
apartment
  flat 192 n.
  chamber 194 n.
apathetic
  inert 175 adj.
  incurious 454 adj.
  inactive 679 adj.
  apathetic 820 adj.
  unastonished 865
    adj.
apathy
  (*see* apathetic)
ape
  imitate 20 vb.
  monkey 365 n.
aperçu
  dissertation 591 n.
  compendium 592 n.
aperient
  cathartic 658 n.
apéritif
  liquor 301 n.
aperture
  orifice 263 n.
apex
  summit 213 n.
aphasia
  speech defect
    580 n.
aphelion
  distance 199 n.
aphonic
  voiceless 578 adj.
aphorism
  maxim 496 n.
  conciseness 569 n.
aphrodisiac
  stimulant 174 n.
  erotic 887 adj.

apiary
  nest 192 n.
  stock farm 369 n.
apical
  topmost 213 adj.
apiculture
  animal husbandry
    369 n.
apish
  imitative 20 adj.
apocalypse
  revelation 975 n.
apocrypha
  scripture 975 n.
apocryphal
  uncertified 474 adj.
apogee
  distance 199 n.
apologetic
  vindicating 927 adj.
  repentant 939 adj.
apologetics,
  apologia
  argument 475 n.
  vindication 927 n.
apologies
  regret 830 n.
apologist
  reasoner 475 n.
  vindicator 927 n.
apologize
  knuckle under
    721 vb.
  regret 830 vb.
apology
  penitence 939 n.
apology for
  pretext 614 n.
  laughing stock
    851 n.
apophthegm
  maxim 496 n.
apoplexy
  blood pressure
    651 n.
apostasy
  (*see* apostatize)
apostate
  changed person
    147 n.
  (*see* apostatize)
apostatize
  apostatize 603 vb.
  relinquish 621 vb.
  schismatize 978 vb.
apostle
  preacher 537 n.

religious teacher
973 n.
apostolate
church ministry
985 n.
apostolic
ecclesiastical
985 adj.
priestly 985 adj.
apostrophe
punctuation 547 n.
apostrophize
speak to 583 vb.
apothecary
druggist 658 n.
apotheosis
deification 982 n.
apotropaic
deprecatory
762 adj.
appal
frighten 854 vb.
appanage
dower 777 n.
apparatus
tool 630 n.
apparatus criticus
commentary 520 n.
apparel
clothing 228 n.
apparent
visible 443 adj.
appearing 445 adj.
manifest 522 adj.
apparentation
consanguinity 11 n.
attribution 158 n.
apparition
appearance 445 n.
ghost 970 n.
appeal
influence 178 vb.
attraction 291 n.
allocution 583 n.
motivate 612 vb.
entreaty 761 n.
deprecate 762 vb.
pleasurableness
826 n.
lovableness 887 n.
legal trial 959 n.
appear
appear 445 vb.
happen 154 vb.
appearance
similarity 18 n.
form 243 n.

appearance 445 n.
appearances
etiquette 848 n.
appear for
deputize 755 vb.
appease
assuage 177 vb.
pacify 719 vb.
appellant
petitioner 763 n.
litigant 959 n.
appellation
nomenclature 561
n.
appellative
name 561 n.
append
add 38 vb.
appendage
adjunct 40 n.
sequel 67 n.
appendix
adjunct 40 n.
sequel 67 n.
extremity 69 n.
appertain
belong 773 vb.
appetence
will 595 n.
desire 859 n.
appetite
eating 301 n.
desire, hunger
859 n.
appetizer
stimulant 174 n.
savouriness 390 n.
applaud
applaud 923 vb.
apple of discord
quarrelsomeness,
casus belli 709 n.
apple of one's eye
favourite 890 n.
appliance
tool 630 n.
applicable
relevant 9 adj.
useful 640 adj.
expedient 642 adj.
applicant
petitioner 763 n.
application
relevance 9 n.
attention 455 n.
interpretation
520 n.

use 673 n.
assiduity 678 n.
request 761 n.
apply
use 673 vb.
request 761 vb.
appoint
employ 622 vb.
decree 737 vb.
commission 751 vb.
appointment
job 622 n.
fitting out 669 n.
(*see* appoint)
appointments
equipment 630 n.
apport
spiritualism 984 n.
apportion
apportion 783 vb.
apposite
relevant 9 adj.
apposition
contiguity 202 n.
appraise
estimate 480 vb.
appraiser
estimator 480 n.
appreciate
grow 36 vb.
know 490 vb.
be dear 811 vb.
honour 866 vb.
appreciation
discrimination
463 n.
estimate 480 n.
gratitude 907 n.
approbation 923 n.
apprehend
expect 507 vb.
understand 516 vb.
arrest 747 vb.
apprehensible
intelligible 516 adj.
apprehensive
nervous 854 adj.
apprentice
beginner 538 n.
bungler 697 n.
apprenticeship
learning 536 n.
apprise
inform 524 vb.
approach
nearness 200 n.
approach 289 vb.

way 624 n.
offer 759 n.
approachable
accessible 289 adj.
approaches
near place 200 n.
approbation
approbation 923 n.
appropriate
relevant 9 adj.
apt 24 adj.
acquire 771 vb.
appropriate 786 vb.
appropriation
taking 786 n.
approval
permission 756 n.
approbation 923 n.
approve
permit 756 vb.
approve 923 vb.
approver
informer 524 n.
accuser 928 n.
approximate
similar 18 adj.
approach 289 vb.
approximation
numerical operation
86 n.
appulse
approach 289 n.
appurtenance
adjunct 40 n.
component 58 n.
appurtenant
ingredient 58 adj.
April fool
dupe 544 n.
laughing stock
851 n.
a priori
rational 475 adj.
a priori knowledge
intuition 476 n.
apriorism
reasoning 475 n.
apron
apron 228 n.
apron strings
subjection 745 n.
apse
church interior
990 n.
apt
relevant 9 adj.
apt 24 adj.

skilful 694 adj.
aptitude
fitness 24 n.
ability 160 n.
aptitude 694 n.
aquamarine
blueness 435 n.
aquarelle
picture 553 n.
aquarium
cattle pen 369 n.
zoo 369 n.
aquatic
seafaring 269 adj.
watery 339 adj.
aquatics
aquatics 269 n.
aquatint
picture 553 n.
engraving 555 n.
aqueduct
conduit 351 n.
aqueous
watery 339 adj.
aquiline
curved 248 adj.
arabesque
pattern 844 n.
arable
soil 344 n.
farm 370 n.
agrarian 370 adj.
arbiter
adviser 691 n.
arbitrage
judgement 480 n.
mediation 720 n.
arbitrament
judgement 480 n.
arbitrary
unconformable 84 adj.
wilful 602 adj.
authoritarian, oppressive 735 adj.
unconditional 744 adj.
lawless 954 adj.
arbitrate
judge 480 vb.
mediate 720 vb.
arboreal
arboreal 366 adj.
arboretum
garden 370 n.
arbour
arbour 194 n.

arc
arc 250 n.
arcade
street 192 n.
emporium 796 n.
Arcadian
artless 699 adj.
arcane
unintelligible 517 adj.
latent 523 adj.
arch
supreme 34 adj.
supporter 218 n.
curve 248 n.
be convex 253 vb.
archaeologist
antiquarian 125 n.
archaeology
palaetiology 125 n.
archaic
olden 127 adj.
archaism
archaism 127 n.
archbishop
ecclesiarch 986 n.
archbishopric
parish 985 n.
archdeacon
ecclesiarch 986 n.
archer
soldiery 722 n.
archery
propulsion 287 n.
sport 837 n.
archetypal
unimitative 21 adj.
archetype
prototype 23 n.
idea 451 n.
archipelago
island 349 n.
architect
producer 167 n.
architectonic
architectural 192 adj.
architectural
architectural 192 adj.
structural 331 adj.
architecture
form 243 n.
structure 331 n.
art 551 n.

architrave
summit 213 n.
archivist
recorder 549 n.
archpriest
ecclesiarch 986 n.
priest 986 n.
archway
doorway 263 n.
Arctic
coldness 380 n.
arcuate
make curved 248 vb.
ardent
(see ardour)
ardour
heat 379 n.
vigour 571 n.
warm feeling 818 n.
arduous
laborious 682 adj.
difficult 700 adj.
area
space 183 n.
region 184 n.
place 185 n.
size 195 n.
arena
theatre 594 n.
battle 718 n.
arena 724 n.
arenaceous
powdery 332 adj.
argent
white 427 adj.
heraldry 547 n.
argonaut
mariner 270 n.
argosy
shipping 275 n.
merchant ship 275 n.
argot
slang 560 n.
arguable
possible 469 adj.
uncertain 474 adj.
argue
argue 475 vb.
confer 584 vb.
argue against
dissuade 613 vb.
argue for
contend 716 vb.
argument
topic 452 n.

argument 475 n.
narrative 590 n.
quarrel 709 n.
argumentative
arguing 475 adj.
aria
tune 412 n.
arid
unproductive 172 adj.
dry 342 adj.
arise
become 1 vb.
begin 68 vb.
ascend 308 vb.
arise from
result 157 vb.
aristocracy
government 733 n.
aristocrat
aristocrat 868 n.
aristocratic
governmental 733 adj.
genteel 868 adj.
arithmetic
mathematics 86 n.
arithmetical
numerical 85 adj.
arithmetical progression
ratio 85 n.
ark
box 194 n.
refuge 662 n.
arm
empower 160 vb.
tool 630 n.
make ready 669 vb.
weapon 723 n.
armada
armed force 722 n.
navy 722 n.
armament
fitting out 669 n.
armed force 722 n.
armature
coil 251 n.
armband
belt 228 n.
armchair
seat 218 n.
armchair critic
theorist 512 n.
armiger
aristocrat 868 n.

arm in arm
conjunct 45 adj.
armistice
lull 145 n.
peace 717 n.
armless
fragmentary 53 adj.
crippled 163 adj.
armlet
belt 228 n.
loop 250 n.
armorial
heraldic 547 adj.
armour
protection 660 n.
safeguard 662 n.
armour 713 n.
weapon 723 n.
armoured car
war-chariot 274 n.
cavalry 722 n.
armoury
heraldry 547 n.
arsenal 723 n.
arms
heraldry 547 n.
war 718 n.
arms, in
infantine 132 adj.
warring 718 adj.
army
multitude 104 n.
army 722 n.
army officer
army officer 741 n.
aroma
fragrance 396 n.
arouse
incite 612 vb.
excite 821 vb.
arpeggio
musical note 410 n.
arrack
liquor 301 n.
arraign
indict 928 vb.
arraignment
accusation 928 n.
arrange
arrange 62 vb.
plan 623 vb.
arrangement
musical piece 412 n.
arras
covering 226 n.

array
order 60 n.
arrangement 62 n.
series 71 n.
multitude 104 n.
dress 228 vb.
decorate 844 vb.
arrears
debt 803 n.
arrest
cessation 145 n.
halt 145 vb.
arrest 747 vb.
arresting
unexpected 508 adj.
arrival
arrival 295 n.
arrive
be present 189 vb.
arrive 295 vb.
prosper 730 vb.
arriviste
made man 730 n.
arrogance
pride 871 n.
insolence 878 n.
arrogant
rash 857 adj.
arrogate
claim 915 vb.
be undue 916 vb.
arrow
speeder 277 n.
indicator 547 n.
missile weapon 723 n.
arsenal
accumulation 74 n.
storage 632 n.
arsenal 723 n.
arsenic
poison 659 n.
arsis
prosody 593 n.
arson
incendiarism 381 n.
art
art 551 n.
skill 694 n.
stratagem 698 n.
art, work of
masterpiece 694 n.
artefact
product 164 n.
art equipment
art equipment 553 n.

arterial
communicating 624 adj.
artery
conduit 351 n.
artesian well
outflow 298 n.
artful
cunning 698 adj.
art gallery
collection 632 n.
arthritic
crippled 163 adj.
diseased 651 adj.
artichoke
tuber 301 n.
article
object 319 n.
reading matter 589 n.
article 591 n.
article oneself
learn 536 vb.
articles
creed 485 n.
conditions 766 n.
articulate
join 45 vb.
phrase 563 vb.
vocal 577 adj.
voice 577 vb.
artifice
contrivance 623 n.
stratagem 698 n.
artificer
producer 167 n.
artisan 686 n.
artificial
simulating 18 adj.
spurious 542 adj.
affected 850 adj.
artificial respiration
revival 656 n.
artificial satellite
space-ship 276 n.
artillery
gun 723 n.
artilleryman
soldiery 722 n.
artisan
artisan 686 n.
artist
producer 167 n.
artist 556 n.
artistic
elegant 575 adj.
well-made 694 adj.

tasteful 846 adj.
artistry
skill 694 n.
good taste 846 n.
artless
ignorant 491 adj.
veracious 540 adj.
inelegant 576 adj.
artless 699 adj.
graceless 842 adj.
innocent 935 adj.
arts
culture 490 n.
asbestos
incombustibility 382 n.
ascend
ascend 308 vb.
ascendancy
power 160 n.
influence 178 n.
ascender
print-type 587 n.
ascending order
increase 36 n.
series 71 n.
ascent
acclivity 220 n.
ascent 308 n.
ascertain
make certain 473 vb.
ascertainment
certainty 473 n.
discovery 484 n.
ascetic
unfeeling person 820 n.
temperate 942 adj.
ascetic 945 n., adj.
monk 986 n.
asceticism
temperance 942 n.
asceticism 945 n.
monasticism 985 n.
ascribe
attribute 158 vb.
grant claims 915 vb.
ascription
attribution 158 n.
aseptic
clean 648 adj.
salubrious 652 adj.
asexual
simple 44 adj.
as good as
equivalent 28 adj.

415

ASH

ash
ash 381 n.
dirt 649 n.

ash can
cleaning utensil
648 n.

ashen
colourless 426 adj.
grey 429 adj.

ashes
corpse 363 n.

ashlar
building material
631 n.

ashram
monastery 986 n.

ashy
grey 429 adj.
colourless 426 adj.

aside
sideways 239 adv.
hint 524 n.
soliloquy 585 n.

asinine
equine 273 adj.
foolish 499 adj.

ask
inquire 459 vb.
request 761 vb.

askew
oblique 220 adj.
distorted 246 adj.

ask for
desire 859 vb.

ask for trouble
be rash 857 vb.

aslant
oblique 220 adj.

asleep
sleepy 679 adj.

asp
reptile 365 n.

aspect
modality 7 n.
appearance 445 n.

asperge
moisten 341 vb.
purify 648 vb.

asperity
roughness 259 n.
irascibility 892 n.

aspersion
moistening 341 n.
detraction 926 n.

asphalt
resin 357 n.
road 624 n.

ASS

asphyxiant
poison 659 n.

aspirant
hoper 852 n.
desirer 859 n.

aspirate
breathe 352 vb.
rasp 407 vb.
speech sound
398 n.
voice 577 vb.

aspiration
motive 612 n.
aspiration 852 n.
desire 859 n.

aspire
hope 852 vb.

asquint
obliquely 220 adv.

ass
beast of burden
273 n.
fool 501 n.

assail
attack 712 vb.

assailant
attacker 712 n.
combatant 722 n.

assassin
murderer 362 n.
ruffian 904 n.

assassinate
murder 362 vb.

assault
knock 279 n.
attack 712 n., vb.

assay
experiment
461 n., vb.
essay 671 vb.

assemblage
(*see* assemble)

assemble
join 45 vb.
compose 56 vb.
bring together
74 vb.
meet 295 vb.

assembly
sociability 882 n.
(*see* assemble)

assembly-line
production 164 n.

assent
assent 488 n., vb.
willingness 597 n.
consent 758 n., vb.

ASS

assert
affirm 532 vb.

assertion
testimony 466 n.

assertive
assertive 532 adj.

assert oneself
influence 178 vb.
be active 678 vb.

assess
price 809 vb.

assessment
estimate 480 n.
tax 809 n.

assessor
estimator 480 n.
jury 957 n.

assets
means 629 n.
estate 777 n.

assiduity
assiduity 678 n.
exertion 682 n.

assign
attribute 158 vb.
transfer 672 vb.
apportion 783 vb.

assignation
social round 882 n.

assignee
recipient 782 n.

assignment
mandate 751 n.
transfer 780 n.
apportionment
783 n.

assimilate
identify 13 vb.
make uniform
16 vb.
liken 18 vb.
make conform 83 vb.
absorb 299 vb.
learn 536 vb.

assimilation
(*see* assimilate)

assist
aid 703 vb.

assistance
instrumentality
628 n.
aid 703 n.

assistant
inferior 35 n.
auxiliary 707 n.

assize
law-court 956 n.

AST

legal trial 959 n.

associate
join 45 vb.
congregate 74 vb.
accompany 89 vb.
colleague 707 n.
society 708 n.
join a party 708 vb.

association
relation 9 n.
group 74 n.
association 706 n.
participation 775 n.
sociality 882 n.

association of ideas
thought 449 n.

assonance
assimilation 18 n.
prosody 593 n.

assortment
accumulation 74 n.
sort 77 n.

assuage
assuage 177 vb.
pacify 719 vb.
relieve 831 vb.

assume
wear 228 vb.
believe 485 vb.
expect 507 vb.
suppose 512 vb.
dissemble 541 vb.
undertake 672 vb.

assumption
supposition 512 n.
receiving 782 n.
taking 786 n.
arrogation 916 n.

assurance
belief 485 n.
affirmation 532 n.
safety 660 n.
promise 764 n.
insolence 878 n.

assure
make certain
473 vb.
convince 485 vb.
give security
767 vb.

assured
believing 485 adj.
safe 660 adj.

asterisk
punctuation 547 n.

asterism
star 321 n.

asteroid
planet 321 n.
asthma
respiratory disease
651 n.
asthmatic
puffing 352 adj.
astigmatism
dim sight 440 n.
astir
busy 678 adj.
astonish
be wonderful
864 vb.
astonishment
wonder 864 n.
astound
surprise 508 vb.
be wonderful 864 vb.
astral
immaterial 320 adj.
celestial 321 adj.
spooky 970 adj.
astral body
immateriality
320 n.
spiritualism 984 n.
astray
deviating 282 adj.
astriction
joinder 45 n.
astringent
compressor 198 n.
pungent 388 adj.
astrolabe
astronomy 321 n.
astrologer
diviner 511 n.
occultist 984 n.
astromancy
astronomy 321 n.
astronaut
aeronaut 271 n.
astronautical
aviational 276 adj.
astronomer
astronomy 321 n.
astute
intelligent 498 adj.
cunning 698 adj.
asylum
madhouse 503 n.
protection 660 n.
refuge, shelter
662 n.
asymmetry
irrelation 10 n.

non-uniformity
17 n.
distortion 246 n.
asymptote
part of speech
564 n.
asyndeton
disjunction 46 n.
atavism
heredity 5 n.
reversion 148 n.
atheism
unbelief 486 n.
irreligion 974 n.
athirst
hungry 859 adj.
athlete
athlete 162 n.
contender 716 n.
athletics
athletics 162 n.
contest 716 n.
sport 837 n.
at home
social gathering
882 n.
atlas
map 551 n.
atmosphere
influence 178 n.
circumjacence 230 n.
atmosphere 340 n.
atmospherics
commotion 318 n.
atoll
island 349 n.
atom
small thing 33 n.
unit 88 n.
minuteness 196 n.
element 319 n.
atomic
simple 44 adj.
minute 196 adj.
atomize
demolish 165 vb.
vaporize 338 vb.
atomizer
pulverizer 332 n.
atonality
discord 411 n.
atone
atone 941 vb.
atonement
atonement 941 n.
divine function
965 n.

atrocious
cruel 898 adj.
heinous 934 adj.
atrocity
cruel act 898 n.
atrophy
helplessness 161 n.
attach
add 38 vb.
connect, affix 45 vb.
attaché case
box 194 n.
attachment
adjunct 40 n.
expropriation
786 n.
love 887 n.
attack
vigorousness 174 n.
spasm 318 n.
essay 671 n.
attack 712 n., vb.
fight 716 vb.
attacker
opponent 705 n.
attacker 712 n.
attain
arrive 295 vb.
acquire 771 vb.
attainable
accessible 289 adj.
possible 469 adj.
attainder (*see*
attaint)
attainment(s)
culture 490 n.
attaint
indict 928 vb.
condemn 961 vb.
attempt
essay 671 n., vb.
attend
accompany 89 vb.
be present 189 vb.
follow 284 vb.
be attentive 455 vb.
doctor 658 vb.
attendance
retinue 67 n.
(*see attend*)
attendant
accompanying
89 adj.
follower 284 n.
attention
attention 455 n.
carefulness 457 n.

attenuate
make smaller
198 vb.
make thin 206 vb.
rarefy 325 vb.
attest
testify 466 vb.
swear 532 vb.
attestant
witness 466 n.
signatory 765 n.
attestation
testimony 466 n.
attic
attic 194 n.
attire
dressing 228 n.
dress 228 vb.
attitude
form 243 n.
affections 817 n.
attitudinize
be affected 850 vb.
attorney
law agent 958 n.
attract
bring together
74 vb.
influence 178 vb.
attract 291 vb.
motivate 612 vb.
attraction
energy 160 n.
influence 178 n.
attraction 291 n.
inducement 612 n.
incentive 612 n.
favourite 890 n.
attractions
lovableness 887 n.
attribute
speciality 80 n.
concomitant 89 n.
attribute 158 vb.
attrition
friction 333 n.
warfare 718 n.
attune
adjust 24 vb.
atypical
abnormal 84 adj.
auburn
brown 430 adj.
red 431 adj.
auction
sale 793 n.
sell 793 vb.

audacity
 courage 855 n.
 rashness 857 n.
 insolence 878 n.
audible
 sounding 398 adj.
 loud 400 adj.
 intelligible 516 adj.
 speaking 579 adj.
audience
 listener 415 n.
 onlookers 441 n.
 allocution 583 n.
 playgoer 594 n.
audit
 inquiry 459 n.
 account 808 vb.
audition
 hearing 415 n.
 listening 415 n.
 exam 459 n.
auditor
 listener 415 n.
 accountant 808 n.
auditorium
 classroom 539 n.
 theatre 594 n.
auger
 sharp point 256 n.
 perforator 263 n.
augment
 augment 36 vb.
 adjunct 40 n.
augur
 diviner 511 n.
augury
 divination 511 n.
 omen 511 n.
august
 great 32 adj.
 worshipful 866 adj.
aunt
 kinsman 11 n.
Aunt Sally
 laughing-stock
 851 n.
aura
 circumjacence
 230 n.
 prestige 866 n.
aural
 auditory 415 adj.
auricle
 ear 415 n.
auricular confession
 secrecy 525 n.
 ministration 988 n.

aurist
 doctor 658 n.
auscultation
 listening 415 n.
auspicate
 auspicate 68 vb.
 divine 511 vb.
auspice(s)
 omen 511 n.
 protection 660 n.
auspicious
 opportune 137 adj.
 presageful 511 adj.
 palmy 730 adj.
austere
 plain 573 adj.
 ascetic 945 adj.
austerities
 penance 941 n.
austerity
 plainness 573 n.
 asceticism 945 n.
autarchy
 independence 744 n.
authentic
 genuine 494 adj.
authenticate
 testify 466 vb.
 endorse 488 vb.
authenticity
 identity 13 n.
 authenticity 494 n.
author
 cause 156 n.
 producer 167 n.
 author 589 n.
 narrator 590 n.
 dissertator 591 n.
authoritarian
 authoritarian
 735 adj.
authoritative
 influential 178 adj.
 certain 473 adj.
 authoritative
 733 adj.
 commanding
 737 adj.
authorities
 evidence 466 n.
authorities, the
 master 741 n.
authority
 influence 178 n.
 credential 466 n.
 informant 524 n.
 authority 733 n.

 permit 756 n.
 jurisdiction 955 n.
authorize
 empower 160 vb.
 commission 751 vb.
 permit 756 vb.
authorship
 causation 156 n.
 writing 586 n.
autobiographer
 narrator 590 n.
autobiography
 biography 590 n.
autochthonous
 native 191 adj.
autocracy
 despotism 733 n.
autocrat
 tyrant 735 n.
 autocrat 741 n.
autocratic
 authoritative
 733 adj.
autograph
 sign 547 vb.
 script 586 n.
automatic
 involuntary
 596 adj.
 mechanical 630 adj.
automation
 production 164 n.
 instrumentality
 628 n.
 mechanics 630 n.
automaton
 machine 630 n.
automobile
 automobile 274 n.
autonomy
 independence
 744 n.
autopsy
 inquest 364 n.
 inspection 438 n.
auto-suggestion
 fantasy 513 n.
autumn
 autumn 129 n.
auxiliary
 additional 38 n.
 aiding 703 adj.
 auxiliary 707 n.
avail
 be useful 640 vb.
available
 on the spot 189 adj.

 accessible 289 adj.
 possible 469 adj.
 provisionary
 633 adj.
 saleable 793 adj.
avail of
 avail of 673 vb.
avalanche
 descent 309 n.
 snow 380 n.
avant-garde
 modernist 126 n.
avarice
 avarice 816 n.
avaricious
 acquiring 771 adj.
 (*see avarice*)
avatar
 transformation
 143 n.
 theophany 965 n.
avenge
 avenge 910 vb.
 punish 963 vb.
avenger
 vindicator 927 n.
avenue
 street 192 n.
aver
 affirm 532 vb.
average
 average 30 n.
 median 30 adj.
 middle 70 n.
 generality 79 n.
 typical 83 adj.
 not discriminate
 464 vb.
 mediocre 732 adj.
averages
 statistics 86 n.
aversion
 unwillingness 598
 n.
 dislike 861 n.
 hateful object
 888 n.
avert
 deflect 282 vb.
 parry 713 vb.
aviary
 nest 192 n.
 zoo 369 n.
aviation
 aeronautics 271 n.
aviator
 aeronaut 271 n.

avidity
rapacity 786 n.
avarice 816 n.

avifauna
bird 365 n.

avocation
pursuit 619 n.

avoid
avoid 620 vb.
parry 713 vb.

avouch
affirm 532 vb.

avow
affirm 532 vb.
confess 526 vb.

avuncular
akin 11 adj.

await
expect, await
507 vb.

awake
attentive 455 adj.

awaken
(see wake)

award
judgement 480 n.
trophy 729 n.
reward 962 n., vb.

aware
sentient 374 adj.
knowing 490 adj.

awareness
intellect 447 n.

awash
drenched 341 adj.

away
absent 190 adj.

awe
fear 854 n.
wonder 864 n.
respect 920 n.

awesome *(see* awe)

awesomeness
prestige 866 n.

awful
not nice 645 adj.
bad 645 adj.

awkward
unconformable
84 adj.
clumsy 695 adj.
ill-bred 847 adj.
graceless 842 adj.

awkward squad
bungler 697 n.

awl
sharp point 256 n.

perforator 263 n.

awning
canopy 226 n.

awry
orderless 61 adj.
oblique 220 adj.

axe
sharp edge 256 n.
dismiss 300 vb.
axe 723 n.
means of execution
964 n.

axiom
certainty 473 n.
axiom 496 n.

axis
pivot 218 n.
association 706 n.

axle
rotator 315 n.

axle-load
weighment 322 n.

ayes, the
assenter 488 n.

azure
blueness 435 n.
heraldry 547 n.

B

baa
ululate 409 vb.

babble
be foolish 499 vb.
mean nothing 515
vb.
chatter 581 n.

babe
ignoramus 493 n.
ninny 501 n.
darling 890 n.
innocent 935 n.
(see baby)

baboon
monkey 365 n.

baby
child 132 n.
little 196 adj.
mandate 751 n.
(see babe)

babyhood
youth 130 n.

babyish
infantine 132 adj.

baby-sit
look after 457
vb.

baby-sitter
keeper 749 n.

bacchante
madman 504 n.

Bacchic
frenzied 503 adj.

bachelor
male 372 n.
celibate 895 n.

bacillus
animalcule 196 n.
infection 651 n.

back
supporter 218 n.
line 227 vb.
rear 238 n.
regress 286 vb.
gamble 618 vb.
patronize 703 vb.
approve 923 vb.

back-bencher
inferior 35 n.
councillor 692 n.
commoner 869 n.

backbone
essential part 5 n.
supporter 218 n.
stamina 600 n.

backbreaking
laborious 682 adj.

backchat
answer 460 n.

backcloth
stage-set 594 n.

backdoor
means of escape
667 n.
stealthy 525 adj.

back down
regress 286 vb.

backer
gambler 618 n.
patron 707 n.

background
concomitant 89 n.
accompanying
89 adj.
rear 238 n.

backing
lining 227 n.

backlog
store 632 n.

back number
archaism 127 n.

back out
regress 286 vb.
resign 753 vb.

back-pedal
retard 278 vb.

back-scratcher
toady 879 n.

back-scratching
flattery 925 n.

back seat
inferiority 35 n.

backside
buttocks 238 n.

back-slapping
sociability 882 n.

backslide
tergiversate 603 vb.
relapse 657 vb.

backslider
offender 904 n.

backstage
stage-set 594 n.

backswept
back 238 adj.

back-talk
sauciness 878 n.

back-to-front
inverted 221 adj.

backward
regressive 286 adj.
unintelligent
499 adj.
unwilling 598 adj.
avoiding 620 adj.

backward-looking
regressive 286 adj.

backwards
backwards 286 adv.

backwash
effect 157 n.
eddy, wave 350 n.

back-water
retard 278 vb.
regress 286 vb.

bacon
meat 301 n.

bacteria
animalcule 196 n.
infection 651 n.

bactericide
prophylactic 658 n.

bacteriology
pathology 651 n.

bad
inferior 35 adj.
decomposed 51 adj.
bad 645 adj.
deteriorated
655 adj.
wrong 914 adj.

bandit
robber 789 n.
outcaste 883 n.
banditry
brigandage 788 n.
band-master
orchestra 413 n.
bandolier
girdle 47 n.
belt 228 n.
arsenal 723 n.
bandsman
orchestra 413 n.
bandy
deformed 246 adj.
bane
bane 659 n.
hateful object
888 n.
baneful
(*see* bane)
bang
hair 259 n.
impel, strike
279 vb.
bang 402 n., vb.
bangle
jewellery 844 n.
banish
exclude 57 vb.
eject 300 vb.
banishment
penalty 963 n.
banister(s)
pillar 218 n.
banjo
harp 414 n.
bank
high land 209 n.
acclivity 220 n.
shore 344 n.
treasury 799 n.
bank down
extinguish 382 vb.
banker
merchant 794 n.
treasurer 798 n.
banknote
paper money 797 n.
bankrupt
fleece 786 vb.
poor man 801 n.
non-payer 805 n.
bankruptcy
insufficiency 636 n.
loss 772 n.
insolvency 805 n.

banner
flag 547 n.
banns
marriage 894 n.
banquet
feasting 301 n.
eat, feed 301 vb.
festivity 837 n.
banshee
demon 970 n.
bant
make thin 206 vb.
starve 946 vb.
bantam
animalcule 196 n.
bantam-weight
pugilist 722 n.
banter
witticism 839 n.
ridicule 851 n., vb.
banterer
humorist 839 n.
banting
fasting 946 n.
bantling
child 132 n.
baptism
reception 299 n.
moistening 341 n.
baptismal
ritual 988 adj.
baptize
auspicate 68 vb.
admit 299 vb.
name 561 vb.
perform ritual
988 vb.
bar
exclude 57 vb.
tavern 192 n.
line 203 n.
close 264 vb.
island 349 n.
restrain 747 vb.
bar 958 n.
barb
sharp point 256 n.
sharpen 256 vb.
thoroughbred 273 n.
barbarian
foreigner 59 n.
extraneous 59 adj.
violent creature
176 n.
ruffian 904 n.
barbarism
neology 560 n.

solecism 565 n.
bad taste 847 n.
barbarity
violence 176 n.
inhumanity 898 n.
barbarous
(*see* barbarian,
barbarism)
barbecue
meal 301 n.
festivity 837 n.
barbed wire
defences 713 n.
barber
beautician 843 n.
barbiturate
soporific 679 n.
bard
musician 413 n.
poet 593 n.
bare
empty 190 adj.
uncover 229 vb.
disclose 526 vb.
plain 573 adj.
unprovided 636 adj.
vulnerable 661 adj.
barefaced
undisguised 522 adj.
barehanded
defenceless 161 adj.
bare-headed
uncovered 229 adj.
respectful 920 adj.
bare minimum
needfulness 627 n.
dueness 915 n.
bareness
bareness 229 n.
bargain
compact 765 n.
make terms 766 vb.
bargain 791 vb.
cheapness 812 n.
barge
boat 275 n.
bargee
boatman 270 n.
barge in
intrude 297 vb.
baritone
resonance 404 n.
vocalist 413 n.
bark
skin 226 n.
sailing-ship 275 n.
ululate 409 vb.

sullenness 893 n.
threaten 900 vb.
barley
provender 301 n.
corn 366 n.
barm
leaven 323 n.
barman
servant 742 n.
barmy
light 323 adj.
unintelligent
499 adj.
barn
storage 632 n.
barnacle
coherence 48 n.
barometer
pneumatics 340 n.
weather 340 n.
baron
nobleman 868 n.
judge 957 n.
baronet
nobleman 868 n.
baronial
noble 868 adj.
barouche
carriage 274 n.
barque
sailing-ship 275 n.
barrack
quarters 192 n.
be obstructive
702 vb.
barrage
bombardment 712 n.
defences 713 n.
barratry
improbity 930 n.
barrel
vat 194 n.
barren
impotent 161 adj.
unproductive
172 adj.
profitless 641 adj.
barricade
obstruct 702 vb.
defences 713 n.
barricades
revolt 738 n.
barrier
exclusion 57 n.
obstacle 702 n.
barrister
lawyer 958 n.

barrow
monticle 209 n.
pushcart 274 n.
tomb 364 n.
barrow-boy
pedlar 794 n.
bar-tender
servant 742 n.
barter
interchange 151 n.,
vb.
barter 791 n.
trade 791 vb.
base
inferiority 35 n.
station 187 n.
base 214 n.
basis 218 n.
rascally 930 adj.
heinous 934 adj.
baseball
ball game 837 n.
base-born
plebeian 869 adj.
baseless
unreal 2 adj.
baseline
place 185 n.
base 214 n.
basement
cellar 194 n.
baseness
improbity 930 n.
bash
strike 279 vb.
bashful
modest 874 adj.
basic
intrinsic 5 adj.
fundamental 156
adj.
important 638 adj.
basilica
church 990 n.
basin
bowl 194 n.
cavity 255 n.
lake 346 n.
basis
basis 218 n.
bask
enjoy 376 vb.
be hot 379 vb.
basket
basket 194 n.
bas relief
rilievo 254 n.

bass
table fish 365 n.
resonance 404 n.
vocalist 413 n.
bassinet
bed 218 n.
pushcart 274 n.
bassoon
flute 414 n.
bast
ligature 47 n.
fibre 208 n.
bastard
spurious 542 adj.
cad 938 n.
bastard 954 adj.
bastardize
disentitle 916 vb.
baste
cook 301 vb.
pinguefy 357 vb.
Bastille
prison 748 n.
bastinado
*corporal
punishment* 963 n.
bastion
protection 660 n.
fortification 713 n.
bat
velocity 277 n.
strike 279 vb.
propel 287 vb.
bird 365 n.
club 723 n.
batch
group 74 n.
bate
bate 37 vb.
blunt 257 vb.
bated breath, with
faintly 401 adv.
bath
vessel 194 n.
ablution 648 n.
bath-chair
pushcart 274 n.
bathe
swim 269 vb.
plunge 313 vb.
drench 341 vb.
clean 648 vb.
bathing beach
pleasure ground
837 n.
bathos
absurdity 497 n.

ridiculousness
849 n.
bathroom
ablution 648 n.
bath salts
cosmetic 843 n.
bathymeter
oceanography 343 n.
bathyscaph
oceanography 343 n.
bathysphere
diver 313 n.
oceanography
343 n.
batman
domestic 742 n.
baton
badge of rule
743 n.
batrachian
frog 365 n.
animal 365 n., adj.
battalion
formation 722 n.
batten
fastening 47 n.
batten on
eat 301 vb.
batter
demolish 165 vb.
obliquity 220 n.
strike, collide
279 vb.
battering-ram
ram 279 n.
battery
electricity 160 n.
formation 722 n.
gun 723 n.
battle
slaughter 362 n.
exert oneself
682 vb.
fight 716 n.
battle 718 n.
battle-axe
axe 723 n.
battle-cry
call 547 n.
**battledore and
shuttlecock**
interchange 151 n.
battlefield
battleground 724 n.
battleground
casus belli 709 n.
battleground 724 n.

battlement
fortification 713 n.
battler
contender 716 n.
combatant 722 n.
battleship
warship 722 n.
battue
slaughter 362 n.
chase 619 n.
batty
crazed 503 adj.
bauble
bauble 639 n.
finery 844 n.
baulk
beam 218 n.
(see balk)
bawd
bawd 952 n.
bawdry
impurity 951 n.
bawl
vociferate 408 vb.
bay
compartment
194 n.
potherb 301 n.
gulf 345 n.
ululate 409 vb.
brown 430 adj.
bayonet
side-arms 723 n.
bayou
lake 346 n.
bays
trophy 729 n.
honours 866 n.
bazaar
sale 793 n.
shop 796 n.
bazooka
gun 723 n.
be
be 1 vb.
be situate 186 vb.
beach
land 295 vb.
shore 344 n.
beachcomber
wanderer 268 n.
wave 350 n.
beachwear
beachwear 228 n.
aquatics 269 n.
beacon
warning 664 n.

danger signal
665 n.
beading
ornamental art
844 n.
beadle
law officer 955 n.
beadledom
governance 733 n.
beady
rotund 252 adj.
beagle
dog 365 n.
hunt 619 vb.
beak
prow 237 n.
projection 254 n.
beaked
curved 248 adj.
beaker
cup 194 n.
be-all and end-all
important matter
638 n.
beam
beam 218 n.
laterality 239 n.
scales 322 n.
flash 417 n.
radiate 417 vb.
smile 835 vb.
beanery
café 192 n.
beanfeast
meal 301 n.
bear
reproduce itself
164 vb.
be fruitful 171
vb.
support 218 vb.
carry 273 vb.
orientate 281 vb.
animal 365 n.
speculate 791 vb.
seller 793 n.
be patient 823 vb.
beard
hair 259 n.
defy 711 vb.
beardless
young 130 adj.
hairless 229 adj.
bear down
charge 712 vb.
bearer
bearer 273 n.

bear fruit
reproduce itself
164 vb.
be successful 727 vb.
beargarden
turmoil 61 n.
arena 724 n.
bearing
relation 9 n.
supporter 218 n.
direction 281 n.
meaning 514 n.
conduct 688 n.
bearish
saleable 793 adj.
ungracious 885 adj.
bear oneself
behave 688 vb.
bear out
corroborate 466 vb.
bearskin
headgear 228 n.
bear up
resist 715 vb.
bear upon
be related 9 vb.
bear with
be patient 823 vb.
beast
animal 365 n.
ruffian 904 n.
beast of burden
beast of burden
273 n.
worker 686 n.
beast of prey
killer 362 n.
noxious animal
904 n.
beat
be superior 34 vb.
periodicity 141 n.
territory 184 n.
strike 279 vb.
oscillate 317 vb.
pulverize 332 vb.
roll 403 vb.
tempo 410 n.
prosody 593 n.
defeat 727 vb.
spank 963 vb.
beat down
cheapen 812 vb.
beaten track
habit 610 n.
beatific
paradisiac 971 adj.

beatify
sanctify 979 vb.
beating
victory 727 n.
corporal
punishment 963 n.
beatitude
happiness 824 n.
beat it up
revel 837 vb.
beat of drum
publication 528 n.
beat off
repel 292 vb.
beat time
time 117 vb.
play music 413 vb.
beat up
strike 279 vb.
attack 712 vb.
beau
fop 848 n.
lover 887 n.
Beaufort scale
anemology 352 n.
beau monde
beau monde 848 n.
beautician
beautician 843 n.
beautiful
beautiful 841 adj.
beautify
make better 654 vb.
beautify 841 vb.
decorate 844 vb.
beauty
symmetry 245 n.
beauty 841 n.
a beauty 841 n.
beauty parlour
beauty parlour
843 n.
beauty treatment
beautification 843 n.
beaver
rodent 365 n.
worker 686 n.
armour 713 n.
beck
stream 350 n.
gesture 547 n.
**beck and call, at
one's**
obedient 739 adj.
serving 742 adj.
beckon
gesticulate 547 vb.

become
become 1 vb.
be turned to 147 vb.
beautify 841 vb.
becoming
existence 1 n.
personable 841 adj.
bed
layer 207 n.
bed 218 n.
garden 370 n.
sleep 679 n.
bed and board
provision 633 n.
bedbug
vermin 365 n.
bed-clothes
coverlet 226 n.
bedevil
bedevil 63 vb.
bedim
darken 418 vb.
bedim 419 vb.
bedizen
dress 228 vb.
decorate 844 vb.
bedlam
turmoil 61 n.
madhouse 503 n.
bedlamite
madman 504 n.
bed of roses
euphoria 376 n.
bed-pan
latrine 649 n.
bedraggled
orderless 61 adj.
dirty 649 adj.
bedridden
sick 651 adj.
bedrock
reality 1 n.
source 156 n.
base 214 n.
chief thing 638 n
bedroom
chamber 194 n.
bee
fly 365 n.
beef
vitality 162 n.
meat 301 n.
beefy
stalwart 162 adj.
fleshy 195 adj.
beehive
stock farm 369 n.

bee-keeper
breeder 369 n.
bee-line
straightness 249 n.
beer
liquor 301 n.
beery
drunken 949 adj.
beestings
milk 301 n.
beetle
be high 209 vb.
hammer 279 n.
fly 365 n.
beetroot
tuber 301 n.
befall
happen 154 vb.
befit
accord 24 vb.
be expedient 642 vb.
befool
befool 542 vb.
beforehand
before 119 adv.
betimes 135 adv.
befoul
make unclean
 649 vb.
befriend
patronize 703 vb.
befriend 880 vb.
beg
beg 761 vb.
be servile 879 vb.
beg, borrow, or steal
find means 629 vb.
beget
generate 164 vb.
begetter
cause 156 n.
producer 167 n.
parent 169 n.
beggar
wanderer 268 n.
beggar 763 n.
impoverish 801 vb.
beggarly
beggarly 801 adj.
beggary
poverty 801 n.
begin
become 1 vb.
begin 68 vb.
undertake 672 vb.
begin again
repeat 106 vb.

revert 148 vb.
beginner
beginner 538 n.
bungler 697 n.
beg off
deprecate 762 vb.
begrime
bedim 419 vb.
begrudge
be loth 598 vb.
refuse 760 vb.
beg the question
reason ill 477 vb.
beguile
mislead 495 vb.
deceive 542 vb.
behalf
benefit 615 n.
behave
behave 688 vb.
behaviour
mien 445 n.
conduct 688 n.
behead
shorten 204 vb.
execute 963 vb.
behind
rear 238 n.
behindhand
late 136 adj.
unprepared 670 adj.
behind the times
antiquated 127 adj.
behold
see 438 vb.
beholden
grateful 907 adj.
beholder
spectator 441 n.
behove
be one's duty
 917 vb.
beige
brown 430 adj.
being
existence 1 n.
affections 817 n.
bejewel
primp 843 vb.
decorate 844 vb.
belabour
strike 279 vb.
flog 963 vb.
belated
late 136 adj.
belay
tie 45 vb.

belch
vomit 300 vb.
breathe 352 vb.
beldam
old woman 133 n.
beleaguer
besiege 712 vb.
belfry
church exterior
 990 n.
belie
negate 533 vb.
belief
belief 485 n.
religious faith
 973 n.
believable
plausible 471 adj.
credible 485 adj.
believe
believe 485 vb.
believer
religionist 973 n.
pietist 979 n.
belittle
underestimate
 483 vb.
hold cheap 922 vb.
detract 926 vb.
bell
ululate 409 vb.
campanology 412 n.
gong 414 n.
bell, book, and
 candle
malediction 899 n.
belle
a beauty 841 n.
belletrist
dissertator 591 n.
bell-hop
courier 531 n.
bellicose
violent 176 adj.
quarrelling 709 adj.
defiant 711 adj.
warring 718 adj.
belligerency
belligerency 718 n.
enmity 881 n.
bellow
vociferate 408 vb.
ululate 409 vb.
be angry 891 vb.
bellows
sufflation 352 n.
heater 383 n.

bell-ringer
campanology 412
 n.
instrumentalist
 413 n.
belly
maw 194 n.
insides 224 n.
be convex 253 vb.
belly-ache
indigestion 651 n.
be discontented
 829 vb.
belly-band
girdle 47 n.
belt 228 n.
belly-flop
plunge 313 n.
bellyful
plenitude 54 n.
redundance 637
 n.
belong
be intrinsic 5 vb.
be related 9 vb.
constitute 56 vb.
belong 773 vb.
belongings
property 777 n.
beloved
loved one 887 n.
below par
imperfect 647 adj.
below the belt
unjust 914 adj.
below the salt
plebeian 869 adj.
below the surface
latent 523 adj.
belt
region 184 n.
compressor 198 n.
belt 228 n.
spank 963 vb.
bemedal
decorate 844 vb.
dignify 866 vb.
bemoan
lament 836 vb.
bemused
abstracted 456
 adj.
bench
seat 218 n.
tribunal 956 n.
bencher
lawyer 958 n.

bench of bishops
synod 985 n.
bend
tie 45 vb.
force 176 vb.
be oblique 220 vb.
angularity 247 n.
curve 248 n.
stoop 311 vb.
heraldry 547 n.
be servile 879 vb.
beneath one
degrading 867 adj.
benediction
thanks 907 n.
prayers 981 n.
benefaction
gift 781 n.
liberality 813 n.
benefactor
patron 707 n.
benefactor 903 n.
benefice
benefice 985 n.
beneficence
benevolence 897 n.
beneficial
beneficial 644 adj.
gainful 771 adj.
beneficiary
beneficiary 776 n.
recipient 782 n.
benefit
benefit 615 n.
utility 640 n.
be expedient 642
vb.
do good 644 vb.
subvention 703 n.
benefit of clergy
non-liability 919 n.
benefit of doubt
acquittal 960 n.
benevolence
goodness 644 n.
benevolence 897 n.
disinterestedness
931 n.
benighted
vespertine 129 adj.
late 136 adj.
ignorant 491 adj.
bent
tendency 179 n.
curved 248 adj.
grass 366 n.
aptitude 694 n.

benthos
ocean 343 n.
ben trovato
plausible 471 adj.
witty 839 adj.
bent upon
desiring 859 adj.
benumb
render insensible
375 vb.
refrigerate 382 vb.
make insensitive
820 vb.
bequeath
dower 777 vb.
bequeath 780 vb.
give 781 vb.
bequest
(see bequeath)
berate
exprobate 924 vb.
bereave
deprive 786 vb.
bereavement
loss 772 n.
beret
headgear 228 n.
beribbon
decorate 844 vb.
dignify 886 vb.
berm
edge 234 n.
berry
fruit 301 n.
berserk
frenzied 503 adj.
angry 891 adj.
berth
quarters 192 n.
dwell 192 vb.
arrive 295 vb.
job 622 n.
beseech
entreat 761 vb.
beset
besiege 712 vb.
besetting
habitual 610 adj.
beside oneself
frenzied 503 adj.
besiege
besiege 712 vb.
besmear
make unclean 649 vb.
besom
cleaning utensil
648 n.

besotted
foolish 499 adj.
enamoured 887 adj.
bespatter
make unclean
649 vb.
best
be superior 34 vb.
best 644 adj.
defeat 727 vb.
bestial
animal 365 adj.
sensual 944 adj.
bestiality
illicit love 951 n.
bestir oneself
exert oneself
682 vb.
best man
bridesman 894 n.
best of, make the
avail of 673 vb.
bestow
place 187 vb.
give 781 vb.
best people
beau monde 848 n.
upper class 868 n.
bestraddle
overlie 266 vb.
bestride
be broad 205 vb.
overlie 266 vb.
dominate 733 vb.
best-seller
book 589 n.
exceller 644 n.
bet
gamble 618 vb.
bête noire
bane 659 n.
hateful object
888 n.
bethink oneself
meditate 449 vb.
betoken
evidence 466 vb.
predict 511 vb.
indicate 547 vb.
betray
deceive 542 vb.
apostatize 603 vb.
fail in duty 918
vb.
betrothal
wooing 889 n.
wedding 894 n.

betrothed
loved one 887 n.
marriageable
894 adj.
better
superior 34 adj.
gambler 618 n.
make better 654 vb.
restored 656 adj.
betterment
benefit 615 n.
improvement 654 n.
betting
gambling 618 n.
bevel
obliquity 220 n.
beverage
potion 301 n.
bevy
group 74 n.
bewail
lament 836 vb.
beware
be warned 664 vb.
bewilder
puzzle 474 vb.
bewitch
delight 826 vb.
excite love 887 vb.
bewitch 983 vb.
bewray
disclose 526 vb.
beyond one's means
dear 811 adj.
beyond price
of price 811 adj.
beyond the pale
excluded 57 adj.
bezel
obliquity 220 n.
bias
influence 178 vb.
tendency 179 n.
obliquity 220 n.
bias 481 vb.
eccentricity 503 n.
motivate 612 vb.
bib
apron 228 n.
Bible
oracle 511 n.
scripture 975 n.
bibliographer
bookman 589 n.
bibliography
list 87 n.
reference book 589 n.

bibliophile
bookman 589 n.
bibulous
drunken 949 adj.
bicameral
parliamentary
692 adj.
bicker
bicker 709 vb.
bicolour
variegated 437 adj.
bicycle
bicycle 274 n.
bid
gambling 618 n.
essay 671 n., vb.
command 737 vb.
offer 759 n., vb.
bid against
oppose 704 vb.
biddable
obedient 739 adj.
bidder
petitioner 763 n.
purchaser 792 n.
bier
bed 218 n.
funeral 364 n.
biform
dual 90 adj.
bifurcate
bisect 92 vb.
diverge 294 vb.
big
great 32 adj.
large 195 adj.
important 638 adj.
bigamist
polygamist 894 n.
bigamy
type of marriage
894 n.
bight
gulf 345 n.
bigness
greatness 32 n.
strength 162 n.
big noise
bigwig 638 n.
bigot
doctrinaire 473 n.
opinionist 602 n.
religionist 979 n.
bigotry
positiveness 473 n.
narrow mind 481
n.

big shot
bigwig 638 n.
big stick
compulsion 740 n.
bigwig
superior 34 n.
bigwig 638 n.
person of repute
866 n.
bikini
beachwear 228 n.
bilateral
dual 90 adj.
contractual 765 adj.
bilboes
fetter 748 n.
bile
resentment 891 n.
bilge
leavings 41 n.
base 214 n.
silly talk 515 n.
swill 649 n.
bilingual
linguistic 557 adj.
bilious
green 432 adj.
yellow 433 adj.
unhealthy 651 adj.
biliousness
indigestion 651 n.
bilk
defraud 788 vb.
not pay 805 vb.
bilker
non-payer 805 n.
bill
list 87 n.
advertise 528 vb.
label 547 n.
spear, axe 723 n.
demand 737 vb.
paper money 797 n.
debt 803 n.
accounts 808 n.
price 809 n., vb.
bill and coo
caress 889 vb.
bill-collector
receiver 782 n.
billet
place 187 vb.
quarters 192 n.
goal 295 n.
billingsgate
slang 560 n.
scurrility 899 n.

bill of exchange
paper money 797 n.
bill of fare
meal 301 n.
billow
swelling 253 n.
wave 350 n.
billowy
curved 248 adj.
bill-sticker
publicizer 528 n.
bind
tie 45 vb.
bring together
74 vb.
compel 740 vb.
fetter 747 vb.
give terms 766 vb.
tedium 838 n.
impose a duty
917 vb.
binder
compressor 198 n.
farm tool 370 n.
binding
ligature 47 n.
wrapping 226 n.
obligatory 917 adj.
bind oneself
promise 764 vb.
bind up
repair 656 vb.
relieve 831 vb.
binge
festivity 837 n.
binnacle
sailing aid 269 n.
binoculars
telescope 442 n.
biographer
chronicler 549 n.
author 589 n.
narrator 590 n.
biography
record 548 n.
biography 590 n.
biology
biology 358 n.
life 360 n.
biotic potential
productiveness
171 n.
biotype
organism 358 n.
bipartisan
cooperative 706 adj.
concordant 710 adj.

bipartite
bisected 92 adj.
biped
animal 365 n.
birch
spank 963 vb.
bird
bird 365 n.
bird in the hand
object 319 n.
possession 773 n.
bird's-eye view
whole 52 n.
view 438 n.
biretta
headgear 228 n.
canonicals 989 n.
birth
origin 68 n.
propagation 164 n.
obstetrics 164 n.
genealogy 169 n.
life 360 n.
nobility 868 n.
birthday
anniversary 141 n.
birthmark
identification
547 n.
birth-pang
obstetrics 164 n.
birthplace
source 156 n.
home 192 n.
birthrate
statistics 86 n.
birthright
dower 777 n.
dueness 915 n.
biscuit
food 301 n.
pastry 301 n.
bisect
bisect 92 vb.
bishop
ecclesiarch 986 n.
bishopric
parish 985 n.
church office 985 n.
bison
cattle 365 n.
bit
small quantity 33
n.
piece 53 n.
perforator 263 n.
fetter 748 n.

bitch
female animal
373 n.
hell-hag 904 n.
bitchy
malevolent 898 adj.
bite
cut 46 vb.
be sharp 256 vb.
mouthful 301 n.
chew 301 vb.
pungency 388 n.
wound 655 vb.
enrage 891 vb.
biter bit
retaliation 714 n.
bitter
liquor 301 n.
unsavoury 391 adj.
sour 393 adj.
unpleasant 827 adj.
resentful 891 adj.
bitter end
finality 69 n.
bitter-ender
opinionist 602 n.
bitterness (*see* bitter)
bitter pill
unsavouriness
391 n.
adversity 731 n.
hateful object
888 n.
bitty
fragmentary 53 adj.
incomplete 55 adj.
bitumen
resin 357 n.
bivouac
place oneself
187 vb.
abode 192 n.
bizarre
unusual 84 adj.
blab
inform 524 vb.
divulge 526 vb.
blabber
informer 524 n.
black
exclude 57 vb.
funereal 364 adj.
dark 418 adj.
blackness 428 n.
black 428 adj.
blacken 428 vb.
bad 645 adj.

dirty 649 adj.
prohibited 757 adj.
black and white
light contrast
417 n.
pied 437 adj.
blackball
exclusion 57 n.
blackberry
fruit 301 n.
blackbird
vocalist 413 n.
black books
odium 888 n.
black cap
condemnation
961 n.
blacken
darken 418 vb.
blacken 428 vb.
shame 867 vb.
defame 926 vb.
blackguard
cuss 889 vb.
ruffian 904 n.
exprobate 924 vb.
blacking
black pigment
428 n.
blackjack
vessel 194 n.
blacklead
lubricant 334 n.
blackleg
nonconformist 84
n.
black-list
disapprobation
924 n.
condemn 961 vb.
black magic
diabolism 969 n.
sorcery 983 n.
blackmail
demand 737 n., vb.
compulsion 740 n.
rapacity 786 n.
fleece 786 vb.
tax 809 n.
threaten 900 vb.
Black Maria
lock-up 748 n.
black mark
reprimand 924 n.
black market
trade 791 n.
illegal 954 adj.

Black Mass
diabolism 969 n.
blackness
darkness 418 n.
blackness 428 n.
black-out
obscuration 418 n.
black out
darken 418 vb.
obliterate 550 vb.
black sheep
offender 904 n.
bladder
bladder 194 n.
blade
sharp edge 256 n.
side-arms 723 n.
blah-blah
empty talk 515 n.
blain
ulcer 651 n.
blame
attribute 158 vb.
blame 924 vb.
accusation 928 n.
guilt 936 n.
blameless
guiltless 935 adj.
blameworthy
discreditable
867 adj.
blameworthy
924 adj.
blanch
lose colour 426 vb.
decolorize 426 vb.
whiten 427 vb.
bland
lenitive 177 adj.
smooth 258 adj.
courteous 884 adj.
blandish
tempt 612 vb.
flatter 925 vb.
blandishment
endearment 889 n.
blank
non-existence 2 n.
zero 103 n.
empty 190 adj.
ignorant 491 adj.
blank cartridge
insubstantial thing
4 n.
false alarm 665 n.
blank cheque
scope 744 n.

blanket
general 79 adj.
coverlet 226 n.
screen 421 vb.
indiscriminate
464 adj.
blare
be loud 400 vb.
stridor 407 n.
blarney
empty talk 515 n.
flattery 925 n.
blasé
sated 863 adj.
blaspheme
be impious 980
vb.
blast
wind, gale 352 n.
loudness 400 n.
bang 402 n., vb.
blight 659 n.
blatancy
ostentation 875 n.
ululant 409 adj.
blather
empty talk 515 n.
blaze
fire 379 n.
light 417 n.
shine 417 vb.
mark 547 vb.
blazer
tunic 228 n.
livery 547 n.
blazonry
heraldry 547 n.
bleach
decolorize 426 vb.
whiten 427 vb.
clean 648 vb.
bleak
adverse 731 adj.
blear
bedim 419 vb.
bleat
ululate 409 vb.
be discontented
829 vb.
bleb
swelling 253 n.
bleed
flow out 298 vb.
void 300 vb.
doctor 658 vb.
fleece 786 vb.
suffer 825 vb.

blemish
　impair 655 vb.
　eyesore 842 n.
　blemish 845 n., vb.
blench
　avoid 620 vb.
　quake 854 vb.
blend
　a mixture 43 n.
　combine 50 vb.
bless
　be auspicious
　　730 vb.
　permit 756 vb.
　thank 907 vb.
　praise 923 vb.
blessed
　good 615 adj.
　palmy 730 adj.
　happy 824 adj.
blessing
　benefit 615 n.
　good 615 n.
　(*see* bless)
blessings
　prosperity 730 n.
blether
　empty talk 515 n.
blight
　decay 51 n.
　destroyer 168 n.
　impair 655 vb.
　blight 659 n.
blighter
　cad 938 n.
blind
　shade 226 n.
　screened 421 adj.
　blind 439 adj., vb.
　distract 456 vb.
　indiscriminating
　　464 adj.
　trickery 542 n.
　deceive 542 vb.
　pretext 614 n.
　stratagem 698 n.
　drunkenness 949
　　n.
blind alley
　obstacle 702 n.
blindfold
　screen 421 vb.
　blind 439 adj., vb.
blinding
　luminous 417 adj.
blindness
　blindness 439 n.

blind side
　blindness 439 n.
　inattention 456 n.
　prejudice 481 n.
　opiniatry 602 n.
blink
　flash 417 n.
　reflection 417 n.
　gaze 438 vb.
　dim sight 440 n.
blinker
　signal light 420 n.
　screen 421 vb.
　blind 439 vb.
bliss
　happiness 824 n.
blissful
　palmy 730 adj.
　pleasurable 826
　　adj.
blister
　swelling 253 n.
blithe
　cheerful 833 adj.
blitz
　havoc 165 n.
　bombardment
　　712 n.
　attack 712 vb.
blizzard
　storm 176 n.
　snow 380 n.
bloat
　enlarge 197 vb.
bloated
　fleshy 195 adj.
bloc
　political party
　　708 n.
block
　bulk 195 n.
　stand 218 n.
　close 264 vb.
　solid body 324 n.
　dunce 501 n.
　obstruct 702 vb.
　parry 713 vb.
　prohibit 757 vb.
blockade
　close 264 vb.
　besiege 712 vb.
　restriction 747 n.
blockage
　stop 145 n.
　obstacle 702 n.
blockhead
　dunce 501 n.

blockish
　unintelligent 499 adj.
block out
　efform 243 vb.
blond
　whitish 427 adj.
　yellow 433 adj.
blood
　consanguinity 11 n.
　breed 77 n.
　genealogy 169 n.
　blood 335 n.
　life 360 n.
　fop 848 n.
　nobility 868 n.
blood bath
　slaughter 362 n.
blood-group
　race 11 n.
blood-guilty
　murderous 362 adj.
　guilty 936 adj.
bloodhound
　dog 365 n.
　detective 459 n.
bloodless
　insubstantial 4 adj.
　weak 163 adj.
　colourless 426 adj.
　guiltless 935 adj.
blood-letting
　killing 362 n.
　surgery 658 n.
blood-money
　atonement 941 n.
blood-pressure
　blood pressure
　　651 n.
bloodshed
　slaughter 362 n.
　warfare 718 n.
bloodshot
　sanguineous
　　335 adj.
　bloodshot 431 adj.
blood-sport
　chase 619 n.
bloodstained
　murderous 362 adj.
　bloodshot 431 adj.
bloodstock
　thoroughbred
　　273 n.
bloodsucker
　taker 786 n.
blood-sucking
　rapacity 786 n.

blood-thirsty
　murderous 362 adj.
　cruel 898 adj.
blood vessel
　conduit 351 n.
bloody
　violent 176 adj.
　sanguineous 335 adj.
　murderous 362 adj.
　bloodshot 431 adj.
　cruel 898 adj.
bloody-mindedness
　obstinacy 602 n.
bloom
　reproduce 164 vb.
　expand 197 vb.
　flower 366 n.
　health 650 n.
bloomer
　mistake 495 n.
bloomers
　trousers 228 n.
　underwear 228 n.
blossom
　product 164 n.
　reproduce itself
　　164 vb.
　be fruitful 171 vb.
　(*see* bloom)
blot
　absorb 299 vb.
　dry 342 vb.
　blacken 428 vb.
　variegate 437 vb.
　mistake 495 n.
　mark 547 n.
　obliterate 550 vb.
　make unclean
　　649 vb.
　eyesore 842 n.
　blemish 845 n., vb.
　slur 867 n.
blotch
　blemish 845 n.
blot out
　destroy 165 vb.
　(*see* blot)
blotter
　cleaning utensil
　　648 n.
blouse
　bodywear 228 n.
blow
　expand 197 vb.
　knock 279 n.
　blow 352 vb.
　deed 676 n.

boiler
  cauldron 194 n.
  heater 383 n.
boisterous
  violent 176 adj.
  windy 352 adj.
bold
  salient 254 adj.
  courageous 855 adj.
  insolent 878 adj.
bolide
  meteor 321 n.
bollard
  fastening 47 n.
boloney
  empty talk 515 n.
Bolshevism
  government 733 n.
bolshie
  disobedient 738 adj.
bolster
  cushion 218 n.
  support 218 vb.
bolt
  fastening 47 n.
  stopper 264 n.
  move fast 277 vb.
  run away 620 vb.
  purify 648 vb.
  deteriorate 655 vb.
  gluttonize 947 vb.
bolt from the blue
  inexpectation
   508 n.
bolt-hole
  tunnel 263 n.
  refuge 662 n.
bolus
  medicine 658 n.
bomb
  destroyer 168 n.
  bang 402 n.
  bomb 723 n.
bombard
  radiate 417 vb.
  fire at 712 vb.
bombardment
  bombardment
   712 n.
bombast
  lining 227 n.
  empty talk 515 n.
  magniloquence
   574 n.
  boast 877 n.
bomber
  air force 722 n.

bomb-proof
  unyielding 162 adj.
bombshell
  inexpectation 508 n.
bona fide
  veracious 540 adj.
bona fides
  probity 929 n.
bonbon *sweet* 392 n.
bond
  relation 9 n.
  bond 47 n.
  fetter 748 n.
  promise 764 n.
  title-deed 767 n.
bondage
  servitude 745 n.
bonehead
  dunce 501 n.
bon enfant
  kind person 897 n.
bone of contention
  casus belli 709 n.
  contention 716 n.
bone-setting
  therapy 658 n.
bone to pick
  resentment 891 n.
bonfire
  fire 379 n.
  celebration 876 n.
bonhomie
  sociability 882 n.
bon mot
  witticism 839 n.
bonnet
  covering 226 n.
  headgear 228 n.
bonny
  beautiful 841 adj.
bon ton
  fashionable 848 adj.
bonus
  extra 40 n.
  incentive 612 n.
  gift 781 n.
bony
  lean 206 adj.
  hard 326 adj.
boo
  vociferate 408 vb.
  disapprove 924 vb.
boob, booby
  ninny 501 n.
booby-trap
  trap 542 n.
  defences 713 n.

boodle
  booty 790 n.
book
  book 589 n.
  account 808 vb.
book-case
  cabinet 194 n.
book-club
  library 589 n.
book-collector
  bookman 589 n.
bookie
  gambler 618 n.
bookish
  instructed 490 adj.
  studious 536 adj.
book-keeper
  computer 86 n.
  accountant 808 n.
book-keeping
  accounts 808 n.
book-learning
  erudition 490 n.
bookmaker
  gambler 618 n.
bookman
  bookman 589 n.
books
  account book
   808 n.
book-shop
  library 589 n.
book-trade
  publication 528 n.
bookworm
  scholar 492 n.
boom
  resound 404 vb.
  ululate 409 vb.
  obstacle 702 n.
  prosperity 730 n.
boomerang
  recoil 280 n.
  missile weapon
   723 n.
boon
  benefit 615 n.
  gift 781 n.
boon companion
  close friend 880 n.
  social person 882 n.
boor
  countryman 869 n.
boorish
  ill-bred 847 adj.
boorishness
  discourtesy 885 n.

boost
  invigorate 174 vb.
  advertise 528 vb.
booster
  publicizer 528 n.
  commender 923 n.
boot
  box 194 n.
  footwear 228 n.
  kick 279 vb.
  ejection 300 n.
booth
  small house 192 n.
  shop 796 n.
bootlicker
  toady 879 n.
booty
  trophy 729 n.
  booty 790 n.
booze
  liquor 301 n.
  get drunk 949 vb.
boozer
  drunkard 949 n.
border
  be near 200 vb.
  contiguity 202 n.
  edging 234 n.
  limit 236 vb.
  decorate 844 vb.
borderland(s)
  contiguity 202 n.
borderline case
  predicament 700 n.
bore
  breadth 205 n.
  pierce 263 vb.
  wave 350 n.
  tedium, bore 838
   n.
boredom
  tedium 838 n.
borer
  sharp point 256 n.
  perforator 263 n.
boring
  tunnel 363 n.
born
  born 360 adj.
borough
  district 184 n.
borrow
  copy 20 vb.
  borrow 785 vb.
borrower
  beggar 763 n.
  debtor 803 n.

bosh
silly talk 515 n.
bosh shot
mistake 495 n.
bosom
interiority 224 n.
bosom 253 n.
affections 817 n.
boss
superior 34 n.
swelling 253 n.
director 690 n.
dominate 733 vb.
master, autocrat 741 n.
bossy
authoritarian 735 adj.
botanical
vegetal 366 adj.
botanist
botanist 368 n.
botany
biology 358 n.
botany 368 n.
botch
misrepresent 552 vb.
repair 656 vb.
be clumsy 695 vb.
botcher
mender 656 n.
bungler 697 n.
bother
hinder 702 vb.
worry 825 n.
torment 827 vb.
bottle
vessel 194 n.
potion 301 n.
preserve 666 vb.
bottleneck
narrowness 206 n.
obstacle 702 n.
bottle up
conceal 525 vb.
bottom
inferiority 35 n.
extremity 69 n.
lowness 210 n.
depth 211 n.
undermost 214 adj.
buttocks 238 n.
marsh 347 n.
bottomless
deep 211 adj.
bottomry
security 767 n.

boudoir
chamber 194 n.
bough
branch 53 n.
foliage 53 n.
boulder
rock 344 n.
boulevard
street 192 n.
bounce
recoil 280 n.
eject 300 vb.
leap 312 vb.
oscillate 317 vb.
elasticity 328 n.
boasting 877 n.
bound
limit 236 vb.
leap 312 n., vb.
restrained 747 adj.
boundary
limit 236 n.
bounder
vulgarian 847 n.
bound for
directed 281 adj.
boundless
infinite 107 adj.
spacious 183 adj.
bounds
region 184 n.
bounteous
liberal 813 adj.
bountiful
giving 781 adj.
bounty
subvention 703 n.
liberality 813 n.
bouquet
bunch 74 n.
fragrance 396 n.
praise 923 n.
bourgeois
commoner 869 n.
bourgeoisie
mediocrity 732 n.
commonalty 869 n.
bourse
bourse 618 n.
mart 796 n.
bout
period 110 n.
periodicity 141 n.
pugilism 716 n.
bovine
animal 365 adj.
unintelligent 499 adj.

bow
prow 237 n.
curve 248 n.
stoop 311 vb.
viol 414 n.
knuckle under 721 vb.
missile weapon 723 n.
trimming 844 n.
courteous act 884 n.
bowdlerize
impair 655 vb.
bow down, — to
stoop 311 vb.
honour 866 vb.
bowels
insides 224 n.
bower
arbour 194 n.
bowl
bowl 194 n.
propel 287 vb.
potion 301 n.
rotate 315 vb.
bowl along
go smoothly 258 vb.
move fast 277 vb.
bowler
thrower 287 n.
bowline
tackling 47 n.
bowl over
disable 161 vb.
fell 311 vb.
surprise 508 vb.
bowls
ball game 837 n.
bowsprit
prow 237 n.
bow to
be inferior 35 vb.
box
small house 192 n.
box 194 n.
fight 716 vb.
boxer
dog 365 n.
pugilist 722 n.
boxing
pugilism 716 n.
box-office
onlookers 441 n.
theatre 594 n.
treasury 799 n.

box up
imprison 747 vb.
boy
youngster 132 n.
boycott
exclusion 57 n.
make unwelcome 883 vb.
disapprobation 924 n.
boy-friend
lover 887 n.
boyhood
youth 130 n.
boyish
young 130 adj.
infantine 132 adj.
brace
duality 90 n.
supporter 218 n.
support 218 vb.
refresh 685 vb.
brace and bit
perforator 263 n.
bracelet(s)
fetter 748 n.
jewellery 844 n.
brace oneself
prepare oneself 669 vb.
bracer
stimulant 174 n.
tonic 658 n.
bracing
salubrious 652 adj.
refreshing 685 adj.
bracket
equalize 28 vb.
classification 77 n.
shelf 218 n.
punctuation 547 n.
bracket with
liken 18 vb.
brackish
salty 388 adj.
bradawl
sharp point 256 n.
brag
boast 877 vb.
braggart
(see **brag**)
braid
tie 45 vb.
ligature 47 n.
weave 222 vb.
braille
writing 586 n.

brain
head 213 n.
render insensible
375 vb.
intellect 447 n.
intellectual 492 n.
brain-child
idea 451 n.
brain-fag
thought 449 n.
fatigue 684 n.
brainless
mindless 448 adj.
foolish 499 adj.
brainpan
head 213 n.
brainstorm
psychopathy 503 n.
excitable state
822 n.
brains trust
interrogation 459
n.
intellectual 492 n.
brainwash
teach 534 vb.
misteach 535 vb.
brain-wave
idea 451 n.
brain-work
thought 449 n.
brain-worker
intellectual 492 adj.
brainy
intelligent 498 adj.
brake
halt 145 vb.
moderator 177 n.
retard 278 vb.
wood 366 n.
restraint 747 n.
bramble
prickle 256 n.
bran
powder 332 n.
rubbish 641 n.
branch
adjunct 40 n.
classification 77 n.
descendant 170 n.
diverge 294 vb.
tree, foliage 366 n.
brand
sort 77 n.
burn 381 vb.
lighter 385 n.
torch 420 n.

identification 547 n.
mark 547 vb.
slur 867 n.
brandish
agitate 318 vb.
show 522 vb.
brash
insolent 878 adj.
brass
orchestra 413 n.
musical instrument
414 n.
monument 548 n.
badge of rank
743 n.
sauciness 878 n.
brasserie
café 192 n.
brass hat
army officer 741 n.
brassière
underwear 228 n.
brass tacks
reality 1 n.
brassy
loud 400 adj.
strident 407 adj.
brat
child 132 n.
bravado
boast 877 n.
brave
soldier 722 n.
brave person 855 n.
courageous 855 adj.
bravery
courage 855 n.
ostentation 875 n.
bravo
desperado 857 n.
ruffian 904 n.
bravura
musical skill 413 n.
brawl
quarrel 709 n.
fight 716 n.
brawler
rioter 738 n.
brawn
vitality 162 n.
brawny
stalwart 162 adj.
bray
pulverize 332 vb.
ululate 409 vb.
braze
agglutinate 48 vb.

brazen
insolent 878 adj.
impenitent 940 adj.
brazier
heater 383 n.
breach
disjunction 46 n.
gap 201 n.
dissension 709 n.
enmity 881 n.
breach of faith
perfidy 930 n.
breach of trust
peculation 788 n.
bread
food 301 n.
cereal 301 n.
bread and butter
food 301 n.
vocation 622 n.
bread and water
unsavouriness
391 n.
fasting 946 n.
breadth
breadth 205 n.
breadth of mind
wisdom 498 n.
breadwinner
worker 686 n.
breadwinning
gainful 771 adj.
break
break 46 vb.
discontinuity 72 n.
lull 145 n.
continuance 146 n.
be brittle 330 vb.
repose 683 n.
quarrel 709 vb.
prosperity 730 n.
depose 752 vb.
not pay 805 vb.
breakable
brittle 330 adj.
break away
schismatize 978 vb.
breakdown
decomposition 51 n.
illness 651 n.
hitch 702 n.
break even
be equal 28 vb.
breakfast
meal 301 n.
break in
intrude 297 vb.

train 534 vb.
habituate 610 vb.
breaking point
casus belli 709 n.
breakneck
speedy 277 adj.
rash 857 adj.
break of
cure 656 vb.
break off
cease 145 vb.
break open
force 176 vb.
break out
begin 68 vb.
be violent 176 vb.
emerge 298 vb.
escape 667 vb.
break the news
inform 524 vb.
breakthrough
success 727 n.
break-up
separation 46 n.
revolution 149 n.
breakwater
safeguard 662 n.
breast
interiority 224 n.
bosom 253 n.
climb 308 vb.
affections 817 n.
breastplate
armour 713 n.
breastwork
defences 713 n.
breath
insubstantial thing
4 n.
breeze 352 n.
life 360 n.
breathe
exude 298 vb.
breathe 352 vb.
live 360 vb.
sound faint 401 vb.
hint 524 vb.
divulge 526 vb.
breathe life into
vitalize 360 vb.
breathe upon
defame 926 vb.
breathing
respiration 352 n.
breathless
agitated 318 adj.
voiceless 578 adj.

hasty 680 adj.
panting 684 adj.
breath-taking
notable 638 adj.
wonderful 864 adj.
bred
(*see* breed)
breech
dress 228 vb.
rear, buttocks 238 n.
breech-cloth
loincloth 228 n.
breeches
breeches 228 n.
breed
character 5 n.
race 11 n.
breed 77 n.
posterity 170 n.
breed stock 369 n.
educate 534 vb.
breeder
producer 167 n.
breeder 369 n.
breeding
etiquette 848 n.
breeding-place
seedbed 156 n.
breeze
breeze 352 n.
blow 352 vb.
quarrel 709 n.
breezy
windy 352 adj.
cheerful 833 adj.
disrespectful 921 adj.
breviary
office-book 988 n.
brevity
shortness 204 n.
conciseness 569 n.
brew
a mixture 43 n.
mix 43 vb.
mature 669 vb.
briar
(*see* brier)
bribable
venal 930 adj.
bribe
bribe 612 vb.
offer 759 vb.
bribery
(*see* bribe)
bric-à-brac
bauble 639 n.

finery 844 n.
brick
pottery 381 n.
building material 631 n.
good man 937 n.
brickbat
piece 53 n.
missile weapon 723 n.
bricks and mortar
building material 631 n.
brick wall
obstacle 702 n.
brickwork
edifice 164 n.
structure 331 n.
bridal
matrimonial 894 adj.
bride
spouse 894 n.
bridegroom
spouse 894 n.
bridesmaid
bridesman 894 n.
bridge
connect 45 vb.
bridge 624 n.
facilitate 701 vb.
card game 837 n.
bridle
fetter 748 n.
brief
brief 114 adj.
short 204 adj.
inform 524 vb.
concise 569 adj.
compendium 592 n.
briefing
advice 691 n.
briefs
underwear 228 n.
brier, briar
prickle 256 n.
tobacco 388 n.
brigade
combine 50 vb.
group 74 n.
formation 722 n.
brigand
robber 789 n.
brigandage
brigandage 788 n.
bright
luminous 417 adj.

intelligent 498 adj.
clean 648 adj.
cheerful 833 adj.
brighten
make bright 417 vb.
brightness
light 417 n.
bright side
pleasurableness 826 n.
brilliance
light 417 n.
hue 425 n.
intelligence 498 n.
beauty 841 n.
ostentation 875 n.
brilliant
gem 844 n.
(*see* brilliance)
brim
fill 54 vb.
brine
season 388 vb.
preserver 666 n.
bring about
cause 156 vb.
carry out 725 vb.
bring back
replace 187 vb.
restitute 787 vb.
bring forth
reproduce itself 164 vb.
bring home to
attribute 158 vb.
impress 821 vb.
bring to
add 38 vb.
bring to a head
mature 669 vb.
bring to bear
relate 9 vb.
use 673 vb.
bring together
mediate 720 vb.
bring to heel
subjugate 745 vb.
bring to life
vitalize 360 vb.
bring to light
detect 484 vb.
manifest 522 vb.
bring up
vomit 300 vb.
educate 534 vb.
brink
extremity 69 n.

nearness 200 n.
edge 234 n.
brinkman
desperado 857 n.
brinkmanship
tactics 688 n.
rashness 857 n.
brisk
vigorous 174 adj.
bristly
sharp 256 adj.
hairy 259 adj.
brittle
ephemeral 114 adj.
brittle 330 adj.
broach
initiate 68 vb.
sharp point 256 n.
pierce 263 vb.
make flow 350 vb.
undertake 672 vb.
broad
general 79 adj.
broad 205 adj.
inexact 495 adj.
impure 951 adj.
broad-based
inclusive 78 adj.
general 79 adj.
broadcast
disperse 75 vb.
cultivate 370 vb.
publish 528 vb.
telecommunication 531 n.
broadcloth
textile 222 n.
broad-minded
wise 498 adj.
free 744 adj.
broadsheet
the press 528 n.
broadside
laterality 239 n.
bombardment 712 n.
gun 723 n.
broadwife
slave 742 n.
brocade
textile 222 n.
brochure
the press 528 n.
book 589 n.
brogue
dialect 560 n.
pronunciation 577 n.

broil
cook 301 vb.
broiler
poultry 365 n.
broke
poor 801 adj.
broke for
deputize 755 vb.
broken
rough 259 adj.
(*see* break)
broken reed
weak thing 163 n.
broken-winded
panting 684 adj.
broker
consignee 754 n.
merchant 794 n.
brokerage
discount 810 n.
bronchitis
respiratory disease
651 n.
bronze
brownness 430 n.
brooch
fastening 47 n.
jewellery 844 n.
brood
group 74 n.
youngling 132 n.
posterity 170 n.
meditate 449 vb.
be dejected 834
vb.
broody
productive 164 adj.
brook
stream 350 n.
be patient 823 vb.
broom
cleaning utensil
648 n.
broth
soup 301 n.
brothel
brothel 951 n.
brothel-keeper
bawd 952 n.
brother
kinsman 11 n.
analogue 18 n.
colleague 708 n.
brotherhood
community 708 n.
sect 978 n.
monk 986 n.

brotherly
friendly 880 adj.
brow
head 213 n.
face 237 n.
projection 254 n.
browbeat
frighten 854 vb.
reprove 924 vb.
brown
brownness 430 n.
browned off
discontented
829 adj.
brown study
thought 449 n.
abstractedness
456 n.
browse
graze 301 vb.
bruise
pulverize 332 vb.
pain 377 n.
wound 655 n., vb.
bruit
publish 528 vb.
brunette
black 428 adj.
brown 430 adj.
brunt, bear the
resist 715 vb.
brush
be contiguous
202 vb.
rear 238 n.
rub 333 vb.
cleaning utensil
648 n.
fight 716 n.
brushwood
fuel 385 n.
brushwork
painting 553 n.
brusque
concise 569 adj.
ungracious 885 adj.
brutal
violent 176 adj.
oppressive 735 adj.
cruel 898 adj.
brutalize
pervert 655 vb.
make insensitive
820 vb.
brute
violent creature
176 n.

animal 365 n.
mindless 448 adj.
ruffian 904 n.
brute fact
reality 1 n.
brute force
strength 162 n.
brute force 735 n.
brutish
discourteous
885 adj.
sensual 944 adj.
bubble
insubstantial thing
4 n.
levity 323 n.
brittleness 330 n.
bubble 355 n., vb.
hiss 406 vb.
bubo
swelling 253 n.
buccaneer
robber 789 n.
buck
leap 312 n., vb.
deer 365 n.
paper money
797 n.
fop 848 n.
bucket
vessel 194 n.
bucket shop
bourse 618 n.
buckle
fastening 47 n.
distort 246 vb.
make concave
255 vb.
buckler
armour 713 n.
buckshot
ammunition 723 n.
buck up
relieve 831 vb.
cheer, be cheerful
833 vb.
bud
reproduce itself
164 vb.
be fruitful 171 vb.
swelling 253 n.
flower 366 n.
budding
young 130 adj.
new 126 adj.
budge
move 265 vb.

budgerow
small house 192 n.
boat 275 n.
budget
bunch 74 n.
correspondence
588 n.
provide 633 vb.
accounts 808 n.
budgetary
monetary 797 adj.
accounting 808 adj.
buff
rub 333 vb.
brown 430 adj.
cleaning cloth
648 n.
buffer
interjacence 231 n.
defence 713 n.
buffer state
interjacence 231 n.
buffet
cabinet 194 n.
strike 279 vb.
wound 655 vb.
buffoon
entertainer 594 n.
humorist 839 n.
buffoonery
foolery 497 n.
bug
vermin 365 n.
bugbear
bane 659 n.
intimidation 854 n.
demon 970 n.
buggy
carriage 274 n.
bugle
horn 414 n.
call 547 n.
build
compose 56 vb.
efform 243 vb.
structure 331 n.
building
edifice 164 n.
production 164 n.
house, housing
192 n.
build-up
increase 36 n.
advertisement
528 n.
build up
strengthen 162 vb.

built-in
  ingredient 58 adj.
  interior 224 adj.
built-up
  urban 192 adj.
bulb
  plant 366 n.
  lamp 420 n.
bulbous
  rotund 252 adj.
bulge
  fill 54 vb.
  swelling 253 n.
  be convex 253 vb.
bulk
  be great 32 vb.
  greater number
    104 n.
  bulk 195 n.
bulkhead
  partition 231 n.
bulky
  substantial 3 adj.
  large 195 adj.
bull
  cattle 365 n.
  solecism 565 n.
  decree 737 n.
  formality 875 n.
bulldog
  dog 368 n.
bulldoze
  demolish 165 vb.
bulldozer
  ram 279 n.
bullet
  ammunition 723 n.
bulletin
  report 524 n.
  news 529 n.
bullet-proof
  invulnerable
    660 adj.
bullion
  bullion 797 n.
bullionist
  moneyer 797 n.
bullish
  buying 792 adj.
bull-ring
  arena 724 n.
bull's-eye
  centrality 225 n.
  lamp 420 n.
bully
  tyrant 735 n.
  oppress 735 vb.

frighten 854 vb.
  desperado 857 n.
  ruffian 904 n.
bulwark
  protection 660 n.
  defence 713 n.
  fortification 713 n.
bumbledom
  governance 733 n.
bump
  swelling 253 n.
  protuberance 254 n.
  collision 279 n.
bumper
  plenitude 54 n.
  potion 301 n.
bumper crop
  plenty 635 n.
bumpiness
  roughness 259 n.
bump into
  collide 217 vb.
bump off
  murder 362 vb.
bumptious
  vain 873 adj.
  insolent 878 adj.
bumpy
  rough 259 adj.
bun
  pastry 301 n.
  hair-dressing 843 n.
bunch
  cohere 48 vb.
  bunch, crowd 74 n.
  party 708 n.
bundle
  bunch 74 n.
  bag 194 n.
  collection 632 n.
bung
  stopper 264 n.
  close 264 vb.
bungalow
  house 192 n.
bungle
  be clumsy 695 vb.
  fail 728 vb.
bungler
  fool 501 n.
  bungler 697 n.
bunion
  swelling 253 n.
bunk
  bed 218 n.
  empty talk 515 n.
  run away 620 vb.

bunker
  storage 632 n.
  obstacle 702 n.
bunkum
  empty talk 515 n.
bunting
  flag 547 n.
buoy
  sailing aid 269 n.
  elevate 310 vb.
buoyancy
  levity 323 n.
buoyant
  swimming 269 adj.
  cheerful 833 adj.
buoy up
  support 218 vb.
burbler
  fool 501 n.
burden
  load 193 vb.
  make heavy 322 vb.
  vocal music 412 n.
  topic 452 n.
  difficulty 700 n.
burdensome
  weighty 322 adj.
  difficult 700 adj.
bureau
  cabinet 194 n.
  workshop 687 n.
bureaucracy
  management 689 n.
  governance 733 n.
bureaucrat
  official 690 n.
burgeon
  reproduce itself
    164 vb.
  expand 197 vb.
burgess
  native 191 n.
burglar
  thief 789 n.
burglary
  stealing 788 n.
burial
  interment 364 n.
buried
  dead 361 adj.
  buried 364 adj.
  secluded 883 adj.
burin
  sculpture 554 n.
  engraving 555 n.
burke
  suppress 165 vb.

burlesque
  misrepresent
    552 vb.
  funny 849 adj.
  satirize 851 vb.
burly
  stalwart 162 adj.
burn
  stream 350 n.
  burn 381 vb.
  shine 417 vb.
  embrown 430 vb.
burner
  furnace 383 n.
burning
  pungent 388 adj.
burning-glass
  optical device
    442 n.
burnish
  smooth 258 vb.
  make bright 417 n.
burn one's fingers
  be rash 857 vb.
burnt offering
  oblation 981 n.
burp
  eruct 300 vb.
burr
  coherence 48 n.
  rasp 407 vb.
  pronunciation
    577 n.
burrow
  dwelling 192 n.
  excavation 255 n.
  make concave
    255 vb.
  pierce 263 vb.
  lurk 523 vb.
bursar
  treasurer 798 n.
bursary
  treasury 799 n.
burst
  break 46 vb.
  be dispersed 75 vb.
  be violent 176 vb.
  open 263 vb.
  spurt 277 n.
  be brittle 330 vb.
  bang 402 n., vb.
  activity 678 n.
bury
  inter 364 vb.
  conceal 525 vb.
  obliterate 550 vb.

bus
bus 274 n.
busby
headgear 228 n.
bush
line 227 vb.
wood 366 n.
bushing
lining 227 n.
bushy
arboreal 366 adj.
dense 325 adj.
business
affairs 154 n.
topic 452 n.
intention 617 n.
business 622 n.
trade 791 n.
business house
workshop 687 n.
corporation 708 n.
businesslike
orderly 60 adj.
businesslike
622 adj.
industrious 678 adj.
expert 694 adj.
bust
bosom 253 n.
meal 301 n.
sculpture 554 n.
bustle
skirt 228 n.
activity 678 n.
bustling
eventful 154 adj.
busy
eventful 154 adj.
busy bee
busy person 678 n.
busybody
inquisitor 453 n.
meddler 678 n.
butcher
killer 362 n.
slaughter 362 vb.
butler
domestic 742 n.
retainer 742 n.
butt
vat 194 n.
collide 279 vb.
objective 617 n.
laughing-stock
851 n.
butter
fat 357 n.

flatter 925 vb.
butterfingers
bungler 697 n.
butterfly
fly 365 n.
variegation 437 n.
butt in
meddle 678 vb.
buttocks
rear 238 n.
button
fastening 47 n.
close 264 vb.
buttonhole
fastening 47 n.
fragrance 396 n.
speak to 583 vb.
ornamentation
844 n.
buttons
courier 531 n.
buttress
supporter 218 n.
corroborate 466 vb.
buy
purchase 792 vb.
buy and sell
trade 791 vb.
buyer
purchaser 792 n.
buy off
bribe 612 vb.
deliver 668 vb.
buzz
resound 404 vb.
ululation 409 n.
obstruct 702 vb.
buzzer
megaphone 400 n.
buzz off
decamp 296 vb.
bygone
past 125 adj.
forgotten 506 adj.
by-pass
avoid 620 vb.
road 624 n.
bypath
deviation 282 n.
path 624 n.
by-play
gesture 547 n.
by-product
sequel 67 n.
product 164 n.
byre
stable 192 n.

cattle pen 369 n.
bystander
spectator 441 n.
byword
maxim 496 n.
laughing-stock
851 n.
object of scorn
867 n.

C

cab
cab 274 n.
cabal
plot 623 n., vb.
cabaret
stage show 594 n.
place of amusement
837 n.
cabbage
leavings 41 n.
vegetable 301 n.
cabbalism
occultism 984 n.
cabby
driver 268 n.
cabin
small house 192 n.
chamber 194 n.
cabinet
cabinet 194 n.
council 692 n.
cable
cable 47 n.
telecommunication
531 n.
cacation
cacation 302 n.
cache
hiding-place 527 n.
store 632 n.
cachet
label 547 n.
repute 866 n.
cackle
ululate 409 vb.
cacophony
stridor 407 n.
discord 411 n.
cactus
prickle 256 n.
plant 366 n.
cad
cad 938 n.
cadastral
metric 465 adj.

cadastre
list 87 n.
cadaver
corpse 363 n.
cadaverous
lean 206 adj.
cadaverous 363 adj.
caddie, caddy
bearer 273 n.
cadence
sound 398 n.
cadenza
musical note 410 n.
cadet
youngster 132 n.
army officer 741 n.
cadge
beg 761 vb.
cadger
idler 679 n.
beggar 763 n.
cadre
classification 77 n.
personnel 686 n.
caesarian operation
obstetrics 164 n.
Caesarism
despotism 733 n.
caesura
interval 201 n.
café
café 192 n.
cage
stable 192 n.
compartment 194
n.
frame 218 n.
lock-up 748 n.
cairn
tomb 364 n.
dog 365 n.
monument 548 n.
cajole
befool 542 vb.
flatter 925 vb.
cake
cohere 48 vb.
pastry 301 n.
be dense 324 vb.
cakes and ale
prosperity 770 n.
calabash
vessel 194 n.
calamity
ill fortune 731 n.
calcify
harden 326 vb.

cannibalize
  repair 656 vb.
cannonade
  bombardment
    712 n.
cannon-ball
  ammunition 723 n.
cannot
  be impotent 161 vb.
canny
  intelligent 498 adj.
  cunning 698 adj.
  cautious 858 adj.
canoe
  row 269 vb.
  rowboat 275 n.
canoeing
  aquatics 269 n.
canoeist
  boatman 270 n.
canon
  precept 693 n.
  decree 737 n.
  scripture 975 n.
  ecclesiarch 986 n.
canonical
  preceptive 693 adj.
  scriptural 975 adj.
  orthodox 976 adj.
canonicals
  canonicals 989 n.
canonist
  jurist 958 n.
  theologian 973 n.
canonization
  dignification 866 n.
  sanctity 979 n.
canonry
  benefice 985 n.
  church office 985 n.
canopy
  canopy 226 n.
cant
  obliquity 220 n.
  falsehood 541 n.
  slang 560 n.
  be affected 850 vb.
cantabile
  musical 412 adj.
cantankerous
  quarrelling 709 adj.
  irascible 892 adj.
cantata
  vocal music 412 n.
canteen
  café 192 n.
  box 194 n.

canter
  gait 265 n.
  ride 267 vb.
canticle
  hymn 981 n.
cantilever
  supporter 218 n.
canto
  subdivision 53 n.
  verse form 593 n.
canton
  district 184 n.
cantor
  choir 413 n.
canvas
  sail 275 n.
  picture 553 n.
canvass
  inquire 459 vb.
  argue 475 vb.
  advertise 528 vb.
  dissert 591 vb.
  vote 605 n., vb.
canvass for
  patronize 703 vb.
canyon
  valley 255 n.
cap
  crown 213 vb.
  headgear 228 n.
  stopper 264 n.
  retaliate 714 vb.
  climax 725 vb.
capability
  ability 160 n.
capable
  possible 469 adj.
  intelligent 498 adj.
capacious
  great 32 adj.
  spacious 183 adj.
capacity
  plenitude 54 n.
  inclusion 78 n.
  ability 160 n.
  room 183 n.
  size 195 n.
  intelligence 498 n.
  function 622 n.
caparison
  coverlet 226 n.
  dress 228 vb.
cape
  cloak 228 n.
caper
  potherb 301 n.
  leap 312 n., vb.

condiment 389 n.
  dance 837 vb.
capillary
  filament 208 n.
capital
  supreme 34 adj.
  summit 213 n.
  deadly 362 adj.
  important 638 adj.
  magistrature 733 n.
  funds 797 n.
  wealth 800 n.
capitalist
  master 741 n.
  rich man 800 n.
capitalize
  use 673 vb.
  profit by 137 vb.
capital levy
  taking 786 n.
  tax 809 n.
capital punishment
  capital punishment
    963 n.
capitulate
  submit 721 vb.
capitulation
  submission 721 n.
capon
  poultry 365 n.
caponize
  unman 161 vb.
caprice
  changeableness
    152 n.
  caprice 604 n.
capricious
  multiform 82 adj.
  transient 114 adj.
  light-minded
    456 adj.
  uncertain 474 adj.
  (*see* **caprice**)
capsicum
  condiment 389 n.
capsize
  invert 221 vb.
capstan
  lifter 310 n.
capsular
  capsular 194 adj.
capsule
  receptacle 194 n.
  medicine 658 n.
captain
  navigate 269 vb.
  mariner 270 n.

direct 689 vb.
  army officer 741 n.
  naval officer 741 n.
caption
  label 547 n.
  letterpress 587 n.
captious
  sophistical 477 adj.
  disapproving
    927 adj.
captivate
  subjugate 745 vb.
captive
  slave 742 n.
  imprisoned 747 adj.
  prisoner 750 n.
captivity
  servitude 745 n.
  detention 747 n.
captor
  possessor 776 n.
  taker 786 n.
capture
  overmaster 727 vb.
  trophy 729 n.
  subjugate 745 vb.
  take 786 vb.
car
  automobile 274 n.
carafe
  vessel 194 n.
caramel
  sweet 392 n.
carapace
  covering 226 n.
  armour 713 n.
carat
  weighment 322 n.
caravan
  procession 71 n.
  small house 192 n.
caravanserai
  inn 192 n.
caraway
  condiment 389 n.
carbuncle
  swelling 253 n.
  redness 431 n.
carcass
  corpse 363 n.
carcinoma
  carcinosis 651 n.
card
  unravel 62 vb.
  label 547 n.
  correspondence
    588 n.

cardboard
paper 631 n.
card game
card game 837 n.
cardigan
vest 228 n.
cardinal
red 431 adj.
important 638 adj.
ecclesiarch 986 n.
cardinal points
compass point
281 n.
card index
sorting 62 n.
cards on the table
disclosure 526 n.
care
carefulness 457 n.
mandate 751 n.
worry 825 n.
love 887 vb.
career
move fast 277 vb.
vocation 622 n.
conduct 688 n.
careerism
selfishness 932 n.
carefree
cheerful 833 adj.
careful
(see care)
careless
inattentive 456 adj.
negligent 458 adj.
indifferent 860 adj.
caress
endearment 889 n.
caress 889 vb.
caret
deficit 55 n.
punctuation 547 n.
caretaker
manager 690 n.
keeper 749 n.
consignee 754 n.
cargo
contents 193 n.
thing transferred
272 n.
merchandise 795 n.
caricature
imitate 20 vb.
misinterpret
521 vb.
misrepresent
552 vb.

laughing-stock
851 n.
satire 851 n.
calumny 926 n.
caries
decay 51 n.
carillon
campanology 412
n.
gong 414 n.
carnage
havoc 165 n.
slaughter 362 n.
carnal
sensual 944 adj.
lecherous 951 adj.
carnal knowledge
coition 45 n.
carnival
festivity 837 n.
pageant 875 n.
carol
vocal music 412 n.
sing 413 vb.
carouse
revel 837 vb.
be sociable 882 vb.
get drunk 949 vb.
carousel
pleasure-ground
837 n.
carp
table fish 365 n.
blame 924 vb.
car park
enclosure 235 n.
carper
detractor 926 n.
carpet
floor-cover 226 n.
reprove 924 vb.
carriage
transport 272 n.
gait 265 n.
carriage 274 n.
mien 445 n.
conduct 688 n.
carriageway
road 624 n.
carrier
supporter 218 n.
carrier 273 n.
courier 531 n.
infection 651 n.
carrion
decay 51 n.
corpse 363 n.

carrot
tuber 301 n.
incentive 612 n.
carry
reproduce itself
64 vb.
support 218 vb.
wear 228 vb.
carry 273 vb.
carry on
do 676 vb.
behave 688 vb.
manage 689 vb.
carry out
carry out 725 vb.
carry-over
remainder 44 n.
carry through
terminate 69 vb.
carry through
725 vb.
cart
carry 273 vb.
cart 274 n.
cartage
transport 272 n.
carte blanche
scope 744 n.
cartel
association 706 n.
corporation 708 n.
carter
driver 268 n.
carrier 273 n.
cartilage
toughness 329 n.
cartography
map 551 n.
carton
small box 194 n.
cartoon
representation
551 n.
satire 851 n.
cartoonist
artist 556 n.
humorist 839 n.
cartouche
script 586 n.
ammunition 723 n.
cartridge
ammunition 723 n.
cartwheel
overturning 221 n.
carve
cut 46 vb.
efform 243 vb.

groove 262 vb.
sculpt 554 vb.
apportion 783 vb.
carver
sharp edge 256 n.
sculptor 556 n.
carving
sculpture 554 n.
cascade
descend 309 vb.
waterfall 350 n.
case
state 7 n.
example 83 n.
case 194 n.
cover 226 vb.
enclosure 235 n.
topic 452 n.
sick person 651 n.
case-harden
toughen 329 vb.
case-hardened
obstinate 602 adj.
impenitent 940
adj.
case-history
record 548 n.
case in point
relevance 9 n.
case-law
legal trial 959 n.
casement
window 263 n.
cash
acquire 771 vb.
money 797 n.
cash book
account book
808 n.
cash box
treasury 799 n.
cashier
depose 752 vb.
treasurer 798 n.
casino
gaming-house
618 n.
cask
vat 194 n.
casket
small box 194 n.
casserole
cauldron 194 n.
dish 301 n.
cassock
tunic 228 n.
vestments 989 n.

cast
number 86 vb.
produce 164 vb.
doff 229 vb.
form 243 vb.
propel 287 vb.
excrement 302 n.
liquefy 337 vb.
heat 381 vb.
dim sight 440 n.
actor 594 n.
castaway
solitary 883 n.
(see derelict)
caste
breed 77 n.
nobility 868 n.
caster
small box 194 n.
wheel 250 n.
castigation
reprimand 924 n.
punishment 963
n.
cast-iron
hard 326 adj.
castle
fort 713 n.
chessman 837 n.
castles in Spain
fantasy 513 n.
aspiration 852 n.
cast lots
divine 511 vb.
gamble 618 vb.
cast-off
excretory 302 adj.
derelict 779 n.
castor oil
cathartic 658 n.
castrate
unman 161 vb.
sterilize 172 vb.
impair 655 vb.
casual
extrinsic 6 adj.
casual 159 adj.
negligent 458 adj.
unintentional
618 adj.
casualty
chance 159 n.
casualty station
hospital 658 n.
casuist
reasoner 475 n.
sophist 477 n.

casus belli
casus belli 709 n.
cat
vomit 300 vb.
cat 365 n.
hell-hag 904 n.
scourge 964 n.
cataclysm
revolution 149 n.
havoc 165 n.
catacomb
cemetery 364 n.
catalectic
short 204 adj.
catalepsy
insensibility 375 n.
catalogue
class 62 vb.
list 87 n., vb.
record 548 n.
catalyst
alterer 143 n.
cat and dog life
dissension 709 n.
cataplasm
surgical dressing
658 n.
catapult
propellant 287 n.
missile weapon
723 n.
cataract
waterfall 350 n.
dim sight 440 n.
catarrh
excretion 302 n.
catastrophe
ruin 165 n.
ill fortune 731 n.
catcall
shrill 407 vb.
catch
fastening 47 n.
rub 333 vb.
vocal music 412 n.
surprise 508 vb.
understand 516 vb.
trap 542 n.
ensnare 542 vb.
represent 551 vb.
hunt 619 vb.
stratagem 698 n.
hitch 702 n.
wrestling 716 n.
desired object
859 n.
favourite 890 n.

catch-all
receptacle 194 n.
catch at
be willing 597 vb.
catching
infectious 653 adj.
catch on
be wont 610 vb.
catchpenny
spurious 542 adj.
trivial 639 adj.
catch the eye
attract notice
455 vb.
catch up
outstrip 277 vb.
hasten 680 vb.
catchword
maxim 496 n.
indication 547 n.
catchy
melodious 410 adj.
catechism
creed 485 n.
orthodoxy 976 n.
catechist
teacher 537 n.
religious teacher
973 n.
catechize
interrogate 459 vb.
catechumen
learner 538 n.
beginner 538 n.
categorical
assertive 532 adj.
categorical
imperative
conscience 917 n.
categorization
arrangement 62 n.
category
classification 77 n.
cater
feed 301 vb.
provide 633 vb.
sell 793 vb.
caterer
caterer 633 n.
caterwaul
shrill 407 vb.
cry 408 vb.
ululate 409 vb.
catgut
viol 414 n.
cathartic
cathartic 658 n.

remedial 658 adj.
cathedral
church 990 n.
catholic
universal 79 adj.
orthodox 976 adj.
Catholicism
Catholicism 976 n.
catholicity
generality 79 n.
cat-o'-nine-tails
scourge 964 n.
cat's-paw
wave 350 n.
dupe 350 n.
tool 630 n.
auxiliary 707 n.
cattle
cattle 365 n.
cattle farm
stock farm 369 n.
cattleman
herdsman 369 n.
catty
malevolent 898
adj.
detracting 926 adj.
catwalk
aircraft 276 n.
bridge 624 n.
caucus
party 708 n.
caudle
potion 301 n.
caul
obstetrics 164 n.
cauldron
cauldron 194 n.
heater 383 n.
causal
causal 156 adj.
instrumental 628
adj.
causation
causation 156 n.
agency 173 n.
cause
cause 156 n., vb.
produce 164 vb.
influence 178 n.
predetermine
608 vb.
motive 612 n.
litigation 959 n.
causeless
causeless 159 adj.
designless 618 adj.

cause-list
legal trial 959 n.
caustic
burning 381 n.
pungent 388 adj.
disapproving 924
adj.
cauterize
burn 381 vb.
doctor 658 vb.
caution
slowness 278 n.
carefulness 457 n.
foresight 510 n.
irresolution 601 n.
warn 664 vb.
caution 858 n.
cautionary
cautionary 664 adj.
cautious
doubting 474 adj.
(see caution)
cavalcade
procession 71 n.
marching 267 n.
cavalier
rider 268 n.
disrespectful
921 adj.
cavalry
rider 268 n.
cavalry 722 n.
cave
dwelling 192 n.
receptacle 194 n.
cavity 255 n.
party 708 n.
caveat
warning 664 n.
cave in
descend 309 vb.
cavern
cavity 255 n.
cavernous
deep 211 adj.
caviar
condiment 389 n.
savouriness 390 n.
cavil
dissent 489 vb.
disapprove 924
vb.
cavity
cavity 255 n.
cavort
leap 312 vb.
dance 837 vb.

caw
ululate 409 vb.
cayenne
condiment 389 n.
cease
cease 145 vb.
be inactive 679 vb.
cease-fire
lull 145 n.
cede
relinquish 621 vb.
ceiling
height 209 n.
roof 226 n.
limit 236 n.
celebrate
proclaim 528 vb.
be cheerful 833 vb.
revel 837 vb.
celebrate 876 vb.
celebrated
known 490 adj.
renowned 866 adj.
celebration
(see celebrate)
celebrity
famousness 866 n.
person of repute
866 n.
celestial
celestial 321 adj.
paradisiac 971 adj.
celibacy
celibacy 895 n.
monasticism 985 n.
celibate
celibate 895 n.
virgin 950 n.
(see celibacy)
cell
electricity 160 n.
compartment 194 n.
enclosure 235 n.
cavity 255 n.
organism 358 n.
party, society
708 n.
lock-up 748 n.
monastery 986 n.
cellar
cellar 194 n.
sink 649 n.
cellaret
cabinet 194 n.
cellist
instrumentalist
413 n.

cello
viol 414 n.
cellular
cellular 194 adj.
cement
bond 47 n.
adhesive 47 n.
agglutinate 48 vb.
solid body 324 n.
building material
631 n.
cemented
firm-set 45 adj.
cemetery
cemetery 364 n.
cenotaph
tomb 364 n.
censer
cauldron 194 n.
scent 396 n.
censor
inquisitor 543 n.
obliterate 550 vb.
disapprove 924
vb.
censorious
disapproving
924 adj.
censurable
discreditable
867 adj.
blameworthy
924 adj.
censure
censure 924 n.
reprimand 924 n.
census
statistics 86 n.
centaur
rara avis 84 n.
rider 268 n.
centenary
hundred 99 n.
anniversary 141 n.
centesimal
multifid 100 adj.
central
median 30 adj.
fundamental
156 adj.
central 225 adj.
inland 344 adj.
important 638 adj.
centrality
centrality 225 n.
centralization
uniformity 16 n.

centrality 225 n.
centre
focus 76 vb.
arena 224 n.
centre 225 n.
converge 293 vb.
centre-line
centrality 225 n.
centre on
converge 293 vb.
centrifugal
unassembled 75 adj.
repellant 292 adj.
divergent 294 adj.
avoiding 620 adj.
centring
location 187 n.
centripetal
convergent 293 adj.
centurion
soldier 722 n.
century
hundred 99 n.
period 110 n.
diuturnity 113 n.
ceramics
pottery 381 n.
sculpture 554 n.
cerate
unguent 357 n.
cereal
cereal 301 n.
corn 366 n.
cerebral
mental 447 adj.
cerebration
thought 449 n.
cerement(s)
grave clothes
364 n.
ceremonial
formality 875 n.
formal 875 adj.
ceremonialist
ritualist 988 n.
ceremonious
formal 875 adj.
respectful 920 adj.
ceremony
formality 875 n.
celebration 876 n.
certain
certain 473 adj.
demonstrated
478 adj.
believing 485 adj.
true 494 adj.

certain, a
one 88 adj.
certainty
certainty 473 n.
positiveness 473 n.
expectation 507 n.
certifiable
insane 503 adj.
certificate
record 548 n.
certification
assent 488 n.
certify
make certain
  473 vb.
inform 524 vb.
affirm 532 vb.
certitude
certainty 473 n.
cess
tax 809 n.
cessation
end 69 n.
cessation 145 n.
quiescence 266 n.
cession
relinquishment
  621 n.
cesspool
sink 649 n.
chad
picture 553 n.
chafe
rub 333 vb.
hurt 827 vb.
be angry 891 vb.
chaff
leavings 41 n.
corn 366 n.
rubbish 641 n.
be witty 839 vb.
ridicule 851 n., vb.
chaffer
bargain 791 vb.
chafing dish
heater 383 n.
chagrin
discontent 829 n.
chain
cable 47 n.
bond 47 n.
series 71 n.
long measure 203
  n.
fetter 748 n.
chain-gang
prisoner 750 n.

chain-reaction
continuity 71 n.
chair
seat 218 n.
rostrum 539 n.
director 690 n.
honour 866 vb.
chairman
director 690 n.
chairmanship
directorship 689 n.
chalcolithic
secular 110 adj.
chalet
house 192 n.
chalice
cup 194 n.
church utensil 990 n.
chalk
mark 547 vb.
chalk up
register 548 vb.
challenge
question 459 n.
dissent 489 n., vb.
negation 533 n.
defiance 711 n.
threat 900 vb.
challenger
opponent 705 n.
contender 716 n.
chamber
chamber 194 n.
chamberlain
retainer 742 n.
chambermaid
domestic 742 n.
chamber-pot
vessel 194 n.
chameleon
changeable thing
  152 n.
variegation 437 n.
chamfer
groove 262 vb.
champagne
wine 301 n.
champion
supreme 34 adj.
exceller 644 n.
proficient 696 n.
patron 707 n.
defender 713 n.
victor 727 n.
vindicator 927 n.
chance
opportunity 137 n.

happen 154 vb.
chance 159 n.
possibility 469 n.
gambling 618 n.
chance it
gamble 618 vb.
chancellor
director 690 n.
chancre
venereal disease
  651 n.
chancy
casual 159 adj.
uncertain 474 adj.
speculative 618 adj.
dangerous 661 adj.
chandelier
lamp 420 n.
chandler
merchant 794 n.
change
difference 15 n.
change 143 n.
  147 n.
vary 152 vb.
money 797 n.
changeable
changeable 143 adj.
changeful 152 adj.
change course
deviate 286 vb.
change front
tergiversate 603 vb.
changeful
(*see* changeable)
change into
become 1 vb.
(*see* convert)
changeless
unchangeable
  153 adj.
changeling
child 132 n.
substitute 150 n.
elf 970 n.
change of mind
tergiversation
  603 n.
change round
modify 143 vb.
change sides
apostatize 603 vb.
channel
groove 262 vb.
passage 305 n.
gulf 345 n.
conduit 351 n.

informant 524 n.
access, path 624 n.
direct 689 vb.
chant
vocal music 412 n.
sing 413 vb.
hymn 981 n.
chantry
church 990 n.
chanty
vocal music 412 n.
chaos
non-uniformity
  17 n.
confusion 61 n.
anarchy 734 n.
chaotic
lawless 954 adj.
(*see* chaos)
chap
person 371 n.
chapel
sect 978 n.
church 990 n.
chaperon
accompany 89 vb.
look after 457 vb.
keeper 749 n.
chaperonage
carefulness 457 n.
chaplain
pastor 986 n.
chaplet
loop 250 n.
chapter
subdivision 53 n.
topic 452 n.
synod 985 n.
chapter and verse
evidence 466 n.
char
burn 381 vb.
embrown 430 vb.
cleaner 648 n.
servant 742 n.
character
character 5 n.
composition 56 n.
sort 77 n.
credential 466 n.
letter 558 n.
acting 594 n.
affections 817 n.
repute 866 n.
probity 929 n.
characteristic
intrinsic 5 adj.

characteristic 5 adj.
speciality 80 n.
special 80 adj.
characterization
representation
551 n.
description 590 n.
characterless
amorphous 244 adj.
disreputable
867 adj.
charade
enigma 530 n.
gesture 547 n.
charcoal
ash 381 n.
fuel 385 n.
charge
fill 54 vb.
empower 160 vb.
load 193 vb.
move fast 277 vb.
heraldry 547 n.
call 547 n.
job 622 n.
management
689 n.
attack 712 n.
ammunition 723 n.
dependant 742 n.
mandate 751 n.
debt 803 n.
price 709 vb.
accusation 928 n.
chargeable
owed 803 adj.
priced 809 adj.
accusable 928 adj.
chargé d'affaires
envoy 754 n.
charge of, take
undertake 672 vb.
charge on, — to, —
with
attribute 158 vb.
charger
plate 194 n.
war-horse 273 n.
chariot
carriage 274 n.
charioteer
driver 268 n.
charitable
liberal 813 adj.
(*see* charity)
charity
giving, gift 781 n.

liberality 813 n.
love 887 n.
benevolence 897 n.
disinterestedness
931 n.
charlatan
sciolist 493 n.
affector 850 n.
charlatanism
sciolism 491 n.
pretension 850 n.
charm
preserver 666 n.
pleasurableness
826 n.
please 826 vb.
beauty 841 n.
lovableness 887 n.
spell 983 n.
talisman 983 n.
bewitch 983 vb.
charmed life
safety 660 n.
charmer
a beauty 841 n.
charms
beauty 841 n.
charnel house
interment 364 n.
chart
itinerary 267 n.
sailing aid 269 n.
map 551 n.
represent 551 vb.
charter
title-deed 767 n.
hire 785 vb.
charwoman
(*see* char)
Charybdis
vortex 315 n.
chase
grassland 348 n.
wood 366 n.
objective 617 n.
chase 619 n.
pursue 619 vb.
chasm
depth 211 n.
cavity 255 n.
chassis
supporter 218 n.
frame 218 n.
chaste
plain 573 adj.
elegant 575 adj.
tasteful 846 adj.

modest 874 adj.
virtuous 933 adj.
pure 950 adj.
chasten
moderate 177 vb.
deject 834 vb.
punish 963 vb.
chastise
punish 963 vb.
chastity (*see* chaste)
chat
rumour 529 n.
converse 584 vb.
chattel
slave 742 n.
property 777 n.
chatter
ululate 409 vb.
chatter 581 n.
chatterbox
chatterer 581 n.
chatty
informative 524
adj.
loquacious 581 adj.
chauffeur
driver 268 n.
chauvinism
prejudice 481 n.
bellicosity 718 n.
chauvinist
militarist 722 n.
(*see* chauvinism)
cheap
cheap 812 adj.
vulgar 847 adj.
cheapen
discount 812 vb.
vulgarize 847 vb.
cheapjack
pedlar 794 n.
cheapness
cheapness 812 n.
(*see* cheap)
cheat
deceive 542 vb.
defraud 788 vb.
knave 938 n.
check
delay 136 n.
halt 145 vb.
counteraction
182 n.
retard 278 vb.
variegate 437 vb.
be careful 457 vb.
comparison 462 n.

make certain
473 vb.
obstacle 702 n.
defeat 728 n.
restraint 747 n.
pattern 844 n.
checkerboard
chequer 437 n.
arena 724 n.
checkers
board game 837 n.
checkmate
be obstructive
702 vb.
victory 727 n.
cheek
laterality 239 n.
sauciness 878 n.
cheeky
impertinent 878 adj.
cheep
ululate 409 vb.
discontent 829 n.
cheer
food 301 n.
vociferate 408 vb.
content 828 vb.
cheer 833 vb.
rejoice 835 vb.
give courage
855 vb.
applaud 923 vb.
cheerful
cheerful 833 adj.
cheerless
cheerless 834 adj.
dejected 834 adj.
cheer up
be cheerful 833 vb.
cheese
milk product 301 n.
cheese-paring
economy 814 n.
parsimony 816 n.
chef
cookery 301 n.
chef d'œuvre
masterpiece 694 n.
chemise
bodywear 228 n.
chemist
druggist 658 n.
chemistry
conversion 147 n.
cheque
paper money 797
n.

chequer
variegate 437 vb.
cherish
look after 457 vb.
preserve 666 vb.
pet 889 vb.
cheroot
tobacco 388 n.
cherry
fruit 301 n.
cherub
child 132 n.
angel 968 n.
chess
board game 837 n.
chess-board
arena 724 n.
chessman
chessman 837 n.
chest
box 194 n.
bosom 253 n.
store 632 n.
Chesterfield
seat 218 n.
chestnut
horse 273 n.
fruit 301 n.
brown 430 adj.
witticism 839 n.
chest of drawers
cabinet 194 n.
chevron
heraldry 547 n.
badge of rank 743 n.
chew
chew 301 vb.
chew over
meditate 449 vb.
chiaroscuro
grey 429 n.
light contrast 417 n.
painting 553 n.
chiasma, chiasmus
inversion 221 n.
chic
elegant 575 adj.
beauty 841 n.
fashionable 848 adj.
chicanery, chicane
trickery 542 n.
cunning 698 n.
chick
youngling 132 n.
chicken
youngling 132 n.

poultry 365 n.
coward 856 n.
chicken-feed
small quantity 33 n.
trifle 639 n.
chicken run
stock farm 369 n.
chicory
potherb 301 n.
chide
reprove 924 vb.
chief
superior 34 n.
supreme 34 adj.
director 690 n.
potentate 741 n.
chieftain
potentate 741 n.
chieftainship
magistrature 733 n.
chiffon
textile 222 n.
finery 844 n.
chiffonier
cabinet 194 n.
chignon
hair-dressing 843 n.
chilblain
ulcer 651 n.
child
child 132 n.
posterity 170 n.
innocent 935 n.
childbed, childbirth
obstetrics 164 n.
childhood
youth 130 n.
childish
young 130 adj.
infantine 132 adj.
foolish 499 adj.
childless
unproductive 172 adj.
childlike
infantine 132 adj.
artless 699 adj.
child of nature
ingenue 699 n.
chill
coldness 380 n.
refrigerate 382 vb.
chilly
cold 380 adj.
a-cold 380 adj.
chime
resonance 404 n.

tune 412 n.
campanology 412 n.
chime in (with)
accord 24 vb.
assent 488 vb.
chimera
insubstantial thing 4 n.
fantasy 513 n.
chimerical
(*see* chimera)
chimes
gong 414 n.
chimney
chimney 263 n.
chimney-sweep
cleaner 648 n.
chimpanzee
monkey 365 n.
chin
face 237 n.
projection 254 n.
china
brittleness 330 n.
pottery 381 n.
chinaware
pottery 381 n.
chink
gap 201 n.
vulnerability 661 n.
chintz
textile 222 n.
chip
cut 46 vb.
piece 53 n.
pulverize 332 vb.
chip on one's shoulder, have a
be discontented 829 vb.
chiromancy
occultism 984 n.
chiropodist
doctor 658 n.
beautician 843 n.
chiropody
therapy 658 n.
beautification 843 n.
chiropractor
doctor 658 n.
chirp
ululate 409 vb.
sing 413 vb.
chirpy
cheerful 833 adj.
chirrup (*see* chirp)

chisel
sharp edge 256 n.
sculpt 554 vb.
chiseller
trickster 545 n.
knave 938 n.
chit
youngster 132 n.
chit-chat
interlocution 584 n.
chitterlings
insides 224 n.
meat 301 n.
chivalrous
courageous 855 adj.
courteous 884 adj.
honourable 929 adj.
chivalry
rider 268 n.
cavalry 722 n.
aristocracy 868 n.
courtesy 884 n.
chive
vegetable 301 n.
chivvy
torment 827 vb.
chlorinate
sanitate 652 vb.
chloroform
render insensible 375 vb.
chock
supporter 218 n.
chocolate
soft drink 301 n.
sweet 392 n.
brownness 430 n.
choice
choice 605 n.
excellent 644 adj.
tasteful 846 adj.
choiceless
choiceless 606 adj.
choir
accord 24 vb.
choir 413 n.
choke
close 264 vb.
stopper 264 n.
kill 362 vb.
extinguish 382 vb.
rasp 407 vb.
choke off
dissuade 613 vb.
choleric
irascible 892 adj.

choose
will 595 vb.
choose 605 vb.
choosy
fastidious 862 adj.
chop
cut 46 vb.
piece 53 n.
shorten 204 vb.
meat 301 n.
trade 791 vb.
chop and change
vary 152 vb.
chopper
sharp edge 256 n.
axe 723 n.
choppiness
roughness 259 n.
wave 350 n.
choppy
rough 259 adj.
chops
laterality 239 n.
choral
musical 412 adj.
chorale
vocal music 412 n.
chord
musical note 410 n.
chords, vocal
voice 577 n.
chore
job 622 n.
labour 682 n.
choreography
composition 56 n.
dancing 837 n.
chorister
choir 413 n.
chorus
periodicity 141 n.
vociferate 402 vb.
choir 413 n.
sing 413 vb.
consensus 488 n.
actor 594 n.
chorus girl
actor 594 n.
chosen few
élite 644 n.
chosen race
particularism 80 n.
chrestomathy
textbook 589 n.
anthology 592 n.
Christ
God the Son 965 n.

christen
auspicate 68 vb.
perform ritual
988 vb.
Christendom
the Church 976 n.
christening
nomenclature
561 n.
Christianity
religious faith 973 n.
chromatic
harmonic 410 adj.
coloured 425 adj.
chromatics
chromatics 425 n.
chromosome
organism 358 n.
chromosphere
sun 321 n.
chronic
lasting 113 adj.
sick person 651 n.
sick 651 adj.
chronicle
record 548 n., vb.
narrative 590 n.
chronicler
chronologist 117 n.
chronicler 549 n.
chronogram
chronology 117 n.
chronological
chronological
117 adj.
chronology
date 108 n.
chronology 117 n.
chronometer
timekeeper 117 n.
sailing aid 269 n.
chrysalis
youngling 132 n.
source 156 n.
nest 192 n.
wrapping 226 n.
chubby
fleshy 195 adj.
chuck
propel 287 vb.
chucker-out
ejector 300 n.
chuckle
ululate 409 vb.
laughter 835 n.
chug
move slowly 278 vb.

chum
colleague 707 n.
chum 880 n.
chummery
quarters 192 n.
chummy
friendly 880 adj.
chump
dunce 501 n.
chunk
piece 53 n.
chunky
fleshy 195 adj.
church
the Church 976 n.
church 990 n.
churchdom
churchdom 985 n.
church-goer
worshipper 981 n.
churchiness
pietism 979 n.
churchman
cleric 986 n.
churchmanship
piety 979 n.
churchwarden
tobacco 388 n.
church officer
986 n.
churchyard
cemetery 364 n.
church exterior
990 n.
churlish
ungracious 885 adj.
churlishness
sullenness 893 n.
churn
rotator 315 n.
rotate 315 vb.
churn out
produce 164 vb.
chute
outlet 298 n.
waterfall 350 n.
chutney
condiment 389 n.
cicerone
guide 520 n.
cider
liquor 301 n.
ci-devant
former 125 adj.
resigning 753 adj.
cigar, cigarette
tobacco 388 n.

cilia
hair 259 n.
cilium
filament 208 n.
cinch
tie 45 vb.
girdle 47 n.
certainty 473 n.
cincture
belt 228 n.
cinder(s)
ash 381 n.
dirt 649 n.
Cinderella
nonentity 639 n.
object of scorn
867 n.
cinema
cinema 445 n.
photography 551 n.
theatre 594 n.
cinematograph
cinema 445 n.
cinematographer
photography 551 n.
cinerary
funereal 364 adj.
grey 429 adj.
cinnamon
condiment 389 n.
brown 430 adj.
cipher
number 85 n.
do sums 86 vb.
zero 103 n.
enigma 530 n.
symbology 547 n.
initials 558 n.
nonentity 639 n.
cipherer
interpreter 520 n.
circle
family 11 n.
group 74 n.
circle 250 n.
circuit 626 n.
circuit
whole 52 n.
electricity 160 n.
outline 233 n.
circle 250 n.
circuition 314 n.
circuit 626 n., vb.
circuitous
deviating 282 adj.
circuitous 314 adj.
roundabout 626 adj.

CIR

circular
  uniform 16 adj.
  continuous 71 adj.
  round 250 adj.
  publication 528 n.
  correspondence
    588 n.
  decree 737 n.
circularity
  continuity 71 n.
  circularity 250 n.
circularize
  publish 528 vb.
circular reasoning
  sophism 477 n.
circulate
  disperse 75 vb.
  circle 314 vb.
  be published
    528 vb.
  mint 797 vb.
circulation
  blood 335 n.
  (*see* circulate)
circumambient
  circumjacent
    230 adj.
circumambulate
  circle 314 vb.
circumambulation
  circuition 314 n.
circumcise
  cut 46 vb.
circumcision
  scission 46 n.
  rite 988 n.
circumference
  circumjacence
    230 n.
  outline 233 n.
  circuit 626 n.
circumjacence
  exteriority 223 n.
  circumjacence
    230 n.
circumlocution
  pleonasm 570 n.
circumlocutory
  prolix 570 adj.
  roundabout 626 adj.
circumnavigate
  navigate 269 vb.
  circle 314 vb.
circumscribe
  circumscribe
    232 vb.
  restrain 747 vb.

CIT

circumspection
  carefulness 457 n.
  caution 858 n.
circumstance
  circumstance 8 n.
  concomitant 89 n.
circumstantial
  circumstantial
    8 adj.
  complete 54 adj.
  diffuse 570 adj.
  descriptive 590 adj.
circumstantiate
  corroborate 466 vb.
circumvallation
  fortification 713 n.
  defences 713 n.
circumvent
  deceive 542 vb.
circumvolution
  rotation 315 n.
circus
  band 74 n.
  zoo 369 n.
  arena 724 n.
  pleasure-ground
    837 n.
cist
  box 194 n.
  tomb 364 n.
cistern
  vat 194 n.
  storage 632 n.
citadel
  refuge 662 n.
  fort 713 n.
citation
  referral 9 n.
  repetition 106 n.
  decoration 729 n.
cite
  exemplify 83 vb.
  repeat 106 vb.
citizen
  native 191 n.
  subject 742 n.
citizenry
  habitancy 191 n.
  social group 371 n.
  commonalty 869 n.
citizenship
  subjection 745 n.
city
  abode 192 n.
  housing 192 n.
city state
  polity 733 n.

CLA

civic
  national 371 adj.
civic centre
  focus 76 n.
civil
  national 371 adj.
  well-bred 848 adj.
  courteous 884 adj.
civil code
  law 953 n.
civilian
  peaceful 717 adj.
  jurist 958 n.
  layman 987 n.
civility
  courtesy 884 n.
civilization
  culture 490 n.
  civilization 654 n.
civilize
  make better 654 vb.
civilized
  well-bred 848 adj.
clack
  mean nothing
    515 vb.
  chatter 581 n.
claim
  territory 184 n.
  affirm 532 vb.
  plead 614 vb.
  require 627 vb.
  demand 737 n., vb.
  possess 773 vb.
  right 913 n.
  claim 915 vb.
claimant
  petitioner 763 n.
  dueness 915 n.
  litigant 959 n.
clairvoyance
  intuition 476 n.
  foresight 510 n.
  divination 511 n.
  psychics 984 n.
clairvoyant
  oracle 511 n.
  (*see* clairvoyance)
clam
  taciturnity 582 n.
clamant
  loud 400 adj.
  crying 408 adj.
clamber
  climb 308 vb.
clammy
  viscid 354 adj.

CLA

clamorous
  (*see* clamour)
clamour
  cry 408 n.
  vociferate 408 vb.
clamp
  affix 45 vb.
  fastening 47 n.
  nippers 778 n.
clan
  group 74 n.
  breed 77 n.
  genealogy 169 n.
  community 708 n.
clandestine
  stealthy 525 adj.
  concealed 525 adj.
clang
  be loud 400 vb.
  resonance 404 n.
clanger
  mistake 495 n.
clannish
  sectional 708 adj.
  sectarian 978 adj.
clannishness
  cooperation 706 n.
  (*see* clannish)
clansman
  kinsman 11 n.
clap
  strike 279 vb.
  venereal disease
    651 n.
  applause 923 n.
claptrap
  empty talk 515 n.
claque
  playgoer 594 n.
  flattery 925 n.
clarification
  demonstration
    478 n.
  (*see* clarify)
clarify
  eliminate 44 vb.
  interpret 520 vb.
  purify 648 vb.
clarinet
  flute 414 n.
clarion call
  loudness 400 n.
clarity
  perspicuity 567 n.
  elegance 575 n.
clash
  contrariety 14 n.

disagreement 25 n.
collide 279 vb.
discord 411 vb.
quarrel 709 n., vb.
battle 718 n.
clasp
　fastening 47 n.
　cohere 48 vb.
　caress 889 vb.
class
　class 62 vb.
　group 74 n.
　classification 77 n.
　contemporary
　　123 n.
　study 536 n.
class-conscious
　sectional 708 adj.
class consciousness
　particularism 80 n.
　pride 871 n.
classes, the
　social group 371 n.
classic
　elegant 575 adj.
　excellent 644 adj.
classifiability
　relation 9 n.
classification
　relation 9 n.
　classification 77 n.
　identification 547 n.
classify
　class 62 vb.
classmate
　chum 880 n.
classroom
　classroom 539 n.
class war
　prejudice 481 n.
classy
　fashionable 848
　　adj.
　genteel 868 adj.
clatter
　loudness 400 n.
clause
　subdivision 53 n.
　phrase 563 n.
　conditions 766 n.
claustral
　sealed off 264 adj.
claw
　rend 46 vb.
　foot 214 n.
　wound 655 vb.
　nippers 778 n.

clay
　softness 327 n.
　soil 344 n.
clean
　make bright
　　417 vb.
　clean 648 adj., vb.
　sanitate 652 vb.
　pure 950 adj.
cleaner
　cleaner 648 n.
clean hands
　probity 929 n.
　innocence 935 n.
cleanliness
　cleanness 648 n.
　hygiene 652 n.
cleanse
　purify 648 vb.
　sanitate 652 vb.
cleanser
　cleanser 648 n.
clean slate
　obliteration 550 n.
clean up
　purify 648 vb.
clear
　unmixed 44 adj.
　displace 188 vb.
　leap 312 vb.
　undimmed 417 adj.
　transparent 422 adj.
　well-seen 443 adj.
　intelligible 516 adj.
　perspicuous
　　567 adj.
　disencumber 701 vb.
　permit 756 vb.
　acquit 960 vb.
clearance
　room 183 n.
　interval 201 n.
　voidance 300 n.
　cacation 302 n.
　permission 756 n.
　acquittal 960 n.
clear-cut
　well-seen 443 adj.
　(*see* clear)
clear-headed
　intelligent 498 adj.
　sober 948 adj.
clearing
　open space 263 n.
clearness
　transparency 422 n.
　(*see* clear)

clear out
　decamp 296 vb.
clear-sighted
　intelligent 498 adj.
cleat
　fastening 47 n.
cleavage
　scission 46 n.
　dissension 709 n.
cleave
　cut, sunder 46 vb.
cleaver
　sharp edge 256 n.
cleave to
　cohere 48 vb.
clef
　notation 410 n.
cleft
　disjunct 46 adj.
　gap 201 n.
　spaced 201 adj.
cleft stick
　dubiety 474 n.
clemency
　lenity 736 n.
　mercy 905 n.
clench
　retain 778 vb.
clergy
　clergy 986 n.
cleric
　cleric 986 n.
clerical
　ecclesiastical
　　985 adj.
　clerical 986 adj.
clerk
　scholar 492 n.
　intellectual 492 n.
　recorder 549 n.
　penman 586 n.
clerkly
　instructed 490 adj.
clever
　intelligent 498 adj.
cliché
　unmeaningness
　　515 n.
　neology 560 n.
　phrase 563 n.
cliché-ridden
　repeated 106 adj.
　feeble 572 adj.
click
　speech sound 398 n.
　sound dead 405 vb.
　understand 516 vb.

client
　follower 284 n.
　dependant 742 n.
　purchaser 792 n.
clientèle
　dependant 742 n.
　purchaser 792 n.
clientship
　subjection 745 n.
cliff
　high land 209 n.
　rock 244 n.
climate
　influence 178 n.
　region 184 n.
　weather 340 n.
climatology
　weather 340 n.
climax
　degree 27 n.
　serial place 73 n.
　summit 213 n.
　crown 213 vb.
　climax 725 vb.
　excitation 821 n.
climb
　ascent 308 n.
　climb 308 vb.
climb-down
　humiliation 872 n.
clime
　region 184 n.
　land 344 n.
clinal
　oblique 220 adj.
clinch
　tie 45 vb.
　ligature 47 n.
　pugilism 716 n.
　carry through
　　725 vb.
　retention 778 n.
clincher
　confutation 479 n.
cling
　cohere 48 vb.
　caress 889 vb.
cling to
　be near 200 vb.
　retain 778 vb.
clinic
　hospital 658 n.
clinician
　doctor 658 n.
clink
　faintness 401 n.
　gaol 748 n.

clinker
ash 381 n.
clip
cut 46 vb.
fastening 47 n.
make smaller
198 vb.
shorten 204 vb.
hair-dressing 843 n.
clipper
sailing-ship 275 n.
speeder 277 n.
clippers
sharp edge 256 n.
clip the wings
disable 161 vb.
hinder 702 vb.
clique
party 708 n.
cliquish, cliquey
biased 481 adj.
sectional 708 adj.
cliquism
prejudice 481 n.
cloak
cloak 228 n.
screen 421 n.
cloak-and-dagger
stealthy 525 adj.
cloakroom
chamber 194 n.
latrine 649 n.
clock
timekeeper 117 n.
clock in
begin 68 vb.
arrive 295 vb.
clock out
end 69 vb.
clockwork
complexity 61 n.
accuracy 494 n.
machine 630 n.
clod
soil 344 n.
countryman 869 n.
clog
footwear 228 n.
encumbrance 702 n.
fetter 748 n.
cloister
enclose 235 vb.
seclusion 883 n.
close
similar 18 adj.
join 45 vb.
cohesive 48 adj.

end 69 n., vb.
cease 145 vb.
near 200 adj.
narrow 206 adj.
close 264 vb.
approach 289 vb.
dense 324 adj.
warm 379 adj.
taciturn 582 adj.
parsimonious
816 adj.
closed door
exclusion 57 n.
closed mind
narrow mind 481 n.
closed shop
exclusion 57 n.
restriction 747 n.
close-fisted
parsimonious
816 adj.
close grips
duel 716 n.
close in
circumscribe 232 vb.
closeness
(*see close*)
close quarters
short distance
200 n.
close season
period 110 n.
close shave
danger 661 n.
escape 667 n.
closet
chamber 194 n.
latrine 649 n.
close-up
short distance
200 n.
photography 551 n.
close with
strike at 712 vb.
consent 758 vb.
closure
stop 145 n.
closure 264 n.
clot
be dense 324 vb.
solid body 324 n.
dunce 501 n.
blood pressure
651 n.
cloth
textile 222 n.
clergy 986 n.

clothe
dress 228 vb.
clothes
clothing 228 n.
clothier
clothier 228 n.
clothing
clothing 228 n.
clotted
semiliquid 354 adj.
cloud
cloud 355 n.
opacity 423 n.
variegate 437 vb.
cloud-burst
rain 350 n.
cloudless
dry 342 adj.
undimmed 417 adj.
palmy 730 adj.
cloudy
cloudy 355 adj.
dim 419 adj.
semitransparent
424 adj.
imperspicuous
568 adj.
clout
strike 279 vb.
repair 656 n., vb.
spank 963 vb.
clove
potherb 301 n.
condiment 389 n.
cloven
(*see cleft*)
cloven hoof
wickedness 934 n.
Mephisto 969 n.
clover
grass 366 n.
euphoria 376 n.
clown
fool 501 n.
entertainer 594 n.
bungler 697 n.
humorist 839 n.
laughing-stock
851 n.
countryman 869 n.
clownish
clumsy 695 adj.
ill-bred 847 adj.
ridiculous 849 adj.
cloy
render insensible
375 vb.

sate 863 vb.
club
focus 76 n.
strike 279 vb.
association 706 n.
party 708 n.
club 723 n.
scourge 964 n.
clubbable
corporate 708 adj.
sociable 882 adj.
clubman
social person 882
n.
club together
cooperate 706 vb.
cluck
ululate 409 vb.
clue
bunch 74 n.
evidence 466 n.
interpretation
520 n.
indication 547 n.
clueless
ignorant 491 adj.
clump
bunch 74 n.
strike 279 vb.
wood 366 n.
clumsy
inelegant 576 adj.
clumsy 695 adj.
graceless 842 adj.
ill-bred 847 adj.
cluster
group 74 n.
congregate 74 vb.
clutch
group 74 n.
youngling 132 n.
clutches
retention 778 n.
coach
train, carriage
274 n.
train, educate
534 vb.
trainer, teacher
537 n.
coachman
driver 268 n.
coadjutor
auxiliary 707 n.
co-agency
concurrence 181 n.
cooperation 706 n.

COA

coagulate
cohere 48 vb.
be dense 324 vb.
coagulum
solid body 324 n.
coal
coal, lighter 385 n.
torch 420 n.
coalesce
be identical 13 vb.
coalescence
junction 45 n.
coal-field
coal 385 n.
coalition
political party 708 n.
society 708 n.
coaming
edge 234 n.
coarse
rough 259 adj.
textural 331 adj.
unsavoury 391 adj.
inelegant 576 adj.
graceless 842 adj.
impure 951 adj.
coarsen
impair 655 vb.
vulgarize 847 vb.
coarseness
moral insensibility 820 n.
plainness 573 n.
coast
laterality 239 n.
go smoothly 258 vb.
voyage 269 vb.
shore 344 n.
coastal
marginal 234 adj.
coastal 344 adj.
coaster
merchant ship 275 n.
coat
layer 207 n.
skin, wrapping 226 n.
coat 226 vb.
tunic, overcoat 228 n.
preserve 666 vb.
coating
layer 207 n.
facing 226 n.
lining 227 n.

COC

coat of arms
heraldry 547 n.
coax
tempt 612 vb.
pet 889 vb.
flatter 925 vb.
cob
saddle-horse 273 n.
waterfowl 365 n.
cobble
paving 226 n.
cobbler
clothier 228 n.
mender 656 n.
cobblestone
paving 226 n.
cobra
reptile 365 n.
cobweb
weak thing 163 n.
filament 208 n.
network 222 n.
dirt 649 n.
cocaine
drug 658 n.
cock
poultry 365 n.
cockade
livery 547 n.
cock-a-hoop
jubilant 833 adj.
cock-and-bull story
fable 543 n.
cock a snook at
be insolent 878 vb.
cockerel
poultry 365 n.
cock-eyed
oblique 220 adj.
distorted 246 adj.
cock fight
duel 716 n.
cockney
native 191 n.
dialectical 560 adj.
cock of the walk
master 741 n.
cockpit
chamber 914 n.
aircraft 276 n.
arena 724 n.
cock-shy
laughing-stock 851 n.
cocksure
believing 485 adj.

COF

cocktail
a mixture 43 n.
potion 301 n.
cocky
prideful 871 adj.
vain 873 adj.
impertinent 878 adj.
cocoon
youngling 132 n.
nest 192 n.
receptacle 194 n.
wrapping 226 n.
coda
sequel 67 n.
musical piece 412 n.
coddle
cook 301 vb.
pet 889 vb.
code
rule 81 n.
enigma 530 n.
symbology 547 n.
writing 586 n.
code of honour
probity 929 n.
codicil
adjunct 40 n.
title-deed 767 n.
codification
law 953 n.
legislation 953 n.
codify
class 62 vb.
coefficient
numerical element 85 n.
concomitant 89 n.
coerce
dominate 733 vb.
compel 740 vb.
coercion
brute force 735 n.
coeval
contemporary 123 n.
synchronous 123 adj.
coexistence
existence 1 n.
accompaniment 89 n.
synchronism 123 n.
concord 710 n.
coextension
equality 28 n.
coffee house
café 192 n.

COI

coffer
box 194 n.
storage 632 n.
treasury 799 n.
coffin
interment 364 n.
cog
notch 260 n.
cogent
powerful 160 adj.
compelling 740 adj.
cogged
toothed 256 adj.
cogitate
think 449 vb.
cogitation, cogitative
(see cogitate)
cognate
relative 9 adj.
akin 11 adj.
similar 18 adj.
cognisance
(see cognizance)
cognition
knowledge 490 n.
cognitive
mental 447 adj.
cognizable
known 490 adj.
legal 953 adj.
cognizance
knowledge 490 n.
intellect 447 n.
cognomen
name 561 n.
cohabit
unite with 45 vb.
wed 894 vb.
cohere
cohere 48 vb.
be dense 324 vb.
coherence
junction 45 n.
coherence 48 n.
sanity 501 n.
coherent
(see coherence)
cohesion
coherence 48 n.
density 324 n.
cohesive
firm-set 45 adj.
cohesive 48 adj.
retentive 778 adj.
coiffure
wig 228 n.
hair-dressing 843 n.

coil
complexity 61 n.
twine 251 vb.
difficulty 700 n.

coin
efform 243 vb.
fake 541 vb.
mint 797 vb.

coinage
coinage 797 n.

coincide
be identical 13 vb.
accompany 89 vb.

coincidence
synchronism 123 n.
eventuality 154 n.
chance 159 n.
(*see* coincide)

coincidental
unintentional
618 adj.

coir
fibre 208 n.

coition, coitus
coition 45 n.
propagation 164 n.

coke
ash 381 n.
coal 385 n.

cold
wintry 129 adj.
coldness 380 n.
respiratory disease
651 n.
indifferent 860 adj.
unkind 898 adj.
pure 950 adj.

cold comfort
discontent 829 n.

cold feet
nervousness 854 n.

cold-shoulder
exclude 57 vb.
disregard 458 vb.
make unwelcome
833 vb.

cold storage
delay 136 n.
refrigerator 384 n.

cold water
moderator 177 n.
dissuasion 613 n.

collaborate
be willing 597 vb.
cooperate 706 vb.

collaboration
cooperation 706 n.

collaborator
tergiversator 603
n.
collaborator 707 n.

collapse
ruin 165 n.
descent 309 n.
illness 651 n.
dilapidation 655 n.
fatigue 684 n.
fail 728 vb.

collar
halter 47 n.
neckwear 228 n.
take 786 vb.

collate
compare 462 vb.

collateral
relative 9 adj.
akin 11 adj.
security 767 n.

collaterality
sonship 170 n.

colleague
colleague 707 n.

colleagueship
association 706 n.

collect
bring together
74 vb.
receive 782 vb.

collectanea
anthology 592 n.

collection
accumulation 74 n.
exhibit 522 n.
collection 632 n.
oblation 981 n.

collective
general 79 adj.
joint possession
775 n.

collectivism
joint possession
775 n.

collectivity
whole 52 n.

collectivization
assemblage 74 n.

collector
receiver 782 n.

collector's piece
exhibit 522 n.
exceller 644 n.
masterpiece 694 n.

college
academy 539 n.

collide
collide 279 vb.

collier
merchant ship
275 n.

colliery
excavation 255 n.

collision
collision 279 n.
convergence 293 n.
quarrel 709 n.

collision course
convergence 293 n.

collocate
place 187 vb.

collocutor
interlocutor 584 n.

collop
piece 53 n.

colloquial
dialectical 560 adj.

colloquialism
slang 560 n.

colloquy
interlocution 584 n.
conference 584 n.

collusion
cooperation 706 n.

collusive, collusory
false 541 adj.
deceiving 542 adj.

colon
insides 224 n.
punctuation 547 n.

colonial
settler 191 n.
subject 745 adj.

colonialism
governance 733 n.
subjection 745 n.

colonist
settler 191 n.
incomer 297 n.

colonize
place oneself
187 vb.
dwell 192 vb.
subjugate 745 vb.
appropriate 786 vb.

colony
crowd 74 n.
polity 733 n.
subject 742 n.

coloration
colour, hue 425 n.

coloratura
vocal music 412 n.

colossal
enormous 32 adj.
huge 195 adj.
tall 209 adj.

colossus
giant 195 n.

colour
tincture 43 n.
mix 43 vb.
sort 77 n.
influence 187 vb.
light 417 n.
colour 425 n., vb.
probability 471 n.
paint 553 vb.

colourable
plausible 471 adj.
ostensible 614 adj.

colour-bar
exclusion 57 n.

colour-blind
dim-sighted 440 adj.
indiscriminating
464 adj.

coloured
coloured 425 adj.
blackish 428 adj.

colourful
luminous 417 adj.
florid 425 adj.
variegated 437 adj.
showy 875 adj.

colouring
hue 425 n.
painting 553 n.

colouring matter
pigment 425 n.

colourless
colourless 426 adj.
mediocre 732 adj.
dull 840 adj.

colours
flag 547 n.

colour up
redden 431 vb.

colt
youngling 132 n.
horse 273 n.
beginner 538 n.

column
pillar 218 n.
cylinder 252 n.
monument 548 n.
formation 722 n.

columnar
supporting 218 adj.
rotund 252 adj.

columnist
chronicler 549 n.
author 589 n.
coma
insensibility 375 n.
sleep 679 n.
comatose
(see coma*)*
comb
tooth 256 n.
clean 648 vb.
combat
contention, fight
716 n.
give battle 718 vb.
combatant
combatant 722 n.
combative
warlike 718 adj.
combination
coherence 48 n.
combination 50 n.
composition 56 n.
assemblage 74 n.
association 706 n.
comb out
unravel 62 vb.
combustible
fuel 385 n.
combustible
385 adj.
combustion
burning 381 n.
come
arrive 295 vb.
come about
happen 154 vb.
be inexpedient
643 vb.
come and go
be active 678 vb.
come-back
compensation 31
n.
revival 656 n.
come by
acquire 771 vb.
comedian
actor 594 n.
humorist 839 n.
come-down
humiliation 872 n.
come down
decrease 37 vb.
descend 309 vb.
comedy
stage play 594 n.

ridiculousness
849 n.
come from
result 157 vb.
come in for
receive 782 vb.
come into
inherit 771 vb.
comely
beautiful 841 adj.
come of age
come of age
134 vb.
come out of
result 157 vb.
come out with
divulge 526 vb.
come round
be periodic 141 vb.
be restored 656 vb.
come short
not suffice 636 vb.
comet
planet 321 n.
come to
be restored 656 vb.
cost 809 vb.
come to a head
climax 725 vb.
come together
congregate 74 n.
come to grief
miscarry 728 vb.
have trouble
731 vb.
come to light
be visible 443 vb.
appear 445 vb.
come to terms
contract 765 vb.
come to the point
be concise 569 vb.
mean 514 vb.
comfit
sweet 392 n.
comfort
euphoria 376 n.
refresh 685 vb.
aid 703 n., vb.
content 828 vb.
relief 831 n.
cheer 833 vb.
give hope 852 vb.
condolence 905 n.
comfortable
comfortable 376
adj.

palmy 730 adj.
content 828 adj.
comforter
shawl 228 n.
comfortless
cheerless 834 adj.
comic
actor 594 n.
humorist 839 n.
funny 849 adj.
coming events
futurity 124 n.
destiny 155 n.
coming out
début 68 n.
comma
punctuation 347 n.
command
be superior 34 vb.
influence 178 vb.
be high 209 vb.
dispose of 673 vb.
precept 693 n.
dominate 733 vb.
command 737 n., vb.
commandant
army officer 741 n.
commandeer
appropriate 786 vb.
commander
army officer 741 n.
naval officer 741 n.
commanding
authoritative
733 adj.
proud 871 adj.
(see command*)*
commandment
(see command*)*
commando
armed force 722 n.
commemorate
honour 866 vb.
celebrate 876 vb.
(see
commemorate*)*
commence
begin 68 vb.
commend
advise 691 vb.
praise 923 vb.
commendable
approvable 923 adj.
commender
commender 923 n.
commensal
mensal 301 adj.

commensurate
relative 9 adj.
numerical 85 adj.
comment
notice 455 vb.
commentary 520 n.
article 591 n.
dissert 591 vb.
commentary
commentary 520 n.
article 591 n.
commentator
interpreter 520 n.
dissertator 591 n.
commerce
trade 791 n.
commercial
trading 791 adj.
vulgar 847 adj.
commercialism
trade 791 n.
commercialize
vulgarize 847 vb.
commination
malediction 899 n.
comminute
break 46 vb.
pulverize 332 vb.
commiseration
pity 905 n.
condolence 905 n.
commissar
tyrant 735 n.
officer 741 n.
autocrat 741 n.
commissariat
provisions 301 n.
provision 633 n.
commission
band 74 n.
job 622 n.
employ 622 vb.
make ready 669 vb.
warrant 737 n., vb.
commission
751 n., vb.
earnings 771 n.
commissionaire
janitor 264 n.
commissioner
official 690 n.
commit
do 676 vb.
commission 751 vb.
commitment
promise 764 n.
duty 917 n.

commit oneself
affirm 532 vb.
promise 764 vb.
incur a duty 917 vb.
committal
transference 272 n.
legal process 959 n.
committee
band 74 n.
consignee 754 n.
commode
cabinet 194 n.
latrine 649 n.
commodious
useful 640 adj.
commodity
object 319 n.
merchandise 795 n.
commodore
naval officer 741 n.
common
typical 83 adj.
frequent 139 adj.
sharing 775 adj.
vulgar 847 adj.
plebeian 869 adj.
common cause
cooperation 706 n.
common denominator
relation 9 n.
commoner
commoner 869 n.
common knowledge
publicity 528 n.
common lot
mediocrity 732 n.
common man
common man 30 n.
everyman 79 n.
common or garden
typical 83 adj.
commonplace
median 30 adj.
topic 452 n.
maxim 496 n.
usual 610 adj.
trivial 639 adj.
dull 840 adj.
commons
provisions 301 n.
commonalty 869 n.
common sense
intelligence 498 n.
sanity 502 n.
common touch
sociability 882 n.
courtesy 884 n.

commonwealth
territory 184 n.
nation 371 n.
polity 733 n.
commotion
commotion 318 n.
excitable state 822 n.
communal
national 371 adj.
sectional 708 adj.
sharing 775 adj.
commune
communicate 524 vb.
converse 584 vb.
communicable
transferable 272 adj.
infectious 653 adj.
communicant
church member 976 n.
worshipper 981 n.
communicate
connect 45 vb.
communicate 524 vb.
offer worship 981 vb.
communication
message 529 n.
correspondence 588 n.
(*see* communicate)
communications
access 624 n.
communicative
loquacious 581 adj.
communion
worship 981 n.
communiqué
report 524 n.
news 529 n.
communist
participator 775 n.
communistic
authoritarian 735 adj.
sharing 775 adj.
community
habitancy 191 n.
social group 371 n.
community 708 n.
sect 978 n.
communize
socialize 775 vb.

commutation
substitution 150 n.
interchange 151 n.
commute
substitute 150 vb.
commuter
traveller 268 n.
rider 268 n.
compact
small 33 adj.
cohesive 48 adj.
case 194 n.
contracted 198 adj.
dense 324 adj.
concise 569 adj.
compact 765 n.
companion
analogue 18 n.
colleague 707 n.
close friend 880 n.
companionable
sociable 882 adj.
companionship
sociality 882 n.
companion-way
entrance 263 n.
company
assembly, band 74 n.
accompaniment 89 n.
personnel 686 n.
association 706 n.
corporation 708 n.
formation 722 n.
comparable
equivalent 28 adj.
compared 462 adj.
comparative
figurative 519 adj.
compare
compare 462 vb.
discriminate 463 vb.
comparison
assimilation 18 n.
comparison 462 n.
compartment
subdivision 53 n.
compartment 194 n.
compass
range 183 n.
sailing aid 269 n.
circle 314 vb.
signpost 547 n.
succeed 727 vb.

compassion
pity 905 n.
compatibility
adaptation 24 n.
concord 710 n.
friendship 880 n.
compatriot
kinsman 11 n.
native 191 n.
compeer
compeer 28 n.
compel
command 737 vb.
compel 740 vb.
compelling
causal 156 adj.
powerful 160 adj.
influential 178 adj.
necessary 596 adj.
compelling 740 adj.
compendious
concise 569 adj.
compendious 592 adj.
compendium
miniature 196 n.
compendium 592 n.
compensate
correlate 12 vb.
compensate 31 vb.
restitute 787 vb.
atone 941 vb.
compère
actor 594 n.
stage-manager 594 n.
compete
do likewise 20 vb.
contend 716 vb.
competence
ability 160 n.
skill 694 n.
wealth 800 n.
jurisdiction 955 n.
competent
(*see* competence)
competition
opposition 704 n.
contention 716 n.
competitive
equal 28 adj.
competitor
compeer 28 n.
contender 716 n.
compilation
composition 56 n.
assemblage 74 n.

dictionary 559 n.
compile
compose 56 vb.
(see compilation)
compiler
etymology 559 n.
anthology 592 n.
complain
be discontented
829 vb.
indict 928 vb.
complainant
accuser 928 n.
complainer
malcontent 829 n.
complain of
be ill 651 vb.
complaint
illness 651 n.
discontent 829 n.
accusation 928 n.
complaisant
lenient 736 adj.
obedient 739 adj.
complement
analogue 18 n.
plenitude 54 n.
personnel 686 n.
complete
make complete
54 vb.
carry through
725 vb.
completeness
whole 52 n.
completeness 54 n.
completion
completion 725 n.
(see completeness)
complex
whole 52 n.
complex 61 adj.
structure 331 n.
complexion
hue 425 n.
mien 445 n.
complexity
complexity 61 n.
(see complex)
compliance
obedience 739 n.
observance 768 n.
compliant
(see compliance)
complicate
bedevil 63 vb.
aggravate 832 vb.

complication
complexity 61 n.
illness 651 n.
(see complexity)
complicity
cooperation 707 n.
participation 775 n.
guilt 936 n.
compliment
honours 866 n.
gratulate 886 vb.
endearment 889 n.
complimentary
uncharged 812 adj.
component
component 58 n.
element 319 n.
comportment
conduct 688 n.
compose
mix 43 vb.
compose, constitute
56 vb.
arrange 62 vb.
assuage 177 vb.
compose music
413 vb.
composed
inexcitable 823 adj.
composer
musician 413 n.
composite
mixed 43 adj.
plural 101 adj.
composition
a mixture 43 n.
composition 56 n.
quid pro quo 150 n.
structure 331 n.
compact 765 n.
compositor
printer 587 n.
compost
fertilizer 171 n.
composure
inexcitability
823 n.
compound
a mixture 43 n.
combination 50 n.
compose 56 vb.
enclosure 235 n.
compromise
770 vb.
comprehend
comprise 78 vb.
know 490 vb.

understand 516 vb.
comprehension
(see comprehend)
comprehensive
comprehensive
52 adj.
complete 54 adj.
general 79 adj.
compress
make smaller
198 vb.
be concise 569 vb.
surgical dressing
658 n.
compression
diminution 37 n.
compression 198 n.
narrowing 206 n.
compendium 592 n.
comprise
comprise 78 vb.
compromise
endanger 661 vb.
pacification 719 n.
compact 765 n.
compromise 770 n.,
vb.
defame 926 vb.
compromising
discreditable
867 adj.
compulsion
necessity 596 n.
compulsion 740 n.
compulsive
compelling 740 adj.
compulsory
compelling 740 adj.
compunction
regret 830 n.
penitence 939 n.
computation
numeration 86 n.
measurement 465 n.
compute
do sums 86 vb.
measure 465 vb.
computer
computer 86 n.
comrade
colleague 707 n.
chum 880 n.
comradeship
cooperation 706 n.
sociality 882 n.
con
meditate 449 vb.

memorize 505 vb.
concatenation
continuity 71 n.
concave
concave 255 adj.
conceal
conceal 525 vb.
concealed
latent 523 adj.
concealment
invisibility 444 n.
concealment 525 n.
concede
assent 488 vb.
permit 756 vb.
conceit
thought 449 n.
idea 451 n.
witticism 839 n.
affectation 850 n.
vanity 873 n.
conceive
be fruitful 171 vb.
vitalize 360 vb.
opine 485 vb.
concentrate
augment 36 vb.
focus 76 vb.
converge 293 vb.
think 449 vb.
be attentive
455 vb.
concentration
condensation 324
n.
assiduity 678 n.
(see concentrate)
concentration camp
prison camp 748 n.
concentric
parallel 219 adj.
central 225 adj.
concept
idea 451 n.
ideality 513 n.
conception
intellect 447 n.
thought 449 n.
idea 451 n.
conceptual
mental 447 adj.
conceptualize
cognize 447 vb.
concern
relation 9 n.
be related 9 vb.
topic 452 n.

CON

function, business
622 n.
importance 638 n.
shop 796 n.
worry 825 n.
concert
accord 24 vb.
music 412 n.
plot 623 vb.
concertina
organ 414 n.
concerto
duet 412 n.
concession
offset 31 n.
compromise 770 n.
discount 810 n.
concessional
given 781 adj.
cheap 812 adj.
concessionnaire
recipient 782 n.
concierge
janitor 264 n.
keeper 749 n.
conciliate
pacify 719 vb.
be courteous
884 vb.
conciliation
(*see* conciliate)
concise
compendious
592 adj.
conciseness
conciseness 569 n.
conclave
council 692 n.
synod 985 n.
conclude
terminate 69 vb.
conclusion
sequel 67 n.
finality 69 n.
opinion 485 n.
completion 725 n.
conclusive
demonstrating
478 adj.
completive 725 adj.
concoct
imagine 513 vb.
fake 541 vb.
plan 623 vb.
concoction
potion 301 n.
maturation 669 n.

CON

concomitant
adjunct 40 n.
concomitant 89 n.
concord
agreement 24 n.
order 60 n.
concord 710 vb.
friendliness 880 n.
concordance
dictionary 559 n.
concordat
treaty 765 n.
concourse
assembly 74 n.
convergence 293 n.
concrete
substantial 3 adj.
material 319 adj.
dense 324 adj.
concreteness
substantiality 3 n.
materiality 319 n.
density 324 n.
concretion
substance 3 n.
condensation 324 n.
solid body 324 n.
concubinage
type of marriage
894 n.
illicit love 951 n.
concubine
kept woman 952 n.
concupiscent
lecherous 951 adj.
concur
concur 181 vb.
assent 488 vb.
concurrence
junction 45 n.
combination 50 n.
concurrence 181 n.
assent 488 n.
cooperation 706 n.
concurrent
concurrent 181 adj.
(*see* concurrence)
concuss
render insensible
375 vb.
concussion
impulse 279 n.
condemn
condemn 961 vb.
punish 963 vb.
condemnable
accusable 928 adj.

CON

condemned
dilapidated 655 adj.
condemned 961 adj.
condensation
condensation 324 n.
solid body 324 n.
condense
make smaller
198 vb.
be dense 324 vb.
be concise 569 vb.
abstract 592 vb.
condescend
be humble 872 vb.
be courteous 884 vb.
condescension
pride 871 n.
humility 872 n.
condign
due 915 adj.
condiment
condiment 389 n.
condition
state 7 n.
teach 534 vb.
give terms 766 vb.
conditional
qualifying 468 adj.
conditional 766 adj.
conditioning
teaching 534 n.
habituation 610 n.
conditions
conditions 766 n.
condole
pity 905 vb.
condolence
(*see* condole)
condone
forgive 909 vb.
condottiere
leader 690 n.
militarist 722 n.
conduce
conduce 156 vb.
tend 179 vb.
aid 703 vb.
conduct
accompany 89 vb.
transfer 272 vb.
play music 413 vb.
mien 445 n.
action 676 n.
conduct 688 n.
manage 689 vb.
conductor
driver 268 n.

CON

orchestra 413 n.
leader 690 n.
conduit
outlet 298 n.
conduit 351 n.
cone
cone 252 n.
confectionery
pastry 301 n.
sweet 392 n.
confederate
colleague 707 n.
corporate 708 adj.
confederation
association 706 n.
polity 733 n.
confer
confer 584 vb.
consult 691 vb.
give 781 vb.
conference
inquiry 459 n.
conference 584 n.
confess
believe 485 vb.
confess 526 vb.
be penitent 939 vb.
confession
creed 485 n.
penance 941 n.
(*see* confess)
confessional
credal 485 adj.
tribunal 956 n.
confessions
biography 590 n.
confidant
adviser 691 n.
close friend 880 n.
confide
inform 524 vb.
divulge 526 vb.
confide in
consult 691 vb.
confidence
positiveness 473 n.
secret 530 n.
safety 660 n.
hope 852 n.
confidence trick
trickery 542 n.
confident
positive 473 adj.
believing 485 adj.
expectant 507 adj.
confidential
concealed 525 adj.

confiding
  credulous 487 adj.
  artless 699 adj.
confine
  circumscribe
    232 vb.
  imprison 747 vb.
confinement
  obstetrics 164 n.
  detention 747 n.
  seclusion 883 n.
confines
  near place 200 n.
confirm
  strengthen 162 vb.
  corroborate 466 vb.
  make certain
    473 vb.
  endorse 488 vb.
  perform ritual
    988 vb.
confiscate
  deprive 786 vb.
confiscatory
  taking 786 adj.
  punitive 963 adj.
conflagration
  fire 379 n.
conflict
  contrariety 14 n.
  quarrel 709 vb.
confluence
  junction 45 n.
  convergence 293 n.
  current 350 n.
conform
  do likewise 20 vb.
  conform 83 vb.
  observe 768 vb.
conformable
  conformable
    83 adj.
conformation
  composition 56 n.
  form 243 n.
conforming
  orthodox 976 adj.
conformist
  conformist 83 n.
conformity
  uniformity 16 n.
  conformity 83 n.
  orthodoxism 976 n.
confound
  derange 63 vb.
  not discriminate
    464 vb.

confute 479 vb.
confraternity
  community 708 n.
confrère
  colleague 707 n.
confront
  be present 189 vb.
  be opposite 240 vb.
  compare 462 vb.
  show 522 vb.
  oppose 704 vb.
  resist 715 vb.
confuse
  bedevil 63 vb.
  puzzle 474 vb.
confused
  mixed 43 adj.
  orderless 61 adj.
  ill-seen 444 adj.
  imperspicuous
    568 adj.
confusion
  medley 43 n.
  confusion 61 n.
  psychopathy
    503 n.
confutation
  confutation 479 n.
  negation 533 n.
congeal
  be dense 324 vb.
  refrigerate 382 vb.
congenial
  agreeing 24 adj.
  pleasant 376 adj.
  concordant 701 adj.
congenital
  genetic 5 adj.
congestion
  crowd 74 n.
  redundance 637 n.
conglomerate
  cohere 48 vb.
  solid body 324 n.
  rock 344 n.
congratulate
  gratulate 886 vb.
congratulation
  rejoicing 835 n.
  congratulation
    886 n.
congregate
  congregate 74 vb.
  meet 295 vb.
congregation
  assembly 74 n.
  worshipper 981 n.

laity 987 n.
congress
  junction 45 n.
  council 692 n.
  parliament 692 n.
congruence,
  congruity
  similarity 18 n.
  conformance 24 n.
congruent
  agreeing 24 adj.
congruity
  (*see* congruence)
conical
  rotund 252 adj.
  convergent 293 adj.
conjecture
  uncertainty 474 n.
  conjecture 512 n.
conjugal
  matrimonial
    894 adj.
conjugate
  parse 564 vb.
conjunct
  conjunct 45 adj.
conjunction
  junction 45 n.
  contiguity 202 n.
  part of speech
    564 n.
conjure
  deceive 542 vb.
  entreat 761 vb.
  practise sorcery
    983 vb.
conjure up
  imagine 513 vb.
conjuror
  conjuror 545 n.
con-man
  trickster 545 n.
connect
  connect 45 vb.
  continuate 71 vb.
connexion
  relation 9 n.
  bond 47 n.
  (*see* connect)
connivance
  cooperation 706 n.
  laxity 734 n.
  permission 756 n.
connive
  disregard 458 vb.
connoisseur
  man of taste 846 n.

connoisseurship
  good taste 846 n.
  fastidiousness
    862 n.
connotation
  connotation 514 n.
connote
  mean 514 vb.
  imply 523 vb.
connubial
  matrimonial
    894 adj.
conquer
  overmaster 727 vb.
conqueror
  victor 727 n.
conquest
  victory 727 n.
  subjection 745 n.
consanguinity
  relation 9 n.
  consanguinity 11 n.
  parentage 169 n.
conscience
  conscience 917 n.
conscienceless
  wicked 934 adj.
  impenitent 940 adj.
conscience-money
  restitution 787 n.
  atonement 941 n.
conscientious
  careful 457 adj.
  observant 768 adj.
  trustworthy 929
    adj.
conscious
  mental 447 adj.
  knowing 490 adj.
conscript
  soldier 722 n.
  compel 740 vb.
conscription
  war measures 718 n.
  compulsion 740 n.
consecrate
  sanctify 979 vb.
consecutive
  sequent 65 adj.
  continuous 71 adj.
consensus
  agreement 24 n.
  consensus 488 n.
consent
  agreement 24 n.
  assent 488 n., vb.
  consent 758 n., vb.

consentient
assenting 488 adj.
consequence
sequel 67 n.
effect 157 n.
importance 638 n.
consequential
caused 157 adj.
ostentatious
875 adj.
conservancy
cleansing 648 n.
conservation
storage 632 n.
preservation 666 n.
conservative
preserving 666 adj.
sectional 708 adj.
cautious 858 adj.
conservatoire
academy 539 n.
conservatory
garden 370 n.
heater 383 n.
conserve
sweet 392 n.
preserve 666 vb.
consider
meditate 449 vb.
inquire 459 vb.
estimate 480 vb.
considerable
substantial 3 adj.
great 32 adj.
many 104 adj.
considerate
thoughtful 449 adj.
disinterested
931 adj.
consideration
quid pro quo 150
n.
meditation 449 n.
courtesy 884 n.
respect 920 n.
consign
send 272 vb.
consignee
agent 686 n.
consignee 754 n.
recipient 782 n.
consignment
thing transferred
272 n.
transfer 780 n.
consignor
transferrer 272 n.

consistence
density 324 n.
consistency
uniformity 16 n.
consistent
rational 475 adj.
(*see* consistency)
consist of
comprise 78 vb.
consolation
relief 831 n.
condolence 905 n.
consolatory
relieving 831 adj.
console
stand 218 n.
cheer 833 vb.
consolidate
bring together
74 vb.
be dense 324 vb.
consolidation
(*see* consolidate)
consonance
agreement 24 n.
consonantal
sounding 398 adj.
consort
concomitant 89 n.
spouse 894 n.
conspectus
generality 79 n.
view 438 n.
compendium 592 n.
conspicuous
well-seen 443 adj.
conspiracy
secrecy 525 n.
plot 623 n.
compact 765 n.
conspirator
planner 623 n.
conspiratorial
stealthy 525 adj.
planning 623 adj.
conspire
combine 50 vb.
(*see* conspiracy)
constabulary
police 955 n.
constancy
uniformity 16 n.
stability 153 n.
loyalty 739 n.
probity 929 n.
constant
identity 13 n.

uniform 16 adj.
regular 81 adj.
unchangeable
153 adj.
constellation
group 74 n.
star 321 n.
consternation
fear 854 n.
constipate
be dense 324 vb.
constipation
condensation 324 n.
indigestion 651 n.
constituency
electorate 605 n.
constituent
part 53 n.
component 58 n.
electorate 605 n.
constituents
contents 193 n.
constitute
constitute 56 vb.
constitution
character 5 n.
composition 56 n.
structure 331 n.
polity 733 n.
law 953 n.
constitutional
habit 610 n.
governmental
733 adj.
legal 953 adj.
constitutionalism
legality 953 n.
constraint
compulsion 740 n.
restraint 747 n.
constrict
make smaller
198 vb.
constriction
narrowing 206 n.
construction
arrangement 62 n.
structure 331 n.
interpretation
520 n.
constructional
structural 331 adj.
constructive
productive 164 adj.
interpretive 520 adj.
constructor
producer 167 n.

construe
interpret 520 vb.
parse 564 vb.
consult
consult 691 vb.
consultant
oracle 511 n.
adviser 691 n.
expert 696 n.
consultation
advice 691 n.
consultative
advising 691 adj.
consume
eat 301 vb.
waste 634 vb.
use 673 vb.
expend 806 vb.
consumer
eater 301 n.
purchaser 792 n.
consummate
great 32 adj.
unite with 45 vb.
complete 54 adj.
carry through
725 vb.
consummation
coition 45 n.
(*see* consummate)
consumption
phthisis 651 n.
(*see* consume)
contact
junction 45 n.
connect 45 vb.
contiguity 202 n.
informant 524 n.
contact man
messenger 531 n.
contagion
influence 178 n.
infection 651 n.
contagious
(*see* contagion)
contain
comprise 78 vb.
container
receptacle 194 n.
storage 632 n.
containment
circumscription
232 n.
contaminate
make unclean
649 vb.
impair 655 vb.

contemplate
  meditate 449 vb.
  intend 617 vb.
contemplation
  attention 455 n.
  (*see* contemplate)
contemplative
  pietist 979 n.
contemporaneity
  present time 121 n.
  synchronism 123 n.
contemporary
  contemporary
   123 n.
contempt
  pride 871 n.
  contempt 922 n.
contemptibility
  despisedness 922 n.
contemptible
  unimportant
   639 adj.
  ridiculous 849 adj.
  discreditable 867
   adj.
  contemptible
   922 adj.
contemptuous
  insolent 878 adj.
  despising 922 adj.
contend
  contend 716 vb.
contender
  athlete 162 n.
  contender 716 n.
  combatant 722 n.
content
  structure 331 n.
  euphoria 376 n.
  content 828 n.,
   adj., vb.
  cheer 833 vb.
contented
  content 828 adj.
contention
  quarrel 709 n.
  contention 716 n.
contentment
  euphoria 376 n.
  content 828 n.
contents
  contents 193 n.
  topic 452 n.
conterminous
  contiguous 202 adj.
contest
  athletics 162 n.

contend 716 vb.
  sport 837 n.
context
  circumstance 8 n.
  relation 9 n.
  concomitant 89 n.
  meaning 514 n.
  connotation 514 n.
contiguity
  junction 45 n.
  contiguity 202 n.
continence
  temperance 942 n.
continent
  region 184 n.
  land 344 n.
  temperate 942 adj.
  pure 950 adj.
continental
  regional 184 adj.
  dweller 191 n.
  inland 344 n.
contingency
  chance 159 n.
  possibility 469 n.
contingent
  extrinsic 6 adj.
  part 53 n.
  casual 159 adj.
  uncertain 474 adj.
  conditional 766 adj.
contingents
  armed force 722 n.
continual
  continuous 71 adj.
  unceasing 146 adj.
continuance
  course of time
   111 n.
  durability 113 n.
  continuance 146 n.
continuate
  continuate 71 vb.
continuation
  sequence 65 n.
  sequel 67 n.
  continuance 146 n.
continue
  run on 71 vb.
  lengthen 203 vb.
  (*see* continuance)
continuity
  continuity 71 n.
  recurrence 106 n.
  continuance 146 n.
continuous
  (*see* continuity)

continuum
  space 183 n.
contort
  distort 246 vb.
contour
  outline 233 n.
  form 243 n.
contraband
  prohibited 757 adj.
  booty 790 n.
contraception
  unproductivity
   172 n.
contract
  become small
   198 vb.
  shorten 204 vb.
  undertaking 672 n.
  compact 765 n.
  make terms 766 vb.
contraction
  contraction 198 n.
contractor
  essayer 671 n.
  signatory 765 n.
contractual
  agreeing 24 adj.
  contractual 765 adj.
contradict
  be contrary 14 vb.
  tell against 467 vb.
  negate 533 vb.
  oppose 704 vb.
contradiction
  (*see* contradict)
contradictory
  negative 533 adj.
contradistinction
  contrariety 14 n.
contra-indication
  counter-evidence
   467 n.
contralto
  vocalist 413 n.
contraposition
  contrariety 14 n.
  contraposition
   240 n.
contraption
  contrivance 623 n.
contrariety
  contrariety 14 n.
  counteraction 182 n.
  contraposition
   240 n.
contrarious
  opposing 704 adj.

contrary
  contrary 14 adj.
  countervailing
   467 adj.
  negative 533 adj.
  adverse 731 adj.
contrast
  contrariety 14 n.
  differ 15 vb.
  non-uniformity
   17 n.
  dissimilarity 19 n.
  compare 462 vb.
contravene
  be contrary 14 vb.
contravention
  lawbreaking 954 n.
  (*see* contravene)
contretemps
  hitch 702 n.
contribute
  concur 181 vb.
  give 781 vb.
contribute to
  add 38 vb.
  conduce 156 vb.
  aid 703 vb.
contribution
  increment 36 n.
  cooperation 706 n.
  giving, offering
   781 n.
contributor
  correspondent
   588 n.
  dissertator 591 n.
  giver 781 n.
contrition
  regret 830 n.
  penitence 939 n.
contrivance
  contrivance 623 n.
  plan 623 n.
  means 629 n.
  tactics 688 n.
contrive
  predetermine
   608 vb.
  find means 629 vb.
contriver
  planner 623 n.
control
  be able 160 n.
  influence 178 n.
  comparison 462 n.
  management 689 n.
  governance 733 n.

rule 733 vb.
restrain 747 vb.
spiritualism 984 n.
controlled
impassive 820 adj.
inexcitable 823 adj.
controller
director 690 n.
control oneself
be temperate
942 vb.
controls
aircraft 276 n.
directorship 689 n.
controversial
uncertain 474 adj.
arguing 475 adj.
controversy
disagreement 25 n.
argument 475 n.
controvert
argue 475 vb.
negate 533 vb.
contumacious
disobedient 738 adj.
contumacy
impenitence 940 n.
contumely
insolence 878 n.
disrespect 921 n.
contusion
wound 655 n.
conundrum
enigma 530 n.
conurbate
urbanize 192 vb.
conurbation
district 184 n.
housing 192 n.
convalesce
be restored 656 vb.
convection
transference 272 n.
convene
bring together
74 vb.
convenience
opportunity 137 n.
euphoria 376 n.
utility 640 n.
expedience 642 n.
leisure 681 n.
facility 701 n.
convenient
(*see* **convenience**)
convent
monastery 986 n.

conventicle
assembly 74 n.
sect 978 n.
church 990 n.
convention
conformity 83 n.
conference 584 n.
practice 610 n.
treaty 765 n.
etiquette 848 n.
conventional
(*see* **convention**)
conventionality
conformity 83 n.
(*see* **convention**)
converge
congregate 74 vb.
focus 76 vb.
converge 293 vb.
conversable
conversing 584 adj.
sociable 882 adj.
amiable 884 adj.
conversant
knowing 490 adj.
conversation
interlocution 584 n.
conversational
conversing 584 adj.
conversations
conference 584 n.
conversazione
social gathering
882 n.
converse
contrariety 14 n.
speak 579 vb.
interlocution
584 n.
converse 584 vb.
conversion
conversion 147 n.
production 164 n.
use 673 n.
convert
modify 143 vb.
changed person
147 n.
convert 147 vb.
convince 485 vb.
learner 538 n.
use 673 n.
make pious 979
vb.
convexity
curvature 248 n.
convexity 253 n.

convey
move 265 vb.
transfer 272 vb.
mean 514 vb.
communicate
524 vb.
convey 780 vb.
conveyance
transport 272 n.
vehicle 274 n.
transfer 780 n.
conveyancer
law agent 958 n.
convict
confute 479 vb.
offender 904 n.
condemn 961 vb.
conviction
positiveness 473 n.
belief 485 n.
convict settlement
prison camp 748 n.
convince
demonstrate 478 vb.
convince 485 vb.
convincing
plausible 471 adj.
credible 485 adj.
conviviality
festivity 837 n.
sociability 882 n.
convocation
council 692 n.
synod 985 n.
convoke
bring together
74 vb.
convolution
convolution 251 n.
convoy
accompany 89 vb.
keeper 749 n.
convulsion
turmoil 61 n.
derangement 63 n.
revolution 149 n.
spasm 318 n.
coo
ululate 409 vb.
caress 889 vb.
cook
cook 301 vb.
domestic 742 n.
cooker
furnace 383 n.
cookery
cookery 301 n.

cool
moderate 177 vb.
refrigerate 382 vb.
refresh 685 vb.
indifferent 860 adj.
inimical 881 adj.
coolant
refrigerator 384 n.
coolie
bearer 273 n.
worker 686 n.
coolness
coldness 380 n.
(*see* **cool**)
coop
stable 192 n.
lock-up 748 n.
cooperation
concurrence 181 n.
instrumentality
628 n.
aid 703 n.
cooperation 706 n.
cooperative
cooperative 706 adj.
corporate 708 adj.
cooperator
collaborator 707 n.
participator 775 n.
coopt
choose 605 vb.
coordinate
regularize 62 vb.
metrology 465 n.
cope
vestments 989 n.
cope with
be equal 28 vb.
copious
diffuse 570 adj.
plenteous 635 adj.
copper
cauldron 194 n.
heater 383 n.
police 955 n.
copperplate
engraving 555 n.
written 586 adj.
coppers
money 797 n.
copse
wood 366 n.
copula
bond 47 n.
copulation
coition 45 n.
propagation 164 n.

copulative
conjunctive 45 adj.
grammatical
564 adj.

copy
copy 20 vb.
copy 22 n.
prototype 23 n.
conform 83 vb.
duplication 91 n.
reproduce 166 vb.
news 529 n.
represent 551 vb.

copycat
imitator 20 n.
conformist 83 n.

copyist
imitator 20 n.
artist 556 n.
penman 586 n.

copyright
dueness 915 n.

copy-writer
publicizer 528 n.

coquetry
affectation 850 n.
love-making
887 n.
wooing 889 n.

coquette
affector 850 n.
court 889 vb.

coral
redness 431 n.
gem 844 n.

cord
cable, ligature 47 n.
line 203 n.
fibre 208 n.

cordage
tackling 47 n.

cordial
tonic 658 n.
felt 818 adj.
friendly 880 adj.
sociable 882 adj.

cordite
explosive 723 n.

cordon bleu
proficient 696 n.
decoration 729 n.

cordon sanitaire
hygiene 652 n.

core
essence 1 n.
essential part 5 n.
centrality 225 n.

co-religionist
colleague 707 n.
church member
976 n.

cork
stopper 264 n.
levity 323 n.

corked
unsavoury 391 adj.

corkscrew
meander 251 vb.
opener 263 n.

cormorant
glutton 947 n.

corn
provender 301 n.
corn 366 n.
ulcer 651 n.
preserve 666 vb.

corner
place 185 n.
angularity 247 n.
cavity 255 n.
hiding-place 527 n.
purchase 792 vb.

corner-boy
rioter 738 n.

cornered
angular 247 adj.
in difficulties
700 adj.

cornering
circuition 314 n.
purchase 792 n.

corner-stone
supporter 218 n.

cornet
cone 252 n.
horn 414 n.
army officer 741 n.

cornucopia
abundance 171 n.

corny
known 490 adj.

corollary
adjunct 40 n.

corona
sun 321 n.
light 417 n.

coronach
lament 836 n.

coronal
ornamentation
844 n.

coronation
dignification 866 n.

coroner
judge 957 n.

coronet
headgear 228 n.
regalia 743 n.

corporal punishment
corporal punish-
ment 963 n.

corporate
corporate 708 adj.

corporation
swelling 253 n.
corporation 708 n.

corporeality
materiality 319 n.

corps
formation 722 n.

corps de ballet
actor 594 n.

corps diplomatique
envoy 754 n.

corpse
corpse 363 n.

corpulence
bulk 195 n.
thickness 205 n.

corpus
whole 52 n.
reading matter
589 n.

corpuscle
small thing 33 n.
blood 335 n.

corral
enclosure 235 n.
imprison 747 vb.

correct
true, accurate
494 adj.
grammatical
564 adj.
elegant 575 adj.
rectify 654 vb.
remedy 658 vb.
fashionable
848 adj.
formal 875 adj.
punish 963 vb.

correction
amendment 654 n.
reprimand 924 n.

corrective
counteracting
182 n.
remedial 658 adj.
punitive 963 adj.

correctness
good taste 846 n.
etiquette 848 n.
formality 875 n.

correlate
compare 462 vb.
(see **correlation**)

correlation
relativeness 9 n.
correlation 12 n.

correlative
interchanged
151 adj.

correspondence
relativeness 9 n.
correlation 12 n.
symmetry 245 n.
correspondence
588 n.

correspondent
respondent 460 n.
informant 524 n.
correspondent
588 n.
recipient 782 n.

correspond to
resemble 18 vb.

corridor
lobby 194 n.
access 624 n.

corrigendum
mistake 495 n.

corroborate
corroborate 466 vb.
demonstrate 478 vb.

corroboration
evidence 466 n.

corrode
impair 655 vb.
hurt 827 vb.

corrosive
destroyer 168 n.
harmful 645 adj.

corrugate
crinkle 251 vb.
fold 261 vb.
groove 262 vb.

corrupt
decompose 51 vb.
misteach 535 vb.
pervert 655 vb.
venal 930 adj.
vicious 934 adj.
make wicked
934 vb.

corruptible
venal 930 adj.

corruption
neology 560 n.
improbity 930 n.
(see corrupt)

corselet
armour 713 n.

corset
compressor 198 n.
supporter 218 n.
underwear 228 n.

cortège
procession 71 n.
obsequies 364 n.

cortex
skin 226 n.

corvée
labour 682 n.
compulsion 740 n.

corvette
warship 722 n.

corybantiasm
frenzy 503 n.

coryphaeus
teacher 537 n.
leader 690 n.

cosh
strike 279 vb.
club 723 n.

cosiness
euphoria 376 n.

cosmetic
cosmetic 843 n.

cosmetician
beautician 843 n.

cosmic
comprehensive
52 adj.
cosmic 321 adj.

cosmology
uranometry 321 n.
cosmography
321 n.

cosmopolitan
universal 79 adj.
urban 192 adj.
beau monde 848 n.
well-bred 848 adj.

cosmos
universe 321 n.

cosset
pet 889 vb.

cost
account 808 vb.
cost 809 n., vb.
dearness 811 n.

coster, — monger
pedlar 794 n.

costive
retentive 778 adj.

costly
destructive 165
adj.
valuable 644 adj.
dear 811 adj.

costs
expenditure 806 n.
cost 809 n.
penalty 963 n.

costume
dress 228 n.

costumier
clothier 228 n.
stage-hand 594 n.

cosy
comfortable
376 adj.

cot
bed 218 n.

coterie
band 74 n.
party 708 n.

cottage
small house 192 n.

cotton
textile 222 n.
fibre 208 n.

cottons
clothing 228 n.

couch
bed, seat 218 n.
sit down 311 vb.

couchant
supine 216 adj.
heraldic 547 adj.

cough
eruct 300 vb.
rasp 407 vb.
respiratory disease
651 n.

coulter
sharp edge 256 n.
farm tool 370 n.

council
assembly 74 n.
adviser 691 n.
council 692 n.
conference 884 n.
synod 985 n.

councillor
councillor 692 n.

counsel
incite 612 vb.
advise 691 vb.
lawyer 958 n.

counsellor
sage 500 n.
adviser 691 n.

count
quantify 26 vb.
comprise 78 vb.
numeration 86 n.
be important
638 vb.
nobleman 868 n.
accusation 928 n.

countenance
face 237 n.
mien 445 n.
patronize 703 vb.
approve 923 vb.

counter
contrary 14 adj.
computer 86 n.
counteract 182 vb.
stand 118 n.
poop 238 n.
retaliate 714 vb.
shop 796 n.

counteract
counteract 182 vb.
tell against 467 vb.

counteractive
contrary 14 adj.

counter attack
retaliation 714 n.

counterbalance
offset 31 n.

counterblast
counteraction
182 n.

counterchange
interchange
151 n., vb.

counter-charge
rejoinder 460 n.

countercheer
disapprobation
924 n.

counterdraw
copy 20 vb.

counter-espionage
secret service
459 n.

counter-evidence
counter-evidence
467 n.

counterfeit
imitation 20 n.
fake 541 vb.
sham 542 n.
spurious 542 adj.

deceive 542 vb.

counterfoil
label 547 n.

counter-irritant
counteraction 182 n.
antidote 658 n.

countermand
abrogate 752 vb.

countermarch
turn back 286 vb.

countermine
defences 713 n.

counterpane
coverlet 226 n.

counterpart
analogue 18 n.
copy, duplicate 22 n.

counterpoint
music 412 n.

counterpoise
equalize 28 vb.
offset 31 n.
counteract 182 vb.
weigh 322 vb.

counter-revolution
reversion 148 n.
revolution 149 n.

counterscarp
fortification 713 n.

countersign
answer 460 n.
endorse 488 vb.

counterspin
evolution 316 n.

counter statement
rejoinder 460 n.

counter-stroke
defence 713 n.
retaliation 714 n.

counter-symptom
contrariety 14 n.

countervail
counteract 182 vb.
tell against 467 vb.

counterweight
offset 31 n.
stabilizer 153 n.
counteract 182 vb.

counting-house
treasury 799 n.

countless
infinite 107 adj.

count out
exclude 57 vb.

countrified
provincial 192 adj.
ill-bred 847 adj.

country
  region 184 n.
  home 192 n.
countryman
  countryman 869 n.
counts
  particulars 80 n.
count upon
  expect 507 vb.
county
  district 184 n.
coup
  deed 676 n.
coup de grâce
  killing 362 n.
  completion 725 n.
coup d'état
  policy 623 n.
  revolt 738 n.
couple
  analogue 18 n.
  join 45 vb.
  unite with 45 vb.
  duality 90 n.
  marry 894 vb.
couplet
  verse form 593 n.
coupling
  joinder, coition
    45 n.
  coupling 47 n.
courage
  courage 855 n.
courier
  guide 520 n.
  courier 531 n.
course
  course of time
    111 n.
  layer 207 n.
  motion 265 n.
  direction 281 n.
  dish 301 n.
  flow 350 vb.
  curriculum 534 n.
  hunt 619 vb.
  route 624 n.
  therapy 658 n.
  arena 724 n.
course of events
  affairs 154 n.
course of law
  legal process 959
    n.
course of time
  course of time
    111 n.

court
  housing 192 n.
  open space 263 n.
  arena 724 n.
  retainer 742 n.
  court 889 vb.
  flatter 925 vb.
courteous
  well-bred 848 adj.
  (see courtesy)
courtesan
  prostitute 952 n.
courtesy
  humility 872 n.
  sociability 882 n.
  courtesy 884 n.
courtesy title
  insubstantial thing
    4 n.
  title 870 n.
courtier
  retainer 742 n.
  flatterer 925 n.
courtly
  well-bred 848 adj.
  courteous 884 adj.
court-martial
  law-court 956 n.
court of law
  law-court 956 n.
courtroom
  courtroom 956 n.
courtship
  love-making 887 n.
  wooing 889 n.
courtyard
  place 185 n.
cousin
  kinsman 11 n.
couturier
  clothier 228 n.
cove
  gulf 345 n.
coven
  assembly 74 n.
  sorcery 983 n.
covenant
  compact 765 n.
  contract 765 vb.
  title-deed 767 n.
Coventry, send to
  exclude 57 vb.
cover
  offset 31 n.
  extend 183 vb.
  receptacle 194 n.
  wrapping 226 n.

cover 226 vb.
  meal, dish 301 n.
  communicate
    524 vb.
  conceal 525 vb.
  hiding-place, dis-
    guise 527 n.
  obliterate 550 vb.
  shelter 662 n.
coverage
  range 183 n.
  publicity 528 n.
cover all cases
  be general
    79 vb.
coverlet
  coverlet 226 n.
covert
  nest 192 n.
  wood 366 n.
  occult 523 adj.
coverts
  plumage 259 n.
covet
  desire 859 vb.
  envy 912 vb.
covetous
  avaricious 816
    adj.
  envious 912 adj.
  selfish 932 adj.
covey
  group 74 n.
covinous
  false 541 adj.
cow
  cattle 365 n.
  frighten 854 vb.
coward
  coward 856 n.
cowardice
  irresolution 601 n.
  cowardice 856 n.
cowardly
  (see cowardice)
cower
  stoop 311 vb.
  quake 854 vb.
cowherd, cowman
  herdsman 369 n.
cowhouse, cowshed
  stable 192 n.
  cattle pen 369 n.
cowl
  covering 226 n.
  headgear 228 n.
  canonicals 989 n.

co-worker
  collaborator 707 n.
cox
  navigator 270 n.
  direct 689 vb.
coxcomb
  vain person 783 n.
coxcombry
  affectation 850 n.
coxswain
  (see cox)
coy
  affected 850 adj.
  modest 874 adj.
cozen
  deceive 542 vb.
cozener
  trickster 545 n.
crab
  table fish 365 n.
  detract 926 vb.
crabbed
  sour 393 adj.
  inelegant 576 adj.
  sullen 893 adj.
crack
  break 46 vb.
  weakness 163 n.
  gap 201 n.
  opening 263 n.
  be brittle 330 vb.
  crackle 402 vb.
  defect 647 n.
  skilful 694 adj.
  witticism 839 n.
crack-brained
  crazed 503 adj.
crack down on
  be severe 735 vb.
cracked
  non-resonant
    405 adj.
  unintelligent
    499 adj.
  imperfect 647 adj.
crackers
  crazed 503 adj.
crackle
  crackle 402 vb.
crackpot
  fool 501 n.
  crank 504 n.
cracksman
  thief 789 n.
crack up
  be fatigued 684 vb.
  praise 923 vb.

cradle
origin 68 n.
nonage 130 n.
seedbed 156 n.
nest 192 n.
basket 194 n.
pet 889 vb.

craft
ship, shipping
275 n.
vocation 622 n.
skill 694 n.

craftiness
(*see* crafty)

craftsman
producer 167 n.
artist 556 n.
artisan 686 n.

craftsmanship
skill 694 n.

crafty
intelligent 498 adj.
deceiving 542 adj.
cunning 698 adj.

crag
high land 209 n.
rock 344 n.

craggy
rough 259 adj.

cragsman
climber 308 n.

cram
fill 54 vb.
load 193 vb.
educate 534 vb.
study 536 vb.
gluttonize 947 vb.

crammer
teacher 537 n.
training school
539 n.

cramp
spasm 318 n.
hinder 702 vb.
restraint 747 n.

cramped
narrow-minded
481 adj.

crane
lifter 310 n.

craniometry
head 213 n.
anthropology 371 n.

cranium
head 213 n.

crank
rotate 315 vb.

eccentricity 503 n.
crank 504 n.

crankiness
(*see* crank,
cranky)

cranky
convoluted 251 adj.
crazed 503 adj.

cranny
compartment 194 n.
hiding-place 527 n.

crapulence
crapulence 949 n.

crash
textile 222 n.
collision 279 n.
descent 309 n.
bang 402 n., vb.
miscarry, fail
728 vb.
insolvency 805 n.

crash-landing
aeronautics 271 n.

crasis
composition 56 n.

crass
unintelligent 499
adj.
vulgar 847 adj.

crate
vehicle 274 n.

crater
bowl 194 n.
cavity 255 n.

cravat
neckwear 228 n.

crave
require 627 vb.
request 761 vb.

craven
coward 856 n.

crawl
pedestrianism
267 n.
move slowly 278 vb.
knuckle under
721 vb.
be servile 879 vb.

crawlers
breeches 228 n.

craze
make mad 503 vb.
fashion 848 n.

crazed
foolish 499 adj.

craziness
eccentricity 503 n.

crazy
distorted 246 adj.
variegated 437
adj.
crazed 503 adj.

creak
stridor 407 n.

creaking, creaky
strident 407 adj.

cream
milk 301 n.
fat 357 n.
select 605 vb.
élite 644 n.
cosmetic 845 n.

creamy
semiliquid 354 adj.
fatty 357 adj.
savoury 390 adj.
whitish 427 adj.

crease
jumble 63 vb.
fold 261 n., vb.

create
cause 156 vb.
produce 164 vb.

creation
non-imitation 21 n.
production 164 n.
universe 321 n.

creative
unimitative 21 adj.
causal 156 adj.
prolific 171 adj.
imaginative
513 adj.

creator
cause 156 n.
producer 167 n.
the Deity 965 n.

creature
product 164 n.
animal 365 n.
person 371 n.
auxiliary 707 n.
dependant 742 n.

creature of habit
habitué 610 n.

crèche
school 539 n.

credal
credal 485 adj.
theological 973 adj.

credence
belief 485 n.

credential
credential 465 n.

credible
plausible 471 adj.
credible 485 adj.

credit
attribute 158 vb.
believe 485 vb.
subvention 703 n.
lend 784 vb.
credit 802 n., vb.
account 808 vb.
repute 866 n.
thank 907 vb.
dueness 915 n.

creditable
approvable 923 adj.

creditor
lender 784 n.
creditor 802 n.

credit side
gain 771 n.

credit-worthy
reputable 866 adj.
deserving 915 adj.

credo
(*see* creed)

credulity
credulity 487 n.
persuasibility 612 n.

credulous
credulous 487 adj.

creed
creed 485 n.

creek
gulf 345 n.
stream 350 n.

creel
basket 194 n.

creep
move slowly 278
vb.
itch 378 vb.
be stealthy 525 vb.

creeper
plant 366 n.

creeps
formication 378 n.
nervousness 854 n.

cremation
interment 364 n.
burning 381 n.

crematorium
interment 364 n.
furnace 383 n.

crenellate
notch 260 vb.

creole
settler 191 n.

crepitate
eruct 300 vb.
crackle 402 vb.
crescendo
increase 36 n.
crescent
housing 192 n.
arc 250 n.
crest
superiority 34 n.
summit 213 n.
plumage 259 n.
heraldry 547 n.
nobility 868 n.
crestfallen
dejected 834 adj.
humbled 872
adj.
cretin
madman 504 n.
cretinous
insane 503 adj.
crevasse
cavity 255 n.
crevice
gap 201 n.
crew
band 74 n.
navigate 269 vb.
mariner 270 n.
personnel 686 n.
crib
copy 22 n.
bed 218 n.
cribble
porosity 263 n.
cribriform
perforated 263
adj.
crick
pang 377 n.
cricket
ball game 837 n.
cri de cœur
lament 836 n.
crier
publicizer 528 n.
seller 793 n.
crime
foul play 930 n.
lawbreaking 954
n.
crime passionel
revenge 910 n.
jealousy 911 n.
crime wave
lawlessness 954 n.

criminal
offender 904 n.
rascally 930 adj.
guilty 936 adj.
**criminal
conversation**
illicit love 951 n.
criminologist
detective 459 n.
criminology
lawbreaking 954 n.
criminous
(*see* **criminal**)
crimp
crinkle 251 vb.
notch 260 vb.
taker 786 n.
thief 789 n.
cringe
stoop 311 vb.
be servile 879 vb.
crinkle
crinkle 251 vb.
fold 261 n., vb.
crinoline
skirt 228 n.
cripple
disable 161 vb.
weaken 163 vb.
sick person 651 n.
crisis
crisis 137 n.
eventuality 154 n.
predicament 700 n.
crisp
crinkle 251 vb.
brittle 330 adj.
criss-cross
crossed 222 adj.
criterion
testing agent 461 n.
comparison 462 n.
critic
estimator 480 n.
dissentient 489 n.
theorist 512 n.
interpreter 520 n.
dissertator 591 n.
malcontent 829 n.
man of taste 846 n.
disapprover 924 n.
critical
crucial 137 adj.
timely 137 adj.
discriminating
463 adj.
judicial 480 adj.

dangerous 661 adj.
discontented
829 adj.
fastidious 862 adj.
criticism
estimate 480 n.
interpretation
520 n.
article 591 n.
advice 691 n.
criticize
discriminate
463 vb.
be discontented
829 vb.
critique
(*see* **criticism**)
croak
ululate 409 vb.
croaker
malcontent 829 n.
crock
vessel 194 n.
sick person 651 n.
crockery
brittleness 330 n.
pottery 381 n.
crock up
be fatigued 684 vb.
crocodile
procession 71 n.
reptile 365 n.
crocodile tears
duplicity 541 n.
croft
farm 370 n.
crofter
husbandman 370 n.
crony
chum 880 n.
crook
render oblique
220 vb.
angulate 247 vb.
knave 938 n.
crooked
oblique 220 adj.
distorted 246 adj.
dishonest 930 adj.
croon
sing 413 vb.
sound faint 401 vb.
crooner
vocalist 413 n.
entertainer 594 n.
croon over
pet 889 vb.

crop
multitude 104 n.
maw 194 n.
shorten 204 vb.
graze 301 vb.
agriculture 370 n.
store 632 n.
hair-dressing 843 n.
cropper
descent 309 n.
crop up
happen 154 vb.
crosier
vestments 989 n.
cross
hybrid 43 n.
counteract 182 vb.
cross 222 n., vb.
bane 659 n.
decoration 729 n.
angry 891 adj.
religious faith
973 n.
talisman 983 n.
crossbow
missile weapon
723 n.
cross-breed
hybrid 43 n.
mix 43 vb.
cross-current
counteraction
182 n.
current 350 n.
cross-examination
interrogation 459
n.
legal trial 959 n.
cross-examiner
questioner 459 n.
cross-eyed
dim-sighted 440
adj.
cross-grained
wilful 602 adj.
sullen 893 adj.
crossing
crossing 222 n.
passage 305 n.
cross out
subtract 39 vb.
obliterate 550 vb.
cross-purposes
misinterpretation
521 n.
cross-question
interrogate 459 vb.

cross-reference
sorting 62 n.
class 62 vb.
crossroad
juncture 8 n.
focus 76 n.
road 624 n.
cross section
example 83 n.
cross the Rubicon
overstep 306 vb.
be resolute 599 vb.
crossways
focus 76 n.
road 624 n.
cross with
unite with 45 vb.
crossword
enigma 530 n.
crotchet
angularity 247 n.
notation 410 n.
punctuation 547 n.
crotchety
wilful 602 adj.
crouch
be low 210 vb.
stoop 311 vb.
be servile 879 vb.
croup
buttocks 238 n.
respiration 352 n.
croupier
treasurer 798 n.
crow
ululate 409 vb.
black thing 428 n.
boast 877 vb.
crowd
great quantity
32 n.
crowd 74 n.
multitude 104 n.
be dense 324 vb.
crown
completeness 54 n.
vertex 213 n.
crown 213 vb.
headgear 228 n.
climax 725 vb.
authority 733 n.
regalia 743 n.
coinage 797 n.
crown all
climax 725 vb.
crow over
triumph 727 vb.

crow to pluck
resentment 891 n.
crozier
(see crosier)
crucial
crucial 137 adj.
fundamental
156 adj.
crucial moment
crisis 137 n.
crucial test
experiment 461 n.
crucible
mixture 43 n.
testing agent 461 n.
crucifix
cross 222 n.
church interior
990 n.
crucifixion
killing 362 n.
suffering 825 n.
crucify *(see*
crucifixion)
crude
inelegant 576 adj.
immature 670 adj.
cruel
violent 176 adj.
cruel 898 adj.
pitiless 906 adj.
cruelty *(see* cruel)
cruet
vessel 194 n.
cruise
water travel 269 n.
cruiser
warship 722 n.
crumb
small thing 33 n.
crumble
break 46 vb.
decompose 51 vb.
be brittle 330 vb.
pulverize 332 vb.
crumbling
antiquated 127 adj.
powdery 332 adj.
crumpet
pastry 301 n.
crumple
jumble 63 vb.
fold 261 vb.
crunch
rend 46 vb.
chew 301 vb.
rasp 407 vb.

crupper
buttocks 238 n.
crusade
war 718 n.
crusader
militarist 722 n.
religionist 979 n.
crusading spirit
philanthropy 901 n.
pietism 979 n.
crush
jumble 63 vb.
crowd 74 n.
demolish 165 vb.
make smaller
198 vb.
pulverize 332 vb.
oppress 735 vb.
humiliate 872 vb.
crusher
pulverizer 332 n.
crushing
forceful 571 adj.
completive 725 adj.
crust
exteriority 223 n.
covering 226 n.
skin 226 n.
mouthful 301 n.
crustacean
animal 365 n.
crusty
irascible 892 adj.
crutch
supporter 218 n.
angularity 247 n.
crux
enigma 530 n.
cry
loudness 400 n.
cry 408 n., vb.
ululation 409 n.
proclaim 528 vb.
rumour 529 n.
weep 836 vb.
fashion 848 n.
cry-baby
weakling 163 n.
cry down
detract 926 vb.
crypt
cellar 194 n.
church interior
990 n.
cryptic
occult 523 adj.
concealed 525 adj.

cabbalistic 984 adj.
crypto
latent 523 adj.
cryptogram
enigma 530 n.
crystal
solid body 324 n.
oracle 511 n.
crystal-gazer
diviner 511 n.
crystalline
transparent 422 adj.
crystallization
condensation 324 n.
crystallize
harden 326 vb.
sweeten 392 vb.
cry up
praise 923 vb.
cub
youngster 132 n.
youngling 132 n.
cubby-hole
compartment 194 n.
cubic
spatial 183 adj.
metric 465 adj.
cubic content
space 183 n.
metrology 465 n.
cubicle
compartment
194 n.
chamber 194 n.
cubit
long measure
203 n.
cuckold
cuckold 952 n.
cuckoldry
illicit love 951 n.
cuckoo
intruder 59 n.
repetition 106 n.
ululation 409 n.
fool 501 n.
crazed 503 adj.
cucumber
vegetable 301 n.
cud
mouthful 301 n.
cuddle
caress 889 vb.
cudgel
strike 279 vb.
club 723 n.
scourge 964 n.

cue
hint 524 n.

cuff
sleeve 228 n.
fold 261 n.
spank 963 vb.

cuirass
armour 713 n.

cuirassier
cavalry 722 n.

cuisine
cookery 301 n.

cul-de-sac
closure 264 n.
obstacle 702 n.

culinary
culinary 301 adj.

cull
select 605 vb.

culminate
be high 209 vb.
crown 213 vb.
climax 725 vb.

culpable
wrong 914 adj.
blameworthy 924 adj.
guilty 936 adj.

culprit
offender 904 n.
accused person 928 n.

cult
practice 610 n.
fashion 848 n.
cult 981 n.
rite 988 n.

cult image
idol 982 n.

cultivable
agrarian 370 adj.

cultivate
cultivate 370 vb.
flatter 925 vb.

cultivated
instructed 490 adj.

cultivation
agriculture 370 n.
culture 490 n.

cultivator
husbandman 370 n.

cultural
educational 534 adj.
improving 654 adj.

culture
culture 490 n.

cultured
instructed 490 adj.
spurious 542 adj.

culvert
drain 351 n.

cumbersome, cumbrous
weighty 322 adj.
clumsy 695 adj.

cumulative
increasing 36 adj.

cumulativeness
continuity 71 n.

cuneiform
letter 558 n.

cunning
skill 694 n.
cunning 698 n., adj.
dishonest 930 adj.

cup
cup 194 n.
liquor 301 n.
doctor 658 vb.
trophy 729 n.
adversity 731 n.

cupboard
cabinet 194 n.
shelf 218 n.

cupful
finite quantity 26 n.

cup-holder
proficient 696 n.

cupidity
avarice 816 n.
desire 859 n.

cupola
roof 226 n.
dome 253 n.

cups
drunkenness 949 n.

cur
dog 365 n.
coward 856 n.
cad 938 n.

curable
restored 656 adj.

curacy
church office 985 n.

curate
pastor 986 n.

curative
remedial 658 adj.

curator
protector 660 n.
keeper 749 n.

curb
moderate 177 vb.

retard 278 vb.
restrain 747 vb.
fetter 748 n.

curd
solid body 324 n.

curdle
be dense 324 vb.

curds
milk product 301 n.

cure
revival 656 n.
cure 656 vb.
remedy, therapy 658 n.
preserve 666 vb.

cure-all
remedy 658 n.

cure of disaccustom
611 vb.

cure of souls
church ministry 985 n.

curfew
restriction 747 n.

curia
council 692 n.

curio
exhibit 522 n.

curiosity
curiosity 453 n.

curious literature
impurity 951 n.

curl
curve 248 n.
loop 250 n.
coil 251 n.
hair 259 n.
hair-dressing 843 n.
primp 843 vb.

curlers
hair-dressing 843 n.

curlicue
coil 251 n.
lettering 586 n.

curling
sport 837 n.

curling-iron
hair-dressing 843 n.

curly
undulatory 251 adj.

currency
generality 79 n.
publicity 528 n.
money 797 n.

current
existing 1 adj.

present 121 adj.
electricity 160 n.
direction 281 n.
current 350 n.
published 528 adj.

curriculum
curriculum 534 n.

curry
cook 301 vb.
rub 333 vb.
condiment 389 n.

curry-comb
rub 333 vb.
groom 369 vb.

curse
influence 178 n.
bane 659 n.
adversity 731 n.
malediction 899 n.
spell 983 n.

cursory
transient 114 adj.
inattentive 456 adj.

curt
concise 569 adj.
taciturn 582 adj.

curtail
subtract 39 vb.
cut 46 vb.
shorten 204 vb.

curtain
end 69 n.
partition 321 n.
fence 235 n.
screen 421 vb.
stage-set 594 n.

curtain-raiser
beginning 68 n.
stage play 594 n.

curtsy
show respect 920 vb.

curvaceous
curved 248 adj.
shapely 841 adj.

curvature
curvature 248 n.

curve
obliquity 220 n.
curve 248 n.
deviate 282 vb.

curvet
equitation 267 n.
leap 312 n., vb.

curvilinear
curved 248 adj.

cushion
seat, cushion 218 n.

line 227 vb.
soften 327 vb.
protection 660 n.

cusp
vertex 213 n.
sharp point 256 n.

cuspidor
bowl 194 n.

cuss
cuss 899 vb.

cussedness
opposition 704 n.
malevolence 898 n.

custodial
tutelary 660 adj.

custodian
protector 660 n.
keeper 749 n.

custody
protection 660 n.
detention 747 n.

custom
tradition 127 n.
habit 610 n.
purchase 792 n.
etiquette 848 n.

customer
person 371 n.
purchaser 792 n.

customs
conduct 688 n.
tax 809 n.

cut
diminution 37 n.
decrement 42 n.
cut 46 vb.
piece 53 n.
gap 201 n.
shorten 204 vb.
form 243 n.
excavation 255 n.
be sharp 256 vb.
groove 262 vb.
engrave 555 vb.
wound 655 n., vb.
portion 783 n.
discount 810 n.
cheapen 812 vb.
hair-dressing 843 n.
make unwelcome 883 vb.

cut above, a
superior 34 adj.

cut a dash
be ostentatious 875 vb.

cut and thrust
foin 712 n.

cutaneous
dermal 226 adj.

cut both ways
tell against 467 vb.
be equivocal 518 vb.

cute
personable 841 adj.

cuticle
skin 226 n.

cutis
skin 226 n.

cutlass
side arms 723 n.

cutlery
sharp edge 256 n.

cutlet
piece 53 n.
(see meat)

cut off
circumscribe 232 vb.
hinder 702 vb.

cut out
be superior 34 vb.
efform 243 vb.

cut out for
fit 24 adj.

cut price
cheap 812 adj.

cutter
clothier 228 n.
boat 275 n.

cut-throat
destructive 165 adj.
murderer 362 n.
ruffian 904 n.

cut through
pierce 263 vb.

cutting
scission 46 n.
excavation 255 n.
sharp 256 adj.
cinema 445 n.

cut up
unhappy 825 adj.

cut up rough
be angry 891 vb.

cybernetics
mechanics 630 n.

cycle
recurrence 106 n.
era 110 n.
regular return 141 n.
bicycle 274 n.

cyclone
vortex 315 n.
weather 340 n.
gale 352 n.

cyclopedia
reference book 589 n.

cygnet
youngling 132 n.
waterfowl 365 n.

cylinder
cylinder 252 n.

cylindrical
rotund 252 adj.
tubular 263 adj.

cynic
misanthrope 902 n.
detractor 926 n.

cynical
indifferent 860 adj.
detracting 926 adj.
(see cynicism)

cynicism
moral insensibility 820 n.
misanthropy 902 n.

cynosural
well-seen 443 adj.

cynosure
prototype 23 n.
focus 76 n.
attraction 291 n.
signpost 547 n.

D

dab
knock 279 n.
proficient 696 n.

dabble
make unclean 649 vb.
amuse oneself 837 vb.

dabbler
sciolist 493 n.

dabbling
smattering 491 adj.

dacoit
robber 789 n.

dad
parent 169 n.

dado
base 214 n.

daemonic, demonic
active 678 adj.
diabolic 969 adj.

daft, daffy
foolish 499 adj.
crazed 503 adj.

dagger
sharp point 256 n.
side-arms 723 n.

daily
often 139 adv.
seasonal 141 adj.
the press 528 n.
usual 610 adj.
servant 742 n.

daily bread
food 301 n.
vocation 622 n.

dainty
small 33 adj.
little 196 adj.
savoury 390 adj.
clean 648 adj.
personable 841 adj.
fastidious 862 adj.

dairy
chamber 194 n.

dais
stand 218 n.
rostrum 539 n.

dale
plain 348 n.

dalesman
dweller 191 n.

dalliance
love-making 887 n.

dally
be inactive 679 vb.
amuse oneself 837 vb.
caress 889 vb.

dam
be akin 11 vb.
maternity 169 n.
close 264 vb.
irrigator 341 n.
lake 346 n.
obstruct 702 vb.

damage
break 46 vb.
harm 645 vb.
impairment 655 n.

damages
offset 31 n.
restitution 787 n.
penalty 963 n.

damaging
harmful 645 adj.
discreditable 867 adj.

damask
textile 222 n.
dame
woman 373 n.
damn
curse, cuss 899 vb.
condemn 961 vb.
damnation
condemnation
961 n.
damnatory
maledictory
899 adj.
damnify
harm 645 vb.
damn the
consequences
be rash 857 vb.
damp
water 339 n.
moisture 341 n.
mute 401 vb.
damper
moderator 177 n.
stopper 264 n.
silencer 401 n.
mute 414 n.
dissuasion 613 n.
moper 834 n.
disapprover 924 n.
damp-proof
dry 342 adj.
damp squib
insubstantial thing
4 n.
disappointment
509 n.
dance
vary 152 vb.
leap 312 vb.
shine 417 vb.
rejoice 835 vb.
dance 837 n., vb.
dance-floor,
dance-hall
place of
amusement 837 n.
dancer
dance 837 n.
dancing
dancing 837 n.
dancing girl
entertainer 594 n.
dandified
fashionable 848 adj.
dandle
caress 889 vb.

dandruff
dirt 649 n.
dandy
fop 848 n.
danegeld
tax 809 n.
danger
probability 471 n.
danger 661 n.
dangerous
dangerous 661 adj.
frightening 854 adj.
malevolent 898 adj.
danger signal
dissuasion 613 n.
danger signal
665 n.
danger-spot
pitfall 663 n.
dangle
come unstuck
49 vb.
hang 217 vb.
oscillate 317 vb.
cause desire
859 vb.
dank
humid 341 adj.
cheerless 834 adj.
dapper
personable 841 adj.
dapple
variegate 437 vb.
dappled
pied 437 adj.
dare
be resolute 599 vb.
face danger 661 vb.
undertake 672 vb.
defy 711 vb.
dare-devil
brave person 855 n.
desperado 857 n.
rash 857 adj.
daring
showy 875 adj.
(*see* dare)
dark
vespertine 129 adj.
dark 418 adj.
black 428 adj.
dark, in the
invisible 444 adj.
ignorant 491 adj.
darken
darken 418 vb.
blur 440 vb.

deject 834 vb.
dark glasses
screen 421 n.
dark horse
unknown thing
491 n.
darkness
ignorance 491 n.
(*see* dark)
darling
darling 890 n.
favourite 890 n.
darn
repair 656 n., vb.
dart
move fast 277 vb.
missile 287 n.
Darwinism
biology 358 n.
dash
small quantity 33 n.
vigorousness 174 n.
spurt 277 n.
move fast 277 vb.
punctuation 547 n.
racing 716 n.
dash at
charge 712 vb.
dashed
humbled 872 adj.
dastard
coward 856 n.
data, datum
evidence 466 n.
date
date 108 n.
chronology 117 n.
lover 887 n.
date up
be sociable 882 vb.
datum (*see* data)
daub
coat 226 vb.
colour 425 vb.
misrepresentation
552 n.
picture 553 n.
paint 553 vb.
dauber
artist 556 n.
bungler 697 n.
daughter
descendant 170 n.
daughterly
filial 170 adj.
daunt
frighten 854 vb.

dauntless
unfearing 855 adj.
dawdle
be late 136 vb.
walk 267 vb.
move slowly 278 vb.
dawdler
slowcoach 278 n.
dawn
precursor 66 n.
beginning 68 n.
morning 128 n.
appear 445 vb.
day
period 110 n.
daybreak
morning 128 n.
daydream
fantasy 513 n.
desire 959 n.
daylight
interval 201 n.
light 417 n.
manifestation
522 n.
disclosure 526 n.
day off
lull 145 n.
day of judgement
finality 69 n.
day of reckoning
revenge 910 n.
punishment 963 n.
days
time 108 n.
era 110 n.
daze
distract 456 vb.
puzzle 474 vb.
dazzle
light 417 n.
shine 417 vb.
blind 439 vb.
blur 440 vb.
distract 456 vb.
impress 821 vb.
be ostentatious
875 vb.
dazzler
a beauty 841 n.
dazzling
excellent 644 adj.
(*see* dazzle)
D-day
start 68 n.
deacon
cleric 986 n.

deactivated
inert 175 adj.
dead
unborn 2 adj.
inert 175 adj.
dead 361 adj.
non-resonant
405 adj.
soft-hued 425 adj.
dead-beat
fatigued 684 adj.
dead body
corpse 363 n.
deaden
render insensible
375 vb.
mute 401 vb.
make mute 578 vb.
make insensitive
820 vb.
relieve 831 vb.
dead end
stopping place
145 n.
obstacle 702 n.
deadfall
trap 542 n.
dead heat
draw 28 n.
synchronism 123 n.
dead letter
ineffectuality 161 n.
abrogation 752 n.
deadlight
screen 421 n.
deadline
limit 236 n.
deadlock
equilibrium 28 n.
stop 145 n.
obstacle 702 n.
defeat 728 n.
deadly
destructive 165 adj.
deadly 362 adj.
toxic 653 adj.
heinous 934 adj.
dead march
obsequies 364 n.
dead-on
accurate 494 adj.
dead-pan
impassive 820 adj.
dead reckoning
navigation 269 n.
dead set at
attack 712 n.

dead spit
analogue 18 n.
dead stop
stop 145 n.
dead-weight
encumbrance 702 n.
dead wood
rubbish 641 n.
deaf
deaf 416 adj.
deafen
be loud 400 vb.
deafen 416 vb.
deaf-mute
deafness 416 n.
aphony 578 n.
deafness
deafness 416 n.
deal
great quantity
32 n.
compact 765 n.
deed 676 n.
portion 783 n.
dealer
merchant 794 n.
deal in
trade 791 vb.
dealings
deed 676 n.
deal with
be related 9 vb.
dissert 591 vb.
dean
ecclesiarch 986 n.
dear
profitless 641 adj.
dear 811 adj.
loved one 887 n.
lovable 887 adj.
darling 890 n.
dearth
scarcity 636 n.
death
extinction 2 n.
death 361 n.
death-bed
decease 361 n.
illness 651 n.
deathblow
end 69 n.
killing 362 n.
defeat 728 n.
death-knell
decease 361 n.
deathless
perpetual 115 adj.

deathliness
quiescence 266 n.
deathly
dying 361 adj.
colourless 426 adj.
death rate
death roll 361 n.
death-rattle
decease 361 n.
death sentence
capital punishment
963 n.
death's head
moper 834 n.
eyesore 842 n.
death-trap
danger 661 n.
death-wish
dejection 834 n.
débâcle
ruin 165 n.
debar
restrain 747 vb.
prohibit 757 vb.
debase
pervert 655 vb.
impair 655 vb.
demonetize 797
vb.
debatable
topical 452 adj.
uncertain 474 adj.
debate
argument 475 n.
conference 584 n.
debater
reasoner 475 n.
debauch
festivity 837 n.
drunkenness 949 n.
debauch 951 vb.
debauched
vicious 934 adj.
debauchee
libertine 952 n.
debauchery
sensualism 944 n.
unchastity 951 n.
debenture
title-deed 767 n.
debility
weakness 163 n.
ill-health 651 n.
debit
debt 803 n.
debouch
emerge 298 vb.

débris
leavings 41 n.
rubbish 641 n.
debt
debt 803 n.
dueness 915 n.
debtor
debtor 803 n.
debunk
ridicule 851 vb.
detract 926 vb.
début
début 68 n.
débutant, -e
beginner 538 n.
spinster 895 n.
decadence
deterioration 655 n.
decamp
decamp 296 vb.
decant
transpose 272 vb.
void 300 vb.
infuse 303 vb.
decanter
vessel 194 n.
transferrer 272 n.
decay
decrease 37 vb.
decay 51 n.
age 131 n.
desuetude 611 n.
dirt 649 n.
dilapidation 655 n.
decease
decease 361 n.
deceit
deception 542 n.
deceitful
false 541 adj.
deceiving 542 adj.
deceive
mislead 495 vb.
deceive 542 vb.
deceiver
deceiver 545 n.
libertine 952 n.
deceiving
disappointing
509 adj.
deceleration
slowness 278 n.
decency
good taste 846 n.
purity 950 n.
decent
not bad 644 adj.

mediocre 732 adj.
ethical 917 adj.
pure 950 adj.
decentralization
non-uniformity 17 n.
laxity 734 n.
deception
(*see* deceptive)
deceptive
simulating 18 adj.
erroneous 495 adj.
disappointing
509 adj.
deceiving 542 adj.
decide
cause 156 vb.
judge 480 vb.
decree 737 vb.
decided
assertive 532 adj.
deciduous
ephemeral 114 adj.
vegetal 366 adj.
decimal
numerical element
85 n.
decimate
render few 105 vb.
slaughter 362 vb.
execute 963 vb.
decipher
decipher 520 vb.
decipherable
intelligible 516 adj.
decipherment
interpretation
520 n.
decision
will 595 n.
(*see* decide)
decisive
crucial 137 adj.
causal 156 adj.
deck
layer 207 n.
overlay 226 vb.
decorate 844 vb.
deckhand
mariner 270 n.
declaim
orate 579 vb.
declaimer
speaker 579 n.
declamation
magniloquence
574 n.
oratory 579 n.

declaration
(*see* declare)
declaratory
meaningful 514 adj.
affirming 532 adj.
declare
divulge 526 vb.
affirm 532 vb.
declare war
go to war 718 vb.
declassify
exclude 57 vb.
declension
grammar 564 n.
declination
bearings 186 n.
descent 309 n.
decline
decrease 37 n., vb.
weakness 163 n.
parse 564 vb.
reject 607 vb.
phthisis 651 n.
deterioration 655 n.
adversity 731 n.
declivity
acclivity 220 n.
decoction
potion 301 n.
decode
decipher 520 vb.
décolleté
uncovering 229 n.
decolorize
decolorize 426 vb.
decompose
decompose 51 vb.
be dispersed 75 vb.
deconsecrate
laicize 987 vb.
decontrol
liberation 746 n.
non-retention 779 n.
décor
stage-set 594 n.
decorate
(*see* decoration)
decoration
improvement 654 n.
decoration 729 n.
badge of rank
743 n.
ornamentation
844 n.
honours 866 n.
decorative
ornamental 844 adj.

decorous
pure 950 adj.
decorum
good taste 846 n.
decoy
trap 542 n.
trickster 545 n.
incentive 612 n.
decrease
decrease 37 n., vb.
deterioration 655
n.
decree
judgement 480 n.
decree 737 n., vb.
legislation 953 n.
decrement
decrement 42 n.
shortcoming 307 n.
loss 772 n.
decrepit
unhealthy 651 adj.
dilapidated 655 adj.
decry
hold cheap 922 vb.
detract 926 vb.
dedicate
offer 759 vb.
give 781 vb.
dignify 866 vb.
sanctify 979 vb.
dedicated
obedient 739 adj.
disinterested
931 adj.
dedication
resolution 599 n.
(*see* dedicated)
deduce
reason 475 vb.
deduction
subtraction 39 n.
decrement 42 n.
reasoning 475 n.
judgement 480 n.
discount 810 n.
deed
deed 676 n.
title-deed 767 n.
prowess 855 n.
deep
great 32 adj.
deep 211 adj.
interior 224 adj.
loud 400 adj.
florid 425 adj.
wise 498 adj.

inexpressible
517 adj.
imperspicuous
568 adj.
deep down
intrinsic 5 adj.
deepen
augment 36 vb.
be deep 211 vb.
blacken 428 vb.
aggravate 832 vb.
deep-freeze
refrigeration 382 n.
preservation 666 n.
deep in
attentive 455 adj.
deep-laid
matured 669 adj.
cunning 698 adj.
deep-rooted
lasting 113 adj.
deep 211 adj.
deep-seated
lasting 113 adj.
interior 224 adj.
deer
speeder 277 n.
coward 856 n.
deface
destroy 165 vb.
obliterate 550 vb.
impair 655 vb.
make ugly 842 vb.
blemish 845 vb.
defaecate
(*see* defecation)
defalcate
be dishonest 930 vb.
defalcation
non-payment 805 n.
defamation
detraction 926 n.
defamatory
detracting 926 adj.
defame
defame 926 vb.
accuse 928 vb.
default
deficit 55 n.
negligence 458 n.
non-payment 805
n.
fail in duty 918 vb.
defaulter
defrauder 789 n.
debtor 803 n.
non-payer 805 n.

defeat
confute 479 vb.
defeat 728 n., vb.
defeatism
dejection 834 n.
hopelessness 853 n.
nervousness 854 n.
defeatist
alarmist 854 n.
(*see* **defeatism**)
defecation
cacation 302 n.
defect
shortcoming 307 n.
insufficiency 636 n.
defect 647 n.
defection
tergiversation 603 n.
dutilessness 918 n.
perfidy 930 n.
defective
insane 503 adj.
(*see* **defect**)
defence
counter-evidence
467 n.
defence 713 n.
defenceless
defenceless 161 adj.
vulnerable 661 adj.
defences
defences 713 n.
defend
patronize 703 vb.
defend 713 vb.
defendant
accused person
928 n.
litigant 959 n.
defender
protector 660 n.
patron 707 n.
defender 713 n.
defensive
avoiding 620 adj.
defending 713 adj.
defer
put off 136 vb.
deference
submission 721 n.
respect 920 n.
deferential
(*see* **deference**)
deferment
delay 136 n.
defiance
affirmation 532 n.

negation 533 n.
opposition 704 n.
defiance 711 n.
sauciness 878 n.
defiant
uncomfortable
84 adj.
deficiency
inferiority 35 n.
insufficiency 636 n.
defect 647 n.
deficient
deficient 307 adj.
unintelligent
499 adj.
deficit
deficit 55 n.
shortcoming 307 n.
defile
gap 201 n.
walk 267 vb.
passage 305 n.
make unclean
649 vb.
impair, pervert
655 vb.
shame 867 vb.
defilement
impurity 951 n.
define
specify 80 vb.
limit 236 vb.
interpret 520 vb.
definite
limited 236 adj.
accurate 494 adj.
definition
interpretation 520 n.
perspicuity 567 n.
definitive
ending 69 adj.
interpretive 520 adj.
deflate
make smaller
198 vb.
ridicule 851 vb.
detract 926 vb.
deflation
finance 797 n.
cheapness 812 n.
deflect
render oblique
220 vb.
deflect 282 vb.
parry 713 vb.
deflection
deviation 282 n.

deflower
unite with 45 vb.
debauch 951 vb.
deform
distort 246 vb.
misrepresent
552 vb.
pervert 655 vb.
make ugly 842 vb.
deformity
deformity 246 n.
ugliness 842 n.
defraud
defraud 788 vb.
be dishonest 930 vb.
de-frost
heat 381 vb.
deft
skilful 694 adj.
defumigate
have no smell
395 vb.
defunct
extinct 2 adj.
dead 361 adj.
defy
negate 533 vb.
be resolute 599 vb.
defy 711 vb.
be insolent 878 vb.
degeneracy
deterioration 655 n.
wickedness 934 n.
degenerate
changed person
147 n.
deteriorate 655 vb.
relapse 657 vb.
vicious 934 adj.
cad 938 n.
degenerative
diseased 651 adj.
degrade
impair, pervert
655 vb.
depose 752 vb.
not respect 921 vb.
degree
relativeness 9 n.
degree 27 n.
series 71 n.
angular measure
247 n.
dehumanize
pervert 655 vb.
make wicked
934 vb.

dehydration
desiccation 342 n.
preservation 666 n.
deification
deification 982 n.
deify
dignify 866 vb.
idolatrize 982 vb.
deign
consent 758 vb.
deism
religion, deism
973 n.
deist
religionist 973 n.
deity
divineness 965 n.
dejected
unhappy 825 adj.
dejection
dejection 834 n.
de jure
due 915 adj.
legal 953 adj.
delay
delay 136 n.
lull 145 n.
be inactive 679 vb.
delectable
pleasurable 826 adj.
delectation
enjoyment 824 n.
delegate
councillor 692 n.
commission 751 vb.
delegate 754 n.
delegation
delegate 754 n.
transfer 780 n.
deleterious
harmful 645 adj.
deletion
obliteration 550 n.
deliberate
slow 278 adj.
predetermined
608 adj.
intended 617 adj.
consult 691 vb.
deliberation
meditation 449 n.
deliberative
advising 691 adj.
delicacy
savouriness 390 n.
discrimination
463 n.

dénouement
eventuality 154 n.
effect 157 n.
evolution 316 n.
denounce
inform 524 vb.
satirize 851 vb.
dispraise 924 vb.
accuse 928 vb.
dense
firm-set 45 adj.
multitudinous
104 adj.
dense 324 adj.
unintelligent
499 adj.
density
materiality 319 n.
density 324 n.
opacity 423 n.
(*see* dense)
dent
concavity 255 n.
notch 260 vb.
dental
toothed 256 adj.
speech sound
398 n.
denticulation
tooth 256 n.
dentist
doctor 658 n.
dentistry
surgery 658 n.
dentition, denture
tooth 256 n.
denudation
uncovering 229 n.
denude
uncover 229 vb.
disclose 526 vb.
denunciation
(*see* denounce)
denunciatory
maledictory
899 adj.
accusing 928 adj.
deny
disbelieve 486 vb.
negate 533 vb.
deny oneself
be temperate
942 vb.
deodorant
inodorousness
395 n.
cleanser 648 n.

deodorize
aerify 340 vb.
purify 648 vb.
depart
depart 296 vb.
depart from
deviate 282 vb.
department
subdivision 53 n.
classification 77 n.
district 184 n.
function 622 n.
departure
start 68 n.
deviation 282 n.
departure 296 n.
(*see* depart)
depend
depend 157 vb.
be uncertain
474 vb.
dependable
trustworthy 929 adj.
dependant
inferior 35 n.
dependant 742 n.
dependence
inferiority 35 n.
subjection 745 n.
dependency
polity 733 n.
subject 742 n.
dependent
inferior 35 adj.
subject 745 adj.
depend on
believe 485 vb.
be subject 745 vb.
depict
represent 551 vb.
describe 590 vb.
deplete
waste 634 vb.
deplorable
bad 645 adj.
regretted 830 adj.
deplore
regret 830 vb.
lament 836 vb.
disapprove 924 vb.
deploy
place 187 vb.
open 263 vb.
dispose of 673 vb.
depopulate
lay waste 165 vb.
void 300 vb.

deport
exclude 57 vb.
deportation
ejection 300 n.
deportee
outcaste 883 n.
deportment
conduct 688 n.
deposal
deposal 752 n.
depose
testify 466 vb.
depose 752 vb.
deprive 786 vb.
deposit
leavings 41 n.
thing transferred
272 n.
store 632 n., vb.
security 767 n.
deposition
testimony 466 n.
deposal 752 n.
depositor
creditor 802 n.
depot
station 187 n.
storage 632 n.
emporium 796 n.
depraved
vicious 934 adj.
depravity
wickedness 934 n.
deprecate
dissuade 613 vb.
deprecate 762
vb.
regret 830 vb.
deprecation
disapprobation
924 n.
(*see* deprecate)
depreciation
decrease 37 n.
underestimation
483 n.
loss 772 n.
detraction 926 n.
depredation
spoliation 788 n.
depress
make concave
255 vb.
depress 311 vb.
deject 834 vb.
depressing
cheerless 834 adj.

depression
valley 255 n.
depression 311 n.
psychopathy 503 n.
deprivation
separation 46 n.
deposal 752 n.
loss 772 n.
expropriation
786 n.
deprive
impoverish 801 vb.
(*see* deprivation)
depth
depth 211 n.
interiority 224 n.
wisdom 498 n.
imperspicuity
568 n.
depth-charge
bomb 723 n.
deputation
commission 751 n.
depute
commission 751 vb.
deputize
substitute 150 vb.
deputize 755 vb.
deputy
substitute 150 n.
deputy 755 n.
derail
derange 63 vb.
displace 188 vb.
derange
derange 63 vb.
make mad 503 vb.
incommode 827
vb.
deranged
insane 503 adj.
derangement
disorder 61 n.
displacement 188 n.
(*see* derange)
derelict
disused 674 adj.
unpossessed
774 adj.
derelict 779 n.
not retained
779 adj.
dereliction
dutilessness 918 n.
derestrict
restore 656 vb.
not retain 779 vb.

deride
ridicule 851 vb.
de rigueur
obligatory 917 adj.
derision
ridicule 851 n.
derisive
derisive 851 adj.
derisory
ridiculous 849 adj.
derivable
attributed 158 adj.
derivation
origin 68 n.
attribution 158 n.
etymology 559 n.
derivative
imitative 20 adj.
effect 157 n.
derive
result 158 vb.
attribute 158 vb.
acquire 771 vb.
derogatory
degrading 867 adj.
detracting 926 adj.
derrick
lifter 310 n.
dervish
ascetic 945 n.
monk 986 n.
descant
vocal music 412 n.
be diffuse 570 vb.
hymn 981 n.
descend
descend 309 vb.
descendant
survivor 41 n.
descendant 170 n.
descent
consanguinity 11 n.
decrease 37 n.
posteriority 120 n.
source 156 n.
genealogy 169 n.
sonship 170 n.
descent 309 n.
plunge 313 n.
theophany 965 n.
describe
represent 551 vb.
describe 590 vb.
description
sort 77 n.
nomenclature
561 n.

description 590 n.
descriptive
expressive 516 adj.
descriptive 590 adj.
descry
see 438 vb.
desecrate
misuse 675 vb.
be impious 980 vb.
desecrator
usurper 916 n.
impious person
980 n.
desert
desert 172 n.
emptiness 190 n.
dryness 342 n.
tergiversate 603 vb.
goodness 644 n.
fail in duty 918 vb.
(*see* deserts)
deserter
coward 856 n.
dutilessness 918 n.
desertion
disobedience 738 n.
perfidy 930 n.
deserts
right 913 n.
dueness 915 n.
reward 962 n.
deserve
deserve 915 vb.
deserved
just 913 adj.
due 915 adj.
deserving
excellent 644 adj.
approvable 923 adj.
déshabillé
informal dress
228 n.
uncovering 229 n.
desiccation
desiccation 342 n.
desideration,
desideratum
requirement 627 n.
desired object
859 n.
design
prototype 23 n.
composition 56 n.
form 243 n.
intention 617 n.
plan 623 n.
pattern 844 n.

designate
future 124 adj.
mark 547 vb.
select 605 vb.
designation
classification 77 n.
nomenclature
561 n.
designer
artist 556 n.
planner 623 n.
designing
selfish 932 adj.
designless
designless 618 adj.
desirability
expedience 642 n.
desirable
expedient 642 adj.
lovable 887 adj.
approvable 923
adj.
desire
motive 612 n.
desire 859 vb.
desired object
859 n.
desist
cease 145 vb.
not act 677 vb.
desk
cabinet 194 n.
stand 218 n.
desolate
lay waste 165 vb.
unproductive
172 adj.
void 300 vb.
secluded 883 adj.
desolation
havoc 165 n.
desert 172 n.
emptiness 190 n.
sorrow 825 n.
despair
hopelessness 853 n.
despatch
(*see* dispatch)
desperado
desperado 857 n.
ruffian 904 n.
desperate
resolute 599 adj.
hopeless 853 adj.
rash 857 adj.
desperation
(*see* desperate)

despicable
contemptible
922 adj.
despise
despise 922 vb.
despoil
lay waste 165 vb.
rob 788 vb.
despoiler
taker 786 n.
despondency
dejection 834 n.
hopelessness 853 n.
despot
tyrant 735 n.
autocrat 741 n.
despotic
oppressive 735 adj.
authoritarian
735 adj.
lawless 954 adj.
despotism
despotism 733 n.
brute force 735 n.
dessert
dish 301 n.
destination
stopping place 145 n.
objective 617 n.
destine
necessitate 596 vb.
predetermine
608 vb.
intend 617 vb.
destined
future 124 adj.
impending 155 adj.
destiny
destiny 155 n.
necessity 596 n.
predetermination
608 n.
destitute
not owning 774 adj.
destitution
poverty 801 n.
destroy
nullify 2 vb.
destroy 165 vb.
destroyer
destroyer 168 n.
violent creature
176 n.
warship 722 n.
destruction
extinction 2 n.
destruction 165 n.

destructive
  destructive 165 adj.
  wasteful 634 adj.
desultory
  orderless 61 adj.
  discontinuous
    72 adj.
  fitful 142 adj.
  light-minded
    456 adj.
detach
  disjoin 46 vb.
  unstick 49 vb.
  send 272 vb.
detachable
  severable 46 adj.
detached
  independent 744 adj.
  disinterested
    931 adj.
detachment
  separation 46 n.
  armed force 722 n.
  inexcitability
    823 n.
  disinterestedness
    931 n.
detail
  small quantity 33 n.
  specify 80 vb.
  send 272 vb.
  describe 590 vb.
  trifle 639 n.
  pattern 844 n.
detailed
  complete 54 adj.
  diffuse 570 adj.
  descriptive 590 adj.
details
  particulars 80 n.
detain
  imprison 747 vb.
  retain 778 vb.
detainee
  prisoner 750 n.
detect
  detect 484 vb.
  understand 516 vb.
  disclose 526 vb.
detection
  discovery 484 n.
detective
  detective 459 n.
detector
  detector 484 n.
détente
  pacification 719 n.

detention
  delay 136 n.
  detention 747 n.
deter
  hinder 702 vb.
  frighten 854 vb.
detergent
  cleanser 648 n.
deteriorate
  decompose 51 vb.
  be weak 163 vb.
deterioration
  deterioration 655
    n.
  relapse 657 n.
determinant
  cause 156 n.
determination
  will 595 n.
  resolution 599 n.
  intention 617 n.
  assiduity 678 n.
determine
  terminate 69 vb.
  will 595 vb.
  be resolute 599 vb.
determinism
  necessity 596 n.
deterrence
  dissuasion 613 n.
  intimidation 854 n.
deterrent
  safeguard 662 n.
  cautionary 664 adj.
  retaliation 714 n.
  weapon 723 n.
  threat 900 n.
detest
  (*see* detestation)
detestation
  hatred 888 n.
dethrone
  depose 752 vb.
dethronement
  deposal 752 n.
detonation
  bang 402 n.
detonator
  ammunition 723 n.
détour
  deviation 282 n.
  circuit 626 n.
detract
  subtract 39 vb.
detraction
  contempt 922 n.
  detraction 926 n.

detriment
  impairment 655 n.
detritus
  leavings 41 n.
  thing transferred
    272 n.
de trop
  superfluous 637 adj.
devalue
  impair 655 vb.
  demonetize 797 vb.
devastate
  lay waste 165 vb.
devastation
  havoc 165 n.
develop
  become 1 vb.
  augment 36 vb.
  result 157 vb.
  photograph 551 vb.
  (*see* development)
development
  increase 36 n.
  propagation 164 n.
  expansion 197 n.
  progression 285 n.
  evolution 316 n.
  improvement 654 n.
deviate
  be oblique 220 vb.
  (*see* deviation)
deviation
  unconformity 84 n.
  deviation 282 n.
deviationism
  unconformity 84 n.
deviationist
  nonconformist 84 n.
device
  heraldry 547 n.
  contrivance 623 n.
  tool 630 n.
  stratagem 698 n.
devil
  cook 301 vb.
  season 388 vb.
  monster 938 n.
  devil 969 n.
  demon 970 n.
devilish
  cruel 898 adj.
  diabolic 969 adj.
  infernal 972 adj.
devil-may-care
  rash 857 adj.
devilry
  cruel act 898 n.

  diabolism 969 n.
devil's advocate
  sophist 477 n.
Devil, the
  Satan 969 n.
devil-worship
  diabolism 969 n.
devious
  deviating 282 adj.
  circuitous 314 adj.
  dishonest 930 adj.
devise
  transfer 272 vb.
  think 449 vb.
  plan 623 vb.
  bequeath 780 vb.
devitalize
  weaken 163 vb.
devoid
  empty 190 adj.
devolution
  commission 751 n.
  transfer 780 n.
devolve
  impose a duty
    917 vb.
devolve on
  be one's duty
    917 vb.
devote
  give 781 vb.
devoted
  unfortunate 731
    adj.
  obedient 739 adj.
  friendly 880 adj.
  disinterested
    931 adj.
  pious 979 adj.
devotee
  habitué 610 n.
  worshipper 981 n.
devotion
  loyalty 739 n.
  love 887 n.
devotional
  religious 973 adj.
  devotional 981 adj.
devotions
  prayers 981 n.
devour
  destroy 165 vb.
  eat 301 vb.
  waste 634 vb.
  fleece 786 vb.
devouring
  gluttonous 947 adj.

devout
religious 973 adj.
pious 979 adj.
devoutness
piety 979 n.
dew
moisture 341 n.
(see dewy)
dewy
humid 341 adj.
clean 648 adj.
dexterity
skill 694 n.
dextral, dextrad
dextral 241 adj.
dhow
sailing-ship 275 n.
diabetes
disease 651 n.
diabolic
evil 616 adj.
cruel 898 adj.
diabolic 969 adj.
infernal 972 adj.
diabolist
diabolist 969 n.
sorcerer 983 n.
diacritical mark
punctuation 547 n.
diadem
regalia 743 n.
jewellery 844 n.
diaeresis
punctuation 547 n.
diagnose
discriminate 463 vb.
diagnosis
classification 77 n.
discrimination
463 n.
pathology 651 n.
medical art 658 n.
diagnostic
distinctive 15 adj.
special 80 adj.
identification 547 n.
diagram
outline 233 n.
representation 551
n.
dial
timekeeper 117 n.
dialect
language 557 n.
dialect 560 n.
dialectic
reasoning 475 n.

dialectical
linguistic 557 adj.
dialectical 560 adj.
dialectics
reasoning 475 n.
dialogue
argument 475 n.
interlocution 584 n.
diameter
dividing line 92 n.
breadth 205 n.
diamond
angular figure
247 n.
hardness 326 n.
gem 844 n.
diapason
loudness 400 n.
musical note 410 n.
diaper
loincloth 228 n.
pattern 844 n.
diaphanous
transparent 422
adj.
diaphragm
partition 231 n.
musical instrument
414 n.
diarist
chronicler 549 n.
narrator 590 n.
diarrhoea
dysentery 651 n.
diary
chronology 117 n.
reminder 505 n.
record 548 n.
biography 590 n.
diatribe
oration 579 n.
censure 924 n.
dibble
farm tool 370 n.
dibs
dibs 797 n.
dice
gambling 618 n.
dicer
gambler 618 n.
dicey
speculative 618 adj.
dick
police 955 n.
dickey
seat 218 n.
apron 228 n.

dictaphone
hearing aid 415 n.
dictate
speak 579 vb.
rule, dominate
733 vb.
dictation
necessity 596 n.
no choice 606 n.
(see dictate)
dictator
autocrat 741 n.
dictatorial
authoritative
733 adj.
compelling 740 adj.
insolent 878 adj.
dictatorship
despotism 733 n.
brute force 735 n.
diction
style 566 n.
dictionary
dictionary 559 n.
dictum
maxim 496 n.
affirmation 532 n.
didactic
educational 534 adj.
advising 691 adj.
diddle
deceive 542 vb.
defraud 788 vb.
die
mould 23 n.
die 361 vb.
die down
decrease 37 vb.
be quiescent 266 vb.
die-hard
unchangeable
153 adj.
opinionist 602 n.
opponent 705 n.
die out
pass away 2 vb.
diet
dieting 301 n.
therapy 658 n.
council 692 n.
be temperate
942 vb.
dietetics
dieting 301 n.
dietician
dieting 301 n.
doctor 658 n.

difference
difference 15 n.
disagreement 25 n.
numerical result
85 n.
heraldry 547 n.
dissension 709 n.
schism 978 n.
difference, see the
discriminate 463 vb.
different
non-uniform
17 adj.
changeful 152 adj.
differential
variant 15 n.
inequality 29 n.
numerical element
85 n.
earnings 771 n.
differentiate
specify 80 vb.
discriminate 463 vb.
differentiation
differentiation 15 n.
comparison 462 n.
difficult
imperspicuous
568 adj.
laborious 682 adj.
difficult 700 adj.
ungracious 885 adj.
difficulty
difficulty 700 n.
obstacle 702 n.
adversity 731 n.
diffidence
modesty 874 n.
diffident
nervous 854 adj.
diffraction
dispersion 75 n.
diffuse
irrelevant 10 adj.
diffuse 570 adj.
(see diffusion)
diffuseness
empty talk 515 n.
diffuseness 570 n.
diffusion
dispersion 75 n.
information 524 n.
dig
excavation 255 n.
make concave
255 vb.
cultivate 370 vb.

DIG

digest
  arrangement 62 n.
  absorb 299 vb.
  eat 301 vb.
  compendium
    592 n.
  mature 669 vb.
digestion
  (*see* digest)
digestive
  remedial 658 adj.
digger
  excavator 255 n.
diggings, digs
  quarters 192 n.
dig in
  place oneself
    187 vb.
digit
  number 85 n.
  feeler 378 n.
dignification
  dignification
    866 n.
dignified
  impressive 821 adj.
  well-bred 848 adj.
  worshipful 866 adj.
  formal 875 adj.
  courteous 884 adj.
dignify
  decorate 844 vb.
  dignify 866 vb.
dignitary
  aristocrat 868 n.
dignity
  elegance 575 n.
  good taste 846 n.
  prestige 866 n.
  title 870 n.
  formality 875 n.
dig one's toes in
  retain 778 vb.
dig out
  extract 304 vb.
digression
  deviation 282 n.
  pleonasm 570 n.
dig up
  exhume 364 vb.
dike
  fence 235 n.
dilapidate
  (*see* dilapidation)
dilapidation
  decay 51 n.
  dilapidation 655 n.

DIM

  poverty 801 n.
dilatation
  expansion 197 n.
dilate
  expand 197 vb.
  sufflate 352 vb.
  be diffuse 570 vb.
dilatory
  late 136 adj.
  slow 278 adj.
dilemma
  dubiety 474 n.
  argumentation
    475 n.
  choice 605 n.
  predicament 700 n.
dilettante
  sciolist 493 n.
  man of taste 846 n.
dilettantism
  good taste 846 n.
  fastidiousness
    862 n.
diligence
  stage-coach 274 n.
  assiduity 678 n.
diligent
  studious 536 adj.
dilly-dally
  be late 136 vb.
  be irresolute 601 vb.
dilute
  weaken 163 vb.
  moisten 341 vb.
dim
  bedim 419 vb.
  dim 419 adj.
  ill-seen 444 adj.
  unintelligent
    499 adj.
dimensional
  metric 465 adj.
dimensions
  size 195 n.
dim-eyed
  dim-sighted 440
    adj.
diminish
  bate 37 vb.
  render few 105 vb.
diminished
  lesser 35 adj.
diminishing returns
  loss 772 n.
diminution
  diminution 37 n.
  contraction 198 n.

DIO

diminutive
  small 33 adj.
  little 196 adj.
dimness
  dimness 419 n.
  invisibility 444 n.
dimple
  cavity 255 n.
dimpled
  fleshy 195 adj.
dim sight
  dim sight 440 n.
dim-witted
  unintelligent
    499 adj.
din
  loudness 400 n.
  be loud 400 vb.
dine
  eat 301 vb.
dine out
  be sociable 882 vb.
diner
  café 192 n.
  eater 301 n.
diner-out
  reveller 837 n.
ding-dong
  equal 28 adj.
  roll 403 n.
  contending 716 adj.
dinghy
  rowboat 275 n.
dingy
  dim 419 adj.
  colourless 426 adj.
  dirty 649 adj.
  graceless 842 adj.
dinkum
  truth 494 n.
dinner
  meal 301 n.
dinner jacket
  informal dress
    228 n.
  tunic 228 n.
dinnerless
  fasting 946 adj.
dint
  make concave
    255 n.
  knock 279 n.
diocesan
  ecclesiastical
    985 adj.
diocese
  parish 985 n.

DIR

Dionysiac
  disorderly 61 adj.
diorama
  spectacle 445 n.
diorism
  discrimination
    463 n.
dip
  acclivity 220 n.
  cavity, valley
    255 n.
  plunge 313 n., vb.
  drench 341 vb.
  snuff out 418 vb.
  bedim 419 vb.
  torch 420 n.
  colour 425 vb.
diphtheria
  respiratory disease
    651 n.
diphthong
  speech sound 398 n.
diploma
  credential 466 n.
diplomacy
  cunning 698 n.
diplomat
  mediator 720 n.
  envoy 754 n.
diplomatist
  mediator 720 n.
  envoy 754 n.
dipper
  ladle 194 n.
  irrigator 341 n.
  obscuration 418 n.
dippy
  crazed 503 adj.
  enamoured 887 adj.
dipsomania
  alcoholism 949 n.
dipsomaniac
  drunkard 949 n.
diptych
  picture 553 n.
dire
  harmful 645 adj.
  adverse 731 adj.
direct
  straight 249 adj.
  send 272 vb.
  orientate 281 vb.
  indicate 547 vb.
  perspicuous
    567 adj.
  veracious 540 adj.
  command 737 vb.

direct action
revolt 738 n.
direction
direction 281 n.
teaching 534 n.
directorship 689 n.
directive
command 737 n.
director
stage-manager
594 n.
director 690 n.
directorial
directing 689 adj.
directorship
directorship 689 n.
directory
list 87 n.
dirge
obsequies 364 n.
musical piece
412 n.
lament 836 n.
dirigible
airship 276 n.
dirigism
governance 733 n.
dirk
side-arms 723 n.
dirt
rubbish 641 n.
dirt 649 n.
impurity 951 n.
dirty
black 428 adj.
dirty 649 adj.
impure 951 adj.
dirty linen
slur 867 n.
dirty look
reproach 924 n.
dirty trick
foul play 930 n.
disability
impotence 161 n.
illness 651 n.
disable
disable 161 vb.
weaken 163 vb.
disabuse
inform 524 vb.
educate 534 vb.
disaccord
disagreement 25 n.
disorder 61 n.
disaccustom
disaccustom 611 vb.

disadvantage
inferiority 35 n.
inexpedience 643 n.
disadvantageous
harmful 645 adj.
disaffection
hatred 888 n.
disagree
(*see* disagreement)
disagreeable
unpleasant 827 adj.
discourteous
885 adj.
disagreement
disagreement
25 n.
unconformity 84 n.
dissent 489 n.
dissension 709 n.
disallow
exclude 57 vb.
refuse 760 vb.
disentitle 916 vb.
disappear
pass away 2 vb.
disappear 446 vb.
be stealthy 525 vb.
disappearance
absence 190 n.
disappearance
446 n.
disappoint
disappoint 509 vb.
miscarry 728 vb.
displease 827 vb.
disappointment
inexpectation 508 n.
(*see* disappoint)
disapprobation
disapprobation
924 n.
disapprove
deprecate 762 vb.
dislike 861 vb.
disapprove 924 vb.
disarm
disable 161 vb.
weaken 163 vb.
pacify 719 vb.
disarmament
impotence 161 n.
pacification 719 n.
disarming
pacificatory
719 adj.
disarray
disorder 61 n.

disaster
ill fortune 731 n.
disastrous
harmful 645 adj.
disavow
negate 533 vb.
reject 607 vb.
disband
disperse 75 vb.
disbelief
unbelief 486 n.
negation 533 n.
non-wonder 865 n.
disbursement
payment 804 n.
expenditure 806 n.
disc
circle 250 n.
gramophone 414 n.
discard
rejection 607 n.
rubbish 641 n.
disuse 674 vb.
discarnate
immaterial 320 adj.
discern *see* 438 vb.
understand 516 vb.
discernible
visible 443 adj.
discernment
sagacity 498 n.
fastidiousness
862 n.
discharge
propulsion 287 n.
outflow 298 n.
ejection 300 n.
dismiss, void
300 vb.
ulcer 651 n.
carry out 725 vb.
deposal 752 n.
pay 804 vb.
do one's duty
917 vb.
acquittal 960 n.
disciple
learner 538 n.
disciplinarian
trainer 537 n.
tyrant 735 n.
disciplinary
punitive 963 adj.
discipline
order 60 n.
dominate 733 vb.
obedience 739 n.

restraint 747 n.
punishment 963 n.
disclaim
negate 533 vb.
resign 753 vb.
not retain 779 vb.
disclaimer
negation 533 n.
disclose
disclose 526 vb.
indicate 547 vb.
disclosure
disclosure 526 n.
discoloration
achromatism 426 n.
discolour
variegate 437 vb.
make ugly 842 vb.
discomfiture
defeat 728 n.
discomfort
suffering, worry
825 n.
incommode 827 vb.
discompose
derange 63 vb.
agitate 318 vb.
incommode 827 vb.
discomposure
disorder 61 n.
worry 825 n.
disconcert
derange 63 vb.
distract 456 vb.
disappoint 509 vb.
disconnect
disjoin 46 vb.
discontinue 72 vb.
disconnectedness
discontinuity 72 n.
disconnexion
disjunction 46 n.
disconsolate
melancholic
834 adj.
hopeless 853 adj.
discontent
displease 827 vb.
discontent 829 n.
resentment 891 n.
discontinuance
discontinuity 72 n.
desuetude 611 n.
abrogation 752 n.
discontinuity
non-uniformity
17 n.

disjunction 46 n.
discontinuity 72 n.
interval 201 n.
discord
disagreement 25 n.
rasp 407 vb.
discord 411 n., vb.
discount
decrement 42 n.
disregard 458 vb.
discount 810 n., vb.
discountenance
disapprove 924 vb.
discourage
deject 834 vb.
frighten 854 vb.
discourse
lecture 534 n.
oration 579 n.
dissertation 591 n.
discourtesy
ill-breeding 847 n.
discourtesy 885 n.
disrespect 921 n.
discover
cause 156 vb.
see 438 vb.
discover 484 vb.
discoverer
precursor 66 n.
detector 484 n.
discovery
discovery 484 n.
disclosure 526 n.
discredit
disbelieve 486 vb.
disrepute 867 n.
discreditable
bad 645 adj.
discreditable
867 adj.
discredited
disapproved
924 adj.
discreet
wise 498 adj.
cautious 858 adj.
discrepancy
difference 15 n.
disagreement 25 n.
discretion
judgement 480 n.
sagacity 498 n.
choice 605 n.
caution 858 n.
discretional
voluntary 597 adj.

unconditional
744 adj.
discriminate
discriminate
463 vb.
select 605 vb.
discrimination
discrimination
463 n.
judgement 480 n.
fastidiousness
862 n.
injustice 914 n.
(see discriminate)
discursive
rational 475 adj.
prolix 570 adj.
discursive 591 adj.
discuss
dissert 591 vb.
discussion
inquiry 459 n.
dissertation 591 n.
disdain
reject 607 vb.
pride 871 n.
contempt 922 n.
disease
disease 651 n.
disembark
land 295 vb.
disembodied
immaterial 320 adj.
disembowel
void 300 vb.
disenchantment
reversion 148 n.
discovery 484 n.
disencumber
disencumber 701 vb.
take away 786 vb.
disendow
impoverish 801 vb.
disengage
liberate 746 vb.
disengaged
leisurely 681 adj.
disengagement
disjunction 46 n.
regression 286 n.
extraction 304 n.
disentangle
simplify 44 vb.
unravel 62 vb.
disencumber 701 vb.
disentitle
deprive 786 vb.

disentitlement
non-ownership
774 n.
loss of right 916 n.
disequilibrium
inequality 29 n.
disestablishment
deposal 752 n.
disesteem
disrespect 921 n.
diseuse
entertainer 594 n.
disfavour
disrepute 867 n.
odium 888 n.
disapprobation
924 n.
disfigure
make ugly 842 vb.
disfranchisement
loss of right 916 n.
disgorge
void, vomit 300 vb.
restitute 787 vb.
pay 804 vb.
disgrace
slur 867 n.
shame 867 vb.
disgraceful
discreditable
867 adj.
heinous 934 adj.
disgruntle
cause discontent
829 vb.
disguise
assimilation 18 n.
dissimilarity 19 n.
disguise 527 n.
dissemble 541 vb.
disgust
cause discontent
829 vb.
dislike 861 n.
dish
plate 194 n.
dish 301 n.
disharmony
discord 411 n.
dissension 709 n.
dishearten
deject 834 vb.
dishevelment
disorder 61 n.
derangement 63 n.
dishonest
dishonest 930 adj.

dishonesty
thievishness 788 n.
improbity 930 n.
lawbreaking 954 n
dishonour
not observe 769 vb
disrepute 867 n.
debauch 951 vb.
dishonourable
discreditable 867
adj.
dishonest 930 adj.
dish-water
swill 649 n.
disillusion
disappoint 509 vb.
regret 830 n.
dejection 834 n.
disincentive
dissuasion 613 n.
disinclination
unwillingness 598 n
disincline
cause dislike
861 vb.
disinfect
sanitate 652 vb.
disinfectant
cleanser 648 n.
prophylactic 658 n.
disinfection
hygiene 652 n.
disingenuous
false 541 adj.
disinherit
not retain 779 vb.
deprive 786 vb.
disintegrate
be disjoined 46 vb.
decompose 51 vb.
disperse 75 vb.
disinter
exhume 364 vb.
disinterested
just 913 adj.
disinterested
931 adj.
disinterment
inquest 364 n.
disinvestment
expenditure 806 n.
disjoin
simplify 44 vb.
disjoin 46 vb.
unstick 49 vb.
disjunct
disjunct 46 adj.

discontinuous
72 adj.
disjunction
discontinuity 72 n.
(see disjoin)
disk
circle 250 n.
(see disc)
dislike
dislike 861 n., vb.
dislocate
derange 63 vb.
disable 161 vb.
distort 246 vb.
dislodge
displace 188 vb.
eject 300 vb.
disloyalty
disobedience 738 n.
dutilessness 918 n.
perfidy 930 n.
dismal
melancholic 834 adj.
cheerless 834 adj.
dismantle
sunder 46 vb.
demolish 165 vb.
uncover 229 vb.
dismay
worry 825 n.
fear 854 n.
dismember
rend 46 vb.
dismiss
be dispersed 75 vb.
dismiss 300 vb.
disregard 458 vb.
dismissal
valediction 296 n.
ejection 300 n.
deposal 752 n.
dismount
unstick 49 vb.
land 295 vb.
disobedience
disobedience 738 n.
disobedient
wilful 602 adj.
disoblige
be malevolent
898 vb.
disorder
disorder 61 n.
derangement 63 n.
negligence 458 n.
disease 651 n.
revolt 738 n.

disorderly
riotous 738 adj.
disorganization
derangement 63 n.
anarchy 734 n.
disorganized
lax 734 adj.
disorientate
derange 63 vb.
disorientation
deviation 282 n.
disown
negate 533 vb.
not retain 779 vb.
disapprove 924 vb.
disparage
hold cheap 922 vb.
detract 926 vb.
disparity
irrelation 10 n.
difference 15 n.
inequality 29 n.
dispassionate
impassive 820 adj.
disinterested
931 adj.
dispatch
punctuality 135 n.
send 272 vb.
kill 362 vb.
report 524 n.
correspondence
588 n.
do 676 vb.
haste 680 n.
effectuation 725 n.
dispatcher
transferrer 272 n.
dispel
disperse 75 vb.
repel 292 vb.
dispensable
superfluous
637 adj.
dispensary
hospital 658 n.
dispensation
management 689 n.
non-retention 779 n.
apportionment
783 n.
non-liability 919 n.
dispense
exempt 919 vb.
(see dispensation)
dispense with
not retain 779 vb.

dispersal
dispersion 75 n.
disperse
disappear 446 vb.
defeat 727 vb.
dispersion
non-coherence 49 n.
dispersion 75 n.
divergence 294 n.
waste 634 n.
dispirit
deject 834 vb.
displace
displace 188 vb.
transpose 272 vb.
displaced person
wanderer 268 n.
outcaste 883 n.
displacement
displacement 188 n.
depth 211 n.
gravity 322 n.
display
exhibit 522 n.
show 522 vb.
ostentation 875 n.
displease
displease 827 vb.
displeasure
annoyance 827 n.
discontent 829 n.
disapprobation
924 n.
disposable
used 673 adj.
disposal
arrangement 62 n.
use 673 n.
non-retention 779 n.
dispose
arrange 62 vb.
motivate 612 vb.
dispose of
dispose of 673 vb.
sell 793 vb.
disposition
temperament 5 n.
arrangement 62 n.
location 187 n.
willingness 597 n.
dispossess
eject 300 vb.
deprive 786 vb.
impoverish 801 vb.
disentitle 916 vb.
dispraise
dispraise 924 vb.

disproof
confutation 479 n.
disproportion
irrelation 10 n.
inequality 29 n.
disproportioned
unsightly 842 adj.
disprove
(see disproof)
disputable
uncertain 474 adj.
disputant
reasoner 475 n.
disputation
argument 475 n.
dispute
disagree 25 vb.
argue 475 vb.
quarrel 709 n.
disqualification
loss of right 916 n.
disqualify
exclude 57 vb.
disable 161 vb.
disentitle 916 vb.
disquiet
worry 825 n.
incommode 827 vb.
disquisition
dissertation 591 n.
disregard
exclude 57 vb.
be incurious 454 vb.
disregard 458 vb.
not use 674 vb.
not respect 921 vb.
disrepair
dilapidation 655 n.
disreputable
vulgar 847 adj.
disreputable
867 adj.
dishonest 930 adj.
disrepute
disrepute 867 n.
odium 888 n.
disrespect
disrepute 867 n.
disrespect 921 n.
disrespectful
insolent 878 adj.
impertinent 878
adj.
disrespectful
921 adj.
disrobe
doff 229 vb.

disruption
destruction 165 n.
dissatisfaction
discontent 829 n.
disapprobation
924 n.
dissatisfy
displease 827 vb.
cause discontent
829 vb.
dissect
sunder 46 vb.
decompose 51 vb.
class 62 vb.
dissemble
make unlike 19 vb.
conceal 525 vb.
dissemble 541 vb.
be affected 850 vb.
dissembler
deceiver 545 n.
dissemination
dispersion 75 n.
publication 528 n.
dissension
dissent 489 n.
dissension 709 n.
dissent
dissent 489 n., vb.
dissension 709 n.
sectarianism 978 n.
dissenter
nonconformist 84 n.
dissentient 489 n.
schismatic 978 n.
dissentient
dissentient 489 n.
dissenting
heterodox 977 adj.
dissert
dissert 591 vb.
dissertation
dissertation 591 n.
disservice
evil 616 n.
inutility 641 n.
dissever
disjoin 46 vb.
dissidence
disagreement 25 n.
dissent 489 n.
dissident
nonconformist 84 n.
dissentient 489 n.
schismatic 978 n.
dissimilar
different 15 adj.

dissimilar 19 adj.
dissimilation
dissimilarity 19 n.
speech sound 398 n.
dissimulate
dissemble 541 vb.
dissimulation
mimicry 20 n.
duplicity 541 n.
dissipation
dispersion 75 n.
prodigality 815 n.
sensualism 944 n.
unchastity 951 n.
dissociation
unwillingness 598 n.
opposition 704 n.
schism 978 n.
dissoluteness
unchastity 951 n.
dissolution
decomposition 51 n.
finality 69 n.
destruction 165 n.
dissolve
decompose 51 vb.
(*see* dissolution)
dissonance
discord 411 n.
dissuade
dissuade 613 vb.
deprecate 762 vb.
dissuasive
dissuasive 613 adj.
distaff
weaving 222 n.
distaff side
womankind 373 n.
distance
distance 199 n.
length 203 n.
outstrip 277 vb.
distant
extraneous 59 adj.
distant 199 adj.
prideful 871 adj.
unsociable 883 adj.
distant past
preterition 125 n.
distaste
dislike 861 n.
distasteful
unpleasant 827 adj.
distemper
colour, pigment
425 n.
disease 651 n.

distend
augment 36 vb.
expand 197 vb.
distension
expansion 197 n.
distich
verse form 593 n.
distil
extract 304 vb.
vaporize 338 vb.
purify 648 vb.
distillation
outflow 298 n.
distillery
vaporizer 338 n.
distinct
separate 46 adj.
loud 400 adj.
well-seen 443 adj.
distinction
differentiation 15 n.
discrimination
463 n.
elegance 575 n.
prestige 866 n.
nobility 868 n.
distinctive
distinctive 15 adj.
special 80 adj.
distinguish
differentiate 15 vb.
see 438 vb.
distinguish 463 vb.
dignify 866 vb.
distinguished
elegant 575 adj.
notable 638 adj.
distort
transform 147 vb.
distort 246 vb.
misinterpret 521 vb.
misteach 535 vb.
misrepresent
552 vb.
pervert 655 vb.
distortion
irrelation 10 n.
falsehood 541 n.
blemish 845 n.
(*see* distort)
distract
distract 456 vb.
distraction
abstractedness
456 n.
excitable state
822 n.

distraint
expropriation
786 n.
distress
give pain 377 vb.
fatigue 684 n., vb.
adversity 731 n.
expropriation
786 n.
distressing
distressing 827 adj.
distress signal
danger signal
665 n.
distribution
apportionment
783 n.
district
subdivision 53 n.
district 184 n.
regional 184 adj.
parish 985 n.
distrust
doubt 486 n.
jealousy 911 n.
disturb
derange 63 vb.
agitate 318 vb.
incommode 827 vb.
disturbance
derangement 63 n.
intempestivity
138 n.
commotion 318 n.
disunion, disunity
dissension 709 n.
disunite
disjoin 46 vb.
disuse
desuetude 611 n.
non-use 674 n.
disused
antiquated 127 adj.
ditch
fence 235 n.
cavity 255 n.
conduit 351 n.
drain 351 n.
disuse 674 vb.
defences 713 n.
ditch-water
swill 649 n.
dither
be irresolute
601 vb.
dithyramb
praise 923 n.

ditto
  identity 13 n.
  repetition 106 n.
  assent 488 vb.
ditty
  vocal music 412 n.
diuretic
  excretory 302 adj.
diurnal
  seasonal 141 adj.
diuturnity
  diuturnity 113 n.
diva
  vocalist 413 n.
  actor 594 n.
divagate
  stray 282 vb.
divan
  seat 218 n.
divaricate
  diverge 294 vb.
dive
  tavern 192 n.
  swim 269 vb.
  plunge 313 n., vb.
diver
  diver 313 n.
  waterfowl 365 n.
diverge
  be oblique 220 vb.
  (*see* divergence)
divergence
  difference 15 n.
  deviation 282 n.
  divergence 294 n.
diverse
  (*see* diversity)
diversification
  variegation 437 n.
diversify
  modify 143 vb.
  variegate 437 vb.
diversion
  change 143 n.
  deviation 282 n.
  trickery, trap 542 n.
  amusement 837 n.
diversity
  multiformity 82 n.
  variegation 437 n.
divert
  deflect 282 vb.
  distract 456 vb.
  misuse 675 vb.
  amuse 837 vb.
divertissement
  stage play 594 n.

  amusement 837 n.
divest
  uncover 229 vb.
  deprive 786 vb.
divide
  sunder 46 vb.
  do sums 86 vb.
  bisect 92 vb.
  partition 231 n.
  vote 605 vb.
  apportion 783 vb.
  schismatize 978 vb.
dividend
  numerical element
    85 n.
  portion 783 n.
dividers
  gauge 465 n.
dividing line
  dividing line 92 n.
divination
  divination 511 n.
  occultism 984 n.
divine
  foresee 510 vb.
  divine 511 vb.
  godlike 965 adj.
  theologian 973 n.
diviner
  diviner 511 n.
  occultist 984 n.
divine right
  authority 733 n.
divinity
  divineness 965 n.
  theology 973 n.
division
  scission 46 n.
  subdivision 53 n.
  classification 77 n.
  district 184 n.
  vote 605 n.
  dissension 709 n.
  formation 722 n.
  apportionment
    783 n.
  schism, sect 978 n.
divorce
  separation 46 n.
  divorce 896 n., vb.
divot
  soil 344 n.
divulgation
  publication 528 n.
divulge
  manifest 522 vb.
  divulge 526 vb.

dizzy
  changeful 152 adj.
  rotary 315 adj.
  light-minded
    456 adj.
  fool 501 n.
do
  operate 173 vb.
  deceive 542 vb.
  suffice 635 vb.
  do 676 vb.
do as others do
  conform 83 vb.
do away with
  destroy 165 vb.
  kill 362 vb.
docile
  studious 536 adj.
  obedient 739 adj.
docility
  learning 536 n.
  persuasibility 612 n.
dock
  subtract 39 vb.
  cut 46 vb.
  stable 192 n.
  shorten 204 vb.
  arrive 295 vb.
  courtroom 956 n.
docker
  boatman 270 n.
docket
  list 87 vb.
  mark 547 vb.
  registration 548 n.
doctor
  mix 43 vb.
  scholar 492 n.
  sage 500 n.
  doctor 658 n., vb.
  relieve 831 vb.
doctrinaire
  doctrinaire 473 n.
  positive 473 adj.
  narrow mind 481 n.
  theorist 512 n.
doctrinal
  credal 485 adj.
doctrine
  creed 485 n.
  theology 973 n.
document
  evidence 466 n.
  corroborate 466 vb.
  record 548 n.
documentary
  evidential 466 adj.

  informative 524 adj.
  descriptive 590 adj.
documentation
  (*see* document)
dodderer
  waverer 601 n.
dodge
  trickery 542 n.
  avoid 620 vb.
  elude 667 vb.
  stratagem 698 n.
dodger
  hider 527 n.
  avoider 620 n.
do duty
  function 622 vb.
  deputize 755 vb.
doer
  doer 676 n.
doff
  doff 229 vb.
do for
  destroy 165 vb.
  murder 362 vb.
  serve 742 vb.
dog
  follow 284 vb.
  dog 365 n.
  pursue 619 vb.
dog-collar
  neckwear 228 n.
  canonicals 989 n.
dog-days
  heat 379 n.
dog-eared
  folded 261 adj.
  dilapidated 655 adj.
dog-fight
  duel 716 n.
dogged
  obstinate 602 adj.
  courageous
    855 adj.
doggedness
  perseverance 600 n.
doggerel
  doggerel 593 n.
  ridiculousness
    849 n.
dog in the manger
  hinderer 702 n.
  egotist 932 n.
dogma
  creed 485 n.
  theology 973 n.
dogmatic
  positive 473 adj.

credal 485 adj.
assertive 532 adj.
dogmatics
theology 973 n.
dogmatism
affirmation 532 n.
opiniatry 602 n.
dogmatist
doctrinaire 473 n.
opinionist 602 n.
dogmatize
dogmatize 473 vb.
do-gooder
philanthropist 901 n.
do in
destroy 165 vb.
doing
happening 154 adj.
operative 173 adj.
doing 676 adj.
doings
affairs 154 n.
deed 676 n.
do-it-yourself
artless 699 adj.
laical 987 adj.
doldrums
weather 340 n.
inactivity 769 n.
dole
gift 781 n.
portion 783 n.
doleful
melancholic 834 adj.
dole out
apportion 783 vb.
be parsimonious
816 vb.
doll
image 551 n.
dollop
piece 53 n.
doll up
primp 843 vb.
dolmen
monument 548 n.
dolt
dunce 501 n.
doltish
unintelligent
499 adj.
domain
territory 184 n.
lands 777 n.
dome
edifice 164 n.
roof 226 n.

dome 253 n.
domestic
native 191 adj.
provincial 192 adj.
interior 224 adj.
domestic 742 n.
domesticate
break in 369 vb.
domesticated
native 191 adj.
domestication
animal husbandry
369 n.
domesticity
quietude 266 n.
domestic science
cookery 301 n.
domicile
abode 192 n.
domiciled
native 191 adj.
dominance
influence 178 n.
dominant
supreme 34 adj.
influential 178 adj.
dominate
influence 178 vb.
dominate 733 vb.
domination
governance 733 n.
domineer
oppress 735 vb.
domineering
authoritative
733 adj.
oppressive 735 adj.
dominion
governance 733 n.
polity 733 n.
domino
cloak 228 n.
disguise 527 n.
plaything 837 n.
don
wear 228 vb.
scholar 492 n.
teacher 537 n.
donation
giving 781 n.
donative
incentive 612 n.
gift 781 n.
donee
recipient 782 n.
done thing
etiquette 848 n.

donkey
beast of burden
273 n.
fool 501 n.
donnish
instructed 490 adj.
severe 735 adj.
fastidious 862 adj.
donor
giver 781 n.
benefactor 903 n.
do-nothing
non-active 677 adj.
idler 679 n.
Don Quixote
crank 504 n.
visionary 513 n.
doodle
play music 413 vb.
be inattentive
456 vb.
doodlebug
bomb 723 n.
doom
fate 596 n.
condemnation
961 n.
punishment 963 n.
doomsday
future state 124 n.
door
doorway 263 n.
access 624 n.
door-keeper,
doorman
janitor 264 n.
doormat
weakling 163 n.
slave 742 n.
doorway
doorway 263 n.
access 624 n.
dope
anaesthetic 375 n.
ninny 501 n.
information 524
n.
drug 658 n.
doctor 658 vb.
dope-addict,
dope-fiend
madman 504 n.
habitué 610 n.
dormant
inert 175 adj.
quiescent 266 adj.
sleepy 679 adj.

dormitory
quarters 192 n.
chamber 194 n.
dormouse
idler 679 n.
dorsal
back 238 adj.
dose
finite quantity 26 n.
medicine 658 n.
portion 783 n.
doss down
sleep 679 vb.
doss-house
inn 192 n.
dossier
record 548 n.
dot
small thing 33 n.
punctuation 547 n.
dower 777 n.
dotage
age 131 n.
folly 499 n.
dotard
old man 133 n.
fool 501 n.
dote
be foolish 499 vb.
be in love 887 vb.
dottle
leavings 41 n.
dotty
foolish 499 adj.
crazed 503 adj.
double
analogue 18 n.
double 91 adj., vb.
repeat 106 vb.
fold 261 vb.
gait 265 n.
turn back 286 vb.
equivocal 578 adj.
double-cross
deceive 542 vb.
be dishonest 930 vb.
double-dealing
duplicity 541 n.
perfidy 930 n.
double Dutch
unintelligibility
517 n.
double-dyed
vicious 934 adj.
double entendre
equivocalness 518 n.
impurity 951 n.

double-harness
duality 90 n.
cooperation 706 n.
double-jointed
flexible 327 adj.
double-strength
strong 162 adj.
intoxicating
949 adj.
doublet
substitute 150 n.
tunic 228 n.
word 559 n.
doubletalk
unmeaningness
515 n.
equivocalness
518 n.
double up
disable 161 vb.
hurt 827 vb.
doubt
dubiety 474 n.
doubt 486 n.
caution 858 n.
doubter
unbeliever 486 n.
doubtful
disreputable
867 adj.
(*see* doubt)
doubting
irresolute 601 adj.
douche
ablution 648 n.
therapy 658 n.
dough
softness 327 n.
pulpiness 356 n.
dibs 797 n.
doughty
courageous 855 adj.
do up
join 45 vb.
repair 656 vb.
dour
obstinate 602 adj.
douse
snuff out 418 vb.
dove
bird 365 n.
mediator 720 n.
innocent 935 n.
dovecote
stable 192 n.
dovetail
join 45 vb.

implant 303 vb.
dowager
widowed spouse
896 n.
dowdy
graceless 842 adj.
dower
dower 777 n.
down
under 210 adv.
hair 259 n.
levity 323 n.
softness 327 n.
dejected 834 adj.
down-at-heel
dilapidated 655 adj.
beggarly 801 adj.
downcast
dejected 834 adj.
downfall
ruin 165 n.
defeat 728 n.
downhill
acclivity 220 n.
sloping 220 adj.
downpour
rain 350 n.
downright
veracious 540 adj.
downs
high land 209 n.
downstairs
under 210 adv.
down to earth
true 949 adj.
down tools
cease 154 vb.
revolt 738 vb.
downtrend
deterioration 655 n.
downtrodden
suffering 825 adj.
downy
fibrous 208 adj.
smooth 258 adj.
downy 259 adj.
soft 327 adj.
comfortable
376 adj.
dowry
dower 777 n.
dowser
inquirer 459 n.
detector 484 n.
diviner 511 n.
dowsing
divination 511 n.

doxology
act of worship
981 n.
hymn 981 n.
doxy
creed 485 n.
kept woman 952 n.
theology 973 n.
doyen
seniority 131 n.
doze
sleep 679 n., vb.
drab
dirty person 649 n.
cheerless 834 adj.
dull 840 adj.
loose woman 952 n.
drachm
weighment 322 n.
Draconian
severe 735 adj.
draft
compose 56 vb.
write 586 vb.
plan 623 n., vb.
armed force 722 n.
paper money 797
n.
drag
counteraction
182 n.
be long 203 vb.
slowness 278 n.
draw 288 vb.
friction 333 vb.
fetter 748 n.
be tedious 838 vb.
dragging
slow 278 adj.
dragging out
protraction 113 n.
dragoman
guide 520 n.
dragon
rara avis 84 n.
violent creature
176 n.
dragon's mouth
danger 661 n.
dragoon
cavalry 722 n.
compel 740 vb.
drag out
extract 304 vb.
drain
receptacle 194 n.
outflow 298 n.

void 300 vb.
dry 342 vb.
drain 351 n.
waste 634 vb.
sink 649 n.
sanitate 652 vb.
loss 772 n.
drainage
voidance 300 n.
desiccation 342 n.
waste 634 n.
cleansing 648 n.
dirt, swill 649 n.
dram
potion 301 n.
metrology 465 n.
drama, dramatics
drama, stage play
594 n.
excitation 821 n.
dramatic
dramatic 594 adj.
impressive 821 adj.
wonderful 864 adj.
showy 875 adj.
dramatis personae
actor 594 n.
personnel 686 n.
dramatist
dramatist 594 n.
dramatize
represent 551 vb.
dramatize 594 vb.
dramaturgy
dramaturgy 594 n.
drape
hang 217 vb.
dress 228 vb.
draper
clothier 228 n.
drapery
pendant 217 n.
robe 228 n.
drapes
covering 226 n.
drastic
vigorous 174 adj.
severe 735 adj.
draught
depth 211 n.
traction 288 n.
potion 301 n.
gravity 322 n.
wind 352 n.
medicine 658 n.
draughts
board game 837 n.

draughtsman
artist 556 n.

draughtsmanship
painting 553 n.

draw
copy 20 vb.
draw 28 n.
be equal 28 vb.
draw 288 n.
attract 291 vb.
extract 304 vb.
represent 551 vb.
paint 553 vb.
describe 590 vb.
gambling 618 n.
receive 782 vb.
desired object 859 n.

draw a blank
fail 728 vb.

draw attention
attract notice 455 vb.

draw back
recede 290 vb.

drawback
obstacle 702 n.
discount 810 n.

drawbridge
bridge 624 n.

drawee
debtor 803 n.

drawer
compartment 194 n.
artist 556 n.
servant 742 n.

drawers
trousers 228 n.
underwear 228 n.

drawing
picture 553 n.

drawing and quartering
capital punishment 963 n.

drawing-room
chamber 194 n.
social gathering 882 n.

drawl
speech defect 580 n.

draw lots
gamble 618 vb.

drawn game
draw 28 n.

draw off
extract 304 vb.

draw out
extract 304 vb.

draw the line
exclude 57 vb.
discriminate 463 vb.
restrain 747 vb.

draw the teeth
disable 161 vb.

draw together
join 45 vb.

draw up
compose 56 vb.
be in order 60 vb.

dray
cart 274 n.

drayman
driver 268 n.

dread
fear 854 n., vb.

dreadful
not nice 645 adj.
frightening 854 adj.

dreadnought
warship 722 n.

dream
insubstantial thing 4 n.
visual fallacy 440 n.
be inattentive 456 vb.
fantasy 513 n.
sleep 679 vb.
desired object 859 n.

dreamer
visionary 513 n.
idler 679 n.

dreamlike
shadowy 419 adj.

dream world
fantasy 513 n.

dreamy
insubstantial 4 adj.
abstracted 456 adj.
imaginary 513 adj.

dreary
cheerless 834 adj.
tedious 838 adj.
dull 840 adj.

dredge
extract 304 vb.

dredger
extractor 304 n.

dregs
leavings 41 n.

extremity 69 n.
rubbish 641 n.

drench
potion 301 n.
drench 341 vb.
medicine 658 n.
sate 863 vb.

dress
dress 228 n., vb.
cook 301 vb.
livery 547 n.
doctor 658 vb.
make ready 669 vb.

dressage
equitation 267 n.

dresser
stand, shelf 218 n.
clothier 228 n.

dressing
dressing 228 n.
condiment 389 n.
surgical dressing 658 n.

dressing station
hospital 658 n.

dressmaker
clothier 228 n.

dress up
dissemble 541 vb.
primp 843 vb.

dressy
fashionable 848 adj.
showy 875 adj.

dribble
small quantity 33 n.
exude 298 vb.
flow 350 vb.

driblet
finite quantity 26 n.

drier
drier 342 n.

drift
accumulation 74 n.
tendency 179 n.
thing transferred 272 n.
direction 281 n.
deviation 282 n.
be uncertain 474 vb.
meaning 514 n.
not act 677 vb.

drifter
fishing-boat 275 n.
idler 679 n.

driftwood
thing transferred 272 n.

drill
make uniform 16 vb.
textile 222 n.
perforator 263 n.
train 534 vb.
habituation 610 n.
ritual 988 n.

drill-sergeant
trainer 537 n.
tyrant 735 n.

drink
potion 301 n.
drink 301 vb.
get drunk 949 vb.

drinker
reveller 837 n.
drunkard 949 n.

drinking bout
drunkenness 949 n.

drink to
toast 876 vb.

drip
be wet 341 vb.
flow, rain 350 vb.
ninny 501 n.

dripping
fat 357 n.

drive
operate 173 vb.
vigorousness 174 n.
ride 267 vb.
impel 279 vb.
propulsion 287 n.
vigour 571 n.
incite 612 vb.
chase 619 n.
access, path 624 n.
haste 680 n.
compel 740 vb.

drive at
mean 514 vb.
aim at 617 vb.

drive-in
doorway 263 n.
approachable 289 adj.

drivel
be foolish 499 vb.
silly talk 515 n.

driveller
fool 501 n.

driver
driver 268 n.
machinist 630 n.

drive out
 eject 300 vb.
drizzle
 rain 350 n., vb.
droll
 witty 839 adj.
 funny 849 adj.
drollery
 foolery 497 n.
 wit 839 n.
 ridiculousness
 849 n.
drone
 fly 265 n.
 roll 403 vb.
 stridor 407 n.
 ululation 409 n.
 musical note 410
 n.
 be loquacious
 581 vb.
 idler 679 n.
drool
 exude 298 vb.
 mean nothing
 515 vb.
droop
 hang 217 vb.
 be ill 651 vb.
 be fatigued 684 vb.
 be dejected 834 vb.
drop
 small thing 33 n.
 decrease 37 n., vb.
 reproduce itself
 164 vb.
 minuteness 196 n.
 pendant 217 n.
 descent 309 n.
 let fall 311 vb.
 moisture 341 n.
 stage-set 594 n.
 disuse 674 vb.
drop a sitter
 lose a chance
 138 vb.
drop in
 arrive 295 vb.
 visit 882 vb.
droplet
 small thing 33 n.
 minuteness 196 n.
drop of the curtain
 finality 69 n.
drop out
 not complete
 726 vb.

droppings
 excrement 302 n.
dropsy
 fluid 335 n.
droshky
 cab 274 n.
dross
 rubbish 641 n.
 dirt 649 n.
drought
 dryness 342 n.
 scarcity 636 n.
 blight 659 n.
 hunger 859 n.
drove
 group 74 n.
drover
 driver 268 n.
drown
 fill 54 vb.
 destroy, suppress
 165 vb.
 founder 313 vb.
 drench 341 vb.
 perish 361 vb.
 kill 362 vb.
 silence 399 vb.
drowse
 be inattentive
 456 vb.
 sleep 679 n.
drowsy
 sleepy 679 adj.
 tedious 838 adj.
drub
 spank 963 vb.
drudge
 busy person 678 n.
 work 682 vb.
 servant 742 n.
drudgery
 assiduity 678 n.
 labour 682 n.
drug
 anaesthetic 375 n.
 drug 658 n.
 poison 659 n.
drugget
 floor-cover 226 n.
druggist
 druggist 658 n.
drug on the market
 superfluity 637 n.
drum
 cylinder 252 n.
 roll 403 vb.
 play music 413 vb.

drum 414 n.
drummer
 instrumentalist
 413 n.
drum out
 eject 300 vb.
drunk
 reveller 837 n.
 drunkard 949 n.
drunkard
 drunkard 949 n.
drunkenness
 intemperance
 943 n.
 drunkenness 949 n.
dry
 dry 342 adj., vb.
 stanch 350 vb.
 sour 393 adj.
 clean 648 vb.
 preserve 666 vb.
 tedious 838 adj.
 hungry 859 adj.
 sober 948 adj.
dryad
 nymph 967 n.
dry-as-dust
 bore 838 n.
dry-cleaner
 cleaner 648 n.
dryer *(see* drier)
dryness
 dryness 342 n.
 tedium 838 n.
 hunger 859 n.
dry-point
 engraving 555 n.
dry rot
 blight 659 n.
dry up
 decrease 37 vb.
 cease 145 vb.
 not suffice 636 vb.
dual
 dual 90 adj.
duality
 duality 90 n.
dub
 name 561 vb.
 dignify 866 vb.
dubiety
 dubiety 474 n.
dubious
 uncertain 474 adj.
 doubting 474 adj.
ducal
 noble 868 adj.

duce
 leader 690 n.
 autocrat 741 n.
duck
 zero 103 n.
 textile 222 n.
 plunge 313 vb.
 drench 341 vb.
 waterfowl 365 n.
 avoid 620 vb.
duck-boards
 paving 226 n.
 bridge 624 n.
ducking
 plunge 313 vb.
ducking-stool
 pillory 964 n.
duckling
 youngling 132 n.
duct
 conduit 351 n.
ductile
 flexible 327 adj.
 wieldy 701 adj.
dud
 loser 728 n.
 unsuccessful
 728 adj.
due
 owed 803 adj.
 due 915 adj.
duel
 duel 716 n.
duellist
 quarreller 709 n.
 combatant 722 n.
dueness
 attribution 158 n.
 dueness 915 n.
 (see duty)
duenna
 keeper 749 n.
dues
 receipt 807 n.
 dueness 915 n.
duet
 duet 412 n.
 cooperation 706 n.
due to
 caused 157 adj.
duffel
 textile 222 n.
duffer
 dunce 501 n.
 bungler 697 n.
dug-out
 old man 133 n.

excavation 255 n.
rowboat 275 n.
defences 713 n.
duke
potentate 741 n.
nobleman 868 n.
dulcet
melodious 410 adj.
pleasurable 826 adj.
dulcify
sweeten 392 vb.
dull
inert 175 adj.
blunt 257 vb.
non-resonant
405 adj.
soft-hued 425 adj.
colourless 426 adj.
unintelligent
499 adj.
tedious 838 adj.
dull 840 adj.
dullard
dunce 501 n.
dullness
dullness 840 n.
(see **dull**)
dumb
unintelligent
499 adj.
voiceless 578 adj.
dumbfound
make mute 578 vb.
be wonderful
864 vb.
dumbness
aphony 578 n.
dumb show
gesture 547 n.
stage play 594 n.
dummy
insubstantial thing
4 n.
prototype 23 n.
substitute 150 n.
ineffectuality 161 n.
sham 542 n.
image 551 n.
dump
storage 632 n.
rubbish 641 n.
disuse 674 vb.
dumps
dejection 834 n.
dumpy
fleshy 195 adj.
short 204 adj.

thick 205 adj.
dun
dim 419 adj.
demand 737 vb.
dunce
dunce 501 n.
dune
monticle 209 n.
dung
fertilizer 171 n.
excrement 302 n.
dungarees
trousers 228 n.
dungeon
cellar 194 n.
prison 748 n.
dunghill
sink 649 n.
duologue
interlocution 584 n.
dupe
befool 542 vb.
dupe 544 n.
loser 728 n.
duplicate
duplicate 22 n.
double 91 adj., vb.
reproduce 166 vb.
duplicity
equivocalness
518 n.
duplicity 541 n.
perfidy 930 n.
durability
toughness 329 n.
durable
lasting 113 adj.
tough 329 adj.
duration
time 108 n.
course of time
111 n.
duress
compulsion 740 n.
dusk
evening 129 n.
half-light 419 n.
dusky
vespertine 129 adj.
dim 419 adj.
dust
oldness 127 n.
overlay 226 vb.
powder 332 n.
trickery 542 n.
clean 648 vb.
dirt 649 n.

dustbin
cleaning utensil
648 n.
sink 649 n.
dust-bowl
desert 172 n.
duster
obliteration 550 n.
cleaning cloth
648 n.
dust-heap
rubbish 641 n.
dustiness
pulverulence 332 n.
dust in the eyes
pretext 614 n.
stratagem 698 n.
dustman
cleaner 648 n.
dustpan
cleaning utensil
648 n.
dusty
powdery 332 adj.
dry 342 adj.
dirty 649 adj.
duteous (see **dutiful**)
dutiable
priced 809 adj.
dutiful
obedient 739 adj.
trustworthy 929
adj.
dutiless
dutiless 918 adj.
duty
necessity 596 n.
function 622 n.
labour 682 n.
tax 809 n.
duty 917 n.
duty-free
non-liable 919 adj.
dwarf
dwarf 196 n.
make smaller
198 vb.
elf 970 n.
dwarfish
dwarfish 196 adj.
dwell
be situate 186 vb.
dwell 192 vb.
be quiescent
266 vb.
dweller
dweller 191 n.

dwelling
dwelling 192 n.
dwell on
emphasize 532 vb.
dwindle
decrease 37 vb.
dye
tincture 43 n.
hue, pigment 425 n.
colour 425 vb.
dyestuff
pigment 425 n.
dying
sick 651 adj.
dyke
fence 235 n.
conduit 351 n.
dynamic
powerful 160 adj.
operative 173 adj.
vigorous 174 adj.
dynamics
motion 265 n.
impulse 279 n.
dynamism
energy 160 n.
vigorousness 174 n.
dynamite
destroyer 168 n.
explosive 723 n.
dynamo
vigorousness 174 n.
dynast
potentate 741 n.
dynastic
ruling 733 adj.
dynasty
sovereign 741 n.
dysentery
dysentery 651 n.
dyspepsia
indigestion 651 n.

E

each other
correlation 12 n.
eager
willing 597 adj.
fervent 818 adj.
desiring 859 adj.
eagle
bird of prey 365 n.
eagle-eyed
seeing 438 adj.
ear
ear 415 n.

earful
oration 579 n.
earl
nobleman 868 n.
earliness
earliness 134 n.
early
past 125 adj.
matinal 128 adj.
early 135 adj.
earmark
label 547 n.
select 605 vb.
require 627 vb.
earn
acquire 771 vb.
deserve 915 vb.
earner
worker 686 n.
recipient 782 n.
earnest
resolute 599 adj.
security 767 n.
fervent 818 adj.
seriousness 834 n.
earnings
earnings 771 n.
receiving 782 n.
reward 962 n.
earphone
hearing aid 415 n.
ear-piercing
strident 407 adj.
ear-ring
pendant 217 n.
jewellery 844 n.
earshot
short distance 200 n.
earth
connect 45 vb.
dwelling 192 n.
world 321 n.
land 344 n.
refuge 662 n.
earthborn
human 371 adj.
earth-bound
imprisoned 747 adj.
earth-dweller
native 191 n.
earthenware
pottery 381 n.
earthly
telluric 321 adj.
earthquake
oscillation 317 n.

earth-shaking
important 638 adj.
earthwork
defences 713 n.
earthy
sensual 944 adj.
ear-trumpet
hearing aid 415 n.
ease
assuage 177 vb.
euphoria 376 n.
repose 683 n.
facility 701 n.
facilitate 701 vb.
relieve 831 vb.
easeful
comfortable 376 adj.
reposeful 683 adj.
easel
art equipment 553 n.
easement
estate 777 n.
ease of mind
content 828 n.
ease oneself
excrete 302 vb.
east
compass point 281 n.
easy
comfortable 376 adj.
intelligible 516 adj.
easy 701 adj.
sociable 882 adj.
easy-going
lenient 736 adj.
indifferent 860 adj.
easy terms
cheapness 812 n.
easy virtue
unchastity 951 n.
eat
eat 301 vb.
eatable
food 301 n.
edible 301 adj.
eat humble pie
recant 603 vb.
be humble 872 vb.
eating house
café 192 n.
eat one's words
recant 603 vb.
eave
roof 226 n.

projection 254 n.
eavesdrop
hear 415 vb.
be curious 453 vb.
eavesdropper
inquisitor 453 n.
informer 524 n.
ebb
decrease 37 n.
recede 290 vb.
flow 350 vb.
deterioration 655 n.
ebb and flow
fluctuation 317 n.
ebony
black thing 428 n.
ebullience
stimulation 174 n.
ebullient
lively 819 adj.
ebullition
excitable state 822 n.
eccentric
unimitative 21 adj.
misfit 25 n.
deviating 282 adj.
crank 504 n.
eccentricity
unconformity 84 n.
(*see* eccentric)
ecclesiastic
ecclesiastical 985 adj.
cleric 986 n.
echo
imitation 20 n.
conform 83 vb.
repetition 106 n.
resonance 404 n.
assent 488 vb.
echoing
loud 400 adj.
resonant 404 adj.
éclat
prestige 866 n.
eclecticism
choice 605 n.
eclipse
be superior 34 vb.
obscuration 418 n.
conceal 525 vb.
ecliptic
zodiac 321 n.
ecology
biology 358 n.

economical
cheap 812 adj.
economical 814 adj.
economics
management 689 n.
economize
economize 814 vb.
economy
order 60 n.
economy 814 n.
ecstasy
frenzy 503 n.
excitable state 822 n.
joy 824 n.
ecstatic
approving 923 adj.
(*see* ecstasy)
ectoplasm
spiritualism 984 n.
ecumenical
universal 79 adj.
eczema
skin disease 651 n.
eddy
vortex 315 n.
eddy 350 n.
edge
vantage 34 n.
nearness 200 n.
edge 234 n.
sharpen 256 vb.
pungency 383 n.
edge, have the
be superior 34 vb.
edge-tool
sharp edge 256 n.
edgy
excitable 822 adj.
edible
edible 301 adj.
edict
decree 737 n.
edification
teaching 534 n.
sanctity 979 n.
edifice
edifice 164 n.
edify
educate 534 vb.
make pious 979 vb.
edifying
pure 950 adj.
edit
interpret 520 vb.
publish 528 vb.
rectify 654 vb.

edition
edition 589 n.
editor
interpreter 520 n.
bookman 589 n.
editorial
interpretive 520 adj.
article 591 n.
educated
instructed 490 adj.
education
culture 490 n.
teaching 534 n.
educational
informative 524 adj.
educational 534 adj.
eel
table fish 365 n.
eerie
frightening 854 adj.
spooky 970 adj.
efface
destroy 165 vb.
obliterate 550 vb.
efface oneself
be modest 874 vb.
effect
sequel 67 n.
eventuality 154 n.
cause 156 vb.
effect 157 n.
product 164 n.
spectacle 445 n.
meaning 514 n.
effective
causal 156 adj.
forceful 571 adj.
expedient 642 adj.
successful 727 adj.
effects
property 777 n.
effectual
(*see* **effective**)
effectuation
agency 173 n.
effectuation 725 n.
effeminacy
weakness 163 n.
effeminate
female 373 adj.
effervesce
hiss 406 vb.
(*see* **effervescence**)
effervescence
bubble 355 n.
excitable state 822 n.

effervescent
bubbly 355 adj.
effete
impotent 161 adj.
deteriorated 655 adj.
efficacious
successful 727 adj.
efficacy
ability 160 n.
agency 173 n.
instrumentality 628 n.
efficient
powerful 160 adj.
operative 173 adj.
businesslike 622 adj.
instrumental 628 adj.
skilful 694 adj.
effigy
copy 22 n.
image 551 n.
effluence
outflow 298 n.
effluvium
gas 336 n.
odour 394 n.
efflux
outflow 298 n.
effort
essay 671 n.
action 676 n.
exertion 682 n.
effortless
easy 701 adj.
effort-wasting
useless 641 adj.
effrontery
insolence 878 n.
effulgence
light 417 n.
effusion
outflow 298 n.
effusive
loquacious 581 adj.
effusiveness
warm feeling 818 n.
egg
source 156 n.
egghead
intellectual 492 n.
sage 500 n.
egg on
incite 612 vb.

egg-shell
brittleness 330 n.
ego
intrinsicality 5 n.
spirit 447 n.
egocentric
selfish 932 adj.
egoism
selfishness 932 n.
egotism
selfishness 932 n.
egregious
unconformable 84 adj.
notable 638 adj.
egress
egress 298 n.
eiderdown
coverlet 226 n.
eights
racing 716 n.
eisteddfod
assembly 74 n.
choir 413 n.
ejaculation
cry 408 n.
voice 577 n.
eject
(*see* **ejection**)
ejection
ejection 300 n.
extraction 304 n.
deposal 752 n.
expropriation 786 n.
eke out
make complete 54 vb.
elaborate
mature 669 vb.
elaboration
elegance 575 n.
improvement 654 n.
élan
vigorousness 174 n.
elapse
elapse 111 vb.
be past 125 vb.
elasticity
recoil 280 n.
elasticity 328 n.
elate
delight 826 vb.
cheer 833 vb.
elation
psychopathy 503 n.

elbow
joint 45 n.
angularity 247 n.
impel 279 vb.
elbow-grease
exertion 682 n.
elbow-room
room 183 n.
scope 744 n.
elder
superior 34 n.
prior 119 adj.
older 131 adj.
old man 133 n.
church officer 986 n.
elderly
aged 131 adj.
eldership
church office 985 n.
El Dorado
fantasy 513 n.
eldritch
spooky 970 adj.
election
vote, choice 605 n.
electioneer
vote 605 vb.
elective, electoral
choosing 605 adj.
elector
electorate 605 n.
electric
dynamic 160 adj.
electric chair
means of execution 964 n.
electricity
electricity 160 n.
electrify
empower 160 vb.
excite 821 vb.
electrocution
capital punishment 963 n.
electron
small thing 33 n.
element 319 n.
electronics
nucleonics 160 n.
electroplate
coat 226 vb.
electrum
bullion 797 n.
eleemosynary
benevolent 897 adj.

elegance
elegance 575 n.
good taste 846 n.
fashion 848 n.
elegist
poet 593 n.
weeper 836 n.
elegy
obsequies 364 n.
poem 593 n.
lament 836 n.
element
component 58 n.
source 156 n.
filament 208 n.
element 319 n.
elemental
simple 44 adj.
elementary
simple 44 adj.
beginning 68 adj.
immature 670 adj.
elements
weather 340 n.
the sacrament 988 n.
elephant
giant 195 n.
elevate
(*see* elevation)
elevation
height 209 n.
elevation 310 n.
excitable state
822 n.
dignification 866 n.
elevator
lifter 310 n.
eleventh hour
lateness 136 n.
occasion, crisis
137 n.
elf
dwarf 196 n.
elf 970 n.
elfin
fairylike 970 adj.
elicit
extract 304 vb.
detect 484 vb.
manifest 522 vb.
elide
(*see* elision)
eligibility
inclusion 78 n.
nubility 894 n.
eligible
expedient 642 adj.

marriageable
894 adj.
eliminate
void 300 vb.
reject 607 vb.
exempt 919 vb.
elimination
destruction 165 n.
(*see* eliminate)
elision
shortening 204 n.
élite
élite 644 n.
upper class 868 n.
elixir
remedy 658 n.
ellipse
arc 250 n.
ellipsis
shortening 204 n.
conciseness 569 n.
elliptical
short 204 adj.
elocution
pronunciation
577 n.
oratory 579 n.
elongate
lengthen 203 vb.
elope
decamp 296 vb.
wed 894 vb.
eloquence
eloquence 579 n.
eloquent
inducive 612 adj.
elucidate
interpret 520 vb.
elude
avoid 620 vb.
elude 667 vb.
elusive
puzzling 517 adj.
avoiding 620 adj.
escaped 667 adj.
elysian
paradisiac 971 adj.
emaciation
thinness 206 n.
emanate
emerge 298 vb.
emanation
egress 298 n.
appearance 445 n.
emancipation
freedom 744 n.
liberation 746 n.

emasculate
unman 161 vb.
emasculation
weakness 163 n.
embalm
inter 364 vb.
be fragrant 396 vb.
preserve 666 vb.
embalmer
interment 364 n.
embank
obstruct 702 vb.
embankment
supporter 218 n.
obstacle 702 n.
embarcation
(*see* embarkation)
embargo
prohibition 757 n.
embark
voyage 269 vb.
embarkation
departure 296 n.
embark on
undertake 672 vb.
embarrass
incommode 827 vb.
embarrassment
predicament 700 n.
annoyance 827 n.
embassy
message 529 n.
envoy 754 n.
embed
place 187 vb.
implant 303 vb.
embellish
make better
654 vb.
decorate 844 vb.
embellishment
ornament 574 n.
ornamentation
844 n.
ember
ash 381 n.
lighter 385 n.
embezzle
defraud 788 vb.
embezzlement
peculation 788 n.
embezzler
defrauder 789 n.
embitter
impair 655 vb.
cause discontent
829 vb.

aggravate 832 vb.
enrage 891 vb.
embittered
resentful 891 adj.
embitterment
aggravation 832 n.
emblazoned
heraldic 547 adj.
emblem
badge 547 n.
emblematic
representing
551 adj.
embodiment
inclusion 78 n.
materiality 319 n.
representation
551 n.
embody
join 45 vb.
(*see* embodiment)
embolden
give courage 855 vb.
emboss
mark 547 vb.
embox
enclose 235 vb.
insert 303 vb.
embrace
unite with 45 vb.
cohere 48 vb.
comprise 78 vb.
enclose 235 vb.
greet 884 vb.
endearment 889 n.
embrasure
window 263 n.
fortification 713 n.
embrocation
balm 658 n.
embroider
variegate 437 vb.
decorate 844 vb.
embroidery
adjunct 40 n.
needlework 844 n.
embroil
enrage 891 vb.
embroilment
complexity 61 n.
embryo
source 156 n.
undevelopment
670 n.
embryonic
beginning 68 adj.
immature 670 adj.

emendator
interpreter 520 n.
mender 656 n.
emerald
greenness 432 n.
emerge
emerge 298 vb.
emergence
egress 298 n.
emergency
crisis 137 n.
needfulness 627 n.
predicament 700 n.
emetic
cathartic 658 n.
bane 659 n.
emigrant
foreigner 59 n.
wanderer 268 n.
emigration
departure 296 n.
egress 298 n.
émigré
wanderer 268 n.
eminence
greatness 32 n.
superiority 34 n.
height 209 n.
importance 638 n.
prestige 866 n.
emissary
messenger 531 n.
envoy 754 n.
emit
emit 300 vb.
emollient
lenitive 177 adj.
soft 327 adj.
lubricant 334 n.
balm 658 n.
remedial 658 adj.
pacificatory 719 adj.
emolument
earnings 771 n.
pay 804 n.
reward 962 n.
emotion
warm feeling 818 n.
emotional
feeling 818 adj.
impressible 819 adj.
excitable 822 adj.
emotionalism
feeling 818 n.
excitability 822 n.

emotive
felt 818 adj.
empalement
(*see* impale)
empanel
list 87 vb.
empathy
imagination 513 n.
emperor
sovereign 741 n.
emphasis
(*see* emphasize)
emphasize
strengthen 162 vb.
emphasize 532 vb.
make important 638 vb.
emphatic
strong 162 adj.
assertive 532 adj.
forceful 571 adj.
empire
polity 733 n.
governance 733 n.
empirical
experimental 461 adj.
empiricism
empiricism 461 n.
emplacement
location, station 187 n.
stand 218 n.
employ
employ 622 vb.
use 673 n., vb.
service 745 n.
employable
useful 640 adj.
employee
worker 686 n.
employer
director 690 n.
master 741 n.
employment
job 622 n.
use 673 n.
service 745 n.
emporium
emporium, shop 796 n.
empower
empower 160 vb.
permit 756 vb.
empowered
authoritative 733 adj.

emptiness
insubstantiality 4 n.
emptiness 190 n.
empty
empty 190 adj.
void 300 vb.
make flow 350 vb.
unprovided 636 adj.
fasting 946 adj.
empty-handed
unprovided 636 adj.
unsuccessful 728 adj.
empty-headed
unthinking 450 adj.
empty talk
empty talk 315 n.
empyreuma
burning 381 n.
emulation
imitation 20 n.
jealousy 911 n.
emulator
opponent 705 n.
contender 716 n.
emulsion
viscidity 354 n.
enable
empower 160 vb.
facilitate 701 vb.
enact
represent 551 vb.
decree 737 vb.
make legal 953 vb.
enamel
coat 226 vb.
colour 425 vb.
enamour
excite love 887 vb.
encamp
place oneself 187 vb.
dwell 192 vb.
encampment
abode 192 n.
encase
cover 226 vb.
insert 303 vb.
encash
receive 782 vb.
enchant
delight 826 vb.
bewitch 983 vb.
enchanter
sorcerer 983 n.
enchantment
excitation 821 n.

joy 824 n.
spell 983 n.
enchantress
a beauty 841 n.
sorceress 983 n.
encircle
circumscribe 232 vb.
circuit 626 vb.
encirclement
circumscription 232 n.
enclose
surround 230 vb.
enclose 235 vb.
enclosed
interior 234 adj.
monastic 986 adj.
enclosure
place 185 n.
receptacle 194 n.
frame 218 n.
circumscription 232 n.
enclosure 235 n.
encomium
praise 923 n.
encompass
surround 230 vb.
encore
repetition 106 n.
applause 923 n.
encounter
meet with 154 vb.
collision 279 n.
fight 716 n., vb.
encourage
aid 703 vb.
cheer 833 vb.
give courage 855 vb.
encouragement
causation 156 n.
encroach
encroach 306 vb.
encroacher
usurper 916 n.
encroachment
overstepping 306 n.
attack 712 n.
encumber
hinder 702 vb.
encumbrance
encumbrance 702 n.
debt 803 n.
encyclical
publication 528 n.
decree 737 n.

encyclopedia
erudition 490 n.
reference book
589 n.
encyclopedic
general 79 adj.
encyclopedist
scholar 492 n.
end
extremity 69 n.
end 69 n., vb.
cease 145 vb.
eventuality 154 n.
decease 261 n.
objective 617 n.
completion 725 n.
endanger
endanger 661 vb.
endearing
lovable 887 adj.
endearment
endearment 889 n.
endeavour
essay 671 n., vb.
endemic
interior 224 adj.
infectious 653 adj.
endless
infinite 107 adj.
perpetual 115 adj.
endogamy
(*see* marriage)
endorse
endorse 488 vb.
sign 547 vb.
approve 923 vb.
endorsement
consent 758 n.
endow
dower 777 vb.
endowment
heredity 5 n.
aptitude 694 n.
end to end
contiguous 202 adj.
endurance
durability 113 n.
perseverance 600 n.
patience 823 n.
endure
be 1 vb.
last 113 vb.
go on 146 vb.
persevere 600 vb.
feel 818 vb.
be patient 823 vb.
suffer 825 vb.

enema
therapy 658 n.
enemy
opponent 705 n.
enemy 881 n.
energetic
(*see* energy)
energize
invigorate 174 vb.
energy
energy 160 n.
power 160 n.
strength 162 n.
vigorousness 174 n.
vigour 571 n.
restlessness 678 n.
enervate
unman 161 vb.
weaken 163 vb.
enfeeble
weaken 163 vb.
enflame
excite 821 vb.
enfold
fold 261 vb.
enforce
compel 740 vb.
enfranchise
liberate 746 vb.
engage
join 45 vb.
employ 622 vb.
undertake 672 vb.
give battle 718 vb.
contract 765 vb.
incur a duty 917 vb.
engage in
undertake 672 vb.
engagement
undertaking 672 n.
battle 718 n.
promise 764 n.
social round 882 n.
duty 917 n.
engagement diary
reminder 505 n.
engender
generate 164 vb.
engine
empower 160 vb.
machine 630 n.
engineer
cause 156 vb.
plan 623 vb.
machinist 630 n.
engraft
add 38 vb.

engrave
cut 46 vb.
groove 262 vb.
engraver
engraver 556 n.
engraving
engraving 555 n.
engross
absorb 299 vb.
cause thought
449 vb.
write 586 vb.
appropriate 786 vb.
engrossment
possession 773 n.
engulf
absorb 299 vb.
enhance
make important
638 vb.
beautify 841 vb.
enhancement
improvement 654 n.
aggravation 832 n.
ornamentation
844 n.
enigma
question 459 n.
unknown thing
491 n.
enigma 530 n.
enigmatic
aphoristic 496 adj.
imperspicuous
568 adj.
enjoin
command 737 vb.
enjoy
unite with 45 vb.
enjoy 376 vb.
dispose of 673 vb.
possess 773 vb.
enjoyable
pleasant 376 adj.
enjoyment
coition 45 n.
sociability 882 n.
(*see* enjoy)
enkindle
excite 821 vb.
enlarge
boast 877 vb.
(*see* enlargement)
enlargement
increase 36 n.
expansion 197 n.
photography 551 n.

liberation 746 n.
enlarge upon
be diffuse 570 vb.
enlighten
inform 524 vb.
educate 534 vb.
enlightened
wise 498 adj.
philanthropic
901 adj.
enlightenment
knowledge 490 n.
wisdom 498 n.
enlist
list 87 vb.
register 548 vb.
employ 622 vb.
go to war 718 vb.
enlistment
registration 548 n.
enliven
invigorate 174 vb.
animate 821 vb.
amuse 837 vb.
enmity
enmity 881 n.
ennoblement
dignification 866 n.
ennui
tedium 838 n.
enormity
greatness 32 n.
hugeness 195 n.
wickedness 934 n.
guilty act 936 n.
enormous
huge 195 adj.
enough
sufficiency 635 n.
enrage
enrage 891 vb.
enrapture
excite love 887 vb.
enrich
decorate 844 vb.
enrol
list 87 vb.
admit 299 vb.
register 548 vb.
ensconce
place 187 vb.
conceal 525 vb.
ensemble
all, whole 52 n.
enshrine
circumscribe 232 vb.
sanctify 979 vb.

ensign
flag 547 n.
army officer 741 n.
ensilage
preservation 666 n.
enslave
oppress 735 vb.
subjugate 745 vb.
enslavement
(*see* enslave)
ensnare
ensnare 542 vb.
take 786 vb.
ensue
ensue 120 vb.
ensure
make certain
473 vb.
predetermine
608 vb.
entail
conduce 156 vb.
entailed
retained 778 adj.
entangle
bedevil 63 vb.
ensnare 542 vb.
entangled
complex 61 adj.
entanglement
crossing 222 n.
entente
agreement 24 n.
concord 710 n.
enter
begin 68 vb.
enter 297 vb.
insert 303 vb.
register 548 vb.
join a party 708
vb.
enter into
imagine 513 vb.
describe 590 vb.
enterprise
vigorousness 174 n.
undertaking 672 n.
restlessness 678 n.
enterprising
speculative 618 adj.
entertain
employ 622 vb.
amuse 837 vb.
be hospitable
882 vb.
entertainer
entertainer 594 n.

entertainment
provision 633 n.
amusement 837 n.
enthral
subjugate 745 vb.
excite love 887 vb.
enthronement
dignification 866 n.
enthusiasm
willingness 579 n.
warm feeling 818 n.
enthusiast
visionary 513 n.
religionist 979 n.
enthusiastic
optimistic 482 adj.
(*see* enthusiasm)
entice
ensnare 542 vb.
tempt 612 vb.
enticing
pleasurable 826 adj.
entire
whole 52 adj.
perfect 646 adj.
entirety
whole 52 n.
entitle
name 561 vb.
grant claims
915 vb.
entitled
deserving 915 adj.
entitlement
dueness 915 n.
entity
unit 88 n.
entomology
zoology 367 n.
entourage
circumjacence
230 n.
entrails
insides 224 n.
entrance
front 237 n.
ingress 297 n.
delight 826 vb.
entrant
incomer 297 n.
contender 716 n.
entreaty
entreaty 761 n.
entrée
reception 299 n.
entrench
stabilize 153 vb.

place oneself
187 vb.
entrenched
vested 153 adj.
entrenchment
defences 713 n.
entrepôt
storage 632 n.
emporium 796 n.
entrust
commission 751 vb.
convey 780 vb.
entry
doorway 263 n.
ingress 297 n.
entwine
enlace 222 vb.
enumerate
specify 80 vb.
enumeration
numeration 86 n.
list 87 n.
enunciate
affirm 532 vb.
enunciation
pronunciation
577 n.
speech 579 n.
enveigle
tempt 612 vb.
envelop
dress 228 vb.
circumscribe
232 vb.
envelope
receptacle 194 n.
covering 226 n.
correspondence
588 n.
envelopment
circumscription
232 n.
envenom
aggravate 832 vb.
excite hate 888 vb.
envenomed
toxic 653 adj.
enviable
approvable 923 adj.
envious
malevolent 898 adj.
envious 912 adj.
environment
circumstance 8 n.
relation 9 n.
circumjacence
230 n.

environs
near place 200 n.
circumjacence
230 n.
envisage
imagine 513 vb.
envoy
messenger 531 n.
envoy 754 n.
envy
be discontented
829 vb.
desire 859 vb.
jealousy 911 n.
envy 912 n., vb.
enzyme
alterer 143 n.
leaven 323 n.
epaulette
livery 547 n.
badge of rank 743 n.
ephemeral
ephemeral 114 adj.
ephemeris
chronology 117 n.
epic
prolix 570 adj.
descriptive 590 adj.
poem 593 n.
epicene
abnormal 84 adj.
equivocal 518 adj.
epicentre
centrality 225 n.
epicure
eater 301 n.
gastronomy 301 n.
glutton 947 n.
epicureanism
gastronomy 301 n.
enjoyment 824 n.
epidemic
universal 79 adj.
plague 651 n.
infectious 653 adj.
epidemiology
pathology 651 n.
epidermis
skin 226 n.
epigram
maxim 496 n.
conciseness 569 n.
witticism 839 n.
epigrammatist
humorist 839 n.
epigraphic
recording 548 adj.

epigraphist
interpreter 520 n.
epigraphy
hermeneutics 520 n.
registration 548 n.
epilepsy
spasm 318 n.
frenzy 503 n.
epilogue
sequel 67 n.
epiphany
revelation 975 n.
episcopacy
church office 985 n.
episcopalian
ecclesiastical
985 adj.
episcopate
church office 985 n.
episode
discontinuity 72 n.
epistemology
knowledge 490 n.
epistle
correspondence
588 n.
epitaph
obsequies 364 n.
phrase 563 n.
description 590 n.
epithet
name 561 n.
epitome
miniature 196 n.
compendium 592 n.
epitomize
shorten 204 vb.
abstract 592 vb.
epoch
era 110 n.
chronology 117 n.
epoch-making
notable 638 adj.
equal
compeer 28 n.
equal 28 adj.
equality
identity 13 n.
equality 28 n.
parallelism 219 n.
equalize
equalize 28 vb.
average out 30 vb.
equanimity
inexcitability 823 n.
equate
identify 13 vb.

equalize 28 vb.
equation
equalization 28 n.
equivalence 28 n.
numerical operation
86 n.
equator
middle 70 n.
dividing line 92 n.
equatorial
telluric 321 adj.
warm 379 adj.
equestrian
rider 268 n.
equestrianism
equitation 267 n.
equidistance
middle 70 n.
parallelism 219 n.
equilateral
uniform 16 adj.
symmetrical 245
adj.
angular figure
247 n.
equilibrium
equilibrium 28 n.
equine
equine 273 adj.
equinox
spring 128 n.
autumn 129 n.
equip
dress 228 vb.
find means 629 vb.
provide 633 vb.
make ready 669
vb.
equipage
carriage 274 n.
equipment
equipment 630 n.
provision 633 n.
fitting out 669 n.
equipoise
equilibrium 28 n.
weighment 322 n.
equitable
just 913 adj.
honourable 929 adj.
equitation
equitation 267 n.
equity
justice 913 n.
equivalence
identity 13 n.
equivalence 28 n.

equivalent
quid pro quo 150 n.
equivocal
uncertain 474 adj.
equivocal 518 adj.
imperspicuous
568 adj.
equivocation
sophistry 477 n.
equivocalness 518 n.
falsehood 541 n.
equivocator
sophist 477 n.
era
era 110 n.
chronology 117 n.
eradicate
destroy 165 vb.
eject 300 vb.
extract 304 vb.
erase
obliterate 550 vb.
clean 648 vb.
erasure
obliteration 550 n.
erect
place 187 vb.
make vertical
215 vb.
elevate 310 vb.
honourable
929 adj.
erectile
elevated 310 adj.
erection
edifice 164 n.
erector
lifter 310 n.
erg
energy 160 n.
ergatocracy
government 733 n.
eristic
reasoner 475 n.
arguing 475 adj.
ermine
skin 226 n.
regalia 743 n.
erode
subtract 39 vb.
rub 333 vb.
impair 655 vb.
Eros
libido 859 n.
love 887 n.
erotic
erotic 887 adj.

eroticism
love 887 n.
err
stray 282 vb.
err 495 vb.
errand
message 529 n.
mandate 751 n.
errand boy
courier 531 n.
erratic
non-uniform 17 adj.
fitful 142 adj.
unstable 152 adj.
deviating 282 adj.
inexact 495 adj.
crazed 503 adj.
erratum
mistake 495 n.
erring
wicked 934 adj.
erroneous
erroneous 495 adj.
error
misjudgement 481 n.
error 495 n.
heterodoxy 977 n.
ersatz
imitative 20 adj.
spurious 542 adj.
eructation
respiration 352 n.
erudition
erudition 490 n.
erupt
attack 712 vb.
(see **eruption**)
eruption
egress 298 n.
voidance 300 n.
skin disease 651 n.
escalade
climb 308 vb.
attack 712 n., vb.
escalator
conveyor 274 n.
lifter 310 n.
escapade
foolery 497 n.
revel 837 n.
escape
outflow, outlet,
egress 298 n.
flow out 298 vb.
escape 667 n., vb.
escape clause
qualification 468 n.

escapism
fantasy 513 n.
escape 667 n.

escapist
visionary 513 n.
avoider 620 n.

escarpment
high land 209 n.
acclivity 220 n.

eschatology
finality 69 n.

eschew
avoid 620 vb.

escort
accompaniment,
concomitant 89 n.
keeper 749 n.

esculent
edible 301 adj.

escutcheon
heraldry 547 n.

esoteric
occult 523 adj.
occultist 984 n.

esoterism
occultism 984 n.

especial
(*see* special)

espial
inspection 438 n.

espionage
secret service
459 n.

esplanade
path 624 n.

espousal
wedding 894 n.

espouse
marry 894 vb.

esprit de corps
prejudice 481 n.
cooperation 706
n.

espy
see 438 vb.

esquire
male 372 n.

essay
experiment 461 n.
article 591 n.
dissertation 591 n.
essay 671 n., vb.
undertaking 672 n.
exert oneself
682 vb.

essayist
dissertator 591 n.

essence
essence 1 n.
essential part 5 n.
extraction 304 n.
goodness 644 n.
cosmetic 843 n.

essential
real 1 adj.
chief thing 638 n.

essentiality
substantiality 3 n.

establish
auspicate 68 vb.
stabilize 153 vb.
place 187 vb.

established
permanent 144 adj.
vested 153 adj.
usual 610 adj.

establishment
location 187 n.
corporation 708 n.

Establishment, the
upper class 868 n.

estate
territory 184 n.
estate, lands 777 n.

esteem
repute 866 n.
respect 920 n., vb.

estimable
approvable 923 adj.

estimate
do sums 86 vb.
measurement 465 n.
estimate 480 n., vb.

estimation
estimate 480 n.
(*see* esteem)

estoppel
hindrance 702 n.

estrange
make enemies
881 vb.

estuary
gulf 345 n.

et cetera
in addition 38 adv.

etch
outline 233 vb.
engrave 555 vb.

etcher
engraver 556 n.

etching
engraving 555 n.
ornamental art
844 n.

eternal
lasting 113 adj.
unceasing 146 adj.
(*see* eternity)

eternalize, eternize
perpetuate 115 vb.

eternal triangle
illicit love 951 n.

eternity
infinity 107 n.
perpetuity 115 n.

ether
heavens 321 n.
gas 336 n.

etherial
insubstantial 4 adj.

ethics
morals 917 n.

ethnic
ethnic 11 adj.
human 371 adj.

ethnic type
mankind 371 n.

ethnology
anthropology 371 n.

ethos
character 5 n.
conduct 688 n.

etiology
attribution 158 n.
science 490 n.
pathology 651 n.

etiquette
etiquette 848 n.
formality 875 n.

etymology
linguistics 557 n.
etymology 559 n.

etymon
word 559 n.

Eucharist
Holy Communion
988 n.

eugenics
biology 358 n.

eulogist
commender 923 n.

eulogy
praise 923 n.

eunuch
eunuch 161 n.

euphemism
trope 519 n.
affectation 850 n.
prudery 950 n.

euphemize
be affected 850 vb.

euphony
melody 410 n.

euphoria
euphoria 376 n.
health 650 n.
content 828 n.

euphuism
trope 519 n.
ornament 574 n.

eurhythmics
exercise 862 n.
dancing 837 n.

eurhythmy
symmetry 245 n.

euthanasia
decease 361 n.
killing 362 n.
euphoria 376 n.

evacuate
decamp 296 vb.

evacuation
cacation 302 n.
relinquishment
621 n.

evacuee
outcaste 883 n.

evade
avoid 620 vb.
elude 667 vb.

evaluate
estimate 480 vb.

evanescence
transientness 114 n.
disappearance
446 n.

evanescent
inconsiderable
33 adj.

evangelical
revelational
975 adj.
orthodox 976 adj.

evangelist
preacher 537 n.
religious teacher
973 n.
pastor 986 n.

evangelistic
scriptural 975 adj.

evangelize
convert 147 vb.

evaporate
be dispersed 75 vb.
vaporize 338 vb.
disappear 446 vb.

evaporation
(*see* evaporate)

evasion
mental dishonesty
543 n.
pretext 614 n.
avoidance 620 n.
stratagem 698 n.
evasive
equivocal 518 adj.
eve
precursor 66 n.
evening 129 n.
even
uniform 16 adj.
regular 81 adj.
flatten 216 vb.
symmetrical
245 adj.
straight 249 adj.
smooth 258 vb.
evening
end 69 n.
evening 129 n.
evening dress
formal dress 228 n.
even-sided
symmetrical
245 adj.
Evensong
church service
988 n.
event
occasion 137 n.
eventuality 154 n.
contest 716 n.
even tenor
uniformity 16 n.
order 60 n.
eventful
eventful 154 adj.
eventuality
juncture 8 n.
futurity 124 n.
occasion 137 n.
eventuality 154 n.
chance 159 n.
eventuate
happen 154 vb.
evergreen
perpetual 115 adj.
young 130 adj.
unchangeable
153 adj.
everlasting
perpetual 115 adj.
everybody
all 52 n.
everyman 79 n.

everyday
typical 83 adj.
usual 610 adj.
every excuse
vindication 927 n.
innocence 935 n.
everyman
prototype 23 n.
common man 30 n.
everyman 79 n.
commoner 869 n.
everyone
(*see* everybody)
everywhere
space 183 n.
eviction
ejection 300 n.
expropriation
786 n.
evidence
evidence 466 n.,
vb.
indication 547 n.
trace 548 n.
evidence against
counter-evidence
467 n.
evident
visible 443 adj.
demonstrated
478 adj.
manifest 522 adj.
evidential
evidential 466 adj.
evil
evil 616 n.
harmful 645 adj.
adversity 731 n.
wickedness 934 n.
evil day
adversity 731 n.
evildoer
evildoer 904 n.
evil eye
malediction 899 n.
spell 983 n.
evil hour
intempestivity
138 n.
evil-speaking
detraction 926 n.
evince
evidence 466 vb.
manifest 522 vb.
eviscerate
void 300 vb.
extract 304 vb.

evocation
remembrance 505 n.
representation
551 n.
description 590 n.
evoke (*see* evocation)
evolution
production 164 n.
motion 265 n.
progression 285 n.
evolution 316 n.
biology 358 n.
evolutionary
evolving 316 adj.
biological 358 adj.
evolutionist
biology 358 n.
evolve
become 1 vb.
result 157 vb.
evolve 316 vb.
(*see* evolution)
evolved from
caused 157 adj.
ewe
sheep 365 n.
ewer
vessel 194 n.
ex
prior 119 adj.
exacerbate
make violent
176 vb.
aggravate 832 vb.
exact
careful 457 adj.
accurate 494 adj.
perspicuous 567 adj.
demand 737 vb.
levy 786 vb.
exacting
difficult 700 adj.
fastidious 862 adj.
exaction
taking 786 n.
tax 809 n.
exactitude
(*see* exactness)
exactness
carefulness 457 n.
accuracy 494 n.
perspicuity 567 n.
exaggeration
overestimation
482 n.
exaggeration 545 n.
boast 877 n.

exalt
elevate 310 vb.
praise 923 vb.
exaltation
warm feeling 818 n.
joy 824 n.
exalted
great 32 adj.
high 209 adj.
examination
meditation 449 n.
exam 459 n.
examination-in-chief
interrogation 459
n.
examination paper
question 459 n.
examine
scan 438 vb.
interrogate 459 vb.
examinee
respondent 460 n.
exam 459 n.
testee 461 n.
examiner
inquisitor 453 n.
inquirer 459 n.
estimator 480 n.
interlocutor 584 n.
example
relevance 9 n.
prototype 23 n.
example 83 n.
warning 664 n.
exasperate
aggravate 832 vb.
enrage 891 vb.
excavation
excavation 255 n.
extraction 304 n.
exceed
be great 32 vb.
overstep 306 vb.
be intemperate
943 vb.
excellence
superiority 34 n.
goodness 644 n.
excellent
great 32 adj.
supreme 34 adj.
perfect 646 adj.
splendid 841 adj.
exceller
exceller 644 n.
excelsior
up 308 adv.

exception
exclusion 57 n.
unconformity 84 n.
qualification 468 n.
rejection 607 n.
deprecation 762 n.
conditions 766 n.

exceptional
non-uniform 17 adj.
disagreeing 25 adj.

excerpt
part 53 n.
abstract 592 vb.
select 605 vb.

excerpts
anthology 592 n.

excess
overactivity 678 n.
cruel act 898 n.
intemperance 943 n.

excessive
exaggerated
546 adj.
superfluous 637 adj.
redundant 637 adj.
dear 811 adj.

exchange
equivalence 28 n.
substitution 150 n.
interchange 151 n.,
vb.
bourse 618 n.
barter, trade
791 vb.
mart 796 n.
finance 797 n.

exchequer
treasury 799 n.

excise
subtract 39 vb.
tax 809 n.

exciseman
receiver 782 n.

excitable
impressible 819 adj.
excitable 822 adj.

excitant
stimulant 174 n.
excitant 821 n.

excitation
(*see* excite)

excite
cause 156 vb.
invigorate 174 vb.
incite 612 vb.
excite 821 vb.
delight 826 vb.

excitement
excitation 821 n.

exclaim
cry 408 vb.
voice 577 vb.
disapprove 924 vb.

exclamation
cry 408 n.
voice 577 n.

exclamation mark
punctuation 547 n.

exclude
make impossible
470 vb.
depose 752 vb.
prohibit 757 vb.
(*see* exclusion)

exclusion
exclusion 57 n.
unconformity 84 n.
ejection 300 n.
rejection 607 n.
(*see* exclude)

exclusive
sectional 708 adj.
sectarian 978 adj.

exclusiveness
particularism 80 n.
sectarianism 978 n.

excommunicate
exclude 57 vb.
curse 899 vb.
condemn 961 vb.

excommunicated
schismatical
978 adj.

excrement, excreta
excrement 302 n.

excrescence
swelling 253 n.
superfluity 637 n.
blemish 845 n.

excretion
excretion 302 n.

excruciate
give pain 377 vb.
torment 827 vb.

exculpation
acquittal 960 n.

excursion
land travel 267 n.
amusement 837 n.

excursionist
traveller 268 n.
reveller 837 n.

excursus
dissertation 591 n.

excusable
vindicable 927 adj.
guiltless 935 adj.

excuse
mental dishonesty
543 n.
pretext 614 n.
vindication 927 n.
extenuate 927 vb.

execrable
bad 645 adj.

execrate
curse 899 vb.
dispraise 924 vb.

execration
hatred 888 n.
malediction 899 n.

executant
musician 413 n.
doer 676 n.

execution
killing 362 n.
effectuation 725 n.
capital punishment
963 n.

executive
agent 686 n.
directing 689 adj.
manager 690 n.

executor
agent 686 n.

exegesis
interpretation
520 n.

exemplar
prototype 23 n.
example 83 n.

exemplary
excellent 644 adj.

exemplify
exemplify 83 vb.

exempt
liberate 746 vb.

exemption
exclusion 57 n.
non-liability 919 n.

exercise
train 534 vb.
prepare oneself
669 vb.
use 673 n., vb.
exercise 682 n.

exert
use 673 vb.

exertion
action 676 n.
exertion 682 n.

exigence
needfulness 627 n.

exhalation
gas 336 n.

exhale
exude 298 vb.
emit 300 vb.
breathe 352 vb.
smell 394 vb.

exhaust
outlet 298 n.
waste 634 n., vb.
fatigue 684 vb.

exhaustion
weakness 163 n.
(*see* exhaust)

exhaustive
complete 54 adj.

exhaust pipe
sufflation 352 n.

exhibit
evidence 466 n.
exhibit 522 n.
advertisement
528 n.

exhibition
spectacle 445 n.
foolery 497 n.
manifestation 522 n.
collection 632 n.

exhibitioner
college student
538 n.

exhibitionism
vanity 873 n.

exhibitionist
vain person 873 n.
showy 875 adj.

exhibitor
exhibitor 522 n.

exhilarate
delight 826 vb.
cheer 833 vb.

exhilarated
pleased 824 adj.

exhilaration
excitable state
822 n.
(*see* exhilarate)

exhort
incite 612 vb.
advise 691 vb.

exhortation
inducement 612 n.

exhume
exhume 364 vb.

exigence
needfulness 627 n.

difficulty 700 n.

exiguity
littleness 196 n.

exile
exclusion 57 n.
displacement 188 n.
ejection 300 n.
outcaste 883 n.
penalty 963 n.

exist
be 1 vb.
be present 189 vb.
live 360 vb.

existence
existence 1 n.
presence 189 n.
life 360 n.

exit
doorway 263 n.
departure 296 n.
egress, outlet 298 n.

exodus
departure 296 n.
egress 298 n.

ex officio
authoritative 733 adj.

exoneration
forgiveness 909 n.
acquittal 960 n.

exorbitance
greatness 32 n.
exaggeration 546 n.

exorcism
malediction 899 n.
sorcery 983 n.

exorcist
sorcerer 983 n.

exorcize
eject 300 vb.
practise sorcery 983 vb.

exordium
prelude 66 n.
beginning 68 n.

exoteric
undisguised 522 adj.

exotic
irrelation 10 n.
extraneous 59 adj.
unconformable 84 adj.
horticultural 370 adj.

expand
lengthen 203 vb.

be broad 205 vb.
(*see* expansion)

expanse
space 183 n.
breadth 205 n.

expansion
increase 36 n.
expansion 197 n.
diffuseness 570 n.

expansionism
overstepping 306 n.
governance 733 n.

expansive
spacious 183 adj.
broad 205 adj.

expatiate
be diffuse 570 vb.
be loquacious 581 vb.

expatriate
exclude 57 vb.
foreigner 59 n.
eject 300 vb.
outcaste 883 n.

expatriation
seclusion 883 n.

expect
expect 507 vb.

expectant
future 124 adj.
expectant 507 adj.
beneficiary 776 n.

expectation
probability 471 n.
expectation 507 n.
hope 852 n.

expectations
dueness 915 n.

expectorant
cathartic 658 n.

expectorate
eruct 300 vb.

expectoration
excretion 302 n.

expedience
utility 640 n.
expedience 642 n.

expedient
operative 173 adj.
contrivance 623 n.

expedite
accelerate 277 vb.
hasten 680 vb.

expedition
velocity 277 n.
haste 680 n.

expel
reject 607 vb.
(*see* expulsion)

expellee
outcaste 883 n.

expend
pay 804 vb.
expend 806 vb.

expendable
superfluous 637 adj.
unimportant 639 adj.

expenditure
waste 634 n.
expenditure 806 n.

expense
(*see* expenditure)

expensive
dear 811 adj.

experience
meet with 154 vb.
knowledge 490 n.
wisdom 498 n.
skill 694 n.
feel 818 vb.

experienced
matured 669 adj.
expert 694 adj.

experiences
biography 590 n.

experiment
experiment 461 n., vb.
essay 671 n.

experimental
experimental 461 adj.
speculative 618 adj.

experimentalist
experimenter 461 n.

experimentation
experiment 461 n.

expert
knowing 490 adj.
expert 694 adj.
proficient, expert 696 n.

expertise
skill 694 n.

expiation
propitiation 941 n.

expiration
respiration 352 n.

expire
end 69 vb.
elapse 111 vb.

die 361 vb.

explain
facilitate 701 vb.

explain away
confute 479 vb.
disbelieve 486 vb.
misteach 535 vb.

explanation
interpretation 520 n.

expletive
pleonasm 570 n.
scurrility 899 n.

explicable
intelligible 516 adj.

explicit
meaningful 514 adj.
intelligible 516 adj.
perspicuous 567 adj.

explode
be dispersed 75 vb.
be brittle 330 vb.
(*see* explosion)

exploit
important matter 638 n.
use 673 vb.
be skilful 694 vb.
success 727 n.

exploitation
(*see* exploit)

exploration
inquiry, search 459 n.
discovery 484 n.

exploratory
precursory 66 adj.
experimental 461 adj.

explore
(*see* exploration)

explorer
inquirer 459 n.
detector 484 n.

explosion
bang 402 n.
excitable state 822 n.
anger 891 n.

explosive
violent 176 adj.
propellant 287 n.
combustible 385 adj.
dangerous 661 adj.
explosive 723 n.

exponent
numerical element
85 n.
interpreter 520 n.
export
transference 272 n.
egress 298 n.
exporter
transferrer 272 n.
merchant 794 n.
expose
uncover 229 vb.
show 522 vb.
disclose 526 vb.
photograph 551 vb.
shame 867 vb.
accuse 928 vb.
exposé
description 590 n.
exposed
defenceless
161 adj.
liable 180 adj.
vulnerable 661 adj.
exposition
interpretation
520 n.
dissertation 591 n.
expositor
interpreter 520 n.
dissertator 591 n.
expository
interpretive
520 adj.
expostulate
reprove 924 vb.
expostulation
deprecation 762 n.
exposure
uncovering 229 n.
visibility 443 n.
discovery 484 n.
vulnerability 661 n.
expound
interpret 520 vb.
teach 534 vb.
express
efform 243 vb.
speeder 277 n.
mean 514 n.
courier 531 n.
affirm 532 vb.
phrase 563 vb.
voice 577 vb.
expression
number 85 n.
form 243 n.

mien 445 n.
meaning 514 n.
word 559 n.
phrase 563 n.
feeling 818 n.
expressionless
impassive 820 adj.
expressive
meaningful
514 adj.
expressive 516 adj.
exprobate
exprobate 924 vb.
expropriation
expropriation 786 n.
penalty 963 n.
expropriator
taker 786 n.
expulsion
exclusion 57 n.
ejection 300 n.
expropriation
786 n.
(*see* **expel**)
expulsive
propulsive 287 adj.
expulsive 300 adj.
expunge
obliterate 550 vb.
expurgate
purify 648 vb.
expurgation
prudery 950 n.
exquisite
painful 377 adj.
savoury 390 adj.
excellent 644 adj.
beautiful 841 adj.
tasteful 846 adj.
fop 848 n.
extant
existing 1 adj.
recorded 548 adj.
extemporaneous
spontaneous
609 adj.
extempore
instantaneously
116 adv.
spontaneous
609 adj.
extemporization
spontaneity 609 n.
extemporize
improvise 609 vb.
be unprepared
670 vb.

extend
extend 183 vb.
enlarge 197 vb.
lengthen 203 vb.
extension
increase 36 n.
adjunct 40 n.
protraction 113 n.
lengthening 203 n.
(*see* **extent**)
extensive
extensive 32 adj.
spacious 183 adj.
extent
quantity 26 n.
degree 27 n.
greatness 32 n.
space 183 n.
length 203 n.
(*see* **extension**)
extenuate
weaken 163 vb.
qualify 468 vb.
extenuate 927 vb.
qualification 468 n.
extenuation
vindication 927 n.
exterior
extrinsic 6 adj.
exteriority 223 n.
exteriority
exteriority 223 n.
exterminate
destroy 165 vb.
extermination
slaughter 362 n.
exterminator
killer 362 n.
extern
externalize 223 vb.
eject 300 vb.
external
extrinsic 6 adj.
appearing 445 adj.
externalize
externalize 223 vb.
materialize 319 vb.
externment
ejection 300 n.
extinct
extinct 2 adj.
past 125 adj.
dead 361 adj.
inactive 679 adj.
extinction
extinction 2 n.
death 361 n.

extinguish
suppress 165 vb.
snuff out 418 vb.
extinguisher
extinguisher 382 n.
extirpation
destruction 165 n.
extol
praise 923 vb.
worship 981 vb.
extort
extract 304 vb.
extortion
expropriation
786 n.
rapacity 786 n.
extortionate
oppressive 735 adj.
dear 811 adj.
avaricious 816 adj.
extortioner
tyrant 735 n.
taker 786 n.
extra
additional 38 adj.
extra 40 n.
superfluity 637 n.
extract
part 53 n.
extract 304 vb.
take, levy 786 vb.
extraction
genealogy 169 n.
extraction 304 n.
extractive
extracted 304 adj.
extradition
transference 272 n.
extrajudicial
illegal 954 adj.
extramarital
extramarital
951 adj.
extramundane
immaterial 320 adj.
divine 965 adj.
extramural
exterior 223 adj.
extraneous
separate 46 adj.
extraneous 59 adj.
extraneousness
extraneousness
59 n.
extraordinary
unusual 84 n.
wonderful 864 adj.

extrapolate
externalize 223 vb.
extra-territorial
exterior 223 adj.
extra-territoriality
non-liability 919 n.
extravagance
exaggeration
546 n.
waste 634 n.
prodigality 815 n.
extravagant
imaginative
513 adj.
dear 811 adj.
extravaganza
ideality 513 n.
extravasation
outflow 298 n.
extraversion
extrinsicality 6 n.
extravert
extrinsicality 6 n.
extreme
complete 54 adj.
ending 69 adj.
(*see* extremes,
extremity)
extremes
exaggeration 546 n.
severity 735 n.
cruel act 898 n.
extremism
reformism 654 n.
extremist
crank 504 n.
exaggeration 546
n.
reformer 654 n.
revolter 738 n.
extremity
extremity 69 n.
vertex 213 n.
limit 236 n.
adversity 731 n.
extricate
disencumber
701 vb.
extrication
extraction 304 n.
liberation 746 n.
extrinsicality
extrinsicality 6 n.
extraneousness
59 n.
extroversion
(*see* extraversion)

extrusion
ejection 300 n.
extrusive
expulsive 300 adj.
exuberance
productiveness
171 n.
redundance 637 n.
exude
exude 298 vb.
emit 300 vb.
be wet 341 vb.
exult
rejoice 835 vb.
exultant
jubilant 833 adj.
exultation
rejoicing 835 n.
eye
orifice 263 n.
eye 438 n.
gaze 438 vb.
eye for an eye
revenge 910 n.
eyeful
spectacle 445 n.
eyeglass
eyeglass 442 n.
eyeless
blind 439 adj.
eyelet
fastening 47 n.
orifice 263 n.
eyelid
shade 226 n.
eye-opener
discovery 484 n.
inexpectation
508 n.
eye-piece
optical device
442 n.
eyesight
vision 438 n.
eyesore
deformity 246 n.
eyesore 842 n.
eyestrain
dim sight 440 n.
eye to eye
concordant 710
adj.
eye-witness
spectator 441 n.
witness 466 n.
eyrie, eyry
nest 192 n.

F

Fabian
reformer 654 n.
Fabianism
slowness 278 n.
reformism 654 n.
Fabian policy
delay 136 n.
fable
fantasy 513 n.
fable 543 n.
narrative 590 n.
fabric
edifice 164 n.
textile 222 n.
structure, texture
331 n.
fabricate
imagine 513 vb.
fake 541 vb.
fabrication
production 164 n.
falsehood 541 n.
fabulous
prodigious 32 adj.
imaginary 513 adj.
façade
exteriority 223 n.
face 237 n.
face
be present 189 vb.
coat 226 vb.
line 227 vb.
face 237 n.
be opposite 240 vb.
mien 445 n.
oppose 704 vb.
be courageous
855 vb.
prestige 866 n.
face about
revert 148 vb.
face both ways
tergiversate
603 vb.
face down
supine 216 adj.
faceless
uniform 16 adj.
face-lift
beautification
843 n.
facetiousness
wit 839 n.
face to face
opposing 704 adj.

F

face value
appearance 445 n.
price 809 n.
facial
exterior 223 adj.
beautification 843 n.
facile
easy 701 adj.
facilitate
facilitate 701 vb.
facilities
means 629 n.
facility 701 n.
scope 744 n.
facility
facility 701 n.
facing
near 200 adj.
facing 226 n.
opposing 704 adj.
facsimile
copy 22 n.
fact
reality 1 n.
certainty 473 n.
truth 494 n.
(*see* facts)
fact-finding
inquiring 459 adj.
faction
dissentient 489 n.
party 708 n.
dissension 709 n.
sect 978 n.
factiousness
quarrelsomeness
709 n.
sectarianism 978 n.
factor
component 58 n.
numerical element
85 n.
cause 156 n.
influence 178 n.
agent 686 n.
manager 690 n.
deputy 755 n.
factorize
simplify 44 vb.
decompose 51 vb.
factors
circumstance 8 n.
factory
workshop 687 n.
factotum
busy person 678 n.
servant 742 n.

falsehood 541 n.
  deception 542 n.
false light
  visual fallacy 440 n.
false modesty
  underestimation
  483 n.
false name
  misnomer 562 n.
false note
  misfit 25 n.
false position
  predicament 700 n.
falsetto
  stridor 407 n.
falsify
  misinterpret
  521 vb.
  be false 541 vb.
falsity
  (*see* **false,**
  falsehood)
falter
  be irresolute
  601 vb.
fame
  publicity 528 n.
  famousness 866 n.
familiar
  known 490 adj.
  usual 610 adj.
  impertinent 878 adj.
  devil 969 n.
familiarity
  knowledge 490 n.
  habit 610 n.
  friendship 880 n.
family
  family 11 n.
  subdivision 53 n.
  breed 77 n.
  genealogy 169 n.
  parental 169 adj.
  posterity 170 n.
  community 708 n.
  nobility 868 n.
family man
  resident 191 n.
family tree
  genealogy 169 n.
famine
  scarcity 636 n.
  hunger 859 n.
famish
  starve 946 vb.
famous
  renowned 866 adj.

fan
  aerify 340 vb.
  ventilation 352 n.
  refrigerator 384 n.
  habitué 610 n.
  refresh 685 vb.
  patron 707 n.
fanatic
  doctrinaire 473 n.
  narrow mind
  481 n.
  biased 481 adj.
  opinionist 602 n.
  religionist 979 n.
fanatical
  positive 473 adj.
fanaticism
  narrow mind 481 n.
  warm feeling 818 n.
  pietism 979 n.
fancier
  breeder 369 n.
  expert 696 n.
fanciful
  imaginary 513 adj.
fancy
  think 449 vb.
  idea 451 n.
  supposition 512 n.
  imagination 513 n.
  caprice 604 n.
  choice 605 n.
  ornamental
  844 adj.
  liking 859 n.
fancy dress
  disguise 527 n.
fancy-work
  ornamental art
  844 n.
fanfare
  celebration 876 n.
fang
  tooth 256 n.
fan out
  expand 197 vb.
  diverge 294 vb.
fantastic
  absurd 497 adj.
  ridiculous 849 adj.
  wonderful 864 adj.
fantastical
  imaginative 513 adj.
fantasy
  insubstantiality 4 n.
  fantasy 513 n.
  aspiration 852 n.

far
  distant 199 adj.
far between
  spaced 201 adj.
farce
  foolery 497 n.
  stage play 594 n.
  ridiculousness
  849 n.
farcical
  (*see* **farce**)
far corner
  rear 238 n.
far cry
  distance 199 n.
fare
  be in a state 7 vb.
  travel 267 vb.
  meal 301 n.
  eat 301 vb.
  price 809 n.
farewell
  valediction 296 n.
far from
  different 15 adj.
farm
  breed stock
  369 vb.
  farm 370 n.
  cultivate 370 vb.
  hire 785 vb.
farmer
  husbandman 370 n.
farming
  agriculture 370 n.
farm out
  lease 784 vb.
farmstead
  house 192 n.
farmyard
  farm 370 n.
farrago
  medley 43 n.
  confusion 61 n.
far-reaching
  extensive 32 adj.
farrow
  youngling 132 n.
  reproduce itself
  164 vb.
far-sighted
  vigilant 457 adj.
  intelligent 498 adj.
farthest point
  extremity 69 n.
fascia
  strip 208 n.

fascinate
  (*see* **fascination**)
fascination
  influence 178 n.
  pleasurableness
  826 n.
  liking 859 n.
  spell 983 n.
fashion
  modality 7 n.
  conformity 83 n.
  modernism 126 n.
  dressing 228 n.
  form 243 n.
  efform 243 vb.
  feature 445 n.
  style 566 n.
  practice 610 n.
  fashion 848 n.
fashionable
  (*see* **fashion**)
fast
  firm-set 45 adj.
  fixed 153 adj.
  speedy 277 adj.
  coloured 425 adj.
  fast 946 n.
  starve 946 vb.
  unchaste 951 adj.
fast-day
  fast 946 n.
fasten
  affix 45 vb.
  close 264 vb.
fastener
  fastening 47 n.
fastening
  fastening 47 n.
fastidious
  discriminating
  463 adj.
  clean 648 adj.
  fastidious 862
  adj.
fat
  fleshy 195 adj.
  expanded 197
  adj.
  fat 357 n.
fatal
  deadly 362 adj.
  harmful 645 adj.
fatalism
  necessity 596 n.
  submission 721 n.
fatalist
  fatalist 596 n.

FAT

fatality
decease 361 n.
necessity 596 n.
fate
destiny 155 n.
cause 156 n.
chance 159 n.
influence 178 n.
fate 596 n.
non-design 618 n.
fathead
dunce 501 n.
father
generate 164 vb.
parent 169 n.
cleric 986 n.
fatherhood
parentage 169 n.
fatherland
home 192 n.
fatherless
defenceless 161
adj.
fatherly
parental 169 adj.
fatherly eye
protection 660 n.
father upon
attribute 158 vb.
fathom
long measure 203
n.
plunge 313 vb.
understand 516 vb.
fatigue
misuse 675 vb.
sleepiness 679 n.
fatigue 684 n., vb.
oppress 735 vb.
be tedious 838 vb.
fatigues
uniform 228 n.
fatling
cattle 365 n.
fat of the land
plenty 635 n.
prosperity 730 n.
fatten
enlarge 197 vb.
feed 301 vb.
pinguefy 357 vb.
breed stock 369 vb.
fatty
fatty 357 adj.
fatuity
absurdity 497 n.
folly 499 n.

FAV

fatuous
absurd 497 adj.
unmeaning 515 adj.
fault
weakness 163 n.
gap 201 n.
blunder 495 n.
defect 647 n.
dispraise 924 vb.
guilty act 966 n.
fault-finder
malcontent 829 n.
fault-finding
fastidious 826 adj.
censure 924 n.
faultiness
inferiority 35 n.
imperfection 647 n.
faultless
perfect 646 adj.
guiltless 935 adj.
**fault on the right
side**
virtues 933 n.
faulty
inexact 495 adj.
inelegant 576 adj.
imperfect 647 adj.
fauna
animality 365 n.
faux pas
mistake 495 n.
favour
vantage 34 n.
influence 178 n.
promote 285 vb.
badge 547 n.
choose 605 vb.
aid 703 n.
be auspicious
730 vb.
liking 859 n.
repute, honours
866 n.
love-token 889 n.
kind act 897 n.
approbation 923 n.
favourable
opportune 137 adj.
promising 852 adj.
approving 923 adj.
favourer
patron 707 n.
favourite
chosen 605 adj.
social person
882 n.

FEA

favourite 890 n.
kept woman 952 n.
favouritism
prejudice 481 n.
injustice 914 n.
fawn
youngling 132 n.
deer 365 n.
brown 430 adj.
be servile 879 vb.
caress 889 vb.
flatter 925 vb.
fawner
toady 879 n.
fear
fear 854 n., vb.
honour 866 vb.
piety 979 n.
fearful
nervous 854 adj.
fearless
unfearing 855 adj.
fear of God
piety 979 n.
fearsome
frightening 854 adj.
feasibility
possibility 469 n.
feast
feasting 301 n.
feed 301 vb.
revel 837 n.
social gathering
882 n.
feast-day
holy-day 988 n.
feasting
gluttony 947 n.
feat
deed 676 n.
prowess 855 n.
feather
sort 77 n.
levity 323 n.
(*see* feathers)
featherbed
euphoria 376 n.
be lenient 736 vb.
feather-brained
foolish 499 adj.
feathering
plumage 259 n.
feather in one's cap
honours 866 n.
feather one's nest
get rich 800 vb.
be selfish 932 vb.

FEE

feathers
plumage 259 n.
wing 271 n.
softness 327 n.
(*see* feather)
feather-weight
levity 323 n.
pugilist 722 n.
feathery
downy 259 adj.
light 323 adj.
feature
character 5 n.
component 58 n.
speciality 80 n.
face 237 n.
form 243 n.
feature 445 n.
show 522 vb.
advertise 528 vb.
dramatize 594 vb.
featureless
uniform 16 adj.
amorphous 244 adj.
feckless
unskilful 695 adj.
unsuccessful 728 adj.
fecundation
propagation 164 n.
fecundity
propagation 164 n.
federal
corporate 708 adj.
federalism
government 733 n.
federation
association 706 n.
polity 733 n.
fee
estate 777 n.
pay 804 n.
reward 962 n., vb.
feeble
weak 163 adj.
lax 734 adj.
feeble-minded
unintelligent
499 adj.
insane 503 adj.
feed
eat 301 vb.
provide 633 vb.
be hospitable
882 vb.
feeder
eater 301 n.
provider 633 n.

feel
 texture 331 n.
 opine 485 vb.
 feel 818 vb.
feeler
 feeler 378 n.
 empiricism 461 n.
feeling
 sense 374 n.
 touch 378 n.
 intuition 476 n.
 opinion 485 n.
 feeling 818 n., adj.
feel like
 be willing 597 vb.
feel one's way
 be tentative 461
 vb.
feel the pulse
 be tentative 461 vb.
feet of clay
 defect 647 n.
 vulnerability 661 n.
feign
 dissemble 541 vb.
 be affected 850 vb.
feint
 stratagem 698 n.
felicitation
 congratulation
 886 n.
felicitous
 apt 24 adj.
 elegant 575 adj.
feline
 cat 365 n.
 stealthy 525 adj.
fell
 demolish 165 vb.
 skin 226 n.
 high land 209 n.
 strike 279 vb.
 fell 311 vb.
 evil 616 adj.
 cruel 898 adj.
felloe, felly
 wheel 250 n.
fellow
 analogue 18 n.
 compeer 28 n.
 concomitant 89 n.
 male 372 n.
 colleague 707 n.
 friend, chum 880 n.
fellow-countryman
 native 191 n.
 friend 880 n.

fellow-creature
 person 371 n.
fellow-feeling
 cooperation 706 n.
 participation 775 n.
 friendliness 880 n.
 benevolence 897 n.
 condolence 905 n.
fellowship
 community 708 n.
 friendship 880 n.
 sociality 882 n.
fellow-traveller
 collaborator 707 n.
felly
 wheel 250 n.
felo de se
 suicide 362 n.
felon
 offender 904 n.
 knave 938 n.
felonious
 lawbreaking
 954 adj.
felony
 lawbreaking 954 n.
female
 female 373 n., adj.
feminine
 generic 77 adj.
 female 373 adj.
feminist
 female 373 adj.
femoral
 crural 267 adj.
fen
 marsh 347 n.
fence
 fence 235 n.
 obstacle 702 n.
 defences 713 n.
 parry 713 vb.
 thief 789 n.
fencer
 combatant 722 n.
fend
 parry 713 vb.
fender
 furnace 383 n.
feoffee
 possessor 776 n.
 beneficiary 776 n.
ferment
 turmoil 61 n.
 conversion 147 n.
 stimulation 174 n.
 commotion 318 n.

leaven 323 n.
 be sour 393 vb.
 excitable state
 822 n.
fern
 plant 366 n.
ferocious
 cruel 898 adj.
ferret
 vermin 365 n.
ferret out
 detect 484 vb.
ferry
 carry 273 vb.
 ship, boat 275 n.
ferryman
 boatman 270 n.
 carrier 273 n.
fertile
 gainful 771 adj.
 rich 800 adj.
fertility
 propagation 164 n.
 productiveness
 171 n.
fertilization
 propagation 164 n.
fertilize
 make fruitful
 171 vb.
 cultivate 370 vb.
fertilizer
 fertilizer 171 n.
ferule
 scourge 964 n.
fervent
 hot 379 adj.
 fervent 818 adj.
 loving 887 adj.
 pietistic 979 adj.
fervour
 heat 379 n.
 warm feeling 818 n.
festal
 amusing 837 adj.
 ritual 988 adj.
fester
 be unclean 649 vb.
 be ill 651 vb.
festering
 toxic 653 adj.
festival
 festivity 837 n.
festive
 sociable 882 adj.
festivity
 meal 301 n.

festivity 837 n.
 celebration 876 n.
festoon
 decorate 844 vb.
fetch
 delight 826 vb.
fetch and carry
 be servile 879 vb.
fetching
 personable 841 adj.
fête
 amusement 837 n.
 pageant 875 n.
 celebration 876 n.
fetid
 fetid 397 adj.
 unclean 649 adj.
fetish
 idol 982 n.
fetishism
 idolatory 982 n.
fetor
 (see fetid)
fetter
 tie 45 vb.
 hinder 702 vb.
 fetter 748 n.
fettle
 state 7 n.
feud
 quarrel 709 n.
 revenge 910 n.
feudal
 governmental
 733 adj.
feudalism
 government 733 n.
feudatory
 subject 745 adj.
 possessor 776 n.
fever
 heat 379 n.
 excitable state
 822 n.
feverish
 agitated 318 adj.
 hasty 680 adj.
 fervent 818 adj.
few
 few 105 adj.
 infrequent 140 adj.
 scarce 636 adj.
few and far between
 discontinuous
 72 adj.
 few 105 adj.
 seldom 140 adv.

fey
  bewitched 983 **adj.**
  psychical 984 **n.**
fiancé, fiancée
  lover, loved one
    887 **n.**
fiasco
  failure 728 **n.**
fiat
  decree 737 **n.**
fib
  untruth 543 **n.**
fibber, fibster
  liar 545 **n.**
fibre
  fibre 208 **n.**
  texture 331 **n.**
fibrous
  fibrous 208 **adj.**
  tough 329 **adj.**
fibula
  fastening 47 **n.**
  jewellery 844 **n.**
fickle
  changeful 152 **adj.**
  unreliable 474 **adj.**
  capricious 604 **adj.**
fiction
  ideality 513 **n.**
  falsehood 541 **n.**
  novel 590 **n.**
fictional
  imaginative
    513 **adj.**
  descriptive 590 **adj.**
fiction-writer
  narrator 590 **n.**
fictitious
  imaginary 513 **adj.**
  untrue 543 **adj.**
fiddle
  viol 414 **n.**
  trickery 542 **n.**
  foul play 930 **n.**
fiddlehead
  coil 251 **n.**
  pattern 844 **n.**
fiddler
  instrumentalist
    413 **n.**
  trickster 545 **n.**
fiddlestick
  viol 414 **n.**
fiddle with
  touch 378 **vb.**
fiddling
  trivial 639 **adj.**

fidelity
  accuracy 494 **n.**
  loyalty 739 **n.**
  probity 929 **n.**
fidgets
  restlessness 678 **n.**
fidgety
  unstable 152 **adj.**
  excitable 822 **adj.**
fiduciary
  monetary 797 **adj.**
fief
  possession 773 **n.**
  lands 777 **n.**
field
  opportunity 137 **n.**
  range 183 **n.**
  region 184 **n.**
  enclosure 235 **n.**
  grassland 348 **n.**
  arena 724 **n.**
  scope 744 **n.**
field day
  pageant 875 **n.**
  special day 876 **n.**
field marshal
  army officer 741 **n.**
field of battle
  battleground 724 **n.**
fieldpiece
  gun 723 **n.**
fields
  land 344 **n.**
  farm 370 **n.**
fiend
  monster 938 **n.**
  devil 969 **n.**
fiendish
  cruel 898 **adj.**
fierce
  active 678 **adj.**
  warlike 718 **adj.**
  irascible 892 **adj.**
  cruel 898 **adj.**
fiery
  fiery 379 **adj.**
  luminous 417 **adj.**
  fervent 818 **adj.**
  excitable 822 **adj.**
fife
  flute 414 **n.**
fifth column
  perfidy 930 **n.**
fifth columnist
  tergiversator 603 **n.**
fifty-fifty
  equal 28 **adj.**

  median 30 **adj.**
  mediocre 732 **adj.**
fight
  fight 716 **n., vb.**
  go to war 718 **vb.**
fight back, fight off
  parry 713 **vb.**
fighter
  combatant 722 **n.**
  air force 722 **n.**
fight for
  defend 713 **vb.**
fighting
  athletic 162 **adj.**
fighting cock
  combatant 722 **n.**
  brave person 855
    n.
fight shy
  be loth 598 **vb.**
  avoid 620 **vb.**
figment
  insubstantial
    thing 4 **n.**
  idea 451 **n.**
  ideality 513 **n.**
figurative
  semantic 514 **adj.**
  figurative 519 **adj.**
  representing
    551 **adj.**
  rhetorical 574 **adj.**
figure
  numbering 85 **n.**
  do sums 86 **vb.**
  outline 233 **n.**
  form 243 **n.**
  feature 445 **n.**
  trope 519 **n.**
  image 551 **n.**
  represent 551 **vb.**
  funds 797 **n.**
  person of repute
    866 **n.**
figurehead
  insubstantial
    thing 4 **n.**
  face, prow 237 **n.**
  nonentity 639 **n.**
figure of fun
  laughing-stock
    851 **n.**
figure of speech
  trope 519 **n.**
  ornament 574 **n.**
figures
  statistics 86 **n.**

filament
  filament 208 **n.**
  lamp 420 **n.**
filch
  steal 788 **vb.**
filcher
  thief 789 **n.**
file
  sorting 62 **n.**
  class 62 **vb.**
  procession 71 **n.**
  receptacle 194 **n.**
  sharpener 256 **n.**
  smoother 258 **n.**
  rub 333 **vb.**
  record 548 **n., vb.**
  formation 722 **n.**
filial
  filial 170 **adj.**
  obedient 739 **adj.**
filiation
  consanguinity 11
    n.
  attribution 158 **n.**
  sonship 170 **n.**
filibeg
  skirt 228 **n.**
filibuster
  delay 136 **n.**
  be loquacious
    581 **vb.**
  hinderer 702 **n.**
filigree
  network 222 **n.**
  ornamental art
    844 **n.**
filings
  powder 332 **n.**
filing system
  sorting 62 **n.**
fill
  fill 54 **vb.**
  load 193 **vb.**
  replenish 633 **vb.**
  sate 863 **vb.**
fillet
  girdle 47 **n.**
  headgear 228 **n.**
  void 300 **vb.**
filling
  contents 193 **n.**
  lining 227 **n.**
fillip
  incentive 612 **n.**
  excitant 821 **n.**
fill out
  expand 197 **vb.**

fill up
replenish 633 vb.
sate 863 vb.

filly
youngling 132 n.
horse 273 n.

film
layer 207 n.
skin, shade 226 n.
opacity 423 n.
dim sight 440 n.
photography 551 n.

film-goer
playgoer 594 n.

films
cinema 445 n.

filmy
opaque 423 adj.

filter
cleaning utensil
648 n.
purify 648 vb.

filth
dirt 649 n.
impurity 951 n.

final
ending 69 adj.
contest 716 n.
completive 725 adj.

finale
end 69 n.
musical piece
412 n.

finality
(see final)

finance
lend 784 vb.
finance 797 n.

financial
monetary 797 adj.

financier
moneyer 797 n.
merchant 794 n.

find
meet with 154 vb.
discovery 484 n.
provide 633 vb.
acquisition 771 n.

find against
condemn 961 vb.

find fault
blame 924 vb.

find guilty
condemn 961 vb.

finding
judgement 480 n.
legal trial 959 n.

find means
find means 629 vb.

find out
discover 484 vb.

fine
small 33 adj.
narrow 206 adj.
rare 325 adj.
textural 331 adj.
dry 342 adj.
transparent
422 adj.
discriminating
463 adj.
accurate 494 adj.
excellent 644 adj.
splendid 841 adj.
penalty 963 n.

fine feeling
good taste 846 n.

fine gentleman
fop 848 n.
proud man 871 n.

finer feelings
moral sensibility
819 n.

finery
finery 844 n.

fine-spun
narrow 206 adj.
textural 331 adj.

finesse
cunning 698 n.

finger
piece 53 n.
finger 378 n.
touch 378 vb.
indicator 547 n.

**finger in the pie,
have a**
meddle 678 vb.

fingerprint
identification 547 n.
trace 548 n.

finial
vertex 213 n.

finicky
fastidious 862 adj.

finish
completion 54 n.
end 69 n., vb.
cease 145 n.
elegance 575 n.
perfection 646 n.

finishing school
training school
539 n.

finish off
carry through
725 vb.

finite
limited 236 adj.

fiord
gulf 345 n.

fire
shoot 287 vb.
dismiss 300 vb.
fire 379 n.
furnace 383 n.
light 417 n.
vigour 571 n.
bombardment
712 n.
warm feeling 818 n.

fire-alarm
danger signal
665 n.

fire-arm
fire-arm 723 n.

firebrand
incendiarism 381 n.
trouble-maker
663 n.
agitator 738 n.

fire-brigade
extinguisher 382 n.

fire-bug
incendiarism 381 n.

fire-eater
desperado 857 n.

fire-engine
extinguisher 382 n.

fire-escape
means of escape
667 n.

firefly
fly 365 n.
glow-worm 420 n.

fireman
extinguisher 382 n.

fire-party
punisher 963 n.

fireplace
furnace 383 n.

fire-proof
incombustible
382 adj.

fireside
focus 76 n.
home 192 n.

fire-station
extinguisher 382 n.

firewood
fuel 385 n.

fireworks
fireworks 420 n.
masterpiece 694 n.
celebration 876 n.

firing line
battle 718 n.
battleground 724
n.

firm
firm-set 45 adj.
fixed 153 adj.
strong 162 adj.
dense 324 adj.
rigid 326 adj.
merchant 794 n.

firmament
heavens 321 n.

firmness
stability 153 n.
hardness 326 n.

first
supreme 34 adj.
first 68 adj.
prior 119 adj.
foremost 283 adj.
best 644 adj.

first aid
therapy 658 n.

first-born
precursor 66 n.
older 131 adj.

First Cause
cause 156 n.

first choice
chief thing 638 n.

first-class
supreme 34 adj.

first draft
plan 623 n.

first-hand
unimitative 21 adj.

first lady
superior 34 n.

first-nighter
playgoer 594 n.

first offence
début 68 n.

first offender
beginner 538 n.

first-rate
best 644 adj.

first water, of the
excellent 644 adj.

firth
gulf 345 n.

fisc
treasury 799 n.

fiscal
monetary 797 adj.
fish
animal, fish 365
n.
hunt 619 vb.
fish day
fast 946 n.
fisher
hunter 619 n.
fishery
stock farm 369 n.
fish for
search 459 vb.
fishiness
improbity 930 n.
fishing
sport 837 n.
fish out of water
misfit 25 n.
fishwife
shrew 892 n.
fishy
animal 365 adj.
dishonest 930 adj.
fissile
brittle 330 adj.
fission
separation 46 n.
decompose 51 vb.
fissionable
severable 46 adj.
fissure
gap 201 n.
fist
finger 378 n.
lettering 586 n.
fisticuffs
quarrel 709 n.
pugilism 716 n.
fistula
ulcer 651 n.
fit
modality 7 n.
adjust 24 vb.
join 45 vb.
cohere 48 vb.
spasm 318 n.
expedient 642 adj.
healthy 650 adj.
right 913 adj.
fit for
useful 640 adj.
fit for nothing
useless 641 adj.
fitfulness
fitfulness 142 n.

fit in
accord 24 vb.
conform 83 vb.
load 193 vb.
fitness
fitness 24 n.
aptitude 694 n.
preparedness 669 n.
fit out
make ready 669
vb.
fits and starts
fitfulness 142 n.
fitter
machinist 630 n.
fitting
cohesive 48 adj.
expedient 642 adj.
fittings
equipment 630 n.
fix
affix 45 vb.
stabilize 153 vb.
repair 656 vb.
predicament 700 n.
fixation
location 187 n.
habituation 610 n.
fixative
adhesive 47 n.
pigment 425 n.
fixed
fixed 153 adj.
still 266 adj.
habitual 610 adj.
fixed interval
regular return
141 n.
fixity
resolution 599 n.
obstinacy 602 n.
fixture
adjunct 40 n.
fixture 153 n.
equipment 630 n.
fizz
vigorousness 174 n.
wine 301 n.
soft drink 301 n.
bubble 355 n., vb.
hiss 406 vb.
fizzer
exceller 644 n.
fizzle
hiss 406 vb.
fizzle out
miscarry 728 vb.

fizzy
windy 352 adj.
bubbly 355 adj.
flabbergast
frighten 854 vb.
be wonderful
864 vb.
flabby
soft 327 adj.
pulpy 356 adj.
flaccidity
weakness 163 n.
flag
be weak 163 vb.
signal, flag 547 n.
be fatigued 684 vb.
greet 884 vb.
flag day
request 671 n.
flagellant
penitent 939 n.
ascetic 945 n.
flagellation
asceticism 945 n.
*corporal
punishment* 963 n.
flageolet
flute 414 n.
flagitiousness
wickedness 934 n.
flag of convenience
stratagem 698 n.
flag of truce
irenics 719 n.
flagon
vessel 194 n.
flagrancy
publicity 528 n.
ostentation 875 n.
flagrant
great 32 adj.
(*see* flagrancy)
flags
paving 226 n.
flagship
warship 722 n.
flagstaff
support 218 n.
flail
hammer 279 n.
cultivate 370 vb.
strike at 712 vb.
flog 963 vb.
flair
odour 394 n.
discrimination
463 n.

aptitude 694 n.
flak
bombardment
712 n.
flake
small thing 33 n.
lamina 207 n.
pulverize 332 vb.
flaky
brittle 330 adj.
flame
fire 379 n.
shine 417 vb.
luminary 420 n.
redness 431 n.
loved one 887 n.
flame-proof
incombustible
382 adj.
flame-thrower
gun 723 n.
flaming
fiery 379 adj.
flange
edge 234 n.
flank
laterality 239 n.
safeguard 660 vb.
flannel
textile 222 n.
warm clothes
381 n.
cleaning cloth
648 n.
flap
come unstuck
49 vb.
pendant 217 n.
hang 217 vb.
covering 226 n.
agitation 318 n.
flapdoodle
empty talk 515 n.
flapper
youngster 132 n.
flaps
wing 271 n.
aircraft 276 n.
flare
be hot 379 vb.
shine 417 vb.
torch 420 n.
signal light 420 n.
flare up
get angry 891 vb.
flash
instant 116 n.

flash 417 n.
luminary 420 n.
news 529 n.
spurious 542 adj.
signal 547 n.

flash-back
remembrance
505 n.

flash in the pan
insubstantial thing
4 n.
brief span 114 n.

flashlight
lamp 420 n.

flashy
ornate 574 adj.
vulgar 847 adj.

flask
vessel 194 n.

flat
uniform 16 adj.
inert 175 adj.
spatial 183 adj.
flat 192 n.
chamber 194 n.
low 210 adj.
flat 216 adj.
unsharpened
257 adj.
marsh 347 n.
unsavoury
391 adj.
non-resonant
405 adj.
discordant 411 adj.
soft-hued 425 adj.
ninny 501 n.
assertive 532 adj.
feeble 572 adj.
dull 840 adj.

flat-foot
police 955 n.

flat-iron
smoother 258 n.

flatness
lowness 210 n.
horizontality 216 n.
(*see* **flat**)

flats
plain 348 n.

flatten
flatten 216 vb.
fell 311 vb.

flatter
imitate 20 vb.
befool 542 vb.
beautify 841 vb.

flatter 925 vb.
(*see* **flattery**)

flatterer
toady 879 n.
flatterer 925 n.

flatter oneself
be vain 873 vb.

flattery
assent 488 n.
servility 879 n.
endearment 889 n.
flattery 925 n.
(*see* **flatter**)

flatulence
gaseity 336 n.
magniloquence
574 n.
indigestion 651 n.

flatulent
feeble 572 adj.

flaunt
show 522 vb.
be ostentatious
875 vb.

flautist
instrumentalist
413 n.

flavour
taste 386 n.
season 388 vb.

flavourless
tasteless 387 adj.

flaw
gale 352 n.
defect 647 n.
blemish 845 n.,
vb.

flawless
perfect 646 adj.

flax
fibre 208 n.

flaxen
yellow 433 adj.

flay
rend 46 vb.
uncover 229 vb.
dispraise 924 vb.

flea
vermin 365 n.

flea-bite
small quantity 33 n.
trifle 639 n.

fleck
small thing 33 n.
(*see* **blemish**)

flection
deviation 282 n.

fledgeling
youngling 132 n.
bird 365 n.

flee
run away 620 vb.

fleece
skin 226 n.
hair 259 n.
fleece 786 vb.
overcharge 811 vb.

fleecy
fibrous 208 adj.
downy 259 adj.

fleet
shipping 275 n.
speedy 277 adj.
navy 722 n.

fleeting
transient 114 adj.

flesh
auspicate 68 vb.
matter 319 n.
mankind 371 n.
sensualism 944 n.

flesh and blood
substance 3 n.
matter 319 n.
animality 365 n.

flesh-pots
feasting 301 n.

fleshy
fleshy 195 adj.
pulpy 356 adj.

flexed
curved 248 adj.

flexibility
softness 327 n.

flexible
conformable 83
adj.
flexible 327 adj.
wieldy 701 adj.

flexion
curvature 248 n.
deviation 282 n.

flexuosity
convolution 251 n.

flibbertigibbet
demon, elf 970 n.

flick
impel 279 vb.
touch 378 vb.

flicker
be transient
114 vb.
flash 417 n.
be dim 419 vb.

flier, flyer
aeronaut 271 n.

flight
group 74 n.
transientness 114 n.
aeronautics 271 n.
departure 296 n.
avoidance 620 n.
air force 722 n.
defeat 728 n.

flightiness
changeableness
152 n.
(*see* **flighty**)

flight of time
course of time
111 n.

flighty
light-minded
456 n.
irresolute 601 adj.

flimsy
brittle 330 adj.

flinch
recoil 280 vb.
feel pain 377 vb.
avoid 620 vb.
quake 854 vb.

flincher
coward 856 n.

fling
propulsion 287 n.
scope 744 n.
dance 837 n.

fling, have one's
be intemperate
943 vb.

flint
lighter 385 n.
tool 630 n.

flinty
hard 326 adj.
territorial 344 adj.

flip
impulse 279 n.
touch 378 vb.

flippancy
wit 839 n.
sauciness 878 n.

flippant
light-minded
456 adj.

flipper
feeler 378 n.

flirt
affector 850 n.
excite love 887 vb.

libertine 952 n.
loose woman 952 n.
flirtation
  love affair 887 n.
  wooing 889 n.
flit
  be transient 114 vb.
  move 265 vb.
  run away 620 vb.
float
  hang 217 vb.
  swim 269 vb.
  cart 274 n.
  raft 275 n.
  be light 323 vb.
floating
  unstable 152 adj.
floating vote
  changeableness
    152 n.
  irresolution 601 vb.
flock
  group 74 n.
  congregate 74 vb.
  be many 104 vb.
  hair 259 n.
  animal 365 n.
  laity 987 n.
floe
  ice 380 n.
flog
  strike 279 vb.
  fatigue 684 vb.
  sell 793 vb.
  flog 963 vb.
flog a dead horse
  waste effort 641 vb.
flood
  crowd 74 n.
  be many 104 vb.
  irrigate 341 vb.
  flow 350 vb.
  plenty 635 n.
flood-gate
  outlet 298 n.
  conduit 351 n.
floor
  layer 207 n.
  base 214 n.
  horizontality 216 n.
  paving 226 n.
  overlay 226 vb.
  strike 279 vb.
  fell 311 vb.
  arena 724 n.
floor-show
  stage show 594 n.

flop
  descend 309 vb.
  failure 728 n.
  (see fatigue)
floppy
  non-adhesive
    49 adj.
  soft 327 adj.
flora and fauna
  organism 358 n.
floral
  vegetal 366 adj.
florescence
  vegetability 366 n.
floriculture
  agriculture 370 n.
florid
  florid 425 adj.
  ornate 574 adj.
  healthy 650 adj.
floruit
  palmy days 730 n.
floss
  hair 259 n.
flotilla
  shipping 275 n.
  navy 722 n.
flotsam
  derelict 779 n.
flotsam and jetsam
  outcaste 883 n.
flounce
  edging 234 n.
  leap 312 vb.
flounder
  leap 312 vb.
  be uncertain
    474 vb.
  be clumsy 695 vb.
  be in difficulty
    700 vb.
flour
  cereal 301 n.
  powder 332 n.
  corn 366 n.
flourish
  coil 251 n.
  show 522 vb.
  publication 528 n.
  ornament 574 n.
  lettering 586 n.
  be healthy 650 vb.
  prosper 730 vb.
  pattern 844 n.
  ostentation 875 n.
floury
  powdery 332 adj.

flout
  despise 922 vb.
flow
  continuity 71 n.
  elapse 111 vb.
  current 350 n.
  flow 350 vb.
flower
  grow 36 vb.
  reproduce itself
    164 vb.
  flower 366 n.
  élite 644 n.
  prosper 730 vb.
flowering
  young 130 adv.
flowery
  vegetal 366 adj.
flowing
  unstable 152 adj.
fluctuate
  be periodic 141 vb.
  vary 152 vb.
fluctuation
  changeableness
    152 n.
  motion 265 n.
  fluctuation 317 n.
flue
  chimney 263 n.
  furnace 383 n.
fluency
  diffuseness 570 n.
  elegance 575 n.
fluent
  flowing 350 adj.
fluff
  levity 323 n.
  be clumsy 695 vb.
fluffy
  downy 259 adj.
fluid
  unstable 152 adj.
  amorphous 244 adj.
  fluid 335 n.
fluidity
  non-coherence 49
    n.
  fluidity 335 n.
  liquefaction 337 n.
  unreliability 474 n.
fluke
  chance 159 n.
  non-design 618 n.
  success 727 n.
fluky
  casual 159 adj.

flummox
  puzzle 474 vb.
flunkey
  domestic 742 n.
  toady 879 n.
fluorescence
  glow 417 n.
flurry
  derange 63 vb.
  rain 350 n.
  gale 352 n.
  distract 456 vb.
flush
  flat 216 adj.
  glow 417 n.
  redness 431 n.
  clean 648 vb.
fluster
  derange 63 vb.
  distract 456 vb.
flute
  groove 262 vb.
  play music 413 vb.
  flute 414 n.
fluting
  furrow 262 n.
  ornamental art
    844 n.
flutter
  fly 271 vb.
  agitation 318 .n
  gambling 618 n.
  nervousness 854 n.
fluvial
  flowing 350 adj.
flux
  liquefaction 337 n.
  current 350 n.
flux and reflux
  fluctuation 317 n.
fly
  be transient 114 vb.
  animalcule 196 n.
  fly 271 vb.
  cab 274 n.
  move fast 277 vb.
  fly 365 n.
  intelligent 498 adj.
  run away 620 vb.
  cunning 698 adj.
flyblown
  unclean 649 adj.
fly-by-night
  avoiding 620 adj.
flying
  transient 114 adj.
  aeronautics 271 n.

flying colours
trophy 729 n.
flying colours, with
successfully
727 adv.
flying saucer
space-ship 276 n.
flying start
spurt 277 n.
fly in the ointment
defect 647 n.
hitch 702 n.
fly-over
traffic contro
305 n.
bridge 624 n.
fly-paper
adhesive 47 n.
trap 542 n.
flyweight
pugilist 722 n.
foal
youngling 132 n.
horse 273 n.
foam
be violent 176 vb.
bubble 355 n., vb.
be excitable 822 vb.
foamy
light 323 adj.
bubbly 355 adj.
fob
pocket 194 n.
focal
central 225 adj.
focalization
convergence 293 n.
focal point
focus 76 n.
centrality 225 n.
focus
bring together
74 vb.
focus 76 n., vb.
centralize 225 vb.
convergence 293 n.
gaze 438 vb.
arena 724 n.
focus the attention
attract notice
455 vb.
fodder
provender 301 n.
foe
enemy 881 n.
foetus
source 156 n.

fog
cloud 355 n.
opacity 423 n.
blur 440 vb.
fogey
(*see* fogy)
foggy
dense 324 adj.
cloudy 355 adj.
opaque 423 adj.
fogy, fogey
crank 504 n.
laughing-stock
851 n.
foible
vice 934 n.
(*see* defect)
foil
bluntness 257 n.
be obstructive
702 vb.
foin
foin 712 n.
parry 713 vb.
fold
stable 192 n.
enclosure 235 n.
fold 261 n., vb.
shelter 662 n.
folder
receptacle 194 n.
foliage
foliage 366 n.
foliate
number 86 vb.
folk
social group 371 n.
folklore
tradition 127 n.
anthropology 371 n.
folksy
sociable 882 adj.
follow
do likewise 20 vb.
come after 65 vb.
conform 83 vb.
result 157 vb.
follow 284 vb.
understand 516 vb.
serve 742 vb.
follow advice
consult 691 vb.
follower
concomitant 89 n.
follower 284 n.
learner 538 n.
dependant 742 n.

lover 887 n.
sectarist 978 n.
follow-through
sequel 67 n.
effectuation 725 n.
follow through
sustain 146 vb.
carry through
725 vb.
folly
folly 499 n.
rashness 857 n.
foment
heat 381 vb.
doctor 658 vb.
aid 703 vb.
fomentation
surgical dressing
658 n.
therapy 658 n.
fond
foolish 499 adj.
crazed 503 adj.
loving 887 adj.
fondle
caress 889 vb.
fondness
(*see* fond)
font
church utensil
990 n.
food
food 301 n.
life 360 n.
provision 633 n.
food for thought
topic 452 n.
foodstuff(s)
food 301 n.
provisions 301 n.
fool
fool 501 n.
madman 504 n.
befool 542 vb.
dupe 544 n.
humorist 839 n.
laughing-stock
851 n.
foolery
foolery 497 n.
folly 499 n.
foolhardiness
rashness 857 n.
foolish
mindless 448 adj.
foolish 499 adj.
crazed 503 adj.

foolishness
(*see* folly)
fool-proof
certain 473 adj.
invulnerable
660 adj.
easy 701 adj.
successful 727 adj.
fool's errand
lost labour 641 n.
fool's paradise
insubstantial thing
4 n.
disappointment
509 n.
aspiration 852 n.
foot
base, foot 214 n.
infantry 722 n.
football
ball game 837 n.
football pool
gambling 618 n.
footfall
gait 265 n.
footgear
footwear 228 n.
foothold
retention 778 n.
footing
circumstance 8 n.
serial place 73 n.
footlight(s)
lighting 420 n.
drama, theatre
594 n.
footloose
travelling 267 adj.
footman
domestic 742 n.
(*see* infantry)
footmark
trace 548 n.
footnote(s)
commentary 520
n.
footpad
robber 789 n.
footpath
path 624 n.
footprint
concavity 255 n.
trace 548 n.
footrule
gauge 465 n.
foot-slogger
infantry 722 n.

509

footsore
 fatigued 684 adj.
footwear
 footwear 228 n.
foozle
 be clumsy 695 vb.
fop
 fop 848 n.
foppery
 fashion 848 n.
 affectation 850 n.
foppish
 fashionable 848
  adj.
 affected 850 adj.
forage
 provender 301 n.
 provide 633 vb.
foray
 attack 712 n.
 brigandage 788 n.
forbear
 precursor 66 n.
 parent 169 n.
 (*see* **forbearance**)
forbearance
 lenity 736 n.
 mercy 905 n.
forbid
 prohibit 757 vb.
forbidden fruit
 incentive 612 n.
forbidding
 cheerless 834 adj.
 sullen 893 adj.
force
 band 74 n.
 energy 160 n.
 strength 162 n.
 vigorousness 174 n.
 force 176 vb.
 cultivate 370 vb.
 meaning 514 n.
 vigour 571 n.
 mature 669 vb.
 misuse 675 n., vb.
 exertion 682 n.
 armed force 722 n.
 compulsion 740 n.
 debauch 951 vb.
forced
 feeble 572 adj.
 inelegant 576 adj.
forced labour
 compulsion 740 n.
forced march
 haste 680 n.

forceful
 strong 162 adj.
 assertive 532 adj.
 forceful 571 adj.
 compelling 740
  adj.
 impressive 821 adj.
force of
 circumstances
 necessity 596 n.
force open
 force 176 vb.
forceps
 extractor 304 n.
 nippers 778 n.
forcible-feeble
 feeble 572 adj.
ford
 pass 305 vb.
forearm
 prepare 669 vb.
forebode
 predict 511 vb.
foreboding
 foresight 510 n.
 prediction 511 n.
 warning 664 n.
forecast
 expectation 507 n.
 predict 511 vb.
forecastle
 prow 237 n.
foreclose
 deprive 786 vb.
foreclosure
 expropriation
  786 n.
 debt 803 n.
forefather
 parent 169 n.
forefathers
 the dead 361 n.
forefinger
 finger 378 n.
forefront
 beginning 68 n.
 front 237 n.
foreglimpse
 foresight 510 n.
foregoing
 preceding 64 adj.
 prior 119 adj.
foregone conclusion
 predetermination
  608 n.
foreground
 front 237 n.

forehead
 head 213 n.
 face 237 n.
foreign
 irrelative 10 adj.
 extraneous 59 adj.
foreigner
 foreigner 59 n.
foreign parts
 extraneousness
  59 n.
foreknowledge
 foresight 510 n.
foreland
 projection 254 n.
foreleg
 leg 267 n.
forelock
 hair 259 n.
foreman
 manager 690 n.
foremast
 prow 237 n.
foremost
 foremost 283 adj.
 important 638 adj.
forename
 name 561 n.
forenoon
 morning 128 n.
forensic
 jurisprudential
  958 adj.
forerun
 come before 64
  vb.
 precede 283 vb.
forerunner
 precursor 66 n.
 messenger 531 n.
foresee
 foresee 510 vb.
foreseeable
 expected 507 adj.
foreshadow
 predestine 155 vb.
foreshorten
 shorten 204 vb.
foresight
 foresight 510 n.
 prediction 511 n.
 preparation 669 n.
forest
 wood 366 n.
forestall
 be early 135 vb.
 foresee 510 vb.

forester
 forestry 366 n.
 gardener 370 n.
forestry
 forestry 366 n.
foretaste
 precursor 66 n.
 foresight 510 n.
foretell
 predict 511 vb.
forethought
 sagacity 498 n.
 foresight 510 n.
forewarn
 predict 511 vb.
 warn 664 vb.
forewarning
 precursor 66 n.
foreword
 prelude 66 n.
forfeit
 loss 772 n.
 disentitle 916 vb.
 penalty 963 n.
forfeiture
 (*see* **forfeit**)
forge
 efform 243 vb.
 furnace 383 n.
 fake 541 vb.
 workshop 687 n.
forge ahead
 progress 285 vb.
forger
 imitator 20 n.
 defrauder 789 n.
forgery
 imitation 20 n.
 sham 542 n.
forget
 forget 506 vb.
forgetful
 forgetful 506 adj.
forgivable
 trivial 639 adj.
 vindicable 927 adj.
forgive
 disregard 458 vb.
forgiveness
 lenity 736 n.
 forgiveness 909 n.
forgo
 relinquish 621 vb.
 not retain 779 vb.
fork
 cross 222 vb.
 diverge 294 vb.

fork out
pay 804 vb.

forlorn
friendless 883 adj.

forlorn hope
armed force 722 n.

form
constitute 56 vb.
conformity 83 n.
seat 218 n.
form 243 n.
appearance 445 n.
practice 610 n.
fashion 848 n.
formality 875 n.

form, bad
ill-breeding 847 n.

formal
conditionate 7 adj.

formal dress
formal dress 228 n.

formalism
ritualism 988 n.

formality
formality 875 n.

format
form 243 n.

formation
group 74 n.
production 164 n.
formation 722 n.

formative
formative 243 adj.

forme
letterpress 587 n.

former
prior 119 adj.
former 125 adj.
resigning 753 adj.

formication
formication 378 n.
skin disease 651 n.

formidable
difficult 700 adj.
frightening 854 adj.

formless
amorphous 244 adj.

formula
rule 81 n.
phrase 563 n.
precept 693 n.

formulary
precept 693 n.
rite 988 n.

formulate
arrange 62 vb.
affirm 532 vb.

fornication
unchastity 951 n.

fornicator
libertine 952 n.

forsake
relinquish 621 vb.

forswear
be false 541 vb.
recant 603 vb.

fort
refuge 662 n.
fort 713 n.

forte
skill 694 n.

forthcoming
impending 155 adj.
veracious 540 adj.

forthright
undisguised 522 adj.

fortification
fortification 713 n.

fortified
defended 713 adj.

fortify
strengthen 162 vb.
safeguard 660 vb.

fortissimo
loud 400 adj.
loudness 400 n.

fortnight
period 110 n.

fortress
fort 713 n.

fortuitous
casual 159 adj.
unintentional 618 adj.

fortunate
prosperous 730 adj.
happy 824 adj.

fortune
eventuality 154 n.
chance 159 n.
fate 596 n.
wealth 800 n.

fortunes
biography 590 n.

fortune-teller
diviner 511 n.

fortune-telling
divination 511 n.

forum
focus 76 n.
arena 724 n.
mart 796 n.

forward
early 135 adj.

send 272 vb.
intelligent 498 adj.

forward-looking
progressive 285 adj.

fosse
fence 235 n.
defences 713 n.

fossil
antiquity 125 n.
old man 133 n.
corpse 363 n.

fossilization
hardening 326 n.

foster
look after 457 vb.
safeguard 660 vb.
pet 889 vb.

fosterling
child 132 n.

foul
collide 279 vb.
windy 352 adj.
fetid 397 adj.
bad 645 adj.
unclean 649 adj.
insalubrious 653 adj.
foul play 930 n.
heinous 934 adj.

foul play
injustice 914 n.
foul play 930 n.

found
stabilize 153 vb.
cause 156 vb.
liquefy 337 vb.
heat 381 vb.

foundation
beginning 68 n.
source 156 n.
basis 218 n.

foundational
fundamental 156 adj.

founder
producer 167 n.
founder 313 vb.
perish 361 vb.
patron 707 n.

foundling
derelict 779 n.

foundry
workshop 687 n.

fount
origin 68 n.
source 156 n.

stream 350 n.
print-type 587 n.
store 632 n.

fountain
source 156 n.
outflow 298 n.

four corners
whole 52 n.

four-in-hand
carriage 274 n.

four-letter word
plainness 573 n.

four-sided
symmetrical 245 adj.

foursome
quaternity 96 n.
dance 837 n.

fourth dimension
time 108 n.

fourth estate
the press 528 n.

fowl
bird 365 n.
hunt 619 vb.

fowler
hunter 619 n.

fox
vermin 365 n.
trickster 545 n.
slyboots 698 n.

fox-trot
dance 837 n., vb.

foxy
cunning 698 adj.
dishonest 930 adj.

foyer
lobby 194 n.
theatre 594 n.

fracas
turmoil 61 n.

fraction
part 53 n.
numerical element 85 n.
fraction 102 n.

fractionize
sunder 46 vb.

fractious
irascible 892 adj.

fracture
break 46 vb.
gap 201 n.
be brittle 330 vb.

fragile
insubstantial 4 adj.
brittle 330 adj.

511

fragment
small thing 33 n.
part, piece 53 n.
fraction 102 n.
pulverize 332 vb.
fragmentary
fragmentary 53 adj.
fragrance
sweetness 392 n.
fragrance 396 n.
frail
ephemeral 114 adj.
brittle 330 adj.
wicked, frail 934
  adj.
unchaste 951 adj.
frailty
vice 934 n.
(see fragile)
frame
mould 23 n.
receptacle 194 n.
frame 218 n.
circumscribe
  232 vb.
outline 233 n., vb.
efform 243 vb.
structure 331 n.
fake 541 vb.
frame of mind
affections 817 n.
frame of reference
referral 9 n.
frame-up
trap 542 n.
false charge 928 n.
framework
frame 218 n.
framing
circumjacent
  230 adj.
franchise
vote 605 n.
frank
undisguised 522 adj.
artless 699 adj.
trustworthy
  929 adj.
frankincense
resin 357 n.
scent 396 n.
frankness
veracity 540 n.
plainness 573 n.
frantic
frenzied 503 adj.
excitable 822 adj.

fraternal
akin 11 adj.
corporate 708 adj.
friendly 880 adj.
fraternity
family 11 n.
community 708 n.
fraternize
concord 710 vb.
be friendly 880 vb.
fratricide
homicide 362 n.
fraud
trickery 542 n.
slyboots 698 n.
peculation 788 n.
fraudulence
deception 542 n.
fraudulent
false 541 adj.
perfidious 930 adj.
fray
rend 46 vb.
rub 333 vb.
fight 716 n.
freak
nonconformist 84 n.
whim 604 n.
freakish
unexpected 508 adj.
(see freak)
freckle
variegate 437 vb.
free
disjoin 46 vb.
escaped 667 adj.
deliver 668 vb.
disencumber
  701 vb.
free 744 adj.
uncharged 812 adj.
free-and-easy
impertinent 878 adj.
freeboard
interval 201 n.
freebooter
robber 789 n.
free-born
free 744 adj.
freedom
opportunity 137 n.
freedom 744 n.
freedom of action
independence 744 n.
free-for-all
turmoil 61 n.
fight 716 n.

free hand
scope 744 n.
freehold
unconditional
  744 adj.
lands 777 n.
free-holder
possessor 776 n.
freelance
worker 686 n.
militarist 722 n.
Freemasonry
society 708 n.
free play
scope 744 n.
free-thinker
irreligionist 971 n.
free thought
antichristianity
  974 n.
free verse
verse form 593 n.
freewheel
go smoothly
  258 vb.
free will
will 595 n.
freeze
halt 145 vb.
render insensible
  375 vb.
refrigerate 382 vb.
preserve 666 vb.
freight
fill 54 vb.
contents 193 n.
load 193 vb.
merchandise 795 n.
freightage
transport 272 n.
freighter
carrier 273 n.
merchant ship
  275 n.
frenzied
angry 891 adj.
frenzy
turmoil 61 n.
commotion 318 n.
frenzy 503 n.
fantasy 513 n.
unmeaningness
  515 n.
excitable state
  822 n.
frequency
degree 27 n.

frequency 139 n.
periodicity 141 n.
oscillation 317 n.
frequent
usual 610 adj.
be wont 610 vb.
frequenter
habitué 610 n.
fresco
picture 553 n.
fresh
new 126 adj.
cold 380 adj.
clean 648 adj.
salubrious 652 adj.
preserved 666 adj.
fresh-air fiend
sanitarian 652 n.
fresh blood
aftercomer 67 n.
freshen
aerify 340 vb.
blow 352 vb.
purify 648 vb.
sanitate 652 vb.
refresh 685 vb.
freshet
stream 350 n.
freshman
college student 538
  n.
freshness
non-imitation 21 n.
(see fresh)
fret
rend 46 vb.
rub 333 vb.
variegate 437 vb.
worry 825 n.
decorate 844 vb.
enrage 891 vb.
fretful
irascible 892 adj.
fretting
ornamental art
  844 n.
Freudianism
psychology 447 n.
friable
brittle 330 adj.
powdery 332 adj.
friar
monk 986 n.
friary
monastery 986 n.
fribble
nonentity 639 n.

amuse oneself
837 vb.

fricative
speech sound 398 n.

friction
collision 279 n.
friction 333 n.
dissension 709 n.

frictionless
wieldy 701 adj.
cooperating 706 adj.
pleasurable 826 adj.

friend
friend 880 n.
kind person 897 n.
sectarist 978 n.

friend at court
patron 707 n.

friendless
friendless 883 adj.

friendliness
irenics 719 n.
friendliness 880 n.
sociability 882 n.

friendly
friendly 880 adj.

friendship
friendship 880 n.
love 887 n.

frieze
textile 222 n.
trimming 844 n.

frigate
warship 722 n.

fright
eyesore 842 n.
fear 854 n.

frighten
raise the alarm
665 vb.
frighten 854 vb.

frigid
cold 380 adj.
inexcitable 823 adj.
pure 950 adj.

frigidaire
provisions 301 n.
refrigerator 384 n.

frigidity
coldness 380 n.
moral insensibility
820 n.

frill
adjunct 40 n.
trimming 844 n.

frills
ornament 574 n.

fringe
edging 234 n.
hair-dressing 843
n.
trimming 844 n.

frippery
bauble 639 n.
finery 844 n.

frisk
search 459 vb.
be cheerful 833 vb.

frisky
leaping 312 adj.
gay 833 adj.

fritter away
waste 634 vb.
be prodigal
815 vb.

frivolity
folly 499 n.
merriment 833 n.

frivolous
light-minded
456 adj.
capricious 604 adj.
(*see* frivolity)

frizz
crinkle 251 vb.

frizzle
fold 261 vb.
be hot 379 vb.

frizzy
undulatory 251 adj.

frock
dress 228 n.

frog
fastening 47 n.
frog 365 n.

frogman
diver 313 n.

frogmarch
impel 279 vb.

frolic
enjoyment 824 n.
amuse oneself
837 vb.

frondescence
vegetability 366 n.
foliage 366 n.

front
exteriority 223 n.
edge 234 n.
front 237 n.
battle 718 n.
battleground 724 n.

frontage
face 237 n.

frontier
extremity 69 n.
farness 199 n.
limit 236 n.

frontiersman
dweller 191 n.

frontispiece
front, face 237 n.

front-page
notable 638 n.

front-rank
supreme 34 adj.

frost
wintriness 380 n.
whiten 427 vb.
blight 659 n.
failure 728 n.

frostbite
coldness 380 n.

frosty
cold 380 adj.

froth
moisture 341 n.
bubble 355 n., vb.
be excitable
822 vb.

frothy
light 323 adj.
bubbly 355 adj.
ornate 574 adj.

frou-frou
sibilation 406 n.

frounce
fold 261 n., vb.

frown
anger 891 n.
be sullen 893 vb.

frowning
adverse 731 adj.

frown on
prohibit 757 vb.
(*see* disapprove)

frowsty
fetid 397 adj.

frowzy
fetid 397 adj.

frozen
still 266 adj.
hard 326 adj.
insensible 375
adj.
a-cold 380 adj.
preserved 666 adj.

frugality
economy 814 n.

frugivorous
feeding 301 adj.

fruit
product 164 n.
fruit 301 n.

fruitful
prolific 171 adj.
successful 727 adj.

fruit-growing
agriculture 370 n.

fruition
use 673 n.
enjoyment 824 n.

fruitless
unproductive
172 adj.
profitless 641 adj.

fruity
fetid 397 adj.

frustration
psychopathy 503
n.
disappointment
509 n.
hindrance 702 n.
failure 728 n.

fry
youngling 132 n.
cook 301 vb.

frying-pan
heater 383 n.

fuddle
inebriate 949 vb.

fuddled
foolish 499 adj.
tipsy 949 adj.

fudge
sweet 392 n.

fuel
propellant 287 n.
oil 357 n.
kindle 381 vb.
fuel 385 n.
provide 633 vb.

fugitive
transient 114 adj.
wanderer 268 n.
escaper 667 n.

fugleman
living model 23 n.
leader 690 n.

fugue
musical piece
412 n.
oblivion 506 n.

fulcrum
pivot 218 n.

fulfil
observe 768 vb.

fulfilment
 completion 725 n.
 enjoyment 824 n.
full
 whole 52 adj.
 plenitude 54 n.
 multitudinous
   104 adj.
 fleshy 195 adj.
 drunk 949 adj.
full blast
 loudness 400 n.
full-blooded
 vigorous 174 adj.
full-blown
 expanded 197 adj.
full circle
 revolution 149 n.
 circuition 314 n.
full dress
 formal dress 228
   n.
fuller
 cleaner 648 n.
full-fed
 gluttonous 947 adj.
full force, in
 strong 162 adj.
full-grown
 grown up 134 adj.
full-length
 comprehensive
   52 adj.
 long 203 adj.
full life
 enjoyment 824 n.
 sensualism 944 n.
full measure
 sufficiency 635 n.
fullness
 greatness 32 n.
 plenitude 54 n.
 plenty 635 n.
full play
 facility 701 n.
 scope 744 n.
full-size
 great 32 adj.
full speed
 speeding 277 n.
full stop
 stop 145 n.
 punctuation 547 n.
fulminate
 be violent 176 vb.
 curse 899 vb.
 threaten 900 vb.

fulsome
 fetid 397 adj.
 unpleasant 827 adj.
 flattering 925 adj.
fumble
 be tentative 461 vb.
 be clumsy 695 vb.
fumbler
 bungler 697 n.
fume
 emit 300 vb.
 gas 336 n.
 vaporize 338 vb.
 be hot 379 vb.
 odour 394 n.
 excitable state
   822 n.
 be angry 891 vb.
fumigation
 fragrance 396 n.
 cleaning 648 n.
fun
 enjoyment 824 n.
 pleasurableness
   826 n.
 merriment 833 n.
 amusement 837 n.
function
 relativeness 9 n.
 number 85 n.
 agency 173 n.
 function 622 vb.
 celebration 876 n.
functional
 correlative 12 adj.
 instrumental
   628 adj.
 useful 640 adj.
functionary
 official 690 n.
 consignee 754 n.
functionless
 useless 641 adj.
fund
 store 632 n., vb.
 funds 797 n.
fundament
 base 214 n.
 rear, buttocks
   238 n.
fundamental
 intrinsic 5 adj.
 fundamental
   156 adj.
 undermost 214 adj.
 supporting 218 adj.
 important 638 adj.

fundamentalism
 scripture 975 n.
fundamentals
 reality 1 n.
 chief thing 638 n.
funeral
 funeral 364 n.
funeral oration
 valediction 296 n.
 obsequies 364 n.
 lament 836 n.
funereal
 funereal 364 adj.
 cheerless 834 adj.
fun-fair
 pleasure-ground
   837 n.
fungus
 plant 366 n.
 dirt 649 n.
funk
 fear 854 n.
 coward 856 n.
funk-hole
 hiding-place 527 n.
 refuge 662 n.
funnel
 tunnel 263 n.
 chimney 263 n.
 conduit 351 n.
funny
 unusual 84 adj.
 funny 849 adj.
fur
 skin 226 n.
 hair 259 n.
 warm clothes
   381 n.
 dirt 649 n.
furbish
 (see **refurbish**)
furious
 destructive 165 adj.
 frenzied 503 adj.
 angry 891 adj.
furl
 fold 261 vb.
furlough
 leisure 681 n.
furnace
 fire 379 n.
 furnace 383 n.
 workshop 687 n.
furnish
 provide 633 vb.
 make ready 669
   vb.

furnishing(s)
 contents 193 n.
 equipment 630 n.
furniture
 equipment 630 n.
 property 776 n.
furore
 commotion 318 n.
furrow
 furrow 262 n.
furry
 hairy 259 adj.
further
 promote 285 vb.
 aid 703 vb.
furtherance
 progression 285 n.
furthermost
 distant 199 adj.
furtive
 stealthy 525 adj.
fury
 violence, violent
   creature 176 n.
 anger 891 n.
 shrew 892 n.
 demon 970 n.
furze
 plant 366 n.
fuse
 heat 381 vb.
 safeguard 662 n.
 ammunition 723 n.
 (see **fusion**)
fuselage
 frame 218 n.
fusillade
 bombardment 712
   n.
fusion
 mixture 43 n.
 combination 50 n.
 liquefaction 337 n.
 association 706 n.
fuss
 excitation 821 n.
fussiness
 fastidiousness
   862 n.
fusspot
 meddler 678 n.
 perfectionist 861 n.
fussy
 active 678 adj.
 fastidious 862 adj.
fust
 deteriorate 655 vb.

fustian
textile 222 n.
empty talk 515 n.
fusty
antiquated 127 adj.
fetid 397 adj.
dirty 649 adj.
futility
ineffectuality 161 n.
absurdity 497 n.
inutility 641 n.
future
unborn 2 adj.
subsequent 120 adj.
futurity 124 n.
impending 155 adj.
future state
future state 124 n.
futuristic
modern 126 adj.
futurity
futurity 124 n.
fuzzy
amorphous 244 adj.
hairy 259 adj.
ill-seen 444 adj.

G

gab
loquacity 581 n.
gabble
stammer 580 vb.
chatter 581 vb.
gable
roof 226 n.
gable-end
extremity 69 n.
gad
wander 267 vb.
gadfly
fly 365 n.
excitant 821 n.
gadget
object 319 n.
contrivance 623 n.
tool 630 n.
gaff
spear 723 n.
gaffer
old man 133 n.
countryman 869 n.
gag
stopper 264 n.
make mute 578 vb.
fetter 748 n.
witticism 839 n.

gaga
foolish 499 adj.
gage
defiance 711 n.
gaggle
group 74 n.
gaiety
merriment 833 n.
gain
increment 36 n.
progression 284 n.
gain 771 n., vb.
gainful
profitable 640 adj.
gainful 771 adj.
gaining time
delay 136 n.
gain on
outstrip 277 vb.
gainsay
negate 533 vb.
gait
gait 265 n.
gaiters
legwear 228 n.
canonicals 989 n.
gala
festivity 837 n.
pageant 875 n.
galactic
cosmic 321 adj.
galaxy
group 74 n.
star 321 n.
gale
gale 352 n.
gale force
storm 176 n.
gall
swelling 253 n.
rub 333 vb.
give pain 377 vb.
sourness 393 n.
malevolence 898 n.
gallant
courageous 855 adj.
showy 875 adj.
courteous 884 adj.
lover 887 n.
gallantry
(*see* gallant)
galleon
ship 275 n.
merchant ship 275 n.
warship 722 n.

gallery
tunnel 263 n.
doorway 263 n.
theatre 594 n.
galley
chamber 194 n.
galley, rowboat 275 n.
gallivant
wander 267 vb.
court 889 vb.
gallon
metrology 465 n.
galloon
trimming 844 n.
gallop
gait 265 n.
ride 267 vb.
move fast 277 vb.
gallows
means of execution 964 n.
gallowsbird
offender 904 n.
Gallup poll
inquiry 459 n.
galore
great quantity 32 n.
galosh
footwear 228 n.
galvanism
excitation 821 n.
gambit
tactics 688 n.
gamble
uncertainty 474 n.
gamble 618 vb.
speculate 791 vb.
gambler
gambler 618 n.
gambling game
gambling game 837 n.
gambol
leap 312 n., vb.
amuse oneself 837 vb.
game
meat 301 n.
animal 365 n.
gamble 618 vb.
chase 619 n.
stratagem 698 n.
contest 716 n.
amusement 837 n.
laughing-stock 851 n.

courageous 855 adj.
gamekeeper
animal husbandry 369 n.
gamesman
player 837 n.
gamesmanship
tactics 688 n.
cunning 698 n.
gamesome
gay 833 adj.
amused 837 adj.
gammer
old woman 133 n.
gammon
meat 301 n.
silly talk 515 n.
deceive 542 vb.
gamut
series 71 n.
musical note 410 n.
gamy
pungent 388 adj.
fetid 397 adj.
gander
waterfowl 365 n.
gang
band 74 n.
personnel 686 n.
party 708 n.
gangplank
bridge 624 n.
gangrene
decay 51 n.
ulcer 651 n.
gangster
murderer 362 n.
offender 904 n.
gang up
congregate 74 vb.
cooperate 706 vb.
gangway
access, bridge 624 n.
gantry
stand 218 n.
gaol
gaol 748 n.
gaol-bird
prisoner 750 n.
offender 904 n.
gaoler
gaoler 749 n.
gap
disjunction 46 n.
discontinuity 72 n.
gap 201 n.
opening 263 n.

GAP

gape
space 201 vb.
open 263 vb.
gaze 438 vb.

gaper
spectator 441 n.
ninny 501 n.

gappy
spaced 201 adj.

garage
stable 192 n.
safeguard 660 vb.

garb
dress 228 vb.

garbage
dirt 649 n.

garble
misinterpret 521 vb.

garden
garden 370 n.

gardener
gardener 370 n.

gardening
agriculture 370 n.
ornamental art 844 n.

garden-party
amusement 837 n.

gardens
pleasure-ground 837 n.

gargle
moisten 341 vb.
cleanser 648 n.

gargoyle
conduit 351 n.
eyesore 842 n.

garish
luminous 417 adj.
vulgar 847 adj.
showy 875 adj.

garland
loop 250 n.
honours 866 n.

garlic
condiment 389 n.

garment
dress 228 n.

garner
store 632 vb.

garnish
adjunct 40 n.
cook 301 vb.
ornamentation 844 n.

garret
attic 194 n.

GAS

garrison
resident 191 n.
defender 713 n.
armed force 722 n.

garrotte, garotte
execute 963 vb.
means of execution 964 n.

garrulous
loquacious 581 adj.

garter
fastening 47 n.
underwear 228 n.
badge of rank 743 n.

gas
gas 336 n.
fuel 385 n.
empty talk 515 n.
be loquacious 581 vb.
execute 963 vb.

gas-bag
bladder 194 n.
chatterer 581 n.

gas-chamber
slaughter-house 362 n.

gaseous
gaseous 336 adj.

gash
cut 46 vb.
wound 655 n.

gasify
gasify 336 vb.

gasket
lining 227 n.

gaskins
legwear 228 n.

gas-mask
armour 713 n.

gasoline
fuel 385 n.

gasometer
gas 336 n.
storage 632 n.

gasp
breathe 352 vb.
rasp 407 vb.
be fatigued 684 vb.

gas-ring
furnace 383 n.

gassy
gaseous 336 adj.

gastronomy
gastronomy 301 n.
gluttony 947 n.

GAW

gasworks
gas 336 n.

gate
doorway 263 n.
onlookers 441 n.

gate-crash
intrude 297 vb.
be sociable 882 vb.

gate-crasher
intruder 59 n.

gate-keeper
janitor 264 n.

gate-money
receipt 807 n.

gather
congregate 74 vb.
expand 197 vb.
fold 261 vb.
store 632 vb.
acquire 771 vb.

gathering
assembly 74 n.
ulcer 651 n.
(see **gather**)

gauche
sinistral 242 adj.
clumsy 695 adj.
ill-bred 847 adj.

gaucherie
ignorance 491 n.

gaucho
herdsman 369 n.

gaudy
florid 425 adj.
ornamented 844 adj.
vulgar 847 adj.
showy 875 adj.

gauge
breadth 205 n.
gauge 465 n., vb.

gaunt
lean 206 adj.

gauntlet
glove 228 n.
defiance 711 n.
armour 713 n.

gauze
transparency 422 n.

gauzy
insubstantial 4 adj.

gawk
gaze 438 vb.
ninny 501 n.

gawky
foolish 499 adj.
clumsy 695 adj.

GEN

gay
gay 833 adj.
amusing 837 adj.
showy 875 adj.

gaze
look, gaze 438 vb.
watch 441 vb.
be curious 453 vb.
be attentive 455 vb.

gazebo
arbour 194 n.

gazelle
deer 365 n.

gazette
journal 528 n.
proclaim 528 vb.
record 548 n.

gazetteer
guide-book 524 n.
reference book 589 n.

gear
clothing 228 n.
equipment 630 n.

gear to
relate 9 vb.
join 45 vb.

geisha girl
entertainer 594 n.

gelatination
condensation 324 n.

geld
unman 161 vb.
sterilize 172 vb.

gelding
horse 273 n.

gelignite
explosive 723 n.

gem
exceller 644 n.
gem 844 n.

gen
information 524 n.

gender
classification 77 n.
grammar 564 n.

gene
heredity 5 n.

genealogy
genealogy 169 n.

general
usual 610 adj.
army officer 741 n.
commonalty 869 n.
(see **generality**)

generalissimo
army officer 741 n.

generality
whole 52 n.
generality 79 n.
indiscrimination
464 n.
inexactness 495 n.
generalization
reasoning 475 n.
generalize
generalize 79 vb.
(*see* generality)
general practitioner
doctor 658 n.
generalship
tactics 688 n.
skill 694 n.
generate
vitalize 360 vb.
generation
race 11 n.
causation 156 n.
propagation 164 n.
generator
electricity 160 n.
producer 167 n.
generic
generic 77 adj.
general 79 adj.
generosity
(*see* generous)
generous
plenteous 635 adj.
giving 781 adj.
liberal 813 adj.
noble 868 adj.
benevolent 897 adj.
disinterested
931 adj.
rewarding 962 adj.
genesis
origin 68 n.
source 156 n.
propagation 164 n.
genetic
genetic 5 adj.
genetics
biology 358 n.
genial
warm 379 adj.
pleasurable 826 adj.
cheerful 833 adj.
genie
demon 970 n.
genital
productive 164 adj.
genitalia
genitalia 164 n.

genius
spirit 447 n.
intellectual 492 n.
intelligence 498 n.
sage 500 n.
exceller 644 n.
fairy 970 n.
genocide
slaughter 362 n.
genotype
breed 77 n.
genre
sort 77 n.
picture 553 n.
genteel
genteel 868 adj.
genteelism
prudery 950 n.
gentile
ethnic 11 adj.
heathen 974 n.
profane 980 adj.
gentility
race 11 n.
nobility 868 n.
gentle
moderate 177 adj.
soft 327 adj.
lenient 736 adj.
noble 868 adj.
gentlefolk
aristocracy 868 n.
gentleman
gentleman 929 n.
good man 937 n.
gentlemanlike
well-bred 848 adj.
gentlemanly
reputable 866 adj.
**gentleman's
agreement**
promise 764 n.
compact 765 n.
**gentleman's
gentleman**
domestic 742 n.
gentleness
pity 905 n.
(*see* gentle)
gentry
aristocracy 868 n.
genuflect
stoop 311 vb.
perform ritual
988 vb.
genuflexion
respects 920 n.

genuine
(*see* genuineness)
genuine article
no imitation 21 n.
genuineness
identity 13 n.
no imitation 21 n.
authenticity 494
n.
genus
group 74 n.
breed 77 n.
geocentric
central 225 adj.
geodesy
geography 321 n.
uranometry 321 n.
geographer
uranometry 321 n.
geography
situation 186 n.
geography 321 n.
geologist
uranometry 321 n.
geology
geography 321 n.
uranometry 321 n.
mineralogy 359 n.
geometer
geometry 465 n.
surveyor 465 n.
**geometrical
progression**
ratio 85 n.
geometry
mathematics 86 n.
geometry 465 n.
George Cross
decoration 729 n.
geriatrics
gerontology 131 n.
medical art 658 n.
germ
source 156 n.
animalcule 196 n.
infection 651 n.
poison 659 n.
germane
apt 24 adj.
germ-carrier
infection 651 n.
germicide
prophylactic 658 n.
poison 659 n.
germinal
causal 156 adj.
generative 171 adj.

germinate
be fruitful 171 vb.
germ-laden
infectious 653 adj.
toxic 653 adj.
gerontology
gerontology 131 n.
gerrymander
be dishonest
930 vb.
gestation
maturation 669 n.
gesticulation
(*see* gesture)
gesticulatory
indicating 547 adj.
gesture
motion 265 n.
gesture 547 n.
gesticulate 547 vb.
get
generate 164 vb.
understand 516 vb.
acquire 771 vb.
receive 782 vb.
get across
communicate
524 vb.
make enemies
881 vb.
get-at-able
accessible 289 adj.
get-away
escape 667 n.
get back
retrieve 656 vb.
get even with
retaliate 714 vb.
get in touch
communicate
524 vb.
get off
escape 667 vb.
court 889 vb.
get on
accord 24 vb.
progress 285 vb.
get rid of
destroy 165 vb.
kill 362 vb.
not retain 779 vb.
get-together
social gathering
882 n.
get up
study 636 vb.
fake 541 vb.

gewgaw
bauble 639 n.
finery 844 n.
geyser
stream 350 n.
heat 379 n.
ghastly
colourless 426 adj.
distressing 827 adj.
frightening 854 adj.
ghetto
seclusion 883 n.
ghost
insubstantial thing 4 n.
immateriality 320 n.
visual fallacy 440 n.
author 589 n.
ghost 970 n.
ghostly
insubstantial 4 adj.
immaterial 320 adj.
spooky 970 adj.
ghoul
monster 938 n.
demon 970 n.
ghoulish
inquisitive 453 adj.
cruel 898 adj.
giant
giant 195 n.
gibber
goblinize 970 vb.
gibberish
unmeaningness 515 n.
slang 560 n.
gibbet
hanger 217 n.
dispraise 924 vb.
means of execution 964 n.
gibbosity
rotundity 252 n.
convexity 253 n.
gibe (*see* jibe)
giblets
meat 301 n.
giddy
changeful 152 adj.
light-minded 456 adj.
crazed 503 adj.
capricious 604 adj.
rash 857 adj.

gift
aptitude 694 n.
acquisition 771 n.
gift 781 n.
no charge 812 n.
(*see* give)
gifted
gifted 694 adj.
gift of the gab
eloquence 579 n.
loquacity 581 n.
gig
carriage 274 n.
boat 275 n.
gigantic
huge 195 adj.
tall 209 adj.
gigantism
hugeness 195 n.
giggle
laughter 835 n.
gigolo
libertine 952 n.
gild
coat 226 vb.
gild 433 vb.
decorate 844 vb.
gill
laterality 239 n.
metrology 465 n.
gillie
animal husbandry 369 n.
gilt
ornamentation 844 n.
gilt-edged
valuable 644 adj.
gimcrack
brittle 330 adj.
gimlet
perforator 263 n.
gimmick
contrivance 623 n.
gin
liquor 301 n.
trap 542 n.
ginger
vigorousness 714 n.
condiment 389 n.
excitant 821 n.
gingerly
careful 457 adj.
gipsy (*see* gypsy)
gird
tie 45 vb.

girder
beam 218 n.
girdle
tie 45 vb.
girdle 47 n.
compressor 198 n.
underwear 228 n.
surround 230 n.
girl
youngster 132 n.
woman 373 n.
girlhood
youth 130 n.
girth
size 195 n.
belt 228 n.
gist
essential part 5 n.
chief part 52 n.
meaning 514 n.
chief thing 638 n.
give
elasticity 328 n.
give 781 vb.
reward 962 vb.
(*see* gift)
give and take
fight 716 n.
compromise 770 n., vb.
give away
disclose 526 vb.
give back
restitute 787 vb.
give birth
reproduce itself 164 vb.
give grounds
justify 927 vb.
give in
submit 721 vb.
given
existing 1 adj.
supposed 512 adj.
givenness
existence 1 n.
given to
habituated 610 adj.
give off
emit 300 vb.
give oneself airs
be vain 873 vb.
give one the slip
elude 667 vb.
give points to
equalize 28 vb.
be unequal 29 vb.

giver
giver 781 n.
give rise to
conduce 156 vb.
give up
cease 145 vb.
submit 721 vb.
not retain 779 vb.
gizzard
maw 194 n.
glacé
cooled 382 adj.
glacial
cold 380 adj.
glaciation
condensation 324 n.
refrigeration 382 n.
glacier
ice 380 n.
glacis
acclivity 220 n.
fortification 713 n.
gladden
please 826 vb.
cheer 833 vb.
glade
valley 255 n.
open space 263 n.
glad eye
wooing 889 n.
gladiator
combatant 722 n.
gladness
joy 824 n.
glamorize
beautify 841 vb.
glamorous
personable 841 adj.
glamour
beauty 841 n.
prestige 866 n.
spell 983 n.
glance
deflect 282 vb.
shine 417 vb.
look 438 n.
gesture 547 n.
glancing
lateral 239 adj.
gland
insides 224 n.
glare
light 417 n.
gaze 438 vb.
anger 891 n.
glass
cup 194 n.

smoothness 258 n.
potion 301 n.
brittleness 330 n.
transparency 422 n.
mirror 442 n.
glasses
eyeglass 442 n.
glassy
brittle 330 adj.
undimmed 417 adj.
transparent 422 adj.
glaucoma
dim sight 440 n.
glaze
facing 226 n.
coat 226 vb.
viscidity 354 n.
gleam
flash 417 n.
incentive 612 n.
glean
cultivate 370 vb.
abstract 592 vb.
take 786 vb.
gleaner
aftercomer 67 n.
husbandman 370 n.
gleanings
anthology 592 n.
earnings 771 n.
glebe
benefice 985 n.
glee
vocal music 412 n.
merriment 833 n.
gleeful
jubilant 833 adj.
gleeman
vocalist 413 n.
glen
valley 255 n.
glengarry
headgear 228 n.
glib
loquacious 581 adj.
glide
go smoothly 258 vb.
move 265 vb.
fly 271 vb.
glider
aeronaut 271 n.
aircraft 276 n.
glimmer
flash 417 n.
half-light 419 n.
be dim 419 vb.

glimpse
look 438 n.
see 438 vb.
knowledge 490 n.
glint
flash 417 n.
glissade
descent 309 n.
glisten, glister
shine 417 vb.
glitter
flash 417 n.
shine 417 vb.
ostentation 875 n.
glittering
ornamented 844 adj.
gloaming
half-light 419 n.
gloat
gaze 438 vb.
rejoice 835 vb.
be malevolent 898 vb.
gloating
revengeful 910 adj.
global
inclusive 78 adj.
universal 79 adj.
ubiquitous 189 adj.
globe
sphere 252 n.
world 321 n.
globe-trotter
traveller 268 n.
globule
sphere 252 n.
gloom
darkness 418 n.
dimness 419 n.
dejection 834 n.
glorification
praise 923 n.
act of worship 981 n.
glorify
advertise 528 vb.
praise 923 vb.
worship 981 vb.
glorious
great 32 adj.
excellent 644 adj.
noteworthy 866 adj.
(see glory)
glory
light 417 n.
trophy 729 n.

prestige, famousness 866 n.
boast 877 vb.
gloss
smoothness 258 n.
commentary 520 n.
ostentation 875 n.
glossarist
interpreter 520 n.
glossary
commentary 520 n.
dictionary 559 n.
gloss over
neglect 458 vb.
conceal 525 vb.
glossy
luminous 417 adj.
splendid 841 adj.
glove
glove 228 n.
glow
glow 417 n.
redness 431 n.
be visible 443 vb.
vigour 571 n.
glower
be angry 891 vb.
glow-worm
glow-worm 420 n.
gloze
misinterpret 521 vb.
flatter 925 vb.
glucose
sweet 392 n.
glue
adhesive 47 n.
agglutinate 48 vb.
viscidity 354 n.
glum
melancholic 834 adj.
glut
superfluity 637 n.
cheapness 812 n.
glutton
desirer 859 n.
sensualist 944 n.
glutton 947 n.
gluttonous
greedy 859 adj.
gluttony
gastronomy 301 n.
gluttony 947 n.
glycerine
lubricant 334 n.
glyptic
formative 243 adj.
glyptic 554 adj.

gnarled
distorted 246 adj.
rough 259 adj.
gnash one's teeth
regret 830 vb.
gnat
fly 365 n.
gnaw
rend 46 vb.
chew 301 vb.
gnome
maxim 496 n.
elf 970 n.
gnomic
aphoristic 496 adj.
gnosticism
deism 973 n.
go
operate 173 vb.
vigorousness 174 n.
move 265 vb.
travel, walk 267 vb.
recede 290 vb.
function 622 vb.
go a-begging
be useless 641 vb.
goad
sharp point 256 n.
impel 279 vb.
excitant 821 n.
enrage 891 vb.
go against
counteract 182 vb.
oppose 704 vb.
go-ahead
vigorous 174 adj.
enterprising 672 adj.
goal
extremity 69 n.
limit 236 n.
goal 295 n.
objective 617 n.
desired object 859 n.
go-as-you-please
free 744 adj.
goat
cattle 365 n.
goatish
lecherous 951 adj.
go back on
not observe 769 vb.
(see tergiversate)
gobbet
mouthful 301 n.

gobble
ululate 409 vb.
gluttonize 947 vb.
go-between
mediator 720 n.
matchmaker 894 n.
bawd 952 n.
goblet
cup 194 n.
goblin
elf 970 n.
go by
elapse 111 vb.
god
the Deity 965 n.
god 966 n.
god-forsaken
secluded 883 adj.
profane 980 adj.
godhead
divineness 965 n.
godless
irreligious 974 adj.
impious 980 adj.
godlike
godlike 965 adj.
godly
pious 979 adj.
go down
descend 309 vb.
founder 313 vb.
godparents
family 11 n.
godsend
benefit 615 n.
prosperity 730 n.
God's own
chosen 605 adj.
goffer
groove 262 vb.
go for
aim at 617 vb.
attack 712 vb.
go-getter
planner 623 n.
busy person 678 n.
goggle
gaze 438 vb.
goggles
eyeglass 442 n.
go in for
undertake 672 vb.
go into
inquire 459 vb.
dissert 591 vb.
go it alone
be free 744 vb.

gold
yellowness 433 n.
exceller 644 n.
money, bullion 797 n.
golden
yellow 433 adj.
valuable 644 adj.
palmy 730 adj.
Golden Age
palmy days 730 n.
happiness 824 n.
golden calf
idol 982 n.
golden rule
precept 693 n.
golden touch
prosperity 730 n.
wealth 800 n.
gold-mine
store 632 n.
wealth 800 n.
gold standard
finance 797 n.
golf
ball game 837 n.
Goliath
giant 195 n.
gondola
rowboat 275 n.
gondolier
boatman 270 n.
carrier 273 n.
gone
past 125 adj.
lost 772 adj.
gong
timekeeper 117 n.
gong 414 n.
decoration 729 n.
good
good 615 n., adj.
excellent 644 adj.
skilful 694 adj.
obedient 739 adj.
benevolent 897 adj.
virtuous 933 adj.
good as one's word
veracious 540 adj.
trustworthy 929 adj.
good behaviour
virtue 933 n.
good books
approbation 923 n.
good breeding
etiquette 848 n.

goodbye
valediction 296 n.
good cheer
food 301 n.
enjoyment 824 n.
good faith
probity 929 n.
good fault
virtues 933 n.
good fellowship
sociability 882 n.
good form
etiquette 848 n.
good for nothing
profitless 641 adj.
vicious 934 adj.
bad man 938 n.
good genius
benefactor 903 n.
good graces
approbation 923 n.
good humour
cheerfulness 833 n.
courtesy 884 n.
good living
gastronomy 301 n.
good-looking
beautiful 841 adj.
good luck
prosperity 730 n.
goodly
good 615 adj.
beautiful 841 adj.
good man
good man 937 n.
good name
repute 866 n.
goodness
(see good)
goodnight
valediction 296 n.
good odour
repute 866 n.
good offices
aid 703 n.
pacification 719 n.
mediation 720 n.
good points
goodness 644 n.
good riddance
rubbish 641 n.
hateful object 888 n.
relief 831 n.
goods
thing transferred 272 n.

property 777 n.
merchandise 795 n.
Good Samaritan
kind person 897 n.
goods and chattels
property 777 n.
good sense
intelligence 498 n.
good-tempered
inexcitable 823 adj.
amiable 884 adj.
good time, have a
rejoice 835 vb.
good turn
kind act 897 n.
goodwill, good will
willingness 597 n.
friendliness 880 n.
benevolence 897 n.
good wishes
congratulation 886 n.
goody-goody
ninny 501 n.
innocent 935 n., adj.
goof
ninny 501 n.
go on
last 113 vb.
go on 146 vb.
progress 285 vb.
goose
table-bird 365 n.
waterfowl 365 n.
ignoramus 493 n.
fool 501 n.
gooseberry, play
look after 457 vb.
gooseflesh
formication 378 n.
nervousness 854 n.
go out of one's way
deviate 282 vb.
be willing 597 vb.
go over
repeat 106 vb.
pass 305 vb.
search 459 vb.
study 536 vb.
go places
travel 267 vb.
(see sociability)
Gordian knot
ligature 47 n.
complexity 61 n.

gore
pierce 263 vb.
blood 335 n.

gorge
valley 255 n.
sate 863 vb.
gluttonize 947 vb.

gorged
full 45 adj.

gorgeous
florid 425 adj.
ornamented 844 adj.
showy 875 adj.

gorgon
rara avis 84 n.
demon 970 n.

gorilla
monkey 365 n.

gormandize
gluttonize 947 vb.

gorse
plant 366 n.

gory
sanguineous 335
adj.
bloodshot 431 adj.

go shares
participate 775 vb.

go-slow
slowness 278 n.

gospel
certainty 473 n.
authenticity 494 n.
revelation 975 n.
scriptural 975 adj.

gospeller
religious teacher
973 n.

gossamer
insubstantial thing
4 n.
weak thing 163 n.

gossip
informer 524 n.
newsmonger 529 n.
be loquacious
581 vb.

gossip-writer
chronicler 549 n.

gossipy
loquacious 581 adj.

go the round
circle 314 vb.

go through
meet with 154 vb.
pass 305 vb.
suffer 825 vb.

go to it
begin 68 vb.

go to law
litigate 959 vb.

go too far
overstep 306 vb.

go to one's head
inebriate 949 vb.

go to pieces
decompose 51 vb.

go to the wall
be destroyed
165 vb.

gouache
art equipment
553 n.

gouge (out)
make concave
255 vb.
extract 304 vb.

gourd
vessel 194 n.
vegetable 301 n.

gourmandise
gastronomy 301 n.

gourmet
eater 301 n.
gastronomy 301 n.
glutton 947 n.

gouty
diseased 651 adj.

govern
manage 689 vb.
rule 733 vb.

governance
power 160 n.
influence 178 n.
(*see* government)

governess
teacher 537 n.
keeper 749 n.

governessy
authoritarian
735 adj.

governing body
director 690 n.

government
management 689 n.
government 733 n.

governor
teacher 537 n.
director 690 n.
potentate 741 n.

governorship
magistrature 733 n.

go with
accord 24 vb.

gown
dress 228 n.

go wrong
err 495 vb.
miscarry 728 vb.

grab
take 786 vb.

grace
elegance 575 n.
permission 756 n.
gift 781 n.
beauty 841 n.
decorate 844 vb.
good taste 846 n.
mercy 905 n.

gracefulness
beauty 841 n.

graceless
clumsy 695 adj.
graceless 842 adj.

grace marks
extra 40 n.
undueness 916 n.

gracious
tasteful 846 adj.
courteous 884 adj.

gradation
degree 27 n.
order 60 n.
series 71 n.

grade
degree 27 n.
graduate 27 vb.
arrange, class 62 vb.
serial place 73 n.
sort 77 n.
acclivity 220 n.
class 538 n.

gradient
acclivity 220 n.

gradual
gradational 27 adj.
slow 278 adj.

gradualism
slowness 278 n.
reformism 654 n.

graduate
graduate 27 vb.
gauge 465 vb.
study 536 vb.
college student
538 n.

graduation
(*see* grade)

gradus
dictionary 559 n.
textbook 589 n.

graffito
script 586 n.

graft
implant 303 vb.
improbity 930 n.

grafting
venal 930 adj.

grain
temperament 5 n.
tendency 179 n.
weighment 322 n.
texture 331 n.
corn 366 n.
pigment 425 n.

graining
ornamental art
844 n.

graminivorous
feeding 301 adj.

grammar
grammar 564 n.
textbook 589 n.

grammarian
linguist 557 n.

gramophone
gramophone 414 n.

gramophone record
repetition 106 n.

granary
storage 632 n.

grand
topping 644 adj.
splendid 841 adj.
proud 871 adj.
(*see* grandeur)

grande dame
proud man 871 n.

grandee
aristocrat 868 n.

grande toilette
formal dress 228 n.

grandeur
greatness 32 n.
prestige 866 n.
ostentation 875 n.

grandfather
parent 169 n.

grandiloquence
magniloquence
574 n.
boasting 877 n.

grandiose
huge 195 adj.
ostentatious 875 adj.

grandstand
view 438 n.
onlookers 441 n.

grange
farm 370 n.

granite
hardness 326 n.

grant
subvention 703 n.
permission 756 n.
gift 781 n.

granted
supposed 512 adj.

grantee
beneficiary 776 n.
recipient 782 n.

grant-in-aid
pay 804 n.

granular
powdery 332 adj.

granulation
texture 331 n.
pulverulence 332 n.

granule
powder 332 n.

grape
fruit 301 n.

grape-shot
ammunition 723 n.

grape-vine
informant 524 n.

graph
mathematics 86 n.

graphic
expressive 516 adj.
representing 551 adj.
painted 553 adj.
descriptive 590 adj.

graphic art
art 551 n.
painting 553 n.

grapple
tie 45 vb.
wrestling 716 n.
contend 716 vb.

grappling iron
coupling 47 n.

grasp
ability 160 n.
range 183 n.
be wise 498 vb.
understand 516 vb.
possession 773 n.
retention 778 n.

grasping
oppressive 735 adj.
avaricious 816 adj.

grass
grass 366 n.
garden 370 n.

grasshopper
vermin 365 n.

grassland
grassland 348 n.

grate
rub 333 vb.
give pain 377 vb.
furnace 383 n.
rasp 407 vb.
discord 411 vb.
pulverize 332 vb.
cause dislike
861 vb.

grateful
pleasurable 826 adj.
grateful 907 adj.

gratification
pleasure 376 n.
(*see* gratify)

gratify
bribe 612 vb.
give 781 vb.
content 828 vb.
reward 962 vb.

grating
network 222 n.
(*see* grate)

gratis
uncharged 812 adj.

gratitude
gratitude 907 n.

gratuitous
voluntary 597 adj.
uncharged 812 adj.
undue 916 adj.

gratuity
extra 40 n.
gift 781 n.

gravamen
accusation 928 n.

grave
great 32 adj.
death 361 n.
tomb 364 n.
inexcitable 823 adj.
serious 834 adj.
heinous 934 adj.

grave-digger
interment 364 n.

gravel
flatten 216 vb.
powder 332 n.
puzzle 474 vb.
be difficult 700 vb.
defeat 727 vb.

graven image
idol 982 n.

graveyard
cemetery 364 n.

gravitate
tend 179 vb.
descend 309 vb.
weigh 322 vb.

gravitation
gravity 322 n.

gravity
attraction 291 n.
gravity 322 n.
seriousness 834 n.

graze
be contiguous
202 vb.
collide 279 vb.
feed 301 vb.
rub 333 vb.
touch 378 n., vb.
wound 655 vb.

grazing
grassland 348 n.
stock farm 369 n.

grease
adhesive 47 n.
lubricant 334 n.
fat 357 n.

grease-paint
stage-set 594 n.
cosmetic 843 n.

greasy
smooth 258 adj.
unctuous 357 adj.

great
great 32 adj.
supreme 34 adj.
powerful 160 adj.
strong 162 adj.
influential 178 adj.
large 195 adj.
important 638 adj.
excellent 644 adj.
worshipful 866 adj.
proud 871 adj.

greatcoat
overcoat 228 n.

great man
bigwig 638 n.

greatness (*see* great)

great thing
chief thing 638 n.

greaves
armour 713 n.

greed
rapacity 786 n.
avarice 816 n.
selfishness 932 n.

gluttony 947 n.

greediness
(*see* greed)

Greek kalends
neverness 109 n.

green
new 126 adj.
young 130 adj.
sour 393 adj.
greenness 432 n.
ignorant 491 adj.
immature 670 adj.
pleasure-ground
837 n.
innocent 935 adj.

greenback
paper money 797
n.

green belt
grassland 348 n.

greenery
plant 366 n.
greenness 432 n.

greenhorn
ninny 501 n.
beginner 538 n.
dupe 544 n.

greenhouse
arbour 194 n.
garden 370 n.

green light
assent 488 n.
permit 756 n.

greens
vegetable 301 n.

greet
speak to 583 vb.
greet 884 vb.

greetings
respects 920 n.

gregarious
sociable 882 adj.

gremlin
hinderer 702 n.
elf 970 n.

grenade
bomb 723 n.

grenadier
soldiery 722 n.

grey
dim 419 adj.
grey 429 n., adj.
neutral 625 adj.
cheerless 834 adj.

greyhound
speeder 277 n.
dog 365 n.

grey matter
  head 213 n.
grid
  electricity 160 n.
  network 222 n.
gridiron
  network 222 n.
  heater 383 n.
grief
  sorrow 825 n.
grievance
  discontent 829 n.
  wrong 914 n.
grieve
  suffer 825 vb.
  sadden 834 vb.
  lament 836 vb.
grievous
  distressing 827 adj.
grill
  network 222 n.
  window 263 n.
  cook 301 vb.
  heater 383 n.
  interrogate 459 vb.
grill-room
  café 192 n.
grim
  serious 834 adj.
  frightening 854 adj.
  ungracious 885 adj.
  sullen 893 adj.
grimace
  distortion 246 n.
grime
  dirt 649 n.
  (*see* grim)
grimy
  dirty 649 adj.
grin
  smile 835 vb.
grin and bear it
  be patient 823 vb.
  be cheerful 833
   vb.
grind
  rend 46 vb.
  sharpen 256 vb.
  pulverize 332 vb.
  rub 333 vb.
  rasp 407 vb.
  study 536 vb.
  labour 682 n.
  oppress 735 vb.
grinder
  tooth 256 n.
  pulverizer 332 n.

grindstone
  sharpener 256 n.
  pulverizer 332 n.
  labour 682 n.
grip
  tie 45 vb.
  fastening 47 n.
  cohere 48 vb.
  bag 194 n.
  handle 218 n.
  skill 694 n.
  retention 778 n.
  impress 821 vb.
gripe
  pang 377 n.
  indigestion 651 n.
gripping
  exciting 821 adj.
grisly
  unsightly 842 adj.
  frightening 854
   adj.
grist
  powder 332 n.
  materials 631 n.
  provision 633 n.
gristle
  toughness 329 n.
grit
  strength 162 n.
  texture 331 n.
  powder 332 n.
  stamina 600 n.
grizzled
  whitish 427 adj.
  grey 429 adj.
  pied 437 adj.
groan
  cry 408 vb.
  weep 836 vb.
groceries
  provisions 301 n.
grog
  liquor 301 n.
groggy
  oscillating 317 adj.
  sick 651 adj.
groom
  animal husbandry
   369 n.
  train 534 vb.
  make ready 669 vb.
groomsman
  bridesman 894 n.
groove
  cut 46 vb.
  place 185 n.

  furrow 262 n.
  habit 610 n.
grope
  be tentative 461 vb.
  be clumsy 695 vb.
grope for
  search 459 vb.
gross
  whole 52 adj.
  unintelligent
   499 adj.
  manifest 522 adj.
  bad 645 adj.
  receive 782 vb.
  vulgar 847 adj.
  heinous 934 adj.
  sensual 944 adj.
grot, grotto
  arbour 194 n.
grotesque
  distorted 246 adj.
  inelegant 576 adj.
  eyesore 842 n.
  ridiculous 849 adj.
grouch
  (*see* grouse)
ground
  situation 186 n.
  base 214 n.
  flatten 216 vb.
  basis 218 n.
  come to rest
   266 vb.
  navigate 269 vb.
  land 344 n.
  evidence 466 n.
  educate 534 vb.
  motive 612 n.
  arena 724 n.
groundless
  unreal 2 adj.
  insubstantial 4 adj.
  causeless 159 adj.
ground-plan
  map 551 n.
grounds
  leavings 41 n.
  pleasure-ground
   837 n.
groundwork
  base 214 n.
  preparation 669 n.
group
  combine 50 vb.
  subdivision 53 n.
  arrange 62 vb.
  series 71 n.

  group 74 n.
  party 708 n.
  formation 722 n.
grouse
  table bird 365 n.
  be discontented
   829 vb.
grouser
  dissentient 489 n.
grout
  coat 226 vb.
grove
  wood 366 n.
grovel
  knuckle under
   721 vb.
  be servile 879 vb.
grow
  become 1 vb.
  grow 36 vb.
  be turned to 147 vb.
  expand 197 vb.
  cultivate 370 vb.
  mature 669 vb.
grower
  producer 167 n.
growing pains
  increase 36 n.
  youth 130 n.
growl
  ululate 409 vb.
  sullenness 893 n.
grown-up
  grown-up 134 adj.
grow on one
  be wont 610 vb.
growth
  increase 36 n.
  swelling 253 n.
  agriculture 370 n.
groyne
  obstacle 702 n.
grub
  animalcule 196 n.
  food 301 n.
  extract 304 vb.
grudge
  be loth 598 vb.
  refuse 760 vb.
  be parsimonious
   816 vb.
  resentment 891 n.
gruel
  cereal 301 n.
gruesome
  unsightly 842 adj.
  frightening 854 adj.

gruff
 hoarse 407 adj.
 ungracious 885
 adj.
 irascible 892 adj.

grumble
 be discontented
 829 vb.

grumpy
 irascible 892 adj.
 sullen 893 adj.

Grundy, Mrs
 prude 950 n.

grunt
 rasp 407 vb.
 ululate 409 vb.

guano
 excrement 302 n.
 fertilizer 171 n.

guarantee
 make certain
 473 vb.
 safeguard 660 vb.
 security 767 n.

guarantor
 patron 707 n.

guard
 surveillance 457 n.
 safeguard 660 vb.
 defender 713 n.
 keeper 749 n.

guarded
 cautious 858 adj.

guardian (see **guard**)

guardian angel
 patron 707 n.
 benefactor 903 n.

gubernatorial
 governmental
 733 adj.

guernsey
 vest 228 n.

guerrilla
 soldier 722 n.
 revolter 738 n.

guess
 not know 491 vb.
 conjecture 512 n.

guesswork
 empiricism 461 n.
 uncertainty 474 n.
 conjecture 512 n.

guest
 resident 191 n.
 friend 880 n.

guffaw
 laughter 835 n.

guidance
 directorship 689 n.
 advice 691 n.

guide
 prototype 23 n.
 rule 81 n.
 itinerary 267 n.
 guide 520 n.
 show 522 vb.
 indication 547 n.
 direct 689 vb.
 adviser 691 n.

guide-book
 guide-book 524 n.

guided missile
 rocket 276 n.

guideless
 vulnerable 661 adj.

guidon
 flag 547 n.

guild
 business 622 n.
 corporation 708 n.
 merchant 794 n.

guile
 duplicity 541 n.
 deception 542 n.
 cunning 698 n.

guileless
 artless 699 adj.
 innocent 935 adj.

guillotine
 means of execution
 964 n.

guilt
 wickedness 934 n.
 guilt 936 n.

guiltless
 guiltless 935 adj.

guilty (see **guilt**)

guilty man
 offender 904 n.

guinea
 coinage 797 n.

guinea-pig
 testee 461 n.

guise
 modality 7 n.
 appearance 445 n.

guitar
 harp 414 n.

gulf
 depth 211 n.
 gulf 345 n.

gull
 befool 542 vb.
 dupe 544 vb.

gullet
 maw 194 n.
 air-pipe 353 n.

gullible
 credulous 487 adj.

gully
 valley 255 n.

gulp
 potion 301 n.
 eat 301 vb.

gum
 adhesive 47 n.
 agglutinate 48
 vb.
 resin 357 n.

gummy
 cohesive 48 adj.
 viscid 354 adj.
 retentive 778 adj.

gumption
 intelligence 498 n.

gun
 gun 723 n.

gunboat
 warship 722 n.

gun-cotton
 explosive 723 n.

gunfire
 bombardment
 712 n.

gunman
 shooter 287 n.
 murderer 362 n.
 ruffian 904 n.

gunner
 shooter 287 n.
 soldiery 722 n.

gunnery
 bombardment
 712 n.
 arm 723 n.

gunny
 textile 222 n.

gunpowder
 explosive 723 n.

gunwale
 edge 234 n.

gurge
 vortex 315 n.

gurgle
 laughter 835 n.

gurk
 eruct 300 vb.

gush
 flow out 298 vb.
 flow 350 vb.
 diffuseness 570 n.

gusher
 outflow 298 n.
 stream 350 n.
 store 632 n.

gushing
 feeling 818 adj.

gust
 breeze 352 n.

gusto
 pleasure 376 n.
 enjoyment 824 n.

gusty
 windy 352 adj.

gut
 void 300 vb.
 extract 304 vb.
 gulf 345 n.
 burn 381 vb.

gutless
 weak 163 adj.

guts
 insides 224 n.
 resolution 599 n.

gutter
 drain 351 n.
 sink 649 n.

guttering
 fitful 142 adj.

guttural
 speech sound 398 n.
 hoarse 407 adj.

guy
 tackling 47 n.
 male 372 n.
 laughing-stock
 851 n.
 satirize 851 vb.

guzzle
 eat 301 vb.
 gluttonize 947 vb.
 get drunk 949 vb.

gymkhana
 contest 716 n.

gymnasium
 academy 539 n.
 arena 724 n.

gymnast
 athlete 162 n.

gymnastics
 athletics 162 n.
 exercise 682 n.
 sport 837 n.

gynaecologist
 doctor 658 n.

gypsy
 wanderer 268 n.
 diviner 511 n.

gyration
rotation 315 n.
gyrocompass
sailing aid 269 n.
gyroscope
rotator 315 n.
gyrostatics
rotation 315 n.

H

habeas corpus
legal process 959 n.
haberdasher
clothier 228 n.
habit
temperament 5 n.
state 7 n.
rule 81 n.
tradition 127 n.
dress 228 n.
habit 610 n.
conduct 688 n.
habitat
abode 192 n.
habitation
abode 192 n.
habit-forming
influential 178 adj.
habitual 610 adj.
habitual
general 79 adj.
repeated 106 adj.
frequent 139 adj.
habitual 610 adj.
habituate
habituate 610 vb.
habitude (*see* habit)
habitué
habitué 610 n.
hack
cut 46 vb.
saddle-horse 273 n.
worker 686 n.
servant 742 n.
hackle
plumage 259 n.
hackneyed
known 490 adj.
usual 610 adj.
haemoglobin
blood 335 n.
haemophilia
haemorrhage 302 n.
haemorrhage
outflow 298 n.
haemorrhage 302 n.

haemorrhoids
swelling 253 n.
haft
handle 218 n.
haggard
lean 206 adj.
suffering 825 adj.
melancholic 834 adj.
unsightly 842 adj.
haggle
make terms 766 vb.
bargain 791 vb.
hagiography
biography 590 n.
hagiology
theology 973 n.
hag-ridden
bewitched 983 adj.
hail
ice 380 n.
allocution 583 n.
greet 884 vb.
applaud 923 vb.
hail-fellow-well-met
sociable 882 adj.
hailstone
ice 380 n.
hair
filament 208 n.
hair 259 n.
hair-cut, hair-do
hair-dressing 843 n.
hairdresser
beautician 843 n.
hairiness
roughness 259 n.
hairless
hairless 229 adj.
hairpin
fastening 47 n.
hair-raising
frightening 854 adj.
hair's breadth
narrowness 206 n.
short distance 200 n.
hair shirt
asceticism 945 n.
interval 201 n.
hair-splitting
discrimination 463 n.
sophistry 477 n.
hair-style
hair-dressing 843 n.

hairy
fibrous 208 adj.
hairy 259 adj.
halberdier
soldiery 722 n.
halcyon days
palmy days 730 n.
hale
draw 288 vb.
healthy 650 adj.
half
part 53 n.
incompleteness 55 n.
bisection 92 n.
half-and-half
equal 28 adj.
mixed 43 adj.
neutral 625 adj.
half-baked
immature 670 adj.
unskilled 695 adj.
half-blood
hybrid 43 n.
half-breed
hybrid 43 n.
half-caste
hybrid 43 n.
half-educated
smattering 491 adj.
half-hearted
unwilling 598 adj.
irresolute 601 adj.
apathetic 820 adj.
indifferent 860 adj.
half-light
evening 129 n.
half-light 419 n.
half-masted
lamenting 836 adj.
half-measures
irresolution 601 n.
insufficiency 636 n.
bungling 695 n.
half-moon
arc 250 n.
half-nelson
retention 778 n.
half-price
cheap 812 adj.
half-starved
fasting 946 adj.
half the battle
chief thing 638 n.
half-tone
light contrast 417 n.

picture 553 n.
half-truth
mental dishonesty 543 n.
half-way
middle point 30 n.
half-wit
fool 501 n.
halitosis
fetor 397 n.
hall
house 192 n.
chamber 194 n.
hallelujah
celebration 876 n.
hymn 981 n.
halliard, halyard
tackling 47 n.
hall-mark
label 547 n.
halloa, halloo
cry 408 vb.
hallow
sanctify 979 vb.
hallowed
divine 965 adj.
hallucination
error 495 n.
psychopathy 503 n.
fantasy 513 n.
deception 542 n.
halo
circumjacence 230 n.
loop 250 n.
honours 866 n.
halt
end 69 n.
stop 145 n.
crippled 163 adj.
move slowly 278 vb.
halter
halter 47 n.
fetter 748 n.
means of execution 964 n.
halve
bisect 92 vb.
apportion 783 vb.
halves
portion 783 n.
ham
buttocks 238 n.
leg 267 n.
meat 301 n.
bungler 697 n.

ham-handed
  clumsy 695 adj.
hamlet
  housing 192 n.
hammer
  hammer 279 n.
  strike at 712 vb.
hammer at
  repeat oneself
    106 vb.
hammer out
  efform 243 vb.
hammock
  pendant 217 n.
  bed 218 n.
hamper
  basket 194 n.
  hinder 702 vb.
hamster
  rodent 365 n.
hamstrung
  crippled 163 adj.
hand
  feeler, finger 378 n.
  indicator 547 n.
  tool 630 n.
  worker 686 n.
  servant 742 n.
handbill
  the press 528 n.
handbook
  guide-book 524 n.
handcuff
  tie 45 vb.
  fetter 748 n.
hand down
  transfer 272 vb.
handfast
  married 894 adj.
handful
  finite quantity 26 n.
  bunch 74 n.
  fewness 105 n.
  hard task 700 n.
handhold
  retention 778 n.
handicap
  equalize 28 vb.
  inferiority 35 n.
  retard 278 vb.
  encumbrance 702 n.
  contest 716 n.
handicraft
  business 622 n.
handiness
  instrumentality
    628 n.

  utility 640 n.
  skill 694 n.
hand in hand
  conjunct 45 n.
handiwork
  product 164 n.
  deed 676 n.
handkerchief
  cleaning cloth
    648 n.
handle
  opportunity 137 n.
  operate 173 vb.
  handle 218 n.
  touch 378 vb.
  tool 630 n.
  use 673 vb.
  manage 689 vb.
handlebar
  handle 218 n.
handmaid
  tool 630 n.
  auxiliary 707 n.
hand on
  transfer 272 vb.
hand-out
  report 524 n.
hand over
  transfer 272 vb.
hand-picked
  chosen 605 adj.
  excellent 644 adj.
handrail
  handle 218 n.
hands
  personnel 686 n.
handshake
  sociability 882 n.
  courteous act
    884 n.
handsome
  liberal 813 adj.
  beautiful 841 adj.
handspring
  overturning 221
    n.
hand to
  transfer 272 vb.
handwriting
  writing 586 n.
handy
  light 323 adj.
  useful 640 adj.
  skilful 694 adj.
  wieldy 701 adj.
handyman
  proficient 696 n.

hang
  come unstuck
    49 vb.
  hang 217 vb.
  appearance 445 n.
  execute 963 vb.
hangar
  stable 192 n.
  air travel 271 n.
hang back
  be loth 598 vb.
hanger
  hanger 217 n.
  side-arms 723 n.
hanger-on
  dependant 742 n.
  toady 879 n.
hang fire
  be inert 175 vb.
  not act 677 vb.
hangings
  covering 226 n.
hangman
  punisher 963 n.
hang on
  persevere 600 vb.
  retain 778 vb.
hang over
  impend 155 vb.
  be high 209 vb.
hangover
  sequel 67 n.
  crapulence 949 n.
hang together
  cohere 48 vb.
  concur 181 vb.
  cooperate 706 vb.
hang upon
  depend 157 vb.
hank
  bunch 74 n.
hanker
  desire 859 vb.
hanky-panky
  foul play 930 n.
hansom
  cab 274 n.
haphazard
  casual 159 adj.
  indiscriminate
    464 adj.
  designless 618 adj.
hapless
  unfortunate 731 adj.
happen
  be 1 vb.
  happen 154 vb.

  chance 159 vb.
happening
  (*see* happen)
happiness
  (*see* happy)
happy
  good 615 adj.
  concordant 710 adj.
  successful 727 adj.
  happy 824 adj.
  pleasurable 826 adj.
  cheerful 833 adj.
happy-go-lucky
  unprepared 670 adj.
happy returns
  congratulation
    886 n.
hara-kiri
  suicide 362 n.
harangue
  diffuseness 570 n.
  oration 579 n.
  dissertation 591 n.
harass
  oppress 735 vb.
  torment 827 vb.
harbinger
  precursor 66 n.
  omen 511 n.
  messenger 531 n.
harbour
  goal 295 n.
  shelter 662 n.
hard
  hard 326 adj.
  imperspicuous
    568 adj.
  laborious 682 adj.
  difficult 700 adj.
  pitiless 906 adj.
  intoxicating
    949 adj.
hard-boiled
  tough 329 adj.
  (*see* hard)
hard case
  ill fortune 731 n.
hard-drinking
  drunken 949 adj.
harden
  härden 326 vb.
  habituate 610 vb.
  make insensitive
    820 vb.
hardened arteries
  blood pressure
    651 n.

hard going
difficulty 700 n.
hard-headed
intelligent 498 adj.
hard-hearted
cruel 898 adj.
hard-hitting
disapproving
924 adj.
hardihood
courage 855 n.
insolence 878 n.
(*see* hardy)
hard labour
penalty 963 n.
hard life
adversity 731 n.
hard lines
ill fortune 731 n.
severity 735 n.
hardness
hardness 326 n.
obstinacy 602 n.
severity 735 n.
inhumanity 898 n.
pitilessness 906 n.
hard on, be
be severe 735 vb.
hardship
adversity 731 n.
hard times
adversity 731 n.
hard to please
discontented
829 adj.
hard up
poor 801 adj.
hard way, the
difficulty 700 n.
hard-working
industrious 678 adj.
hardy
stalwart 162 adj.
healthy 650 adj.
courageous 855 adj.
hare
speeder 277 n.
move fast 277 vb.
hare-brained
light-minded
456 adj.
harem
womankind 373 n.
hark
(*see* hearken)
hark back
turn back 286 vb.

harlequinade
stage play 594 n.
wit 839 n.
harlot
prostitute 952 n.
harlotry
unchastity 951 n.
social evil 951 n.
harm
harm 645 vb.
impairment 655 n.
harmful
destructive 165 adj.
inexpedient 643 adj.
harmful 645 adj.
adverse 731 adj.
harmless
weak 163 adj.
beneficial 644 adj.
humble 872 adj.
innocent 935 adj.
harmonic
musical note 410 n.
harmonious
melodious 410 adj.
(*see* harmony)
harmonize
compose music 413
vb.
(*see* harmony)
harmony
agreement 24 n.
combination 50 n.
symmetry 245 n.
melody 410 n.
consensus 488 n.
concord 710 n.
harness
tackling 47 n.
break in 369 vb.
equipment 630 n.
make ready 669 vb.
fetter 748 n.
harness, in
doing 676 adj.
harp
harp 414 n.
harper
instrumentalist
413 n.
harpoon
sharp point 256 n.
spear 723 n.
harpsichord
piano 414 n.
harpy
taker 876 n.

hell-hag 904 n.
harridan
eyesore 842 n.
harrow
farm tool 370 n.
frighten 854 vb.
harry
attack 712 vb.
torment 827 vb.
be malevolent
898 vb.
harsh
strident 407 adj.
discordant 411 adj.
oppressive 735 adj.
paining 827 adj.
pitiless 906 adj.
hart
deer 365 n.
harum-scarum
disorderly 61 adj.
rash 857 adj.
harvest
product 164 n.
abundance 171 n.
agriculture 370 n.
store 632 n., vb.
earnings 771 n.
harvester
husbandman 370 n.
has-been
archaism 127 n.
loser 728 n.
hash
confusion 61 n.
dish 301 n.
be clumsy 695 vb.
hashish
poison 659 n.
hasp
fastening 47 n.
hassock
cushion 218 n.
haste
non-preparation
670 n.
haste 680 n.
hasten
be early 135 vb.
accelerate 277
vb.
hasten 680 vb.
hasty
hasty 680 adj.
irascible 892 adj.
hat
headgear 228 n.

hatch
group 74 n.
doorway 263 n.
breed stock 369 vb.
plan 623 vb.
mature 669 vb.
hatchery
stock farm 369 n.
hatches
lock-up 748 n.
hatchet
sharp edge 256 n.
axe 723 n.
hatching
obscuration 418 n.
maturation 669 n.
hatchment
heraldry 547 n.
hatchway
doorway 263 n.
hate
hatred 888 n.
resentment 891 n.
(*see* hatred)
hateful
not nice 645 adj.
hateful 888 adj.
hatefulness
odium 888 n.
hatless
uncovered 229 adj.
hatred
phobia 854 n.
enmity 881 n.
hatred 888 n.
hatter
clothier 228 n.
hat-trick
triplication 94 n.
success 727 n.
haughty
proud, prideful
871 adj.
insolent 878 adj.
haul
traction 288 n.
haulage
transport 272 n.
traction 288 n.
haulier
carrier 273 n.
haunch
buttocks 238 n.
haunt
focus 76 n.
recur 139 vb.
district 184 n.

abode 192 n.
dwell 192 vb.
cause thought
  449 vb.
be wont 610 vb.
frighten 854 vb.
goblinize 970 vb.
haunted
nervous 854 adj.
spooky 970 adj.
haunting
remembered
  505 adj.
pleasurable 826 adj.
hauteur
pride 871 n.
have
comprise 78 vb.
befool 542 vb.
possess 773 vb.
have a hold on
influence 178 vb.
have at
strike at 712 vb.
have everything
be complete 54 vb.
haven
goal 295 n.
shelter 662 n.
have-nots
poor man 801 n.
lower classes 869 n.
have one's say
affirm 532 vb.
haver
be loquacious
  581 vb.
haversack
bag 194 n.
haves, the
rich man 800 n.
upper class 868 n.
havoc
havoc 165 n.
hawk
eruct 300 vb.
bird of prey
  365 n.
rasp 407 vb.
hunt 619 vb.
sell 793 vb.
hawker
pedlar 794 n.
hawser
cable 47 n.
hay
provender 301 n.

grass 366 n.
haymaker
knock 279 n.
hayseed
ingenue 699 n.
countryman 869 n.
haystack
store 632 n.
haywire
orderless 61 adj.
hazard
chance 159 n.
gambling 618 n.
danger 661 n.
obstacle 702 n.
hazardous
speculative
  618 adj.
dangerous 661 adj.
haze
cloud 355 n.
uncertainty 474 n.
hazel
brown 430 adj.
hazy
cloudy 355 adj.
ill-seen 444 adj.
uncertain 474 adj.
head
extremity 69 n.
classification 77 n.
energy 160 n.
vertex, head 213 n.
face 237 n.
be in front 237 vb.
outstrip 277 vb.
precede 283 vb.
topic 452 n.
intelligence 498 n.
director 690 n.
master 741 n.
headache
pang 377 n.
worry 825 n.
head-count
numeration 86 n.
headdress
headgear 228 n.
header
plunge 313 n.
head for
navigate 269 vb.
headgear
headgear 228 n.
heading
classification 77 n.
label 547 n.

headlamp, headlight
radiation 417 n.
lamp 420 n.
headland
projection 254 n.
headline
advertisement
  528 n.
make important
  638 vb.
excitant 821 n.
(see **heading***)*
headlong
violently 176 vb.
hasty 680 adj.
rash 857 adj.
headman
director 690 n.
headmaster
teacher 537 n.
head off
dissuade 613 vb.
head-on
fore 237 adj.
head over heels
inverted 221 adj.
headphone
telecommunication
  531 n.
headpiece
intelligence 498 n.
(see **head***)*
headquarters
focus 76 n.
headstone
supporter 218 n.
obsequies 364 n.
headstrong
wilful 602 adj.
rash 857 adj.
head-up
vertical 215 adj.
head-waters
source 156 n.
headway
progression 285 n.
head-work
thought 449 n.
heady
exciting 821 adj.
intoxicating
  949 adj.
heal
cure 656 vb.
remedy 658 vb.
healer
mender 656 n.

doctor 658 n.
health
vitality 162 n.
health 650 n.
salubrity 652 n.
celebration 876 n.
healthy
(see **health***)*
heap
accumulation 74
  n.
multitude 104 n.
monticle 209 n.
store 632 n., vb.
hear
hear 415 vb.
learn 536 vb.
try a case 959 vb.
heard
sounding 398 adj.
loud 400 adj.
hearer
listener 415 n.
hearing
hearing 415 n.
listening 415 n.
legal trial 959 n.
hearing aid
hearing aid 415
  n.
hearken
hear 415 vb.
obey 739 vb.
hearsay
evidence 466 n.
rumour 529 n.
hearse
funeral 364 n.
heart
essence 1 n.
essential part 5 n.
interiority 224 n.
centrality 225 n.
life 360 n.
spirit 447 n.
chief thing 638 n.
affections 817 n.
courage 855 n.
heart-ache
suffering 825 n.
dejection 834 n.
heartbroken
unhappy 825 adj.
heartburn
indigestion 651 n.
heartburning
discontent 829 n.

resentment 891 n.
heart disease
  heart disease 651 n.
hearten
  invigorate 174 vb.
  give courage
    855 vb.
heartfelt
  felt 818 adj.
hearth
  home 192 n.
  furnace 383 n.
heartiness
  (*see* **hearty**)
heartless
  impassive 820 adj.
heart's blood
  life 360 n.
heart-sinking
  dejection 834 n.
heart-throb
  loved one 887 n.
heart-whole
  free 744 adj.
  indifferent 860 adj.
hearty
  vigorous 174 adj.
  healthy 650 adj.
  felt 818 adj.
  cheerful 833 adj.
  sociable 882 adj.
heat
  dryness 342 n.
  heat 379 n.
  contest 716 n.
  excitable state
    822 n.
  libido 859 n.
  excite love 887 vb.
  anger 891 n.
heater
  heater 383 n.
heath
  plain 348 n.
  plant, wood 366 n.
heathen
  heathen 974 n.
heathenism
  antichristianity
    974 n.
  idolatry 982 n.
heather
  plant 366 n.
heave
  be periodic 141 vb.
  propel 287 vb.
  vomit 300 vb.

breathe 352 vb.
heaven
  heaven 971 n.
heaven-born
  worshipful 866 adj.
heavenly
  celestial 321 adj.
  topping 644 adj.
  pleasurable 826 adj.
  paradisiac 971 adj.
heavens
  heavens 321 n.
heaven-sent
  opportune 137 adj.
heave to
  navigate 269 vb.
heaviness
  sleepiness 679 n.
heavy
  inert 175 adj.
  weighty 322 adj.
  dense 324 adj.
  odorous 394 adj.
  unintelligent
    499 adj.
  laborious 682 adj.
  melancholic
    834 adj.
  dull 840 adj.
  heinous 934 adj.
heavy-eyed
  sleepy 679 adj.
heavy-handed
  oppressive 735 adj.
heavyweight
  pugilist 722 n.
heavy with
  productive 164 adj.
hecatomb
  oblation 981 n.
heckle
  be obstructive
    702 vb.
heckler
  dissentient 489 n.
  hinderer 702 n.
hectic
  red 431 adj.
hector
  threaten 900 vb.
hedge
  set off 31 vb.
  fence 235 n.
  wood 366 n.
  obstacle 702 n.
  be cautious 858
    vb.

hedgehog
  prickle 256 n.
hedonism
  pleasure 376 n.
  sensualism 944 n.
heebiejeebies
  alcoholism 949 n.
heed
  carefulness 457 n.
  observe 768 vb.
heedless
  inattentive 456 adj.
heedlessness
  rashness 857 n.
heel
  extremity 69 n.
  base, foot 214 n.
  be oblique 220 vb.
  rear 238 n.
  cad 938 n.
heel over
  be inverted 221
    vb.
heel-tap
  leavings 41 n.
hefty
  stalwart 162 adj.
hegemony
  influence 178 n.
  authority 733 n.
  prestige 866 n.
heifer
  youngling 132 n.
  cattle 365 n.
height
  height 209 n.
  high land 209 n.
  summit 213 n.
  metrology 465 n.
heighten
  augment 36 vb.
  elevate 310 vb.
heinous
  heinous 934 adj.
heir
  survivor 41 n.
  aftercomer 67 n.
  descendant 170 n.
  beneficiary 776 n.
heirloom
  dower 778 n.
heirship
  sonship 170 n.
helicopter
  aircraft 276 n.
heliocentric
  celestial 321 adj.

heliograph
  signal 547 n.
heliotrope
  purple 434 n., adj.
helix
  coil 251 n.
hell
  depth 211 n.
  suffering 825 n.
  hell 972 n.
hell-bent
  rash 857 adj.
  intending 617 adj.
hell-born
  diabolic 969 adj.
hell-cat
  hell-hag 904 n.
hell-hag
  hell-hag 904 n.
  monster 938 n.
hellish
  damnable 645 adj.
  infernal 972 adj.
helm
  sailing aid 269 n.
  directorship 689 n.
helmet
  armour 713 n.
helmsman
  navigator 270 n.
  director 690 n.
helot
  slave 742 n.
helotry
  servitude 745 n.
help
  utility 640 n.
  be expedient 642
    vb.
  facilitate 701 vb.
  aid 703 n., vb.
  servant 742 n.
helper
  auxiliary 707 n.
  servant 742 n.
helpful
  willing 597 adj.
  cooperative 706
    adj.
helpless
  impotent 161 adj.
  weak 163 adj.
hem
  surround 230 vb.
  edging 234 n.
  flank 239 vb.
  fold 261 vb.

he-man
athlete 162 n.
male 372 n.
brave person 855 n.

hemisphere
bisection 92 n.
region 184 n.
sphere 252 n.

hemistich
verse form 593 n.

hemline
edging 234 n.

hemp
fibre 208 n.

hen
poultry 365 n.

hen battery
stock farm 369 n.

henchman
auxiliary 707 n.
retainer 742 n.

hencoop, henhouse
stable 192 n.
cattle pen 369 n.

henna
orange 436 n.

henotheism
deism 973 n.

hen party
womankind 373 n.

henpeck
bicker 709 vb.

heptagon
angular figure 247 n.

herald
precursor 66 n.
precede 283 vb.
omen 511 n.
proclaim 528 vb.
messenger 531 n.

heraldry
heraldry 547 n.

herb
potherb 301 n.
medicine 658 n.

herbaceous
vegetal 366 adj.

herbage
grass 366 n.

herbal
vegetal 366 adj.
botany 368 n.

herbalist
botanist 368 n.
doctor 658 n.

herbivorous
feeding 301 adj.

Herculean
great 32 adj.
huge 195 adj.
laborious 682 adj.

Herculean task
hard task 700 n.

Hercules
athlete 162 n.

herd
group 74 n.
cattle 365 n.
herdsman 369 n.
imprison 747 vb.

herd instinct
crowd 74 n.

herdsman
herdsman 369 n.

hereafter
sequel 67 n.
future state 124 n.

hereditary
inherited 157 adj.
filial 170 adj.

heredity
heredity 5 n.
recurrence 106 n.
reversion 148 n.
affections 817 n.

heresy
heterodoxy 977 n.

heresy-hunting
orthodox 976 adj.
pietism 979 n.

heretic
nonconformist 84 n.
unbeliever 486 n.

heretical
heterodox 977 adj.

heritable
inherited 157 adj.
proprietary 777 adj.

heritage
possession 773 n.
dower 777 n.

hermaphrodite
eunuch 161 n.

hermaphroditism
abnormality 84 n.

hermeneutics
hermeneutics 520 n.

hermit
solitary 883 n.
ascetic 945 n.
pietist 979 n.

hermitage
monastery 986 n.

hero
brave person 855 n.
favourite 890 n.
good man 937 n.

heroic
olden 127 adj.
courageous 855 adj.
worshipful 866 adj.

heroics
prowess 855 n.
ostentation 875 n.

heroine
brave person 855 n.

heroism
prowess 855 n.

hero-worship
wonder 864 n., vb.
praise 923 n.

herpes
skin disease 651 n.

herring
table fish 365 n.

hesitant
doubting 474 adj.

hesitate
be inactive 679 vb.
(see **hesitation***)*

hesitation
doubt 486 n.
unwillingness 598 n.
nervousness 854 n.
caution 858 n.

hessian
textile 222 n.

hetaera
kept woman 952 n.

heteroclite
abnormal 84 adj.
grammatical 564 adj.

heterodoxy
heterodoxy 977 n.

heterogeneity
non-uniformity 17 n.
multiformity 82 n.

hew
cut 46 vb.
efform 243 vb.

hexagon
angular figure 247 n.

heyday
palmy days 730 n.

hiatus
interval 201 n.
opening 263 n.

hibernation
sleep 679 n.

hiccup
eruct 300 vb.
drunkenness 949 n.

hidden
concealed 525 adj.
secluded 883 adj.
cabbalistic 984 adj.

hidden hand
influence 178 n.
trouble-maker 663 n.

hide
skin 226 n.
strike 279 vb.
lurk 523 vb.
conceal 525 vb.
safeguard 660 vb.
flog 963 vb.

hidebound
obstinate 602 adj.

hideosity
eyesore 842 n.

hideous
ugly 842 adj.

hide-out
hiding-place 527 n.

hiding
corporal punishment 963 n.

hiding-place
hiding-place 527 n.

hierarchy
series 71 n.
clergy 986 n.

hieratic
scriptural 975 adj.
priestly 985 adj.

hierocracy
Churchdom 985 n.

hieroglyphics
enigma 530 n.

hierophant
religious teacher 973 n.

higgle
make terms 766 vb.
bargain 791 vb.

high
great 32 adj.
high 209 adj.
fetid 397 adj.
unclean 649 adj.

proud 871 adj.
high and mighty
  prideful 871 adj.
highball
  liquor 301 n.
highbrow
  instructed 490 adj.
  intellectual 492 n.
high-caste
  worshipful 866 adj.
high-class
  genteel 868 adj.
High Command
  master 741 n.
High Commission
  envoy 754 n.
high day
  holy-day 988 n.
higher critic
  theologian 973 n.
higher criticism
  interpretation 520 n.
highest
  supreme 34 adj.
  topmost 213 adj.
highfalutin
  ornate 574 adj.
  ostentatious
  875 adj.
high-fidelity
  accurate 494 adj.
high-flown
  rhetorical 574 adj.
high hand
  violence 176 n.
high-handed
  oppressive 735 adj.
high-hat
  prideful 871 adj.
high jinks
  revel 837 n.
highland
  high land 209 n.
high-level
  important 638 adj.
high life
  festivity 837 n.
  (*see* high living)
highlight
  publish 528 vb.
  indicate 547 vb.
high living
  sensualism 944 n.
highly-coloured
  expressive 516 adj.
high mightiness
  pride 871 n.

high-minded
  disinterested
  931 adj.
highness
  sovereign 741 n.
high-pitched
  strident 407 adj.
high-powered
  strong 162 adj.
high pressure
  vigorousness 174 n.
high-priority
  important 638 adj.
highroad
  road 624 n.
high society
  beau monde 848 n.
high-sounding
  ostentatious
  875 adj.
high spirits
  merriment 833 n.
high-strung
  lively 819 adj.
  excitable 822 adj.
high time
  opportunity 137 n.
  lateness 136 n.
high treason
  perfidy 930 n.
high-up
  superior 34 n.
high-water mark
  limit 236 n.
  gauge 465 n.
highway
  road 624 n.
  facility 701 n.
highwayman
  robber 789 n.
high words
  quarrel 709 n.
hijack
  steal 788 vb.
hike
  walk 267 vb.
hiker
  pedestrian 268 n.
hilarity
  merriment 833 n.
hill
  high land 209 n.
  acclivity 220 n.
hillbilly
  countryman 869 n.
hillman
  dweller 191 n.

hillock
  monticle 209 n.
hillside
  acclivity 220 n.
hilly
  alpine 209 adj.
hilt
  handle 218 n.
hind
  back 238 adj.
  deer 365 n.
hinder
  disable 161 vb.
  back 238 adj.
  retard 278 vb.
  hinder 702 vb.
  (*see* hindrance)
hinderer
  hinderer 702 n.
hindmost
  ending 69 adj.
  back 238 adj.
hindquarters
  buttocks 238 n.
hindrance
  delay 136 n.
  hindrance 702 n.
  hinderer 702 n.
hindsight
  remembrance 505 n.
hinge
  joint 45 n.
  fastening 47 n.
  pivot 218 n.
hinge on
  depend 157 vb.
hint
  hint 524 n., vb.
  indication 547 n.
hinterland
  land 344 n.
hip (*see* hips)
hippodrome
  arena 724 n.
hips
  buttocks 238 n.
hipshot
  crippled 163 adj.
hire
  employ 622 vb.
  hire 785 vb.
  lease 784 vb.
hireling
  servant 742 n.
  venal 930 adj.
hirer
  lender 784 n.

hirsute
  hairy 259 adj.
hiss
  sibilation 406 n.
  ululate 409 vb.
  disapprobation
  924 n.
historian
  antiquarian 125 n.
  chronicler 549 n.
  narrator 590 n.
historic
  olden 127 adj.
  renowned 866 adj.
historical
  past 125 adj.
  true 494 adj.
  descriptive 590 adj.
historicity
  reality 1 n.
  truth 494 n.
history
  preterition 125 n.
  record 548 n.
  narrative 590 n.
histrionics
  exaggeration 546 n.
  acting 594 n.
  ostentation 875 n.
hit
  strike 279 vb.
  discover 484 vb.
  success 727 n.
  favourite 890 n.
hit and miss
  empiricism 461 n.
hitch
  tie 45 vb.
  ligature 47 n.
  hitch 702 n.
hitch-hike
  ride 267 vb.
hit off
  represent 551 vb.
hit on
  discover 484 vb.
hive
  dwelling 192 n.
  stock farm 369 n.
  storage 632 n.
  activity 678 n.
hive off
  be dispersed 75 vb.
  schismatize 978 vb.
hoar
  white 427 adj.
  grey 429 adj.

hoard
store 632 n., vb.
safeguard 660 vb.
be parsimonious
816 vb.
hoarder
niggard 816 n.
hoarding
exhibit 522 n.
advertisement
528 n.
hoar-frost
wintriness 380 n.
hoarse
hoarse 407 adj.
voiceless 578 adj.
hoary
immemorial
127 adj.
grey 429 adj.
hoax
rumour 529 n.
trickery 542 n.
hoaxable
credulous 487 adj.
hob
stand 218 n.
hobble
tie 45 vb.
move slowly
278 vb.
impair 655 vb.
fetter 747 vb.
hobby
business 622 n.
amusement 837 n.
hobby-horse
vehicle 274 n.
hobgoblin
elf 970 n.
hobnob
be friendly 880 vb.
hobo
wanderer 268 n.
Hobson's choice
necessity 596 n.
no choice 606 n.
hock
leg 267 n.
wine 301 n.
hocus
trickery 542 n.
hocus-pocus
unmeaningness
515 n.
sleight 542 n.
spell 983 n.

hod
shovel 274 n.
hoe
farm tool 370 n.
hog
pig 365 n.
appropriate 786 vb.
be selfish 932 vb.
glutton 947 n.
hoggish
unclean 649 adj.
selfish 932 adj.
hogwash
silly talk 515 n.
swill 649 n.
hoist
elevate 310 vb.
flag 547 n.
hold
cohere 48 vb.
comprise 78 vb.
go on 146 vb.
influence 178 n.
cellar 194 n.
base 214 n.
handle 218 n.
support 218 vb.
opine 485 vb.
affirm 532 vb.
storage 632 n.
wrestling 716 n.
lock-up 748 n.
retention 778 n.
hold-all
bag 194 n.
hold cheap
underestimate
483 vb.
hold cheap 922 vb.
hold down
dominate 733 vb.
holder
receptacle 194 n.
handle 218 n.
possessor 776 n.
hold fast
cohere 48 vb.
hold forth
orate 579 vb.
hold hands
caress 889 vb.
hold in
restrain 747 vb.
hold in common
socialize 775 vb.
holding
territory 184 n.

farm 370 n.
hold office
function 622 vb.
rule 733 vb.
hold on
retain 778 vb.
hold one's own
be equal 28 vb.
hold out
resist 715 vb.
offer 759 vb.
hold over
put off 136 vb.
hold the baby
deputize 755 vb.
hold together
cooperate 706 vb.
hold up
put off 136 vb.
hinder 702 vb.
rob 788 vb.
hole
cavity 255 n.
pierce 263 vb.
refuge 662 n.
hole-and-corner
stealthy 525 adj.
holiday
leisure 681 n.
amusement 837 n.
holiday camp
pleasure-ground
837 n.
holiday-maker
traveller 268 n.
reveller 837 n.
holier than thou
prideful 871 adj.
disapproving
924 adj.
pietistic 979 adj.
holiness (*see* holy)
hollow
insubstantial 4
adj.
empty 190 adj.
cavity 255 n.
furrow 261 n.
resonant 404 adj.
hypocritical
541 adj.
holocaust
havoc 165 n.
oblation 981 n.
holster
case 194 n.
arsenal 723 n.

holy
divine, godlike
965 adj.
sanctified 979 adj.
devotional 981 adj.
Holy Communion
Holy Communion
988 n.
holy-day
holy-day 988 n.
Holy Ghost
Holy Ghost 965 n.
Holy Grail
church utensil
990 n.
holy horror
false piety 980 n.
Holy of Holies
holy place 990 n.
Holy Spirit
Holy Ghost 965 n.
holy war
philanthropy 901 n.
homage
submission 721 n.
loyalty 739 n.
respects 920 n.
home
native 191 adj.
house, home 192 n.
home, at
knowing 490 adj.
habituated 610 adj.
home-coming
return 286 n.
homefolks
family 11 n.
home ground
focus 76 n.
home-keeping
unsociable 883 adj.
homeland
home 192 n.
homeless
alone 88 adj.
displaced 188 adj.
travelling 267 adj.
home-life
seclusion 883 n.
homely
comfortable
376 adj.
plain 573 adj.
ugly 842 adj.
plebeian 869 adj.
home-made
artless 699 adj.

homeopath
doctor 658 n.
homeopathic
small 33 adj.
medical 658 adj.
homeopathy
medical art 658 n.
home rule
independence
744 n.
homesickness
desire 859 n.
homespun
textile 222 n.
artless 699 adj.
homestead
home 192 n.
home-truth
veracity 540 n.
censure 924 n.
homeward-bound
regressive 286 adj.
homework
study 536 n.
preparation 669 n.
homicide
homicide 362 n.
homiletics
teaching 534 n.
homily
lecture 534 n.
oration 579 n.
homing
regressive 286 adj.
incoming 297 adj.
homogeneity
uniformity 16 n.
homonym
word 559 n.
homonymous
semantic 514 adj.
homo sapiens
mankind 371 n.
homosexual
nonconformist 84 n.
homunculus
dwarf 196 n.
hone
sharpen 256 vb.
honest
genuine 494 adj.
ethical 917 adj.
honourable
929 adj.
honesty (*see* **honest**)
honey
sweet 392 n.

darling 890 n.
honeycomb
porosity 263 n.
pierce 263 vb.
sweet 392 n.
honeymoon
concord 710 n.
wedding 894 n.
honeymooners
spouse 894 n.
honeypot
focus 76 n.
honk
ululate 409 vb.
danger signal
665 n.
honorarium
reward 962 n.
honorary
uncharged 812 adj.
honorific
title 870 n.
celebrative
876 adj.
honour
decoration 729 n.
prestige 866 n.
title 870 n.
celebrate 876 vb.
pay respects
884 vb.
probity 929 n.
purity 950 n.
worship 981 n., vb.
honourable
honourable
929 adj.
honours
victory 727 n.
honours 866 n.
hooch
liquor 301 n.
hood
covering 226 n.
headgear 228 n.
screen 421 n., vb.
hoodlum
ruffian 904 n.
hoodoo
sorcery 983 n.
hoodwink
blind 439 vb.
deceive 542 vb.
hoof
foot 214 n.
hook
coupling 47 n.

hanger 217 n.
take 786 vb.
hook and eye
fastening 47 n.
**hook, line, and
sinker**
all 52 n.
hook-up
association 706 n.
hooligan
ruffian 904 n.
hoop
bond 47 n.
circle 250 n.
hoot
ululate 409 vb.
laugh 835 vb.
disapprove 924 vb.
hooter
megaphone 400 n.
signal 547 n.
hop
leap 312 n., vb.
be agitated 318 vb.
dancing 837 n.
hope
hope 852 n., vb.
hopeful
youngster 132 n.
probable 471 adj.
promising 852 adj.
hopeless
impossible 470 adj.
hopeless 853 adj.
unpromising
853 adj.
hop it
decamp 296 vb.
hopper
vat 194 n.
hops
liquor 301 n.
horde
multitude 104 n.
army 722 n.
rabble 869 n.
horizon
distance 199 n.
limit 236 n.
view 438 n.
horizontality
horizontality
216 n.
hormone
stimulant 174 n.
horn
cone 252 n.

megaphone 400 n.
horn 414 n.
hornet
shrew 892 n.
noxious animal
904 n.
hornet's nest
bane 659 n.
pitfall 663 n.
horny
hard 326 adj.
horny-handed
labouring 682 adj.
horology
chronometry 117 n.
horoscope
destiny 155 n.
prediction 511 n.
horrible
not nice 645 adj.
frightening 854 adj.
horrid
not nice 645 adj.
horrific
frightening 854 adj.
horrify
displease 827 vb.
frighten 854 vb.
horror
eyesore 842 n.
fear 854 n.
horrors
melancholy 834 n.
alcoholism 949 n.
hors de combat
impotent 161 adj.
hors d'œuvre
dish 301 n.
horse
horse 273 n.
cavalry 722 n.
horse-dealing
barter 791 n.
horseman
rider 268 n.
cavalry 722 n.
horsemanship
equitation 267 n.
horse-play
fight 716 n.
horse-power
energy 160 n.
horse sense
intelligence 498 n.
horsewhip
flog 963 vb.
scourge 964 n.

horsy
equine 273 adj.
hortatory
inducive 612 adj.
horticulture
agriculture 370 n.
hosanna
hymn 981 n.
hose
legwear 228 n.
conduit 351 n.
extinguisher 382 n.
hosier
clothier 228 n.
hosiery
legwear 228 n.
hospitable
(*see* hospitality)
hospital
hospital 658 n.
hospitality
friendliness 880 n.
sociability 882 n.
hospitalize
doctor 658 vb.
host
multitude 104 n.
army 722 n.
social person 882 n.
the sacrament
988 n.
hostage
security 767 n.
hostel
quarters 192 n.
hostess
social person 882 n.
hostile
attacking 712 adj.
adverse 731 adj.
(*see* hostility)
hostilities
belligerency 718 n.
hostility
enmity 881 n.
disapprobation
924 n.
hot
hot 379 adj.
pungent 388 adj.
fervent 818 adj.
lecherous 951 adj.
hot air
empty talk 515 n.
hotbed
seedbed 156 n.
infection 651 n.

hot-blooded
violent 176 adj.
hotchpotch
medley 43 n.
dish 301 n.
hotel
inn 192 n.
hotelier
caterer 633 n.
hot-gospeller
religionist 979 n.
hothead
desperado 857 n.
hot-headed
rash 857 adj.
hot-house
garden 370 n.
heater 383 n.
hound
dog 365 n.
be malevolent
898 vb.
cad 938 n.
hound on
incite 612 vb.
hour
juncture 8 n.
period 110 n.
clock time 117 n.
hourglass
timekeeper 117 n.
narrowing 206 n.
hourly
periodic 110 adj.
house
genealogy 169 n.
place 187 vb.
abode, house 192 n.
playgoer 594 n.
houseboat
small house 192 n.
boat 275 n.
housebreaker
thief 789 n.
housebreaking
stealing 788 n.
housecoat
informal dress
228 n.
household
family 11 n.
group 74 n.
known 490 adj.
householder
resident 191 n.
housekepeer
resident 191 n.

caterer 633 n.
manager 690 n.
housekeeping
management 689
n.
houseless
displaced 188 adj.
houseman
doctor 658 n.
domestic 742 n.
house of cards
weak thing 163 n.
house party
social gathering
882 n.
housetop
roof 226 n.
house-trained
well-bred 848 adj.
house-warming
social gathering
882 n.
housewife
resident 191 n.
case 194 n.
manager 690 n.
housework
labour 682 n.
housing
housing 192 n.
housings
coverlet 226 n.
hover
impend 155 vb.
be near 200 vb.
be high 209 vb.
fly 271 vb.
howdah
seat 218 n.
howl
ululate 409 vb.
lament 836 n.
howler
mistake 495 n.
absurdity 497 n.
how the land lies
circumstance 8 n.
hoyden
youngster 132 n.
hub
focus 76 n.
centrality 225 n.
wheel 250 n.
chief thing 638 n.
hubbub
commotion 318 n.
loudness 400 n.

hubris
pride 871 n.
insolence 878 n.
huckster
bargain 791 vb.
pedlar 794 n.
huddle
confusion 61 n.
jumble 63 vb.
crowd 74 n.
conference 584 n.
hue
hue 425 n.
hue and cry
chase 619 n.
huff
resentment 891 n.
huff 891 vb.
huffy
irascible 892 adj.
hug
cohere 48 vb.
make smaller
198 vb.
be near 200 vb.
greet 884 vb.
caress 889 vb.
huge
enormous 32 adj.
huge 195 adj.
hugger-mugger
stealthy 525 adj.
hug oneself
be content 828 vb.
rejoice 835 vb.
hulk
ship 275 n.
hulks
prison 748 n.
hull
ship 275 n.
uncover 229 vb.
hullabaloo
turmoil 61 n.
loudness 400 n.
hum
sound faint 401
vb.
resound 404 vb.
ululate 409 vb.
sing 413 vb.
human
human 371 adj.
human being
person 371 n.
hum and haw
stammer 580 vb.

be irresolute
601 vb.
humane
benevolent 897 adj.
humanism
philanthropy 901 n.
humanist
philanthropist
901 n.
humanitarian
philanthropist
901 n.
humanitarianism
benevolence 897 n.
philanthropy 901 n.
humanities
culture 490 n.
humanity
mankind 371 n.
benevolence 897 n.
pity 905 n.
humanize
be lenient 736 vb.
human nature
mankind 371 n.
humble
inconsiderable
33 adj.
impress 821 vb.
plebeian 869 adj.
humiliate 872 vb.
respectful 920 adj.
(see humility)
humbug
falsehood 541 n.
deceive 542 vb.
affectation 850 n.
humdrum
plain 573 adj.
humidity
moisture 341 n.
humiliation
adversity 731 n.
humiliation 872 n.
indignity 921 n.
humility
humility 872 n.
modesty 874 adj.
disinterestedness
931 n.
hummock
monticle 209 n.
humorist
humorist 839 n.
humorous
funny 849 adj.
(see humour)

humour
temperament 5 n.
whim 604 n.
affections 817 n.
please 826 vb.
wit 839 n.
flatter 925 vb.
humourless
serious 834 adj.
dull 840 adj.
humoursome
capricious 604 adj.
sullen 893 adj.
hump
monticle 209 n.
carry 273 vb.
hunch
intuition 476 n.
supposition 512 n.
hundred per cent
perfect 646 adj.
hunger
rapacity 786 n.
hunger 859 n.
hunger-strike
fast 946 n.
hungry
hungry 859 adj.
hunk
piece 53 n.
hunt
oscillate 317 vb.
search 459 n.
chase 619 n.
hunter
timekeeper 117 n.
thoroughbred 273 n.
hunter 619 n.
huntsman
hunter 619 n.
hunt with the hounds
do likewise 20 vb.
hurdle
leap 312 vb.
obstacle 702 n.
hurdler
jumper 312 n.
hurdles
racing 716 n.
hurdy-gurdy
organ 414 n.
hurl
propel 287 vb.
hurly-burly
commotion 318 n.
hurrah
rejoicing 835 n.

hurricane
storm 176 n.
gale 352 n.
hurried
brief 114 adj.
hurry
move fast 277 vb.
activity 678 n.
haste 680 n.
hurt
pain 377 n.
impair 655 vb.
hurt 827 vb.
huff 891 vb.
husband
store 632 vb.
spouse 894 n.
husbandman
husbandman 370 n.
countryman 869 n.
husbandry
agriculture 370 n.
management 689 n.
economy 814 n.
hush
quietude 266 n.
silence 399 n., vb.
hush-hush
concealed 525 adj.
hush up
keep secret 525 vb.
husk
skin 226 n.
corn 366 n.
rubbish 641 n.
huskiness
aphony 578 n.
husky
stalwart 162 adj.
hoarse 407 adj.
hussy
loose woman 952
n.
hustings
rostrum 539 n.
vote 605 n.
hustle
activity 678 n.
hasten 680 vb.
hustler
busy person 678 n.
hut
small house 192 n.
hutch
stable 192 n.
hybrid
hybrid 43 n.

hydra-headed
reproductive
166 adj.
hydrant
conduit 351 n.
hydro
hospital 658 n.
hydrocele
fluid 335 n.
hydrocephalic
diseased 651 adj.
hydrography
geography 321 n.
hygrometry 341 n.
oceanography
343 n.
hydrometer
density 324 n.
hygrometry 341 n.
hydrophobia
frenzy 503 n.
hydroponics
agriculture 370 n.
hydrotherapy
therapy 658 n.
hyena
noxious animal
904 n.
hygiene
health 650 n.
hygiene 652 n.
prophylactic 658 n.
hymn
praise 923 vb.
hymn 981 n.
hymnal
hymnal 988 n.
hyp
psychopathy 503 n.
hyperaesthesia
sensibility 374 n.
hyperbola
curve 248 n.
hyperbole
expansion 197 n.
exaggeration 546 n.
ornament 574 n.
hyperbolical
exaggerated
546 adj.
hypercriticism
fastidiousness
862 n.
censure 924 n.
hyperphysical
paranormal 984
adj.

535

hypersonic
  speedy 277 adj.
hypertension
  blood pressure
  651 n.
hypertrophy
  size 195 n.
hyphen
  bond 47 n.
  punctuation 547 n.
hyphenate
  join 45 vb.
hypnosis
  insensibility 375 n.
hypnotic
  influential 178 adj.
  inducive 612 adj.
  somnific 679 adj.
hypnotist
  motivator 612 n.
hypnotize
  render insensible
  375 vb.
hypochondria
  psychopathy 503 n.
  melancholy 834 n.
hypochondriac
  insane 503 adj.
  madman 504 n.
  moper 834 n.
hypocrisy
  duplicity 541 n.
  deception 542 n.
hypocrite
  deceiver 545 n.
  slyboots 698 n.
  affector 850 n.
hypomania
  psychopathy 503 n.
hypothecation
  security 767 n.
hypothesis
  supposition 512 n.
hypothetical
  suppositional
  512 adj.
  imaginary 513 adj.
hysteria
  psychopathy 503 n.
hysteric
  madman 504 n.
hysterical
  insane 503 adj.
  excitable 822 adj.
hysterics
  excitable state
  822 n.

hysteron proteron
  inversion 221 n.

I

ice
  smoothness 258 n.
  ice 380 n.
  refrigeration 382 n.
  refrigerator 384 n.
  preserve 666 vb.
ice age
  era 110 n.
iceberg
  ice 380 n.
  unfeeling person
  820 n.
  solitary 883 n.
iced
  cooled 382 adj.
ice-sheet
  ice 380 n.
ichor
  blood 335 n.
icicle
  ice 380 n.
  unfeeling person
  820 n.
icing
  sweet 392 n.
icon
  image 551 n.
  picture 553 n.
iconoclasm
  destruction 165 n.
iconoclast
  destroyer 168 n.
  violent creature
  176 n.
  religionist 979 n.
iconography
  representation
  551 n.
iconolatry
  cult 981 n.
  idolatry 982 n.
ictus
  prosody 593 n.
icy
  cold 380 adj.
id
  spirit 447 n.
idea
  idea 451 n.
  opinion 485 n.
ideal
  prototype 23 n.

ideational 451 adj.
  imaginary 513 adj.
  perfection 646 n.
  desired object
  859 n.
idealism
  immateriality
  320 n.
  fantasy 513 n.
  fastidiousness
  862 n.
  disinterestedness
  931 n.
idealist
  visionary 513 n.
  perfectionist 862 n.
  philanthropist
  901 n.
idealistic
  improving 654 adj.
  (see idealism)
ideality
  supposition 512 n.
  ideality 513 n.
idealize
  imagine 513 vb.
  overrate 482 vb.
ideals
  morals 917 n.
  disinterestedness
  931 n.
ideate
  think 449 vb.
  imagine 513 vb.
identical
  identical 13 adj.
identification
  identity 13 n.
  comparison 462 n.
  identification 547 n.
identification papers
  label 547 n.
identify
  (see identification)
identity
  identity 13 n.
  self 80 n.
  authenticity 494 n.
idiocy
  unintelligence
  499 n.
  insanity 503 n.
idiom
  speciality 80 n.
  connotation 514 n.
  dialect 560 n.
  phrase 563 n.

  speech 579 n.
idiomatic
  special 80 adj.
  semantic 514 adj.
  linguistic 557 adj.
idiosyncrasy
  temperament 5 n.
  speciality 80 n.
idiot
  fool 501 n.
  madman 504 n.
idiotic
  (see idiocy)
idle
  be inattentive
  456 vb.
  unused 674 adj.
  lazy 679 adj.
idleness
  inactivity 679 n.
idler
  slowcoach 278 n.
  idler 679 n.
idol
  image 551 n.
  person of repute
  866 n.
  favourite 890 n.
  idol 982 n.
idolater
  idolater 982 n.
idolatry
  love 887 n.
  cult 981 n.
  idolatry 982 n.
idolization
  deification 982 n.
idolize
  love 887 vb.
  idolatrize 982 vb.
idyllic
  pleasurable 826 adj.
ignis fatuus
  visual fallacy
  440 n.
ignite
  kindle 381 vb.
igniter
  lighter 385 n.
ignition
  burning 381 n.
ignoble
  discreditable
  867 adj.
  plebeian 869 adj.
ignominy
  disrepute 867 n.

ignoramus
 ignoramus 493 n.
ignorance
 ignorance 491 n.
ignorant
 ignorant 491 adj.
 inexpectant 508 adj.
 (*see* ignorance)
ignore
 disregard 458 vb.
 reject 607 vb.
 make unwelcome
  833 vb.
ill
 evil 616 n.
 sick 651 adj.
ill-advised
 unwise 499 adj.
 inexpedient
  643 adj.
ill-breeding
 ill-breeding 847 n.
ill-conceived
 unwise 499 adj.
ill-conditioned
 bad 645 adj.
 sullen 893 adj.
 malevolent 898 adj.
ill-defined
 amorphous 244 adj.
 ill-seen 444 adj.
ill-disciplined
 disobedient 738 adj.
ill-done
 bungled 695 adj.
illegal
 prohibited 757 adj.
 dishonest 930 adj.
 illegal 954 adj.
illegality
 illegality 954 n.
illegibility
 unintelligibility
  517 n.
illegitimacy
 bastardy 954 n.
 illegality 954 n.
ill fame
 disrepute 867 n.
ill-fated
 unfortunate
  731 adj.
ill-favoured
 ugly 842 adj.
ill feeling
 enmity 881 n.
 hatred 888 n.

ill-furnished
 unprovided 636 adj.
ill-health
 ill-health 651 n.
ill-humour
 resentment 891 n.
 sullenness 893 n.
illicit
 (*see* illegal)
illimitable
 infinite 107 adj.
illiterate
 uninstructed
  491 adj.
 ignoramus 493 n.
ill-mannered
 (*see* ill-breeding)
ill-natured
 malevolent 898 adj.
illness
 illness 651 n.
illogical
 illogical 477 adj.
 erroneous 495 adj.
illogicality
 irrelevance 10 n.
 sophism 477 n.
ill-omened
 inopportune
  138 adj.
 unpromising
  853 adj.
ill-spent
 profitless 641 adj.
ill-timed
 ill-timed 138 adj.
ill-treat
 misuse 675 vb.
illuminant
 lighter 385 n.
 luminary 420 n.
illuminate
 make bright 417 vb.
 colour 425 vb.
 interpret 520 vb.
 manifest 522 vb.
 decorate 844 vb.
illumination
 lighting 420 n.
 knowledge 490 n.
 ornamental art
  844 n.
 revelation 975 n.
illuminations
 fireworks 420 n.
ill-usage
 misuse 675 n.

ill-used
 suffering 825 adj.
illusion
 visual fallacy 440 n.
 sleight 542 n.
illusionism
 mimicry 20 n.
illusionist
 conjuror 545 n.
illusory
 deceiving 542 adj.
illustrate
 (*see* illustration)
illustration
 example 83 n.
 interpretation
  520 n.
 picture 553 n.
 ornamental art
  844 n.
illustrative
 expressive 516 adj.
illustrator
 artist 556 n.
illustrious
 renowned 866 adj.
ill-will
 malevolence 898 n.
ill-wisher
 trouble-maker
  663 n.
 enemy 881 n.
ill wishes
 malediction 899 n.
image
 copy 22 n.
 reflection 417 n.
 ideality 513 n.
 metaphor 519 n.
 image 551 n.
 idol 982 n.
imagery
 imagination 513 n.
 metaphor 519 n.
image-worship
 idolatry 982 n.
imaginary
 unreal 2 adj.
 insubstantial 4 adj.
 imaginary 513 adj.
imagination
 imagination 513 n.
imaginative
 imaginative 513 adj.
 descriptive 590 adj.
imagine
 suppose 512 vb.

 imagine 513 vb.
imbalance
 inequality 29 n.
imbecile
 foolish 499 adj.
 fool 501 n.
 insane 503 adj.
imbecility
 (*see* imbecile)
imbibe
 absorb 299 vb.
 drink 301 vb.
imbroglio
 complexity 61 n.
 predicament 700 n.
imbrue
 infuse 303 vb.
 drench 341 vb.
imbue
 infuse 303 vb.
 drench 341 vb.
 educate 534 vb.
imitate
 liken 18 vb.
 imitate 20 vb.
 represent 551 vb.
imitation
 imitation 20 n.
 sham 542 n.
 representation
  551 n.
imitative
 simulating 18 vb.
 imitative 20 adj.
 unthinking 450 adj.
imitativeness
 mimicry 20 n.
immaculate
 perfect 646 adj.
 clean 648 adj.
 pure 950 adj.
immanence
 intrinsicality 5 n.
immateriality
 insubstantiality 4 n.
 immateriality
  320 n.
 unimportance
  639 n.
immature
 early 135 adj.
immaturity
 incompleteness
  55 n.
 youth, nonage
  130 n.
 imperfection 647 n.

non-preparation
670 n.
immeasurable
infinite 107 adj.
immediacy
haste 680 n.
immediate
instantaneous
116 n.
immemorial
immemorial
127 adj.
permanent 144 adj.
worshipful 866 adj.
immemorial usage
tradition 127 n.
immense
infinite 107 adj.
immensity
greatness 32 n.
immersion
insertion 303 n.
plunge 313 n.
moistening 341 n.
immigrant
foreigner 59 n.
settler 191 n.
incomer 297 n.
immigration
ingress 297 n.
imminent
early 135 adj.
impending 155 adj.
immobility
stability 153 n.
quiescence 266 n.
inaction 677 n.
immoderate
violent 176 adj.
immoderation
intemperance 943 n.
immodesty
impurity 951 n.
immolation
killing 362 n.
oblation 981 n.
immoral
dishonest 930 adj.
immoralism
impiety 980 n.
immoralist
bad man 938 n.
immorality
wickedness 934 n.
unchastity 951 n.
immortal
perpetual 115 adj.

renowned 866 adj.
immortality
perpetuity 115 n.
famousness 866 n.
immortalize
perpetuate 115 vb.
honour 866 vb.
immortals
god 966 n.
immovables
property 777 n.
immunity
hygiene 652 n.
safety 660 n.
non-liability 919 n.
immunization
hygiene 652 n.
prophylactic 658 n.
immure
imprison 747 vb.
immutable
antiquated 127 adj.
imp
child 132 n.
implant 303 vb.
elf, demon 970 n.
impact
influence 178 n.
collision 279 n.
impair
disable 161 vb.
harm 645 vb.
impair 655 vb.
impale
kill 362 vb.
pierce 263 vb.
execute 963 vb.
impart
inform 524 vb.
impartial
wise 498 adj.
impartiality
equality 28 n.
justice 913 n.
disinterestedness
931 n.
impassable
impracticable
470 adj.
impasse
closure 264 n.
obstacle 702 n.
impassioned
forceful 571 adj.
fervent 818 adj.
impassive
impassive 820 adj.

indifferent 860 adj.
unastonished
865 adj.
impatience
haste 680 n.
excitability 822 n.
irascibility 892 n.
impeachment
accusation 928 n.
impeccable
perfect 646 adj.
innocent 935 adj.
impecunious
poor 801 adj.
impede
hinder 702 vb.
impediment
speech defect
580 n.
hindrance 702 n.
impedimenta
thing transferred
272 n.
encumbrance 702 n.
impel
impel 279 vb.
propel 287 vb.
impend
be to come 124 vb.
impend 155 vb.
impending
approaching
289 adj.
impenetrable
closed 264 adj.
dense 324 adj.
unintelligible
517 adj.
thick-skinned
820 adj.
impenitence
impenitence 940 n.
imperative
necessary 596 adj.
commanding
737 adj.
obligatory 917 adj.
imperceptible
minute 196 adj.
invisible 444 adj.
imperceptive
insensible 375 adj.
imperfect
uncompleted
726 adj.
imperfection
inferiority 35 n.

shortcoming 307 n.
imperfection 647 n.
blemish 845 n.
imperial
ruling 733 adj.
imperialism
governance 733 n.
imperil
endanger 661 vb.
imperious
authoritative
733 adj.
proud 871 adj.
insolent 878 adj.
imperishable
perpetual 115 adj.
impermanence
transientness 114 n.
impermeable
closed 264 adj.
impersonal
impassive 820 adj.
indifferent 860 adj.
disinterested
931 adj.
impersonation
representation
551 n.
impersonator
imitator 20 n.
imperspicuity
imperspicuity
568 n.
impertinence
sauciness 878 n.
rudeness 885 n.
imperturbability
inexcitability
823 n.
non-wonder 865 n.
impervious
dense 324 adj.
opaque 423 adj.
impracticable
470 adj.
unintelligent
499 adj.
thick-skinned
820 adj.
impetuosity
vigorousness 174 n.
haste 680 n.
excitability 822 n.
rashness 857 n.
impetus
spurt 277 n.
impulse 279 n.

impiety
irreligion 974 n.
impiety 980 n.
impinge
collide 279 vb.
encroach 306 vb.
impious
impious 980 adj.
impish
fairylike 970 adj.
implacable
resolute 599 adj.
pitiless 906 adj.
revengeful 910 adj.
implant
implant 303 vb.
implausible
improbable 472 adj.
implement
tool 630 n.
carry out 725 vb.
implicate
accuse 928 vb.
implication
relation 9 n.
meaning 514 n.
implicit
intrinsic 5 adj.
tacit 523 adj.
implore
entreat 761 vb.
imply
be intrinsic 5 vb.
evidence 466 vb.
mean 514 vb.
imply 523 vb.
indicate 547 vb.
impolite
discourteous
885 adj.
impolitic
inexpedient
643 adj.
imponderability
insubstantiality 4 n.
immateriality
320 n.
levity 323 n.
import
add 38 vb.
transference 272 n.
admit 299 vb.
meaning 514 n.
importance
importance 638 n.
important
crucial 137 adj.

fundamental
156 adj.
importation
(see import)
imported
extraneous 59 adj.
incoming 297 adj.
importer
merchant 794 n.
importunate,
importunity
(see importune)
importune
request 761 vb.
impose
add 38 vb.
deceive 542 vb.
command 737 vb.
command respect
920 vb.
imposing
impressive 821 adj.
imposition
bane 659 n.
tax 809 n.
penalty 963 n.
impossible
impossible 470 adj.
difficult 700 adj.
wonderful 864 adj.
impost
tax 809 n.
impostor
impostor 545 n.
knave 938 n.
imposture
deception 542 n.
impotence
impotence 161 n.
unproductivity
172 n.
impound
imprison 747 vb.
impoverish
make insufficient
636 vb.
impoverish 801 vb.
impoverishment
poverty 801 n.
impracticable
impracticable
470 adj.
impractical
irrelevant 10 adj.
misjudging 481 adj.
imprecision
inexactness 495 n.

impregnable
invulnerable
660 adj.
impregnate
generate 164 vb.
make fruitful
171 vb.
infuse 303 vb.
impresario
stage manager
594 n.
impress
impress 821 vb.
command respect
920 vb.
(see impression,
impress on)
impression
copy 22 n.
idea 451 n.
intuition 476 n.
opinion 485 n.
feeling 818 n.
impressionable
sentient 374 adj.
impressible 819 adj.
excitable 822 adj.
impressionistic
descriptive 590 adj.
impressive
great 32 adj.
forceful 571 adj.
felt 818 adj.
impressive 821 adj.
(see impression)
impressiveness
spectacle 445 n.
ostentation 875 n.
impress on
cause thought
449 vb.
emphasize 532 vb.
engrave 555 vb.
imprimatur
permit 756 n.
orthodoxism 976 n.
imprint
identification 547 n.
label 547 n.
imprison
imprison 747 vb.
imprisonment
detention 747 n.
improbability
improbability 472 n.
improbity
thievishness 788 n.

improbity 930 n.
impromptu
spontaneity 609 n.
non-preparation
670 n.
improper
unapt 25 adj.
not nice 645 adj.
vulgar 847 adj.
wrong 914 adj.
impropriety
inaptitude 25 n.
bad taste 847 n.
guilty act 936 n.
improve
(see improvement)
improvement
increase 36 n.
progression 285 n.
improvement 654 n.
improve on
be superior 34 vb.
improver
reformer 654 n.
improvidence
non-preparation
670 n.
improvident
prodigal 815 adj.
improvisation
spontaneity 609 n.
non-preparation
670 n.
improvise
make ready 699
vb.
imprudence
rashness 857 n.
impudent
impertinent 878 adj.
impugn
negate 533 vb.
impulse
energy 160 n.
impulse 279 n.
motive 612 n.
feeling 818 n.
desire 859 n.
impulsive
spontaneous
609 adj.
excitable 822 adj.
impunity
non-liability 919 n.
impurity
uncleanness 649 n.
impurity 951 n.

imputation
attribution 158 n.
slur 867 n.
inability
impotence 161 n.
unskilfulness 695 n.
inaccessible
removed 199 adj.
impracticable
470 adj.
inaccuracy
inexactness 495 n.
inaction
inertness 175 n.
inaction 677 n.
inactivity 679 n.
inactive
apathetic 820 adj.
inactivity
quiescence 266 n.
non-use 674 n.
inactivity 679 n.
leisure 681 n.
inadequacy
insufficiency 636 n.
imperfection 647 n.
inadmissible
excluded 57 adj.
wrong 914 adj.
inadvertence
inattention 456 n.
inadvisability
inexpedience 643
n.
inalienable
retained 788 adj.
due 915 adj.
inamorata
loved one 887 n.
in and out system
periodicity 141 n.
inane (*see* **inanity**)
inanimate
inorganic 359 adj.
dead 361 adj.
mindless 448 adj.
inactive 679 adj.
inanition
weakness 163 n.
inanity
insubstantial thing
4 n.
unmeaningness
515 n.
inapplicability
irrelevance 10 n.
inutility 641 n.

inappreciable
inconsiderable
33 adj.
inappropriate
inexpedient
643 adj.
undue 916 adj.
inaptitude
inaptitude 25 n.
inexpedience 643 n.
inarticulate
voiceless 578 adj.
stammering 580 adj.
artless 699 adj.
inattention
inattention 456 n.
inattentive
unthinking 450 adj.
hasty 680 adj.
inaudibility
silence 399 n.
faintness 401 n.
deafness 416 n.
inaugural
precursory 66 adj.
beginning 68 adj.
inaugurate
auspicate 68 vb.
inauguration
début 68 n.
mandate 751 n.
inauspicious
inopportune
138 adj.
adverse 731 adj.
unpromising
853 adj.
inborn
genetic 5 adj.
inbred
genetic 5 adj.
with affections
817 adj.
incalculable
multitudinous
104 adj.
infinite 107 adj.
casual 159 adj.
incandescence
heat 379 n.
glow 417 n.
incantation
sorcery 983 n.
incapable
powerless 161 adj.
incapacitate
disable 161 vb.

incapacity
inaptitude 25 n.
unskilfulness 695 n.
incarceration
detention 747 n.
incarnate
manifest 522 vb.
incarnation
materiality 319 n.
theophany 965 n.
incautious
rash 857 adj.
incendiary
violent 176 adj.
incendiarism 381 n.
incense
scent 396 n.
enrage 891 vb.
flattery 925 n.
oblation 981 n.
incensed
angry 891 adj.
incentive
incentive 612 n.
incessant
frequent 139 adj.
unceasing 146 adj.
incest
illicit love 951 n.
inch
move slowly
278 vb.
inchoate
amorphous 244 adj.
uncompleted
726 adj.
incidence
eventuality 154 n.
incident
circumstantial
8 adj.
eventuality 154 n.
incidental
extrinsic 6 adj.
accompanying
89 adj.
eventuality 154 n.
casual 159 adj.
incineration
burning 381 n.
incinerator
furnace 383 n.
incipient
beginning 68 adj.
incise
cut 46 vb.
engrave 555 vb.

incision
scission 46 n.
wound 655 n.
incisive
assertive 532 adj.
forceful 571 adj.
incite
influence 178 vb.
incite 612 vb.
inclemency
storm 176 n.
pitilessness 906 n.
inclination
tendency 179 n.
obliquity 220 n.
willingness 597 n.
liking 859 n.
incline
tend 179 vb.
acclivity 220 n.
render oblique
220 vb.
choose 605 vb.
motivate 612 vb.
inclose
(*see* **enclosure**)
inclosure
(*see* **enclosure**)
include
add 38 vb.
comprise 78 vb.
inclusion
inclusion 78 n.
participation 775 n.
inclusiveness
whole 52 n.
generality 79 n.
incognito
unknown 491 adj.
anonymous 562 adj.
incognizance
ignorance 491 n.
incoherence
unintelligibility
517 n.
incoherent
orderless 61 adj.
income
earnings 771 n.
receipt 807 n.
incomer
incomer 297 n.
incoming
incoming 297 adj.
incommensurable
correlative 10 adj.
disagreeing 25 adj.

incommode
hinder 702 vb.
incommode 827 vb.
incommunicable
inexpressible
517 adj.
incommunicado
concealed 525 adj.
imprisoned 747 adj.
incomparable
unimitated 21 adj.
supreme 34 adj.
incompatibility
disagreement 25 n.
enmity 881 n.
incompetence
inaptitude 25 n.
unintelligence
499 n.
unskilfulness 695 n.
incomplete
incomplete 55 adj.
deficient 307 adj.
uncompleted
726 adj.
incomprehensible
unintelligible
517 adj.
incomprehension
ignorance 491 n.
incompressible
rigid 326 adj.
inconceivable
unthought 450 adj.
impossible 470 adj.
unintelligible
517 adj.
inconclusive
illogical 477 adj.
confuted 479 adj.
incongruent
irrelative 10 adj.
incongruous
disagreeing 25 adj.
unconformable
84 adj.
inconsequence
irrelevance 10 n.
unimportance
639 n.
inconsequential
irrelevant 10 adj.
unimportant
639 adj.
inconsiderable
inconsiderable
33 adj.

inconsiderate
inattentive 456 adj.
discourteous
885 adj.
inconsistency
changeableness
152 n.
(see inconsistent)
inconsistent
contrary 14 adj.
disagreeing 25 adj.
illogical 477 adj.
inconspicuous
ill-seen 444 adj.
inconstancy
(see inconstant)
inconstant
non-uniform 17 adj.
fitful 142 adj.
capricious 604 adj.
incontestable
undisputed 473 adj.
incontinence
intemperance
943 n.
unchastity 951 n.
incontinent
intemperate
943 adj.
unchaste 951 adj.
incontrovertible
undisputed 473 adj.
inconvenience
inexpedience 643 n.
hinder 702 vb.
obstacle 702 n.
inconvenient
ill-timed 138 adj.
incorporate
join 45 vb.
combine 50 vb.
absorb 299 vb.
material 319 adj.
corporate 708 adj.
incorporation
(see incorporate)
incorporeality
immateriality
320 n.
incorrect
inelegant 576 adj.
wrong 914 adj.
incorrigibility
obstinacy 602 n.
impenitence 940 n.
incorrigible
wicked 934 adj.

incorruptibility
probity 929 n.
innocence 935 n.
incorruptible
perpetual 115 adj.
honourable
929 adj.
increase
increase 36 n.
product 164 n.
propagation 164 n.
improvement 654 n.
incredible
unbelieved 486 adj.
incredulity
unbelief 486 n.
increment
increment 36 n.
addition 38 n.
adjunct 40 n.
gain 771 n.
incriminate
blame 924 vb.
accuse 928 vb.
incrust
coat 226 vb.
incubate
generate 164 vb.
breed stock 369 vb.
mature 669 vb.
incubator
seedbed 156 n.
incubus
gravity 322 n.
encumbrance 702 n.
worry 825 n.
demon 970 n.
inculcate
educate 334 vb.
inculpation
censure 924 n.
accusation 928 n.
incumbency
job 622 n.
benefice 985 n.
church office 985 n.
incumbent
resident 191 n.
possessor 776 n.
beneficiary 776 n.
obligatory 917 adj.
cleric 986 n.
incunabula
origin 68 n.
edition 589 n.
incur
meet with 154 vb.

be liable 180 vb.
acquire 771 vb.
incurable
deadly 362 adj.
impracticable
470 adj.
obstinate 602 adj.
bad 645 adj.
sick 651 adj.
unpromising
853 adj.
incuriosity
incuriosity 454 n.
moral insensibility
820 n.
indifference 860 n.
incursion
ingress 297 n.
attack 712 n.
incurvation
concavity 255 n.
indebtedness
debt 803 n.
gratitude 907 n.
dueness 915 n.
indecent
impure 951 adj.
indecision
dubiety 474 n.
irresolution 601 n.
indecisive
uncertain 474 adj.
indefatigability
stamina 600 n.
assiduity 678 n.
indefeasible
vested 153 adj.
undisputed 473 adj.
indefinable
inexpressible
517 adj.
indefinite
general 79 adj.
imperspicuous
568 adj.
indelible
fixed 153 adj.
remembered
505 adj.
indelicacy
bad taste 847 n.
impurity 951 n.
indemnification
compensation 31 n.
restitution 787 n.
indemnify oneself
recoup 31 vb.

indemnity
offset 31 n.
restitution 787 n.
payment 804 n.
indent
crinkle 251 vb.
notch 260 vb.
demand 737 vb.
indentation
convolution 251 n.
notch 260 n.
indenture
compact 765 n.
title deed 767 n.
independence
irrelation 10 n.
independence 744 n.
independent
revolter 738 n.
indeterminacy
non-design 618 n.
indeterminate
causeless 159 adj.
uncertain 474 adj.
index
relate 9 vb.
class 62 vb.
list 87 n., vb.
finger 378 n.
indicator 547 n.
record 548 n., vb.
index expurgatorius
prohibition 757 n.
disapprobation 924 n.
Indian summer
revival 656 n.
indicate
mean 514 vb.
(see indication)
indication
evidence 466 n.
hint 524 n.
indication 547 n.
indicative
evidential 466 adj.
indicating 547 adj.
indict
indict 928 vb.
litigate 959 vb.
indictment
accusation 928 n.
indifference
incuriosity 454 n.
no choice 606 n.
moral insensibility 820 n.

indifference 860 n.
disinterestedness 931 n.
indifferent
irrelative 10 adj.
not bad 644 adj.
indifferent 860 adj.
indigence
poverty 801 n.
indigenous
native 191 adj.
indigestible
tough 329 adj.
indigestion
indigestion 651 n.
indignation
resentment 891 n.
disapprobation 924 n.
indignation meeting
malcontent 829 n.
indignity
indignity 921 n.
indigo
blue pigment 435 n.
indirect
oblique 220 adj.
deviating 282 adj.
roundabout 626 adj.
indiscernible
invisible 444 adj.
indiscipline
anarchy 734 n.
disobedience 738 n.
dutilessness 918 n.
indiscreet
unwise 499 adj.
indiscretion
disclosure 526 n.
rashness 857 n.
indiscriminate
indiscriminate 464 adj.
indiscrimination
generality 79 n.
indiscrimination 464 n.
no choice 606 n.
indispensable
necessary 596 adj.
important 638 adj.
indisposed
unwilling 598 adj.
sick 651 adj.
indisposition
ill-health 651 n.

indissoluble
indivisible 52 adj.
indistinct
ill-seen 444 adj.
stammering 580 adj.
indistinctness
faintness 401 n.
(see indistinct)
indistinguishable
identical 13 adj.
equivalent 28 adj.
invisible 444 adj.
indite
write 586 vb.
individual
unimitative 21 adj.
special 80 adj.
unit 88 n.
person 371 n.
individualism
particularism 80 n.
selfishness 932 n.
individualist
egotist 932 n.
individuality
speciality 80 n.
unconformity 84 n.
(see individual)
individualize
specify 80 vb.
indivisibility
simpleness 44 n.
unity 88 n.
indoctrinate
educate 534 vb.
indolence
sluggishness 679 n.
indomitable
persevering 600 adj.
courageous 855 adj.
indoor
interior 224 adj.
indubitable
undisputed 473 adj.
induce
influence 178 vb.
inducement
attraction 291 n.
inducement 612 n.
induct
auspicate 68 vb.
inductive
rational 475 adj.
indulge
(see indulgence)

indulgence
lenity 736 n.
permission 756 n.
forgiveness 909 n.
intemperance 943 n.
indulgent
benevolent 897 adj.
induration
hardening 326 n.
industrial
businesslike 622 adj.
industrialism
business 622 n.
industrialist
producer 167 n.
industrialization
business 622 n.
industrious
vigorous 174 adj.
studious 536 adj.
industrious 678 adj.
industry
production 164 n.
business 622 n.
assiduity 678 n.
inebriation
drunkenness 949 n.
inedible
tough 329 adj.
unsavoury 391 adj.
ineffable
inexpressible 517 adj.
ineffaceable
(see indelible)
ineffective
powerless 161 adj.
feeble 572 adj.
unsuccessful 728 adj.
ineffectual
useless 641 adj.
unskilful 695 adj.
ineffectuality
ineffectuality 161 n.
inefficacy
inutility 641 n.
inefficient
powerless 161 adj.
useless 641 adj.
unskilful 695 adj.
inelastic
rigid 326 adj.
inelegant
inelegant 576 adj.
clumsy 695 adj.

ineligible
rejected 607 adj.
inept
unapt 25 adj.
absurd 497 adj.
inequality
dissimilarity 19 n.
inequality 29 n.
inequitable
unjust 914 adj.
inequity
injustice 914 n.
ineradicable
characteristic 5
adj.
fixed 153 adj.
inerrancy
certainty 473 n.
inert
inert 175 adj.
quiescent 266 adj.
inertia
inertness 175 n.
inaction 677 n.
inactivity 679 n.
inessential
irrelevance 10 n.
trifle 639 adj.
inestimable
valuable 644 adj.
inevitable
impending 155 adj.
certain 473 adj.
necessary 596 adj.
inexact
(see inexactness)
inexactness
inexactness 495 n.
inexcitability
inertness 175 n.
moral insensibility
820 n.
inexcitability 823 n.
inexcitable
tranquil 266 adj.
inexcusable
heinous 934 adj.
guilty 936 adj.
inexhaustible
full 54 adj.
plenteous 635 adj.
inexorable
pitiless 906 adj.
inexpectation
inexpectation 508 n.
inexpedient
hindering 702 adj.

inexpensive
cheap 812 adj.
inexperience
unskilfulness 695 n.
innocence 935 n.
inexperienced
unhabituated
611 adj.
inexpert
unskilled 695 adj.
inexpiable
heinous 934 adj.
inexplicability
unintelligibility
517 n.
inexplicable
causeless 159 adj.
inexpressible
inexpressible
517 adj.
in extenso
wholly 52 adv.
inextricable
firm-set 45 adj.
cohesive 48 adj.
infallibility
certainty 473 n.
positiveness 473 n.
infallible
certain 473 adj.
accurate 494 adj.
veracious 540 adj.
infamous
disreputable
867 adj.
heinous 934 adj.
infamy
(see infamous)
infancy
youth, nonage
130 n.
helplessness 161 n.
infant
child 132 n.
infanticide
homicide 362 n.
infantile
infantine 132 adj.
foolish 499 adj.
infantry
infantry 722 n.
infatuate
make mad 503 vb.
(see infatuation)
infatuation
credulity 487 n.
folly 499 n.

love 887 n.
infect
infiltrate 297 vb.
excite 821 vb.
(see infection)
infection
influence 178 n.
transference 272 n.
infection 651 n.
poison 659 n.
infectious
influential 178 adj.
transferable
272 adj.
diseased 651 adj.
infectious 653 adj.
infer
reason 475 n.
imply 523 vb.
inference
sequence 65 n.
(see infer)
inferential
rational 475 n.
inferior
inferior 35 n., adj.
nonentity 639 n.
bad 645 adj.
mediocre 732 adj.
commoner 869 n.
(see inferiority)
inferiority
inequality 29 n.
inferiority 35 n.
subjection 745 n.
inferiority complex
jealousy 911 n.
infernal
diabolic 969 adj.
infernal 972 adj.
inferno
turmoil 61 n.
hell 972 n.
inferred
attributed 158 adj.
infest
be many 104 vb.
incommode 827 vb.
infested
full 54 adj.
insalubrious 653 adj.
infidel
unbeliever 486 n.
profane 980 adj.
infidelity
unbelief 486 n.
illicit love 951 n.

irreligion 974 n.
infiltrate
infiltrate 297 vb.
infiltration
mixture 43 n.
ingress 297 n.
infinite
multitudinous
104 adj.
infinite 107 adj.
infinitesimal
minute 196 adj.
infinity
infinity 107 n.
infirm
unhealthy 651 adj.
infirmary
hospital 658 n.
infirmity
ill-health 651 n.
vice 934 n.
infix
interjection 231 n.
implant 303 vb.
inflame
heat 381 vb.
aggravate 832 vb.
inflamed
violent 176 adj.
diseased 651 adj.
inflammability
burning 381 n.
excitability 822 n.
inflammable
combustible
385 adj.
inflammation
heating 381 n.
ulcer 651 n.
inflated
ostentatious
875 adj.
inflation
increase 36 n.
magniloquence
574 n.
finance 597 n.
dearness 811 n.
inflationary
monetary 797 adj.
inflect
parse 564 vb.
inflection
(see inflexion)
inflexibility
hardness 326 n.
resolution 599 n.

pitilessness 906 n.
inflexion
  pronunciation
    577 n.
infliction
  adversity 731 n.
  suffering 825 n.
  punishment 963 n.
inflow
  ingress 297 n.
  current 350 n.
influence
  modify 143 vb.
  power 160 n.
  influence 178 n.,
    vb.
  bias 481 vb.
  teach 534 vb.
  inducement 612 n.
  authority 733 n.
  prestige 866 n.
influential
  great 32 adj.
  (see **influence**)
influx
  ingress 297 n.
in force
  powerful 160 adj.
inform
  inform 524 vb.
  divulge 526 vb.
  accuse 928 vb.
informal
  (see **informality**)
informal dress
  informal dress
    228 n.
informality
  unconformity 84 n.
  laxity 734 n.
  non-observance
    769 n.
informant
  informant 524 n.
information
  information 524 n.
  disclosure 526 n.
  message 529 n.
  accusation 928 n.
informative
  informative 524 adj.
  loquacious 581 adj.
informer
  informer 524 n.
  accuser 928 n.
infraction
  disobedience 738 n.

infrequency
  infrequency 140 n.
infrequent
  discontinuous
    72 adj.
  fitful 142 adj.
infringement
  overstepping 306 n.
  disobedience 738 n.
  undueness 916 n.
infuriate
  make violent
    176 vb.
  enrage 891 vb.
infuse
  infuse 303 vb.
infusion
  potion 301 n.
  solution 337 n.
ingenious
  imaginative 513 adj.
  skilful 694 adj.
ingenue
  ingenue 699 n.
ingenuity
  cunning 698 n.
ingenuous
  artless 699 adj.
  honourable 929 adj.
ingest
  absorb 299 vb.
  eat, drink 301 vb.
inglorious
  mediocre 732 adj.
  unsuccessful
    728 adj.
  inglorious 867 adj.
ingot
  bullion 797 n.
ingraft
  implant 303 vb.
ingratiating
  servile 879 adj.
  flattering 925 adj.
ingratitude
  ingratitude 908 n.
ingredient
  part 53 n.
  component 58 n.
  element 319 n.
ingress
  ingress 297 n.
ingrown
  firm-set 45 adj.
  interior 224 adj.
inhabit
  dwell 192 vb.

possess 773 vb.
inhabitant
  dweller 191 n.
inhale
  breathe 352 vb.
  smoke 388 vb.
in hand
  stored 632 adj.
inharmonious
  discordant 411 adj.
inhere
  be intrinsic 5 vb.
  belong 773 adj.
inherent
  ingredient 58 adj.
inherit
  inherit 771 vb.
inheritance
  dower 777 n.
  transfer 780 n.
inherited
  genetic 5 adj.
  acquired 771 adj.
inhibition
  prohibition 757 n.
inhibitor
  counteraction
    182 n.
inhospitable
  unsociable 883 adj.
inhospitality
  unsociability 883 n.
inhuman
  (see **inhumanity**)
inhumanity
  inhumanity 898 n.
  wickedness 934 n.
inhumation
  interment 364 n.
inimical
  opposing 704 adj.
  inimical 881 adj.
inimitable
  unimitated 21 adj.
  supreme 34 adj.
iniquitous
  unjust 914 adj.
iniquity
  wickedness 934 n.
initial
  first 68 adj.
  sign 547 vb.
  initials 558 n.
initiate
  initiate 68 vb.
  train 534 vb.
  beginner 538 n.

initiation
  learning 536 n.
  rite 988 n.
initiative
  vigorousness 174 n.
inject
  infuse 303 vb.
injection
  insertion 303 n.
  therapy 658 n.
injudicious
  unwise 499 adj.
injunction
  precept 693 n.
  command 737 n.
  legal process 959 n.
injure
  harm, ill-treat
    645 vb.
  hurt 827 vb.
  do wrong 914 vb.
injurious
  harmful 645 adj.
  insolent 878 adj.
  detracting 926 adj.
injury
  wound 655 n.
  injustice 914 n.
injustice
  injustice 914 n.
  guilty act 936 n.
inkling
  hint 524 n.
inky
  black 428 adj.
inlaid
  ornamented 844 adj.
inland
  interior 224 adj.
in-laws
  family 11 n.
inlay
  line 227 vb.
  insert 303 vb.
  variegate 437 vb.
inlet
  gulf 345 n.
inmate
  resident 191 n.
inmost
  (see **innermost**)
inmost being
  interiority 224 n.
inn
  inn 192 n.
inner
  interior 224 adj.

inner being
essence 1 n.
inner man
spirit 447 n.
affections 817 n.
innermost
interior 224 adj.
innings
period 110 n.
innkeeper
caterer 633 n.
innocence
artlessness 699 n.
innocence 935 n.
purity 950 n.
acquittal 960 n.
innocent
ingenue 699 n.
innocent 935 n., adj.
good man 937 n.
(*see* innocence)
innocuous
salubrious 652 adj.
innocent 935 adj.
innovation
newness 126 n.
change 143 n.
innuendo
hint 524 n.
detraction 926 n.
innumerable
multitudinous
104 adj.
inoculate
implant 303 vb.
doctor 658 vb.
inoculation
prophylactic 658 n.
inoffensive
humble 872 adj.
innocent 935 adj.
in one piece
whole 52 adj.
inoperable
deadly 362 adj.
impracticable
470 adj.
inoperative
non-active 677 adj.
inopportune
inopportune 138
adj.
inorganic
inorganic 359 adj.
mindless 448 adj.
inpatient
sick person 651 n.

in preparation
incomplete 55 adj.
input
requirement 627 n.
inquest
inquest 364 n.
inquiry 459 n.
inquietude
changeableness
152 n.
inquire
inquire 459 vb.
study 536 vb.
inquirer
inquirer 459 n.
inquiry
inquiry 459 n.
experiment 461 n.
dissertation 591 n.
legal trial 959 n.
inquiry agent
detective 459 n.
inquisition
inquiry 459 n.
severity 735 n.
inquisitive
inquisitive 453 adj.
inquisitor
inquisitor 453 n.
questioner 459 n.
inroad
ingress 297 n.
impairment 655 n.
attack 712 n.
ins and outs
particulars 80 n.
insane
insane 503 adj.
(*see* insanity)
insanitary
insalubrious
653 adj.
insanity
insanity 503 n.
insatiability
rapacity 786 n.
gluttony 947 n.
insatiate
greedy 859 adj.
inscribe
record 548 vb.
write 586 vb.
inscription
commentary 520
n.
indication 547 n.
monument 548 n.

inscrutable
unintelligible
517 adj.
impassive 820 adj.
insect
vermin 365 n.
cad 938 n.
insecticide
poison 659 n.
insecurity
danger 661 n.
vulnerability 661 n.
insemination
propagation 164 n.
inseminator
producer 167 n.
insensate
insensible 375 adj.
thick-skinned
820 adj.
insensibility
insensibility 375 n.
non-wonder 865 n.
insensible
impassive 820 adj.
(*see* insensibility)
insensitive
thick-skinned
820 adj.
inseparable
firm-set 45 adj.
indivisible 52 adj.
concomitant 89 adj.
insert
load 193 vb.
insertion
piece 53 n.
insertion 303 n.
inset
insertion 303 n.
insert 303 vb.
inshore
near 200 adj.
inside
interiority 224 n.
imprisoned 747 adj.
inside job
plot 623 n.
inside out
inverted 221 adj.
insides
insides 224 n.
insidious
occult 523 adj.
deceiving 542 adj.
insight
intellect 447 n.

discrimination
463 n.
intuition 476 n.
imagination 513 n.
interpretation
520 n.
insignia
badge 547 n.
insignificance
unimportance
639 n.
insincerity
duplicity 541 n.
affectation 850 n.
flattery 925 n.
insinuate
imply 523 vb.
inform, hint 524 vb.
insinuate oneself
infiltrate 297 vb.
insinuation
insertion 303 n.
detraction 926 n.
insipid
tasteless 387 adj.
feeble 572 adj.
dull 840 adj.
insist
emphasize 532 vb.
compel 740 vb.
insistence (*see* insist)
insistent
assertive 532 adj.
forceful 571 adj.
requesting 761 adj.
insobriety
drunkenness 949 n.
insolence
insolence 878 n.
insoluble
impracticable
470 adj.
puzzling 517 adj.
insolvency
debt 803 n.
insolvency 805 n.
insomnia
restlessness 678 n.
insouciance
moral insensibility
820 n.
indifference 860 n.
insouciant
light-minded
456 adj.
inspection
inspection 438 n.

surveillance 457 n.
inquirer 459 n.
inspector
 estimator 480 n.
 manager 690 n.
inspiration
 causation 156 n.
 intuition 476 n.
 contrivance 623 n.
 excitation 821 n.
 revelation 975 n.
inspirational
 intuitive 476 adj.
 revelational
  975 adj.
inspire
 cheer 833 vb.
 (*see* inspiration)
inspired
 forceful 571 adj.
 revelational
  975 adj.
inspiring
 causal 156 adj.
 influential 178 adj.
inspirit
 animate 821 vb.
 cheer 833 vb.
instability
 changeableness
  152 n.
 excitability 822 n.
install
 auspicate 68 vb.
 commission 751 vb.
installation
 location 187 n.
 workshop 687 n.
instalment
 part 53 n.
 incompleteness
  55 n.
instance
 example 83 n.
 request 761 n.
instant
 brief span 114 n.
 instant 116 n.
 requesting 761 adj.
instantaneous
 instantaneous
  116 adj.
instant, be
 emphasize 532 vb.
in statu pupillari
 young 130 adj.
 subject 745 adj.

instead
 instead 150 adv.
instep
 foot 214 n.
instigation
 inducement 612 n.
instigator
 motivator 612 n.
instil
 infuse 303 vb.
instinct
 tendency 179 n.
 non-intellect 448 n.
 incogitance 450 n.
 intuition 476 n.
 habit 610 n.
 non-design 618 n.
instinctive
 involuntary 596 adj.
instincts
 affections 817 n.
institute
 auspicate 68 vb.
 cause 156 vb.
 academy 539 n.
institution
 academy 539 n.
 practice 610 n.
 rite 988 n.
institutionalism
 orthodoxism 976 n.
instruct
 (*see* instruction)
instruction
 information 524 n.
 teaching 534 n.
 command 737 n.
instructive
 informative 524 adj.
instructor
 teacher, trainer
  537 n.
instrument
 tool 630 n.
 agent 686 n.
 title-deed 767 n.
instrumental
 musical 412 adj.
 mechanical 630 adj.
 used 673 adj.
instrumentalist
 instrumentalist
  413 n.
instrumentality
 agency 173 n.
 instrumentality
  628 n.

instrumentation
 composition 56 n.
insubordination
 anarchy 734 n.
 disobedience 738 n.
insubstantial
 unreal 2 adj.
 insubstantial 4 adj.
 immaterial 320 adj.
 brittle 330 adj.
insufferable
 intolerable 827 adj.
insufficiency
 shortcoming 307 n.
 insufficiency 636 n.
insufficient
 (*see* insufficiency)
insular
 separate 46 adj.
 regional 184 adj.
 insular 349 adj.
insularity
 island 349 n.
 prejudice 481 n.
insulate
 set apart 46 vb.
insulation
 protection 660 n.
insult
 rudeness 885 n.
 indignity 921 n.
insuperable
 impracticable
  470 adj.
insupportable
 intolerable 827
  adj.
insurance
 calculation of
  chance 159 n.
 security 767 n.
insure
 prepare 669 vb.
 give security
  767 vb.
insurgent
 revolter 738 n.
insurmountable
 impracticable
  470 adj.
insurrection
 revolt 738 n.
insurrectional
 resisting 715 adj.
intact
 intact 52 adj.
 preserved 666 adj.

intaglio
 sculpture 554 n.
intake
 requirement 627 n.
 waste 634 n.
intangibility
 insubstantiality 4 n.
intangible
 immaterial 320 adj.
integer
 number 85 n.
 unit 88 n.
integral
 whole 52 adj.
 numerical element
  85 n.
integrate
 make complete
  54 vb.
integration
 combination 50 n.
 completeness 54 n.
 unity 88 n.
 association 706 n.
integrity
 virtue 933 n.
integument
 layer 207 n.
 skin 226 n.
intellect
 intellect 447 n.
intellectual
 mental 447 adj.
 intellectual 492 n.
intellectualism
 intellect 447 n.
intelligence
 secret service
  459 n.
 intelligence 498 n.
 news 529 n.
intelligent
 intelligent 498 adj.
intelligentsia
 intellectual 492 n.
intelligible
 semantic 514 adj.
 intelligible 516 adj.
 perspicuous
  567 adj.
intemperance
 intemperance
  943 n.
intemperate
 intemperate
  943 adj.
 drunken 949 adj.

intempestivity
irrelation 10 n.
intempestivity
138 n.
intend
predestine 155 vb.
mean 514 vb.
will 595 vb.
predetermine
608 vb.
desire 859 vb.
intense
great 32 n.
vigorous 174 adj.
intensification
increase 36 n.
aggravation 832 n.
intensify
enlarge 197 vb.
aggravate 832 vb.
intensity
degree 27 n.
greatness 32 n.
intent
attentive 455 adj.
resolute 599 adj.
(*see* intention)
intention
connotation 514 n.
intention 617 n.
plan 623 n.
intentional
volitional 595 adj.
intended 617 adj.
intentness
attention 455 n.
inter
inter 364 vb.
interaction
correlation 12 n.
interbreeding
mixture 43 n.
intercalation
interjection 231 n.
intercede
mediate 720 vb.
intercept
converge 293 vb.
obstruct 702 vb.
intercession
mediation 720 n.
deprecation 762 n.
intercessor
mediator 720 n.
interchange
correlation 12 n.

substitution 150 n.
interchange 151 n.,
vb.
interchangeability
equivalence 28 n.
intercommunicate
connect 45 vb.
intercommunication
bond 47 n.
contiguity 202 n.
information 524 n.
intercommunion
public worship
981 n.
interconnexion
correlation 12 n.
bond 47 n.
intercourse
coition 45 n.
sociality 882 n.
interdependence
correlation 12 n.
interdict
prohibition 757 n.
interest
relation 9 n.
increment 36 n.
product 164 n.
influence 178 n.
curiosity 453 n.
attract notice
455 vb.
importance 638 n.
gain 771 n.
interest 803 n.
impress 821 vb.
amuse 837 vb.
interested
inquisitive 453 adj.
selfish 932 adj.
interests
affairs 154 n.
interfere
counteract 182 vb.
meddle 678 vb.
obstruct 702 vb.
interference
(*see* interfere)
interfusion
mixture 43 n.
interim
lull 145 n.
interior
intrinsic 5 adj.
interiority 224 n.
inland 344 adj.
picture 553 n.

interjacence
interjacence 231 n.
interject
(*see* interjection)
interjection
interjection 231 n.
insertion 303 n.
allocution 583 n.
interlace
enlace 222 vb.
interlard
mix 43 vb.
put between 231 vb.
interleave
put between 231 vb.
interlineation
interjection 231 n.
interlock
correlate 12 n.
join 45 vb.
interlocking
correlative 12 adj.
complexity 61 n.
interlocution
interlocution 584 n.
interlocutor
interlocutor 584 n.
interloper
intruder 59 n.
interlude
lull 145 n.
stage play 594 n.
intermarriage
type of marriage
894 n.
intermeddle
meddle 678 vb.
intermediary
interjacent 231 adj.
mediator 720 n.
intermediate
middle 70 adj.
interjacent 231 adj.
interment
interment 364 n.
interminable
long 203 adj.
intermingle
mix 43 vb.
intermission
lull 145 n.
intermit
be discontinuous
72 vb.
intermittent
discontinuous
72 adj.

fitful 142 adj.
intermixture
mixture 43 n.
intern
imprison 747 vb.
internal
interior 224 adj.
international
comprehensive
52 adj.
unpossessed
774 adj.
sharing 775 adj.
internationalize
socialize 775 vb.
internecine
destructive 165 adj.
internee
interiority 224 n.
internment
detention 747 n.
interpellation
interrogation 459 n.
question 459 n.
interpenetration
interjacence 231 n.
interplay
correlation 12 n.
interchange 151 n.
interpolate
put between 231 vb.
interpolation
interjection 231 n.
interpose
put between 231 vb.
interpret
account for 158 vb.
interpret 520 vb.
interpretation
interpretation
520 n.
interpreter
interpreter 520 n.
inter-racial
ethnic 11 adj.
interregnum
interval 201 n.
anarchy 734 n.
interrelation
correlation 12 n.
interrogation
interrogation
459 n.
interrogative
inquiring 459 adj.
interrogator
questioner 459 n.

interrupt
  intrude 297 vb.
interrupter
  hinderer 702 n.
interruption
  discontinuity 72 n.
  intempestivity
    138 n.
  interval 201 n.
  hindrance 702 n.
intersection
  joint 45 n.
  access, road 624 n.
interspace
  interval 201 n.
intersperse
  put between 231 vb.
interstellar
  cosmic 321 n.
interstice
  gap 201 n.
interstitial
  interior 224 adj.
intertwine
  enlace 222 vb.
interval
  discontinuity 72 n.
  period 110 n.
  lull 145 n.
  interval 201 n.
intervene
  meddle 678 vb.
  mediate 720 vb.
intervention
  hindrance 702 n.
  mediation 720 n.
interview
  exam 459 n.
  interrogate 459 vb.
interviewer
  interlocutor 584 n.
interweave
  enlace 222 vb.
  put between 231 vb.
interworking
  agency 173 n.
intestine
  insides 224 n.
in the running
  contending 716 adj.
intimacy
  relation 9 n.
  coition 45 n.
  friendship 880 n.
  sociability 882 n.
intimate
  interior 224 adj.

knowing 490 adj.
  inform, hint 524 vb.
  indicate 547 vb.
  close friend 880 n.
intimidate
  frighten 854 vb.
  threaten 900 b.
intimidation
  intimidation 854 n.
intolerable
  intolerable 827 adj.
intolerance
  exclusion 57 n.
  prejudice 481 n.
  severity 735 n.
  prohibition 757 n.
intonation
  sound 398 n.
  voice 577 n.
intone
  sing 413 vb.
intoxicant
  poison 659 n.
intoxicate
  delight 826 vb.
intoxicated
  drunk 949 adj.
intoxication
  excitable state
    822 n.
  drunkenness 949 n.
intractability
  obstinacy 602 n.
intractable
  difficult 700 adj.
intransigence
  obstinacy 602 n.
intrench
  encroach 306 vb.
intrepidity
  courage 855 n.
intricacy
  complexity 61 n.
  convolution 251 n.
intricate
  difficult 700 adj.
  (see intricacy)
intrigant
  planner 623 n.
intrigue
  plot 623 n., vb.
  impress 821 vb.
  love affair 887 n.
intriguer
  slyboots 698 n.
intrinsic
  intrinsic 5 adj.

intrinsicality
  essence 1 n.
  intrinsicality 5 n.
introduce
  initiate 68 vb.
  precede 283 vb.
  insert 303 vb.
  befriend 880 vb.
introduction
  prelude 66 n.
  insertion 303 n.
  teaching 534 n.
introductory
  precursory 66 adj.
intromit
  insert 303 vb.
introspection
  meditation 449 n.
introspective
  thoughtful 449
    adj.
introversion
  interiority 224 n.
introverted
  intrinsic 5 adj.
intrude
  intrude 297 vb.
  meddle 678 vb.
intruder
  intruder 59 n.
  incomer 297 n.
intrusion
  inaptitude 25 n.
  (see intrude)
intrusive
  irrelative 10 adj.
  extraneous 59 adj.
intuition
  intuition 476 n.
  conjecture 512 n.
  spontaneity 609 n.
intuitive
  intuitive 476 adj.
intumescence
  expansion 197 n.
inundate
  overlie 226 vb.
  irrigate 341 vb.
  (see inundation)
inundation
  waterfall 350 n.
  redundance 637 n.
inure
  train 534 vb.
  habituate 610 vb.
inutility
  inutility 641 n.

invade
  irrupt 297 vb.
  attack 712 vb.
  wage war 718 vb.
invalid
  powerless 161 adj.
  weakling 163 n.
  sick person 651 n.
invalidate
  disable 161 vb.
  weaken 163 vb.
  confute 479 vb.
  abrogate 752 vb.
invalidism
  ill-health 651 n.
invaluable
  valuable 644 adj.
invariable
  characteristic 5 adj.
  uniform 16 adj.
  unchangeable
    153 adj.
  usual 610 adj.
invasion
  ingress 297 n.
  attack 712 n.
invective
  scurrility 899 n.
inveigh
  curse 899 vb.
inveigle
  ensnare 542 vb.
invent
  imagine 513 vb.
invention
  causation 156 n.
  discovery 484 n.
  untruth, fable 543 n.
inventiveness
  non-imitation 21 n.
  productiveness
    171 n.
  thought 449 n.
  imagination 513 n.
inventor
  producer 167 n.
  detector 484 n.
inventory
  list 87 n., vb.
  contents 193 n.
inversion
  inversion 221 n.
invert
  invert 221 vb.
invertebrate
  weak 163 adj.
  animal 365 n.

invest
 circumscribe
 232 vb.
 store 632 vb.
 besiege 712 vb.
 expend 806 vb.
investigation
 inquiry 459 n.
investigator
 inquirer 459 n.
 detective 459 n.
invest in
 purchase 792 vb.
investiture
 mandate 751 n.
investment
 (*see* invest)
investor
 creditor 802 n.
inveteracy
 tradition 127 n.
inveterate
 immemorial
 127 adj.
 habitual 610 adj.
invidious
 unpleasant 827 adj.
invigilate
 invigilate 457 vb.
invigilator
 keeper 749 n.
invigorate
 invigorate 174 vb.
 refresh 685 vb.
 animate 821 vb.
 cheer 833 vb.
invincible
 unbeaten 727 adj.
inviolate
 permanent 144 adj.
invisibility
 invisibility 444 n.
 disappearance
 446 n.
invitation
 inducement 612 n.
 offer 759 n.
 request 761 n.
 courteous act
 884 n.
invite
 be hospitable
 882 vb.
inviting
 accessible 289 adj.
 pleasurable
 826 adj.

invocation
 allocution 583 n.
 prayers 981 n.
invoice
 list 87 n.
 accounts 808 n.
invoke
 speak to 583 vb.
 entreat 761 vb.
involuntariness
 non-design 618 n.
involuntary
 involuntary 596 adj.
 compelling 740 adj.
involve
 be intrinsic 5 vb.
 bedevil 63 vb.
 make likely
 471 vb.
 imply 523 vb.
 accuse 928 vb.
involved
 convoluted 251 adj.
 imperspicuous
 568 adj.
involvement
 complexity 61 n.
 affairs 154 n.
 participation 775 n.
 feeling 818 n.
invulnerable
 invulnerable
 660 adj.
inward
 intrinsic 5 adj.
 interior 224 adj.
 incoming 297 adj.
inward-looking
 intrinsic 5 adj.
inwrought
 intrinsic 5 adj.
 interior 224 adj.
ion
 element 319 n.
I.O.U.
 title deed 767 n.
irascibility
 quarrelsomeness
 709 n.
 irascibility 892 n.
irate
 angry 891 adj.
irenic
 pacificatory
 719 adj.
irenics
 irenics 719 n.

iridescence
 variegation 437 n.
iridescent
 iridescent 437 adj.
iris
 eye 438 n.
irk
 bore 838 n.
 be tedious 838 vb.
irksome (*see* irk)
iron
 strength 162 vb.
 smoother 258 n.
 hardness 326 n.
 (*see* iron out)
iron curtain
 exclusion 57 n.
iron heel
 brute force 735 n.
ironical
 figurative 519 adj.
 derisive 851 adj.
ironist
 humorist 839 n.
 affector 850 n.
iron out
 unravel 62 vb.
 facilitate 701 vb.
iron ration
 insufficiency 636 n.
 fasting 946 n.
irons
 supporter 218 n.
 fetter 748 n.
irons in the fire
 business 622 n.
irony
 affectation 850 n.
 ridicule 851 n.
irradiation
 light 417 n.
 lighting 420 n.
irrational
 illogical 477 adj.
irreconcilability
 irrelation 10 n.
 contrariety 14 n.
irreconcilable
 opponent 705 n.
 malcontent 829 n.
 inimical 881 adj.
irrecoverable
 lost 772 adj.
irredeemable
 unpromising
 853 adj.
 impenitent 940 adj.

irredentism
 patrotism 901 n.
irredentist
 patriot 901 n.
irreducible
 simple 44 adj.
 unchangeable
 153 adj.
irrefutable
 undisputed 473 adj.
irregular
 multiform 82 adj.
 distorted 246 adj.
 soldier 722 n.
 wrong 914 adj.
 (*see* irregularity)
irregularity
 non-uniformity
 17 n.
 unconformity 84 n.
 fitfulness 142 n.
 illegality 954 n.
irrelation
 irrelation 10 n.
irrelevance
 irrelevance 10 n.
 unimportance
 639 n.
irrelevant
 misplaced 118 adj.
irreligion
 irreligion 974 n.
 impiety 980 n.
irremediable
 bad 645 adj.
 harmful 645 adj.
irremovable
 fixed 153 adj.
irreplaceable
 important 638 adj.
 valuable 644 adj.
irrepressible
 wilful 602 adj.
 independent
 744 adj.
 lively 819 adj.
irreproachable
 perfect 646 adj.
 guiltless 935 adj.
irresistible
 strong 162 adj.
 influential 178 adj.
 compelling
 740 adj.
irresolute
 irresolute 601 adj.
 choiceless 606 adj.

irresponsible
capricious 604 adj.
lawless 954 adj.
irretrievable
lost 772 adj.
irreverence
non-wonder 865 n.
impiety 980 n.
irreversible
unchangeable
153 adj.
progressive 285 adj.
necessary 596 adj.
irrevocable
necessary 596 adj.
irrigable
dry 342 n.
irrigate
irrigate 341 vb.
irritable
irascible 892 adj.
irritant
excitant 821 n.
irritate
give pain 377 vb.
aggravate 832 vb.
enrage 891 vb.
irritation
painfulness 827 n.
resentment 891 n.
irrupt
irrupt 297 vb.
irruption
ingress 297 n.
attack 712 n.
island
island 349 n.
seclusion 883 n.
islander
dweller 191 n.
isle (*see* **island**)
ism
creed 485 n.
isolate
set apart 46 vb.
seclude 883 vb.
isolated
alone 88 adj.
isolation
irrelation 10 n.
separation 46 n.
unity 88 n.
seclusion 883 n.
isolationist
independent
744 adj.
solitary 883 n.

issue
kinsman 11 n.
effect 157 n.
posterity 170 n.
outflow 298 n.
emerge 298 vb.
topic 452 n.
publish 528 vb.
completion 725 n.
mint 797 vb.
litigation 959 n.
isthmus
narrowness 206 n.
land 344 n.
bridge 624 n.
italic
lettering 586 n.
italicize
emphasize 532 vb.
itch
attraction 291 n.
formication 378 n.
curiosity 453 n.
skin disease 651 n.
desire 859 n.
item
adjunct 40 n.
part 53 n.
itemize
list 87 vb.
items
particulars 80 n.
list 87 n.
iterate
repeat 106 vb.
iterative
repeated 106 adj.
itinerant
travelling 267 adj.
itinerary
itinerary 267 n.
ivory
white thing 427 n.
ivory tower
seclusion 883 n.
izzat
prestige 866 n.

J

jab
knock 279 n.
wound 655 n.
jabber
chatter 581 n.
jack
lifter 310 n.

jackal
dependant 742 n.
toady 879 n.
noxious animal
904 n.
jacket
skin 226 n.
tunic 228 n.
Jack-in-office
official 690 n.
insolent person
878 n.
Jack-in-the-box
inexpectation
508 n.
jackpot
acquisition 771 n.
jack up
elevate 310 vb.
jade
saddle-horse 273 n.
greenness 432 n.
fatigue 684 vb.
gem 844 n.
sate 863 vb.
loose woman 952
n.
jadedness
fatigue 684 n.
satiety 863 n.
jagged
rough 259 adj.
jail
gaol 748 n.
jailer
gaoler 749 n.
jam
affix 45 vb.
crowd 74 n.
sweet 392 n.
predicament 700 n.
jamb
pillar 218 n.
jammy
viscid 354 adj.
jangle
rasp 407 vb.
discord 411 vb.
janitor
janitor 264 n.
japan
coat 226 vb.
resin 357 n.
black pigment
428 n.
jape
witticism 839 n.

jar
disagree 25 vb.
vessel 194 n.
rasp 407 vb.
discord 411 vb.
dissension 709 n.
displease 827 vb.
jargon
unmeaningness
515 n.
slang 560 n.
jasper
variegate 437 vb.
jaundice
yellowness 433 n.
bias 481 vb.
jaundiced
biased 481 adj.
melancholic
834 adj.
jaunt
land travel 267 n.
jaunty
cheerful 833 adj.
impertinent 878 adj.
javelin
spear 723 n.
missile weapon
723 n.
jaw
be loquacious
581 vb.
chatter 581 n.
(*see* **jaws**)
jaw-breaker
word 559 n.
jaws
maw 194 n.
orifice 263 n.
jaywalker
bungler 697 n.
jazz
music 412 n.
jealous
resentful 891 adj.
(*see* **jealousy**)
jealousy
imitation 20 n.
contention 716 n.
jealousy 911 n.
jeans
trousers 228 n.
jeep
automobile 274 n.
jeer
ridicule 851 vb.
despise 922 vb.

JEJ

jejune
lean 206 adj.
feeble 572 adj.

jellyfish
weakling 163 n.
coward 856 n.

jeopardy
danger 661 n.

jerk
move 265 vb.
impulse 279 n.
agitate 318 vb.

jerkiness
fitfulness 142 n.

jerks, the
spasm 318 n.

jersey
textile 222 n.
vest 228 n.

jest
witticism 839 n.

jester
humorist 839 n.

jesuitry
sophistry 477 n.

jet
propellant 287 n.
outflow 298 n.
stream 350 n.
black thing 428 n.

jetsam
derelict 779 n.

jettison
eject 300 vb.
not retain 779 vb.

jetty
projection 254 n.
shelter 662 n.

jewel
exceller 644 n.
gem 844 n.

jewellery
jewellery 844 n.

jib
prow 237 n.
sail 275 n.
deviate 282 vb.
avoid 620 vb.

jibe
satirize 851 vb.
indignity 921 n.

jiffy
instant 116 n.

jig
dance 837 n.

jiggle
agitate 318 vb.

JOI

jilt
tergiversator 603 n.
relinquish 621 vb.

jim-jams
alcoholism 949 n.

jingle
resonance 404 n.
doggerel 593 n.

jingler
poet 593 n.

jingoism
bellicosity 718 n.
boasting 877 n.

jink
avoid 620 vb.

Jinn
demon 970 n.

jitterbug
dance 837 n., vb.

jitters
agitation 318 n.
nervousness 854 n.

jive
dance 837 n., vb.

job
job, function 622 n.
undertaking 672 n.
hard task 700 n.
foul play 930 n.

jobbery
improbity 930 n.

jockey
rider 268 n.

jockeyship
trickery 542 n.

jocularity
merriment 833 n.

jog
walk 267 vb.
agitate 318 vb.
gesticulate 547 vb.

jog-trot
gait 265 n.

joie de vivre
cheerfulness 833 n.

join
join 45 vb.
agglutinate 48 vb.
bring together
74 vb.
meet 295 vb.

joinder
joinder 45 n.

join in
cooperate 706 vb.
participate 775 vb.
be sociable 882 vb.

JOT

join issue
argue 475 vb.

joint
joint 45 n.
angularity 247 n.
meat 301 n.
corporate 708 adj.

jointness
joint possession
775 n.

joint, out of
orderless 61 adj.

joint-stock
corporate 708 adj.

jointure
dower 777 n.

joist
beam 218 n.

joke
witticism 839 n.

joker
nonconformist 84 n.
humorist 839 n.

jollification
revel 837 n.

jollity
merriment 833 n.

jolly
navy man 722 n.
gay 833 adj.

jolt
be rough 259 vb.
move slowly
278 vb.
impulse 279 n.
inexpectation
508 vb.

Jonah
moper 834 n.

jorum
bowl 194 n.

josh
ridicule 851 vb.

joss
idol 982 n.

joss-house
temple 990 n.

joss-stick
scent 396 n.

jostle
be contiguous
202 vb.
obstruct 702 vb.

jot
small quantity 33 n.

jot down
record 548 vb.

JUD

jottings
reading matter
589 n.

journal
chronology 117 n.
the press, journal
528 n.
record 548 n.
biography 590 n.
account book 808 n.

journalese
neology 560 n.

journalism
publicity 528 n.

journalist
publicizer 328 n.
author 589 n.

journalize
account 808 vb.

journey
travel 267 vb.

journeyman
artisan 686 n.

joust
contest, duel 716 n.

jouster
combatant 722 n.

joviality
merriment 833 n.

joy
joy 824 n.

joyful, joyous
happy 824 adj.
gay 833 adj.

joy-ride
easy thing 701 n.

jubilant
jubilant 833 adj.

jubilate
rejoice 835 vb.
celebrate 876 vb.

jubilation
(see jubilate)

jubilee
period 110 n.
anniversary 141 n.
rejoicing 835 n.

judge
judge 957 n.
(see judgement)

judge and jury
tribunal 956 n.

judgement
discrimination
463 n.
judgement 480 n.
opinion 485 n.

551

decree 737 n.
legal trial 959 n.
judgement day
future state 124 n.
judgement seat
tribunal 956 n.
judicature
jurisdiction 955 n.
judicial
judicial 480 adj.
curial 956 adj.
judiciary
jurisdictional
955 adj.
judicious
discriminating
463 adj.
judicial 480 adj.
wise 498 adj.
judo
wrestling 716 n.
jug
vessel 194 n.
juggle
sleight 542 n.
juggler
conjuror 545 n.
slyboots 698 n.
jugglery (see juggle)
juice
fluid 335 n.
moisture 341 n.
juicy
fluidal 335 adj.
humid 341 adj.
pulpy 356 adj.
savoury 390 adj.
ju-jitsu
wrestling 716 n.
juke box
gramophone 414 n.
julep
liquor 301 n.
sweet 392 n.
jumble
medley 43 n.
confusion 61 n.
jumble 63 vb.
jump
interval 201 n.
spurt 277 n.
leap 312 n., vb.
agitation 318 n.
jump a claim
appropriate 786 vb.
jump at
be willing 597 vb.

desire 859 vb.
jumper
vest 228 n.
jumper 312 n.
**jump on the
bandwagon**
do likewise 20 vb.
conform 83 vb.
jumps
agitation 318 n.
nervousness 854 n.
jump the gun
be early 135 vb.
jump the queue
precede 283 vb.
jumpy
agitated 318 adj.
nervous 854 adj.
junction
junction 45 n.
road, railroad
624 n.
juncture
juncture 8 n.
occasion, crisis
137 n.
jungle
confusion 61 n.
wood 366 n.
jungliness
ill-breeding 847 n.
jungly
arboreal 366 adj.
junior
inferior 35 n.
young 130 adj.
youngster 132 n.
junk
sailing-ship 275 n.
rubbish 641 n.
junket
milk product 301 n.
revel 837 vb.
junta, junto
party 708 n.
juridical
judicial 480 adj.
jurisdictional
955 adj.
jurisconsult
jurist 958 n.
jurisdiction
authority 733 n.
jurisdiction 955 n.
jurisprudence
jurisprudence
953 n.

jurist
jurist 958 n.
juror (see juryman)
jury
estimator 480 n.
jury 957 n.
juryman
jury 957 n.
jussive
commanding
737 adj.
just
just 913 adj.
disinterested
931 adj.
legal 953 adj.
just cause
vindication 927 n.
justice
justice 913 n.
probity 929 n.
judge 957 n.
justiciable
accusable 928 adj.
jurisdictional
955 adj.
justifiable
deserving 915 adj.
vindicable 927 adj.
justification
pretext 614 n.
vindication 927 n.
justify
demonstrate
478 vb.
(see justification)
jut
jut 254 vb.
jute
fibre 208 n.
textile 222 n.
jutting
salient 254 adj.
juvenile
young 130 adj.
infantine 132 adj.
immature 670 adj.
juvenilia
reading matter
589 n.
juxtapose
juxtapose 202 vb.

K

kailyard
dialectical 560 adj.

kale
vegetable 301 n.
kaleidoscope
multiformity 82 n.
changeable thing
152 n.
variegation 437 n.
optical device
442 n.
kalends
date 108 n.
kaput
defeated 728 adj.
karma
fate 596 n.
katatonia
psychopathy 503 n.
keel
stabilizer 153 n.
base 214 n.
ship 275 n.
keelhaul
punish 963 vb.
keen
sharp 256 adj.
lament 836 n., vb.
desiring 859 adj.
keener
funeral 364 n.
weeper 836 n.
keen-eyed
seeing 438 adj.
keen on
enamoured 887 adj.
keep
go on 146 vb.
dwell 192 vb.
provisions 301 n.
provide 633 vb.
fort 713 n.
defend 713 vb.
celebrate 876 vb.
keep accounts
number 86 vb.
keep an eye
safeguard 660 vb.
keep away
avoid 620 vb.
keep back
keep secret 525 vb.
keeper
surveillance 457 n.
protector 660 n.
keeper 749 n.
keep faith
observe faith
768 vb.

keep holy
celebrate 876 vb.
sanctify 979 vb.
keep in
imprison 747 vb.
retain 778 vb.
keep in hand
store 632 vb.
not use 674 vb.
keep in step
synchronize 123 vb.
keep on
go on 146 vb.
keep oneself to oneself
be unsocial 883 vb.
keep order
safeguard 660 vb.
keep out
exclude 57 vb.
restrain 747 vb.
keepsake
reminder 505 n.
keep time
time 117 vb.
synchronize 123 vb.
keep up with
be equal 28 vb.
keep up with the Joneses
afford 800 vb.
keg
vat 194 n.
kelpie
demon 970 n.
kennel
group 74 n.
stable 192 n.
lock-up 748 n.
kenning
name 561 n.
kept woman
kept woman 952 n.
kerb
limit 236 n.
road 624 n.
kerchief
headgear 228 n.
kernel
essential part 5 n.
centrality 225 n.
kerosene
oil 357 n.
fuel 385 n.
kersey
textile 222 n.

ketch
sailing-ship 275 n.
kettle
cauldron 194 n.
heater 383 n.
kettle of fish
predicament 700 n.
key
crucial 137 adj.
influential 178 adj.
opener 263 n.
musical note 410 n.
interpretation 520 n.
translation 520 n.
important 638 adj.
keyboard
piano 414 n.
keyed up
expectant 507 adj.
keyhole
orifice 263 n.
key man
bigwig 638 n.
keynote
prototype 23 n.
musical note 410 n.
chief thing 638 n.
keystone
summit 213 n.
supporter 218 n.
khaki
uniform 228 n.
brownness 430 n.
kibbutz
farm 370 n.
joint possession 775 n.
kibe
ulcer 651 n.
kick
kick 279 vb.
recoil 280 n., vb.
propulsion 287 n.
resist 715 vb.
disobey 738 vb.
joy 824 n.
kick back
retaliate 714 vb.
kick-off
start 68 n.
kickshaw
bauble 639 n.
kid
child 132 n.
youngling 132 n.
befool 542 vb.

kidder
deceiver 545 n.
kidding
deception 542 n.
kid gloves
cleanness 648 n.
lenity 736 n.
kidnap
take away 786 vb.
steal 788 vb.
kidnapper
taker 786 n.
thief 789 n.
kidney
sort 77 n.
meat 301 n.
kill
kill 362 vb.
success, victory 727 n.
killer
killer 362 n.
murderer 362 n.
ruffian 904 n.
killing
deadly 362 adj.
laborious 682 adj.
kill-joy
hinderer 702 n.
ascetic 944 n.
kill time
amuse oneself 837 vb.
kill with kindness
pet 889 vb.
kiln
furnace 383 n.
kilt
skirt 228 n.
fold 261 vb.
kimono
informal dress 228 n.
kin
kinsman 11 n.
breed 77 n.
kind
sort 77 n.
benevolent 897 adj.
kindergarten
nonage 130 n.
school 539 n.
kindheartedness
benevolence 897 n.
kindle
cause 156 vb.

kindle 381 vb.
feel 818 vb.
kindling
fuel 385 n.
kindness
love 887 n.
benevolence 897 n.
kindred
relative 9 adj.
consanguinity 11 n.
kinsman 11 n.
kinetic
dynamic 160 adj.
kinetics
motion 265 n.
king
sovereign 741 n.
kingdom
polity 733 n.
kingdom come
future state 124 n.
kingly
ruling 733 adj.
worshipful 866 adj.
noble 868 adj.
king-maker
director 690 n.
king-pin
bigwig 638 n.
kingship
government 733 n.
magistrature 733 n.
kink
coil 251 n.
eccentricity 503 n.
kinsfolk
kinsman 11 n.
kinship
relation 9 n.
consanguinity 11 n.
similarity 18 n.
parentage 169 n.
kinsman
kinsman 11 n.
kiosk
shop 796 n.
kipper
dry 342 vb.
season 388 vb.
preserve 666 vb.
kirk
church 990 n.
kirk session
synod 985 n.
kirtle
skirt 228 n.

kismet
  fate 596 n.
kiss
  touch 378 vb.
  caress 889 vb.
kissable
  personable 841 adj.
kit
  accumulation 74 n.
  viol 414 n.
  equipment 630 n.
kitbag
  bag 194 n.
kitchen
  cookery 301 n.
  heater 383 n.
kitchener
  furnace 383 n.
kitchen garden
  farm 370 n.
kite
  airship 276 n.
  bird of prey 365 n.
  cleaner 648 n.
kite-flying
  empiricism 461 n.
kitten
  youngling 132 n.
  cat 365 n.
kittenish
  infantine 132 adj.
  amused 837 adj.
kitty
  store 632 n.
  joint possession
    775 n.
klaxon
  megaphone 400 n.
kleptomania
  mania 503 n.
  thievishness 788 n.
knack
  habit 610 n.
  aptitude 694 n.
knacker
  killer 362 n.
knacker's yard
  slaughter-house
    362 n.
knapsack
  bag 194 n.
knave
  knave 938 n.
knavery
  improbity 930 n.
knavish
  (*see* **knavery**)

knead
  efform 243 vb.
  soften 327 vb.
  rub 333 vb.
knee
  joint 45 n.
  leg 267 n.
knee-deep
  deep 211 adj.
knee-high
  dwarfish 196 adj.
kneel
  stoop 311 vb.
  be servile 879 vb.
  show respect 920 vb.
kneeler
  cushion 218 n.
  church utensil
    990 n.
knees
  seat 218 n.
knell
  ruin 165 n.
  obsequies 364 n.
  lament 836 n.
  condemnation
    961 n.
  (*see* **finality**)
knickerbockers
  breeches 228 n.
knickers
  breeches 228 n.
  underwear 228 n.
knick-knack
  bauble 639 n.
  finery 844 n.
knife
  cut 46 vb.
  sharp edge 256 n.
knife-edge
  narrowness 206 n.
knight
  rider 268 n.
  cavalry 722 n.
  brave person 855 n.
  dignify 866 vb.
  gentleman 929 n.
knight-errant
  crank 504 n.
  visionary 513 n.
  defender 713 n.
  combatant 722 n.
  philanthropist
    901 n.
knight-errantry
  disinterestedness
    931 n.

knightly
  courageous 855
    adj.
  courteous 884 adj.
knight's move
  obliquity 220 n.
knit
  tie 45 vb.
  weave 222 vb.
knitting
  needlework 844 n.
knob
  handle 218 n.
  swelling 253 n.
knobbly
  rough 259 adj.
knock
  knock 279 n.
  propulsion 287 n.
  bang 402 n.
knock-about
  dramatic 594 adj.
  ridiculousness
    849 n.
knock down
  demolish 165 vb.
  fell 311 vb.
knock-down
arguments
  confutation 479 n.
knocker
  hammer 279 n.
  detractor 926 n.
knock off
  cease 145 vb.
knock out
  render insensible
    375 vb.
knock-out
  exceller 644 n.
  victory 727 n.
knot
  tie 45 vb.
  ligature 47 n.
  complexity 61 n.
  crowd, band 74 n.
  long measure 203 n.
  solid body 324 n.
  garden 370 n.
knotted
  rough 259 adj.
knotty
  difficult 700 adj.
knotty point
  enigma 530 n.
knout
  scourge 964 n.

know
  know 490 vb.
  understand 516
    vb.
  befriend 880 vb.
know-all
  doctrinaire 473 n.
  wiseacre 500 n.
  vain person 873 n.
know-how
  means 629 n.
  skill 694 n.
knowing
  cunning 698 adj.
knowledge
  knowledge 490 n.
knowledgeable
  instructed 490 adj.
known as
  named 561 adj.
know-nothing
  ignoramus 493 n.
know one's place
  conform 83 vb.
  be modest 874 vb.
know what's what
  discriminate
    463 vb.
  be wise 498 vb.
knuckle
  joint 45 n.
knuckle-duster
  club 723 n.
knuckle under
  knuckle under
    721 vb.
kohl
  cosmetic 843 n.
kolkhoz
  farm 370 n.
  joint possession
    775 n.
kosher
  edible 301 adj.
  ritual 988 adj.
koumiss
  milk 301 n.
kowtow
  be servile 879 vb.
  show respect
    920 vb.
kraal
  dwelling 192 n.
kudos
  approbation 923 n.
kulakism
  sedition 738 n.

L

laager
 fort 713 n.
label
 label 547 n.
labial
 (*see* speech sound)
laboratory
 workshop 687 n.
laborious
 industrious 678 adj.
 laborious 682 adj.
 difficult 700 adj.
labour
 obstetrics 164 n.
 emphasize 532 vb.
 job 622 n.
 labour 682 n.
 personnel 686 n.
 hard task 700 n.
labour camp
 compulsion 740 n.
laboured
 inelegant 576 adj.
 matured 669 adj.
labourer
 producer 167 n.
 worker 686 n.
labour force
 personnel 686 n.
labouring
 in difficulties
  700 adj.
labour of love
 voluntary work
  597 n.
labour-saving
 leisurely 681 adj.
 wieldy 701 adj.
 economical 814 adj.
labour under
 be in a state 7 vb.
labyrinth
 meandering 251 n.
 enigma 530 n.
lac
 resin 357 n.
lace
 mix 43 vb.
 tie 45 vb.
 network, textile
  222 n.
 needlework 844 n.
lacerate
 rend 46 vb.
 wound 655 vb.

laches
 negligence 458 n.
 dutilessness 918 n.
lack
 deficit 55 n.
 shortcoming 307 n.
 scarcity 636 n.
 imperfection 647 n.
lackadaisical
 indifferent 860 adj.
lackey
 dependant 742 n.
 domestic 742 n.
lacking
 absent 190 adj.
 deficient 307 adj.
lack-lustre
 colourless 426 adj.
 dejected 834 adj.
laconic
 concise 569 adj.
lacquer
 facing 226 n.
 resin 357 n.
lactescence
 semitransparency
  424 n.
 whiteness 427 n.
lacuna
 interval 201 n.
 opening 263 n.
lad
 youngster 132 n.
ladder
 disjunction 46 n.
 series 71 n.
 ascent 308 n.
 means of escape
  667 n.
lade
 load 193 vb.
laden
 full 54 adj.
ladies' man
 lover 887 n.
lading
 contents 193 n.
 gravity 322 n.
ladle
 ladle 194 n.
lady
 woman 373 n.
 spouse 894 n.
Lady Bountiful
 benefactor 903 n.
lady-killer
 libertine 952 n.

ladylike
 well-bred 848 adj.
lag
 be late 136 vb.
 slowness 278 n.
 follow 284 vb.
 fall short 307 vb.
 offender 904 n.
laggard
 lazy 679 adj.
lagoon
 gulf 345 n.
 lake 346 n.
laid up
 sick 651 adj.
 disused 674 adj.
lair
 dwelling 192 n.
 refuge 662 n.
laisser faire
 be lax 734 vb.
 freedom 744 n.
laity
 laity 987 n.
lake
 lake 346 n.
lake-dwelling
 lacustrine 346 adj.
lama
 priest 986 n.
lamb
 youngling 132 n.
 reproduce itself
  164 vb.
 sheep 365 n.
 innocent 935 n.
lambent
 luminous 417 adj.
lame
 disable 161 vb.
 crippled 163 adj.
 impair 655 vb.
lame dog
 weakling 163 n.
 unlucky person
  731 n.
lament
 regret 830 vb.
 lament 836 n., vb.
 disapprove 924 vb.
lamentable
 bad 645 adj.
lamentation
 obsequies 364 n.
 lamentation 836 n.
lamina
 lamina 207 n.

lamination
 stratification 207 n.
lamp
 lamp 420 n.
lampoon
 satire 851 n.
 calumny 926 n.
lampooner
 humorist 839 n.
lamp-post
 high structure
  209 n.
 stand 218 n.
lance
 pierce 263 vb.
 spear 723 n.
lancer
 soldiery 722 n.
 cavalry 722 n.
lancet
 sharp point 256 n.
 perforator 263 n.
land
 region 184 n.
 land 295 vb.
 land 344 n.
 lands 777 n.
land-bridge
 bridge 624 n.
landed
 territorial 344 adj.
 proprietary
  777 adj.
landes
 plain 348 n.
landfall
 arrival 295 n.
landholder
 owner 776 n.
landing
 vertex 213 n.
 arrival 295 n.
 descent 309 n.
landing ground
 air travel 271 n.
landlady
 owner 776 n.
land-locked
 interior 224 adj.
 inland 344 adj.
 lacustrine 346 adj.
landlord
 caterer 633 n.
 owner 776 n.
landmark
 spectacle 445 n.
 signpost 547 n.

land-mass
region 184 n.

landowner
owner 776 n.

lands
farm 370 n.
lands 777 n.

landscape
spectacle 445 n.
picture 553 n.

landslide
revolution 149 n.
ruin 165 n.

lane
street 192 n.
route, path 624 n.

language
language 557 n.
dialect 560 n.
speech 579 n.

languid
feeble 572 adj.
(*see* **languish, languor**)

languish
be weak 163 vb.
be ill 651 vb.
be fatigued 684 vb.
be dejected 834 vb.

languor
weakness 163 n.
sluggishness 679 n.
fatigue 684 n.

lank
long 203 adj.

lanky
long 203 adj.
tall 209 adj.

lantern
lamp 420 n.

lanyard
cable 47 n.

Laodicean
moderate 625 n.
indifferent 860 adj.

lap
period 110 n.
seat 218 n.
enclose 235 vb.
outstrip 277 vb.
drink 301 vb.
circuition 314 n.
moisten 341 vb.
pet 889 vb.

lapel
fold 261 n.

lapidary
funereal 364 adj.
engraver 556 n.

lapis lazuli
blueness 435 n.
gem 844 n.

lapse
elapse 111 vb.
deviation 282 n.
deteriorate 655 vb.
be wicked 934 vb.

lapsed
irreligious 974 adj.

lapse of time
course of time 111 n.

lapsus calami
solecism 565 n.

lap up
absorb 299 vb.

larboard
sinistrality 242 n.

larceny
stealing 788 n.

lard
cook 301 vb.
fat 357 n.

larder
provisions 301 n.
storage 632 n.

large
great 32 adj.
extensive 183 adj.
large 195 adj.

large, at
escaped 667 adj.
free 744 adj.

large-scale
large 195 adj.

largesse
liberality 813 n.

lariat
halter 47 n.

lark
climber 308 n.
vocalist 413 n.
revel 837 n.

larrup
spank 963 vb.

larva
youngling 132 n.

larynx
air-pipe 353 n.
voice 577 n.

lasciviousness
unchastity 951 n.

lash
tie 45 vb.
stimulant 174 n.
filament 208 n.
incite 612 vb.
animate 821 vb.
flog 963 vb.
scourge 964 n.

lash out
be violent 176 vb.

lassitude
fatigue 684 n.

lasso
halter 47 n.
missile weapon 723 n.

last
mould 23 n.
ending 69 adj.
stay 144 vb.

last ditcher
opinionist 602 n.

lasting
lasting 113 adj.

last lap
end 69 n.

last minute
lateness 136 n.
crisis 137 n.

last-minute
hasty 680 adj.

last post
obsequies 364 n.
call 547 n.

last resort
refuge 662 n.

last rites
obsequies 364 n.

last straw
redundance 637 n.
annoyance 827 n.

last things
finality 69 n.

last touch
completion 725 n.

last word
modernism 126 n.

last words
valediction 296 n.

latch
fastening 47 n.

late
former 125 adj.
vespertine 129 adj.
late 136 adj.
ill-timed 138 adj.
slow 278 adj.

dead 361 adj.

late-comer
lateness 136 n.

latency
inertness 175 n.
invisibility 444 n.
latency 523 n.

lateness
lateness 136 n.

latent
(*see* **latency**)

laterality
laterality 239 n.

latest
present 121 adj.

latest, the
modernism 126 n.
fashion 848 n.

lath
lamina 207 n.
strip 208 n.

lathe
rotator 315 n.

lather
lubricant 334 n.
bubble 355 n.
clean 648 vb.

latitude
region 184 n.
breadth 205 n.
scope 744 n.

latitude and longitude
bearings 186 n.
coordinate 465 n.

latrine
latrine 649 n.

latter-day
modern 126 adj.

lattice
network 222 n.
window 263 n.

laud
praise 923 vb.
worship 981 vb.

laudable
approvable 923 adj.

laudanum
anaesthetic 375 n.

laudatory
approving 923 adj.

laugh
be cheerful 833 vb.
laughter 835 n.

laughable
ridiculous 849 adj.

laughing matter
  laughter 835 n.
laughing-stock
  laughing-stock
  851 n.
laughter
  laughter 835 n.
  festivity 837 n.
launch
  initiate 68 vb.
  navigate 269 vb.
  ship, boat 275 n.
  propel 287 vb.
launch out
  be diffuse 570 vb.
launch out at
  attack 712 vb.
launder
  clean 648 vb.
laundress
  cleaner 648 n.
laundry
  ablution 648 n.
laurels
  trophy 729 n.
lava
  rock 344 n.
  ash 381 n.
lavatory
  ablution 648 n.
  latrine 649 n.
lavender
  scent 396 n.
  prophylactic 658
  n.
lavish
  liberal 813 adj.
  prodigal 815 adj.
law
  rule 81 n.
  necessity 596 n.
  habit 610 n.
  decree 737 n.
  compulsion 740 n.
  law 953 n.
law-abiding
  peaceful 717 adj.
  obedient 739 adj.
lawbreaker
  offender 904 n.
lawbreaking
  lawbreaking
  954 n., adj.
law-court
  law-court 956 n.
lawful
  legal 953 adj.

law-giver
  director 690 n.
  legislation 953 n.
lawless
  anarchic 734 adj.
  lawless 954 adj.
law-making
  legislation 953 n.
lawn
  textile 222 n.
  garden 370 n.
laws
  polity 733 n.
lawsuit
  litigation 959 n.
lawyer
  lawyer 958 n.
lax
  weak 163 adj.
  (see laxity)
laxative
  cathartic 658 n.
laxity
  negligence 458 n.
  laxity 734 n.
  lenity 736 n.
  non-observance
  769 n.
lay
  reproduce itself
  164 vb.
  assuage 177 vb.
  place 187 vb.
  vocal music 412
  n.
  gamble 618 vb.
  unskilled 695 adj.
  laical 987 adj.
lay aside
  disuse 674 vb.
lay bare
  disclose 526 vb.
lay-by
  stable 192 n.
lay by
  store 632 vb.
lay down
  let fall 311 vb.
  suppose 512 vb.
lay down the law
  dogmatize 473 vb.
  decree 737 vb.
layer
  layer 207 n.
  gambler 618 n.
layette
  clothing 228 n.

lay figure
  insubstantial thing
  4 n.
  mould 23 n.
lay in
  store 632 vb.
lay low
  fell 311 vb.
layman
  ignorance 491 n.
  layman 987 n.
lay off
  dismiss 300 vb.
lay oneself open
  be liable 180 vb.
lay open
  uncover 229 vb.
lay out
  flatten 216 vb.
  inter 364 vb.
  expend 806 vb.
lay-out
  arrangement 62 n.
lays
  poem 593 n.
lay the foundations
  auspicate 68 vb.
  prepare 669 vb.
lay to
  navigate 269 vb.
lay under
  contribution
  levy 786 vb.
lay up
  store 632 vb.
  disuse 674 vb.
lay waste
  lay waste 165 vb.
laze
  be inactive 679 vb.
laziness
  sluggishness 679 n.
lazy (*see* laziness)
lea
  grassland 348 n.
leach
  drench 341 vb.
  purify 648 vb.
leachy
  porous 263 adj.
lead
  vantage 34 n.
  halter 47 n.
  come before
  64 vb.
  sailing aid 269 n.
  precede 283 vb.

gauge 465 n.
  hint 524 n.
  print-type 578 n.
  actor 594 n.
  direct 689 vb.
leaded
  spaced 201 adj.
leaden
  weighty 322 adj.
  grey 429 adj.
  tedious 838 adj.
leader
  superior 34 n.
  precursor 66 n.
  article 591 n.
  leader 690 n.
leadership
  superiority 34 n.
  authority 733 n.
leader-writer
  dissertator 591 n.
leading
  influential 178 adj.
  foremost 283 adj.
  directing 689 adj.
leading article
  article 591 n.
leading case
  precept 693 n.
leading light
  sage 500 n.
  bigwig 638 n.
leading strings
  nonage 130 n.
  teaching 534 n.
  subjection 745 n.
  fetter 748 n.
leadsman
  navigator 270 n.
lead to
  tend 179 vb.
  conduce 156 vb.
leaf
  lamina 207 n.
  foliage 366 n.
leafless
  uncovered 229 adj.
leaflet
  the press 528 n.
league
  combination 50 n.
  long measure 203 n.
  association 706 n.
  compact 765 n.
leak
  decrement 42 n.
  outflow 298 n.

LEA

be wet 341 vb.
disclosure 526 n.
waste 634 vb.
non-retention
   779 n.

leakage
decrease 37 n.
loss 772 n.
(see leak)

leaky
porous 263 adj.
disclosing 526 adj.

lean
tend 179 vb.
lean 206 adj.
be oblique 220 vb.
underfed 636 adj.

leaning
willingness 597 n.
liking 859 n.

leanness
scarcity 636 n.

lean-to
small house 192 n.

leap
leap 312 n., vb.
rejoice 835 vb.

leap-frog
overstepping
   306 n.

leap in the dark
uncertainty 474 n.
gambling 618 n.

leaps and bounds
progression 285 n.

learn
memorize 505 vb.
understand 516 vb.
learn 536 vb.

learned
instructed 490 adj.

learner
learner 538 n.

learning
knowledge 490 n.
learning 536 n.

lease
lease 784 vb.
hire 785 vb.

lease-holder
possessor 776 n.

leash
halter 47 n.

least
lesser 35 adj.

least one can do
dueness 915 n.

LEE

leather
skin 226 n.
toughness 329 n.
cleaning cloth
   648 n.

leathery
tough 329 adj.

leave
depart 296 vb.
relinquish 621 vb.
leisure 681 n.
permission 756 n.
bequeath 780 vb.

leave behind
outstrip 277 vb.

leave in the lurch
fail in duty 918 vb.

leaven
alterer 143 n.
convert 147 vb.
influence 178 n.,
   vb.
leaven 323 n.
qualify 468 vb.

leave off
disuse 674 vb.

leave out
exclude 57 vb.

leave-taking
valediction 296 n.

leavings
leavings 41 n.

lecher
libertine 952 n.

lechery
unchastity 951 n.

lectern
rostrum 539 n.

lecture
lecture 534 n.
dissertation 591 n.
reprimand 924 n.

lecture-hall
classroom 539 n.
conference 584 n.

lecturer
teacher 537 n.
speaker 579 n.

ledge
shelf 218 n.
projection 254 n.

ledger
account book
   808 n.

lee
laterality 239 n.
shelter 662 n.

LEG

leer
court 889 vb.

lees
leavings 41 n.
rubbish 641 n.

lee shore
pitfall 663 n.

leeway
deviation 282 n.

leeway, make up
recoup 31 vb.

left
remaining 41 adj.
sinistrality 242 n.
political party
   708 n.

left-handed
sinistral 242 adj.
clumsy 695 adj.

leftish
moderate 177 adj.

left-overs
leavings 41 n.

leg
stand 218 n.
leg 267 n.

legacy
sequel 67 n.
dower 777 n.

legal
legal 953 adj.

legal adviser
law agent, jurist
   958 n.

legal code
law 953 n.

legalize
make legal 953 vb.

legal profession
bar 958 n.

legatory
beneficiary 776 n.

legate
envoy 754 n.

legatee
beneficiary 776 n.

legation
envoy 754 n.

legend
commentary 520 n.
phrase 563 n.
narrative 590 n.
(see fable)

legendary
imaginary 513 adj.

legerdemain
sleight 542 n.

LEN

leggings
legwear 228 n.

leggy
crural 267 adj.

legibility
intelligibility 516 n.

legion
multitude 104 n.
army 722 n.

legionary
soldier 722 n.

legislate
decree 737 vb.
make legal 953 vb.

legislation
legislation 953 n.

legislative
legal 953 adj.

legislative assembly
parliament 692 n.

legislator
director 690 n.

legitimacy
authority 733 n.
legality 953 n.

legitimate
genuine 494 adj.
legal 953 adj.

legitimist
defender 713 n.

legitimize
make legal 953 vb.

leg-pull
trickery 542 n.

leg-puller
humorist 839 n.

leg-up
elevation 310 n.
aid 703 n.

leisure
leisure 681 n.
amusement 837 n.

leisurely
slow 278 adj.
leisurely 681 adj.

leitmotiv
topic 452 n.

lemma
argumentation
   475 n.

lemon
sourness 393 n.
yellowness 433 n.

lemonade
soft drink 301 n.

lend
provide 633 vb.

LEN

lend 784 vb.
  credit 802 vb.
lend colour to
  make likely 471 vb.
lender
  creditor 802 n.
length
  quantity 26 n.
  piece 53 n.
  size 195 n.
  distance 199 n.
  interval 201 n.
  length 203 n.
  diffuseness 570 n.
length and breadth
  all 52 n.
lengthen
  augment 36 vb.
  continuate 71 vb.
lengthy
  long 203 adj.
  prolix 570 adj.
lenient
  moderate 177 adj.
  lenient 736 adj.
lenitive
  moderator 177 n.
  lenitive 177 adj.
  balm 658 n.
  pacificatory
   719 adj.
lenity
  softness 327 n.
  (see **lenient**)
lens
  optical device
   442 n.
Lent
  fast 946 n.
lenticular
  convex 253 adj.
leonine
  animal 365 adj.
  beautiful 841 adj.
leopard
  cat 365 n.
leopard's spots
  fixture 153 n.
leper
  dirty person 649 n.
  outcaste 883 n.
leprechaun
  elf 970 n.
leprosy
  skin disease 651 n.
leprous
  unclean 649 adj.

LET

lesion
  wound 655 n.
lessee
  possessor 776 n.
lessen
  bate 37 vb.
  become small
   198 vb.
lesson
  lecture 534 n.
  study 536 n.
  warning 664 n.
lessor
  lender 784 n.
let
  obstacle 702 n.
  permit 756 vb.
  lease 784 vb.
let alone
  avoid 620 vb.
let down
  disappoint 509 vb.
let fall
  let fall 311 vb.
  hint 524 vb.
let fly
  be violent 176 vb.
  fire at 712 vb.
let go
  relinquish 621 vb.
  not retain 779 vb.
lethal
  deadly 362 adj.
lethal chamber
  means of execution
   964 n.
lethargy
  sluggishness 679 n.
  moral insensibility
   820 n.
Lethe
  oblivion 506 n.
let in
  admit 299 vb.
let off
  shoot 287 vb.
let-off
  acquittal 960 n.
let out
  enlarge 197 vb.
  lengthen 203 vb.
letter
  letter 558 n., vb.
  correspondence
   588 n.
letter-bag
  mails 531 n.

LEV

lettering
  lettering 586 n.
  letterpress 587 n.
letter of credit
  paper money 797 n.
letter of the law
  severity 735 n.
letterpress
  letterpress 587 n.
letters
  erudition 490 n.
  lettering 586 n.
  correspondence
   588 n.
letters patent
  warrant 737 n.
letter-writer
  correspondent
   588 n.
lettuce
  vegetable 301 n.
let up
  cease 145 vb.
let well alone
  be cautious 858 vb.
leucoderma
  skin disease 651 n.
levant
  run away 620 vb.
  not pay 805 vb.
levée
  social gathering
   882 n.
level
  degree 27 n.
  equality 28 n.
  serial place 73 n.
  demolish 165 vb.
  layer 207 n.
  horizontality
   216 n.
  smooth 258 vb.
  aim 281 vb.
  fell 311 vb.
level crossing
  railroad 624 n.
level-headedness
  sagacity 498 n.
leveller
  destroyer 168 n.
levelness
  uniformity 16 n.
lever
  handle, pivot 218
   n.
  lifter 310 n.
  tool 630 n.

LIB

leverage
  scope 744 n.
levigate
  smooth 258 vb.
  rub 333 vb.
levitation
  elevation 310 n.
  levity 323 n.
Levite
  priest 986 n.
levity
  insubstantiality 4
   n.
  levity 323 n.
  folly 499 n.
  merriment 833 n.
levy
  assemblage 74 n.
  armed force 722 n.
  levy 786 vb.
  tax 809 n.
lewd
  impure 951 adj.
  lecherous 951 adj.
lexical
  verbal 559 adj.
lexicographer
  linguist 557 n.
  etymology 559 n.
lexicology
  etymology 559 n.
lexicon
  dictionary 559 n.
  reference book
   589 n.
lexigraphy
  letter 558 n.
  word 559 n.
liability
  tendency 179 n.
  liability 180 n.
  vulnerability 661 n.
  duty 917 n.
  penalty 963 n.
liable
  subject 745 adj.
  (see **liability**)
liaison
  relation 9 n.
  bond 47 n.
  love affair 887 n.
liar
  liar 545 n.
libation(s)
  drinking 301 n.
  drunkenness 949 n.
  oblation 981 n.

libel
calumny 926 n.
false charge 928 n.
libeller
defamer 926 n.
liberal
plenteous 635 adj.
expending 806 adj.
prodigal 815 adj.
(*see* liberality)
liberalism
freedom 744 n.
liberality
giving 781 n.
liberality 813 n.
benevolence 897 n.
liberalize
liberate 746 vb.
liberate
disencumber 701 vb.
liberation
extraction 304 vb.
deliverance 668 n.
liberation 746 n.
libertarianism
freedom 744 n.
libertine
libertine 952 n.
liberty
freedom, scope
 744 n.
permission 756 n.
libidinous
lecherous 951 adj.
libido
libido 859 n.
librarian
bookman 589 n.
library
library 589 n.
collection 632 n.
libration
oscillation 317 n.
librettist
dramatist 594 n.
author 589 n.
libretto
vocal music 412 n.
reading matter
 589 n.
stage play 594 n.
licence
anarchy 734 n.
permit 756 n.
license
liberate 746 vb.
permit 756 vb.

licensee
consignee 754 n.
licentious
anarchic 734 adj.
lecherous 951 adj.
lawless 954 adj.
lick
eat 301 vb.
moisten 341 vb.
touch 378 vb.
defeat 727 vb.
lick and a promise
incompleteness
 55 n.
lick into shape
efform 243 vb.
educate 534 vb.
lickspittle
toady 879 n.
lid
covering 226 n.
stopper 264 n.
lido
pleasure ground
 837 n.
lie
be situate 186 vb.
dwell 192 vb.
be horizontal
 216 vb.
be false 541 vb.
untruth 543 n.
lieder
vocal music 412 n.
lie-detector
detector 484 n.
lie down
be horizontal
 216 vb.
repose 683 vb.
liegeman
dependant 742 n.
lie in
reproduce itself
 164 vb.
lie in wait
ambush 527 vb.
lie low
elude 667 vb.
lie to
navigate 269 vb.
lie under
be liable 180 vb.
lieutenant
auxiliary 707 n.
army officer 741 n.
naval officer 741 n.

deputy 755 n.
lie with
unite with 45 vb.
life
existence 1 n.
vitality 162 n.
life 360 n.
biography 590 n.
vocation 622 n.
life-belt
safeguard 662 n.
life-blood
essential part 5 n.
life 360 n.
lifeboat
safeguard 662 n.
life-giving
generative 171 adj.
lifeguard
protector 660 n.
defender 713 n.
life-jacket
safeguard 662 n.
lifeless
dead 361 adj.
inactive 679 adj.
lifelike
lifelike 18 adj.
life-line
safeguard 662 n.
lifelong
lasting 113 adj.
lifemanship
tactics 688 n.
skill 694 n.
life-preserver
safeguard 662 n.
life-saving
deliverance 668 n.
life sentence
diuturnity 113 n.
life-size
large 195 adj.
lifetime
period 110 n.
diuturnity 113 n.
life to come
future state 124 n.
life with
accompaniment
 89 n.
life-work
vocation 622 n.
lift
carry 273 vb.
lifter 310 n.
elevate 310 vb.

steal 788 vb.
relieve 831 vb.
lifter
lifter 310 n.
thief 789 n.
ligament
ligature 47 n.
ligature
ligature 47 n.
light
light 323 adj.
fire 379 n.
kindle 381 vb.
lighter 385 n.
light 417 n.
luminary 420 n.
illuminate 420 vb.
soft-hued 425 adj.
appearance 445 n.
truth 494 n.
interpretation
 520 n.
funny 849 adj.
unchaste 951 adj.
light and shade
light contrast 417 n.
lighten
lighten 323 vb.
make bright 417 vb.
disencumber 701 vb.
lighter
boat 275 n.
torch 420 n.
light-grasp
range 183 n.
optics 417 n.
light-headed
frenzied 503 adj.
light-hearted
cheerful 833 adj.
lighthouse
signal light 420 n.
signpost 547 n.
lighting
lighting 420 n.
light-minded
changeful 152 adj.
lightness
levity 323 n.
unchastity 951 n.
lightning
velocity 277 n.
flash 417 n.
light of nature
intuition 476 n.
light rein
lenity 736 n.

light relief
ridiculousness
849 n.

lights
knowledge 490 n.
intelligence 498 n.

lights out
obscuration 418 n.
call 547 n.

light up
make bright 417 vb.

light wave
radiation 417 n.

light-weight
light 323 adj.
nonentity 639 n.
pugilist 722 n.

like
similar 18 adj.
appetize 390 vb.
be friendly 880 vb.
love 887 vb.

likeable
lovable 887 adj.

like for like
retaliation 714 n.

likelihood
probability 471 n.

likely
probable 471 adj.
credible 485 adj.

like-minded
assenting 488 adj.

liken
liken 18 vb.
compare 462 vb.

likeness
similarity 18 n.
copy 22 n.
metaphor 519 n.

likes of, the
analogue 18 n.

liking
liking 859 n.

lilac
purple 434 adj.

lilt
sing 413 vb.

lily
white thing 427 n.

limb
piece 53 n.
leg 267 n.
tree, foliage 366 n.

limber
flexible 327 adj.
gun 723 n.

limber up
prepare oneself
669 vb.

limbo
prison 748 n.
hell 972 n.

lime
adhesive 47 n.
bleacher 426 n.
green 432 adj.
ensnare 542 vb.

limelight
lighting 420 n.
advertisement
528 n.
theatre 594 n.

limelight, in the
manifest 522 adj.

limerick
doggerel 593 n.
impurity 951 n.

limit
finite quantity
26 n.
extremity 69 n.
edge 234 n.
limit 236 n., vb.
restriction 747 n.

limitary
limited 236 adj.
restraining 747 adj.

limitation
limit 236 n.
qualification 468 n.
restriction 747 n.

limitless
infinite 107 adj.

limousine
automobile 274 n.

limp
move slowly
278 vb.
soft 327 adj.

limpet
coherence 48 n.

limpid
transparent 422 adj.
perspicuous 567 adj.

linage
letterpress 587 n.

linchpin
fastening 47 n.

linctus
medicine 658 n.

line
race 11 n.
cable 47 n.

continuity 71 n.
breed 77 n.
genealogy 169 n.
line 203 n.
line 227 vb.
groove 262 vb.
direction 281 n.
vocation 622 n.
tactics 688 n.
formation 722 n.
merchandise 794 n.

lineage
genealogy 169 n.
nobility 868 n.

line ahead
line 203 n.

lineal
filial 170 n.

lineament
outline 233 n.
feature 445 n.

linear
straight 249 adj.

linear measure
long measure 203 n.

lined
furrowed 262 adj.

line-drawing
picture 553 n.

linen
textile 222 n.
bodywear 228 n.

liner
ship 275 n.

lines
feature 445 n.
poem 593 n.
railroad 624 n.
defences 713 n.

line up
assemblage 74 n.

linger
be late 136 vb.

lingerer
slowcoach 278 n.

lingerie
underwear 228 n.

lingo
language 557 n.
dialect 560 n.

lingua franca
language 557 n.
dialect 560 n.

linguist
linguist 557 n.

linguistic
linguistic 557 adj.

linguistics
linguistics 557 n.

liniment
unguent 357 n.
balm 658 n.

lining
lining 227 n.

link
relation 9 n.
connect 45 vb.
bond 47 n.

linkage
(*see* link)

linoleum
floor-cover 226 n.

linotype
print 587 n.

lintel
summit 213 n.
doorway 263 n.

lion
cat 365 n.
bigwig 638 n.
brave person 855 n.
favourite 890 n.

lionize
honour 866 vb.

lion's share
main part 52 n.
undueness 916 n.

lip
edge 234 n.
projection 254 n.
sauciness 878 n.

lip-read
hear 415 vb.
translate 520 vb.

lipstick
cosmetic 843 n.

liquefaction
fluidity 335 n.
liquefaction 337 n.

liqueur
liquor 301 n.

liquid
liquor 301 n.
fluid 335 n.
speech sound 398 n.
transparent
422 adj.

liquidation
destruction 165 n.
slaughter 362 n.
payment 804 n.

liquidator
receiver 782 n.
treasurer 798 n.

liquidity
fluidity 335 n.
funds 797 n.
liquor
liquor 301 n.
fluid 335 n.
lisp
speech defect 580 n.
list
specify 80 vb.
list 87 n., vb.
obliquity 220 n.
edging 234 n.
listen (to)
hear 415 vb.
be attentive 455 vb.
listener
listener 415 n.
listen in
hear 415 vb.
listless
weakly 163 adj.
inattentive 456 adj.
dejected 834 adj.
lists
duel 716 n.
arena 724 n.
litany
prayers 981 n.
literal
narrow-minded 481 adj.
accurate 494 adj.
semantic 514 adj.
interpretive 520 adj.
literal 558 adj.
literal-minded
narrow-minded 481 adj.
literary
instructed 490 adj.
stylistic 566 adj.
literate
instructed 490 adj.
literati
intellectual 492 n.
literature
writing 586 n.
reading matter 589 n.
lithe
flexible 327 adj.
lithograph
print 587 vb.
litigant
litigant 959 n.

litigation
litigation 959 n.
litigious
quarrelling 709 adj.
litigating 959 adj.
litmus paper
testing agent 461 n.
litotes
underestimation 483 n.
litter
confusion 61 n.
jumble 63 vb.
youngling 132 n.
bed 218 n.
rubbish 641 n.
litterer
dirty person 649 n.
little
small 33 adj.
little 196 adj.
unimportant 639 adj.
contemptible 922 adj.
little man
common man 30 n.
littoral
coastal 344 adj.
liturgy
ritual 988 n.
live
dynamic 160 adj.
vigorous 174 adj.
alive 360 adj.
live 360 vb.
live and let live
not act 677 vb.
livelihood
vocation 622 n.
liveliness
vitality 162 n.
moral sensibility 819 n.
cheerfulness 833 n.
livelong
lasting 113 adj.
lively
lively 819 adj.
(*see* liveliness)
liver
insides 224 n.
meat 301 n.
liverish
irascible 892 adj.
liverishness
indigestion 651 n.

livery
livery 547 n.
liveryman
merchant 794 n.
livestock
cattle 365 n.
live wire
electricity 160 n.
vigorousness 174 n.
livid
blackish 428 adj.
purple 434 adj.
blue 435 adj.
angry 891 adj.
living
benefice 985 n.
living being
life 360 n.
living space
room 183 n.
living wage
sufficiency 635 n.
lixivium
solution 337 n.
lizard
reptile 365 n.
load
fill 54 vb.
load 193 vb.
contents 193 n.
gravity 322 n.
loadstone
attraction 291 n.
loaf
cereal 301 n.
be inactive 679 vb.
loafer
idler 679 n.
loam
soil 344 n.
loan
lending 784 n.
borrowing 785 n.
loan-word
neology 560 n.
loathing
dislike 861 n.
hatred 888 n.
loathsome
not nice 645 adj.
hateful 888 adj.
lobby
lobby 194 n.
incite 612 vb.
lobbyist
motivator 612 n.
petitioner 763 n.

lobe
ear 415 n.
lobster
table fish 365 n.
local
regional 184 adj.
native 191 n.
provincial 192 adj.
near 200 adj.
local colour
accuracy 494 n.
locality
district 184 n.
region 184 n.
localize
place 187 vb.
restrain 747 vb.
locate
place 187 vb.
location
location 187 n.
loch
lake 346 n.
lock
fastening 47 n.
hair 259 n.
stopper 264 n.
close 264 vb.
conduit 351 n.
locker
box 194 n.
locket
jewellery 844 n.
lock-out
exclusion 57 n.
strike 145 n.
lock, stock, and barrel
all 52 n.
lock up
imprison 747 vb.
lock-up
lock-up 748 n.
locomotion
motion 265 n.
locomotive
locomotive 274 n.
vehicular 274 adj.
locum tenens
substitute 150 n.
doctor 658 n.
locus classicus
example 83 n.
locust
destroyer 168 n.
vermin 365 n.
glutton 947 n.

locution
word 559 n.
phrase 563 n.

lodestar
attraction 291 n.
signpost 547 n.

lodge
place 187 vb.
small house 192 n.
dwell 192 vb.

lodger
resident 191 n.

lodging(s)
quarters 192 n.

lodgement
location 187 n.

loft
attic 194 n.
propel 287 vb.

lofty
high 209 adj.
proud 871 adj.

log
sailing aid 269 n.
raft 275 n.
fuel 385 n.
gauge 465 n.
register 548 vb.

logarithm
mathematics 86 n.

log-book
record 548 n.

loggia
lobby 194 n.

logic
reasoning 475 n.
necessity 596 n.

logical
relevant 9 adj.
philosophic 449 adj.
rational 475 adj.
necessary 596 adj.

logicality
relevance 9 n.

logic-chopping
sophistry 477 n.

logician
reasoner 475 n.

logistics
provision 633 n.
fitting out 669 n.

loin
rear 238 n.

loincloth
loincloth 228 n.

loins
genitalia 164 n.

loiter
be late 136 vb.
be stealthy 525 vb.

loiterer
slowcoach 278 n.

loll
be horizontal 216 vb.
be inactive 679 vb.
repose 683 vb.

lone
alone 88 adj.
unsociable 883 adj.

lonely
alone 88 adj.
empty 190 adj.
friendless 883 adj.
secluded 883 adj.

lone wolf
solitary 883 n.

long
lasting 113 adj.
long 203 adj.
prolix 570 adj.
desire 859 vb.

longevity
diuturnity 113 n.
age 131 n.

long-headed
intelligent 498 adj.

longimetry
long measure 203 n.

longing
desire 859 n.

longinquity
distance 199 n.

longitude
length 203 n.

long-legged
tall 209 adj.

long measure
long measure 203 n.

long odds
improbability 472 n.

long-range
distant 199 adj.

long rope
scope 744 n.

long run
protraction 113 n.

longshoreman
boatman 270 n.

long-standing
lasting 113 adj.
immemorial 127 adj.

long-suffering
patience 823 n.

long-term
lasting 113 adj.

long-winded
prolix 570 adj.
loquacious 581 adj.

loo
latrine 649 n.

look
similarity 18 n.
form 243 n.
look 438 n.
mien 445 n.

look after
look after 457 vb.
safeguard 660 vb.

look askance
disapprove 924 vb.

look blue
be discontented 829 vb.

look daggers
threaten 900 vb.

look down on
despise 922 vb.

looker-on
spectator 441 n.

look for
search 459 vb.
expect 507 vb.

look for trouble
make quarrels 709 vb.

look forward
expect 507 vb.

look in
enter 297 vb.
visit 882 vb.

looking back
reversion 148 n.
tergiversation 603 n.

looking-glass
mirror 442 n.

look into
be attentive 455 vb.

look like
resemble 18 vb.

look of things
circumstance 8 n.

look on
be present 189 vb.
not act 677 vb.

look-out
view 438 n.
surveillance 457 n.

expectation 507 n.
warner 664 n.

look out
be cautious 858 vb.

look silly
be ridiculous 849 vb.

look the other way
avoid 620 vb.

look twice
be cautious 858 vb.

look up
visit 882 vb.

look up to
respect 920 vb.

loom
impend 156 vb.
weave 222 vb.
be dim 419 vb.
be visible 443 vb.

loon
madman 504 n.

loop
loop 250 n.
circuit 626 n.

loophole
window 263 n.
contrivance 623 n.
means of escape 667 n.
fortification 713 n.

loose
disjoin 46 vb.
non-adhesive 49 adj.
unstable 152 adj.
pendent 217 adj.
lax 734 adj.

loose end, at a
leisurely 681 adj.

loose liver
sensualist 944 n.
libertine 952 n.

loosen, looseness
(*see* loose)

loot
rob 788 vb.
booty 790 n.

looting
spoliation 788 n.

lop
shorten 204 vb.

lope
gait 265 n.
move fast 277 vb.

lop-sided
unequal 29 adj.
(*see* oblique)

loquacity
  diffuseness 570 n.
  loquacity 581 n.
lord
  nobleman 868 n.
  title 870 n.
  master 741 n.
  owner 776 n.
lord it
  dominate 733 vb.
  be proud 871 vb.
lordly
  authoritarian
    735 adj.
  liberal 813 adj.
  proud 871 adj.
lordship
  aristocracy 868 n.
Lord's Supper
  Holy Communion
    988 n.
Lord's Table
  altar 990 n.
lore
  tradition 127 n.
  erudition 490 n.
  learning 536 n.
lorgnette
  eyeglass 442 n.
lorry
  automobile 274 n.
lose
  misplace 188 vb.
  be defeated 728 vb.
  lose 772 vb.
lose consciousness
  be impotent 161 vb.
lose control
  be lax 734 vb.
lose face
  lose repute 867 vb.
lose ground
  regress 286 vb.
lose numbers
  decrease 37 vb.
loser
  bungler 697 n.
  loser 728 n.
lose the scent
  be uncertain
    474 vb.
lose the thread
  be unrelated 10 vb.
  be inattentive
    456 vb.
lose the way
  stray 282 vb.

lose weight
  become small
    198 vb.
losing
  profitless 641 adj.
losing game
  defeat 728 n.
losing side
  loser 728 n.
loss
  decrement 42 n.
  waste 634 n.
  loss 772 n.
loss, at a
  doubting 474 adj.
losses
  failure 728 n.
loss-making
  profitless 641 adj.
lost cause
  defeat 728 n.
lot
  great quantity 32 n.
  all 52 n.
  bunch 74 n.
  multitude 104 n.
  chance 159 n.
  territory 184 n.
  fate 596 n.
  plenty 635 n.
  portion 783 n.
loth
  unwilling 598 adj.
lotion
  cleanser 648 n.
  cosmetic 833 n.
lottery
  gambling 618 n.
loud
  crying 408 adj.
  florid 425 adj.
  (see loudness)
loud-hailer
  megaphone 400 n.
loudness
  loudness 400 n.
  bang 402 n.
  resonance 404 n.
loud pedal
  megaphone 400 n.
loud-speaker
  megaphone 400 n.
  hearing aid 415 n.
lough
  lake 346 n.
lounge
  chamber 194 n.

  be inactive 679 vb.
lounger
  idler 679 n.
lour
  (see lower)
louse
  vermin 365 n.
  cad 938 n.
lousy
  not nice 645 adj.
  unclean 649 adj.
lout
  bungler 697 n.
  ruffian 904 n.
loutish
  discourteous
    885 adj.
lovable
  amiable 884 adj.
  lovable 887 adj.
love
  zero 103 n.
  liking 859 n.
  love 887 n., vb.
  lover, loved one
    887 n.
  pet, caress 889 vb.
  darling 890 n.
  disinterestedness
    931 n.
love affair
  love affair 887 n.
love all
  draw 28 n.
love-child
  bastardy 954 n.
love-feast
  public worship
    981 n.
love, in
  enamoured 887 adj.
loveless
  indifferent 860 adj.
  unwanted 860 adj.
love-letter
  wooing 889 n.
lovely
  a beauty 841 n.
  beautiful 841 adj.
  lovable 887 adj.
love-making
  wooing 889 n.
  love-making 887 n.
lover
  lover 887 n.
loverlike
  loving 887 adj.

love-sickness
  love 887 n.
love to
  be wont 610 vb.
love-token
  love-token 889 n.
loving care
  carefulness 457 n.
loving-kindness
  benevolence 897 n.
low
  inferior 35 adj.
  low 210 adj.
  muted 401 adj.
  ululate 409 vb.
  dejected 834 adj.
  vulgar 847 adj.
  humble 872 adj.
  rascally 930 adj.
low-born
  plebeian 869 adj.
low-brow
  uninstructed
    491 adj.
  ignoramus 493 n.
low-class
  plebeian 869 adj.
low-down
  information 524 n.
  rascally 930 adj.
lower
  inferior 35 adj.
  be low 210 vb.
  hang 217 vb.
  depress 311 vb.
  vulgarize 847 vb.
  humiliate 872 vb.
lower classes
  lower classes 869
    n.
lowering
  impending 155 adj.
lower oneself
  demean oneself
    867 vb.
lowlander
  dweller 191 n.
lowlands
  lowness 210 n.
  plain 348 n.
low-level
  unimportant
    639 adj.
lowliness
  humility 872 n.
low-lying
  low 210 adj.

lowness
lowness 210 n.
base 214 n.
  (*see* low)
low water
scarcity 636 n.
poverty 801 n.
loyal
patriotic 901 adj.
trustworthy 929 adj.
  (*see* loyalty)
loyalist
defender 713 n.
loyalty
willingness 597 n.
loyalty 739 n.
observance 768 n.
duty 917 n.
probity 929 n.
disinterestedness
  931 n.
lozenge
angular figure
  247 n.
medicine 658 n.
lubber
ninny 501 n.
bungler 697 n.
lubberly
clumsy 695 adj.
lubricant
lubricant 334 n.
lubricate
smooth 258 vb.
lubricate 334 vb.
lubrication
lubrication 334 n.
unctuousness 357 n.
lucid
sane 502 adj.
perspicuous 567 adj.
luck
opportunity 137 n.
chance 159 n.
non-design 618 n.
prosperity 730 n.
luckless
unfortunate 731 adj.
lucky
opportune 137 adj.
successful 727 adj.
prosperous 730 adj.
happy 824 adj.
lucky dip
confusion 61 n.
lucky dog
made man 730 n.

lucrative
gainful 771 adj.
lucre
money 797 n.
Luddite
rioter 738 n.
ludicrous
absurd 497 adj.
ridiculous 849 adj.
lug
draw 288 vb.
ear 415 n.
luggage
thing transferred
  272 n.
property 777 n.
lugger
sailing-ship 275 n.
lugubrious
cheerless 834 adj.
lukewarm
neutral 625 adj.
indifferent 860 adj.
lull
discontinuity 72 n.
lull 145 n.
assuage 177 vb.
silence 399 n., vb.
inactivity 679 vb.
repose 683 n.
peace 717 n.
please 826 vb.
lullaby
vocal music 412 n.
soporific 679 n.
lumbar
back 238 adj.
lumber
leavings 41 n.
move slowly
  278 vb.
wood 366 n.
rubbish 641 n.
be clumsy 695 vb.
encumbrance 702 n.
lumberjack
forestry 366 n.
lumber-room
chamber 194 n.
collection 632 n.
luminary
luminary 420 n.
sage 500 n.
luminescence
glow 417 n.
luminosity
light 417 n.

luminous
luminous 417 adj.
lump
bulk 195 n.
solid body 324 n.
lumpish
inactive 679 adj.
lump together
not discriminate
  464 vb.
lumpy
rough 259 adj.
lunacy
insanity 503 n.
lunar
celestial 321 adj.
lunate
curved 248 adj.
lunatic
insane 503 adj.
madman 504 n.
lunatic asylum
madhouse 503 n.
lunch
meal 301 n.
eat 301 vb.
lung
  (*see* lungs)
lunge
foin 712 n.
strike at 712 vb.
lungs
respiration 352 n.
voice 577 n.
lunik
space-ship 276 n.
lurch
walk 267 vb.
fluctuation 317 n.
deviate 282 vb.
lure
tempt 612 vb.
desired object
  859 n.
lurid
florid 425 adj.
lurk
lurk 523 vb.
elude 667 vb.
lurker
hider 527 n.
lurking
latent 523 adj.
stealthy 525 adj.
luscious
savoury 309 adj.
pleasurable 826 adj.

lush
prolific 171 adj.
vegetal 366 adj.
lust
libido 859 n.
unchastity 951 n.
lustful
desiring 859 adj.
lecherous 951 adj.
lustiness
vigorousness 174 n.
lustration
cleansing 648 n.
penance 941 n.
lustre
prestige 866 n.
lustreless
colourless 426 adj.
lustrous
luminous 417 adj.
lusty
strong 162 adj.
vigorous 174 adj.
lute
adhesive 47 n.
harp 414 n.
luxuriance
productiveness
  171 n.
vegetability 366 n.
plenty 635 n.
luxuriate
enjoy 376 vb.
be intemperate
  943 vb.
luxurious
ostentatious
  875 adj.
  (*see* luxury)
luxury
extra 40 n.
euphoria 376 n.
superfluity 637 n.
prosperity 730 n.
intemperance 943 n.
lye
solution 337 n.
cleanser 648 n.
lying
falsehood 541 n.
untrue 543 adj.
lying-in
obstetrics 164 n.
lymph
blood 335 n.
lynch
execute 963 vb.

lynching
capital punishment
963 n.
lynch law
lawlessness 954 n.
lynx-eyed
vigilant 457 adj.
lyre
harp 414 n.
lyric
vocal music 412 n.
musicianly 413 adj.
poetic 593 adj.
lyrical
excitable 822 adj.
rejoicing 835 adj.
approving 923 adj.

M

ma'am
woman 373 n.
macabre
frightening
854 adj.
spooky 970 adj.
macadam
road 624 n.
mace
potherb 301 n.
condiment 389 n.
club 723 n.
badge of rule
743 n.
macerate
soften 327 vb.
drench 341 vb.
machicolation
notch 260 n.
fortification 713 n.
machination
plot 623 n.
stratagem 698 n.
machine
produce 164 vb.
machine 630 n.
machine-minded
mechanical 630 adj.
machinery
complexity 61 n.
machine 630 n.
machinist
machinist 630 n.
mackerel
table fish 365 n.
mackintosh
overcoat 228 n.

macrocosm
universe 321 n.
macroscopic
large 195 adj.
visible 443 adj.
maculate
variegate 437 vb.
maculation
maculation 437 n.
blemish 845 n.
mad
insane 503 adj.
madcap
desperado 857 n.
rash 857 adj.
madden
make mad 503 vb.
enrage 891 vb.
maddening
annoying 827 adj.
madder
red pigment 431 n.
made of
composing 56 adj.
madhouse
madhouse 503 n.
madman
fool 501 n.
madman 504 n.
madness
insanity 503 n.
madrigal
vocal music 412 n.
maelstrom
vortex 315 n.
pitfall 663 n.
maffick
rampage 61 vb.
rejoice 835 vb.
magazine
accumulation 74 n.
journal 528 n.
storage 632 n.
arsenal 723 n.
fire-arm 723 n.
mage, magian, Magi
sorcerer 983 n.
maggot
vermin 365 n.
ideality 513 n.
maggoty
unclean 649 adj.
magic
influence 178 n.
thaumaturgy 864 n.
fairylike 970 adj.
sorcery 893 n.

magician
conjuror 545 n.
sorcerer 983 n.
magisterial
skilful 694 adj.
ruling 733 adj.
magistracy
magistrature 733 n.
judge 957 n.
magistrate
judge 957 n.
magnanimous
disinterested
931 adj.
magnate
aristocrat 868 n.
magnet
attraction 291 n.
incentive 612 n.
magnetic needle
indicator 547 n.
magnetism
attraction 291 n.
magnification
increase 36 n.
vision 438 n.
(see magnify)
magnificence
beauty 841 n.
ornamentation
844 n.
ostentation 875 n.
magnificent
excellent 644 adj.
splendid 841 adj.
magnify
augment 36 vb.
enlarge 197 vb.
make important
638 vb.
praise 923 vb.
worship 981 vb.
magnifying glass
eyeglass 442 n.
magniloquence
magniloquence
574 n.
affectation 850 n.
magnitude
quantity 26 n.
degree 27 n.
greatness 32 n.
size 195 n.
magsman
trickster 545 n.
mahogany
brownness 430 n.

mahout
rider, driver 268 n.
maid
domestic 742 n.
(see maiden)
maiden
first 68 adj.
spinster 895 n.
virgin 950 n.
maidenhood
celibacy 895 n.
purity 950 n.
maidenly
unwedded 895 adj.
pure 950 adj.
maid-of-all-work
busy person 678 n.
domestic 742 n.
mail
send 272 vb.
mails 531 n.
armour 713 n.
mailbag
mails 531 n.
mail-clad
defended 713 adj.
mailed fist
lawlessness 954 n.
maim
disable 161 vb.
impair 655 vb.
main
great 32 adj.
supreme 34 adj.
conduit 351 n.
main chance
benefit 615 n.
gain 771 n.
main force
strength 162 n.
mainland
land 344 n.
main part
main part 32 n.
chief part 52 n.
mainsail
sail 275 n.
mainspring
cause 156 n.
motive 612 n.
machine 630 n.
mainstay
supporter 218 n.
main stream
tendency 179 n.
maintain
sustain 146 vb.

MAI

support 218 vb.
affirm 532 vb.
provide 633 vb.
maintenance
subvention 703 n.
(*see* maintain)
maize
corn 366 n.
majestic
impressive 821 adj.
beautiful 841 adj.
proud 871 adj.
formal 875 adj.
(*see* majesty)
majesty
greatness 32 n.
authority 733 n.
sovereign 741 n.
prestige 866 n.
nobility 868 n.
major
superior 34 adj.
older 131 adj.
grown up 134 adj.
important 638 adj.
army officer 741 n.
majority
main part 32 n.
greater number
104 n.
adultness 134 n.
major suit
skill 694 n.
make
character 5 n.
composition 56 n.
constitute 56 vb.
sort 77 n.
produce 164 vb.
efform 243 vb.
structure 331 n.
estimate 480 vb.
compel 740 vb.
gain 771 vb.
make a will
bequeath 780 vb.
make-believe
imitate 20 vb.
fantasy 513 n.
sham 542 n.
untrue 543 adj.
make certain
make certain
473 vb.
make do with
substitute 150 vb.
avail of 673 vb.

MAK

make eyes
court 889 vb.
make free with
appropriate 786 vb.
make good
succeed 727 vb.
make hay
prosper 730 vb.
make into
convert 147 vb.
make it up
make peace 719 vb.
make light of
do easily 701 vb.
be indifferent
860 vb.
make love
love 887 vb.
caress 889 vb.
make merry
revel 837 vb.
ridicule 851 vb.
make money
prosper 730 vb.
get rich 800 vb.
make much of
love 887 vb.
pet 889 vb.
make one of
be included 78 vb.
join a party
708 vb.
make or mar
influence 178 vb.
make out
see 438 vb.
demonstrate
478 vb.
understand 516 vb.
maker
producer 167 n.
make sense
be intelligible
516 vb.
makeshift
inferior 35 adj.
substitute 150 n.
imperfection 647 n.
unprepared 670 adj.
make short work of
destroy 165 vb.
do easily 701 vb.
make sure
make certain
473 vb.
make terms
make terms 766 vb.

MAL

make the best of
(*see* make the
most of)
make the most of
be ostentatious
875 vb.
make trouble
cause discontent
829 vb.
make up
constitute 56 vb.
imagine 513 vb.
primp 843 vb.
make-up
composition 56 n.
affections 817 n.
cosmetic 843 n.
make water
excrete 302 vb.
make way
avoid 620 vb.
makeweight
offset 31 n.
gravity 322 n.
make worse
aggravate 832 vb.
maladministration
bungling 695 n.
malady
disease 651 n.
malaise
suffering 825 n.
malapropism
misnomer 562 n.
solecism 565 n.
malaria
malaria 651 n.
malcontent
dissentient 489 n.
malcontent 829 n.
male
vitality 162 n.
male 372 n., adj.
malediction
malediction 899 n.
detraction 926 n.
malefactor
offender 904 n.
malevolence
enmity 881 n.
malevolence 898 n.
malformation
deformity 246 n.
malice
malevolence 898 n.
malicious
malevolent 898 adj.

MAN

malign
adverse 731 adj.
malevolent 898 adj.
defame 926 vb.
malignant
hating 888 adj.
malevolent 898 adj.
malignity
(*see* malevolence)
malinger
fail in duty 918 vb.
malingerer
impostor 545 n.
dutilessness 918 n.
malleable
flexible 327 adj.
impressible 819 adj.
mallet
hammer 279 n.
malnutrition
disease 651 n.
malpractice
guilty act 936 n.
maltreat
misuse 675 vb.
torment 827 vb.
malversation
misuse 675 n.
peculation 788 n.
mamilla
bosom 253 n.
mammal
animal 365 n.
Mammon
money 797 n.
mammoth
giant 195 n.
animal 365 n.
mammy
keeper 749 n.
man
adult 134 n.
mankind 371 n.
male 372 n.
worker 686 n.
defend 713 vb.
domestic 742 n.
chessman 837 n.
brave person 855 n.
manacle
tie 45 vb.
fetter 748 n.
manage
arrange 62 vb.
be able 160 vb.
look after 457 vb.
undertake 672 vb.

567

manage 689 vb.
manageable
 wieldy 701 adj.
management
 management 689 n.
 director 690 n.
manager
 doer 676 n.
 agent 686 n.
 manager 690 n.
 consignee 754 n.
managerial
 directing 689 adj.
man and wife
 spouse 894 n.
man-at-arms
 soldier 722 n.
mandarin
 fruit 301 n.
 official 690 n.
mandate
 job 622 n.
 mandate 751 n.
mandatory
 commanding
 737 adj.
mane
 hair 259 n.
man-eater
 animal 365 n.
 noxious animal
 904 n.
manège
 equitation 267 n.
manful
 courageous 855
 adj.
mange
 skin disease 651 n.
 animal disease
 651 n.
manger
 bowl 194 n.
mangle
 compressor 198 n.
 smoother 258 n.
 dry 342 vb.
 wound 655 vb.
mangy
 hairless 229 adj.
man-handle
 move 265 vb.
manhole
 orifice 263 n.
manhood
 adultness 134 n.
 manliness 855 n.

man-hours
 labour 682 n.
mania
 mania 503 n.
 psychopathy 503 n.
 warm feeling 818 n.
maniac
 madman 504 n.
manic
 insane 503 adj.
manicure
 beautification
 843 n.
manicurist
 beautician 843 n.
manifest
 list 87 n.
 appearing 445 adj.
 manifest 522 adj.,
 vb.
manifestation
 manifestation
 522 n.
 disclosure 526 n.
manifesto
 publication 528 n.
manifold
 multiform 82 adj.
man in the street
 common man 30 n.
 social group 371 n.
manipulate
 operate 173 vb.
 touch 378 vb.
 fake 541 vb.
 motivate 612 vb.
 manage 689 vb.
manipulation
 (*see* manipulate)
manipulator
 motivator 612 n.
mankind
 mankind 371 n.
manliness
 (*see* manly)
manly
 grown up 134 adj.
 manly 162 adj.
 male 372 adj.
 courageous 855 adj.
manna
 food 301 n.
 subvention 703 n.
mannequin
 living model 23 n.
manner
 sort 77 n.

style 566 n.
 conduct 688 n.
mannered
 affected 850 adj.
mannerism
 speciality 80 n.
 style 566 n.
 affectation 850 n.
mannerless
 discourteous
 885 adj.
mannerly
 courteous 884 adj.
manners
 etiquette 848 n.
 courtesy 884 n.
manners and customs
 practice 610 n.
mannish
 male 372 adj.
manoeuvrable
 wieldy 701 adj.
manoeuvre
 be cunning 698
 vb.
 wage war 718 vb.
manoeuvrer
 slyboots 698 n.
man of action
 doer 676 n.
man of business
 expert 696 n.
 consignee 754 n.
man of prayer
 worshipper 981 n.
man of property
 owner 776 n.
man of straw
 insubstantial thing
 4 n.
 nonentity 639 n.
man of the people
 commoner 869 n.
man on the spot
 delegate 754 n.
manor
 house 192 n.
 lands 777 n.
man-o'-war
 warship 722 n.
man-power
 means 629 n.
 personnel 686 n.
man's estate
 adultness 134 n.
mansion
 house 192 n.

man-size
 large 195 adj.
manslaughter
 homicide 362 n.
mantilla
 shawl 228 n.
mantle
 wrapping 226 n.
 cloak 228 n.
mantology
 divination 311 n.
manual
 piano 414 n.
 textbook 589 n.
manufacture
 production 164 n.
 produce 164 vb.
 business 622 n.
manufacturer
 producer 167 n.
manumission
 liberation 746 n.
manure
 fertilizer 171 n.
manuscript
 script 586 n.
 book 589 n.
many
 many 104 adj.
many-sided
 multiform 82 adj.
 skilful 694 adj.
map
 itinerary 267 n.
 map 551 n.
mar
 impair 655 vb.
 be clumsy 695 vb.
marathon
 lasting 113 adj.
 distance 199 n.
maraud
 rob 788 vb.
marauder
 robber 789 n.
marble
 smoothness 258 n.
 white thing 427 n.
 variegate 437 vb.
marbles
 plaything 837 n.
marbling
 maculation 437 n.
march
 motion, gait 265 n.
 itinerary 267 n.
 walk 267 vb.

progression 285 n.
route 624 n.
Iarcher
 dweller 191 n.
 pedestrian 268 n.
 agitator 738 n.
Iarches
 limit 236 n.
Iare
 horse 273 n.
Iargarine
 fat 357 n.
Iargin
 remainder 41 n.
 room 183 n.
 edge 234 n.
 redundance 637 n.
Iarginal
 inconsiderable
  33 adj.
 marginal 234 adj.
Iarginalia
 commentary 520
  n.
Iarina
 stable 192 n.
Iarine
 seafaring 269 adj.
 shipping 275 n.
 navy man 722 n.
Iariner
 mariner 270 n.
Iarionette(s)
 image 551 n.
 stage-play 594 n.
Iarital
 matrimonial
  894 adj.
Iaritime
 seafaring 269 adj.
 oceanic 343 adj.
Iarjoram
 potherb 301 n.
Iark
 character 5 n.
 sort 77 n.
 speciality 80 n.
 feature 445 n.
 indication 547 n.
 mark 547 vb.
 trace 548 n.
 objective 617 n.
 blemish 845 n.
Iark, beside the
 irrelevant 10 adj.
Iark down
 cheapen 812 vb.

market
 sell 793 vb.
 mart 796 n.
marketable
 saleable 793 adj.
marketer
 purchaser 792 n.
market garden
 farm 370 n.
market, in the
 saleable 793 adj.
market-place
 arena 724 n.
 (*see* market)
markings
 identification 547 n.
mark out
 set apart 46 vb.
marksman
 shooter 287 n.
 proficient 696 n.
mark time
 time 117 vb.
 be quiescent 266 vb.
 await 507 vb.
mark, up to the
 expert 694 adj.
marl
 soil 344 n.
marmoreal
 glyptic 554 adj.
maroon
 brown 430 adj.
 derelict 779 n.
marplot
 bungler 677 n.
 hinderer 702 n.
marquee
 canopy 226 n.
marquetry
 chequer 437 n.
marriage
 marriage 894 n.
marriageable
 grown up 134 adj.
 marriageable
  894 adj.
marrow
 substance 3 n.
 essential part 5 n.
 vegetables 301 n.
marry
 marry, wed 894
  vb.
marsh, marshland
 marsh 347 n.
 dirt 649 n.

marshal
 arrange 62 vb.
marshalling yard
 railroad 624 n.
marshy
 marshy 347 adj.
 pulpy 356 adj.
 dirty 649 adj.
martial
 warlike 718 adj.
martial law
 government 733 n.
 anarchy 734 n.
martinet
 tyrant 735 n.
martyr
 kill 362 vb.
 torment 827 vb.
 pietist 979 n.
martyrdom
 death 361 n.
 killing 362 n.
 pain 377 n.
 suffering 825 n.
 disinterestedness
  931 n.
marvel
 wonder 864 vb.
marvellous
 prodigious 32 adj.
 excellent 644 adj.
 wonderful 864 adj.
Marxism
 materiality 319 n.
 antichristianity
  974 n.
Marxist
 revolutionist 149 n.
mascara
 cosmetic 843 n.
mascot
 talisman 983 n.
masculine
 generic 77 adj.
 manly 162 adj.
 male 372 adj.
masculinity
 male 372 n.
mash
 soften 327 vb.
 pulverize 332 vb.
 pulpiness 356 n.
masher
 pulverizer 332 n.
mask
 screen 421 n., vb.
 conceal 525 vb.

disguise 527 n.
masochism
 abnormality 84 n.
mason
 efform 243 vb.
masonry
 building material
  631 n.
masque
 drama 594 n.
mass
 quantity 26 n.
 main part 32 n.
 chief part 52 n.
 accumulation 74 n.
 crowd 74 n.
 general 79 adj.
 greater number
  104 n.
 size, bulk 195 n.
 matter 319 n.
 gravity 322 n.
 solid body 324 n.
 Holy Communion
  988 n.
massacre
 slaughter 362 n.,
  vb.
massage
 friction 333 n.
 touch 378 n., vb.
 surgery 658 n.
 beautification 843 n.
massed
 multitudinous
  104 adj.
 dense 324 adj.
masses, the
 social group 371 n.
 commonalty 869 n.
masseur, masseuse
 (*see* massage)
massif
 high land 209 n.
massive
 great 32 adj.
 large 195 adj.
 weighty 322 adj.
mass-meeting
 assembly 74 n.
mass production
 uniformity 16 n.
 reproduction 166 n.
 productiveness
  171 n.
massy
 weighty 322 adj.

dense 324 adj.
master
  mariner 270 n.
  sage 500 n.
  understand 516 vb.
  learn 536 vb.
  teacher 537 n.
  proficient 696 n.
  victor 727 n.
  overmaster 727 vb.
  master 741 n.
  owner 776 n.
masterful
  authoritarian
    735 adj.
master-key
  opener 263 n.
masterless
  independent 744
    adj.
  unpossessed
    774 adj.
masterly
  skilful 694 adj.
master-mariner
  mariner 270 n.
master-mind
  intellectual 492 n.
masterpiece
  perfection 646 n.
  masterpiece 694 n.
  a beauty 841 n.
master spirit
  sage 500 n.
master-stroke
  masterpiece 694 n.
  success 727 n.
mastery
  knowledge 490 n.
  skill 694 n.
  victory 727 n.
mastication
  eating 301 n.
mastiff
  dog 368 n.
mat
  enlace 222 yb.
  floor-cover 226 n.
matador
  combatant 722 n.
match
  analogue 18 n.
  resemble 18 vb.
  compeer 28 n.
  pair 90 vb.
  lighter 385 n.
  contest, duel 716 n.

  marriage 894 n.
match against
  oppose 704 vb.
matchless
  supreme 34 adj.
  best 644 adj.
match-maker
  match-maker 894 n.
match-winner
  victor 727 n.
match-winning
  successful 727 adj.
mate
  analogue 18 n.
  unite with 45 vb.
  pair 90 vb.
  colleague 707 n.
  chum 880 n.
  spouse 894 n.
material
  real 1 adj.
  substantiality 3 n.
  textile 222 n.
  matter 319 n.
  important 638 adj.
materialism
  materiality 319 n.
materialistic
  selfish 932 adj.
materiality
  materiality 319 n.
  importance 638 n.
materialization
  manifestation 522 n.
materialize
  materialize 319 vb.
  be visible 443 vb.
  appear 445 vb.
materials
  means 629 n.
  materials 631 n.
maternal
  parental 169 adj.
  benevolent 897 adj.
maternity
  maternity 169 n.
matey
  friendly 880 adj.
mathematical
  statistical 86 adj.
mathematician
  computer 86 n.
  reasoner 476 n.
mathematics
  mathematics 86 n.
mating
  coition 45 n.

matins
  church service
    988 n.
matriarch
  family 11 n.
  maternity 169 n.
matrimonial
  matrimonial
    894 adj.
matrimony
  marriage 894 n.
matrix
  mould 23 n.
matron
  adult 134 n.
  maternity 169 n.
  nurse 658 n.
  spouse 894 n.
matronly
  grown up 134 adj.
  parental 169 adj.
matt
  soft-hued 425 adj.
matted
  hairy 259 adj.
matter
  substantiality 3 n.
  matter 319 n.
  solid body 324 n.
  topic 452 n.
  be important
    638 vb.
  ulcer 651 n.
matter of course
  practice 610 n.
  non-wonder 865 n.
matter of fact
  reality 1 n.
  certainty 473 n.
matter-of-fact
  narrow-minded
    481 adj.
matter-of-factness
  plainness 573 n.
matters
  affairs 154 n.
matting
  network 222 n.
  floor-cover 226 n.
mattress
  cushion 218 n.
maturation
  (*see* mature)
mature
  be complete 54 vb.
  perfect 646 vb.
  make better 654 vb.

  mature 669 vb.
maturity
  adultness 134 n.
  completion 725 n.
matutinal
  matinal 128 adj.
maudlin
  foolish 499 adj.
  tipsy 949 adj.
maul
  impair, wound
    655 vb.
maunder
  be foolish 499 vb.
  be diffuse 570 vb.
mausoleum
  tomb 364 n.
mauve
  purple 434 n.
maw
  maw 194 n.
mawkish
  feeling 818 adj.
maxim
  maxim 496 n.
  precept 693 n.
maximalism
  reformism 654 n.
maximalist
  reformer 654 n.
maximize
  exaggerate 546 vb.
maximum
  greatness 32 n.
  plenitude 54 n.
  summit 213 n.
mayor
  councillor 692 n.
mayoralty
  magistrature 733 n
maze
  complexity 61 n.
  meandering 251 n.
  enigma 530 n.
mead
  liquor 301 n.
  grassland 348 n.
meadow
  grassland 348 n.
meagre
  little 196 adj.
  lean 206 adj.
  underfed 636 adj.
  economical 814
    adj.
meal
  meal 301 n.

cereal 301 n.
corn 366 n.
mean
average 30 n.
middle 70 n., adj.
intend 617 vb.
parsimonious
816 adj.
plebeian 869 adj.
humble 872 adj.
meander
meander 251 vb.
meaning
meaning 514 n.
interpretation
520 n.
meaningful
meaningful 514 adj.
intelligible 516 adj.
meaningless
unmeaning 515 adj.
meanness
parsimony 816 n.
mean nothing
mean nothing
515 vb.
means
contrivance 623 n.
instrumentality
628 n.
means 629 n.
funds 797 n.
measly
bad 645 adj.
diseased 651 adj.
measurable
numerable 86 adj.
measure
finite quantity 26 n.
moderation 177 n.
size 195 n.
tempo 410 n.
gauge 465 n.
estimate 480 vb.
prosody 593 n.
deed 676 n.
portion 783 n.
measured
periodical 141 adj.
moderate 177 adj.
measure for measure
retaliation 714 n.
measurement
measurement 465 n.
(*see* **measure**)
measures
policy 623 n.

action 676 n.
meat
meat 301 n.
food 301 n.
Mecca
focus 76 n.
mechanic
machinist 630 n.
mechanical
involuntary 596 adj.
mechanical 630 adj.
mechanics
mechanics 630 n.
mechanism
machine 630 n.
mechanization
instrumentality
628 n.
medal
badge 547 n.
decoration 729 n.
medallion
jewellery 844 n.
medallist
proficient 696 n.
meddle
meddle 678 vb.
obstruct 702 vb.
mediate 720 vb.
meddler
meddler 678 n.
hinderer 702 n.
meddlesome
inquisitive 453 adj.
meddling 678 adj.
medial
middle 70 adj.
median
average 30 n.
mediate
mediate 720 vb.
mediation
mediation 720 n.
mediator
mediator 720 n.
match-maker 894 n.
mediatory
mediatory 720 adj.
medical
medical 658 adj.
medical treatment
therapy 658 n.
medicate
cure 656 vb.
doctor 658 vb.
medicinal
remedial 658 adj.

medicine
medicine 658 n.
medicine-man
doctor 658 n.
sorcerer 983 n.
medieval
olden 127 adj.
mediocre
mediocre 732 adj.
modest 874 adj.
mediocrity
moderation 177 n.
mid-course 625 n.
nonentity 639 n.
mediocrity 732 n.
meditate
meditate 449 vb.
intend 617 vb.
meditation
meditation 449 n.
worship, prayers
981 n.
mediterranean
middle 70 adj.
medium
average 30 n.
instrumentality
628 n.
psychic 984 n.
medley
medley 43 n.
confusion 61 n.
meed
portion 783 n.
meek
obedient 739 n.
humble 782 adj.
meet
congregate 74 vb.
meet with 154 vb.
touch 378 vb.
(*see* **meeting**)
meet half-way
compromise 770
vb.
meeting
junction 45 n.
assembly 74 n.
convergence 293 n.
social gathering
882 n.
meeting place
focus 76 n.
meeting-point
junction 45 n.
megalith
monument 548 n.

megalithic
large 195 adj.
megalomania
mania 503 n.
megaphone
megaphone 400 n.
hearing aid 415 n.
megaton
weighment 322 n.
megrims
spasm 318 n.
animal disease
651 n.
melancholia
psychopathy 503 n.
melancholy 834 n.
melancholic
melancholic 834
adj.
melancholy
bad 645 adj.
unhappy 825 adj.
melancholy 834 n.
cheerless 834 n.
melancholic
834 adj.
mêlée
turmoil 61 n.
fight 716 n.
mellifluous
melodious 410 adj.
elegant 575 adj.
mellow
soften 327 vb.
soft-hued 425 adj.
get better 654 vb.
mature 669 vb.
melodic
musical 412 adj.
melodious
melodious 410 adj.
melodrama
stage play 594 n.
excitation 821 n.
melodramatic
dramatic 594 adj.
exciting 821 adj.
melody
sweetness 392 n.
tune 412 n.
melon
fruit 301 n.
melt
decrease 37 vb.
be dispersed 75 vb.
liquefy 337 vb.
disappear 446 vb.

waste 634 vb.
melting
  soft 327 adj.
melting-pot
  mixture 43 n.
melt into
  shade off 27 vb.
  be turned to 147 vb.
member
  part 53 n.
  component 58 n.
  genitalia 164 n.
  participator 775 n.
membership
  inclusion 78 n.
  association 706 n.
  participation 775 n.
membrane
  layer 207 n.
memento
  reminder 505 n.
memoir
  record 548 n.
memoirs
  remembrance
  505 n.
  biography 590 n.
memorable
  remembered
  505 adj.
  notable 638 adj.
memorandum
  reminder 505 n.
  record 548 n.
memorial
  reminder 505 n.
  report 524 n.
  monument 548 n.
  trophy 729 n.
memorialize
  request 761 vb.
memorize
  memorize 505 vb.
  learn 536 vb.
memory
  memory 505 n.
  famousness 866 n.
menace
  hateful object
  888 n.
  threat 900 n.
menagerie
  zoo 369 n.
  collection 632 n.
mend
  rectify 654 vb.
  repair 656 vb.

mendacity
  falsehood 541 n.
Mendelian
  inherited 157 adj.
mender
  mender 656 n.
mendicancy
  poverty 801 n.
mendicant
  beggar 763 n.
menfolk
  male 372 n.
menial
  inferior 35 n., adj.
  worker 686 n.
  servant 742 n.
mensal
  mensal 301 adj.
mensurable
  numerable 86 adj.
  measured 465 adj.
mensuration
  measurement 465 n.
mental
  mental 447 adj.
  insane 503 adj.
mental disease
  insanity 503 n.
mental hospital
  madhouse 503 n.
  hospital 658 n.
mental hygiene
  sanity 502 n.
mentality
  intellect 447 n.
mental reservation
  mental dishonesty
  543 n.
mention
  referral 9 n.
  notice 455 vb.
  speak 579 vb.
mentor
  sage 500 n.
  teacher 537 n.
  adviser 691 n.
menu
  meal 301 n.
mephitic
  fetid 397 adj.
  toxic 653 adj.
mercantile
  trading 791 adj.
mercenary
  militarist 722 n.
  avaricious 816 adj.
  venal 930 adj.

selfish 932 adj.
mercer
  clothier 228 n.
mercerize
  toughen 329 vb.
merchandise
  merchandise
  795 n.
merchant
  merchant 794 n.
merchantman
  merchant ship
  275 n.
merciful
  lenient 736 adj.
  pitying 905 adj.
merciless
  severe 735 adj.
  pitiless 906 adj.
mercurial
  changeful 152 adj.
  unstable 152 adj.
  speedy 277 adj.
  light-minded
  456 adj.
  irresolute 601 adj.
  capricious 604 adj.
mercy
  mercy 905 n.
mere
  inconsiderable
  33 adj.
  simple 44 adj.
  lake 346 n.
meretricious
  spurious 542 adj.
  ornate 574 adj.
  vulgar 847 adj.
  unchaste 951 adj.
meretriciousness
  spectacle 445 n.
merge
  mix 43 vb.
  combine 50 vb.
  be turned to
  147 vb.
  cooperate 706 vb.
merger
  combination 50 n.
  association 706 n.
meridian
  noon 128 n.
  summit 213 n.
merit
  goodness 644 n.
  deserve 915 vb.
  virtues 933 n.

meritless
  unentitled 916 adj.
meritorious
  deserving 915 adj.
  approvable 923 adj.
mermaid
  sea-nymph 343 n.
merriment
  merriment 833 n.
  amusement 837 n.
merry
  (*see* merriment)
merry-andrew
  entertainer 594 n.
merry-maker
  reveller 837 n.
merry-making
  (*see* merriment)
mescalin
  drug 658 n.
mesh
  space 201 vb.
  network 222 n.
meshwork
  network 222 n.
mesmerize
  render insensible
  375 vb.
  frighten 854 vb.
mess
  medley 43 n.
  jumble 63 vb.
  chamber 194 n.
  feasting 301 n.
  eat 301 vb.
  predicament 700 n.
message
  message 529 n.
mess can, mess tin
  cauldron 194 n.
messenger
  messenger 531 n.
messenger boy
  courier 531 n.
Messiah
  leader 690 n.
  religious teacher
  973 n.
messianic
  redemptive 965 adj.
messianism
  aspiration 852 n.
messing
  mensal 301 adj.
messmate
  eater 301 n.
  chum 880 n.

messroom
chamber 194 n.
messy
orderless 61 adj.
dirty 649 adj.
mestizo
hybrid 43 n.
met
assembled 74 adj.
metagalactic
cosmic 321 adj.
metal
hardness 326 n.
mineral 359 n.
metallic
strident 407 adj.
metamorphic
multiform 82 adj.
metamorphosis
transformation 143 n.
metaphor
metaphor 519 n.
ornament 574 n.
metaphorical
semantic 514 adj.
figurative 519 adj.
metaphysician
philosopher 449 n.
metaphysics
philosophy 449 n.
occultism 984 n.
metapsychological
paranormal 984 adj.
metapsychology
psychology 447 n.
mete
measure 465 vb.
apportion 783 vb.
metempsychosis
transformation 143 n.
transference 272 n.
meteor, meteorite
meteor 321 n.
meteoric
speedy 277 adj.
meteorological
celestial 321 adj.
meteorologist
weather 340 n.
meteorology
weather 340 n.
meter
gauge 465 n.
method
order 60 n.

rule 81 n.
way 624 n.
methodize
regularize 62 vb.
methodology
order 60 n.
Methuselah
old man 133 n.
metic
foreigner 59 n.
settler 191 n.
meticulous
careful 457 adj.
accurate 494 adj.
fastidious 862 adj.
metre
long measure 203 n.
prosody 593 n.
metric
metric 465 adj.
metrical
metric 465 adj.
poetic 593 adj.
metrics
measurement 465 n.
prosody 593 n.
metric system
metrology 465 n.
metrology
metrology 465 n.
metronome
timekeeper 117 n.
metropolis
magistrature 733 n.
metropolitan
urban 192 adj.
central 225 adj.
ecclesiarch 986 n.
mettle
vigorousness 174 n.
resolution 599 n.
mettlesome
vigorous 174 adj.
lively 819 adj.
courageous 855 adj.
meum et tuum
property 777 n.
mew
ululate 409 vb.
imprison 747 vb.
mews
flat, stable 192 n.
mezzotint
engraving 555 n.
miasma
infection 651 n.

poison 659 n.
microbe
animalcule 196 n.
microcosm
miniature 196 n.
universe 321 n.
microfilm
camera 442 n.
record 548 n.
micrology
micrology 196 n.
micrometer
micrology 196 n.
micron
long measure 203 n.
micro-organism
animalcule 196 n.
microphone
megaphone 400 n.
hearing aid 415 n.
microscope
micrology 196 n.
microscope 442 n.
microscopic
minute 196 adj.
ill-seen 444 adj.
mid
middle 70 adj.
Midas touch
prosperity 730 n.
wealth 800 n.
midday
noon 128 n.
midden
rubbish 641 n.
sink 649 n.
middle
middle 70 n., adj.
centrality 225 n.
interjacent 231 adj.
Middle Ages
antiquity 125 n.
middle class
median 30 adj.
middleman
mediator 720 n.
consignee 754 n.
tradesman 794 n.
middle-of-the-road
neutral 625 adj.
middle term
average 30 n.
middling
median 30 adj.
not bad 644 adj.
mediocre 732 adj.

midge
animalcule 196 n.
midget
dwarf 196 n.
midland
inland 344 adj.
midline
middle 70 n.
midnight
midnight 129 n.
midriff
partition 231 n.
midshipman
naval officer 741 n.
mid-stream
mid-course 625 n.
midsummer
summer 128 n.
midwife
obstetrics 164 n.
doctor 658 n.
midwifery
obstetrics 164 n.
medical art 658 n.
midwinter
winter 129 n.
mien
mien 445 n.
conduct 688 n.
might
greatness 32 n.
strength 162 n.
be possible 469 vb.
might and main
exertion 682 n.
mightiness
(see **might, mighty**)
mighty
great 32 adj.
powerful 160 adj.
influential 178 adj.
worshipful 866 adj.
migraine
pang 377 n.
migrant
foreigner 59 n.
incomer 297 n.
bird 365 n.
migration
departure 296 n.
migratory
travelling 267 adj.
milch-cow
abundance 171 n.
store 632 n.

mild
warm 379 adj.
lenient 736 adj.
amiable 884 adj.
mildew
dirt 649 n.
blight 659 n.
mile
long measure
203 n.
mileage
distance 119 n.
milestone
degree 27 n.
serial place 73 n.
signpost 547 n.
militancy
bellicosity 718 n.
(*see* militant)
militant
active 678 adj.
defiant 711 adj.
militarist 722 n.
inimical 881 adj.
militarism
bellicosity 718 n.
militarist
militarist 722 n.
military
warlike 718 adj.
militate against
counteract 182 vb.
oppose 704 vb.
militia
army 722 n.
milk
milk 301 n.
extract 304 vb.
milk and water
insipidity 387 n.
milkiness
semitransparency
424 n.
milkmaid
herdsman 369 n.
milkman
seller 793 n.
milksop
weakling 163 n.
ninny 501 n.
milky
edible 301 adj.
semitransparent
424 adj.
whitish 427 adj.
Milky Way
star 321 n.

mill
notch 260 vb.
pulverizer 332 n.
pulverize 332 vb.
workshop 687 n.
millennial
secular 110 adj.
future 124 adj.
paradisiac 971 adj.
millennium
future state 124 n.
aspiration 852 n.
milliner
clothier 228 n.
millinery
dressing 228 n.
milling
edging 234 n.
millionaire
rich man 800 n.
million, for the
intelligible 516 adj.
easy 701 adj.
mill-pond
lake 346 n.
millstone
encumbrance 702
n.
milt
fertilizer 171 n.
mime
mimicry 20 n.
imitate 20 vb.
gesticulate 547 vb.
actor 594 n.
stage play 594 n.
act 594 vb.
mimetic
dramatic 594 adj.
mimic
imitate 20 vb.
represent 551 vb.
actor 594 n.
satirize 851 vb.
mimicry
mimicry 20 n.
(*see* mime,
mimic)
minatory
cautionary 664 adj.
threatening 900 adj.
mince
rend 46 vb.
pulverize 332 vb.
mind
be careful 457 vb.
look after 457 vb.

intellect, spirit
447 n.
opinion 485 n.
intention 617 n.
minded
intending 617 adj.
minder
machinist 630 n.
mindful
careful 457 adj.
remembering
505 adj.
mindless
mindless 448 adj.
foolish 499 adj.
mind's eye
imagination 513 n.
mine
great quantity
32 n.
demolish 165 vb.
excavation 255 n.
extract 304 vb.
store 632 n.
bomb 723 n.
mine-field
defences 713 n.
miner
excavator 255 n.
extractor 304 n.
mineral
soft drink 301 n.
mineral 359 n.
mineralogy
mineralogy 359 n.
mingle
mix 43 vb.
mingy
parsimonious
816 adj.
miniature
small 33 adj.
miniature 196 n.
picture 553 n.
minim
notation 410 n.
metrology 465 n.
minimal
small 33 adj.
lesser 35 adj.
minimalism
reformism 654 n.
minimalist
moderate 625 n.
reformer 654 n.
minimize
bate 37 vb.

underestimate
483 vb.
detract 926 vb.
minimum
small quantity
33 n.
sufficiency 635 n.
mining
extraction 304 n.
minister
agent 686 n.
envoy 754 n.
pastor 986 n.
ministerial
instrumental
628 adj.
governmental
733 adj.
minister to
conduce 156 vb.
minister to 703 vb.
ministration
ministration 988 n.
ministry
clergy 986 n.
mink
skin 226 n.
minnow
animalcule 196 n.
minor
inconsiderable
33 adj.
lesser 35 adj.
youngster 132 n.
unimportant
639 adj.
minority
fewness 105 n.
nonage 130 n.
minster
church 990 n.
minstrel
musician 413 n.
entertainer 594 n.
minstrelsy
musical skill 413 n.
poetry 593 n.
mint
mould 23 n.
potherb 301 n.
mint 797 vb.
mint condition, in
new 126 adj.
minting
coinage 797 n.
minus
non-existent 2 adj.

subtracted 39 adj.
indebted 803 adj.
minuscule
letter 558 n.
minute
period 110 n.
record 548 vb.
(see minuteness)
minute-book
record 548 n.
minuteness
minuteness 196 n.
carefulness 457 n.
minutiae
particulars 80 n.
trifle 639 n.
minx
youngster 132 n.
loose woman 952 n.
miracle
prodigy 864 n.
miracle-making
thaumaturgy 864 n.
miraculous
unusual 84 adj.
impossible 470 adj.
wonderful 864 adj.
mirage
visual fallacy
440 n.
fantasy 513 n.
deception 542 n.
mire
marsh 347 n.
mirror
resemble 18 vb.
imitate 20 vb.
copy 22 n.
reflection 417 n.
mirror 442 n.
mirth
merriment 833 n.
miry
marshy 347 adj.
misadventure
ill fortune 731 n.
misalliance
misfit 25 n.
misanthrope
misanthrope 902 n.
misanthropy
misanthropy 902 n.
misapplication
solecism 565 n.
misuse 675 n.
misapplied
irrelevant 10 adj.

misappropriation
misuse 675 n.
peculation 788 n.
misbegotten
deformed 246 adj.
bastard 956 adj.
misbehaviour
conduct 688 n.
guilty act 936 n.
miscalculation
misjudgement 481
n.
mistake 495 n.
miscall
misname 562 vb.
miscarriage
failure 728 n.
miscarry
be unproductive
172 vb.
miscarry 728 vb.
miscast
mismatch 25 vb.
miscegenation
mixture 43 n.
type of marriage
894 n.
miscellaneous
mixed 43 adj.
miscellany,
miscellanea
medley 43 n.
reading matter
589 n.
mischance
ill fortune 731 n.
mischief
destruction 165 n.
impairment 655 n.
mischief-maker
trouble-maker
663 n.
agitator 738 n.
mischievous
harmful 645 adj.
malevolent 898 adj.
(see mischief)
misconceive
misjudge 481 vb.
misinterpret
521 vb.
misconception
misjudgement 481
n.
misconduct
bungling 695 n.
guilty act 936 n.

misconstruction
error 495 n.
misinterpretation
521 n.
misconstrue
misinterpret
521 vb.
misdate
misdate 118 vb.
misdeed
guilty act 936 n.
misdemeanant
offender 904 n.
misdemeanour
guilty act 936 n.
lawbreaking 954 n.
misdescribe
misrepresent
552 vb.
misdirect
mislead 495 vb.
misdirection
misteaching 535 n.
misuse 675 n.
misdoing
wrong 914 n.
guilty act 936 n.
mise-en-scène
stage set 594 n.
miser
niggard 816 n.
miserable
unimportant
639 adj.
melancholic
834 adj.
miserly
parsimonious
816 adj.
avaricious 816 adj.
misery
adversity 731 n.
sorrow 825 n.
moper 834 n.
misfeasance
lawbreaking 954 n.
misfire
bungling 695 n.
misfit
irrelation 10 n.
misfit 25 n.
displacement 188 n.
misfortune
ill fortune 731 n.
misgiving
doubt 486 n.
nervousness 854 n.

misguidance
error 495 n.
misteaching 535 n.
misguided
misjudging 481 adj.
mistaken 495 adj.
mishap
ill fortune 731 n.
mishit
bungling 695 n.
misinformation
untruth 543 n.
misinterpret
misjudge 481 vb.
blunder 495 vb.
misinterpret
521 vb.
misjoinder
misfit 25 n.
misjudge
mistime 138 vb.
misinterpret
521 vb.
misjudgement
misjudgement 481
n.
error 495 n.
mislaid
misplaced 188 adj.
mislay
derange 63 vb.
lose 772 vb.
mislead
mislead 495 vb.
befool 542 vb.
mismanage
(see mismanage-
ment)
mismanagement
misuse 675 n.
bungling 695 n.
mismatch
mismatch 25 vb.
misnomer
name 561 n.
misnomer 562 n.
misogynist
celibate 895 n.
misanthrope 902 n.
misplace
derange 63 vb.
misplace 188 vb.
misplaced
irrelevant 10 adj.
unapt 25 adj.
misprint
mistake 495 n.

575

mispronounce
solecize 565 vb.
stammer 580 vb.
misquote
misinterpret
521 vb.
misrepresent
distort 246 vb.
misinterpret
521 vb.
satirize 851 vb.
misrepresentation
misteaching 535 vb.
falsehood 541 n.
untruth 543 n.
misrepresentation
552 n.
misrule
anarchy 734 n.
oppress 735 vb.
miss
youngster 132 n.
fall short 307 vb.
blunder 495 vb.
fail 728 vb.
lose 772 vb.
regret 830 vb.
missal
office-book 988 n.
miss, give it a
not act 677 vb.
misshapen
amorphous 244 adj.
deformed 246 adj.
unsightly 842 adj.
missile
missile 287 n.
missing
non-existent
2 adj.
absent 190 adj.
required 627 adj.
lost 772 adj.
missing link
incompleteness
55 n.
discontinuity 72 n.
completion 725 n.
mission
vocation 622 n.
mandate 751 n.
envoy 754 n.
philanthropy 901 n.
church ministry
985 n.
missionary
preacher 537 n.

religious teacher
973 n.
pastor 986 n.
missionary spirit
philanthropy 901 n.
missive
correspondence
588 n.
miss out
exclude 57 vb.
misstatement
inexactness 495 n.
untruth 543 n.
mist
cloud 355 n.
opacity 423 n.
blur 440 vb.
invisibility 444 n.
uncertainty 474 n.
mistake
mistake 495 n.
solecism 565 n.
mistaken
misjudging 481 adj.
misteach
misinterpret 521 vb.
misteach 535 vb.
mistiming
intempestivity
138 n.
mistitle
misname 562 n.
mistress
master 741 n.
owner 776 n.
loved one 887 n.
kept woman 952 n.
mistrust
doubt 486 n.
mistrustful
doubting 474 adj.
unbelieving
486 adj.
misty
cloudy 355 adj.
dim 419 adj.
opaque 423 adj.
semitransparent
424 adj.
ill-seen 444 adj.
misunderstand
err 495 vb.
misinterpret 521 vb.
misuse 675 n.
misuse
waste 634 vb.
misuse 675 n., vb.

prodigality 815 n.
mite
small quantity 33 n.
child 132 n.
vermin 365 n.
mitigate
moderate 177 vb.
qualify 468 vb.
relieve 831 vb.
extenuate 927 vb.
mitre
vestments 989 n.
mitten
glove 228 n.
mix
mix 43 vb.
jumble 63 vb.
be sociable 882 vb.
mixed bag
non-uniformity
17 n.
mix it
fight 716 vb.
mixture
mixture 43 n.
composition 56 n.
medicine 658 n.
mnemonic
reminder 505 n.
moan
cry 408 vb.
be discontented
829 vb.
moat
fence 235 n.
conduit 351 n.
defences 713 n.
mob
rampage 61 vb.
crowd 74 n.
multitude 104 n.
charge 712 vb.
rabble 869 n.
disapprove 924 vb.
mobility
changeableness
152 n.
mobilization
assemblage 74 n.
war measures
718 n.
mob law
anarchy 734 n.
lawlessness 954 n.
mock
simulating 18 adj.
spurious 542 adj.

laughing-stock
851 n.
ridicule 851 vb.
shame 867 vb.
mocker
(*see* mock)
mockery
insubstantial thing
4 n.
(*see* mock)
mock-heroic
derisive 851 adj.
mock-modest
affected 850 adj.
modal
conditionate
7 adj.
circumstantial
8 adj.
modality
modality 7 n.
mode
modality 7 n.
musical note 410 n.
way 624 n.
fashion 848 n.
model
copy, duplicate
22 n.
prototype 23 n.
living model 23 n.
miniature 196 n.
little 196 adj.
efform 243 vb.
image 551 n.
represent 551 vb.
sculpt 554 vb.
plan 623 n.
paragon 646 n.
perfect 646 adj.
modeller
sculptor 556 n.
moderate
median 30 adj.
moderate 177 adj.,
vb.
qualify 468 vb.
moderate 625 n.
relieve 831 vb.
moderation
counteraction
182 n.
underestimation
483 n.
irenics 719 n.
temperance 942 n.
(*see* moderate)

moderator
moderator 177 n.
church officer
986 n.
modern
modern 126 adj.
fashionable 848 adj.
modernism
modernism 126 n.
modernize
modernize 126 vb.
modify 143 vb.
revolutionize
149 vb.
restore 656 vb.
modest
mediocre 732 adj.
humble 872 adj.
disinterested
931 adj.
(*see* modesty)
modesty
modesty 874 n.
purity 950 n.
modicum
small quantity 33 n.
portion 783 n.
modification
change 143 n.
qualification 468 n.
modify
(*see* modification)
modish
fashionable 848 adj.
modiste
clothier 228 n.
modulate
adjust 24 vb.
modulation
change 143 n.
modus operandi
way 624 n.
conduct 688 n.
mohair
textile 222 n.
moiety
part 53 n.
bisection 92 n.
moist
humid 341 adj.
moisten
moisten 341 vb.
moisture
moisture 341 n.
moke
beast of burden
273 n.

mokes
network 222 n.
molar
tooth 256 n.
molasses
sweet 392 n.
mole
projection 254 n.
rodent 365 n.
safeguard 662 n.
defences 713 n.
molecule
element 319 n.
molehill
monticle 209 n.
molest
be obstructive
702 vb.
torment 827 vb.
mollification
moderation 177 n.
softness 327 n.
pacification 719 n.
mollusc
animal 365 n.
mollycoddle
ninny 501 n.
molten
liquefied 337 adj.
fiery 379 adj.
moment
brief span 114 n.
instant 116 n.
occasion 137 n.
cause 156 n.
importance 638 n.
momentary
transient 114 adj.
momentous
crucial 137 adj.
eventful 154 adj.
influential 178 adj.
important 638 adj.
momentum
impulse 279 n.
monarch
sovereign 741 n.
possessor 776 n.
monarchy
government 733 n.
monastery
monastery 986 n.
monasticism
seclusion 883 n.
celibacy 895 n.
monasticism 985
n.

monetary
monetary 797 adj.
money
money 797 n.
wealth 800 n.
money-bag,
money-box
storage 632 n.
money-changer
moneyer 797 n.
money for jam
easy thing 701 n.
money-grubber
niggard 816 n.
money-grubbing
acquisition 771 n.
(*see* money-
grubber)
money-lender
lender 784 n.
money-making
wealth 800 n.
money market
finance 797 n.
money's worth
price 809 n.
monger
seller 793 n.
tradesman 794 n.
mongoose
rodent 365 n.
mongrel
hybrid 43 n.
monitor
inquire 459 vb.
adviser 691 n.
monitory
cautionary 664 adj.
monk
monk 986 n.
monkey
imitator 20 n.
monkey 365 n.
monkey-trick
foolery 497 n.
monochromatic
coloured 425 adj.
monocle
eyeglass 442 n.
monodrama
stage play 594 n.
monogamy
type of marriage
894 n.
monogram
label 547 n.
initials 558 n.

monograph
dissertation 591 n.
monolith
uniformity 16 n.
unit 88 n.
monolithic
simple 44 adj.
indivisible 52 adj.
(*see* monolith)
monologue
oration 579 n.
soliloquy 585 n.
monomachy
duel 716 n.
monomania
eccentricity 503 n.
opiniatry 602 n.
monopolist
restriction 747 n.
egotist 932 n.
monopolistic
restraining 747 adj.
possessing 773 adj.
avaricious 816 adj.
selfish 932 adj.
monopolize
appropriate 786 vb.
monopoly
exclusion 57 n.
corporation 708 n.
restriction 747 n.
possession 773 n.
monosyllabic
concise 569 adj.
taciturn 582 adj.
monosyllable
word 559 n.
monotheism
deism 973 n.
monotone
uniformity 16 n.
musical note 410 n.
monotony
uniformity 16 n.
continuity 71 n.
recurrence 106 n.
tedium 838 n.
monsoon
rain 350 n.
wind 352 n.
monster
eyesore 842 n.
prodigy 864 n.
monster 938 n.
monstrosity
deformity 246 n.
prodigy 864 n.

monstrous
huge 195 adj.
ugly 842 adj.
wonderful 864 adj.
heinous 934 adj.
month
period 110 n.
monthly
seasonal 141 adj.
monument
antiquity 125 n.
reminder 505 n.
monument 548 n.
trophy 729 n.
monumental
enormous 32 adj.
recording 548 adj.
moo
ululate 409 vb.
mood
temperament 5 n.
grammar 564 n.
affections 817 n.
moody
melancholic 834 adj.
irascible 892 adj.
sullen 893 adj.
moon
changeable thing 152 n.
follower 284 n.
moon 321 n.
luminary 420 n.
be inattentive 456 vb.
moonlight
moon 321 n.
moonshine
insubstantial thing 4 n.
pretext 614 n.
moor
tie 45 vb.
place 187 vb.
navigate 269 vb.
(*see* moorland)
mooring(s)
cable 47 n.
moorland
high land 209 n.
marsh 347 n.
moot
uncertain 474 adj.
argue 475 vb.
propound 512 vb.
moot point
topic 452 n.

question 459 n.
mop
cleaning utensil 648 n.
mop and mow
goblinize 970 vb.
mope
be dejected 834 vb.
moper
moper 834 n.
mop up
destroy 165 vb.
dry 342 vb.
carry through 725 vb.
moraine
thing transferred 272 n.
soil 344 n.
moral
maxim 496 n.
commentary 520 n.
precept 693 n.
ethical 917 adj.
pure 950 adj.
morale
obedience 739 n.
manliness 855 n.
morality
(*see* morals)
moralize
teach 534 vb.
make better 654 vb.
moralizing
advice 691 n.
morals
conduct 688 n.
morals 917 n.
virtue 933 n.
purity 950 n.
morass
marsh 347 n.
moratorium
lull 145 n.
non-payment 805 n.
morbidity
ill-health 651 n.
mordancy
(*see* mordant)
mordant
pungent 388 adj.
forceful 571 adj.
disapproving 924 adj.
mordent
musical note 410 n.

more so
superior 34 adj.
crescendo 36 adv.
more than enough
redundance 637 n.
morganatic
matrimonial 894 adj.
morgue
interment 364 n.
moribund
dying 361 adj.
sick 651 adj.
morion
headgear 228 n.
armour 713 n.
Mormon
polygamist 894 n.
morning
beginning 68 n.
morning 128 n.
earliness 135 n.
morocco
skin 226 n.
moron
fool 501 n.
madman 504 n.
moronic
insane 503 adj.
moroseness, morosity
unsociability 883 n.
sullenness 893 n.
misanthropy 902 n.
morphia
drug 658 n.
morphology
form 243 n.
linguistics 557 n.
morrow
futurity 124 n.
morse
telecommunication 531 n.
signal 547 n.
morsel
small quantity 33 n.
piece 53 n.
mouthful 301 n.
mortal
ephemeral 114 adj.
deadly 362 adj.
person 371 n.
mortality
transientness 114 n.
death, death roll 361 n.

mortar
adhesive 47 n.
gun 723 n.
mortgage
security 767 n.
debt 803 n.
mortgagee
creditor 802 n.
mortgagor
debtor 803 n.
mortician
interment 364 n.
mortification
decay 51 n.
annoyance 827 n.
regret 830 n.
humiliation 872 n.
asceticism 945 n.
mortify
cause discontent 829 vb.
mortise
join 45 vb.
mortuary
interment 364 n.
mosaic
non-uniformity 17 n.
chequer 437 n.
ornamental art 844 n.
mosque
temple, church 990 n.
mosquito
fly 365 n.
mossy
vegetal 366 adj.
mote
small thing 33 n.
dirt 649 n.
motel
inn 192 n.
moth
destroyer 168 n.
blight 659 n.
moth-ball
preserver 666 n.
moth-eaten
antiquated 127 adj.
dilapidated 655 adj.
mother
maternity 169 n.
pet 889 vb.
motherhood
family 11 n.
maternity 169 n.

motherland
home 192 n.

motherly
parental 169 adj.
loving 887 adj.

mother superior
nun 986 n.

mother tongue
language 557 n.

mother-wit
intelligence 498 n.

motif
topic 452 n.
pattern 844 n.

motion
motion 265 n.
cacation 302 n.
topic 452 n.
gesture 547 n.
activity 678 n.

motionless
still 266 adj.
inactive 679 adj.

motivate
motivate 612 vb.

motivation
motive 612 n.

motive
moving 265 adj.
motive 612 n.

motiveless
designless 618 n.

motive power
energy 160 n.

motley
non-uniformity 17 n.
multiform 82 adj.

motor
automobile 274 n.
machine 630 n.

motor-car
automobile 274 n.

motoring
land travel 267 n.

motorist
driver 268 n.

motorway
road 624 n.

mottle
variegate 437 vb.

motto
maxim 496 n.
heraldry 547 n.

moue
distortion 246 n.

mould
modality 7 n.

mould 23 n.
decay 51 n.
sort 77 n.
efform 243 vb.
structure 331 n.
soil 344 n.
sculpt 554 vb.
dirt 649 n.
decorate 844 vb.

moulder
decompose 51 vb.
deteriorate 655 vb.

moulding
ornamental art 844 n.

moult
doff 229 vb.

mound
monticle 209 n.
defences 713 n.

mount
support 218 vb.
ride 267 vb.
saddle-horse 273 n.
ascend 308 vb.
elevate 310 vb.
prepare 669 vb.

mountain
high land 209 n.

mountaineer
dweller 191 n.
climber 308 vb.

mountainous
great 32 adj.
huge 195 adj.
alpine 209 adj.

mountebank
entertainer 594 n.

mourn
lament 836 vb.

mourner
funeral 364 n.
weeper 836 n.

mournful
melancholic 834 adj.

mournfulness
sorrow 825 n.

mourning
funeral dress 228 n.
obsequies 364 n.
funereal 364 adj.

mouse
animalcule 196 n.

mouse-like
humble 872 adj.

mouser
hunter 619 n.

moustache,
moustachio
hair 259 n.

mousy
colourless 426 adj.
grey 429 adj.

mouth
maw 194 n.
orifice 263 n.
voice 577 vb.

mouthful
mouthful 301 n.
oration 579 n.

mouthpiece
air-pipe 353 n.
speaker 579 n.
deputy 755 n.

movable
moving 265 adj.
property 777 n.

move
operate 173 vb.
move 265 vb.
transpose 272 vb.
propound 512 vb.
gesture 547 n.
essay 671 n.
deed 676 n.
tactics 688 n.
stratagem 698 n.
excite 821 vb.

moveable
(*see* movable)

movement
motion 265 n.
cacation 302 n.
musical piece 412 n.
activity 678 n.
party, society 708 n.

mover
motivator 612 n.
adviser 691 n.

move with the times
modernize 126 vb.
progress 285 vb.

movie
cinema 445 n.

moving staircase
conveyor 274 n.
lifter 310 n.

mow
cut 46 vb.
shorten 204 vb.
cultivate 370 vb.

mow down
slaughter 362 vb.

mower
husbandman 370 n.

Mrs Grundy
etiquette 848 n.
prude 950 n.

Mr X
no name 562 n.

much
great quantity 32 n.
many 104 adj.

much of, make
make important 638 vb.

muck
rubbish 641 n.
dirt 649 n.

muck-raker
defamer 926 n.

muck up
make unclean 649 vb.

mucky
dirty 649 adj.

mucous
viscid 354 adj.

mucus
semiliquidity 354 n.

mud
marsh 347 n.
dirt 649 n.

muddle
confusion 61 n.
derange 63 vb.
not discriminate 464 vb.

muddy
humid 341 adj.
marshy 347 adj.
dirty 649 adj.
make unclean 649 vb.

mud-slinging
detraction 926 n.

muff
glove 228 n.
be clumsy 695 vb.
bungler 697 n.

muffin
pastry 301 n.

muffle
cover 226 vb.
mute 401 vb.
conceal 525 vb.

muffled
non-resonant 405 adj.

muffler
shawl 228 n.
warm clothes 381 n.
mufti
informal dress
228 n.
theologian 973 n.
mug
cup 194 n.
face 237 n.
ninny 501 n.
study 536 vb.
mulatto
hybrid 43 n.
mulct
punish 963 vb.
mule
hybrid 43 n.
footwear 228 n.
opinionist 602 n.
muleteer
driver 268 n.
mulish
equine 273 adj.
obstinate 602 adj.
mull
textile 222 n.
study 536 vb.
mullet
table fish 365 n.
multicoloured
variegated 437 adj.
multifarious
multiform 82 adj.
multiform
multiform 82 adj.
changeful 152 adj.
multilateral
lateral 239 adj.
contractual 765 adj.
multilingual
linguistic 557 adj.
multiple
numerical element
85 n.
plural 101 adj.
many 104 adj.
multiplication
numerical operation
86 n.
propagation 164 n.
multiplication table
counting instrument
86 n.
multiplicity
plurality 101 n.
multitude 104 n.

multiply
be many 104 vb.
(*see* multiplica-
tion)
multipurpose
general 79 adj.
useful 640 adj.
multiracial
mixed 43 adj.
multitude
crowd 74 n.
multitude 104 n.
mum
voiceless 578 adj.
taciturn 582 adj.
mumble
chew 301 vb.
stammer 580 vb.
mumbo-jumbo
god 966 n.
spell 983 n.
mummery
foolery 497 n.
sham 542 n.
ostentation 875 n.
mummify
inter 364 vb.
preserve 666 vb.
mummy
corpse 363 n.
munch
chew 301 vb.
mundane
irreligious 974 adj.
municipal
regional 184 adj.
municipality
jurisdiction 955 n.
municipalize
appropriate
786 vb.
munificence
liberality 813 n.
muniment
record 548 n.
title-deed 767 n.
muniment room
recorder 549 n.
munitions
means 629 n.
arm 723 n.
mural
picture 553 n.
murder
murder 362 vb.
murderer
murderer 362 n.

murderous
murderous 362 adj.
murk
darkness 418 n.
dimness 419 n.
murky
opaque 423 adj.
murmur
faintness 401 n.
discontent 829 n.
murrain
plague 651 n.
animal disease
681 n.
muscle
power 160 n.
exertion 682 n.
muscle-bound
rigid 326 adj.
muscular
stalwart 162 adj.
muse
meditate 449 vb.
museum
exhibit 522 n.
collection 632 n.
museum piece
archaism 127 n.
exhibit 522 n.
laughing-stock
851 n.
mush
semiliquidity 354 n.
pulpiness 356 n.
mushroom
upstart 126 n.
new 126 adj.
radiation 417 n.
mushy
soft 327 adj.
pulpy 356 adj.
music
music 412 n.
musical
musical 412 adj.
stage play 594 n.
musical instrument
musical instrument
414 n.
musical notation
notation 410 n.
music hall
theatre 594 n.
musician
musician 413 n.
musicianship
musical skill 413 n.

musk
scent 396 n.
musket
fire-arm 723 n.
musketeer
soldiery 722 n.
musketry
propulsion 287 n.
bombardment
712 n.
arm 723 n.
muslin
textile 222 n.
mussel
table fish 365 n.
must, a
requirement 627
n.
mustard
condiment 389 n.
yellowness 433 n.
muster
assemblage 74 n.
statistics 86 n.
number 86 vb.
muster-roll
list 87 n.
musty
fetid 397 adj.
dirty 649 adj.
mutability
changeableness
152 n.
mutation
change 143 n.
conversion 147 n.
mute
funeral 364 n.
silent 399 adj.
silencer 401 n.
taciturn 582 adj.
weeper 836 n.
mutilate
make ugly 842 vb.
torture 963 vb.
mutilation
impairment 655 n.
mutineer
revolter 738 n.
mutinous
dutiless 918 adj.
(*see* mutiny)
mutiny
strike 145 n.
dutilessness 918 n.
mutism
aphony 578 n.

er
nd faint 401 vb.
nmer 580 vb.
on
at 301 n.
ial
relative 12 adj.
erchanged
1 adj.
ial assistance
peration 706 n.
ality
relation 12 n.
erchange 151 n.
ialize
ialize 775 vb.
zle
able 161 vb.
ke mute 587 vb.
der 702 vb.
e-arm 723 n.
ter 748 n.
pia, myosis
n sight 440 n.
pic
n-sighted 440 adj.
iad
ltitude 104 n.
rh
in 357 n.
nt 396 n.
teries
igion 973 n.
e 988 n.
terious
usual 84 adj.
zzling 517 adj.
cult 523 adj.
tery
known thing
91 n.
cret, enigma
30 n.
ge play 594 n.
e 988 n.
stic
xpressible
17 adj.
igious 973 adj.
tist 979 n.
votional 981 adj.
stical
ine 968 adj.
ee mystic)
sticism
editation 449 n.
ligion 973 n.

mystification
sophistry 477 n.
unintelligibility
517 n.
concealment 525 n.
mystify
puzzle 474 vb.
mystique
prestige 866 n.
cult 981 n.
myth
fantasy 513 n.
fable 543 n.
mythical, mythic
imaginary 513 adj.
theotechnic 966 adj.
mythological
olden 127 adj.
imaginary 513 adj.
mythology
tradition 127 n.
anthropology 371 n.
fable 543 n.

N

nab
arrest 747 vb.
take 786 vb.
nadir
zero 103 n.
lowness 210 n.
nag
saddle-horse 273 n.
incite 612 vb.
bicker 709 vb.
enrage 891 vb.
nail
affix 45 vb.
fastening 47 n.
hanger 217 n.
perforator 263 n.
pierce 263 vb.
nails
nippers 778 n.
naïve
foolish 499 adj.
artless 699 adj.
naked
uncovered 229 adj.
undisguised 522 adj.
vulnerable 661 adj.
name
name 561 n., vb.
repute 866 n.
name-giver
nomenclator 561 n.

nameless
anonymous 562 adj.
inglorious 867 adj.
name-plate
label 547 n.
namesake
name 561 n.
naming
nomenclature
561 n.
nanny
domestic 742 n.
keeper 749 n.
nap
hair 259 n.
texture 331 n.
sleep 679 n., vb.
nape
rear 238 n.
napless
hairless 229 adj.
nappy
loincloth 228 n.
downy 259 adj.
narcissism
vanity 873 n.
Narcissus
vain person 873 n.
narcosis
helplessness 161 n.
insensibility 375 n.
narcotic
anaesthetic 375 n.
drug 658 n.
nark
informer 524 n.
narration
description 590 n.
narrative
record 548 n.
narrative 590 n.
narrator
narrator 590 n.
narrow
make smaller
198 vb.
narrow 206 adj.
narrow-minded
481 adj.
restraining 747 adj.
narrow-mindedness
narrow mind 481
n.
narrowness
narrowness 206 n.
narrow squeak
escape 667 n.

nasal
speech sound 398 n.
nasality
stridor 407 n.
nascent
beginning 68 adj.
nastiness
discourtesy 885 n.
(*see* nasty)
nasty
unsavoury 391 adj.
fetid 397 adj.
not nice 645 adj.
unclean 649 adj.
malevolent 898 adj.
natal
first 68 adj.
natation
aquatics 269 n.
nation
nation 371 n.
national
ethnic 11 adj.
native 191 adj.
national 371 adj.
subject 742 n.
nationalism
particularism 80 n.
patriotism 901 n.
nationalist
patriot 901 n.
nationalistic
biased 481 adj.
nationality
race 11 n.
subjection 745 n.
(*see* nationalism)
nationalize
socialize 775 vb.
appropriate 786 vb.
native
genetic 5 adj.
intrinsic 5 adj.
native 191 n., adj.
native state
undevelopment
670 n.
nativity
origin 68 n.
natural
real 1 adj.
lifelike 18 adj.
material 319 adj.
probable 471 adj.
true, genuine
494 adj.
fool 501 n.

descriptive 590 adj.
usual 610 adj.
artless 699 adj.
natural history
biology 358 n.
naturalist
biology 358 n.
naturalistic
representing
551 adj.
naturalization
conformity 83 n.
conversion 147 n.
reception 299 n.
habituation 610 n.
naturalized
native 191 adj.
naturalness
plainness 573 n.
artlessness 699 n.
natural selection
biology 358 n.
nature
character 5 n.
composition 56 n.
matter 319 n.
habit 610 n.
affections 817 n.
nature study
biology 358 n.
naught
zero 103 n.
(see nought)
naughtiness
disobedience 738 n.
naughty
unchaste 961 adj.
nausea
voidance 300 n.
dislike 861 n.
nauseate
be unpalatable
391 n.
cause dislike
861 vb.
nauseated
vomiting 300 adj.
nauseous
hateful 888 adj.
nautch-girl
entertainer 594 n.
nautical
seafaring 269 adj.
seamanlike 270 adj.
marine 275 adj.
naval
seafaring 269 adj.

warlike 718 adj.
nave
middle 70 n.
church interior
990 n.
navel
centrality 225 n.
navigable
deep 211 adj.
seafaring 269 adj.
navigate
navigate 269 vb.
navigator
navigator 270 n.
navvy
worker 686 n.
navy
navy 722 n.
nay
negation 533 n.
refusal 760 n.
near
akin 11 adj.
near 200 adj.
approach 289 vb.
nearness
nearness 200 n.
neat
unmixed 44 adj.
orderly 60 adj.
elegant 575 adj.
clean 648 adj.
skilful 694 adj.
personable 841
adj.
intoxicating
949 adj.
neaten
unravel 62 vb.
beautify 841 vb.
nebula
star 321 n.
cloud 355 n.
nebulosity
(see nebulous)
nebulous
celestial 321 adj.
cloudy 355 adj.
necessaries
requirement 627 n.
necessary
necessary 596 adj.
necessitarian
fatalist 596 n.
necessitate
necessitate 596 vb.
compel 740 vb.

necessitous
necessitous 627 adj.
poor 801 adj.
necessitude
necessity 596 n.
necessity
destiny 155 n.
necessity 596 n.
no choice 606 n.
needfulness 627 n.
compulsion 740 n.
neck
supporter 218 n.
caress 889 vb.
neck and neck
equal 28 adj.
synchronous
123 adj.
neckband
neckwear 228 n.
necklace
neckwear 228 n.
jewellery 844 n.
necrology
death roll 361 n.
necromancy
sorcery 983 n.
necropolis
cemetery 364 n.
nectar
liquor 301 n.
savouriness 390 n.
need
deficit 55 n.
shortcoming 307 n.
requirement 627 n.
needful
required 627 adj.
neediness
poverty 801 n.
needle
sharp point 256 n.
indicator 547 n.
enrage 891 vb.
needles
nervousness 854 n.
needless
superfluous 637 adj.
needlework
needlework 844 n.
needy
poor 801 adj.
ne'er-do-well
bad man 938 n.
nefarious
disreputable
867 adj.

heinous 934 adj.
negate
(see negation)
negation
contrariety 14 n.
negation 533 n.
rejection 607 n.
refusal 760 n.
negative
nullify 2 vb.
unsuccessful
728 adj.
(see negation)
neglect
negligence 458 n.
dilapidation 655 ▶
not use 674 vb.
not observe 769
vb.
neglectful
negligent 458 adj
négligé
informal dress
228 n.
negligence
negligence 458 n.
laxity 734 n.
indifference 860 n
(see neglect)
negligent
negligent 458 adj.
forgetful 506 adj.
(see negligence)
negligible
unimportant
639 adj.
negotiable
transferable
272 adj.
possible 469 adj.
transferred 780 a⊄
negotiate
cooperate 706 vb.
make terms 766 ▶
bargain 791 vb.
negotiation
conference 584 n.
(see negotiate)
negotiator
mediator 720 n.
envoy 754 n.
negress
negro 428 n.
negro
negro 428 n.
neigh
ululate 409 vb.

eighbour
be near 200 vb.
friend 880 n.
eighbourhood
region 184 n.
near place 200 n.
eighbourly
sociable 882 adj.
emesis
retaliation 714 n.
revenge 910 n.
punishment 963 n.
eolithic
secular 110 adj.
eological
neological 560 adj.
eologism
neology 560 n.
eology
neology 560 n.
eophyte
changed person
147 n.
beginner 538 n.
eoterism
newness 126 n.
ephew
kinsman 11 n.
s plus ultra
extremity 69 n.
perfection 646 n.
epotism
injustice 914 n.
improbity 930 n.
erve
strengthen 162 vb.
give courage 855 vb.
sauciness 878 n.
erveless
impotent 161 adj.
feeble 572 adj.
erve-racking
distressing 827 adj.
frightening 854 adj.
erves
psychopathy 503 n.
nervousness 854 n.
ervous
agitated 318 adj.
irresolute 601 adj.
nervous 854 adj.
ervous disorder
psychopathy 503 n.
ervousness
(*see* nervous)
ervy
(*see* nerves)

nest
group 74 n.
seedbed 156 n.
nest 192 n.
dwell 192 vb.
refuge 662 n.
nest-egg
store 632 n.
nestle
dwell 192 vb.
caress 889 vb.
nestling
youngling 132 n.
Nestor
sage 500 n.
net
remaining 41 adj.
bring together
74 vb.
network 222 n.
enclosure 235 n.
trap 542 n.
take 786 vb.
nether
low 210 adj.
nether-world
the dead 361 n.
nettle
prickle 256 n.
huff 891 vb.
network
correlation 12 n.
gap 201 n.
network 222 n.
neurologist
doctor 658 n.
neurosis
psychopathy 503 n.
neurotic
insane 503 adj.
madman 504 n.
neuter
generic 77 adj.
eunuch 161 n.
impotent 161 adj.
neutral
median 30 adj.
grey 429 adj.
choiceless 606 adj.
neutral 625 adj.
peaceful 717 adj.
disinterested
931 adj.
neutralization
counteraction 182 n.
neutralize
disable 161 vb.

counteract 182 vb.
remedy 658 vb.
never
never 109 adv.
never-ending
perpetual 115 adj.
uncompleted
726 adj.
never-failing
successful 727 adj.
never-never system
borrowing 785 n.
new
first 68 adj.
new 126 adj.
new-born
new 126 adj.
infantine 132 adj.
new broom
busy person 678 n.
new-comer
incomer 297 n.
newfangled
modern 126 adj.
neological 560 adj.
new leaf
amendment 654 n.
new look
modernism 126 n.
newly-wed
spouse 894 n.
married 894 adj.
new man
changed person
147 n.
newness
non-imitation 21
n.
newness 126 n.
news
information 524 n.
news 529 n.
newsman
newsmonger 529 n.
newsmonger
inquisitor 453 n.
newsmonger 529 n.
newspaper
the press 528 n.
newsprint
stationery 586 n.
paper 631 n.
newsreel
cinema 445 n.
news 529 n.
news-value
news 529 n.

newsy
informative 524
adj.
loquacious 581 adj.
next
sequent 65 adj.
subsequent 120 adj.
next door
near place 200 n.
next of kin
kinsman 11 n.
next step
progression 285 n.
next world
the dead 361 n.
nexus
bond 47 n.
niagara
waterfall 350 n.
nib
stationery 586 n.
nibble
mouthful 301 n.
eat 301 vb.
nice
pleasant 376 adj.
savoury 390 adj.
discriminating
463 adj.
clean 648 adj.
pleasurable 826 adj.
fastidious 862 adj.
amiable 884 adj.
nicety
discrimination
463 n.
niche
place 185 n.
compartment 194 n.
nick
notch 260 n., vb.
mark 547 vb.
nickname
name 561 n.
misnomer 562 n.
nick of time
occasion 137 n.
nicotine
tobacco 388 n.
niece
kinsman 11 n.
niffy
fetid 397 adj.
niggard
niggard 816 n.
niggardly
insufficient 636 adj.

niggler
  detractor 926 n.
nigh
  nigh 200 adv.
night
  darkness 418 n.
  (*see* evening)
nightcap
  nightwear 228 n.
  potion 301 n.
  soporific 679 n.
night club
  place of amusement
  837 n.
nightfall
  evening 129 n.
nightgown, nightshirt
  nightwear 228 n.
nightingale
  vocalist 413 n.
nightly
  vespertine 129 adj.
nightmare
  fantasy 513 n.
  worry 825 n.
night-time
  evening 129 n.
nihilism
  anarchy 734 n.
  sedition 738 n.
nihilist
  destroyer 168 n.
nihilistic
  violent 176 adj.
nihil obstat
  permit 756 n.
nil
  zero 103 n.
nimble
  speedy 277 adj.
nimble-witted
  intelligent 498 adj.
nincompoop
  ninny 501 n.
nine days' wonder
  insubstantial thing
  4 n.
  brief span 114 n.
  prodigy 864 n.
**nine points of the
law**
  possession 773 n.
ninny
  ninny 501 n.
nip
  make smaller
  198 vb.

shorten 204 vb.
  potion 301 n.
  pang 377 n.
  touch 378 vb.
  refrigerate 382 vb.
  blight 659 n.
nip in the bud
  suppress 165 vb.
nippers
  extractor 304 n.
  nippers 778 n.
nipple
  bosom 253 n.
nippy
  active 678 adj.
nirvana
  extinction 2 n.
  heaven 971 n.
nit
  vermin 365 n.
no
  refusal 760 n.
Noah's Ark
  medley 43 n.
  cattle pen 369 n.
nob
  head 213 n.
  aristocrat 868 n.
nobble
  impair 655 vb.
nobility
  genealogy 169 n.
  élite 644 n.
  aristocracy 868 n.
  disinterestedness
  931 n.
noble
  impressive 821 adj.
  splendid 841 adj.
  well-bred 848 adj.
  worshipful 866 adj.
  nobleman 868 n.
  proud 871 adj.
  (*see* nobility)
nobleman
  nobleman 868 n.
nobody
  nobody 190 n.
  nonentity 639 n.
nobody's
  unpossessed
  774 adj.
nobody's darling
  hateful object
  888 n.
nobody's fool
  sage 500 n.

no business
  irrelation 10 n.
no change
  identity 13 n.
  permanence 144 n.
nocturnal
  dark 418 adj.
  vespertine 129 adj.
nod
  oscillate 317 vb.
  be inattentive
  456 vb.
  assent 488 n., vb.
  hint 524 n.
  sleep 679 vb.
  consent 758 vb.
nodding
  pendent 217 adj.
node
  joint 45 n.
nodosity
  swelling 253 n.
  roughness 259 n.
noes, the
  dissentient 489 n.
nog
  liquor 301 n.
noggin
  cup 194 n.
  potion 301 n.
noise
  sound 398 n.
  loudness 400 n.
  rumour 529 n.
noise abatement
  faintness 401 n.
noiseless
  silent 399 adj.
noises off
  mimicry 20 n.
  dramaturgy 594 n.
noisome
  fetid 397 adj.
  bad 645 adj.
  unclean 649 adj.
  baneful 659 adj.
noisy
  loud 400 adj.
no joke
  reality 1 n.
  important matter
  638 n.
nomad
  extraneous 59 adj.
  wanderer 268 n.
nomadism
  wandering 267 n.

no man's land
  territory 184 n.
  emptiness 190 n.
  non-ownership
  774 n.
nom de plume
  misnomer 562 n.
nomenclature
  identification 547
  nomenclature
  561 n.
nominal
  insubstantial 4 ad
  verbal 559 adj.
  trivial 639 adj.
nomination
  mandate 751 n.
nominee
  delegate 754 n.
  consignee 754 n.
non-acceptance
  refusal 760 n.
non-adhesive
  non-adhesive
  49 adj.
nonage
  nonage 130 n.
  helplessness 161 n
non-aggression
  peace 717 n.
non-appearance
  invisibility 444 n.
non-attendance
  absence 190 n.
nonce-word
  word 559 n.
  neology 560 n.
nonchalance
  negligence 458 n.
  inexcitability 823
  indifference 860 n
non-combatant
  pacifist 717 n.
non-committal
  avoiding 620 adj.
  neutral 625 adj.
nonconformist
  nonconformist 84
  dissentient 489 n.
  non-observant
  769 adj.
  schismatic 978 n.
nonconformity
  unconformity 84 n
  sectarianism 978 n
non-cooperation
  opposition 704 n.

sistance 715 n.	**non-profitmaking**	**north**	notice 455 vb.
sobedience 738 n.	disinterested	compass point	record 548 vb.
-cooperator	931 adj.	281 n.	correspondence
ssentient 489 n.	**non-recurrent**	**northern lights**	588 n.
ponent 705 n.	discontinuous	glow 417 n.	paper money 797 n.
descript	72 adj.	**northwester**	**notebook**
conformable	**non-residence**	gale 352 n.	reminder 505 n.
34 adj.	absence 190 n.	**nose**	record 548 n.
-design	**nonsense**	face, prow 237 n.	**note of hand**
iance 159 n.	silly talk 515 n.	protuberance 254 n.	title-deed 767 n.
on-design 618 n.	**non sequitur**	smell 394 vb.	paper money
ne	irrelevance 10 n.	**nose-dive**	797 n.
ero 103 n.	sophism 477 n.	aeronautics 271 n.	**note of interrogation**
nentity	**non-starter**	plunge 313 n.	punctuation 547 n.
onentity 639 n.	slowcoach 278 n.	**nosegay**	**notepaper**
bject of scorn	loser 728 n.	bunch 74 n.	stationery 586 n.
867 n.	**non-stop**	fragrance 396 n.	paper 631 n.
nesuch	continuous 71 adj.	**nose out**	**notes**
aragon 646 n.	unceasing 146 adj.	be curious 453 vb.	commentary 520 n.
-existence	**non-U**	**nostalgia**	**noteworthy**
on-existence 2 n.	ill-bred 847 adj.	regret 830 n.	notable 638 adj.
-fulfilment	plebeian 869 adj.	melancholy 834 n.	noteworthy 866
hortcoming 307 n.	**non-violence**	**nostril**	adj.
on-completion	peace 717 n.	orifice 263 n.	**nothing**
726 n.	**non-voting**	air-pipe 353 n.	non-existence 2 n.
-functional	choiceless 606 adj.	**nostrum**	zero 103 n.
seless 641 adj.	**noodle**	contrivance 623 n.	trifle 639 n.
rnamental 844	ninny 501 n.	remedy 658 n.	**nothingness**
adj.	**nook**	**nosy, nosey**	insubstantiality 4 n.
n-inflammable	compartment 194	inquisitive 453 adj.	zero 103 n.
ncombustible	n.	**Nosy Parker**	**notice**
382 adj.	hiding-place 527 n.	inquisitor 453 n.	period 110 n.
n-involvement	**noon, noonday**	**notability**	see 438 vb.
voidance 620 n.	noon 128 n.	importance 638 n.	attention 455 n.
eace 717 n.	**noose**	**notable**	article 591 n.
isinterestedness	halter 47 n.	notable 638 adj.	warning 664 n.
931 n.	means of execution	person of repute	**noticeable**
n-observance	964 n.	866 n.	visible 443 adj.
egligence 458 n.	**no other**	noteworthy 866 adj.	manifest 522 adj.
on-observance	identity 13 n.	**notary**	**notification**
769 n.	**no quarter**	notary 958 n.	information 524 n.
n-partisan	pitilessness 906 n.	**notation**	publication 528 n.
ndependent	**norm**	numerical operation	**notify**
744 adj.	rule 81 n.	86 n.	communicate
n-party	paragon 646 n.	notation 410 n.	524 vb.
ssented 488 adj.	**normal**	**notch**	proclaim 528 vb.
n-payment	median 30 adj.	cut 46 vb.	**notion**
on-payment 805 n.	typical 83 adj.	gap 201 n.	idea 451 n.
nplus	(see normality)	notch 260 n., vb.	supposition 512 n.
uzzle 474 vb.	**normality**	**not done**	**notional**
redicament 700 n.	sanity 502 n.	unconformable	ideational 451 adj.
n-practising	right 913 n.	84 adj.	suppositional
religious 974 adj.	**normalize**	unwonted 611 adj.	512 adj.
mpious 980 adj.	regularize 62 vb.	**note**	**not mind**
n-professional	**normative**	ululation 409 n.	acquiesce 488 vb.
nskilled 695 adj.	regular 81 adj.	character 5 n.	be indifferent 860
ayman 987 n.	formative 243 adj.	musical note 410 n.	vb.

585

notoriety
 publicity 528 n.
 disrepute 867 n.
nought
 zero 103 n.
noun
 part of speech
 564 n.
nourish
 feed 301 vb.
 aid 703 vb.
nourishment
 food 301 n.
nous
 intelligence 498 n.
nouveau riche
 upstart 126 n.
nova
 star 321 n.
novel
 new 126 adj.
 novel 590 n.
novelist
 author 589 n.
 narrator 590 n.
novelty
 (*see* novel)
novice
 ignoramus 493 n.
 beginner 538 n.
 bungler 697 n.
 monk, nun 986 n.
 layman 987 n.
novitiate
 learning 536 n.
 preparation
 669 n.
nowhere
 absent 190 adj.
no wiser
 uninstructed
 491 adj.
noxious
 harmful 645 adj.
 insalubrious
 653 adj.
nozzle
 orifice 263 n.
nuance
 differentiation
 15 n.
 degree 27 n.
 discrimination
 463 n.
nub
 essential part 5 n.
 swelling 253 n.

nubile
 marriageable
 894 adj.
nuclear
 dynamic 160 adj.
nucleate
 be dense 324 vb.
nucleonics
 nucleonics 160 n.
nucleus
 centrality 225 n.
 element 319 n.
 solid body 324 n.
nude
 stripper 229 n.
 uncovered 229 adj.
nudge
 knock 279 n.
 hint 524 n., vb.
nudist
 stripper 229 n.
 sanitarian 652 n.
nudity
 bareness 229 n.
nugatory
 unimportant
 639 adj.
nugget
 bullion 797 n.
nuisance
 meddler 678 n.
 annoyance 827 n.
null
 non-existent 2 adj.
 unmeaning 515
 adj.
null and void
 powerless 161 adj.
 abrogated 752 adj.
nullification
 abrogation 752 n.
nullify
 (*see* nullification)
nullity
 zero 103 n.
numb
 inert 175 adj.
 insensible 375 adj.
number
 quantity 26 n.
 number 85 n.
 plurality 101 n.
 label 547 n.
numberless
 infinite 107 adj.
number one
 self 80 n.

numbness
 (*see* numb)
numeral
 number 85 n.
numeration
 numeration 86 n.
numerical
 numerical 85 adj.
numerous
 many 104 adj.
numinous
 frightening 854 adj.
 divine 965 adj.
numismatics
 money 797 n.
numskull
 dunce 501 n.
nun
 nun 986 n.
nuncio
 envoy 754 n.
nunnery
 monastery 986 n.
nuptial
 matrimonial
 894 adj.
nurse
 look after 457 vb.
 train 534 vb.
 nurse 658 n.
 doctor 658 vb.
 preserve 666 vb.
 minister to 703 vb.
 domestic 742 n.
 keeper 749 n.
 pet 889 vb.
nursemaid
 keeper 749 n.
nursery
 nonage 130 n.
 child 132 n.
 seedbed 156 n.
 training school
 539 n.
nurseryman
 gardener 370 n.
nursery rhyme
 doggerel 593 n.
nursing
 therapy 658 n.
nursing home
 hospital 658 n.
nursling
 child 132 n.
nurture
 support 218 n.
 food 301n.

 educate 534 vb.
nut
 fastening 47 n.
 madman, crank
 504 n.
nutriment
 food 301 n.
nutrition
 eating 301 n.
 food 301 n.
nutritional
 remedial 658 adj.
nutritionist
 doctor 658 n.
nutritious
 nourishing 301 ad
 salubrious 652 ad
nutshell
 small quantity 33
nuzzle
 caress 889 vb.
nylon
 fibre 208 n.
 textile 222 n.
nymphomania
 abnormality 84 n.
 libido 859 n.

O

oaf
 elf 970 n.
oafish
 unintelligent
 499 adj.
oak
 strength 162 n.
 tree 366 n.
oar
 boatman 270 n.
 propellant 278 n.
oarsman
 boatman 270 n.
oasis
 land 344 n.
oath
 testimony 466 n.
 oath 532 n.
 promise 764 n.
 scurrility 899 n.
oatmeal
 cereal 301 n.
oats
 provender 301 n.
 corn 366 n.
obduracy
 obstinacy 602 n.

occupancy
 presence 189 n.
 possession 773 n.
occupant
 possessor 776 n.
 resident 191 n.
occupation
 presence 189 n.
 business, job 622 n.
 action 676 n.
 (*see* occupy)
occupational disease
 habit 610 n.
occupier
 resident 191 n.
 possessor 776 n.
occupy
 fill 54 vb.
 be present 189 vb.
 dwell 192 vb.
 cause thought
  449 vb.
 employ 622 vb.
 possess 773 vb.
 appropriate 786 vb.
occur
 happen 154 vb.
occurrence
 eventuality 154 n.
ocean
 ocean 343 n.
ocean-going
 seafaring 269 adj.
 oceanic 343 adj.
oceanography
 geography 321 n.
 oceanography
  343 n.
ochre
 brown paint 430 n.
octave
 period 110 n.
 musical note 410 n.
octavo
 edition 589 n.
octet
 over five 99 n.
 duet 412 n.
octopus
 fish 365 n.
 tyrant 735 n.
octroi
 tax 809 n.
ocular
 seeing 438 adj.
oculist
 eyeglass 442 n.

 doctor 658 n.
odd
 unequal 29 adj.
 remaining 41 adj.
 unusual 84 adj.
 numerical 85 adj.
 crazed 503 adj.
oddity
 misfit 25 n.
 eccentricity 503 n.
 crank 504 n.
odd man out
 misfit 25 n.
 dissentient 489 n.
oddment(s)
 adjunct 40 n.
 medley 43 n.
odds
 difference 15 n.
 inequality 29 n.
 vantage 34 n.
 dissension 709 n.
odds and ends
 leavings 41 n.
 medley 43 n.
ode
 poem 593 n.
odious
 hateful 888 adj.
odium
 disrepute 867 n.
 odium 888 n.
odium theologicum
 narrow mind 481 n.
odour
 odour 394 n.
odour, bad
 odium 888 n.
odourless
 odourless 395 adj.
oecumenicalism
 (*see*
  ecumenicalism)
oedema
 swelling 253 n.
oedematous
 expanded 197 adj.
oesophagus
 maw 194 n.
oestrus
 libido 859 n.
off
 decomposed
  51 adj.
 unpleasant 827 adj.
offal
 insides 224 n.

 meat 301 n.
 rubbish 641 n.
 dirt 649 n.
off-centre
 irrelevant 10 adj.
 deviating 282 adj.
off-chance
 possibility 469 n.
off colour
 sick 651 adj.
off-day
 failure 728 n.
offence
 resentment 891 n.
 guilty act 936 n.
offend
 displease 827 vb.
 cause dislike
  861 vb.
offender
 offender 904 n.
offensive
 fetid 397 adj.
 attack 712 n.
 unpleasant 827 adj.
 impertinent 878 adj.
offer
 incentive 612 n.
 provide 633 vb.
 offer 759 n., vb.
 make terms 766 vb.
offering
 offering 781 n.
 oblation 981 n.
offertory
 oblation 981 n.
off form
 imperfect 647 adj.
off guard
 inexpectant 508
  adj.
off-hand
 negligent 458 adj.
 spontaneous
  609 adj.
 disrespectful
  921 adj.
office
 job, function 622 n.
 workshop 687 n.
 authority 733 n.
 duty 917 n.
 jurisdiction 955 n.
 church service
  988 n.
office-bearer
 official 690 n.

office-book
 office-book 988 n.
office, in
 authoritative
  733 adj.
officer
 official 690 n.
 officer 741 n.
offices, good
 aid 703 n.
 mediation 720 n.
official
 genuine 494 adj.
 businesslike
  622 adj.
 official 690 n.
 authoritative
  733 adj.
 governmental
  733 adj.
 formal 875 adj.
officiate
 function 622 vb.
 perform ritual
  988 vb.
officiousness
 overactivity 678 n.
off-load
 displace 188 vb.
off-peak
 small 33 adj.
off-pitch
 discordant 411 adj.
offscourings
 leavings 41 n.
 dirt 649 n.
offset
 offset 31 n.
 remainder 41 n.
 counteract 182 vb.
offshoot
 subdivision 53 n.
 descendant 170 n.
 sect 978 n.
offside
 unconformable
  84 adj.
 illegal 954 adj.
offspring
 kinsman 11 n.
 effect 157 n.
 posterity 170 n.
off the peg
 ready-made
  669 adj.
off-white
 whitish 427 adj.

ogle
gaze 438 vb.
wooing 889 n.

ogre
giant 195 n.
intimidation 854 n.
demon 970 n.

oil
propellant 287 n.
lubricant 334 n.
oil 357 n.
fuel 385 n.
balm 658 n.
facilitate 701 vb.

oils
art equipment
553 n.

oil-well
store 632 n.

oily
smooth 258 adj.
unctuous 357 adj.
flattering 925 adj.

ointment
unguent 357 n.
balm 658 n.

O.K.
in order 60 adv.
assent 488 n.

old, olden
past 125 adj.
olden 127 adj.
aged 131 adj.

old age
age 131 n.

olden days
preterition 125 n.

old-fashioned
antiquated
127 adj.

old fogy
old man 133 n.
fool 501 n.

old hand
expert 696 n.

old maid
spinster 895 n.
virgin 950 n.

Old Moore
oracle 511 n.

old school
habit 610 n.

old school tie
livery 547 n.

old stager
actor 594 n.
expert 696 n.

old story
repetition 106 n.

old-world
olden 127 adj.

oligarchy
government 733 n.

olive-branch
irenics 719 n.

ologies and isms
science 490 n.

Olympian
aristocrat 868 n.
genteel 868 adj.

Olympics
contest 716 n.

omega
extremity 69 n.

omen
omen 511 n.
danger signal
665 n.

ominous
presageful 511 adj.
cautionary 664 adj.
unpromising
853 adj.
threatening 900 adj.

omission
exclusion 57 n.
negligence 458 n.
non-observance
769 n.

omit
(*see* omission)

omnibus
comprehensive
52 adj.
bus, stage-coach
274 n.

omnicompetent
state
despotism 733 n.

omnipotence
power 160 n.

omniscience
knowledge 490 n.

omnivorous
feeding 301 adj.
gluttonous 947 adj.

on and on
forever 115 adv.

once
singly 88 adv.
not now 122 adv.
seldom 140 adv.

once bitten
cautious 858 adj.

once-over
inspection 438 n.

oncoming
approaching
289 adj.

one
simple 44 adj.
unit 88 n.
person 371 n.

one after another
following 284 n.

one and only
unimitated 21 adj.

one and the same
identical 13 adj.

one-dimensional
longitudinal 203 adj.

one-eyed
dim-sighted 440 adj.

one-horse
trivial 639 adj.

one in a million
exceller 644 n.

oneness
identity 13 n.
simpleness 44 n.
unity 88 n.

one of
ingredient 58 adj.

one of the best
favourite 890 n.

one or two
fewness 105 n.

one-piece
uniform 16 adj.

onerous
difficult 700 adj.
(*see* heavy)

one-sided
biased 481 adj.
unjust 914 adj.

one-time
former 125 adj.

one-track mind
narrow mind 481 n.

one up
superior 34 adj.

one-upmanship
superiority 34 n.
tactics 688 n.

onion
vegetable 301 n.
condiment 389 n.

onlooker
spectator 441 n.

only
one 88 adj.

only-begotten
one 88 adj.

onset
approach 289 n.
attack 712 n.

onslaught
attack 712 n.
censure 924 n.

on tap
provisionary
633 adj.

on the make
acquiring 771 adj.
selfish 932 adj.

ontology
existence 1 n.
philosophy 449 n.

onus
demonstration
478 n.
duty 917 n.
guilt 936 n.

onward
forward 285 adv.

ooze
move slowly
278 vb.
exude 298 vb.
moisture 341 n.
marsh 347 n.
flow 350 vb.

opacity
opacity 423 n.
imperspicuity
568 n.

opalescent, opaline
semitransparent
424 adj.
iridescent 437 adj.

opaque
(*see* opacity)

open
disjoin, cut 46 vb.
begin 68 vb.
auspicate 68 vb.
uncover 229 vb.
open 263 adj., vb.
visible 443 adj.
uncertain 474 adj.
manifest 522 vb.

open air
exteriority 223 n.
salubrity 652 n.

open arms
friendliness 880 n.

open country
plain 348 n.

opener
opener 263 n.
open-eyed
attentive 455 adj.
open fire
shoot 287 vb.
fire at 712 vb.
open house
liberality 813 n.
opening
prelude 66 n.
début 68 n.
opportunity 137 n.
gap 201 n.
open into
connect 45 vb.
open letter
publicity 528 n.
open question
uncertainty 474 n.
open secret
knowledge 490 n.
publicity 528 n.
open sesame
spell 983 n.
open to
vulnerable 661 adj.
open up
disclose 526 vb.
open verdict
dubiety 474 n.
opera
stage play 594 n.
operable
possible 469 adj.
medical 658 adj.
opera glass
telescope 442 n.
operate
function 622 vb.
manage 689 vb.
(*see* operation)
operatic
musical 412 adj.
operation
instrumentality 628 n.
surgery 658 n.
undertaking 672 n.
labour 682 n.
operational
operative 173 adj.
warlike 718 adj.
operative
powerful 160 adj.
operative 173 adj.
worker 686 n.

operator
machinist 676 n.
doer 630 n.
ophthalmia
dim sight 440 n.
ophthalmologist
eyeglass 442 n.
doctor 658 n.
opiate
soporific 679 n.
opine
opine 485 vb.
(*see* opinion)
opiniatry
opiniatry 602 n.
opinion
idea 451 n.
opinion 485 n.
supposition 512 n.
opinionated
positive 473 adj.
opinionist
doctrinaire 473 n.
opinionist 602 n.
opium
anaesthetic 375 n.
drug 658 n.
opium-eater
idler 679 n.
opponent
opponent 705 n.
opportune
apt 24 adj.
opportune 137 adj.
opportunism
expedience 642 n.
improbity 930 n.
opportunist
enterprising 672 adj.
egotist 932 n.
opportunity
opportunity 137 n.
scope 744 n.
oppose
(*see* opposition)
opposite
opposite 240 adj.
opposite number
correlation 12 n.
compeer 28 n.
opposition
counteraction 182 n.
opposition 704 n.
resistance 715 n.
oppress
oppress 735 vb.

torment 827 vb.
oppression
severity 735 n.
dejection 834 n.
oppressive
warm 379 adj.
inimical 881 adj.
oppressor
tyrant 735 n.
opt
choose 605 vb.
optical
seeing 438 adj.
optical illusion
visual fallacy 440 n.
optician
eyeglass 442 n.
doctor 658 n.
optics
optics 417 n.
optimism
cheerfulness 833 n.
hope 852 n.
optimistic
optimistic 482 adj.
optimum
best 644 adj.
option
choice 605 n.
optional
choosing 605 adj.
opulent
rich 800 adj.
opus
musical piece 412 n.
oracle
sage 500 n.
oracle 511 n.
equivocalness 518 n.
oracular
uncertain 474 adj.
aphoristic 496 adj.
wise 498 adj.
predicting 511 adj.
equivocal 518 adj.
imperspicuous 568 adj.
oral
vocal 577 adj.
speaking 579 adj.
orange
fruit 301 n.
orange 436 n., adj.

oration
oration 579 n.
orator
speaker 579 n.
oratorical
figurative 519 adj.
rhetorical 574 adj.
eloquent 579 n.
oratorio
vocal music 412 n.
oratory
style 566 n.
oratory 579 n.
church 990 n.
orb
circle 250 n.
regalia 743 n.
orbit
fly 271 vb.
circuition 314 n.
rotate 315 vb.
orbital
circuitous 314 adj.
orchard
farm, garden 370 n.
orchestra
orchestra 413 n.
orchestrate
arrange 62 vb.
compose music 413 vb.
ordain
decree 737 vb.
ecclesiasticize 985 vb.
ordained
clerical 986 adj.
ordeal
experiment 461 n.
suffering 825 n.
order
order 60 n.
serial place 73 n.
community 708 n.
decoration 729 n.
command 737 n., vb.
title 870 n.
monk 986 n.
ritual, rite 988 n.
order, keep
rule 733 vb.
restrain 747 vb.
orderless
orderless 61 adj.
amorphous 244 adj.

orderly
orderly 60 adj.
regular 81 adj.
businesslike 622 adj.
servant 742 n.
order, out of
orderless 61 adj.
orders, in
clerical 986 adj.
ordinal
numerical 85 adj.
ordinance
precept 693 n.
legislation 953 n.
rite 988 n.
ordinand
cleric 986 n.
ordinary
median 30 adj.
typical 83 adj.
usual 610 adj.
mediocre 732 adj.
unastonishing
865 adj.
ordnance
gun 723 n.
ordure
excrement 302 n.
ore
materials 631 n.
organ
organ 414 n.
the press 528 n.
tool 630 n.
organic
structural 331 adj.
organic nature
organism 358 n.
organism
life 360 n.
organist
instrumentalist
413 n.
organization
composition 56 n.
arrangement 62 n.
structure 331 n.
organism 358 n.
plan 623 n.
corporation 708 n.
organizational
arranged 62 adj.
structural 331 adj.
organizer
planner 623 n.
orgasm
spasm 318 n.

orgiastic
disorderly 61 adj.
sensual 944 adj.
orgy
feasting 301 n.
plenty 635 n.
sensualism 944 n.
oriel
window 263 n.
orientation
direction 281 n.
orifice
orifice 263 n.
origin
origin 68 n.
source 156 n.
genealogy 169 n.
original
irrelative 10 adj.
prototype 23 n.
first 68 adj.
nonconformist 84 n.
new 126 adj.
laughing-stock
851 n.
(*see* originality)
originality
non-imitation 21 n.
imagination 513 n.
originate
initiate 68 vb.
produce 164 vb.
originator
producer 167 n.
planner 623 n.
orison
prayers 981 n.
ormolu
ornamental art
844 n.
ornament
ornament 574 n.
ornamentation
844 n.
ornamental
useless 641 adj.
ornamental
844 adj.
ornamentation
ostentation 875 n.
(*see* ornament)
ornate
ornate 574 adj.
splendid 841 adj.
affected 850 adj.
ornithology
zoology 367 n.

orphan
survivor 41 n.
derelict 779 n.
deprive 786 vb.
orphaned
alone 88 adj.
orthodox
orthodox 976 adj.
(*see* orthodoxy)
orthodoxism
orthodoxism 976 n.
orthodoxy
conformity 83 n.
certainty 473 n.
creed 485 n.
orthodox 976 n.
orthography
letter 558 n.
orthopaedist
doctor 658 n.
orthopaedy
therapy 658 n.
oscillate
oscillate 317 vb.
oscillation
periodicity 141 n.
changeableness
152 n.
oscillation 317 n.
ossification
condensation 324 n.
hardening 326 n.
ossified
antiquated 127 adj.
ostensible
appearing 445 adj.
ostensible 614 adj.
ostentation
affectation 850 n.
vanity 873 n.
ostentation 875 n.
osteopath
doctor 658 n.
osteopathy
therapy 658 n.
ostler
animal husbandry
369 n.
servant 742 n.
ostracism
exclusion 57 n.
unsociability 883 n.
disapprobation
924 n.
ostracize
make unwelcome
883 vb.

ostrich
visionary 513 n.
other
extrinsicality 6 n.
different 15 adj.
other ranks
inferior 35 n.
nonentity 639 n.
other side
opposition 704 n.
enemy 881 n.
otherworldliness
sanctity 979 n.
otherworldly
immaterial 320 adj.
imaginative 513 adj.
pious 979 adj.
otiose
useless 641 adj.
inactive 679 adj.
ottoman
seat 218 n.
ounce
small quantity
33 n.
oust
eject 300 vb.
depose 752 vb.
deprive 786 vb.
ouster
loss of right 916 n.
out
absent 190 adj.
eject 300 vb.
inexact 495 adj.
out-and-out
completely 54 adv.
out-argue
confute 479 vb.
outbid
bargain 791 vb.
outbreak
egress 298 n.
excitable state
822 n.
outburst
excitable state
822 n.
outcaste
exclude 57 vb.
reject 607 vb.
disreputable
867 adj.
derelict 779 n.
outcaste 883 n.
outclass
be superior 34 vb.

defeat 727 vb.
outcome
  effect 157 n.
outcropping
  visible 443 adj.
outcry
  cry 408 n.
outdistance
  outstrip 277 vb.
outdoor
  exterior 233 adj.
outdoors
  salubrity 652 n.
outer, outermost
  exterior 223 adj.
outface
  be courageous
    855 vb.
  be insolent 878 vb.
outfall
  outflow 298 n.
outfit
  all 52 n.
  component 58 n.
  clothing 228 n.
  equipment 630 n.
outfitter
  clothier 228 n.
outflow
  outflow 298 n.
  waste 634 n.
out for
  intending 617 adj.
outgoing
  former 125 adj.
  resigning 753 adj.
outgoings
  expenditure 806 n.
outgrow
  disaccustom 611 vb.
outgrown
  unwonted 611 adj.
out-Herod Herod
  exaggerate 546 vb.
outhouse
  small house 192 n.
  chamber 194 n.
outing
  land travel 267 n.
  amusement 837 n.
outlandish
  extraneous 59 adj.
  unusual 84 adj.
outlast
  outlast 113 vb.
outlaw
  robber 789 n.

outcaste 883 n.
  offender 904 n.
  make illegal 954 vb.
outlawry
  brigandage 788 n.
  lawlessness 954 n.
  condemnation
    961 n.
outlay
  expenditure 806 n.
outlet
  outlet 298 n.
outline
  incompleteness
    55 n.
  outline 233 n., vb.
  form 243 n.
  appearance 445 n.
  compendium 592 n.
outlive
  outlast 113 vb.
outlook
  futurity 124 n.
  destiny 155 n.
  spectacle 445 n.
  expectation 507 n.
outlying
  exterior 223 adj.
outmanoeuvre
  be superior 34 vb.
  deceive 542 vb.
outmatch
  be superior 34 vb.
outnumber
  be many 104 vb.
  superabound 637 vb.
out of character
  unapt 25 adj.
out of date
  anachronistic
    118 adj.
  antiquated 127 adj.
out of doors
  exteriority 223 n.
  air 340 n.
out of fashion
  antiquated 127 adj.
out of favour
  disliked 861 adj.
out of keeping
  unconformable
    84 adj.
out of love
  hating 888 adj.
out of luck
  unfortunate
    731 adj.

out of order
  irrelevant 10 adj.
  useless 641 adj.
out of place
  misplaced 188 adj.
out of pocket
  losing 772 adj.
out of proportion
  irrelative 10 adj.
out of season
  anachronistic
    118 adj.
out of shape
  distorted 246 adj.
out of sorts
  sick 651 adj.
out of step
  non-uniform 17 adj.
  unconformable
    84 adj.
out of the question
  impossible 470 adj.
  rejected 607 adj.
outpace
  outstrip 277 vb.
outplay
  be superior 34 vb.
  defeat 727 vb.
outpoint
  be superior 34 vb.
outpost
  farness 199 n.
outpouring
  outflow 298 n.
  diffuseness 570 n.
  plenty 635 n.
output
  production 164 n.
outrage
  huff 891 vb.
  cruel act 898 n.
  indignity 921 n.
outrageous
  cruel 898 adj.
  disrespectful
    921 adj.
  heinous 934 adj.
outrank
  be superior 34 vb.
outrival
  be superior 34 vb.
outrun
  outstrip 277 vb.
outset
  start 68 n.
outshine
  be superior 34 vb.

outside
  exteriority 223 n.
  appearance 445 n.
outsider
  misfit 25 n.
  intruder 59 n.
  nonconformist 84 n.
  outcaste 883 n.
outsize
  huge 195 adj.
outskirts
  farness 199 n.
outspoken
  undisguised 522 adj.
  veracious 540 adj.
outstanding
  superior 34 adj.
  remainder 41 n.
  notable 638 adj.
outstrip
  outstrip 277 vb.
out to
  intending 617 adj.
out-turn
  production 164 n.
outvote
  reject 607 vb.
outward
  extrinsic 6 adj.
  exterior 223 adj.
outward bound
  outgoing 298 adj.
outweigh
  weigh 322 vb.
outwit
  be superior 34 vb.
  befool 542 vb.
outworn
  antiquated 127 adj.
oval
  arc 250 n.
  round 250 adj.
ovary
  genitalia 164 n.
ovation
  celebration 876 n.
  applause 923 n.
oven
  cookery 301 n.
  furnace 383 n.
oven-ready
  ready-made
    669 adj.
overact
  exaggerate 546 vb.
overactivity
  overactivity 678 n.

over-age
  antiquated 127 adj.
overall
  inclusive 78 adj.
  apron 228 n.
  trousers 228 n.
overawe
  dominate 733 vb.
  command respect
  920 vb.
overbalance
  tumble 309 vb.
overbearing
  oppressive 735 adj.
  proud 871 adj.
overburden
  make heavy 322
  vb.
overcast
  cheerless 834 adj.
  sullen 893 adj.
overcharge
  dearness 811 n.
overcoat
  overcoat 228 n.
overcome
  overmaster 727 vb.
over-confidence
  rashness 857 n.
over-confident
  optimistic 482 adj.
overcrowded
  assembled 74 adj.
overdo
  exaggerate 546 vb.
overdone
  tough 329 adj.
  exaggerated
  546 adj.
  affected 850 adj.
overdose
  redundance 637 n.
  satiety 863 n.
overdraft
  debt 803 n.
  insolvency 805 n.
overdraw
  be in debt 803 vb.
overdrawn
  indebted 803 adj.
overdrive
  power 160 n.
  fatigue 684 vb.
overdue
  late 136 adj.
  important 638 adj.
  just 913 adj.

overeat
  gluttonize 947 vb.
over-emphasis
  exaggeration 546 n.
overestimate
  overestimation
  482 n.
overexpose
  darken 418 vb.
over-extension
  overactivity 678 n.
overfamiliar
  impertinent 878 adj.
overfed
  gluttonous 947 adj.
overfeed
  sate 863 vb.
overflow
  be many 104 vb.
  outflow 298 n.
  encroach 306 vb.
  waterfall 350 n.
  drain 351 n.
  redundance 637 n.
overflowing
  great 32 adj.
  full 54 adj.
overhang
  hang 217 vb.
  jut 254 vb.
  overlie 226 vb.
overhaul
  outstrip 277 vb.
  search 459 vb.
  repair 656 vb.
overheads
  cost 809 n.
overhear
  hear 415 vb.
overlap
  continuity 71 n.
  be contiguous
  202 vb.
  stratification 207 n.
  covering 226 n.
  encroach 306 vb.
overlie
  overlie 226 vb.
overload
  load 193 vb.
  make heavy 322 vb.
overlook
  be high 209 vb.
  neglect 458 vb.
  not use 674 vb.
overlord
  superior 34 n.

  master 741 n.
overlying
  superior 34 adj.
overmaster
  overmaster 727 vb.
over-mighty
  powerful 160 adj.
  influential 178 adj.
over-modesty
  prudery 950 n.
over-nice
  fastidious 862 adj.
overpaid
  rich 800 adj.
overpaint
  coat 226 vb.
  obliterate 550 vb.
overpayment
  redundance 637 n.
  undueness 916 n.
overplus
  remainder 41 n.
  redundance 637 n.
over-population
  crowd 74 n.
overpower
  be strong 162 vb.
  overmaster 727 vb.
overpowering
  impressive 821 adj.
overpraise
  overrate 482 vb.
  flatter 925 vb.
over-priced
  dear 811 adj.
overprint
  obliterate 550 vb.
over-proof
  intoxicating
  949 adj.
overrate
  overrate 482 vb.
overrated
  unimportant
  639 adj.
overreach
  deceive 542 vb.
  be cunning 698 vb.
override
  overmaster 727
  vb.
  oppress 735 vb.
overriding
  supreme 34 adj.
  important 638 adj.
overrule
  abrogate 752 vb.

overruling
  supreme 34 adj.
  authoritative
  733 adj.
overrun
  encroach 306 vb.
  appropriate 786 vb.
oversea
  extraneous 59 adj.
overseer
  manager 690 n.
overset
  overturning 221 n.
overshadow
  be superior 34 vb.
  darken 418 vb.
  dominate 733 vb.
oversight
  negligence 458 n.
  management 689 n.
oversize
  huge 195 adj.
oversleep
  lose a chance
  138 vb.
  fail in duty 918 vb.
overspill
  redundance 637 n.
overstep
  overstep 306 vb.
overt
  undisguised
  522 adj.
overtake
  outstrip 277 vb.
overtax
  oppress 735 vb.
overthrow
  revolution 149 n.
  fell 311 vb.
  overmaster 727 vb.
overtime
  protraction 113 n.
  exertion 682 n.
overtone
  musical note
  410 n.
overtop
  be superior 34 vb.
  crown 213 vb.
overtrick
  remainder 41 n.
overtrump
  overmaster 727 vb.
overture
  musical piece
  412 n.

irenics 719 n.
offer 759 n.
overturn
demolish 165 vb.
invert 221 vb.
overweening
proud 871 adj.
insolent 878 adj.
overweigh
be many 104 vb.
overweight
inequality 29 n.
make heavy
322 vb.
overwhelm
be many 104 vb.
be strong 162 vb.
superabound
637 vb.
defeat 727 vb.
impress 821 vb.
overwhelming
prodigious 32 adj.
impressive 821 adj.
wonderful 864 adj.
overwork
misuse 675 vb.
fatigue 684 vb.
over-wrought
fervent 818 adj.
owe
be in debt 803 vb.
owe nothing to
be unrelated
10 vb.
owing
owed 803 adj.
due 915 adj.
owing to
caused 157 adj.
attributed 158 adj.
owl
fool 501 n.
owlish
unintelligent
499 adj.
own
confess 526 vb.
possess 773 vb.
owner
master 741 n.
owner 776 n.
ownerless
unpossessed
774 adj.
ownership
possession 773 n.

594

own generation,
one's
contemporary
123 n.
ox
cattle 365 n.
oxygen
air 340 n.
oyster
taciturnity 582 n.
ozone
salubrity 652 n.

P

pabulum
food 301 n.
pace
synchronize
123 vb.
gait 265 n.
walk 267 vb.
velocity 277 n.
pacemaker
leader 690 n.
pacer
pedestrian 268 n.
pachyderm
animal 365 n.
pachydermatous
thick-skinned
820 adj.
pacific
peaceful 717 adj.
pacification
pacification 719 n.
pacificator, pacifier
mediator 720 n.
pacifism
peace 717 n.
pacifist
pacifist 717 n.
pacify
pacify 719 vb.
pack
fill 54 vb.
group 74 n.
load 193 vb.
line 227 vb.
dog 365 n.
package
bunch 74 n.
inclusion 78 n.
(*see* pack)
packet
bunch 74 n.
small box 194 n.

pack-horse
beast of burden
273 n.
packing
contents 193 n.
lining 227 n.
pact
compact 765 n.
pad
foot 214 n.
line 227 n.
stationery 586 n.
padded
soft 327 adj.
expanded 197 adj.
padded cell
madhouse 503 n.
padding
lining 227 n.
softness 327 n.
paddle
walk 267 vb.
row, swim
269 vb.
spank 963 vb.
paddling
aquatics 269 n.
paddock
enclosure 235 n.
padlock
fastening 47 n.
lock-up 748 n.
pad out
be diffuse 570 vb.
padre
cleric 986 n.
paean
hymn 981 n.
paederast
libertine 952 n.
paedeutics
teaching 534 n.
pagan
heathen 974 n.
profane 980 adj.
idolater 982 n.
paganism
idolatry 982 n.
page
courier 531 n.
retainer 742 n.
pageant, pageantry
pageant 875 n.
pagination
numeration 86 n.
pagoda
temple 990 n.

pail
vessel 194 n.
pain
pain 377 n.
suffering 825 vb.
painfulness 827 n.
painful
painful 377 adj.
paining 827 adj.
pain-killer
anaesthetic 375 n.
relief 831 n.
pain-killing
lenitive 177 adj.
painless
easy 701 adj.
pleasurable 826 adj.
pains
obstetrics 164 n.
carefulness 457 n.
painstaking
careful 457 adj.
paint
coat 226 vb.
pigment 425 n.
paint 553 vb.
describe 590 vb.
cosmetic 843 n.
decorate 844 vb.
painted
florid 425 adj.
false 541 adj.
painter
cable 47 n.
artist 556 n.
painting
representation
551 n.
picture 553 n.
paints
art equipment
553 n.
pair
analogue 18 n.
unite with 45 vb.
combine 50 vb.
group 74 n.
duality 90 n.
pairing
coition 45 n.
pal
chum 880 n.
palace
house 192 n.
magistrature 733 n.
paladin
combatant 722 n.

philanthropist
901 n.
palaeography
palaetiology 125 n.
hermeneutics 520 n.
linguistics 557 n.
palaeolithic
secular 110 adj.
primal 127 adj.
palaeontologist
antiquarian 125 n.
palaeontology
palaetiology 125 n.
palaestra
arena 724 n.
palaestric
contending 716 adj.
palaetiology
palaetiology 125 n.
palanquin
vehicle 274 n.
palatable
tasty 386 adj.
savoury 390 adj.
palatal
speech sound 398 n.
palate
taste 386 n.
palatial
architectural
192 adj.
palaver
chatter 581 n.
conference 584 n.
pale
region 184 n.
fence 235 n.
soft-hued 425 adj.
colourless 426 adj.
whitish 427 adj.
palette
art equipment
553 n.
palindrome
inversion 221 n.
paling
fence 235 n.
palinode
recantation 603 n.
palisade
defences 713 n.
pall
funeral 364 n.
be unpalatable
391 n.
screen 421 n.
be tedious 838 vb.

sate 863 vb.
vestments 989 n.
palladium
refuge 662 n.
pall-bearer
funeral 364 n.
pallet
bed 218 n.
palliate
moderate 177 vb.
qualify 468 vb.
extenuate 927 vb.
palliative
moderator 177 n.
pallor
achromatism 426 n.
pally
friendly 880 adj.
palm
long measure 203 n.
feeler 378 n.
trophy 729 n.
palmate
notched 260 adj.
palmer
traveller 268 n.
pietist 979 n.
palmistry
divination 511 n.
palm off
deceive 542 vb.
palmy days
palmy days 730 n.
palp
feeler 378 n.
touch 378 vb.
palpable
substantial 3 adj.
material 319 adj.
tactual 378 adj.
palpation
touch 378 n.
palpitation
agitation 318 n.
feeling 818 n.
palsied
aged 131 adj.
(*see* palsy)
palsy
helplessness 161 n.
agitation, spasm
318 n.
palter
be irresolute 601 vb.
paltry
inconsiderable
33 adj.

unimportant
639 adj.
pamper
pet 889 vb.
pamphlet
the press 528 n.
book 589 n.
pamphleteer
publicizer 528 n.
dissertator 591 n.
pan
scales 322 n.
panacea
remedy 658 n.
panache
plumage 259 n.
ostentation 875 n.
pandar
bawd 952 n.
(*see* pander)
pandemic
universal 79 adj.
plague 651 n.
pandemonium
turmoil 61 n.
loudness 400 n.
pander
provide 633 vb.
please 826 vb.
be impure 951 vb.
(*see* pandar)
pander to
minister to 703 vb.
be servile 879 vb.
flatter 925 vb.
pane
transparency 422 n.
panegyric
praise 923 n.
panel
band 74 n.
list 87 n.
lamina 207 n.
panelling
lining 227 n.
ornamental art
844 n.
pang
pang 377 n.
panic
fear 854 n., vb.
be cowardly 856 vb.
pannier
basket 194 n.
skirt 228 n.
panoply
armour 713 n.

panorama
generality 79 n.
spectacle 445 n.
pansy
weakling 163 n.
pant
breathe 352 vb.
be fatigued 684 vb.
pantaloons
trousers 228 n.
pantheism
deism 973 n.
pantheist
religionist 971 adj.
pantheon
temple 990 n.
panther
cat 365 n.
pantomime
mimicry 20 n.
gesture 547 n.
stage play 594 n.
pantry
chamber 194 n.
provisions 301 n.
pants
trousers 228 n.
underwear 228 n.
pap
bosom 253 n.
food 301 n.
pulpiness 356 n.
insipidity 387 n.
papacy
churchdom 985 n.
papal
ecclesiastical
985 adj.
paper
insubstantial 4 adj.
thinness 206 n.
overlay 226 vb.
line 227 vb.
the press 528 n.
stationery 586 n.
dissertation 591 n.
paperback
edition 589 n.
paperchase
racing 716 n.
paper over the
cracks
not suffice 636 vb.
papers
record 548 n.
paper war
quarrel 709 n.

papery
 brittle 330 adj.
papistry
 Catholicism 976 n.
pappy
 pulpy 356 adj.
paprika
 condiment 389 n.
papyrus
 stationery 586 n.
parable
 metaphor 519 n.
 lecture 534 n.
parabola
 curve 248 n.
parachute
 descend 309 vb.
 safeguard 662 n.
parade
 assemblage 74 n.
 show 522 vb.
parade ground
 arena 724 n.
paradigm
 prototype 23 n.
 grammar 564 n.
paradisal
 paradisiac 971 adj.
paradise
 happiness 824 n.
paradox
 argumentation
  475 n.
 inexpectation 508 n.
paragon
 paragon 646 n.
 prodigy 864 n.
paragraph
 subdivision 53 n.
 phrase 563 n.
parallel
 analogue 18 n.
 region 184 n.
 parallelism 219 n.
 compare 462 vb.
parallel course
 accompaniment
  89 n.
parallelism
 parallelism 219 n.
 symmetry 245 n.
paralogism
 sophism 477 n.
paralyse
 disable 161 vb.
 render insensible
  375 vb.

prohibit 757 vb.
paralysis
 inertness 175 n.
 insensibility 375 n.
paramnesia
 oblivion 506 n.
paramount
 supreme 34 adj.
 authoritative
  733 adj.
paramountcy
 superiority 34 n.
paramour
 lover 887 n.
paranoia
 psychopathy 503 n.
paranoiac
 madman 504 n.
paranormal
 paranormal
  984 adj.
parapet
 fortification 713 n.
paraphernalia
 medley 43 n.
 equipment 630 n.
 property 777 n.
paraphrase
 translation 520 n.
paraphrastic
 interpretive 520 adj.
parapsychology
 psychology 447 n.
 psychics 984 n.
parasite
 idler 679 n.
 dependant 742 n.
 beggar 763 n.
 toady 879 n.
parasitical
 inferior 35 adj.
 residing 192 adj.
parasol
 shade 226 n.
paratrooper
 aeronaut 271 n.
 armed force 722 n.
parboil
 cook 301 vb.
parcel
 piece 53 n.
 apportion 783 vb.
parch
 dry 342 vb.
 be hot 379 vb.
parchment
 stationery 586 n.

pardon
 forgiveness 909 n.
 acquittal 960 n.
pare
 cut 46 vb.
 shorten 204 vb.
paregoric
 remedial 658 adj.
parent
 kinsman 11 n.
 parent 169 n.
parentage
 source 156 n.
 parentage 169 n.
parenthesis
 irrelevance 10 n.
 discontinuity 72 n.
parenthood
 propagation 164 n.
 parentage 169 n.
pariah
 outcaste 883 n.
paring
 leavings 41 n.
pari passu
 equally 28 adv.
 synchronously
  123 adv.
parish
 parish 985 n.
parishioner
 native 191 n.
 layman 987 n.
parish pump
 trifle 639 n.
parity
 similarity 18 n.
 equality 28 n.
park
 place oneself
  187 vb.
 enclosure 235 n.
 grassland 348 n.
 pleasure-ground
  837 n.
parking-meter
 timekeeper 117 n.
Parkinson's law
 expansion 197 n.
parlance
 style 566 n.
 speech 579 n.
parley
 interlocution
  584 n.
 conference 584 n.
 make terms 766 vb.

parliament
 parliament 692 n.
parliamentarian
 councillor 692 n.
parlour
 chamber 194 n.
parochial
 regional 184 adj.
 provincial 192 adj.
 narrow-minded
  481 adj.
parodist
 humorist 839 n.
parody
 mimicry 20 n.
 misrepresentation
  552 n.
 satire 851 n.
parole
 promise 764 n.
parolee
 prisoner 750 n.
paronomasia
 equivocalness
  518 n.
 ornament 574 n.
paroxysm
 spasm 318 n.
 frenzy 503 n.
parricide
 homicide 362 n.
parrot
 imitator 20 n.
 repeat 106 vb.
parry
 repel 292 vb.
 parry 713 vb.
 resist 715 vb.
parse
 parse 564 vb.
parsec
 long measure 203 n.
parsimony
 insufficiency 636 n.
 parsimony 816 n.
parson
 cleric 986 n.
parsonage
 parsonage 986 n.
part
 disjoin 46 vb.
 part 53 n.
 incompleteness
  55 n.
 component 58 n.
 fraction 102 n.
 diverge 294 vb.

PAR

acting 594 n.
function 622 n.
portion 783 n.
partake
eat 301 vb.
partial
incomplete 55 adj.
desiring 859 adj.
(see partiality)
partiality
prejudice 481 n.
liking 859 n.
injustice 914 n.
participate
be instrumental
628 vb.
feel 818 vb.
(see participation)
participation
association 706 n.
cooperation 706 n.
participation 775 n.
participator
participator 775 n.
particle
small thing 33 n.
element 319 n.
particoloured
variegated 437 adj.
particular
special 80 adj.
eventuality 154 n.
careful 457 adj.
descriptive 590 adj.
fastidious 862 adj.
particularism
particularism 80 n.
sectarianism 978 n.
particularity
(see particular)
particularize
specify 80 vb.
be diffuse 570 vb.
particulars
particulars 80 n.
parting
separation 46 n.
dividing line 92 n.
partition 231 n.
departure 296 n.
partisan
patron 707 n.
sectional 708 adj.
revolter 738 n.
sectarian 978 adj.
partisanship
prejudice 481 n.

PAS

partition
separation 46 n.
dividing line 92 n.
partition 231 n.
apportionment
783 n.
partner
join 45 vb.
concomitant 89 n.
cooperate 706 vb.
colleague 707 n.
participator 775 n.
partnership
corporation 708 n.
participation 775 n.
(see partner)
part of speech
word 559 n.
part of speech
564 n.
parts
genitalia 164 n.
region 184 n.
aptitude 694 n.
parturition
obstetrics 164 n.
part with
not retain 779 vb.
party
band 74 n.
person 371 n.
party 708 n.
signatory 765 n.
social gathering
882 n.
party line
policy 623 n.
tactics 688 n.
party man
sectarist 978 n.
party-minded
biased 481 adj.
sociable 882 adj.
sectarian 978 adj.
party spirit
cheerfulness 833 n.
sectarianism 978 n.
party to
assenting 488 adj.
party-wall
partition 231 n.
parvenu
upstart 126 n.
pash
love 887 n.
pass
elapse 111 vb.

PAS

opener 263 n.
excrete 302 vb.
passage 305 n.
overstep 306 vb.
sleight 542 n.
access 624 n.
predicament 700 n.
foin 712 n.
permit 756 n., vb.
approve 923 vb.
make legal 953 vb.
passable
not bad 644 adj.
mediocre 732 adj.
passage
lobby 194 n.
motion 265 n.
land travel 267 n.
water travel 269 n.
passage 305 n.
anthology 592 n.
pass book
account book 808 n.
pass by
elapse 111 vb.
(see pass)
passenger
thing transferred
272 n.
idler 679 n.
encumbrance 702 n.
pass for
resemble 18 vb.
pass into
shade off 27 vb.
be turned to 147 vb.
passion
affections 817 n.
warm feeling
818 n.
love 887 n.
anger 891 n.
passionate
fervent 818 adj.
excitable 822 adj.
loving 887 adj.
passionless
impassive 820 adj.
indifferent 860 adj.
passive
inert 175 adj.
inexcitable 823 adj.
passivity
inaction 677 n.
(see passive)
pass muster
suffice 635 vb.

PAS

pass on
transfer 272 vb.
communicate
524 vb.
pass out
be impotent 161 vb.
emerge 298 vb.
pass over
disregard 458 vb.
reject 607 vb.
passport
credential 466 n.
permit 756 n.
pass the buck
transfer 272 vb.
be exempt 919 vb.
pass the time
amuse oneself
837 vb.
password
identification 547 n.
permit 756 n.
past
preterition 125 n.
antiquated 127 adj.
paste
adhesive 47 n.
agglutinate 48 vb.
sham 542 n.
finery 844 n.
pastel
soft-hued 425 adj.
pasteurize
purify 648 vb.
sanitate 652 vb.
pastiche, pasticcio
a mixture 43 n.
picture 553 n.
pastime
amusement 837 n.
past-master
proficient 696 n.
pastor
pastor 986 n.
pastoral
agrarian 370 adj.
priestly 985 adj.
pastry
pastry 301 n.
past tense
preterition 125 n.
pasture
provender 301 n.
graze, feed 301 vb.
grassland 348 n.
stock farm 369 n.
farm 370 n.

pasty
  pastry 301 n.
  pulpy 356 adj.
  colourless 426 adj.
pat
  apt 24 adj.
  touch 378 n.
  caress 889 vb.
patch
  adjunct 40 n.
  piece 53 n.
  variegate 437 vb.
  dirt 649 n.
  repair 656 n., vb.
  cosmetic 843 n.
patcher
  mender 656 n.
patchiness
  non-uniformity 17 n.
  maculation 437 n.
  imperfection 647 n.
patchwork
  variegation 437 n.
patchy
  discontinuous
    72 adj.
  (*see* patchiness)
patent
  manifest 522 adj.
patented
  proprietary 777 adj.
patentee
  beneficiary 776 n.
paterfamilias
  parent 179 n.
paternal
  parental 169 adj.
  benevolent 897 adj.
paternalism
  despotism 733 n.
paternity
  parentage 169 n.
path
  passage 305 n.
  trace 548 n.
  path 624 n.
pathetic
  unimportant
    639 adj.
  felt 818 adj.
  distressing 827 adj.
pathological
  diseased 651 adj.
pathologist
  doctor 658 n.
pathology
  pathology 651 n.

  medical art 658 n.
pathos
  painfulness 827 n.
patience
  perseverance 600 n.
  patience 823 n.
patient
  sick person 651 n.
  (*see* patience)
patina
  hue 425 n.
patois
  dialect 560 n.
pat on the back
  applause 923 n.
patriarch
  family 11 n.
  old man 133 n.
  parent 169 n.
patriarchal
  olden 127 adj.
  primal 127 adj.
patrician
  aristocrat 868 n.
  genteel 868 adj.
patricide
  homicide 362 n.
patrilinear
  parental 169 adj.
patrimony
  possession 773 n.
  dower 777 n.
patriot
  defender 713 n.
  patriot 901 n.
patriotic
  (*see* patriotism)
patriotism
  patriotism 901 n.
  disinterestedness
    931 n.
patrol
  safeguard 660 vb.
  armed force 722 n.
  restrain 747 vb.
patron
  protector 660 n.
  patron 707 n.
  defender 713 n.
  friend 880 n.
  benefactor 903 n.
patronage
  influence 178 n.
  protection 660 n.
  approbation 923 n.
patronize
  choose 605 vb.

  patronize 703 vb.
  be proud 871 vb.
  befriend 880 vb.
patronizing
  prideful 871 adj.
patter
  faintness 401 n.
  empty talk 515 n.
  slang 560 n.
  be loquacious
    581 vb.
pattern
  prototype 23 n.
  composition 56 n.
  example 83 n.
  form 243 n.
  structure 331 n.
  paragon 646 n.
  pattern 844 n.
patty
  pastry 301 n.
paucity
  fewness 105 n.
  scarcity 636 n.
paunch
  maw 194 n.
paunchy
  fleshy 195 adj.
pauper
  poor man 801 n.
pauperism
  poverty 801 n.
pauperize
  impoverish 801 vb.
pause
  discontinuity 72 n.
  lull 145 n.
  repose 683 n.
pave
  overlay 226 vb.
  smooth 258 vb.
pavement
  paving 226 n.
  road, path 624 n.
pave the way
  prepare 669 vb.
pavilion
  canopy 226 n.
paw
  foot 214 n.
  feeler 378 n.
pawn
  dupe 544 n.
  tool 630 n.
  slave 742 n.
  security 767 n.
  borrow 785 vb.

  chessman 837 n.
pawnbroker
  lender 784 n.
pawnshop
  pawnshop 784 n.
pay
  coat, overlay
    226 vb.
  earnings 771 n.
  pay 804 n., vb.
  reward 962 n., vb.
payable
  due 915 adj.
payee
  recipient 782 n.
payer
  pay 804 n.
pay for
  defray 804 vb.
paying
  profitable 640 adj.
  gainful 771 adj.
payload
  contents 193 n.
paymaster
  treasurer 798 n.
payment
  quid pro quo 150 n.
  payment 804 n.
pay-off
  end 69 n.
  pay 804 n.
pay out
  lengthen 203 vb.
  retaliate 714 vb.
payroll
  list 87 n.
  personnel 686 n.
peace
  quietude 266 n.
  peace 717 n.
  pleasurableness
    826 n.
peaceful
  tranquil 266 adj.
  peaceful 717 adj.
  obedient 739 adj.
  pleasurable
    826 adj.
peace-lover
  pacifist 717 n.
peacemaker
  mediator 720 n.
peacemaking
  pacification 719 n.
peace offering
  irenics 719 n.

PEA

peach
divulge 526 vb.
peacock
fop 848 n.
vain person 873 n.
peak
summit 213 n.
shade 226 n.
peaky
lean 206 adj.
sick 651 adj.
peal
loudness 400 n.
resonance 404 n.
campanology 412 n.
gong 414 n.
pearl
white thing 427 n.
a beauty 841 n.
pearlies
clothing 228 n.
pearly
soft-hued 425 adj.
whitish 427 adj.
grey 429 adj.
iridescent 437 adj.
pearly king
fop 848 n.
peasant
husbandman 370 n.
countryman 869 n.
peat
fuel 385 n.
pebble
hardness 326 n.
peccadillo
trifle 639 n.
guilty act 936 n.
peccant
diseased 651 adj.
guilty 936 adj.
peck
eat 301 vb.
bicker 709 vb.
peckish
hungry 859 adj.
peculation
peculation 788 n.
peculator
defrauder 789 n.
peculiar
special 80 adj.
unusual 84 adj.
crazed 503 adj.
peculiarity
temperament 5 n.
(*see* **peculiar**)

PEE

pecuniary
monetary 797 adj.
pedagogic
educational
534 adj.
pedagogue
scholar 492 n.
teacher 537 n.
pedagogy
teaching 534 n.
pedal
footed 214 adj.
mute 414 n.
pedant
narrow mind 481 n.
scholar 492 n.
perfectionist 862 n.
pedantry
narrow mind 481 n.
erudition 490 n.
accuracy 494 n.
fastidiousness
862 n.
peddle
sell 793 vb.
peddler (*see* **pedlar**)
pedestal
stand 218 n.
pedestrian
pedestrian 268 n.
prosaic 593 adj.
pedestrian crossing
traffic control
305 n.
pedestrianism
motion 265 n.
pediatrics
medical art 658 n.
pedicure
beautification
843 n.
pedigree
genealogy 169 n.
nobility 868 n.
pediment
summit 213 n.
pedlar
pedlar 794 n.
peek (*see* **peep**)
peel
unstick 49 vb.
layer 207 n.
skin 226 n.
uncover, doff
229 vb.
peep
look 438 n.

PEN

be curious 453 vb.
peephole
window 263 n.
Peeping Tom
inquisitor 453 n.
peep-show
spectacle 445 n.
peer
compeer 28 n.
scan 438 vb.
be dim-sighted
440 vb.
nobleman 868 n.
peerage
aristocracy 868 n.
peerless
best 644 adj.
peevish
irascible 892 adj.
sullen 893 adj.
peg
fastening 47 n.
hanger 217 n.
stopper 264 n.
potion 301 n.
peg at
persevere 600 vb.
pejorative
depreciating
483 adj.
word 559 n.
detracting 926 adj.
pellet
ammunition 723 n.
pellicle
skin 226 n.
pellucid
transparent
422 adj.
pelt
skin 226 n.
move fast 277 vb.
rain 350 vb.
lapidate 712 vb.
peltry
skin 226 n.
pen
enclosure 235 n.
stationery 586 n.
write 586 vb.
imprison 747 vb.
lock-up 748 n.
penal
punitive 963 adj.
penal code
law 953 n.
penalty 963 n.

PEN

penalize
make illegal 954 vb.
punish 936 vb.
penal servitude
penalty 963 n.
penalty
penalty 963 n.
penance
penance 941 n.
asceticism 945 n.
penchant
tendency 179 n.
pencil
stationery 586 n.
pendant
pendant 217 n.
jewellery 844 n.
pendency
pendency 217 n.
pendent
pendent 217 adj.
pendulous
pendent 217 adj.
pendulum
timekeeper 117 n.
pendant 217 n.
oscillation 317 n.
penetralia
interiority 224 n.
penetrate
pierce 263 vb.
infiltrate 297 vb.
impress 821 vb.
penetrating
pungent 388 adj.
felt 818 adj.
penetration
ingress 297 n.
passage 305 n.
pen-friend
correspondent
588 n.
peninsula
region 184 n.
projection 254 n.
land 344 n.
penis
genitalia 164 n.
penitence
penitence 939 n.
penitent
penitent 939 n.
ascetic 945 n.
penitential
atoning 941 adj.
penitentiary
prison 748 n.

atoning 941 adj.
pen-knife
　sharp edge 256 n.
penman
　penman 586 n.
penmanship
　lettering 586 n.
pen-name
　misnomer 562 n.
pennant
　flag 547 n.
penniless
　poor 801 adj.
pennyweight
　small quantity
　　33 n.
　weighment 322 n.
penny-wise
　parsimonious
　　816 adj.
penology
　punishment 963 n.
pension
　quarters 192 n.
　resignation 753 n.
　pay 804 n.
pensioner
　dependant 742 n.
　recipient 782 n.
pension off
　disuse 674 vb.
　not retain 779 vb.
pensive
　thoughtful 449 adj.
penthouse
　flat 192 n.
　attic 194 n.
penultimate
　ending 69 adj.
penumbra
　half-light 419 n.
penurious
　poor 801 adj.
　parsimonious
　　816 adj.
penury
　poverty 801 n.
people
　place oneself
　　187 vb.
　dwell 192 vb.
　nation 371 n.
　social group 371 n.
　subject 742 n.
　commonalty 869 n.
pep
　vigorousness 174 n.

pepper
　season 388 vb.
　condiment 389 n.
　wound 655 vb.
　fire at 712 vb.
pepper-and-salt
　grey 429 adj.
　chequer 437 n.
peppery
　pungent 388 adj.
　irascible 892 adj.
peppy
　vigorous 174 adj.
pep-talk
　stimulant 174 n.
peptic
　remedial 658 adj.
perambulate
　walk 267 vb.
perambulator
　pushcart 274 n.
perceive
　cognize 447 vb.
per cent
　ratio 85 n.
percentage
　extra 40 n.
　ratio 85 n.
　discount 810 n.
percept
　idea 451 n.
perception
　vision 438 n.
　intellect 447 n.
　sagacity 498 n.
perceptual
　mental 447 adj.
perch
　place oneself
　　187 vb.
　nest 192 n.
　dwell 192 vb.
　sit down 311 vb.
　repose 683 vb.
percolate
　infiltrate 297 vb.
　exude 298 vb.
　flow 350 vb.
　purify 648 vb.
percolator
　cauldron 194 n.
percussion
　impulse 279 n.
　musical instrument
　　414 n.
perdition
　ruin 165 n.

loss 772 n.
peremptory
　assertive 532 adj.
　commanding
　　737 adj.
　obligatory 917 adj.
perennial
　lasting 113 adj.
perfect
　perfect 646 adj.,
　　vb.
　mature 669 vb.
　carry through
　　725 vb.
　(see **perfection**)
perfectibility
　improvement 654 n.
perfection
　goodness 644 n.
　perfection 646 n.
perfectionism
　carefulness 457 n.
　discontent 829 n.
　fastidiousness
　　862 n.
perfectionist
　perfectionist 862 n.
perfective
　completive 725 adj.
perfidious (see
　perfidy)
perfidy
　tergiversation
　　603 n.
　dutilessness 918 n.
　perfidy 930 n.
perflation
　sufflation 352 n.
perforate
　pierce 263 vb.
perforation
　perforation 263 n.
perform
　be instrumental
　　628 vb.
　do one's duty
　　917 vb.
　(see **performance**)
performance
　production 164 n.
　dramaturgy 594 n.
　action, deed 676 n.
　effectuation 725 n.
performer
　entertainer 594 n.
　doer 676 n.
　agent 686 n.

perfume
　odour 394 n.
　scent 396 n.
　cosmetic 843 n.
perfumery
　fragrance 396 n.
perfunctory
　deficient 307 adj.
　unwilling 598 adj.
　hasty 680 adj.
　uncompleted
　　726 adj.
perfusion
　surgery 658 n.
pergola
　arbour 194 n.
peril
　danger 661 n.
perimeter
　outline 233 n.
period
　end 69 n.
　period 110 n.
　limit 236 n.
　phrase 563 n.
periodic
　discontinuous
　　72 adj.
　periodic 110 adj.
periodical
　regular 81 adj.
　journal 528 n.
　book 589 n.
　(see **periodicity**)
periodicity
　recurrence 106 n.
　periodicity 141 n.
peripatetic
　pedestrian 268 n.
peripeteia
　eventuality 154 n.
peripheral
　unimportant
　　639 adj.
periphery
　distance 199 n.
　outline 233 n.
　enclosure 235 n.
periphrasis
　pleonasm 570 n.
periscope
　optical device 442 n.
perish
　decompose 51 vb.
　perish 361 vb.
perishable
　ephemeral 114 adj.

perjurer
liar 545 n.
perjury
falsehood 541 n.
untruth 543 n.
perks
reward 962 n.
perk up
be refreshed 685 vb.
be cheerful 833 vb.
perky
cheerful 833 adj.
vain 783 adj.
permanence
permanence 144 n.
stability 153 n.
permanent
(*see* permanence)
permanent way
railroad 624 n.
permeable
porous 263 adj.
permeate
(*see* permeation)
permeation
mixture 43 n.
presence 189 n.
interjacence 231 n.
permissible
permitted 756 adj.
permission
permission 756 n.
permit
be lax 734 vb.
permit 756 n., vb.
permutation
change 143 n.
pernicious
harmful 645 adj.
pernickety
fastidious 862 adj.
peroration
end 69 n.
oration 579 n.
peroxide
pigment 425 n.
bleacher 426 n.
perpend
meditate 449 vb.
perpendicular
vertical 215 adj.
straight 249 adj.
perpetrate
do 676 vb.
do wrong 914 vb.
perpetrator
doer 676 n.

perpetual
existing 1 adj.
(*see* perpetuity)
perpetuate
perpetuate 115 vb.
perpetuation
continuance 146 n.
perpetuity
continuity 71 n.
permanence 144 n.
perplex
puzzle 474 vb.
perplexity
dubiety 474 n.
difficulty 700 n.
perquisite
earnings 771 n.
receipt 807 n.
persecute
(*see* persecution)
persecuted
suffering 825 adj.
persecution
pursuit 619 n.
severity 735 n.
cruel act 898 n.
persecutor
opinionist 602 n.
tyrant 735 n.
punisher 963 n.
perseverance
perseverance 600 n.
persevere
stay 144 vb.
exert oneself
682 vb.
persiflage
witticism 839 n.
ridicule 851 n.
persistence
continuance 146 n.
perseverance
600 n.
persistent
lasting 113 adj.
unyielding 162 adj.
person
self 80 n.
object 319 n.
person 371 n.
personable
personable 841 adj.
personage
person 371 n.
bigwig 638 n.
persona grata
favourite 896 n.

personal
intrinsic 5 adj.
special 80 adj.
human 371 adj.
proprietary
777 adj.
impertinent 878 adj.
personal effects
property 777 n.
personal equation
speciality 80 n.
personality
speciality, self
80 n.
spirit 447 n.
affections 817 n.
personalty
property 777 n.
personate
represent 551 vb.
act 594 vb.
personification
metaphor 519 n.
representation
551 n.
acting 594 vb.
personify
materialize 319 vb.
manifest 522 vb.
personnel
personnel 686 n.
perspective
relativeness 9 n.
range 183 n.
length 203 n.
depth 211 n.
convergence 293 n.
view 438 n.
perspicacious
(*see* perspicacity)
perspicacity
vision 438 n.
sagacity 498 n.
perspicuity
intelligibility 516 n.
perspicuity 567 n.
perspiration
excretion 302 n.
perspire
exude 298 vb.
persuade
convince 485 vb.
motivate 612 vb.
persuasibility
credulity 487 n.
persuasibility
612 n.

persuasion
influence 178 n.
belief 485 n.
inducement 612 n.
persuasive
plausible 471 adj.
inducive 612 adj.
pert
cheerful 833 adj.
impertinent 878 adj.
pertain
be related 9 vb.
belong 773 vb.
pertinacity
perseverance 600 n.
pertinence
relevance 9 n.
fitness 24 n.
pertness
sauciness 878 n.
perturbation
excitation 821 n.
perusal
study 536 n.
pervade
pervade 189 vb.
pervasion
presence 189 n.
pervasive
ubiquitous 189 adj.
perverse
wilful 602 adj.
perversion
distortion 246 n.
misteaching 535 n.
falsehood 541 n.
misuse 675 n.
perversity
(*see* perverse)
pervert
nonconformist
84 n.
distort 246 vb.
mislead 495 vb.
pervert 655 vb.
make wicked
934 vb.
libertine 952 n.
(*see* perversion)
pessimism
underestimation
483 n.
hopelessness 853 n.
pessimist
alarmist 854 n.
pest
plague 651 n.

bane 659 n.
hateful object
888 n.
noxious animal
904 n.
pester
meddle 678 vb.
torment 827 vb.
pesticide
poison 569 n.
pestilence
plague 651 n.
pestilent
infectious 653 adj.
baneful 659 adj.
pestilential
toxic 653 adj.
pestle
hammer 279 n.
pulverizer 332 n.
pet
pet, caress 889 vb.
darling 890 n.
anger 891 n.
petal
flower 366 n.
peter out
cease 145 vb.
petition
request 761 n., vb.
litigation 959 n.
prayers 981 n.
petitionary
devotional 981 adj.
petitioner
petitioner 763 n.
litigant 959 n.
petrifaction
condensation
324 n.
hardening 326 n.
petrify
harden 326 vb.
frighten 854 vb.
petrol, petroleum
propellant 287 n.
fuel 385 n.
petticoat
bodywear 228 n.
pettifogger
trickster 545 n.
lawyer 958 n.
pettifogging
sophistical 477 adj.
rascally 930 adj.
pettish
irascible 892 adj.

petty
inconsiderable
33 adj.
little 196 adj.
unimportant
639 adj.
petulance
sauciness 878 n.
irascibility 892 n.
pew
seat 218 n.
church interior
990 n.
phalanx
coherence 48 n.
multitude 104 n.
solid body 324 n.
army, formation
722 n.
phallus
genitalia 164 n.
phantasm
visual fallacy
440 n.
ghost 970 n.
phantasmagoria
visual fallacy 440 n.
spectacle 445 n.
phantom
ghost 970 n.
pharisaical
hypocritical
541 adj.
pharmaceutics
medical art 658 n.
pharmacist
druggist 658 n.
pharmacopoeia
medicine 658 n.
pharmacy
hospital 658 n.
phase
modality 7 n.
time 117 vb.
synchronize 123 vb.
appearance 445 n.
phenomenal
appearing 445 adj.
wonderful 864 adj.
phenomenon
eventuality 154 n.
appearance 445 n.
prodigy 864 n.
philander
court 889 vb.
philanderer
lover 887 n.

libertine 952 n.
philanthropic
philanthropic
901 adj.
philanthropist
philanthropist 901 n.
philanthropy
philanthropy 901 n.
disinterestedness
931 n.
philharmonic
musical 412 adj.
Philistine
ignorance 491 n.
artless 699 adj.
vulgarian 847 n.
philologist
linguist 557 n.
etymology 559 n.
philology
linguistics 557 n.
etymology 559 n.
grammar 564 n.
philoprogenitive
generative 171 adj.
philosopher
philosopher 449 n.
sage 500 n.
philosophic
philosophic 449 adj.
patient 823 adj.
content 828 adj.
philosophize
meditate 449 vb.
reason 475 vb.
philosophy
philosophy 449 n.
philtre
spell 983 n.
magic instrument
983 n.
phlegm
sluggishness 679 n.
moral insensibility
820 n.
phlegmatic
impassive 820 adj.
phobia
psychopathy 503 n.
phobia 854 n.
hatred 888 n.
phoenix
rara avis 84 n.
phoenix-like
restored 656 adj.
phoneme
word 559 n.

phone-tapping
listening 415 n.
phonetic
sounding 398 adj.
vocal 577 adj.
phonetician
acoustics 398 n.
linguist 557 n.
phonetics
acoustics 398 n.
phoney (*see* phony)
phonology
acoustics 398 n.
etymology 559 n.
phony, phoney
imitative 20 adj.
spurious 542 adj.
untrue 543 adj.
phosphorescence
glow 417 n.
photo
(*see* photograph)
photogenic
representing
551 adj.
beautiful 841 adj.
photograph
photography 551 n.
photographic
lifelike 18 adj.
accurate 494 adj.
photography
photography 551 n.
photon
element 319 n.
radiation 417 n.
photoplay
cinema 445 n.
photosphere
sun 321 n.
photostat
photography 551 n.
phrase
word 559 n.
phrase 563 n.
phrasemonger
stylist 575 n.
phraseology
phrase 563 n.
style 566 n.
phthisis
phthisis 651 n.
physic
cure 656 vb.
medicine 658 n.
physical
real 1 adj.

Column 1 (HY)

material 319 adj.
sensuous 376 adj.
ysical wreck
dilapidation 655 n.
ysician
doctor 658 n.
ysics
physics 319 n.
ysiognomy
face 237 n.
feature 445 n.
ysiotherapy
therapy 658 n.
ysique
vitality 162 n.
animality 365 n.
anist
instrumentalist
  413 n.
ano
muted 401 adj.
piano 414 n.
dejected 834 adj.
anoforte, pianola
piano 414 n.
broch
musical piece 412 n.
cador
killer 362 n.
caresque
descriptive 590 adj.
rascally 930 adj.
ccolo
flute 414 n.
ck
sharp point 256 n.
extractor 304 n.
choice 605 n.
élite 644 n.
take 786 vb.
ck-a-back
bearing 273 adj.
ck a bone with
bicker 709 vb.
ckaxe
sharp point 256 n.
perforator 263 n.
extractor 304 n.
cker and chooser
perfectionist 862 n.
cket
tie 45 vb.
be obstructive
  702 vb.
armed force 722 n.
cketing
hindrance 702 n.

Column 2 (PIE)

pick holes
  dispraise, blame
  924 vb.
  detract 926 vb.
pickings
  earnings 771 n.
pickle
  state 7 n.
  season 388 vb.
  store 632 vb.
  preserver 666 n.
  predicament 700 n.
pick-me-up
  stimulant 174 n.
  tonic 658 n.
pick out
  extract 304 vb.
  select 605 vb.
pickpocket
  thief 789 n.
pick the brains
  interrogate 459 vb.
pick up
  detect 484 vb.
  get better 654 vb.
  arrest 747 vb.
pick-up
  gramophone 414 n.
  prostitute 952 n.
Pickwickian
  absurd 497 adj.
picnic
  meal 301 n.
  amusement 837 n.
pictorial
  representing
  551 adj.
picture
  imagine 513 vb.
  represent 551 vb.
  picture 553 n.
  describe 590 vb.
picture-gallery
  art equipment
  553 n.
picture, in the
  informed 524 adj.
picturesque
  impressive 821 adj.
  beautiful 841 adj.
  ornamental 844 adj.
picture-writing
  writing 586 n.
pidgin
  dialect 560 n.
pie
  pastry 301 n.

Column 3 (PIG)

  print-type 587 n.
piebald
  pied 437 adj.
piece
  piece 53 n.
  unit 88 n.
  portion 783 n.
  loose woman 952 n.
piece, collector's
  (*see* collector's
  piece)
pièce de résistance
  dish 301 n.
piecegoods
  textile 222 n.
piecemeal
  piecemeal 53 adv.
piece, of a
  uniform 16 adj.
piece together
  make complete
  54 vb.
piecework
  labour 682 n.
pied
  pied 437 adj.
pier
  supporter 218 n.
pierce
  pierce 263 vb.
piercing
  loud 400 adj.
  strident 407 adj.
pietism
  pietism 979 n.
piety
  religion 973 n.
  piety 979 n.
  worship 981 n.
piffle
  silly talk 515 n.
pig
  pig 365 n.
  dirty person 649 n.
  glutton 947 n.
pigeon
  bird 365 n.
pigeon-hole
  classification 77 n.
  put off 136 vb.
  compartment 194 n.
piggery
  stock farm 369 n.
pig-headed
  obstinate 602 adj.
pig in a poke
  uncertainty 474 n.

Column 4 (PIL)

  gambling 618 n.
piglet
  youngling 132 n.
pigment
  pigment 425 n.
pigmentation
  hue 425 n.
pigmy
  dwarf 196 n.
pigskin
  skin 226 n.
pigsticking
  chase 619 n.
pigsty
  cattle pen 369 n.
pigtail
  hair 259 n.
pi-jaw
  empty talk 515 n.
pike
  road 624 n.
  soldiery 722 n.
  spear 723 n.
pilaster
  pillar 218 n.
pilau, pilaff
  dish 301 n.
pile
  accumulation 74 n.
  edifice 164 n.
  pillar 218 n.
  texture 331 n.
  store 632 vb.
  wealth 800 n.
pile-driver
  ram 279 n.
pile on
  add 38 vb.
piles
  swelling 253 n.
pile-up
  collision 279 n.
pilfer
  steal 788 vb.
pilferer
  thief 789 n.
pilgrim
  traveller 268 n.
  pietist 979 n.
pilgrimage
  land travel 267 n.
  piety 979 n.
pilgrimage, place of
  focus 76 n.
  holy place 990 n.
pill
  medicine 658 n.

pithy
meaningful 514 adj.
concise 569 adj.
compendious
  592 adj.
pitiable
unimportant
  639 adj.
pitiable 905 adj.
contemptible
  922 adj.
pitiful
unimportant
  639 adj.
pitying 905 adj.
pitiable 905 adj.
pitilessness
severity 735 n.
pitilessness 906 n.
pittance
finite quantity
  26 n.
insufficiency
  636 n.
receipt 807 n.
pity
pity 905 n., vb.
pivot
influence 178 n.
pivot 218 n.
chief thing 638 n.
pivotal
important 638 adj.
pivot on
depend 157 vb.
pixie, pixy
elf 970 n.
placability
mercy 905 n.
placard
exhibit 522 n.
advertisement
  528 n.
placate
pacify 719 vb.
place
degree 27 n.
serial place 73 n.
specify 80 vb.
region 184 n.
place 185 n.
situation 186 n.
place 187 vb.
abode 192 n.
placement, placing
arrangement 62 n.
location 187 n.

placidity
inexcitability 823 n.
placket
pocket 194 n.
plagiarism
imitation 20 n.
copy 22 n.
plagiarist
imitator 20 n.
plagiarize
fake 541 vb.
borrow 785 vb.
plague
plague 651 n.
bane 659 n.
annoyance 827 n.
plague-spot
sink 649 n.
infection 651 n.
plague-stricken
diseased 651 adj.
plaguy
not nice 645 adj.
annoying 827 adj.
plaid
shawl 228 n.
chequer 437 n.
plain
simple 44 adj.
horizontality 216 n.
land 344 n.
plain 348 n.
well-seen 443 adj.
intelligible 516 adj.
undisguised 522
  adj.
assertive 532 adj.
veracious 540 adj.
plain 573 adj.
artless 699 adj.
ugly 842 n.
plain-clothes man
detective 459 n.
police 955 n.
plain living
temperance 942 n.
asceticism 945 n.
plain man
ingénue 699 n.
plainness
simpleness 44 n
unsavouriness
  391 n.
(see plain)
plain sailing
navigation 269 n.
easy thing 701 n.

plainsman
dweller 191 n.
plain speaking
intelligibility 516 n.
plain-spoken
intelligible 516 adj.
plaint
accusation 928 n.
plaintiff
accuser 928 n.
litigant 959 n.
plaintive
lamenting 836 adj.
plait
crossing 222 n.
weave 222 vb.
hair 259 n.
plan
structure 331 n.
map 551 n.
intention 617 n.
plan 623 n., vb.
preparation 669 n.
tactics 688 n.
plane
horizontally 216 n.
sharp edge 256 n.
smoother 258 n.
planet, planetoid
planet 321 n.
planetarium
astronomy 321 n.
plangency
resonance 404 n.
lamentation 836 n.
plangent
(see plangency)
plank
lamina 207 n.
shelf 218 n.
policy 623 n.
planner
theorist 512 n.
planner 623 n.
expert 696 n.
plan out
plan 623 vb.
plant
place 187 vb.
implant 303 vb.
plant 366 n.
trap 542 n.
cultivate 370 vb.
workshop 687 n.
plantation
habitancy 191 n.
(see farm)

planter
settler 191 n.
husbandman
  370 n.
plash
sound faint 401 vb.
sibilation 406 n.
plasma
blood 335 n.
plasmic
formative 243 adj.
plaster
adhesive 47 n.
coat 226 vb.
surgical dressing
  658 n.
plastic
formative 243 adj.
impressible 819
  adj.
plasticity
softness 327 n.
plastic surgery
beautification
  843 n.
plate
mould 23 n.
plate 194 n.
coat 226 vb.
photography 551 n.
trophy 729 n.
plateau
high land 209 n.
plain 348 n.
platform
stand 218 n.
rostrum 539 n.
policy 623 n.
arena 724 n.
platitude
unmeaningness
  515 n.
platoon
formation 722 n.
platter
plate 194 n.
plaudits
applause 923 n.
plausible
plausible 471 adj.
credible 485 adj.
hypocritical
  541 adj.
ostensible 614 adj.
vindicable 927 adj.
play
operate 173 vb.

flow 350 vb.
play music 413 vb.
variegate 437 vb.
stage play 594 n.
action 676 n.
easy thing 701 n.
scope 744 n.
amusement 837 n.
play-act
dissemble 541 vb.
act 594 vb.
be affected 850 vb.
play ball
cooperate 706 vb.
playboy
reveller 837 n.
play down
underestimate 483 vb.
player
instrumentalist 413 n.
actor 594 n.
gambler 618 n.
player 837 n.
playful
gay 833 adj.
amused 837 adj.
innocent 935 adj.
playgoer
playgoer 594 n.
play gooseberry
look after 457 vb.
playground
arena 724 n.
pleasure-ground 837 n.
playhouse
theatre 594 n.
playing field
arena 724 n.
playmate
colleague 707 n.
chum 880 n.
play safe
be cautious 858 vb.
playsuit
beachwear 228 n.
plaything
bauble 639 n.
plaything 837 n.
playtime
festivity 837 n.
play to the gallery
be affected 850 vb.
be ostentatious 875 vb.

play upon words
absurdity 497 n.
be equivocal 518 vb.
playwright
dramatist 594 n.
plea
argument 475 n.
pretext 614 n.
litigation 959 n.
plead
argue 475 vb.
plead 614 vb.
pleader
reasoner 475 n.
law agent 958 n.
pleasance
pleasure-ground 837 n.
pleasant
pleasant 376 adj.
pleasurable 826 adj.
witty 839 adj.
pleasantry
wit 839 n.
please
please 826 vb.
content 828 vb.
pleasurable
pleasurable 826 adj.
pleasure
pleasure 376 n.
amusement 837 n.
pleasure-ground
pleasure-ground 837 n.
pleasure-loving
sensuous 376 adj.
pleat
fold 261 n., vb.
plebeian
commonalty 869 n.
plebeian 869 adj.
plebiscite
vote 605 n.
decree 737 n.
pledge
thing transferred 272 n.
oath 532 n.
promise 764 n., vb.
security 767 n.
toast 876 vb.
pledgee
creditor 802 n.
plenary
complete 54 adj.

plenipotentiary
delegate, envoy 754 n.
plenitude
plenitude 54 n.
plentiful
great 32 adj.
plenteous 635 adj.
plenty
great quantity 32 n.
store 632 n.
plenty 635 n.
prosperity 730 n.
pleonasm
pleonasm 570 n.
pleonastic
prolix 570 adj.
superfluous 637 adj.
plethora
redundance 637 n.
satiety 863 n.
pliable
flexible 327 adj.
pliancy
conformity 83 n.
softness 327 n.
persuasibility 612 n.
pliant
(see pliancy)
pliers
nippers 778 n.
plight
state 7 n.
adversity 731 n.
plinth
base 214 n.
stand 218 n.
plod
walk 267 vb.
move slowly 278 vb.
persevere 600 vb.
plot
garden 370 n.
topic 452 n.
narrative 590 n.
dramaturgy 594 n.
plot 623 n., vb.
stratagem 698 n.
compact 765 n.
plotter
planner 623 n.
slyboots 698 n.
plough
groove 262 vb.
cultivate 370 vb.

disapprove 924 vb.
plough back
economize 814 vb.
ploughman
husbandman 370 n.
ploy
job 622 n.
pluck
rend 46 vb.
uncover 229 vb.
draw 288 vb.
agitate 318 vb.
touch 378 vb.
deceive 542 vb.
fleece 786 vb.
courage 855 n.
disapprove 924 vb.
plucked
unsuccessful 728 adj.
plucky
courageous 855 adj.
plug
repeat oneself 106 vb.
stopper 264 n.
stanch 350 vb.
emphasize 532 vb.
plum
redness 431 n.
desired object 859 n.
plumage
plumage 259 n.
plumb
vertical 215 adj.
plunge 313 vb.
measure 465 vb.
plumbing
conduit 351 n.
cleansing 648 n.
plumb-line
verticality 215 n.
plume
headgear 228 n.
plumage 259 n.
plume oneself
be vain 873 vb.
plummet
sailing aid 269 n.
diver 313 n.
plump
fleshy 195 adj.
plump for
choose 605 vb.
plunder
rob 788 vb.

booty 790 n.

plunge
aquatics 269 n.
plunge 313 n., vb.
gambling 618 n.
ablution 648 n.

plunger
diver 313 n.
gambler 618 n.

plunging
deep 211 adj.

plurality
plurality 101 n.

plus
in addition 38 adv.

plush
rich 800 adj.
ornamental 844 adj.

plutocracy
government 733 n.

plutocrat
rich man 800 n.

pluvial
rainy 350 adj.

ply
be periodic 141 vb.
layer 207 n.
function 622 vb.
do 676 vb.
work 682 vb.

pneumatic
soft 327 adj.
gaseous 336 adj.

pneumatics
anemology 352 n.

pneumonia
respiratory disease
  651 n.

poach
cook 301 vb.
steal 788 vb.

poacher
thief 789 n.

pocked
mottled 437 adj.

pocket
pocket 194 n.
insert 303 vb.
receive 782 vb.

pocket-money
receipt 807 n.

pocket-size
little 196 adj.

pock-mark
cavity 255 n.

pod
skin 226 n.

podgy
fleshy 195 adj.

podium
seat, stand 218 n.

poem
poem 593 n.

poet
poet 593 n.

poetic
poetic 593 adj.

poetic justice
retaliation 714 n.

poetics
poetry 593 n.

poetry
poetry 593 n.

pogrom
slaughter 362 n.

poignant
painful 377 adj.

point
relevance 9 n.
degree 27 n.
place 185 n.
minuteness 196 n.
sharpen 256 vb.
aim 281 vb.
topic 452 n.
argument 475 n.
punctuation 547 n.
gesticulate 547 vb.
use 673 n.

point a moral
teach 534 vb.

point at issue
question 459 n.

pointer
dog 365 n.
indicator 547 n.

pointless
irrelevant 10 adj.
useless 641 adj.

point of view
view 438 n.
appearance 445 n.
idea 451 n.

point out
indicate 547 vb.

points
vantage 34 n.

point-to-point
racing 716 n.

point, to the
relevant 9 adj.

poise
conduct 688 n.
inexcitability 823 n.

poison
destroyer 168 n.
murder 362 vb.
impair 655 vb.
poison 659 n.

poisoner
murderer 362 n.

poisonous
deadly 362 adj.
not nice 645 adj.
toxic 653 adj.
baneful 659 adj.

poison pen
defamer 926 n.

poke
pocket 194 n.
pierce 263 n.

poke fun
ridicule 851 vb.

poker
card game 837 n.

poker-faced
unintelligible
  517 adj.
impassive 820 adj.

poky
restraining
  747 adj.
graceless 842 adj.

polar
telluric 321 adj.
cold 380 adj.

polarity
contrariety 14 n.
contraposition
  240 n.
opposition 704 n.

pole
extremity 69 n.
farness 199 n.
pivot 218 n.

pole-axe
slaughter 362 vb.
axe 723 n.

polecat
fetor 397 n.

polemic
argument 475 n.

polemics
argument 475 n.
contention 716 n.

pole star
directorship 689 n.

police
rule 733 vb.
restrain 747 vb.
police 955 n.

police action
war 718 n.

policeman
protector 660 n.
police 955 n.

police state
despotism 733 n.

police-station
lock-up 748 n.

policy
sagacity 498 n.
policy 623 n.
tactics 688 n.

polish
smoothness 258 n.
make bright
  417 vb.
elegance 575 n.
cleanness 648 n.

polish off
carry through
  725 vb.

polite
elegant 575 adj.
courteous 884 adj.
respectful 920 adj.

politic
wise 498 adj.
expedient 642 adj.

political
governmental
  733 adj.

politician
manager 690 n.
political party
  708 n.

politics
tactics 688 n.

polity
polity 733 n.

poll
numeration 86 n.
shorten 204 vb.
vote 605 n., vb.

pollard
shorten 204 vb.

pollination
propagation 164 n.

pollster
inquirer 459 n.

pollution
uncleanness 649 n.
infection 351 n.

polo
ball game 837 n.

poltergeist
elf, ghost 970 n.

poltergeistery
  spiritualism 984 n.
poltroonery
  cowardice 856 n.
polyandry
  type of marriage
    894 n.
polychromatic
  variegated 437 adj.
polygamy
  type of marriage
    894 n.
polyglot
  linguist 557 n.
polyhedron
  angular figure
    247 n.
polypus
  swelling 253 n.
polysyllabic
  diffuse 570 adj.
polysyllable
  speech sound
    398 n.
  word 559 n.
polytechnic
  trade school 539 n.
polytheism
  deism 973 n.
pomander
  scent 396 n.
pomiculture
  agriculture 370 n.
pommel
  handle 218 n.
pomp
  pride 871 n.
  ostentation 875 n.
pomposity
  magniloquence
    574 n.
  ostentation 875 n.
pompous
  vain 873 adj.
  (*see* **pomposity**)
ponce
  libertine 952 n.
pond
  lake 346 n.
ponder
  meditate 449 vb.
ponderous
  weighty 322 adj.
  inelegant 576 adj.
poniard
  sharp point 256 n.
  side-arms 723 n.

pontiff
  priest 986 n.
pontifical
  positive 473 adj.
  ecclesiastical
    985 adj.
pontificals
  vestments 989 n.
pontificate
  dogmatize 473 vb.
pontoon
  bridge 624 n.
pony
  saddle-horse 273 n.
pony-tail
  hair-dressing 843 n.
poodle
  dog 365 n.
poodlefake
  caress 889 vb.
pooh-pooh
  hold cheap 922 vb.
pool
  lake 346 n.
  store 632 vb.
  joint possession
    775 n.
poop
  poop 238 n.
poor
  unproductive
    172 adj.
  unimportant
    639 adj.
  bad 645 adj.
  unfortunate
    731 adj.
  poor 801 adj.
  unhappy 825 adj.
poorly
  sick 651 adj.
poor opinion
  disapprobation
    924 n.
poor quality
  inferiority 35 n.
poor relation
  inferior 35 n.
pope
  ecclesiarch 986 n.
pop-eyed
  wondering 864 adj.
pop-gun
  bang 402 n.
  toy gun 723 n.
popinjay
  fop 848 n.

pop out
  jut 254 vb.
  emerge 298 vb.
poppet
  darling 890 n.
popple
  \ *crinkle* 251 vb.
  flow 350 vb.
poppy
  soporific 679 n.
poppycock
  empty talk 515 n.
pop-shop
  pawnshop 784 n.
populace
  habitancy 191 n.
  commonalty 869 n.
popular
  general 79 adj.
  native 191 adj.
  reputable 866 adj.
popularity
  repute 866 n.
  lovableness 887 n.
  approbation 923 n.
popularize
  be intelligible
    516 vb.
  facilitate 701 vb.
populate
  dwell 192 vb.
population
  habitancy 191 n.
  social group 371 n.
populous
  multitudinous
    104 adj.
pop up
  happen 154 vb.
porcelain
  pottery 381 n.
porch
  doorway 263 n.
porcine
  animal 365 adj.
porcupine
  prickle 256 n.
pore
  outlet 298 n.
  scan 438 vb.
  be attentive 455 vb.
pork
  meat 301 n.
porker
  pig 365 n.
pornography
  impurity 951 n.

porosity
  porosity 263 n.
porpoise
  fish 365 n.
porridge
  cereal 301 n.
porringer
  bowl 194 n.
port
  stable 192 n.
  sinistrality 242 n.
  window 263 n.
  goal 295 n.
  wine 301 n.
  mien 445 n.
portable
  light 323 adj.
portal
  doorway 263 n.
portend
  predict 511 vb.
portent
  omen 511 n.
porter
  janitor 264 n.
  bearer 273 n.
porterage
  transport 272 n.
portfolio
  title-deed 767 n.
  jurisdiction
    955 n.
porthole
  window 263 n.
portico
  lobby 194 n.
  pillar 218 n.
portion
  part 53 n.
  fraction 102 n.
  participation
    775 n.
  dower 777 n.
  portion 783 n.
portly
  fleshy 195 adj.
portmanteau
  box 194 n.
portrait
  copy 22 n.
  picture 553 n.
portraiture
  representation
    551 n.
portray
  paint 553 vb.
  (*see* **portrayal**)

portrayal
representation 551 n.
description 590 n.
pose
be example 23 vb.
interrogate 459 vb.
be affected 850 vb.
poser
living model 23 n.
enigma 530 n.
affector 850 n.
poseur
affector 850 n.
position
state 7 n.
arrange 62 vb.
serial place 73 n.
station 187 n.
job 622 n.
prestige 866 n.
positive
real 1 adj.
positive 473 adj.
believing 485 adj.
positiveness
affirmation 532 n.
positivism
materiality 319 n.
possess
possess 773 vb.
excite 821 vb.
possession
possession 773 n.
property 777 n.
excitation 821 n.
possessive
greedy 859 adj.
jealous 911 adj.
selfish 932 adj.
possessor
master 741 n.
possessor 776 n.
possibility
opportunity 137 n.
possibility 469 n.
probability 471 n.
possible
accessible 289 adj.
possible 469 adj.
(*see* possibility)
post
subsequent 120 adj.
situation 186 n.
place 187 vb.
pillar 218 n.
send 272 vb.

mails 531 n.
register 548 vb.
correspondence 588 n.
job 622 n.
commission 751 vb.
account 808 vb.
postal
epistolary 588 adj.
postbag
correspondence 588 n.
postcard
correspondence 588 n.
post-christian
irreligious 974 adj.
postdate
misdate 118 vb.
posted
informed 524 adj.
poster
advertisement 528 n.
posterior
subsequent 120 adj.
back, buttocks 238 adj.
posterity
aftercomer 67 n.
posterity 170 n.
postern
back 238 adj.
doorway 263 n.
post-haste
speeding 277 n.
posthumous
subsequent 120 adj.
postilion
driver 268 n.
posting
transference 272 n.
mandate 751 n.
postman
mails 531 n.
post-mortem
inquest 364 n.
post-office
mails 531 n.
postpone
put off 136 vb.
not complete 726 vb.
postponement
(*see* postpone)
postposition
sequence 65 n.

postscript
adjunct 40 n.
sequel 67 n.
postulant
nun 986 n.
postulate
axiom 496 n.
supposition 512 n.
posture
form 243 n.
mien 445 n.
be affected 850 vb.
post-war
peaceful 717 adj.
posy
bunch 74 n.
pot
vessel 194 n.
shorten 204 vb.
pottery 381 n.
abstract 592 vb.
preserve 666 vb.
trophy 729 n.
potation
drinking 301 n.
potato
tuber 301 n.
pot-bellied
fleshy 195 adj.
potboiler
reading matter 589 n.
potboiling
trivial 639 adj.
potency
power 160 n.
strength 162 n.
potent
generative 171 adj.
vigorous 174 adj.
intoxicating 949 adj.
(*see* potency)
potentate
potentate 741 n.
potential
unreal 2 adj.
energy 160 n.
electricity 160 n.
(*see* potentiality)
potentiality
ability 160 n.
possibility 469 n.
latency 523 n.
potherb
potherb 301 n.

condiment 389 n.
pot-hole
cavity 255 n.
pothouse
tavern 192 n.
pot-hunter
contender 716 n.
potion
potion 301 n.
pot-luck
meal 301 n.
pot-pourri
medley 43 n.
scent 396 n.
potsherd
piece 53 n.
potted
short 204 adj.
potter
epitomizer 592 n.
pottery
pottery 381 n.
pot-valiant
drunk 949 adj.
pouch
pocket 194 n.
receive 872 vb.
poultice
surgical dressing 658 n.
poultry
poultry 365 n.
pounce
spurt 277 n.
descent 309 n.
plunge 313 n.
pounce on
surprise 508 vb.
attack 712 vb.
pound
enclosure 235 n.
pulverize 332 vb.
lock-up 748 n.
pound of flesh
severity 735 n.
interest 803 n.
pour
let fall 311 vb.
flow, rain 350 vb.
pour in
irrupt 297 vb.
pour out
void 300 vb.
pout
be convex 253 vb.
jut 254 vb.
gesture 547 n.

poverty
scarcity 636 n.
non-ownership
774 n.
poverty 801 n.
poverty-stricken
beggarly 801 adj.
powder
overlay 226 vb.
powder 332 n.
pulverize 332 vb.
explosive 723 n.
primp 843 vb.
powder and shot
ammunition 723 n.
powdery
powdery 332 adj.
power
intrinsicality 5 n.
power 160 n.
strength 162 n.
vigour 571 n.
instrumentality
628 n.
authority 733 n.
**power behind the
throne**
influence 178 n.
powered
dynamic 160 adj.
mechanical 630 adj.
powerful
influential 178 adj.
loud 400 adj.
(*see* power)
powerless
powerless 161 adj.
weak 163 adj.
powerlessness
anarchy 734 n.
power of attorney
mandate 751 n.
power of speech
eloquence 579 n.
power of the purse
finance 797 n.
powers that be
master 741 n.
power vacuum
anarchy 734 n.
pow-wow
conference 584 n.
pox
venereal disease
651 n.
practicable
possible 469 adj.

practical
intelligent 498 adj.
expedient 642 adj.
used 673 adj.
practical joke
foolery 497 n.
practice
practice 610 n.
plot 623 n.
medical art 658 n.
preparation 669 n.
exercise 682 n.
foul play 930 n.
practice, in
prepared 669 adj.
practise
train 534 vb.
habituate 610 vb.
(*see* practice)
practising
orthodox 976 adj.
practitioner
agent 686 n.
expert 696 n.
pragmatic
useful 640 adj.
pragmatism
expedience 642 n.
prairie
plain 348 n.
praise
praise 923 n., vb.
praiseworthy
excellent 644 adj.
approvable 923 adj.
pram
push cart 274 n.
prance
walk 267 vb.
ride 267 vb.
be ostentatious
875 vb.
prandial
mensal 301 adj.
prank
revel 837 n.
primp 843 vb.
prankish
capricious 604 adj.
amused 837 adj.
prate
empty talk 515 n.
prattle
empty talk 515 n.
chatter 581 n.
prawn
table fish 365 n.

pray
entreat 761 vb.
worship 981 vb.
prayer
entreaty 761 n.
prayers 981 n.
prayer-book
office-book 988 n.
prayer-meeting
public worship
981 n.
prayers
prayers 981 n.
pray for
patronize 703 vb.
pre-
prior 119 adj.
preach
teach 534 vb.
orate 579 vb.
preacher
preacher 537 n.
pastor 986 n.
preachiness
pietism 979 n.
preaching office
church ministry
985 n.
preamble
prelude 66 n.
prearrangement
predetermination
608 n.
prebendary
ecclesiarch 986 n.
precarious
unreliable 474 adj.
unsafe 661 adj.
precautionary
preparatory 669
adj.
precede
precede 283 vb.
precedence
precedence 64 n.
seniority 131 n.
precedent
non-imitation
21 n.
precursor 66 n.
example 83 n.
guide 520 n.
precept 693 n.
precept
maxim 496 n.
advice 691 n.
precept 693 n.

preceptor
teacher 537 n.
precession
precession 283 n.
precinct
place 185 n.
inclosure 235 n.
preciosity
ornament 574 n.
affectation 850 n.
precious
valuable 644 adj.
of price 811 adj.
affected 850 adj.
precious stone
gem 844 n.
precipice
high land 209 n.
verticality 215 n.
precipitance
haste 680 n.
rashness 857 n.
precipitate
leavings 41 n.
propel 287 vb.
eject 300 vb.
hasten 680 vb.
rash 857 adj.
precipitation
condensation 324 n.
precipitous
vertical 215 adj.
précis
compendium 592 n.
precise
accurate 494 adj.
pietistic 979 adj.
precisian
perfectionist 862 n.
religionist 979 n.
precision
accuracy 494 n.
preclude
exclude 57 vb.
restrain 747 vb.
precocity
anticipation 135 n.
precognition
foresight 510 n.
psychics 984 n.
preconception
prejudgement 481 n.
precursor
precursor 66 n.
priority 119 n.
predator
taker 786 n.

predatory
taking 786 adj.
thieving 788 adj.
predecessor
precursor 66 n.
predestinarian
fatalist 596 n.
predestination
fate 596 n.
predetermination
608 n.
destiny 155 n.
predestine
predestine 155 vb.
necessitate 596 vb.
predetermination
necessity 596 n.
predetermination
608 n.
predetermine
predestine 155 vb.
predetermine
608 vb.
plan 623 vb.
predial
proprietary 777 adj.
predicament
predicament 700 n.
predicate
attribute 158 vb.
predication
affirmation 532 n.
predict
indicate 547 vb.
(see prediction)
predictable
future 124 adj.
prediction
prediction 511 n.
warning 664 n.
predigested
edible 301 adj.
ready-made
669 adj.
predilection
liking 859 n.
love 887 n.
predispose
bias 481 vb.
motivate 612 vb.
predisposition
tendency 179 n.
predominance
superiority 34 n.
authority 733 n.
predominate
overmaster 727 vb.

pre-eminence
superiority 34 n.
precedence 64 n.
pre-empt
exclude 57 vb.
be early 135 vb.
preen
primp 843 vb.
preen oneself
be vain 873 vb.
prefabricate
produce 164 vb.
preface
prepose 64 vb.
prelude 66 n.
prefatory
precursory 66 adj.
prefect
officer 741 n.
prefer
promote 285 vb.
choose 605 vb.
preferable
superior 34 adj.
chosen 605 adj.
preference
choice 605 n.
preferment
progression 285 n.
church office 985 n.
prefigure
predict 511 vb.
indicate 547 vb.
prefix
prepose 64 vb.
precursor 66 n.
pregnancy
propagation 164 n.
pregnant
productive 164 adj.
meaningful 514 adj.
concise 569 adj.
pregnant with
impending 155 adj.
presageful 511 adj.
prehension
retention 778 n.
prehistorian
antiquarian 125 n.
prehistoric
former 125 adj.
olden 127 adj.
prehistory
antiquity 125 n.
prejudgement
prejudgement
481 n.

prejudice
prejudice, bias
481 n.
dislike 861 n.
injustice 914 n.
prejudicial
harmful 645 adj.
prelacy
churchdom 985 n.
prelate
ecclesiarch 986 n.
preliminaries
preparation 669 n.
preliminary
prelude 66 n.
precursory 66 adj.
prelude
prelude 66 n.
prelusory
(see prelude)
premature
ill-timed 138 adj.
unsuccessful
728 adj.
premeditation
predetermination
608 n.
premier
director 690 n.
première
début 68 n.
dramaturgy 594 n.
premiership
directorship 689 n.
premise
supposition 512 n.
premises
place 185 n.
shop 796 n.
premium
receipt 807 n.
premonition
foresight 510 n.
warning 664 n.
prenomen
name 561 n.
prentice
beginner 538 n.
immature 670 adj.
preoccupation
abstractedness
456 n.
preoccupied
distracted 456 adj.
preoccupy
cause thought
449 vb.

possess 773 vb.
prep
study 536 n.
preparation
provision 633 n.
preparation 669 n.
preparatory
preparatory
669 adj.
prepare
train 534 vb.
plan 623 vb.
prepare 669 vb.
preponderance
superiority 34 n.
authority 733 n.
preposition
adjunct 40 n.
part of speech
564 n.
prepossessing
personable 841 adj.
lovable 887 adj.
prepossession
prejudice 481 n.
preposterous
absurd 497 adj.
ridiculous 849 adj.
prerequisite
requirement 627 n.
prerogative
vantage 34 n.
freedom 744 n.
right 913 n.
dueness 915 n.
presage
omen 511 n.
threaten 900 vb.
presageful
presageful 511 adj.
presbyter
church officer
986 n.
presbyterate
church office 985 n.
presbytery
synod 985 n.
parish 985 n.
prescience
foresight 510 n.
prescribe
doctor 658 vb.
advise 691 vb.
prescript
decree 737 n.
prescription
tradition 127 n.

excellent 644 adj.
make ready 669 vb.
prime minister
director 690 n.
primer
textbook 589 n.
primeval
primal 127 adj.
priming
ammunition 723 n.
primitive
primal 127 adj.
earliness 135 n.
primness
prudery 950 n.
(see prim)
primogenital
filial 170 adj.
primogeniture
seniority 131 n.
sonship 170 n.
primordial
primal 127 adj.
primp
primp 843 vb.
primrose path
deterioration 655 n.
facility 701 n.
primum mobile
cause 156 n.
prince
potentate 741 n.
aristocrat 868 n.
princely
ruling 733 adj.
liberal 813 adj.
noble 868 adj.
prince of
paragon 646 n.
principal
supreme 34 adj.
teacher 537 n.
director 690 n.
principality
polity 733 n.
principle
essential part 5 n.
rule 81 n.
element 319 n.
idea 451 n.
opinion 485 n.
axiom 496 n.
principles
creed 485 n.
probity 929 n.
print
photography 551 n.

printing 555 n.
letterpress 587 n.
printer
printer 587 n.
printing
printing 555 n.
print-type
print-type 587 n.
prior
prior 119 adj.
ecclesiarch 986 n.
priority
precedence 64 n.
priority 119 n.
seniority 131 n.
chief thing 638 n.
priory
monastery 986 n.
prise, prize
force 176 vb.
prism
chromatics 425 n.
variegation 437 n.
optical device
442 n.
prismatic
variegated 437 adj.
prison
prison 748 n.
seclusion 883 n.
prisoner
prisoner 750 n.
accused person
928 n.
pristine
former 125 adj.
privacy
seclusion 883 n.
private
inferior 35 n.
soldiery 722 n.
possessed 773 adj.
secluded 883 adj.
privateer
warship 722 n.
private parts
genitalia 164 n.
privation
loss 772 n.
poverty 801 n.
privilege
permit 756 vb.
right 913 n.
non-liability 919 n.
privy
knowing 490 adj.
latrine 649 n.

privy purse
receipt 807 n.
prize
trophy 729 n.
acquisition 771 n.
booty 790 n.
desired object
859 n.
love 887 vb.
reward 962 n.
prize-fight
pugilism 716 n.
prize-fighter
pugilist 722 n.
prize-money
reward 962 n.
prize-winner
proficient 696 n.
pro
deputy 755 n.
probability
probability 471 n.
probable
probable 471 adj.
credible 485 adj.
probation
essay 671 n.
probationary
experimental
461 adj.
probationer
beginner 538 n.
offender 904 n.
probative
evidential 466 adj.
demonstrating
478 adj.
probe
perforator 263 n.
inquiry 459 n.
experiment 461 n.
probity
morals 917 n.
probity 929 n.
problem
topic 452 n.
question 459 n.
enigma 530 n.
difficulty 700 n.
worry 825 n.
problematical
uncertain 474 adj.
difficult 700 adj.
proboscis
projection 254 n.
procedure
policy 623 n.

way 624 n.
ritual 988 n.
proceed
travel 267 vb.
progress 285 vb.
proceeding
deed 676 n.
proceedings
record 548 n.
proceeds
earnings 771 n.
receipt 807 n.
process
convert 147 vb.
motion 265 n.
way 624 n.
action 676 n.
procession
procession 71 n.
pageant 875 n.
process-server
law officer 955 n.
proclaim
proclaim 528 vb.
honour 866 vb.
proclamation
publication 528 n.
call 547 n.
proclivity
tendency 179 n.
proconsul
officer 741 n.
procrastinate
put off 136 vb.
not act 677 vb.
procreation
propagation 164 n.
productiveness
171 n.
proctor
law agent 958 n.
proctorship
management 689 n.
procurator
consignee 754 n.
law agent 958 n.
procure
cause 156 vb.
acquire 771 vb.
be impure 951 vb.
procurement
acquisition 771 n.
procuress
bawd 952 n.
prod
stimulant 174 n.
impel 279 vb.

incentive 612 n.
prodigal
wasteful 634 adj.
prodigal 815 n.,
adj.
prodigality
prodigality 815 n.
(*see* prodigal)
prodigal son
prodigal 815 n.
penitent 939 n.
prodigious
prodigious 32 adj.
wonderful 864 adj.
prodigy
exceller 644 n.
prodigy 864 n.
produce
cause 156 vb.
product 164 n.
lengthen 203 vb.
dramatize 594 vb.
producer
producer 167 n.
stage-manager
594 n.
product
numerical result
85 n.
product 164 n.
production
product 164 n.
dramaturgy 594 n.
production line
workshop 687 n.
productive
prolific 171 adj.
gainful 771 adj.
productivity
productiveness
171 n.
plenty 635 n.
profanation
misuse 675 n.
impiety 980 n.
profane
maledicent 899 adj.
not respect 921 vb.
irreligious 974 adj.
profane 980 n.
laical 987 adj.
profanity
scurrility 899 n.
impiety 980 n.
profess
believe 485 vb.
teach 534 vb.

professing
affirmative 532 adj.
profession
creed 485 n.
affirmation 532 n.
vocation 622 n.
professional
instructed 490 adj.
businesslike 622
adj.
expert 696 n.
professionalism
skill 694 n.
professor
scholar 492 n.
teacher 537 n.
proffer
offer 759 vb.
proficiency
skill 694 n.
proficient
knowing 490 adj.
proficient 696 n.
profile
outline 233 n., vb.
laterality 239 n.
feature 445 n.
description 590 n.
profit
increment 36 n.
benefit 615 n.
gain 771 n.
profitable
prolific 171 adj.
(*see* profit)
profit by
profit by 137 vb.
use 673 vb.
profiteer
prosper 730 vb.
overcharge 811 vb.
profitless
profitless 641 adj.
losing 772 adj.
profligate
vicious 934 adj.
libertine 952 n.
profound
great 32 adj.
deep 211 adj.
wise 498 adj.
felt 818 adj.
profundity
thought 448 n.
(*see* profound)
profuse
diffuse 570 adj.

liberal 813 adj.
profusion
great quantity 32 n.
plenty 635 n.
prodigality 815 n.
progenitor
source 156 n.
parent 169 n.
progeny
posterity 170 n.
prognosis
prediction 511 n.
medical art 658 n.
prognostic
foreseeing 510 adj.
omen 511 n.
programme
policy 623 n.
plan 623 n., vb.
progress
increase 36 n.
motion 265 n.
travel 267 vb.
progression 285 n.
improvement 654 n.
progression
series 71 n.
ratio 85 n.
(*see* progress)
progressive
progressive 285 adj.
reformer 654 n.
prohibit
restrain 747 vb.
prohibit 757 vb.
prohibition
temperance 942 n.
(*see* prohibit)
prohibitionist
abstainer 942 n.
prohibitive
dear 811 adj.
project
externalize 223 vb.
jut 254 vb.
plan 623 n., vb.
undertaking 672 n.
projectile
missile 287 n.
ammunition 723 n.
projection
distortion 246 n.
projection 254 n.
image, map 551 n.
projector
optical device
442 n.

planner 623 n.
prole
(*see* proletarian)
prolegomena
prelude 66 n.
dissertation 591 n.
proletarian
commoner 869 n.
proletariat
lower classes
869 n.
commonalty 869 n.
proliferate
reproduce 164 vb.
be fruitful 171 vb.
prolific
productive 164 adj.
prolific 171 adj.
prolix
prolix 570 adj.
prologue
prelude 66 n.
oration 579 n.
actor 594 n.
prolong
lengthen 203 vb.
promenade
street 192 n.
pedestrianism
267 n.
pageant 875 n.
prominence
prominence 254 n.
elevation 310 n.
importance 638 n.
prestige 866 n.
prominent
salient 254 adj.
well-seen 443 adj.
(*see* prominence)
promiscuity
indiscrimination
464 n.
unchastity 951 n.
promiscuous
mixed 43 adj.
orderless 61 adj.
promise
oath 532 n.
be auspicious
730 vb.
promise 764 n., vb.
compact 765 n.
promissory
promissory 764 adj.
promontory
projection 254 n.

land 344 n.
promote
 tend 179 vb.
 promote 285 vb.
 make likely 471 vb.
 be instrumental
  628 vb.
 make better
  654 vb.
 aid 703 vb.
 dignify 866 vb.
promoter
 planner 623 n.
prompt
 speedy 277 adj.
 hint 524 n., vb.
 incite 612 vb.
 advise 691 vb.
prompter
 reminder 505 n.
 motivator 612 n.
 adviser 691 n.
promptitude
 punctuality 135 n.
promulgate
 proclaim 528 vb.
 decree 737 vb.
prone
 supine 216 adj.
proneness
 tendency 179 n.
prong
 sharp point 256 n.
pronounce
 affirm 532 vb.
 voice 577 vb.
pronounced
 well-seen 443 adj.
 vocal 577 adj.
pronouncement
 publication 528 n.
pronunciation
 pronunciation
  577 n.
proof
 sealed off 264 adj.
 demonstration
  478 n.
 letterpress 587 n.
 invulnerable
  660 adj.
 resisting 715 adj.
prop
 supporter 218 n.
 elevate 310 vb.
propaganda
 argument 475 n.

publicity 528 n.
propagandist
 publicizer 528 n.
 preacher 537 n.
 motivator 612 n.
propagate
 generate 164 vb.
 publish 528 vb.
propel
 propel 287 vb.
propellant
 propellant 287 n.
 explosive 723 n.
propeller
 propellant 287 n.
 rotator 317 n.
propensity
 tendency 179 n.
 liking 859 n.
proper
 characteristic 5 adj.
 relevant 9 adj.
 possessed 773 adj.
 right 913 adj.
 virtuous 933 adj.
property
 ability 160 n.
 stage-set 594 n.
 property 777 n.
prophecy
 prediction 511 n.
 revelation 975 n.
prophesy
 predict 511 vb.
prophet
 sage 500 n.
 oracle 511 n.
 preacher 537 n.
 warner 664 n.
 religious teacher
  973 n.
prophylactic
 hygiene 652 n.
 prophylactic 658 n.
prophylaxis
 (see **prophylactic**)
propinquity
 nearness 200 n.
propitiate
 pacify 719 vb.
 atone 941 vb.
propitious
 opportune 137 adj.
 aiding 703 adj.
 promising 852 adj.
proportion
 correlation 12 n.

ratio 85 n.
 symmetry 245 n.
 portion 783 n.
**proportional, propor-
 tionable, propor-
 tionate**
 (see **proportion**)
proportions
 size 195 n.
proposal
 supposition 512 n.
 intention 617 n.
 plan 623 n.
 advice 691 n.
 offer 759 n.
propose
 propound 512 vb.
 intend 617 vb.
 advise 691 vb.
 court 889 vb.
proposition
 topic 453 n.
 supposition 512 n.
 (see **proposal**)
propound
 propound 512 vb.
 (see **propose**)
proprietary
 proprietary 777 adj.
proprietor
 owner 776 n.
propriety
 fitness 24 n.
 good taste 846 n.
 right 913 n.
propulsion
 propulsion 287 n.
prorogation
 delay 136 n.
prorogue
 put off 136 vb.
prosaic
 prosaic 593 adj.
 dull 840 adj.
proscenium
 front 237 n.
proscribe
 prohibit 757 vb.
 condemn 961 vb.
proscription
 prohibition 757 n.
 condemnation
  961 n.
 penalty 963 n.
prose
 plainness 573 n.
 prose 593 n.

prosecute
 do 676 vb.
prosecution
 accusation 928 n.
 legal trial 959 n.
proselyte
 changed person
  147 n.
 learner 538 n.
proselytize
 convert 147 vb.
 teach 534 vb.
prosing, prosy
 prolix 570 adj.
 loquacious 581 adj.
prosody
 prosody 593 n.
prospect
 futurity 124 n.
 spectacle 445 n.
 search 459 vb.
 probability 471 n.
 prediction 511 n.
prospective
 future 124 adj.
prospector
 inquirer 459 n.
prospectus
 list 87 n.
 policy 623 n.
prosper
 prosper 730 vb.
prosperity (see **prosper, prosperous**)
prosperous
 prosperous 730 adj.
 rich 800 adj.
 happy 824 adj.
prostitute
 pervert 655 vb.
 prostitute 952 n.
prostitution
 misuse 675 n.
 social evil 951 n.
prostrate
 supine 216 adj.
 flatten 216 vb.
prostrate oneself
 stoop 311 vb.
 show respect
  920 vb.
prostration
 (see **prostrate**)
protagonist
 actor 594 n.
protean
 multiform 82 adj.

changeful 152 adj.
protect
　patronize 703 vb.
　befriend 880 vb.
　(*see* protection)
protection
　surveillance 457 n.
　protection 660 n.
　safeguard 662 n.
　restriction 747 n.
protectionism
　restriction 747 n.
protector
　protector 660 n.
　defender 713 n.
protectorate
　polity 733 n.
protégé
　dependant 742 n.
protest
　oppose 704 vb.
　resistance 715 n.
　deprecation 762 n.
　disapprobation
　924 n.
protestant
　dissentient 489 n.
Protestantism
　Protestantism
　976 n.
protester
　agitator 738 n.
proto-
　past 125 adj.
protocol
　etiquette 848 n.
　formality 875 n.
proton
　element 319 n.
protoplasm
　organism 358 n.
prototype
　prototype 23 n.
protozoon
　animalcule 196 n.
protract
　put off 136 vb.
　lengthen 203 vb.
protractor
　gauge 465 n.
protrude
　jut 254 vb.
protuberance
　protuberance 254 n.
proud
　proud 871 adj.
　insolent 878 adj.

prove
　demonstrate
　478 vb.
proven
　trustworthy 929 adj.
provenance
　origin 68 n.
provender
　provender 301 n.
　provision 633 n.
proverb
　maxim 496 n.
proverbial
　known 490 adj.
　aphoristic 496 adj.
provide
　store 632 vb.
　provide 633 vb.
　give 781 vb.
providence
　divineness 965 n.
provident
　foreseeing 510 adj.
providential
　opportune 137 adj.
　divine 965 adj.
province
　district 184 n.
　function 622 n.
provincial
　provincial 192 adj.
　narrow-minded
　481 adj.
　plebeian 869 adj.
proving ground
　testing agent 461 n.
provision
　means 629 n.
　provision 633 n.
　fitting out 669 n.
　conditions 766 n.
provisional
　experimental
　461 adj.
　conditional
　766 adj.
provisions
　provisions 301 n.
proviso
　qualifications
　468 n.
　conditions 766 n.
provisory
　conditional 766 adj.
provocation
　excitation 821 n.
　resentment 891 n.

provocative
　defiant 711 adj.
　impure 951 adj.
　(*see* provocation,
　provoke)
provoke
　cause 156 vb.
　incite 612 vb.
　torment 827 vb.
prow
　prow 237 n.
prowess
　skill 694 n.
　prowess 855 n.
prowl
　be stealthy 525 vb.
proximate
　near 200 adj.
proximity
　nearness 200 n.
proxy
　substitute 150 n.
　consignee 754 n.
prude
　prude 950 n.
　(*see* prudish)
prudence
　sagacity 498 n.
　foresight 510 n.
　caution 858 n.
prudery
　modesty 874 n.
prudish
　prudish 950 adj.
prune
　subtract 39 vb.
　shorten 204 vb.
prurience
　curiosity 453 n.
　desire, libido
　859 n.
pry
　inquisitor 453 n.
　be curious 453 vb.
psalm
　hymn 981 n.
psalmist,
　psalmodist
　worshipper 981 n.
psalmody
　act of worship
　981 n.
　hymn 981 n.
psalter
　hymnal 988 n.
pseudo
　spurious 542 adj.

pseudonym
　misnomer 562 n.
psi
　psychics 984 n.
psyche
　intellect, spirit
　447 n.
psychiatry
　psychology 447 n.
　therapy 658 n.
psychic
　psychic 447 adj.
　psychic 984 n.
　psychical 984 adj.
psychic bid
　gambling 618 n.
psychoanalysis
　psychology 447 n.
　therapy 658 n.
psychological
　psychic 447 adj.
　behaving 688 adj.
psychologist
　psychologist 447 n.
psychology
　psychology 447 n.
　psychics 984 n.
psychopath
　madman 504 n.
psychopathist
　doctor 658 n.
psychopathy
　psychopathy 503 n.
psychosis
　psychopathy 503 n.
psychotherapy
　insanity 503 n.
　therapy 658 n.
psychotic
　insane 503 adj.
　madman 504 n.
pub
　tavern 192 n.
pub-crawl
　drunkenness 949 n.
puberty
　(*see* adultness)
pubescence
　hair 259 n.
public
　social group 371 n.
　national 371 adj.
　known 490 adj.
　formal 875 adj.
publican
　caterer 633 n.
　receiver 782 n.

publication
 publication 528 n.
 book 589 n.
public convenience
 latrine 649 n.
public domain
 joint possession
 775 n.
public house
 tavern 192 n.
publicist
 dissertator 591 n.
publicity
 knowledge 490 n.
 publicity 528 n.
 ostentation 875 n.
publicity agent
 publicizer 528 n.
public spirit
 patriotism 901 n.
publish
 publish 528 vb.
publisher
 bookman 589 n.
puce
 brown 430 adj.
 purple 434 adj.
pucker
 fold 261 n., vb.
puckish
 fairylike
 970 adj.
puddle
 shallowness 212 n.
 lake 346 n.
puerile
 trivial 639 adj.
puerility
 folly 499 n.
puff
 breeze 352 n.
 blow, breathe
 352 vb.
 advertisement
 528 n.
 praise 923 vb.
puffed-up
 prideful 871 adj.
puffy
 expanded 197 adj.
 windy 352 adj.
pug
 foot 214 n.
pugilism
 pugilism 716 n.
pugilist
 pugilist 722 n.

pugnacious
 (*see* pugnacity)
pugnacity
 bellicosity 718 n.
puisné
 subsequent 120 adj.
 young 130 adj.
puissant
 powerful 160 adj.
puke
 vomit 300 vb.
pukka
 genuine 494 adj.
pule
 cry 408 vb.
 weep 836 vb.
pull
 influence 178 n.
 traction 288 n.
 attraction 291 n.
 extract 304 vb.
pull down
 fell 311 vb.
pullet
 poultry 365 n.
pulley
 wheel 250 n.
pull one's leg
 ridicule 851 vb.
pull one's punches
 avoid 620 vb.
pull out
 open 263 vb.
 start out 296 vb.
 extract 304 vb.
pullover
 vest 228 n.
pull strings
 influence 178 vb.
pull through
 be restored 656 vb.
pull-through
 cathartic 658 n.
pull together
 concur 181 vb.
pullulate
 be many 104 vb.
 be fruitful 171 vb.
pull up
 halt 145 vb.
pull-up
 stopping place
 145 n.
 café 192 n.
pulp
 demolish 165 vb.
 soften 327 vb.

pulpit
 rostrum 539 n.
 church utensil
 990 n.
pulpy
 soft 327 adj.
 pulpy 356 adj.
pulsate
 be periodic 141 vb.
 oscillate 317 vb.
pulsation
 (*see* pulse)
pulse
 periodicity 141 n.
 oscillation 317 n.
pulverize
 pulverize 332 vb.
pulverulence
 pulverulence 332 n.
pumice stone
 cleanser 648 n.
pummel
 strike 279 vb.
pump
 footwear 228 n.
 irrigator 341 n.
 make flow 350 vb.
 interrogate 459 vb.
pump out
 make smaller
 198 vb.
 sufflate 352 vb.
pump-room
 hospital 658 n.
 place of amusement
 837 n.
pun
 equivocalness
 518 n.
 witticism 839 n.
punch
 mould 23 n.
 vigorousness 174 n.
 perforator 263 n.
 knock 279 n.
 printing 555 n.
 vigour 571 n.
punctilio
 etiquette 848 n.
 formality 875 n.
punctilious
 observant 768 adj.
 formal 875 adj.
 trustworthy 929 adj.
punctual
 early 135 adj.
 accurate 494 adj.

 observant 768 adj.
punctuate
 variegate 437 vb.
 mark 547 vb.
punctuation
 punctuation 547 n.
puncture
 perforation 263 n.
pungency
 sourness 393 n.
 vigour 571 n.
pungent
 pungent 388 adj.
 forceful 571 adj.
punish
 punish 963 vb.
punishable
 punishable 963 adj.
punishment
 punishment 963 n.
punitive
 punitive 963 adj.
punitive action
 retaliation 714 n.
punkah
 ventilation 352 n.
punster
 humorist 839 n.
punt
 rowboat 275 n.
 gamble 618 vb.
punter
 boatman 270 n.
 gambler 618 n.
puny
 weak 163 adj.
 unimportant
 639 adj.
pupil
 eye 438 n.
 learner 538 n.
pupillage
 nonage 130 n.
puppet
 dupe 544 n.
 image 551 n.
 nonentity 639 n.
 slave 742 n.
puppy
 youngling 132 n.
 insolent person
 878 n.
purchase
 purchase 792 n.,
 vb.
purchaser
 purchaser 792 n.

purdah
womankind 373 n.
seclusion 883 n.
(*see* screen)
pure
unmixed 44 adj.
genuine 494 adj.
clean 648 adj.
salubrious 652 adj.
innocent 935 adj.
pure 950 adj.
purgation
penance 941 n.
purgative
excretory 302 adj.
cathartic 658 n.
purgatorial
paining 827 adj.
atoning 941 adj.
purgatory
suffering 825 n.
penance 941 n.
purge
slaughter 362 n.,
vb.
purify 648 vb.
cathartic 658 n.
purification
cleansing 648 n.
purify
purify 648 vb.
sanitate 652 vb.
purist
perfectionist 862 n.
puritan
prude 950 n.
religionist 979 n.
puritanical
severe 735 adj.
serious 834 adj.
prudish 950 adj.
puritanism
(*see* puritan)
purity
simpleness 44 n.
good taste 846 n.
virtue 933 n.
purity 950 n.
sanctity 979 n.
purlieu
district 184 n.
near place 290 n.
purloin
steal 788 vb.
purple patch
ornament 574 n.
eloquence 579 n.

purport
meaning 514 n.
purpose
intention 617 n.
purposeful
resolute 599 adj.
purposeless
designless 618 adj.
useless 641 adj.
purr
ululate 409 vb.
be pleased 824 vb.
purse
pocket 194 n.
make smaller
198 vb.
funds 797 n.
purser
provider 633 n.
purse-strings
finance 797 n.
pursue
pursue 619 vb.
(*see* pursuit)
pursuer
hunter 619 n.
pursuit
sequence 65 n.
pursuit 619 n.
business 622 n.
pursy
fleshy 195 adj.
purulent
toxic 653 adj.
purvey
provide 633 vb.
purveyor
caterer 633 n.
purview
range 183 n.
pus
ulcer 651 n.
push
impulse 279 n.
propulsion 287 n.
ejection 300 n.
motivate 612 vb.
push-button
instrumental
628 adj.
pushcart
pushcart 274 n.
pushful, pushing
vigorous 174 adj.
active 678 adj.
push-over
victory 727 n.

pusillanimity
cowardice 856 n.
puss
cat 365 n.
pussyfoot
be stealthy 525 vb.
abstainer 942 n.
put
firm-set 45 adj.
place 187 vb.
put aside
set apart 46 vb.
putative
attributed 158 adj.
supposed 512 adj.
put away
divorce 896 vb.
put back
replace 187 vb.
turn back 286 vb.
put by
store 632 vb.
put down
suppress 165 vb.
kill 362 vb.
put down to
attribute 158 vb.
put first
make important
638 vb.
put off
put off 136 vb.
be neglectful
458 vb.
cause dislike
861 vb.
put on
wear 228 vb.
be affected 850 vb.
put one's finger on
detect 484 vb.
put out
derange 63 vb.
disable 161 vb.
extinguish 382 vb.
enrage 891 vb.
putrefaction
decay 51 n.
putrefy
deteriorate 655 vb.
putrid
fetid 397 adj.
put right
inform 524 vb.
rectify 654 vb.
putsch
revolt 738 n.

putt
insert 303 vb.
puttees
legwear 228 n.
put to music
compose music
413 vb.
put to rights
regularize 62 vb.
putty
adhesive 47 n.
put up
dwell 192 vb.
put-up
predetermined
608 adj.
put-up job
predetermination
608 n.
put upon
oppress 735 vb.
put up to
incite 612 vb.
put up with
acquiesce 488 vb.
be patient 823 vb.
puzzle
puzzle 474 vb.
enigma 530 n.
pyjamas
nightwear 228 n.
pyramid
edifice 164 n.
high structure
209 n.
pyre
interment 364 n.
pyrotechnics
fireworks 420 n.
Pyrrhic
dear 811 adj.
python
compressor 198 n.
reptile 365 n.
pyx
small box 194 n.

Q

Q.E.D.
argumentation
475 n.
quack
ululate 409 vb.
impostor 545 n.
be loquacious
581 vb.

bungler 697 n.
quackery
  sciolism 491 n.
  pretension 850 n.
quadrangle
  place 185 n.
quadrennial
  seasonal 141 adj.
quadrennium
  quaternity 96 n.
quadriga
  carriage 274 n.
quadrilateral
  angular figure
    247 n.
quadrille
  dance 837 n.
  card game 837 n.
quadruped
  horse 273 n.
  animal 365 n.
quadruple
  quadruple 97 vb.
quaff
  revel 837 vb.
  drink 301 vb.
  get drunk 949 vb.
quagmire
  marsh 347 n.
quail
  table bird 365 n.
  be cowardly
    856 vb.
quaint
  ornamental 844 adj.
  ridiculous 849 adj.
quaintness
  ridiculousness
    849 n.
quake
  quake 854 vb.
Quaker
  sectarist 978 n.
qualification
  fitness 24 n.
  ability 160 n.
  qualification 468 n.
  aptitude 694 n.
  conditions 766 n.
qualified
  fit 24 adj.
  expert 694 adj.
qualify
  mix 43 vb.
  moderate 177 vb.
  discriminate
    463 vb.

qualify 468 vb.
qualities
  affections 817 n.
quality
  character 5 n.
  superiority 34 n.
  sort 77 n.
  goodness 644 n.
  nobility 868 n.
qualm
  nervousness 854 n.
qualms of conscience
  penitence 939 n.
quandary
  predicament 700 n.
quantification
  measurement
    465 n.
quantify
  quantify 26 vb.
  measure 465 vb.
quantitative
  quantitative
    26 adj.
quantities
  great quantity 32 n.
quantity
  quantity 26 n.
  multitude 104 n.
quantum
  finite quantity 26 n.
  element 319 n.
  portion 783 n.
quarantine
  hygiene 652 n.
  prophylactic 658 n.
  detention 747 n.
  seclusion 883 n.
quarrel
  disagreement 25 n.
  quarrel 709 n., vb.
  enmity 881 n.
quarrelsome
  quarrelling 709 adj.
quarrelsomeness
  irascibility 892 n.
quarry
  source 156 n.
  excavation 255 n.
  extract 304 vb.
  objective 617 n.
  store 632 n.
  workshop 687 n.
quarter
  rend 46 vb.
  quadrisect 98 vb.
  district 184 n.

place 187 vb.
  compass point
    281 n.
  mercy 905 n.
quarterings
  heraldry 547 n.
quartermaster
  provider 633 n.
quarters
  quarters 192 n.
quartet
  quaternity 96 n.
  duet 412 n.
quarto
  edition 589 n.
quash
  abrogate 752 vb.
quasi
  similar 18 adj.
  misnamed 562 adj.
quaternion
  quaternity 96 n.
quatrain
  verse form 593 n.
quaver
  notation 410 n.
  sing 413 vb.
  stammer 580 vb.
  quake 854 vb.
quay
  stable 192 n.
  shelter 662 n.
quean
  woman 373 n.
queasy
  disliking 861 adj.
queen
  sovereign 741 n.
queenly
  impressive 821 adj.
  worshipful 866 adj.
Queen's Counsel
  lawyer 958 n.
queer
  nonconformist 84 n.
  abnormal 84 adj.
  crazed 503 adj.
  sick 651 adj.
queerness
  eccentricity 503 n.
Queer Street
  poverty 801 n.
quell
  suppress 165 vb.
  subjugate 745 vb.
quench
  suppress 165 vb.

snuff out 418 vb.
  sate 863 vb.
quern
  pulverizer 332 n.
querulous
  irascible 892 adj.
query
  question 459 n.
quest
  pursuit 619 n.
  undertaking 672 n.
question
  question 459 n.
  interrogate 459 vb.
  doubt 486 n.
  negate 533 vb.
questionable
  uncertain 474 adj.
  disreputable
    867 adj.
question and answer
  interrogation
    459 n.
  interlocution 584 n.
questioner
  questioner 459 n.
questionnaire
  question 459 n.
question paper
  question 459 n.
question time
  interrogation 459 n.
queue
  procession 71 n.
queue up
  await 507 vb.
quibble
  argue 475 vb.
  sophistry 477 n.
  pretext 614 n.
quick
  speedy 277 adj.
  alive 360 adj.
  intelligent 498 adj.
  active 678 adj.
quick-change
  changeful 152 adj.
quicken
  invigorate 174 vb.
  accelerate 277 vb.
  animate 821 vb.
quicksand
  marsh 347 n.
  pitfall 663 n.
quicksilver
  changeable thing
    152 n.

quick-witted
intelligent 498 adj.
quid
mouthful 301 n.
tobacco 388 n.
quiddity
essence 1 n.
quid pro quo
substitute 150 n.
interchange 151 n.
retaliation 714 n.
reward 962 n.
quiescence
quiescence 266 n.
peace 717 n.
quiescent
apathetic 820 adj.
quiet
assuage 177 vb.
quietude 266 n.
silence 399 n.
soft-hued 425 adj.
peaceful 717 adj.
inexcitable 823 adj.
secluded 883 adj.
quietism
quietude 266 n.
inexcitability 823 n.
quietude
(*see* quiet)
quietus
end 69 n.
killing 362 n.
quiff
hair 259 n.
hair-dressing 843 n.
quill
plumage 259 n.
stationery 586 n.
quilt
coverlet 226 n.
quinine
antidote 658 n.
quinquennium
period 110 n.
quintessence
essential part 5 n.
quintet
duet 412 n.
orchestra 413 n.
quip
witticism 839 n.
quipu
counting instrument 86 n.
quire
letterpress 587 n.

paper 631 n.
quirk
whim 604 n.
quisling
tergiversator 603 n.
revolter 738 n.
quit
depart 296 vb.
resign 753 vb.
fail in duty 918 vb.
quite
completely 54 adv.
quittance
payment 804 n.
quitter
tergiversator 603 n.
coward 856 n.
quiver
case 194 n.
be agitated 318 vb.
arsenal 723 n.
quake 854 vb.
Quixotry
rashness 857 n.
quiz
gaze 438 vb.
interrogation 459 n.
quizzical
derisive 851 adj.
quoin
press 587 n.
quoit
missile 287 n.
quondam
former 125 adj.
quorum
finite quantity 26 n.
sufficiency 635 n.
quota
finite quantity 26 n.
portion 783 n.
quotable
relevant 9 adj.
pure 950 adj.
quotation
referral 9 n.
anthology 592 n.
quote
exemplify 83 vb.
(*see* quotation)
quotidian
seasonal 141 adj.

quotient
numerical element 85 n.

R

rabbi
theologian 973 n.
rabbit
vermin 365 n.
testee 461 n.
coward 856 n.
rabble
crowd 74 n.
rabble 869 n.
rabble-rouser
agitator 738 n.
Rabelaisian
impure 951 n.
rabid
frenzied 503 adj.
angry 891 adj.
rabies
frenzy 503 n.
race
race 11 n.
genealogy 169 n.
speeding 277 n.
current 350 n.
racing 716 n.
race-course
arena 724 n.
race-horse
speeder 277 n.
racial
ethnic 11 adj.
human 371 adj.
racialism, racism
prejudice 481 n.
raciness
(*see* racy)
racing
racing 716 n.
rack
shelf 218 n.
cloud 355 n.
torture 963 vb.
racket
loudness 400 n.
foul play 930 n.
racketeer
be dishonest 930 vb.
rack-rent
overcharge 811 vb.
raconteur
narrator 590 n.

racy
savoury 390 adj.
impure 951 adj.
radar
telecommunication 531 n.
radiance
light, glow 417 n.
radiant
divergent 294 adj.
luminous 417 adj.
radiating 417 adj.
cheerful 833 adj.
radiate
emit 300 vb.
(*see* radiation)
radiation
dispersion 75 n.
radiation 417 n.
radiator
heater 383 n.
radical
intrinsic 5 adj.
complete 54 adj.
fundamental 156 adj.
important 638 adj.
reformer 654 n.
radicalism
reformism 654 n.
radiesthesia
discovery 484 n.
radio
telecommunication 531 n.
radio-activity
radiation 417 n.
radiogram
gramophone 414 n.
message 529 n.
radio-location
bearings 186 n.
radioscopy
optics 417 n.
radio-therapy
therapy 658 n.
radius
range 183 n.
breadth 205 n.
raffia
fibre 208 n.
raffle
gambling 618 n.
raft
raft 275 n.
rafter(s)
beam 218 n.

roof 226 n.
rag
  torment 827 vb.
  ridicule 851 vb.
rage
  violence 176 n.
  excitable state
    822 n.
  fashion 848 n.
  libido 859 n.
  anger 891 n.
ragged
  uncovered 229 adj.
raggedness
  non-uniformity
    17 n.
  poverty 801 n.
rags
  clothing 228 n.
  rubbish 641 n.
rag, tag, and bobtail
  commonalty 869 n.
raid
  irrupt 299 vb.
  attack 712 n.
  rob 788 vb.
raider
  attacker 712 n.
  robber 789 n.
raiding
  brigandage 788 n.
rail
  handle 218 n.
  carry 273 vb.
  exprobate 924 vb.
railing
  fence 235 n.
raillery
  ridicule 851 n.
railroad, railway
  railroad 624 n.
raiment
  clothing 228 n.
rain
  descend 309 vb.
  rain 350 n., vb.
rainbow
  arc 250 n.
  variegation 437 n.
raincoat
  overcoat 228 n.
rainfall
  rain 350 n.
rain-gauge
  hygrometry 341 n.
rainproof
  dry 342 adj.

rainy
  rainy 350 adj.
rainy day
  adversity 731 n.
raise
  make vertical
    215 vb.
  elevate 310 vb.
  breed stock 369 vb.
raise Cain
  be angry 891 vb.
raise one's voice
  vociferate 400 vb.
  emphasize 532 vb.
raise steam
  make ready 669 vb.
raise the alarm
  raise the alarm
    665 vb.
rake
  obliquity 220 n.
  farm tool 370 n.
  search 459 vb.
  fire at 712 vb.
  libertine 952 n.
rake in
  bring together
    74 vb.
rake-off
  decrement 42 n.
  receipt 807 n.
rake up
  retrospect 505 vb.
rakish
  oblique 220 adj.
  lecherous 951 adj.
rally
  assemblage 74 n.
  congregate 74 vb.
  call 547 n.
  get better 645 vb.
  contest 716 n.
  ridicule 851 vb.
  give courage
    855 vb.
rallying point
  focus 76 n.
ram
  ram 279 n.
  collide 279 vb.
  sheep 365 n.
  charge 712 vb.
ramble
  pedestrianism
    267 n.
  stray 282 vb.
  be insane 503 vb.

  be diffuse 570 vb.
rambler
  wanderer 268 n.
rambling
  unstable 152 adj.
  (see ramble)
ramification
  branch 53 n.
  descendant 170 n.
  divergence 294 n.
rammer
  ram 279 n.
ramp
  obliquity 220 n.
  ascent 308 n.
  leap 312 vb.
  trickery 542 n.
  get angry 891 vb.
rampage
  rampage 61 vb.
  anger 891 n.
rampant
  vertical 215 adj.
  heraldic 547 adj.
rampart
  fortification 713 n.
  defence 713 n.
ramrod
  fire-arm 723 n.
ramshackle
  dilapidated 655 adj.
ranch
  breed stock 369 vb.
  farm 370 n.
rancher
  herdsman 369 n.
rancid
  unsavoury 391 adj.
  decomposed 51 adj.
rancorous
  revengeful 910 adj.
  (see rancour)
rancour
  resentment 891 n.
  malevolence 898 n.
random
  orderless 61 adj.
  casual 159 adj.
  indiscriminate
    464 adj.
  designless 618 adj.
randy
  lecherous 951 adj.
range
  arrange 62 vb.
  series 71 n.
  range 183 n.

  plain 348 n.
  furnace 383 n.
  arena 724 n.
  scope 744 n.
range-finder
  direction 281 n.
  telescope 442 n.
range oneself with
  join a party 708 vb.
ranger
  keeper 749 n.
ranging
  extensive 32 adj.
  free 744 adj.
rank
  degree 27 n.
  class 62 vb.
  serial place 73 n.
  fetid 397 adj.
  estimate 480 vb.
  nobility 868 n.
  heinous 934 adj.
rank and file
  commonalty 869 n.
ranker
  commoner 869 n.
ranking
  noteworthy 866 adj.
rankle
  hurt 827 vb.
rankness
  (see rank)
ransack
  search 459 vb.
  rob 788 vb.
ransom
  deliverance 668 n.
  purchase 792 vb.
  penalty 963 n.
ransom, hold to
  overcharge 811 vb.
rant
  empty talk 515 n.
  magniloquence
    574 n.
rap
  knock 279 n.
  crackle 402 vb.
rapacious
  (see rapacity)
rapacity
  rapacity 786 n.
  avarice 816 n.
  gluttony 947 n.
rape
  stealing 788 n.
  rape 951 n.

rapidity
velocity 277 n.
rapids
waterfall 350 n.
rapier
side-arms 723 n.
rapine
spoliation 788 n.
rap over the knuckles
reprimand 924 n.
rapport
relation 9 n.
concord 710 n.
rapprochement
concord 710 n.
pacification 719 n.
rapscallion
knave 938 n.
rapt
abstracted 456 adj.
raptorial
taking 786 adj.
rapture
joy 824 n.
love 887 n.
rapturous
pleased 824 adj.
rara avis
rara avis 84 n.
infrequency 140 n.
rare
few 105 adj.
infrequent 140 adj.
culinary 301 adj.
rare 325 adj.
scarce 636 adj.
excellent 644 adj.
rarefy
rarefy 325 vb.
rarity
rarity 325 n.
(*see* **rare**)
rascal
knave 938 n.
rascality
improbity 930 n.
rascally
rascally 930 adj.
rase
obliterate 550 vb.
rash
skin disease 651 n.
(*see* **rashness**)
rasher
meat 301 n.
rashness
haste 680 n.

rashness 857 n.
rasp
pulverize 332 vb.
rub 333 vb.
rasp 407 vb.
raspberry
reprimand 924 n.
rasping
hoarse 407 adj.
rat
rodent 365 n.
tergiversator 603 n.
apostatize 603 vb.
noxious animal
 904 n.
ratan
(*see* **rattan**)
rat-catcher
hunter 619 n.
ratchet
notch 260 n.
rate
degree 27 n.
class 62 vb.
velocity 277 n.
estimate 480 n.
price 809 n., vb.
exprobate 924 vb.
ratification
assent 488 n.
ratifier
signatory 765 n.
ratify
endorse 488 vb.
make legal 953 vb.
rating
measurement
 465 n.
navy man 722 n.
tax 809 n.
reprimand 924 n.
(*see* **rate**)
ratio
relativeness 9 n.
ratio 85 n.
ratiocination
reasoning 475 n.
ration
provisions 301 n.
portion 783 n.
rational
mental 447 adj.
philosophic 449 adj.
rational 475 adj.
sane 502 adj.
rationale
attribution 158 n.

rationalism
reasoning 475 n.
antichristianity
 974 n.
rationalist
reasoner 475 n.
rationalization
arrangement 62 n.
plan 623 n.
rationalize
reason 475 vb.
plan 623 vb.
rations
provisions 633 n.
ratline
tackling 47 n.
rat race
activity 678 n.
rattan
club 723 n.
ratter
tergiversator 603 n.
hunter 619 n.
rattle
derange 63 vb.
respiration 352 n.
crackle 402 vb.
distract 456 vb.
chatterer 581 n.
bauble 639 n.
frighten 854 vb.
rattled
irresolute 601 adj.
ratty
angry 891 adj.
raucous
hoarse 407 adj.
discordant 411 adj.
ravage
havoc 165 n.
lay waste 165 vb.
ravaged
unsightly 842 adj.
rave
be insane 503 vb.
mean nothing
 515 vb.
be pleased 824 vb.
ravel
bedevil 63 vb.
enlace 222 vb.
raven
black thing 428 n.
omen 511 n.
be hungry 859 vb.
ravenous
hungry 859 adj.

ravine
valley 255 n.
raving
pleased 824 adj.
(*see* **rave**)
ravish
take away 786 vb.
delight 826 vb.
debauch 951 vb.
raw
new 126 adj.
young 130 adj.
uncovered 229 adj.
culinary 301 adj.
painful 377 adj.
cold 380 adj.
unhabituated
 611 adj.
immature 670 adj.
unskilled 695 adj.
sensitive 819 adj.
raw-boned
lean 206 adj.
raw deal
ill fortune 731 n.
(*see* **injustice**)
raw material
source 156 n.
materials 631 n.
undevelopment
 670 n.
ray
flash 417 n.
radiation 417 n.
rayon
fibre 208 n.
raze
demolish 165 vb.
fell 311 vb.
razor
sharp edge 256 n.
razor edge
danger 661 n.
reach
ability 160 n.
distance 199 n.
arrive 295 vb.
stream 350 n.
reach-me-downs
clothing 228 n.
reach to
extend 183 vb.
react
be active 678 vb.
(*see* **reaction**)
react against
dislike 861 vb.

reaction
 compensation 31 n.
 effect 157 n.
 recoil 280 n.
 retaliation 714 n.
 feeling 818 n.
reactionary
 tergiversating
  603 adj.
 opponent 705 n.
reactor
 nucleonics 160 n.
read
 gauge 465 vb.
 interpret 520 vb.
 decipher 520 vb.
 indicate 547 vb.
reader
 teacher 537 n.
 textbook 589 n.
 bookman 589 n.
readership
 publicity 528 n.
 lecture 534 n.
readiness
 tendency 179 n.
 intelligence 498 n.
 preparedness 669 n.
 completion 725 n.
reading
 erudition 490 n.
 lecture 534 n.
 study 536 n.
reading matter
 reading matter
  589 n.
readjustment
 restoration 656 n.
read off
 gauge 465 vb.
ready
 on the spot 189 adj.
 intelligent 498 adj.
 prepared 669 adj.
 obedient 739 adj.
 consenting 758 adj.
ready-made
 ready-made
  669 adj.
ready reckoner
 counting instrument
  86 n.
reagent
 testing agent 461 n.
real
 real 1 adj.
 substantial 3 adj.

 material 319 adj.
 true 494 adj.
real estate
 lands 777 n.
realism
 accuracy 494 n.
 veracity 540 n.
 representation
  551 n.
realist
 materiality 319 n.
realistic
 lifelike 18 adj.
 wise 498 adj.
 descriptive 590 adj.
reality
 reality 1 n.
 truth 494 n.
realizable
 possible 469 adj.
realization
 eventuality 154 n.
 discovery 484 n.
 representation
  551 n.
 feeling 818 n.
realize
 copy 20 vb.
 materialize
  319 vb.
 imagine 513 vb.
 understand 516 vb.
 carry out 725 vb.
 (see realization*)*
real-life
 descriptive 594 adj.
realm
 function 622 n.
 polity 733 n.
realpolitik
 tactics 688 n.
real presence
 the sacrament
  988 n.
real thing
 reality 1 n.
 no imitation 21 n.
 authenticity 494 n.
realty
 lands 777 n.
ream
 paper 631 n.
reamer
 perforator 263 n.
 tobacco 388 n.
reanimate
 vitalize 360 vb.

reap
 cultivate 370 vb.
 take 786 vb.
reaper
 husbandman 370 n.
reaping
 product 164 n.
reappear
 be restored 656 vb.
reappearance
 recurrence 106 n.
rear
 sequel 67 n.
 make vertical
  215 vb.
 rear, buttocks 238 n.
 leap 312 vb.
 breed stock 369 vb.
 educate 534 vb.
rearing
 animal husbandry
  369 n.
rearmost
 back 238 adj.
rearrange
 modify 143 vb.
rear up
 get angry 891 vb.
reason
 intellect 447 n.
 reasoning 475 n.
 sanity 502 n.
reasonable
 moderate 177 adj.
 plausible 471 adj.
 rational 475 adj.
 wise 498 adj.
 sane 502 adj.
 just 913 adj.
reasonableness
 moderation 177 n.
 justice 913 n.
reasoner
 reasoner 475 n.
reasoning
 reasoning 475 n.
reassemble
 repair 656 vb.
reassure
 give courage
  855 vb.
reawakening
 revival 656 n.
rebarbative
 disliked 861 adj.
rebate
 discount 810 n.

rebel
 nonconformist 84 n.
 revolt 738 vb.
 fail in duty 918 vb.
 schismatic 978 n.
rebellion
 revolt 738 n.
rebellious
 dutiless 918 adj.
rebirth
 revival 656 n.
rebound
 recoil 280 n.
 elasticity 328 n.
rebuff
 repulsion 292 n.
 rejection 607 n.
 resistance 715 n.
 defeat 728 n., vb.
 refusal 760 n.
rebuke
 reprimand 924 n.
rebut
 (see rebuttal*)*
rebuttal
 rejoinder 460 n.
 negation 533 n.
recalcitrance
 resistance 715 n.
recalcitrant
 unwilling 598 adj.
 disobedient 738 adj.
recall
 retrospect 505 vb.
 recant 603 vb.
 abrogation 752 n.
recant
 negate 533 vb.
recantation
 recantation 603 n.
 abrogation 752 n.
recanter
 tergiversator 603 n.
recapitulation
 repetition 106 n.
recapture
 retrieve 656 vb.
recast
 modify 143 vb.
 rectify 654 vb.
recede
 regress 286 vb.
 recede 290 vb.
receipt
 cookery 301 n.
 remedy 658 n.
 precept 693 n.

receipt 807 n.
receipts
earnings 771 n.
receive
admit 299 vb.
receive 782 vb.
receiver
telecommunication
531 n.
receiver 782 n.
thief 789 n.
recension
amendment 654 n.
recent
new 126 adj.
receptacle
receptacle 194 n.
reception
reception 299 n.
hearing 415 n.
receiving 782 n.
social gathering
882 n.
receptive
studious 536 adj.
willing 597 adj.
receiving 782 adj.
recess
lull 145 n.
compartment 194 n.
recession
decrease 37 n.
recession 290 n.
deterioration 655 n.
recessional
hymn 981 n.
recessive
receding 290 adj.
réchauffée
dish 301 n.
recidivism
reversion 148 n.
tergiversation 603 n.
relapse 657 n.
recidivist
tergiversator 603 n.
offender 904 n.
recipe
cookery 301 n.
contrivance 623 n.
precept 693 n.
recipient
recipient 782 n.
reciprocal
correlative 12 adj.
numerical element
85 n.

reciprocate
correlate 12 vb.
be periodic 141 vb.
cooperate 706 vb.
reciprocation
correlation 12 n.
interchange 151 n.
fluctuation 317 n.
reciprocity
correlation 12 n.
concord 710 n.
recitation
oration 579 n.
recite
repeat 106 vb.
(*see* recital)
reck
be careful 457 vb.
reckless
rash 857 adj.
reckon
expect 507 vb.
(*see* reckoning)
reckoning
numeration 86 n.
measurement 465 n.
price 809 n.
reclaim
make better 654 vb.
retrieve 656 vb.
claim 915 vb.
recline
be horizontal
216 vb.
sit down 311 vb.
repose 683 vb.
recluse
solitary 883 n.
recognition
knowledge 490 n.
dueness 915 n.
approbation 923 n.
recognizable
intelligible 516 adj.
manifest 522 adj.
recognizance
security 767 n.
recognize
identify 13 vb.
see 438 vb.
remember 505 vb.
recoil
recoil 280 n.
elasticity 328 n.
dislike 861 adj.
recollection
remembrance 505 n.

recommend
incite 612 vb.
patronize 703 vb.
recommendation
credential 466 n.
advice 691 n.
recompense
reward 962 n., vb.
reconcile
pacify 719 vb.
content 828 vb.
reconciliation
pacification 719 n.
propitiation 941 n.
recondite
puzzling 517 adj.
concealed 525 adj.
reconditioning
repair 656 n.
reconnaissance
inspection 438 n.
reconnoitre
scan 438 vb.
reconsideration
amendment 654 n.
reconstitute
restore 656 vb.
reconstruction
conjecture 512 n.
restoration 656 n.
record
superiority 34 n.
gramophone 414 n.
record 548 n., vb.
narrative 590 n.
best 644 adj.
conduct 688 n.
record-breaker
exceller 644 n.
recorder
flute 414 n.
recorder 549 n.
recording
musical piece 412 n.
record-keeper
recorder 549 n.
record-player
gramophone 414 n.
recount
communicate
524 vb.
describe 590 vb.
recoup
recoup 31 vb.
retrieve 656 vb.
recoupment
acquisition 771 n.

recourse
contrivance 623 n.
recourse to, have
avail of 673 vb.
recover
recoup 31 vb.
retrieve 656 vb.
re-cover
repair 656 vb.
recovery
revival 656 n.
taking 786 n.
restitution 787 n.
recreant
tergiversator 603 n.
knave 938 n.
recreation
refreshment 685 n.
amusement 837 n.
recrimination
dissension 709 n.
accusation 928 n.
recrudescence
relapse 657 n.
recruit
invigorate 174 vb.
beginner 538 n.
employ 622 vb.
refresh 685 vb.
auxiliary 707 n.
soldier 722 n.
recruitment
war measures 718 n.
(*see* recruit)
rectangle
angular figure
247 n.
rectification
amendment 654 n.
rectify
regularize 62 vb.
rectify 654 vb.
rectilinear
straight 249 adj.
rectitude
probity 929 n.
rector
pastor, cleric
986 n.
rectory
parsonage 986 n.
rectum
insides 224 n.
recumbent
supine 216 adj.
recuperation
refreshment 685 n.

recur
recur 139 vb.
(*see* **recurrence**)

recurrence
recurrence 106 n.
periodicity 141 n.
relapse 657 n.

recusancy
dissent 489 n.
refusal 760 n.

recusant
dissentient 489 n.

red
revolutionist 149 n.
red 431 adj.
revolter 738 n.

redactor
bookman 589 n.

red, be in the
be in debt 803 vb.

red-blooded
courageous 855 adj.

red-brick
regional 184 adj.

Red Cross
doctor 658 n.

redden
redden 431 vb.

redeem
pay 804 vb.
(*see* **redemption**)

redeemer
purchaser 792 n.
benefactor 903 n.

redemption
deliverance 668 n.
purchase 792 n.
divine function
  965 n.

red flag
danger signal
  665 n.

red-handed
murderous 362 adj.
guilty 936 adj.

red herring
irrelevance 10 n.
hinderer 702 n.

redintegration
repair 656 n.

red, in the
indebted 803 adj.

redivivus
restored 656 adj.

red-letter day
important matter
  638 n.

red light
danger signal 665 n.

red-light district
brothel 951 n.

redolence
odour 394 n.

redouble
double 91 vb.
invigorate 174 vb.

redoubtable
frightening 854 adj.

redound
tend 179 vb.

redress
remedy 658 n.
justice 913 n.

red tape
delay 136 n.

reduce
decompose 51 vb.
render few 105 vb.
abstract 592 vb.
subjugate 745 vb.
starve 946 vb.
(*see* **reduction**)

reduce to
convert 147 vb.

reductio ad absurdum
confutation 479 n.

reduction
diminution 37 n.
miniature 196 n.
contraction 198 n.
shortening 204 n.
photography 551 n.
discount 810 n.

redundance
plenty 635 n.
redundance 637 n.

redundant
useless 641 adj.

reduplication
duplication 91 n.
reproduction 166 n.

re-echo
resound 404 vb.

reed
weak thing 163 n.
flute 414 n.

reedy
strident 407 adj.

reef
fold 261 vb.
rock 344 vb.
pitfall 663 n.

reefer
tobacco 388 n.

reek
odour 394 n.
fetor 397 n.

reel
rotate 315 vb.
oscillate 317 vb.
dance 837 n.

reel off
be loquacious
  581 vb.

reeve
tie 45 vb.

reface
repair 656 vb.

refection
meal 301 n.
refreshment 685 n.

refer
indicate 547 vb.
consult 691 vb.
(*see* **refer to**)

referable
relative 9 adj.
attributed 158 adj.

referee
estimator 480 n.
mediator 720 n.

reference
relation 9 n.
referral 9 n.
class 62 vb.
credential 466 n.
connotation
  514 n.

reference system
sorting 62 n.

referendum
vote 605 n.

refer to
be related 9 vb.
attribute 158 vb.
mean 514 vb.

refill
plenitude 54 n.
replenish 633 vb.

refine
purify 648 vb.
(*see* **refinement**)

refined
tasteful 846 adj.
pure 950 adj.

refinement
elegance 575 n.
civilization 654 n.
good taste 846 n.
fastidiousness
  846 n.

refiner
cleaner 648 n.

refinery
workshop 687 n.

refit
repair 656 vb.

reflation
expansion 197 n.

reflect
resemble 18 vb.
retrospect 505 vb.
(*see* **reflection**)

reflection
analogue 18 n.
copy 22 n.
reflection 417 n.
meditation 449 n.
image 551 n.
detraction 926 n.

reflect on
shame 867 vb.

reflector
lamp 420 n.
telescope 442 n.

reflex
recoil 280 n.
spontaneity 609 n.
habituation 610 n.

reflex action
necessity 596 n.

reflexive
reverted 148 adj.

reflux
return 286 n.
current 350 n.

reform
transform 147 vb.
tergiversate 603 vb.
amendment 654 n.
philanthropize
  897 vb.

reformation
amendment 654 n.

reformatory
school 539 n.
amendment 654 n.
prison 748 n.

reformed
repentant 939 adj.

reformer
reformer 654 n.

refraction
reflection 417 n.

refractor
telescope 442 n.

refractory
wilful 602 adj.

disobedient 738 adj.
refrain
repetition 106 n.
periodicity 141 n.
tune 412 n.
verse form 593 n.
avoid 620 vb.
not act 677 vb.
be temperate
942 vb.
refresh
invigorate 174 vb.
revive 656 vb.
refresher
tonic 658 n.
refreshment 685 n.
refresher course
study 536 n.
refreshment
meal 301 n.
refreshment 685 n.
pleasurableness
826 n.
relief 831 n.
refrigeration
refrigeration 382 n.
preservation 666 n.
refrigerator
refrigerator 384 n.
refuel
store 632 vb.
replenish 633 vb.
refuge
refuge 662 n.
fort 713 n.
refugee
foreigner 59 n.
wanderer 268 n.
outcaste 883 n.
refund
restitution 787 n.
refurbish
repair 656 vb.
refusal
rejection 607 n.
refusal 760 n.
refuse
waste 634 n.
rubbish 641 n.
(*see* refusal)
refutation
confutation 479 n.
regain
retrieve 656 vb.
regal
ruling 733 adj.
impressive 821 adj.

regale
eat 301 vb.
refresh 685 vb.
regalia
regalia 743 n.
regard
relation 9 n.
look 438 n.
attention 455 n.
repute 866 n.
love 887 vb.
respect 920 n., vb.
regardless
inattentive 456 adj.
rash 857 adj.
regards
respects 920 n.
regatta
racing 716 n.
(*see* aquatics)
regency
governance 733 n.
commission 751 n.
regenerate
repentant 939 adj.
(*see* regeneration)
regeneration
conversion 147 n.
revival 656 n.
regent
potentate 741 n.
regicide
homicide 362 n.
revolter 738 n.
régime
dieting 301 n.
governance 733 n.
regiment
formation 722 n.
dominate 733 vb.
regimentals
uniform 228 n.
regimentation
compulsion 740 n.
region
region 184 n.
regional
regional 184 adj.
provincial 192 adj.
register
accord 24 vb.
class 62 vb.
list 87 n.
notice 455 vb.
indicate 547 vb.
record 548 n.
account book 808 n.

registrar
recorder 549 n.
registration
registration 548 n.
registry
registration 548 n.
regnal
ruling 733 adj.
regnant
ruling 733 adj.
regress
regression 286 n.
regression
change 143 n.
reversion 148 n.
regression 286 n.
regret
disappointment
509 n.
sorrow 825 n.
regret 830 n., vb.
disapprove 924 vb.
penitence 939 n.
regretful
unhappy 825 adj.
regrettable
regretted 830 adj.
regular
regular 81 adj.
frequent 139 adj.
soldier 722 n.
shapely 841 adj.
regularity
uniformity 16 n.
order 60 n.
rule 81 n.
symmetry 245 n.
regularize
regularize 62 vb.
regulate
adjust 24 vb.
regulation
rule 81 n.
legislation 953 n.
rehabilitation
restoration 656 n.
restitution 787 n.
vindication 927 n.
rehash
repetition 106 n.
rehearsal
repetition 106 n.
dramaturgy 594 n.
preparation 669 n.
reign
date 108 n.
governance 733 n.

reimburse
restitute 787 vb.
pay 804 vb.
rein
halter 47 n.
moderator 177 n.
reincarnation
transformation
143 n.
reinforce
augment 36 vb.
strengthen 162 vb.
aid 703 vb.
reinforcement
auxiliary 707 n.
rein in
restrain 747 vb.
reinstate
replace 187 vb.
reinstatement
reversion 148 n.
restitution 787 n.
reissue
repetition 106 n.
reiterate
repeat 106 vb.
reject
inferior 35 n.
rubbish 641 n.
not use 674 vb.
disapprove 924 vb.
(*see* rejection)
rejection
rejection 607 n.
refusal 760 n.
rejoice
rejoice 835 vb.
revel 837 vb.
rejoicing
celebration 876 n.
rejoin
meet 295 vb.
answer 460 vb.
rejoinder
rejoinder 460 n.
wit 839 n.
rejuvenation
revival 656 n.
rekindle
revive 656 vb.
animate 821 vb.
relapse
tergiversation
603 n.
relapse 657 n., vb.
relate
attribute 158 vb.

related
  akin 11 adj.
relater
  narrator 590 n.
relation
  relation 9 n.
  kinsman 11 n.
  correlation 12 n.
relationship
  relation 9 n.
  consanguinity 11 n.
relative
  relative 9 adj.
  kinsman 11 n.
  comparative 27 adj.
relative quantity
  degree 27 n.
relativity
  relativeness 9 n.
relax
  weaken 163 vb.
  keep calm 823 vb.
  show mercy 905 vb.
relaxation
  repose 683 n.
  liberation 746 n.
  amusement 837 n.
relaxed
  tranquil 266 adj.
relay
  telecommunication 531 n.
  auxiliary 707 n.
release
  disjoin 46 vb.
  liberation 746 n.
  non-retention 779 n.
releasee
  beneficiary 776 n.
  recipient 782 n.
relegate
  displace 188 vb.
  transpose 272 vb.
relegation
  transference 272 n.
  ejection 300 n.
relent
  be moderate 177 vb.
  show mercy 905 vb.
  forgive 909 vb.
relentless
  severe 735 adj.
  pitiless 906 adj.
relevance
  relevance 9 n.

fitness 24 n.
  meaning 514 n.
relevant
  important 638 adj.
reliability
  credit 802 n.
  (*see* **reliable**)
reliable
  unchangeable 153 adj.
  probable 471 adj.
  certain 473 adj.
  credible 485 adj.
  genuine 494 adj.
  observant 768 adj.
  trustworthy 929 adj.
reliance
  belief 485 n.
  expectation 507 n.
relic
  antiquity 125 n.
  archaism 127 n.
  reminder 505 n.
  trace 548 n.
  talisman 983 n.
relics
  church utensil 990 n.
relict
  survivor 41 n.
  widowed spouse 896 n.
relief
  contrariety 14 n.
  aftercomer 67 n.
  substitute 150 n.
  moderation 177 n.
  outline 233 n.
  form 243 n.
  rilievo 254 n.
  feature 445 n.
  sculpture 554 n.
  deliverance 668 n.
  refreshment 685 n.
  aid 703 n.
  relief 831 n.
  kind act 897 n.
relieve
  come after 65 vb.
  assuage 177 vb.
  remedy 658 vb.
  aid 703 vb.
  relieve 831 vb.
  cheer 833 vb.
  (*see* **relief**)
relieved
  comfortable 376 adj.

relieve of
  take away 786 vb.
religion
  religion 973 n.
  piety 979 n.
  public worship 981 n.
religionism
  pietism 979 n.
religiosity
  pietism 979 n.
religious
  observant 768 adj.
  trustworthy 929 adj.
  divine 965 adj.
  religious 973 adj.
  pious 979 adj.
  monk 986 n.
religious mania
  mania 503 n.
religiousness
  piety 979 n.
religious truth
  orthodoxy 976 n.
reline
  repair 656 vb.
relinquish
  cease 145 vb.
  be irresolute 601 vb.
  relinquish 621 vb.
  disuse 674 vb.
  abrogate 752 vb.
  resign 753 vb.
  not retain 779 vb.
relinquished
  empty 190 adj.
relinquishment
  (*see* **relinquish**)
reliquary
  church utensil 990 n.
relish
  taste 386 n.
  condiment 389 n.
  savouriness 390 n.
  feeling 818 n.
  enjoyment 824 n.
  liking 859 n.
relive
  be restored 656 vb.
reload
  replenish 663 vb.
reluctance
  slowness 278 n.
  unwillingness 598 n.
reluctantly
  unwillingly 598 adv.

disapprovingly 924 adj.
rely
  hope 852 vb.
rely on
  believe 485 vb.
remade
  restored 656 adj.
remain
  last 113 vb.
  stay 144 vb.
  go on 146 vb.
  dwell 192 vb.
remainder
  difference 15 n.
  remainder 41 n.
  piece 53 n.
  numerical result 85 n.
  posteriority 120 n.
  effect 157 n.
  book 589 n.
  superfluity 637 n.
  dower 777 n.
  sell 793 vb.
remainder, leave a
  be unequal 29 vb.
remainderman
  beneficiary 776 n.
remaindership
  possession 773 n.
remaining
  separate 46 adj.
remains
  remainder 41 n.
  trace 548 n.
  reading matter 589 n.
remake
  reproduce 166 vb.
  restore 656 vb.
remand
  put off 136 vb.
  detention 747 n.
remand home
  school 539 n.
remark
  notice 455 n.
  affirmation 532 n.
  affirm 532 vb.
  speech 579 n.
remarkable
  prodigious 32 adj.
  noteworthy 866 adj.
remedial
  lenitive 177 adj.
  remedial 658 adj.

remedy
moderator 177 n.
means 629 n.
remedy 658 n., vb.

remember
remember 505 vb.

remembrance
remembrance 505 n.
celebration 876 n.

remind
remind 505 vb.
hint 524 vb.

reminder
reminder 505 n.
record 548 n.

reminiscence
remembrance 505 n.
narrative 590 n.

remiss
negligent 458 adj.
lax 734 adj.

remission
lull 145 n.
forgiveness 909 n.

remit
send 272 vb.
forgive 909 vb.

remittance
transference 272 n.
payment 804 n.

remittent
periodical 141 adj.
fitful 142 adj.

remitter
transferrer 272 n.

remnant
leavings 41 n.
fewness 105 n.

remonstrance
deprecation 762 n.
reprimand 924 n.

remonstrate
(*see* **remonstrance**)

remorse
regret 830 n.
pity 905 n.
penitence 939 n.

remorseless
pitiless 906 adj.

remote
distant 199 adj.

removal
displacement 188 n.
transference 272 n.
departure 296 n.
extraction 304 n.
deposal 752 n.

remove
serial place 73 n.
destroy 165 vb.
(*see* **removal**)

remover
destroyer 168 n.

remuneration
earnings 771 n.
reward 962 n.

remunerative
profitable 640 adj.
gainful 771 adj.

renaissance
revival 656 n.

rend
rend 46 vb.
wound 655 vb.

render
liquefy 337 vb.
translate 520 vb.
give 781 vb.

rendering
translation 520 n.

rendezvous
focus 76 n.
meet 295 vb.
social round 882 n.

renegade
tergiversator
603 n.
knave 938 n.

renew
(*see* **renewal**)

renewal
repetition 106 n.
repair, revival
656 n.

rennet
condensation 324 n.

renounce
recant 603 vb.
relinquish 621 vb.
not retain 779 vb.

renovate
make better 654 n.

renovation
newness 126 n.
reproduction 166 n.
repair 656 n.

renown
famousness 866 n.

rent
gap 201 n.
hire 785 vb.
price 809 n.

rental
price 809 n.

rent-collector
receiver 782 n.

renter
possessor 776 n.
lender 784 n.

rentier
receiver 782 n.

rent-roll
receipt 807 n.

renunciation
recantation 603 n.
relinquishment
621 n.

reorganize
transform 147 vb.
rectify 654 vb.

rep
textile 222 n.
drama 594 n.

repair
repair 656 n., vb.

repairer
mender 656 n.

reparation
restitution 787 n.
atonement 941 n.

repartee
answer 460 n.
witticism 839 n.

repast
meal 301 n.

repatriation
restitution 787 n.

repay
restitute 787 vb.

repayable
owed 803 adj.

repeal
abrogation 752 n.

repeat
do likewise 20 vb.
repetition 106 n.
memorize 505 vb.
emphasize 532 vb.

repeated
frequent 139 adj.

repeater
timekeeper 117 n.
pistol 723 n.

repel
repel 292 vb.
parry 713 vb.
excite hate 888 vb.

repellent
repellent 292 adj.
ugly 842 adj.
hateful 888 adj.

repent
(*see* **repentance**)

repentance
penitence 939 n.

repercussion
effect 157 n.
recoil 280 n.

repertoire, repertory
list 87, n.
collection 632 n.
merchandise 795 n.

repetition
repetition 106 n.
reproduction 166 n.

repetitious
repeated 106 adj.
prolix 570 adj.

repetitive
continuous 71 adj.

repetitive job
habituation 610 n.

repine
be discontented
829 vb.
regret 830 vb.

replace
substitute 150 vb.
replace 187 vb.
restore 656 vb.

replaceable
superfluous 637 adj.

replenish
replenish 633 vb.

replete
full 54 adj.

repletion
satiety 863 n.

replica
copy 22 n.

reply
answer 460 n., vb.
rejoinder 460 n.

report
loudness 400 n.
bang 402 n.
report 524 n.
communicate
524 vb.
news 529 vb.
record 548 n.
describe 590 vb.

reporter
informant 524 n.
newsmonger 529 n.
narrator 590 n.

report on
estimate 480 vb.

reports
record 548 n.
repose
leisure 681 n.
repose 683 n., vb.
reposeful
comfortable 376 adj.
reposeful 683 adj.
reprehend
(*see* reprehension)
reprehension
reprimand 924 n.
censure 924 n.
reprehensible
blameworthy
924 adj.
represent
describe 590 vb.
deputize 755 vb.
(*see*
representation)
representation
manifestation
522 n.
representation
551 n.
drama 594 n.
vote 605 n.
representative
typical 83 adj.
agent 686 n.
consignee 754 n.
delegate 754 n.
repress
subjugate 745 vb.
repression
restraint 747 n.
prohibition 757 n.
repressive
restraining 747 adj.
reprieve
delay 136 n.
deliverance 668 n.
forgiveness 909 n.
acquittal 960 n.
reprimand
reprimand 924 n.
reprint
copy 20 vb.
duplicate 22 n.
edition 589 n.
reprisal
retaliation 714 n.
reproach
slur 867 n.
object of scorn
867 n.

reproach 924 n.
accusation 928 n.
reproachful
resentful 891 adj.
disapproving
924 adj.
reprobate
exprobate 924 vb.
bad man 938 n.
impious person
980 n.
reprobation
reprimand 924 n.
reproduce
repeat 106 vb.
reproduction
copy 22 n.
propagation 164 n.
reproduction 166 n.
reprove
warn 664 vb.
reprove 924 vb.
reptile
reptile 365 n.
bane 659 n.
republic
polity 733 n.
republicanism
government 733 n.
repudiate
(*see* repudiation)
repudiation
dissent 489 n.
rejection 607 n.
non-observance
769 n.
non-payment 805 n.
divorce 896 n.
repugnance
dislike 861 n.
hatred 888 n.
repulse
repulsion 292 n.
defeat 728 n.
refusal 760 n.
repulsive
repellent 292 adj.
ugly 842 adj.
hateful 888 adj.
reputable
reputable 866 adj.
reputation
(*see* repute)
repute
importance 638 n.
credit 802 n.
repute 866 n.

request
request 761 n., vb.
requiem
obsequies 364 n.
lament 836 n.
require
not suffice 636 vb.
(*see* requirement)
requirement
requirement 627 n.
conditions 766 n.
requisite
necessary 596 adj.
requirement 627 n.
requisition
demand 737 n., vb.
request 761 n., vb.
requital
retaliation 714 n.
thanks 907 n.
reward 962 n.
rescind
abrogate 752 vb.
rescript
answer 460 n.
decree 737 n.
rescue
deliverance 668 n.
defend 713 vb.
rescuer
defender 713 n.
research
inquiry 459 n.
experiment 461 n.,
vb.
study 536 n.
resemblance
similarity 18 n.
resent
(*see* resentment)
resentful
malevolent 898 adj.
(*see* resentment)
resentment
enmity 881 n.
resentment 891 n.
jealousy 911 n.
reservation
qualification 468 n.
doubt 486 n.
registration 548 n.
reserve
be early 135 vb.
substitute 150 n.
enclosure 235 n.
taciturnity 582 n.
store 632 vb.

modesty 874 n.
seclusion 883 n.
reserve, in
prepared 669 adj.
reserves
extra 40 n.
armed force 722 n.
funds 797 n.
reservist
soldier 722 n.
reservoir
irrigator 341 n.
lake 346 n.
storage 632 n.
reshape
transform 147 vb.
reside
dwell 192 vb.
residence
place 185 n.
abode, house 192 n.
resident
settler 191 n.
resident 191 n.
envoy 754 n.
resident alien
foreigner 59 n.
residual
remainder 41 n.
remaining 41 adj.
residue, residuum
remainder 41 n.
resign
not retain 779 vb.
(*see* resignation)
resignation
relinquishment
621 n.
resignation 753 n.
patience 823 n.
resile
recant 603 vb.
resilient
cheerful 833 adj.
resin
resin 357 n.
resist
give battle 718 vb.
(*see* resistance)
resistance
electricity 160 n.
counteraction
182 n.
hardness 326 n.
resistance 715 n.
resister
opponent 705 n.

res judicata
judgement 480 n.
resolute
resolute 599 adj.
courageous 855 adj.
resolution
decomposition 51 n.
vigorousness 174 n.
resolution 599 n.
intention 617 n.
resolve
resolution 599 n.
predetermination
608 n.
resonance
roll 403 n.
resonance 404 n.
resort
focus 76 n.
contrivance 623 n.
resort to
congregate 74 vb.
avail of 673 vb.
resound
(*see* resonance)
resource
contrivance 623 n.
resourceful
imaginative 513 adj.
cunning 698 adj.
resources
means 629 n.
wealth 800 n.
respect
relation 9 n.
fear 854 n.
respect 920 n., vb.
respectability
mediocrity 732 n.
repute 866 n.
respectable
reputable 866 adj.
respected 920 adj.
respectful
courteous 884 adj.
respectful 920 adj.
respective
relative 9 adj.
respects
respects 920 n.
respiration
respiration 352 n.
respire
breathe 352 vb.
be refreshed 685 vb.
respite
delay 136 n.

lull 145 n.
acquit 960 vb.
resplendent
splendid 841 adj.
respond
answer 460 vb.
cooperate 706 vb.
feel 818 vb.
respondent
testee 461 n.
interlocutor 584 n.
litigant 959 n.
response
effect 157 n.
answer 460 n.
feeling 818 n.
responsibility
liability 180 n.
mandate 751 n.
duty 917 n.
responsible
causal 156 adj.
observant 768 adj.
dutied 917 adj.
trustworthy
929 adj.
responsive
answering 460 adj.
impressible 819 adj.
responsiveness
feeling 818 n.
rest
lull 145 n.
cease 145 vb.
stability 153 n.
supporter 218 n.
inaction 677 n.
leisure 681 n.
repose 683 n., vb.
restaurant
café 192 n.
restaurateur
caterer 633 n.
restful
reposeful 683 adj.
rest home
hospital 658 n.
resthouse
inn 192 n.
restitution
restitution 787 n.
dueness 915 n.
vindication 927 n.
restive
wilful 602 adj.
discontented
829 adj.

restlessness
restlessness 678 n.
restoration
improvement 654 n.
restoration 656 n.
restitution 787 n.
restorative
tonic 658 n.
refreshing 685 adj.
restore
make complete
54 vb.
remedy 658 vb.
(*see* restoration)
restrain
dissuade 613 vb.
hinder 702 vb.
retain 778 vb.
(*see* restraint)
restraint
moderation 177 n.
counteraction
182 n.
restraint 747 n.
restrict
(*see* restriction)
restriction
limit 236 n.
qualification 468 n.
restriction 747 n.
result
sequel 67 n.
effect 157 n.
product 164 n.
completion 725 n.
resultant
remaining 41 adj.
resume
abstract 592 vb.
(*see* resumption)
résumé
compendium 592 n.
resumption
start 68 n.
repetition 106 n.
taking 786 n.
resurgence
revival 656 n.
resurrection
revival 656 n.
resuscitate
revive 656 vb.
animate 821 vb.
retail
communicate
524 vb.
sell 793 vb.

retailer
provider 633 n.
tradesman 794 n.
retain
tie 45 vb.
retain 778 vb.
retainer
inferior 35 n.
retainer 742 n.
reward 962 n.
retaliate
answer 460 vb.
(*see* retaliation)
retaliation
retaliation 714 n.
retard
retard 278 vb.
retardation
delay 136 n.
slowness 278 n.
retarded
unintelligent
499 adj.
retch
vomit 300 vb.
retention
coherence 48 n.
retention 778 n.
retentive
retentive 778 adj.
reticence
taciturnity 582 n.
reticulate
space 201 vb.
cross 222 vb.
reticulation
network 222 n.
reticule
bag 194 n.
retina
eye 438 n.
retinue
procession 71 n.
retainer 742 n.
retire
recede 290 vb.
run away 620 vb.
resign 753 vb.
retired
former 125 adj.
resigning 753 adj.
secluded 833 adj.
retirement
recession 290 n.
resignation 753 n.
retiring
modest 874 adj.

unsociable 883 adj.
retold
repeated 106 adj.
retort
vessel 194 n.
answer 460 n., vb.
testing agent 461 n.
witticism 839 n.
retouch
repair 656 vb.
retrace
revert 148 vb.
retrospect 505 vb.
retrace one's steps
turn back 286 vb.
retract
recant 603 vb.
retractable
drawing 288 adj.
retral
back 238 adj.
retreat
focus 76 n.
regression 286 n.
meditation 449 n.
defeat 728 n.
seclusion 883 n.
prayers 981 n.
retrench
(*see* retrenchment)
retrenchment
diminution 37 n.
restriction 747 n.
economy 814 n.
retribution
retaliation 714 n.
punishment 963 n.
retrieval
restoration 656 n.
retrieve
recoup 31 vb.
retrieve 656 vb.
retriever
dog 365 n.
retroaction
counteraction
182 n.
retroactive
reverted 148 adj.
retrocession
restoration 656 n.
retroflexion
curvature 248 n.
retrograde
regressive 286 adj.
deteriorate 655 vb.
relapse 657 vb.

retrogression
regression 286 n.
deterioration 655 n.
retrospect
remembrance
505 n.
retrospection
remembrance
505 n.
retroussé
curved 248 adj.
retroversion
inversion 221 n.
return
recurrence 106 n.
product 164 n.
recoil 280 n.
return 286 n.
vote 605 vb.
reject 607 vb.
retaliate 714 vb.
restitution 787 n.
receipt 807 n.
returns
list 87 n.
record 548 n.
reunion
concord 710 n.
social gathering
882 n.
revanchism
revengefulness
910 n.
reveal
disclose 526 vb.
publish 528 vb.
revealed
revelational
975 adj.
revealing
transparent 422 adj.
reveille
call 547 n.
revel
revel 837 n., vb.
celebration 876 n.
intemperance 943 n.
revelation
discovery 484 n.
truth 494 n.
inexpectation
508 n.
prediction 511 n.
disclosure 526 n.
revelation 975 n.
reveller
reveller 837 n.

revenge
revenge 910 n.
jealousy 911 n.
punishment 963 n.
revengeful
malevolent 898 adj.
revengeful 910 adj.
revenue
receipt 807 n.
reverberation
recoil 280 n.
resonance 404 n.
revere
honour 866 vb.
respect 920 vb.
reverence
respect 920 n., vb.
worship 981 n.
reverend
worshipful 866 adj.
cleric 986 n.
reverent
respectful 920 adj.
worshipping
981 adj.
reverie
thought 449 n.
abstractedness
456 n.
fantasy 513 n.
reversal
reversion 148 n.
inexpectation
508 n.
abrogation 752 n.
reverse
contrariety 14 n.
revert 148 vb.
back 238 adj.
contraposition
240 n.
defeat 728 n.
reversion
return 286 n.
reversion 148 n.
transfer 780 n.
reversioner
beneficiary 776 n.
revert
revert 148 vb.
revert to
repeat oneself
106 vb.
revetment
facing 226 n.
revictual
replenish 633 vb.

review
assemblage 74 n.
inspection 438 n.
meditate 449 vb.
estimate 480 n.,
vb.
journal 528 n.
article 591 n.
rectify 654 vb.
pageant 875 n.
reviewer
bookman 589 n.
dissertator 591 n.
revile
curse 899 vb.
exprobate 924 vb.
revise
modify 143 vb.
(*see* revision)
reviser
alterer 143 n.
reformer 654 n.
revision
study 536 n.
amendment 654 n.
revitalize
revive 656 vb.
revival
strengthening
162 n.
revival 656 vb.
revivalism
public worship
981 n.
revivalist
antiquarian 125 n.
pastor 986 n.
revive
repeat 106 vb.
refresh 685 vb.
animate 821 vb.
(*see* revival)
reviver
tonic 658 n.
revocation
recantation 603 n.
revoke
abrogate 752 vb.
not retain 779 vb.
revolt
revolt 738 n., vb.
cause dislike
861 vb.
fail in duty 918 vb.
revolting
not nice 645 adj.
disliked 861 adj.

631

revolution
regular return
141 n.
revolution 149 n.
rotation 315 n.
revolt 738 n.
revolutionary
modern 126 adj.
revolutionary
149 adj.
reformer 654 n.
revolter 738 n.
revolutionize
modify 143 vb.
revolutionize
149 vb.
revolve
rotate 315 vb.
meditate 449 vb.
revolver
pistol 723 n.
revue
stage show 594 n.
revulsion
recoil 280 n.
reward
incentive 612 n.
trophy 729 n.
honours 866 n.
thanks 907 n.
reward 962 vb.
rewarding
rewarding 962 adj.
rhapsodical
imaginative 513 adj.
rhapsodist
crank 504 n.
rhapsody
absurdity 497 n.
ideality 513 n.
rhetoric
oratory 579 n.
ostentation 875 n.
rhetorical
exaggerated
546 adj.
rhetorical 574 adj.
rhetorical figure
trope 519 n.
rhetorician
speaker 579 n.
rheum
excrement 302 n.
rheumatic
crippled 163 adj.
rheumatoid
diseased 651 adj.

rheumy
excretory 302 adj.
rhinoceros
animal 365 n.
rhomb
magic instrument
983 n.
rhombus
angular figure
247 n.
rhumb
compass point
281 n.
rhyme
poetry 593 n.
rhymer, rhymester
poet 593 n.
rhyming
poetic 593 adj.
rhyming slang
slang 560 n.
rhythm
recurrence 106 n.
symmetry 245 n.
tempo 410 n.
prosody 593 n.
rhythmic
periodical 141 adj.
(see **rhythm**)
rib
(see **ribs**)
ribald
vulgar 847 adj.
derisive 851 adj.
impure 951 adj.
ribaldry
(see **ribald**)
riband
ligature 47 n.
strip 208 n.
ribbon
ligature 47 n.
trimming 844 n.
honours 866 n.
ribbons
fetter 748 n.
finery 844 n.
ribs
frame 218 n.
laterality 239 n.
rice
corn 366 n.
rich
prolific 171 adj.
nourishing 301 adj.
fatty 357 adj.
savoury 390 adj.

florid 425 adj.
ornate 574 adj.
rich 800 adj.
ornamental
844 adj.
riches
wealth 800 n.
rick
derange 63 vb.
store 632 n.
rickety
weak 163 adj.
lean 206 adj.
diseased 651 adj.
rickshaw
pushcart, cab
274 n.
ricochet
recoil 280 n., vb.
rid
eject 300 vb.
deliver 668 vb.
riddable
extricable 668 adj.
riddance
deliverance 668 n.
liberation 746 n.
riddle
porosity 263 n.
pierce 263 vb.
enigma 530 n.
ride
land travel 267 n.
path 624 n.
rider
rider 268 n.
gravity 322 n.
ride roughshod
kick 279 vb.
ridge
high land 209 n.
roof 226 n.
ridicule
laughter 835 n.
ridicule 851 n., vb.
contempt 922 n.
ridiculous
absurd 497 adj.
amusing 837 adj.
ridiculous 849 adj.
riding
land travel 267 n.
equitation 267 n.
rife
existing 1 adj.
riff-raff
rabble 869 n.

rifle
groove 262 vb.
fire-arm 723 n.
steal 788 vb.
rifleman
soldiery 722 n.
rift
gap 201 n.
dissension 709 n.
rig
dressing 228 n.
fake 541 vb.
make ready
669 vb.
rigging
tackling 47 n.
right
dextrality 241 n.
true 494 adj.
accurate 494 adj.
expedient 642 adj.
right 913 n.
dueness 915 n.
right about turn
be inverted 221 vb.
right arm
power 160 n.
right ascension
bearings 186 n.
righteous
just 913 adj.
virtuous 933 adj.
rightful
right 913 adj.
due 915 adj.
right hand
dextrality 241 n.
auxiliary 707 n.
right itself
equalize 28 vb.
cure 656 vb.
right man
fitness 24 n.
expert 696 n.
rightness
truth 494 n.
right 913 n.
right of way
access 624 n.
rights
freedom 744 n.
right 913 n.
right time
opportunity 137 n.
right-winger
political party
708 n.

rigid
 unyielding 162 adj.
 rigid 326 adj.
 obstinate 602 adj.
rigidity
 (*see* rigid)
rigmarole
 unmeaningness
 515 n.
rigor
 spasm 318 n.
rigorist
 opinionist 602 n.
 tyrant 735 n.
rigorous
 severe 735 adj.
 fastidious 862 adj.
 pitiless 906 adj.
rigour
 accuracy 494 n.
 severity 735 n.
rig out
 dress 228 vb.
rile
 enrage 891 vb.
rilievo
 rilievo 254 n.
rill
 stream 350 n.
rim
 edge 234 n.
rime
 wintriness 380 n.
rind
 skin 226 n.
ring
 outline 233 n.
 circle 250 n.
 be loud 400 vb.
 resonance 404 n.
 association 706 n.
 pugilism 716 n.
 arena 724 n.
 restriction 747 n.
 jewellery 844 n.
 love-token 889 n.
ring a bell
 be remembered
 505 vb.
ringing
 resonant 404 adj.
 campanology 412 n.
ringleader
 leader 690 n.
 agitator 738 n.
ringlet
 loop 250 n.

 hair 259 n.
ringside seat
 near place 200 n.
rink
 pleasure-ground
 837 n.
rinse
 drench 341 vb.
 clean 648 vb.
rinsings
 dirt 649 n.
riot
 turmoil 61 n.
 plenty 635 n.
 superabound 637 vb.
 revolt 738 n.
rioter
 rioter 738 n.
riotous
 riotous 738 adj.
 sensual 944 adj.
 lawless 954 adj.
rip
 rend 46 vb.
 move fast 277 vb.
 wave 350 n.
 libertine 952 n.
riparian
 coastal 344 adj.
ripe
 matured 669 adj.
ripen
 mature 669 vb.
ripeness
 (*see* ripe)
ripening
 young 130 adj.
 maturation 669 n.
riposte
 answer 460 n., vb.
 parry 713 vb.
ripple
 shallowness 212 n.
 convolution 251 n.
 wave 350 n.
riproaring
 loud 400 adj.
rise
 increase 36 n.
 beginning 68 n.
 be high 209 vb.
 acclivity 220 n.
 ascent 308 n.
 prosper 730 vb.
 revolt 738 vb.
rise above
 be superior 34 vb.

rising
 aged 131 adj.
 influential 178 adj.
 prosperous 730 adj.
 revolt 738 n.
rising generation
 youth 130 n.
 posterity 170 n.
rising man
 made man 730 n.
risk
 gambling 618 n.
 possibility 469 n.
 danger 661 n.
 speculate 791 vb.
risk it
 chance 159 vb.
 face danger 661 vb.
risk-taker
 gambler 618 n.
risk-taking
 calculation of
 chance 159 n.
risky
 speculative
 618 adj.
 dangerous 661 adj.
risqué
 impure 951 adj.
rite
 rite 988 n.
ritual
 formality 875 n.
 ritual 988 n., adj.
 (*see* rite)
ritzy
 rich 800 adj.
 dear 811 adj.
rival
 compeer 28 n.
 opponent 705 n.
 enemy 881 n.
 (*see* rivalry)
rivalry
 imitation 20 n.
 opposition 704 n.
 jealousy 911 n.
 envy 912 n.
river
 stream 350 n.
river-bed
 conduit 351 n.
riverine
 coastal 344 adj.
rivet
 affix 45 vb.
 fastening 47 n.

riviera
 shore 344 n.
rivulet
 stream 350 n.
road
 street 192 n.
 road 624 n.
roadhouse
 tavern 192 n.
road map
 itinerary 267 n.
roads
 stable 192 n.
roadside
 edge 234 n.
 accessible 289 adj.
roadstead
 stable 192 n.
roadworthy
 transferable
 272 adj.
roam
 wander 267 vb.
roan
 horse 273 n.
 brown 430 adj.
 pied 437 adj.
roar
 vociferate 408 vb.
 ululate 409 vb.
 be angry 891 vb.
roaring trade
 prosperity 730 n.
roast
 cook 301 vb.
 heat 381 vb.
rob
 rob 788 vb.
 impoverish 801 vb.
robber
 robber 789 n.
robbery
 stealing 788 n.
robe
 robe 228 n.
 dress 228 vb.
robot
 machine 630 n.
 slave 742 n.
robust
 stalwart 162 adj.
 healthy 650 adj.
rock
 fixture 153 n.
 assuage 177 vb.
 oscillate 317 vb.
 hardness 326 n.

rock 344 n.
refuge 662 n.
pitfall 663 n.
pet 889 vb.
rock-bottom
base 214 n.
basis 218 n.
rocket
rocket 276 n.
missile 287 n.
signal light 420 n.
missile weapon
  723 n.
reprimand 924 n.
rocketry
aeronautics 271 n.
rocket 276 n.
rocking chair
seat 218 n.
rocky
unstable 152 adj.
hard 326 adj.
rod
long measure 203 n.
cylinder 252 n.
incentive 612 n.
rodent
rodent 365 n.
rodomontade
empty talk 515 n.
magniloquence
  574 n.
roe
fertilizer 171 n.
deer 365 n.
rogation
prayers 981 n.
rogue
ruffian 904 n.
knave 938 n.
roguery
improbity 930 n.
roguish
gay 833 adj.
witty 839 adj.
roister
rampage 61 vb.
revel 837 vb.
roisterer
reveller 837 n.
role
acting 594 n.
function 622 n.
roll
bunch 74 n.
list 87 n.
textile 222 n.

coil 251 n.
twine 251 vb.
cylinder 252 n.
smooth 258 vb.
go smoothly 258 vb.
hair 259 n.
fold 261 vb.
rotation 315 n.
fluctuation 317 n.
loudness 400 n.
roll 403 n., vb.
record 548 n.
roll-call
statistics 86 n.
nomenclature 561 n.
roller
girdle 47 n.
ligature 47 n.
wheel 250 n.
smoother 258 n.
pulverizer 332 n.
wave 350 n.
rollick
be cheerful 833 vb.
amuse oneself
  837 vb.
rollicking
gay 833 adj.
roll in
irrupt 297 vb.
rolling
alpine 209 adj.
undulatory 251 adj.
rolling-pin
cylinder 252 n.
smoother 258 n.
rolling-stock
train 274 n.
rolling stone
wanderer 268 n.
roll on
elapse 111 vb.
roll up
congregate 74 vb.
fold 261 vb.
Roman Catholicism
Catholicism 976 n.
romance
ideality 513 n.
be false 541 vb.
fable 543 n.
novel 590 n.
love affair 887 n.
Roman holiday
slaughter 362 n.
Romanism
Catholicism 976 n.

romantic
imaginative 513 adj.
feeling 818 adj.
impressible 819 adj.
romanticism
fantasy 513 n.
romanticize
imagine 513 vb.
romp
be cheerful 833 vb.
revel 837 n.
rompers
breeches 228 n.
rood
cross 222 n.
roof
home 192 n.
roof 226 n.
overlay 226 vb.
shelter 662 n.
rook
chessman 837 n.
room
room 183 n.
dwell 192 vb.
chamber 194 n.
scope 744 n.
rooms
quarters 192 n.
roomy
spacious 183 adj.
roost
nest 192 n.
dwell 192 vb.
sit down 311 vb.
sleep 679 vb.
rooster
poultry 365 n.
root
numerical element
  85 n.
stabilize 153 vb.
source 156 n.
base 214 n.
tuber 301 n.
vociferate 408 vb.
word 559 n.
applaud 923 vb.
rooted
firm-set 45 adj.
fixed 153 adj.
still 266 adj.
rootless
unstable 152 adj.
displaced 188 adj.
root out
destroy 165 vb.

extract 304 vb.
rope
tie 45 vb.
cable 47 n.
scope 744 n.
fetter 748 n.
rope's end
scourge 964 n.
ropes, know the
be expert 694 vb.
ropy
thick 205 adj.
semiliquid 354 adj.
bad 645 adj.
rosary
prayers 981 n.
rose
fragrance 396 n.
redness 431 n.
rosette
badge 547 n.
rose-water
scent 396 n.
rosin
resin 357 n.
roster
list 87 n.
rostrate
angular 247 adj.
curved 248 adj.
rostrum
stand 218 n.
rostrum 539 n.
rosy
red 431 adj.
healthy 650 adj.
promising 852 adj.
rot
decay 51 n.
silly talk 515 n.
dilapidation 655 n.
blight 659 n.
rota
list 87 n.
regular return
  141 n.
rotary
rotary 315 adj.
rotation
regular return
  141 n.
rotation 315 n.
rotator
rotator 315 n.
rotten
antiquated 127 adj.
weakened 163 adj.

not nice 645 adj.
vicious 934 adj.
(*see* rot)
rotter
cad 938 n.
rotund
rotund 252 adj.
roué
libertine 952 n.
rouge
red pigment 431 n.
cosmetic 843 n.
rough
non-uniform 17 adj.
incomplete 55 adj.
rough 259 adj.
hoarse 407 adj.
graceless 842 adj.
cruel 898 adj.
ruffian 904 n.
(*see* roughness)
roughage
dieting 301 n.
rough-and-tumble
turmoil 61 n.
fight 716 n.
rough diamond
ingenue 699 n.
vulgarian 847 n.
good man 937 n.
roughen
roughen 259 vb.
rough-hewn
incomplete 55 adj.
immature 670 adj.
rough house
turmoil 61 n.
fight 716 n.
roughness
violence 176 n.
roughness 259 n.
(*see* rough)
roulette
gambling game
837 n.
round
whole 52 n.
period 110 n.
make curved
248 vb.
round 250 adj.
unsharpened
257 adj.
circle 314 vb.
vocal music 412 n.
habit 610 n.
business 622 n.

circuit 626 n., vb.
pugilism 716 n.
ammunition 723 n.
roundabout
deviating 282 adj.
circuitous 314 adj.
prolix 570 adj.
road 624 n.
roundabout 626 adj.
rounded
smooth 258 adj.
shapely 841 adj.
roundel
circle 250 n.
rounders
ball game 837 n.
roundhouse
chamber 194 n.
lock-up 748 n.
round on
retaliate 714 vb.
round-robin
deprecation 762 n.
roundsman
traveller 268 n.
round the bend
crazed 503 adj.
round the clock
all along 113 adv.
round trip
reversion 148 n.
circuition 314 n.
round up
bring together
74 vb.
rouse
incite 612 vb.
excite 821 vb.
rouse oneself
be active 678 vb.
rout
crowd 74 n.
disperse 75 vb.
multitude 104 n.
defeat 728 n., vb.
revel 837 n.
rabble 869 n.
route
itinerary 267 n.
way, route 624 n.
direct 689 vb.
route-map
itinerary 267 n.
routine
uniformity 16 n.
order 60 n.
regular return 141 n.

practice 610 n.
business 622 n.
conduct 688 n.
ritual 988 n.
rove
wander 267 vb.
rover
wanderer 268 n.
row
turmoil 61 n.
series 71 n.
row (*a boat*)
269 vb.
loudness 400 n.
rowboat
rowboat 275 n.
rowdiness
loudness 400 n.
rowdy
violent 176 adj.
ruffian 904 n.
rowel
sharp point 256 n.
rower
boatman 270 n.
rowing
aquatics 269 n.
royal
ruling 733 adj.
noble 868 adj.
ostentatious
875 adj.
royalty
authority 733 n.
sovereign 741 n.
receipt 807 n.
rub
be contiguous
202 vb.
rub 333 vb.
give pain 377 vb.
hindrance 702 n.
painfulness 827 n.
rubber
elasticity 328 n.
silencer 401 n.
contest 716 n.
rubber stamp
assent 488 n.
rubber-stamp
endorse 488 vb.
rubbery
tough 329 adj.
rubbish
leavings 41 n.
silly talk 515 n.
rubbish 641 n.

rubbish-heap
sink 649 n.
rubbishy
trivial 639 adj.
profitless 641 adj.
rub down
smooth 258 vb.
groom 369 vb.
rubicundity
redness 431 n.
rub in
emphasize 532 vb.
make important
638 vb.
rub out
murder 362 vb.
obliterate 550 vb.
rubric
precept 693 n.
rite 988 n.
rub shoulders with
be contiguous
202 vb.
rub the wrong way
make quarrels
709 vb.
ruby
redness 431 n.
ruck
average 30 n.
fold 261 vb.
rucksack
bag 194 n.
ruction
turmoil 61 n.
rudder
poop 238 n.
sailing aid 269 n.
directorship 689 n.
ruddy
florid 425 adj.
red 431 adj.
healthy 650 adj.
rude
violent 176 adj.
inelegant 576 adj.
graceless 842 adj.
discourteous 885
adj.
rudery
rudeness 885 n.
rudiment
beginning 68 n.
rudimental
immature 670 adj.
rudimentary
beginning 68 adj.

rue
regret 830 vb.
rueful
regretting 830 adj.
ruff
neckwear 228 n.
ruffian
ruffian 904 n.
ruffianism
inhumanity 898 n.
ruffle
jumble 63 vb.
roughen 259 vb.
enrage 891 vb.
rug
floor-cover 226 n.
coverlet 226 n.
rugged
stalwart 162 adj.
graceless 842 adj.
ruggedness
non-uniformity 17 n.
roughness 259 n.
ruin
antiquity 125 n.
ruin 165 n.
waste 634 vb.
dilapidation 655 n.
adversity 731 n.
loss 772 n.
impoverish 801 vb.
ruination
ruin 165 n.
ruinous
destructive 165 adj.
harmful 645 adj.
dilapidated 655 adj.
rule
order 60 n.
rule 81 n.
line 203 n.
judge 480 vb.
precept 693 n.
governance 733 n.
rule of thumb
empiricism 461 n.
rule out
exclude 57 vb.
make impossible
470 vb.
ruler
gauge 465 n.
potentate 741 n.
rulership
magistrature 733 n.
rules and regulations
practice 610 n.

ruling
judgement 480 n.
ruling class
upper class 868 n.
rum
unusual 84 adj.
liquor 301 n.
ridiculous 849 adj.
rumble
roll 403 vb.
rumbling
voidance 300 n.
rumbustious
disorderly 61 adj.
loud 400 adj.
ruminant
animal 365 adj.
thoughtful 449 adj.
rumination
eating 301 n.
meditation 449 n.
rummage
search 459 vb.
rummy
unusual 84 adj.
rumour
rumour 529 n.
fable 543 n.
rump
remainder 41 n.
buttocks 238 n.
rumple
jumble 63 vb.
fold 261 vb.
rumpus
turmoil 61 n.
run
series 71 n.
recurrence 106 n.
continuance 146 n.
pedestrianism
267 n.
voyage 269 vb.
move fast 277 vb.
flow out 298 vb.
liquefy 337 vb.
flow 350 vb.
chase 619 vb.
run away 620 vb.
path 624 n.
manage 689 vb.
run after
pursue 619 vb.
desire 859 vb.
run amuck
lay waste 165 vb.
be violent 176 vb.

be excitable
822 vb.
run away
run away 620 vb.
escape 667 vb.
runaway
speedy 277 adj.
avoider 620 n.
escaper 667 n.
coward 856 n.
run counter
counteract 182 vb.
tell against
467 vb.
run down
decrease 37 vb.
pursue 619 vb.
dispraise 924 vb.
rung
degree 27 n.
stand 218 n.
ascent 308 n.
runic
literal 558 adj.
written 586 adj.
run in one's head
cause thought
449 vb.
run low
decrease 37 vb.
runnel
stream 350 n.
conduit 351 n.
runner
pedestrian 268 n.
speeder 277 n.
courier 531 n.
contender 716 n.
running
continuous 71 adj.
running sore
bane 659 n.
loss 772 n.
runny
non-adhesive
49 adj.
fluidal 335 adj.
run off
void 300 vb.
run of the mill
average 30 n.
run on
continuate 71 vb.
be loquacious
581 vb.
run over
collide 279 vb.

run riot
be violent 176 vb.
superabound
637 vb.
be excitable 822 vb.
runt
animalcule 196 n.
dwarf 196 n.
run the gauntlet
face danger 661 vb.
run to seed
waste 634 vb.
runty
dwarfish 196 adj.
run upon, run on
requirement 627 n.
runway
air travel 271 n.
run wild
be violent 176 vb.
rupture
separation 46 n.
rend 46 vb.
gap 201 n.
wound 655 n.
dissension 709 n.
rural
regional 184 adj.
provincial 192 adj.
ruse
trickery 542 n.
rush
crowd 74 n.
spurt 277 n.
commotion 318 n.
non-preparation
670 n.
attack 712 n.
rush at
charge 712 vb.
rushed
hasty 680 adj.
rush hour
crowd 74 n.
rush in, rush into
irrupt 297 vb.
rush-light
torch 420 n.
rush to conclusions
misjudge 481 vb.
rusk
cereal 301 n.
russet
brown 430 adj.
red 431 adj.
rust
decay 51 n.

oldness 127 n.
destroyer 168 n.
blunt 257 vb.
desuetude 611 n.
dilapidation 655 n.
blight 659 n.
inaction 677 n.
rustic
dweller 191 n.
provincial 192 adj.
agrarian 370 adj.
countryman 869 n.
rustication
seclusion 883 n.
rusticity
ill-breeding 847 n.
rustiness
unskilfulness 695 n.
(*see* rust)
rustle
sibilation 406 n.
rustler
thief 789 n.
rustle up
make ready 699 vb.
rusty
antiquated 127 adj.
unsharpened
257 adj.
strident 407 adj.
clumsy 695 adj.
(*see* rust,
rustiness)
rusy
cunning 698 adj.
rut
furrow 262 n.
habit 610 n.
libido 859 n.
ruthless
cruel 898 adj.
pitiless 906 adj.
rutting, ruttish
lecherous 951 adj.
rutty
rough 259 adj.
furrowed 262 adj.
rye
liquor 301 n.
corn 366 n.

S

sabbatarian
religionist 979 n.
sabbath
repose 683 n.

holy-day 988 n.
sabbatical
reposeful 683 adj.
sable
skin 226 n.
black 428 adj.
sabotage
disable 161 vb.
hindrance 702 n.
dutilessness 918 n.
saboteur
hinderer 702 n.
sabre
kill 362 vb.
side-arms 723 n.
sabre-rattling
intimidation
854 n.
saccharine
sweet 392 n.
sacerdotal
priestly 985 adj.
clerical 986 adj.
sachet
scent 396 n.
sack
bag 194 n.
dismiss 300 n.
deposal 752 n.
spoliation 788 n.
sackcloth
asceticism 945 n.
sackcloth and ashes
lamentation 836 n.
sacking
textile 222 n.
sacrament
the sacrament
988 n.
sacramental
devotional 981 adj.
priestly 985 adj.
sacred
worshipful 866 adj.
divine 965 adj.
devotional 981 adj.
sacrifice
decrement 42 n.
loss 772 n.
offering 781 n.
cheapen 812 vb.
be disinterested
931 vb.
propitiation 941 n.
oblation 981 n.
sacrificer
worshipper 981 n.

sacrificial
losing 772 adj.
atoning 941 adj.
devotional 981 adj.
sacrilege
impiety 980 n.
sacrilegious
disrespectful
921 adj.
profane 980 adj.
sacristy
church interior
990 n.
sacrosanct
worshipful 866 adj.
sanctified 979 adj.
sad
funereal 364 adj.
bad 645 adj.
unhappy 825 adj.
melancholic
834 adj.
sadden
sadden 834 vb.
saddle
affix 45 vb.
seat 218 n.
meat 301 n.
saddle with
impose a duty
917 vb.
sadism
abnormality 84 n.
inhumanity 898 n.
sadist
monster 938 n.
sadistic
cruel 898 adj.
sadness
sorrow 825 n.
dejection 834 n.
safari
land travel 267 n.
safe
hiding-place 527 n.
storage 632 n.
safe 660 adj.
treasury 799 n.
cautious 858 adj.
safe-conduct
protection 660 n.
permit 756 n.
safe-deposit
storage 632 n.
treasury 799 n.
safeguard
protection 660 n.

safeguard 662 n.
safe-keeping
protection 660 n.
safety
bicycle 274 n.
safety 660 n.
safety belt
safeguard 662 n.
safety first
caution 858 n.
safety valve
safeguard 662 n.
means of escape
667 n.
sag
be weak 163 vb.
hang 217 vb.
be curved 248 vb.
be dejected 834 vb.
saga
narrative 590 n.
sagacious
(*see* sagacity)
sagacity
sagacity 498 n.
sage
potherb 301 n.
wise 498 adj.
sage 500 n.
teacher 537 n.
sail
water travel 269 n.
swim 269 vb.
ship, sail 275 n.
sailing-ship
sailing-ship 275 n.
sailor
mariner 270 n.
navy man 722 n.
sailorlike, sailorly
seamanlike 270 adj.
saint
good man 937 n.
pietist 979 n.
sainthood
sanctity 979 n.
St John's
Ambulance
doctor 658 n.
saintly
virtuous 933 adj.
pious 979 adj.
saints, the
church member
976 n.
St Vitus's dance
spasm 318 n.

sake of, for the
  in aid of 703 adv.
salaam
  respects 920 n.
salacity
  unchastity 951 n.
salad
  a mixture 43 n.
salad days
  youth 130 n.
salamander
  rara avis 84 n.
  reptile 365 n.
  heater 383 n.
salami
  meat 301 n.
salariat
  upper class 868 n.
salary
  earnings 771 n.
  receipt 807 n.
sale
  sale 793 n.
salesman
  seller 793 n.
salesmanship
  inducement 612 n.
  sale 793 n.
sales talk
  inducement 612 n.
salient
  region 184 n.
  projection 254 n.
  salient 254 adj.
  manifest 522 adj.
  battleground 724 n.
salient point
  chief thing 638 n.
saline
  salty 388 adj.
saliva
  excrement 302 n.
sallow
  colourless 426 adj.
  unhealthy 651 adj.
sally
  emerge 298 vb.
  attack 712 n., vb.
  witticism 839 n.
sally-port
  outlet 298 n.
salon
  social gathering
    882 n.
saloon
  tavern 192 n.
  chamber 194 n.

salt
  pungency 388 n.
  season 388 vb.
  condiment 389 n.
  preserve 666 vb.
  wit 839 n.
saltatory
  leaping 312 adj.
salt away
  store 632 vb.
salt of the earth
  élite 644 n.
  good man 937 n.
saltpetre
  explosive 723 n.
salty
  witty 839 adj.
salubrious
  healthy 650 n.
salubrity
  salubrity 652 n.
salutary
  beneficial 644 adj.
salutation
  allocution 583 n.
  respects 920 n.
salute
  speak to 583 vb.
  courteous act 884 n.
  congratulation
    886 n.
  endearment 889 n.
  show respect
    920 vb.
salvage
  restoration 656 vb.
  deliverance 668 n.
salvation
  preservation 666 n.
  deliverance 668 n.
salvationism
  pietism 979 n.
salvationist
  sectarist 978 n.
  religionist 979 n.
salve
  unguent 357 n.
  balm 658 n.
salvo
  bang 402 n.
  qualification 468 n.
  bombardment 712 n.
sal volatile
  tonic 658 n.
Samaritan, Good
  kind person 897 n.
  benefactor 903 n.

same (*see* **sameness**)
same mind
  consensus 488 n.
sameness
  identity 13 n.
  uniformity 16 n.
  equivalence 28 n.
same time
  synchronism 123 n.
samovar
  cauldron 194 n.
sampan
  sailing ship 275 n.
sample
  prototype 23 n.
  part 53 n.
  example 83 n.
  experiment 461 vb.
  exhibit 522 n.
sampling
  empiricism 461 n.
sanative
  remedial 658 adj.
sanatorium
  hospital 658 n.
sanctification
  (*see* **sanctify**)
sanctify
  sanctify 979 vb.
  idolatrize 982 vb.
sanctimonious
  hypocritical
    541 adj.
  pietistic 979 adj.
sanctimony
  false piety 980 n.
sanction
  endorse 488 vb.
  compulsion 740 n.
  approbation 923 n.
sanctions
  compulsion 740 n.
sanctity
  sanctity 979 n.
sanctuary
  refuge 662 n.
  holy place 990 n.
sanctum
  chamber 194 n.
  holy place 990 n.
sand
  desert 172 n.
  powder 332 n.
sandal
  footwear 228 n.
sandbank
  island 349 n.

sandiness
  (*see* **sandy**)
sandpaper
  sharpener 256 n.
sandwich
  put between 231 vb.
  mouthful 301 n.
sandwich-man
  publicizer 528 n.
sandy
  powdery 332 adj.
  red 431 adj.
sane
  wise 498 adj.
  sane 502 adj.
sang froid
  inexcitability
    823 n.
sanguinary
  sanguineous
    335 adj.
  murderous 362 adj.
  bloodshot 431 adj.
sanguine
  red 431 adj.
  optimistic 482 adj.
sanhedral
  ecclesiastical
    985 adj.
sanhedrim
  council 692 n.
sanitary
  salubrious 652 adj.
sanitary inspector
  sanitarian 652 n.
sanitation
  hygiene 652 n.
  prophylactic 658 n.
sanity
  sanity 502 n.
sap
  essential part 5 n.
  weaken 163 vb.
  demolish 165 vb.
  excavation 255 vb.
  fluid 335 n.
  ninny 501 n.
sapless
  dry 342 n.
sapling
  young plant 132 n.
  tree 366 n.
sapper
  excavator 255 n.
  soldiery 722 n.
sapphire
  blueness 435 n.

sappy
fluidal 335 adj.
pulpy 356 adj.

sarcasm
ridicule 851 n.
reproach 924 n.

sarcastic
(*see* sarcasm)

sarcophagus
interment 364 n.

sardine
table fish 365 n.

sardonic
derisive 851 adj.

sartorial
dressed 228 adj.

sash
girdle 47 n.
frame 218 n.

Satan
Satan 969 n.

satanic
evil 616 adj.
diabolic 969 adj.

Satanism
diabolism 969 n.

satchel
bag 194 n.

sate, satiate
make insensitive
820 vb.
be tedious 838 vb.
sate 863 vb.

satellite
concomitant 89 n.
space-ship 276 n.
follower 284 n.
auxiliary 707 n.
dependant 742 n.

satellite status
subjection 745 n.

satiety
sufficiency 635 n.
superfluity 637 n.
tedium 838 n.
satiety 863 n.

satin
textile 222 n.
smoothness 258 n.

satiny
smooth 258 adj.
textural 331 adj.

satire
satire 851 n.
calumny 926 n.

satirical
funny 849 adj.

derisive 851 adj.
disrespectful
921 adj.

satirist
humorist 839 n.
detractor 926 n.

satirize (*see* satire)

satisfaction
sufficiency 635 n.
content 828 n.
atonement 941 n.

satisfactory
sufficient 635 adj.
not bad 644 adj.

satisfy
suffice 635 vb.
content 828 vb.

saturate
fill 54 vb.
drench 341 vb.

saturation
satiety 863 n.

Saturnalia
turmoil 61 n.
festivity 837 n.

Saturnian
primal 127 adj.
planetary 321 adj.

saturnine
serious 834 adj.
ugly 842 adj.

satyr
libertine 952 n.

sauce
stimulant 174 n.
season 388 vb.
condiment 389 n.
sauciness 878 n.

saucer
plate 194 n.

saucy
disrespectful
921 adj.

saunter
move slowly 278 vb.

sausage
meat 301 n.

savage
violent creature
176 n.
wound 655 vb.
ingenue 699 n.
attack 712 vb.
severe 735 adj.
vulgarian 847 n.
cruel 898 adj.
ruffian 904 n.

savagery
inhumanity 898 n.

savant
scholar 492 n.
expert 696 n.

save
store 632 vb.
preserve 666 vb.
deliver 668 vb.
not use 674 vb.
retain 778 vb.
economize 814 vb.

saving clause
qualification
468 n.

saving grace
virtues 933 n.

savings
store 632 n.
economy 814 n.

saviour
preserver 666 n.
benefactor 903 n.

savoir faire
skill 694 n.
etiquette 848 n.

savour
taste 386 n., vb.
appetize 390 vb.

savouriness
savouriness 390 n.

savour of
resemble 18 vb.

savoury
tasty 386 adj.
savouriness 390 n.

saw
cut 46 vb.
notch 260 n.
rasp 407 vb.
maxim 496 n.

sawdust
powder 332 n.

saw-edge
roughness 259 n.

sawney
ninny 501 n.

saw the air
gesticulate 547 vb.

saxophone
horn 414 n.

say
affirm 532 vb.
speak 579 vb.

saying
maxim 496 n.
phrase 563 n.

say of
attribute 158 vb.

say-so
affirmation 532 n.

scab
nonconformist 84 n.
cure 656 vb.
cad 938 n.

scabbard
case 194 n.
arsenal 723 n.

scabby
unclean 649 adj.

scabrous
impure 951 adj.

scaffold
structure 331 n.
means of execution
964 n.

scaffolding
frame 218 n.

scalar
gradational 27 adj.

scalawag, scallywag
bad man 938 n.

scald
burning 381 n.
wound 655 n.

scalding
hot 379 adj.
paining 827 adj.

scale
degree 27 n.
series 71 n.
covering, skin
226 n.
climb 308 vb.
musical note 410 n.
opacity 423 n.
gauge 465 n.

scale down
bate 37 vb.

scalene
unequal 29 adj.

scales
scales 322 n.
gauge 465 n.

scallop
crinkle 251 vb.
notch 260 n., vb.
cook 301 vb.

scallywag
(*see* scalawag)

scalp
head 213 n.
uncover 229 n.
trophy 729 n.

scalpel
  sharp edge 256 n.
scaly
  layered 207 adj.
  dermal 226 adj.
scamp
  neglect 458 vb.
  not complete
    726 vb.
  bad man 938 n.
scan
  scan 438 vb.
  be attentive 455 vb.
  inquire 459 vb.
  poetize 593 vb.
scandal
  slur 867 n.
  calumny 926 n.
scandalize
  displease 827 vb.
  incur blame 924 vb.
  defame 926 vb.
scandalized
  disapproving
    924 adj.
scandal-monger
  newsmonger 529 n.
  defamer 926 n.
scandalous
  discreditable
    867 adj.
  detracting 926 adj.
scansion
  prosody 593 n.
scant
  make insufficient
    636 vb.
  (*see* scanty)
scantiness
  scarcity 636 n.
  (*see* scanty)
scanty
  small 33 adj.
  few 105 adj.
  short 204 adj.
scapegoat
  substitute 150 n.
  unlucky person
    731 n.
  sufferer 825 n.
  oblation 981 n.
scapegrace
  bad man 938 n.
scar
  high land 209 n.
  mark 547 vb.
  trace 548 n.

  wound 655 n.
  trophy 729 n.
  blemish 845 n.,
    vb.
scarab
  talisman 983 n.
scarce
  infrequent 140 adj.
  scarce 636 adj.
scarcity
  scarcity 636 n.
  (*see* scarce)
scare
  false alarm 665 n.
  frighten 854 vb.
scarecrow
  thinness 206 n.
  eyesore 842 n.
scaremonger
  alarmist 854 n.
scarf
  shawl 228 n.
  neckwear 228 n.
scarify
  rend 46 vb.
  wound 655 vb.
scarlet
  heinous 934 adj.
scarp
  acclivity 220 n.
  fortification 713 n.
scathe
  harm 645 vb.
  impairment 655 n.
scatheless
  perfect 646 adj.
scatological
  impure 951 adj.
scatter
  jumble 63 vb.
  dispersion 75 n.
  diverge 294 vb.
  let fall 311 vb.
  waste 634 vb.
scatter-brained
  light-minded
    456 adj.
scatterbrains
  fool 501 n.
scattering
  reflection 417 n.
  (*see* scatter)
scatty
  foolish 499 adj.
  crazed 503 adj.
scavenger
  cleaner 648 n.

scenario
  narrative 590 n.
  stage play 594 n.
scene
  spectacle 445 n.
  exhibit 522 n.
  stage-set 594 n.
  arena 724 n.
  excitable state
    822 n.
scenery
  beauty 841 n.
  (*see* scene)
scenic
  beautiful 841 adj.
  ornamental
    844 adj.
  showy 875 adj.
scent
  smell 394 vb.
  scent 396 n.
  detect 484 vb.
  trace 548 n.
  cosmetic 843 n.
scent, on the
  pursuing 619 adj.
sceptic
  unbeliever 486 n.
sceptical
  doubting 474 adj.
  dissenting 489 adj.
scepticism
  doubt 486 n.
  irreligion 974 n.
sceptre
  regalia 743 n.
schedule
  list 87 n., vb.
  plan 623 vb.
schematic
  orderly 60 adj.
  planned 623 adj.
schematize
  regularize 62 vb.
scheme
  plan 623 n.
  plot 623 vb.
  be cunning 698 vb.
schemer
  slyboots 698 n.
scheming
  (*see* scheme)
schism
  schism 978 n.
schismatic
  quarrelling 709 adj.
  schismatic 978 n.

schizoid
  insane 503 adj.
  madman 504 n.
schizophrenia
  psychopathy 503 n.
schnapps
  liquor 301 n.
scholar
  scholar 492 n.
  learner 538 n.
scholarly
  instructed 490 adj.
  studious 536 adj.
scholarship
  erudition 490 n.
scholastic
  intellectual 492 n.
  educational 534 adj.
  theologian 973 n.
scholasticism
  theology 973 n.
scholiast
  interpreter 520 n.
scholium
  commentary 520 n.
school
  group 74 n.
  educate, train
    534 vb.
  school 539 n.
schoolbook
  textbook 589 n.
schoolboy
  youngster 132 n.
  learner 538 n.
schooled
  instructed 490 adj.
schoolfellow
  chum 880 n.
schoolgoer
  learner 538 n.
schooling
  teaching 534 n.
schoolman
  reasoner 475 n.
  theologian 973 n.
schoolmaster,
  schoolmistress
  teacher 537 n.
schoolroom
  classroom 539 n.
schooner
  sailing-ship 275 n.
science
  physics 319 n.
  science 490 n.
  skill 694 n.

scientific
  accurate 494 adj.
scientist
  intellectual 492 n.
scimitar
  side-arms 723 n.
scintillate
  shine 417 vb.
  be witty 839 vb.
scintillation
  flash 417 n.
sciolism
  sciolism 491 n.
sciolist
  sciolist 493 n.
scion
  young plant 132 n.
  descendant 170 n.
scissors
  sharp edge 256 n.
sclerosis
  hardening 326 n.
scoff
  ridicule 851 vb.
  contempt 922 n.
scoffer
  unbeliever 486 n.
  detractor 926 n.
scold
  bicker 709 vb.
  shrew 892 n.
  exprobate 924 vb.
scolding
  reprimand 924 n.
scollop
  edging 234 n.
  notch 260 n.
scone
  pastry 301 n.
scoop
  ladle 194 n.
  extractor 304 n.
  news 529 n.
scoot
  move fast 277 vb.
scooter
  bicycle 274 n.
scope
  range 183 n.
  meaning 514 n.
  function 622 n.
  scope 744 n.
scorbutic
  unclean 649 adj.
scorch
  move fast 277 vb.
  burn 381 vb.

scorched earth
  havoc 165 n.
scorcher
  speeder 277 n.
score
  rend 46 vb.
  numerical result
    85 n.
  list 87 n., vb.
  groove 262 vb.
  music 412 n.
  register 548 vb.
  obliterate 550 vb.
  wound 655 vb.
  accounts 808 n.
score-board,
  score-sheet
  record 548 n.
score off
  be superior 34 vb.
  humiliate 872 vb.
scorn
  reject 607 vb.
  disrespect 921 n.
  contempt 922 n.
scornful
  (*see* scorn)
scorpion
  noxious animal
    904 n.
scotch
  disable 161 vb.
  wound 655 vb.
  hinder 702 vb.
scotch-tape
  adhesive 47 n.
scot-free
  uncharged 812 adj.
  non-liable 919 adj.
scoundrelism
  improbity 930 n.
scour
  search 459 vb.
  clean 648 vb.
scourge
  bane 659 n.
  oppress 735 vb.
  flog 963 vb.
  scourge 964 n.
scourings
  leavings 41 n.
  rubbish 641 n.
scout
  scan 438 vb.
  spectator 441 n.
  inquirer 459 n.
  reject 607 vb.

scowl
  look 438 n.
  sullenness 893 n.
scraggy
  lean 209 adj.
scram
  decamp 296 vb.
scramble
  confusion 61 n.
  bedevil 63 vb.
  cook 301 vb.
  haste 680 n.
scrap
  small thing 33 n.
  piece 53 n.
  disuse 674 vb.
  fight 716 n., vb.
scrap-book
  reminder 505 n.
  record 548 n.
scrape
  stoop 311 vb.
  rub 333 vb.
  touch 378 vb.
  rasp 407 vb.
  predicament 700 n.
  be parsimonious
    816 vb.
  guilty act 936 n.
scrap of paper
  unreliability 474 n.
  perfidy 930 n.
scrappy
  incomplete 55 adj.
scraps
  leavings 41 n.
  rubbish 641 n.
scratch
  inferior 35 adj.
  rend 46 vb.
  be rough 259 vb.
  rub 333 vb.
  touch, itch 378 vb.
  faintness 401 n.
  rasp 407 vb.
  trifle 639 n.
  wound 655 n., vb.
  unprepared 670 adj.
  unskilled 695 adj.
  resign 753 vb.
scratch out
  obliterate 550 vb.
scratchy
  irascible 892 adj.
scrawl
  unintelligibility
    517 n.

script 586 n.
scrawny
  lean 206 adj.
scream
  cry 408 vb.
screaming
  whopping 32 adj.
  loud 400 adj.
  florid 425 adj.
scree
  thing transferred
    272 n.
screech
  stridor 407 n.
  rasp 407 vb.
  cry 408 vb.
  ululate 409 vb.
screed
  script 586 n.
  dissertation 591 n.
screen
  canopy 226 n.
  partition 231 n.
  porosity 263 n.
  screen 421 n., vb.
  opacity 423 n.
  cinema 445 n.
  disguise 527 n.
  pretext 614 n.
  purify 648 vb.
  safeguard 660 vb.
screw
  affix 47 vb.
  fastening 45 n.
  distort 246 vb.
  coil 251 n.
  propellant 287 n.
  be parsimonious
    816 vb.
screw loose
  eccentricity 503 n.
scribble
  unintelligibility
    517 n.
  lettering 586 n.
scribe
  recorder 549 n.
  penman 586 n.
  theologian 973 n.
scrimmage
  fight 716 n., vb.
scrimp
  shorten 204 vb.
  niggard 816 n.
scrip
  bag 194 n.
  title-deed 767 n.

script
script 586 n.
lettering 586 n.
stage play 594 n.
scriptural
scriptural 975 adj.
scripturality
orthodoxy 976 n.
scripture
credential 466 n.
scripture 975 n.
script-writer
dramatist 594 n.
scrofulous
unclean 649 adj.
scroll
list 87 n.
coil 251 n.
lettering 586 n.
scroll-work
pattern 844 n.
scrounge
beg 761 vb.
scrub
rub 333 vb.
wood 366 n.
clean 648 vb.
scrubbing-brush
roughness 159 n.
cleaning utensil
648 n.
scrubby
arboreal 366 adj.
scruff
rear 238 n.
scruffy
unclean 649 adj.
scrum
crowd 74 n.
fight 716 n.
scruple
small quantity 33 n.
weighment 322 n.
doubt 486 n.
scrupulosity
pietism 979 n.
scrupulous
careful 457 adj.
honourable 929 adj.
scrutineer
inquirer 459 n.
scrutinize
scan 438 vb.
(*see* **scrutiny**)
scrutiny
attention 455 n.
inquiry 459 n.

scud
move fast 277 vb.
cloud 355 n.
scuffle
fight 716 n., vb.
scull
row 269 vb.
scullery
chamber 194 n.
sculpt
sculpt 554 vb.
sculptor
sculptor 556 n.
sculpture
sculpture 554 n.
scum
leavings 41 n.
layer 207 n.
dirt 649 n.
rabble 869 n.
scumble
coat 226 vb.
paint 553 vb.
scupper
drain 351 n.
slaughter 362 vb.
scurf
dirt 649 n.
scurfy
unclean 649 adj.
scurrility
scurrility 899 n.
(*see* **scurrilous**)
scurrilous
maledicent 899 adj.
disrespectful
921 adj.
scurry
move fast 277 vb.
hasten 680 vb.
scurvy
rascally 930 adj.
scutcheon
(*see* **escutcheon**)
scuttle
vessel 194 n.
pierce 263 vb.
plunge 313 vb.
run away 620 vb.
haste 680 n.
fail in duty 918 vb.
scythe
sharp edge 256 n.
farm tool 370 n.
sea
ocean 343 n.
wave 350 n.

seaboard
shore 344 n.
seafarer
mariner 270 n.
seafaring
seafaring 269 adj.
sea-going
seafaring 269 adj.
seal
mould 23 n.
close 264 vb.
endorse 488 vb.
label 547 n.
sealed book
unknown thing
491 n.
secret 530 n.
sealed off
sealed off 264 adj.
sea-legs
equilibrium 28 n.
sealing-wax
adhesive 47 n.
seal up
imprison 747 vb.
seam
joint 45 n.
dividing line 92 n.
layer 207 n.
seaman
mariner 270 n.
seamanlike
seamanlike
270 adj.
seamanship
navigation 268 n.
seamless
whole 52 adj.
seamstress
clothier 228 n.
séance
spiritualism 984 n.
sea-power
navy 722 n.
sear
dry 342 vb.
make insensitive
820 vb.
search
search 459 n., vb.
searcher
inquirer 459 n.
searching
inquisitive 453 adj.
paining 827 adj.
searchlight
lamp 420 n.

search-party
search 459 n.
seashore
shore 344 n.
seasick
vomiting 300 adj.
seaside
shore 344 n.
pleasure-ground
837 n.
season
time 108 n.
regular return
141 n.
season 388 vb.
habituate 610 vb.
preserve 666 vb.
mature 669 vb.
social round 882 n.
seasonable
timely 137 adj.
seasonal
seasonal 141 adj.
seasoned
expert 694 adj.
seasoning
condiment 389 n.
seat
equilibrium 28 n.
station 187 n.
seat 218 n.
buttocks 238 n.
seating
room 183 n.
seat oneself
sit down 311 vb.
seaworthy
seafaring 269 adj.
secateur
sharp edge 256 n.
secede
(*see* **secession**)
secession
dissent 489 n.
schism 978 n.
seclude
imprison 747 vb.
(*see* **seclusion**)
secluded
tranquil 266 adj.
concealed 525 adj.
seclusion
separation 46 n.
farness 199 n.
seclusion 883 n.
second
inferior 35 n., adj.

SEC

instant 116 n.
endorse 488 vb.
patronize 703 vb.
secondary
unimportant
  639 adj.
second-best
inferior 35 adj.
second chance
mercy 905 n.
second childhood
age 131 n.
folly 499 n.
seconder
patron 707 n.
second fiddle
inferior 35 n.
second-hand
imitative 20 adj.
used 673 adj.
second nature
habit 610 n.
second-rate
inferior 35 adj.
mediocre 732 adj.
second sight
foresight 510 n.
psychics 984 n.
second string
inferior 35 n.
second thought(s)
amendment 654 n.
regret 830 n.
caution 858 n.
secrecy
secrecy 525 n.
taciturnity 582 n.
secret
unknown thing
  491 n.
unintelligibility
  517 n.
secret 530 n.
  (*see* secrecy)
secretariat
workshop 687 n.
management 689 n.
secretary
recorder 549 n.
deputy 755 n.
secrete
conceal 525 vb.
  (*see* secretion)
secretive
cautious 858 adj.
secret service
secret service 459 n.

SED

sect
sect 978 n.
sectarian
biased 481 adj.
sectional 708 adj.
sectarist 978 n.
sectarianism
sectarianism 978 n.
sectary
dissentient 489 n.
sectarist 978 n.
section
subdivision 53 n.
classification 77 n.
sectional
sectional 708 adj.
sectarian 978 adj.
sector
subdivision 53 n.
arc 250 n.
battleground 724 n.
secular
secular 110 adj.
lasting 113 adj.
laical 987 adj.
secularize
laicize 987 vb.
secure
tie 45 vb.
safeguard 660 vb.
give security
  767 vb.
securities
estate 777 n.
security
safety 660 n.
security 767 n.
sedate
inexcitable 823 adj.
serious 834 adj.
sedation
moderation 177 n.
sedative
soporific 679 n.
sedilia
church interior
  990 n.
sediment
leavings 41 n.
marsh 347 n.
semiliquidity 354 n.
dirt 649 n.
sedimentary
remaining 41 adj.
sedimentation
condensation
  324 n.

SEE

sedition
sedition 738 n.
seditious
disobedient 738 adj.
seduce
debauch 951 vb.
make wicked
  934 vb.
seducer
libertine 952 n.
seduction
  (*see* seduce)
seductive
pleasurable 826
  adj.
lovable 887 adj.
sedulity
assiduity 678 n.
sedulous
  (*see* sedulity)
see
see, scan 438 vb.
understand 516 vb.
church office 985 n.
seed
reproduce itself
  164 n.
source 156 n.
fertilizer 171 n.
select 605 vb.
seedbed
seedbed 156 n.
garden 370 n.
seeding
sorting 62 n.
seedling
young plant 132 n.
seed-time
spring 128 n.
seedy
weak 163 adj.
sick 651 adj.
dilapidated 655 adj.
beggarly 801 adj.
see fit
will 595 vb.
seeing
vision 438 n.
visibility 443 n.
seek
search 459 vb.
pursue 619 vb.
seeker
inquirer 459 n.
hunter 619 n.
seem
resemble 18 vb.

SEI

appear 445 vb.
seeming
appearance 445 n.
seemliness
good taste 846 n.
seep
infiltrate 297 vb.
exude 298 vb.
seepage
outflow 298 n.
seer
sage 500 n.
oracle 511 n.
visionary 513 n.
sorcerer 983 n.
see red
be violent 176 vb.
get angry 891 vb.
see-saw
fluctuation 317 n.
be irresolute
  601 vb.
seethe
be hot 379 vb.
hiss 406 vb.
seething mass
confusion 61 n.
see through
understand 516 vb.
segment
piece 53 n.
subdivision 53 n.
segregate
sanitate 652 vb.
  (*see* segregation)
segregation
separation 46 n.
seclusion 883 n.
seignorial
proprietary 777 adj.
seisin
possession 773 n.
seismic
revolutionary
  149 adj.
violent 176 adj.
important 638 adj.
seismology
oscillation 317 n.
seize
halt 145 vb.
take 786 vb.
seizure
spasm 318 n.
blood pressure
  651 n.
taking 786 n.

select
set apart 46 vb.
excellent 644 adj.
(see selection)

selection
accumulation 74 n.
discrimination
463 n.
anthology 592 n.
choice 605 n.

selective
discriminating
463 adj.

self
intrinsicality 5 n.
self 80 n.

self-absorption
selfishness 932 n.

self-advertisement
boasting 877 n.

self-assertion
insolence 878 n.

self-conceit
vanity 873 n.

self-condemnation
penitence 939 n.

self-confidence
positiveness 473 n.

self-conscious
affected 850 adj.

self-consideration
selfishness 932 n.

self-contained
complete 54 adj.
independent 744 adj.

self-control
moderation 177 n.
restraint 747 n.
temperance 942 n.

self-defence
defence 713 n.
vindication 927 n.

self-denial
disinterestedness
931 n.
temperance 942 n.

self-determination
independence 744 n.

self-discipline
temperance 942 n.

self-esteem
vanity 873 n.

self-evident
certain 473 adj.
manifest 522 adj.

self-expression
independence 744 n.

self-glory
boasting 877 n.

self-governing
independent 744 adj.

self-government
government 733 n.

self-importance
vanity 873 n.

self-indulgence
selfishness 932 n.
sensualism 944 n.

self-interest
selfishness 932 n.

selfish
greedy 859 adj.
selfish 932 adj.

selfishness
selfishness 932 n.

selfless
disinterested
931 adj.

self-love
vanity 873 n.

self-opinion
opiniatry 602 n.

self-possession
inexcitability 823 n.

self-preservation
selfishness 931 n.

self-reliance
courage 855 n.

self-reproach
regret 830 n.
penitence 939 n.

self-respecting
proud 871 adj.

self-restraint
restraint 747 n.
temperance 942 n.

self-sacrifice
disinterestedness
931 n.

selfsame
identical 13 adj.

self-satisfied
vain 873 adj.

self-seeker
egotist 932 n.

self-styled
misnamed 562 adj.

self-sufficiency
completeness 54 n.
independence 744 n.

self-support
independence 744 n.

self-taught
studious 536 adj.

self-will
obstinacy 602 n.

sell
trickery 542 n.
sell 793 vb.

sell an idea to
convince 485 vb.

seller
seller 793 n.
pedlar 794 n.

seller's market
scarcity 636 n.

selvedge
edging 234 n.

semanteme
word 559 n.

semantics
meaning 514 n.
linguistics 557 n.

semaphore
telecommunication
531 n.
indicator 547 n.
gesticulate 547 vb.

semasiological
semantic 514 adj.

semasiology
meaning 514 n.
etymology 559 n.

semblance
similarity 18 n.
appearance 445 n.

semeiology
hermeneutics 520 n.

semen
fertilizer 171 n.

semester
period 110 n.

semi
fragmentary
53 adj.
incomplete 55 adj.
bisected 92 adj.

semicircular
curved 248 adj.

semidarkness
half-light 419 n.

semiliquidity
semiliquidity 354 n.

semi-literate
smattering 491 adj.

seminal
causal 156 adj.
generative 171 adj.

seminar
class 538 n.
conference 584 n.

seminarist
college student
538 n.
cleric 986 n.

seminary
academy 539 n.

semi-skilled
unskilled 695 adj.

semitransparency
semitransparency
424 n.

semivowel
speech sound 398 n.

sempstress
clothier 228 n.

senate
parliament 692 n.

senator
councillor 692 n.

senatorial
parliamentary
692 adj.

send
send 272 vb.
emit 300 vb.

send after
pursue 619 vb.

send down
eject 300 vb.

sender
transferrer 272 n.

send-off
valediction 296 n.

send out
emit 300 vb.

send packing
dismiss 300 vb.

senescence
age 131 n.

senility
age 131 n.
folly 499 n.

senior
older 131 adj.
old man 133 n.
master 741 n.

seniority
superiority 34 n.
seniority 131 n.

sensation
sense 374 n.
news 529 n.
feeling 818 n.
prodigy 864 n.

sensational
exciting 821 adj.
wonderful 864 adj.

showy 875 adj.
sensationalism
 publicity 528 n.
 exaggeration 546 n.
 excitation 821 n.
sense
 sense 374 n.
 intuit 476 vb.
 intelligence 498 n.
 meaning 514 n.
 feeling 818 n.
senseless
 insensible 375 adj.
 absurd 497 adj.
sense of duty
 duty 917 n.
sense of honour
 probity 929 n.
sense of humour
 wit 839 n.
sense perception
 feeling 818 n.
senses
 sanity 502 n.
sensibility
 sensibility 374 n.
sensible
 material 319 adj.
 sentient 374 adj.
 wise 498 adj.
sensitive
 discriminating
  463 adj.
 sensitive 819 adj.
sensitive plant
 moral sensibility
  819 n.
sensitivity
 sensibility 374 n.
 accuracy 494 n.
 moral sensibility
  819 n.
sensory
 feeling 818 adj.
sensual
 sensuous 376 adj.
 sensual 944 adj.
sensuality
 materiality 319 n.
 pleasure 376 n.
 sensualism 944 n.
sensuous
 sensuous 376 adj.
 feeling 818 adj.
sentence
 period 110 n.
 phrase 563 n.

penalty 963 n.
sententious
 judicial 480 adj.
 aphoristic 496 adj.
sentient
 sentient 374 adj.
 feeling 818 adj.
sentience
 feeling 818 n.
sentiment
 opinion 485 n.
 feeling 818 n.
 love 887 n.
sentimental
 feeling 818 adj.
 impressible 819 adj.
 loving 887 adj.
sentimentality
 moral sensibility
  819 n.
 love 887 n.
sentimental value
 lovableness 887 n.
sentinel, sentry
 surveillance 457 n.
 warner 664 n.
sentry-go
 surveillance 457 n.
separability
 non-coherence
  49 n.
separable
 severable 46 adj.
separate
 separate 46 adj.
 (*see* separation)
separation
 separation 46 n.
 gap 201 n.
 liberation 746 n.
 divorce 896 n.
 sectarianism 978 n.
sepsis
 infection 651 n.
sept
 race 11 n.
 breed 77 n.
septic
 toxic 653 adj.
septicaemia
 infection 651 n.
septic tank
 latrine 649 n.
septum
 partition 231 n.
sepulchral
 funereal 364 adj.

resonant 404 adj.
sepulchre
 tomb 364 n.
sequel
 sequel 67 n.
 posteriority 120 n.
 effect 157 n.
sequence
 sequence 65 n.
 following 284 n.
sequester
 set apart 46 vb.
 seclude 883 vb.
sequestration
 expropriation
  786 n.
 seclusion 883 n.
seraglio
 womankind 373 n.
seraphic
 angelic 968 adj.
 pietistic 979 adj.
sere
 lean 206 adj.
 deteriorated
  655 adj.
serenade
 sing 413 vb.
 wooing 889 n.
serendipity
 chance 159 n.
 discovery 484 n.
serene
 (*see* serenity)
serenity
 inexcitability
  823 n.
 content 828 n.
serf
 slave 742 n.
serfdom
 servitude 745 n.
serial
 continuous 71 adj.
 recurrence 106 n.
 reading matter
  589 n.
serialization
 sequence 65 n.
 continuity 71 n.
serialize
 publish 528 vb.
serial order
 relativeness 9 n.
series
 sequence 65 n.
 series 71 n.

accumulation
 74 n.
continuance 146 n.
serious
 great 32 adj.
 intending 617 adj.
 important 638 adj.
 dangerous 661 adj.
 serious 834 adj.
seriousness
 warm feeling 818 n.
 (*see* serious)
sermon
 lecture 534 n.
 oration 579 n.
sermonize
 be pious 979 vb.
serpent
 reptile 365 n.
 sibilation 406 n.
 noxious animal
  904 n.
serpentine
 snaky 251 adj.
serration
 roughness 259 n.
 notch 260 n.
serried
 assembled 74 adj.
 dense 324 adj.
serum
 blood 335 n.
servant
 servant 742 n.
servant-class
 plebeian 869 adj.
serve
 follow 284 vb.
 function 622 vb.
 be expedient
  642 vb.
 serve 742 vb.
 (*see* service)
server
 thrower 287 n.
 ritualist 988 n.
serve rightly
 retaliate 714 vb.
service
 provision 633 n.
 utility 640 n.
 obedience 739 n.
 service 745 n.
 kind act 897 n.
 church service
  988 n.
 (*see* serve)

serviceable
instrumental
628 adj.
useful 640 adj.
serviceman
soldier 722 n.
servicing
preservation 666 n.
servile
plebeian 869 adj.
(*see* servility)
servility
servility 879 n.
serving man
domestic 742 n.
servitude
submission 721 n.
servitude 745 n.
sesquipedalian
long 203 adj.
diffuse 570 adj.
sessions
law-court 956 n.
legal trial 959 n.
set
decrease 37 vb.
firm-set 45 adj.
series 71 n.
band 74 n.
stabilize 153 vb.
tend 179 vb.
place 187 vb.
hang 217 vb.
form 243 n.
sharpen 256 vb.
be dense 324 vb.
current 350 n.
print 587 vb.
stage-set 594 n.
obstinate 602 adj.
collection 632 n.
party 708 n.
contest 716 n.
hair-dressing 843 n.
decorate 844 vb.
set about
begin 68 vb.
set against
dissuade 613 vb.
make quarrels
709 vb.
set apart
set apart 46 vb.
set aside
abrogate 752 vb.
set at ease
content 828 vb.

set at naught
hold cheap 922 vb.
setback
disappointment
509 n.
adversity 731 n.
set down
record 548 vb.
set fair
be auspicious
730 vb.
set forth
start out 296 vb.
set free
liberate 746 vb.
set going
move 265 vb.
set off
correlate 12 vb.
initiate 68 vb.
beautify 841 vb.
set-off
offset 31 n.
set on
incite 612 vb.
attack 712 vb.
set on edge
give pain 377 vb.
set out
arrange 62 vb.
start out 296 vb.
show 522 vb.
set right
rectify 654 vb.
set sail
voyage 269 vb.
set-square
gauge 465 n.
sett
paving 226 n.
settee
seat 218 n.
set the fashion
motivate 612 vb.
set the pace
motivate 612 vb.
setting
situation 186 n.
circumjacence
230 n.
print 587 n.
settle
place oneself
187 vb.
dwell 192 vb.
descend 309 vb.
pay 804 vb.

settled
ending 69 adj.
vested 153 adj.
located 187 adj.
positive 473 adj.
settle for
bargain 791 vb.
settlement
station 187 n.
habitancy 191 n.
dower 777 n.
transfer 780 n.
payment 804 n.
settler
settler 191 n.
incomer 297 n.
set to music
compose music
413 vb.
set up
stabilize 153 vb.
place 187 vb.
make vertical
215 vb.
set-up
composition 56 n.
structure 331 n.
set watch
invigilate 457 vb.
seventh heaven
happiness 824 n.
sever
disjoin 46 vb.
severable
severable 46 adj.
several
plurality 101 n.
many 104 adj.
severance (*see* sever)
severe
vigorous 174 adj.
violent 176 adj.
severe 735 adj.
paining 827 adj.
pitiless 906 adj.
severity
severity 735 n.
inhumanity 898 n.
(*see* severe)
sew
tie 45 vb.
sewage
leavings 41 n.
swill 649 n.
sewer
receptacle 194 n.
drain 351 n.

fetor 397 n.
cleanser 648 n.
sink 649 n.
insalubrity 653 n.
sewerage
cleansing 648 n.
sex
classification 77 n.
impurity 951 n.
sex appeal
beauty 841 n.
lovableness 887 n.
sex-crazy, sex-mad
lecherous 951 adj.
sexless
impotent 161 adj.
sexologist
doctor 658 n.
sextant
gauge 465 n.
sextet
over five 99 n.
duet 412 n.
sexton
interment 364 n.
church officer
986 n.
sexual
generic 77 adj.
sexual abnormality
abnormality 84 n.
sexual desire
libido 859 n.
sexual intercourse
coition 45 n.
sexy
impure 951 adj.
shabby
dilapidated 655 adj.
beggarly 801 adj.
disreputable
867 adj.
shack
small house 192 n.
shackle
halter 47 n.
fetter 748 n., vb.
shade
differentiate 15 vb.
degree 27 n.
small quantity
33 n.
shade 226 n.
dimness 419 n.
hue 425 n.
conceal 525 vb.
paint 553 vb.

refresh 685 vb.
ghost 970 n.
shade off
shade off 27 vb.
shade, throw into the
be superior 34 vb.
shadiness
improbity 930 n.
shadow
insubstantial thing
4 n.
imitation 20 n.
concomitant 89 n.
follow 284 vb.
dimness 419 n.
screen 421 vb.
colour 425 vb.
hunter 619 n.
close friend 880 n.
shadow-boxing
ideality 513 n.
shadow cabinet
futurity 124 n.
shadowless
undimmed 417 adj.
shadowy
insubstantial 4 adj.
immaterial 320 adj.
shadowy 419 adj.
uncertain 474 adj.
shady
cold 380 adj.
shadowy 419 adj.
shaft
pillar 218 n.
handle 218 n.
excavation 255 n.
tunnel 263 n.
missile weapon
723 n.
shaggy
hairy 259 adj.
shake
mix 43 vb.
derange 63 vb.
weaken 163 vb.
oscillate 317 vb.
be agitated 318 vb.
musical note 410 n.
impress 821 vb.
frighten, quake
854 vb.
shake hands
make peace 719 vb.
greet 887 vb.
shaken
irresolute 601 adj.

shake off
unstick 49 vb.
shake-up
revolution 149 n.
shaky
unsafe 661 adj.
shale
lamina 207 n.
shallow
inconsiderable
33 adj.
foolish 499 adj.
(see shallowness)
shallowness
shallowness 212 n.
sciolism 491 n.
shallows
shallowness 212 n.
sham
sham 542 n.
spurious 542 adj.
shamanism
sorcery 983 n.
shamble
move slowly
278 vb.
shambles
confusion 61 n.
slaughter 362 n.
slaughter-house
362 n.
shame
slur 867 n.
shame 867 vb.
humiliation 872 n.
shameful
discreditable
867 adj.
heinous 934 adj.
shameless
thick-skinned
820 adj.
insolent 878 adj.
dishonest 930 adj.
unchaste 951 adj.
shamiana
canopy 226 n.
shammer
impostor 545 n.
shampoo
friction 333 n.
ablution 648 n.
shamrock
grass 366 n.
heraldry 547 n.
shandy
liquor 301 n.

shanghai
take away 786 vb.
shank
stand 218 n.
leg 267 n.
shanty
small house 192 n.
shape
sort 77 n.
form 243 n.
efform 243 vb.
structure 331 n.
feature 445 n.
shapeless
amorphous 244 adj.
shapely
shapely 841 adj.
share
part 53 n.
sharp edge 256 n.
participation
775 n.
share out
apportion 783 vb.
sharer
participator 775 n.
shares
apportionment
783 n.
sharing
equal 28 adj.
shark
lender 784 n.
taker 786 n.
sharp
sharp 256 adj.
pungent 388 adj.
musical note 410 n.
discordant 411 adj.
intelligent 498 adj.
cunning 698 adj.
painful 827 adj.
irascible 892 adj.
sharpen
sharpen 256 vb.
sharpener
sharpener 256 n.
sharper
trickster 545 n.
sharp-eyed
attentive 455 adj.
vigilant 457 adj.
sharpness
sourness 393 n.
(see sharp)
sharp point
sharp point 256 n.

sharp practice
trickery 542 n.
sharpshooter
soldier 722 n.
sharp-tempered
irascible 892 adj.
shatter
break 46 vb.
demolish 165 vb.
be brittle 330 vb.
shattering
notable 638 adj.
shatter-proof
unyielding 162 adj.
shave
be near 200 vb.
shorten 204 vb.
smooth 258 vb.
hair-dressing 843 n.
shaved, shaven
hairless 229 adj.
shaving
small thing 33 n.
lamina 207 n.
shavings
piece 53 n.
rubbish 641 n.
shawl
shawl 228 n.
she
female 373 n., adj.
sheaf
bunch 74 n.
shear
shorten 204 vb.
groom 369 vb.
fleece 786 vb.
shears
sharp edge 256 n.
farm tool 370 n.
sheath
case 194 n.
covering 226 n.
sheathe
replace 187 vb.
cover 226 vb.
insert 303 vb.
shed
decrease 37 vb.
small house 192 n.
doff 229 vb.
emit 300 vb.
let fall 311 vb.
disaccustom 611 vb.
relinquish 621 vb.
sheep
imitator 20 n.

laity 987 n.
sheepfold
cattle pen 369 n.
sheepish
weak 163 adj.
sheep's eyes
desire 859 n.
wooing 889 n.
sheer
simple 44 adj.
vertical 215 adj.
transparent 422 adj.
sheer off
recede 290 vb.
sheet
lamina 207 n.
coverlet 226 n.
letterpress 587 n.
paper 631 n.
sheet anchor
safeguard 662 n.
sheets
tackling 47 n.
sheikh
potentate 741 n.
shelf
shelf 218 n.
storage 632 n.
shell
mould 23 n.
emptiness 190 n.
exterior 223 n.
covering, skin 226 n.
uncover 229 vb.
structure 331 n.
fire at 712 vb.
missile weapon 723 n.
seclusion 883 n.
shellac
resin 357 n.
shelter
stable 192 n.
dwell 192 vb.
hiding-place 527 n.
shelter 662 n.
shelve
put off 136 vb.
be oblique 220 vb.
avoid 620 vb.
shepherd
herdsman 369 n.
protector 660 n.
direct 689 vb.
pastor 986 n.

sherbet
soft drink 301 n.
sheriff
law officer 955 n.
shibboleth
identification 457 n.
shield
screen 421 n., vb.
safeguard 660 vb.
armour 713 n.
defend 713 vb.
shift
period 110 n.
change 143 n.
vary 152 vb.
displacement 188 n.
transpose 272 vb.
trickery 542 n.
pretext 614 n.
labour 682 n.
stratagem 698 n.
shifty
cunning 698 adj.
shillelagh
club 723 n.
shilly-shally
be irresolute 601 vb.
shimmer
flash 417 n.
shin
leg 267 n.
shindy
fight 716 n.
shine
shine 417 vb.
shine on
patronize 703 vb.
be auspicious 730 vb.
shingle
laminate 207 vb.
roof 226 n.
shore 344 n.
building material 631 n.
hair-dressing 843 n.
shingles
skin disease 651 n.
shining light
sage 500 n.
shiny
luminous 417 adj.
clean 648 adj.
ship
carry 273 vb.
ship 275 n.

shipment
transport 272 n.
thing transferred 272 n.
shipper
carrier 273 n.
shipping
shipping 275 n.
shipshape
orderly 60 adj.
well-made 694 adj.
shipwreck
ruin 165 n.
shipyard
workshop 687 n.
shire
district 184 n.
shirk
avoid 620 vb.
fail in duty 918 vb.
shirker
coward 856 n.
shirt
bodywear 228 n.
shirty
angry 891 adj.
shiver
break 46 vb.
be brittle 330 vb.
be cold 380 vb.
quake 854 vb.
shivers
nervousness 854 n.
shoal
group 74 n.
shallow 212 adj.
shock
bunch 74 n.
collision 279 n.
agitation 318 n.
inexpectation 508 n.
suffering 825 n.
displease 827 vb.
fear 854 n.
incur blame 927 vb.
shockable
prudish 950 adj.
shock-absorber
moderator 177 n.
shocked
disapproving 924 adj.
shocker
novel 590 n.
monster 938 n.
shock-headed
hairy 259 adj.

shocking
not nice 645 adj.
distressing 827 adj.
wonderful 864 adj.
discreditable 867 adj.
heinous 934 adj.
shock-proof
tough 329 adj.
shock tactics
attack 712 n.
shock troops
attacker 712 n.
shoddy
bad 645 adj.
bad taste 847 n.
shoe
footwear 228 n.
shoo off
dismiss 300 vb.
shoot
young plant 132 n.
kick 279 vb.
shoot 287 vb.
pass 305 vb.
kill 362 vb.
tree 366 n.
fire at 712 vb.
shooter
shooter 287 n.
shooting star
meteor 321 n.
shop
topic 452 n.
workshop 687 n.
purchase 392 vb.
shop 796 n.
shop-assistant
seller 793 n.
shopkeeper
tradesman 794 n.
shopper
purchaser 792 n.
shopping
buying 792 adj.
shopping centre
emporium 796 n.
shopping list
requirement 627 n.
shop-soiled
imperfect 647 adj.
blemished 845 adj.
shop-steward
leader 690 n.
shop-window
exhibit 522 n.
mart 796 n.

shore
 shore 344 n.
shore up
 support 218 vb.
shorn
 short 204 adj.
short
 brief 114 adj.
 dwarfish 196 adj.
 short 204 adj.
 deficient 307 adj.
 brittle 330 adj.
 concise 569 adj.
 taciturn 582 adj.
 scarce 636 adj.
 ungracious 885 adj.
shortage
 deficit 55 n.
 shortcoming 307 n.
short circuit
 escape 667 n.
 hitch 702 n.
shortcoming
 shortcoming 307 n.
 insufficiency 636 n.
 (*see* shortage)
short commons
 insufficiency 636 n.
 fasting 946 n.
short cut
 short distance
  200 n.
shorten
 shorten 204 vb.
shortfall
 deficit 55 n.
shorthand
 writing 586 n.
short-lived
 ephemeral 114 adj.
shorts
 trousers 228 n.
short shrift
 pitilessness 906 n.
short-sighted
 dim-sighted 440
  adj.
short supply
 scarcity 636 n.
short-tempered
 irascible 892 adj.
short-term
 brief 114 adj.
shot
 shooter 287 n.
 bang 402 n.
 iridescent 437 adj.

 photography 551 n.
 ammunition 723 n.
shotgun
 fire-arm 723 n.
shot in the dark
 empiricism 461 n.
 conjecture 512 n.
shoulder
 supporter 218 n.
 carry 273 vb.
 impel 279 vb.
shout
 vociferate 408 vb.
 be rude 885 vb.
shout down
 affirm 532 vb.
 make mute 578 vb.
shove
 move 265 vb.
 impulse 279 n.
shovel
 ladle 194 n.
 shovel 274 n.
show
 be visible 443 vb.
 spectacle 445 n.
 appear 445 vb.
 demonstrate
  478 vb.
 exhibit 522 n.
 show 522 vb.
 deception 542 n.
 stage play 594 n.
 pageant 875 n.
show business
 drama 594 n.
showcase
 exhibit 522 n.
showdown
 disclosure 526 n.
shower
 descend 309 vb.
 let fall 311 vb.
 rain 350 n., vb.
 ablution 648 n.
showery
 rainy 350 adj.
show fight
 defy 711 vb.
showiness
 ostentation 875 n.
showman
 exhibitor 522 n.
 stage-manager
  594 n.
showmanship
 publicity 528 n.

show of hands
 vote 605 n.
show off
 be vain 873 vb.
 be ostentatious
  875 vb.
show, on
 undisguised 522 adj.
show one's hand
 divulge 526 vb.
show piece
 exhibit 522 n.
showplace
 exhibit 522 n.
showroom
 exhibit 522 n.
show signs
 indicate 547 vb.
show up
 disclose 526 vb.
 shame 867 vb.
showy
 vulgar 847 adj.
 showy 875 adj.
shrapnel
 missile weapon
  723 n.
shred
 small thing 33 n.
 piece 53 n.
shredded
 fragmentary
  53 adj.
shrew
 quarreller 709 n.
 shrew 892 n.
shrewd
 intelligent 498 adj.
 cunning 698 adj.
shrewd idea
 conjecture 512 n.
shrewish
 irascible 892 adj.
shriek
 stridor 407 n.
 cry 408 vb.
shrift
 forgiveness 909 n.
 penance 941 n.
 church ministry
  985 n.
shrill
 loud 400 adj.
 shrill 407 vb.
shrimp
 dwarf 196 n.
 animalcule 196 n.

shrine
 temple 990 n.
shrink
 decrease 37 vb.
 become small
  198 vb.
 recoil 280 vb.
 avoid 620 vb.
shrinkage
 decrement 42 n.
shrinking
 modest 874 adj.
shrive
 perform ritual
  988 vb.
shrivel
 deteriorate 655 vb.
shrivelled
 lean 206 adj.
shroud
 tackling 47 n.
 grave clothes 364 n.
 conceal 525 vb.
shrub
 tree 366 n.
shrubbery
 wood 366 n.
shrug
 gesture 547 n.
 be indifferent
  860 vb.
shrunk
 contracted 198 adj.
shuck
 skin 226 n.
 uncover 229 vb.
shudder
 agitation 318 n.
 quake 854 vb.
shuffle
 mix 43 vb.
 jumble 63 vb.
 interchange 151 n.,
  vb.
 vary 151 vb.
 gait 265 n.
 walk 267 vb.
 move slowly
  278 vb.
 tergiversate 603 vb.
shun
 avoid 620 vb.
 dislike 861 vb.
shunt
 deflect 282 vb.
shut
 close 264 vb.

649

shut down
  cease 145 vb.
shut in
  surround 230 vb.
  imprison 747 vb.
shutter
  covering, shade
    226 n.
shuttle
  weaving 222 n.
  fluctuation 317 n.
shuttlecock
  waverer 601 n.
shut up
  cease 145 vb.
  make mute 578 vb.
shy
  unwilling 598 adj.
  avoid 620 vb.
  lapidate 712 vb.
  modest 874 adj.
  unsociable 883 adj.
shyster
  trickster 545 n.
  lawyer 958 n.
sibilation
  sibilation 406 n.
sick
  vomiting 300 adj.
  sick 651 adj.
  suffering 825 adj.
sick-bed
  illness 651 n.
  hospital 658 n.
sicken
  be ill 651 vb.
  displease 827 vb.
  cause dislike 861 vb.
sickener
  superfluity 637 n.
  bane 659 n.
sickening
  unsavoury 391 n.
  disliked 861 adj.
sickle
  sharp edge 256 n.
  farm tool 370 n.
sick list
  sick person 651 n.
sickly
  unhealthy 651 adj.
sickness
  illness 651 n.
sick of
  sated 863 adj.
sick-room
  hospital 658 n.

side
  race 11 n.
  situation 186 n.
  laterality 239 n.
  party 708 n.
  pride 871 n.
  ostentation 875 n.
side against
  oppose 704 vb.
side-arms
  side-arms 723 n.
sideboard
  cabinet 194 n.
side-dish
  dish 301 n.
sideline
  laterality 239 n.
side-pressure
  obliquity 220 n.
sidereal
  celestial 321 adj.
sideslip
  deviation 282 n.
side-splitting
  funny 849 adj.
sidestep
  laterality 239 n.
  deviation 282 vb.
  avoidance 620 n.
sidetrack
  deflect 282 vb.
  avoid 620 vb.
sidewalk
  road 624 n.
  path 624 n.
side with
  patronize 703 vb.
sidle
  be oblique 220 vb.
  deviate 282 vb.
sienna
  brown paint 430 n.
sierra
  high land 209 n.
sieve
  sorting 62 n.
  porosity 263 n.
  cleaning utensil
    648 n.
  (*see* sift)
sift
  exclude 57 vb.
  class 62 vb.
  discriminate
    463 vb.
  select 605 vb.
  purify 648 vb.

sigh
  respiration 352 n.
  breathe 352 vb.
  sound faint 401 vb.
  be dejected 834 vb.
  lamentation 836 n.
sigh for
  desire 859 vb.
sight
  aim 281 vb.
  vision 438 n.
  spectacle 445 n.
  eyesore 842 n.
sightless
  blind 439 adj.
sights
  direction 281 n.
sight-seeing
  curiosity 453 n.
sightseer
  spectator 441 n.
  inquisitor 453 n.
sign
  evidence 466 n.
  endorse 488 vb.
  omen 511 n.
  indication 547 n.
  badge, label 547 n.
  gesture 547 n.
  letter 588 n.
  contract 765 vb.
  prodigy 864 n.
signal
  communicate
    524 vb.
  message 529 n.
  signal 547 n., vb.
  notable 638 adj.
signalize
  indicate 547 vb.
  celebrate 876 vb.
signalling
  telecommunication
    531 n.
signatory
  signatory 765 n.
signature
  assent 488 vb.
  identification
    547 n.
sign-board
  label 547 n.
significance
  meaning 514 n.
  importance 638 n.
significant
  evidential 466 adj.

signification
  connotation 514 n.
  indication 547 n.
signify
  mean 514 vb.
sign language
  mimicry 20 n.
  gesture 547 n.
sign off
  resign 753 vb.
sign on
  join a party
    708 vb.
signpost
  signpost 547 n.
silence
  silence 399 n., vb.
  confute 479 vb.
  taciturnity 582 n.
silencer
  silencer 401 n.
  non-resonance
    405 n.
silent
  stealthy 525 adj.
  (*see* silence)
silhouette
  outline 233 n., vb.
  feature 445 n.
  picture 553 n.
silk
  textile 222 n.
  smoothness 258 n.
silky
  smooth 258 adj.
  textural 331 adj.
sill
  shelf 218 n.
silly
  absurd 497 adj.
  foolish 499 adj.
silly season
  absurdity 497 n.
silly talk
  silly talk 315 n.
silo
  preserver 666 n.
silt
  leavings 41 n.
  fertilizer 171 n.
  soil 344 n.
silty
  semiliquid 354 adj.
silver
  coat 266 vb.
  money, bullion
    797 n.

silvery
white 427 adj.
similar
(see similarity)
similarity
similarity 18 n.
simile
analogue 18 n.
comparison 462 n.
metaphor 519 n.
ornament 574 n.
simmer
cook 301 vb.
simony
improbity 930 n.
simper
smile 835 n.
be affected 850 vb.
simple
simple 44 adj.
foolish 499 adj.
intelligible 516 adj.
plain 573 adj.
elegant 575 adj.
medicine 658 n.
artless 699 adj.
easy 701 adj.
plebeian 869 adj.
simplemindedness
artlessness 699 n.
simpleton
ignoramus 493 n.
ninny 501 n.
simplicity
(see simple)
simplification
intelligibility
516 n.
facility 701 n.
simplify
decompose 51 vb.
(see simplification)
simulacrum
sham 542 n.
(see image)
simulation
assimilation 18 n.
mimicry 20 n.
duplicity 541 n.
simulator
imitator 20 n.
simultaneity
synchronism 123 n.
(see simultaneous)
simultaneous
accompanying
89 adj.

instantaneous
116 adj.
sin
wickedness 934 n.
be wicked 934 vb.
impiety 980 n.
sincere
(see sincerity)
sincerity
veracity 540 n.
artlessness 699 n.
probity 929 n.
sinciput
head 213 n.
sinecure
inaction 677 n.
easy thing 701 n.
sinecurist
idler 679 n.
sine die
never 109 adv.
sine qua non
concomitant 89 n.
requirement 627 n.
chief thing 638 n.
conditions 766 n.
sinews
vitality 162 n.
sinewy
stalwart 162 adj.
sinful
wicked 934 adj.
impious 980 adj.
sing
resound 404 vb.
sing 413 vb.
singable
melodious 410 adj.
singe
burn 381 vb.
embrown 430 vb.
singer
vocalist 413 n.
single
simple 44 adj.
one 88 adj.
unwedded 895 adj.
single combat
duel 716 n.
single file
procession 71 n.
single-handed
alone 88 adj.
singlemindedness
attention 455 n.
perseverance
600 n.

singleness
unity 88 n.
(see single)
single out
set apart 46 vb.
singlet
bodywear 228 n.
singleton
unit 88 n.
sing small
be humble
872 vb.
sing-song
music 412 n.
singular
(see singularity)
singularity
irrelation 10 n.
speciality 80 n.
unity 88 n.
sinister
sinistrality 242 n.
presageful 511 adj.
adverse 731 adj.
frightening
854 adj.
sink
decrease 37 vb.
suppress 165 vb.
receptacle 194 n.
founder 313 vb.
drain 351 n.
sink 649 n.
fail 728 vb.
sinkage
depth 211 n.
gravity 322 n.
sinker
diver 313 n.
gravity 322 n.
sink in
infiltrate 297 vb.
cause thought
449 vb.
sinless
innocent 935 adj.
sinner
offender 904 n.
bad man 938 n.
impious person
980 n.
sin-offering
oblation 981 n.
sinuosity
convolution 251 n.
sinus
cavity 255 n.

sinusitis
respiratory disease
651 n.
sip
mouthful 301 n.
drink 301 vb.
siphon
transferrer 272 n.
transpose 272 vb.
conduit 351 n.
sir
male 372 n.
title 870 n.
sire
generate 164 vb.
parent 169 n.
master 741 n.
sired
born 360 adj.
siren
timekeeper 117 n.
megaphone 400 n.
motivator 612 n.
danger signal
665 n.
sissy
weakling 163 n.
coward 856 n.
sister
kinsman 11 n.
nurse 658 n.
nun 986 n.
sisterhood
family 11 n.
community 708 n.
sit
sit down 311 vb.
be inactive 679 vb.
sit down
sit down 311 vb.
site
situation 186 n.
place 187 vb.
sit loose to
be indifferent
860 vb.
sit on
suppress 165 vb.
sit on the fence
be uncertain
474 vb.
sit pretty
be content 828 vb.
sitter
living model 23 n.
testee 461 n.
easy thing 701 n.

sit tight
be quiescent 266 vb.
sitting-room
chamber 194 n.
situation
circumstance 8 n.
situation 186 n.
station 187 n.
job 622 n.
predicament 700 n.
sit up
be attentive 455 vb.
sixth sense
intuition 476 n.
size
make uniform
16 vb.
degree 27 n.
adhesive 47 n.
size 195 n.
viscidity 354 n.
size of it
similarity 18 n.
size up
estimate 480 vb.
sizzle
hiss 406 vb.
skate
go smoothly
258 vb.
sled 274 n.
skedaddle
decamp 296 vb.
skein
bunch 74 n.
skeletal
lean 206 adj.
structural 331 adj.
skeleton
thinness 206 n.
frame 218 n.
outline 233 n.
structure 331 n.
compendium 592 n.
sketch
incompleteness 55 n.
outline 233 n., vb.
picture 553 n.
description 590 n.
compendium 592 n.
sketchy
incomplete 55 adj.
skewer
sharp point 256 n.
perforator 263 n.
skewness
obliquity 220 n.

ski
go smoothly
258 vb.
sled 274 n.
skid
go smoothly 258 vb.
deviate 282 vb.
fetter 748 n.
skiddy
smooth 258 adj.
skier
pedestrian 268 n.
skiff
boat 275 n.
skilful
skilful 694 adj.
skill
skill 694 n.
skilled worker
expert 696 n.
skim
be near 200 vb.
be contiguous
202 vb.
move fast 277 vb.
purify 648 vb.
skimmings
leavings 41 n.
skimp
neglect 458 vb.
be parsimonious
816 vb.
skimpy
short 204 adj.
skin
rend 46 vb.
layer 207 n.
exteriority 223 n.
skin 226 n.
uncover 229 vb.
fleece 786 vb.
skin and bone
thinness 206 n.
skin-deep
inconsiderable
33 adj.
shallow 212 adj.
exterior 223 adj.
skin disease
skin disease 651 n.
skinflint
niggard 816 n.
skinny
lean 206 adj.
skip
leap 312 n., vb.
escape 667 vb.

not complete
726 vb.
skipper
mariner 270 n.
skirl
stridor 407 n.
skirmish
fight 716 n., vb.
skirmisher
soldier 722 n.
skirt
be near 200 vb.
base 214 n.
skirt 228 n.
edge 234 n.
pass 305 vb.
circuit 626 vb.
skirting
edging 234 n.
skit
satire 851 n.
skittish
capricious 604 adj.
lively 819 adj.
skittles
ball game 837 n.
skive
cut 46 vb.
skivvy
domestic 742 n.
skulduggery
improbity 930 n.
skulk
be stealthy 525 vb.
skulker
hider 527 n.
skull
head 213 n.
skull-cap
headgear 228 n.
skunk
vermin 365 n.
fetor 397 n.
cad 938 n.
sky
summit 213 n.
elevate 310 vb.
heavens 321 n.
skylarker
reveller 837 n.
skylight
window 263 n.
sky-line
distance 199 n.
edge 234 n.
sky-rocket
rocket 276 n.

skyscraper
high structure
209 n.
slab
lamina 207 n.
slabby
marshy 347 adj.
slack
non-adhesive 49 adj.
weak 163 adj.
be loth 598 vb.
lazy 679 adj.
lax 734 adj.
slacker
avoider 620 n.
slacks
trousers 228 n.
slack, take up the
recoup 31 vb.
slag
ash 381 n.
rubbish 641 n.
slake
sate 863 vb.
slam
close 264 vb.
strike 279 vb.
bang 402 n., vb.
slander
calumny 926 n.
false charge 928 n.
slanderer
defamer 926 n.
slang
slang 560 n.
cuss 899 vb.
slanging match
scurrility 899 n.
slangy
dialectical 560 adj.
slant
obliquity 220 n.
view 438 n.
slap
spank 963 vb.
slapdash
negligent 458 adj.
rash 857 adj.
slap-happy
rash 857 adj.
slap in the face
refusal 760 n.
slapstick
ridiculousness
849 n.
slash
cut, rend 46 vb.

notch 260 vb.
dispraise 924 vb.
slat
strip 208 n.
slate
stationery 586 n.
dispraise 924 vb.
slattern
dirty person 649 n.
slaughter
slaughter 362 n.,
vb.
slaughter-house
slaughter-house
362 n.
slave
work 682 vb.
slave 742 n.
prisoner 750 n.
slave-born
plebeian 869 adj.
slave camp
prison camp 748 n.
slave-driver
tyrant 735 n.
slaver
merchant ship
275 n.
exude 298 vb.
excrement 302 n.
slave-raider
thief 789 n.
slavery
servitude 745 n.
slave to, a
subject 745 adj.
slavey
domestic 742 n.
slavish
imitative 20 adj.
servile 879 adj.
slay
kill 362 vb.
slayer
killer 362 n.
sled
sled 274 n.
sledge
sled 274 n.
hammer 279 n.
sleek
smooth 258 adj.
personable 841 adj.
sleep
be quiescent 266 vb.
be inattentive
456 vb.

sleep 679 n., vb.
sleeper
railroad 624 n.
idler 679 n.
sleepiness
(*see* **sleepy**)
sleeping
latent 523 n.
inactive 679 adj.
sleeping partner
nonentity 639 n.
idler 679 n.
sleepless
active 678 adj.
sleep off
be refreshed
685 vb.
be sober 948 vb.
sleep on it
meditate 449 vb.
sleep-walking
sleep 679 n.
sleep with
unite with 45 vb.
sleepy
sleepy 679 adj.
fatigued 684 adj.
sleet
ice 380 n.
sleety
cold 380 adj.
sleeve
sleeve 228 n.
sleigh
sled 274 n.
sleight
sleight 542 n.
skill 694 n.
slender
small 33 adj.
narrow 206 adj.
shapely 841 adj.
sleuth
detective 459 n.
slew
rotate 315 vb.
slice
cut 46 vb.
piece 53 n.
lamina 207 n.
deflect 282 vb.
slick
skilful 694 adj.
slicker
trickster 545 n.
slide
fastening 47 n.

obliquity 220 n.
go smoothly
258 vb.
deviate 282 vb.
optical device 442 n.
photography 551 n.
slide-rule
gauge 465 n.
slight
inconsiderable
33 adj.
disregard 458 vb.
underestimate
483 vb.
trivial 639 adj.
indignity 921 n.
detract 926 vb.
slim
small 33 adj.
narrow 206 adj.
shapely 841 adj.
slime
marsh 347 n.
sling
surgical dressing
658 n.
lapidate 712 vb.
missile weapon
723 n.
slinger
thrower 287 n.
soldiery 722 n.
slink
be stealthy 525 vb.
slinky
narrow 206 adj.
slip
come unstuck 49 vb.
young plant 132 n.
bodywear 228 n.
go smoothly
258 vb.
descent 309 n.
viscidity 354 n.
mistake 495 n.
slip into, slip on
wear 228 vb.
slipper
footwear 228 n.
slipperiness
unreliability
474 n.
(*see* **slippery**)
slippery
non-adhesive
49 adj.
smooth 258 adj.

unsafe 661 adj.
dishonest 930 adj.
slips
workshop 687 n.
slipshod
orderless 61 adj.
lax 734 adj.
slip-stream
wind 352 n.
slipway
smoothness 258 n.
road 624 n.
slit
rend 46 vb.
gap 201 n.
slither
move 265 vb.
sliver
piece 53 n.
slobber
exude 298 vb.
excrete 302 vb.
slog
propel 287 vb.
persevere 600 vb.
exert oneself
682 vb.
slogan
maxim 496 n.
call 547 n.
slogger
busy person 678 n.
sloop
warship 722 n.
slop
flow out 298 vb.
let fall 311 vb.
slope
high land 209 n.
obliquity 220 n.
slopping
full 54 adj.
sloppy
orderless 61 adj.
feeble 572 adj.
slops
clothing 228 n.
swill 649 n.
slopshop
clothier 228 n.
slot
receptacle 194 n.
groove 262 vb.
orifice 263 n.
trace 548 n.
sloth
sluggishness 679 n.

slot-machine
treasury 799 n.
slouch
move slowly
278 vb.
sloucher
slowcoach 278 n.
slough
leavings 41 n.
excrement 302 n.
marsh 347 n.
sloven
dirty person 649 n.
slovenly
orderless 61 adj.
dirty 649 adj.
clumsy 695 adj.
slow
anachronistic
118 adj.
late 136 adj.
slow 278 adj.
unintelligent
499 adj.
leisurely 681 adj.
tedious 838 adj.
slowcoach
slowcoach 278 n.
idler 679 n.
slow down
decelerate 278 vb.
slow-motion
slowness 278 n.
slow 278 adj.
sludge
leavings 41 n.
slug
slowcoach 278 n.
strike 279 vb.
ammunition 723 n.
sluggard
idler 679 n.
sluggish
inert 175 adj.
apathetic 820 adj.
sluice
irrigator 341 n.
drench 341 vb.
conduit 351 n.
clean 648 vb.
slum
housing 192 n.
insalubrity 653 n.
poverty 801 n.
eyesore 842 n.
slumber
sleep 679 n., vb.

slum-dweller
poor man 801 n.
slummer
philanthropist
901 n.
slummy
dilapidated 655 adj.
unclean 649 adj.
slump
decrease 37 n.
deterioration 655 n.
adversity 731 n.
slur
slur 867 n.
calumny 926 n.
slush
marsh 347 n.
slut
loose woman
952 n.
sluttish
dirty 649 adj.
sly
stealthy 525 adj.
cunning 698 adj.
slyboots
slyboots 698 n.
smack
sailing ship 275 n.
taste 386 n.
spank 963 vb.
smack of
resemble 18 vb.
small
small 33 adj.
weak 163 adj.
little 196 adj.
small arms
fire-arm 723 n.
small beer
nonentity 639 n.
trifle 639 n.
smaller
contracted 198 adj.
small fry
nonentity 639 n.
smallholder
husbandman 370 n.
small hours
morning 128 n.
lateness 136 n.
smallness
(*see* small)
small talk
chatter 581 n.
smarm
flatter 925 vb.

smart
speedy 277 adj.
pang 377 n.
intelligent 498 adj.
suffer 825 vb.
witty 839 adj.
fashionable
848 adj.
smart aleck
wiseacre 500 n.
smarten
decorate 844 vb.
smarting
painful 377 adj.
resentful 891 adj.
smart under
feel 818 vb.
smash
break 46 vb.
collision 279 n.
strike 279 vb.
propel 287 vb.
smash hit
exceller 644 n.
smashing
topping 644 adj.
smatterer
sciolist 493 n.
smattering
sciolism 491 n.
smattering 491 adj.
smear
overlay 226 vb.
bedim 419 vb.
make unclean
649 vb.
calumny 926 n.
smear-word
calumny 926 n.
smell
odour 394 n.
stink 397 vb.
trace 548 n.
smelling salts
tonic 658 n.
smelly
fetid 397 adj.
smelt
heat 381 vb.
smile
laughter 835 n.
smile on
patronize 703 vb.
be auspicious
730 vb.
smiles
cheerfulness 833 n.

smirch
defame 926 vb.
smirk
smile 835 vb.
be affected 850 vb.
smite
strike 279 vb.
smithereens
small thing 33 n.
smithy
workshop 687 n.
smitten
enamoured 887 adj.
smock
bodywear 228 n.
smocking
needlework 844 n.
smog
cloud 355 n.
smoke
emit 300 vb.
vaporize 338 vb.
dry 342 vb.
season, smoke
388 vb.
be hot 397 vb.
make opaque
423 vb.
preserve 666 vb.
smoke out
eject 300 vb.
smoker
tobacco 388 n.
smoke-screen
screen 421 n.
opacity 423 n.
concealment 525 n.
smoke-signal
telecommunication
531 n.
smoke-stack
chimney 263 n.
smoky
opaque 423 adj.
dirty 649 adj.
smooth
uniform 16 adj.
non-adhesive
49 adj.
flatten 216 vb.
hairless 229 adj.
smooth 258 adj.,
vb.
rub 333 vb.
flattering 925 adj.
smooth citizen
slyboots 698 n.

smoothness
lubrication 334 n.
cunning 698 n.
(*see* smooth)
smooth-running
wieldy 701 adj.
smother
cover 226 vb.
murder 362 vb.
conceal 525 vb.
smoulder
be hot 379 vb.
lurk 523 vb.
be inactive 679 vb.
resent 891 vb.
smouldering
sullen 893 adj.
smudge
blacken 428 vb.
blemish 845 n., vb.
smuggle
steal 788 vb.
smuggler
thief 789 n.
smugness
content 828 n.
smut
ash 381 n.
dirt 649 n.
impurity 951 n.
snack
meal 301 n.
snack-bar
café 192 n.
snaffle
take 786 vb.
steal 788 vb.
snag
hitch 702 n.
snail
slowcoach 278 n.
snake
reptile 365 n.
bane 659 n.
slyboots 698 n.
noxious animal
902 n.
snake in the grass
latency 523 n.
trouble-maker
663 n.
snaky
snaky 251 adj.
cunning 698 adj.
snap
break 46 vb.
discontinue 72 vb.

be brittle 330 vb.
crackle 402 vb.
photography 551 n.
spontaneous
609 adj.
sullenness 893 n.
snap one's fingers
defy 711 vb.
snappish
irascible 982 adj.
snappy
speedy 277 adj.
personable 841 adj.
snapshot
photography 551 n.
snare
trap 542 n.
snarl
distortion 246 n.
ululate 409 vb.
sullenness 893 n.
snatch
take 786 vb.
snatcher
taker 786 n.
sneak
be stealthy 525 vb.
coward 856 n.
sneaking
servile 879 adj.
sneer
contempt 922 n.
detraction 926 n.
sneeze
breathe 352 vb.
sibilation 406 n.
snick
cut 46 vb.
sniff
breathe 352 vb.
smell 394 vb.
sniff at
despise 922 vb.
sniffy
puffing 352 adj.
despising 922 adj.
snifter
potion 301 n.
snigger
laughter 835 n.
snip
cut 46 vb.
piece 53 n.
snipe
fire at 712 vb.
sniper
shooter 287 n.

snitch
informer 524 n.
snivel
weep 836 vb.
snob
proud man 871 n.
snobbery
etiquette 848 n.
pride 871 n.
snobbish
affected 850 adj.
despising 922 adj.
snood
headgear 228 n.
snook
sauciness 878 n.
snoop
scan 438 vb.
spectator 441 n.
be curious 453 vb.
detective 459 n.
be stealthy 525 vb.
snoopy
inquisitive 453 adj.
snooty
insolent 878 adj.
snooze
sleep 679 n., vb.
snore
rasp 407 vb.
snort
breathe 352 vb.
rasp 407 vb.
ululate 409 vb.
contempt 922 n.
snorter
potion 301 n.
snout
projection 254 n.
snow
snow 380 n.
snowball
grow 36 vb.
accumulation 74 n.
snow 380 n.
snowflake
snow 380 n.
snowman
brief span 114 n.
snow-shoe
sled 274 n.
snowy
cold 380 adj.
white 427 adj.
snub
unsharpened
257 adj.

humiliate 872 vb.
be rude 885 vb.
reprimand 924 n.
snuff
suppress 165 vb.
tobacco 388 n.
smell 394 vb.
snuff-box
tobacco 388 n.
snuffle
breathe 352 vb.
snug
adjusted 24 adj.
comfortable
376 adj.
reposeful 683 adj.
snuggle
caress 889 vb.
soak
fill 54 vb.
drench 341 vb.
overcharge 811 vb.
drunkard 949 n.
soak into, soak
through
infiltrate 297 vb.
soak up
absorb 299 vb.
so-and-so
no name 562 n.
soap
cleanser 648 n.
flatter 925 vb.
soap-box
rostrum 539 n.
soapy
flattering 925 adj.
soar
be high 209 vb.
fly 271 vb.
ascend 308 vb.
sob
rasp 407 vb.
cry 408 vb.
lamentation
836 vb.
sober
moderate 177 adj.
soft-hued 425 adj.
sane 502 adj.
plain 573 adj.
serious 834 adj.
deject 834 vb.
cautious 858 adj.
sober 948 adj.
sobered
repentant 939 adj.

sobriety
moderation 177 n.
sanity 502 n.
seriousness 834 n.
sobriety 948 n.
sob-story
lament 836 n.
sobstuff
lament 836 n.
so-called
spurious 542 adj.
misnamed 562 adj.
sociability
sociability 882 n.
sociable
amiable 884 adj.
social
national 371 adj.
corporate 708 adj.
social gathering
882 n.
social circle
sociality 882 n.
social class
community 708 n.
social climber
social person
882 n.
social conscience
philanthropy
901 n.
social engineering
sociology 901 n.
social group
social group 371 n.
socialism
government 733 n.
joint possession
775 n.
sociology 901 n.
socialistic
sharing 775 adj.
socialite
beau monde 848 n.
social person 882 n.
sociality
sociality 882 n.
social round
social round 882 n.
social science
sociology 901 n.
social service
sociology 901 n.
social worker
reformer 654 n.
societal
national 371 adj.

society
accompaniment
89 n.
association 706 n.
society 708 n.
beau monde 848 n.
sociality 882 n.
sociology
sociology 901 n.
sock
legwear, footwear
228 n.
strike 279 vb.
socket
place 185 n.
receptacle 194 n.
cavity 255 n.
sod
soil 344 n.
soda
soft drink 301 n.
soda-fountain
café 192 n.
sodality
association 706 n.
sodden
drenched 341 adj.
drunken 949 adj.
sodomite
libertine 952 n.
sodomy
illicit love 951 n.
sofa
seat 218 n.
soft
weak 163 adj.
soft 327 adj.
comfortable
376 adj.
muted 401 adj.
foolish 499 adj.
lenient 736 adj.
soft drink
soft drink 301 n.
soften
soften 327 vb.
extenuate 927 vb.
(*see* soft)
softness
softness 327 n.
pulpiness 356 n.
(*see* soft)
soft pedal
silencer 401 n.
mute 401 vb.
underestimate
483 vb.

soft soap
flattery 925 n.
soft-spoken
courteous 884 adj.
soft spot
defect 647 n.
softy
ninny 501 n.
soggy
pulpy 356 adj.
soi-disant
misnamed 562 adj.
vain 873 adj.
soil
soil 344 n.
make unclean
649 vb.
blemish 845 vb.
soirée
social gathering
882 n.
sojourn
dwell 192 vb.
sojourner
dweller 191 n.
solace
relief 831 n.
amuse 837 vb.
solar
celestial 321 adj.
solar system
sun 321 n.
solder
join 45 vb.
adhesive 47 n.
soldier
soldier 722 n.
soldier of fortune
militarist 722 n.
soldiery
soldiery 722 n.
sole
one 88 adj.
foot 214 n.
solecism
solecism 565 n.
solecistic
neological 560 adj.
ungrammatical
565 adj.
solemn
great 32 adj.
serious 834 adj.
formal 875 adj.
solemnity
formality 875 n.
rite 988 n.

solemnize
do 676 vb.
celebrate 876 vb.
solicitation
inducement 612 n.
request 761 n.
solicitor
law agent 958 n.
solicitous
careful 457 adj.
desiring 859 adj.
solicitude
carefulness 457 n.
worry 825 n.
solid
substantial 3 adj.
cohesive 48 adj.
thick 205 adj.
material 319 adj.
solid body 324 n.
dense 324 adj.
solidarity
cooperation 706 n.
association 706 n.
concord 710 n.
solid body
solid body 324 n.
solidification
condensation
324 n.
solidify
cohere 48 vb.
be dense 324 vb.
solidity
substantiality 3 n.
materiality 319 n.
density 324 n.
solid vote
consensus 488 n.
soliloquy
soliloquy 585 n.
solitary
alone 88 adj.
solitary 883 n.
unsociable 883 adj.
solitude
seclusion 883 n.
solo
unit 88 n.
soloist
musician 413 n.
solstice
winter 129 n.
solubility
liquefaction 337 n.
soluble (*see*
solubility)

solution
solution 337 n.
interpretation
520 n.
solve
decipher 520 vb.
solvent
liquefaction 337 n.
moneyed 800 adj.
sombre
black 428 adj.
cheerless 834 adj.
some
plurality 101 n.
someone
person 371 n.
somersault
overturning 221 n.
something
object 319 n.
something over
extra 40 n.
sometime
former 125 adj.
somnambulism
sleep 679 n.
somnambulist
visionary 513 n.
somnolence
sleepiness 679 n.
son
descendant 170 n.
sonant
speech sound 398 n.
vocal 577 adj.
sonata, sonatina
musical piece
412 n.
sone
sound 398 n.
son et lumière
lighting 420 n.
song
vocal music 412 n.
songful
musicianly
413 adj.
poetic 593 adj.
songster
bird 365 n.
vocalist 413 n.
sonic
sounding 398 adj.
sonic barrier
sound 398 n.
sonnet
verse form 593 n.

sonority
sound 398 n.
resonance 404 n.
sonorous
ornate 574 adj.
sonship
sonship 170 n.
soon
betimes 135 adv.
soot
black thing 428 n.
dirt 649 n.
soothe
assuage 177 vb.
please 826 vb.
soothsayer
oracle 511 n.
sorcerer 983 n.
sooty
dark 418 adj.
opaque 423 adj.
dirty 649 adj.
sop
mouthful 301 n.
potion 301 n.
moisture 341 n.
incentive 612 n.
sophism
sophism 477 n.
sophist
sophist 477 n.
sophisticate
mix 43 vb.
man of taste
846 n.
sophistication
mixture 43 n.
culture 490 n.
skill 694 n.
good taste 846 n.
sophistry
sophistry 477 n.
deception 542 n.
soporific
soporific 679 n.
tedious 838 adj.
sopping
drenched 341 adj.
soppy
foolish 499 adj.
soprano
vocalist 413 n.
sorcerer
sorcerer 983 n.
occultist 984 n.
sorcery
sorcery 983 n.

sore
ulcer 651 n.
diseased 651 adj.
sensitive 819 adj.
painfulness 827 n.
resentful 891 adj.
sore point
resentment 891 n.
sorority
community 708 n.
sorrow
adversity 731 n.
sorrow 825 n.
lament 836 vb.
sorry
unhappy 825 adj.
repentant 939 adj.
sorry sight
painfulness 827 n.
sort
sort 77 n.
discriminate
463 vb.
sorter
mails 531 n.
sortie
attack 712 n.
sortilege
divination 511 n.
sort out
exclude 57 vb.
S.O.S.
danger signal
665 n.
sot
drunkard 949 n.
soteriology
theology 973 n.
sottish
drunken 949 adj.
sotto voce
faintly 401 adv.
soul
essential part 5 n.
interiority 224 n.
life 360 n.
spirit 447 n.
affections 817 n.
soulful
feeling 818 adj.
soulless
impassive 820 adj.
soul-stirring
exciting 821 adj.
sound
unyielding 162 adj.
plunge 313 vb.

gulf 345 vb.
sound 398 n.
interrogate 459 vb.
be tentative 461 vb.
measure 465 vb.
genuine 484 adj.
perfect 646 adj.
healthy 650 adj.
soundless
silent 399 adj.
sound mind
sanity 502 n.
soundproof
silent 399 adj.
non-resonant
405 adj.
sound-tape
hearing aid 415 n.
soup
soup 301 n.
soupçon
small quantity 33 n.
sour
sour 393 adj.
sullen 893 adj.
source
origin 68 n.
source 156 n.
informant 524 n.
store 632 n.
sour grapes
jealousy 911 n.
sourness
malevolence 898 n.
(see sour)
souse
plunge 313 vb.
drench 341 vb.
souvenir
reminder 505 n.
sou'wester
overcoat 228 n.
gale 352 n.
sovereign
supreme 34 adj.
remedial 658 adj.
sovereign 741 n.
sovereignty
superiority 34 n.
soviet
council 692 n.
sovietism
government 733 n.
sow
disperse 75 vb.
pig 365 n.
cultivate 370 vb.

657

sower
  husbandman 370 n.
sow one's wild oats
  be intemperate
  943 vb.
sow the seed
  prepare 669 vb.
sozzled
  tipsy 949 adj.
spa
  hygiene 652 n.
  hospital 658 n.
space
  space 183 n.
  room 193 n.
  distance 199 n.
  interval 201 n.
  opening 263 n.
space-man
  aeronaut 271 n.
space-ship, space
  station
  space-ship 276 n.
space-traveller
  traveller 268 n.
spacious
  great 32 adj.
  spacious 183 adj.
spade
  ladle 194 n.
  shovel 274 n.
span
  connect 45 vb.
  bond 47 n.
  duality 90 n.
  period 110 n.
  be broad 205 vb.
  overlie 226 vb.
  measure 465 vb.
  bridge 624 n.
spangle
  variegate 437 vb.
  finery 844 n.
spaniel
  dog 365 n.
spank
  strike 279 vb.
  spank 963 vb.
spanner in the works
  hitch 702 n.
spar
  bicker 709 vb.
  pugilism 716 n.
spare
  additional 38 n.
  extra 40 n.
  remaining 41 adj.

lean 206 adj.
  be lenient 736 vb.
  not retain 779 vb.
  show mercy 905 vb.
spare diet
  fasting 946 n.
spare hours, spare
  time
  opportunity 137 n.
spare part
  extra 40 n.
spark
  electricity 160 n.
  fire 379 n.
  flash 417 n.
  fop 848 n.
sparkle
  shine 417 vb.
  be witty 839 vb.
spark off
  initiate 68 vb.
sparse
  few 105 adj.
  scarce 636 adj.
Spartan
  severe 735 adj.
  temperate 942 adj.
spasm
  fitfulness 142 n.
  spasm 318 n.
  blood pressure
  651 n.
  excitation 821 n.
spasmodic
  discontinuous
  72 adj.
  (*see* spasm)
spate
  great quantity
  32 n.
  redundance 637 n.
spatial
  spatial 183 adj.
spatter
  disperse 75 vb.
  emit 300 vb.
spawn
  youngling 132 n.
  reproduce itself
  164 vb.
spawning
  prolific 171 adj.
speak
  signal 547 vb.
  speak 579 vb.
speakeasy
  tavern 192 n.

speaker
  speaker 579 n.
speak for
  deputize 755 vb.
speak for itself
  be intelligible
  516 vb.
speaking tube
  hearing aid 415 n.
speak one's mind
  be truthful 540 vb.
speak to
  speak to 583 vb.
spear
  pierce 263 vb.
  spear 723 n.
spearhead
  front 237 n.
  leader 690 n.
  attacker 712 n.
special
  characteristic 5 adj.
  special 80 adj.
  unconformable
  84 adj.
special
  correspondent
  informant 524 n.
  newsmonger 529 n.
specialism
  knowledge 490 n.
  skill 694 n.
specialist
  scholar 492 n.
  expert 696 n.
speciality
  speciality 80 n.
specialization
  speciality 80 n.
specialize
  study 536 vb.
specialized
  instructed 490 adj.
  expert 694 adj.
special pleading
  sophistry 477 n.
specie
  coinage 797 n.
species
  subdivision 53 n.
  breed 77 n.
specific
  special 80 adj.
  remedy 658 n.
specification
  classification 77 n.
  particulars 80 n.

description 590 n.
specify
  specify 80 vb.
  name 561 vb.
specimen
  prototype 23 n.
  example 83 n.
specious
  plausible 471 adj.
  ostensible 614 adj.
  ostentatious 875 adj.
speck, speckle
  small thing 33 n.
  variegate 437 vb.
spectacle
  spectacle 445 n.
  stage show 594 n.
  pageant 875 n.
spectacles
  eyeglass 442 n.
spectacular
  showy 875 adj.
spectator
  spectator 441 n.
spectral
  variegated 437 adj.
  spooky 970 adj.
spectre
  ghost 970 n.
spectroscope
  chromatics 425 n.
  optical device
  442 n.
spectroscopy
  optics 417 n.
spectrum
  variegation 437 n.
  colour 425 n.
speculate
  (*see* speculation)
speculation
  meditation 449 n.
  empiricism 461 n.
  conjecture 512 n.
  gambling 618 n.
speculative
  philosophic 449 adj.
  thoughtful 449 adj.
  experimental
  461 adj.
  suppositional
  512 adj.
  speculative 618 adj.
  dangerous 661 adj.
speculator
  experimenter 461 n.
  gambler 618 n.

speech
  language 557 n.
  speech, oration
  579 n.
speech defect
  speech defect 580 n.
speechless
  silent 399 adj.
  voiceless 578 adj.
speechless, be
  be taciturn 582 vb.
speech-making
  oratory 579 n.
speech sound
  speech sound
  398 n.
speed
  motion 265 n.
  velocity 277 n.
  facilitate 701 vb.
speedometer
  velocity 277 n.
speed-rate
  velocity 277 n.
speed-up
  spurt 277 n.
speedy
  speedy 277 adj.
speleology
  mineralogy 359 n.
  sport 837 n.
spell
  period 110 n.
  influence 178 n.
  mean 514 vb.
  imply 523 vb.
  spell 558 vb.
  spell 983 n.
spellbinder
  speaker 579 n.
  sorcerer 983 n.
spellbound
  bewitched 983 adj.
spelling
  letter 558 n.
spell out
  decipher 520 vb.
spend
  emit 300 vb.
  waste 634 vb.
  expend 806 vb.
spender
  prodigal 815 n.
spending spree
  prodigality 815 n.
spendthrift
  prodigal 815 n.

spent
  fatigued 684 adj.
sperm
  genitalia 164 n.
  fertilizer 171 n.
spermatic
  generative 171 adj.
spermatozoa
  genitalia 164 n.
spew
  eject, vomit 300 vb.
sphere
  region 184 n.
  sphere 252 n.
  function 622 n.
spherical
  rotund 252 adj.
sphericity
  convexity 253 n.
sphinxlike
  puzzling 517 adj.
spica
  prickle 256 n.
spice
  stimulant 174 n.
  season 388 vb.
  condiment 389 n.
  appetize 390 vb.
spicery
  condiment 389 n.
spick and span
  clean 648 adj.
spicy
  pungent 388 adj.
  savoury 390 adj.
  fragrant 396 adj.
  impure 951 adj.
spider
  planner 623 n.
  weaving 222 n.
spiderman
  elevation 310 n.
spider's web
  ambush 527 n.
spidery
  lean 206 adj.
spike
  sharp point 256 n.
  stopper 264 n.
spiky
  sharp 256 adj.
spill
  overturning 221 n.
  flow out 298 vb.
  let fall 311 vb.
spillway
  waterfall 350 n.

spilt milk
  loss 772 n.
spin
  rotation 315 n.
spinal
  back 238 adj.
spindle
  pivot 218 n.
  rotator 315 n.
spindle-shaped
  round 250 adj.
spindly
  lean 206 adj.
spine
  supporter 218 n.
  rear 238 n.
  prickle 256 n.
spineless
  impotent 161 adj.
  weak 163 adj.
spinner
  weaving 222 n.
spinney
  wood 366 n.
spinster
  spinster 895 n.
spinsterhood
  celibacy 895 n.
spiracle
  air-pipe 353 n.
spiral
  coil 251 n.
  ascend 308 vb.
  rotation 315 n.
spire
  vertex 213 n.
  church exterior
  990 n.
spirit
  temperament 5 n.
  vigorousness 174 n.
  life 360 n.
  spirit 447 n.
  meaning 514 n.
  vigour 571 n.
  affections 817 n.
  courage 855 n.
  ghost 970 n.
spirit away
  steal 788 vb.
spirited
  lively 819 adj.
  courageous
  855 adj.
spiritless
  apathetic 820 adj.
  cowardly 856 adj.

spirit of the age
  tendency 179 n.
spirits
  liquor 301 n.
  cheerfulness 833 n.
spiritual
  immaterial 320 adj.
  psychic 447 adj.
  religious 973 adj.
spiritualism
  spiritualism 984 n.
spiritualist
  occultist 984 n.
spiritualistic
  psychic 447 adj.
  psychical 984 adj.
spirituality
  sanctity 979 n.
spiritual life
  sanctity 979 n.
spirituous
  intoxicating 949 adj.
spirt
  (see spurt)
spit
  sharp point 256 n.
  perforator 263 n.
  pierce 263 vb.
  emit, eruct 300 vb.
  excrement 302 n.
  hiss 406 vb.
spit and polish
  formality 875 n.
spite
  resentment 891 n.
  revengefulness
  910 n.
  detraction 926 n.
spiteful
  (see spite)
spitfire
  shrew 892 n.
spit out
  eject 300 vb.
spittle
  excrement 302 n.
spittoon
  bowl 194 n.
splash
  small quantity
  33 n.
  moisten 341 vb.
  advertise 528 vb.
splay
  diverge 294 vb.
spleen
  insides 224 n.

sullenness 893 n.
splendid
  excellent 644 adj.
  splendid 841 adj.
  ostentatious
    875 adj.
splendour
  light 417 n.
  beauty 841 n.
  prestige 866 n.
  ostentation 875 n.
splenetic
  (*see* spleenful)
splice
  tie 45 vb.
  marry 894 vb.
splint
  surgical dressing
    658 n.
splinter
  break 46 vb.
  piece 53 n.
  be brittle 330 vb.
splinter group
  dissentient 489 n.
split
  bisect 92 vb.
  gap 201 n.
  open 263 vb.
  be brittle 330 vb.
  divulge 526 vb.
  dissension 709 n.
  apportion 783 vb.
split hairs
  discriminate
    463 vb.
split second
  instant 116 n.
split the difference
  average out 30 vb.
splutter
  hiss 406 vb.
spoil
  lay waste 165 vb.
  impair 655 vb.
  be lenient 736 vb.
  booty 790 n.
  pet 889 vb.
spoiler
  robber 789 n.
spoiling for
  willing 597 adj.
spoilsport
  hinderer 702 n.
  disapprover 924 n.
spoke
  divergence 294 n.

spokesman
  interpreter 520 n.
  messenger 531 n.
  speaker 579 n.
spoliation
  spoliation 788 n.
sponge
  porosity 263 n.
  absorb 299 vb.
  drier 342 n.
  obliteration 550 n.
  cleaning utensil
    648 n.
  beg 761 vb.
  be servile 879 vb.
sponger
  idler 679 n.
  toady 879 n.
sponging house
  prison 748 n.
spongy
  porous 265 adj.
  pulpy 356 adj.
sponsor
  patronize 703 vb.
sponsorship
  aid 703 n.
spontaneity
  spontaneity 609 n.
  non-preparation
    670 n.
  feeling 818 n.
spontaneous
  involuntary 596 adj.
  voluntary 597 adj.
  artless 699 adj.
  (*see* spontaneity)
spoof
  deceive 542 vb.
spoon
  ladle 194 n.
  caress 889 vb.
spoonerism
  absurdity 497 n.
  ridiculousness
    849 n.
spoonfeed
  be lax 734 vb.
  be lenient 736 vb.
spoor
  trace 548 n.
sporadic
  unassembled
    75 adj.
  infrequent 140 adj.
sport
  misfit 25 n.

athletics 162 n.
  wear 228 vb.
  exercise 682 n.
  merriment 833 n.
  sport 837 n.
  laughing-stock
    851 n.
  good man 937 n.
sporting
  (*see*
    sportsmanlike)
sportive
  gay 833 adj.
  amused 837 adj.
sportsman
  hunter 619 n.
  player 837 n.
  gentleman 929 n.
sportsmanlike
  honourable 929 adj.
sportsmanship
  probity 929 n.
spot
  place 185 n.
  variegate 437 vb.
  detect 484 vb.
  blemish 845 n.
spotless
  perfect 646 adj.
  pure 950 adj.
spotlight
  lighting 420 n.
  manifest 522 vb.
  theatre 594 n.
spotter
  spectator 441 n.
spotty
  mottled 347 adj.
spouse
  spouse 894 n.
spout
  orifice 263 n.
  flow 350 vb.
  conduit 351 n.
sprain
  disable 161 vb.
  distort 246 vb.
sprat
  animalcule 196 n.
sprawl
  be horizontal
    216 vb.
  repose 683 vb.
sprawl over
  be dispersed 75 vb.
spray
  vaporizer 338 n.

irrigator 341 n.
  bubble 355 n.
  foliage 366 n.
spread
  grow 36 vb.
  dispersion 75 n.
  range 183 n.
  overlay 226 vb.
  progress 285 vb.
  meal 301 n.
  advertisement
    528 n.
spree
  revel 837 n.
sprig
  young plant 132 n.
  foliage 366 n.
sprightly
  cheerful 833 adj.
spring
  spring 128 n.
  source 156 n.
  coil 251 n.
  spurt 277 n.
  recoil 280 n.
  leap 312 n., vb.
  elasticity 328 n.
  stream 350 n.
  motive 612 n.
  machine 630 n.
springboard
  recoil 280 n.
  lifter 310 n.
spring-clean
  clean 648 vb.
springe
  trap 542 n.
spring from
  result 157 vb.
spring up
  begin 68 vb.
  ascend 308 vb.
  leap 312 vb.
springy
  soft 327 adj.
  elastic 328 adj.
sprinkle
  emit 300 vb.
  let fall 311 vb.
  moisten 341 vb.
  variegate 437 vb.
sprinkler
  irrigator 341 n.
  extinguisher 382 n.
sprint
  spurt 277 n.
  racing 716 n.

sprout
grow 36 vb.
young plant 132 n.
reproduce itself
164 vb.
expand 197 vb.
spruce
clean 648 adj., vb.
sprung
elastic 328 adj.
spry
active 678 adj.
spume
bubble 355 n., vb.
spur
branch 53 n.
projection 254 n.
sharp point 256 n.
accelerate 277 vb.
impel, kick 279 vb.
incentive 612 n.
hasten 680 vb.
animate 821 vb.
spurious
false 541 adj.
spurious 542 adj.
bastard 954 adj.
spurn
kick 279 vb.
reject 607 vb.
despise 922 vb.
spur of the moment
spontaneity 609 n.
spurt
vigorousness 174 n.
accelerate 277 vb.
progression 285 n.
flow out 298 vb.
flow 350 n.
haste 680 n.
sputnik
space-ship 276 n.
sputter
emit 300 vb.
hiss 406 vb.
be dim 419 vb.
sputum
excrement 302 n.
spy
see, scan 438 vb.
be curious 453 vb.
secret service 459 n.
detective 459 n.
informer 524 n.
spy-ring
secret service
459 n.

squab
youngling 132 n.
thick 205 adj.
squabble
quarrel 709 n.
squad
band 74 n.
squadron
shipping 275 n.
formation 722 n.
air force 722 n.
navy 722 n.
squalid
unclean 649 adj.
beggarly 801 adj.
disreputable
867 adj.
squall
gale 352 n.
cry 408 n.
weep 836 vb.
squalor
uncleanness 649 n.
squander
waste 634 vb.
misuse 675 vb.
be prodigal 815 vb.
squandermania
prodigality 815 n.
square
equal 28 adj.
regular 81 adj.
make conform
83 vb.
quadruple 97 vb.
angular figure
247 n.
unsharpened
257 adj.
bribe 612 vb.
honourable 929 adj.
square accounts
with
pay 804 vb.
square peg in a
round hole
misfit 25 n.
square with
accord 24 vb.
squash
suppress 165 vb.
flatten 216 vb.
pulpiness 356 n.
social gathering
882 n.
squashy
soft 327 adj.

pulpy 356 adj.
squat
place oneself
187 vb.
dwarfish 196 adj.
short 204 adj.
low 210 adj.
encroach 306 vb.
sit down 311 vb.
appropriate
786 vb.
squatter
intruder 59 n.
resident 191 n.
usurper 916 n.
squaw
spouse 894 n.
squawk
ululation 409 n.
squeak
sound faint 401 vb.
ululate 409 vb.
discontent 829 n.
squeaker
informer 524 n.
squeaky
strident 407 adj.
squeal
divulge 526 vb.
squealer
informer 524 n.
squeamish
disliking 861 adj.
fastidious 862 adj.
squeeze
compression 198 n.
restriction 747 n.
caress 889 vb.
squeeze out
extract 304 vb.
squelch
be wet 341 vb.
squelchy
soft 327 adj.
marshy 347 n.
squib
satire 851 n.
squinny
gaze, scan 438 vb.
squint
obliquity 220 n.
look 438 n.
squire
accompany 89 vb.
retainer 742 n.
serve 742 vb.
lover 887 n.

squirearchy
aristocracy 868 n.
squirm
wriggle 251 vb.
feel pain 377 vb.
be servile 879 vb.
squirt
emit 300 vb.
stab
pierce 263 vb.
wound 655 n., vb.
stabilimeter
stabilizer 153 n.
stability
stability 153 n.
stabilize
stabilize 153 vb.
stabilizer
stabilizer 153 n.
stable
group 74 n.
stable 192 n.
inexcitable 823 adj.
(*see* stability)
stack
store 632 n., vb.
stadium
arena 724 n.
staff
supporter 218 n.
employ 622 vb.
personnel 686 n.
director 690 n.
army officer 741 n.
domestic 742 n.
staff college
training school
539 n.
staff-work
arrangement 62 n.
management
689 n.
stag
deer 365 n.
gambler 618 n.
stage
juncture 8 n.
degree 27 n.
stand 218 n.
stage-coach 274 n.
rostrum 539 n.
drama, theatre
594 n.
dramatize 594 vb.
arena 724 n.
stage-craft
dramaturgy 594 n.

stage-fright
fear 854 n.
acting 594 n.
stage-manager
stage-manager 594 n.
stage-struck
dramatic 594 adj.
stagger
move slowly 278 vb.
tumble 309 vb.
oscillate 317 vb.
surprise 508 vb.
impress 821 vb.
staggers
spasm 318 n.
stagnant, stagnate
(*see* stagnation)
stagnation
unproductivity 172 n.
quiescence 266 n.
inactivity 679 n.
stag-party
male 372 n.
stagy
affected 850 adj.
showy 875 adj.
staid
inexcitable 823 adj.
serious 834 adj.
stain
tincture 43 n.
pigment 425 n.
decolorize 426 vb.
blemish 845 n., vb.
slur 867 n.
stained glass
variegation 437 n.
stainless
clean 648 adj.
innocent 935 adj.
stair
degree 27 n.
ascent 308 n.
staircase
ascent 308 n.
stake
furnace 383 n.
gambling 618 n.
endanger 661 vb.
security 767 n.
stake, at
unsafe 661 adj.
stake-money
security 767 n.

stake out
limit 236 vb.
stakes
contest 716 n.
stalactite
pendant 217 n.
stale
antiquated 127 adj.
fatigued 684 adj.
tedious 838 adj.
stalemate
draw 28 n.
stop 145 n.
obstacle 702 n.
stalk
supporter 218 n.
gait 265 n.
walk 267 vb.
foliage 366 n.
hunt 619 vb.
stalker
hunter 619 n.
stalking horse
ambush 527 n.
stall
put off 136 vb.
stable 192 n.
seat 218 n.
parry 713 vb.
shop 796 n.
stallion
horse 273 n.
stalls
onlookers 441 n.
stalwart
stalwart 162 adj.
stamina
stamina 600 n.
stammer
speech defect 580 n.
stamp
character 5 n.
mould 23 n.
form 243 n.
make concave 255 vb.
walk 267 vb.
knock 279 n.
endorse 488 vb.
label 547 n.
engrave 555 vb.
mint 799 vb.
stampede
frighten 854 vb.
stamp on
suppress 165 vb.

stance
form 243 n.
stanch
dry 342 vb.
stanch 350 vb.
obstruct 702 vb.
stand
be in a state 7 vb.
stay 144 vb.
be situate 186 vb.
place 187 vb.
be vertical 215 vb.
stand 218 n.
be quiescent 266 vb.
resistance 715 n.
defray 804 vb.
be patient 823 vb.
standard
uniform 16 adj.
prototype 23 n.
degree 27 n.
median 30 adj.
general 79 adj.
typical 83 adj.
stand 218 n.
flag 547 n.
standardization
uniformity 16 n.
standardize
regularize 62 vb.
make conform 83 vb.
stand by
be present 189 vb.
await 507 vb.
patronize 703 vb.
stand-by
auxiliary 707 n.
stand down
resign 753 vb.
stand for
be 1 vb.
mean 514 vb.
deputize 755 vb.
stand-in
substitute 150 n.
deputy 755 n.
standing
state 7 n.
serial place 73 n.
permanent 144 adj.
vertical 215 adj.
prestige 866 n.
standing water
lake 346 n.
stand off
recede 290 vb.

stand-offish
unsociable 883 adj.
stand on ceremony
show respect 920 vb.
stand out
jut 254 vb.
be visible 443 vb.
stand pat
stay 144 vb.
standstill
stop 145 n.
lull 145 n.
stand to
be liable 180 vb.
stand to reason
be reasonable 475 vb.
stand up
be vertical 215 vb.
stand up to
support 218 vb.
defy 711 vb.
stanza
verse form 593 n.
staple
fastening 47 n.
main part 52 n.
texture 331 n.
important 638 adj.
star
star 321 n.
be brittle 330 vb.
actor 594 n.
exceller 644 n.
badge of rank 743 n.
desired object 859 n.
favourite 890 n.
starboard
dextrality 241 n.
starch
harden 326 vb.
clean 648 vb.
Star Chamber
law-court 956 n.
starchy
rigid 326 adj.
formal 875 adj.
stardom
prestige 866 n.
stare
gaze 438 vb.
wonder 864 vb.
star-gazer
astronomy 321 n.

stark
 uncovered 229 adj.
 plain 573 adj.
starless
 unlit 418 adj.
starlight
 luminary 420 n.
starry-eyed
 happy 824 adj.
stars
 influence 178 n.
 fate 596 n.
start
 vantage 34 n.
 start 68 n.
 open 263 vb.
 departure 296 n.
 agitation 318 n.
 inexpectation
 508 n.
starter
 contender 716 n.
starting-point
 start 68 n.
 departure 296 n.
startle
 raise the alarm
 665 vb.
 frighten 854 vb.
 be wonderful
 864 vb.
start up
 initiate 68 vb.
 operate 173 vb.
starvation
 fasting 946 n.
starve
 make thin 206 vb.
 be parsimonious
 816 vb.
 starve 946 vb.
state
 state 7 n.
 affirm 532 vb.
 polity 733 n.
 formality 875 n.
state control
 governance 733 n.
statecraft
 management 689 n.
statehood
 nation 371 n.
 independence 744 n.
stateless person
 outcaste 883 n.
stately
 impressive 821 adj.

 formal 875 adj.
 proud 871 adj.
statement
 list 87 n.
 topic 452 n.
 report 524 n.
 affirmation 532 n.
 accounts 808 adj.
state of affairs
 affairs 154 n.
state of war
 belligerency 718 n.
statesman
 sage 500 n.
 manager 690 n.
statesmanlike
 wise 498 adj.
 skilful 694 adj.
statesmanship
 sagacity 498 n.
 tactics 688 n.
static
 quiescent 266 adj.
station
 serial place 73 n.
 stopping place
 145 n.
 situation 186 n.
 nobility 868 n.
stationary
 inactive 679 adj.
stationer
 bookman 589 n.
stationery
 stationery 586 n.
statism
 despotism 733 n.
statistical
 statistical 86 adj.
statistician
 computer 86 n.
 accountant 808 n.
statistics
 statistics 86 n.
statuary
 sculpture 554 n.
statue
 monument 548 n.
 sculpture 554 n.
statuesque
 tall 209 adj.
 beautiful 841 adj.
statu pupillari, in
 young 130 adj.
 subject 745 adj.
stature
 height 209 n.

status
 state 7 n.
 circumstances 8 n.
 prestige 866 n.
status quo
 permanence 144 n.
 reversion 148 n.
statute
 legislation 953 n.
statutory
 preceptive 693 adj.
 legal 953 adj.
staunch
 unyielding 162 adj.
 resolute 599 adj.
 trustworthy 929 adj.
stave in
 make concave
 255 vb.
 pierce 263 vb.
stave off
 obstruct 702 vb.
stay
 delay 136 n.
 stay 144 vb.
 cease 145 vb.
 dwell 192 vb.
 supporter 218 n.
 support 218 vb.
 be quiescent
 266 vb.
 visit 882 vb.
stay-at-home
 quiescent 266 adj.
 unsociable 883 adj.
staying power
 stamina 600 n.
stay put
 be quiescent 266 vb.
stays
 supporter 218 n.
 underwear 228 n.
stead
 utility 640 n.
 aid 703 n.
steadfast
 fixed 153 adj.
steadfastness
 perseverance
 600 n.
steady
 uniform 16 adj.
 regular 81 adj.
 support 218 vb.
 still 266 adj.
 persevering 600 adj.
 lover 887 n.

steak
 meat 301 n.
steal
 be stealthy 525 vb.
 steal 788 vb.
steal a march
 be early 135 vb.
stealing
 stealing 788 n.
stealth
 cunning 698 n.
 (see secrecy)
stealthy
 stealthy 525 adj.
steam
 stimulation 174 n.
 propellant 287 n.
 emit 300 vb.
 cook 301 vb.
 vaporize 338 vb.
 heat 379 n.
steam-engine
 locomotive 274 n.
steamer
 ship 275 n.
steam-roller
 demolish 165 vb.
 locomotive 274 n.
steamy
 vaporific 338 adj.
steel
 strengthen 162 vb.
 sharp edge 256 n.
 hardness 326 n.
 make insensitive
 820 vb.
steely
 hard 326 adj.
 cruel 898 adj.
steep
 high land 209 n.
 deep 211 adj.
 vertical 215 adj.
 sloping 220 adj.
 drench 341 vb.
steepen
 ascend 308 vb.
steeple
 church exterior
 990 n.
steeplechase
 racing 716 n.
steeple-jack
 climber 308 n.
steer
 navigate 269 vb.
 cattle 365 n.

direct 689 vb.
steerage
  lower classes 869 n.
steer clear
  deviate 282 vb.
steersman
  navigator 270 n.
  director 690 n.
steersmanship
  directorship 689 n.
stellar
  celestial 321 adj.
stem
  stanch 350 vb.
  foliage 366 n.
stench
  fetor 397 n.
stencil
  duplicate 22 n.
stenographer
  recorder 549 n.
stenography
  writing 586 n.
stentorian
  loud 400 adj.
  crying 408 adj.
step
  degree 27 n.
  stand 218 n.
  gait 265 n.
step by step
  by degrees 27 adv.
stepfather
  parent 169 n.
step, in
  agreeing 24 adj.
step into the shoes of
  substitute 150 vb.
stepmother
  maternity 169 n.
stepmotherly
  unkind 898 adj.
steppe
  horizontality 216 n.
  plain 348 n.
stepping-stone
  bridge 624 n.
steps
  series 71 n.
  ascent 308 n.
  policy 623 n.
step up
  augment 36 vb.
  invigorate 174 vb.
stereoscopic
  seeing 438 adj.

visible 443 adj.
stereotype
  uniformity 16 n.
  copy 22 n.
  print 587 vb.
stereotyped
  unchangeable 153 adj.
sterile
  unproductive 172 adj.
  profitless 641 adj.
  salubrious 652 adj.
sterility (*see* sterile)
sterilization
  prophylactic 658 n.
  (*see* sterilize)
sterilize
  unman 161 vb.
  sterilize 172 vb.
  sanitate 652 vb.
sterling
  genuine 494 adj.
  virtuous 933 adj.
  monetary 797 n.
stern
  buttocks 238 n.
  poop 238 n.
  serious 834 adj.
  sullen 893 adj.
  unkind 898 adj.
stern-sheets
  poop 238 n.
sternway
  water travel 269 n.
stertorous
  puffing 352 adj.
  hoarse 407 adj.
stethoscope
  hearing aid 415 n.
stevedore
  bearer 273 n.
stew
  a mixture 43 n.
  dish 301 n.
  cook 301 vb.
  heat 381 vb.
  excitable state 822 n.
  brothel 951 n.
steward
  provider 633 n.
  manager 690 n.
  treasurer 798 n.
stewardship
  management 689 n.

stick
  cohere 48 vb.
  halt 145 vb.
  supporter 218 n.
  pierce 263 vb.
  club 723 n.
  scourge 964 n.
stick at nothing
  be resolute 599 vb.
sticker
  coherence 48 n.
stickiness
  (*see* sticky)
stick in the throat
  make mute 578 vb.
stick it out
  persevere 600 vb.
stickler
  opinionist 602 n.
stick one's neck out
  be rash 857 vb.
stick out
  jut 254 vb.
stick up for
  patronize 703 vb.
sticky
  cohesive 48 adj.
  retentive 778 adj.
sticky wicket
  predicament 700 n.
stiff
  unyielding 162 adj.
  crippled 163 adj.
  rigid 326 adj.
  ninny 501 n.
  obstinate 602 adj.
  clumsy 695 adj.
  severe 735 adj.
  formal 875 adj.
stiffen
  harden 326 vb.
stiffener
  supporter 218 n.
stiff-necked
  obstinate 602 adj.
stifle
  suppress 165 vb.
  kill 362 vb.
  be hot 379 vb.
  extinguish 382 vb.
  silence 399 vb.
stigma
  label 547 n.
  slur 867 n.
stigmata
  indication 547 n.

stigmatize
  mark 547 vb.
  defame 926 vb.
stiletto
  sharp point 256 n.
still
  assuage 177 vb.
  still 266 adj.
  vaporizer 338 n.
  silent 399 adj.
  photography 551 n.
stillborn
  dead 361 adj.
  unsuccessful 728 adj.
still life
  picture 553 n.
still-room
  provisions 301 n.
stilt
  stand 218 n.
stilted
  ornate 574 adj.
  affected 850 adj.
stimulant
  stimulant 174 n.
  liquor 301 n.
  drug 658 n.
  excitant 821 n.
stimulate
  incite 612 vb.
stimulation
  stimulation 174 n.
  excitation 821 n.
stimulus
  (*see* stimulant)
sting
  pang 377 n.
  pungency 388 n.
  wound 655 vb.
  enrage 891 vb.
stinginess
  insufficiency 636 n.
  parsimony 816 n.
stink
  fetor 397 n.
stint
  finite quantity 26 n.
  period 110 n.
  make insufficient 636 vb.
  labour 682 n.
  be parsimonious 816 vb.
stipend
  subvention 703 n.

stipendiary
recipient 782 n.
receiving 782 adj.
stipple
variegate 437 vb.
stipulation
requirement 627 n.
conditions 766 n.
stir
mix 43 vb.
commotion 318 n.
excite 821 vb.
stirring
eventful 154 adj.
stirrup
supporter 218 n.
stitch
tie 45 vb.
pang 377 n.
needlework 844 n.
stitch in time
anticipation 135 n.
stoat
vermin 365 n.
stock
race 11 n.
typical 83 adj.
genealogy 169 n.
pillar 218 n.
neckwear 228 n.
soup 301 n.
usual 610 adj.
store 632 n.
merchandise 795 n.
stockade
enclosure 235 n.
defences 713 n.
stock exchange
bourse 618 n.
mart 796 n.
stock-farm
stock-farm 369 n.
stockings
legwear 228 n.
stock-in-trade
equipment 630 n.
merchandise 795 n.
stockman
herdsman 369 n.
stockpile
store 632 vb.
stock-room
storage 632 n.
stocks
pillory 964 n.
stocky
short 204 adj.

stodgy
semiliquid 354 adj.
dull 840 adj.
stoic
unfeeling person
820 n.
stoical
impassive 820 adj.
patient 823 adj.
stoicism
philosophy 449 n.
inexcitability
823 n.
stoke
kindle 381 vb.
stoker
driver 268 n.
stole
shawl 228 n.
stolen goods
booty 790 n.
stolid
unintelligent
499 n.
impassive 820 adj.
stomach
maw 194 n.
be patient 823 vb.
liking 859 n.
stone
missile 287 n.
rock 344 n.
lapidate 712 vb.
unfeeling person
820 n.
gem 844 n.
stone-cutting
sculpture 554 n.
stone's throw
short distance
200 n.
stonewall
parry 713 vb.
stonework
structure 331 n.
stoning
capital punishment
963 n.
stony
unproductive
172 adj.
rough 259 adj.
insensible 375 adj.
stooge
nonentity 639 n.
auxiliary 707 n.
dependant 742 n.

stook
bunch 74 n.
cultivate 370 vb.
stool
seat 218 n.
excrement 302 n.
stool-pigeon
informer 524 n.
stoop
stoop 311 vb.
plunge 313 n., vb.
be servile 879 vb.
stop
end 69 n., vb.
stop 145 n.
close 264 vb.
stanch 350 vb.
obstacle 702 n.
prohibit 757 vb.
stop-gap
substitute 150 n.
stop-over
itinerary 267 n.
stoppage
strike 145 n.
hitch 702 n.
stopper
stopper 264 n.
stopping-place
stopping-place
145 n.
stop up
obstruct 702 vb.
stopwatch
timekeeper 117 n.
storage
storage 632 n.
store
great quantity 32 n.
accumulation 74 n.
store 632 n., vb.
acquire 771 vb.
shop 796 n.
store-house
storage 632 n.
storekeeper
provider 633 n.
tradesman 794 n.
store-room
storage 632 n.
storey
compartment 194 n.
layer 207 n.
stork
obstetrics 164 n.
storm
turmoil 61 n.

storm 176 n.
commotion 318 n.
gale 352 n.
overmaster 727 vb.
take 786 vb.
be angry 891 vb.
storm in a tea-cup
overestimation
482 n.
storm troops
attacker 712 n.
stormy
violent 176 adj.
windy 352 adj.
story
narrative 590 n.
story-teller
liar 545 n.
narrator 590 n.
stout
strong 162 adj.
fleshy 195 adj.
thick 205 adj.
liquor 301 n.
stove
furnace 383 n.
stow
load 193 vb.
stowage
room 183 n.
storage 632 n.
stowaway
intruder 59 n.
hider 527 n.
straddle
be broad 205 vb.
overlie 266 vb.
strafe
bombardment
712 n.
exprobate 924 vb.
straggle
be dispersed 75 vb.
stray 282 vb.
straggler
wanderer 268 n.
straggling
orderless 61 adj.
straight
simple 44 adj.
continuous 71 adj.
straightness 249 n.
honourable 929 adj.
straighten
straighten 249 vb.
straighten out
unravel 62 vb.

straight-faced
  serious 834 adj.
straightforward
  veracious 540 adj.
  trustworthy 929
    adj.
strain
  race 11 n.
  breed 77 n.
  weaken 163 vb.
  genealogy 169 n.
  force 176 n.
  distortion 246 n.
  pain 377 n.
  be loud 400 vb.
  be false 541 vb.
  style 566 n.
  purify 648 vb.
  misuse 675 vb.
  exertion 682 n.
  fatigue 684 n., vb.
strainer
  sorting 62 n.
  cleaning utensil
    648 n.
strain off
  transpose 272 vb.
  void 300 vb.
strait
  narrowness 206 n.
  gulf 345 n.
  restraining 747 adj.
strait-jacket
  compressor 198 n.
  fetter 748 n.
strait-laced
  prudish 950 adj.
strand
  cable 47 n.
  fibre 208 n.
  hair 259 n.
  shore 344 n.
strange
  extraneous 59 adj.
  unusual 84 adj.
stranger
  foreigner 59 n.
strangle
  kill 362 vb.
stranglehold
  retention 778 n.
strangler
  murderer 362 n.
strangulation
  compression 198 n.
  capital punishment
    963 n.

strap
  tie 45 vb.
strap-hanger
  rider 268 n.
strapping
  stalwart 162 adj.
stratagem
  tactics 688 n.
  stratagem 698 n.
strategic
  warlike 718 adj.
strategist
  planner 623 n.
  slyboots 698 n.
strategy
  policy 623 n.
  tactics 688 n.
  warfare 718 n.
stratification
  stratification 207 n.
stratosphere
  atmosphere 340 n.
stratum
  layer 207 n.
straw
  insubstantial thing
    4 n.
  trifle 639 n.
straw vote
  inquiry 459 n.
stray
  be dispersed 75 vb.
  wanderer 268 n.
  stray 282 vb.
  err 495 vb.
  derelict 779 n.
streak
  line 203 n.
  flash 417 n.
  striation 437 n.
stream
  group 74 n.
  classification 77 n.
  be wet 341 adj.
  stream 350 n.
  flow, rain 350 vb.
streamer
  advertisement 528 n.
  trimming 844 n.
streamline
  rectify 654 vb.
streamlined
  speedy 277 adj.
streams
  great quantity 32 n.
street
  street 192 n.

  road 624 n.
streetwalker
  prostitute 952 n.
strength
  strength 162 n.
  stamina 660 n.
strengthen
  augment 36 vb.
  strengthen 162 vb.
  corroborate 466 vb.
strenuous
  industrious 678 adj.
stress
  distortion 246 n.
  emphasize 532 vb.
  pronunciation
    577 n.
  prosody 593 n.
  exertion 682 n.
  difficulty 700 n.
stretch
  period 110 n.
  space, range 183 n.
  lengthen 203 vb.
  elasticity 328 n.
stretch a point
  be lax 734 vb.
  exempt 919 vb.
stretcher
  bed 218 n.
  vehicle 274 n.
stretcher-bearer
  nurse 658 n.
stretcher-case
  sick person 651 n.
strew
  disperse 75 vb.
striate
  groove 262 vb.
striation
  striation 437 n.
stricken
  suffering 825 adj.
strict
  severe 735 adj.
  orthodox 976 adj.
strictness
  severity 735 n.
stricture
  reprimand 924 n.
  censure 924 n.
stride
  gait 265 n.
  walk 267 vb.
  progression 285 n.
stridency
  (*see* strident)

strident
  strident 407 adj.
  discordant 411 adj.
stride, take in one's
  be expert 694 vb.
  do easily 701 vb.
strife
  quarrel 709 n.
  contention 716 n.
strike
  strike 145 n.
  cease 145 vb.
  strike 279 vb.
  cause thought
    449 vb.
  discovery 484 n.
  impress 821 vb.
strike a balance
  average out 30 vb.
strike at
  strike at 712 vb.
strike off
  exclude 57 vb.
  eject 300 vb.
strike oil
  have luck 730 vb.
  get rich 800 vb.
strike, on
  inactive 679 adj.
strike out
  obliterate 550 vb.
striker
  revolter 738 n.
strike work
  cease 145 vb.
  revolt 738 vb.
striking
  wonderful 864 adj.
string
  tie 45 vb.
  cable 47 n.
  viol 414 n.
stringency
  severity 735 n.
stringent
  severe 735 adj.
strings
  orchestra 413 n.
  conditions 766 n.
string together
  connect 45 vb.
stringy
  fibrous 208 adj.
  tough 329 adj.
strip
  rend 46 vb.
  line 203 n.

lamina 207 n.
strip 208 n.
uncover, doff
  229 vb.
deprive 786 vb.
stripe
  striation 437 n.
  corporal
  punishment 963 n.
stripling
  youngster 132 n.
stripper
  stripper 229 n.
strive
  essay 671 vb.
  exert oneself
  682 vb.
  contend 716 vb.
stroke
  instant 116 n.
  knock 279 n.
  spasm 318 n.
  touch 378 n., vb.
  blood pressure
  651 n.
  deed 676 n.
  caress 889 vb.
  corporal
  punishment 963 n.
stroll
  pedestrianism
  267 n.
stroller
  wanderer 268 n.
strolling
  travelling 267 adj.
strong
  strong 162 adj.
  fetid 397 adj.
  assertive 532 adj.
  forceful 571 adj.
  invulnerable
  660 adj.
  intoxicating
  949 adj.
strong-arm man
  combatant 722 n.
strong-box
  treasury 799 n.
stronghold
  fort 713 n.
strongly-worded
  assertive 532 adj.
strong-room
  treasury 799 n.
strop
  sharpener 256 n.

structural
  supporting 218 adj.
  structural 331 adj.
structure
  composition 56 n.
  structure 331 n.
  pattern 844 n.
struggle
  be violent 176 vb.
  exertion 682 n.
  contest 716 n.
struggler
  contender 716 n.
strum
  play music 413 vb.
  mean nothing
  515 vb.
strut
  supporter 218 n.
  gait 265 n.
  be proud 871 vb.
stub
  unsharpened
  257 adj.
  label 547 n.
stubble
  leavings 41 n.
  roughness 259 n.
  corn 366 n.
stubborn
  unyielding 162 adj.
  obstinate 602 adj.
stubby
  short 204 adj.
  thick 205 adj.
  unsharpened
  257 adj.
stucco
  facing 226 n.
stuck
  firm-set 45 adj.
stuck up
  prideful 871 adj.
stud
  fastening 47 n.
  stock-farm 369 n.
  variegate 437 vb.
student
  scholar 492 n.
  learner 538 n.
studio
  workshop 687 n.
studious
  studious 536 adj.
study
  musical piece 412 n.
  scan 438 vb.

meditation 449 n.
topic 452 n.
be attentive 455 vb.
study 536 n., vb.
dissertation 591 n.
workshop 687 n.
stuff
  essential part 5 n.
  fill 54 vb.
  load 193 vb.
  textile 222 n.
  line 227 vb.
  matter 319 n.
  texture 331 n.
  silly talk 515 n.
  rubbish 641 n.
  merchandise 795 n.
  gluttonize 947 vb.
stuff and nonsense
  silly talk 515 n.
stuffing
  contents 193 n.
  lining 227 n.
stuffy
  warm 397 adj.
  dull 840 adj.
stultify oneself
  stultify oneself
  695 vb.
stumble
  tumble 309 vb.
  blunder 495 vb.
stumble on
  chance 159 vb.
stumbling
  clumsy 695 adj.
stumbling-block
  obstacle 702 n.
stump
  remainder 41 n.
  leg 267 n.
  puzzle 474 vb.
stumpy
  short 204 adj.
stun
  render insensible
  375 vb.
  deafen 416 vb.
  impress 821 vb.
  frighten 854 vb.
stunning
  topping 644 adj.
stunt
  shorten 204 vb.
  deed 676 n.
  be ostentatious
  875 vb.

stunted
  dwarfish 196 adj.
stupefaction
  wonder 864 n.
stupefy
  render insensible
  375 vb.
  impress 821 vb.
stupendous
  wonderful 864 adj.
stupid
  unintelligent
  499 adj.
stupor
  insensibility 375 n.
  wonder 864 n.
sturdy
  stalwart 162 adj.
stutter
  stammer 580 vb.
  quake 854 vb.
sty
  stable 192 n.
  sink 649 n.
stye
  swelling 253 n.
style
  modality 7 n.
  sort 77 n.
  name 561 n., vb.
  style 566 n.
  elegance 575 n.
  way 624 n.
  fashion 848 n.
styled
  formed 243 adj.
stylet
  perforator 263 n.
stylish
  elegant 575 adj.
  fashionable 848 adj.
stylist
  stylist 575 n.
stylized
  formed 243 adj.
stylo, stylus
  stationery 586 n.
stymie
  obstruct 702 vb.
suave
  courteous 884 adj.
suavity
  courtesy 884 n.
sub
  inferior 35 adj.
subaltern
  inferior 35 n.

667

army officer 741 n.
sub-branch
  branch 53 n.
sub-clause
  subdivision 53 n.
subconscious
  spirit 447 n.
  psychic 447 adj.
subdivision
  subdivision 53 n.
subdivisional
  regional 184 adj.
subdual
  victory 727 n.
subdue
  subjugate 745 vb.
  restrain 747 vb.
subdued
  moderate 177 adj.
  dejected 834 adj.
subgrade
  inferior 35 adj.
sub-group
  subdivision 53 n.
sub-head
  classification 77 n.
sub-human
  animal 365 adj.
subject
  living model 23 n.
  prototype 23 n.
  liable 180 adj.
  topic 452 n.
  testee 461 n.
  subject 742 n.
  subject 745 adj.
  subjugate 745 vb.
subjection
  subjection 745 n.
subjective
  intrinsic 5 adj.
subjectivity
  fantasy 513 n.
subject-matter
  topic 452 n.
subjoin
  add 38 vb.
  place after 65 vb.
subjugate
  subjugate 745 vb.
sublet
  lease 784 vb.
sublimate
  vaporize 338 vb.
  purify 648 vb.
sublimated
  pure 950 adj.

sublime
  great 32 adj.
  impressive 821 adj.
  (*see* sublimity)
subliminal
  psychic 447 adj.
sublimity
  height 209 n.
  beauty 841 n.
  prestige 866 n.
sublunary
  telluric 321 adj.
submarine
  deep 211 adj.
  diver 313 n.
  warship 722 n.
submariner
  diver 313 n.
  navy man 722 n.
submerge
  plunge 313 vb.
  drench 341 vb.
  obliterate 550 vb.
submerged
  deep 211 adj.
submergence
  descent 309 n.
  plunge 313 n.
submersion
  moistening 341 n.
submission
  argument 475 n.
  submission 721 n.
  entreaty 761 n.
  servility 879 n.
submissive
  (*see* submission)
submit
  acquiesce 488 vb.
  propound 512 vb.
  submit 721 vb.
  be defeated 728 vb.
  (*see* submission)
subnormal
  inferior 35 adj.
subordinate
  inferior 35 n.
  servant 742 n.
subordination
  inferiority 35 n.
  subjection 745 n.
suborn
  bribe 612 vb.
subpoena
  legal process 959 n.
subscribe
  sign 547 vb.

contract 765 vb.
  pay 804 vb.
subscriber
  assenter 488 n.
  signatory 765 n.
subscribe to
  endorse 488 vb.
subscription
  offering 781 n.
  giving 781 n.
subsection
  classification 77 n.
subsequent
  subsequent 120 adj.
subserve
  be instrumental
  628 vb.
subservience
  submission 721 n.
  (*see* subservient)
subservient
  aiding 703 adj.
  servile 879 adj.
subside
  decrease 37 vb.
subsidence
  descent 309 n.
subsidiary
  inferior 35 n., adj.
  additional 38 adj.
  unimportant
  639 adj.
  aiding 703 adj.
subsidize
  aid 703 vb.
subsidy
  subvention 703 n.
subsist
  be 1 vb.
subsistence
  existence 1 n.
subsistence level
  poverty 801 n.
subsoil
  soil 344 n.
substance
  substance 3 n.
  main part 32 n.
  matter 319 n.
  meaning 514 n.
  chief thing 638 n.
  wealth 800 n.
substandard
  inferior 35 adj.
substantial
  substantial 3 adj.
  great 32 adj.

substantiate
  demonstrate 478 vb.
substantive
  real 1 adj.
  part of speech
  564 n.
substitute
  substitute 150 n.,
  vb.
  deputy 755 n.
substitution
  (*see* substitute)
substratum
  layer 207 n.
  base 214 n.
  basis 218 n.
substructure
  base 214 n.
subsume
  class 62 vb.
  number with 78 vb.
subterfuge
  pretext 614 n.
  stratagem 698 n.
subterranean
  deep 211 adj.
  concealed 525 adj.
subtle
  rare 325 adj.
  intelligent 498 adj.
  cunning 698 adj.
subtlety
  discrimination
  463 n.
  cunning 698 n.
subtopia
  mediocrity 732 n.
subtraction
  subtraction 39 n.
suburb
  district 184 n.
  housing 192 n.
suburban
  regional 184 adj.
  urban 192 adj.
suburbanite
  dweller 191 n.
  native 191 n.
suburbia
  habitancy 191 n.
  mediocrity 732 n.
  (*see* suburb)
suburbs
  circumjacence
  230 n.
subvention
  subvention 703 n.

subversion
revolution 149 n.
overturning 221 n.
subversive
revolutionary
149 adj.
subvert
revolutionize
149 vb.
demolish 165 vb.
subway
tunnel 263 n.
succeed
succeed 727 vb.
prosper 730 vb.
possess 773 vb.
success
success 727 n.
successful
successful 727 adj.
succession
sequence 65 n.
series 71 n.
posteriority 120 n.
successive
continuous 71 adj.
(*see* succession)
successor
aftercomer 67 n.
beneficiary 776 n.
successorship
futurity 124 n.
succinct
concise 569 adj.
succour
remedy 658 n., vb.
aid 703 n., vb.
succuba
demon 970 n.
succulent
savoury 390 adj.
succumb
be fatigued 684 vb.
knuckle under
721 vb.
suck
absorb 299 vb.
drink 301 vb.
extract 304 vb.
sucker
young plant 132 n.
orifice 263 n.
dupe 544 n.
suckling
child 132 n.
suck up to
flatter 925 vb.

suction
reception 299 n.
sudden
instantaneous
116 adj.
unexpected 508 adj.
suds
bubble 355 n.
sue
request, entreat
761 vb.
claim 915 vb.
indict 928 vb.
suet
fat 357 n.
suffer
permit 756 vb.
be patient 823 vb.
suffer 825 vb.
sufferance
lenity 736 n.
permission 756 n.
sufferer
sick person 651 n.
sufferer 825 n.
suffering
pain 377 n.
adversity 731 n.
painfulness 827 n.
suffice
suffice 635 vb.
sate 863 vb.
sufficiency
sufficiency 635 n.
sufficient
contenting 828 adj.
(*see* sufficiency)
suffix
adjunct 40 n.
affix 45 n.
part of speech
564 n.
sufflation
sufflation 352 n.
suffocate
suppress 165 vb.
kill 362 vb.
suffocating
warm 379 adj.
suffragan
ecclesiarch 986 n.
suffrage
vote 605 n.
sugar
sweet 392 n.
sugar-candy
sweet 392 n.

sugar-daddy
lover 887 n.
sugar the pill
sweeten 392 vb.
sugary
sweet 392 adj.
suggest
propound 512 vb.
imply 523 vb.
(*see* suggestion)
suggestibility
persuasibility 612 n.
suggestible
sentient 374 adj.
suggestio falsi
mental dishonesty
543 n.
suggestion
small quantity 33 n.
hint 524 n.
advice 691 n.
(*see* suggest)
suggestive
evidential 466 adj.
suppositional
512 adj.
impure 951 adj.
suicidal
destructive 165 adj.
rash 857 adj.
suicide
suicide 362 n.
sui generis
special 80 adj.
unconformable
84 adj.
suit
accord 24 vb.
sort 77 n.
dress 228 n.
request 761 n.
beautify 841 vb.
wooing 889 n.
litigation 959 n.
suitable
fit 24 adj.
expedient 642 adj.
suitcase
box 194 n.
suite
flat 192 n.
follower 284 n.
suiting
dress 228 n.
suitor
petitioner 763 n.
lover 887 n.

litigant 959 n.
sulk
be discontented
829 vb.
be sullen 893 vb.
sulks
discontent 829 n.
sullenness 893 n.
sulky
discontented
829 adj.
sullen 893 adj.
sullen
discontented
829 adj.
ungracious 885 adj.
sullen 893 adj.
malevolent 898 adj.
sully
make unclean
649 vb.
shame 867 vb.
sultanate
polity 733 n.
sultry
warm 379 adj.
sum
add 38 vb.
all 52 n.
numerical result
85 n.
summarize
be concise 569 vb.
abstract 592 vb.
summary
brief 114 adj.
concise 569 adj.
compendium 592 n.
summation
addition 38 n.
summer
summer 128 n.
palmy days 730 n.
summerhouse
arbour 194 n.
summing up
estimate 480 n.
legal trial 959 n.
summit
height 209 n.
summit 213 n.
conference 584 n.
summon
command 737 vb.
litigate 959 vb.
summons
call 547 n.

legal process 959 n.
summum bonum
good 615 n.
sump
sink 649 n.
sumptuary
monetary 797 adj.
sumptuary law
economy 814 n.
sumptuous
ostentatious 875 adj.
sum up
shorten 204 vb.
judge, estimate
480 vb.
try a case 959 vb.
sun
sun 321 n.
dry 342 vb.
sunburn
burning 381 n.
brownness 430 n.
Sunday
holy-day 988 n.
sunder
sunder 46 vb.
sundial
timekeeper 117 n.
sundown
evening 129 n.
sun-dry
preserve 666 vb.
sundry
many 104 adj.
sunlight
sun 321 n.
light 417 n.
sunny
dry 342 adj.
warm 379 adj.
undimmed 417 adj.
pleasurable 826 adj.
cheerful 833 adj.
sunny side
pleasurableness
826 n.
sunrise
morning 128 n.
sunset
evening 129 n.
sunshine
salubrity 652 n.
palmy days 730 n.
sunspot
maculation 437 n.
sun-tan
brownness 430 n.

sun-worshipper
sanitarian 652 n.
sup
eat, drink 301 vb.
taste 386 vb.
super
superior 34 adj.
topping 644 adj.
superabundance
great quantity 32 n.
redundance 637 n.
superannuated
antiquated 127 adj.
superannuation
age 131 n.
non-use 674 n.
(*see* resignation)
superb
excellent 644 adj.
supercharged
dynamic 160 adj.
supercilious
prideful 871 adj.
despising 922 adj.
supererogation
superfluity 637 n.
superficial
insubstantial 4 adj.
spatial 183 adj.
shallow 212 adj.
exterior 223 adj.
negligent 458 adj.
superfluity
great quantity 32 n.
superfluity 637 n.
superfluous
remaining 41 adj.
superfluous 637 adj.
superhuman
divine 965 adj.
superimpose
add 38 vb.
superintendence
management 689 n.
superintendent
manager 690 n.
superior
superior 34 n., adj.
prideful 871 adj.
(*see* superiority)
superiority
superiority 34 n.
precedence 64 n.
seniority 131 n.
goodness 644 n.
superlative
supreme 34 adj.

excellent 644 adj.
superman
exceller 644 n.
paragon 646 n.
supermarket
emporium 796 n.
supernatural
abnormal 84 adj.
divine 965 adj.
spooky 970 adj.
magical 983 adj.
paranormal
984 adj.
supernaturalism
occultism 984 n.
supernumerary
extra 40 n.
superfluous 637 adj.
superscription
label 547 n.
supersede
substitute 150 vb.
eject 300 vb.
depose 752 vb.
not retain 779 vb.
supersensory
immaterial 320 adj.
supersession
(*see* supersede)
supersonic
speedy 277 adj.
superstition
credulity 487 n.
ignorance 491 n.
heterodoxy 977 n.
superstitious
(*see* superstition)
supervene
ensue 120 vb.
happen 154 vb.
supervise
manage 689 vb.
supervisor
manager 690 n.
supervisory
directing 689 adj.
supine
supine 216 adj.
inactive 679 adj.
apathetic 820 adj.
supper
meal 301 n.
supplant
substitute 150 vb.
eject 300 vb.
supple
flexible 327 adj.

supplement
increment 36 n.
augment 36 vb.
adjunct 40 n.
make complete
54 vb.
sequel 67 n.
suppliant
petitioner 763 n.
supplication
entreaty 761 n.
prayers 981 n.
supplier
provider 633 n.
supplies
provision 633 n.
subvention 703 n.
supply
store 632 n.
provide 633 vb.
support
sustain 146 vb.
support 218 n., vb.
corroborate
466 vb.
aid 703 n., vb.
auxiliary 707 n.
approve 923 vb.
supporter
supporter 218 n.
patron 707 n.
supporting role
inferiority 35 n.
suppose
opine 485 vb.
suppose 512 vb.
supposition
topic 452 n.
(*see* suppose)
suppositional
suppositional
512 adj.
imaginary 513 adj.
suppress
suppress 165 vb.
counteract 182 vb.
obliterate 550 vb.
make mute 578 vb.
suppression
destruction 165 n.
abrogation 752 n.
prohibition 757 n.
suppressio veri
mental dishonesty
543 n.
suppurate
be ill 651 vb.

suppurating
toxic 653 adj.
suppuration
infection 651 n.
supremacy
governance 733 n.
(*see* supreme)
supreme
supreme 34 adj.
topmost 213 adj.
important 638 adj.
surcharge
price 809 n.
surcingle
girdle 47 n.
sure
certain 473 adj.
expectant 507 adj.
safe 660 adj.
trustworthy 929 adj.
sure-footed
vigilant 457 adj.
skilful 694 adj.
sure thing
certainty 473 n.
surety
security 767 n.
suretyship
security 767 n.
surf
wave 350 n.
bubble 355 n.
surface
space 183 n.
shallowness 212 n.
exteriority 223 n.
emerge 298 vb.
texture 331 n.
be visible 443 vb.
surfeit
superfluity 637 n.
satiety 863 n.
surf-riding
aquatics 269 n.
surge
vortex 315 n.
eddy 350 n.
flow 350 vb.
surgeon
doctor 658 n.
surgery
surgery 658 n.
surly
ungracious 885 adj.
surmise
opinion 485 n.
conjecture 512 n.

surmount
be high 209 vb.
crown 213 vb.
climb 308 vb.
surmountable
possible 469 adj.
surname
name 561 n., vb.
surpass
be superior 34 vb.
surpassing
great 32 adj.
excellent 644 adj.
surplus
remainder 41 n.
superfluity 637 n.
surprise
inexpectation
508 n.
surrender
relinquish 621 vb.
submission 721 n.
surreptitious
stealthy 525 adj.
surround
surround 230 vb.
circumscribe
232 vb.
surroundings
circumjacence
230 n.
surveillance
surveillance 457 n.
survey
inspection 438 n.
estimate 480 n., vb.
dissertation 591 n.
surveyor
surveyor 465 n.
survival
existence 1 n.
durability 113 n.
life 360 n.
**survival of the
fittest**
biology 358 n.
survive
outlast 113 vb.
be restored 656 vb.
survivor
survivor 41 n.
escaper 667 n.
susceptibility
liability 180 n.
persuasibility
612 n.
vulnerability 661 n.

moral sensibility
819 n.
susceptible
impressible 819 adj.
suspect
be uncertain
474 vb.
opine 485 vb.
unbelieved 486 adj.
offender 904 n.
accused person
928 n.
suspend
put off 136 vb.
hang 217 vb.
abrogate 752 vb.
suspender
hanger 217 n.
suspense
lull 145 n.
dubiety 474 n.
expectation 507 n.
suspension
elasticity 328 n.
abrogation 752 n.
suspicion
hint 524 n.
suspicious
nervous 854 adj.
jealous 911 adj.
sustain
sustain 146 vb.
support 218 vb.
aid 703 vb.
sustenance
food 301 n.
sutler
provider 633 n.
suttee
suicide 362 n.
oblation 981 n.
suture
joinder 45 n.
dividing line 92 n.
suzerain
sovereign 741 n.
suzerainty
governance 733 n.
svelte
narrow 206 adj.
shapely 841 adj.
swab
cleaning utensil
648 n.
surgical dressing
658 n.
navy man 722 n.

swaddle
tie 45 vb.
dress 228 vb.
swag
booty 790 n.
swagger
gait 265 n.
be proud 871 vb.
boasting 877 n.
swallow
absorb 299 vb.
mouthful 301 n.
eat 301 vb.
swallow whole
not discriminate
464 vb.
swamp
fill 54 vb.
drench 341 vb.
marsh 347 n.
swampy
marshy 347 adj.
swan
waterfowl 365 n.
swank
be affected 850 vb.
vanity 873 n.
swanker
proud man 871 n.
swanky
fashionable
848 adj.
swansong
end 69 n.
lament 836 n.
swap
interchange 151 n.,
vb.
barter 791 n.
swarm
crowd 74 n.
be many 104 vb.
be fruitful 171 vb.
swarthy
blackish 428 adj.
swashbuckler
insolent person
878 n.
swastika
cross 222 n.
talisman 983 n.
swat
strike 279 vb.
swathe
tie 45 vb.
cover 266 vb.
trace 548 n.

sway
influence 178 n.
oscillate 317 vb.
vary 152 vb.
power 160 n.
governance 733 n.

swear
swear 532 vb.
promise 764 vb.
cuss 899 vb.

swear by
believe 485 vb.
praise 923 vb.

swear off
recant 603 vb.

swear-word
scurrility 899 n.

sweat
exude 298 vb.
be hot 379 vb.
labour 682 n.

sweater
vest 228 n.

sweep
range 183 n.
curvature 248 n.
move fast 277 vb.
scan 438 vb.
clean 648 vb.

sweeper
cleaner 648 n.

sweeping
comprehensive
  52 adj.

sweepings
leavings 41 n.
rubbish 641 n.
dirt 649 n.

sweepstake
gambling 618 n.

sweet
savoury 390 adj.
sweet 392 n., adj.
melodious 410 adj.
pleasurable
  826 adj.
lovable 887 adj.

sweeten
sweeten 392 vb.

sweetheart
loved one 887 n.
darling 890 n.

sweetmeat
sweet 392 n.

sweetness
fragrance 396 n.
(*see* sweet)

swell
expand 197 vb.
be convex 253 vb.
wave 350 n.
loudness 400 n.
fop 848 n.

swelled head
vanity 873 n.

swelling
swelling 253 n.

swell the ranks
accrue 38 vb.
be included 78 vb.

swelter
be hot 379 vb.

swerve
deviation 282 n.
recede 290 vb.

swift
speedy 277 adj.

swiftness
velocity 277 n.

swill
drink 301 vb.
swill 649 n.

swim
swim 269 vb.

swimming
aquatics 269 n.

swimsuit
beachwear 228 n.

swindle
deceive 542 vb.
peculation 788 n.
be dishonest
  930 vb.

swindler
defrauder 789 n.

swine
pig 365 n.
knave, cad 938 n.

swing
periodicity 141 n.
range 183 n.
hang 217 vb.
oscillate 317 vb.
music 412 n.

swinish
sensual 944 adj.

swipe
knock 279 n.
propulsion 287 n.

swirl
vortex 315 n.
eddy 350 n.

swish
sibilation 406 n.

switch
interchange 151 vb.
hair 259 n.
transpose 272 vb.
club 723 n.
hair-dressing
  843 n.

switchback
obliquity 220 n.
undulatory 251 adj.

switch off
terminate 69 vb.
snuff out 418 vb.

switch on
initiate 68 vb.

swivel
gun 723 n.

swizz
trickery 542 n.

swollen
expanded 197 adj.
convex 253 adj.
prideful 871 adj.

swoon
be impotent 161 vb.
fatigue 684 n.
(*see* insensibility)

swoop
descend 309 vb.
plunge 313 n.

sword
combatant 722 n.
side-arms 723 n.

swordsman
combatant 722 n.

swot
study 536 vb.
learner 538 n.

sybarite
sensualist 944 n.

sycophancy
servility 879 n.
flattery 925 n.

sycophant
toady 879 n.
flatterer 925 n.

syllabic
literal 558 adj.

syllable
speech sound 368 n.
word 559 n.

syllabus
list 87 n.
compendium 592 n.

syllogism
argumentation
  475 n.

sylph
fairy 970 n.

symbiosis
life 360 n.
cooperation 706 n.

symbol
metaphor 519 n.
indication 547 n.
image 551 n.

symbolic
representing
  551 adj.
ritual 988 adj.

symbolism
(*see* symbol,
  symbolic)

symbolization
symbology 547 n.
(*see* symbolize)

symbolize
mean 514 vb.
represent 551 vb.

symbology
symbology 547 n.

symmetry
correlation 12 n.
symmetry 245 n.

sympathetic
agreeing 24 adj.
(*see* sympathy)

sympathize
(*see* sympathy)

sympathizer
patron 707 n.
collaborator 707 n.

sympathy
participation 775 n.
feeling 818 n.
friendliness 880 n.
pity 905 n.

symphonic
musical 412 adj.

symphony
musical piece
  412 n.

symposium
argument 475 n.
interlocution 584 n.
social gathering
  882 n.

symptom
concomitant 89 n.
evidence 466 n.
indication 547 n.

symptomatic
evidential 466 adj.
indicating 547 adj.

synagogue
 church 990 n.
synchronism
 synchronism 123 n.
synchronization
 synchronism 123 n.
synchronize
 accompany 89 vb.
 synchronize 123 vb.
syncopation
 tempo 410 n.
 music 412 n.
syncopator
 musician 713 n.
syncope
 helplessness 161 n.
syncretism
 mixture 43 n.
 combination 50 n.
syndicalism
 government 733 n.
syndicate
 corporation 708 n.
synod
 council 692 n.
synoecism
 association 706 n.
synonym
 substitute 150 n.
 connotation 514 n.
synonymity
 (*see* synonym)
synonymous
 semantic 514 adj.
synopsis
 whole 52 n.
 generality 79 n.
 list 87 n.
 compendium
 592 n.
synoptical
 inclusive 78 adj.
syntax
 composition 56 n.
 grammar 564 n.
synthesis
 combination 50 n.
synthesize
 compose 56 vb.
syphilis
 venereal disease
 651 n.
syringe
 irrigator 341 n.
syrup
 soft drink 301 n.
 sweet 392 n.

system
 order 60 n.
 rule 81 n.
systematic
 philosophic
 449 adj.
 rational 475 adj.
 businesslike
 622 adj.
 (*see* system)
systematize
 regularize 62 vb.
 plan 623 vb.

T

tab
 label 547 n.
 mark 547 vb.
tabby
 cat 365 n.
 mottled 437 adj.
tabernacle
 temple, church
 990 n.
table
 list 87 n.
 stand 218 n.
 eating, meal 301 n.
 register 548 vb.
tableau
 spectacle 445 n.
 stage show 594 n.
table d'hôte
 meal 301 n.
table fish
 table fish 365 n.
tableland
 high land 209 n.
 plain 348 n.
table manners
 eating 301 n.
tablet
 mouthful 301 n.
tabloid
 the press 528 n.
 medicine 658 n.
taboo
 exclusion 57 n.
 prohibition 757 n.
tabular
 arranged 62 adj.
tabula rasa
 obliteration 550 n.
tabulate
 class 62 vb.
 list 87 vb.

tacit
 tacit 523 adj.
taciturn
 taciturn 582 adj.
 unsociable 883 adj.
tack
 tie 45 vb.
 fastening 47 n.
 navigate 269 vb.
 direction 281 n.
 deviate 282 vb.
tackle
 tackling 47 n.
 equipment 630 n.
 undertake 672 vb.
tacky
 viscid 354 adj.
tact
 discrimination
 463 n.
 skill 694 n.
tactful
 discriminating
 463 adj.
tactical
 (*see* tactics)
tactician
 planner 623 n.
tactics
 policy 623 n.
 tactics 688 n.
tactile
 tactual 378 adj.
tactless
 indiscriminating
 464 adj.
 discourteous
 885 adj.
tactual
 tactual 378 adj.
tadpole
 youngling 132 n.
 frog 365 n.
tag
 label 547 n.
 mark 547 vb.
tag on
 add 38 vb.
tail
 sequel 67 n.
 extremity 69 n.
 pursue 619 vb.
 nonentity 639 n.
tail off
 decrease 37 vb.
tailor
 clothier 228 n.

 efform 243 vb.
tail-piece
 sequel 67 n.
tails
 formal dress 228 n.
taint
 badness 645 n.
 infection 651 n.
 impair 655 vb.
 slur 867 n.
take
 comprise 78 vb.
 overmaster
 727 vb.
 subjugate 745 vb.
 arrest 747 vb.
 take 786 vb.
take aback
 navigate 269 vb.
 surprise 508 vb.
take advantage of
 use 673 vb.
 be skilful 694 vb.
take after
 resemble 18 vb.
take amiss
 resent 891 vb.
take apart
 sunder 46 vb.
take aside
 speak to 583 vb.
take back
 recoup 31 vb.
 recant 603 vb.
take cover
 be stealthy 525 vb.
take down
 depress 311 vb.
take effect
 operate 173 vb.
 be successful
 727 vb.
take heed
 be warned 664 vb.
take in
 make smaller
 198 vb.
 admit 299 vb.
 understand 516 vb.
 befool 542 vb.
take in hand
 undertake 672 vb.
take it out of
 be malevolent
 898 vb.
take liberties
 be free 744 vb.

taken bad
  sick 651 adj.
take off
  doff 229 vb.
  fly 271 vb.
  satirize 851 vb.
take offence
  resent 891 vb.
take-over
  transference 272 n.
take-over bid
  offer 759 n.
  purchase 792 n.
take place
  happen 154 vb.
take root
  be wont 610 vb.
take shape
  become 1 vb.
take sides
  join a party 708 vb.
take steps
  do 676 vb.
take stock
  estimate 480 vb.
  account 808 vb.
take the lead
  initiate 68 vb.
  precede 283 vb.
take time
  have leisure 681 vb.
  be cautious 858 vb.
take to
  be in love 887 vb.
take up
  undertake 672 vb.
  befriend 880 vb.
takings
  earnings 771 n.
  receipt 807 n.
tale
  numeration 86 n.
  narrative 590 n.
  novel 590 n.
tale-bearer
  informer 524 n.
talent
  intelligence 498 n.
talent scout
  inquirer 459 n.
tale of woe
  lament 836 n.
talisman
  talisman 983 n.
talk
  inform 524 vb.
  rumour 529 n.

  speak 579 vb.
  be loquacious 581 vb.
  interlocution 584 n.
talkative
  loquacious 581 adj.
talk big
  boast 877 vb.
talker
  chatterer 581 n.
  interlocutor 584 n.
talk it over
  confer 584 vb.
talks
  conference 584 n.
talk to oneself
  soliloquize 585 vb.
tall
  whopping 32 adj.
  tall 209 adj.
tall order
  hard task 700 n.
tallow
  fat 357 n.
tall story
  fable 543 n.
tall talk
  insubstantial thing 4 n.
tally
  numeration 86 n.
  label 547 n.
  accounts 808 n.
talon
  nippers 778 n.
tambourine
  drum 414 n.
tame
  break in 369 vb.
  train 534 vb.
  feeble 572 adj.
tamper
  impair 655 vb.
  meddle 678 vb.
tamper with
  bribe 612 vb.
tan
  toughen 329 vb.
  burning 381 n.
  brown 430 adj.
  spank 963 vb.
tang
  projection 254 n.
  taste 386 n.
tangency
  contiguity 202 n.

tangent
  ratio 85 n.
tangential
  contiguous 202 adj.
tangible
  substantial 3 adj.
  tactual 378 adj.
tangle
  complexity 61 n.
  bedevil 63 vb.
tank
  vat 194 n.
  war-chariot 274 n.
  lake 346 n.
  storage 632 n.
tankard
  cup 194 n.
tantalize
  disappoint 509 vb.
  cause desire 859 vb.
tantamount
  equivalent 28 adj.
tantrum
  anger 891 n.
tap
  pierce 263 vb.
  strike 279 vb.
  outlet 298 n.
  extract 304 vb.
  conduit 351 n.
  touch 378 vb.
tape
  strip 208 n.
taped
  measured 465 adj.
tape-machine
  recording instrument 549 n.
tape-measure
  gauge 465 n.
taper
  shade off 27 vb.
  be narrow 206 vb.
  converge 293 vb.
  torch 420 n.
tape-recorder
  recording instrument 549 n.
tapestry
  covering 226 n.
  picture 553 n.
  needlework 844 n.
tapping
  extraction 304 vb.
tap-room
  tavern 192 n.

taproot
  source 156 n.
tapster
  servant 742 n.
tap the line
  hear 415 vb.
tar
  mariner 270 n.
  resin 357 n.
tardy
  late 136 adj.
  lazy 679 adj.
tare
  discount 810 n.
target
  direction 281 n.
  objective 617 n.
tariff
  restriction 747 n.
  price, tax 809 n.
tarmac
  paving 226 n.
tarnish
  make unclean 649 vb.
  blemish 845 n.
tarry
  be late 136 vb.
  move slowly 278 vb.
tart
  pastry 301 n.
  sour 393 adj.
  irascible 892 adj.
  prostitute 952 n.
tartan
  chequer 437 n.
task
  job 622 n.
  labour 682 n.
  fatigue 684 vb.
  hard task 700 n.
  duty 917 n.
tassel
  pendant 217 n.
taste
  eat 301 n.
  taste 386 n., vb.
  elegance 575 n.
  good taste 846 vb.
tasteful
  elegant 575 adj.
  tasteful 846 adj.
tasteless
  weak 163 adj.
  inelegant 576 adj.
tastelessness
  insipidity 387 n.

bad taste 847 n.
tasty
tasty 386 adj.
savoury 390 adj.
tatters
piece 53 n.
tatters, in
dilapidated 655 adj.
tattle
be loquacious
581 vb.
tattler
informer 524 n.
chatterer 581 n.
tattoo
pierce 263 vb.
roll 403 n., vb.
variegate 437 vb.
mark 547 vb.
pageant 875 n.
tattooer
beautician 843 n.
tattooing
ornamental art
844 n.
tatty
dilapidated
655 adj.
taunt
enrage 891 vb.
indignity 921 n.
accusation 928 n.
taut
rigid 326 adj.
tauten
make smaller
198 vb.
tautology
repetition 106 n.
redundance 637 n.
tavern
tavern 192 n.
tawdry
vulgar 847 adj.
tawny
brown 430 adj.
red 431 adj.
tax
oppress 735 vb.
levy 786 vb.
tax 809 n., vb.
taxable
priced 809 adj.
taxation
tax 809 n.
tax-collector
receiver 782 n.

tax-free
uncharged 812 adj.
non-liable 919 adj.
taxi
move 265 vb.
cab 274 n.
taxidermy
zoology 367 n.
taxonomy
arrangement 62 n.
tax with
accuse 928 vb.
tea
meal 301 n.
soft drink 301 n.
teach
convince 485 vb.
educate 534 vb.
teachable
studious 536 adj.
teachableness
persuasibility 612 n.
teacher
teacher 537 n.
teaching
teaching 534 n.
tea-drinker
sober person 948 n.
team
group, band 74 n.
team-mate
collaborator
707 n.
team spirit
cooperation 706 n.
concord 710 n.
teamwork
cooperation 706 n.
tear
rend 46 vb.
lamentation 836 n.
tear down
fell 311 vb.
tearful
unhappy 825 adj.
lamenting 836 adj.
tea-room
café 192 n.
tear up
abrogate 752 vb.
tease
tempt 612 vb.
torment 827 vb.
be witty 839 vb.
enrage 891 vb.
teaser
enigma 530 n.

humorist 839 n.
teat
bosom 253 n.
technical
trivial 639 adj.
well-made 694 adj.
technicality
trifle 639 n.
technical knowledge
skill 694 n.
technical term
name 561 n.
technician
artisan 686 n.
expert 696 n.
technicology
mechanics 630 n.
technique
way 624 n.
skill 694 n.
technocracy
government 733 n.
technology
science 490 n.
tectonic
structural 331 adj.
tectonics
structure 331 n.
tedious
tedious 838 adj.
dull 840 adj.
tedium
tedium 838 n.
(*see* tedious)
teed up
prepared 669 adj.
teem
reproduce itself
164 vb.
be fruitful 171 vb.
teen-ager
youngster 132 n.
teeter
be irresolute
601 vb.
teeth
vigorousness 174 n.
weapon 723 n.
teething troubles
beginning 68 n.
teetotal
temperate 942 adj.
teetotalism
temperance 942 n.
teetotaller
abstainer 942 n.
sober person 948 n.

teetotum
rotator 315 n.
telecommunication
telecommunication
531 n.
telegram
message 529 n.
telegraph
telecommunication
531 n.
telegraph boy
courier 531 n.
telegraphic
concise 569 adj.
telepathy
psychics 984 n.
telephone
hearing aid 415 n.
communication
531 n.
teleprinter
telecommunication
531 n.
recording
instrument 549 n.
telescope
shorten 204 vb.
telescope 442 n.
telescopic
distant 199 adj.
visible 443 adj.
televiewer
telecommunication
531 n.
televise
communicate
524 vb.
television
spectacle 445 n.
telecommunication
531 n.
tell
number 86 vb.
influence 178 vb.
inform 524 vb.
divulge 526 vb.
command 737 vb.
tell against
tell against 467 vb.
teller
computer 86 n.
treasurer 798 n.
tell fortunes
divine 511 vb.
telling
influential 178 adj.
impressive 821 adj.

tell off
reprove 924 vb.
tell-tale
informer 524 n.
indicating 547 adj.
telluric
telluric 321 adj.
temerity
rashness 857 n.
temper
temperament 5 n.
mix 43 vb.
composition 56 n.
strengthen 162 vb.
moderate 177 vb.
hardness 326 n.
toughen 329 vb.
mature 669 vb.
affections 817 n.
anger 891 n.
temperament
temperament 5 n.
affections 817 n.
excitability 822 n.
temperamental
capricious 604 adj.
excitable 822 adj.
temperance
temperance 942 n.
asceticism 945 n.
temperate
moderate 177 adj.
warm 379 adj.
cold 380 adj.
sober 948 adj.
(*see* **temperance**)
temperature
heat 379 n.
tempered
strong 162 adj.
moderate 177 adj.
tempest
storm 176 n.
tempestuous
disorderly 61 adj.
windy 352 adj.
angry 891 adj.
temple
laterality 239 n.
temple 990 n.
tempo
tempo 410 n.
temporal
transient 114 adj.
chronological
117 adj.
laical 987 adj.

temporality
benefice 985 n.
temporary
ephemeral 114 adj.
temporize
put off 136 vb.
tempt
attract 291 vb.
tempt 612 vb.
cause desire
859 vb.
temptation
inducement 612 n.
tempter
motivator 612 n.
tempting
savoury 390 adj.
tempt providence
be rash 857 vb.
tenable
rational 475 adj.
invulnerable
660 adj.
tenacious
cohesive 48 adj.
resolute 599 adj.
tenacity
retention 778 n.
(*see* **tenacious**)
tenant
resident 191 n.
dwell 192 vb.
tend
conduce 156 vb.
tend 179 vb.
groom 369 vb.
serve 742 vb.
tendency
tendency 179 n.
aptitude 694 n.
tendentious
tending 179 adj.
intended 617 adj.
tender
ship 275 n.
soft-hued 425 adj.
offer 759 n., vb.
(*see* **tenderness**)
tenderize
soften 327 vb.
tenderness
weakness 163 n.
softness 327 n.
sensibility 374 n.
moral sensibility
819 n.
painfulness 827 n.

love 887 n.
tender spot
moral sensibility
819 n.
tending
liable 180 adj.
tenement
housing 192 n.
estate 777 n.
tenet
creed 485 n.
precept 693 n.
tenor
modality 7 n.
tendency 179 n.
direction 281 n.
vocalist 413 n.
meaning 514 n.
tense
time 108 n.
rigid 326 adj.
grammar 564 n.
excitable 822 adj.
tensile
elastic 328 adj.
tension
lengthening 203 n.
discontent 829 n.
tent
dwelling 192 n.
canopy 226 n.
tentacle
nippers 778 n.
tentative
experimental
461 adj.
cautious 858 adj.
tenterhooks, on
expectant 507 adj.
tenuity
insubstantiality
4 n.
thinness 206 n.
tenuous
(*see* **tenuity**)
tenure
possession 773 n.
estate 777 n.
tepid
warm 379 adj.
teratogenesis
abnormality 84 n.
teratology
thaumaturgy 864 n.
tergiversation
change 143 n.
unreliability 474 n.

tergiversation
603 n.
term
end 69 n.
serial place 73 n.
period 110 n.
limit 236 n.
word 559 n.
name 561 n., vb.
termagant
shrew 892 n.
terminal
extremity 69 n.
ending 69 adj.
stopping place
145 n.
distant 199 adj.
terminate
terminate 69 vb.
termination
end 69 n.
terminology
nomenclature
561 n.
terminus
extremity 69 n.
stopping place
145 n.
limit 236 n.
termite
vermin 365 n.
term of art
neology 560 n.
name 561 n.
terms
conditions 766 n.
terms of reference
function 622 n.
terrace
housing 192 n.
terracotta
pottery 381 n.
terra firma
land 344 n.
terrain
region 184 n.
arena 724 n.
terrapin
reptile 365 n.
terrestrial
native 191 n.
telluric 321 adj.
terrible
frightening
854 adj.
terrier
dog 365 n.

terrific
 excellent 644 adj.
terrify
 frighten 854 vb.
territorial
 territorial 344 adj.
 soldier 722 n.
territory
 territory 184 n.
 lands 777 n.
terror
 fear 854 n.
 intimidation 854 n.
 ruffian 904 n.
terrorism
 violence 176 n.
 intimidation 854 n.
terrorist
 revolter 738 n.
terrorize
 oppress 735 vb.
 frighten 854 vb.
terse
 short 204 adj.
terseness
 conciseness 569 n.
test
 experiment 461 n.,
  vb.
 hard task 700 n.
testament
 title-deed 767 n.
testamentary
 proprietary 777 adj.
testamentary
 disposition
 transfer 780 n.
testator
 transferrer 272 n.
test case
 prototype 23 n.
 experiment 461 n.
tested
 trustworthy
  929 adj.
testee
 testee 461 n.
tester
 experimenter 461 n.
testicle
 genitalia 164 n.
testifier
 informant 524 n.
testify
 testify 466 vb.
testimonial
 credential 466 n.

monument 458 n.
testimony
 testimony 466 n.
testing agent
 testing agent 461 n.
test-tube
 testing agent 461 n.
testy
 irascible 892 adj.
tetchy
 irascible 892 adj.
tête-à-tête
 interlocution 584 n.
tether
 tie 45 vb.
 halter 47 n.
 fetter 747 vb.
tetrarch
 potentate 741 n.
text
 topic 452 n.
 reading matter
  589 n.
 precept 693 n.
textbook
 reading matter
  589 n.
textile
 textile 222 n.
textual
 scriptural 975 adj.
textural
 textural 331 adj.
texture
 texture 331 n.
 pattern 844 n.
thank
 thank 907 vb.
 reward 962 vb.
thankful
 content 828 adj.
 grateful 907 adj.
thankfulness
 gratitude 907 n.
thankless
 profitless 641 adj.
 unthanked 908 adj.
thanksgiving
 rejoicing 835 n.
 thanks 907 n.
thatch
 roof 226 n.
thaumaturgy
 thaumaturgy 864 n.
 sorcery 983 n.
thaw
 liquefaction 337 n.

liquefy 337 vb.
theatre
 region 184 n.
 theatre 594 n.
 arena 724 n.
 place of amusement
  837 n.
theatre-goer
 playgoer 594 n.
theatricality
 dramaturgy 594 n.
 acting 594 n.
 affectation 850 n.
theatricals
 dramaturgy 594 n.
theft
 stealing 788 n.
theism
 deism 973 n.
theist
 religionist 973 n.
theme
 topic 452 n.
theocracy
 theocracy 965 n.
 churchdom 985 n.
theodolite
 gauge 465 n.
theogony
 god 966 n.
theologian
 theologian 973 n.
theology
 theology 973 n.
theophany
 manifestation
  522 n.
 theophany 965 n.
 revelation 975 n.
theorem
 topic 452 n.
 argumentation
  475 n.
theoretical
 mental 447 adj.
 suppositional
  512 adj.
theorist
 theorist 512 n.
theorize
 account for 158 vb.
 suppose 512 vb.
theory
 idea 451 n.
 supposition 512 n.
theosophist
 occultist 984 n.

theosophy
 religion 973 n.
therapeutics
 therapy 658 n.
therapy
 therapy 658 n.
therm
 thermometry 379 n.
thermae
 hospital 658 n.
thermodynamics
 thermometry 379 n.
thermometer
 thermometry 379 n.
thermometry
 thermometry 379 n.
thermostat
 thermometry 379 n.
thesaurus
 list 87 n.
 dictionary 559 n.
thesis
 topic 452 n.
 dissertation 591 n.
thick
 middle 70 n.
 thick 205 adj.
 dense 324 adj.
 semiliquid 354 adj.
 cloudy 355 adj.
thicken
 be broad 205 vb.
 be dense 324 vb.
thickener
 condensation
  324 n.
thicket
 wood 366 n.
thickhead
 dunce 501 n.
thickness
 thickness 205 n.
 layer 207 n.
 density 324 n.
 (*see* thick)
thick of things
 middle 70 n.
 activity 678 n.
thick on the ground
 multitudinous
  104 adj.
thickset
 stalwart 162 adj.
 dense 324 adj.
thick-skinned
 thick-skinned
  820 adj.

thief
thief 789 n.
thieve
steal 788 vb.
thievery
thievishness 788 n.
thigh
leg 267 n.
thin
insubstantial 4 adj.
weaken 163 vb.
lean 206 adj.
transparent 422 adj.
insufficient 636 adj.
thing
object 319 n.
thing of the past
archaism 127 n.
things
clothing 228 n.
property 777 n.
thingummybob
no name 562 n.
think
think 449 vb.
imagine 513 vb.
thinkable
possible 469 adj.
think about
meditate 449 vb.
think alike
cooperate 706 vb.
think back
retrospect 505 vb.
think better of it
tergiversate
603 vb.
thinker
philosopher 449 n.
sage 500 n.
theorist 512 n.
thinking
wise 498 adj.
think well of
respect 920 vb.
approve 923 vb.
thinness
thinness 206 n.
(*see* thin)
thin on the ground
few 105 adj.
thin out
be dispersed 75 vb.
thin-skinned
sensitive 819 adj.
thin time, have a
suffer 825 vb.

third
treble 94 adj.
third estate
commonalty 869 n.
thirst
dryness 342 n.
hunger 859 n.
thirsty
hungry 859 adj.
drunken 949 adj.
thistle
prickle 256 n.
plant 366 n.
thistledown
hair 259 n.
levity 323 n.
thong
ligature 47 n.
thorax
bosom 253 n.
thorn
prickle 256 n.
thorn in the flesh
bane 659 n.
thorny
sharp 256 adj.
thorough
complete 54 adj.
careful 457 adj.
resolute 599 adj.
thoroughbred
unmixed 44 adj.
thoroughbred 273 n.
well-bred 848 adj.
thoroughfare
road 624 n.
thoroughgoing
(*see* thorough)
thoroughness
(*see* thorough)
thought
thought 449 n.
idea 451 n.
opinion 485 n.
worry 825 n.
thoughtful
thoughtful 449 adj.
wise 498 adj.
thoughtless
unthinking 450 adj.
inattentive 456 adj.
unwise 499 adj.
thraldom
servitude 745 n.
thrash
strike 279 vb.
defeat 727 vb.

flog 963 vb.
thread
connect 45 vb.
cable 47 n.
ligature 47 n.
line 203 n.
fibre 208 n.
pass 305 vb.
threadbare
beggarly 801 adj.
threat
danger 661 n.
intimidation 854 n.
threat 900 n.
threaten
impend 155 vb.
warn 664 vb.
threaten 900 vb.
three-dimensional
spatial 183 adj.
metric 465 adj.
threefold
treble 94 adj.
three Rs, the
curriculum 534 n.
threesome
three 93 n.
thresh
strike 279 vb.
cultivate 370 vb.
thresher
farm tool 370 n.
threshold
limit 236 n.
doorway 263 n.
thrift
economy 814 n.
thriftless
prodigal 815 adj.
thrifty
economical 814 adj.
thrill
pang 377 n.
excitation 821 n.
joy 824 n.
please 826 vb.
thriller
novel 590 n.
thrive
prosper 730 vb.
throat
orifice 263 n.
air-pipe 353 n.
throaty
hoarse 407 adj.
throb
spasm 318 n.

give pain 377 vb.
show feeling 818 vb.
throe
spasm 318 n.
pang 377 n.
thrombosis
blood pressure
651 n.
throne
seat 218 n.
regalia 743 n.
tribunal 956 n.
throng
crowd 74 n.
multitude 104 n.
throttle
close 264 vb.
retard 278 vb.
throughput
production 164 n.
transference 272 n.
throw
impulse 279 n.
propel 287 vb.
gambling 618 n.
throw away
waste 634 vb.
misuse 675 vb.
throw-back
recurrence 106 n.
reversion 148 n.
relapse 657 n.
throw down
demolish 165 vb.
fell 311 vb.
thrower
thrower 287 n.
throw fits
be agitated 318 vb.
be excitable
822 vb.
throw in one's teeth
accuse 928 vb.
throw light on
interpret 520 vb.
throw mud
defame 926 vb.
throw out
eject 300 vb.
throw-out
rubbish 641 n.
throw over
tergiversate 603 vb.
relinquish 621 vb.
throw overboard
lighten 323 vb.
disuse 674 vb.

throw up
  vomit 300 vb.
  resign 753 vb.
thrum
  edging 234 n.
  play music 413 vb.
thrummer
  instrumentalist
    413 n.
thrush
  vocalist 413 n.
thrust
  energy 160 n.
  vigorousness 174 n.
  impulse 279 n.
  propellant 287 n.
  foin 712 n.
thruster
  busy person 678 n.
thrustful
  vigorous 174 adj.
thud
  non-resonance
    405 n.
thug
  murderer 362 n.
  robber 789 n.
  ruffian 904 n.
thuggee
  homicide 362 n.
  stealing 788 n.
thumb-nail
  small 33 adj.
  compendium 592 n.
thumbscrew
  instrument of
    torture 964 n.
thumbs down
  condemnation
    961 n.
thumbs up
  acquittal 960 n.
thump
  strike 279 vb.
  non-resonance
    405 n.
thumper
  whopper 195 n.
thumping
  whopping 32 adj.
thunder
  storm 176 n.
  loudness 400 n.
  malediction 899 n.
thunderbolt
  missile weapon
    723 n.

thunder-clap
  inexpectation
    508 n.
thunderous
  loud 400 adj.
thunderstruck
  wondering 864 adj.
thwart
  oblique 220 adj.
  be obstructive
    702 vb.
thwarted
  impotent 161 adj.
  disappointed
    509 adj.
thyme
  scent 396 n.
thyrotoxic
  active 678 adj.
tiara
  headgear 228 n.
  regalia 743 n.
tibia
  leg 267 n.
tic
  spasm 318 n.
tick
  instant 116 n.
  oscillate 317 vb.
  sound faint
    401 vb.
  mark 547 vb.
  credit 802 n.
ticket
  credential 466 n.
  label 547 n.
  policy 623 n.
  permit 756 n.
ticket-holder
  incomer 297 n.
tickle
  itch 378 vb.
  tempt 612 vb.
  amuse 837 vb.
ticklish
  unreliable 474 adj.
  sentient 374 adj.
  unsafe 661 adj.
tick off
  register 548 vb.
  reprove 924 vb.
tidal
  periodical 141 adj.
  flowing 350 adj.
tide
  time 108 n.
  current 350 n.

tide over
  pass time 108 vb.
  navigate 269 vb.
  triumph 727 vb.
tideway
  current 350 n.
tidiness
  carefulness 457 n.
tidings
  news 529 n.
tidy
  orderly 60 adj.
  careful 457 adj.
  clean 648 adj.
tie
  draw 28 n.
  be equal 28 vb.
  tie 45 vb.
  bond 47 n.
  neckwear 228 n.
  fetter 747 vb.
tie down
  give terms 766 vb.
tier
  series 71 n.
  layer 207 n.
tie-up
  relation 9 n.
tiff
  bicker 709 vb.
tiger
  violent creature
    176 n.
  striation 437 n.
  brave person
    855 n.
  noxious animal
    904 n.
tight
  firm-set 45 adj.
  cohesive 48 adj.
  full 54 adj.
  sealed off 264 adj.
  parsimonious
    816 adj.
tight corner
  predicament 700 n.
tighten
  make smaller
    198 vb.
tightener
  compressor 198 n.
tight-fisted
  parsimonious
    816 adj.
tight-lipped
  taciturn 582 adj.

tights
  legwear 228 n.
tightwad
  niggard 816 n.
tile
  roof 226 n.
  headgear 228 n.
  building material
    631 n.
till
  while 108 adv.
  cultivate 370 vb.
  treasury 799 n.
tillage
  agriculture 370 n.
tiller
  handle 218 n.
  husbandman 370 n.
tilt
  obliquity 220 n.
  canopy 226 n.
  contest, duel
    716 n.
tilt at
  charge 712 vb.
timber
  wood 366 n.
timbre
  sound 398 n.
  voice 577 n.
timbrel
  drum 414 n.
time
  time 108 n.
  era 110 n.
  time 117 vb.
  tempo 410 n.
time and place
  situation 186 n.
time being
  present time 121 n.
timed
  synchronous
    123 adj.
time-fuse
  timekeeper 117 n.
time-honoured
  immemorial
    127 adj.
timekeeper
  timekeeper 117 n.
timeless
  perpetual 115 adj.
timelessness
  neverness 109 n.
time limit
  limit 236 n.

timely
apt 24 adj.
timely 137 adj.
expedient 642 adj.
time of day
clock time 117 n.
time off
leisure 681 n.
time of life
age 131 n.
timepiece
timekeeper 117 n.
time-saving
economy 814 n.
timescale
gauge 465 n.
time-server
tergiversator 603 n.
egotist 932 n.
time-serving
expedience 642 n.
selfish 932 adj.
time-signal
timekeeper 117 n.
signal 547 n.
times, the
present time 121 n.
time-switch
timekeeper 117 n.
timetable
chronology 117 n.
guide-book 524 n.
time up
finality 69 n.
timid
nervous 854 adj.
modest 874 adj.
timidity, timidness
(*see* timid)
timing
chronometry 117 n.
tempo 410 n.
timocracy
rich man 800 n.
(*see* government)
timorous
nervous 854 adj.
tin
small box 194 n.
preserve 666 vb.
tincture
small quantity 33 n.
tincture 43 n.
tinder
lighter 385 n.
tinge
tincture 43 n.

mix 43 vb.
hue 425 n.
tingle
formication 378 n.
tin god
autocrat 741 n.
tinker
mender 656 n.
repair 656 vb.
meddle 678 vb.
be unskilful
695 vb.
tinkle
sound faint 401 vb.
tinny
strident 407 adj.
tinsel
sham 542 n.
bauble 639 n.
finery 844 n.
bad taste 847 n.
tint
hue 425 n.
paint 553 vb.
tintinnabulation
gong 414 n.
tiny
small 33 adj.
little 196 adj.
tip
extra 40 n.
prepose 64 vb.
extremity 69 n.
obliquity 220 n.
invert 221 vb.
hint 524 n.
advice 691 n.
reward 962 n., vb.
tip-and-run
escaped 667 adj.
tip-off
hint 524 n.
tippet
cloak 228 n.
tipple
get drunk 949 vb.
tipster
gambler 618 n.
tipsy
tipsy 949 adj.
tip the scale
be unequal 29 vb.
weigh 322 vb.
tiptilted
curved 248 adj.
tiptoe
be stealthy 525 vb.

tip-top
topmost 213 adj.
best 644 adj.
tirade
oration 579 n.
censure 924 n.
tire
fatigue 684 vb.
be tedious 838 vb.
tired
sleepy 679 adj.
tireless
industrious 678 adj.
tirelessness
perseverance 600 n.
tiresome
tedious 838 adj.
tissue
textile 222 n.
texture 331 n.
cleaning cloth
648 n.
tissue-paper
thinness 206 n.
tit
saddle-horse 273 n.
titanic
huge 195 adj.
titbit
mouthful 301 n.
news 529 n.
savouriness 390 n.
tit for tat
retaliation 714 n.
tithe
trifle 639 n.
tax 809 n.
titillate
amuse 837 vb.
cause desire
859 vb.
titivate
beautify 841 vb.
title
label 547
name 561 n., vb.
decoration 729 n.
title 870 n.
dueness 915 n.
title-deed
title-deed 767 n.
title-holder
exceller 644 n.
title-page
beginning 68 n.
titter
laughter 835 n.

tittle
small quantity 33 n.
tittle-tattle
rumour 529 n.
chatter 581 n.
titular
verbal 559 adj.
named 561 adj.
toad
frog 365 n.
toady
toady 879 n.
toady to
flatter 925 vb.
toast
cereal, potion
301 n.
drink 301 vb.
a beauty 841 n.
toast 876 n.
favourite 890 n.
toast-master
nomenclator 561 n.
tobacco
tobacco 388 n.
tobacco-pipe
tobacco 388 n.
to be
future 124 adj.
toboggan
sled 274 n.
toccata, toccatina
musical piece 412 n.
to come
future 124 adj.
impending 155 adj.
tocsin
gong 414 n.
danger signal
665 n.
today
present time 121 n.
toddle
walk 267 vb.
toddler
child 132 n.
toddy-shop
tavern 192 n.
to-do
turmoil 61 n.
toe
extremity 69 n.
base, foot 214 n.
toe the line
acquiesce 488 vb.
toff
fop 848 n.

toga
 tunic 228 n.
toggery, togs
 clothing 228 n.
 finery 844 n.
toil
 labour 682 n.
toiler
 worker 686 n.
toilet
 dressing 228 n.
 latrine 649 n.
 beautification 843 n.
toiletry
 cosmetic 843 n.
toilsome
 laborious 682 adj.
token
 insubstantial thing
   4 n.
 reminder 505 n.
 indication 547 n.
 badge 547 n.
 trivial 639 adj.
tolerable
 not bad 644 adj.
 mediocre 732 adj.
tolerance
 strength 162 n.
 permission 756 n.
 patience 823 n.
tolerate
 consent 758 vb.
 forgive 909 vb.
 (see toleration)
toleration
 laxity 734 n.
 lenity 736 n.
 permission 756 n.
 patience 823 n.
to let
 offering 759 adj.
toll
 roll 403 vb.
 levy 786 vb.
 tax 809 n.
tomahawk
 axe 723 n.
tomb
 tomb 364 n.
tomboy
 youngster 132 n.
Tom, Dick, and
 Harry
 everyman 79 n.
tomfoolery
 foolery 497 n.

tommyrot
 silly talk 515 n.
Tom Tiddler's
 ground
 territory 184 n.
tom-tom
 drum 414 n.
tonal
 harmonic 410 adj.
 vocal 577 adj.
tonality
 melody 410 n.
tone
 strength 162 n.
 musical note 410 n.
 hue 425 n.
 style 566 n.
 voice 577 n.
tone-deaf
 deaf 416 n.
 indiscriminating
   464 adj.
tone down
 moderate 177 vb.
 decolorize 426 vb.
 misrepresent
   552 vb.
toneless
 discordant 411 adj.
tongs
 nippers 778 n.
tongue
 projection 254 n.
 language 557 n.
 voice 577 n.
tongue in cheek
 deception 542 n.
 mental dishonesty
   543 n.
tongue-in-cheek
 affected 850 adj.
tongue-tied
 voiceless 578 adj.
 taciturn 582 adj.
tonic
 salubrious 652 adj.
 tonic 658 n.
 excitant 821 n.
tonic effect
 stimulation 174 n.
tonnage
 size 195 n.
tonsure
 bareness 229 n.
 canonicals 989 n.
tontine
 gambling 618 n.

tool
 dupe 544 n.
 means 629 n.
 tool 630 n.
 decorate 844 vb.
tool-using
 mechanical 630 adj.
too much
 redundance 637 n.
 satiety 863 n.
toot, tootle
 play music 413 n.
 danger signal
   665 n.
tooth
 tooth 256 n.
 taste 386 n.
tooth for a tooth
 revenge 910 n.
toothless
 aged 131 adj.
 unsharpened
   257 adj.
toothpick
 cleaning utensil
   648 n.
top
 superiority 34 n.
 summit 213 n.
 covering 226 n.
 stopper 264 n.
 climb 308 vb.
 rotator 315 n.
 bubble 355 n.
top drawer
 élite 644 n.
top-drawer
 genteel 868 adj.
tope
 get drunk 949 vb.
toper
 drunkard 949 n.
top-flight
 notable 638 adj.
top-heavy
 unequal 29 adj.
 unsafe 661 adj.
top-hole
 topping 644 adj.
topiarism
 ornamental art
   844 n.
topic
 topic 452 n.
topical
 modern 126 adj.
 topical 452 adj.

topicality
 present time 121 n.
topknot
 hair 259 n.
top-level
 superior 34 adj.
topmost
 supreme 34 adj.
 topmost 213 adj.
topography
 situation 186 n.
 guide-book 524 n.
top, on
 superior 34 adj.
top people
 bigwig 638 n.
topping
 topping 644 adj.
topple down
 tumble 309 vb.
top-sawyer
 proficient 696 n.
top-secret
 concealed 525 adj.
 important 638 adj.
tops, the
 favourite 890 n.
topsy-turvy
 orderless 61 adj.
 inverted 221 adj.
top up
 replenish 633 vb.
tor
 high land 209 n.
torch
 lamp, torch 420 n.
 lighter 385 n.
torch-bearer
 preparer 669 n.
toreador
 killer 362 n.
toreutics
 ornamental art
   844 n.
torment
 pain 377 n.
 oppress 735 vb.
 suffering 825 n.
 torment 827 vb.
 torture 963 vb.
tornado
 gale 352 n.
torpedo
 suppress 165 vb.
 bomb 723 n.
torpedo-boat
 warship 722 n.

torpid
inert 175 adj.
apathetic 820 adj.
torpor
helplessness 161 n.
(*see* **torpid**)
torrent
velocity 277 n.
stream 350 n.
torrid
hot, warm 379 adj.
torso
piece 53 n.
sculpture 554 n.
tort
guilty act 936 n.
lawbreaking 954 n.
tortfeasor
offender 904 n.
tortoise
slowcoach 278 n.
tortoise-shell
variegation 437 n.
tortuous
convoluted 251 adj.
sophistical 477 adj.
torture
distort 246 vb.
give pain 377 vb.
oppress 735 vb.
suffering 825 n.
torment 827 vb.
torture 963 vb.
torture-chamber
lock-up 748 n.
torturer
punisher 963 n.
tosh
silly talk 515 n.
to spare
superfluous 637 adj.
toss
propel 287 vb.
oscillate 317 vb.
tot
potion 301 n.
total
addition 38 n.
all 52 n.
inclusive 78 adj.
numerical result
85 n.
totalizator
gaming-house
618 n.
totalitarianism
brute force 735 n.

totality
whole 52 n.
tote
carry 273 vb.
gaming house
618 n.
totem
idol 982 n.
to the point
important 638 adj.
totter
move slowly
278 vb.
tumble 309 vb.
oscillate 317 vb.
tottering
unstable 152 adj.
touch
be related 9 vb.
be situate 186 vb.
texture 331 n.
touch 378 n., vb.
discrimination
463 n.
meddle 678 vb.
skill 694 n.
excite 821 vb.
touch and go
unstable 152 adj.
unsafe 661 adj.
touch-down
air travel 271 n.
descend 309 vb.
touch-hole
orifice 263 n.
furnace 383 n.
touch off
initiate 68 vb.
kindle 381 vb.
touch on
relate 9 vb.
notice 455 vb.
touchstone
testing agent 461 n.
touch up
colour 425 vb.
make better 654 vb.
repair 656 vb.
touchwood
lighter 385 n.
touchy
sensitive 819 adj.
irascible 892 adj.
tough
strong 162 adj.
tough 329 adj.
difficult 700 adj.

thick-skinned
820 adj.
ruffian 904 n.
pitiless 906 adj.
toughen
toughen 329 vb.
toupee
wig 228 n.
tour
travel 267 vb.
circuition 314 n.
tour de force
masterpiece 694 n.
tourism
land travel 267 adj.
sport 837 n.
tourist
traveller 268 n.
tournament, tourney
contest, duel
716 n.
pageant 875 n.
tourniquet
compressor 198 n.
surgical dressing
658 n.
tousle
jumble 63 vb.
tousled
orderless 61 adj.
tout
request 761 vb.
petitioner 763 n.
seller 793 n.
tout ensemble
all 52 n.
tow
fibre 208 n.
traction 288 n.
towel
cleaning cloth
648 n.
tower
be great 32 vb.
house 192 n.
be high 209 vb.
ascend 308 vb.
fort 713 n.
tower of silence
tomb 364 n.
tower of strength
refuge 662 n.
tower over
be superior 34 vb.
tow-line, tow-rope
cable 47 n.
traction 288 n.

town
abode, housing
192 n.
beau monde 848 n.
town-crier
publicizer 528 n.
townee, townsman
native 191 n.
town-plan
urbanize 192 vb.
township
district 184 n.
towny
urban 192 adj.
toxic
toxic 653 adj.
baneful 659 adj.
toxicology
poison 659 n.
toxophilite
shooter 287 n.
toy
little 196 adj.
bauble 639 n.
plaything 837 n.
amuse oneself
837 vb.
caress 889 vb.
toy gun
toy gun 723 n.
trace
copy 20 vb.
small quantity 33 n.
effect 157 n.
outline 233 n., vb.
trace 548 n.
tracery
pattern 844 n.
traces
fetter 748 n.
trace to
attribute 158 vb.
trachea
air-pipe 353 n.
tracing
copy 22 n.
track
direction 281 n.
trace 548 n.
pursue 619 vb.
path, railroad
624 n.
arena 724 n.
tracker
hunter 619 n.
track, off the
mistaken 495 adj.

tract
region 184 n.
dissertation 591 n.
tractability
persuasibility 612 n.
tractable
wieldy 701 adj.
tractarian
dissertator 591 n.
tractile
drawing 288 adj.
flexible 327 adj.
traction
traction 288 n.
tractor
vehicle 274 n.
traction 288 n.
trade
interchange 151 vb.
business 622 n.
trade 791 n., vb.
sell 793 vb.
trade-mark
label 547 n.
trader
merchant ship
   275 n.
merchant 794 n.
tradesman
artisan 686 n.
tradesman 794 n.
trades union
society 708 n.
trading centre
emporium 796 n.
tradition
tradition 127 n.
narrative 590 n.
traditional
immemorial 127
   adj.
orthodox 976 adj.
traditionalism
conformity 83 n.
traditionalist
the orthodox 976 n.
traduce
defame 926 vb.
traffic
motion 265 n.
passing along 305 n.
trade 791 n., vb.
trafficator
indicator 547 n.
traffic control
traffic control
   305 n.

trafficker
merchant 794 n.
traffic light
signal light 420 n.
tragedian
actor 594 n.
tragedy
stage play 594 n.
evil 616 n.
tragic
dramatic 594 adj.
distressing 827 adj.
tragi-comic
dramatic 594 adj.
trail
be dispersed 75 vb.
be long 203 vb.
hang 217 vb.
follow 284 vb.
draw 288 vb.
trace 548 n.
pursue 619 vb.
path 624 n.
trailer
small house 192 n.
cinema 445 n.
train
procession 71 n.
pendant 217 n.
rear 238 n.
train 274 n.
follower 284 n.
train 534 vb.
habituate 610 vb.
trained
expert 694 adj.
trainee
beginner 538 n.
trainer
breeder 369 n.
trainer 537 n.
training
exercise 682 n.
training school
training school
   539 n.
traipse
(see trapes)
trait
temperament 5 n.
feature 445 n.
traitor
tergiversator 603 n.
dutilessness 918 n.
knave 938 n.
trajectory
route 624 n.

tram, tram-car
tram 274 n.
trammel
fetter 747 vb.
fetter 748 n.
tramp
gait 265 n.
walk 267 vb.
wanderer 268 n.
merchant ship
   275 n.
idler 679 n.
beggar 763 n.
trample
flatten 216 vb.
oppress 735 vb.
trampoline
lifter 310 n.
trance
insensibility 375 n.
fantasy 513 n.
sleep 679 n.
tranquil
tranquil 266 adj.
inexcitable 823 adj.
tranquillize
assuage 177 vb.
pacify 719 vb.
tranquillizer
moderator 177 n.
drug 658 n.
transaction(s)
affairs 154 n.
deed 676 n.
transcend
be great 32 vb.
   (see
   transcendence)
transcendence
extrinsicality 6 n.
non-imitation 21 n.
superiority 34 n.
perfection 646 n.
transcendental
inexpressible
   517 adj.
divine 965 adj.
transcribe
copy 20 vb.
write 586 vb.
transcript
copy 22 n.
transection
crossing 222 n.
transept
church interior
   990 n.

transfer
duplicate 22 n.
displace 188 vb.
transference 272 n.
carry 273 vb.
convey 780 vb.
transferable
transferable
   272 adj.
transferee
recipient 782 n.
transference
transference 272 n.
(see **transfer)**
transferrer
transferrer 272 n.
transfiguration
transformation
   143 n.
conversion 147 n.
theophany 965 n.
transfix
pierce 263 vb.
transformation
transformation
   143 n.
conversion 147 n.
improvement 654 n.
transfusion
transference 272 n.
surgery 658 vb.
transgress
disobey 738 vb.
(see **transgression)**
transgression
overstepping 306 n.
non-observance
   769 n.
guilty act 936 n.
transience
(see **transient)**
transient
transient 114 adj.
unstable 152 adj.
short 204 adj.
transit
motion 265 n.
passage 305 n.
transition
change 143 n.
transformation
   143 n.
transference 272 n.
transitional
converted 147 adj.
transitory
transient 114 adj.

translate
ecclesiasticize
985 vb.
(see translation)
translation
transference 272 n.
translation 520 n.
translator
interpreter 520 n.
transliteration
imitation 20 n.
translation 520 n.
translucent
semitransparent
424 adj.
transmigration
transformation
143 n.
transference 272 n.
transmission
transference 272 n.
transfer 780 n.
transmit
transfer 272 vb.
send 272 vb.
communicate
524 vb.
transmitter
telecommunication
531 n.
transmutation
transformation
143 n.
transom
beam 218 n.
window 263 n.
transparency
transparency 422 n.
photography 551 n.
transparent
transparent 422 adj.
perspicuous
567 adj.
artless 699 adj.
transpire
emerge, exude
298 vb.
transplant
implant 303 vb.
transplantation
transference 272 n.
transport
displace 188 vb.
transport 272 n.
carry 273 vb.
vehicle 274 n.
warm feeling 818 n.

transportation
penalty 963 n.
transpose
interchange 151 vb.
transpose 272 vb.
transubstantiation
transformation
143 n.
the sacrament
988 n.
transverse
oblique 220 adj.
crossed 222 adj.
transvestism
abnormality 84 n.
trap
receptacle 194 n.
carriage 274 n.
surprise 508 vb.
trap 542 n.
ensnare 542 vb.
pitfall 663 n.
take 786 vb.
trapan
(see trepan)
trapdoor
doorway 263 n.
pitfall 663 n.
trapes, traipse
wander 267 vb.
dirty person 649 n.
trapper
hunter 619 n.
trappings
coverlet 226 n.
equipment 630 n.
trash
rubbish 641 n.
trashy
feeble 572 adj.
trivial 639 adj.
trauma
wound 655 n.
travail
obstetrics 164 n.
labour 682 n.
adversity 731 n.
travel
motion 265 n.
land travel 267 n.
traveller
traveller 268 n.
travelogue
oration 579 n.
description 590n.
traverse
beam 218 n.

pass 305 vb.
tell against 467 vb.
oppose 704 vb.
defences 713 n.
travesty
misinterpretation
521 n.
misrepresentation
552 n.
satire 851 n.
trawl
network 222 n.
draw 288 vb.
hunt 619 vb.
trawler
fishing-boat 275 n.
hunter 619 n.
tray
receptacle 194 n.
plate 194 n.
treacherous
deceiving 542 adj.
unsafe 661 adj.
malevolent 898
adj.
perfidious 930 adj.
treachery
perfidy 930 n.
treacle
viscidity 354 n.
sweet 392 n.
treacly
viscid 354 adj.
tread
stand 218 n.
gait 265 n.
walk 267 vb.
ascent 308 n.
tread down
oppress 735 vb.
treadmill
labour 682 n.
bore 838 n.
tread on the heels
be near 200 vb.
follow 284 vb.
treason
sedition 738 n.
perfidy 930 n.
treasonable
perfidious 930 adj.
treasure
store 632 n., vb.
exceller 644 n.
preserve 666 vb.
funds 797 n.
honour 866 vb.

treasure-house
storage 632 n.
treasury 799 n.
treasurer
treasurer 798 n.
accountant 808 n.
treasure-trove
acquisition 771 n.
treasury
anthology 592 n.
storage 632 n.
treasury 799 n.
treat
modify 143 vb.
dissert 591 vb.
remedy, doctor
658 vb.
make terms 766 vb.
give 781 vb.
amusement 837 n.
treatise
dissertation 591 n.
treatment
change 143 n.
therapy 658 n.
use 673 n.
treaty
treaty 765 n.
treaty-maker
signatory 765 n.
treaty-making
conditions 766 n.
treble
treble 94 vb.
tree
tree 366 n.
trek
land travel 267 n.
trekker
traveller 268 n.
trellis
network 222 n.
tremble
be agitated 318 vb.
quake 854 vb.
tremolo
musical note 410 n.
tremor
oscillation 317 n.
agitation 318 n.
nervousness 854 n.
tremulous
agitated 318 adj.
trench
fence 235 n.
excavation 255 n.
conduit 351 n.

defences 713 n.
trenchancy
  vigour 571 n.
trenchant
  forceful 571 adj.
  disapproving
    924 adj.
trencher
  plate 194 n.
trencherman
  eater 301 n.
trenches
  battleground 724 n.
trench upon
  encroach 306 vb.
trend
  tendency 179 n.
  liability 180 n.
trepan
  perforator 263 n.
  pierce 263 vb.
  doctor 658 vb.
trephine
  doctor 658 vb.
trepidation
  fear 854 n.
trespass
  intrude 279 vb.
  be undue 916 vb.
  lawbreaking 954 n.
trespasser
  offender 904 n.
  usurper 916 n.
tresses
  hair 259 n.
trestle
  frame 218 n.
trews
  trousers 228 n.
triable
  legal 953 adj.
triad
  three 93 n.
trial
  experiment 461 n.
  bane 659 n.
  preparation 669 n.
  suffering 825 n.
  legal trial 959 n.
triangle
  angular figure
    247 n.
  gong 414 n.
triangulation
  measurement 465 n.
tribal
  ethnic 11 adj.

native 191 n.
  national 371 n.
tribe
  race 11 n.
  group 74 n.
  breed 77 n.
  multitude 104 n.
  community 708 n.
tribesman
  kinsman 11 n.
tribulation
  suffering 825 n.
tribunal
  tribunal 956 n.
tribune
  rostrum 539 n.
tributary
  stream 350 n.
  subject 745 adj.
tribute
  service 745 n.
  offering 781 n.
  tax 809 n.
  thanks 907 n.
  dueness 915 n.
tributes
  praise 923 n.
trichology
  hair-dressing 843 n.
trick
  trickery 542 n.
  befool 542 vb.
  habit 610 n.
  stratagem 698 n.
  foul play 930 n.
trickery
  trickery 542 n.
trickle
  small quantity 33 n.
  move slowly
    278 vb.
  flow 350 vb.
tricks of the trade
  trickery 542 n.
trickster
  trickster 545 n.
tricky
  cunning 698 adj.
tricolour
  flag 547 n.
trident
  authority 733 n.
tried
  expert 694 adj.
  trustworthy 929 adj.
trier
  essayer 671 n.

contender 716 n.
trifle
  insubstantial thing
    4 n.
  be inattentive
    456 vb.
  trifle 639 n.
  amuse oneself
    837 vb.
trifler
  nonentity 639 n.
trifle with
  hold cheap 922 vb.
trifling
  inconsiderable
    33 adj.
trigger
  tool 630 n.
  fire-arm 723 n.
trigger-happy
  rash 857 adj.
trigger off
  cause 156 vb.
trigonometry
  mathematics 86 n.
  angular measure
    247 n.
trill
  roll 403 n., vb.
  sing 413 vb.
  voice 577 vb.
trilogy
  three 93 n.
trim
  state 7 n.
  equalize 28 vb.
  orderly 60 adj.
  shorten 204 vb.
  dress 228 n.
  form 243 n.
  tergiversate 603 vb.
  clean 648 vb.
  personable 841 adj.
  decorate 844 vb.
trimmer
  tergiversator
    603 n.
trimming
  trimming 844 n.
trimmings
  adjunct 40 n.
trinity
  triality 93 n.
  Trinity 965 n.
trinket
  plaything 837 n.
  finery 844 n.

trio
  three 93 n.
  duet 412 n.
trip
  land travel 267 n.
  walk 267 vb.
  tumble 309 vb.
  blunder 495 vb.
  ensnare 542 vb.
  be clumsy 695 vb.
  hinder 702 vb.
  dance 837 vb.
tripartite
  trifid 95 adj.
tripe
  insides 224 n.
  silly talk 515 n.
triple
  treble 94 vb.
triplet
  three 93 n.
triplication
  triplication 94 n.
tripod
  stand 218 n.
  oracle 511 n.
tripper
  traveller 268 n.
triptych
  picture 553 n.
trireme
  warship 722 n.
trisection
  trisection 95 n.
trite
  known 490 adj.
  usual 610 adj.
triturate
  pulverize 332 vb.
triumph
  victory 727 n.
  triumph 727 vb.
  rejoice 835 vb.
  celebration 876 n.
triumphal
  celebrative 876 adj.
  gratulatory 886 adj.
triumphant
  successful 727 adj.
  jubilant 833 adj.
  celebrative 876 adj.
triune
  three 93 adj.
trivet
  stand 218 n.
trivial
  trivial 639 adj.

TRO

trodden
flat 216 adj.
troglodyte
dweller 191 n.
Trojan Horse
trap 542 n.
stratagem 698 n.
troll
demon 970 n.
trolley
pushcart 274 n.
tram 274 n.
trollop
prostitute 952 n.
trombone
horn 414 n.
troop
congregate 74 vb.
formation 722 n.
trooper
cavalry 722 n.
troops
armed force 722 n.
troopship
warship 722 n.
trope
trope 519 n.
trophy
trophy 729 n.
booty 790 n.
tropical
hot 379 adj.
figurative 519 adj.
trot
gait 265 n.
ride 267 vb.
move fast 277 vb.
troth
promise 764 n.
trot out
repeat 106 vb.
trotter
foot 214 n.
thoroughbred 273 n.
troubadour
musician 413 n.
poet 593 n.
trouble
derange 63 vb.
exertion 682 n.
adversity 731 n.
worry 825 n.
incommode 827 vb.
trouble-maker
trouble-maker
663 n.
agitator 738 n.

TRU

trouble-shooter
mediator 720 n.
troublesome
laborious 682 adj.
annoying 827 adj.
trouble spot
pitfall 663 n.
trough
bowl 194 n.
cavity 255 n.
trounce
defeat 727 vb.
reprove 924 vb.
spank 963 vb.
troupe
band 74 n.
trouper
actor 594 n.
trousers
trousers 228 n.
trousseau
clothing 228 n.
store 632 n.
trout
table fish 365 n.
trowel
shovel 274 n.
farm tool 370 n.
truancy
absence 190 n.
dutilessness 918 n.
truant
avoider 620 n.
(*see* truancy)
truce
lull 145 n.
peace 717 n.
truck
automobile 274 n.
pushcart 274 n.
barter 791 n.
truckle
be servile 879 vb.
truckman
driver 268 n.
truculence
rudeness 885 n.
trudge
move slowly
278 vb.
true
straight 249 adj.
true, accurate
494 adj.
trustworthy 929 adj.
true-blue
obedient 739 adj.

TRU

patriotic 901 adj.
true faith
orthodoxy 976 n.
true saying
maxim 496 n.
true to life
lifelike 18 adj.
true to type
typical 83 adj.
truffle
tuber 301 n.
truism
maxim, axiom
496 n.
trump
be superior 34 vb.
masterpiece 694 n.
overmaster 727 vb.
good man 937 n.
trumpery
bauble 639 n.
trivial 639 adj.
trumpet
megaphone 400 n.
horn 414 n.
proclaim 528 vb.
trumpeter
instrumentalist
413 n.
trump up
fake 541 vb.
truncate
shorten 204 vb.
truncated
incomplete 55 adj.
truncheon
club 723 n.
trundle
propel 287 vb.
rotate 315 vb.
trunk
piece 53 n.
box 194 n.
supporter 218 n.
tree 366 n.
communicating
624 adj.
trunks
legwear 228 n.
beachwear 228 n.
trunnion
pivot 218 n.
truss
tie 45 vb.
bunch 74 n.
trust
belief 485 n.

TUC

association 706 n.
mandate 751 n.
hope 852 n., vb.
trustee
consignee 754 n.
treasurer 798 n.
trusteeship
commission 751 n.
trustful
believing 485 adj.
trustworthy
credible 485 adj.
trustworthy
929 adj.
truth
truth 494 n.
maxim 496 n.
orthodoxy 976 n.
truthful
true 494 adj.
veracious 540 adj.
truthfulness
veracity 540 n.
try
taste 386 vb.
experiment 461 vb.
judge 480 vb.
tempt 612 vb.
essay 671 n., vb.
torment 827 vb.
trying
annoying 827 adj.
try-out
experiment 461 n.
tub
vat 194 n.
ablution 648 n.
tubby
fleshy 195 adj.
thick 205 adj.
tube
cylinder 252 n.
tunnel, tube 263 n.
railroad 624 n.
tuber
tuber 301 n.
tuberculosis
phthisis 651 n.
tub-thumper
speaker 579 n.
agitator 738 n.
tubular
tubular 263 adj.
tuck
fold 261 n., vb.
tuck in
place 187 vb.

eat 301 vb.

tuck up
  place 187 vb.
  shorten 204 vb.

tuff
  ash 381 n.

tuft
  hair 259 n.

tufty
  hairy 259 adj.

tug
  boat 275 n.
  traction 288 n.
  attraction 291 n.

tugboat
  traction 288 n.

tug-of-war
  opposition 704 n.
  contest 716 n.

tuition
  teaching 534 n.

tumble
  jumble 63 vb.
  tumble 309 vb.

tumble-down
  dilapidated 655 adj.

tumbler
  cup 194 n.
  entertainer 594 n.

tumbril
  cart 274 n.
  means of execution
   964 n.

tumescence
  convexity 253 n.

tummy
  maw 194 n.

tumour
  carcinosis 651 n.

tumult
  turmoil 61 n.
  loudness 400 n.

tumultuous
  disorderly 61 adj.
  loud 400 adj.

tun
  vat 194 n.

tundra
  plain 348 n.

tune
  adjust 24 vb.
  synchronize
   123 vb.
  tune 412 n.
  play music 413 vb.

tuneful
  melodious 410 adj.

tuneless
  discordant 411 adj.

tunic
  tunic 228 n.

tunnel
  tunnel 263 n.
  pierce 263 vb.
  descend 309 vb.
  railroad 624 n.

tu quoque
  rejoinder 460 n.

tu quoque
  argument
  accusation 928 n.

turban
  headgear 228 n.

turbid
  opaque 423 adj.

turbot
  table fish 365 n.

turbulence
  turmoil 61 n.
  commotion 318 n.
  excitability 822 n.

tureen
  bowl 194 n.

turf
  soil 344 n.
  grassland 348 n.
  racing 716 n.
  arena 724 n.

turfy
  soft 327 adj.
  vegetal 366 adj.

turgid
  rhetorical 574 adj.

turkey
  table bird 365 n.

Turkish bath
  ablution 648 n.

turmeric
  condiment 389 n.

turmoil
  turmoil 61 n.
  violence, storm
   176 n.
  commotion 318 n.
  activity 678 n.

turn
  period 110 n.
  change 143 n.
  tendency 179 n.
  efform 243 vb.
  make round 250 n.
  blunt 257 vb.
  fold 261 vb.
  land travel 267 n.

deviate 282 vb.
  circuition 314 n.
  rotation 315 n.
  be sour 393 vb.
  circuit 626 vb.
  aptitude 694 n.
  parry 713 vb.

turn a blind eye
  disregard 458 vb.

turn away
  dismiss 300 vb.
  refuse 760 vb.

turncoat
  tergiversator
   603 n.

turn down
  invert 221 vb.
  refuse 760 vb.

turned-up
  curved 248 adj.

turning
  circuition 314 n.

turning point
  juncture 8 n.
  crisis 137 n.
  reversion 148 n.

turn into
  convert 147 vb.
  translate 520 vb.

turnip
  tuber 301 n.

turnkey
  gaoler 749 n.

turn of the tide
  reversion 148 n.
  return 286 n.

turn on
  depend 157 vb.
  operate 173 vb.

turn out
  happen 154 vb.
  eject 300 vb.
  search 459 vb.

turn-out
  dressing 228 n.
  carriage 274 n.

turn over
  fold 261 vb.
  transfer 272 vb.
  sell 793 vb.

turnover
  pastry 301 n.
  receipt 807 n.

turnpike
  road 624 n.

turnspit
  domestic 742 n.

turnstile
  recording
   instrument 549 n.
  treasury 799 n.

turntable
  rotator 315 n.

turn tail
  run away 620 vb.

turn the corner
  get better 654 vb.

turn the tables
  tell against 467 vb.
  retaliate 714 vb.

turn to
  be turned to 147 vb.

turn to account
  use 673 vb.

turn turtle
  be inverted 221 vb.

turn-up
  fold 261 n.

turn up
  happen 151 vb.
  arrive 295 vb.

turn up one's nose
  despise 922 vb.

turpitude
  wickedness 934 n.

turquoise
  blueness 435 n.

turret
  fort 713 n.

turtle
  reptile 365 n.

tusk, tush
  tooth 256 n.

tusker
  pig 365 n.

tussle
  contention 716 n.

tussler
  contender 716 n.

tussock
  monticle 209 n.

tutelage
  teaching 534 n.
  subjection 745 n.

tutelary
  tutelary 660 adj.

tutelary genius
  patron 707 n.

tutor
  teach 534 vb.
  teacher 537 n.
  keeper 749 n.

tutorial
  teaching 534 n.

educational 534 n.
tut-tut
　deprecation 762 n.
tutu
　skirt 228 n.
tuxedo
　informal dress
　　228 n.
twaddle
　absurdity 497 n.
　silly talk 515 n.
twang
　stridor 407 n.
　play music 413 vb.
　speech defect 580 n.
tweak
　give pain 377 vb.
　touch 378 vb.
tweeds
　clothing 228 n.
tweeny
　domestic 742 n.
tweezers
　nippers 778 n.
twelvemonth
　period 110 n.
Twelve Tables
　precept 693 n.
twice-born, the
　upper class 868 n.
twice-told
　repeated 106 adj.
twice-told tale
　bore 838 n.
twiddle
　touch 378 vb.
twig
　foliage 366 n.
　understand 516 vb.
twilight
　evening 129 n.
　half-light 419 n.
　deterioration 655 n.
twill
　fold 261 vb.
twin
　kinsman 11 n.
　analogue 18 n.
　double 91 vb.
twine
　tie 45 vb.
　fibre 208 n.
　enlace 222 vb.
　twine 251 vb.
twinge
　pang 377 n.
　suffering 825 n.

twinkle
　flash 417 n.
　laughter 835 n.
twirl
　rotate 315 vb.
twist
　complexity 61 n.
　enlace 222 vb.
　distortion 246 n.
　twine 251 vb.
　eccentricity 503 n.
　misrepresentation
　　552 n.
　defect 647 n.
twister
　trickster 545 n.
twists and turns
　meandering 251 n.
twit
　ridicule 851 vb.
　accuse 928 vb.
twitch
　move 265 vb.
　spasm 318 n.
　feel pain 377 vb.
twitter
　agitation 318 n.
　ululate 409 vb.
two
　duality 90 n.
two-a-penny
　trivial 639 adj.
two-edged
　equivocal 518 adj.
two-faced
　hypocritical
　　541 adj.
two-fold
　double 91 adj.
two minds, of
　irresolute 601 adj.
two of a kind
　analogue 18 n.
two strings to one's
　bow
　means 629 n.
two voices, speak
　with
　be equivocal 518 vb.
two-way
　correlative 12 adj.
tycoon
　autocrat 741 n.
tyke
　dog 365 n.
tympanum
　ear 415 n.

type
　character 5 n.
　analogue 18 n.
　example 83 n.
　form 243 n.
　person 371 n.
　image 551 n.
　write 586 vb.
　print-type 587 n.
typescript
　script 586 n.
　book 589 n.
typesetting
　print 587 n.
typhoon
　gale 352 n.
typical
　general 79 adj.
　typical 83 adj.
　figurative 519 adj.
typify
　mean 514 vb.
　represent 551 vb.
typographer
　engraver 556 n.
　printer 587 n.
typography
　print 587 n.
tyrannical
　violent 176 adj.
　cruel 898 adj.
　(see tyranny)
tyrannicide
　homicide 362 n.
tyrannize
　be violent 176 vb.
　oppress 735 vb.
tyranny
　influence 178 n.
　despotism 733 n.
　brute force 735 n.
　arrogation 916 n.
tyrant
　tyrant 735 n.
　autocrat 741 n.
tyre
　wheel 250 n.
tyro
　beginner 538 n.

U

U
　well bred 848 adj.
　genteel 868 adj.
ubiquitous
　universal 79 adj.

ubiquitous 189 adj.
udder
　bladder 194 n.
　bosom 253 n.
uglify
　make ugly 842 vb.
ugly
　dangerous 661 adj.
　ugly 842 adj.
ugly customer
　ruffian 904 n.
ukase
　decree 737 n.
ukelele
　harp 414 n.
ulcer
　ulcer 651 n.
　bane 659 n.
ulceration
　ulcer 651 n.
　painfulness 827 n.
ulterior
　extraneous 59 adj.
ultimate
　ending 69 adj.
　distant 199 adj.
ultimate point
　extremity 69 n.
ultimatum
　period 110 n.
　demand 737 n.
　conditions 766 n.
ultra
　extremely 32 adv.
ultramarine
　blue pigment 435 n.
ultramontane
　ecclesiastical
　　985 adj.
ultra vires
　unwarranted
　　916 adj.
ululation
　ululation 409 n.
umber
　brown paint 430 n.
umbilical
　central 225 adj.
umbilicus
　centre 225 n.
umbrage
　resentment 891 n.
umbrella
　shade 226 n.
　shelter 662 n.
umpire
　estimator 480 n.

mediator 720 n.
mediate 720 vb.
unabashed
 insolent 878 adj.
unable
 powerless 161 adj.
unabridged
 intact 52 adj.
 long 203 adj.
unacclimatized
 extraneous 59 adj.
unaccompanied
 alone 88 adj.
unaccountable
 causeless 159 adj.
 wonderful 864 adj.
unaccustomed
 unhabituated
 611 adj.
unacquaintance
 ignorance 491 n.
unadmired
 unrespected
 921 adj.
unadorned
 plain 573 adj.
 artless 699 adj.
unadulterated
 unmixed 44 adj.
 pure 950 adj.
unadvisable
 inexpedient
 643 adj.
unaesthetic
 graceless 842 adj.
unaffected
 intact 52 adj.
 elegant 575 adj.
 artless 699 adj.
 non-liable 919 adj.
unalike
 dissimilar 19 adj.
unalloyed
 unmixed 44 adj.
unambiguous
 perspicuous
 567 adj.
unambitious
 apathetic 820 adj.
 modest 874 adj.
unamiable
 unkind 898 adj.
unanimity
 agreement 24 n.
 consensus 488 n.
unanimous
 (*see* **unanimity**)

unannounced
 unexpected 508 adj.
unanswerable
 demonstrated
 478 adj.
unappeasable
 violent 176 adj.
 revengeful 910 adj.
unappetizing
 unsavoury 391 adj.
unapproachable
 removed 199 adj.
 impracticable
 470 adj.
unarmed
 defenceless 161 adj.
 peaceful 717 adj.
unashamed
 impenitent 940 adj.
unasked
 voluntary 597 adj.
unaspiring
 indifferent 860 adj.
unassailable
 invulnerable
 660 adj.
unassimilated
 extraneous 59 adj.
 unsociable 883 adj.
unassuming
 humble 872 adj.
 modest 874 adj.
unattached
 separate 46 adj.
 independent
 744 adj.
unattractive
 unpleasant 827 adj.
 unwanted 860 adj.
unauthorized
 unwarranted
 916 adj.
unavoidable
 certain 473 adj.
 necessary 596 adj.
 obligatory 917 adj.
unaware
 ignorant 491 adj.
 inexpectant
 508 adj.
unbalance
 derange 63 vb.
unbalanced
 unwise 499 adj.
 owed 803 adj.
unbaptized
 heathenish 974 adj.

unbearable
 intolerable 827 adj.
unbeatable
 unbeaten 727 adj.
unbecoming
 graceless 842 adj.
 discreditable
 867 adj.
unbelief
 unbelief 486 n.
unbelievable
 unbelieved 486 adj.
 wonderful 864 adj.
unbeliever
 unbeliever 486 n.
unbend
 repose 683 vb.
 show mercy
 905 vb.
unbending
 rigid 326 adj.
 resolute 599 adj.
 obstinate 602 adj.
unbiased
 judicial 480 adj.
 just 913 adj.
unbiblical
 heterodox 977 adj.
unbidden
 unwanted 860 adj.
unbind
 disjoin 46 vb.
 deliver 668 vb.
unblemished
 perfect 646 adj.
unblest
 unfortunate
 731 adj.
 profane 980 adj.
unblest with
 not owning 774 adj.
unblushing
 thick-skinned
 820 adj.
 impenitent 940 adj.
unborn
 unborn 2 adj.
unbosom oneself
 divulge 526 vb.
unbounded
 infinite 107 adj.
unbowed
 vertical 215 adj.
unbreakable
 unyielding 162 adj.
unbreeched
 infantine 132 adj.

unbridled
 anarchic 734 adj.
 unconfined 744 adj.
unbriefed
 uninstructed
 491 adj.
unbroken
 uniform 16 adj.
 intact 52 adj.
 continuous 71 adj.
 unhabituated
 611 adj.
unburden
 disencumber 701 vb.
unbutton
 doff 229 vb.
unbuttoned
 sociable 882 adj.
uncalculating
 rash 857 adj.
uncalled for
 undue 916 adj.
uncanny
 spooky 970 adj.
 magical 983 adj.
uncaring
 indifferent 860 adj.
unceasing
 unceasing 146 adj.
 persevering 600 adj.
uncensorious
 approving 923 adj.
unceremonious
 discourteous
 885 adj.
uncertain
 fitful 142 adj.
 unstable 152 adj.
 uncertain 474 adj.
 capricious 604 adj.
 speculative 618 adj.
uncertainty
 doubt 486 n.
 ignorance 491 n.
 (*see* **uncertain**)
unchain
 liberate 746 vb.
unchallengeable
 undisputed 473 adj.
unchangeability
 permanence 144 n.
unchangeable
 unchangeable
 153 adj.
unchanging
 uniform 16 adj.
 permanent 144 adj.

uncharitable
unkind 898 adj.
uncharted
unknown 491 adj.
unchaste
unchaste 951 adj.
unchivalrous
discourteous
885 adj.
uncial
letter 558 n.
uncircumcised
heathenish 974 adj.
uncircumscribed
spacious 183 adj.
uncivil
discourteous
885 adj.
uncivilized
artless 699 adj.
plebeian 869 adj.
unclad
uncovered 229 adj.
unclaimed
unpossessed 774 adj.
not retained
779 adj.
unclassified
mixed 43 adj.
orderless 61 adj.
uncle
kinsman 11 n.
unclean
unclean 649 adj.
uncleanliness
insalubrity 653 n.
uncleanness
impurity 951 n.
(*see* **unclean**)
unclinch
be disjoined 46 vb.
not retain 779 vb.
uncloak
uncover 229 vb.
disclose 526 vb.
unclose
disclose 526 vb.
unclothe
uncover 229 vb.
unclouded
undimmed 417 adj.
well-seen 443 adj.
unclubbable
unsociable 883 adj.
uncoil
unravel 62 vb.
straighten 249 vb.

evolve 316 vb.
uncomfortable
suffering 825 adj.
unpleasant 827 adj.
uncommitted
neutral 625 adj.
independent
744 adj.
uncommon
special 80 adj.
infrequent 140 adj.
uncomplaining
patient 823 adj.
uncomplicated
simple 44 adj.
artless 699 adj.
easy 701 adj.
uncomplimentary
disrespectful
921 adj.
disapproving
924 adj.
uncompromising
obstinate 602 adj.
severe 735 adj.
unconcealed
manifest 522 adj.
unconcern
indifference 860 n.
unconcerned
irrelative 10 adj.
(*see* **unconcern**)
unconditional
unconditional
744 adj.
obligatory 917 adj.
unconfined
unconfined 744 adj.
unconformable
unconformable
84 adj.
unconformity
unconformity 84 n.
uncongealed
fluid 335 adj.
liquefied 337 adj.
uncongenial
disagreeing 25 adj.
cheerless 834 adj.
unconnected
irrelative 10 adj.
unconquerable
unbeaten 727 adj.
independent
744 adj.
unconscionable
great 32 adj.

unconscious
insensible 375 adj.
ignorant 491 adj.
involuntary
596 adj.
sleepy 679 adj.
unconscious, the
spirit 447 n.
unconstitutional
unwarranted
916 adj.
illegal 954 adj.
uncontested
undisputed 473 adj.
uncontrollable
violent 176 adj.
frenzied 503 adj.
wilful 602 adj.
excitable 822 adj.
unconventional
unconformable
84 adj.
free 744 adj.
unconvincing
improbable
472 adj.
uncooperative
unwilling 598 adj.
hindering 702 adj.
uncoordinated
orderless 61 adj.
uncork
open 263 vb.
uncorroborated
uncertified 474 adj.
uncounted
many 104 adj.
uncouth
inelegant 576 adj.
ill-bred 847 adj.
uncovenanted
unexpected 508 adj.
uncover
open 263 vb.
disclose 526 vb.
uncritical
indiscriminating
464 adj.
uncrowned king
influence 178 n.
unction
lubrication 334 n.
unguent 357 n.
pietism 979 n.
unctuous
unctuous 357 adj.
flattering 925 adj.

uncultured
uninstructed
491 adj.
plebeian 869 adj.
uncurl
straighten 249 vb.
undamaged
intact 52 adj.
undated
anachronistic
118 adj.
undaunted
resolute 599 adj.
unfearing 855 adj.
undeceive
inform 524 vb.
displease 827 vb.
undeceived
regretting 830 adj.
undecided
doubting 474 adj.
irresolute 601 adj.
undeclared
tacit 523 adj.
undefeated
unbeaten 727 adj.
undefiled
pure 950 adj.
undefined
amorphous 244 adj.
shadowy 419 adj.
uncertain 474 adj.
undemocratic
authoritarian
735 adj.
undeniable
undisputed 473 adj.
under
inferior 35 adj.
low 210 adj.
subject 745 adj.
under a cloud
unprosperous
731 adj.
under-age
young 130 adj.
under arms
warring 718 adj.
underbred
ill-bred 847 adj.
undercarriage
frame 218 n.
underclothes
underwear 228 n.
under control
obedient 739 adj.
restrained 747 adj.

under cover
latent 523 adj.
concealed 525 adj.
undercover agent
secret service
459 n.
undercurrent
current 350 n.
latency 523 n.
undercut
meat 301 n.
cheapen 812 vb.
under discipline
restrained 747 adj.
underdog
inferior 35 n.
unlucky person
731 n.
underdone
immature 670 adj.
uncompleted
726 adj.
underestimate
underestimate
483 vb.
underexposure
achromatism 426 n.
underfed
underfed 636 adj.
hungry 859 adj.
underfoot
low 210 adj.
undergo
meet with 154 vb.
feel 818 vb.
suffer 825 vb.
undergraduate
college student
538 adj.
underground
deep 211 adj.
tunnel 263 n.
buried 364 adj.
underground
activities
sedition 738 n.
undergrowth
wood 366 n.
underhand
occult 523 adj.
stealthy 525 adj.
dishonest 930 adj.
underhung
salient 254 adj.
underlie
be low 210 vb.
lurk 523 vb.

underline
emphasize 532 vb.
mark 547 vb.
underlinen
underwear 228 n.
underling
inferior 35 n.
servant 742 n.
underlying
undermost 214 adj.
undermine
weaken 163 vb.
demolish 165 vb.
descend 309 vb.
impair 655 vb.
undermost
base 214 adj.
undernourished
underfed 636 adj.
underpaid
cheap 812 adj.
underpants
underwear 228 n.
underpass
tunnel 263 n.
bridge 624 n.
underpin
support 218 vb.
underpriced
cheap 812 adj.
underprivileged, the
poor man 801 n.
lower classes 869 n.
underrate
underestimate
483 vb.
hold cheap 922 vb.
undersea
deep 211 adj.
undershot
salient 254 adj.
underside
lowness 210 n.
undersigned, the
signatory 765 n.
undersized
small 33 adj.
dwarfish 196 adj.
lean 206 adj.
undersong
vocal music 412 n.
understaffed
unprovided 636 adj.
understand
know 490 vb.
be wise 498 vb.
understand 516 vb.

understanding
agreement 24 n.
intellect 447 n.
intelligence 498 n.
concord 710 n.
compact 765 n.
understatement
underestimation
483 n.
understood
tacit 523 adj.
usual 610 adj.
understrapper
inferior 35 n.
nonentity 639 n.
understudy
substitute 150 n.
actor 594 n.
deputy 755 n.
undersurface
lowness 210 n.
undertake
undertake 672 vb.
promise 764 vb.
undertaker
interment 364 n.
doer 676 n.
undertaking
undertaking 672 n.
promise 764 n.
undertone
faintness 401 n.
undertow
current 350 n.
undervaluation
underestimation
483 n.
undervitaminized
underfed 636 adj.
unhealthy 651 adj.
underwater
deep 211 adj.
underwear
underwear 228 n.
underweight
light 323 adj.
underworld
the dead 361 n.
lower classes 869 n.
offender 904 n.
hell 972 n.
underwrite
give security
767 vb.
underwriting
calculation of
chance 159 n.

security 767 n.
undeserving
unentitled 916 adj.
undesigned
unintentional
618 adj.
undesirability
inexpedience 643 n.
undesirable
unwanted 860 adj.
bad man 938 n.
undeveloped
latent 523 adj.
immature 670 adj.
undevelopment
undevelopment
670 n.
undeviating
uniform 16 adj.
straight 249 adj.
undifferentiated
simple 44 adj.
indiscriminate
464 adj.
undigested
immature 670 adj.
undignified
vulgar 847 adj.
undiluted
unmixed 44 adj.
Undine
sea-nymph 343 n.
undiscerning
unwise 499 adj.
undisciplined
disorderly 61 adj.
disobedient 738 adj.
undisguised
undisguised 522 adj.
artless 699 adj.
undismayed
unfearing 655 adj.
undisputed
undisputed 473 adj.
undistinguished
mediocre 732 adj.
undistorted
symmetrical
245 adj.
undistracted
attentive 455 adj.
undisturbed
tranquil 266 adj.
undivided
intact 52 adj.
undo
disjoin 46 vb.

revert 148 **vb.**
destroy 165 **vb.**
counteract 182 **vb.**
doff 229 **vb.**
undoing
ruin 165 **n.**
undoubting
believing 485 **adj.**
undress
informal dress
228 **n.**
uncover 229 **vb.**
undue
undue 916 **adj.**
undulation
convolution 251 **n.**
oscillation 317 **n.**
wave 350 **n.**
undulatory
periodical 141 **adj.**
undulatory 251 **adj.**
undutiful
dutiless 918 **adj.**
unearned
unwarranted
916 **adj.**
unearth
exhume 364 **vb.**
unearthly
immaterial 320 **adj.**
spooky 970 **adj.**
uneasiness
worry 825 **n.**
discontent 829 **n.**
nervousness 854 **n.**
uneatable
unsavoury 391 **adj.**
uneconomic
wasteful 634 **adj.**
unedifying
discreditable
867 **adj.**
uneducated
uninstructed
491 **adj.**
unemotional
impassive 820 **adj.**
unemployable
useless 641 **adj.**
unused 674 **adj.**
unemployment
inactivity 679 **n.**
adversity 731 **n.**
unending
perpetual 115 **adj.**
unendurable
intolerable 827 **adj.**

unenjoyable
tedious 838 **adj.**
unenlightened
ignorant 491 **adj.**
unwise 499 **adj.**
unequal
unequal 29 **adj.**
unequalled
best 644 **adj.**
unerring
certain 473 **adj.**
accurate 494 **adj.**
successful 727 **adj.**
unethical
dishonest 930 **adj.**
uneven
non-uniform
17 **adj.**
unequal 29 **adj.**
fitful 142 **adj.**
rough 259 **adj.**
imperfect 647 **adj.**
uneventful
tranquil 266 **adj.**
unexampled
unusual 84 **n.**
unexceptionable
not bad 644 **adj.**
unexpected
unexpected 508 **adj.**
unexpended
remaining 41 **adj.**
unexpired
remaining 41 **adj.**
unexplained
causeless 159 **adj.**
puzzling 517 **adj.**
unexpressed
tacit 523 **adj.**
unexpurgated
intact 52 **adj.**
unfactual
erroneous 495 **adj.**
unfading
lasting 113 **adj.**
coloured 425 **adj.**
unfailing
unceasing 146 **adj.**
unfair
unjust 914 **adj.**
dishonest 930 **adj.**
unfaith
unbelief 486 **n.**
perfidy 930 **n.**
unfaithful
unbelieving
486 **adj.**

perfidious 930 **adj.**
extramarital
951 **adj.**
unfallen
innocent 935 **adj.**
unfaltering
persevering 600 **adj.**
unfamiliar
unusual 84 **adj.**
unknown 491 **adj.**
unfashionable
unwonted 611 **adj.**
ill-bred 847 **adj.**
unfathomable
deep 211 **adj.**
unintelligible
517 **adj.**
unfavourable
adverse 731 **adj.**
disapproving
924 **adj.**
unfeeling
impassive 820 **adj.**
unfeigned
veracious 540 **adj.**
unfetter
liberate 746 **vb.**
unfilial
disobedient 738 **adj.**
unkind 898 **adj.**
dutiless 918 **adj.**
unfinished
fragmentary
53 **adj.**
incomplete 55 **adj.**
unfit
disable 161 **vb.**
useless 641 **adj.**
unfitting
inexpedient 643 **adj.**
unflagging
persevering
600 **adj.**
industrious 678 **adj.**
unflappable
inexcitable 823 **adj.**
unflattering
true 494 **adj.**
disrespectful
921 **adj.**
unfledged
new 126 **adj.**
infantine 132 **adj.**
immature 670 **adj.**
unflinching
resolute 599 **adj.**
courageous 855 **adj.**

unfold
become 1 **vb.**
result 157 **vb.**
uncover 229 **vb.**
open 263 **vb.**
evolve 316 **vb.**
disclose 526 **vb.**
unforeseen
unexpected 508 **adj.**
unforgettable
remembered
505 **adj.**
unforgivable
heinous 934 **adj.**
unforgiving
revengeful 910 **adj.**
unforthcoming
unsociable 883 **adj.**
unfortified
defenceless 161 **adj.**
vulnerable 661 **adj.**
unfortunate
unfortunate
731 **adj.**
unhappy 825 **adj.**
unfounded
erroneous 495 **adj.**
unfranchised
subject 745 **adj.**
unentitled 916 **adj.**
unfree
subject 745 **adj.**
unfriendliness
unsociability 883 **n.**
(*see* **unfriendly**)
unfriendly
inimical 881 **adj.**
ungracious 885 **adj.**
unfrock
depose 752 **vb.**
unfruitful
unproductive
172 **adj.**
unfurl
lengthen 203 **vb.**
evolve 316 **vb.**
disclose 526 **vb.**
unfurnished
unprovided 636 **adj.**
ungainly
clumsy 695 **adj.**
ungenerous
selfish 932 **adj.**
ungentlemanly
ill-bred 847 **adj.**
ungodly
irreligious 974 **adj.**

ungovernable
violent 176 adj.
wilful 602 adj.
ungoverned
anarchic 734 adj.
independent 744 adj.
ungracious
ungracious 885 adj.
ungrammatical
ungrammatical
565 adj.
ungrateful
ungrateful 908 adj.
ungrown
immature 670 adj.
ungrudging
liberal 813 adj.
unguarded
vulnerable 661 adj.
unguent
lubricant 334 n.
unguent 357 n.
unguessed
unexpected
508 adj.
latent 523 adj.
ungulate
footed 214 adj.
unhackneyed
unimitated 21 adj.
new 126 adj.
unhallowed
profane 980 adj.
unhappy
bungled 695 adj.
unfortunate
731 adj.
unhappy 825 adj.
dejected 834 adj.
unhealthy
unhealthy 651 adj.
insalubrious
653 adj.
unheard of
new 126 adj.
unhearing
deaf 416 adj.
inattentive 456 adj.
unheeding
inattentive 456 adj.
unhelpful
unwilling 598 adj.
hindering 702 adj.
unheralded
unexpected 508 adj.
unheroic
cowardly 856 adj.

inglorious 867 adj.
unhinge
derange 63 vb.
make mad 503 vb.
unhistorical
erroneous 495 adj.
unholy
profane 980 adj.
unhurried
slow 278 adj.
leisurely 681 adj.
unhurt
perfect 646 adj.
unhygienic
insalubrious
653 adj.
unicorn
rara avis 84 n.
unidentified
unknown 491 adj.
unification
combination 50 n.
unity 88 n.
uniform
dress, uniform
228 n.
livery 547 n.
badge of rank
743 n.
(*see* uniformity)
uniformity
uniformity 16 n.
continuity 71 n.
unify
combine 50 vb.
(*see* unification)
unilateral
irrelative 10 adj.
independent
744 adj.
unimaginative
unthinking 450 adj.
narrow-minded
481 adj.
thick-skinned
820 adj.
unastonished
865 adj.
unimpeachable
undisputed 473 adj.
unimportance
unimportance
639 n.
uninhabitable
empty 190 adj.
uninhabited
secluded 883 adj.

uninquisitive
incurious 454 adj.
uninspired
feeble 572 adj.
tedious 838 adj.
unintellectual
mindless 448 adj.
unthinking 450 adj.
unintentional
involuntary
596 adj.
spontaneous
609 adj.
unintentional
618 adj.
uninterested
incurious 454 adj.
choiceless 606 adj.
indifferent 860 adj.
uninteresting
dull 840 adj.
uninterrupted
continuous 71 adj.
uninvited
unwanted 860 adj.
friendless 883 adj.
uninvited guest
intruder 59 n.
uninviting
unpleasant 827 adj.
union
junction 45 n.
coition 45 n.
combination 50 n.
association 706 n.
society 708 n.
marriage 894 n.
unique
non-uniform 17 adj.
unimitated 21 adj.
special 80 adj.
unison
melody 410 n.
concord 710 n.
unit
group 74 n.
unit 88 n.
formation 722 n.
unitarianism
philosophy 449 n.
unitary
one 88 n.
unite
join 45 vb.
bring together
74 vb.
converge 293 vb.

united
concordant
710 adj.
unity
identity 13 n.
uniformity 16 n.
unity 88 n.
concord 710 n.
universal
comprehensive
52 adj.
universal 79 adj.
ubiquitous
189 adj.
cosmic 321 adj.
universal aunt
servant 742 n.
universality
generality 79 n.
indiscrimination
464 n.
(*see* universal)
universe
universe 321 n.
university
academy 539 n.
unjust
unjust 914 adj.
unjustifiable
blameworthy
924 adj.
guilty 936 adj.
unkempt
orderless 61 adj.
dirty 649 adj.
unkind
unkind 898 adj.
unknown quantity
unknown thing
491 n.
secret 530 n.
unladylike
ill-bred 847 adj.
unlamented
hated 888 adj.
unlatch
open 263 vb.
unlawful
illegal 954 adj.
unlearn
forget 506 vb.
unlearned
uninstructed
491 adj.
artless 699 adj.
unleash
liberate 746 vb.

unlettered
uninstructed
491 adj.
unlicensed
unwarranted
916 adj.
unlicked cub
undevelopment
670 n.
vulgarian 847 n.
unlike
dissimilar 19 adj.
unlikely
improbable 472 adj.
unlimited
infinite 107 adj.
unconditional
744 adj.
unload
displace 188 vb.
transpose 272 vb.
disencumber
701 vb.
unlock
open 263 vb.
liberate 746 vb.
unlooked for
unexpected 508 adj.
unloose
disjoin 46 vb.
liberate 746 vb.
unlovely
ugly 842 adj.
unlucky
unsuccessful
728 adj.
unfortunate
731 adj.
unmake
revert 148 vb.
destroy 165 vb.
unman
unman 161 vb.
sterilize 172 vb.
frighten 854 vb.
unmanageable
wilful 602 adj.
unmanly
female 373 adj.
cowardly 856 adj.
unmannerly
discourteous
885 adj.
unmarried
unwedded 895 adj.
unmask
disclose 526 vb.

unmatched
best 644 adj.
unmeaning
unmeaning 515 adj.
unmeant
unmeant 515 adj.
unintentional
618 adj.
unmeasured
plenteous 635 adj.
unmentionable
inexpressible
517 adj.
impure 951 adj.
unmerited
unwarranted
916 adj.
unmindful
inattentive 456 adj.
ungrateful 908 adj.
unmistakable
certain 473 adj.
manifest 522 adj.
unmitigated
complete 54 adj.
unmoor
navigate 269 vb.
start out 296 vb.
unmoved
apathetic 820 adj.
pitiless 906 adj.
unmusical
discordant 411 adj.
deaf 416 adj.
unnamed
anonymous 562 adj.
unnatural
abnormal 84 adj.
impossible 470 adj.
affected 850 adj.
unkind, cruel
898 adj.
unnecessary
superfluous 637 adj.
unimportant
639 adj.
unnerve
frighten 854 vb.
unnoticeable
inconsiderable
33 adj.
unnumbered
infinite 107 adj.
unobservant
inattentive 456 adj.
unobtrusive
modest 874 adj.

unoccupied
empty 190 adj.
unpossessed
774 adj.
unorganized
orderless 61 adj.
lax 734 adj.
unpack
uncover 229 vb.
unpacking
displacement 188 n.
transference 272 n.
unpaid
owed 803 adj.
uncharged 812 adj.
unpalatable
unsavoury 391 adj.
unpleasant 827 adj.
unparalleled
unusual 84 adj.
unpardonable
heinous 934 adj.
unparliamentary
maledicent 899 adj.
unpatriotic
misanthropic
902 adj.
unpick
disjoin 46 vb.
unpin
unstick 49 vb.
unplaced
defeated 728 adj.
unpleasant
unpleasant 827 adj.
unpleasantness
dissension 709 n.
discourtesy 885 n.
unpleasing
unpleasant 827 adj.
unpolished
inelegant 576 adj.
artless 699 adj.
unpopular
disliked 861 adj.
friendless 883 adj.
hated 888 adj.
unpopularity
odium 888 n.
unpractical
useless 641 adj.
unprecedented
first 68 adj.
new 126 adj.
wonderful 864 adj.
unpredictable
changeful 152 adj.

uncertain 474 adj.
capricious 604 adj.
unprejudiced
just 913 adj.
unprepared
inexpectant 508 adj.
spontaneous
609 adj.
unprepared 670 adj.
unpretentious
plain 573 adj.
humble 872 adj.
modest 874 adj.
unprincipled
dishonest 930 adj.
wicked 934 adj.
unprivileged
unentitled 916 adj.
unproductive
unproductive
172 adj.
unprofessional
non-observant
769 adj.
unprofitable
profitless 641 adj.
losing 772 adj.
unpromising
unpromising
853 adj.
unpropitious
inopportune
138 adj.
unpromising
853 adj.
unprosperous
unprosperous
731 adj.
unprotected
vulnerable 661 adj.
unproved
uncertified 474 adj.
unprovoked
spontaneous
609 adj.
unpunctual
late 136 adj.
ill-timed 138 adj.
unqualified
unmixed 44 adj.
complete 54 adj.
unskilled 695 adj.
unentitled 916 adj.
unquestionable
undisputed 473 adj.
unquestioning
believing 485 adj.

unravel
simplify 44 vb.
unravel 62 vb.
evolve 316 vb.
liberate 746 vb.
unreal
unreal 2 adj.
imaginary 513 adj.
unrealistic
misjudging 481 adj.
unreality
immateriality
320 n.
error 495 n.
unrealized
unreal 2 adj.
unknown 491 adj.
unreason
non-intellect 448 n.
intuition 476 n.
folly 499 n.
unreasonable
illogical 477 adj.
unwise 499 adj.
unreasoning
mindless 448 adj.
unwise 499 adj.
unrecognized
unknown 491 adj.
unrefined
indiscriminating
464 adj.
ill-bred 847 adj.
unreflecting
unthinking 450 adj.
unreformed
impenitent 940 adj.
unrehearsed
spontaneous
609 adj.
unprepared 670 adj.
unrelated
irrelative 10 adj.
unrelenting
pitiless 906 adj.
revengeful 910 adj.
unreliable
changeful 152 adj.
unreliable 474 adj.
unbelieved 486 adj.
irresolute 601 adj.
capricious 604 adj.
unsafe 661 adj.
unrelieved
uniform 16 adj.
unremitting
unceasing 146 adj.

unrepentant
impenitent 940 adj.
unrepresentative
abnormal 84 adj.
unrepresented
absent 190 adj.
unrequited
unthanked 908 adj.
unreserved
undisguised
522 adj.
veracious 540 adj.
unresisting
peaceful 717 adj.
submitting 721 adj.
unresponsive
impassive 820 adj.
indifferent 860 adj.
unrest
changeableness
152 n.
discontent 829 n.
unrestrained
unconfined 744 adj.
unrestraint
intemperance
943 n.
unrestricted
unconditional
744 adj.
unrewarding
profitless 641 adj.
unriddle
decipher 520 vb.
unrighteous
wrong 914 adj.
wicked 934 adj.
unrigorous
inexact 495 adj.
unripe
sour 393 adj.
immature 670 adj.
unrivalled
supreme 34 adj.
unroll
lengthen 203 vb.
evolve 316 vb.
unromantic
true 494 adj.
inexcitable 823 adj.
unruffled
orderly 60 adj.
smooth 258 adj.
inexcitable 823 adj.
unruly
violent 176 adj.
wilful 602 adj.

unsafe
unsafe 661 adj.
unsaid
tacit 523 adj.
unsaleable
cheap 812 adj.
unsanctified
profane 980 adj.
unsanctioned
unwarranted
916 adj.
unsatisfactory
disappointing
509 adj.
bad 645 adj.
disapproved 924 adj.
unsavoury
unsavoury 391 adj.
unsay
recant 603 vb.
unscathed
perfect 646 adj.
unschematic
orderless 61 adj.
unscholarly
uninstructed
491 adj.
unschooled
uninstructed
491 adj.
unscientific
illogical 477 adj.
erroneous 495 adj.
unscramble
simplify 44 vb.
unravel 62 vb.
unscriptural
heterodox 977 adj.
unscrupulous
dishonest 930 adj.
unseal
disclose 526 vb.
unseasonable
ill-timed 138 adj.
unseeing
blind 439 adj.
inattentive 456 adj.
unseemly
inexpedient 643 adj.
wrong 914 n.
unseen
invisible 444 adj.
unknown 491 adj.
modest 874 adj.
unselective
indiscriminating
464 adj.

unselfishness
benevolence 897 n.
disinterestedness
931 n.
unsentimental
inexcitable
823 adj.
unserviceable
useless 641 adj.
unsettle
derange 63 vb.
unsettled
unstable 152 adj.
unshapely
unsightly 842 adj.
unsheathe
uncover 229 vb.
unshriven
impenitent 940 adj.
unsightly
unsightly 842 adj.
unsigned
anonymous 562 adj.
unskilful
unskilful 695 adj.
unsleeping
persevering 600 adj.
industrious 678 adj.
unsmiling
serious 834 adj.
sullen 893 adj.
unsociable
unsociable 883 adj.
sullen 893 adj.
unsophisticated
artless 699 adj.
unsorted
indiscriminate
464 adj.
unsound
erroneous 495 adj.
unhealthy 651 adj.
unsparing
oppressive 735 adj.
liberal 813 adj.
unspeakable
inexpressible
517 adj.
unspent
unused 674 adj.
unspirited
inexcitable 823 adj.
unspiritual
material 319 adj.
sensual 944 adj.
unspoken
tacit 523 adj.

unsportsmanlike
unjust 914 adj.
unstable
unstable 152 adj.
capricious 604 adj.
unsteady
fitful 142 adj.
unstable 152 adj.
unsterilized
infectious 653 adj.
unstick
unstick 49 vb.
unstinting
liberal 813 adj.
unsuccessful
profitless 641 adj.
unsuccessful
728 adj.
unsuitable
unapt 25 adj.
unsullied
clean 648 adj.
unsung
inglorious 867 adj.
unsure
uncertain 474 adj.
unsurpassed
supreme 34 adj.
unsusceptible
impassive 820 adj.
unsuspected
latent 523 adj.
unsuspecting
credulous 487 adj.
inexpectant 508 adj.
unsuspicious
artless 699 adj.
unswerving
straight 249 adj.
unsympathetic
disliking 861 adj.
pitiless 906 adj.
unsystematic
orderless 61 adj.
fitful 142 adj.
untangle
unravel 62 vb.
untaught
uninstructed
491 adj.
unteachable
obstinate 602 adj.
untenable
illogical 477 adj.
unbelieved 486 adj.
untenanted
unpossessed 774 adj.

unthinking
unthinking 450 adj.
unthrifty
prodigal 815 adj.
untidy
non-uniform
17 adj.
orderless 61 adj.
jumble 63 vb.
negligent 458 adj.
untie
disjoin 46 vb.
disencumber
701 vb.
untimely
irrelative 10 adj.
ill-timed 138 adj.
untold
infinite 107 adj.
untouchable
derelict 779 n.
(see outcaste)
untouched
intact 52 adj.
non-liable 919 adj.
untoward
inopportune
138 adj.
adverse 731 adj.
untraceable
lost 772 adj.
untraditional
modern 126 adj.
untrammelled
unconfined 744 adj.
untried
new 126 adj.
unknown 491 adj.
unused 674 adj.
untrodden
new 126 adj.
untrue
erroneous 495 adj.
false 541 adj.
untrue 543 adj.
untrustworthy
unreliable 474 adj.
dishonest 930 adj.
untruth
untruth 543 n.
untruthfulness
falsehood 541 n.
unused
unused 674 adj.
unusual
unusual 84 adj.
wonderful 864 adj.

unutterable
inexpressible
517 adj.
unvaried
unceasing 146 adj.
(see uniform)
unvarnished
genuine 494 adj.
artless 699 adj.
unveil
uncover 229 vb.
disclose 526 vb.
unverified
uncertified 474 adj.
suppositional
512 adj.
unversed
ignorant 491 adj.
unviable
impracticable
470 adj.
unvoiced
tacit 523 adj.
unwanted
rejected 607 adj.
superfluous 637 adj.
unused 674 adj.
unwanted 860 adj.
unwarlike
peaceful 717 adj.
unwarranted
wrong 914 adj.
unwarranted
916 adj.
unwary
rash 857 adj.
unwavering
persevering 600 adj.
unwearied
industrious 678 adj.
unwedded
unwedded 895 adj.
unwelcome
unpleasant 827 adj.
unwanted 860 adj.
unwell
sick 651 adj.
unwholesome
insalubrious
653 adj.
unwieldy
clumsy 695 adj.
unwilling
unwilling 598 adj.
refusing 760 adj.
unwind
evolve 316 vb.

unwisdom
folly 499 n.
unwise
unwise 499 adj.
unwitting
ignorant 491 adj.
involuntary 596
adj.
unwomanly
male 372 adj.
unwonted
unwonted 611 adj.
unworkable
impracticable
470 adj.
unworldly
honourable 929 adj.
pious 979 adj.
unworthy
inferior 35 adj.
discreditable
867 adj.
unwrap
uncover 229 vb.
unwritten
tacit 523 adj.
unyielding
unyielding 162 adj.
obstinate 602 adj.
resisting 715 adj.
up against it
in difficulties
700 adj.
up-and-coming
prosperous
730 adj.
up and doing
doing 676 adj.
up-and-down
undulatory 251 adj.
up and up
crescendo 36 adv.
upbraid
exprobate 924 vb.
upbringing
teaching 534 n.
up-end
make vertical
215 vb.
upgrade
dignify 866 vb.
upheaval
revolution 149 n.
havoc 165 n.
uphill
ascending 308 adj.
difficult 700 adj.

uphold
support 218 vb.
corroborate 466 vb.
upholstered
rich 800 adj.
upholstery
lining 227 n.
equipment 630 n.
upkeep
support 218 n.
preservation 666 n.
upland
high land 209 n.
plain 348 n.
uplift
support 218 n.
elevation 310 n.
improvement 654 n.
upper
superior 34 adj.
upper class
upper class 868 n.
uppercut
knock 279 n.
upper hand
vantage 34 n.
victory 727 n.
uppermost
supreme 34 adj.
topmost 213 adj.
uppish
prideful 871 adj.
upraise, uprear
elevate 310 vb.
upright
vertical 215 adj.
just 913 adj.
honourable 929 adj.
uproar
turmoil 61 n.
loudness 400 n.
uproarious
violent 176 adj.
loud 400 adj.
gay 833 adj.
uproot
displace 188 vb.
eject 300 vb.
extract 304 vb.
uprush
increase 36 n.
spurt 277 n.
ups and downs
fluctuation 317 n.
upset
derange 63 vb.
overturning 221 n.

distract 456 vb.
incommode 827 vb.
enrage 891 vb.
upshot
effect 157 n.
upside down
inverted 221 adj.
upstage
stage set 594 n.
insolent 878 adj.
upstanding
vertical 215 adj.
upstart
upstart 126 n.
made man 730 n.
insolent person
878 n.
upswing
improvement 654 n.
up-to-date
modern 126 adj.
progressive 285 adj.
uptrend
improvement 654 n.
urban
urban 192 adj.
urbane
well-bred 848 adj.
courteous 884 adj.
urbanity
(*see* urbane)
urbanize
urbanize 192 vb.
urchin
youngster 132 n.
elf 970 n.
urge
impel 279 vb.
affirm 532 vb.
incite 612 vb.
hasten 680 vb.
advise 691 vb.
request 761 vb.
animate 821 vb.
urgency
needfulness 627 n.
importance 638 n.
haste 680 n.
urgent
important 638 adj.
hasty 680 adj.
compelling 740 adj.
requesting 761 adj.
urinal
latrine 649 n.
urine
excrement 302 n.

urn
vessel 194 n.
interment 364 n.
usable
useful 640 adj.
usage
connotation 514 n.
habit 610 n.
use 673 n.
use
habit 610 n.
utility 640 n.
use 673 n., vb.
used up
impotent 161 adj.
use for, have no
not use 674 vb.
despise 922 vb.
useful
useful 640 adj.
expedient 642 adj.
useless
superfluous 637 adj.
useless 641 adj.
unused 674 adj.
uselessness
ineffectuality 161 n.
(*see* useless)
user
habit 610 n.
(*see* operator)
use up
waste 634 vb.
expend 806 vb.
usher
teacher 537 n.
usherette
stage-hand 594 n.
usher in
precede 283 vb.
admit 299 vb.
usual
regular 81 adj.
usual 610 adj.
unastonishing
865 adj.
usufruct
enjoyment 824 n.
usurer
lender 784 n.
usurious
lending 784 adj.
avaricious 816 adj.
usurp
encroach 306 vb.
appropriate 786 vb.
(*see* usurpation)

usurpation
arrogation 918 n.
lawlessness 954 n.
usurper
impostor 545 n.
usurper 916 n.
usury
lending 784 n.
interest 803 n.
uterine
akin 11 adj.
uterus
genitalia 164 n.
utilitarian
useful 640 adj.
philanthropist
901 n.
utilitarianism
expedience 642 n.
philanthropy 901 n.
utility
utility 640 n.
utilization
utility 640 n.
use 673 n.
Utopia
fantasy 513 n.
Utopian
visionary 513 n.
reformer 654 n.
utter
complete 54 adj.
voice 577 vb.
speak 579 vb.
mint 797 vb.
utterance
voice 577 n.
speech 579 n.
uttermost
limit 236 n.
U-turn
return 286 n.
circuition 314 n.
uxoriousness
love 887 n.

V

vacancy
insubstantiality
4 n.
emptiness 190 n.
job 622 n.
(*see* vacant)
vacant
unthinking 450 adj.
(*see* vacancy)

697

vacate
displace 188 vb.
relinquish 621 vb.
abrogate 752 vb.
vacation
leisure 681 n.
vaccination
hygiene 652 n.
prophylactic 658 n.
vacillate
(*see* vacillation)
vacillation
changeableness
152 n.
fluctuation 317 n.
vacuity, vacuous
(*see* vacancy,
vacant)
vacuum
non-existence 2 n.
emptiness 190 n.
rarity 325 n.
vade mecum
guide-book 524 n.
vagabond
wanderer 268 n.
knave 938 n.
vagabondage
wandering 267 n.
vagary
whim 604 n.
vagina
genitalia 164 n.
vagrancy
wandering 267 n.
vagrant
wanderer 268 n.
vague
insubstantial 4 adj.
shadowy 419 adj.
uninstructed
491 adj.
equivocal 518 adj.
vain
insubstantial 4 adj.
unsuccessful
728 adj.
vain 873 adj.
vainglorious
(*see* vainglory)
vainglory
pride 871 n.
boasting 877 n.
vain, in
profitless 641 adj.
vair
skin 226 n.

heraldry 547 n.
vale
valley 255 n.
valediction
valediction 296 n.
valentine
love-token 889 n.
valet
clothier 228 n.
clean 648 vb.
domestic 742 n.
valetudinarian
sick person 651 n.
valiant
courageous
855 adj.
valid
genuine 494 adj.
useful 640 adj.
validate
corroborate
466 vb.
make legal 953 vb.
validation
assent 488 n.
validity
authenticity 494 n.
valley
valley 255 n.
valour
courage 855 n.
valuable
profitable 640 adj.
valuable 644 adj.
valuables
estate 777 n.
valuation
estimate 480 n.
value
equivalence 28 n.
quid pro quo 150 n.
estimate 480 vb.
importance 638 n.
account 808 vb.
honour 866 vb.
valueless
trivial 639 adj.
profitless 641 adj.
valuer
estimator 480 n.
vamp
improvise 609 vb.
repair 656 vb.
excite love 887 vb.
vampire
noxious animal
904 n.

demon 970 n.
vampirism
rapacity 786 n.
van
front 237 n.
cart 274 n.
armed force 722 n.
Vandal
destroyer 168 n.
vulgarian 847 n.
vandalism
destruction 165 n.
vane
changeable thing
152 n.
weather 340 n.
vanguard
front 237 n.
armed force 722 n.
vanish
pass away 2 vb.
disappear 446 vb.
vanishing point
minuteness 196 n.
disappearance
446 n.
vanity
insubstantiality 4 n.
folly 499 n.
inutility 641 n.
affectation 850 n.
vanity 873 n.
Vanity Fair
fashion 848 n.
vanity 873 n.
vanquish
overmaster 727 vb.
vantage
vantage 34 n.
success 727 n.
vantage ground
influence 178 n.
vapid
tasteless 387 adj.
vaporization
vaporization 338 n.
vaporize
vaporize 338 vb.
vapour
emit 300 vb.
gas 336 n.
cloud 355 n.
mean nothing
515 vb.
vapourish
melancholic
834 adj.

variability
non-uniformity
17 n.
changeableness
152 n.
variance
dissension 709 n.
variant
variant 15 n.
variation
difference 15 n.
change 143 n.
variegation
variegation 437 n.
ornamental art
844 n.
variety
difference 15 n.
non-uniformity
17 n.
sort 77 n.
multiformity 82 n.
stage show 594 n.
various
(*see* variety)
varnish
facing 226 n.
smooth 258 vb.
resin 357 n.
conceal 525 vb.
cleanser 648 n.
vary
modify 143 vb.
vary 152 vb.
vary as
be related 9 vb.
correlate 12 vb.
vase
vessel 194 n.
vaseline
unguent 357 n.
vassal
subject 742 n.
subject 745 adj.
vassalage
subjection 745 n.
vast
enormous 32 adj.
spacious 183 adj.
huge 195 adj.
vastness
greatness 32 n.
hugeness 195 n.
vat
vat 194 n.
vaudeville
stage show 594 n.

vault
cellar 194 n.
dome 253 n.
leap 312 n., vb.
tomb 364 n.
storage 632 n.

vaunt
boast 877 n., vb.

vector
infection 651 n.

veer
vary 152 vb.
deviate 282 vb.

vegetability
vegetability 366 n.
non-intellect 448 n.

vegetable
vegetable 301 n.
mindless 448 adj.

vegetal
vegetal 366 adj.

vegetarian
eater 301 n.
abstainer 942 n.

vegetarianism
temperance 942 n.

vegetate
be 1 vb.
pass time 108 vb.
be inactive 679 vb.

vegetation
vegetability 366 n.

vehemence
vigorousness 174 n.
warm feeling 818 n.

vehement
(*see* vehemence)

vehicle
vehicle 274 n.

vehicular
vehicular 274 adj.

veil
shade 226 n.
screen 421 vb.
conceal 525 vb.

veil, take the
take orders 986 vb.

vein
temperament 5 n.
conduit 351 n.
variegate 437 n.
style 566 n.
store 632 n.
affections 817 n.

vellum
stationery 586 n.

velocity
velocity 277 n.

velvet
textile 222 n.
smoothness 258 n.

velvet glove
lenity 736 n.

velvety
downy 259 adj.
soft 327 adj.

venal
venal 930 adj.

vend
sell 793 vb.

vendetta
quarrel 709 n.
revenge 910 n.

vendible
saleable 793 adj.
merchandise 795 n.

vendor
seller 793 n.

veneer
facing 226 n.
disguise 527 n.

venerable
aged 131 adj.
respected 920 adj.

veneration
respect 920 n.
piety 979 n.

venereal
diseased 651 adj.

venery
unchastity 951 n.

vengeance
revenge 910 n.

venial
trivial 639 adj.
forgiven 909 adj.

venison
meat 301 n.

venom
poison 659 n.
malevolence 898 n.

venomous
toxic 653 adj.

vent
outlet 298 n.
void 300 vb.
air-pipe 353 n.
divulge 526 vb.

ventilate
aerify 340 vb.
dissert 591 vb.
refresh 685 vb.
(*see* ventilation)

ventilation
ventilation 352 n.
refrigeration 382 n.
(*see* ventilate)

ventilator
ventilation 352 n.
refrigerator 384 n.

ventriloquism
mimicry 20 n.
sleight 542 n.

ventriloquist
conjuror 545 n.

venture
be tentative 461 vb.
essay 671 vb.
undertaking 672 n.
speculate 791 vb.

venturesome
speculative 618 adj.
enterprising 672 adj.

veracious
(*see* veracity)

veracity
veracity 540 n.

verandah
lobby 194 n.

verb
part of speech 564 n.

verbal
verbal 559 adj.
grammatical 564 adj.

verbiage
empty talk 515 n.
diffuseness 570 n.

verbosity
diffuseness 570 n.

verdant
green 432 adj.

verdict
judgement 480 n.
legal trial 959 n.

verdure
grass 366 n.

verge
tend 179 vb.
nearness 200 n.
edge 234 n.

verge on
approach 289 vb.

verger
church officer 986 n.

verification
experiment 461 n.

demonstration
478 n.

verify
corroborate 466 vb.
make certain 473 vb.
(*see* verification)

verisimilitude
probability 471 n.
truth 494 n.
accuracy 494 n.

veritable
true 494 adj.

vermifuge
antidote 658 n.

vermilion
red pigment 431 n.

vermin
vermin 365 n.
cad 938 n.

verminous
insalubrious 653 adj.

vernacular
native 191 adj.
language 557 n.
dialect 560 n.
plainness 573 n.

vernal
vernal 128 adj.

versatile
multiform 82 adj.
skilful 694 adj.

verse
subdivision 53 n.
poetry 593 n.

versed in
expert 694 adj.

versification
poetry 593 n.

versify
poetize 593 vb.

version
translation 528 n.

vers libre
verse form 593 n.

versus
in opposition 704 adj.

vertebral
back 238 adj.

vertebrate
animal 365 n.

vertex
vertex 213 n.

vertical
vertical 215 adj.

vertiginous
  high 209 adj.
vertigo
  rotation 315 n.
verve
  vigorousness
    174 n.
  vigour 571 n.
very
  greatly 32 adv.
vesicle
  bladder 194 n.
  swelling 253 n.
vessel
  vessel 194 n.
  ship 275 n.
  pottery 381 n.
vest
  bodywear 228 n.
  vest 228 n.
  give 781 vb.
vestal
  spinster 895 n.
  virgin 950 n.
vested
  vested 153 adj.
  located 187 adj.
vested interest
  dueness 915 n.
vestibule
  lobby 194 n.
vestige
  remainder 41 n.
  trace 548 n.
vestigial
  remaining 41 adj.
vestimentary
  vestimental
    989 adj.
vestments
  clothing 228 n.
  vestments 989 n.
vestry
  council 692 n.
  synod 985 n.
vestryman
  church officer
    986 n.
vet
  animal husbandry
    369 n.
  estimate 480 vb.
  doctor 658 n.
veteran
  old man 133 n.
  expert 696 n.
  soldier 722 n.

veterinary surgeon
  animal husbandry
    369 n.
veto
  prohibition 757 n.
vex
  (*see* vexation)
vexation
  annoyance 827 n.
  anger 891 n.
vexatious
  annoying 827 adj.
  litigating 959 adj.
viability
  life 360 n.
  possibility 469 n.
viaduct
  bridge 624 n.
vial
  vessel 194 n.
via media
  mid-course 625 n.
viands
  food 301 n.
vibrant
  vigorous 174 adj.
vibrate
  oscillate 317 vb.
  resound 404 vb.
  show feeling
    818 vb.
vibration
  oscillation 317 n.
  resonance 404 n.
vicar
  deputy 755 n.
  pastor 986 n.
vicarage
  parsonage 986 n.
vicarious
  substituted
    150 adj.
vice
  deputy 755 n.
  nippers 778 n.
  vice 934 n.
viceroy
  potentate 741 n.
vice versa
  correlatively
    12 adv.
vicinity
  nearness 200 n.
vicious
  malevolent
    898 adj.
  vicious 934 adj.

vicissitude
  changeable thing
    152 n.
vicissitudes
  affairs 154 n.
victim
  dupe 544 n.
  sufferer 825 n.
  laughing-stock
    851 n.
  oblation 981 n.
victimize
  befool 542 vb.
  oppress 735 vb.
  punish 963 vb.
victor
  victor 727 n.
Victoria Cross
  decoration 729 n.
Victorian
  antiquated 127 adj.
  prudish 950 adj.
victorious
  successful 727 adj.
victory
  victory 727 n.
victual
  food 301 n.
  provide 633 vb.
victualler
  provider 633 n.
vie
  be good 644 vb.
  contend 716 vb.
view
  view 438 n.
  spectacle 445 n.
  estimate 480 vb.
  opinion 485 n.
  manifestation
    522 n.
  picture 553 n.
  beauty 841 n.
viewer
  spectator 441 n.
viewership
  publicity 528 n.
view, in
  visible 443 adj.
viewpoint
  opinion 485 n.
viewy
  believing 485 adj.
vigil
  carefulness 457 n.
  church service
    988 n.

vigilant
  attentive 455 adj.
  vigilant 457 adj.
  tutelary 660 adj.
  prepared 669 adj.
vignette
  picture 553 n.
  description 590 n.
vigorous
  great 32 adj.
  (*see* vigour)
vigour
  energy 160 n.
  vigorousness 174 n.
  vigour 571 n.
vile
  bad 645 adj.
  rascally 930 adj.
  heinous 934 adj.
vilification
  detraction 926 n.
vilify
  dispraise 924 vb.
  defame 926 vb.
villa
  house 192 n.
villadom
  housing 190 n.
  habitancy 191 n.
village
  district 184 n.
  housing 192 n.
village green
  focus 76 n.
villager
  dweller 191 n.
villain
  knave 938 n.
villainous
  ugly 842 adj.
  rascally 930 adj.
  vicious 934 adj.
villainy
  improbity 930 n.
  wickedness 934 n.
villein
  countryman 869 n.
vim
  vigorousness 174 n.
vindicate
  claim 915 vb.
  vindicate 927 vb.
vindication
  avenger 910 n.
  vindication 927 n.
vindictive
  resentful 891 adj.

VIN

revengeful 910
  adj.
vine
  plant 366 n.
vinegar
  sourness 393 n.
vineyard
  farm 370 n.
vintage
  date 108 n.
  product 164 n.
  agriculture 370 n.
  savoury 390 adj.
  store 632 n.
  goodness 644 n.
  excellent 644 adj.
violate
  force 176 vb.
  disobey 738 vb.
  debauch 951 vb.
  (*see* violation)
violation
  rape 951 n.
violator
  usurper 916 n.
  impious person
   980 n.
violence
  violence 176 n.
  misuse 675 n.
violent
  violent 176 adj.
  fervent 818 adj.
  lawless 954 adj.
violet
  fragrance 396 n.
  blueness 435 n.
  modesty 844 n.
violin, viola
  viol 414 n.
V.I.P.
  person 371 n.
  bigwig 638 n.
viper
  reptile 635 n.
  noxious animal
   904 n.
virago
  athlete 162 n.
  shrew 892 n.
virgin
  new 126 adj.
  virgin 950 n.
virginal
  pure 950 adj.
virginity
  purity 950 n.

VIS

virgin soil
  unknown thing
   491 n.
  undevelopment
   670 n.
virile
  athlete 162 adj.
  male 372 adj.
virility
  vitality 162 n.
virtu
  good taste 846 n.
virtual
  intrinsic 5 adj.
  possible 469 adj.
virtue
  ability 160 n.
  goodness 644 n.
  manliness 855 n.
  virtue 933 n.
  purity 950 n.
virtuosity
  skill 694 n.
virtuoso
  musician 413 n.
  proficient 696 n.
virtuous
  virtuous 933 adj.
virulence
  poison 659 n.
  malevolence 898 n.
virus
  infection 651 n.
visa
  credential 465 n.
visage
  face 237 n.
  feature 445 n.
viscera
  insides 224 n.
viscid
  viscid 354 adj.
viscidity
  semiliquidity 354 n.
visibility
  visibility 443 n.
visible
  visible 443 adj.
  manifest 522 adj.
vis inertiae
  counteraction
   182 n.
vision
  vision 438 n.
  visual fallacy
   440 n.
  fantasy 513 n.

VIT

  manifestation
   522 n.
  aspiration 852 n.
visionary
  insubstantial 4 adj.
  misjudging 481 adj.
  visionary 513 n.
  imaginative
   513 adj.
  imaginary 513 adj.
  hoper 852 n.
  philanthropist
   901 n.
visit
  presence 189 n.
  enter 297 vb.
  visit 882 vb.
  punish 963 vb.
visitant
  wanderer 268 n.
visitation
  inquiry 459 n.
  bane 659 n.
  punishment 963 n.
visitor
  resident 191 n.
  incomer 297 n.
  social person
   882 n.
visor
  screen 421 n.
  armour 713 n.
vista
  view 438 n.
visual
  seeing 438 adj.
visualize
  imagine 513 vb.
vital
  alive 360 adj.
  required 627 adj.
  cheerful 833 adj.
vital concern
  important matter
   638 n.
vitality
  vitality 162 n.
  life 360 n.
  cheerfulness 833 n.
vitalize
  vitalize 360 vb.
vitamin
  tonic 658 n.
vitaminous
  nourishing 301 adj.
vitamins
  dieting 301 n.

VOC

vitiate
  impair, pervert
   655 vb.
vitiation
  deterioration
   655 n.
vitreous
  transparent
   422 adj.
vitrify
  harden 326 vb.
vitriolic
  maledicent 899 adj.
vituperation
  scurrility 899 n.
viva
  exam 459 n.
vivacious
  lively 819 adj.
vivacity
  vigour 571 n.
  cheerfulness 833 n.
vivid
  lifelike 18 adj.
  expressive 516 adj.
  forceful 571 adj.
  descriptive 590 adj.
vivify
  vitalize 360 vb.
  animate 821 vb.
vivisection
  killing 362 n.
  pain 377 n.
vixen
  vermin 365 n.
  shrew 892 n.
viz.
  namely 80 adv.
vocable
  word 559 n.
vocabulary
  dictionary 559 n.
  style 566 n.
vocal
  vocal 577 adj.
vocal chords
  voice 577 n.
vocalic
  vocal 477 adj.
vocalist
  vocalist 413 n.
vocation
  vocation 622 n.
  church ministry
   985 n.
vocative
  vocative 583 adj.

vociferation
loudness 400 n.
cry 408 n.

vogue
fashion 848 n.

vogue-word
neology 560 n.

voice
publish 528 vb.
grammar 564 n.
voice 577 n., vb.

voiceless
voiceless 578 adj.

void
space 183 n.
emptiness 190 n.
void 300 vb.
abrogate 752 vb.

voidance
voidance 300 n.

volatile
transient 114 adj.
light 323 adj.
vaporific 338 adj.
excitable 822 adj.

volatilize
rarefy 325 vb.
vaporize 338 vb.

volcanic
violent 176 adj.
fiery 379 adj.

volcano
furnace 383 n.
pitfall 663 n.

volition
will 595 n.

volley
strike 279 vb.
shoot 287 vb.
bombardment 712 n.

volt, voltage
electricity 160 n.

volte-face
return 286 n.
tergiversation 603 n.

volubility
loquacity 581 n.

volume
quantity 26 n.
space 183 n.
metrology 465 n.
book 589 n.

volumetric
spatial 183 adj.

voluminous
great 32 adj.

voluntary
musical piece 412 n.
voluntary 597 adj.

volunteer
voluntary work 597 n.
be willing 597 vb.
undertake 672 vb.

voluptuary
sensualist 944 n.

voluptuous
pleasurable 826 adj.
sensual 944 adj.

volute
coil 251 n.

vomit
vomit 300 vb.

voodoo
sorcery 983 n.

voracious
gluttonous 947 adj.

voracity
gluttony 947 n.

vortex
vortex 315 n.
eddy 350 n.
pitfall 663 n.

votary
lover 887 n.
worshipper 981 n.

vote
vote 605 n., vb.

vote against, vote down
oppose 704 vb.

vote-catching
flattering 925 adj.

voted
assented 488 adj.

vote for
endorse 488 vb.
vote 605 vb.

voter
electorate 605 n.

voting list
electorate 605 n.

votive
promissory 764 adj.
devotional 981 adj.

votive offering
oblation 981 n.

voucher
credential 466 n.
receipt 807 n.

vouchsafe
consent 758 vb.
give 781 vb.

vow
affirm 532 vb.
promise 764 n., vb.
offering 781 n.

vowel
speech sound 398 n.
voice 577 n.

voyage
water travel 267 n.
passage 305 n.

voyager
traveller 268 n.

voyeurism
curiosity 453 n.
impurity 951 n.

vulcanize
toughen 329 vb.
heat 381 vb.

vulgar
inelegant 576 adj.
vulgar 847 adj.
plebeian 869 adj.
showy 875 adj.
impure 951 adj.

vulgarian
vulgarian 847 n.

vulgarism
slang 560 n.

vulgarity
(*see* **vulgar**)

vulgarize
impair 655 vb.
cheapen 812 vb.
vulgarize 847 vb.

vulgate
interpretation 520 n.

vulnerable
defenceless 161 adj.
vulnerable 661 adj.

vulture
cleaner 648 n.
tyrant 735 n.
glutton 947 n.

vulva
genitalia 164 n.

W

wad
line 227 vb.
stopper 264 n.

wadding
lining 227 n.

waddle
gait 265 n.
walk 267 vb.

wade
walk 267 vb.
swim 269 vb.

waders
legwear 228 n.

wade through
study 536 vb.

wafer
adhesive 47 n.
pastry 301 n.
the sacrament 988 n.

waffle
cereal 301 n.
mean nothing 515 vb.

waft
carry 273 vb.

waftage
transport 272 n.

wag
oscillate 317 vb.
humorist 839 n.

wage
employ 622 vb.
earnings 771 n.
(*see* **wages**)

wage-earner
worker 686 n.

wager
gambling 618 n.

wages
pay 804 n.
receipt 807 n.

waggish
witty 839 adj.

wagon
cart 274 n.

wagoner, waggoner
carrier 273 n.

waif
wanderer 268 n.
derelict 779 n.
outcaste 883 n.

wail
cry 408 vb.
lamentation 836 n.

wainscot
base 214 n.
lining 227 n.

waist
narrowing 206 n.
bodywear 228 n.

waistcoat
vest 228 n.
waistline
centrality 225 n.
wait
pass time 108 vb.
await 507 vb.
wait and see
be tentative 461 vb.
not act 677 vb.
wait-and-see policy
caution 858 n.
waiter
servant 742 n.
waiting-room
lobby 194 n.
wait on
accompany 89 vb.
minister to 703 vb.
visit 882 vb.
waits
choir 413 n.
waive
not use 674 vb.
resign 753 vb.
not retain 779 vb.
waiver
relinquishment
621 n.
loss of right 916 n.
wake
effect 157 n.
eddy 350 n.
obsequies 364 n.
trace 548 n.
lament 836 n.
wakeful
vigilant 457 adj.
walk
gait 265 n.
pedestrianism
267 n.
walk 267 vb.
vocation 622 n.
path 624 n.
walker
pedestrian 268 n.
walkie-talkie
telecommunication
531 n.
walk of life
conduct 688 n.
walk out with
court 889 vb.
walk-over
easy thing 701 n.
victory 727 n.

wall
separation 46 n.
supporter 218 n.
partition 231 n.
fortification 713 n.
wallet
case 194 n.
wall-eye
dim sight 440 n.
wallflower
rejection 607 n.
wallop
potion 301 n.
spank 963 vb.
wallow
plunge 313 vb.
marsh 347 n.
swill 649 n.
be unclean 649 vb.
be intemperate
943 vb.
wallow in
enjoy 376 vb.
superabound
637 vb.
wallpaper
lining 227 n.
waltz
dance 837 n., vb.
wampum
coinage 797 n.
wan
dim 419 adj.
colourless 426 adj.
melancholic
834 adj.
wand
badge of rule
743 n.
magic instrument
983 n.
wander
wander 267 vb.
be inattentive
456 vb.
be insane 503 vb.
be diffuse 570 vb.
wanderer
wanderer 268 n.
wanderlust
wandering 267 vb.
wane
decrease 37 n., vb.
deteriorate 655 vb.
wangle
trickery 542 n.
contrivance 623 n.

want
deficit 55 n.
shortcoming 307 n.
requirement 627 n.
scarcity 636 n.
desire 859 n., vb.
wanting
absent 190 adj.
deficient 307 adj.
unintelligent
499 adj.
wanton
capricious 604 adj.
amuse oneself
837 vb.
caress 889 vb.
unchaste 951 adj.
loose woman 952 n.
war
dissension 709 n.
war 718 n.
warble
sing 413 vb.
war-cry
defiance 711 n.
ward
district 184 n.
hospital 658 n.
dependant 742 n.
detention 747 n.
warden
protector 660 n.
keeper 749 n.
warder
gaoler 749 n.
ward off
parry 713 vb.
wardrobe
cabinet 194 n.
clothing 228 n.
wardship
nonage 130 n.
subjection 745 n.
ware
product 164 n.
merchandise 795 n.
warehouse
storage 632 n.
warfare
warfare 718 n.
(*see* war)
warhead
ammunition 723 n.
war-horse
war-horse 273 n.
wariness
caution 858 n.

warlike
warlike 718 adj.
warlock
sorcerer 983 n.
war-lord
militarist 722 n.
warm
summery 128 adj.
warm 379 adj.
heat 381 vb.
rich 800 adj.
fervent 818 adj.
excite 821 vb.
friendly 880 adj.
warmed-up
repeated 106 adj.
war-monger
militarist 722 n.
warmth
heat 379 n.
redness 431 n.
excitable state
822 n.
friendliness 880 n.
anger 891 n.
warm to
befriend 880 vb.
warm up
heat 381 vb.
make ready
669 vb.
warn
hint 524 vb.
warn 664 vb.
reprove 924 vb.
warning
omen 511 n.
warning 664 n.
(*see* warn)
warn off
prohibit 757 vb.
warp
weaving 222 n.
distortion 246 n.
bias 481 vb.
warpaint
cosmetic 843 n.
warpath
warfare 718 n.
warped
distorted 246 adj.
warrant
credential 466 n.
warrant 737 n.
mandate 751 n.
permit 756 n., vb.
justify 927 vb.

wayfarer
traveller 268 n.
waylay
ensnare 542 vb.
ambush 527 vb.
be cunning 698 vb.
waymark
signpost 547 n.
way of life
conduct 688 n.
way out
outlet 298 n.
means of escape
667 n.
ways and means
means 629 n.
wayside
accessible 289 adj.
way, under
forward 285 adv.
wayward
wilful 602 adj.
capricious 604 adj.
way-worn
fatigued 684 adj.
weak
small 33 adj.
weak 163 adj.
moderate 177 adj.
watery 339 adj.
lax 734 adj.
weaken
weaken 163 vb.
impair 655 vb.
weak-kneed
irresolute 601 adj.
weakling
weakling 163 n.
coward 856 n.
weakly
weak 163 adj.
weakness
tendency 179 n.
liability 180 n.
irresolution 601 n.
imperfection 647 n.
ill-health 651 n.
vulnerability 661 n.
liking 859 n.
weal
good 615 n.
blemish 845 n.
weald
plain 348 n.
wealth
abundance 171 n.
money 797 n.

wealth 800 n.
wealthy
rich 800 adj.
wean from
disaccustom
611 vb.
weanling
child 132 n.
weapon
tool 630 n.
weapon 723 n.
wear
last 113 vb.
clothing 228 n.
wear 228 vb.
wear and tear
dilapidation 655 n.
weariness
fatigue 684 n.
wearisome
laborious 682 adj.
tedious 838 adj.
wear out
deteriorate 655 vb.
impair 655 vb.
weary
laborious 682 adj.
fatigue 684 vb.
weasel
vermin 365 n.
weather
storm 176 n.
navigate 269 vb.
weather 340 n.
wind 352 n.
colour 425 vb.
mature 669 vb.
weather-beaten
dilapidated 655 adj.
weathercock
changeable thing
152 n.
indicator 547 n.
waverer 601 n.
weathered
soft-hued 425 adj.
weather eye
carefulness 457 n.
weather-wise
predicting 511 adj.
weave
textile 222 n.
weave 222 vb.
pass 305 vb.
pattern 844 n.
weaver
weaving 222 n.

web
complexity 61 n.
network 222 n.
stratagem 698 n.
webbing
network 222 n.
wed
wed 894 vb.
wedding
wedding 894 n.
wedge
piece 53 n.
supporter 218 n.
interjection 231 n.
stopper 264 n.
wedlock
marriage 894 n.
weed
render few 105 vb.
tobacco 388 n.
weed out
eject 300 vb.
weeds
clothing 228 n.
weedy
lean 206 adj.
week
period 110 n.
week-end
pass time 108 vb.
visit 882 vb.
weekly
seasonal 141 adj.
weep
flow out 298 vb.
weep 836 vb.
weeper
weeper 836 n.
weep for
pity 905 vb.
weepy
unhappy 825 adj.
weevil
vermin 365 n.
weft
weaving 222 n.
weigh
influence 178 vb.
weigh 322 vb.
meditate 449 vb.
estimate 480 vb.
be important
638 vb.
weighing-machine
scales 322 n.
weighment
weighment 322 n.

weight
substantiality 3 n.
influence 178 n.
size, bulk 195 n.
gravity, scales
322 n.
make heavy
322 vb.
importance 638 n.
encumbrance 702 n.
weighting
compensation
31 n.
weightless
light 323 adj.
weight of numbers
greater number
104 n.
weights and
measures
metrology 465 n.
weighty
great 32 adj.
weighty 322 adj.
important 638 adj.
weir
waterfall 350 n.
weird
fate 596 n.
wonderful 864 adj.
spooky 970 adj.
welcome
reception 299 n.
assent 488 vb.
pleasurable
826 adj.
desired 859 adj.
friendliness 880 n.
congratulation
886 n.
weld
join 45 vb.
agglutinate 48 vb.
welfare
good 615 n.
prosperity 730 n.
welfare state
sociology 901 n.
welfare work
sociology 901 n.
well
greatly 32 adv.
receptacle 194 n.
flow out 298 vb.
stream 350 n.
store 632 n.
healthy 650 adj.

well-behaved
  obedient 739 adj.
  amiable 884 adj.
well-being
  euphoria 376 n.
  prosperity 730 n.
well-born
  noble 868 adj.
well-bred
  well-bred 848 adj.
  genteel 868 adj.
well-disposed
  aiding 703 adj.
well-drawn
  descriptive 590 adj.
well-dressed
  fashionable
  848 adj.
Wellerism
  witticism 839 n.
well-fed
  feeding 301 adj.
well-founded
  certain 473 adj.
  true 494 adj.
well-inclined
  approving 923 adj.
well-intentioned
  friendly 880 adj.
well-laid
  cunning 698 adj.
well-lined
  full 54 adj.
well-made
  well-made 694 adj.
well-mannered
  well-bred 848 adj.
well-meaning
  innocent 935 adj.
well-meant
  benevolent 897 adj.
well-off
  rich 800 adj.
well-read
  instructed 490 adj.
well-spent
  successful 727 adj.
well-spoken
  well-bred 848 adj.
well-timed
  timely 137 adj.
well-to-do
  rich 800 adj.
well-turned
  shapely 841 adj.
well-wisher
  patron 707 n.

  friend 880 n.
well-worn
  dilapidated 655 adj.
welsh
  run away 620 vb.
  not pay 805 vb.
welsher
  avoider 620 n.
  non-payer 805 n.
welt
  edge 234 n.
  spank 963 vb.
welter
  confusion 61 n.
  be wet 341 vb.
welter-weight
  pugilist 722 n.
wen
  swelling 253 n.
wench
  youngster 132 n.
  woman 373 n.
  loose woman 952 n.
wenching
  unchastity 951 n.
wend
  travel 267 vb.
werewolf
  demon 970 n.
west
  compass point
  281 n.
wet
  watery 339 adj.
  moisture 341 n.
  rainy 350 adj.
  ninny 501 n.
wet blanket
  moderator 177 n.
  moper 834 n.
  bore 838 n.
wet-nurse
  provider 633 n.
whack
  strike 279 vb.
  fatigue 684 vb.
  spank 963 vb.
whack at
  essay 671 n.
whale
  giant 195 n.
whalebone
  supporter 218 n.
  underwear 228 n.
whaler
  fishing boat 275 n.
  hunter 619 n.

wharf
  stable 192 n.
  storage 632 n.
what-have-you
  no name 562 n.
wheal
  swelling 253 n.
wheat
  corn 366 n.
wheedle
  tempt 612 vb.
  induce 612 vb.
  pet 889 vb.
  flatter 925 vb.
wheel
  wheel 250 n.
  rotate 315 vb.
  directorship 689 n.
wheel about,
  wheel round
  turn back 286 vb.
wheelbarrow
  pushcart 274 n.
wheeled
  vehicular 274 adj.
wheels within
  wheels
  complexity 61 n.
  machine 630 n.
wheeze
  respiration 352 n.
  breathe 352 vb.
  idea 451 n.
  contrivance 623 n.
wheezy
  puffing 352 adj.
whelp
  youngling 132 n.
  reproduce itself
  164 vb.
when and where
  situation 186 n.
whereabouts
  situation 186 n.
where the shoe
  pinches
  moral sensibility
  819 n.
  painfulness 827 n.
wherewithal
  means 629 n.
wherret
  torment 827 vb.
wherry
  boat 275 n.
wherryman
  boatman 270 n.

whet
  sharpen 256 vb.
  cause desire
  859 vb.
whetstone
  sharpener 256 n.
whey
  milk product 301 n.
whiff
  breeze 352 n.
  odour 394 n.
  indication 547 n.
while away
  pass time 108 vb.
  have leisure 681 vb.
whilom
  former 125 adj.
whim
  whim 604 n.
whimper
  cry 408 vb.
  weep 836 vb.
whimsey
  whim 604 n.
whimsical
  crazed 503 adj.
  capricious 604 adj.
  ridiculous 849 adj.
whine
  cry 408 vb.
  ululate 409 vb.
  be discontented
  829 vb.
  lamentation 836 vb.
  be servile 879 vb.
whinny
  ululate 409 vb.
whip
  driver 268 n.
  strike 279 vb.
  agitate 318 vb.
  incentive 612 n.
  defeat 727 vb.
  flog 963 vb.
  scourge 964 n.
whip hand
  vantage 34 n.
  victory 727 n.
whipper-in
  hunter 619 n.
whippersnapper
  youngster 132 n.
whippet
  animalcule 196 n.
  dog 365 n.
whipping-boy
  substitute 150 n.

title-deed 767 n.
bequeath 780 vb.
will and pleasure
command 737 n.
willies
nervousness 854 n.
willing
willing 597 adj.
obedient 739 adj.
cheerful 833 adj.
willingness
assent 488 n.
persuasibility 612 n.
(see will, willing)
will-o'-the-wisp
glow-worm 420 n.
visual fallacy
440 n.
incentive 612 n.
willowy
narrow 206 adj.
shapely 841 adj.
will-power
will 595 n.
wilt
deteriorate 655 vb.
be dejected 834 vb.
wily
cunning 698 adj.
wimple
headgear 228 n.
win
victory 727 n.
win 727 vb.
acquire, gain
771 vb.
wince
recoil 280 vb.
feel pain 377 vb.
suffer 825 vb.
winch
lifter 310 n.
wind
insubstantial thing
4 n.
disable 161 vb.
rotate 315 vb.
gas 336 n.
wind 352 n.
detect 484 vb.
empty talk 515 n.
indigestion 651 n.
windbag
chatterer 581 n.
windbreak
wood 366 n.
shelter 662 n.

winded
panting 684 adj.
winder
rotator 315 n.
windfall
acquisition 771 n.
receiving 782 n.
wind-gauge
anemology 352 n.
wind in
draw 288 vb.
windiness
gaseity 336 n.
wind 352 n.
winding
meandering 251 n.
convoluted 251 adj.
winding sheet
grave clothes 364 n.
windlass
traction 288 n.
lifter 310 n.
windmill
rotator 315 n.
window
window 263 n.
transparency 422 n.
window-dressing
ostentation 875 n.
window-shopper
purchaser 792 n.
windpipe
respiration 352 n.
air-pipe 353 n.
windscreen
screen 421 n.
windshield
screen 421 n.
wind-sock
anemology 352 n.
indicator 847 n.
windswept
orderless 61 adj.
wind-tunnel
anemology 352 n.
testing agent 461 n.
wind up
operate 173 vb.
invigorate 174 vb.
elevate 310 vb.
fear 854 n.
wind-up
finality 69 n.
windy
windy 352 adj.
diffuse 570 adj.
nervous 854 adj.

wine
wine 301 n.
wineglass
cup 194 n.
winepress
farm tool 370 n.
wing
adjunct 40 n.
laterality 239 n.
plumage 259 n.
wing 271 n.
fly 271 vb.
wound 655 vb.
shelter 662 n.
hinder 702 vb.
wings
aircraft 276 n.
livery 547 n.
stage-set 594 n.
wink
hint 524 n., vb.
indication 547 n.
gesture 547 n.
wink at
disregard 458 vb.
permit 756 vb.
(see connive)
winkle out
extract 304 vb.
winner
exceller 644 n.
victor 727 n.
winning
acquiring 771 adj.
amiable 884 adj.
winning hit
success 727 n.
winning position
vantage 34 n.
winning-post
objective 617 n.
winnings
gain 771 n.
receipt 807 n.
winning ways
lovableness 887 n.
winnow
discriminate 463 vb.
select 605 vb.
purify 648 vb.
winnowing fan
farm tool 370 n.
win one's spurs
succeed 727 vb.
have repute 866 vb.
win over
convince 485 vb.

winsome
lovable 887 adj.
winter
pass time 108 vb.
winter 129 n.
wintriness 380 n.
wintriness
storm 176 n.
wintriness 380 n.
wintry
wintry 129 adj.
wipe
clean 648 vb.
wipe out
nullify 2 vb.
destroy 165 vb.
slaughter 362 vb.
wire
cable 47 n.
filament 208 n.
message 529 n.
telecommunication
531 n.
wire-drawn
long 230 adj.
narrow 206 adj.
fibrous 208 adj.
wireless
telecommunication
531 n.
wire-puller
influence 178 n.
motivator 612 n.
wires
influence 178 n.
wiry
stalwart 162 adj.
wisdom
erudition 490 n.
wisdom 498 n.
wise
wise 498 adj.
foreseeing 510 adj.
wiseacre
wiseacre 500 n.
wisecrack
witticism 839 n.
wise man
sage 500 n.
adviser 691 n.
wish
desire 859 n., vb.
desired object
859 n.
wishful
illogical 477 adj.
desiring 859 adj.

wish-fulfilment
content 828 n.

wishful thinking
credulity 487 n.
desire 859 n.

wish one joy
gratulate 886 vb.

wish well
be benevolent
897 vb.

wishy-washy
tasteless 387 adj.
feeble 572 adj.

wisp
insubstantial thing
4 n.
piece 53 n.
filament 208 n.

wispy
hairy 259 adj.

wistful
desiring 859 adj.

wit
wit 839 n.
humorist 839 n.

witch
sorceress 983 n.

witchcraft
sorcery 983 n.

witch-doctor
sorcerer 983 n.

witchery
pleasurableness
826 n.
sorcery 983 n.

witch-hunt
inquiry, search
459 n.

witching
magical 983 adj.

with child
productive 164 adj.

withdraw
recede 290 vb.
depart 296 vb.
extract 304 vb.
recant 603 vb.
resign 753 vb.
take 786 vb.
schismatize 978 vb.

withdrawal
seclusion 883 n.
(*see* withdraw)

wither
deteriorate 655 vb.

withered
weakened 163 adj.

lean 206 adj.
(*see* wither)

withering
disapproving
924 adj.

withhold
restrain 747 vb.
refuse 760 vb.

within one's means
cheap 812 adj.

within reach
on the spot 189 adj.
accessible 289 adj.

with interest
in addition 38 adv.

**without a leg to
stand on**
powerless 161 adj.

without complaints
content 828 adj.

without end
perpetual 115 adj.

without issue
unproductive
172 adj.

without notice
unexpectedly
508 adv.

without omission
inclusive 78 adj.

without strings
unconditional
744 adj.

withstand
counteract 182 vb.
oppose 704 vb.
resist 715 vb.

with young
productive 164 adj.

witness
be present 189 vb.
see 438 vb.
testimony 466 n.
witness 466 n.
signatory 765 n.

witness-box
courtroom 956 n.

wits
intelligence 498 n.

witticism
witticism 839 n.
ridicule 851 n.

witty
aphoristic 496 adj.
witty 839 adj.

wive
wed 894 vb.

wizard
sage 500 n.
proficient 696 n.
sorcerer 983 n.

wizardry
skill 694 n.
sorcery 983 n.

wizened
dwarfish 196 adj.
lean 206 adj.

woad
blue pigment
435 n.

wobble
vary 152 vb.
oscillate 317 vb.

wobbler
waverer 601 n.

woe
sorrow 825 n.

wold
high land 209 n.
plain 348 n.

wolf
eat 301 vb.
noxious animal
904 n.
gluttonize 947 vb.

**wolf in sheep's
clothing**
impostor 545 n.

wolfish
cruel 898 adj.
gluttonous 947 adj.

woman
adult 134 n.
woman 373 n.

woman-hater
misanthrope 902 n.

womanhood
adultness 134 n.

womanish
female 373 adj.
cowardly 856 adj.

womankind
womankind 373 n.

womanize
be impure 951 vb.

womanizer
libertine 952 n.

womanly
female 373 adj.

womb
seedbed 156 n.
genitalia 164 n.

womenfolk
womankind 373 n.

wonder
be uncertain 474 vb.
not know 491 vb.
exceller 644 n.
wonder 864 n., vb.
prodigy 864 n.

wonderful
wonderful 864 adj.

wonderland
fantasy 513 n.
pleasure-ground
837 n.
prodigy 864 n.

wonderman
exceller 644 n.
paragon 646 n.
prodigy 864 n.

wonder-working
thaumaturgy 864 n.

wont
habit 610 n.
use 673 n.

woo
be in love 887 vb.
court 889 vb.

wood
wood 366 n.
wooden 366 adj.

woodcut
engraving 555 n.

woodcutter
forestry 366 n.

wooded
arboreal 366 adj.

wooden
wooden 366 adj.
impassive 820 adj.

woodenness
obstinacy 602 n.

woodland
wood 366 n.

woodman
forestry 366 n.

wood-wind
flute 414 n.

woodwork
structure 331 n.

wooer
lover 887 n.

wooing
love-making 887 n.
wooing 889 n.

wool
fibre 208 n.
textile 222 n.

wool-gathering
abstracted 456 adj.

woollens
clothing 228 n.
warm clothes 381 n.
woollies
underwear 228 n.
warm clothes
381 n.
woolly
hairy 259 adj.
woolsack
tribunal 956 n.
word
information 524 n.
news, message
529 n.
oath 532 n.
word 559 n.
phrase 563 n.
command 737 n.
word and a blow
irascibility 892 n.
wordbook
dictionary 559 n.
word-for-word
interpretive
520 adj.
wordiness
diffuseness 570 n.
loquacity 581 n.
word in the ear
hint 524 n.
wordless
voiceless 578 adj.
word list
dictionary 559 n.
Word of God
scripture 975 n.
word of honour
promise 764 n.
word of mouth
message 529 n.
speech 579 n.
word-painting
description 590 n.
word-play
equivocalness
518 n.
wit 839 n.
words
reading matter
589 n.
quarrel 709 n.
word-spinning
diffuseness 570 n.
eloquence 579n.
wordy
prolix 570 adj.

work
agency 173 n.
operate 173 vb.
book 589 n.
business 622 n.
function 622 vb.
be expedient 642 vb.
action 676 n.
be busy 678 vb.
labour 682 n.
workable
operative 173 adj.
possible 469 adj.
workaday
businesslike 622 adj.
work against
counteract 182 vb.
oppose 704 vb.
worked up
angry 891 adj.
worker
producer 167 n.
busy person 678 n.
worker 686 n.
workhouse
workshop 687 n.
working classes
personnel 686 n.
working day
period 110 n.
job 622 n.
working life
labour 682 n.
working model
image 551 n.
workings
structure 331 n.
working to rule
slowness 278 n.
workman
worker 686 n.
workmanlike
industrious 678 adj.
well-made 694 adj.
workmanship
(*see* skill)
work of art
composition 56 n.
**work of
supererogation**
voluntary work
597 n.
work on
(*see* work upon)
work out
do sums 86 vb.
mature 669 vb.

work-out
exercise 682 n.
work over
pass 305 vb.
workpeople
personnel 686 n.
workroom
workshop 687 n.
works
structure 331 n.
machine 630 n.
workshop 687 n.
workshop
workshop 687 n.
work-shy
lazy 679 adj.
work together
cooperate 706 vb.
work up into
effort 243 vb.
work upon
influence 178 vb.
motivate 612 vb.
world
whole 52 n.
multitude 104 n.
space 183 n.
world 321 n.
mankind 371 n.
sociality 882 n.
world-beater
superior 34 n.
worldling
egotist 932 n.
impious person
980 n.
worldly
material 319 adj.
telluric 321 adj.
worldly wisdom
selfishness 932 n.
world of nature
matter 319 n.
world's end
extremity 69 n.
farness 199 n.
world-shaking
revolutionary
149 adj.
world-shattering
important 638 adj.
world-stuff
substantiality 3 n.
world-wide
extensive 32 adj.
universal 79 adj.
spacious 183 adj.

ubiquitous 189 adj.
worm
destroyer 168 n.
coil 251 n.
wriggle 251 vb.
blight 659 n.
cad 938 n.
worm-eaten
dilapidated 655 adj.
worm into
enter 297 vb.
wormwood
unsavouriness
391 n.
worn
dilapidated
655 adj.
used 673 adj.
fatigued 684 adj.
unsightly 842 adj.
worn out
impotent 161 adj.
dilapidated 655 adj.
worry
chew 301 vb.
adversity 731 n.
worry 825 n.
incommode 827 vb.
nervousness 854 n.
worse for wear
dilapidated 655 adj.
worsen
deteriorate 655 vb.
aggravate 832 vb.
worship
honour 866 vb.
worship 981 n., vb.
worshipful
worshipful 866 adj.
respected 920 adj.
worshipper
worshipper 981 n.
worship, place of
temple 990 n.
worst
be superior 34 vb.
defeat 727 vb.
worsted
textile 222 n.
worst intentions
malevolence 898 n.
worst, the
ill fortune 731 n.
wort
plant 366 n.
worth
equivalent 28 adj.

quid pro quo 150 n.
price 809 n.
virtues 933 n.
worth, be
cost 809 vb.
worthless
profitless 641 adj.
bad 645 adj.
contemptible
922 adj.
worth nothing
cheap 812 adj.
worth-while
good 615 adj.
important 638 adj.
expedient 642 adj.
beneficial 644 adj.
worthy
excellent 644 adj.
reputable 866 adj.
would-be
misnamed 562 adj.
hoping 852 adj.
wound
strike 279 vb.
wound 655 n., vb.
huff 891 vb.
woven
crossed 222 adj.
textural 331 adj.
wrack
ruin 165 n.
wraith
ghost 970 n.
wrangle
disagreement 25 n.
argue 475 vb.
bicker 709 vb.
wrangler
computer 86 n.
quarreller 709 n.
wrap
tie 45 vb.
cover 226 vb.
enclose 235 vb.
warm clothes 381 n.
wrapper
receptacle 194 n.
wrapping 226 n.
shawl 228 n.
wrapping
wrapping 226 n.
wrath
anger 891 n.
wreath
loop 250 n.
trophy 729 n.

ornamentation
844 n.
wreathe
enlace 222 vb.
twine 251 vb.
wreck
destroy 165 vb.
dilapidation 655 n.
wreckage
ruin 165 n.
wrecker
destroyer 168 n.
trouble-maker
663 n.
wrecking activities
destruction 165 n.
wrench
disjoin 46 vb.
force 176 vb.
extractor 304 n.
nippers 778 n.
wrest
distort 246 vb.
misinterpret 521 vb.
wrestle
wrestling 716 n.
wrestler
athlete 162 n.
combatant 722 n.
wretch
unlucky person
731 n.
sufferer 825 n.
knave 938 n.
wretched
unimportant
639 adj.
unhappy 825 adj.
wriggle
wriggle 251 vb.
wriggle out of
plead 614 vb.
fail in duty 918 vb.
wring
give pain 377 vb.
levy 786 vb.
wringer
drier 342 n.
wring out
dry 342 vb.
wrinkle
grow old 131 vb.
convolution 251 n.
crinkle 251 vb.
stratagem 698 n.
wrist
joint 45 n.

wristband
sleeve 228 n.
wristwatch
timekeeper 117 n.
writ
warrant 737 n.
security 767 n.
write
communicate
524 vb.
record 548 vb.
write 586 vb.
write back
answer 460 vb.
write down
record 548 vb.
write off
relinquish 621 vb.
writer
penman 586 n.
author 589 n.
dissertator 591 n.
write to
correspond 588 vb.
write up
dissert 591 vb.
praise 923 vb.
write-up
publicity 528 n.
writhe
wriggle 251 vb.
be agitated 318 vb.
suffer 825 vb.
writing
composition 56 n.
writing 586 n.
writing materials
stationery 586 n.
writing on the wall
danger signal
665 n.
threat 900 n.
writing room
stationery 586 n.
writings
reading matter
589 n.
wrong
erroneous 495 n.
evil 616 n., adj.
oppress 735 vb.
wrong 914 n., adj.
do wrong 914 vb.
foul play 930 n.
lawbreaking 954 n.
wrongdoer
evildoer 904 n.

wrongdoing
wickedness 934 n.
lawbreaking 954 n.
wrongful
wrong 914 adj.
wrong-headed
misjudging 481 adj.
erroneous 495 n.
wrongheadedness
obstinacy 602 n.
wrong side
contrariety 14 n.
rear 238 n.
wrong time
intempestivity 138 n.
wrong 'un
bad man 938 n.
wrought
matured 669 adj.
wrought work
ornamental art
844 n.
wry
oblique 220 adj.
distorted 246 adj.
wynd
street 192 n.

X

xebec
sailing ship 275 n.
xenophobe
enemy 881 n.
xenophobia
prejudice 481 n.
phobia 854 n.
hatred 888 n.
X-ray
radiation 417 n.
photography 551 n.
X-shaped
crossed 222 adj.
xylophone
piano 414 n.

Y

yacht
sailing-ship 275 n.
yachter, yachtsman
boatman 270 n.
yachting
water travel 269 n.
aquatics 269 n.
yak
cattle 365 n.

YAM

yam
tuber 301 n.
yap
ululate 409 vb.
yard
enclosure 235 n.
open space 263 n.
workshop 687 n.
yardstick
gauge 465 n.
yarn
fibre 208 n.
fable 543 n.
narrative 590 n.
yarner
narrator 590 n.
yashmak
cloak 228 n.
yaw
navigate 269 vb.
deviate 282 vb.
yawl
sailing-ship 275 n.
yawn
sleep 679 vb.
be fatigued 684 vb.
yawning
open 263 adj.
sleepy 679 adj.
yawp, yaup
ululate 409 vb.
yea
assent 488 n.
yea and nay
changeableness 152 n.
year
date 108 n.
period 110 n.
yearling
youngling 132 n.
yearly
seasonal 141 adj.
yearn
be dejected 834 vb.
desire 859 vb.
yearning
love 887 n.
years
diuturnity 113 n.
age 131 n.
years of discretion
adultness 134 n.
yeast
leaven 323 n.
yeasty
light 323 adj.

YOK

bubbly 355 adj.
yegg, yeggman
thief 789 n.
yell
cry 408 vb.
yellow
yellow 433 adj.
gild 433 vb.
cowardly 856 adj.
yellow press
the press 528 n.
yellow streak
cowardice 856 n.
yelp
ululate 409 vb.
yen
desire 859 n.
yeoman
husbandman 370 n.
cavalry 722 n.
countryman 869 n.
yeomanry
army, cavalry 722 n.
yes
assent 488 n.
yes-man
assenter 488 n.
toady 879 n.
yesterday
preterition 125 n.
yet to come
unborn 2 adj.
future 124 adj.
yield
be inferior 35 vb.
reproduce itself 164 vb.
acquiesce 488 vb.
submit 721 vb.
consent 758 vb.
not retain 779 vb.
yodel
sing 413 vb.
yoghurt, yogurt
milk product 301 n.
yogi
ascetic 945 n.
yoke
affix 45 vb.
coupling 47 n.
duality 90 n.
pair 90 vb.
hanger 217 n.
break in 369 vb.
servitude 745 n.

ZER

yoked
combined 50 adj.
yoke-fellow
collaborator 707 n.
yokel
countryman 869 n.
young
new 126 adj.
young 130 adj.
immature 670 adj.
youngling
youngling 132 n.
youngster
youngster 132 n.
youth
beginning 68 n.
youth 130 n.
youngster 132 n.
youthful
young 130 adj.
strong 162 adj.
Yule-tide
festivity 837 n.

Z

zany
laughing-stock 851 n.
zeal
willingness 597 n.
zealot
doctrinaire 473 n.
narrow mind 481 n.
religionist 979 n.
zealotry
opiniatry 602 n.
zealous
willing 597 adj.
zebra
striation 437 n.
zebra crossing
traffic control 305 n.
zeitgeist
tendency 179 n.
zenana
womankind 373 n.
zenith
summit 213 n.
zephyr
breeze 352 n.
vest 228 n.
zero
smallness 33 n.
zero 103 n.
coldness 380 n.

ZYM

zero hour
start 68 n.
date 108 n.
zest
vigorousness 174 n.
enjoyment 824 n.
zetetic
inquiring 459 adj.
ziggurat
high structure 209 n.
zigzag
obliquity 220 n.
be oblique 220 vb.
meander 251 vb.
deviating 282 adj.
deviate 282 vb.
Zion
holy place 990 n.
zip
move fast 277 vb.
zippy
speedy 277 adj.
zodiac
zodiac 321 n.
zodiacal
celestial 321 adj.
zombie
corpse 363 n.
ghost 970 n.
zone
set apart 46 vb.
girdle 47 n.
region 184 n.
layer 208 n.
belt 228 n.
land 344 n.
zoo
medley 43 n.
zoo 369 n.
collection 632 n.
zoological
biological 358 adj.
zoology
biology 358 n.
zoology 367 n.
zoom
move fast 277 vb.
ascend 308 vb.
zoomorphic
animal 365 adj.
zoomorphism
idolatry 982 n.
zoophyte
animal 365 n.
zymogen
leaven 323 n.

MORE ABOUT PENGUINS

Penguinews, which appears every month, contains details of all the new books issued by Penguins as they are published. From time to time it is supplemented by *Penguins in Print*, which is a complete list of all books published by Penguins which are in print. (There are well over three thousand of these.)

A specimen copy of *Penguinews* will be sent to you free on request, and you can become a subscriber for the price of the postage – 4s. for a year's issues (including the complete lists) if you live in the United Kingdom, or 8s. if you live elsewhere. Just write to Dept EP, Penguin Books Ltd, Harmondsworth, Middlesex, enclosing a cheque or postal order, and your name will be added to the mailing list.

Some other books published by Penguins are described on the following pages.

Note: *Penguinews* and *Penguins in Print*
are not available in the U.S.A. or Canada

USAGE AND ABUSAGE

ERIC PARTRIDGE

Which is to be preferred – *nom de plume*, pseudonym, or pen-name? What are neologisms, disguised conjunctions, and fused participles? How should one set about writing a précis? More generally, where does usage end and abusage begin?

Language is everybody's business, and enters into almost every part of human life. Yet it is all too often misused: directness and clarity disappear in a whirl of clichés, euphemisms, and woolliness of expression. This book wittily attacks linguistic abusage of all kinds, and at the same time offers helpfully constructive advice on the proper use of English. Eric Partridge is well known for his books on words, and this is the most comprehensive of them all.

'A very valuable supplement to Fowler' – Sir Harold Nicolson in the *Daily Telegraph*

'As a handy linguistic reference book and provocative commentary on the present state of English writing, it could scarcely be improved on' – Peter Quennell in the *Daily Mail*

THE PENGUIN DICTIONARY
OF QUOTATIONS

J. M. AND M. J. COHEN

This dictionary is designed for the casual reader. It sets out to give him the common stock of quotations from Shakespeare, the Bible, and *Paradise Lost*, side by side with remarks and stray lines by almost unknown writers who have enriched the language with only a single phrase. Foreign languages are quoted in the original where the quotation is generally remembered in its foreign form, but an English translation is always provided. Modern authors have been drawn on for what the compilers believe to be their memorable sayings, and the ancients have been pruned of many lines that have gone into previous dictionaries of quotations, but which are now almost certainly forgotten. The reader, the writer, the after-dinner speaker, the crossword-puzzle solver, and the browser – all will find what they want among the 12,000 or so quotations of this dictionary.

THE PELICAN GUIDE TO
ENGLISH LITERATURE

EDITED BY BORIS FORD

What this work sets out to offer is a guide to the history and traditions of English Literature, a contour-map of the literary scene. It attempts, that is, to draw up an ordered account of literature that is concerned, first and foremost, with value for the present, and this as a direct encouragement to people to read for themselves.

Each volume sets out to present the reader with four kinds of related material:

(i) An account of the social context of literature in each period.

(ii) A literary survey of the period.

(iii) Detailed studies of some of the chief writers and works in the period.

(iv) An appendix of essential facts for reference purposes.

The *Guide* consists of seven volumes, as follows:

1. *The Age of Chaucer*

2. *The Age of Shakespeare*

3. *From Donne to Marvell*

4. *From Dryden to Johnson*

5. *From Blake to Byron*

6. *From Dickens to Hardy*

7. *The Modern Age*

THE USES OF LITERACY

RICHARD HOGGART

We are often reminded that we do not know how 'the other half' lives. By this vivid and detached piece of social analysis Mr Hoggart seeks to remedy this ignorance. When he began his researches into what the 'masses' read about (and sing about) in these times he found that popular literature must be related to the life and values of the people for whom it is produced. Drawing partly from his own boyhood experience, he portrays in fascinating detail the working-class of northern England, and their assumptions, attitudes, and morals.

Mass literacy has opened new worlds to new readers. How far has it also been exploited to debase standards and behaviour? Have the magazines, books, and films 'for the million' proved on balance a social benefit or a social danger?

'Packed with vivid detail and written with deep feeling . . . absorbing and important' – Raymond Mortimer

'Required reading for anyone concerned with the modern cultural climate' – *The Times Literary Supplement*

'Unusual and important . . . I urge you to read this book, which is wise and courageous' – John Connell

FIVE HUNDRED YEARS OF PRINTING

S. H. STEINBERG

Since this book first appeared in 1955 it has established itself as a standard work, been published in a hardback edition, and been translated into German and Italian. For this fully revised edition there are many new illustrations, which have now been worked into the body of the text for greater ease of reference.

Five Hundred Years of Printing traces the close inter-relation between printing and culture. The author's erudite but highly readable survey takes in not only a long time-span but also particular topics like censorship, best-sellers, popular series, and the connexion between printing and education, language and literature. Here indeed, as Beatrice Warde writes in her foreword, 'are the five hundred years of printing as a creator of changes in human lives'.

'A concise and scholarly but entertaining account of the story of the relation between printing and civilization' – *British Printer*

THE CHANGING ENGLISH LANGUAGE

BRIAN FOSTER

The English language is a complex, adaptable, ever-expanding web that absorbs new words easily and uses them unashamedly. Old words have a habit of turning up with new meanings, and what is slang to one generation is common usage to another.

Doctor Foster examines many aspects of the English language in this book. Different meanings and spellings between Britain and America; how words and phrases have been culled from foreign tongues and used readily in English; and, most importantly, how our language has developed in response to the needs of the modern world.

This is a fascinating glimpse into the origin and history of some of our oldest – and newest – words and phrases. With wit and erudition, Doctor Foster introduces us to some of the delightful nuances and oddities of the English language.

THE PENGUIN COMPANION TO LITERATURE

This reference work signposts all the important literatures of the ancient and modern world. The standard entries are arranged alphabetically by authors and consist of biographical sketches, critical assessments and selective bibliographies of editions, translations in English, biographies, critical studies, etc. In addition there are entries describing literary forms and genres, styles and schools, conventions and traditions, particularly where these are likely to be unfamiliar to Western readers.

The work is arranged as follows:

VOLUME 1: English and Commonwealth (in preparation)
VOLUME 2: European Edited by Anthony Thorlby
VOLUME 3: American and Latin American Edited by Malcolm Bradbury, Eric Mottram, and Jean Franco
VOLUME 4: Classical and Byzantine, Oriental and African Edited by D. R. Dudley, and D. M. Lang

THE COMPLETE PLAIN WORDS

ERNEST GOWERS

Sir Ernest Gowers wrote *The Complete Plain Words* as a result of an invitation from the Treasury, which was concerned about the prevailing standards of official English.

Apart from two chapters on grammar and punctuation, this excellent guide is wholly concerned with 'the choice and arrangement of words in such a way as to get an idea as exactly as possible out of one mind into another'.

It is not only for civil servants that clarity of expression is important. It is equally vital in dictating a business letter, preparing a minute, writing an advertisement, or reporting a crime. Without a trace of pomposity or pudder, *The Complete Plain Words* gently administers the medicine we all require. Reconstructed from the material in two earlier booklets, this reference work can rank with such authoritative books as *The King's English* and *A Dictionary of Modern English Usage*.

NOT FOR SALE IN THE U.S.A.